Dr. Albert Sears, an English professor at Silver Lake College, is the author of these entries: pp. 58-59 "Casablanca" Felicia Hemans; p. 183 "Homes of England, The" Felicia Hemans; p. 283 "Monk, The" Matthew Gregory Lewis; pp. 398-399 sensibility

# Encyclopedia of
# Literary Romanticism

ANDREW MAUNDER

Facts On File
An imprint of Infobase Publishing

Encyclopedia of Literary Romanticism

Facts On File, Inc.
An imprint of Infobase Publishing
132 West 31st Street
New York NY 10001

**Library of Congress Cataloging-in-Publication Data**

Encyclopedia of literary romanticism / [edited by] Andrew Maunder.
p. cm.
Includes bibliographical references and index.
ISBN 978-0-8160-7417-4 (hc : alk. paper) 1. English literature—19th
century—History and criticism—Encyclopedias. 2. English literature—18th
century—History and criticism—Encyclopedias. 3. Romanticism—Great
Britain—Encyclopedias. I. Maunder, Andrew.
PR457.E53 2010
820.9'145—dc22          2009037040

Facts On File books are available at special discounts when purchased in bulk
quantities for businesses, associations, institutions, or sales promotions.
Please call our Special Sales Department in New York at (212) 967-8800
or (800) 322-8755.

You can find Facts On File on the World Wide Web at http://www.factsonfile.com

Text design by Erik Lindstrom
Composition by Hermitage Publishing Services
Cover printed by Sheridan Books, Inc., Ann Arbor, Mich.
Book printed and bound by Sheridan Books, Inc., Ann Arbor, Mich.
Date printed: September 2010
Printed in the United States of America

10 9 8 7 6 5 4 3 2 1

This book is printed on acid-free paper and contains 30 percent postconsumer
recycled content.

# CONTENTS

# INTRODUCTION

The joy, the triumph, the delight, the madness!
The boundless, overflowing, bursting gladness,
The vaporous exultation not to be confined!
Ha! Ha! The animation of delight
Which wraps me, like an atmosphere of light,
And bears me as a cloud is borne by its own wind.
Percy Bysshe Shelley,<br>*Prometheus Unbound* (1820)

These lines written by the young idealist Percy Bysshe Shelley (1792–1822) celebrate the spirit of change that many historians and literary critics see as central to what we have come to call "Romanticism." The Romantic period in British literature has traditionally been seen as running from about 1789 (the outbreak of the French Revolution) to the passing of the 1832 Reform Act in Britain, which substantially extended the democratic rights of men to vote. As Shelley's lines remind us, these years have been characterized as ones of adventure and possibility, in which poets, painters, philosophers, and musicians rose en masse to the challenge of envisioning a new world order. In *Prometheus Unbound* Shelley invokes the figure from ancient Greek mythology who faced excruciating torture after daring to give humankind the secret of fire and who, by doing so, opened up a world of endless possibilities. This sense of optimism is echoed in another text by Shelley, "A Defence of Poetry" (1821), which sums up a feeling, widespread among the poet's contemporaries, that the time in which they were living would be regarded as something out of the ordinary by later generations: ". . . our own will be a memorable age in

intellectual achievements, and we live among such philosophers and poets as surpass beyond comparison any who have appeared since the last national struggle for civil and religious liberty" (Shelley 117).

With the possible exception of William Blake (1757–1827), Shelley was the most revolutionary of the writers who have come to be labelled "Romantic." He was expelled from Oxford University for writing a pamphlet called *The Necessity of Atheism.* He was against monarchy—a stance most famously expressed in his poem "England in 1819"—and called himself a "democrat"—a scandalous thing to do in early 19th-century Britain. He abandoned his wife and ran away with Mary Godwin, a daughter of the freethinkers William Godwin and Mary Wollstonecraft, author of *A Vindication of the Rights of Woman* (1792). Although they later married, the couple's behavior was deemed shocking, and they exiled themselves in Switzerland. It was here that they met another literary celebrity, Lord Byron, infamous as much for his scandalous domestic life as for his acclaimed narrative poem *Childe Harold's Pilgrimage* (1812–18). It was here also that Mary began to write one of the most famous of all Romantic novels, *Frankenstein* (1818), at the same time that another house guest, John Polidori, who was Byron's personal physician, began writing his own gothic tale, "The Vampyre" (1818).

As the list of names above reminds us, a whole range of authors and texts have at some stage been grouped together under the label "Romanticism." The *Encyclopedia of Literary Romanticism* introduces you to some of these writers and their works, as well as to other personalities, texts, and events of this exciting period.

## ROMANTICISM AND ROMANTIC WRITERS

What is Romanticism and what does it encompass? Answering this question poses a challenge for anyone trying to define the concept beyond its (corrupted) modern connotation involving candlelit dinners and boxes of chocolates. In literary terms, *Romanticism* tends to be deployed as a convenient label for literary texts written at the end of the 18th and early 19th century, but like all literary terms—such as *modernist* or *realist*—it can be difficult to define precisely. As Sharon Ruston has noted: "It is doubtful whether writers at the time would have felt that they had much in common with each other in terms of their politics, religious beliefs and aesthetic theories" (1). As is evident in the essays in the present volume, some Romantic writers were fired by opposition to the rationalism of the Enlightenment, some by the ideals of the French Revolution, others by admiration for "sublime" natural phenomena—mountains, rivers, storms—and still others by the mysteries of Orientalism and the East.

The first use of the word *romantic* in a literary sense seems to have emerged in Britain in the 1600s to mean something written in French, one of the Romance languages (as opposed to the more clinical Latin). It was associated with quest narratives in which knights rescued ladies from fire-breathing dragons. A century later, in 1755, Dr. Samuel Johnson, editor of the famous *Dictionary*, described "Romantick" as "resembling the tales or romances; wild . . . improbable; false . . . ; fanciful; full of wild scenery" (quoted in Honour 24). Some parts of this definition stuck, particularly the associations with the power of the imagination, the ability of artistic works to stir the emotions, and also the sublimity of nature. The impact on the reader, observer, or listener was central to the suggestion made in 1810 by E. T. A Hoffman that the composer Beethoven was a *romantischer* because his music "sets in motion the lever of fear, of awe, of horror, of suffering, and awakens that infinite longing which is the essence of Romanticism" (quoted in Honour 24). Hoffman's comment is a reminder that the term *Romanticism* also came to be applied to other areas of artistic expression, notably music and painting, with some overlap. The scope of the present volume does not permit detailed treatment of these "sister arts." Suffice to say that in music Brahms, Strauss, Liszt, Mendelssohn, Schumann, Schubert, and Chopin were also given the label "Romantic." In painting Constable, Delacroix, Friedrich, Fuseli, Gericault and Turner, are perhaps the best known, and in all cases the tag has been used to denote work that seemed new and experimental, personal and sometimes patriotic, and that represented a break with the formal styles of the past. As the 19th century moved on, the label started to be applied to an identifiable literary "movement" or "school," members of which "wandered lonely as a cloud" in the search for truth, beauty, and visionary experience and valued spontaneity, powerful feeling, and the artist's individual response to the experience of life. The notion of "Romanticism" as designating a particular body of literary work—mostly poetry—gained further currency during the early 20th century, when it gradually began to be taught in schools and universities as "a period of cultural expression" denoting a particular (politically radical) "spirit of the age" but also associated with "the myth of the isolated genius (as male poet) at odds with a materialistic society" (Miles 7). The Bristol poet Thomas Chatterton (1752–70), who killed himself in a freezing garret before his 18th birthday and was dubbed "the marvelous boy" by William Wordsworth, is one who fits the mold of what we sometimes imagine a Romantic poet to be.

In terms of British literature it has been customary to start with and make a distinction between a "first generation" of Romantic poets: William Blake (1757–1827), William Wordsworth (1770–1850), and Samuel Taylor Coleridge (1772–1834) and a younger (more cosmopolitan and more idolized) "second generation": Lord Byron (1788–1824), Percy Bysshe Shelley, and John Keats (1795–1821), whose careers were cut short when they died young in the early 1820s. In their own day, critics did not immediately call them "Romantics" but used different labels, tending to describe Wordsworth and Coleridge, among others, as "Lake Poets" (or "Lakeists") because of their links with the Lake District in northwest England, and in particular with the village of Grasmere. In turn, and as a result of their unconventional lifestyles and irreverent ideas, Shelley and Byron were sometimes seen by conservative critics to be part of a "Satanic School" of poetry; Keats's lower-class status (his father hired out horses and was also a London innkeeper) led to the snobbish label "Cockney School" being applied to his work.

Yet despite the tendency to group them together in anthologies of poetry, it is mistaken to suggest that these six figures therefore formed a coherent, self-styled ideological movement, possessing similar ideas and ambitions. Coleridge and Wordsworth were initially close friends who worked together on the important collection *Lyrical Ballads* (1798) and also planned to set up a "Pantisocracy" in a rural outpost of North America. But Coleridge (who carried with him something of a sense of inferiority) could also be critical of Wordsworth, particularly what he regarded as the latter's inflated sense of his importance as the "Head and founder of a *Sect* in poetry" (Coleridge, 2:1013). On one occasion he was moved to complain to the poet Robert Southey (1774–1843) about the "radical Difference" in their "theoretical opinions respecting Poetry" (2:830). Lord Byron was scathing about "Johnny Keats's p—a bed poetry" (quoted in Ricks 78), which seemed to be based on imitations of earlier poets (Milton, Spenser, and Shakespeare). In turn, Keats piously complained of the "unmanly depravity which Byron so publicly assumes to feel or tries to make others feel" (quoted in Ricks 76). Elsewhere, Thomas Love Peacock's (1785–1866) attack on the "typical" Romantic poet as a dreamy figure, arrogant and out of touch with real life— "a waster in his own time" (Peacock 2001, 694) prompted Shelley to write "A Defence of Poetry," in which he claimed a social role for poets as "the unacknowledged legislators of the world" (Shelley 535). Taken together, these personal and ideological squabbles are revealing because they remind us that the writing of any period or "movement" involves debate and discussion, rather than complete agreement. In the case of the Romantic period, the concept of a "war of ideas," a term often used to describe the intellectual ferment of the time, seems particularly apt.

As will be obvious from the contents of this volume, these six poets were not the only figures at work in the period, despite their continued prominence in secondary school and college syllabuses today, nor were they the most admired at the time. Blake in particular was a fairly marginal figure. In Scotland Robert Burns (1759–1796), James MacPherson (1736–1796) and Sir Walter Scott (1771–1832) were the much more famous "chieftains" of a regional Romanticism, which celebrated their country's national character via the Scottish past which, they believed, would speak to and guide the present day (Porter 5). Scott's *Lay of the Last Minstrel* (1805) and his best-selling *Marmion* (1808) also suggested to publishers that epic romance could be profitable, a fact reinforced by the way in which the readers of the early 1800s devoured Byron's *The Giaour* (1813) and Tom Moore's *Lalla Rookh* (1817). At the same time, and as other essays in this volume remind us, this was also the age not only of other popular poets— William Cowper (1731–1800), Robert Southey (1774–1843), Mary Robinson (1757–1800), Charlotte Smith (1749–1806), and John Clare (1793–1864)—but also of novelists like Ann Radcliffe (1764–1823), Frances Burney (1752–1840), and Jane Austen (1775–1817), as well as the Irish writers Maria Edgeworth (1767–1849) and Sydney Owenson (Lady Morgan) (c. 1776–1859). The novel had emerged during the 18th century as an important new genre, and just as it is not possible to reduce poetry to a single recognizable aesthetic, so the same can be said of the period's works of fiction.

For a long time the novel was very much the poor relation to poetry and drama—a "lesser" art form. This point is made by Marilyn Butler when she notes: "The six major poets attempted drama but none completed a novel, except Shelley. . . . Until 1814, when Walter Scott's *Waverley* appeared, it seemed to be taken for granted that the novel was a woman's form which treated daily life and domestic concerns by means of a favourite plot, a young woman's (or, more rarely, a young man's) preparation for marriage" (Butler 61–62). Anyone, so received wisdom had it, could write a novel; no special education or learning was needed. However, to belittle or ignore the novels of these years is to overlook the ways in which seeing and representing lives and landscapes had been extended—first by the gothic novel, then by the so-called regional novel and the historical novel. Butler also charts the emergence of a "novel of ideas" developed in the 1790s by William Godwin, author of *Caleb Williams* (1794), and then by Mary Shelley's *Frankenstein* (1818) and James Hogg's *Private Memoirs and Confessions of a Justified Sinner* (1824)—texts teeming with what Butler calls "Romantic irrationality": "All their protagonists are obsessives seized with a pernicious idea, a notion which leads to the disintegration not only of the hero but of his loved ones and of the entire civic order: they seem to have been read as—and intended for—allegories of revolution" (Butler 62–63). The most famous novelist of the early 19th century, Jane Austen, has traditionally been seen to shun all of this mess, maintaining a ladylike pose of disinterestedness. Yet, as the contributors to this volume reveal, even she demonstrates a familiarity with the upheavals of her time and the social and cultural changes taking place.

One of the things this volume does to is to recognize these "Romantic misfits," as Robert Miles terms them, writers not traditionally grouped under the Romantic umbrella but very much present on the period's literary landscape, sharing ideas and influencing one another. Indeed, since Harold Bloom's book *The Anxiety of Influence* (1973) and its argument that "every poem is a reading of another poem" (93), the influence of different writers across and between contemporaries, between generations, and between countries has been an important part of our understanding of what literary Romanticism involves, a point of which contemporary critics were well aware. "Mr Wordsworth," wrote William Hazlitt in his *Lectures on the English Poets* (1818), "is at the head of what has been denominated the 'Lake School of Poetry.'. . . [It] has its origin in the French Revolution or rather in those sentiments and opinions which produced that revolution, and which sentiments and opinions were directly imported into this country in translations from German . . ." (Hazlitt 161). Hazlitt's point is that British Romantic writers were not always as original as they liked to pretend but drew on the works and techniques not just of

their fellow countrymen but occasionally those of controversial German writers such as Johann Wolfgang von Goethe (1749–1832), Johann Christoph Friedrich von Schiller (1759–1805), Novalis (Georg Friedrich Philipp von Hardenberg, or Friedrich Leopold, baron von Hardenberg, 1772–1801), Gottfried August Burger (1748–1794), and E. T. A. Hoffman (1776–1822)—writers whose novels, plays, and ballads were rich in ideas about the supernatural, about rebellion and social change, about regional pride, and about the importance of individualism. It was not only Germany, of course. France, too, had writers interested in the same ideas—Stendhal (Marie-Henri Beyle, 1783–1842) and Victor Hugo (1802–1885), for example. In Sweden Erik Stagnelius (1793–1823) was another one of those flying the Romantic flag.

The Romantics also had a special interest in the art, culture, myths, and mysteries of the ancient world, inspired partly by the French general Napoleon Bonaparte's failed bid to conquer Egypt and partly by a revived interest in the classics of ancient Greece and Rome. Keats's "Hyperion" and *Endymion* are notable examples, as is Shelley's famous sonnet "Ozymandias," which was inspired by the head of a massive statue discovered by archaeologist Giovanni Belzoni and exhibited in London in 1820. But this interest was also provoked by travel. According to Robin Jarvis, the Romantic period was "a period that coined the word 'tourist,' and in which increasing numbers of people were travelling for pleasure both within Britain and especially, post-Waterloo [1815], on the Continent" (Jarvis 187). Shelley and Byron both spent long periods out of Britain, but even within the country, travel was a popular pastime. For the would-be writer, experience of new sights and sounds was useful because it could provoke self-discovery and "an intensified inwardness," which was not only a means of disassociating oneself from the common herd of tourists but could prompt literary creativity (187).

Other writers were interested in the more recent historical past. Thomas Chatterton famously produced a stash of poems which he said he had transcribed from old manuscripts in a Bristol church and which were by the "lost" priest-poet Thomas Rowley, who supposedly lived in the 15th century. Chatterton was later exposed as a fraud, but many people wanted to believe the poems were authentic. Elsewhere, a revival of interest in older English and Scottish ballad forms prompted Keats to write "La Belle Dame Sans Merci" (1819). Sir Walter Scott helped set the popular taste and seemed to make the past come alive in historical novels such as *Rob Roy* (1817) and *Ivanhoe* (1819), which seemed lifelike in their detailed evocation of the past—even though they were hardly accurate. The medieval period was often used as color for gothic horror stories of persecution and imprisonment, including Clara Reeve's *The Old English Baron* (1778), Matthew Gregory Lewis's shocker *The Monk* (1796), and Charles Maturin's melodrama *Bertram* (1816). These were texts that helped shaped the conventions of the guilty male outsider, seen in works such as Byron's *Manfred* (1817) and Mary Shelley's *Frankenstein* (1818), but that were also parodied by Jane Austen in *Northanger Abbey* (1817) and by Thomas Love Peacock in *Nightmare Abbey* (1818), the latter drawing on the gothic to mock the ideas and pomposity of various Romantic intellectuals.

## BOUNDARIES AND CONTEXTS

Defining the boundaries—geographical *and* generic—of Romantic literature is difficult. A number of different "Romanticisms" exist and coexist. These different constructions of the term are the result of modern critical positions being constantly formed and held, challenged and subverted, but also of the vast range of writings from the period itself that bear its traces. Having said this, it *is* possible to pick out some recurring motifs. For example, Stuart Curran makes the point that the writers generally considered to be Romantics (Wordsworth, Coleridge, etc.) were "simply mad for poetry" (Curran 15). They shared a sense that existing efforts in the genre were often lazy, predictable, and insincere. They wanted to restore meaning to poetry and reverse the sterile conventionalities that produced (as they saw it) formulaic verse. They had no master plan, but in his introduction to the *Norton Anthology of English Literature,* M. H. Abrams flags five "critical principles" to which they adhered. According to Abrams, Romantic poetry is, first, notable for an idea that

poetry is not an "imitation of human life" but a representation of "the inner feelings of the author."

Second, the act of writing of poetry should be "spontaneous—that is, arising from impulse, and free from all rules and the artful manipulation of means to foreseen ends" (Abrams 7). A favourite image here was the poet as a skylark, soaring gracefully over the landscape.

Third, there was reverence for nature, seen as imbued with the spirit of God and unsullied by man. According to Abrams, the reader is often presented with natural objects "corresponding to an inner or a spiritual world [which] served also as the under structure for a tendency . . . to write symbolist poetry in which a rose, a sunflower, a mountain, a cave, or a cloud is presented as an object with significance beyond itself" (9). Thus, Wordsworth writes in "Lines written a Few Miles above Tintern Abbey" (1798) how "Nature" has become "[t]he anchor of my purest thoughts, the nurse / The guide, the guardian of my heart, and soul / Of all my moral being" (Abrams 109–111).

Fourth, Abrams notes a tendency to elevate "humble and rustic life," including "the ignominious, the outcast, and the delinquent" as a way of enlarging the reader's "imaginative sympathies" (9–10).

And fifth, there is the sense of a "supernatural" dimension, often reworking tales of mystery and magic, "set in the distant past or in faraway places, or both . . ." (11).

To Abrams's list we might add the cult of the child, a figure deemed to possess an unspoilt freshness and promise together with an extra-imaginative sense of vision; and also James Buzzard's idea of "sensation," which is "premised on its being not only intense but also unique, always 'for the first time'" (Buzzard 23).

Many of these elements are famously embodied in Wordsworth and Coleridge's *Lyrical Ballads*, which burst onto the scene in 1798. As Samuel Baudry points out in his essay in the present volume, this was the collection that "marked the onslaught of the battle of taste which accompanied the first decades of the 19th century." Trying to explain the impact of *Lyrical Ballads*, the critic William Hazlitt compared the collection to "the turning up of the fresh soil" (Hazlitt 1958; 14). This image was very deliberate, since Hazlitt was making reference to Wordsworth's "levelling" (that is, dem-ocratic) interest in the working "rustic" people of the countryside (as opposed to ladies and gentle-men). The collection is full of peasants, beggars, leech gatherers, shepherds, and others on the mar-gins of society. Some years later, when Coleridge recalled the driving forces behind the collection, he remembered how Wordsworth planned "to give the charm of novelty to the things of everyday," and this included "characters and incidents . . . as will be found in every village and its vicinity, where there is a meditative and feeling mind to seek after them . . ."—presumably Wordsworth's (Coleridge 2:6). Wordsworth himself claimed that he wanted poetry to shake off the "gaudy and inane phraseol-ogy" of popular poetry via a series of "experiments" (quoted in Miles 64). Coleridge, meanwhile, was to direct his attention to "persons and characters supernatural, or at least romantic" to which he was to give "human interest and a semblance of truth" (Coleridge 2:6) Coleridge's "The Rime of the Ancient Mariner" is perhaps the most celebrated example of this artistic mission. In his *Biographia Literaria* (1817), Coleridge writes:

> During the first year that Mr Wordsworth and I were neighbours our conversations turned frequently on the two cardinal points of poetry, the power of exciting the sympa-thy of the reader by a faithful adherence to the truth of nature, and the power of giv-ing the interest of novelty by the modifying colours of imagination. The sudden charm, which accidents of light and shade, which moonlight or sunset diffused over a known and familiar landscape, appeared to rep-resent the practicality of combining both. These are the poetry of nature. (Coleridge 2:5)

In declaring their poetic manifesto, Word-sworth and Coleridge, like others of their genera-tion, were self-consciously turning their back on existing ways of thinking that had emerged dur-ing the Enlightenment or the Age of Reason that emerged in Europe and America after the 1680s. Like the Romantics, the thinkers of the Enlighten-ment championed progress and liberty, but they also championed knowledge and understanding acquired through "reason," which was based on evidence and proof rather than religion or super-stition. The physical world was seen as "orderly, symmetrical and regular" (Halstead 10). "Natural" man was designed to act rationally and was also naturally good. If free from all artificial restraints—including the laws of church or state—and edu-cated in the right way, he or she would work for the benefit of others. In Britain John Locke (1632–1704) was one of the most famous exponents of this theory, and he emphasized the importance of "empiricism," "a belief in the world we can see and touch, or, in other words, we can experience" (Ruston 24). Also influential were Adam Smith (1723–90), David Hume (1711–66), and Jeremy Bentham (1748–1832), who themselves had been influenced by the French philosophers Voltaire (François-Marie Arouet) (1694–1778) and Denis Diderot (1713–84).

"Reason," however, could not provide all the answers—a point made by another philosopher, the Swiss-born Jean-Jacques Rousseau (1712–78). His famous declaration "Man is born free, but today he is everywhere in chains" (Rousseau 1954, 2) sat well with the growing dislike of oppressive government that was gaining impetus through the 18th century. Rousseau, however, rejected the worship of reason and mechanistic science, argu-ing that impulse and emotion were more powerful and that everyone was different. This was the key change as far as it affected the new younger gen-eration of writers and thinkers of the 1780s and 1790s. As Sharon Ruston puts it: "Rather than being primarily concerned with the rational, the Romantic period was fascinated with the irrational, the superstitious and mysterious; with madness, with feelings and with the imagination" (Ruston 23). The new emphasis was also much more on the subjective and the personal: "Myself alone. I feel my heart and I know men. I am not made like any of the ones I have seen," wrote Rous-seau in *The Confessions*. "If I am worth no more, at least I am different" (Rousseau 5). It is perhaps no coincidence that autobiography was another genre that acquired new importance at this time—encouraging the sense that the "artist" or "genius" had a special story to tell. There is a definite autobiographical flavour to some of the most famous Romantic works—not simply Wordsworth's famous poem *The Prelude* (subtitled *Growth of a Poet's Mind*) but also Mary Wollstonecraft's travelogue *Letters Written in Sweden, Norway, and Denmark* (1796) and Thomas De Quincey's *Confessions of An English Opium Eater* (1821). All exhibit to greater or lesser degree a belief, characteristic of many of those traditionally considered Romantics, in the uniqueness of the writer's own experience, originality, and individuality and in some cases, of course, their monumental self-absorption.

These shifts in intellectual thought—from head to heart—took place at a time when Britain—and indeed the rest of Europe—was going through difficult years. By the 1780s many held the view that freedom and justice were being trampled by repressive governments. Romantic writers can thus be seen as being fired by the major events of their day, including the revolutionary upheavals taking place on both sides of the Atlantic. This connectedness was a notion expounded by Thomas Love Peacock, who, in 1818, in "An Essay on Fashionable Literature," wrote of literary texts as objects born out of the historical moment: "As every age has its own character, manners and amusements, which are influenced even in their lightest forms by the fundamental features of the time, the moral and political character of the age of nation may be read by an attentive observer even in its lightest literature" (Peacock 8: 265). Such comments are significant because in some circles there has persisted the idea that Romantic writers were largely self-referential, not really interested in the events of the world around them—a charge levied at Wordsworth by Peacock, who described the poet as a "morbid dreamer . . . studiously ignorant of history society and human nature" (quoted in Ruston 107), and, of course, also levied at Jane Austen. This view was shared by some 20th-century critics as well. In *The Oxford Book of Light Verse*, produced in 1936, Auden suggested that, save for Byron, the Romantic poets "turned away from the life of their time to the contemplation of their own emotions and the creation of imaginary worlds: Wordsworth to nature, Keats . . . to a world of pure poetry, Shelley to a future Golden Age" (Auden x). For much of the mid-20th century, readings of texts based

on "New Criticism"—that is to say, readings that focused on form and language (especially symbol and imagery), claiming for literature a certain kind of scientific objectivity while simultaneously providing a retreat from the realm of social conflict—were much to the fore.

In fact, there were few Romantic writers who did not take an interest in political events and who were not engaged on some level with society around them—even John Keats, a writer generally seen as the most apolitical of the poets (Motion xxv). Romantic texts were produced during some of the most interesting but turbulent years in British history (1789–1832). One way to think of Romanticism is as "a period of political polarization, with politically radical writers such as William Godwin (1756–1836), Mary Wollstonecraft (1759–97), James Leigh Hunt (1784–1859) and John Thelwall (1764–1834) living in fear of imprisonment, their writings represented in the (conservative) Tory press as unpatriotic, immoral, blasphemous and seditious" (Russton 2–3). "Jacobins," a name associated with a French Revolutionary group, was the catch-all label bestowed by the Tory press for all radicals and would-be reformers, and these were the people whom the unpopular "Gagging Acts" of the late 1790s were designed to constrain. Then there were those such as William Blake, George Crabbe, William Cowper, and John Clare, who wrote about industrial and rural poverty, the breakup of old ways of life, and the laissez-faire capitalism that was turning "free" men into slaves. And far from being divorced from society, Wordsworth, in an unctuous 1801 letter to the politician Charles James Fox, explained that the poems "The Brothers" and "Michael" (copies of which he had sent to Fox) were "faithful copies from Nature . . . written with a view to show that men who do not wear fine clothes can feel deeply" (quoted in Knight 2:139). Alarmed at the destruction of family life "among the lower orders of society," Wordsworth attributed this breakdown to "the spreading of manufactures through every part of the country, by the heavy taxes upon postage, by workhouses, houses of industry, and the invention of soup-shops, &c," added to which was the "increasing disproportion between the price of labour and the necessaries of life." (quoted in

Knight 2:137). A few years later, Wordsworth's *The Prelude* (1805) described the British government as "vermin" who "leagu'd / Their strength perfidiously, to undermine / Justice, and make an end of liberty" (*Prelude* 10.654–657).

Wordsworth's comment about "liberty" reminds us that a key event of the period was the French Revolution in 1789. Although its literary influence is sometimes overstated, few writers could escape its implications. Blake was a fervent sympathizer, but Wordsworth was the only poet to visit France during the Revolutionary period. He landed at Calais on July 13, 1790, his arrival coinciding with the first anniversary of the storming of Paris's infamous Bastille prison, an event often seen as marking the moment when the Revolution really got underway. Wordsworth observed the celebrations of the people as they danced, drank, and sang into the night. It was as if a new age had begun: "France standing on top of golden hours / And human nature seeming born again" (*Prelude* b. 341–342). "Bliss was it in that dawn to be alive," he later recalled (*Prelude* 11.109). Earlier, in 1789, Richard Price, a British preacher, had suggested that the examples of the American and French Revolutions both demonstrated "the ardour for liberty catching and spreading . . . the dominion of kings changed for the dominion of laws, and the dominion of priests giving way to the dominion of reason and conscience" (quoted in McCalman 18).

The French Revolution had other implications beyond the political. It also sharpened historical consciousness, causing observers to reflect on past civilizations such as the Roman Empire. Moreover, the mood was not always celebratory. Many conservatives, including the orator and statesman Edmund Burke (1729–1797), thought the French Revolution posed a threat to Britain's "good order" (Burke 124). The massacre of prisoners in Paris in September 1792 and the execution of King Louis XVI and Queen Marie Antoinette in 1793 also provoked widespread revulsion, shaking many people's faith in the ideals of liberty, which the Revolution had seemed to promise—and doubly so when France began to flex her military might and launched a foreign policy of aggression toward her European neighbours. Coleridge's "Fears in Solitude" (1798) is one expression of disillusionment

about the way things were turning out, while in *Letters Containing a Sketch of the Politics of France* (1795), Helen Maria Williams (1762–1827) wrote of liberty as a virtuous young damsel "fallen into the hands of monsters, ignorant of her charms" (quoted in Cobban 368). As these and other works discussed in the present volume reveal, the impact of the Revolution on writers and thinkers of the time should not underestimated. Hugh Honour notes: "It revealed the complexity of what had previously seemed to be simple ideas—that ideals of personal and political liberty, for example, were not identical and could be mutually exclusive. It demonstrated the frailty of reason and the force of passion, the insufficiency of theories, and the power of circumstances to shape events" (19).

Back in Britain the "mad" King George III and his idle, spendthrift sons—immortalized by Shelley in his sonnet "England in 1819"—were viewed by some as being at the root of that country's problems. A kind of anarchy—symbolized by the king's lost mind—was spreading downward from the top. (Recent historians have made the point that that the king was not literally "mad" at all but suffering from porphyria, a metabolic imbalance affecting the nervous system.) In one of many gossipy newspaper accounts he was said to have addressed a tree, talking to it as if it were the king of Prussia. In Britain during the 1790s and early 1800s, economic, commercial, and political competition on the world stage from Germany and France—led for some of the time by Napoleon Bonaparte (whose staggering success and reputation as a man of "action" caused him to be viewed variously as an icon, a Byronic pirate, a wanderer, a Faust figure who had overreached himself, or a latter-day Julius Caesar)—together with the difficulties in maintaining Britain's overseas rule, did not always engender a sense of patriotism. Rather, it helped foster a sense that the country was being exhausted by expensive wars. It was not until the Battle of Waterloo in 1815, when British and German forces under the duke of Wellington defeated Napoleon I, that 23 years of almost uninterrupted war in Europe ended.

Nonetheless "change"—and bullishness about its possibilities—was part of the "Spirit of the Age" (to use William Hazlitt's famous phrase). It seemed to be everywhere. When Wordsworth returned to England at the end of 1792, he "found the air yet busy with the stir / Of a contention which had been raised up / Against the traffickers in Negro blood" (*Prelude* 1805, 10:204–206). An industrial revolution was evident in all most parts of the country, altering forever the look and sound of the country. People migrated from the countryside to the towns, creating large urban centres—Manchester, Birmingham, Liverpool Newcastle—and turning small towns into massive centres of wealth, activity, noise, and poverty. The campaigner Richard Oastler would later write indignantly of the "Yorkshire slavery" of male, female, and children mill workers "doomed to labour from morning to night for one who cares not how soon . . . weak and tender frames are stretched to breaking" (quoted in McCalman 145). By 1790 London, with its population of 1 million (and growing), had become the largest urban community in the world and the center of a rapidly expanding trade network, covering and claiming large parts of the globe, including Australia, New Zealand, and India—the seeming exoticism of which also provided a rich subject for writers. In London in 1791, the pamphleteer Thomas Paine (1737–1809) published his vision of the postrevolutionary state, *Rights of Man,* and had to flee the country, fearing prosecution. In the year 1792 Mary Wollstonecraft published *A Vindication of the Rights of Woman,* a powerful treatise arguing that women should not be raised to be weak, decorative, useless objects, but should instead be raised as rational creatures capable of contributing to the fulfilment of human virtue. For some, like clergyman Richard Polwhele, author of the poem "The Un-Sex'd Females" (1798), this was simply one step too far, but Wollstonecraft was joined by a growing band of women writers, including the poets Anna Barbauld (1743–1825) and Amelia Opie (1769–1853), the essayist and educator Hannah More (1745–1833), and the dramatists Elizabeth Inchbald (1753–1821) and Joanna Baillie (1762–1851)—women whose work was often praised and contained by the epithet *feminine,* but could also be read as *political.*

This interest in the historical and cultural contexts of Romantic writing forms part of a wider trend within literary studies by situating literature within history. Although this kind of work was initially associated most frequently with the study of Shakespeare and the English Renaissance, any period can be examined in this way. The transitional or "innovative" state of the late-18th and early 19th society in which Romantic writers operated has been seen to offer a good deal of potential for this kind of approach. A useful summary of the poetic activity of the period comes from Marilyn Butler. She argues that the Romantic poets fall into three groups:

> The first expresses a challenge from the still disenfranchised middle and provincial classes in the half-century before the French Revolution: it includes Blake and the early Wordsworth and Coleridge. The second, from the mid-1790s to about 1815 (the years when Britain was at war with post-revolutionary France), continues to use similar provincial landscapes and an accessible "natural" tone, but drastically revises the oppositional message in favour of a religiously orthodox, politically loyal one. This phase includes the mature work of Wordsworth and Coleridge. The third, from about 1812 to 1824, is much less distinctively provincial and democratic; indeed the poetic models of Byron and Shelley are as aristocratic as their social origins, though this does not prevent them challenging the policies of the British government more boldly and directly than their predecessors. (Butler 40–41)

Since the 1980s, work by Butler, Jerome McGann, Marjorie Levinson, Tim Fulford, and James Chandler has been influential in that it has helped set a precedent for viewing literary texts by Wordsworth, Austen, et. al. from the perspective of these wider social, economic, and political contexts, linking, for example, the events and characters of Jane Austen's 1818 novel *Persuasion* to the question of representation in all kinds of writings—newspaper reports, political speeches, journalism, medical texts, conduct books, novels—produced by her contemporaries. Thus, what some of the essays in the present volume emphasize is the extent to which Romantic writers are connected to the contemporary world, given the rise of a consumerist society, in that their poems or novels can be can be said to have been partly shaped by the social structures and ideological sources of the late 18th and early 19th centuries; urbanization and industrialisation; the destruction of the countryside; the debates over the slave trade; and conflict between the old and the new, between men and women, and between the declining older landowning classes and a new powerful social group—the professional middle class. A point made by many contributors is the extent to which poets such as Wordsworth and Blake quite clearly draw attention to their characters' positions within a society that is on the cusp of modernity and to the impingement of society on the development of the individual, male and female. By the end of his life, Wordsworth was railing against the spread of mass tourism and the arrival in the Lake District of one of the technologies of the Industrial Revolution in his poem "Suggested by the Proposed Kendal and Windermere Railway" (1844).

The emphasis on the female role in Romantic creativity is a relatively new development. As recently as 1997, Paula Feldman, an influential critic on women's writing, could justifiably claim of female Romantic poets that "their influence and even their existence has been largely unacknowledged . . . throughout most of the 20th century." A handful of male writers constituted the Romantic canon, with "[t]he women . . . so effectively 'not there' that they were even excluded from consideration as 'minor' poets," appearing in accounts of the period "at best as footnotes and at worst solely in familial relation to the 'major' male writers" (Feldman xxv; xxxii). Thirteen years later (2010), the situation has altered sharply. One of the biggest changes in critical understanding of Romanticism has been that prompted by the "rediscovery" of lost (female) voices and by feminist studies, and this is reflected in the present volume.

Before the 1980s the relative lack of serious studies of the Romantic writing by women originated out of two things: the belief that women had, at best, a modest talent for writing (see Lord Byron's patronizing comment of women writers that "as authoresses they can do no great harm" [quoted in Wu xix]); and the sense that their

works were not for "all time" but "of their time"—derivative, gushing, sentimental, prosaic, domestic, unambitious. *Cloying* was the term used by the late-19th century critic William Michael Rossetti to describe the "feminine poetry" of Felicia Hemans (1793–1835)—generally reckoned to be one of the most widely read poets of her day (Armstrong 15). In 1820 the *Edinburgh Review*—one of a number of influential journals to emerge during the period—was bestowing high praise when it reported: "The verses of Mrs Hemans appear the spontaneous offspring of intense and noble feeling, governed by a clear understanding, and fashioned into elegance by an exquisite delicacy and precision of taste." Moreover: "With more than the force of many of her masculine competitors she never ceases to be strictly *feminine* in the whole current of her thought and feeling, nor approaches by any chance, the verge of that free and intrepid course of speculation of which the boldness is more conspicuous than the wisdom, but into which some of the most remarkable among the female literati of our times have freely and fearlessly plunged" (quoted in Hemans p. 2).

This faintly dismissive attitude continued for much of the 20th century, and it was rare to find female poets featured in anthologies of Romantic verse. By the 1990s, however, the work of Roger Lonsdale, Duncan Wu, Stuart Curran, Andrew Ashfield, and Anne K. Mellor (among others) showed the possibility of extending the notion of "literary Romanticism" to include questions of female authorship, female identity and creativity, and also the kind of female social or political engagement that the *Edinburgh Review* seemed to disapprove of. As Paula Feldman points out, works such as Anna Laetitia Barbauld's "Eighteen Hundred and Eleven," Charlotte Smith's "Beachy Head" and Mary Tighe's "Psyche" "are virtuoso performances that can stand unblushingly alongside the most admired works by men of the period" (Feldman xxxi).

It has since become clear that allocating women writers a separate space that restricts itself to discussing women's roles or analyzing their representation in literary works underestimates their impact on the public and on other authors. Daniel Robinson, for example, terms Charlotte Smith's sonnets "the most copiously imitated poems of the last quarter of the century," their impact being felt by Coleridge and others (Robinson 114). In 1833 Wordsworth admitted that Smith "was a lady to whom English verse is under greater obligations than are likely to be either acknowledged or remembered" (quoted in Behrendt 196). Male-dominated criticism centered on the "big six" Romantic writers (Blake, Wordsworth, Coleridge, Byron, Shelley, Keats) is on the wane. The more modern tendency is to see the relative scarcity of information about women's roles in the Romantic movement as something that needs rectifying and makes women-centered studies more necessary.

Significantly, one of the most recent works on the Wordsworths is Frances Wilson's acclaimed *The Ballad of Dorothy Wordsworth* (2008), which overturns traditional views of its subject as an eccentric maiden aunt—"the perfect, selfless and sexless complement to her self-absorbed and humourless sibling" (10). An earlier book, Paula Byrne's *Perdita: The Life of Mary Robinson* (2004), is a detailed analysis of the life and work of another figure airbrushed out of literary historiography in which Byrne argues that Robinson's work, including her *Letter to the Women of England on the Injustice of Mental Subordination*, is worthy of as much attention as Mary Wollstonecraft's *A Vindication of the Rights of Woman*. If nothing else, such work reveals that it is very far from true that literary Romanticism lacks influential and interesting women participants.

## ABOUT THIS BOOK

The essays included in this volume cover writers and texts from the last quarter of the 18th century to the 1830s. By its very nature, any reference work dealing with such a range of writing can only offer a slice of the many different types of work produced during these years. This book is no exception, and the various readings offered here are intended to whet the reader's appetite. Special effort has been made to include writers who have been neglected as well as those who have long been regarded as central to the topic. The vast majority of those featured here were born in Great Britain or Ireland, or settled there. Writers featured include all the major Romantic poets and prose writers, as well as those who seem to stretch the boundaries of the

period but are also frequently regarded as Romantic, including Thomas Gray (1716–71), who influenced the generation of Romantic poets after him; and "Victorians" such as Elizabeth Barrett Browning (1806–61) and Emily Bronte (1818–48), whose status as "Romantics" has been much discussed. The book also brings together information on the historical and cultural contexts of British literary Romanticism, with essays on industrialism, the monarchy, the American and French Revolutions, childhood, slavery, the British Empire, science, and more. It also contains close analyses of individual poems, plays, and novels, as well as general overviews of particular subgenres (for example, the gothic novel, historical fiction, the "Lake School"). Most entries have further reading suggestions. Overall, the contents are intended to demonstrate something of the scope of British literary Romanticism in a way that is accessible to students and inspires them to return to the original texts.

### Further Reading

Abrams, M. H. *The Norton Anthology of English Literature.* 5th ed. Vol. 2. New York: Norton, 1986.

Armstrong, Isobel. "The Gush of the Feminine: How Can We Read Women's Poetry of the Romantic Period?" In *Romantic Women Writers: Voices and Countervoices,* edited by Theresa M. Kelley and Paula M. Feldman, 13–32. Hanover, N.H.: University of New England Press, 1995.

Auden, W. H. ed. *W. H. Auden's Book of Light Verse: An Anthology.* Oxford: Oxford University Press, 1938.

Behrendt, Stephen C. "Charlotte Smith, Women Poets and the Culture of Celebrity." In *Charlotte Smith and British Romanticism,* edited by Jacqueline Labbe, 189–202. London: Pickering and Chatto, 2008.

Bloom, Harold. *The Anxiety of Influence: A Theory of Poetry.* New York: Oxford University Press, 1973.

Burke, Edmund. *Reflections on the Revolution in France.* Edited by Connor Cruise O'Brien. London: Penguin, 1968.

Butler, Marilyn. "Romanticism in England." In *Romanticism in National Context,* edited by Roy Porter, and Mikulas Teich, 37–68. Cambridge: Cambridge University Press, 1988.

Buzzard, James. *The Beaten Track: European Tourism, Literature and Ways to Culture 1800–1918.* Oxford: Oxford University Press, 1993.

Cobban, A. *The Debate on the French Revolution 1789–1800.* London: Black, 1960.

Coleridge, Samuel Taylor. *Biographia Literaria; or Sketches of My Literary Life and Opinions.* 2 vols. edited by James Engell and W. Jackson Bate. Princeton, N.J.: Princeton University Press, 1982.

———. *Collected Letters.* 6 vols. Edited by Leslie Earl Griggs. Oxford: Clarendon Press, 1956–71.

Curran, Stuart. *Poetic Form and British Poetry.* New York: Oxford University Press, 1986.

Duncan, James, and Derek Gregory. *Writes of Passage: Reading Travel Narrative.* London: Routledge, 1999.

Feldman, Paula, ed. *British Women Poets of the Romantic Era: An Anthology.* London: John Hopkins University Press, 1997.

Hazlitt, William. *Lectures on the English Poets.* In *The Complete Works of William Hazlitt.* 5 vols. Edited by O. P. Howe. London: J. M. Dent, 1931.

Halstead, John B. *Romanticism* London: Macmillan, 1969.

———. *Selected Essays.* Edited by George Sampson. Cambridge: Cambridge University Press, 1958.

Hemans, Felicia. *The Domestic Affections.* Edited by Jonathan Wordsworth. New York: Woodstock, 1995.

Honour, Hugh. *Romanticism.* London: Penguin, 1979.

Jarvis, Robin. "Self-Discovery from Byron to Raban: The Long Afterlife of Romantic Travel." *Studies in Travel Writing* 9 (2005): 185–204.

Knight, William. *Letters of the Wordsworth Family from 1787–1855.* 3 vols. Boston: Ginn and Company, 1907.

McCalman, Lain, ed. *The Oxford Companion to the Romantic Age.* Oxford: Oxford University Press, 1999.

Miles, Robert. *Romantic Misfits.* London: Palgrave, 2008.

Motion, Andrew. *John Keats.* London: Faber, 1997.

Peacock, Thomas Love. *The Halliford Edition of the Works of Thomas Love Peacock.* 10 vols. Edited by H. F. B. Brett Smith and Gabriel Wells. London: Constable: 1924–34.

———. "The Four Ages of Poetry." In *The Norton Anthology of Theory and Criticism,* edited by V. B. Leitch, 684–694. New York: Norton, 2001.

Porter, Roy, and Mikulas Teich, eds. *Romanticism in National Context.* Cambridge: Cambridge University Press, 1988.

Robinson, Daniel. "Reviving the Sonnet: Women Romantic Poets and the Sonnet Claim." *European Romantic Review* 6 (1995): 98–127.

Rousseau, Jean-Jacques. *The Confessions and Correspondence.* Edited by Christopher Kelly, Roger D. Masters, and Peter G. Stillman. Hanover, N.H.: University Press of New England, 1995.

———. *The Social Contract.* Translated by W. Kendall. Chicago: Henry Regnery Co., 1954.

Ruston, Sharon. *Romanticism.* New York: Contiuum, 2007.

Scholes, Robert. *Textual Power: Literary Theory and the Teaching of English.* London: Yale University Press, 1985.

Shelley, Percy Bysshe. *Shelley's Poetry and Prose.* New York: Norton, 1977.

Wilson, Frances. *The Ballad of Dorothy Wordsworth. A Life.* London: Faber, 2008.

Wu, Duncan, ed. *Romantic Women Poets. An Anthology.* Oxford: Blackwell, 1997.

## Absentee, The  Maria Edgeworth (1812)

The last book in MARIA EDGEWORTH's series *Tales of Fashionable Life*, *The Absentee* tells the story of the Clonbronies, a family of Irish absentee landlords who, through the intervention of their son, Lord Colambre, return to Ireland to take their proper place as responsible landowners. *The Absentee* is also a "national" novel—a work of fiction that ideally depicts a "modern society with all its parts functioning in their real-life relations to one another" and a form that takes the novel's central character and places him or her in the appropriate social context. Though *The Absentee* is the story of one family's reformation, it has wider implications for political reformation in Ireland and England.

The novel opens with Colambre fresh from Cambridge University and waiting to come of age in London. His initiation into his parents' fashionable life disgusts and dismays him. His mother, once a good and valued lady patroness on her Irish estates, has become a woman whose social-climbing ambitions threaten to ruin their estate. Colambre' father, Lord Clonbrony, is similarly degraded in London, the absence of his Dublin friends forcing him to associate with men of dubious character and education.

Colambre's disillusionment with fashionable life results in a quest for a more purposeful existence. Armed with his friend Sir James Brooke's motto "deeds not words," he searches for his vocation on an undercover mission to the family estates. Colambre finds a thriving estate at Colambre, capably managed by the significantly named Mr. Burke. This is not the case at his family's main property Clonbrony where the corrupt agents Old Nick and St. Dennis Garraghty take advantage of Lord Clonbrony's absence to embezzle rents and terrorize the tenants. The abuses suffered by the Clonbrony tenants are exemplified by the Garraghty brothers' plot to evict Widow O'Neil in favor of one of their minions.

Ousting corrupt agents, however, is only a part of saving the Clonbrony estate. The reformation that Colambre orchestrates forms the foundation for an improved society, a new direction for the nation that the novel presents. Colambre requires a partner to consolidate this shift, to transmit new ideals to a next generation. His eventual partner, his impoverished Catholic cousin Grace Nugent, can be seen to represent Ireland's original ruling class supplanted by the English colonists (like Edgeworth's own family), many of whom rule over their estates in absentia. Their marriage suggests a new model for a union between England and Ireland that is based on not just mutual respect but also a more equal and reciprocal relationship.

See also *BELINDA; CASTLE RACKRENT*.

### Further Reading

Beesemyer, Irene. "'I thought I never set my eyes on a finer figure of a man': Maria Edgeworth Scrutinizes Masculinity in *Castle Rackrent, Ennui,* and *The Absentee*." In *New Essays on Maria Edgeworth,* edited by Julie Nash, 109–129. Aldershot, Eng.: Ashgate, 2006.

Butler, Marilyn. *Maria Edgeworth: A Literary Biography.* Oxford: Clarendon, 1972.

Corbett, Mary Jean. "Public Affections and Familial Politics." *ELH* 61 (1994): 877–897.

Edgeworth, Maria. *The Absentee.* Oxford: Oxford University Press, 2001.

—Megan Woodworth

### "Adonais" Percy Bysshe Shelley (1821)

"Adonais" is a pastoral elegy consisting of 55 Spenserian stanzas (eight iambic pentameters plus an iambic hexameter rhyming *ababbcbcc*) in which PERCY BYSSHE SHELLEY laments the death of JOHN KEATS. It is preceded by a preface detailing the occasion of its composition, the place of burial of the young poet in Rome, the condemnation in the anonymous review of Keats's ENDYMION published in the *Quarterly* (attributed by Shelley to ROBERT SOUTHEY) accused of having provoked the young man's death, and an homage to artist Joseph Severn for taking care of Keats till his final breath. The young poet was, however, too sick with tuberculosis and had to stop in Rome (September 1820), where he died in February 1821. Shelley started writing the elegy immediately upon learning of Keats's death (April 1821). Although he judged the poem "better than anything that I have yet written, & worthy both of him & of me" and even "a highly wrought piece of art," it sold very poorly (about 100 copies). It is now recognized for its artistry and Shelley's mastery of the genre of the pastoral elegy, already illustrated by the ancient Greek poet Moschus's "Elegy for Bion" and the Elizabethan Edmund Spenser's "Astrophel" on the death of Sir Philip Sidney.

Critics have come to agree on the scholar Earl Wasserman's interpretation of the poem's structure: three sections consisting respectively of 17, 21, and 17 stanzas (although Donald Reiman distinguishes three parts of nine, three, and nine stanzas in the middle section). Michael Scrivener thus sums up the argument "part one (stanzas 1–17) is a lamentation; part two (18–38) offers several consolations to the mourners; part three (39–55) is the triumphant celebration of Adonais's spirit immortally reborn in the living imagination as his spirit returns to the 'One'" (Scrivener 273).

The name given to Keats in the elegy, Adonais, has been identified as a syncretic mix between the Greek god Adonis and the Hebrew name for God: Adonai. Indeed, the poem contains many references to the fertility rites with which Adonis was associated in antiquity. However, the reference to the only God of the Bible may be explained by Shelley's Neoplatonism, which is at its peak in the elegy. At any rate, the mingling of the two references testifies to the syncretism of the second generation of Romantics who were fond of merging various mythologies. Earl Wasserman, Ross Woodman, and Milton Wilson all see the poem as the triumph of Shelley's idealism and the clearest example of his choice of the afterlife over life. Michael Scrivener, to the contrary, tries to reconcile Shelley the radical with Shelley the Platonist in his reading of the poem: ". . . Shelley wanted death to provide what life had not, but he unwaveringly maintained his scepticism on the issue. Desire for immortality is clearly present in Adonais, particularly in the third part, but the Neoplatonic One to which the postmortal spirit returns . . . must be understood as a poetically useful fiction" and sees *Adonais* as "another defense of imagination" (Scrivener 272–273).

Of course, Adonais's eternal life is also Keats's continued (albeit posthumous) existence through his verse, thanks to Shelley's elegy. Lamented by Urania (the muse of astrology), an allegory of poetry symbolically embodying his mother, the dead Keats is implicitly compared to Christ after the crucifixion. The poem mimics ancient fertility rites by announcing and performing the resurrection of the dead poet: the flowers in the poem growing on and out of a corpse are a built-in metaphor of the elegy itself, which revives the memory of John Keats, allowing his poetry to live forever through the homage paid by a fellow poet.

Despite its terrible reception by critics, who deemed it unreadable and sometimes unintelligible, Shelley not only had a very high opinion of "Adonais"—"I confess I should be surprised if that poem were born to an immortality of oblivion"—he also went to the trouble of supervising the printing of it in Pisa rather than send the manuscript to England. The whole process took him 27 days, which shows the high hopes he had put in the work. Unappreciated, like Keats, by the literary public of the day, Shelley, "Who in another's fate now wept his own" (l. 300), wished to share the same undying fame he believed would accrue to Keats. Two years later, after a tempest caused his fishing boat to wreck, Shelley was buried in the same Roman cemetery described in the preface in these words: "It might make one in love with death, to think that one should be buried in so sweet a place."

## Further Reading

Bloom, Harold. *Shelley's Mythmaking.* New Haven, Conn.: Yale University Press, 1959.

Peck, Walter Edwin. *Shelley: His Life and Work.* London: Ernest Benn Limited, 1927.

Scrivener, Michael. *Radical Shelley: The Philosophical Anarchism and Utopian Thought of Percy Bysshe Shelley.* Princeton, N.J.: Princeton University Press, 1982.

Shelley, Percy Bysshe. *Shelley's Poetry and Prose.* Edited by Donald H. Reiman and Neil Fraistat. New York: Norton, 2001.

Wasserman, Earl. *Shelley: A Critical Reading.* Baltimore, Md.: Johns Hopkins University Press, 1971.

Wilson, Milton. *Shelley's Later Poetry.* New York: Columbia University Press, 1959.

Woodman, Ross. *The Apocalyptic Vision in the Poetry of Shelley.* Toronto: Toronto University Press, 1964.

—Aurelie Thiria-Meulemans

## "Ae Fond Kiss"  Robert Burns (1791)

Ever since ROBERT BURNS composed "Ae Fond Kiss" in December 1791 and published it the following year in *The Scots Musical Museum*, the song has remained one of the poet's most popular works. Written from a male perspective, "Ae Fond Kiss" represents the parting of two lovers who will never meet again. In 1809, WALTER SCOTT described the song's fourth stanza (lines 13–16) as "exquisitely affecting," stating that it "contains the essence of a thousand love tales" (quoted in Low 1974, 208). Many contemporary critics have agreed with Scott's assessment of "Ae Fond Kiss." G. Ross Roy has called it "one of the greatest love songs in

the language" (Roy 32), while David Daiches has stated that the song is "among his masterpieces of its kind; in it, with the skill so characteristic of his love poetry at its best, [Burns] reduces everything to one basic and overpowering emotion, the emotion of having loved and now having to part" (Daiches 235).

One undeniable attraction readers have had to "Ae Fond Kiss" is its thinly veiled autobiographical content. In December 1791 a very intriguing and peculiar relationship in Burns's life was coming to an end. He had met Agnes Maclehose in December 1787 in Edinburgh during his visit there to oversee the republication of his collection *Poems, Chiefly in the Scottish Dialect*. Originally published in Kilmarnock in 1786, this collection had earned Burns an almost immediate fame and had prompted his Edinburgh trip. Once in the Scottish capital, he found himself encountering a very different social set than he had been accustomed to in Kilmarnock. Edinburgh's "high society" of aristocrats, literati, and other prominent people feted the "ploughman poet" in high style. Agnes Maclehose, a married gentlewoman with poetic leanings, was a member of this class who was drawn to Burns. Their meeting and subsequent relationship not only produced "Ae Fond Kiss" but also a number of letters, poems, and songs that testified to their passionate feelings for each other.

Owing to social conventions of the day, the relationship between Burns and Maclehose was doomed from the start. Not only was there a profound class difference separating the pair, but Maclehose was unhappily married with little option for divorce. She was the mother of three children, and her husband had left her in Scotland and emigrated to Jamaica. Consequently, she was unable to pursue other socially legitimate relationships (although her husband quickly acquired a mistress in Jamaica). Burns, meanwhile, was in the midst of considerable difficulties in his relationships with women at this time in his life; he had already fathered four children, two of them with Jean Armour. During his time in Edinburgh, he and Jean were estranged, although she was caring for their children in Ayrshire. Given the similarity of their interests, it seems almost inevitable that

Burns and Maclehose were drawn to each other upon meeting at the house of a mutual friend. As the academic and author Carol McGuirk has remarked, "[Maclehose] and the poet understood each other very well. They were drawn together by their shared consciousness of being on the fringes of polite society" (Burns 1993, 270). Their meeting initiated a heated correspondence between the two that lasted until December 1791; over the course of this letter exchange, Burns and Maclehose engaged in "a kind of verbal sexuality, in which they . . . proceeded to consummate their love in discourse" (Daiches 235).

In their letters the pair assumed names drawn from the language of pastoral poetry; McGuirk comments that "they both needed this fresh start in a pastoral world" (Burns 1993, 270). Using the name Sylvander, Burns addressed letters, poems, and songs to Clarinda, his fictional name for Maclehose. "Ae Fond Kiss" was the last work in this remarkable series, recording Burns's disappointment that Clarinda was leaving not only Sylvander but Scotland as well. Maclehose had decided to depart for Jamaica in order to join her husband, but this did not end happily for her. By December 1791 Burns had reconciled with Jean and was living with her and his children in Dumfries and working as an excise collector. The song records his disappointment about the futility of his relationship with Maclehose and, as the Burns editor James Kinsley notes, was "probably suggested by [Robert] Dodsley's *The Parting Kiss*: 'One fond kiss before we part, / Drop a tear and bid adieu; / Tho' we sever, my fond Heart / Till we meet shall pant for you'" (Burns 1968, 3:1,379). The Burns editors Andrew Noble and Patrick Scott Hogg suggest that if Dodsley's song "[were] the ore, Burns has transmuted it into one of his most golden lyrics" (Burns 2001, 375).

"Ae Fond Kiss" displays Burns's impressive ability to work within Scottish and English traditions. Unlike many of his other popular works, the song contains only a limited number of Scots words (six) and employs much conventional 18th-century poetic diction. The first stanza records the speaker's emphatic distress upon the prospect of parting with his lover: "Ae fond kiss, and then we sever; / Ae farewell, and then for

ever! / Deep in heart-wrung tears I'll pledge thee, / Warring sighs and groans I'll wage thee" (Burns 1968, 2:591, ll. 1–4). Burns's use of sentimental imagery ("heart-wrung tears," "warring sighs and groans") is amplified over the course of the song, particularly in the second stanza, where the "star of hope" (l. 6) offers the speaker "nae cheerful twinkle" (l. 7). Instead, he finds that "dark despair around benights me" (l. 8). The middle of the poem (particularly the fourth stanza) introduces the cause of the speaker's despair, highlighting the inevitability and impossibility of his love for "Nancy," as he calls her (l. 10): "Had we never lov'd sae kindly, / Had we never lov'd sae blindly! / Never met—or never parted, / We had ne'er been broken-hearted" (ll. 13–16). Agreeing with Walter Scott's judgment of the song, Kinsley claims that the song "owes its popularity" to these lines (Burns 1968, 3:1,379).

In his analysis of "Ae Fond Kiss," Roy states that "these lines [13–16] were written after Burns realized that nothing could ever come of his feelings for Clarinda; with great art he avoided overstepping the bounds of nostalgia into maudlin sentimentality" (Roy 32). John Purser disagrees, arguing that "'Ae fond kiss' considered as a poem is something of a mixed bag. 'Warring sighs and groans,' 'Peace Enjoyment Love and Pleasure' are not the stuff of personal feeling. They are standard guff of cheap valentine and they have their source in the kind of stuff Dodsley was writing" (Purser 332). An important element to recognize about "Ae Fond Kiss," though, is the fact that it is a song written to a specific tune. That tune is "Rory Dall's Port," and the tempo is meant to be "slow and tender" (Burns 1968, 2:591). As Kinsley explains, "Rory Dall was the cognomen of the harpers of Macleod of Skye. 'Port' is [a] Gaelic" word for Celtic song (Burns 1968, 3:1,379). As with so many of his other songs, Burns adapted or wrote lyrics to fit existing folk melodies; Purser comments that the tune "Rory Dall's Port" is "truly lovely, perfectly shaped and balanced by a varied symmetry" (Purser 331). As a result, Purser claims that "once you sing ['Ae Fond Kiss'], it all coheres, the good and the mediocre" (332).

The song's last stanza repeats the plaintive farewell of the first, gaining urgency and added sadness in the speaker's desire for "ae fond kiss" before he and his lover "sever" (line 21). The parting of Burns and Maclehose truly was sad in at least a sentimental way: Each had to deny the other in order to conform to social obligations. However, their split had occurred even before Burns wrote "Ae Fond Kiss," when Maclehose discovered that Burns had impregnated her maid, Jenny Clow. Such a glaring intrusion of sexuality offended "Clarinda," who not long after decided to join her husband in Jamaica. She promptly returned to Scotland, though, when she found that her husband not only refused to leave his mistress but would not even greet his wife at the port.

Burns lived out the remainder of his life in Dumfries, dying at the age of 37 in 1796. "Clarinda" never forgot the poet, whom she outlived by 45 years. Writing in her journal about 40 years after Burns sent her "Ae Fond Kiss," Maclehose recorded the following: "This day I can never forget. Parted with Burns, in the year 1791, never more to meet in this world. Oh, may we meet in Heaven!" (quoted in Low 1996, 108). Such sentiments testify to the enduring power of love songs like Burns's "Ae Fond Kiss."

**Further Reading**

Burns, Robert. *The Canongate Burns: The Complete Poems and Songs of Robert Burns.* Edited by Andrew Noble and Patrick Scott Hogg. Edinburgh: Canongate Classics, 2001.

———. *The Poems and Songs of Robert Burns.* 3 vols. Edited by James Kinsley, Oxford: Oxford University Press, 1968.

———. *Robert Burns: Selected Poems.* Edited by Carol McGuirk. New York: Penguin, 1993.

Daiches, David. *Robert Burns.* 1950. Reprint, Glasgow: Humming Earth, 2009.

Low, Donald. "Nature's Social Union and Man's Dominion: Robert Burns after Two Hundred Years." In *Love and Liberty, Robert Burns: A Bicentenary Celebration,* edited by Kenneth Simpson, 105–110. East Lothian, Scotland: Tuckwell, 1996.

———, ed. *Critical Essays on Robert Burns.* London: Routledge and Kegan Paul, 1975.

———, ed. *Robert Burns: The Critical Heritage.* London: Routledge and Kegan Paul, 1974.

Purser, John. "'The Wee Apollo': Burns and Oswald." 326–333.

Roy, G. Ross. "Robert Burns: A Self-Portrait." *Critical Essays* 13–38.

—Corey E. Andrews

## "Alice Fell" William Wordsworth (1807)

A work of 60 lines arranged in 15 stanzas of four lines each, "Alice Fell" first appeared in WILLIAM WORDSWORTH's *Poems, in Two Volumes* (1807). Like "WE ARE SEVEN" (published in *Lyrical Ballads,* 1798), the poem features a lengthy verbal exchange between an adult male speaker and a very young female child. But the orphan Alice Fell, unlike the little girl of "We Are Seven," has experienced an immediate, heart-wrenching crisis. The speaker first recounts how he helps to resolve this crisis and then describes the compassionate act he performs for Alice in the hope that his benefaction may open a new day for the impoverished child.

While traveling at night by chaise (a closed vehicle drawn by horses), the speaker hears "a lamentable sound" (l. 4) on the wind and commands his driver to stop the carriage (ll. 9–10). The mournful voice, though, has quieted, and the journey resumes amid silence (ll. 11–14). Almost at once, the cryptic sound resumes. The speaker now investigates outside and finds Alice, who weeps because her treasured cloak is caught in one of the chaise's wheels (ll. 17–28). Adult and child work successfully to free the garment (l. 31); this achieved, the two sit together in the chaise as it continues on toward Durham (a city in northern England and home to a celebrated Romanesque cathedral). But the cloak has been nearly destroyed. Alice sobs inconsolably as she tells her companion that she is "fatherless and motherless" (l. 44) and so considers herself a child of the town and its people: "And I to Durham, Sir, belong" (l. 45). Upon arriving in Durham, the speaker entrusts Alice to an innkeeper and provides money to replace the child's ruined garment (ll. 53–56). The poem closes high-spiritedly: "Proud Creature was she the next day, / The little Orphan, Alice Fell!" (ll. 59–60).

Because the speaker acts out of a sense of noblesse oblige, "Alice Fell" raises questions regarding class relations during the Romantic period in England. Although it closely retells a personal anecdote that Robert Grahame, a Glasgow lawyer and friend, shared with William and DOROTHY WORDSWORTH in February 1802 (Wordsworth 2002, 70), the author imagines the plight of the poor in miniature without envisioning an answer for poverty beyond random upper-class altruism facilitated by individual wealth. Still, the poem's speaker intervenes effectively and with alacrity in the crisis at hand and so brightens Alice's dark life, at least for the moment. "Alice Fell" thus hints at conflicts in Wordsworth's social thinking and perhaps indicates that the poet had taken a step away from his youthful radicalism and a step toward the Tory conservatism of his later years.

### Further Reading

Wordsworth, Dorothy. *The Grasmere and Alfoxden Journals.* Edited by Pamela Woof. Oxford: Oxford University Press, 2002.

Wordsworth, William. *The Major Works.* Edited by Stephen Gill. Oxford: Oxford University Press, 2000.

———. *Poems, in Two Volumes, and Other Poems, 1800–1807.* Edited by Jared Curtis. Ithaca, N.Y., and London: Cornell University Press, 1983.

—Tim Ruppert

## Almqvist, Carl Jonas Love (1793–1866)

Born on November 28, 1793, in Ed, near Stockholm, Sweden, Carl Jonas Love Almqvist's life was replete with scandals and unsuccessful projects, but his literary legacy, in both its quantity and diversity, is matched by few in Swedish literature. After graduating from Uppsala University in 1815, Almqvist worked as a clerk in Stockholm (1815–23). After a failed attempt to live as a farmer (1824–25), he returned to the Swedish capital and eventually became the principal of a boys' school (1829–40). He became a well-known writer around mid-1830s, and during the 1840s he worked as a journalist for a number of liberal periodicals. He fled to the United States in 1851 after being accused of poisoning his creditor. He died in Branen, Germany, while traveling back to Sweden, on September 26, 1866.

Throughout his life Almqvist was a politically controversial and radical writer, perhaps more so than his British Romantic counterparts. One of his recurring themes was the fostering of the nation: Almqvist advocated a national revival through the education of youth and promotion of patriotic sentiments. He was characteristically outspoken in the novel *It's Alright* (*Det går an*, 1839), which attacks the traditional view of marriage as determined by legal obligations and sanctioned by the church; it also exposes the economic politics that prevented women from gaining true independence. These aspects of the novel generated a fierce debate on the nature of marriage. In addition, Almqvist was interested in religious mysticism, the result of an interest in the 18th-century Swedish mystic Emanuel Swedenborg and a familial background in the Herrnhut-Moravian Church, a Protestant revival movement that preaches an intimate relationship to Christ. Metaphysical drama *Amorina* (1839), which provides one example of his mystical orientation, incest motifs, madness, religious fervor, and social critique merge together into a "poetic fugue" of unusual intensity.

Almqvist's most studied work is *The Book of the Briar Rose* (*Törnrosens bok*, 1832–40). Published in 13 volumes, it consists of poems, several novels, short stories, essays, and musical and dramatic pieces; thus, it is paradoxically encyclopedic and fragmentary at the same time. On the one hand, the multitude of genres embodies the idea of poetry as total literature; on the other, this totalizing tendency is constantly counteracted by such fragmentizing elements as metafictional comments and changes of narrator and genre. Of these texts, the novel *The Queen's Diadem* (*Drottningens juvelsmycke,* 1834) stands out. The central figure is a poetical character Tintomara, an androgynous ballet dancer who is both destructive and a source of confusion.

### Further Reading

Hermansson, Gunilla. *At fortælle verden: En studie i C.J.L. Almqvists Törnrosens bok.* Hellerup, Denmark: Spring, 2006.

Romberg, Bertil. *Carl Jonas Love Almqvist: Liv och verk.* Stockholm: Ordfront, 1993.

———. *Carl Jonas Love Almquist.* Translated by Sten Liden. Boston: Twayne Publishers, 1977.

Svedjedal, Johan. *Carl Jonas Love Almqvists författarliv 1793–1833*. Stockholm: Wahlström & Widstrand, 2007.

—Ljubica Miočević

### *America: A Prophecy* William Blake (1793)

WILLIAM BLAKE's method of composite art, consisting of the combination of poem text and illustrations, together with the themes he develops in *America*, link this long poem both to VISIONS OF THE DAUGHTERS OF ALBION and to the other continental prophecies (Albion, *Europe: A Prophecy* and *The Song of Lus*). The poem focuses on revolution as the apocalyptic revelation of God in history to rescue oppressed mankind from despotism. In doing so it superimposes the AMERICAN REVOLUTION of the 1770s on events in France in the 1780s. America becomes the site of the experience of a revolutionary energy that will inspire all subsequent revolts.

Thematically, *America* follows *Visions of the Daughters of Albion* insofar as the struggle is directed against political and sexual repression at the same time. It also leads up to *Europe* because the historical revolution moves from the American colonies enslaved by the British king George III (see MONARCHY) to the European countries ruled by political absolutism. Blake's intense engagement with the sociopolitical atmosphere of his time is exhibited by many references to historical events. However, the poem is visionary rather than realistic, thus taking on a more universal significance. Contemporary figures, such as the king, George Washington, and Benjamin Franklin are mythologized: George III, for example, becomes Albion's Angel, an advocate of Urizen, the spirit of oppression, repression, and all restrictions on freedom.

Orc is the central character, embodying the force of revolution/revelation opposing Urizen's despotic, patriarchal power. He is often associated with Jesus Christ as described in the Gospel according to Matthew—namely, the supreme fighter, whose sword will put an end to all injustices. Blake's Orc is the highest transgressor, the vitalistic demon of revolt who wants to create a new world relying on unbounded energy, as it is not angels but demons that are godlike in the poet's imagination. The snake, which is both Jesus' early Christian icon and a phallic symbol in ancestral religions, is also Orc's icon. It is depicted on the flags of the American rebels, whose rescue from British oppression runs parallel to the young demon's emancipation from his mother through a fierce embrace (Preludium). In the later plates illustrating the poem, Blake portrays the awful conditions of the American colonies via the violent struggle that Orc and his fellow demons wage against the angels of political and religious conservatism while devastating flames are raging. Fire has a double meaning in Blake's poetics: As another of Orc's symbols, it recalls the fire of the Apocalypse, foreshadowing a new world to come; but it can also be the symbol of counterrevolution, if revolt should not be raised to the level of a mental fight for the spiritual rebirth of mankind. Counterrevolutionary power appears in Urizen's guise in the last plate, overshadowing Orc's fire and the hopes he embodies. But Urizen is not the winner: Orc will rise again 12 years later, in 1789, in *Europe*.

### Further Reading

Behrendt, Stephen. "This Accursed Family: Blake's *America* and the American Revolution." *The Eighteenth Century: Theory and Interpretation* 27 (1986): 26–51.

Corti, Claudia. *Rivoluzione e rivelazione: William Blake tra profeti, radicali e giacobini*. Napoli: Giannini, 2000. In

Erdman, David. "Blake: Prophet Against Empire," Princeton, N.J.: Princeton University Press, 1977.

—Valeria Pellis

## American Revolution

Though the term is often used interchangeably with the American War of Independence, the American Revolution was also an ideological revolution that began long before independence was declared in 1776 and continued beyond the Peace of Paris in 1783. While most of the philosophies and ideologies that informed the Revolution can be traced to the intellectual period known as the Enlightenment, its focus on the natural rights of individual citizens and an emerging sense of nationalism were profound influences on the Romantic movement.

The road to American independence can be traced to the 1760s and the aftermath of the Seven Years' War (1757–63) between Great Britain and France that effectively ejected the French from North America. By bringing colonizer and colonists into close proximity, the Seven Years' War led to disillusionment on both sides. British generals and officials saw the colonists as unhelpful, even uninterested, in the war effort and believed it unfair that Britain alone shouldered the expense of their defense. This, coupled with the enormous cost of the war, prompted Parliament, who had up to this point allowed the thirteen colonies to essentially govern themselves without much interference, to create a series of taxation acts, beginning with the Stamp Act in 1765. "No taxation without representation" became the rallying cry of this early period of the Revolution, but the distancing that occurred between colony and mother country was more complex.

Americans were increasingly disgusted with Britain in the years following the Seven Years' War. The year 1763 saw an end to Britain's policy of benevolent noninterference and an increase in the military and bureaucratic establishment populated with men more interested in lining their own pockets than attending to the concerns of the colonists they were meant to protect and serve. Furthermore, as the historian William H. Goetzmann notes, the Stamp Act affected the rising elite—merchants, lawyers, and writers whose documents were required to bear the king's stamp; these were the same men who found the corruption of the king's representatives to be in direct contravention of their concept of the classical republican roots of British society.

The American colonists defined themselves as Englishmen and believed they were entitled the same rights as freeborn Englishmen. Indeed, they regarded themselves as better citizens because they were less corrupted by the excesses of imperial wealth and the luxury evident in English high society. Their desire for a more accountable, virtuous government was motivated by a love of liberty, an old English value that the Americans claimed for their own. The British attempted to subdue their discontented colonists with harsh regulations and surveillance, solutions that only enraged the colonists and forced their ideological revolution to its logical, armed conclusion.

The fighting started at Concord and Lexington in 1775, but war was not officially declared until July 4, 1776, with the Declaration of Independence. Early on, British victory seemed certain; however, General Burgoyne's stunning loss at Saratoga, New York, in October 1777 signaled a turning of the tide in favor of the colonial armies and their allies, which included France from 1778 with the Treaty of Amity and Commerce. Facing highly motivated citizen soldiers by land and a French navy intent on revenge by sea, an undermanned, underfunded, and overconfident Britain soon found itself facing the loss of most of its North American colonies, while the French threatened invasion at home. Hostilities effectively ended after an exhausted southern army under the command of General Cornwallis surrendered to the American general George Washington at Yorktown, Virginia, in 1781, though fighting continued and peace negotiations were not concluded until 1783 in Paris. The American Revolution continued beyond the end of the war as the men who came to be known as the Founding Fathers had to determine how the new American nation should be governed.

The quest for American self-definition and self-government began with the Declaration of Independence, in which Thomas Jefferson summoned the authority of natural law and of the English liberal and Scottish Enlightenment traditions: "We hold these truths to be self-evident, that all men are created equal, that they are endowed by their Creator with certain inalienable Rights, that among these are Life, Liberty and the pursuit of Happiness.—That to secure these rights, Governments are instituted among men, deriving their just powers from the consent of the governed,—That whenever any form of Government becomes destructive of these ends, it is the Right of the People to alter or to abolish it, and to institute new Government . . ." The Declaration goes on the enumerate the wrongs committed by the king and Parliament and the ways in which their tyrannical impingement on the rights of the American colonists has forced them to this point and made their declaration inevitable. With this as their ideological framework, the Founding Fathers later structured the government of the United States with the U.S. Constitution in 1787.

The Founding Fathers' desire to form a more perfect union in the name of and for the people is both the apotheosis of Lockean (see LOCKE, JOHN) and Enlightenment political and social philosophy and forms the foundation of the Romantic movement. Though in this case, as in the FRENCH REVOLUTION, "the people" excluded significant segments of the population, including women, Native Americans, and African-American slaves, belief in the fundamental and inalienable rights of individuals and opposition to tyranny provided inspiration to rising generations of writers, philosophers, and revolutionaries. These individuals, who included the Romantics, sought to complete 18th-century revolutions and extend the rights claimed by the American colonists to the women, native peoples, and slaves excluded by Enlightenment precedent.

### Further Reading

Dickinson, H. T. *Britain and the American Revolution.* London: Longman, 1989.

Conway, Stephen. *The British Isles and the War of American Independence.* Oxford: Oxford University Press, 2000.

Goetzmann, William H. *Beyond the Revolution: A History of American Thought from Paine to Pragmatism.* New York: Basic Books, 2009.

Gould, Eliga H. *The Persistence of Empire: British Political Culture in the Age of Empire.* Chapel Hill: University of North Carolina Press, 2000.

Marshall, P. J. *The Making and Unmaking of Empires*: Britain, India and America c. 1750–1783. Oxford: Oxford University Press, 2005.

White, R. S. *Natural Rights and the Birth of Romanticism in the 1790s.* Houndsmills: Palgrave, 2005.

—Megan Woodworth

## "Anecdote for Fathers" William Wordsworth (1798)

WILLIAM WORDSWORTH stages a conversation between a father and his son Edward in this short poem from LYRICAL BALLADS. At first glance the dialogue seems like a model teaching moment:

The father questions his son about the relative merits of Liswyn Farm, the pastoral locale where they are currently situated, and Kilve, the speaker's channel-side home. The son answers that he would rather be at Kilve but cannot give a reason why. The father persists "five times" in asking, "Why? Edward, tell me why?" (l. 48). Struggling to formulate a reason, Edward notices a weather vane on housetop and grasps at this arbitrary object to explain: "At Kilve there was no weather-cock, / And that's the reason why" (ll. 55–56). As the poem closes, the speaker realizes that he has learned much more from the child than the child has learned from him, a typical outcome of many of Wordsworth's poems featuring children.

The subtitle of the poem, "shewing how the art of lying may be taught," points blame at the father for pushing the son to answer a question that he is unable to answer. The scholar Alan Richardson explains that the father's question "implies a cognitive response" but "demands instead the performative response of a catechism" (Richardson 68). The five-year-old son does not have the capacity to rationalize his predilection for Kilve over Liswyn farm. Edward is much more like the young Wordsworth described in "LINES WRITTEN A FEW MILES ABOVE TINTERN ABBEY" who thoughtlessly "like a roe / . . . bounded o'er the mountains" and reveled in the "dizzy raptures" of nature than the adult Wordsworth who, in "Tintern Abbey," mediates the experience of nature with his imagination, learns other lessons from it, and hears "the still sad music of humanity." The boy is not like his father, who experiences the happy day walking on the farm to the degree that he can "bear / To think, and think, and think again" (13–14) but instead gains pleasure from the first-hand experience of the natural world.

While the poem surely teaches the overt moral of "how the art of lying may be taught," as Susan Wolfson suggests, it also "parodies all logic-minded attempts to apply instruments of analysis [the weather vane] to the flow of obscure and elusive moods" (Wolfson). In other words, Wordsworth's choice of the weathervane points to the limits of reason and science to explain some parts of human experience, a lesson many Romantic writers were eager to teach. The poem also highlights the importance of conversation to foster learning. The back-and-forth of the dialogue stresses the importance of community in determining truth, a feature of other *Lyrical Ballads* such as "WE ARE SEVEN" and "The THORN." While scholars often stress individualism's importance to the movement, "Anecdote for Fathers" points to the significance of community, an issue that interested many Romantic writers because of its resonance with the FRENCH REVOLUTION's ideal of *fraternité*.

### Further Reading

Richardson, Alan. *Literature, Education, and Romanticism: Reading as Social Practice, 1780–1832.* New York: Cambridge University Press, 1994.

Wolfson, Susan J. *The Questioning Presence: Wordsworth, Keats, and the Interrogative Mode in Romantic Poetry.* Ithaca, N.Y.: Cornell University Press, 1986.

Wordsworth, William. *Lyrical Ballads, and Other Poems, 1797–1800.* Edited by James Butler and Karen Green. Ithaca, N.Y.: Cornell University Press, 1992.

—Robert C. Hale

### *Animal Magnetism, a Farce*  Elizabeth Inchbald (1788)

First produced on stage in 1788 in the presence of its author, the novelist, dramatist, and actress ELIZABETH INCHBALD (1753–1821), *Animal Magnetism, a Farce* was a comedic response to the then-fashionable therapeutic and diagnostic practice of the Austrian physician Franz Anton Mesmer (1734–1815). *The Monthly Mirror* of July 1797 suggests that the play may have been translated from the French. *Les docteurs modernes* and *Baquet de santé*, two French-language satires on Mesmer's practice, had enjoyed some success in Paris in 1784, and Inchbald may well have initially considered a Continental market for her farce, possibly in Paris, where Mesmer had opened a practice in 1778. The composer Wolfgang Amadeus Mozart, who knew Mesmer in Vienna, also included an allusion to Mesmer's practice in *Cosi fan tutte*, produced in the Austrian capital in 1789 and in London in 1811.

In England Inchbald's three-act farce initially enjoyed a moderate success in productions at the Theatre Royal and Covent Garden, as well as in Dublin, but it lapsed into obscurity toward the end of the first quarter of the 19th century. *Animal Magnetism* was revived in 1848, in part through the enthusiasm of Charles Dickens (1812–70), and it was produced sporadically by the novelist and his associates, primarily in support of charitable causes, until 1857.

Animal magnetism or mesmerism, as Mesmer's practice was popularly known, was an early precursor of modern hypnotism. It was based on the erroneous assumption that personal health and mental equilibrium are bound to an intangible and universal fluid whose qualities of balance and movement resemble those of conventional magnetism. Mesmer, as a therapist, claimed to vary, replenish, and manipulate the fluid content of his patients, either by theatrically directing his eyes, hands, or a wand toward those parts of the body that were afflicted with pain, paralysis, or unwonted movement; or by having his patients touch iron rods or other objects which he had previously invested with his own potent magnetism. Patients claimed that Mesmer and his followers—a small group of wealthy or noble acolytes who paid dearly for access to the alleged secrets of the fashionable treatment—cured them of neuralgia, tumors, fever, and even blindness, and they were able to diagnose disorders concealed beneath the skin without recourse to dangerous exploratory surgery. Skeptics claimed that the cures were at best temporary, or that the patients were conscious dupes if not naïfs deluded. The hysterical and convulsive crises associated with Mesmer's alleged cures, and the collapse of some patients into trance further aroused suspicion of what mesmerism might become in the hands of an unscrupulous practitioner. Rumours of sexual abuses committed on entranced female subjects, and of patients of both sexes instructed in trance to commit crimes or transfer personal property, dogged practitioners of mesmerism (and, later, of conventional hypnotism also) well into the 19th century. The French medical establishment, in the form of several royal commissions, conducted as scientific an investigation as was possible without the cooperation of Mesmer himself and concluded in 1784 that the practice was at best erroneous and at worst an injurious abuse of susceptible imaginations.

Inchbald's play draws less on an accurate representation of the animal magnetism practiced by Mesmer and his followers and more on the enduring associations of mesmerism with charlatanry and the deceiving of gullible minds. Following the lead of popular prejudice, the mesmerist in Inchbald's farce, the celebrated Dr. Mystery—"author and first discover of that healing and sublime Art Animal Magnetism" [sic]—is depicted as a calculating and theatrical deceiver. His elderly victim, styled simply as the Doctor, is correspondingly all too willing to believe in the personal and financial benefits allegedly associated with the modern panacea of animal magnetism. The farcical thrust of the play is derived not merely from this familiar interface of charlatanry and gullibility but from an evident inversion of customary roles. The Doctor, far from being a patient seeking relief, is a bitter and outcast practitioner of conventional medicine who has been refused a diploma by "the faculty," as he admits, because "a dozen or two of my patients have died under my hands."

Dr. Mystery, however, is not Mesmer, nor even a doctor; he is La Fluer, the disguised servant of the Marquis de Lancy, a nobleman seeking amorous congress with Constance, ward and intended bride to the elderly quack. Dr. Mystery inducts the gullible physician into a parody of mesmeric practice, presenting him with a magnetized wand that has the alleged capability to force the reluctant Constance to love her guardian. Much ironic value is gained from the manner in which Constance and her maid, Lisette, knowingly respond to the Doctor's inept use of Mystery's wand, transferring their extravagantly voiced love from the quack to his manservant as quickly as the wand changes hands. The Marquis de Lancy, meanwhile, is introduced into the house by Dr. Mystery as a patient in extremis, seeking a magnetic cure at the hands of the Doctor, and—apparently dying under the treatment—he changes places with La Fluer. The latter revives miraculously, as soon as the Doctor signs a contract conveying Constance to de Lancy in marriage, and once the disguised characters are revealed for who they are, the farce reaches a conventional resolution in the triumph of romance for, as de Lancy concludes, "there is no Magnetism, like the powerful Magnetism of love."

*Animal Magnetism* is thus not a polemic on Mesmer's practice but, rather, an opportunist farce that takes advantage of the currency of recognizable mesmeric terms and gestures in order to advance a fairly standard plot of romantic intrigue, disguise, and topical ironic humour. Its revival in the mid-19th century, ironically, was probably more associated with the renewed interest in, and skepticism about, trance states than was ever the case when Inchbald's farce was first performed in 1788.

## Further Reading

"Biographical Sketch of Mrs Inchbald." *Monthly Mirror* 4 (July 1797): 11–14. Available online. URL: http://www2.shu.ac.uk/corvey/CW3/ContribPage.cfm?Contrib=376. Accessed on March 19, 2009.

Forrest, Derek. *Hypnotism: A History.* London: Penguin, 1999.

Gauld, Alan. *A History of Hypnotism.* Cambridge: Cambridge University Press, 1995.

Inchbald, Elizabeth. *Animal Magnetism, a Farce in Three Acts,* as performed at the Theatre Royal, Covent Garden. (Dublin: Printed for P. Byron, [1789?]).

———. *The Diaries and Papers of Elizabeth Inchbald from the Folger Shakespeare Library and the London Library.* (Marlborough: Adam Matthew Publications, 2009). Microform, four reels.

———. *The Farce of Animal Magnetism. In Three Acts,* as performed at the Theatre Royal, Smoke Alley. (n.p.: Printed for the booksellers, 1792).

Mulvey, Roberts, Marie. "Knebworth Private Theatricals, 1850–2000." *The Dickensian,* 97, no. 1 (Spring 2001): 90–91.

—William Hughes

## annuals and gift books

Annuals and gift books were collections of short stories, poetry, and engravings that appeared for the most part from the 1820s to the 1850s. The British annual industry originated with the publication in 1822 of the Anglo-German Rudolph Ackermann's *Forget-Me-Not*. Ackermann (1764–1834) received his main inspiration from similar collections that were popular at the time in France and Germany, but the roots of the genre can also be traced to the personal albums and pocketbooks of the early 19th

century in England. In these books, people, usually women, would transcribe their favorite poems
and other literary pieces into a decorative volume
to give as a remembrance to a friend or loved one.
An early commercial example of such a book is
ROBERT SOUTHEY's *Annual*, published in 1799 and
1800, which collected poems from various poets
for publication but did not include the illustrations
that would become such a prominent feature of the
later gift books.

In the few years following the publication of
Ackermann's *Forget-Me-Not*, a small number of
rivals appeared, notably *Friendship's Offering, or
the Annual Remembrancer*, in 1823; and *The Literary Souvenir, or Cabinet of Poetry and Romance*,
edited by Alaric Watts, in 1824. These annuals
were generally published in early November so as
to be available for purchase as gifts for the Christmas and the New Year holidays. Consequently, the
books are generally associated with the year following publication, such as *The Literary Souvenir* for
1825. The number of annuals steadily increased
each year until, by 1831, more than 60 different
productions were in circulation. The most successful of them was *The Keepsake*, founded by Charles
Heath, a prominent engraver. *The Keepsake* was
produced annually for the years 1828–57, surpassing Ackermann's *Forget-Me-Not*, the last volume
of which was for the year 1847. The only other
annual to exceed 20 volumes was *Friendship's Offering*, which was available from 1824 until 1844.

Such a large number of rival volumes necessarily led to considerable competition among editors to secure suitable talent to fill their pages. In
this regard the standard was really set by Charles
Heath, who hired a new editor, Frederic Mansel
Reynolds, for the *Keepsake* in 1828, and the two
gentlemen traveled the country that year to secure
contributors from among the literary world's elite.
They offered large sums of money to SIR WALTER
SCOTT, WILLIAM WORDSWORTH, and SAMUEL
TAYLOR COLERIDGE, for example, all of whom
contributed to the *Keepsake* (in addition to other
annuals) despite the qualms they and many other
established writers had about damaging their literary reputations by associating with what they
perceived to be a less dignified industry. Another
popular poet of the time, THOMAS MOORE, was

greatly perturbed to discover the unauthorized
inclusion of some of his lines despite his repeated
rejection of Heath's offers. Nevertheless, *The Keepsake* for 1829 offered works by an unprecedented
collection of writers, including Scott, Wordsworth,
Coleridge, Moore, LETITIA ELIZABETH LANDON,
FELICIA HEMANS, ROBERT SOUTHEY, MARY SHEL-
LEY, and PERCY BYSSHE SHELLEY. Editors quickly
decided, however, that securing such a large number of famous writers was not actually necessary for
financial success, and although later contributors
to the annuals included Alfred Tennyson and Robert and ELIZABETH BARRETT BROWNING, subsequent editions of *The Keepsake* and other annuals
typically included much fewer big names.

The particular significance given to the name
recognition of contributors, especially in the earlier editions of the annuals, resulted in somewhat
relaxed standards for the literary merit of the
actual compositions included in the volume. Writers such as Scott or Wordsworth, who considered
the gift book beneath their standards, often submitted work that had previously been rejected by
other publishers or of which they were not particularly proud. Other writers, working under the strict
guidelines imposed by the editors, would actually
compose pieces especially for the annuals. Often,
however, these writers would be commissioned to
compose a short story or poem to complement an
engraving that had already been secured. As a consequence, the selections would occasionally appear
stilted or unnatural, and their relationship to the
accompanying embellishment would seem forced.
Mary Shelley is just one writer who acknowledged
the pressure of these conditions, and a number
of the 19 stories she contributed to the *Keepsake*
involved some literary concessions on her part.
Thus, although many famous authors contributed
to the annuals, most of the works found in them do
not qualify among the best known or most appreciated of their careers.

In many ways, however, the identity of the
contributors to the annuals, as well as the quality of
their actual offerings, was of less significance than
the general appearance of the book itself. Designed
to appeal to the middle-class consumer intent on
appearing fashionable, the gift books boasted gilt
edges; delicate bindings of leather or silk, often

vibrantly red or purple; and, most important, elegant engravings utilizing the most recent steel-plate technology. Steel plates were more durable than the copper plates they replaced and allowed for crisper images. To take advantage of this new development, editors persuaded some of the most prominent artists of the time to contribute their work. For example, J. M. W. Turner, from whom Heath commissioned 120 pictures during this period for his different publishing ventures, contributed 17 illustrations for the *Keepsake* from 1828 to 1837. Other artists included Robert Smirke, C. R. Leslie, and Richard Westall. Ironically, such details were employed to emulate the hand-crafted books often found in gentleman's libraries, but they were created in very modern factories using the latest equipment to produce thousands of identical volumes for the marketplace.

The middle-brow tone of the gift books was further encouraged by their subject matter. Selections overwhelmingly depicted sentimental domestic scenes, replete with weeping lovers, mothers, and children. These stories and poems have also been seen to perpetuate the conventions and standards for morals and behavior. Sacrifice, devotion, and filial piety were celebrated virtues. Some publishers actually considered it their responsibility to protect their readers from impropriety; their works were designed to offer a sanctuary from the worries of the outside world. At the same time, however, the increased focus on the experiences of women and the preponderance of female contributors (and, increasingly, editors) for the annuals began to be viewed as a more subversive phenomenon, occurring as it did at a time when women had little access to public careers. Further, the recurring use of exotic locales and story lines offered temporary escape from the increasingly rule-bound lifestyle of the middle-class and its emphasis on etiquette and codes of behavior.

Although the quality of the contributions to the annuals has frequently been disparaged, their importance, especially for writers of fiction, should not be overlooked. With the gift books arose a venue wherein writers of short stories and poems could find an increased audience, one that perhaps required the flashy trappings of the exquisitely presented books to arouse an interest in the literature included inside, and the proliferation of these annuals allowed for greater numbers of writers, whether beginners or veterans, to explore the possibilities offered by the genre.

## Further Reading

Booth, Bradford Allen, ed. *A Cabinet of Gems.* Berkeley: University California Press, 1938.

Boyle, Andrew. *An Index to the Annuals: The Authors 1820–1850.* Worcester, Mass.: A. Boyle, 1967.

Faxon, Frederick. *Literary Annuals and Gift Books: A Bibliography 1823–1903. Reprinted with Supplementary Essays by Eleanore Jamieson and Iain Bain.* Pinner, Middlesex, Eng.: Private Libraries Association, 1973.

Ledbetter, Kathryn. "Lucrative Requests: British Authors and Gift Book Editors." *Papers of the Bibliographical Society of America* 2 (1994): 207–216.

———. "'White Vellum and Gilt Edges': Imaging the *Keepsake*." *Studies in the Literary Imagination* 30, no. 2 (1997): 35–49.

—L. Adam Mekler

## "Arabella Stuart" Felicia Hemans (1828)

"Arabella Stuart" is the first poem in FELICIA HEMANS's popular collection RECORDS OF WOMAN, WITH OTHER POEMS (1828). Hemans based this poem on the story of Lady Arabella (1575–1615), King Henry VII's great-granddaughter, who was imprisoned because of her possible claim to the English throne at a time of disputed succession. When she secretly married William Seymour (1588–1660) in 1610, she was confined, and her attempt to escape was thwarted. Using dramatic monologue, biblical allusions, and natural imagery, Hemans adopts Arabella's persona to trace her agonies, starting with her hope of escape, her recapture and imprisonment in the Tower of London, and her subsequent relapse into depression and death. Professor Susan Wolfson asserts that Hemans's source for the historical details was Isaac D'Israeli's *Curiosities of Literature* (1823), which provided Arabella's papers to the public (Hemans 331).

In this poem about memory and absence, the speaker begins by describing her cherished hope of reuniting with her husband. Despite her depressing surroundings, Arabella soothes herself with positive thoughts and promises to resist her conditions and preserve her former beauty, sympathizing with her lover's imprisonment but thankful for his life. The poem's tone and pace lift with the approach of her long-awaited escape but fall when she is unable to reunite with her husband and is reimprisoned. Arabella's hopes gradually shatter, leading her to question the power of love and the "justice" that allows her captors to live freely while she remains in everlasting oppression. She also begins to question whether her husband/lover loves her, whether he remembers her, and where he is. As her miseries increase, her thoughts become egocentric: she laments the irony of being a noble woman but imprisoned, unlike the peasants who freely love and live. When she finally loses all hope and calls on death, it seems as hard to attain as freedom. But it finally approaches, and she is able to make peace with her faith. Before she dies, she apologizes for the suffering her husband had endured for her sake, advising him to seek happiness but bidding him to remember her. Arabella's final wish is to take farewell of him in person, but she believes that her words will still reach his heart, and thus she looks forward to their reunion in the afterlife.

The opening lines confuse distinctions between memory, dream and experience by asserting her experience to be a dream (Armstrong 31). Through Arabella's increasing delirium, Hemans illustrates the disintegration of a woman's psyche. Arabella's birth and her closeness to the throne deny her private fulfillment; her relatives, Queen Elizabeth I and later King James, are also her oppressors. Thus, Arabella's "oppressed subjectivity" (Kelly 203) eventually causes her death. Through narrating a true, tragic tale of female suffering, the poem indirectly raises some vital questions pertaining to the Romantic movement, such as the role of hope, the nature of faith, the reality of justice and destiny, and the prospect of death as a final escape from life's agonies and means of reunion with loved ones.

**Further Reading**

Armstrong, Isobel. "The Gush of the Feminine: How Can We Read Women's Poetry of the Romantic Period." *Romantic Women Writers: Voices and Countervoices,* edited by Paula R. Feldman and Theresa M. Kelley, 13–32. Hanover, N.H.: University Press of New England, 1995.

Hemans, Felicia Dorothea Browne. *Felicia Hemans: Selected Poems, Letters, Reception Materials.* Edited by Susan J. Wolfson. Princeton, N.J.: Princeton University Press, 2000.

Kelly, Gary. "Death and the Matron: Felicia Hemans, Romantic Death, and the Founding of the Modern Liberal State." In *Felicia Hemans: Reimagining Poetry in the Nineteenth Century,* edited by Nanora Sweet and Julie Melnyk, 196–211. Basingstoke, Eng.: Palgrave, 2001.

—Mariam Radhwi

## "Ascent of Snowdon, The" William Wordsworth (1805, 1850)

In this passage, which begins the closing section of *The PRELUDE,* WILLIAM WORDSWORTH's long and much-revised poem written in blank verse, the poet presents a SUBLIME vision from a mountaintop, with moonlight breaking through clouds and illuminating mists that stretch to and obscure the sea. In Romantic literature, visions such as these typically presage a transcendental experience in which the human psyche is overwhelmed by nature and often, through this experience, intuits something of the Deity or experiences some other universal truth. In this poem, which examines the growth of the poet's mind, Wordsworth meditates on several ideas worked through earlier in *The Prelude.* The ambiguity of much of his language has made it a much-discussed passage without critical consensus. There are, nonetheless, aspects about which an analysis may be fairly clear.

The circumstances that inspired this segment occurred when Wordsworth and his friend Robert Jones were touring North Wales during the summer of 1791. They rose early to see the sunrise "from the top of Snowdon," the highest mountain in Wales and England (at 3,560 feet [1,085 metres]), having enlisted the assistance of the local shepherd as their guide. Wordsworth describes the atmosphere as a warm summer night humid with looming storms and visibility so poor that they were

"Hemmed round on every side with fog and damp" (1805, l. 16). Undaunted by the weather, they proceed with the ascent. Moonlight breaks through, and the vision that follows begins the conclusion of *The Prelude*.

Wordsworth sees a brightening on the ground followed by a "light" that "fell like a flash" (ll. 35–39). This image recalls the "Imagination" speech earlier in *The Prelude* (Book VI) when the poet and fellow travelers realized that they had crossed the Alps, experiencing flashes of light like those that occurred "when the light of sense / Goes out, in flashes that have shown to us / The inner world" (VI, ll. 600–601). Instances like these indicate an exploration of the imagination's interaction with the natural world, an interaction that indicates the mind's transcendence. The clouds break, the moon fills the sky, and the ground is covered in mist, which coalesces with the sea itself, out of which rise the "dusky backs" of hills and over which shoot elemental forms of vapors while torrents resound through a blue chasm. In this chasm, Wordsworth contends, "Nature lodged / The soul, the imagination of the whole" (ll. 64–65). This is the vision of the ascent itself, the imagery of which provides the ground from which he writes of "The perfect image of a mighty mind, / Of one that feeds upon infinity," (ll. 69–70) and of human minds issuing "from the Deity" (l. 106). The human mind has perceived and experienced the effects of nature and its own interaction with nature. Also, it ruminates upon its ability to experience the Deity and, leading to "The sense of God" (l. 73), considers its ability to create in the sense described by Coleridge in chapter 13 of the *Biographia Literaria*. The creative imagination is the highest faculty of mind, enabling poets to participate in "truth in moral judgments; and delight / That fails not, in the external universe" (ll. 125–126).

After this comes Wordsworth's introspective examination in which he contends that he has always opted for acting out of the morally good and for perceiving through the imagination and not through the "universe of death" (l. 160) or the lack of imaginative vision, asserting this as the result of early habituation. Love, he says, specifically a platonic "higher love," is that which keeps us from being mere "dust" and that from which

issues "truth and beauty." This "higher love" is "intellectual"—spiritual—and must exist with "imagination," which he defines as a higher reason. Throughout *The Prelude* the imagination, he contends, has been "the moving soul" of his poetic journey which he details from birth through his growth as an adult, culminating in the ability to intuit eternal life, sustained in life by thoughts of "infinity and God" (l. 205).

The "Snowdon" passage, then, could be seen as *The Prelude*'s closing epiphany, apocalypse, or moment of transcendent truth in which the poet's mind, symbolized by the moonlight, breaks through the mists that shroud the consciousness from the clarity of transcendent apperception. What the mind then is able to grasp is the means by which it—or its highest mode, the creative imagination—interacts with nature in the world and leads itself to God, to move humanity positively in imaginative ability and consequently in moral capacity. The passage is one of the great moments in high Romanticism, reflecting the human psyche's yearning for not only understanding of the universe's mysteries but also its capacity to pierce the veil of the everyday to envision, through the creative imagination, truths that are eternal.

## Further Reading

Owen, W. J. B. "The Descent from Snowdon." *Wordsworth Circle* 16, no. 2 (Spring 1985): 65–74.

Schell, Richard. "Wordsworth Revisions of the Ascent of Snowdon." *Philological Quarterly* 54, no. 3 (Summer 1975): 592–603.

Stallknecht, Newton P. "Nature and Imagination in Wordsworth's Meditation upon Mt. Snowdon." *PMLA* 53, no. 3 (September 1937): 835–847.

Wordsworth, Jonathan. "The Climbing of Snowdon." In *Bicentenary Wordsworth Studies*, edited by Jonathan Wordsworth, Ithaca, N.Y. and London: 1970.

Wordsworth, William. *The Prelude 1799, 1805, 1850: William Wordsworth.* Edited by Jonathan Wordsworth, M. H. Abrams, and Stephen Gill. New York: W. W. Norton & Company, 1979.

———. *The Prelude.* Edited by Ernest de Selincourt, revised by Helen Darbishire. Oxford: Oxford University Press, 1959.

—Donna Berliner

## "Auld Lang Syne" Robert Burns (1796)

"Auld Lang Syne" is surely ROBERT BURNS's best-known song, often sung (incorrectly) in modern English-speaking nations each New Year's Eve and at other social occasions. He contributed it to James Johnson's *Scots Musical Museum* in 1788, intimating that he was only partly responsible for its composition. The truth of this is ultimately unclear, although he also gave this impression in a letter to Anna Dunlop, dated December 17, 1788. Anna Dunlop (1730–1815) enjoyed a long correspondence with Burns and he respected her opinion of his writings. Enclosing a copy, he wrote: "[I]s not the Scotch phrase *Auld lang syne* exceedingly expressive? There is an old song and tune which has often thrilled through my soul. . . . Light be the turf on the breast of the heaven-inspired poet who inspired this glorious fragment! There is more of the fire of native genius in it than in half a dozen of modern English Bacchanalians" (quoted in Lindsay). Burns's version remained unpublished until six months after his death in 1796, when it featured in the fifth volume of the *Museum*. It also appeared in George Thomson's *Scottish Airs* (1799).

Some, apparently including Thomson, have concluded that Burns was substantially responsible for the song himself, while some lines nonetheless appear to date back as far as the 16th century. Burns's song consists of a four-line chorus and five four-line verses. The words concern the Romantic themes of solidarity and common humanity in the face of life's trials and time's passing: "We twa hae paidl'd in the burn, / Frae morning sun till dine; / But seas between us braid hae roar'd, / Sin auld lang syne. / And there's a hand, my trusty fiere! / And gie's a hand o' thine! / And we'll tak a right gude-willie-waught, / For auld lang syne" (ll. 17–24). This final verse highlights the song's complicated linguistic and cultural hybridity. It is obviously tempting to view "Auld Lang Syne" as an expression of Scottish identity and as a well-known example of the collection of Scots' songs as part of an 18th-century "Scottish cultural revival" that enjoyed a wide influence over British Romanticism (see SCOTT, SIR WALTER; MACPHERSON, JAMES). Yet, amid what might appear as "authentic" Scots dialect, a term like *gude-willie* is actually old English.

Maurice Lindsay's *The Burns Encyclopedia* traces the genealogy of "Auld Lang Syne" back to an anonymous ballad from 1568, "Auld Kyndnes foryett," through a 1711 ballad probably by Sir Robert Ayton, to a song by Ramsay about returning warriors that was published in *Scots Songs* (1720). Ramsay's song also appeared in an earlier volume of the *Scots Musical Museum,* accompanied by the tune that partnered Burns's version (which first featured in *Playford's Original Scotch Tunes* in 1700). George Thomson, however, published the words to a different tune that Lindsay affirms is the one we know today. He traces this familiar tune back to its inclusion in William Shield's ballad-opera *Rosina* (1783), through late-18th-century incarnations in which it was known as "The Miller's Wedding" and "The Miller's Daughter," and to its use as "The Duke of Buccleugh's Tune" in the song collection *Appollo's Banquet* (1690).

### Further Reading

Burns, Robert. *Burns: Poems and Songs.* Edited by James Kinsley. London: Oxford University Press, 1969.

Lindsay, Maurice. "Auld Lang Syne." *Robert Burns Country: The Burns Encyclopedia.* Available online. URL: http://www.robertburns.org/encyclopedia/AuldLangSyne.5.shtml. Downloaded on March 23, 2008.

—Steve Van Hagen

## Austen, Jane (1775–1817)

The seventh of eight children, Jane Austen was born on December 16, 1775, to the Reverend George and Cassandra Leigh Austen. Both parents came from prominent families but had to supplement their income by boarding pupils, running a dairy, and raising poultry. Austen and her older sister, Cassandra, received very little formal education, but they were immersed in a rich, intellectual environment. Guided and encouraged by her father and brothers, Austen gained knowledge in the classics and was a voracious reader. Unlike Elizabeth Bennet, the heroine of her most famous novel, *PRIDE AND PREJUDICE* (1813), Austen practiced the pianoforte nearly every day of her life. Cassandra developed a talent for art and is responsible for two of the only three drawings in existence of her famous sister. Two of their brothers graduated from Oxford University and became clergymen; one of them, Henry, would also become a banker and handle all of the negotiations for his sister's publications. (It was her father, however, who first solicited publication for *First Impressions / Pride and Prejudice*, but Cadell & Davies in London refused to read the manuscript.) Two other brothers distinguished themselves in naval service, especially Frank, who served under the great hero of the Napoleonic wars, Admiral HORATIO NELSON. Austen's brother Edward was adopted by their cousin Thomas Knight, whose name Edward took.

Austen never married, something which has preoccupied some critics. How could the mastermind of some of the greatest romantic novels of all time die a spinster? It is not as though she had not fallen in love. She often did. Even at age 40, when she first realized that the pain in her back was more than rheumatism, she flirted with a medical doctor who was attending to her brother, even while she was carrying a torch for a Mr. Philips. She wrote about these "conquests" in a letter to Cassandra and added: "Life is to be wrung, squeezed fully; if events yield little, imagination must work them up."

Austen was full of élan and romance and dance. She was apparently a happy person who saw the world full of foibles and antics and often said, "I could die of laughter." She was serious about marriage a few times. Thomas Langlois LeFroy, who one day would be the Lord Chief Justice of Ireland, was studying law at Trinity College in Dublin when he decided to visit his aunt and uncle, who were neighbors to the Austens. After several dances at a ball, the couple were attracted; however, like Elizabeth Bennet, Austen, although a "gentleman's daughter" had very little money. Like Edward Ferrars and John Willoughby in *SENSE AND SENSIBILITY* (1811), Tom was whisked out of harm's way and sent packing to Ireland, leaving Austen saddened but not devastated.

Austen also had a 24-hour engagement with Harris Bigg-Wither. At the time the Austens were living in Bath, a city their daughter detested. In 1802, during a visit to old friends in her father's previous parish, she and Cassandra renewed their acquaintances with the Bigg-Withers, who had been friends of their youth. After one week, Harris proposed to Austen, and she accepted. We do not know why she consented and even less why she rescinded the next day. She was 27; he was 21, wealthy, and able to give her a good life in the country away from Bath. All we do know is that she wrote to her niece Fanny in 1814: "Anything is preferred or endured rather than marrying without Affection."

Despite this, Austen's life appears to have been very full. Besides close relationships with her mother, her brothers and their families, and her sister, her thoughts rarely ran far from her novels. Much has been made of her writing on "the little bit (two Inches wide) of Ivory," as if she wrote on the sly. Actually, she often stitched together small pieces of paper so that she could work out scenes in her novels. She also had little notebooks, which she could quickly put aside when guests arrived without making them feel as if they were intruding. She did compose on broadsheets as well and meticulously revised and revised, which she did behind closed doors; her time, privacy, and quiet were zealously protected by her sister and mother. She saw herself as a writer; it was what defined her, even if her books were published anonymously to protect her identity. Austen's reputation rests on a small number of works: *Sense and Sensibility* (1811), *Pride and Prejudice* (1813), *Mansfield Park* (1814), *Emma* (1815), and *Northanger Abbey* and *Persuasion* (both published posthumously in 1817). There are also several lesser known and incomplete works, unpublished in Austen's lifetime: *Lady Susan, The Watsons,* and *Sanditon,* as well as juvenilia. Contrary to myth, she was popular in her own day; her works were well-received, and several sold out their editions. Perhaps the shining moment of her career as an author was when she was invited to the royal residence on November 13, 1815. She was told that the Prince Regent, later King George IV (see MONARCHY), was a devoted fan, and she probably hoped to be received by him. Instead, she was met by his librarian, Mr. Clarke, who requested that she dedicate her next book to the regent, which she did with *EMMA*.

Another momentous tribute came from the premier novelist of the day, SIR WALTER SCOTT.

Austen claimed not to like him because "He has Fame & Profit enough as a Poet, and should not be taking the bread out of other people's mouths" (Le Faye 277); nevertheless, she was grateful to receive his approbation. In an unsigned review in 1815, Scott not only praised *Emma* as a new kind of novel, he identified it as "the art of copying from nature as she really exists in the common walks of life, and presenting to the reader, instead of the splendid scenes of an imaginary world, a correct and striking representation of that which is daily taking place around him" (Southam 63). In Scott's Journal entry for 14 March 1826, he admits: "The big bow-wow strain I can do myself, like any one now going; but the exquisite touch which renders ordinary commonplace things and characters interesting from the truth of the description and the sentiment, is denied to me" (Southam 106). and recognized 'a truth of painting in her writings ... They do not, it is true, get above the middle classes of society, but there she is inimitable' (Southam 106). Austen knew well the world of the pseudo-gentry and could reproduce with great accuracy and integrity their lives in the parlor and the ballroom, as well as in such grandiose estates as Pemberley, Northanger Abbey, and Mansfield Park. And although we can learn much about the manners of the period from her books, she was more Romantic than neoclassical (see NEOCLASSICISM) in creating situations that scraped away social veneer and exposed elementary emotions and humanity in her characters to themselves and to each other.

There has been a tendency to try and read Austen herself into her novels, a form of analysis that can be overdone. One of the criticisms made of Austen—at least until recently—was that her novels seem divorced from the political, social, and artistic upheavals taking place at the time she was writing. The aim of Marilyn Butler's important book *Jane Austen and the War of Ideas* (1975) was to challenge this ladylike image of Austen. Butler tried to situate Austen within the conflicts that characterized culture during the aftermath of the FRENCH REVOLUTION. As she explained: "For good or ill her 20th century readers seem agreed that Jane Austen stands aside from the ideological convulsions that accompanied and followed the French Revolution. . . . The purpose of this study is to show that her manner as a novelist is broadly that of a conservative Christian moralist of the 1790s" (Butler 162). According to Butler, "All of Jane Austen's novels belong generically to a movement that defines itself by its opposition to revolution" (123).

Since Butler's book was published, critics have agreed that although Austen seems an unlikely Romanticist, her novels engage with many of the prominent intellectual and aesthetic ideas of the time, even though this engagement may not be immediately apparent. Is Austen "a more openly Condition-of-England writer than is generally recognised?" asks the author Roger Sales (xi). Sales goes on to suggest that PERSUASION (1818), which is partly about the mismanagement of an estate, can be read symbolically as being about the mismanagement of a kingdom—that is, Britain. Elsewhere, NORTHANGER ABBEY (1818) satirizes the contemporary vogue for GOTHIC fiction.

Austen also pokes fun at the author William Gilpin (1724–1804) for his "principles of picturesque beauty," although she did admire his work. Keen on the country over the city, Austen has her heroines finding refreshment and strength in nature, and, like Gilpin, she captures the delight of nature simply, with an economy of words, in verbal pictures that would have pleased WILLIAM COWPER, whose poetry frequents her works. One example of picturesque writing can be found in MANSFIELD PARK (1814) when the party is touring Mr. Rushworth's Sotherton Court: "A considerable flight of steps landed them in the wilderness, which was a planted wood of about two acres, and though chiefly of larch and laurel, and beech cut down, and though laid out with too much regularity, was darkness and shade and natural beauty compared with the bowling-green and the terrace." Austen preferred untamed nature to human-made symmetry. This was reflected not only in her portraits of nature but also in her style of writing, which resisted the formal style of 18th-century novels such as the epistolary or the picaresque. Instead, her narrative flows as naturally as a stream over stones and around bends—sometimes smooth, sometimes rough, sometimes in eddies, but always in motion as if driven by its own energy.

Austen died on July 18, 1817, age 41. Scholars still do not know whether she died of Addison's disease or Hodgkin's lymphoma. Her final novel, *Persuasion,* was published posthumously in 1817. She was not well known as a novelist, and it was not until the 1870s that her reputation began to rise.

See also LOVE AND FRIENDSHIP.

## Further Reading

Austen-Leigh, James Edward. *A Memoir of Jane Austen, and Other Family Recollections.* Edited by Kathryn Sutherland. Oxford: Oxford University Press, 2002.

Butler, Marilyn. *Jane Austen and the War of Ideas.* Oxford: Oxford University Press, 1987.

Grey, David J. *The Jane Austen Handbook.* London: Athlone Press, 1986.

Honan, Park. *Jane Austen: Her Life.* New York: Fawcett Columbine, 1987.

Kirkham, Margaret. *Jane Austen, Feminism and Fiction.* London: Athlone Press, 1997.

Laski, Marghanita. *Jane Austen and Her World.* New York: Viking, 1969.

Le Faye, Deirdre. *Jane Austen's Letters.* London: Folio Society, 2003.

Littlewood, Ian, ed. *Jane Austen: Critical Assessments.* 4 vols. Mountfieldd: Helm, 1998.

Lynch, Deidre, ed. *Janeites: Austen's Disciples and Devotees.* Princeton, N.J.: Princeton University Press, 2000.

Nokes, David. *Jane Austen: A Life.* Berkeley, CA: University of California Press, 1998.

Sales, Roger. *Jane Austen and Representations of Regency England.* London: Routledge, 1994.

Southam, Brian, ed. *Jane Austen: The Critical Heritage 1870–1940.* London: Routledge, 1987.

Sulloway, Alison G. *Jane Austen and the Province of Womanhood* (Philadelphia: University of Pennsylvania Press, 1989.

Tanner, Tony. *Jane Austen.* London: Macmillan, 1986.

Tomalin, Claire. *Jane Austen: A Life.* New York: Vintage, 1999.

Wiltshire, John. *Recreating Jane Austen.* Cambridge: Cambridge University Press, 2001.

—Brenda Ayres

## "Badger, The" John Clare (ca. 1820)

In accounts of Romantic literature, JOHN CLARE is often presented as an atypical figure. Clare, in contrast to many other poets, was largely uneducated and worked the land in order to make a living as a youth and a young man. His poetry and use of language can seem more primitive than other Romantics, and this is clearly evident in "The Badger."

This poem is unusual in that two forms of it exist, one consisting of five stanzas and the other of only three, missing the first and last stanzas. The reason for this is unclear and somewhat odd because the first stanza of the five-stanza version details a fine description of the "shaggy hide and sharp nose" of the badger. This stanza also outlines the badger's "grunting" awkwardness and lumbering characteristics, the implication being that the badger is not perceived as a fighting animal. However, once baited, the badger fights courageously and valiantly. The ungainly, clumsy animal becomes a veritable fighting machine for whom "everyone's a foe." Like most animals and wildlife, the badger will go calmly about its business until faced with adversity, at which point his instinct for survival is aroused and he "fights with dogs for hours and beats them all." That which one sees, or perceives, is not necessarily that which lies beneath the exterior; nature itself is rarely violent, unless provoked. In this case the provocation comes from men who cruelly "bait him all the day," unnecessarily and deliberately inciting the otherwise harmless beast to fight hard and long for his survival.

Unlike the dreamlike and imaginative poetry of many Romantics, "The Badger" is very much more down-to-earth and realistic. Clare describes vividly how the badger is "kicked and torn and beaten" and eventually "leaves his hold and crackles, groans and dies." The poet's words are harsh and brutal, and there is not much left to the imagination, but two things occur here. First, there is a strong sense of sympathy for the badger as Clare conveys his situation. Exhausted and broken, the badger falls to his foes; the valiant fighter loses his battle for survival—a battle he should never have had to fight. Second, the vividness of the words also projects the sense that the poet is truly at one with and a part of nature. As such, Clare's work sits on the periphery of the Romantic ideal, erring more toward primitivism and reality than the "imaginative spontaneity" and "emotional self-expression" (Drabble 872) more usually associated with the Romantics. "The Badger," in particular, exudes a sense of Clare's intrinsic connection to and empathy with the badger's plight, as opposed to the arguably somewhat more remote observations of other Romantic authors.

### Further Reading

Bate, Jonathan. *John Clare: A Biography.* London: Picador, 2003.

Drabble, Margaret, ed. *The Oxford Companion to English Literature.* Oxford: Oxford University Press, 2000.

The John Clare Society Web site. Available online. URL: www.johnclare.org.uk. Accessed on June 21, 2009.

—Pauline Guerin

## Baillie, Joanna (1762–1851)

In 1798 an anonymous volume entitled *A Series of Plays: in which it is attempted to delineate the stronger passions of the mind* appeared in London. The plays created an immediate sensation and drew comparisons to the dramatic works of Shakespeare and other renaissance dramatists. Of the likely candidates for authorship noted by contemporaries—a list that included MATTHEW GREGORY LEWIS and ANN RADCLIFFE—Joanna Baillie was not mentioned, but this is not at all surprising. Though Baillie had published a collection, *Poems: Wherein It is Attempted to Describe Certain Views of Nature and Rustic manners,* in 1790 (see "STORM-BEAT MAID, THE" and "REVERIE, A"), it had gone virtually unnoticed. Indeed, little about her life suggested she was on the brink on launching a literary career that would span the next five decades and influence the careers of such writers as WILLIAM WORDSWORTH, LORD BYRON, and SIR WALTER SCOTT.

Born on September 11, 1762, the youngest of three children of the Reverend James Baillie and his wife Dorthea, Joanna Baillie grew up in Scotland, primarily in the town of Hamilton, where her father was appointed minister in 1766. In 1772 she and her sister Agnes began attending boarding school in Glasgow. While there, Joanna was noted for her abilities in music, mathematics, argumentation, and drawing, suggesting the strong analytic cast of mind that reveals itself in her later imaginative works. In 1775 Baillie's father was appointed professor of divinity at Glasgow University, but he died after holding the post for little more than two years. As a result, Baillie, her mother, and Agnes moved to London in 1784 to live with her brother Matthew, who had embarked on a very successful practice as a medical doctor; this would ultimately lead him to become personal physician to King George IV. Baillie never married and lived with her sister in London for the rest of her life. She died on February 23, 1851.

Though Joanna Baillie wrote more than 25 dramas, three substantial collections of poetry, and a treatise on the nature of Christ, her best known and most influential works—the plays *De Monfort* and *BASIL: A TRAGEDY,* as well as a theoretical work, "An Introductory Discourse"—are all from the 1798 volume. In the "Introductory Discourse," Baillie explains that her intention in the *Plays on the Passions* is to reveal "the human mind under the dominion of those strong and fixed passions, which seemingly unprovoked by outward circumstances, will from small beginnings brood within the breast, till . . . all the fair gifts of nature are borne down" (86). In *De Monfort,* for example, the protagonist's personality contracts to a single passion, revenge, with disastrous consequences. Inflamed by the desire to avenge a stain on his honor, De Monfort kills his innocent rival, Rezenvelt, and then is consumed by isolation and then by what seems to be madness. Baillie's purpose in representing the progress of such passions is to engage the "sympathetick curiosity" (74) of her audience, which will lead to moral or ethical growth: "From it we are taught the properties and decencies of ordinary life . . . [and by] examining others, we know ourselves" (74). Baillie's emphasis on the relationship between literature, character psychology, and daily life clearly connects her with other Romantic era writers, most notably William Wordsworth whose PREFACE TO *LYRICAL BALLADS* (1800) she may have influenced.

Because of Baillie's interest in character psychology, some critics have identified her works as closet dramas—that is, plays intended to be read rather than performed. Baillie rejected this conception and worked throughout her life to encourage their performance. *De Manfort* premiered at Druny Lane in 1800 with Sarah Siddens, and Walter Scott produced *The Family Legend* in Edinburgh in 1810.

### Further Reading

Baillie, Joanna. *Plays on the Passions.* Edited by Peter Duthie. Peterborough, Ont., and Orchard Park, N.Y.: Broadview Press, 2001.

Burroughs, Catherine B. *Closet Stages: Joanna Baillie and the Theater Theory of British Romantic Women Writers.* Philadelphia: University of Pennsylvania Press, 1997.

Crochunis, Thomas C. *Joanna Baillie, Romantic Dramatist: Critical Essays.* London: Routledge, 2004.

Forbes, Aileen. "'Sympathetic Curiosity' in Joanna Baillie's Theater of the Passions." *European Romantic Review* 14 (2003): 31–48.

Slagle, Judith Bailey. *Joanna Baillie, a Literary Life.* Madison, N.J.: Fairleigh Dickinson University Press, 2002.

—J. Hunter Morgan

## Barbauld, Anna Laetitia (1743–1825)

A poet, educational pioneer, essayist, and literary critic, Anna Barbauld, eldest of two children, was born on June 20, 1743, at Kibworth Harcourt, Leicestershire, to the Reverend John Aikin, a schoolmaster, and Jane Jennings Aikin. The Aikinses were Dissenters, and Anna, a prodigy who could read by the age of three, was raised in an environment valuing education and freedom of thought. She received a better education than many girls of the period; her father taught her classics, and she read widely. In 1758 the Aikinses moved to Warrington, Lancashire, when the Reverend Barbauld accepted a position at the local Dissenting academy. The social circle at Warrington, which included the theologian Joseph Priestley and his wife Mary, provided important encouragement for Anna's literary development, reading and discussing her early poems.

In 1772 Anna Aikin began her publishing career, contributing songs to her brother John's *Essays on Song-Writing* (1772) and hymns to William Enfield's *Hymns for Public Worship* (1772). Her own volume of *Poems* came out at the end of the year and was reviewed positively overall, although the *Monthly Review* suggested that the poems lacked "femininity" and that the author might have been better off educated "more under the direction of a mother, than of a father." The book went through four editions in the first year. Anna also began her career as an essayist, publishing *Miscellaneous Pieces in Prose* (1773) with her brother, though most of the pieces were by Anna herself. This work, too, was well received.

In 1774 Anna Letitia Aikin married Rochemont Barbauld, whom she had met when he was a student at Warrington. Thereafter, she published under her married name. The Barbaulds took up the management of a progressive school for boys at Palgrave, where Anna taught geography and history. Unable to have children, they adopted her

brother's third son, Charles Rochement Aikin. During this period, inspired by her work with the boys at the school and by her son, Anna Barbauld wrote the books that established her as a key figure in education and children's literature: a series of graduated readers titled *Lessons for Children* (1778–79) and *Hymns in Prose for Children* (1781). The readers have a direct yet sympathetic tone demonstrating respect for the child's intelligence, and the *Hymns* present a kind and loving God, a change from the fear-inspiring religious texts of the Puritans. Some contemporaries thought it a waste of Barbauld's talents to pursue educational work, but she influenced the pedagogical theorist Richard Edgeworth, father of the novelist MARIA EDGEWORTH, and her books for children continued to be used until well into the 19th century.

The Barbaulds gave up the school at Palgrave in 1785, due to Rochemont's ill health, and embarked on a tour of France, after which they settled in London in 1786. There, Anna Barbauld became very active in political commentary. Her upbringing in Dissenting circles gave her a keen interest in the idea of liberty and in the connection between education and democracy. Among the pamphlets she published were *Civic Sermons to the People* (1792; published anonymously), explaining the principles of democratic government; and *Sins of Government, Sins of the Nation* (1793), against war with the French Republic. She also published an antislavery poem, "EPISTLE TO WILLIAM WILBERFORCE" (1791). Barbauld became one of the prominent public intellectuals of the day and was a regular contributor to the periodical press. From 1796 to 1806, her brother edited the *Monthly Magazine,* for which she wrote poems and essays. From 1803 to 1809 she also wrote for the *Annual Review* (under the editorship of her nephew Arthur Aikin) and in 1809 began writing for *The Monthly Review* (until 1815), producing more than 300 reviews. Barbauld's political engagement continued to the end of her career with the final poem published before her death, "EIGHTEEN HUNDRED AND ELEVEN" (1811), a bleak vision of Britain's future given its continuation of the war against France.

In 1802 the Barbaulds moved to Stoke Newington, north of London, close to her brother's family. To her poetry and essay production Barbauld added a series of editing projects that made significant contributions to literary history and criticism. In 1804 she published an edition of the letters of Samuel Richardson. Despite difficulties caused by her husband's mental illness and subsequent suicide in 1808 (he had attacked her earlier that year, causing a separation), Barbauld completed the 50-volume *British Novelists* (1810), comprising an essay on the history of the novel and 20 novels with prefatory introductions. She continued to write until her death on March 9, 1825, at Stoke Newington. Her niece, Lucy Aikin, posthumously published her *Works*, with a memoir (1825) and *A Legacy for Young Ladies* (1826).

Barbauld was included in Richard Samuel's painting *The Nine Living Muses of Great Britain* (1779), and young poets such as WILLIAM WORDS-SWORTH admired her. In her latter years and after her death, however, her reputation suffered greatly. "Eighteen Hundred and Eleven" had been attacked by critics who judged it unpatriotic and unfeminine. Elsewhere, however, Barbauld's seniority meant that she came to represent the passing generation for younger poets; she was mocked by SAMUEL TAYLOR COLERIDGE, both privately (recorded in anecdotes) and in a public lecture in 1813. CHARLES LAMB made her a byword for all that stifles the imagination of the child in an oft-quoted 1802 letter to Coleridge. Finally, to counter any lingering notion of Barbauld's radicalism, Lucy Aikin's memoir downplayed Barbauld's political activism.

For a long time "Mrs. Barbauld" existed only as a vague figure associated with feminine propriety and moralistic writings for children. Since the 1980s critics been reexamining her work, recognizing her as very much a central figure in literary Romanticism. Her poems and essays take up concerns shared by many Romantic writers: the nature of liberty, the relationship between the individual and the state, the nature of the (female) artist (see "WASHING DAY"), and the status of women (for example, "The RIGHTS OF WOMAN"). In her writing for children, she plays a role in changing constructions of the child, so much a part of Romantic literature. Never mind posing as a muse: Barbauld holds her own as an influential figure of the Romantic period.

See also "SUMMER EVENING'S MEDITATION, A."

## Further Reading

Barbauld, Anna Letitia. *Anna Letitia Barbauld: Selected Poetry and Prose.* Edited by William McCarthy and Elizabeth Kraft. Peterborough, Ont., and Orchard, Park, N.Y.: Broadview Press, 2001.

DeRosa, Robin. "A Criticism of Contradictions: Anna Leticia Barbauld and the 'Problem' of Nineteenth-Century Women's Writing." In *Women as Sites of Culture: Women's Roles in Cultural Formation from the Renaissance to the Twentieth Century,* edited by Susan Shifrin, 221–231. Aldershot, Eng.: Ashgate, 2002.

Eger, Elizabeth. "Representing Culture: 'The Nine Living Muses of Great Britain' (1779)." In *Women, Writing, and the Public Sphere 1700–1830,* edited by Elizabeth Eger, Charlotte Grant, Cliona O'Gallchoir, and Penny Warburton, 104–132. Cambridge: Cambridge University Press, 2001.

Janowitz, Anne. *Women Romantic Poets: Anna Barbauld and Mary Robinson.* Tavistock, Eng.: Northcote House, 2004.

Keach, William. "Barbauld, Romanticism, and the Survival of Dissent." *Essays and Studies* 51 (1998): 44–61.

McCarthy, William. "A 'High-Minded Christian Lady': The Posthumous Reception of Anna Laetitia Barbauld." In *Romanticism and Women Poets: Opening the Doors of Reception,* edited by Harriet Kramer Linkin and Stephen C. Behrendt, 165–191. Lexington: University Press of Kentucky, 1999.

Rodgers, Betsy. *Georgian Chronicle: Mrs. Barbauld and Her Family.* London: Methuen, 1958.

—Terri Doughty

## *Basil: A Tragedy* Joanna Baillie (1798)

*Basil* is one of the *Plays on the Passions*, part of JOANNA BAILLIE's self-described "noble design" to write a comedy and a tragedy on each of the major emotions. *Basil* (the tragedy on love) appeared in a volume with *The Trial* (the comedy on love) and *De Monfort* (the tragedy on hatred). The volume gained considerable popularity and was rereleased in five editions, establishing Baillie's reputation as one of Britain's leading Romantic playwrights.

The play follows the fortunes of Count Basil, an army general moving his troops through the city of Padua on his way to assist General Pescara against French forces. Although he is young, his sagacity, charisma, and courage in battle have won him fame far beyond his years, but his blinding love for Victoria causes him to neglect his duties. Basil first spies Victoria, the duke of Padua's daughter, as she and her maidens go to a religious shrine. He accepts her invitation to an evening masquerade, even though it means delaying his troops' movements for a day. The young Victoria coquettishly glories in testing the hero's intense passion, though often rebuked by her attendant, Lady Albini. Baillie's signature treatment of the older female character is well evident in this secondary character, who provides noble, sensible, and dignified instruction to her wayward charge.

Basil's delay in Padua, meanwhile, suits the machinations of the tyrannous duke, who publicly supports Pescara but has privately supported the French king. The duke's minions foment unrest among the soldiers so that Basil faces a full-scale mutiny upon his return from the ball. In speeches notable for their beautiful rhetoric and high moral tone, he wins his soldiers to his side once again and later promises his elder kinsman Count Rosinberg that he will move the troops the next day. Curious about her sway over Basil, however, Victoria invites him to a morning hunt, so Basil unwisely delays his troops yet again. At the close of the hunt, a messenger brings news that the pending battle has just been fought unexpectedly early. Fortunately, Pescara's forces carried the day against Charles V of France, but Basil is devastated to learn that he had left his allies in the lurch. They had engaged in deadly combat with high losses while he and his men lingered in luxury.

Typical of Romantic dramas, the main conflicts in *Basil* are internalized: Baillie reveals the bleak and tragic slippage of identity as Basil alternates between allegiance to the masculine *comitatus* and his desire to play the lover. Victoria, too, is entangled in competing versions of feminine identities. Unable to establish a unified and stable self, Basil retires to a gloomy cave and shoots himself. His men find him and crowd around to express their sorrow as he dies. Victoria arrives too late. When Rosinberg scorns her love as foolish coquetry, she announces her intention of retiring to a nearby

convent where she can watch over Basil's grave to the end of her days.

**Further Reading**

Baillie, Joanna. *Plays on the Passions*. Edited by Peter Duthie. Peterborough, Ont., and Orchard Park, N.Y.: Broadview Press, 2001.

Burroughs, Catherine B. *Closet Stages: Joanna Baillie and the Theater Theory of British Romantic Women Writers*. Philadelphia: University of Pennsylvania Press, 1997.

Slagle, Judith Bailey. *Joanna Baillie, a Literary Life*. Madison, N.J.: Fairleigh Dickinson University Press, 2002.

—Tammy Durant

### "Bastille: A Vision, The"  Helen Maria Williams (1790)

Appearing in the novel *Julia* (1790), HELEN MARIA WILLIAMS's 96-line poem "The Bastille, A Vision" concerns an Englishman who, while confined in the famous French prison, foresees a new world in which freedom and happiness replace tyranny and pain as the principal conditions of earthly life. According to Neil Fraistat and Susan S. Lanser, the piece stands as Williams's "first published response to the [French] Revolution" (Williams 20) and reflects its author's altruistic and idealistic feelings regarding the collapse of the ancien régime in France. Fraistat and Lanser also speculate that the poem in part registers "the sufferings of the worthy du Fossés," a French family with whom Williams had been intimate since the mid-1780s (20).

The poem's first two stanzas introduce a speaker so agonized by his incarceration in the Bastille that he prays for death to wrest him from its nightmare (ll. 1–16). Mercifully, the prisoner falls asleep (l. 20), at which time an otherworldly being appears (l. 22). Although strange and solemn, the apparition benevolently offers to "ope the book of fate" (l. 59) to show the astonished speaker how "Freedom's sacred temple" will "rise" (l. 63), so beginning a new golden age in which all people, inspired by liberty and guided by "Philosophy" (l. 89), shall finally unite. The apparition foretells renewal and contentment for all social classes;

even "the peasant" (l. 81) will rear his family knowing that "Freedom guards his straw-roof'd cot, / And all his useful toils are blest" (ll. 87–88). The poem closes with the promise that Freedom and Philosophy together shall "renovate the gladden'd earth" (l. 96).

As contemporary political commentary, "The Bastille, A Vision" presents in verse what Williams, in the fourth of her LETTERS FROM FRANCE (1790–96), asserts in prose: "If the splendour of a despotic throne can only shine like the radiance of lightning, while all around is involved in gloom and horror, in the name of heaven let its baleful lustre be extinguished for ever" (Williams 74). As a work of Romantic prophecy, the poem exemplifies many of the aesthetic principles and ideological aims (especially the creation of new human communities through art) traditionally associated with the literature of vision in England.

### Further Reading

Williams, Helen Maria. "Letter IV." In *Letters Written in France,* edited by Neil Fraistat and Susan S. Lanser, 73–77. Peterborough, Ont., and Orchard Park, N.Y.: Broadview Press, 2001.

———. "The Bastille, A Vision." In *Letters Written in France,* edited by Neil Fraistat and Susan S. Lanser, 203–206. Peterborough, Ont., and Orchard Park, N.Y.: Broadview Press, 2001.

—Tim Ruppert

## "Battle of Blenheim, The"  Robert Southey (1798)

This famous poem was written in 1798 for the *Morning Post,* a newspaper that opposed the ongoing war with France. Comprising 11 stanzas, the poem is symptomatic of the 23-year-old ROBERT SOUTHEY's youthful pacifism, according to which victory is pointless and war is never justifiable. To support his idea, Southey looks back to the beginning of the 18th century and the much-celebrated Anglo-Austrian victory over France at Blenheim in Bavaria (August 13, 1704).

The ballad-style poem opens on a peaceful summer evening; an old peasant, Kaspar, is resting in front of his cottage after a hard day's labour. Playing by a stream, his grandchildren, Wilhelmine and Peterkin, find "something large and round" (l. 8). Upon closer inspection this is revealed to be a man's skull—from the body of one of the thousands of soldiers who died in the "great victory" (l. 18), which took place on the very same site. Kaspar's response is matter-of-fact; he is used to finding them: "For there's many here about; / And often when I go to plough, / The ploughshare turns them out!" (ll. 21–23). Asked by his grandchildren to explain the war and its causes, Kaspar falters: "'It was the English,' Kaspar cried, / 'Who put the French to rout; / But what they fought each other for, / I could not well make out;. . . .'" (ll. 31–34). All he can remember is that the outcome was reckoned by "everybody" to be "a famous victory" (ll. 35, 36), and he appears to accept this received wisdom. However, as the poem progresses, we are given an insight into the havoc wreaked by the battle. Kaspar's father was forced to flee his home with his wife and child, and his house was burned down. Yet this was not unusual, and indeed, he was one of the lucky ones: "With fire and sword the country round / Was wasted far and wide, / And many a childing mother then, / And new-born baby died; . . ." (ll. 43–46). "But," as Kaspar blithely points out, "things like that, you know, must be / A every famous victory" (ll. 47–48). So, too, the rotting, unburied bodies left on the field of battle "had to be." This "shocking sight" (l. 49) was a small price to pay, and it brought plaudits to the English commander, John Churchill, duke of Marlborough, and his Austrian counterpart, Prince Eugene of Savoy.

Like other Romantic poets, Southey believed that children had a special insight that supposedly wiser adults lacked (see CHILDHOOD). Thus, he shows Wilhelmine suggesting that the whole event was "a very wicked thing!" (l. 57). "Nay . . . nay . . . my little girl," her grandfather says (l. 59), and he quotes again History's official verdict: "It was a famous victory" (l. 60). "But what good came of it at last?" asks "little Peterkin" (ll. 63–64). His grandfather is unable to answer this difficult—yet obvious—question, admitting, "Why, that I cannot tell" (l. 65), but again repeating, parrot-like, "'twas a famous victory'" (l. 66). By this point in the poem, the battle is no longer "great" but simply "famous," reflecting Southey's belief that the causes of war rarely involve important moral principles but invariably hinge on trivial or spurious reasons that are soon forgotten. Kaspar's uncovering of skulls while he ploughs and sows his crop suggests the waste of human life and thought. The ploughing of the fields suggests rebirth and renewal, but the reappearance of the skulls is a reminder that the dead lie uneasily in their mass, makeshift graves in a foreign field. The rightful memorial to the battle is not the magnificent palace built in Oxfordshire by a grateful nation for the British commander Marlborough but this corner of Bavaria where the dead troops rise to the surface as if determined not to be forgotten.

The tone of the poem is heavily ironic. Why should such slaughter be mythologized? Why should its leaders be glorified? Interestingly, as Southey got older, he lost much of his radical edge and his opinion on Blenheim changed. He described it as "the greatest victory which had ever done honour to British arms" (quoted in Speck 180).

## Further Reading

Robert Southey Page. Available online. URL: http://www.accd.edu/sac/English/BAILEY/southey.htm. Accessed on January 12, 2008.

Southey, Robert. *Poetical Works.* 5 vols. Edited by Lynda Pratt et al. (London: Pickering and Chatto, 2004).

Speck, W. A. *Robert Southey: Entire Man of Letters* (New Haven, Conn., and London: Yale University Press, 2006).

—Andrew Maunder

## "Beachy Head" Charlotte Smith (1807)

One of CHARLOTTE SMITH's two famous long blank-verse poems, *"Beachy Head"*—written in 1806, shortly before Smith's death—situates the speaker on the same Sussex cliffs featured in "The EMIGRANTS." This elevated position allows Smith to survey the landscape and, by extension, society using a multifaceted approach, including botany, archeology, anthropology, and sociology. Reflecting much of the same attention to nature and the imagination as many of her Romantic contemporaries, Smith alternates between imagining the past—of the nation and of the community's

residents—and illuminating the present, with an attention to a smuggling trade born of open imperial ports and an impoverished rural working class. Within her historical narration of the invasions and excursions of past British military forces, Smith embeds a clear condemnation of the attitudes and motivations behind war, an obvious critique of the continuing Napoleonic Wars occurring during the time of the poem's composition (see BONAPARTE, NAPOLEON). The poem also often employs nature in a typical Romantic metaphor for the human condition, seeming to argue that in a life connected to nature, one can find the idyllic circumstances lost through industrialization and rampant consumerism. Smith, however, often undercuts this image of idealized country life through a host of subtle images that point to the corruption, alienation, or stagnation of a life lived solely in nature. The poem offers what amounts to an alternative history of the community as well as an evolutionary argument about social changes.

Tension plays a crucial role in Smith's poetry, made manifest here in a focus on both physical and sociological history and the celebration of nature, with a simultaneous focus on its inadequacies. Theresa M. Kelley argues that this tension springs from the problem of "writing history when its records and concerns work at so many discordant levels" (Kelley 290). Unlike many of Smith's other works, the speaker's voice in "Beachy Head" is not as easily mistaken for the author, instead resembling "a grander voice of the historian whose reach goes back in space and time" (297). Smith's choice to write about history and science engages with a Romantic interrogation not only of a woman's role within the literary community but also of female education. Smith's balance in "Beachy Head" between domesticity, manifested in her focus on the incomings and outgoings of the community and an expansive intellectual view argues that women have the capacity to engage skillfully in both spheres. Donelle R. Ruwe argues that Smith's use of botany in "Beachy Head," a science often considered the province of women during the 19th century, articulates the material and concrete nature of the female artistic imagination and relationship with nature, which she contrasts with the encompassing, all-consuming, sublime approach of male poets. Smith's balance between the historic and the personal emphasizes her artistic ability and her engagement with sweeping social issues of interest to her readers.

### Further Reading

Kelley, Theresa M. "Romantic Histories: Charlotte Smith and *Beachy Head.*" *Nineteenth-Century Literature* 59, no. 3 (2004): 281–314.

Ruwe, Donelle R. "Charlotte Smith's Sublime: Feminine Poetics, Botany, and *Beachy Head.*" *Prism(s): Essays in Romanticism* 7 (1999): 117–132.

Smith, Charlotte Turner. *Beachy Head: with other poems.* London: J. Johnson, 1807.

—Caralyn Bolte

## Beckford, William (1760–1844)

William Beckford, author of *Vathek*, was born on October 1, 1760, probably at Fonthill, Wiltshire, where he was baptized in January 1761 (some sources, however, give London as his place of birth). He was the only child of the colorful politician and Jamaican plantation owner William Beckford, often known as Alderman Beckford, and his wife Maria; the senior Beckford was twice Lord Mayor of London. As heir to an immense fortune made from SLAVERY and sugar, Beckford was raised in a mansion of nouveau-riche extravagance at Fonthill, a 4,000-acre country estate. Unusually, he was never sent to school, and apart from being tutored in the gentlemanly disciplines—French, dancing, music (allegedly with the child prodigy Mozart), classics, art, and the principles of architecture—he was at liberty to please himself and spent his time reading the *Arabian Nights* and writing imitations of it, wandering in the parkland, and daydreaming in the mansion's apartments (one of which was decorated in the Eastern style). His tutor John Lettice first encouraged Beckford to write and try out many different styles.

At 14 Beckford was provided with a drawing master, Alexander Cozens. He became strongly attached to Cozens, whose experimental theories of art and facility for telling oriental tales were a significant although not necessarily positive influence. In 1776, age 16, Beckford wrote *L'Esplendente*, an autobiographical tale that prefigures his most famous work, VATHEK, in some of its motifs. In 1777 he wrote the satirical *Biographical Memoirs of Extraordinary Painters*, which was published in 1780 with Lettice's help.

After his father's sudden death in 1777, his mother sent Beckford to study in Geneva, where, although he learned several languages, including Arabic, and attended lectures on natural science and law, he applied himself more diligently to his social life and to exploring the Swiss wilderness. A visit to the monastery of the Grande Chartreuse (in the footsteps of his literary hero Thomas Gray) kindled in him a lifelong love of Roman Catholicism. He continued experimenting with literary styles and wrote *The Long Story* and *Hylas*. He also fell in love with a young man, which prompted Maria Beckford to bring him home.

In 1779, after a secluded spell at Fonthill during which he wrote in a wild Romantic style, Beckford was sent on a rehabilitational tour of England. Here his sexuality took a dark turn when he became infatuated with the 11-year-old son of Viscount Courtenay. In 1780 Maria sent him on a Grand Tour to Europe, where he was dazzled by Italian music and architecture as well as the sexual freedom the Continent afforded. Notes from the tour became *Dreams, Waking Thoughts, and Incidents*, published in 1783 and instantly suppressed by his family. Back in England, Beckford courted a reputation as an amoral extrovert. Still obsessed with young Courteney, he had become entangled with an emotionally unstable married cousin, Louisa, who acted as his handmaiden and confidante. At a lavish coming-of-age party at Fonthill in 1781, Maria introduced him to a suitable wife, Lady Margaret Gordon. Soon afterward, Beckford seduced Courteney.

At an atmospheric Christmas party at Fonthill, which Beckford later claimed inspired him to write *Vathek*, he met Reverend Samuel Henley, who began to help him edit his works. *Vathek* was written in French in 1782 and subsequently translated into English and edited, with footnotes, by Henley. Beckford started writing some accompanying "Episodes" without which he insisted *Vathek* should not to be published.

Beckford married Margaret Gordon in 1783, and despite losing two babies, the couple were happy. He became a member of Parliament but, disliking the House of Commons, petitioned for a barony and thus a seat in the House of Lords. His ambition was derailed, however, when he was caught in bed with Courteney, and a press campaign against him drove him into exile with his wife and a newborn daughter.

In Geneva in 1786 a second daughter was born, but the birth killed Lady Margaret, and the children were taken back to England to be brought up by Maria. Beckford thenceforth showed little interest in them. At this time Henley backhandedly released his version of *Vathek* for publication, passing it off as an original Arabic text. Although critics saw through the claim to authenticity, Henley's footnotes were singled out for praise in the book's many good reviews. Beckford retaliated by publishing the French text in Lausanne, with his name as original author clearly established. An extensively revised version was published in Paris in 1787. *Vathek* was to go through nine editions in Beckford's lifetime.

En route to Jamaica in 1787, Beckford disembarked in Portugal for a prolonged stay. There his extravagant expenditure, anti-English sentiments, and devotion to the Catholic Church ensured that he was embraced by Portuguese high society but virtually shunned by English ex-patriots. This pained him as he was still ambitious for a peerage. Of his numerous romantic attachments to boys, one, with Gregorio Franchi, became long-term. From this sojourn and a decadent season in Madrid came material for *Italy; with Sketches of Spain and Portugal* (1834). There followed a period in Switzerland and revolutionary France, where Beckford ingratiated himself with the National Assembly, his reputation in England thenceforth becoming further tainted.

Beckford was a prolific house and garden designer, and a visit to two Portuguese monasteries in 1793 won him over completely to the Gothic style in architecture. In 1796 he returned to England to build Fonthill Abbey. He employed the royal architect James Wyatt to create a cathedral-like structure with a central tower 276 feet high. Shoddily constructed, the building fell down several times during its erection.

The abbey made a significant impact on the Gothic revival of the 19th century and was widely admired for its "sublimity." It was painted by John Constable and Joseph Turner and inspired Charles Barry and Augustus Pugin's designs for the palace of Westminster. Although sugar revenues (from the colonies) were declining, Beckford continued to spend lavishly, assembling a spectacular collection of books and art. Consequently, he was forced to sell Fonthill Abbey in 1822. Three years later the great tower collapsed.

In 1796 and 1797 Beckford wrote two sentimental novels, *Modern Novel Writing, or The Elegant Enthusiast* and *Azemia*, in lighthearted competition with his half sister, the novelist Elizabeth Hervey. After Maria died in 1798, Beckford's daughters spent some time living near their father; ever the detached parent, Beckford later cut off the elder for marrying for love. An isolated figure despite his huge entourage (which included a dwarf for entertainment), he relied on Gregorio Franchi to procure him art, antiques, and boys.

In 1822 Beckford moved to Bath, where he bought up several farms to make a pleasure garden, complete with a 120-foot neoclassical tower. In 1834, taking material from *Dreams, Waking Thoughts, and Incidents* and early letters and journals and mixing it liberally with invention, he produced *Italy; with Sketches of Spain and Portugal*, which was an instant success. The following year he published *Recollections of an Excursion to the Monasteries of Alcobaça and Batalha*. Both works established Beckford as a travel writer of note, but despite his late literary laurels, he became increasingly embittered. He shunned Franchi at the latter's death; Beckford himself died of influenza on May 2, 1844.

As a writer, Beckford was remarkably erratic. On the one hand, *Vathek* is the work of an eccentric genius. A critic writing in *A New Review* for June/July 1786 called the novel "a literary comet"; its "wild and sublime . . . machinery" felt altogether "new." At only 21 years of age, Beckford displayed "the caustick quickness of Voltaire, the easy sportiveness of Ariosto; the sombrous grotesque of Dante; and the terrific greatness of Milton." His early immersion in oriental texts had given him an instinct for their beauties and grotesqueries, which he recreated with the confidence of a master. Reflected in the novel's brattish, over-reaching, sadistic characters are both the personalities who shaped Beckford's dark emotional life and his own appetites and fantasies writ large. Unsurprisingly, he was something of a model for the Romantic movement. LORD BYRON acknowledged *Vathek* in his 1813 poem *THE GIAOUR*, which added to the popularity of Beckford's work and legitimised orientalism for the Romantic generation. Beckford's terrifying chasms, valleys, and moonlit ruins prefigure the sublime gothic landscapes of ANN RADCLIFFE, and the evocation of infernal halls made possible the supernatural elements in the gothic novels of MATTHEW GREGORY LEWIS and his followers.

*Italy; with Sketches of Spain and Portugal,* on the other hand, comes from the pen of an urbane and carefree raconteur, one with impressive political contacts and friends in high (European) places. The descriptions of social customs and manners are vivid, and there is much lampooning of foreign pretentiousness. *Recollections of an Excursion to the Monasteries of Alcobaca and Batalha* is considered by some to be Beckford's finest piece of writing. For the Beckford biographer Malcolm Jack it is an "unflaggingly zestful" exercise in touristic observation which, despite moments of "Romantic recreation," never "[crosses] the line of exuberance into the merely gushing, the prose holds us back with a slight tautness" (Jack 93, 92). The observations are astutely described by Rose Macaulay as having been made "by someone who saw sharply, beautifully, with the artist's eye" (Macaulay 142).

Interest in Beckford's work did not wane in the 20th century. The "Episodes" that were to have accompanied *Vathek* were published in 1912. *The Long Story* was published as *The Vision* in 1930. *The Journal of William Beckford in Portugal and Spain 1787–1788,* published by Boyd Alexander in 1954, provides a more immediately compelling account of the early Continental travels before the tidying up and straightening out of the 1830s revisions. Alexander also published Beckford's midlife correspondence (1957), which gives insight into his day-to-day life as the "Abbot" of Fonthill Abbey.

**Further Reading**

Beckford, William. *Dreams, Waking Thoughts and Incidents by William Beckford of Fonthill.* 1783. Reprint Stroud, Eng.: Nonsuch, 2006

———. *Italy: With Sketches of Spain and Portugal by the Author of "Vathek."* London: R. Bentley, 1834.

———. *The Journal of William Beckford in Spain and Portugal 1787–1788.* Edited by Alexander Boyd. London: Hart-Davis, 1954.

———. *Life at Fonthill, 1807—1822: From the Correspondence of William Beckford.* Edited by Boyd Alexander. Stroud, Eng.: Nonsuch, 2006.

———. *Recollections of an Excursion to the Monasteries of Alcobaça and Batalha by the Author of "Vathek."* London: R. Bentley, 1835.

Beckford, William. *Vathek.* 1786. Reprint, Oxford: Oxford University Press, 1998.

Graham, Kenneth W., ed. *Vathek and the Escape from Time: Bicentenary Revaluations.* New York: AMS, 1990.

Macaulay, Rose. *They Went to Portugal.* London: Penguin, 1985.

Jack, Malcolm. *William Beckford: An English Fidalgo.* New York: AMS Press, 1996.

Mowl, Timothy. *William Beckford: Composing For Mozart.* London: John Murray Ltd., 1998.

—Maria Purves

## Beddoes, Thomas Lovell (1803–1849)

A late Romantic poet and playwright, Thomas Lovell Beddoes was one of four children of the physician Thomas Beddoes and his wife, Anna (who was the sister of MARIA EDGEWORTH). He was born in Clifton, England, on July 20, 1803, and was five when his father died, leaving Thomas Jr. and his siblings in the care of their mother and of Davies Giddy, a politician, patron of the arts and sciences, and later president of the Royal Society. Beddoes attended a grammar school in Bath and proceeded from there to study at the private Charterhouse School, where he distinguished himself in classics. His unmethodical reading, including PERCY BYSSHE SHELLEY's poetry and Elizabethan and Jacobean drama, helped to lay the foundations for his distinctly morbid literary imagination.

Beddoes won critical attention with the publication of his first collection of verse, *Improvisatore, in Three Fyttes* (1821), published while he was still an undergraduate at Pembroke College, Oxford University. His first attempt to revive Jacobean drama for the 19th century came in 1822 with *The Brides' Tragedy*. These early successes led Beddoes to work, between 1823 and 1825, on a string of gloomy verse tragedies (*The Second Brother, Torrismond, Love's Arrow Poisoned,* and *The Last Man*), of which only fragments remain. Following a bout of illness that caused the temporary loss of his hair, Beddoes convalesced on a trip through Italy in 1824. He graduated from Oxford with a B.A. on his return to England in 1825.

At Oxford Beddoes had developed a keen interest in the natural sciences, especially in physiology and chemistry, and in the fall of his graduating year he left for the University of Göttingen, Germany, to continue his study of these subjects. For the next few years he remained at Göttingen, where he finished the first version of his five-act blank-verse drama, *Death's Jest-Book, or, The Fool's Tragedy.* His friends' unflattering criticism of the play precipitated acute depression, and in the following years he became increasingly suicidal, obsessively redrafting *Death's Jest-Book.* In 1820 Beddoes was forced to leave Göttingen over charges of misconduct, but he was able to continue his studies at Würzburg, where he was awarded a doctorate in medicine in 1831. In the following years he lived in Strasbourg and Zurich, where he became involved with the burgeoning movement for German unification (Germany at this time was a collection of small, independent states). His political agitation in favor of this cause took the form of public speeches as well as of numerous articles and poems, which he penned for radical newspapers.

Beddoes kept on revising the expanding *Death's Jest-Book* for much of the 1830s, planning at one point to integrate it into a larger literary project called *The Ivory Gate.* His growing fame as a satirist and orator led to his being expelled from Zurich in 1840 and forced to wander between Frankfurt, Berlin, and Baden (in Switzerland). Returning to Frankfurt in the mid-1840s, he eventually resumed scientific work, but an accident

causing blood poisoning soon led to a six-month hospitalization. Following this last disappointment, he travelled to Basel, where he attempted suicide by opening an artery in his leg. His life was saved, but the healing process was accompanied by complications and his leg had to be amputated. Another suicide attempt, probably by poison, resulted Beddoes's death on January 26, 1849.

Beddoes left the bulk of his manuscripts, including a large number of drafts for *Death's Jest-Book,* to T. F. Kelsall, one of his few close friends, to "print or not as *he* thinks fit" (Beddoes 683). Kelsall quickly secured publication of *Death's Jest-Book* (1850) and edited his friend's *Poems Posthumous and Collected* (1851). The poems that Beddoes wrote in the late 1820s and early 1830s are arguably his finest (including the much-anthologized "Dream Pedlary"); these intensely lyrical pieces characteristically combine a late-Romantic subjectivity with a Victorian sense for the drama of a poem's voice and tone of address. His first neo-Jacobean dramas, written around the same time, anticipate the morbid imagination of Beddoes's later works, especially *Death's Jest-Book.*

Beddoes's life was famously one of unmitigated disappointment. "Failure," as Christopher Ricks, one of Beddoes's most appreciative critics, points out, "became what he was best at" (Ricks 135). Most prominent among Beddoes's frustrations was his failure to complete his much-labored-over *Death's Jest-Book.* Nonetheless, this long play is incontestably his masterpiece, offering an extraordinary blend of verse and prose genres. *Death's Jest-Book,* modeled on medieval renderings of the allegorical Dance of Death, draws on many traditions, especially on German Romanticism and the eclectic medievalism of Ludwig Tieck. Beddoes had originally intended the play to stage a triumph over Death, but his lack of success in staging this optimistic climax led him to present Death as triumphant in all surviving versions of the play.

Beddoes's works are richly intertextual, frequently drawing on alchemical, kabbalistic, and Islamic sources to effect a visionary tone of voice that stands in marked contrast to the near-nihilism of many of his pieces. But his writings also indulge in a pastiche of lower registers and of the burlesque, a mixture particularly admired by the Victorian poet Robert Browning, who found in Beddoes's works inspiration for his own dramatic monologues. Beddoes's professional interest in anatomy and physiology likewise exerted a formative influence on the imagery and the sombrely detached tone of his poems.

Beddoes is one of the transitional figures of 19th-century English literature, connecting the high tide of English Romanticism and the Victorian age without being easily attributed to either. After a period of relative neglect in the 19th-century, the 1935 edition of *The Works of Thomas Lovell Beddoes,* edited by H. W. Donner, signaled a turning point in the critical recognition of Beddoes's writings. His most prominent champions in the second half of the 20th century have included Northrop Frye and Christopher Ricks. His reputation, as well as his popularity, have continued to grow in recent years, and several monographs have illuminated key aspects of his creative oeuvre. The year 2003 saw the publication of the first number of the *Journal of the Thomas Lovell Beddoes Society.*

**Further Reading**

Allard, James Robert. *Romanticism, Medicine, and the Poet's Body.* Aldershot, Eng.: Ashgate, 2007.

Beddoes, Thomas Lovell. *The Works of Thomas Lovell Beddoes.* Edited by H. W. Donner. Oxford: Oxford University Press, 1935.

Berns, Ute, and Michael Bradshaw, eds. *The Ashgate Research Companion to Thomas Lovell Beddoes.* Aldershot, Eng.: Ashgate, 2007.

Bradshaw, Michael. *Resurrection Songs: The Poetry of Thomas Lovell Beddoes.* Aldershot, Eng.: Ashgate, 2001.

Donner, H. W. *Thomas Lovell Beddoes. The Making of a Poet.* Oxford: Basil Blackwell, 1935.

Frye, Northrop. "Yorick: The Romantic Macabre." In *A Study of English Romanticism.* New York: Random House, 1968, 51–85.

Ricks, Christopher. "Thomas Lovell Beddoes: A Dying Start." In *The Force of Poetry.* Oxford: Oxford University Press, 1984, 135–162.

Thompson, James R. *Thomas Lovell Beddoes.* Boston: Twayne Publishers, 1985.

—Benjamin Kohlmann

## *Belinda* Maria Edgeworth (1801)

In *Belinda* the Anglo-Irish novelist MARIA EDGEWORTH explores female independence, reason, and equality through her young heroine's entrance into society. Avoiding the lures of status, wealth, fashion, and the other perils of London society and the marriage market, Belinda Portman is tempted by the exciting suitor, Mr. Vincent but discovers that a good marriage requires compatibility of taste, education, and temperament. She ultimately finds happiness with a man who is her equal, Clarence Hervey, but, initially, his own mysterious relationship with Virginia, a young woman he has been educating as the 'perfect' wife threatens to prevent their match.

The 18th-century novel was deeply concerned with proper female behavior. In response to MARY WOLLSTONECRAFT's championing of proper education in VINDICATION OF THE RIGHTS OF WOMAN (1792), conservatives worried about the effects of reason and independence on femininity. Edgeworth presents the perils of the extremes and introduces several characters who symbolize different attitudes. The shallow Lady Delacour's hedonism and self-centredness demonstrates how even just claims to independence of thought can result in marital discord. Lord Delacour interprets her desire for equality as an assault on his masculinity, and their stubborn refusal to communicate causes a serious breach. Taking Lady Delacour's professed desire for mental liberty further, the outrageous Harriet Freke objects to all conventions—"whatever is is wrong" (Edgeworth 230). Mrs. Freke's absurd behavior, which challenges the physical limitations of femininity, provides comic relief. By laughing at her, Edgeworth dismisses fears about the physically masculine woman as an alarmist overreaction.

Edgeworth uses the character of Virginia St. Pierre to explore the consequences of insufficient education. Inspired by JEAN-JACQUES ROUSSEAU's Sophie in *Émile* (1763), Clarence Hervey searches for an uncorrupted alternative to simpering society women. Clarence initially delights in Virginia's unspoiled sensibility, but upon meeting Belinda he realizes that an uncultivated woman is an unsuitable companion for a rational man.

Edgeworth's version of companionate marriage requires husbands and wives to be equals, with parity of education and mental accomplishment. Belinda is a rational heroine with the ability to learn from the mistakes of others, making her an ideal partner for a man of sense. Belinda learns the importance of remaining cool in emotional situations and draws a distinction between being in love and loving. Passionate love is potentially detrimental to marriage, as demonstrated by Belinda's sister and cousins, who all marry to socioeconomic advantage by manipulating their suitors. Critics of the time found Belinda's apparent coldness disconcerting, even unfeminine, but her imperviousness to all-consuming love not only saves her from a disastrous connection with Mr. Vincent but allows her a certain amount of independence. Furthermore, Edgeworth suggests that reason and passion are not mutually exclusive through Belinda and Hervey's marriage.

ANNA LAETITIA BARBAULD included *Belinda* in a 50-volume series of re-prints called "British Novelists" (1810) on the condition that Edgeworth make significant alterations to colonial characters. In addition to rendering her heroine and hero more conventional, Edgeworth demoted Mr. Vincent, the wealthy Creole, from Belinda's husband-presumptive to a mere suitor, while Juba, his African servant, is not permitted to marry his English farm girl. This conservative editing perhaps suggests just how ahead of its time *Belinda* was.

See also CASTLE RACKRENT.

**Further Reading**

Edgeworth, Maria. *Belinda* (1802 edition). Edited by Kathryn Kirkpatrick. Oxford: Oxford World's Classics, 1999.

Kirkpatrick, Kathryn. "The Limits of Liberal Feminism in Maria Edgeworth's *Belinda*." In *Jane Austen and Mary Shelley and Their Sister.* Edited by Laura Dabundo. Lanham, Md.: University Press of America, 2000.

Richard, Jessica. "'Games of Chance': *Belinda*, Education, and Empire." In *An Uncomfortable Authority: Maria Edgeworth and Her Contexts,* edited by Heidi Kaufman, 192–211. Newark, Del.: University of Delaware Press, 2004.

Weiss, Deborah. "The Extraordinary Ordinary Belinda: Maria Edgeworth's Female Philosopher." *Eighteenth-Century Fiction* 19 (2007): 441–461.

—Megan Woodworth

## *Bertram, or, The Castle of St. Aldobrand*
**Charles Robert Maturin** (1816)

*Bertram,* CHARLES ROBERT MATURIN's contribution to the stage genre of GOTHIC sensationalism, was the most popular of his works in his own lifetime. Through the direct influence of LORD BYRON and SIR WALTER SCOTT, it was produced at Drury Lane by EDMUND KEAN. Bertram, a robber and Byronic hero-villain, is washed ashore after a storm. The prior of the nearby monastery sends Bertram to the castle of St. Aldobrand for shelter, where it transpires that Aldobrand's wife, Imogine, is the woman Bertram once loved. After an assignation with Imogine, Bertram kills Aldobrand. Imogine subsequently exiles herself to a cave, where her son dies mysteriously and she becomes insane. As the curtain falls, she dies in Bertram's arms; he stabs himself, saying, "I died no felon death— / A warrior's weapon freed a warrior's soul" (Maturin ).

In the character of Bertram, Maturin created an antihero anticipating his most famous creation, Melmoth the Wanderer (the title character of his novel published in 1820). Bertram's initial fall from grace, precipitated by Aldobrand, is unexplained, but as the leader of a band of robbers he is clearly a reprobate. However, his reckless determination to avenge himself on his enemy and his passion for Imogine combine to make him attractive, if disturbing.

The play adheres to accepted conventions of gothic in its setting of monastery, castle, and rugged landscape; in its excessive and violent emotion; and in the pervading atmosphere of evildoing, presaged by the storm and maintained by the repeated fear of something "That seems in truth not earthly" (321). *Bertram* is particularly interesting, however, in its Romanticist treatment of the boundaries of the self, with the emotional immoderation of Bertram and Imogine resulting in disintegrating selfhood, both identity and sanity crumbling. Bertram has already lost sight of himself as the play begins, telling the prior: "I was a man, I know not what I am— / What others' crimes and injuries have made me" (331). However, after the murder of Aldobrand, he seems to regain himself, determined to demonstrate at least a ruffian's code of justice. His final words suggest that his death paradoxically completes and redeems him, allowing him to regain his identity. For Imogine the reverse is true. In the apotheosis of her crisis, she cries: "Nay—let me think—what am I? No, what was I? I was the honoured wife of Aldobrand; I am the scorned minion of a ruffian" (352). Defining herself by her relationships with men, after the death of her husband she feels revulsion for his murderer and wishes for death.

*Bertram* is known now mostly through SAMUEL TAYLOR COLERIDGE's contemptuous comments. His review, included in *BIOGRAPHIA LITERARIA*, described the play as "an insult to common decency" (Coleridge 1997; 350), accusing it of immorality and blasphemy as well as implausibility. However, his comments are considered to be partly due to the recent failure of his play *Remorse* and his contempt for the British public for their debased taste in drama. Despite Coleridge's dismay at the play's success with the public, *Bertram* remains not only an interesting example of staged melodrama but a fascinating exploration of the interiority of identity and selfhood.

### Further Reading

Coleridge, Samuel Taylor. *Biographia Literaria.* Edited by Nigel Leask. London: Everyman, 1997.

Maturin, Charles R. *Bertram, or, The Castle of St Aldobrand.* In *Seven Gothic Dramas.* Edited by Jeffrey Cox. Athens: Ohio University Press, 1992.

——— *Melmoth the Wanderer.* Edited by Victor Sage. London: Penguin Classics, 2001.

—Serena Trowbridge

## *Biographia Literaria* Samuel Taylor Coleridge (1817)

*Biographia Literaria* is often described as SAMUEL TAYLOR COLERIDGE's literary autobiography. However, it is not just autobiography but also Coleridge's statement about his literary and philosophical beliefs and poetic theory. The work presents his theories of the imagination; of the art of poetry; and of the philosophy of Immanuel Kant, Johann Fichte, and Friedrich Schelling.

The *Biographia Literaria*'s five chapters on WILLIAM WORDSWORTH convey a clear idea of Coleridge's theory about poetry. He begins with an account of the genesis of the *LYRICAL BALLADS* and a division of labor between himself and his collaborator, Wordsworth. He then gives his idea of a poem and poetry. The nature of a poem leads to an account of the nature of poetry. The poet, according to Coleridge, is a man of passion and sensibility. It is this passion that links the poet to the state of childhood. Thus, the characteristics of a poem are passion, sensibility, metre, figurative language, and simplicity. There is an order, a specific pattern, and it is this pattern that is essential to a poem. The excitement from which poetry results is a blend of two things; one excites and the other refines the mind of the reader. It is in this polarity that the essence of poetry is to be found.

True poetry also conveys the voice of experience and the feelings of the poet. It is the imagination ("that synthetic and magical power") that gives organic form to poetry. Imagination controls the reason and understanding of the poem. One of Coleridge's greatest contributions to literary theory is his distinction between imagination and fancy. In chapter 13 of the *Biographia*, Coleridge gives his definitions of *fancy* and *imagination*. Fancy, for Coleridge, was the passive and mechanical collation of facts, similes, metaphors, and ideas and is inferior to imagination. Imagination is organic and gives language a concrete form and shape. It is a "modifying," "co-adunating" and "esemplastic" power shaping everything into one. The primary imagination is the agency of knowing. It perceives and creates before association can take place. The primary imagination precedes the secondary. The secondary imagination reconciles all the experiences and knowledge perceived by the primary imagination. It involves the active participation of the will, whereas the primary imagination is involuntary perception. Writing in the *Biographia*, Coleridge says that a great poet has to necessarily be at the same time a "profound philosopher." When he begins the application of his critical principles in chapter 14 of the *Biographia*, he defines poetry in terms of the imagination. Throughout chapter 15 of the *Biographia*, it is Shakespeare who is Coleridge's example of the poet whose work exhibits the poetic perspective on the real level.

## Further Reading

Christensen, Jerome C. "Coleridge's Marginalia Method in the *Biographia Literaria*." *PMLA* 92 (1977): 928–940.

Leask, Nigel. *The Politics of Imagination in Coleridge's Thought*. London: Macmillan, 1988.

Milnes, Tim. "Eclipsing Art: Method and Metaphysics in Coleridge's *Biographia Literaria*." *Journal of the History of Ideas* 60 (1999): 125–147.

—Nishi Pulugurtha

## Blake, William (1757–1827)

While the works of William Blake did not achieve great popularity or recognition during his own lifetime, he is now acknowledged as one of the most influential artists and writers of all time. His works, which combine poetry with highly charged visual art, have not only inspired other writers and visual artists; they have become a source of inspiration within the realm of popular culture as well. And yet, despite the magnitude of his influence over the passage of centuries and ongoing critical controversies surrounding his work, Blake's body of work has remained distinctly unique, defying any certain classification. The most recognizable attributes of his works—the display of radical social and religious views; a penchant for commentary on the rapidly changing cultural landscape resulting from industrialization and the drive for economic progress; the employment of myth and allegory; evidence of the influence of classicism; the use of gothic elements; and, most important, passionate emphasis of the significance of imagination and the power of the individual—are the same characteristics that have come to define Romanticism and the countless works that fall under this heading. Despite Blake's own aversion to classification or abstraction and despite the various places where his work strays from that of other Romantics, his name remains firmly linked to this cultural movement almost 200 years after his death.

William Blake was born into a middle-class family in London on November 28, 1757. His father was James Blake, a hosier. Blake was the third of seven children, two of whom died as infants. He left school at a young age, receiving instruction from his mother, to whom he grew close, and taking up drawing classes in addition to reading poetry. Religion and spirituality, which would later be key concerns in his poems and artwork, were important and influential factors in Blake's life even as a young boy. It is believed that his parents were Dissenters who separated from the established Anglican church, and this element of the family background seems to have had a strong and lasting influence on Blake, who would sustain an interest in religion, mysticism, and dissent throughout his career. Early in his life, he found inspiration in the Bible, a source that would be evident in his later and most well-known works. He also found inspiration in classical literature, Greek mythology, and the artwork of the Renaissance artists Michelangelo, Raphael, and Albrecht Dürer. As a young man he engraved images of antiques that his father purchased for him and spent his time studying other classical works of art.

In 1772 Blake was apprenticed to James Basire, an engraver who practiced old-fashioned methods of printmaking. He worked under Basire for seven years, copying images from churches and architecture in London, which formed the foundation for his unique artistic style. In 1779 he joined the Royal Academy, a London art institution, but he preferred classical works of art to the more modern examples of oil painting promoted at the academy, finding the newer methods to be representative of the same materialistic culture he sought to repudiate. Biographers have noted that one year after joining the academy, in 1780, Blake was either caught up in or willingly joined a mob storming London's Newgate Prison. Whether he voluntarily joined the fray or was inadvertently swept up in the crowd, the experience is thought to have been another key influence in his already developing interest in revolution and rebellion.

In 1782 Blake met and married Catherine Boucher, the illiterate daughter of a local gardener. He taught her how to read, write, and engrave, and she began assisting him in the printing of his works. Blake's first collection of poems, a series of works entitled *Poetical Sketches*, made up primarily of poems the author had written as an adolescent, was printed a year later in 1783 with the help of his wife and his friends. The following year he opened a printing shop with his wife and brother after the death of their father, and they began working with Joseph Johnson, a radical publisher and bookseller who was believed to have held frequent meetings with dissidents of the day such as MARY WOLL-STONECRAFT, WILLIAM GODWIN, Joseph Priestley, Richard Price, and THOMAS PAINE. Blake also became interested in the AMERICAN REVOLUTION and FRENCH REVOLUTION during this time, showing support for those fighting for reform.

In 1788, with the assistance of his wife Catherine, Blake made an important artistic discovery in the invention of relief etching, a reversal of traditional methods of printmaking. The new method—which consisted of inscribing text and imagery onto a copper plate, etching to create a relief, printing onto paper, and then hand coloring with watercolor paint—produced the illuminated manuscripts that became the primary format for the majority of Blake's works. It also subsequently became one of the most utilized printmaking methods for books and artwork of the period. The process allowed for a unique presentation of poetry, imagery, and philosophy, whereby the work as a whole functioned as a unique piece of art. This individualized process allowed Blake to work in protestation of the mass production of books, which was now possible in light of mechanical advancements stemming from the Industrial Revolution (see INDUSTRIAL-ISM). However, his painstaking and time-consuming method of producing books, which turned out unique, handmade works of art, did not allow for the production of large quantities of works, and this limited production is commonly cited as one of the primary reasons for Blake's failure to achieve financial success or popularity during his own lifetime.

Over the next several years Blake continued to work using this method, self-publishing both illuminated and nonilluminated works, including what later became known as his Prophetic Books. Produced by Blake between 1789 and 1820, the Prophetic Books included *Tiriel; The Book of Thel;* AMERICA: A PROPHECY; *Europe: A Prophecy;* VISIONS OF THE DAUGHTERS OF ALBION; *The Book of Urizen; The Book of Ahania; The Book of Los; Song of Los; Vala, or The Four Zoas; Milton: A Poem;* and JERUSALEM: THE EMANATION OF THE GIANT ALBION. The books, which contained invented

mythology based in part on the Bible and Greek mythology, became the subject of intense critical debate. Many scholars and critics provided interpretations that highlighted Blake's concern with topics such as the American and French Revolutions, SLAVERY; and the necessity of the development of a new religion or spirituality, which would replace dogma with visionary experience and imagination. Works such as *Tiriel* (1789), which tells the story of a blind old king whose sons rebel against him and who, in turn, abandons his own parents, seemed to speak out in favor of revolution and announce the necessity of dissent. *Visions of the Daughters of Albion* (1793) presented his disdain for enforced chastity and marriage without love. In accordance with the statement Blake had hoped to make by his choice of production methods, works like *Milton: A Poem* (1811) and *Jerusalem: The Emanation of the Giant Albion* (written 1804–20) seemed indicative of his disgust for the Industrial Revolution and its widespread effects (see INDUSTRIALISM).

In addition to his Prophetic Books, Blake's other works, such as *All Religions Are One* and *There is No Natural Religion* (both ca. 1788) drew on similar themes, taking care to highlight the idea of imagination as a uniting human force. Printed in 1789, *Songs of Innocence,* one of Blake's most famous works, seemed at first glance to be concerned only with the depiction of a simple world of innocence and purity, but it actually contained poems originating from a burlesque novel and social commentary that he had written earlier. While it is unclear if Blake originally planned to produce a corresponding work, he referred back to his collection *Songs of Innocence* in 1794 when he printed *Songs of Experience.* Together with its counterpart, the new volume highlighted the differences between the Old Testament vision of God and the New Testament version and referred to the clash of good and evil, using them as symbols to draw further attention to the disparities between the new material world and the old natural world, which seemed to be facing abandonment. In the two collections Blake utilized imagery that highlighted the contrast between the innocence and sublime beauty of the natural world and the bleakness of the material world that resulted from industrialization and cultural change.

This contrast created a dialogue about the imminent threat of the extinction of true spirituality in contemporary times.

As in the preface to *Milton: A Poem* entitled "And did those feet in ancient time," poems such as "The CHIMNEY SWEEPER," "The TYGER," and "LONDON" in *Songs of Experience* suggested the author's negative opinion of the Industrial Revolution and the materialism that was associated with industrial progress. Other works printed during this period, such as *The Book of Thel* (printed in 1789), employed similar tactics to those utilized in *Songs of Innocence* and *Songs of Experience*, using allegory to suggest the necessity of a return to innocence.

Blake began to compose *The French Revolution,* a history of the revolution, in 1791 but never completed it. Instead, *The Marriage of Heaven and Hell* was printed between 1790 and 1793. The text, consisting almost entirely of prose, presented Hell not in traditional terms but rather as the antithesis to the overwhelming repression that Blake believed to be present in popular religion. Collectively his body of work evidenced his defiance of materialism and the laws of reason, his views on mass production and the changing cultural landscape, and his challenge of religious conventions of the day. In addition to creating his own works, Blake illustrated other texts, including William Hayley's poetry, JOHN MILTON's *Paradise Lost,* and Mary Wollstonecraft's *Original Stories from Real Life.* He also provided illustrations for biblical texts such as the Book of Job and was commissioned to produce illustrations for Dante's *Inferno,* but he died in 1827 before completing the project.

At the time of his death (August 12, 1827), Blake was still relatively unknown. Although he had some followers who considered him a genius, he was by and large considered a radical and an eccentric—some would even say a madman. From a young age Blake claimed to have experienced visions. He acknowledged matter-of-factly that these visions continued to occur throughout his life. They were primarily religious in nature: He saw angels in trees, witnessed processions of monks and priests in empty churches, and even noted that he was able to communicate with his deceased brother. If those who were doubtful were able to overlook these admissions, there was still the mat-

ter of his views, which diverged greatly from popular notions of the day. He was against slavery and was a proponent of sexual equality, condemning enforced chastity and marriage without love. He presented his social and political ideals through the mystical allegories contained in his texts. However, his ideas were not readily welcomed. It has been suggested that after the death of his wife Catherine, the inheritors of many of his manuscripts considered them far too radical, destroying a large number of his works and editing sexual imagery from those that remained.

Today Blake is known as one of the most significant writers and artists of his generation, having influenced countless other artists, writers, and thinkers across genres and geographic boundaries. While many critics and scholars have attributed the start of the Romantic period to the publication of SAMUEL TAYLOR COLERIDGE and WILLIAM WORDSWORTH's *Lyrical Ballads* in 1798 (see *PREFACE TO LYRICAL BALLADS*), there are many who trace the start of the Romantic movement to William Blake. These supporters contend that the plain verse of Coleridge and Wordsworth's *Lyrical Ballads,* which brought literature to the people, was evident in Blake's early works, which predated *Lyrical Ballads* and showed evidence of this same concern for simplicity of language and accessibility. It remains uncertain how much direct contact Blake had with other Romantic writers, artists and thinkers. Yet despite the fact that Blake himself would have frowned on fixed classification, he remains linked to the group. As with the works of the Romantics, Blake's works centered on the promotion and cultivation of the human imagination, which was argued to be "being" itself, and his progressive political, cultural, and religious views also became common markers of Romantic thought.

Influenced by a period of cultural revolutions, including the French and American Revolutions, and by economic change that came in the shape of the Industrial Revolution as England's economy moved from agriculture to manufacturing, Blake's work responded to the drastic social changes taking place. His ideas defied the popular tenets of reason, bridging the logic-driven age of Enlightenment and the new Romantic age, shifting focus onto the potential of the individual and the power and significance of human emotion and imagination, and supporting a renewed interest in nature that allowed for a new definition of spirituality.

See also SONGS OF INNOCENCE AND OF EXPERIENCE.

## Further Reading

Beer, John. *Romantic Consciousness: Blake to Mary Shelley.* New York: Palgrave Macmillan, 2003.

Bentley, G. E. *The Stranger from Paradise: A Biography of William Blake.* New Haven, Conn.: Yale University Press, 2001.

Blake, William. *The Complete Poetry and Prose of William Blake.* Edited by Harold Bloom, David Erdman, and Sir William Golding. Berkeley: University of California Press, 2008.

Bloom, Harold. *Blake's Apocalypse.* New York: Doubleday, 1963.

Bronowski, Jacob. *William Blake and the Age of Revolution.* London: Routledge and K. Paul, 1972.

Damon, S. Foster. *A Blake Dictionary: The Ideas and Symbols of William Blake.* Providence, R.I.: Brown University Press, 1988.

Erdman, David V. *Blake: Prophet against Empire: A Poet's Interpretation of the History of His Own Times.* Princeton, N.J.: Princeton University Press, 1977.

Frye, Northrop. *Fearful Symmetry: A Study of William Blake.* Princeton, N.J.: Princeton University Press, 1947.

Grant, John E., and Mary Lynn Johnson. *Blake's Poetry and Designs.* New York and London: W. W. Norton, 2007.

Green, Matthew J. A. *Visionary Materialism in the Early Works of William Blake: The Intersection of Enthusiasm and Empiricism.* New York: Palgrave Macmillan, 2005.

Jackson, Noel. *Science and Sensation in Romantic Poetry.* New York: Cambridge University Press, 2008.

Makdisi, Saree. *William Blake and the Impossible History of the 1790s.* Chicago: University of Chicago Press, 2002.

Marshall, Peter. *William Blake: Visionary Anarchist.* London: Freedom Press, 1994.

Williams, Nicholas M. *Ideology and Utopia in the Works of William Blake.* New York: Cambridge University Press, 2006.

—Jennifer Banach Palladino

**Blessington, countess of** See GARDINER, MARGUERITE.

## "Blond Eckbert" ("Auburn Egbert") Ludwig Tieck (1797)

LUDWIG TIECK's "Blond Eckbert" ("Der blonde Eckbert," 1797, in *Volksmärchen*) was the first Romantic fairy tale. An early English translation as "Auburn Egbert" appeared in *Popular Tales and Romances of the Northern Nations* (1823). The story uses motifs and narrative structures of the folk tale. While the natural world and the marvellous are kept separate, the two levels become increasingly and confusingly intertwined in Tieck's story, which creates narrative ambiguity. This is furthered by the male protagonist's descent into paranoia and madness until the reader no longer knows whether the events described are real or just figments of Eckbert's imagination.

The tale opens with a description of Eckbert's situation in life: He and his wife Bertha almost never leave their castle in the Harz Mountains, and they have only one friend, Philipp Walther. Their extreme isolation, emphasized by their childlessness, points to their inability to achieve mature, adult roles in society.

One evening Eckbert decides to reveal their secret to Walther—namely, the story of Bertha's childhood. In this story, as the daughter of a poor shepherd, she is clumsy as a child and useless at household chores. She regularly flees into compensatory fantasies, and when her father threatens to beat her, she runs away from home. This constitutes another flight from reality as it leads her into a fairy-tale landscape where she meets a strange old woman, who takes her in. Bertha cares for the woman's little dog and bird, whose song of *Waldeinsamkeit* ("wood solitude") emphasizes the idyllic timelessness of this existence: not only is the song repeated over and over again, but it is also repetitive in itself, thus performing a circular movement.

The old woman treats Bertha like a daughter and finally entrusts her with the secret of the bird, whose eggs are filled with pearls and gems. Being left to her own devices, Bertha again begins to live in a dream world, this time of knights and courtly love, and one day she decides to turn her dreams into reality. When the woman is away from home,

Bertha takes the bird but leaves the little dog behind to starve, and she returns into the world. Serving as a constant reminder of her guilt, the bird has to die, too, when its song changes and becomes accusatory. Bertha's story, though, seems to end happily for she has found a knight of her own in Eckbert.

The telling of this tale does not have the desired effect: Instead of strengthening the friendship with Walther, it turns him into an ominous figure because he knows the name of the small dog, Strohmian, which Bertha has forgotten. At the shock of recognition, she falls ill and dies. Eckbert, meanwhile, deems the former friend too dangerous and murders him. Wracked by guilt, he seeks society and amusements to divert himself. When he befriends a young man, Hugo, he once again tries to strengthen a friendship by telling his secret, yet this strategy fails a second time: Hugo suddenly seems to turn into Walther. Horrified, Eckbert flees until he reaches the idyllic valley of Bertha's childhood, where he is confronted by the old woman. This figure has been interpreted as the spirit of revenge, the personification of nature, or the incarnation of hostile fate, for while Eckbert loses all sense of reality, she reveals that she was both Walther and Hugo—and, moreover, that Bertha was Eckbert's sister. Just like her, Eckbert dies from the shock of recognition, while the little dog barks and the bird sings of wood solitude.

## Further Reading

Ewton, Ralph W. "Childhood without End: Tieck's 'Der blonde Eckbert.'" *German Quarterly* 46 (1973): 410–427.

Mathäs, Alexander. "Self-Perfection-Narcissism-Paranoia: Ludwig Tieck's 'Der blonde Eckbert.'" *Colloquia Germanica* 34, nos. 3–4 (2001): 237–255.

Rippere, Victoria L. "Ludwig Tieck's 'Der blonde Eckbert': A Psychological Reading." *PMLA* 85 (1970): 473–486.

Tatar, Maria. "Unholy Alliances: Narrative Ambiguity in Tieck's 'Der blonde Eckbert.'" *MLN* 102 (1987): 608–626.

Tieck, Ludwig. "Eckbert the Blond." In *Spells of Enchantment: The Wondrous Fairy Tales of Western Culture,* edited by Jack Zipes, 281–295. New York: Viking, 1991.

—Sandra Martina Schwab

## Boaden, James (1762–1839)

A drama critic, biographer, and translator, James Boaden (b. May 23, 1762; d. February 16, 1839) was to have had a career as a merchant, but after time spent as a clerk the young Boaden took up Journalism, becoming editor of *The Oracle* newspaper in 1789. He was initially a critic but also wrote of a small number of original plays of his own, most of which in the GOTHIC and melodramatic vein. *The Secret Tribunal* (1795), a covert comment on the British political situation of the 1790s, is possibly the most notable, due to the influence that the Inquisition-like tribunal of the title had on both ANN RADCLIFFE's *The Italian* and MATTHEW GREGORY LEWIS's *The MONK*. In his triple role as enthusiastic and stagestruck spectator, editor, and (under the pseudonym of Thespis) keen theater criticism contributor to the newspaper *The Oracle* (1789–98), Boaden was aware of the rapidly shifting tastes of late 18th-century audiences, who were more and more inclined toward illegitimate dramatic forms that emphasized spectacles and dramatic sensationalism. During the 1790s he adapted three of the most popular gothic novels to the stage. Initially, it was Radcliffe's *The Romance of the Forest* and *The Italian,* adapted respectively as *Fontainville Forest* (1794), which popularized the vogue for onstage ghosts, and *The Italian Monk* (1797), whose hodgepodge title shrewdly alludes to *The Monk*. Later, Boaden's interest in Lewis's sensational novel was further exploited in *Aurelio and Miranda* (1798), which ambitiously tried to stage—and, rather unwisely, aimed to sanitize—its controversial fictional source.

Boaden's activity as an adapter was limited to the 1790s. He subsequently moved on to the realm of Shakespeare—and thence to the safeguarding of the national dramatic heritage—with the publication of the scholarly *An Inquiry into the Authenticity of Various Pictures and Prints, Which from the Decease of the Poet to Our Own Times Have Been Offered to the Public as Portraits of Shakespeare* (1824) and *On the Sonnets of Shakespeare* (1837). As an amateur Shakespearian philologist, he was instrumental in exposing William Henry Ireland's *Vortigern* forgeries (*A Letter to George Steevens, Esq. Containing a Critical Examination of the Papers of Shakespeare, published by Mr. Samuel Ireland,* 1796), a critical activity for which he has attracted the attention of a small cadre of present-day scholars. His thespian biographies—an invaluable, though hardly impartial, repository of solid criticism mixed with anecdotes and factual information, in the spirit of his work at *The Oracle*—still provide useful insights into contemporary production, the theories of mise-en-scène, and the aesthetic discourse of the age: *Memoirs of the Life of John Philip Kemble, Esq., Including a History of the Stage from the Time of Garrick to the Present Period* (1825); *Memoirs of Mrs Siddons* (1827); *The Life of Mrs Jordan* (1831); *Memoirs of Mrs Inchbald* (1833) and *The Private Correspondence of David Garrick with the Most Celebrated Persons of His Time* (1831).

In later life Boaden was financially hard-up. He had a private income (courtesy of his wealthy family) but by 1830 was forced to apply for assistance to the Royal Literary Fund. He faced imprisonment for debt in 1835 and took up residence in the Fleet Prison (a debtor's prison). He and his wife, Sarah, had nine children, and his family was clearly a heavy expense. In the 1830s Boaden found it difficult to get his work published. Today his role in the formation of the Romantic dramatic canon is long overdue for a critical reappraisal.

## Further Reading

Backscheider, Paula R. "Reflections on the Importance of Romantic Drama." *Texas Studies in Literature and Language* 41 (1999): 311–329.

Cohan, Steven. "Introduction." In *The Plays of James Boaden,* edited by Steven Cohan, iii–xxxvii. New York and London: Garland, 1980.

Miles, Robert. "Trouble in the Republic of Letters: The Reception of the Shakespeare Forgeries." *Studies in Romanticism* 44 (2005): 317–340.

Reno, Robert Princeton. "James Boaden's *Fontainville Forest* and Matthew G. Lewis' *The Castle Spectre:* Challenges of the Supernatural Ghost on the Late Eighteenth-Century Stage." *Eighteenth-Century Life* 9 (1984): 94–106.

Saggini, Francesca. "Radcliffe's Novels and Boaden's Dramas: Bringing the Configurations of the Gothic on Stage." Available online. URL: http://www.unipr.it/ arpa/dipling/GT/Saggini/saggini.html. Downloaded on 28 January 2008.

—Francesca Saggini

## Bonaparte, Napoleon (Napoleon I) (1769–1821)

Viewed by many British radicals as a king-destroying savior and by myriad conservatives as a sinisterly overreaching tyrant, the Corsican-born Napoleon Bonaparte was a pivotal and polarizing international figure during much of the Romantic period. While liberal-minded writers such as WILLIAM HAZLITT and LORD BYRON found much to admire in Bonaparte insofar as he represented a force against Europe's monarchies (Bainbridge 138–139), loyalist authors such as WILLIAM WORDSWORTH came to revile the ambitious French leader as a threat to Great Britain and her principal values (a position famously expressed in the Lake Poet's 1802 sonnet "I griev'd for Buonaparte"). Napoleon caused great conflict and change throughout Europe, and his rise to self-conferred imperial power in 1804 stirred many British Romantics to respond to political realities on the Continent, just as the FRENCH REVOLUTION and the Reign of Terror elicited artistic response, in the early 1790s.

Bonaparte's mystique, enhanced by martial brilliance, charisma, and bravado, intensified the Romantics' individual responses, whether damning or affirming. As the literary scholar Simon Bainbridge notes, Wordsworth's *The Convention of Cintra* (published in 1809) likens Napoleon to Satan, the prideful and malicious agent of bedlam depicted in JOHN MILTON's influential 1667 poem *Paradise Lost.* After Napoleon's decisive loss at Waterloo (1815), the illustrator George Cruikshank (1792–1878) rendered an image of Boney (a derogatory name for Bonaparte) in which the victor of Marengo (1800), Austerlitz (1805), and Jena (1806) bears horns and dark wings and, looking heavenward, speaks verses from Milton's epic (Bainbridge 183–185). Byron, on the other hand, in his "Ode to Napoleon Bonaparte" (1814), asks whether the fallen emperor, after his first exile to Elba, might still achieve the dignity of Promethean defiance (ll. 136–144).

Following Bonaparte's death on St. Helen's on May 5, 1821 (of stomach cancer, according to the biographer Martyn Lyons), LEIGH HUNT's radical newspaper the *Examiner* proclaimed Napoleon "the supreme figure of the Romantic period" (quoted in

Bainbridge 9). Whether exaggerated or accurate, this assertion casts light on the contemporary relevance of Napoleon Bonaparte to the English as a people and to the Romantics as the voice of their age.

See also "NAPOLEON'S FAREWELL"; WATERLOO.

**Further Reading**

Bainbridge, Simon. *Napoleon and English Romanticism.* Cambridge: Cambridge University Press, 1995.

Byron, George Gordon Byron, Baron. "Ode to Napoleon Buonaparte." In *Lord Byron: The Major Works,* edited by Jerome J. McGann, 253–257. Oxford: Oxford University Press, 2000.

Day, Frank. "Napoleon (Bonaparte)." In *Encyclopedia of Romanticism: Culture in Britain, 1780s–1830s,* edited by Laura Dabundo, 399–402. New York: Garland, 1992.

Lyons, Martyn. *Napoleon Bonaparte and the Legacy of the French Revolution.* New York: St. Martin's Press, 1994.

—Tim Ruppert

## Bride of Abydos, The Lord Byron (1813)

Following THE GIAOUR (1813) and preceding *The CORSAIR* and *Lara* (both 1814), *The Bride of Abydos* is among the tremendously popular Eastern tales upon which LORD BYRON's early authorial fame largely rested, tapping into a contemporary interest in ORIENTALISM. Byron wrote the poem swiftly, completing the work in less than a week in November 1813. According to Peter W. Graham, *The Bride of Abydos* went through 11 editions by 1815, indicating the poem's success in England's mid-Regency literary market (Graham 82).

In *The Bride,* Byron dramatizes what befalls two younger characters when they come into conflict with a patriarch whose authority extends over both family and court. The youths here are the fiery Selim and the beautiful Zuleika, who believe themselves at first to be brother and sister; the patriarch is their father Giaffir, whose resolution to marry his daughter away promises to divide Selim and Zuleika forever. Threatened with the loss of his beloved Zuleika, Selim seizes this double opportunity both to save Zuleika and to move

against Giaffir, who openly reviles him. That night (the last night of life for both), he takes his sister to a secret weapon cache near the coast. Amid the stores of pilfered armaments, Selim makes several crucial disclosures, including that he and Zuleika are in fact cousins, not siblings; that Giaffir reared him as a son (though never loved him as such) after murdering his real father, Zuleika's uncle; and that he leads a group of pirates, a clandestine outlawry that has given him both a sense of freedom from the state and the means to overthrow Giaffir. As Selim offers to bear Zuleika away for good, her father's forces attack, and Selim falls mortally to the rushing night waters and the ravaging sea birds. Giaffir has crushed a would-be insurrectionist, but political authoritarianism gets the better of individual passion only for a moment as we discover, with Giaffir, that Zuleika could not live without her Selim and has died, leaving her father childless and heartbroken.

Notwithstanding its myriad aesthetic flaws, *The Bride of Abydos* invites serious consideration as a work epitomizing the conventions and biases of Romantic orientalism. Furthermore, the poem offers in Selim an early image of the Byronic hero, a figure who reappears (in more sophisticated avatars) in CHILDE HAROLD'S PILGRIMAGE, cantos 3 and 4 (1816 and 1818, respectively), MANFRED: A DRAMATIC POEM (1817), CAIN: A MYSTERY (1821), and *The Island* (1823). *The Bride* also casts light on the form, content, and style of 1816's *The Siege of Corinth* and *Parisina,* the best crafted and most thoughtful of Byron's Eastern tales. An adaptation of *The Bride* appeared in a lavish 1818 Drury Lane production, a fact illustrating the Eastern tales' ongoing popularity with the British public (Elfenbein 80).

**Further Reading**

Byron, George Gordon Byron, Baron. *Lord Byron: The Complete Poetical Works.* Vol. 3. Edited by Jerome J. McGann. Oxford: Oxford University Press, 1981.

Elfenbein, Andrew. *Byron and the Victorians.* Cambridge: Cambridge University Press, 1995.

Graham, Peter W. *Lord Byron.* New York: Twayne, 1998.

—Tim Ruppert

## *Bride of Lammermoor, The*  Sir Walter Scott
(1819)

*The Bride of Lammermoor* is a historical novel by SIR WALTER SCOTT, set in Scotland in the reign of Queen Anne (1702–14); together with *A Legend of Montrose*, it comprised the third series of Scott's *Tales of My Landlord*. The novel is shorter and more focused than usual (the author E. M. Forster called it "lean and tragic") and shows traces of GOTHIC fiction in its focus on doomed love, oppressive parents, murder, and madness, together with supernatural elements, windswept castle settings, and brooding North Sea landscapes.

In the same way that SAMUEL TAYLOR COLERIDGE would claim that he had only hazy memories of composing "KUBLA KHAN" on account of the drugs he had taken, so the story of writing of *The Bride of Lammermoor* has gained a similarly mythic status, although the truth of it has been disputed. Scott's son-in-law and biographer J. G. Lockhart described in his *Memoirs of the Life of Sir Walter Scott* (1837–38) that Scott experienced violent stomach pains during the writing of the novel, had to dictate it from his bed, and wrote it in a kind of trance. Later he claimed not to remember "one single incident, character, or conversation it contained." Nor, he felt, was it up to his usual standard being "gross and grotesque; but still the worst of it made me laugh, and I trusted the good-natured public would not be less indulgent" (quoted in Sutherland 221).

Like many of Scott's fictional writings, *The Bride of Lammermoor* takes as its starting point an actual tragedy told to Scott by his aunt, Margaret Swinton. In 1699 Janet Dalrymple, a daughter of Viscount Stair and part of an aristocratic family sympathetic to the Covenanters, secretly engaged herself to a Lord Rutherford, a Royalist. When her parents arranged a match with a favored suitor, she confessed her love for Rutherford and was forced by her ambitious, tyrannical mother to break the engagement. On her wedding night Janet seriously wounded her approved husband in an apparent fit of madness and later died without recovering her sanity.

In *The Bride of Lammermoor* Scott takes the basic premise but shifts the action forward to the years leading up to the union of Scotland and England in 1707, and in so doing he commemorates what the scholar Jane Millgate calls "the dying moments of Scotland's identity as a separate nation" (Millgate 173). The characters operate on both a personal and symbolic level. Edgar, the young, brooding, impoverished master of Ravenswood, buries his father and sees his estate pass to the astute Sir William Ashton, part of Scotland's new governing class, supporters of the English monarchy.

Ravenswood, punished for his family's backing the wrong side in the Glorious Revolution of 1688, which saw the Catholic James II deposed, is left with only the dilapidated Wolf's Crag castle to live in, attended by his faithful servant Caleb Balderstone. When Ravenswood falls in love with Ashton's daughter Lucy, her father initially agrees. However, her monstrous mother takes measures to prevent the match and arranges one with a Whig aristocrat, the laird of Bucklaw—with horrible results. Lucy gives way over the marriage, tricked into believing Ravenswood has abandoned her. Outwardly calm, she stabs her husband on their wedding night and dies shortly afterward. The next day, in his hurry to confront his enemies, Ravenswood gallops to his death on quicksand on the seashore.

The tragedy of Lucy Ashton and Ravenswood, which in effect is about family strife, is set against the possibility of civil war—between the forces of the Jacobites (supported by the French) and the English government, whose effective power in Scotland is becoming weaker. Like other novels in the WAVERLEY series, *The Bride of Lammermoor* is written with an English audience in mind. *Lammermoor* is an Anglicanisation of the Scotch *Lammermuir*. The novel announces itself as a series of documents, relating to stories and legend of local events and people. Dick Tinto, a local man, hands over a handful of notes and sketches—"loose scraps, partly scratched over with his pencil, partly with his pen, where outlines of caricatures, sketches of turrets, mills, old gables, and dovecots, disputed the ground with his written memoranda" (25). He explains that he has heard the story from an old woman "while I was taking sketches on the coast of East Lothian and Berwickshire, I was seduced into the mountains of Lammermoor by the account I received of some remains of antiquity in that district. Those with which I was most struck were the ruins of an ancient castle in which that Elizabeth-chamber, as you call it, once existed. I resided for two or three days at a farm house in the neighbourhood, where the aged goodwife was well acquainted with the history of the castle and the events which had taken place in it" (25). The novel thus makes a great play of its foundations in "fact."

The ending has prompted the most critical comment. Scott's young female characters can often seem rather flat and one-dimensional. However, in Lucy Ashton he presents a startling portrait of female powerlessness. Scott offers familiar gothic motifs of confinement, repression, regression, and entrapment—the captive woman under threat. Lucy tries to hold out against the life-denying investment in status and conventionality that her mother has made a kind of mantra. In this respect the author encapsulates much of what feminist critics might say about the suppression of women's speech and desires. On the other hand, as the story progresses we also get a sense that here, as in other novels, Scott cannot think beyond the restraints of a patriarchal culture and the representations this involves. The options for Lucy are limited: madness or death, but not before she takes revenge: "Here they found the unfortunate girl seated, or rather crouched like a hare upon its form—her head-gear dishevelled, her night-clothes torn and dabbled with blood, her eyes glazed, and her features convulsed into wilt paroxysm of insanity. When she saw herself discovered, she gibbered, made mouths, and pointed at them with bloody fingers, with the frantic gestures of an exulting demoniac" (337–8). Lucy dies shortly afterwards without recovering her sanity: "Convulsion followed convulsion, till they closed in death, without her being able to utter a word explanatory of the fatal scene" (367). The ending of the novel is chilling. The vision of family life presented is a bleak one; the domestic is a space of safety but also of danger, whose boundaries are shifting and unstable. Parents are inadequate, and violence, or the possibility of violence, is always lurking.

The novel was a popular subject for stage adaptation. The most famous version is Gaetano Donizetti's 1835 opera *Lucia di Lammermoor*, which focuses on the latter part of the book.

## Further Reading

Brown, David. *Walter Scott and the Historical Imagination.* London: Routledge & Kegan Paul, 1979.

Edwards, Dudley. "Scott as a Contemporary Historian." In *Walter Scott: The Long Forgotten Melody,* edited by Alan Bold, Totowa, N.J.: Barnes & Noble, 1983.

Lockhart, John G. "Selections taken from *Memoirs of the Life of Sir Walter Scott,* (1837)." In *Walter Scott: The Critical Heritage,* edited by John O. Hayden, London: Routledge & Keagan Paul, 1970.

Millgate Jane. *Walter Scott: The Making of a Novelist.* Toronto: Toronto University Press, 1984.

Scott, Walter. Sir *The Bride of Lammermoor.* Oxford: Oxford University Press, 1991.

———. *The Journal of Sir Walter Scott.* Edited by W. E. K. Anderson. Edinburgh: Canongate, 1998.

Sutherland, John. *The Life of Walter Scott: A Critical Biography.* Oxford: Blackwell, 1995.

—Alison Thomas

## Brontë, Emily Jane (1818–1848)

Emily Jane Brontë was born on July 30, 1818, at Thornton in Yorkshire, the fifth of six children of the Reverend Patrick and Maria Brontë. Less than two years later, in February 1820, her father was appointed perpetual curate of Haworth, the small Yorkshire village where she would spend almost the entirety of her short life. She died on December 19, 1848.

Even though Brontë is first and foremost a poet, she is known principally through her only novel, *Wuthering Heights* (1847), published under the pseudonym Ellis Bell a year before her death in December 1848 from consumption. However, the poetic grandeur of vision that characterizes this dark, strange, and disturbing work of fiction has its origin in Brontë's poetic oeuvre: a body of writing consisting of over 200 poems that explores the complexities of human existence, religion, selfhood, death, nature, terror and power—themes that resonate throughout *Wuthering Heights.*

While Brontë began writing at an early age, collaborating with her younger sister Anne (1820–49) in creating the prose saga of two imaginary islands in the south Pacific, Gondal and Gaaldine, it was not until 1846 that her work was to first enter the public realm. Her eldest sister, Charlotte (1816–55), who discovered Emily's poems hidden in her rosewood writing desk, succeeded in convincing her introverted sibling that her poems merited publication. In May 1846, as part of a joint venture, but with Emily reluctantly giving her consent, the three sisters published, at their own expense, *Poems by Currer, Ellis, and Acton Bell.*

Despite the fact that Brontë is sometimes regarded as chronologically Victorian, in terms of literary history she is most often thought of as a true child of the Romantics. Almost without exception, critics, scholars, and biographers alike have set her among the writers of the Romantic period for contrast and comparison, particularly the male canonical poets. However, while she would have read or been aware of WILLIAM WORDSWORTH, SAMUEL TAYLOR COLERIDGE, LORD BYRON, PERCY BYSSHE SHELLEY, and JOHN KEATS—as well as earlier 18th-century writers, such as James Thomson and WILLIAM COWPER—her poetic voice did not become synonymous with the concerns of these artists, yet she, too, was interested in the inner world of the human psyche, in dualisms, and the divided self.

## Further Reading

Barker, Juliet. *The Brontës.* New York: St. Martin's, 1994.

Brontë, Emily. *The Complete Poems of Emily Jane Brontë.* Edited by C. W. Hatfield. New York: Columbia University Press, 1941.

Davies, Stevie. *Emily Brontë: Heretic.* London: The Women's Press, 1994.

Gérin, Winifred. *Emily Brontë.* Oxford: Oxford University Press, 1971.

Gezari, Janet. *Last Things: Emily Jane Brontë.* Oxford University Press, 2007.

Gordon, Felicia. *A Preface to the Brontës.* Harlow, Eng.: Longman, 1989.

Thormählen, Marianne. *The Brontës and Religion.* Cambridge: Cambridge University Press, 1999.

—Keith O'Sullivan

## Browning, Elizabeth Barrett (1806–1861)

The poet Elizabeth Barrett Browning was the eldest of 12 children born to Edmund Barrett Moulton-Barrett and Mary Graham Clarke. She was born Elizabeth Barrett Moulton-Barrett on March 6, 1806, in County Durham, England. Unusually for a girl, she studied Greek and Latin with her eldest brother. At age 15 she developed the first of her health problems, which affected her throughout her adult life. Her illness freed Barrett from many of the demands placed on young women, giving her time to read and write. Her father supported her writing, paying to publish her first work, an epic poem entitled *The Battle of Marathon* (1820). Barrett brought out three collections of poems before the 1844 two-volume *Poems* that established her as a major poet. *The Athenaeum* proposed her as a candidate for the poet laureateship upon the death of WILLIAM WORDSWORTH in 1850.

In 1845 Barrett began a correspondence with the poet Robert Browning, and ultimately, in the face of her father's disapproval, the two eloped to Italy. The couple had one child, Robert Wiedemann Barrett Browning, born in 1849. Elizabeth Barrett Browning continued to publish, with major works including *Sonnets from the Portuguese,* a sonnet cycle written for Browning and published in 1850 in a revised version of the 1844 *Poems; Casa Guidi Windows* (1851), a two-part work introducing more political topics in her writing, here the unification of Italy; *Aurora Leigh* (1856), an epic about the making of a woman poet; and *Poems before Congress* (1860), more political poems published just before her death on June 29, 1861.

Barrett Browning's reputation fell as her husband's rose throughout the latter part of the 19th and into the 20th century, due mostly to critical rejection of her political poems and a fascination with her elopement. The 1934 Hollywood film *The Barretts of Wimpole Street* (remade in 1957) illustrates the prurient interest in her life. In the 1980s, feminist scholars revisited Barrett Browning, focusing especially on *Aurora Leigh*'s challenge to traditional notions of femininity and situating her in a tradition of female poets. More recently, scholars have become interested in the Barrett family's West Indian connections, exploring issues of race, gender, and SLAVERY in her writing. A key poem is the dramatic monologue "The Runaway Slave at Pilgrim's Point" (1847).

Barrett Browning works within many of the forms and with themes common in literary Romanticism; however, she forges a strong feminist voice that questions many of the conventions. Generally, dominant themes in her poetry include social ones—sympathizing with the dispossessed, dissecting gender roles; political ones—analyzing power relations both personal (between daughters and fathers or women and lovers) and public (between forces of democracy and imperialism); and literary ones—focusing on the function of the poet, particularly the woman poet. Barrett Browning feminizes a number of traditional poetic forms: the ballad, the sonnet, and the epic. As a young woman, she had admired LORD BYRON, but in the ballad "The Romaunt of the Page" (1844) she deconstructs her youthful fantasy of running away to become his page. Similarly, she wrote about both FELICIA HEMANS ("Felicia Hemans," 1838) and LETITIA ELIZABETH LANDON ("LEL's Last Question," 1844), in part to distance herself from the limits of the Romantic poetess.

### Further Reading

Avery, Simon, and Rebecca Stott. *Elizabeth Barrett Browning.* Harlow, Eng.: Pearson Education, 2003.

Barrett Browning, Elizabeth. *Aurora Leigh and Other Poems.* Edited by John Robert Glosney Bolton and Julia Bolton Holloway. London: Penguin, 1995.

Leighton, Angela. Victorian *Women Poets: Writing against the Heart.* Charlottesville: University Press of Virginia, 1992.

Mermin, Dorothy. *Elizabeth Barrett Browning: The Origins of a New Poetry.* Chicago: University of Chicago Press, 1989.

Stone, Marjorie. *Elizabeth Barrett Browning.* Basingstoke, Eng.: Macmillan, 1995.

—Terri Doughty

### Bürger, Gottfried August (1747–1794)

A lecturer in aesthetics at the University of Göttingen, Gottfried August Bürger is best remembered for his stories of Baron Münchausen and his ballad poem "Lenore," a supernatural tale published in 1773. Bürger was born in on December 31, 1747, in Molmerswende near Halberstadt (in what is now Germany), where his father was the clergyman. By all accounts he was a wild and rebellious teenager, regularly in disgrace with his respectable family. In 1768 he attended the University of Göttingen as a law student, but he was more attracted to literary circles than legal ones. In 1771 his first poems were published, which helped to get him noticed. The turning point came in 1773 when his long poem "Lenore" was published in the *Musenalmanach* (an annual collection of poetry published at Göttingen, 1770–75). The poem's appearance was timely. It coincided with—and was partly prompted by—a revival of interest in old ballads that had begun in 1760 when Thomas Percy's *Reliques of Ancient English Poetry* and JAMES MACPHERSON's *Fragments of Ancient Poetry* both appeared. Other popular collections included David Herd's *The Ancient and Modern Scots Songs, Heroic Ballads, etc* (1769) and SIR WALTER SCOTT's MINSTRELSY OF THE SCOTTISH BORDER (1802–03). In Great Britain, Bürger's ballad was translated by Scott for magazine publication in 1796, using two lines of a translation that William Taylor of Norwich and done in 1794, and the Scotsman would later claim that this was the work that made him want to become a poet.

The other reason for the popularity of "Lenore" was its subject matter. Its publication in Britain coincided with the craze for GOTHIC and supernatural tales. Though not exactly a vampire poem, "Lenore" deals with people returning from the dead and love that transcends death. In Germany there was a well-established folkloric tradition of *der Nachtzehrer,* or "night waster"—that is, a dead person who rises from the grave to wreak revenge on family and friends. The poem's opening lines immediately signal its "weird" subject matter: "Up rose Lenore as the red morn wore, / From weary visions starting; / "Art faithless, William, or, / William, art dead? / 'Tis long since thy departing" (ll. 1–4). Driven by grief at the failure of her lover to return from the war, Leonore wishes to die. Wilhelm, however, appears to claim her, and they ride through the night on his ghostly horse to the grave that is to be their wedding bed.

In its emphasis on the "uncanny"—the dead who are alive and the forces of good and evil battling it out for Leonore's soul—the poem also anticipated and influenced other gothic and Romantic writers. JOHANN WOLFGANG VON GOETHE depicted an ancient Greek vampire in "The Bride of Corinth" (1797). As well as MATTHEW LEWIS, whose best seller The MONK appeared in 1796, a translation of the poem appearing in the *Monthly Magazine* (March 1796) intrigued CHARLES LAMB, who drew it to the attention of SAMUEL TAYLOR COLERIDGE. "The RIME OF THE ANCIENT MARINER" has been seen as Coleridge's "tribute to Bürger" (Bürger ii), and in 1816 Coleridge wrote "CHRISTABEL," often regarded as the first British vampire poem. Bürger thus had a major impact in Britain though not everyone was equally impressed but his ability to touch an audience was admitted. Writing in 1798, WILLIAM WORDSWORTH told Coleridge: "As to Bürger, I am yet so far from that admiration of which he has excited in you; but I am by nature slow to admire. . . . In one point I entirely coincide with you, in your feeling concerning his versification. In 'Lenore' the concluding double rhymes [create] . . . both a delicious and pathetic effect: 'Patience, patience, when the heart is breaking; / With thy God there is no question-making: / Of thy body thou art quit and free: / Heaven keep thy soul eternally!' I accede, too, to your opinion that Bürger is always the poet; he is never the mobbist, one of those dim drivellers with which our island has teemed for so many years" (Wordsworth 234).

In some respects Bürger did not live up to the promise of this early work, and he was dogged by difficulties in his personal life. In 1774 he married Dorette Leonhart, but he developed a passion for his wife's sister Auguste, addressing many poems to her (as "Molly"). His attempts to make money from farming failed, and he made ends meet by private tutoring. His wife died in 1784, and in 1785 married his sister-in-law, only for her to die the following year. In 1789 he was made a professor at Göttingen University, but the post was unpaid. This was followed in 1790 by his third marriage to a onetime fan, Elise Hahn, but this marriage failed. In poor health and in straitened financial circumstances, Bürger was a broken man when he died on June 8, 1794.

Though he wrote other poems (Scott translated several into English) and had several of them set to music, it his ballad poems for which Bürger is best remembered. "Des Pfarrers Tochter von Taubenhain" (translated by William Taylor as "The Lass of Fair Wone") was an important inspiration for Wordsworth's "The THORN." Bürger is seen as one of the founders of German Romantic ballad literature, which embodies the revival of interest in folk songs and traditional tales in the late 1700s.

### Further Reading

Bürger, Gottfried August. *Lenore.* Translated by J. T. Stanley. Edited by Jonathan Wordsworth. 1796. Facsimile reprint, Otley, Eng.: Woodstock Books, 2000.

Little, William. *Gottfried August Bürger.* Boston: Twayne Publishers, 1974.

Wordsworth, William. *The Letters of William and Dorothy Wordsworth: The Early Years, 1787–1805.* Edited by Ernest de Selincourt. Oxford: Oxford University Press, 1967.

—Mark Harris

## Burke, Edmund (1729–1797)

Edmund Burke, one of the most influential political theorists and aestheticians of the 18th century, was born on January 12, 1729, in Dublin, the offspring of a mixed Protestant-Roman Catholic marriage. Having attended Trinity College, Dublin, he began to study law in London in the early 1750s. In 1755 he briefly considered applying for a position in Great Britain's colonies, but he obeyed his father's advice to stay in England. In 1757 A *PHILOSOPHICAL ENQUIRY INTO THE ORIGIN OF OUR IDEAS OF THE SUBLIME AND BEAUTIFUL,* on which Burke had been working since he was 19, was published to great acclaim (not least Samuel Johnson's). This work popularized the idea, derived in part from Longinus's classical treatise *On the Sublime,* of two fundamental aesthetic experiences: the SUBLIME and the beautiful, and identified their specific characteristics across a number of artistic mediums. Burke's preference for the sublime, with its power to overwhelm and awe us, made a profound impact on English and Continental Romanticism. In Britain his doctrine of the sublime nourished a growing preoccupation with the pictorial and literary attractions of landscape as, for example, in ANN RADCLIFFE's GOTHIC novel *The MYSTERIES OF UDOLPHO*, while on the Continent, Immanuel Kant's influential *Critique of Judgment* (1790) contained traces of Burke's influence.

In 1757 Burke married Jane Mary Nuget, the daughter of his physician. The couple's finances were initially insecure, and he was forced to take on a post in the English government of Ireland. His firsthand experience of Irish-Catholic suffering and deprivation moved Burke to enter politics, becoming a Whig Member of Parliament in December 1765. However, his view of the nature of government was in essence conservative and guided by a belief in established hierarchies and a deeply ingrained distrust of democracy. His criticism of the British handling of its American colonies led to his notable *Speech on American Taxation* (1774), which famously called for the abrogation of tea duties. The Revolutionary War (1775–83) seriously upset his political convictions, believing as he did in Britain's rightful legal supremacy over its colonies.

Burke's political career was troubled in the 1780s by his attempts to impeach Warren Hastings, governor general of Bengal, whom he believed to be solely responsible for English misrule in India. His relentlessness in this matter, often unfairly attributed to his unstable mental health, alienated many of his party friends. In 1789 he was among the first to acknowledge and to describe the reverberations of the FRENCH REVOLUTION in England. *Reflections on the Revolution in France,* his most widely read political work today, harshly condemned the Jacobins' efforts to replace the aristocratic and monarchical government (so cherished by Burke) with more democratic principles. While Burke's view of the moral authority of monarchy is essentially nostalgic, his *Reflections* were considered by many to be prophetic of the French Reign of Terror. With its rhapsodies on the beauty of French court life, *Reflections* provoked THOMAS PAINE's radical treatise *The RIGHTS OF MAN* (1791). Burke's celebration of the "delightful horror" of the sublime in his *Philosophical Enquiry* (Burke, 1:243) clearly did not extend to the tremendous political and social disruptions brought about by the French Revolution.

**Further Reading**
Bruyn, Frans de. *The Literary Genres of Edmund Burke.* Oxford: Clarendon Press, 1996.
Burke, Edmund. *The Correspondence of Edmund Burke.* 10 vols. Edited by Thomas W. Copeland. Cambridge: Cambridge University Press, 1958–78.
———. *The Writings and Speeches of Edmund Burke.* 9 vols. Edited by Paul Langford et al. Oxford: Clarendon Press, 1981–2000.
Ferguson, Frances. *Solitude and the Sublime: Romanticism and the Aesthetics of Individuation.* London: Routledge, 1992.
Furniss, Tom. *Edmund Burke's Aesthetic Ideology: Language, Gender, and Political Economy in Revolution.* Cambridge: Cambridge University Press, 1993.
Macpherson, C. B. *Burke.* Oxford: Oxford University Press, 1980.

—Benjamin Kohlmann

## Burney, Frances (Fanny Burney) (1752–1840)

Born on June 13, 1752, the novelist, playwright, journal writer, and diarist Frances (Fanny) Burney was the third child of Charles Burney (1726–1814), a composer, musicologist, and travel writer, with whom she lived until her marriage in 1793. Among her siblings were James Burney, author of the five-volume *A Chronological History of the Discoveries in the South Sea or Pacific Ocean* (1803–17). Her half sister, Sarah Harriet (1772–1844), was herself a rather successful writer, the author of a handful of popular novels in the epistolary style. A strong literary tradition thus characterizes the Burney family, starting from Charles Burney, whose cultural aspirations were to mould Frances's career substantially.

Despite his own modest upbringing, Charles Burney, an esteemed musicologist and highly paid music teacher in fashionable circles, established himself as a respected man of letters and popular society host. The most prominent figures of the day started to gather in his London drawing room in St. Martin's Street, near Leicester Square, and soon he and his young family became firm friends with the artist Joshua Reynolds, the actor David Garrick, and the highly-polished intellectual circle of the so-called Streatham Worthies, headed by

Hester Thrale (later PIOZZI) and Samuel Johnson. Throughout his life, Burney strived hard to maintain this newly gained, prestigious social status, adroitly manoeuvring his way into polite society through a network of influential friendships. (His 1781 grand portrait in his doctoral robes, painted by Reynolds, is an interesting reminder of his self-esteem.) As the author of a well-received multivolume *History of Music* (1776–89), for which Frances had acted as an amanuensis, he projected part of his literary ambitions—and social insecurities—onto his promising daughter, whose popular literary debut novel, *EVELINA, or, A Young Lady's Entrance into the World* (1778), opened the doors of fame and fashion to her and, through this means, also to her father.

The totally unexpected and by all means extraordinary success of *Evelina* (more than 2,000 copies sold by the time of its fourth reprint) thus turned the family's celebrity spotlight on Frances, whose childhood had been spent rather demurely, without apparent inclination for either original writing or public display. In reality, as the author confessed many years later in the heavily edited *Memoirs of Doctor Burney* (1832), in 1767, on the eve of her 15th birthday, she had burned in a bonfire a selection of "Elegies, Odes, Plays, Songs, Stories, Farces—nay Tragedies and Epic Poems," (quoted in Patten) which included the manuscript of *The History of Caroline Evelyn,* the blueprint of *Evelina.* This first foray into the world of letters testifies that Frances always intended to try her pen at different genres and styles—from high comedy through serious drama, on the page as much as the stage, free from the current strictures surrounding *genre* or gender.

Thus, when *Evelina* was published, Frances Burney was hardly a novice in the province of letters. Since at least 1768 she had kept a diary addressed to an artfully constructed and self-denying alter ego, "Miss Nobody," behind which she shielded her budding literary ambitions. Diary and journal writing were to accompany Burney throughout her long life, often circulated in the small circle of her close friends through her favourite correspondent, Samuel "Daddy" Crisp, who also acted as one of her early literary mentors. She authored at least 20 volumes of highly informative and entertaining autobiographical writings, which have since been edited by the McGill Burney Centre. As a unique repository of opinions and events from the age of George III, the collection covers the whole spectrum of Burney's long and eventful life—from the very public narratives of the king's mental illness (see MONARCHY) and the pan-European conflicts she witnessed in the company of her husband, the French general Alexandre D'Arblay (whom she married in 1793), to her most intimate joys and distresses, including the shocking mastectomy she underwent without anaesthetic in 1811.

Frances's all-round literary ambitions were soon revealed by her subsequent achievement, the comedy *The Witlings* (1778), a rewriting of some of the themes she had already dealt with in *Evelina.* In point of fact, female financial independence and the fragility of women's reputations are recurrently addressed, albeit from different perspectives, in both her narrative and dramatic work, from her second blockbuster novel *Cecilia, or, Memoirs of a Heiress* (1782) to her last unperformed comedy, *A Busy Day* (ca. 1801). However, much to her dismay, Burney's theatrical ambition was to be quickly, yet firmly curbed by her two "fathers," Charles Burney and Samuel Crisp. Despite the encouragement she had received to try her hand at playwriting (Hester Thrale had been openly supportive of any dramatic plan, as had the celebrated playwright Richard B. Sheridan, who had authoritatively enjoined her to send to him anything she might write, with the promise of accepting it "unsight, unseen," as she breathlessly recorded in her journal), and in the face of the applause received for the pace and brilliant dialogue of her debut novel, theater for an up-and-coming young lady novelist was off limits. Association with the stage would bring moral taint on her as a female and social degradation as a lady author. Arguably, loath to batter his now established social standing with the supposedly harmful professional ambitions of his celebrity daughter, the elder Burney suddenly found himself at risk of possible social regression, and of sliding back amid that "very low Race of Mortals" (in Hester Thrale's words) out of which he had managed to surface. In this way, young Frances was bound to experience firsthand the strictures on female reputation faced by the protagonists of her novels, as hinted in the partly autobiographical *Camilla, or, A Picture of Youth* (quoted in Harmon 3, 1796), whose young heroine is educated in the difficult way not only of the world but also of the family.

Burney continued to write plays in the solitude of her gloomy days as second Keeper of the Robes (1786–91) to Queen Charlotte; similarly, the aborted negotiations to bring one of her comedies to the Covent Garden stage offered solace after the untimely death of her beloved sister, Susan (1800). However, it was the published novels (and the ensuing commercial success) that were to turn Burney into one of the leading women of letters of the age, and certainly one of the highest paid. Her novels allowed her the purchase of a family home—self-referentially named Camilla Cottage to vindicate her independence from both her family's monies and encroachments—and finally, permitted her to establish herself independently of her domineering father. Something of her determination is apparent in the epistolary preface to her final novel, the aptly named *The WANDERER, or, Female Difficulties* (1814), perhaps her most broad-ranging work and an ambitious female version of the historical novel. In a retrospective judgment on her whole career Burney writes, "So early was I impressed myself with ideas that fastened degradation to this class of composition, which . . . I struggled against the propensity which, . . . had impelled me to its toils. The passion, however, though resisted, was not annihilated" (Burney xvi). Burney is here referring to her early troubled negotiations with authorship and novel writing. However, it would be tempting to say that, just like "in defiance of every self-effort, *Evelina* struggled herself into life" (Burney xvi), so did her plays, albeit without the public acknowledgement given by print.

Burney—who died in Bath on January 6, 1840—may be called a "dramatic novelist" in the vein of Samuel Richardson and JANE AUSTEN: Her novels, fraught with references to the stage (from Shakespeare, to whom she turns in search of cultural aggrandizement, to the Georgian playwrights), share with the plays of the time a number of recurrent themes. Her narrative technique, which strongly relies on dialogue and visualization,

also adapts clearly recognizable dramatic situations and stock resolutions to the page. One of the greatest achievements of contemporary Burney scholarship is to have restored the author to her place in the history of the novel and recognized her full dignity as a playwright. Her four comedies (*The Witlings, The Woman-Hater, Love and Fashion, A Busy Day,* the latter three composed around the period 1800–02) have recently received long-overdue critical and editorial attention and have at last received the honor of performance they were denied in the author's lifetime. It is now high time that Burney's historical tragedies (*Edwy and Elgiva, Hubert de Vere, The Siege of Pevensey,* and the fragment *Elberta,* all of which were composed during her service at court) were reassessed in the context of Romantic dramaturgy and placed along with the work of now canonical women dramatists such as JOANNA BAILLIE.

### Further Reading

Burney, Frances. *Complete Plays of Frances Burney.* 2 vols. Edited by Peter Sabor. London: Pickering and Chatto, 1995.

———. *Evelina, or, The History of a Young Lady's Entrance into the World.* Edited by Margaret Anne Doody. London and New York: Penguin Books, 1994.

———. *Journals and Letters.* Edited by Peter Sabor and Lars E. Troide. London: Penguin, 2001.

———. *The Wanderer.* London: Pandora, 1988.

Doody, Margaret Anne. *Frances Burney: The Life in the Works.* New Brunswick, N.J.: Rutgers University Press, 1988.

Greenfield, Susan C. *Mothering Daughters: Novels and the Politics of Family Romance: Frances Burney to Jane Austen.* Detroit: Wayne State University Press, 2002.

Hemlow, Joyce. *The History of Fanny Burney.* London: Oxford University Press, 1958.

Patten, Valerie. "Frances Burney." Available online. URL: http://www.chawton.org/library/biographies/ burney_f.html. Accessed 23 December 2009.

Sabor, Peter, ed. *The Cambridge Companion to Frances Burney.* Cambridge: Cambridge University Press, 2007.

—Francesca Saggini

## Burns, Robert (1759–1796)

Robert Burns, generally regarded as the national bard of Scotland, was born on January 25, 1759, at Alloway in Ayrshire. He was the eldest child of William Burnes, a tenant farmer, and his wife Agnes Broun Burnes. Like his younger brother Gilbert, Burns was educated at Alloway's village school, then at home by his father. In 1766 William Burnes moved his family to a nearby farm, Mount Oliphant, and the young Burns first began experimenting with rhyme and song here in 1774. The following year he furthered his education, learning mathematics and surveying at Hugh Rodger's school in Kirkoswald. In 1777 the Burnes family moved again, this time to Lochlea, Tarbolton, on the north bank of the Ayr. In 1781 the would-be poet worked as a flax dresser in Irvine, but he returned to Lochlea the next year when the shop where he had been working burnt down. In 1783, as a writ of sequestration was served on William Burnes, Robert and Gilbert rented Mossgiel, a 118-acre farm near Mauchline. They moved there the following year when their father died, determined to succeed as tenant farmers. Robert gained a local reputation as an aspiring poet and became deputy grand master of the St. James (Tarbolton) Masonic Lodge.

Burns's sexual promiscuity in this period began to produce the inevitable consequences. In 1785 his daughter Elizabeth was born to Betty Paton, his mother's servant. By 1786 another woman, Jean Armour, was also pregnant by Burns. He made plans to marry her, but in late April 1786 her father refused to accept him as a son-in-law. Burns then sent the copy for *Poems, Chiefly in the Scottish Dialect* to the printer while indulging in women and alcohol in equally excessive measure to divert his mind from Jean. Famously, he hoped to emigrate to Jamaica on the volume's proceeds. The collection was more successful than he could have anticipated, and although only 612 copies were issued, the book's critical acclaim saw Burns feted in Edinburgh. A second subscription sold 2,876 copies, and his fame spread south, resulting in a London edition in November 1787. Consequently, Burns canceled his emigration plans and married Jean the next year. Meanwhile, in 1787 he met James Johnson, a music engraver who had embarked on a project of researching and printing the words and

music of every known Scottish song. Burns joined him, not just collecting and revising extant songs but adding originals. Between 1787 and his death nine years later, he contributed 330 revised and new songs both to the six-volume *Scots Musical Museum* (1787–1803) and to George Thomson's five-volume *Select Scottish Airs* (1793–1818).

After his marriage to Jean in 1788, Burns accepted a commission as an exciseman (or tax collector) at a salary of 50 pounds per year. The job, however, entailed a lot of horseback riding and, still burdened by the strains of tenant farming, he became ill with depression, headaches, and exhaustion. He moved to Dumfries in November 1791, and an expanded two-volume edition of his *Poems* was published in Edinburgh in February 1793, including "TAM O' SHANTER," arguably his greatest individual work. Yet although Burns's poetry continued to be acclaimed, he could never earn enough to support his ever-expanding family (apart from Jean, at least one other woman bore his child), and the famine that struck Dumfries in 1796 hit him and those closest to him hard. He died on July 21, 1796 after becoming ill with rheumatic fever.

From the first publication of *Poems* in 1786, Burns was promoted as a "natural genius." Despite the fact that poets had been promoted in similar terms throughout the century, this was an idea bound up with the Romantic vogue for primitivism fired by publications such as William Duff's 1767 *Essay on Original Genius*. The title page of *Poems* bore the legend (attributed to an anonymous source): "The Simple Bard, unbroken by rules of Art, / He pours the wild effusions of the heart: / And if inspir'd, 'tis Nature's pow'rs inspire; / Her's all the melting thrill, and her's the kindling fire."

He was also famously characterized, in an 1786 review by Henry MacKenzie, as the "Heav'n-taught ploughman" (quoted in Low 267). The truth was certainly more complicated. Burns's use of Scots dialect, like his use of the Scots form of "standard habbie," tends to emphasize the influence of a native Scots tradition—writers such as William Dunbar (ca. 1460–ca. 1530) and Robert Fergusson (1750–74). Yet as a young man he read writers as diverse as William Shakespeare, JOHN LOCKE, Alexander Pope, James Thomson, Tobias Smollett,

Laurence Sterne, THOMAS GRAY, and WILLIAM COWPER. He continued to admire many of them and to write poetry in "standard" English, throughout his life. On the one hand, as David Fairer and Christine Gerrard remark, "it was the broad Scots dialect that liberated Burns with its rhythmic energy and vivid vocabulary" (Fairer and Gerrard 492). Yet Burns's "Scots dialect" was not always quite as "Scottish" as it might appear: As the same critics also observe, "Some of his finest songs . . . speak English with a Scottish accent" (492).

Burns's themes are often those beloved of the Romantics more generally. Although immensely proud of his Scottish heritage, he was a celebrant of the laboring poor everywhere. This is seen nowhere better than in "Song—For A' That and A' That" (sometimes known, alternatively, as "A Man's a Man for a' That" or as "Is there, for honest Poverty"), one of the age's great poetic statements of egalitarianism. Burns is a great poet and songwriter of love (one has only to think, for instance, of "O My Luve's Like a Red, Red Rose"), while "TAM O' SHANTER" combines a knowledge of neoclassical mock-heroic with a love of GOTHIC folklore and myth. Burns's influence on Romanticism was incalculable: Almost every major British Romantic paid him homage, including WILLIAM WORDSWORTH and SAMUEL TAYLOR COLERIDGE, whose LYRICAL BALLADS (1798) shows a deep Burnsian influence. The critical attention consistently paid to him for two centuries also reflects this degree of importance. While Burns is clearly particularly identified with Scottish culture, his ability to reach a wider constituency is amply demonstrated by the annual singing of "AULD LANG SYNE" throughout the English-speaking world each New Year's Eve to see out the passing year and welcome the new one.

See also "AE FOND KISS"; "DESPONDENCY: AN ODE"; "EPISTLE TO J. LAPRAIK"; "MAN WAS MADE TO MOURN: A DIRGE"; "TO A MOUNTAIN DAISY"; "TO A MOUSE."

**Further Reading**
Burns, Robert. *Burns: Poems and Songs*. Edited by James Kinsley. London: Oxford University Press, 1969.

———. *Robert Burns: Complete Letters*. Edited by James MacKay. Darvel: Alloway Publishing, 1987.

Douglas, Hugh. *Robert Burns: The Tinder Heart*. Stroud, Eng.: Sutton Publishing, 1996.

Fairer, David. *English Poetry of the Eighteenth Century, 1700–1789*. Harlow and London: Longman, 2003, 179–185.

Fairer, David, and Christine Gerrard, eds. *Eighteenth-Century Poetry: An Annotated Anthology*. 2nd ed. Oxford: Blackwell, 2004, 492–510.

Lindsay, Maurice. *The Burns Encyclopedia*. 3rd ed. London: Robert Hale, 1996.

Low, Donald A., ed. *Robert Burns: The Critical Heritage*. London: Routledge, 1995.

MacKay, James, ed. *A Biography of Robert Burns*. Edinburgh: Mainstream, 1992.

McGuirk, Carol, ed. *Critical Essays on Robert Burns*. New York: G. K. Hall; London: Prentice Hall, 1998.

Wu, Duncan, ed. *Romanticism: An Anthology*. 3rd ed. Oxford: Blackwell, 2006, 260–276.

—Steve Van Hagen

## Byron, George Gordon Byron, Lord
(1788–1824)

Famously described by Lady CAROLINE LAMB as "mad—bad—and dangerous to know," Lord Byron has received as much, if not more, attention for his provocative but short life as for his innovative, politically engaged, and daring poetry. Born on January 22, 1788, to Catherine Gordon and Captain John "Mad Jack" Byron, Byron was known simply as George Gordon in deference to his mother's higher social standing (she was 13th laird of Gight in her own right, while Mad Jack was merely the nephew of a baron and a fortune-hunting army officer) and the possibility of expectations for the young boy from her family. His early years were spent in Scotland, and though relatively obscure they were far from quiet. His parents' tempestuous marriage, strained by John Byron's spendthrift tendencies and erratic behavior and Catherine's sense of disappointed hopes, ended with Mad Jack's death in France in 1791.

Young Byron's life changed dramatically when a series of family deaths made him the sixth baron Byron in 1798. He moved from Aberdeen to Nottingham and his ancestral home, the crumbling Newstead Abbey. His change of circumstances

came with certain educational and social expectations but few resources to fund them, and financial
difficulties plagued him until the sale of Newstead
in 1818. Byron was sent to Harrow in 1801 and
then to Cambridge in 1805, and though he was not
a great scholar, he always had a certain linguistic
precocity. He read voraciously from an early age
and began writing occasional verse as a teenager.
These early poems were collected and privately
published in 1806 as *Fugitive Pieces,* a collection
that would eventually evolve into *Hours of Idleness* (July 1807). While not necessarily important
in themselves, these juvenile productions proved
a catalyst to a more serious literary career. *Hours
of Idleness* was ravaged by Henry Brougham in the
*Edinburgh Review,* the most important literary journal of the period. After counseling young Byron
to "forthwith abandon poetry" and "turn his talents . . . to better account," Brougham goes on to
inform his lordship that poetry requires more than
"the mere rhyming of the final syllable" (Brougham
28). But if Byron was not unique for having composed "very poor verses" in his youth, his mature
work certainly set him apart. Enraged by the anonymous review, he retaliated with *English Bards and
Scotch Reviewers* (1809), a long poem that takes to
task not only "the critic's starch decree" (l. 402)
but the entire literary establishment. This satire was ultimately a double-edged sword: Though
it made his literary reputation, the attack on his
political allies (both Byron and the *Review* were
Whig) proved embarrassing later.

Byron's education was completed with a Grand
Tour somewhat restricted by the Napoleonic Wars
(see BONAPARTE, NAPOLEON). Byron and his companion, John Cam Hobhouse, a Cambridge friend,
landed in Lisbon in July 1809. After seeking adventure in the midst of the Peninsular War, Byron and
Hobhouse departed Cadiz for Gibraltar, from where
they traveled to Malta and further east. They
toured parts of the Ottoman Empire (Albania and
Turkey) before exploring Greece, a country that
was to inspire Byron throughout his life. His travels
provided the settings and circumstances for much
of his mature writing, including the first two cantos
of *CHILDE HAROLD'S PILGRIMAGE* (1812). Like all
of Byron's works, this long narrative poem is partly
autobiographical. But while he was describing the

places and people he encountered, he was also hiding certain elements of his voyage as the relaxed
sexual mores of the East allowed him the freedom
to pursue affairs with young men. As the literary
historian Fiona MacCarthy observes, *Childe Harold*
is "filtered through the tormented sensibility of the
young traveler, originally named 'Childe Burun,'
responsive to yet alienated from his surroundings
by some undisclosed and undisclosable wrong-
doing. This was to be a pilgrimage of the divided
self" (MacCarthy 105). Byron drew on his sense of
himself as an outsider, the product of his physical
deformity (he was born with a clubfoot) and his
bisexuality, feelings complicated by his early Calvinist religious indoctrination. This work inaugu-
rated both a period of incredible fame and a long
professional relationship with his new publisher,
John Murray.

Of his meteoric success, Byron noted, "I
awoke one morning and found myself famous"
(quoted in Moore, 347). His success gained him
entry to Holland House, the center of Whig
intellectual life, where he was introduced to the
women of Melbourne House, including Lady
Caroline Lamb and Annabella Milbanke. While
attention was initially directed to Byron as a poet-
genius, to his legions of adoring female fans admiration spread from his verses to his person. Letters
with demands ranging from advice and signed
books to locks of hair and private meetings poured
in. Over the next few years, Murray published
Byron's wildly popular oriental tales: THE GIAOUR
(1813), *The BRIDE OF ABYDOS* (1813), *The COR-
SAIR* (1814), and *Lara* (1814). These poems featured more of the dark, brooding, tormented
Byronic heroes that fascinated his female readers,
who conflated protagonist and poet. Meanwhile,
Byron engaged in a series of high-profile affairs,
the first and most tempestuous of which was with
Lady Caroline Lamb. Though the affair lasted only
nine months, the consequences would reverberate far beyond. Lady Caroline became obsessed
with Byron; stalked him; and, when he would not
take her back, wrote a novelization of their affair,
GLENARVON (1816), which included a transcription of Byron's parting letter.

During his years of fame in London, Byron
grew close to his half sister Augusta Leigh. The

child of his father's first marriage, Augusta was raised by her maternal relations and did not meet Byron until 1804. Their relationship was believed to become rather more than fraternal, and Byron even contemplated eloping to the Continent with her. Though it is unclear how far their intimacy extended, Augusta's third daughter, Medora, born 1814, believed that Byron was her father. In order to save his sister's reputation, and indeed his own, Byron and Augusta separated, though their relationship remained of tremendous importance to him, and he would explore incest in the verse drama MANFRED: A DRAMATIC POEM (1817). It was Augusta who urged Byron to marry and helped him select women to court, including his eventual wife, Anna Isabella (Annabella) Milbanke. Byron first met Annabella in early 1812, though he dismissed her as "too good for a fallen spirit to know or wish to know" (Byron 1973, 2: 175–176). He revised this opinion enough to offer marriage to her in October 1812 but was refused. However, despite her rational and serious turn of mind—she enjoyed mathematics and was devoutly religious—she was no more immune to Byron's charms than other women. They married on January 2, 1815, but it was not a happy marriage. Annabella did not deal well with Byron's moodiness and violent outbursts, and Byron was simply miserable, often seeking solace in the company of his sister. Money problems and debt collectors further complicated their uneasy domestic circumstances. Their daughter, Ada Augusta was born on December 10, 1815. Three months later, in February 1816, Lady Byron left her husband, fearing for his sanity and her safety. While Byron initially thought the separation was to be temporary, the situation became official and acrimonious with the interference of Lady Caroline. Amid rumors of incest and more serious crimes, he retreated once again to the Continent in April 1816, never to see England again.

Byron traveled through Europe with an entourage consisting of his Grand Tour travelling companion, Hobhouse, and his personal physician, JOHN POLIDORI, in a replica of Napoleon's coach. Canto III of *Childe Harold* records this journey through Belgium, including a visit to the battlefield at Waterloo where Napoleon's ambitions had been finally put to rest by a decisive allied victory

the year before. From here Byron and company traveled to Switzerland, where they encountered PERCY BYSSHE SHELLEY, Mary Godwin (later MARY WOLLSTONECRAFT SHELLEY), and Claire Clairmont (with whom Byron had had an affair in London that produced a daughter, Allegra, born in 1817). Shelley, who recognized the extent of his friend's talent, was to have a profound influence on Byron and his poetry. Urging that Byron's powers "be exerted to their full extent," Shelley suggested writing an epic on an important political topic, such as the FRENCH REVOLUTION. While Shelley's encouragement was important, Byron would take his earnest suggestion in an entirely different, and ironic, direction in DON JUAN (1819–24).

Byron moved on to Italy in 1818, taking up residence in Venice, where he composed the fourth and final canto of *Childe Harold*. While there, he received a copy of John Hookham Frere's mock-heroic poem whose very long title is now abbreviated as *Whistlecraft* (1817–18). This Arthurian work, heavily written in ottava rima, was influenced by the Italian poets Francesco Berni and Luigi Pulci. Its influence on Byron can be seen in his subsequent works, including *Beppo* (1818), a comic treatment of adultery, and *Don Juan*. As the biographer Caroline Franklin notes, ottava rima proved a better form for Byron's double-edged poetic persona than the Spenserian stanzas of Childe Harold or the Popean couplets of his early work (Franklin 2000, 114–115).

Though not a conventional epic on the French Revolution, Byron's comic-satiric masterpiece *Don Juan* is deeply concerned with exposing the flaws of the ancien regime. Initially designed to be the length of the first canto of *Childe Harold*, *Don Juan* took on a life of its own, spanning 16 completed cantos and a fragment of a 17th. The first two cantos of this determinedly risqué work were published anonymously on July 15, 1819, though Byron's authorship was readily discernible. The poem drew fire from *Blackwood's Magazine*, which, though forced to acknowledge the its genius, deplored its utter disregard for "Love—honor—patriotism—religion" and despaired that Byron was "no longer a human being . . . but a cool unconcerned fiend . . . treating well nigh with derision the most pure of virtues and the most odious of vices" (168). Other reviews were not as kind: the *British Critic* declared that "the versification and morality are about upon a par" and pronounced *Don Juan* "a narrative of degrading debauchery in doggerel rhyme" ("Remarks" 259). The controversy, coupled with Byron's determination to continue despite the outcry, eventually led to the disintegration of his long publishing relationship with John Murray. Moral outrage was not Murray's only concern. Because the publication was anonymous, it was more vulnerable to pirating. Cheap editions produced by radical presses cut into Murray's profits on elaborate quarto editions; it also made the poem a tool in radical campaigns to expose the hypocrisy of elite culture. Ironically, while Byron wrote this gleeful, libertine satire, he had decided that he had had enough of libertinism and began a relationship with Teresa Guiciolli that would last until his death six years later.

Byron and Shelley met again at Pisa in 1821. Shelley hoped Byron would join him and LEIGH HUNT in their new periodical, *The Liberal.* His death at sea in July 1822 put an end to this collaboration, but not to Byron's involvement in radical politics. Though his career in the House of Lords had fizzled out after two speeches, Byron, like his contemporaries in the literary public sphere, was deeply politically engaged. Usually he made his contributions as one of Shelley's "unacknowledged legislators," choosing to share ideas in verse rather than in government or an activist society, but Byron saw his choice as somewhat unsatisfactory: "I do think the preference of *writers* to *agents*—the mighty stir made about scribbling and scribes by themselves and others—a sign of effeminacy, degeneracy, and weakness. Who would write, who had anything better to do?" (Byron 1966, 2:345).

In the final years of his life, Byron switched from the life of contemplation to one of action in his involvement in the Greek war of independence. In 1823 he was approached by the London Greek Committee for financial and perhaps literary support for the cause of Greek independence. The Greeks' fight against tyranny captured his imagination, and he rapidly began making plans to travel to Greece and actively engage in the fight, leading his own group of private soldiers. He was also embroiled in discussions about a post-independence government. It is quite likely that, had he lived, Byron may have had some role in ruling Greece. However, a fever coupled with the excessive bleeding prescribed by his physicians resulted his death on April 19, 1824, age 36, in Missolonghi.

Though a legendary figure, Byron was not always regarded as a great poet. Among his Romantic contemporaries, his satirical and ironic style is markedly different from their concern with myth, nature, and imagination. Early in his career, with *English Bards and Scotch Reviewer,* Byron expressed his distaste for "That mild apostate from poetic rule" (l. 176), WILLIAM WORDSWORTH, whom he accuses of showing, "both by precept and example, . . . That prose is verse, and verse is merely prose" (ll. 181–182), as well as for SAMUEL TAYLOR COLERIDGE. Instead, he marks his preference for the early 18th-century poets Alexander Pope, John Dryden, William Congreve, and Thomas Otway, championing an Augustan (or 18th-century) sensibility instead of the new Romantic concern with natural feelings and settings. His unwillingness to conform to poetic and moral expectations of the Romantic period led many 20th-century critics, particularly those modernists who associated popularity with bad art, to question whether Byron truly was a canon-worthy poet, let alone a Romantic. Byron's reputation for satire complicated his place in literary history even for those who acknowledged his genius. M. H. Abrams left Byron out of his study of Romantic literature because "in his greatest work he speaks with an ironic countervoice and deliberately opens a satirical perspective on . . . his Romantic contemporaries" (Abrams 13). However with the emergence of feminist, New Historicist, postcolonial, and gender criticism, critics such as Jerome McGann, Marilyn Butler, Nigel Leask, Caroline Franklin, Susan Wolfson, and others have begun to explore Byron's works in context and provide a better understanding of Byron's engagement in revolutionary and gender politics and Romanticism as well as his important place in literary history.

See also *CAIN: A MYSTERY; DEFORMED TRANSFORMED, THE; MANFRED: A DRAMATIC POEM;* "NAPOLEON'S FAREWELL"; "PRISONER OF CHILLON, THE"; "SHE WALKS IN BEAUTY."

**Further Reading**

Abrams, M. H. *Natural Supernaturalism: Tradition and Revolution in Romantic Literature.* New York: Norton, 1973.

Brougham, Henry P. Review of *Hours of Idleness. Edinburgh Review* 11 (February 1808): 285–288. In *Byron: The Critical Heritage,* edited by Andrew Rutherford, 27–32. New York: Barnes and Noble, 1970.

Byron, George Gordon Byron, Baron. *The Complete Poetical Works.* 7 vols. Edited by Jerome J. McGann. Oxford: Clarendon, 1980–93.

———. *The Works of Lord Byron. Letters and Journals.* 13 vols. Edited by Rowland E. Prothero. New York: Octagon, 1966.

Franklin, Caroline. *Byron.* London: Routledge, 2007.

———. *Byron: A Literary Life.* London: Palgrave, 2000.

———. *Byron's Heroines.* Oxford: Clarendon. 1992.

MacCarthy, Fiona. *Byron: Life and Legend.* New York: Farrar, Straus and Giroux, 2003.

McGann, Jerome. *Byron and Romanticism.* Cambridge: Cambridge University Press, 2002.

"Remarks on Don Juan." *Blackwood's Magazine* 5 (August 1819): 512–518. In *Byron: The Critical Heritage,* edited by Andrew Rutherford. 166–173. New York: Barnes and Noble, 1970.

Review of *Don Juan. British Critic* 2nd ser., 12 (August 1819): 197. In *Byron: The Critical Heritage,* edited by Andrew Rutherford, 258–259. New York: Barnes and Noble, 1970.

Moore, Thomas. *Letters and Journals of Lord Byron with Notices of His Life.* 2 vols. London: John Murray, 1830.

Thorslev, Peter L. *The Byronic Hero: Types and Prototypes.* Minneapolis: University of Minnesota Press, 1962.

—Megan Woodworth

## Cain: A Mystery Lord Byron (1821)

Perhaps more defiant than any other work in LORD BYRON's corpus, *Cain: A Mystery* reveals Byron's skepticism of orthodoxy and the religious doctrine of predestination. The biblical character Cain struggles with the conflict between the mind and body and between free will and predestination as he questions his family's religion, encounters Lucifer, and kills his brother. Cain's state has been compared to Byron's (or, rather, how Byron saw himself)—that is, to have been born fallen. Byron, some biographers have suggested, saw his clubfoot as God's condemnation. By the play's end, his protagonist will bear the visible evidence of his damnation on his body for all to see: the mark of Cain.

Knowing that *Cain* would cause controversy, Byron prefaced the work with a defense—one that might calm his readership when faced with a work that some might deem heretical. Yet despite his attempts to reassure his audience, *Cain* caused quite a stir in England in 1821. Cain, whom Byron attempted to portray sympathetically, offends through his iconoclasm and blasphemy. Throughout the drama, he struggles with mind/body dualism. Perhaps reflecting Byron's angst-ridden struggle with his disability, the drama wrestles with the issue of whether this man—"poor clay"—can transcend his physical limitations by his mental faculties.

The drama also asks whether the God of Adam—the God who permitted the Fall—is truly good. Cain rejects his family's perspective on the Tree of Knowledge—that the serpent lied and that the Tree brought about death: "The snake spoke *truth*; it *was* the tree of knowledge; / It *was* the tree of life: knowledge is good, / And life is good; and how can both be evil" (1.1.36–38)? Furthermore, he rejects the God of Adam: "Cursed be / He who invented life that leads to death!" (2.2.18–19). Eve rebukes Cain for his blasphemy, and Cain's family departs shortly thereafter, leaving him in solitude to question God and cast blame upon the Deity for his depravity.

In the preface, Byron reminds his audience that the Genesis account does not relate Lucifer to the serpent. Accordingly, Lucifer tells Cain that "the snake *was* the snake— / No more" and claims that he did not have involvement with the Fall (1.1.220–221). The snake, Cain believes, does not lie to Eve. Eve was told that she would have knowledge, and knowledge was what she received. Byron's text also interrogates the idea of the "Fortunate Fall." This view holds that the Fall was necessary for humanity to have a better life. Cain questions this interpretation by recalling the story of "a lamb stung by a reptile" and how his father nursed the lamb back to health (2.2.290–305). Rejecting the idea of the "Fortunate Fall" that is implicit in the story, Cain argues, "But I thought, that 'twere / A better portion for the animal / Never to have been *stung at all*" (2.2. 300–2). Cain sees nothing fortunate about his condition and believes that he should not be held responsible or punished for Eve's actions. Cain also hints that God has been guilty of entrapment: "The tree was planted, and why not for him? / If not, why place him near it, where it grew, / The fairest in the centre?" (1.1.72–74).

Doubting the claims of his family and the goodness of their God, Cain must choose between God and Lucifer. While Cain is alone, Lucifer appears before him and manages to confuse him about whether God is good or evil—a benevolent father or a tyrant. Cain begins to consider Lucifer a friend of humankind in the fight against a deceitful, tyrannical God and chooses to follow him, if not wholly out of worship, then out of a desire for knowledge. However, Cain is not a pupil in the traditional sense. Lucifer never introduces new thoughts into Cain's mind; he only encourages the rebellious and blasphemous thoughts that Cain is already entertaining. He cannot give answers that Cain does not already know. In this sense, Lucifer may be simply a psychological projection of Cain's making. In other words, Lucifer may represent the portion of Cain's psyche that encourages his skepticism.

Lucifer guides Cain through a review of past, present, and future worlds. Lucifer reveals how in the past the earth was filled with supra-human creatures. The earth has already been created and destroyed numerous times prior to Adam and Eve. How, Cain seems to ask, could a God who is proclaimed to be good actually create the world multiple times, with each time resulting in death? Lucifer claims that "all [are] doom'd to death, and wretched" (2.1.47). This doom is the very thing that plagues Cain, prompting him to ask what death is. Lucifer, however, only answers Cain's questions with more questions. In fact, Lucifer cannot understand death since he is immortal. From this realization Cain deduces of the Tree of Knowledge: "It was a lying tree—for we *know* nothing. / At least it *promised knowledge* at the *price* / Of death—but *knowledge* still: but what *knows* man?" (1.2.61–63). Lucifer offers a final consolation to Cain's discontent: "*One good* gift has the fatal apple given, / Your *reason*" (2.2.459–460). The Tree of Knowledge did give humankind knowledge—of death and toil.

Because he realizes the fallen state of the world, Cain detests the notion of procreation if all are destined for death. He wants no children of his own if they are merely going to suffer and,

ultimately, die: "Here let me die: for to give birth to those / Who can but suffer many years, and die, / Me thinks is merely propagating death, / And multiplying murder" (2.1.67–71). The undesirability and futility of perpetuating humankind plagues him so much that he longs for death and even contemplates killing his son Enoch (3.1.122–126).

Upon returning to the earth, Cain, who is more dissatisfied than ever because his questions remain unanswered, joins his family. Unlike Lucifer, he retains some goodness even after visiting other worlds. Unfortunately, he is still susceptible to his sinful nature, which overpowers him more than he would have imagined possible. When Abel insists that he and Cain offer a sacrifice to God, Cain refuses and rejects Abel's God. Angered by his brother's persistence, Cain murders Abel in a moment of rage and experiences a remorse that makes him beg for death. When he acknowledges what has happened, he blames Eve for his sin because it was she who originally ate the fruit of the Tree of Knowledge, thus bringing sin into the world. As a way of demonstrating justice, God places a mark upon the forehead of Cain.

Biographical or psychoanalytic readings of the text remain popular, the idea being that the ideas and characters function as expressions of Byron's own anxieties or ideas. Ultimately Cain stands as the defeated challenger to the God of his family. He cannot grasp that which he seeks—knowledge of death and God. No doubt Byron identified with Cain in multiple ways. Both challenged orthodoxy, led lives in defiance to the norm, and were criticized and adored simultaneously. Both felt damned for something outside of their control—that is, their depravity/disability. Both bore distinct marks from God on their bodies—Cain, a mark on his forehead, and Byron, a clubfoot—that signify their damnation.

Critics have also taken note of the duality of Lucifer and God (Manicheaism) presented throughout the drama, attributing the belief to Byron, despite his denial. When Cain asks, "Ye do not dwell together," Lucifer responds, "No, we reign together; but our dwellings are asunder" (2.2.372–375). He even claims equality with God: "To the two great double mysteries! The two Principles!" (2.2.404). Lucifer would certainly need to use dualistic language in order to convince others of his alleged equality with God. Prior to the play's action, Lucifer deemed himself equal to but fully independent of God, and such blasphemy had led to a battle between God and Lucifer in which Lucifer was defeated. As the victor, argues Lucifer, God wrote history from his perspective: "He as conqueror will call the conquer'd / *Evil*; but what will be the *good* he gives? / Were I the victor, *his* works would be deem'd / The only evil ones" (2.2.443–446). Lucifer encourages Cain to question God. In response, Cain relies solely on his reason, which leaves him unsatisfied.

**Further Reading**

Byron, George Gordon Byron, Baron. *Byron: Complete Poetical Works*. Edited by Frederick Page. New York: Oxford University Press, 1970.

—Mark Westmoreland

### Caleb Williams (Things as They Are; or, The Adventures of Caleb Williams) William Godwin (1794)

There are aspects of *Caleb Williams* that are commonly found in the 18th-century novel: the picaresque narrative, the reliance on coincidence, and the pervasive use of formal language. Yet this is also a novel published at a time of great political and philosophical turmoil, and it sets out to engage with some of the great debates of its time, particularly politics and the relations between the classes. Caleb is a man of peasant stock who becomes a social outcast, and the plot turns on his struggle for survival, recalling some of WILLIAM WORDSWORTH's characters, mistreated by a society in which they have no place.

WILLIAM GODWIN's central concerns in the novel are the twin concepts of tyranny and liberty. He creates two characters to represent the misuse of power: Barnabas Tyrrel, the arrogant English squire; and Falkland, the gentleman and scholar. Falkland is provoked into murdering Tyrrel, his oppressor, and, fearful of the consequences, allows others to take the blame. Falkland shares his guilty secret with an employee, Caleb Williams, and then abuses his position of power by binding Caleb to

secrecy. From that time on Caleb is a prisoner of an agreement, and Falkland is as much an oppressor as Tyrrel had been before. One form of tyranny has been replaced by another.

Caleb is unjustly charged with theft and committed to prison, where he is held without trial. This would have been seen as topical in Britain in 1794, for this was the year when the government, fearing revolution and sedition, suspended habeas corpus. After Caleb escapes from prison, he adopts a variety of disguises, thus securing temporary freedom. He is eventually recaptured and committed to prison again, but as Falkland declines to press charges, he is acquitted. Though a free man in the eyes of the law, Caleb continues to be pursued by Falkland, who fears Caleb for what he knows about Tyrell's murder. Falkland is eventually brought to justice, by which time he is a broken man, worn out by his own guilt and his pursuit of Caleb. Falkland dies, but his death haunts Caleb, who now sees himself as a murderer.

Godwin originally wrote a different conclusion, one in which Caleb is not believed, Falkland lives as a free man, and Caleb is returned to prison. But in either case Caleb fails to find complete freedom since he is either a victim of injustice or else he is a victim of his own conscience. Godwin thus examines tyranny in a number of forms. There is the individual power of men like Tyrrel and Falkland; the officially sanctioned tyranny of the legal system; and the less obvious tyranny of the class system in which a gentleman such as Falkland is more likely to be believed than a peasant such as Caleb.

**Further Reading**

Godwin, William. *Caleb Williams*. Edited by Gary Handwerk and A. A. Markley. (Peterborough, Ont., and Orchard Park, N.Y.: Broadview Press, 2000).

—Irene Wiltshire

### "Calendar, A" Sara Coleridge (1834)

Despite her distinctive writing style and breathtaking imagery, SARA COLERIDGE remains known today more for being the daughter of SAMUEL TAYLOR COLERIDGE as well as editor of his works and less for her own poems and writings. In 1834 Coleridge released a collection entitled *Pretty Lessons in Verse for Good Children,* which included the poem "A Calendar." She used the verses, some of which were in Latin, to instruct her young children, and the entire work was quite popular upon publication. Today, "A Calendar" is one of the few poems known to those outside of the academic community, as it is used in many primary schools to help children memorize the months of the year. It has also been mistitled "The Months" in several publications, including many elementary education handbooks and Kathy Weller's 2007 illustrated edition, *The Months: Fun with Friends All Year 'Round.*

The poem describes the 12 months through 12 rhymed couplets, a pattern of memorization that many educational specialists agree is ideal for younger children. "A Calendar" is straightforward and simple, although it does highlight Coleridge's ability to paint exquisite mental pictures. Each month is described through the eyes of a child, noting the changes in flowers and temperature that seem so dramatic to a young child.

While many biographers try to pull Coleridge into the early Victorian period, her poetry is essentially Romantic. "A Calendar" focuses primarily on nature to describe the changing months, referencing "pretty lambs," "sheaves of corn," and "dancing daffodils." Also, this poem is written for children, not for adults, and that in itself is a Romantic quality. The child was first seen as separate from the adult during the Romantic period. Prior to the Romantic period, children were to act as little adults. Raising and educating children in the upper classes was the duty of wet nurses and governesses (see MARY WOLLSTONECRAFT's *A VINDICATION OF THE RIGHTS OF WOMAN*). By the time of such early Romantics as WILLIAM BLAKE, CHILDHOOD was upheld as the ideal state of man, still enveloped in innocence. The social atmosphere was perfect for the publication of a book of children's verses, and Coleridge's poems were welcomed because of that.

**Further Reading**

Coleridge, Sara. *Collected Poems.* Edited by Peter Swaab. Manchester, Eng.: Carcanet, 2007.

Low, Dennis. *The Literary Protégées of the Lake Poets.* Aldershot, Eng.: Ashgate, 2006.

Mudge, Bradford Keyes. *Sara Coleridge, a Victorian Daughter: Her Life and Essays.* New Haven, Conn.: Yale University Press, 1989.

—Melissa Ann Greggs-West

## "Casabianca" Felicia Hemans (1826)

Both popular and reviled, FELICIA HEMANS's poem "Casabianca," first published in 1826 in the *Monthly Magazine,* might initially strike readers as sentimental and simplistic. Although out of fashion for most of the 20th century, the poem (and Hemans's place in early 19th-century literary culture) is receiving renewed scholarly interest at the beginning of the 21st century.

Like a number of Hemans's poems, "Casabianca" is based on a historical event, focusing on a particular person's role in history. In such poems Hemans frequently appends her own note to the historical context. In the case of "Casabianca," she makes clear to the reader that the poem is named after a 13-year-old boy who died in the battle of the Nile in 1798. She assumes her reader understands that the battle was a victory for the British admiral HORATIO NELSON, who was fighting NAPOLEON BONAPARTE's forces in Egypt, and that Casabianca was on a French vessel. The historical context is important because Hemans creates sympathy for the dead boy, who is not on the British "side."

Hemans's poems are interested in national identity, history, and politics, often emphasizing the role of domestic affections in such affairs. In Hemans's time, history and politics were considered masculine and outside the domain of a female poet. In "Casabianca" she transgresses her traditional female role and assumes authority to comment on the historical event; in doing so, she critiques a masculine world view that supports the violence of war. The last lines of "Casabianca" emphasize the role of the heart in world affairs. Such purpose is instilled in the domestic sphere, and many 19th-century readers believed Hemans was the exemplary female domestic poet. In a poem that shows the absence of the domestic realm and its affections, Hemans represents a crisis in patriarchal culture, especially when Casabianca repeatedly cries out for his father, who never responds because he is already dead. Hemans criticizes the glory of war, showing its cost to home and family, which for her equivocal to transcend national identity and politics.

Perhaps because Hemans wrote the poem in a conventional ballad stanza with regular meter and rhyme, "Casabianca" became a favorite for school recitation throughout the 19th century. Its history in education may partially account for its falling out of fashion in the early 20th century. Its apparent regularity, however, should not conceal some of its formal subtlety, such as Hemans's use of caesura in dramatic lines, such as line 19, when the "booming shots" interrupt the boy's speech, and line 34, when Casabianca has been killed. Nonetheless, the form of "Casabianca" made it an easy poem to ridicule through parody, and this may also account for its becoming unfashionable in the early 1900s.

**Further Reading**

Hemans, Felicia. *Felicia Hemans: Selected Poems, Letters, and Reception Materials.* Edited by Susan J. Wolfson. Princeton, N.J.: Princeton University Press, 2000.

———. *Felicia Hemans: Selected Poems, Prose, and Letters.* Edited by Gary Kelly. Peterborough, Ont., and Orchard Park, N.Y.: Broadview Press, 2002.

Lootens, Tricia. "Hemans and Home: Victorianism, Feminine 'Internal Enemies,' and the Domestication of National Identity." *PMLA* 109 (1994): 238–253.

Mellor, Anne D. *Romanticism & Gender.* New York: Routledge, 1993.

Robson, Catherine. "Standing on the Burning Deck: Poetry, Performance, History." *PMLA* 120 (2005): 148–162.

Sweet, Nanora, and Julie Melnyk, eds. *Felicia Hemans: Reimagining Poetry in the Nineteenth Century.* Houndsmills, Eng.: Palgrave, 2001.

—Albert Sears

## *Castle Rackrent* **Maria Edgeworth** (1800)

An 1800 reviewer of *Castle Rackrent* praised it as "a very pleasant, good-humoured, and successful representation of the eccentricities of our Irish neighbours," a description which for many readers still sums up this influential novel (quoted in Belanger 240). Billed as "an Hiberian Tale, taken from Facts and from the manners of the Irish Squires before the year 1782," the novel has been labeled the first provincial novel and the first "big house" novel. The literary scholar Franco Moretti has suggested that *Castle Rackrent* should be seen as a precursor to the works of SIR WALTER SCOTT and the modern historical novel.

The novel's central character is Thady Quirk, a native Irish servant, who has purportedly "undertaken to publish the memoirs of the Rackrent family," owners of the estate on which he has worked for most of his life. "Honest Thady," as he calls himself, relates stories about the successive generations of family members he has served: the alcoholic Sir Patrick; Sir Murtagh, a "great lawyer," who refuses—"out of honor"—to pay Sir Patrick's debts; and Sir Kit, who gambles away his inheritance and eventually (in a curious reversal of fortunes) has to sell the estate to Thady's unscrupulous son, Jason.

Thady is the novel's most striking character, and MARIA EDGEWORTH claimed he almost took possession of her when she was writing the novel: "When, for mere amusement, without any ideas of publishing," she wrote to a friend, "I began to write a family history as Thady would tell it, he seemed to stand beside me and dictate and I wrote as fast as my pen could go" (quoted in Edgeworth 240–241). Thady is an interesting storyteller on several levels. He is made to speak in an Irish vernacular—a deliberate choice on Edgeworth's part. In an editorial she explains that she prefers "a plain unvarnished tale" of the kind Thady Quirk offers over "the most highly ornamented narrative" (2). Rather like WILLIAM WORDSWORTH and his call for a new kind of poetic language based on the words of ordinary men and women, Edgeworth seems to reject sophisticated or flowery literary language. "Those who are used to literary manufacture know," she tells us, "how much is often sacrificed to the rounding of a period or the pointing of an antithesis" (3). Overly complex writing seems to her to be deliberately obtuse and even deceitful. She offers an alternative linguistic style based on Thady's "plain unvarnished" language—despite the fact that his colloquialisms may seem difficult for metropolitan or non-Irish audiences to under-stand. But the novel is more sophisticated than it might first appear. There is also the central ques-tion: How reliable is Thady as a narrator? As the novel goes on, it appears that Thady cannot—or does want to—tell the complete story. Some read-ers have suggested that rather than being a some-what dim albeit loyal servant, he is actually a cunning and self-serving man who knows how to get what he wants, despite not appearing to. Thus a question hanging over the end of the book is whether the interests of the family have been well served by their servants.

This is a valid question because the story of the Rackrents is one of decline and decay. As James Newcomer notes: "What is memorable about *Castle Rackrent* is an atmosphere" which consists of "whiskey, decay, rot, guttering candles, tobacco, damp, horse dung, and dust. . . . [I]t is an amalgam of improvidence, stupidity, cupid-ity, pride, subservience, animosity, sentimentality, brutality, and perversity" (Newcomer 154–155). Despite their class and supposed gentility, the Rackrent men appear barbarous and (self-)destruc-tive, not least in the ways in which they treat their wives. Notable is Sir Kit, who, short of money and heavily in debt, marries "the grandest heiress in England" (Edgeworth 23) to restore his family's fortunes. Having secured his wife's money, he also demands her diamond cross. When she refuses he locks her up for seven years, and she is freed only when he dies. After Sir Kit's death, Thady comments: "Her diamond cross was, they say, at the bottom of it all; and it was a shame for her, being his wife, not to show more duty, and to have given it up when he condescended to ask so often for such a bit of a trifle in his distresses, especially when he all along made it no secret he married for money" (83).

Lady Kit's determination to keep her own valuables leads to the loss of all her independ-ence—a fate that befalls several other women in the novel. The women are important only as appendages to their husbands, so much so that the first Rackrent wives—those of Sir Murtagh and Sir Kit—are not given first names in Thady's narration. They exist only within the context of, and as possessions of, the Rackrent family.

Although the novel announces itself as realist, it has been suggested that there are strong Gothic overtones, not least in its stories of female impris-onment and abuse. According to Karl J. Winter, female GOTHIC novels "represent the terrifying aspects of life for women in a patriarchal culture" and "are concerned with violence done to familial bonds that is frequently directed against women" (Winter 13, 18). Edgeworth clearly captures something of this.

Another important context for *Castle Rackrent* is the historical. The 1790s saw violent demon-strations against British rule and the unsuccessful United Irishmen's Rebellion of 1798. The contro-versial Act of Union, which "united" Great Britain and Ireland, was passed in 1800, the year *Rackrent* was published. The novel's publication was thus timely, and it announces itself as "tales of other times," imparted "to those totally unacquainted with Ireland," being "for the information of the ignorant English reader." But as well as informing readers about the Irish character, the novel is also interested in ideas of governance and rule and how these can be misused. The Rackrents' Irish tenants clearly suffer for their masters' follies. Edgeworth herself was worried about the novel being read as a political text or as an as an attack on the union with Ireland (still imminent when she was writing the novel). As the editor Marilyn Butler notes, just before the novel was published, Edgeworth inserted an extensive glossary of words and phrases at the end of the novel, flagging up its status as a sociological rather than political document (Edge-worth 4–5). Nonetheless, Castle *Rackrent* can be read within the context of the British Empire and Ireland's status as a British colony.

See also ABSENTEE, THE.

## Further Reading

Belanger, Jacqueline. "Educating the Reading Public: British Critical Reception of Maria Edgeworth's Early Irish Writing." *Irish University Review* 28, no. 2 (1998): 240–255.

Edgeworth, Maria. *Castle Rackrent and Ennui.* Edited by Marilyn Butler. London: Penguin, 1992.

Ferguson, Moira. *Subject to Others: British Women, Writers and Colonial Slavery, 1670–1834.* New York: Rout-ledge, 1992.

Newcomer, James. *Maria Edgeworth, the Novelist, 1767–1849: A Bicentennial Study.* Fort Worth: Texas Christian University Press, 1967.

Winter, Kari J. *Subjects of Slavery, Agents of Change: Women and Power in Gothic Novels and Slave Narratives, 1790–1865.* Athens: University Press of Georgia, 1992.

—Mark Hughes

## celebrity

A thriving celebrity culture shaped new possibilities and perils for authors in the Romantic period. Such enormously successful writers as GEORGE GORDON, LORD BYRON; SIR WALTER SCOTT; and THOMAS MOORE became internationally famous, and their celebrity glamorized authorship as a profession. But to many contemporary observers, the culture of celebrity substituted momentary popular applause for more lasting forms of fame, eroding the traditional ground of literary reputation.

In the late 18th and early 19th centuries, the reading public developed a widespread fascination with the lives and personalities of authors, due in part to the rising cultural prestige of ideas of genius, creativity, and self-expression. Striving for visibility in a rapidly expanding print marketplace, writers adeptly employed authorship as a public performance, often making the writer's persona, visual image, and personal history integral to the appeal of his or her works. Perhaps the greatest celebrity of the age, Lord Byron bewitched audiences by blurring the line between his own character and the dark, brooding heroes of his poetry, beginning with the publication of *CHILDE HAROLD'S PILGRIMAGE*, cantos 1 and 2, in 1812. Byron's powerfully passionate poetry combined with his nobility and an aura of eroticism to create an incendiary mix. At the height of his fame in 1814, his "Eastern tale" *The CORSAIR* reportedly sold 10,000 copies in one day, a stunning figure at the time. Encouraging his readers to form an intimate, emotional bond with the personality they perceived in the poems, Byron followed a trail blazed by earlier writers. As shown by the literary historians Judith Pascoe and Sarah Zimmerman, women writers such as CHARLOTTE SMITH or MARY ROBINSON used their own story and image to draw in sympathetic readers of their writing. The critic Tom Mole notes that 18th-century celebrities such as Laurence Sterne pioneered the self-promotional techniques through which an authorial personality like Byron's becomes both a legend and a reproducible commodity.

As now, the line between celebrity and notoriety was often faint. A writer's identity and image could circulate dangerously outside of his or her control, as Byron discovered when his separation from his wife in 1816 became a full-blown tabloid scandal. Gossip about the private lives of writers was standard fare in newspapers and periodical reviews, which frequently traded in politically motivated "personality" attacks. Tell-all biographies about any kind of celebrity were popular—lives of actors and actresses frequently saw print, for example—and authors were no exception, especially in the wake of James Boswell's unprecedentedly frank *Life* of Samuel Johnson (1791). Celebrity writers could also be the embarrassed subjects of satires and romans à clef by their contemporaries. The public exposure celebrity entailed was particularly dangerous for women writers, especially given the common cultural equation for women of fame and illicit sexuality. Yet women were also among the Romantic era's leading literary personalities—for instance, the actress-turned-poet and novelist Mary Robinson, the Anglo-Irish novelist SYDNEY OWENSON (Lady Morgan), and the poet LETITIA ELIZABETH LANDON, all of whom were highly visible figures in prominent literary and social circles. Other famous women writers, such as the hugely popular poet FELICIA HEMANS, maintained a careful distance from the literary "scene." Caught between their ambition for public success and cultural norms that identified women with domesticity, many women writers reflected directly in their writing on the dilemma of what Hemans calls in one typical poem "WOMAN AND FAME."

Authors and critics in the Romantic period sought to distinguish between the ephemerality of modern celebrity and a classical rhetoric of fame as immortality. Developing institutions such as the public lecture and the periodical press changed the terms on which writers met their public.

Some argued that in the highly commercialized, competitive, and fast-paced literary scene of the 19th century, momentary celebrity was the only fame possible: In his 1823 article "The Periodical Press," WILLIAM HAZLITT commented that "literary immortality is now let on short leases, and we must all be content to succeed by rotation" (Hazlitt 358). Indeed, the culture of celebrity brought so many names before the public's attention that it could produce in effect a kind of anonymity. In an 1823 canto of his satiric epic DON JUAN, Byron wryly describes a London literary scene thronging with "ten thousand living authors" and the "eighty greatest living poets / as every magazine has it's" (11:154). Writers often complained that celebrity authorship demanded pandering to a fickle public of consumers or parading before the public's gaze. The literary scholar Andrew Bennett has argued that Romantic poets countered the perceived transience and commercial orientation of popular fame by emphasizing instead a "culture of posterity" in which neglect or misunderstanding by one's contemporaries comes to seem almost the precondition of posthumous fame.

By the early 19th century, celebrity authorship drove an extensive commercial industry churning out memoirs, appreciations, portraits, busts, and other souvenirs of famous writers, living and dead—most prominently in the cult of Shakespeare. The curiosity readers felt about writers found expression in such increasingly popular practices as collecting autographs and visiting scenes associated with writers or their books. By the middle of the 19th century, tourists were flocking to WILLIAM WORDSWORTH's Lake Country and the Scottish locales popularized by ROBERT BURNS and Sir Walter Scott.

Such influential essays as Peter Manning's "Childe Harold in the Marketplace" and Sonia Hofkosh's "The Writer's Ravishment" have emphasized how Romantic myths of authorial originality and autonomy are challenged by a focus on celebrity, which makes evident instead the collaborative construction of an authorial identity through the exchanges among writers, publishers, and readers. Hofkosh's essay also explores the gendered terms of fame and fame discourse, a subject as well of Susan Wolfsan's important work on Hemans and JOHN

KEATS in Borderlines and elsewhere. Ian Duncan's Modern Romance and the Transformation of the Novel discusses the national "romance of the author" that has developed around Scott. The recent essay collection Janeites: Jane Austen's Disciples and Devotees spotlights yet another emerging focus of criticism: the motivations of the fans who respond to celebrities so passionately.

## Further Reading

Bennett, Andrew. Romantic Poets and the Culture of Posterity. Cambridge: Cambridge University Press, 1999.

Byron, George Gordon Byron, Baron. Don Juan. Edited by T. G. Steffan, E. Steffan, and W. W. Pratt. New York: Penguin, 2005.

Duncan, Ian. Modern Romance and the Transformations of the Novel: The Gothic, Scott, Dickens. Cambridge: Cambridge University Press, 1992.

Hazlitt, William. "The Periodical Press." Edinburgh Review 71 (May 1823): 349–378.

Higgins, David. Romantic Genius and the Literary Magazine: Biography, Celebrity, Politics. New York: Routledge, 2005,

Hofkosh, Sonia. "The Writer's Ravishment: Women and the Romantic Author—The Example of Byron." In Romanticism and Feminism, edited by Anne K. Mellor, 93–114. Bloomington: Indiana University Press, 1988.

Lynch, Deidre, ed. Janeites: Austen's Disciples and Devotees. Princeton, N.J.: Princeton University Press, 2000.

Manning, Peter. "Childe Harold in the Marketplace: From Romaunt to Handbook." MLQ 52 (1991): 170–190.

Mole, Tom. Byron's Romantic Celebrity: Industrial Culture and the Hermeneutic of Intimacy. Basingstoke, Eng.: Palgrave, 2007.

Pascoe, Judith. Romantic Theatricality: Gender, Poetry and Spectatorship. Ithaca, N.Y.: Cornell University Press, 1997.

Wolfson, Susan. Borderlines: The Shiftings of Gender in British Romanticism. Stanford, Calif.: Stanford University Press, 2006.

Zimmerman, Sarah M. Romanticism, Lyricism, and History. New York: State University of New York Press, 1999.

—Eric Eisner

## Charterhouse of Parma, The
### Stendhal (1839)

The diplomat Marie-Henri Beyle (1783–1842), known as STENDHAL, began writing—or rather dictating—his most famous novel in November 1838, finishing it seven weeks later. Traces of the novel's rapid composition are apparent in its complicated, somewhat meandering, plot but it attracted—and has continued to attract—many readers drawn along by its swashbuckling style. The novelist Henry James found *The Charterhouse of Parma* to be "among the dozen finest novels we possess."

The plot of *The Charterhouse of Parma* can suggest a soap opera or miniseries as it includes romance, ambition, intrigue, and sexual frustration. The hero, a headstrong young man named Fabrice Del Dongo, is an idealist and admirer of NAPOLEON BONAPARTE. He is born in the early 1790s, the time when Napoleon was "at the head of that youthful army which but a short time before had crossed the Bridge of Lodi, and taught the world that after so many centuries Caesar and Alexander had a successor" (19). Bewitched by Napoleon and prompted by a spirit of rebellion against his father—a man of "boundless hatred for the new ideas"—Fabrice runs away to join Napoleon's army for the battle of Waterloo. "I will go forth to conquer or to die beside that Man of Destiny" he announces (44). Fabrice is naive, however, and the brutishness and chaos of warfare is far from what he expects: "Suddenly they all moved off full gallop. A few minutes later Fabrice saw, twenty paces ahead of him, a ploughed field at the surface of which was moving in a singular fashion. The furrows were full of water, and the soil very damp, that formed the ridges between those furrows kept flying off in little black lumps three or four feet into the air" (46). After Waterloo Fabrice goes back Milan, where he becomes caught up in a series of romantic exploits, the result of his impetuous nature and the machinations of his fascinating aunt, Gina Pietranera, duchess of Sanseverina, and her married lover, Count Mosca. Amid the political chicanery of the (largely fictionalized) court of Parma of the 1820s, Fabrice is imprisoned for the murder of a lover's guardian (he later escapes via a long rope); becomes a bishop; and falls in love with the innocent, spiritual, if rather dull Clelia Conti.

Alongside the novel's breathless plot, Stendhal allows his readers to understand his hero's psychology. Fabrice is a master of self-deception whose lack of self-awareness is stunning. He shares Stendhal's idealism—as a young man, the author had also followed Napoleon into Italy, Austria, and Russia—and it is an idealism that is common to many protagonists of Romantic novels. However, Fabrice never entirely shakes this off; he tends to judge his actions against the poems and novels he has read, as if they will provide him with the key to living and loving. This is shown to have tragic results. At the close of the story, Fabrice, alone in his religious retreat—the "charterhouse" referred to in the novel's title—has died. He is still young and has also inadvertently caused the deaths of Clelia and their illegitimate child, thanks to an ill-planned scheme that went wrong.

### Further Reading
Stendhal. *The Charterhouse of Parma.* Translated by C. K. Scott, Moncrieff. London: Everyman, 1992.

—Matthew Harris

## Chatterton, Thomas (1752–1770)

Thomas Chatterton produced a prodigious amount of writing in his extremely short life, writing that is sometimes seen as heralding the Romantic age, but he is known almost as much for the Romantic aspects of his life and death as for what he wrote. Almost all the leading Romantic poets hailed him as a forerunner both for his writings and for his life story, but later scholars have challenged the Romantic nature of both his life and works.

Born in Bristol, England, on November 20, 1752, three months after the death of his father, a writing teacher, Chatterton chafed in his provincial surroundings, unhappy with the commercialism, coarseness, and violence of his city, though fiercely loyal to its past, real and imagined. Instead of being sent to a grammar school, where he might have studied Greek and Latin, he attended Colston's, a school training boys for practical work in local businesses. Upon leaving school, in 1767 he was apprenticed to a local lawyer, John Lambert. He spent six days a week transcribing legal documents, work that he loathed, but the workload was actually quite light, and he was able to spend a large part of his working hours on his own historical pursuits and writings. He also liked to wander the streets of Bristol, looking at its medieval ruins, and was especially fascinated by his local church, St. Mary Redcliff, with which his family had a connection, his great uncle having been the sexton there.

Because of the family connection, his father was able to obtain a large number of old church documents, which he brought home to be used for domestic purposes, as book covers and lining papers. The young Chatterton became fascinated with these documents, especially with the story of a 15th-century mayor of Bristol named William Canynge. Eventually he developed an imaginary history set at the time of Canynge and focusing on an invented character, the priest and poet Thomas Rowley. As Chatterton imagined the story, Canynge was a wealthy merchant with spiritual ideals who was the great benefactor of St. Mary Redcliff and a generous patron of Rowley, who served as his personal scholar, adviser, historian, confessor, and writer. Chatterton began producing pseudomedieval writings of various sorts, attributing most of them to Rowley but also putting Canynge and other characters forward as authors of histories, biographies, genealogies, poetry, and drama.

Chatterton's first Rowleyan publication appeared in a local paper, *Felix Farley's Bristol Journal.* It purported to be an account of the opening of the old Bristol bridge in 1247, which Chatterton rightly judged would be of interest because in 1768, when he produced it, a new bridge was being opened in Bristol. His account of the 1247 celebrations caught the attention of two local antiquarians, George Catcott and William Barrett, who were soon convinced that Chatterton had access to a great many medieval manuscripts, which he obligingly produced for them. Seeking an outlet for his work beyond Bristol, he wrote to the writer Horace Walpole, whose medieval novel *The Castle of Otranto* had appeared just a few years before, but Walpole dismissed Chatterton's works as fakes.

In 1770, feeling that he could no longer remain a legal copyist in Bristol, Chatterton convinced his employer that he was unbalanced and even suicidal; he was therefore allowed to escape from his apprenticeship. He then moved to London, where he supported himself with his pen, writing satires in verse and prose on political subjects and on general subjects, such as religion and greed. He also composed a musical play, *The Revenge,* for which he was paid, though it was never performed, and wrote home to his mother and sister saying how well he was doing and sending them gifts. Some commentators say he was just putting on a brave front to cover up his poverty and lack of success, but others say he was in fact beginning to make his way in the world of London journalism and publishing.

On August 24, 1770, Chatterton—still months from his 18th birthday—was found dead in his attic room of a drug overdose. At the time it was assumed he had committed suicide, presumably out of despair over his lack of success as a writer. Horace Walpole was even blamed for having driven him to this desperate act by refusing to support him the year before. In the late 20th century, however, scholars suggested that the overdose may have been accidental.

Though he was hardly known in his lifetime, after his death Chatterton twice became a cause célèbre. First a controversy raged over whether his Rowley poems were genuinely medieval; then, when it was generally accepted that they were not, the notion arose that he had been an unrecognized poetic genius, his life tragically cut short. The Romantic poets seized on this notion, looking to Chatterton as their harbinger and speculating on what he might have accomplished had he lived. WILLIAM WORDSWORTH called him the "marvellous boy," JOHN KEATS dedicated *ENDYMION* to his memory, SAMUEL TAYLOR COLERIDGE wrote a poem about him, and ROBERT SOUTHEY edited his works. Later the Pre-Raphaelites also looked to him; Henry Wallis painted a famous portrait of his death scene, and Dante Gabriel Rossetti said he had been the "day-spring" of the Romantic movement. However, he fell out of favor in the early 20th century, and later in the century critics tried to show his connections to his own neoclassical age, playing down the notion that he was a Romantic forerunner and comparing him instead to Jonathan Swift, Alexander Pope, and Charles Churchill.

Those who see Chatterton as part of the Romantic movement associate him with the GOTHIC revival and also point to his experimentations with verse forms, along with his taste for strong emotions and exotic locations, notably in his *African Eclogues* (1770). He himself distinguished his rugged Rowleyan poems from the affected elegance fashionable in his own day. As to the enduring worth of his poetry, critical opinion is mixed, but his Rowleyan poetic drama *Aella* (1770) generally wins praise for its bold heroism and its sad minstrel songs. Among his non-Rowleyan works, the *African Eclogues* are also praised. Chatterton's imaginative creation of the medieval Rowleyan world has also been cause for admiration. But more than for any of his works, Chatterton is remembered as the boy forger who for a while, at least, fooled some of the most serious scholars in the land and as the prototype of the Romantic hero and unrecognized genius.

**Further Reading**

Chatterton, Thomas. *The Complete Works of Thomas Chatterton: A Bicentenary Edition.* 2 vols. Edited by Donald S. Taylor and Benjamin B. Hoover. Oxford: Clarendon Press, 1971.

Groom, Nick, ed. *Thomas Chatterton and Romantic Culture.* London: Macmillan, 1999.

Kelly, Linda. *The Marvellous Boy: The Life and Myth of Thomas Chatterton.* London: Weidenfeld & Nicolson, 1971.

Meyerstein, E. H. W. *A Life of Thomas Chatterton.* London: Ingpen & Grant, 1930.

Russett, Margaret *Fictions and Fakes: Forging Romantic Authority, 1760–1845.* Cambridge: Cambridge University Press, 2006.

Taylor, Donald S. *Thomas Chatterton's Art: Experiments in Imagined History.* Princeton, N.J.: Princeton University Press, 1978.

—Sheldon Goldfarb

## *Childe Harold's Pilgrimage: A Romaunt*
### Lord Byron (1812–1819)

Any study of this poem should begin with its title. From medieval times, a young noble in line to be knighted was addressed as "Childe" plus his first name. Even though LORD BYRON denied that the poem was autobiographical (MacCarthy 160), most scholars have pointed out myriad parallels between the youth of "Albion's isle" first introduced in canto 1 and Byron, beginning with the author's initial intention to title the poem "Childe Burun," the spelling of his family's name during the Norman Conquest. The poem's subtitle, *Romaunt*, means a "romantic tale." The word evolved into *Romant*, then *Romans*, and finally *Romance*, but Romantics endeared to an idealistic notion of medievalism, including SIR WALTER SCOTT in *IVANHOE* (1819) and *The Fair Maid of Perth* (1828) and Byron, used the archaic spelling.

Like most aristocrats who turned 21, Byron went on his own pilgrimage from 1809 to 1810. For most Englishmen, this meant travel through the Continent, but because of the Napoleonic Wars (1803–15), much of Europe was too dangerous, so he and his friend from Cambridge, John Cam Hobhouse, toured Portugal, Spain, Malta, Albania, Greece, and Turkey (for a detailed itinerary, see Byron 1966, xxi–xxiv). When he returned to England, he had written a travelogue, the first 4,000 lines of *Childe Harold*.

Cantos 1 and 2 were published by John Murray, who was just beginning his career as a publisher. They were available for sale on March 3, 1812, at a price of 50 shillings per copy, roughly half the weekly income of a typical gentleman (St. Clair 6). The first edition sold out in three days, and Byron uttered those famous words, "I woke up one morning and found myself famous."

Although he did become an overnight sensation, during the following four years Byron also became known as the most dissolute man in Britain. His wife won legal separation and custody of their daughter Ada, and he was forced out of England. On April 25, 1816, he wrote with bitterness to his friend MARGUERITE GARDINER countess of Blessington: "Exiled from my country by a species of ostracism—the most humiliating to a proud mind, when *daggers* and not shells were used to ballot, inflicting mental wounds more deadly and difficult to be healed than all that the body could suffer" (Byron 1966, 67). He completed the first three stanzas of canto 3 while seasick (MacCarthy 283) and heartsick; began an eight-year journey through Switzerland, Italy, and Greece. Having formed friendships with PERCY BYSSHE SHELLEY and MARY SHELLEY, he gave them canto 3 to deliver to Murray when they left for England in August 1816.

Ready to depart for Venice in spring 1817, Byron thought he was finished with the poem and turned his attention to MANFRED. But while aboard his ship, he penned three more stanzas, which began canto 4. On January 8, 1818, his traveling companion, Hobhouse, to whom Byron dedicated this canto, carried it to Murray. (For a detailed description of what Byron saw as a tourist and how it is integrated into this canto, see Andrew Rutherford's article on Hobhouse and Byron.)

All four cantos of *Childe Harold* are written in Spenserian stanzas: eight lines of iambic pentameter (five feet, or sets, of unstressed/stressed syllables) followed by an Alexandrine, which is a line of iambic hexameter (six feet of unstressed/stressed syllables) with a caesura, or a break in thought in the middle of each line. The rhyme scheme for the entire poem is *ababbcbcc*.

*Childe Harold* gave rise to the Byronic hero, a type of character who became a permanent fixture in the annals of literary history. Sardonic, he sees himself like a god whose dominion is earth, as conveyed in the second stanza in canto 3: "Once more upon the waters! Yet once more! / And the waves bound beneath me as a steed / That knows his rider" (3.2.10–12). To WILLIAM WORDSWORTH nature was "The anchor of my purest thoughts, the nurse, / The guide, the guardian of my heart, and soul / Of all my moral being" ("LINES WRITTEN A FEW MILES ABOVE TINTERN ABBEY," ll. 111–113); to JOHN KEATS it led to introspection and melancholy; and to Percy Shelley it was the transformer into ecstasy. But to Byron, as he perceived the mountains as friends and he held "companionship" with all other forms of nature (3.13), it filled him with a sense of superiority; from his mountaintop, "He who surpasses or subdues mankind, / Must look down on the hate of those below" (3.45.397–400). The Byronic hero's attitudes of ascendancy and self-aggrandizement isolate him from others: "But soon he knew himself the most unfit / Of men to herd with Man, with whom he held / Little in

common" (3.12.100–102). He not only does not see himself a member of the common herd, he refuses to recognize and appreciate any authority: He was "untaught to submit / His thoughts to others" and "would not yield dominion of his mind" (3.12.7–12). The Byronic hero, in short, is arrogant, conceited, self-exiled, lonely, bitter, and cynical. Byron portrays NAPOLEON BONAPARTE as a Byronic hero: In canto 3, Napoleon is "Conqueror and Captive of the Earth" and has made "monarchs' necks thy footstool," but like Childe Harold and Byron, he cannot conquer himself (3.37–38). The Byronic hero is unable to escape his thoughts; he is the "wandering outlaw of his own dark mind" (3.3.20). This world-weariness that pervades *Childe Harold* also characterizes a man who has expended a profligate youth, as depicted in Byron's last book of poetry, *DON JUAN,* finished just before his death. A German Romantic writer and contemporary of Byron, Jean Paul, called this exhaustion of life *Weltschmerz.* Byron's Childe Harold has "grown agéd in this world of woe, / In deeds, not years" (3.5.37–38). This mood is also apparent in the third book of poetry that completes Byron's trilogy of life, *Manfred,* with a man so worn out from life that he just wants to die, and he refuses to submit himself to God or to any form of religion for redemption. Byron himself was feeling that there was nothing left for him to experience, even though he was still a young man.

It is also worth considering the historical and intellectual context. Byron had been born into a world of turmoil. With the Treaty of Ildefonso in 1796, France forced Spain into an alliance against Great Britain. After several debilitating defeats, the Spanish monarch fled, and Napoleon established his brother on the throne. The Spanish rose up against Napoleon, united with Portugal, and made way for the British generals Arthur Wellesley (who would become better known as the duke of Wellington) and Sir John Moore to advance through the Peninsula and finally into Spain to drive out Napoleon. Byron was in Portugal and Spain witnessing the revolts when he wrote canto 1.

The Convention of Cintra (August 13, 1808), largely negotiated by the British, allowed the French to leave Portugal without further conflict and reparation. Byron sharply criticizes this policy in cantos 1.18 and 2.13. Philip Martin identifies the Byronic hero as the disillusioned "post-revolutionary intellectual" (Martin 77). Overtly, the poem does reflect a politically volatile period in European history, observed by a Romantic who realizes the futility of his faith in mankind to better the world. Although the Byron scholar Drummard Bone reads the end of the fourth canto as reconciliation between man and his natural environment (Bone 155–156), covertly the poem reflects an interior landscape of unsettling turbulence. This is not just the mirror of one individual's heart, soul, and mind or else the poem would have found only a small audience interested in Byron's autobiography. *Childe Harold* resonates with readers who have exerted their own Promethean defiance toward God, and like Prometheus, bound to a rock, we "of the breast which fain no more would feel, / Wrung with the wounds which kill not, but ne'er heal" (3.8.67–68).

## Further Reading

Blessington, Marguerite. *Journal and Conversations between Lord Byron and the Countess of Blessington.* Cincinnati, Ohio: Lorenzo Stratton, 1851.

Bone, Drummond. "*Childe Harold IV, Don Juan* and *Beppo.*" In *The Cambridge Companion to Byron,* edited by Drummond Bone, 151–170. Cambridge University Press, 2004.

Bruffree, Kenneth A. "The Synthetic Hero and the Narrative Structure of *Childe Harold* III." *Studies in English Literature, 1500–1900* 6, no. 4 (Autumn 1966): 669–678.

Byron, George Gordon Byron, Baron. "*Childe Harold's Pilgrimage.* Canto the Fourth." *British Review and London Critical Journal* 12, no. 23 (August 1888): 1–34.

———. *The Works of George Gordon Byron.* 13 vols. Edited by Ernest Hartley Coleridge. New York: Octagon Books, 1966.

MacCarthy, Fiona. *Byron: Life and Legend.* New York: Farrar, Straus and Giroux, 2002.

Martin, Philip W. "Heroism and History: *Childe Harold* I and II and the Tales." In *The Cambridge Companion to Byron,* edited by Drummond Bone, 77–98. Cambridge University Press, 2004.

Rutherford, Andrew. "The Influence of Hobhouse on *Childe Harold's Pilgrimage,* Canto IV." *Review of English Studies,* new ser., 12, no. 48 (November 1961): 391–397.

St. Clair, William. "The Impact of Byron's Writings: An Evaluative Approach." In *Byron: Augustan and Romantic,* edited by Andrew Rutherford, 1–25. London: Macmillan, 1990.

Stein, Harold. "A Note on the Versification of *Childe Harold.*" *Modern Language Notes* 42, no. 1 (January 1927): 34–35.

—Brenda Ayres

## childhood

The figure of the British Romantic child is typically depicted as an innocent, imaginative, pastoral, androgynous, and universal being embodying the paradox of creative effort and organic inspiration aspired to by adult poets. Often referenced yet infrequently defined, constructions of the Romantic child are nevertheless key in interpreting the cultural change that characterizes the period.

In some ways the Romantic child was born before even the Romantic movement, rooted as it is in Rousseauian philosophy of education. Following JOHN LOCKE (1632–1704) in directly challenging Calvinist doctrines of original sin, JEAN-JACQUES ROUSSEAU (1712–78) nevertheless argued that Locke's definition of the child as tabula rasa (blank slate) should not have resulted in the careful instruction in adult rationalism propounded by Locke, but rather in a course of action designed to preserve the child's natural, uneducated state for as long as possible (Coveney 4). Debates over this rejection of original sin resulted in fundamental pedagogical division, but the very fact that childhood became a locus of conflict in the late 18th and early 19th centuries implies that the emerging recognition of childhood as a unique state of human existence opened significant new avenues of discourse in the period.

Philippe Ariès's seminal *Centuries of Childhood: a Social History of Family Life* (1962), argues that childhood as a class-transcendent social category arose in the 18th century, and before that children were mostly treated as incomplete adults. While the details of Ariès's claims have been much disputed, it does appear that at the very least, children emerged as a new audience for literary marketing in the late 18th century. Authors such as MARY WOLLSTONECRAFT (1759–97), Sarah Trimmer (1741–1810), the sister and brother ANNA LAETITIA BARBAULD (1743–1825) and John Aikin (1747–1822), CHARLOTTE SMITH (1749–1806), MARIA EDGEWORTH (1767–1849), and FELICIA HEMANS (1793–1835) wrote best-selling didactic children's fiction in the conviction that children needed moral and rational education in order to become moral adults. This perspective is also evident in the children's hymns by Isaac Watts (1674–1748), Barbauld, and others. CHARLES LAMB's (1775–1834) denouncement of these popular writers as "the cursed Barbauld Crew, those Blights and Blasts of all that is Human in man and child" (quoted in Clarke 91) certainly reflects the attitude of canonical writers such as WILLIAM BLAKE (1757–1827) and WILLIAM WORDSWORTH (1770–1850), who are typically associated with the Romantic child, and may actually reveal less rejection of conventional adult morality than it does the Rousseauian insistence that even books could stifle a child's natural development. In discussions of the conflicting perspectives on childhood in the period, popular authors who wrote for children are frequently compared with now-canonical authors who resolutely wrote only *about* children. Thus, it is important to remember that the term *Romantic child* as it is typically used—and thus as it is defined here—refers primarily to the symbolic opinions of a vocal minority.

Of that vocal minority, Wordsworth's depictions of childhood are perhaps the most commonly referenced. "The child is father of the man; / And I could wish my days to be / Bound each to each by natural piety," Wordsworth declares in lines 7–9 of "My Heart Leaps Up" (1808), which celebrates the continuity of the past, present, and future joy he felt when glimpsing a rainbow. The Wordsworthian child functions as an exemplum of the best of human nature, a fact that resulted in notable tensions in some of his poetry. For example, "ODE: INTIMATIONS OF MORTALITY FROM RECOLLECTIONS OF EARLY CHILDHOOD" (1807) reveals the poet struggling to reconcile the notion that infants arrive on earth "trailing clouds of glory" (l. 65) yet soon "Shades of the prison-house begin to close / Upon the growing Boy" (ll. 68–69) with his determination to remain optimistic about adult human nature even in the face of mortality and philosophical doubt. This theme also arises in "LINES WRITTEN A FEW MILES ABOVE TINTERN ABBEY" (1798) and, perhaps most pointedly of all, in *The Prelude* (1850 version). In the aforementioned poems Wordsworth compares his own childhood and adult sensibilities, but his treatment of childhood also embodies a tension when the subject is a child other than his past self. The five so-called Lucy Poems (1798–1801), "LUCY GRAY" (1800), and "WE ARE SEVEN" (1798) all share an engagement with childhood death. Wordsworth both grieves childhood death and memorializes it as fitting, since it returns children wholly to the nature that they already inhabited so much more perfectly than adults.

William Blake also engages questions of death in his portrayals of children, but his poetry is characterized by a deep social concern for the suffering child, which is mostly absent from Wordsworth. Blake's child figures are victims of the social order castigated in *Songs of Experience*'s "HOLY THURSDAY" (1794); and in the separate poems, both entitled "The CHIMNEY SWEEPER," that appear in *Songs of Innocence* (1789) and *Songs of Experience*. SONGS OF INNOCENCE AND OF EXPERIENCE nuance the construction of child-as-exemplum because instead of simply glorifying innocence and bemoaning experience, the works seek to complicate the relationship between those typically polarized concepts. As the scholar Roni Natov argues, childlike imagination "is where Blake saw the harmony of Innocence and Experience resolve in higher Innocence. For him, Innocence and Wisdom were natural partners, while Ignorance resided with Experience and with those who, in their denial of the worldliness of the world, ultimately denied the spiritual as well" (Natov 12). The children within Blake's poetic universe are at times able to transcend their suffering through imagination, but these portrayals nevertheless demand that the reader critically examine a world which would heap such suffering on a child.

Perhaps a common trait of Romanticism is the notion that art can and should be harnessed to revolution, and the Romantic focus on children had significant influence in the massive Victorian reform of child welfare advocated in literature by ELIZABETH BARRETT BROWNING (1806–61), Charles Dickens (1812–70), and many others. Yet in *Romanticism and the Vocation of Childhood* (2001), Judith Plotz traces how several Romantic writers actually appropriated and totalized childhood for symbolic purposes while neglecting the needs of real children in their spheres. For example, the essayist THOMAS DE QUINCEY (1785–1859) made a sort of industry out of pathos-laden depictions of suffering children. Likewise, despite his avid writing for a juvenile audience, Charles Lamb portrayed chimney sweeps without revealing any sense of obligation to the reality of their plight, instead reframing them in terms of a poetic idealization of childhood imagination.

Probably no one else celebrated childhood to the extent of Wordsworth or exposed the abuses inflicted on it to the degree of Blake, Lamb, or De Quincey, yet the figure of the child appears in some way or another in the works of nearly every author of the period. In her sonnet "TO THE SOUTH DOWNS," CHARLOTTE SMITH depicts childhood as the ideal state, in harmony with nature. Elsewhere, LORD BYRON depicts *DON JUAN*'s coming of age in the eponymous poem, and he describes Don Juan's second lover, Haidée, as a child of nature entirely untouched by the corrupting elements of the civilized world. Likewise, in "FROST AT MIDNIGHT" (1798), SAMUEL TAYLOR COLERIDGE (1772–1834) celebrates the fact that his child will be raised outside the city and thus will be truly able to express his natural childhood identity. In fact, Coleridge applied neo-Rousseauian principles to the parenting of his son, HARTLEY COLERIDGE (1796–1849), even more than to his poetry. JOHN KEATS (1795–1821) also had constructions of childhood projected onto him, albeit posthumously. While childhood was not a central part of Keats's poetry, his untimely death made him the embodiment of the frail, tragic genius that was a significant part of Romantic iconography. Wordsworth, Coleridge, and Keats himself had already dedicated verses to THOMAS CHATTERTON (1752–70), the 18th-century writer who died as a teenager due to what was believed to be starvation-induced suicide. Romantic constructions of genius bore a striking resemblance to Romantic constructions of childhood, suggesting that the Romantic hero and the Romantic child share an inheritance.

Fiction writers also engage the Romantic child. While the Brontë sisters technically published their major novels in the Victorian era, many critics consider them members of the Romantic ethos. EMILY BRONTË (1818–48) creates amalgams of the child of nature and the Byronic hero in both Heathcliff and Catherine of *Wuthering Heights* (1847), while her sister Charlotte (1816–55) exposes the dehumanizing aspects of British boarding schools in *Jane Eyre* (1847). MARY SHELLEY (1797–1851) uses the symbol of the child metaphorically in *FRANKENSTEIN* (1816), for though Victor Frankenstein fashions his creature as a grown man, he repeatedly describes him as his progeny—an offspring whose lack of childhood is a significant contributor to his catastrophically unnatural existence.

Ensuring every individual a proper childhood became a topic of utmost importance in the Romantic era, but what qualified as a proper childhood proved more difficult to define. Depictions of Romantic childhood in canonical fiction and poetry aimed at adult audiences are often read in simple contrast to the definitions of childhood undergirding popular didactic children's literature of the day, an interpretive tendency that risks overshadowing the unifying fact that all such considerations of the child in literature were new developments of the period. Definitions of Romanticism and its canon continue to shift, yet the figure of the child proves an important common denominator across a broad spectrum of Romantic writing.

**Further Reading**

Aikin, John, and Anna Letitia Barbauld. *Evenings at Home; or, the Juvenile Budget Opened.* Cork: J. Connor, 1794.

Ariès, Philippe. *Centuries of Childhood.* Translated by Robert Baldick. London: Cape, 1962.

Blake, William. *Songs of Innocence and of Experience.* San Marino, Calif.: Huntington Library, 2008.

Brontë, Charlotte. *Jane Eyre.* Edited by Stevie Davies. New York: Penguin Books, 2006.

Brontë, Emily. *Wuthering Heights.* Edited by Alison Booth. New York: Pearson Longman, 2009.

Byron, George Gordon Byron, Baron. *Don Juan.* Edited by T. G. Steffan, E. Steffan, and W. W. Pratt. New York: Penguin, 2004.

Chatterton, Thomas. *Poems Supposed to Have Been Written at Bristol by Thomas Rowley and Others in the Fifteenth Century.* Edited by Thomas Tyrwhitt. London: Routledge/Thoemmes Press, 1993.

Clarke, Norma. "'The Cursed Barbauld Crew': Women Writers and Writing for Children in the Late Eighteenth Century." In *Opening the Nursery Door: Reading, Writing, and Childhood 1600–1900,* edited by Mary Hilton, Morag Styles, and Victor Watson, 91–103. London: Routledge, 1997.

Coleridge, Samuel Taylor. *Coleridge's Poetry and Prose.* Edited by Nicholas Halmi, Paul Magnuson, and Raimonda Modiano. New York: Norton, 2004.

Coveney, Peter. *Poor Monkey: The Child in Literature.* London: Rockliff, 1957.

De Quincey, Thomas. *The Collected Writings of Thomas De Quincey.* Edited by David Masson. New York: AMS Press, 1968.

Edgeworth, Maria. *The Novels and Selected Works of Maria Edgeworth.* Edited by Marilyn Butler, et. al. London: Pickering and Chatto, 1999.

Hemens, Felicia. *Felicia Hemans: Selected Poems, Letters, Reception Materials.* Edited by Susan J. Wolfson. Princeton, N.J.: Princeton University Press, 2000.

Keats, John. *Keats's Endymion: A Critical Edition.* Edited by Stephen Steinhoff. Troy, N.Y.: Whitston Pub. Co., 1987.

Knoepflemacher, U. C. "Mutations of the Wordsworthian Child of Nature." In *Nature and the Victorian Imagination,* edited by by U. C. Knoepflemacher and G. B. Tennyson. 391–425. Berkeley: University of California Press, 1977.

Lamb, Charles, and Mary Lamb. *The Works of Charles and Mary Lamb.* 7 vols. Edited by E. V. Lucas. London: Methuen, 1903–05.

McGavran, James Holt. *Literature and the Child: Romantic Continuations, Postmodern Contestations.* Iowa City: University of Iowa Press, 1999.

Natov, Roni. *The Poetics of Childhood.* New York: Routledge, 2003.

Rousseau, Jean-Jacques. *Emile, or, Treatise on Education.* Translated by William H. Payne. Amherst, N.Y.: Prometheus Books, 2003.

Trimmer, Sarah. *Fabulous Histories Designed for the Instruction of Children, Respecting Their Treatment of Animals.* London: Printed by T. Bensley for T. Longman, G. G. J. and J. Robinson, and J. Johnson, 1788.

Watts, Isaac. *Divine Songs Attempted in Easy Language for the Use of Children.* London: Oxford University Press, 1971.

Wollstonecraft, Mary. *Original Stories from Real Life, 1791.* Washington, D.C.: Woodstock Books, 2001.

Wordsworth, William. *Selected Poems.* Edited by Stephen Gill. London: Penguin, 2004.

Plotz, Judith. *Romanticism and the Vocation of Childhood.* New York: Palgrave, 2001.

Smith, Charlotte. *The Works of Charlotte Smith.* Edited by Stuart Curran. London: Pickering and Chatto, 2005.

Shelley, Mary. *Frankenstein, or, The Modern Prometheus.* Edited by Maurice Hindle. New York: Penguin, 2003.

—Katherine L. Carlson

## "Chimney Sweeper, The" William Blake
### (1789, 1794)

The practice of selling small boys, usually between the ages of four and seven, to labour as "climbing boys" in the narrow, twisted flues of town houses was common in WILLIAM BLAKE's London. The boys, sold in groups from poorhouses or traded by individual parents for 20 or 30 shillings, were entered into a seven-year apprenticeship under an adult sweep. Few survived these seven years without incurring, at best, the disabling deformities caused by constantly cramping a growing body into vents around 7 inches square, and at worst, "sooty warts" or cancer of the scrotum. Blake's two poems from SONGS OF INNOCENCE AND OF EXPERIENCE, and indeed the integral illustrations so crucial to his overall artistic vision, are simultaneously a poignant indictment on the plight of the boys and a critique of the moral and religious hypocrisy endemic in a society that permits such brutal exploitation of the children in their care. The two versions of "The Chimney Sweeper" also reflect the volume's contrasting notions of "innocence" and "experience" while setting up a tension between the two that is never wholly reconciled or that is, perhaps, irreconcilable.

The first and perhaps best-known version of "The Chimney Sweeper," from *Songs of Innocence* (1789) is narrated from the viewpoint of a young, innocent sweep. His is a naive and accepting innocence that never seeks to question or challenge the social conditions that keep him, and others like him, bonded and begrimed in cruel and perilous labour. His slight and inconsequential status is emphasized inasmuch as his own story is related matter-of-factly in the opening quatrain. The sweep's mother died, and he was "sold" by his father before his lisping, childish tongue could articulate the street cry associated with his trade. His unpunctuated "weep weep weep weep" (l. 3) is both a pun on tearfulness and a reinforcement of his artlessness. In the next line the sweep states "your chimneys I sweep and in soot I sleep," the correct enunciation of "sweep" indicating his maturity in the trade and thus implicating the reader (and wider society) in the continued suffering of boys like himself.

The quick transfer of emphasis from the narrator's own story to that of his friend, Tom Dacre, in the second quatrain effectively engages the reader's sympathy as the qualities of selflessness and humanity are shown to prevail in the direst situations. The narrator's lack of self-interest is evident throughout the remainder of the poem as the focus is squarely on his concern for Tom, who "cried" when his hair, "curl'd like a lambs back," was "shav'd" (ll. 5–6). Aside from the biblical imagery of the shorn and sacrificial, innocent lamb, the ritual haircut had a dehumanising and reductive function. A part of the boy's identity was clipped away, and he became one with the homogeneous mass of sweeps. The narrator offers his colleague a paradoxical consolation inasmuch as with a "bare" head, the "soot cannot spoil" his "white hair" (ll. 7–8). The binary opposition of black "soot" and "white hair" sets up an incongruity in the notion of the pure boy spending his life in proximity with dirt.

Tom's rectitude is further reinforced by his dream. He sees "thousands of sweepers," all "lock'd up in coffins of black"—in a figurative sense their constricted working environment and constant covering of soot—who are "set free" by an "Angel" to laugh and sport on a heavenly "green plain" (ll. 11–15). That the narrator and Tom have been indoctrinated into and absorbed the teachings of the Bible is clear from the language and imagery utilized. The boys "wash in the river and shine in the sun" (l. 16): baptised in the waters of life with earthly cares sloughed away, they wear the raiment of the sun becoming "naked & white" (l. 17). Effectively, Tom's ecstatic vision is one of deferred gratification, joyously anticipating the life to come "if he'd be a good boy" (l. 19) and work hard for his masters. In the final quatrain, despite going to work on a "dark" (sweeps typically worked from the hours before dawn to midday) and "cold" morning, Tom is "happy & warm" within (l. 23), secure in the knowledge that if he does his "duty" he "need not fear harm" (l. 24) as a celestial home awaits.

Although Blake's closing remark seems to be imbued with cynicism, such worldly wisdom is anathema to the innocence of the narrator. Moreover, the guileless acceptance of religious and social conditioning is doubly affecting given that many of the sweeps were charity boys and wards of the church, their simple faith rendering them complicit with the institution instrumental in their continuing exploitation. The overall impression of Blake's integral artwork is one of stifling confinement. In a narrow border at the foot of the page, an angel releases a boy from his coffin while a group of naked boys run and play. This idyll, though, is compressed by the sheer, even threatening, weight of words above. Like a vast volume of soot in a filthy chimney, the words appear to be capable of falling at any moment to crush and suffocate the boys below. The illustration, perhaps, functions as a visual commentary on the double bind of acceptance and complicity. The dream of a future paradise may be comforting in the short term, yet a purblind and unquestioning concurrence with the prevailing doctrine—and, thus, the hypocrisy at the heart of church charity provision—is equally dangerous in the maintenance of a system that condones this abuse of small boys.

The counterpoint poem in *Songs of Experience* (1794) is, from the outset, scathing and combative in tone and characterized by harsh language and bleak imagery. The narrator is, yet again, a sweep, though this time he is mired in worldly awareness, bitter and contemptuous of the religion that fuels and sustains the boys' world of "misery" (l. 12).

In the first quatrain, the sweep on his rounds is a "little black thing" (l. 1); the use of "thing" depersonalizes the boy, rendering him inconsequential, almost subhuman. His cries of "weep, weep" (l. 2) are explicitly interpreted in a literal sense as signal of distress or "woe" (l. 8) rather than a childish mispronunciation of his business. The narrator also openly questions the whereabouts of his colleague's parents who, having knowingly sold their son into unremitting torment, have "gone to church to pray" (l. 4).

In a reversal of the original version of "The Chimney Sweep," the narrator switches the emphasis to his own story in the second quatrain and sustains this viewpoint for the remainder of the poem. Rather than craving a future paradise like Tom Dacre, he reflects on his youthful happiness in the earthly sphere, when he played on the "heath" and "smil'd among the winters snow" (ll. 5–6)[sic]. The innocence and purity of his early life contrasts here with the "clothes of death" (l. 7), or the black soot, that his parents effectively endowed him with when they bartered him into his apprenticeship. In the final quatrain the narrator reflects that because he appears "happy, & dance & sing" (l. 9)—an ironic allusion, perhaps, to the chimney sweeps' annual holiday on May 1, when they were gaudily decorated and paraded through the streets of London—his parents believe they have done him "no injury" (l. 10). The closing couplet, though, is fiercely critical of the religious establishment—"God," "Priest & King" (l. 11)—that keeps people in their place, who "make up a heaven of our misery" (l. 12) and promise a reward in the afterlife in exchange for pain and suffering in the present.

The integrated artwork to Blake's compact and compelling verse highlight the boys' plight. Unlike the press of words in the earlier version, the poem is contained in the first half of the page, which is dominated by a bleak, snowy street scene peopled only by the small, black figure of a boy with a bag of soot on his back. His dark presence provides an immediate focus for the picture, in stark contrast to the predominantly cold, blue colour palette. In Blake's illustration, the lonely, arduous, predawn world of the "climbing boy" is movingly exposed.

## Further Reading

Ackroyd, Peter. *Blake*. London: Sinclair-Stevenson, 1995.

Blake, William. *Songs of Innocence and of Experience*. Edited by Geoffrey Keynes. Oxford: Oxford University Press, 1970.

Eaves, Maurice. *The Cambridge Companion to William Blake* Cambridge: Cambridge University Press, 2003.

Myrone, Martin. *"Seen in my visions": A Descriptive Catalogue of Pictures by William Blake*. London: Tate Publishing, 2009.

Roberts, Jonathan. *William Blake's Poetry*. London: Continuum Publishing, 2007.

—Diane Mason

## "Christabel" Samuel Taylor Coleridge (1797, 1800)

This poem focuses on the power of good and evil and the loss of innocence. In part 1, written in 1797 in Somerset, we meet Christabel praying under the trees at midnight for the safety of her betrothed lover. When she finds a stranger, Geraldine, who claims to have been abducted by a gang of warriors and then abandoned in the woods, she brings the woman into her father's castle for shelter and protection. This is an innocent act on Christabel's part, motivated solely by love and charity. The reader, however, is alerted to Geraldine's evil powers by her inability to pass through the gate without help from Christabel, the moaning of the sleeping mastiff, and the sudden flame that shoots out from the embers of a dying fire. In her innocence, or naïveté, Christabel extends her hospitality by inviting Geraldine into her bedchamber. During the remainder of the night she is in some way corrupted by the stranger, who admits to supernatural powers.

In part 2 of the poem, written in 1800 in Cumbria after SAMUEL TAYLOR COLERIDGE's return from Germany, there is a change in both mood and direction. Knowing that she has lost her innocence, Christabel now seeks purification and redemption. This can only be achieved by expelling Geraldine from her father's home, but her father, Sir Leoline, feels it his bound duty to protect Geraldine since her father, Lord Roland, was a youthful friend of his. He is torn between his love for his own daughter on the one hand and loyalty to his friend on the other. Since Christabel is under the influence of Geraldine's supernatural powers, she is unable to explain her fears to her father without appearing jealous. She must then learn that it is easier to bring evil into her home than it is to be rid of it. This may be seen as the central dilemma and moral of the tale. The difficulty of resolving this dilemma may be one reason why Coleridge failed to complete the poem, though plans were made for a third part.

The poem is overlaid with GOTHIC elements: the medieval castle with its moat, the clock striking midnight, the hooting owls, the howling mastiff, moonlight, and mists. It is also believed to have been influenced by GOTTFRIED AUGUST BÜRGER's ballad poem "Lenore," a supernatural tale published in 1773. In his preface to the poem, Coleridge drew attention to the versification, which generally comprises four stress rhyming couplets. There were plans to include the poem in the second edition of LYRICAL BALLADS, but Coleridge's collaborator, WILLIAM WORDSWORTH, famously canceled these arrangements. Nonetheless, the gothic elements together with the poem's psychological insights make it a cornerstone of Romantic poetry. While still in manuscript form it was read and admired by SIR WALTER SCOTT and LORD BYRON. The poem exerted a strong influence on 19th-century writers, including JOHN KEATS and EMILY BRONTË.

## Further Reading

Coleridge, Samuel Taylor, *Biographia Literaria*. Edited by Nigel Leask. London: Dent, 1997.
———. *Coleridge's Notebooks: A Selection*. Edited by Seamus Perry. Oxford: Oxford University Press, 2003.
———. *The Complete Poems*. Edited by William Keach. Harmondsworth: Penguin, 1997.
Wordsworth, Dorothy, *The Grasmere and Alfoxden Journals*. Edited by Pamela Woof. Oxford: Oxford University Press, 2002.

—Irene Wiltshire

## Clare, John (1793–1864)

John Clare, widely regarded today as the greatest working-class poet England has produced, as well as a major poet of English Romanticism, was born in rural Helpstone, Northamptonshire, on July 13, 1793. His father, Parker Clare—himself the son of a Scotsman—was an uneducated flail thresher, farm labourer, and sometime rustic wrestler and ballad singer. A sickly child, Clare paid for his schooling for three months of the year (until the age of 12) by threshing alongside his father. By the time he left school, his love of ballads had already inspired him to attempt his own poetry, and James Thomson's *The Seasons* (1730), which he probably first encountered in 1806, was an important early influence. After working with horses for a year, he became a plowboy, enduring swooning fits during this period. Rejecting opportunities to become first a shoemaker's apprentice and then a solicitor's clerk, Clare became a gardener before joining the Eastern Regiment of the Northamptonshire militia (the home guard charged with repelling any Napoleonic invasion) in 1812. Eighteen months later he returned home and aspired to a relationship with his childhood sweetheart, Mary Joyce; nothing came of this, although he continued to be haunted by longing for her throughout his life. After a spell as a lime burner (someone who burns lime before it is spread on fields), he married Martha Turner (whom he called Patty of the Vale) in 1820, and they had eight children.

Two months before his marriage, Clare's *POEMS DESCRIPTIVE OF RURAL LIFE AND SCENERY* was published (heavily edited) by John Taylor of the firm Taylor & Hessey. Although such editorial interventions would become a feature of Taylor's relationship with Clare, the volume met with some success. Subsequent books—such as *The Village Minstrel, and Other Poems* (1821) and *The SHEPHERD'S CALENDAR* (1827) did not fare as well, and *The Rural Muse* (1835) sold hardly at all. Clare became depressed, probably engaged in a number of affairs, and may have attempted suicide.

In 1832 the Clares moved to Northborough, three miles from Helpston, a move that proved traumatic (as recorded in Clare's fine lyric "The Flitting"). By 1837 Clare's sanity was failing under the illusion that his marriage to Patty had been preceded by an espousal to Mary Joyce. He was put under Dr. Matthew Allen's care at the private asylum of High Beech at Epping Forest, where he stayed for four years. In July 1841 he walked the 80 miles home over a period of three-and-a-half days, and during the next five months he finished *Don Juan* and *Child Harold,* both of which were begun under the delusion that he actually was LORD BYRON. He similarly suffered spells of thinking that he was the duke of Wellington, Lord HORATIO NELSON, and William Shakespeare while also tormented by hallucinations of Mary. He was certified in December 1841 and taken to St. Andrew's County Lunatic Asylum, where he remained until his death. The regime at St. Andrews was enlightened, and he enjoyed the freedom to walk into Northampton town; he was not only encouraged to write, but continued to produce work that critics have subsequently regarded as amongst his best. In particular he wrote ballads, often addressed to Mary. He died on May 20, 1864.

Clare, "the miniaturist, the inhabiter of locality" (Bate xx) is one of England's foremost poets of the regional and the natural world. He is a great poet of love, memory, and loss, and of protest at the revocation of old ways and customs. This tendency manifested itself especially in protests against enclosure. As his biographer John Lucas observes, "nothing affected Clare so adversely, deeply and permanently as the act of Parliament, passed in 1809, by which Helpstone became an enclosed space. His world was literally changed out of recognition" (Lucas 8). The circumstances both of his early life and of his promotion by Taylor have identified Clare for posterity with the vogue for "natural genius" that endured throughout the 18th and 19th centuries. Famously, he was identified in the extended title of *Poems Descriptive of Rural Life and Scenery* as "John Clare, A Northamptonshire Peasant" (which is also the inscription on the monument erected to him in Helpstone five years after his death). Indeed, "Poets are born not made"—the English translation of *poeta nascitur non fit,* the Latin phrase most associated with the phenomenon of the labouring poet as "natural genius"—is written on Clare's tombstone. He is arguably additionally identified with the Romantic vogue for primitivism through his use of Northamptonshire dialects, utilizing spellings that were both individualized and idiosyncratic. Even today, the issue of whether Clare's

poems should be read as they appear in his manuscripts—as finally presented to the world in the Clarendon Press editions edited by Eric Robinson, David Powell, and P. M. S. Dawson (1984–2003)—remains critically controversial.

Clare was prolific, writing "over three and a half thousand poems" (Bate xxii), so the scale and range of his achievement is difficult to summarize briefly. Undeniably, however, "The Flitting" and the two late lyrics both entitled "I AM" are among his most noteworthy poems about identity. His numerous poems about the natural world, and about small animals and birds' nests in particular, are often characterized by great attention to material details as the poet-speaker describes the size, color, and texture of the birds' eggs. While Clare experimented with a many verse forms, he never abandoned the traditions of oral ballads and songs, and he was a gifted enough musician to transcribe the tunes of 200 ballads (Lucas 6).

After a period of relative decline following his death, Clare's reputation grew throughout the 20th century, particularly after Arthur Symons's 1908 edition of Clare's work. He has been the subject of many subsequent studies, and the rise of ecocriticism has attributed particular importance to him, understandably, given Clare's concern for locality, the natural world, and the ecosystem. There are flourishing John Clare Societies on both sides of the Atlantic. The publication, meanwhile, of Jonathan Bate's highly regarded *John Clare: A Biography* (2003) arguably restored its subject to a prominence Clare had not enjoyed since his first success in the 1820s.

See also "BADGER, THE."

**Further Reading**

Barrell, John. *The Idea of Landscape and the Sense of Place 1730–1840: An Approach to the Poetry of John Clare.* Cambridge: Cambridge University Press, 1972.

Bate, Jonathan. *John Clare: A Biography.* New York: Farrar, Strauss and Giroux; London: Picador, 2003.

Clare, John. *The Early Poems of John Clare 1804–1822.* 2 vols. Edited by David Powell and Eric Robinson. Oxford: Clarendon Press, 1989.

———. *The Letters of John Clare.* Edited by Mark Storey. Oxford: Oxford University Press, 1985.

————. *John Clare's Autobiographical Writings.* Edited by Eric Robinson. Oxford: Oxford University Press, 1983.

————. *John Clare: Poems of the Middle Period, 1822–1837.* 5 vols. Edited by P. M. S. Dawson, David Powell, and Eric Robinson. Oxford: Clarendon Press, 1996–2003.

————. *John Clare: Selected Poems.* Edited by Jonathan Bate. New York: Farrar, Strauss and Giroux; London: Faber and Faber, 2003b.

Goodridge, John, and Simon Kovesi, eds. *John Clare: New Approaches.* Helpston, Eng.: John Clare Society, 2000.

Grainger, Margaret, ed. *The Natural History Prose Writings of John Clare.* Oxford: Oxford University Press, 1983.

Lucas, John. *John Clare.* Plymouth, Eng.: Northcote House, 1994.

Powell, David, and Eric Robinson, eds. *The Later Poems of John Clare.* 2 vols. Oxford: Clarendon Press, 1984.

—Steve Van Hagen

## "Clod and the Pebble, The"  William Blake
(1794)

WILLIAM BLAKE produced "The Clod and the Pebble," one of the *Songs of Experience*, in his illuminated printing method as part of the collected *SONGS OF INNOCENCE AND OF EXPERIENCE* in 1794 and in later printings.

While *Songs of Innocence and of Experience* develops the opposition of innocence and experience across an entire collection of poems, "The Clod and the Pebble" exemplifies the concept of contrary states within a single poem. Precisely structured and symmetrical, the poem devotes six lines to each figure, and the last line spoken by the pebble mirrors the clod's last line. The clod is the first to speak and describes love as completely selfless: "Love seeketh not Itself to please / Nor for itself hath any care; / But for another gives its ease, / And builds a Heaven in Hells despair" (ll. 1–4). Following the clod's statement, a narrator explains that the clod sings his lines as he is "Trodden with the cattles feet" (l. 6). The pebble of the brook—who, as the narrator says, "warble[s] out"

his "metres meet" (l. 8)—responds with an idea of love that stands in direct opposition to that of the clod: "Love seeketh only Self to please, / To bind another to Its delight: / Joys in another's loss of ease, / And builds a Hell in Heavens despite" (ll. 9–12). The poem supports neither the selfish view of love expressed by the pebble nor the clod's selfless view of love in any obvious way. The two contraries are simply set against one another.

At first glance, the clod seems to describe a virtuous, innocent idea of love, since its only interest is to please another. By contrast, the pebble's view of love involves the malicious enjoyment of power over another as it "binds another in Its delight" (l. 10), but the similarity of the pebble's last line to that of the clod prompts some readers to look again at the clod's view of love. Upon reexamination, these readers see the pebble's last line as a sarcastic critique of the clod and note that the clod's view lacks any mention of pleasure in love or in giving. Since it "builds a Heaven in Hells despair," the clod's view represents an unhappy kind of love that may lead to repression or to the kind of self-righteousness exhibited by the "Religious" view in Blake's *The MARRIAGE OF HEAVEN AND HELL,* (1793), by Urizen in *The [First] Book of Urizen* (1794), or by Satan in *MILTON: A POEM* (1804–10). The clod's view of love appears as a denigration or denial of a person's humanity, rather than a healthy expression of desire, like that of the speaker of "The GARDEN OF LOVE" in *Songs of Experience.*

The tone of the illustration is quite at odds with the contentious mood of the poem. Above the text, four sheep and two oxen enjoy a drink from a brook. They seem to stand with their forefeet in the water and their hind feet on the bank behind them, so presumably they may be standing on both the clod and the pebble at the same time. Beneath the text and on the other side of the brook, a duck, two frogs, and a worm play in and around the water, and a vine sprouts up the right side of the text. All of these creatures in the illustration seem to be enjoying a peaceful coexistence. They simply live their lives according to their own natures. Both the clod and the pebble, however, are engaged in the analysis of abstractions and are isolated from each other in their opposition.

As a poem in experience, then, both sides, the clod and the pebble, turn love into an abstraction, rather than enjoy the concrete act of fellowship or companionship, as demonstrated by the plants and animals in the illustration. The clod and the pebble are more interested in a debate over their views of an abstract concept, and neither has a realistic approach to the actual experience of love.

**Further Reading**

Blake, William. *The Complete Poetry and Prose of William Blake*. Rev. ed. Edited by David V. Erdman. Commentary by Harold Bloom. Garden City, N.Y.: Anchor, 1982.

———. *The Illuminated Blake*. Edited by David V. Erdman. Garden City, N.Y.: Anchor-Doubleday, 1974.

———. *Songs of Innocence and of Experience*. Edited by Andrew Lincoln. Princeton, N.J.: William Blake Trust/Princeton University Press, 1991.

Frosch, Thomas R. "The Borderline of Innocence and Experience." In *Approaches to Teaching Blake's Songs of Innocence and of Experience*, edited by Robert F. Gleckner and Mark L. Greenberg, 74–79. New York: Modern Language Association of America, 1989.

Hirsch, E. D., Jr. *Innocence and Experience: An Introduction to Blake*. New Haven, Conn., and London: Yale University Press, 1964.

Leader, Zachary. *Reading Blake's Songs*. London and Boston: Routledge and Kegan Paul, 1981.

—John H. Jones

## Cobbett, William (1763–1835)

Contemporary with a version of the English Romantic movement that reacted against the ideologies of INDUSTRIALISM by depicting the ideality of rural, peasant communities (as in the poetry of JOHN CLARE and GEORGE CRABBE), William Cobbett branched off from Romanticism into an emerging tradition of social reform. Born in Farnham, Surrey, on March 9, 1763, and "bred," as Cobbett himself said, "at the plough-tail," he was a farm labourer until 1783, when he moved to London. Enlisting in the army at 19 and stationed in New Brunswick, Canada, he set about teaching himself math, logic, and how to read and write. After uncovering and exposing corruption at senior military ranks, he was forced out of the army, whereupon he went to revolutionary France (see FRENCH REVOLUTION) and then to North America. He rejected democratic sensibilities in both France and America, and in 1800 he returned to England, where, in 1802, he started a Tory-friendly newspaper, the POLITICAL REGISTER. Two years later, however, he had become a fierce proponent of radicalism and, though to modern eyes he advocated a strange fusion of political attitudes (despite his radicalism, he was vehemently opposed to increasing suffrage, education reform, and empowering the working classes), he remained a radical until his death. Twice tried for sedition, he was sentenced to two years in Newgate Prison (1810-12). He championed parliamentary and tax reforms (even as a parliamentarian late in his life), fought for the regulation of business and industry, rallied against newspaper taxes, and above all, opposed corruption in the public sector. Fearing arrest again, he fled to the United States in 1817, staying there until November 1819.

Cobbett is best remembered for his Romantic critique of capitalism. In 1821 he toured Britain on horseback, recording his observations on rural England from its politics and people to its houses and weather. These were published in a series of articles in the *Political Register* (which had reached a readership of 40,000) and later in 1830 as a book, *RURAL RIDES*. He wrote of England returning to a decentralized, paternalistic, rural, and deeply religious past, giving us an image of the past that Karl Marx would later refer to as "feudal socialism." The idealization of regional folk traditions was part and parcel of a crusade against the poverty he saw as endemic within the contemporary wage system and capitalism, especially agrarian capitalism. In medieval England, he said, "every labouring man was clothed in good woolen cloth, and all had plenty of meat and bread and beer." *Rural Rides* is a statement of England's decline and a warning about the social effects of rapacious industrialism, anticipating the work of Thomas Carlyle (1795–1881), John Ruskin (1819–1900), and William Morris (1834–96). However, it primarily conveys a Romantic reaction to the directions of social change that England was following. As Raymond Williams says in his important biography, "In Cobbett and Blake, in Shelley and Carlyle, for all their individual differences, there is this characteristic intensity of denunciation of what is happening in their world, and also this characteristic confidence that these evils cannot last, that something radically new must come" (William 58).

Cobbett was elected a member of Parliament in 1832. He was immensely popular in his day: It was said that after he died on his farm of influenza on June 18, 1835, 8,000 people attended his funeral.

### Further Reading

Cobbett, William. *Advice to Young Men.* Oxford: Oxford University Press, 1980.

———. *Cottage Economy.* Oxford: Oxford University Press, 1979.

———. *The English Gardener.* Oxford: Oxford University Press, 1979.

———. *Life and Adventures of Peter Porcupine.* Port Washington, N.Y.: Kennikat Press, 1970.

———. *Rural Rides.* London: Penguin, 2005.

Cole, G. D. H. *The Life of William Cobbett.* 3rd ed. London: Home & Van Thal, 1947.

Dyck, Ian. *William Cobbett and Rural Popular Culture.* Cambridge: Cambridge University Press, 1992.

Williams, Raymond. *Cobbett.* Oxford: Oxford University Press, 1983.

———. *The Country and the City.* New York: Oxford University Press, 1975.

—Rob Breton

## Cockney School

In the early 19th century, three works announced the formation of a new school of poetry, which would come to be called the Cockney School: LEIGH HUNT's "Young Poets," published in the *Examiner*, 1817; WILLIAM HAZLITT's *The Round Table: A Collection of Essays on Literature, Men, and Manners* (1818); and Hunt's *Foliage, or Poems Original and Translated* (1818). One connecting link between the authors was class. Cockney writers were primarily middle class; suburban; radical in politics; radical in aesthetics; and, for the most part, not educated at Oxford or Cambridge University. The Tory literary establishment was not at all pleased, resulting in vitriolic attacks in the periodicals, most notably those by John Gibson Lockhart in the *Quarterly* Review and *Blackwood's Magazine*. Lockhart attacked Hunt for his lack of education, especially in Latin and Greek (a classical education being the mark of a "gentleman"), his inability to read French, and his reading of foreign literature only in translation. Lockhart slammed the work of other "Cockney" writers—notably Hazlitt, JOHN KEATS, CHARLES LAMB, and John Hamilton Reynolds, plus others who centered around Hunt's Hampstead home—as "confectionary" and called Hunt's *The Story of Rimini* (1816), an exemplar of Cockneyism, significant for its lewdness, pretentiousness, and gaudiness. Nature poetry for Hunt and the Cockneys was not the sublime and restorative nature of WILLIAM WORDSWORTH and the LAKE SCHOOL; it was the mere nature of city gardens. What Hunt praised as a "free and idiomatic" aesthetic, Lockhart and the Tories thought unsettling in perhaps more than an aesthetic sense: Cockney literary license could undermine the stability of English values.

The imaginative literature that one sensibility perceived as a return to literary greatness in the English line, from Geoffrey Chaucer to JOHN MILTON, another sensibility saw as a hodgepodge of poetic disruptions, dissonances, and slang, aesthetically as well as thematically dangerous if not subversive in a time when Britain feared that French instability and aggression would destabilize its institutions and undermine the British way of life. While the older Romantics were trying to come to terms with their disillusionment with the ideals of the FRENCH REVOLUTION, many of the younger Romantics rebelled. Even the upper-class PERCY BYSSHE SHELLEY and LORD BYRON advocated social and political reform, but when newly comfortable middle-class suburban writers such as Leigh Hunt and associates advocated a social agenda, the established classes saw it as a challenge to king and country.

Fear of Cockneyism did not endure for long. The passage of the REFORM ACT (1832) and of other social legislation aiming to ameliorate the conditions of the possibly revolutionary masses palliated anxieties. Aesthetically, time was bringing changes in literary taste and practice; even Byron recognized that poetry of the Cockney John Keats was no longer "spoilt by Cockneyfying and Suburbing," (Byron v. 146) while their purported use of jargon and everyday subject-matter as well as their violations of the traditional English poetic line was, with time, becoming less feared and more commonplace.

### Further Reading

Byron, Lord. *The Works of Lord Byron with His Letters and Journals and his Life.* Vol. 5. Edited by Thomas Moore. London: John Mung, 1833.

Cox, Jeffrey. *Poetry and Politics in the Cockney School: Keats, Shelley, Hunt and their Circle.* Cambridge: Cambridge University Press, 1998.

———. "Leigh Hunt's Cockney School: The Lakers' 'Other.'" *Romanticism on the Net: An Electronic Journal Devoted to Romantic Studies* 14 (May 1999). Available online. URL: http://erudit.org/revue/ron/1999/v/n14/005859ar.html. Downloaded on May 25, 2009.

Dawson, P. M. S. "Byron, Shelley, and the 'New School.'" In *Shelley Revalued: Essays from the Gregynog Conference,* edited by Kelvin Everest, 89–108. Totowa, N.J.: Barnes & Noble, 1983.

Holden, Anthony. *The Wit in the Dungeon: The Remarkable Life of Leigh Hunt.* New York: Little, Brown & Co., 2005.

Hunt, Leigh. *Leigh Hunt: Selected Writings.* Edited by David Jesson-Dibley. New York: Routledge, 2003.

Jones, Elizabeth. "The Cockney School of Poetry: Keats in the Suburbs." In *The Persistence of Poetry: Bicentennial Essays on Keats,* edited by Robert M. Ryan, 120–131. Amherst: University of Massachusetts Press, 1998.

Kucich, Greg. "'The Wit in the Dungeon': Leigh Hunt and the Insolent Politics of Cockney Coteries." *Romanticism on the Net: An Electronic Journal Devoted to Romantic Studies* 14 (May 1999). Available online. URL: http://www.erudit.org/revue/ron/1999/v/n14/005850ar.html. Downloaded on December 22, 2009.

Roe, Nicholas. *Fiery Heart: The First Life of Leigh Hunt.* London: Pimlico, 2005.

———, ed. *Leigh Hunt: Life, Poetics, Politics.* London and New York: Routledge, 2003.

Thompson, James R. *Leigh Hunt.* Boston: Twayne, 1977.

Wu, Duncan. "Keats and the 'Cockney School.'" In *The Cambridge Companion to Keats,* edited by Susan J. Wolfson, Cambridge: Cambridge University Press, 2001.

—Donna Berliner

## *Coelebs in Search of a Wife* Hannah More
### (1808)

HANNAH MORE's only novel is a didactic and religious one whose plot is succinctly captured by its title. The orphaned Charles, as he is called in the story (the name *Coelebs* means "bachelor," from the Latin root meaning "celibate"), sets out at age 23 to meet a close friend of his late father, not knowing that this friend, Mr. Stanley, is father to the young woman both parents hoped Charles would someday marry. Unbeknownst to either Charles or the young woman, Lucilla, both were raised and educated by their parents according to similar plans in order to form each as a fitting marriage companion for the other. The various people and events Charles encounters in his journey to the Stanley home and following his arrival help to fulfill this parental scheme by revealing to Charles various less-than-ideal marriage partners, parenting styles, educational programs, aesthetic tastes, and religious views, none of which match the standards he finds in the Stanley home (which naturally match his own). The thinly plotted novel is filled with few events, a number of colorful characters, various cautionary vignettes, the requisite love rival, and many protracted speeches and conversations about various topics, particularly marriage and the weighty choice—one with eternal consequences—of a marriage partner.

*Coelebs in Search of a Wife* plays an important part in the late 18th- and early 19th-century concept of the "companionate marriage," an idea that had grown in popularity since the publication of Samuel Richardson's novel, *Clarissa* (1747–48). Indeed, *Coelebs in Search of a Wife* is in other respects the heir of Samuel Richardson's work: In its didactic purpose it attempts to elevate the novel from a mode of base entertainment to a respectable art form of moral and literary merit. Also like Richardson's novels, *Coelebs in Search of a Wife* draws heavily on the traditions of the conduct book or advice manual, periodical essay, and spiritual autobiography. Indeed, the work arguably shares more features with these genres than with that of the novel form.

Nevertheless, the contribution of *Coelebs in Search of a Wife* to the rise of the novel is considerable, despite its being overlooked in ensuing years of literary criticism. Even with its flaws in characterization and plot, the work employs many of the features that had come to characterize the novel by this time in its development. More important, however, the commercial and critical success of the novel (it went through 12 editions in the first year alone) helped to elevate the reputation of a genre that was still so disdained by polite audiences and literary critics that many serious authors still refused to call their works of fiction *novels* (preferring instead terms such as *history* or *true account*). The praises heaped on *Coelebs in Search of a Wife* by conservative and religious antinovel critics helped to redeem the genre's reputation, paving the way for the artistic heights and literary respect it would achieve later in the 19th century.

## Further Reading

Demers, Patricia. *The World of Hannah More.* Lexington: University of Kentucky Press, 1996.

Jay, Elisabeth. *The Religion of the Heart: Anglican Evangelicalism and the Nineteenth-Century Novel.* Oxford: Clarendon Press, 1979.

More, Hannah. *Coelebs in Search of a Wife: Comprehending Observations on Domestic Habits and Manners, Religion and Morals.* Edited by Patricia Demers. Peterborough, Ont., and Orchard Park, N.Y.: Broadview Press, 2007.

Pickering, Samuel J. *The Moral Tradition in English Fiction, 1785–1850.* Hanover: University Press of New Hampshire, 1976.

Prior, Karen Swallow. *Hannah More's Coelebs in Search of a Wife: A Review of Criticism and a New Analysis.* Lewiston, N.Y.: Edwin Mellen Press, 2003.

—Karen Swallow Prior

## Coleridge, Hartley (1796–1849)

The poet Hartley Coleridge was the eldest surviving child of SAMUEL TAYLOR COLERIDGE and his wife Sarah (née Fricker). He was born on September 19, 1796, in Kingsdown, Bristol, but three months after his birth the family moved to the Lake District. The young Hartley was extremely intelligent, even precocious, and his lively curiosity was encouraged by his father as part of his and WILLIAM WORDSWORTH's belief that children should develop freely under the influence of nature. The two men were delighted with what they saw. Wordsworth later included Hartley as the "six years' darling of a pygmy size" in his "ODE: INTIMATIONS OF IMMORTALITY FROM RECOLLECTIONS OF EARLY CHILDHOOD" (1807), while in 1800 his proud father described him as "all Health & extacy—He is a Spirit dancing on an aspen Leaf—unwearied in Joy, from morning to night indefatigably joyous" (Coleridge *Letters* 2000, 1:844). Samuel Taylor Coleridge's poem "FROST AT MIDNIGHT" likewise captures something of the father's high hopes for his young son. Perhaps inevitably, the attention lavished on Hartley by the adults around him, together with lack of contact with "ordinary" children his own age, led to difficulties in forming easy and sustainable relationships. He was a dreamy child, living in the realms of the imagination, part of which came to be embodied in an imaginary world he called Ejuxria. "It is a cruel thing to breed up boys alone," he recalled in later life (quoted in Reeves, 140).

In 1808 Hartley was sent away with his younger brother, Derwent, to school in Ambleside, spending the weekends with the Wordsworth family. Academically gifted, he progressed to Merton College, Oxford University, graduating in 1818 before becoming a junior fellow of the college in 1819. By this time he was harboring poetic ambitions, believing that success and publication was a way of attracting attention, particularly from women. This was tied in to what would nowadays be termed "low self-esteem." Hartley was short in stature, no good at sports, and acutely conscious of it. Accordingly, he looked for ways to compensate for his massive feelings of inferiority—feelings that were not helped by having Samuel Taylor Coleridge as a parent. It was also at this point that his alcoholism seems to have taken hold, a condition from which he would suffer to a greater or lesser degree for the rest of his life. Eventually this led to his being expelled from Oxford in 1820 for breaking college rules and generally consorting with "unsuitable" company.

From Oxford Coleridge went to London to try and establish a literary career. Initially he was successful, getting articles accepted in the *London Magazine,* but this was short-lived, and by 1822 he had run out of money. On his father's advice, he returned to the Lake District to teach at his former school, run by the Reverend James Dawes. When, in 1826, he took over the running of the school, it failed. He returned to writing, this time with more success, publishing essays regularly in *Blackwood's Magazine* and adopting a recognizable style: droll, eccentric, whimsical, and slightly distanced from the world.

In 1833 Coleridge finally overcame his fear of comparisons with his father (who would die in 1834) and plucked up courage to publish a single volume of poems. Since its publication, Hartley's small trickle of verses has, to quote Lisa Gee been "drowned out by the Niagara of his father's virtuosity." (Coleridge *Bricks* 2000, xi), but the poems were well-received in their own day. Contemporary critics saw traces not of the senior Coleridge but of Wordsworth and LYRICAL BALLADS. In an echo of the sentiments expressed in Wordsworth's "LINES WRITTEN A FEW MILES ABOVE TINTERN ABBEY," Hartley Coleridge's poetic ambition is summed up in "A Task Ad Libitum," in which he writes of how "the humbler spirit / Hears in the daily round of household things / A low sweet melody, inaudible / To the gross sense of worldlings." Like Wordsworth, Coleridge wanted his readers to appreciate the small things overlooked amid the hustle and bustle of everyday life. Unlike PERCY BYSSHE SHELLEY or LORD BYRON, Coleridge's work is not overtly political, although his poem "Prometheus" can be usefully compared with the former's *PROMETHEUS UNBOUND.* Instead, it tends to be gentle and domestic. Nor are the poems intellectually pretentious or lofty: Some of them are narrated in the comfortable, cosy, persona that Coleridge adopted for his journalistic work—for example, "The Old Bachelor." Yet others are extremely personal,

hinting at inner torment, unhappiness, a sense of unworthiness, isolation, and longing for love, but also stoicism—for example, "Long Time a Child" and "Let me not deem that I was made in vain / Or that my being was an accident"). Two often-repeated—and unanswerable—questions in his poems are: "What is the meaning of life?" "Where do I fit into it?"

Poetically, Hartley Coleridge was a talented sonneteer in the Petrachan tradition, as well as being a quick one. He was able to draft a poem in 10 minutes, scribbling frantically as if possessed. As his brother Derwent noted: "He never kneaded or pounded his thoughts; they always came out cap-à-pie, like a troop in quick march" (Coleridge 1851, cxxxiii). Afterwards, he would decide if the poem was worth keeping or not. He also composed outdoors, and stories were told of how, like ROBERT BURNS, he would knock at the doors of strangers' houses while out walking to beg for paper and pencil in order to write down a poem that had suddenly appeared in his head. His best work thus conveys a sense of spontaneity—a much-valued Romantic trait. Other poems are satiric, notably the Wordsworth parody "He lived amid'st th'untrodden ways."

Hartley never married and lived in Grasmere (1833–40) and Rydal (1840–49) in a succession of rented rooms, cared for by a succession of landladies and servants. Nonetheless, he was regarded with affection by his neighbors who nicknamed him "Li'le Hartley" and reputedly much preferred him to the grander William Wordsworth. He died, age 52, on January 6, 1849. Summing his adult son up, his father wrote: "If you can conceive, in connection with an excellent heart, sound religious principles, a mind constitutionally religious, and lastly an active and powerful intellect—if you can conceive, I say in connection with all these, not a *mania,* not a *derangement* but an *idiocy* of Will or rather of Volition, you will have formed a tolerably correct conception of Hartley Coleridge" (quoted in Reeves 141). More recently, Louis de Bernières, in his introduction to a new collection of republished poems, has described him as "an archetypal genius ... an eccentric without actually being mad ... compulsively creative ... passionately intelligent ... He had a child-like nature and a very sophisticated ability to examine things from an interested distance" (Coleridge, *Bricks*, 2000, ix). Neglected for too long, the work of Hartley Coleridge is ripe for rediscovery.

**Further Reading**

Coleridge, Hartley. *Bricks without Mortar. The Selected Poems of Hartley Coleridge*. Edited by Lisa Gee. London: Picador, 2000.
———. *Poems By Hartley Coleridge, With A Memoir of his Life by His Brother (Derwent Coleridge)*. London: Edward Moxon, 1851.
Coleridge, Samuel Taylor. *Collected Letters of Samuel Taylor Coleridge: 1785–1800*. 6 vols. Edited by Earl Leslie Griggs. Oxford: Oxford University Press, 2000.
Reeves, James, ed. *Five Late Romantic Poets*. London: Heinemann, 1974.

—Matthew Gascoyne

## Coleridge, Samuel Taylor (1772–1834)

In addition to being seen as one of the six leading poets of the Romantic period, Samuel Taylor Coleridge was also a prominent philosopher, journalist, lecturer, proto-Freudian, and literary critic of the 1790s and the first decades of the 19th century. Although best known today for his poetry, Coleridge was an important thinker who, among other things, coined the term *unconscious*, gave us the phrase "the suspension of disbelief," and made important distinctions between symbol and allegory, fancy and imagination, and reason and understanding. His wildly original and frequently nightmarish poetry had a powerful influence on WILLIAM WORDSWORTH, MARY ROBINSON, LORD BYRON, JOHN KEATS, and Edgar Allan Poe. His remarks on William Shakespeare's *Hamlet* and JOHN MILTON's Satan initiated questions about those characters that readers and critics still consider essential to understanding them.

The youngest of 10 children of John Coleridge and his second wife, Ann Bowdon, Samuel Taylor Coleridge was born in Ottery St. Mary, Devonshire on October 21, 1772. John Coleridge, was the parish vicar and headmaster of the town's grammar school. A precocious child, Samuel read books ranging from the Bible to *The Arabian Nights*, devel-

oping early the rich inner life that would inform his writing and thinking throughout his life. He was especially close to his father until the latter's unexpected death in 1781. Coleridge had a more difficult relationship with his mother, who, in 1782, sent the 10-year-old boy to Christ's Hospital School in London, a well-known and highly regarded charity school. This lonely period, during which he thought of himself as an orphan, is recalled poignantly in his poem "FROST AT MIDNIGHT" (1798). In his *BIOGRAPHIA LITERARIA* (1817), however, Coleridge stresses the significant influence of his "very severe" grammar master, Reverend James Bowyer, who instructed him extensively in the classics while also assigning the works of Shakespeare and Milton. Recognizing Coleridge's scholarly potential, Bowyer also impressed upon him the importance of plain but precise diction in his English compositions. At Christ's Hospital, Coleridge made friends with CHARLES LAMB, who, in his essay "Christ's Hospital Five-and-Thirty Years Ago," described Coleridge as an inspired and inspiring lecturer and reciter of poetry even in adolescence. As a young man, he also greatly admired the sonnets of William Lisle Bowles, a poet whom he occasionally would imitate.

In October 1791, having completed his education at Christ's Hospital, Coleridge earned a scholarship to enter Jesus College, Cambridge University, where he enrolled with the intention of becoming a parson like his father. His first year at Cambridge was full of promise: He won an award for a poem on the slave trade that he wrote in Greek and became involved in the intellectual life there. Soon he was caught up in political and religious controversies instigated by the FRENCH REVOLUTION and the dissenting Unitarian movement. But major disappointments followed quickly: The university dismissed Unitarian pamphleteer and don William Frend, whom Coleridge had supported; his modest resources ran out, and he found himself desperate for money; and he was further undone by an unsuccessful love affair. In a fit of panic and depression, he fled Cambridge for London, and despite his support of the French Revolution, he enlisted in the 15th Light Dragoons under the name Silas Tomkyn Comberbache. Hopelessly inept as a horseman, Coleridge found himself nursing fellow dragoons suffering from smallpox. Before long (less than five months), the influence of his brother George's money and his brother Tom's rank (colonel) persuaded the army to declare S. T. Comberbache insane and discharge him. Contrite, Coleridge briefly returned to Cambridge in April 1794. By the end of the year, however, he had abandoned his degree, having found a new friend in ROBERT SOUTHEY, who shared his political views and literary tastes. He also began his formal career as a writer, collaborating with Southey on the drama *The Fall of Robespierre* and publishing in the *Morning Chronicle* a series of politically charged "Sonnets on Eminent Characters," which commented on such figures as EDMUND BURKE, Joseph Priestley, WILLIAM GODWIN, and the politician William Pitt.

Together, Coleridge and Southey embarked on an elaborate scheme to marry two sisters, emigrate to America, and found a utopian society on the banks of the Susquehanna River in Pennsylvania. Coleridge coined the term *pantisocracy* (rule by all) to describe their plans for a community based on shared governance and common property. According to plan, he became engaged to Sarah Fricker, the sister of Southey's fiancée, Edith. Dutifully, throughout the winter of 1794–95, Coleridge lectured on radical politics and religion to raise money for emigration; short of money himself, Southey opted to return to Oxford and abandoned pantisocracy altogether. Although he was stung and disappointed, Coleridge went through with his marriage to Sarah in October 1795 and moved with her to Clevedon. There, he composed "The EOLIAN HARP" (1769), which captures his tender feelings for his wife—feelings that would change—and conveys the characteristic philosophical speculation and imaginative vision colored with a religious sensibility that was peculiar to him among the Romantic poets. This poem is a descriptive-meditative poem, an important innovation of Romantic poetry for its mix of blank verse and conversational language to convey lyrical insights, much in the way an ode would do. Coleridge would write other poems, which he called "conversation poems," in this style, including "THIS LIME-TREE BOWER MY PRISON" (1797), "FEARS IN SOLITUDE" (1798), "Frost at Midnight," and "The Nightin-

gale" (1798). His descriptive-meditative poems also provided a model for Wordsworth's "LINES WRITTEN A FEW MILES ABOVE TINTERN ABBEY."

Still absorbed by politics and religion, Coleridge published his lectures and, in 1796, wrote the short-lived radical Christian newspaper the *Watchman*. He devoted most of its 10 issues to opposing Prime Minister Pitt's war policies. This year he also published his first volume of poetry, *Poems on Various Subjects,* which sold well and includes his long apocalyptic blank-verse poem "Religious Musings" and a series of poems he called "effusions." He moved his wife and newborn son, HARTLEY COLERIDGE, named after the philosopher David Hartley, to Nether Stowey, Somerset, close to his friend Thomas Poole, who was instrumental in helping William Wordsworth and his sister, DOROTHY WORDSWORTH, rent the nearby Alfoxden house. Coleridge had met Wordsworth previously in political circles, and the two men had struck up an instant mutual admiration. The four-mile walk between Alfoxden and Nether Stowey over the Quantock Hills and the many subsequent conversations between the two men would solidify their friendship and engender their famous collaboration. Convinced of Wordsworth's genius, Coleridge shared his humanitarian values, and delighted in his company.

To earn money, Coleridge continued lecturing and preaching to Unitarian congregations; he also brought out a second volume of poems in 1797 that included verses by Charles Lamb and Charles Lloyd. He began writing for the *Morning Post*, having reconciled somewhat with Southey, who ran the poetry department and also wrote for the paper. The friendship between Coleridge and Wordsworth became a catalyst for both men's literary ambitions: although he considered Wordsworth the greater poet, Coleridge wrote his greatest poetry during the years of his closest intimacy with his friend. Wordsworth, too, gained from Coleridge (the more incisive reader of literature), the sense that his own poetry should derive from a set of sound critical principles. Their talks concentrated on what Coleridge described later in the *Biographia Literaria* as "the poetry of nature" (1997; 179). Together, they distinguished "two cardinal points of poetry": sympathy and imagination. Starting with some initial collaboration on "The RIME OF THE ANCIENT MARINER," the rest of the LYRICAL BALLADS (1798) volume began to take shape, with the two poets intending to write two different kinds of poems: Wordsworth's poems were subjects "chosen from ordinary life," while Coleridge's were about "incidents and agents . . . in part at least supernatural." Coleridge's main contributions ended up being "The Ancient Mariner" and "The Nightingale," along with a couple of excerpts from a tragedy, *Osorio,* that he was writing at the time. But it is "The Rime of the Ancient Mariner" that attracted the most attention for its deliberately archaic language and fantastic situations and characters. It combined the influence of the ballad revival with Coleridge's characteristic atmosphere of nightmarish guilt and penance. Today regarded as his greatest poem, "The Ancient Mariner" was so harshly attacked that Wordsworth moved it from the opening poem to the closing poem of the first volume for the second edition of *Lyrical Ballads* in 1800. For that edition, Coleridge made some changes to the language and called it "The Ancient Mariner: A Poet's Reverie" to try to account for its strangeness.

Around this time, Coleridge also found himself becoming increasingly dependent on opium as relief for various physical and emotional ailments (see Wordsworth's "ODE TO DUTY"). During the autumn of 1797 he probably composed a draft of "KUBLA KHAN," written, as he would later claim, partially under the influence of an opium trance. It is one of the most innovative poems of the period, but Coleridge would not publish the poem until 1816. He did recite it to friends and share it with other poets such as MARY ROBINSON, who read it before her death in 1800 and wrote a poem about it. "Kubla Khan," however, was not fully appreciated until the 20th century.

By the end of the century, Coleridge's religious and political views were changing. Although he was moving toward a ministry, his interest in philosophy made him increasingly ambivalent about Unitarianism; he would eventually settle on the more traditional Anglican Church. His growing concerns about France's military expansionism led to an all-out renunciation of the French Revolution when the French invaded the democratic

cantons of Switzerland in 1798. While getting *Lyrical Ballads* ready for publication, Coleridge recast himself somewhat as a British patriot with the publication of the small volume *Fears in Solitude* (1798), which includes the title poem, "FRANCE: AN ODE," and "Frost at Midnight." This productivity earned him an annuity from John and Tom Wedgwood part of the famous family of pottery manufacturers intended to give him more time to write. Taking advantage of this opportunity, Coleridge and the Wordsworths left England for a nine-month period of study in Germany; at the University of Göttingen Coleridge studied German literature and philosophy and attended lectures by distinguished professors. While in Germany (1798–99), Coleridge received news that his second son, Berkeley, had died; his delayed return to the family and subsequent abandonment of them to join the Wordsworths, who had settled in England's Lake District, began the slow, painful deterioration of his marriage. He would father two more children, Derwent and SARA COLERIDGE, before he and Sarah separated permanently in 1807.

Coleridge lived for a time with the Wordsworths and then moved his family to the Lake District to be near them. However, the relationship between the two men became strained, beginning perhaps with Wordsworth's decision not to include the incomplete "CHRISTABEL" in the second edition of *Lyrical Ballads.* "Christabel" is Coleridge's most bizarre and erotic poem, with its suggestions of witchcraft, vampirism, and lesbianism. His opium addiction became difficult for all concerned, and his intense erotic fascination with Sara Hutchinson, the sister of Wordsworth's new wife, made the Wordsworth family uncomfortable. His reading of the German philosopher Kant, his hearing Wordsworth recite "ODE: INTIMATIONS OF IMMORTALITY," and his feelings for Sara Hutchinson (or "Asra," as he called her), all combined to inspire the writing of "DEJECTION: AN ODE," the last of Coleridge's great poems. After parting from the Wordsworth household, he spent several unsettled years working as a journalist in London and from 1804 to 1806 worked as secretary to a government functionary in Malta. On a visit to his old friends in 1807, he was moved by Wordsworth's recitation of an early version of *The PRELUDE,* dedicated to him, and wrote in response "To William Wordsworth."

Sadly, tensions between Coleridge and the Wordsworth-Hutchinson circle culminated in a rift that they never fully repaired. But Coleridge found a new family when, in 1816, he sought out the doctor James Gillman to help him with his opium addiction. He lived with Gillman and his family while receiving treatment for the rest of his life. Meanwhile, despite his persistent bad health, depression, and opium addiction, he managed a fairly successful career for a few years. He began a new, more philosophical journal called *The Friend*, which ran for only 28 weekly issues; he gave a series of successful London lectures on literature, Milton, and Shakespeare; he studied the philosophy of Kant; and he revised his early play *Osorio* (1797) as *Remorse*, which had a successful run at Drury Lane theatre in 1813. Additionally, Lord Byron encouraged him to finally publish "Kubla Khan" and "Christabel" in 1816. The next year Coleridge published his monumental *Biographia Literaria*, which includes his famous explanation of the imagination and definition of a poet as well as his objections to the principles in Wordsworth's PREFACE TO LYRICAL BALLADS with an earnest defense of Wordsworth's poetry. He also produced a new volume of poetry called *Sybilline Leaves*, which included the heavily revised version of the "Ancient Mariner," with marginal glosses. Also in 1816, he published two political-religious works. In *The Statesman's Manual* he argues for social and political principles derived from the Bible instead of utilitarian solutions, while his *Lay Sermon* expresses a concern for the unfettered growth of capitalism and commercialism. Both were received poorly, and Coleridge was attacked and parodied mercilessly as an impenetrable philosopher by such writers as WILLIAM HAZLITT in the press, THOMAS LOVE PEACOCK in *NIGHTMARE ABBEY*, and Byron in *DON JUAN*.

Coleridge's final years were fairly productive, although they were filled with a mixture of personal disappointment and happiness. Chief among the disappointments was his son Hartley's alcoholism, expulsion from Oxford, and general aimlessness. He was pleased, however, by the marriage of his daughter Sara to her cousin Henry Nelson Coleridge. H. N. Coleridge would record Coleridge's famous *Table Talk* (ideas and opinions expressed in conversations with friends [1836]), and the couple would become important editors of Coleridge's work after his death. In 1821 an anonymous translation of JOHANN WOLFGANG VON GOETHE's *FAUST* appeared that some scholars now believe to have been written by Coleridge. He had the honor of being named an associate of the Royal Society of Literature in 1824 and received an accompanying annuity. From his home, he continued to give lessons in philosophy that helped him complete his spiritual treatise *Aids to Reflection* (1824), which found an audience and built his reputation as "the Sage of Highgate." Younger writers such as Keats, Thomas Carlyle, and John Stuart Mill met with him; and American writers such as Ralph Waldo Emerson and Edgar Allan Poe read his work.

In 1828 Coleridge and Wordsworth reconciled and toured the Rhine Valley together; in that year he also published his *Poetical Works*. His dissenting views long behind him, Coleridge's final major publication, *On the Constitution of Church and State* (1830), comfortably asserts the value of a relationship between the two but argues for the need for the additional cultural influence of a class he calls the "clerisy," which includes intellectuals, theologians, poets, and professors of the "liberal arts and sciences." In the eyes of the public this was his most successful work.

In March 1834 a third edition of Coleridge's *Poetical Works* appeared, with the help of H. N. Coleridge. Four months later, Coleridge died of congestive heart failure on July 25, 1834. Before his death he received a deathbed visit from the great love of his life, Sara Hutchinson. He never completed his *Opus Maximum*, a massive project on Christianity and philosophy that finally appeared in a scholarly edition in 2002. Indeed, for the rest of the 19th century, it was Coleridge the Christian philosopher, not the poet, who had the greatest influence on the Victorian period. The 20th century, starting with John Livingston Lowes's groundbreaking *The Road to Xanadu* (1927), saw revived interest in Coleridge's poetry.

### Further Reading
Ashton, Rosemary. *The Life of Samuel Taylor Coleridge: A Critical Biography*. Oxford: Blackwell, 1996.

Bate, Walter Jackson. *Coleridge.* New York: Macmillan, 1968.

Beer, John. *Coleridge's Poetic Intelligence.* London: Macmillan, 1977.

Burwick, Frederick, ed. *The Oxford Handbook of Samuel Taylor Coleridge.* Oxford: Oxford University Press, 2009.

Coleridge, Samuel Taylor. *The Collected Works of Samuel Taylor Coleridge.* 16 vols. Princeton, N.J.: Princeton University Press, 1971–2001. *Biographia Literaria.* Edited by Nigel Leask. London: Everyman, 1997.

Fruman, Norman. *Coleridge, the Damaged Archangel.* New York: George Braziller, 1971.

Holmes, Richard. *Coleridge: Darker Reflections.* London: HarperCollins, 1998.

———. *Coleridge: Early Visions.* London: Hodder & Stoughton, 1989.

Lowes, John Livingston. *The Road to Xanadu: A Study in the Ways of the Imagination.* Boston: Houghton Mifflin, 1927.

Magnuson, Paul. *Coleridge and Wordsworth: A Lyrical Dialogue.* Princeton, N.J.: Princeton University Press, 1987.

McFarland, Thomas. *Coleridge and the Pantheist Tradition.* Oxford: Clarendon Press, 1969.

McKusick, James C. *Coleridge's Philosophy of Language.* New Haven, Conn.: Yale University Press, 1986.

Newlyn, Lucy, ed. *The Cambridge Companion to Coleridge.* Cambridge: Cambridge University Press, 2002.

Roe, Nicholas. *Wordsworth and Coleridge: The Radical Years.* Oxford: Clarendon Press, 1988.

Woodring, Carl. *Politics in the Poetry of Coleridge.* University of Wisconsin Press, 1961.

—Daniel Robinson

## Coleridge, Sara (1802–1852)

The only daughter of SAMUEL TAYLOR COLERIDGE and Sarah Fricker, Sara Coleridge described her relationship with her father as a "lifelong separation," as she never lived with him for more than a few weeks at a time and did not see him at all between the ages of 10 and 20. Sara was considered not only beautiful but brilliant, and her mother encouraged her intellectual pursuits. By the time she was 23, she and her brother Derwent had published two translations (one of which was initially attributed to her aunt's husband, ROBERT SOUTHEY), and she later wrote a children's book of verse (1834) and a fairy tale (1837).

After becoming secretly engaged to her first cousin, Henry Nelson Coleridge, Sara married him in 1829, in spite of financial difficulties and opposition from her mother. Unfortunately, she emulated her father not only in literary ability but in an opium addiction which contributed to her physical deterioration. Her health was also affected by repeated pregnancies: She had three miscarriages and gave birth to four living children, only two of whom survived (a set of twins died within hours of being born).

Samuel Taylor Coleridge's death in 1834 prompted widespread criticism about his personal life, including his separation from his wife and his drug use. He was also accused of plagiarism. In order to repair his reputation, Sara and Henry brought out new editions of his work, a project Sara continued after Henry's death in 1843. She contributed her own essays to these editions and spent four years working on the *BIOGRAPHIA LITERARIA.* An invalid for the last twenty years of her life, Sara Coleridge died in 1852 of breast cancer.

### Further Reading

Lefebure, Molly. *The Bondage of Love: A Life of Mrs Samuel Taylor Coleridge.* New York: Norton, 1987.

Mudge, Bradford Keyes. *Sara Coleridge, A Victorian Daughter: Her Life and Essays.* New Haven, Conn.: Yale University Press, 1989.

—Tracey S. Rosenberg

## "Complaint of a Forsaken Indian Woman, The"  William Wordsworth (1798)

As its title indicates, this poem is a complaint, a lyric poem in which a speaker laments his or her situation and seeks relief. This is one of several poems from *LYRICAL BALLADS* (1798) that explores the relationship between a mother and her child, in this case a son. Also a dramatic monologue, the poem presents the perspective of a Native American mother who has been deserted by her tribe in winter and is left to die in the snow because she is too weak to keep up with the tribe's pace. The poem opens with the woman lamenting her state in the winter conditions as she appreciates the beauty of the Northern Lights. She comments on the dying fire (which parallels her impending death) and regrets that she did not have the strength to stay with her tribe. In her exile she recalls the actual separation from her son and the son's desperate response when the tribe gave him to another woman. She imaginatively constructs a representation of her son and consoles him as if he were actually with her in exile: "Then do not weep and grieve for me; / I feel I must have died with thee" (ll. 53–54); she reassures him that she would have died with him even if she had continued. From imaginatively consoling her son, she imagines (almost hallucinates) a reunion with him before abruptly acknowledging that she is still in her camp: her "fire is dead" (l. 65), and "The wolf is come" (l. 67). She shifts attention to her own active desire to die with her child in her arms—"if I / For once could have thee close to me, / With happy heart I then would die" (ll. 66–67)—before acknowledging that she will indeed die alone and without him: "I shall not see another day" (l. 80).

In the PREFACE TO LYRICAL BALLADS, WILLIAM WORDSWORTH claims that one of his primary purposes with the collection is to investigate the workings of the mind. He says "Complaint" depicts the mind's "fluctuations" by examining "the last struggles of a human being, at the approach of death, cleaving in solitude to life and society" (quoted in Wu 499). As the scholar James Averill explains, Wordsworth's interest is in "a person at psychological extremes" (156). The mother's abrupt shifts from despair to hope to shame to jealousy to pride to resignation realistically capture this woman's sorrow and confusion. Stephen Bidlake examines the woman's situation in more social terms, commenting that the mother "longs for the interdefinitive exchange of speech that is the life of men and women in society. The inability of the wind to carry her voice to her tribespeople is merely her utterance's expression of its own impotence to consummate its spoken desire" (192). The Indian woman is typical of Wordsworth's female narrators because, like the speakers of "The Female Vagrant," "THE THORN," and "The Mad Mother," she is a psychologically complex social outcast lamenting her position in the world.

**Further Reading**

Averill, James H. *Wordsworth and the Poetry of Human Suffering.* Ithaca, N.Y.: Cornell University Press, 1980.

Bidlake, Stephen. "'Hidden Dialog' in 'The Mad Mother' and 'The Complaint of the Forsaken Indian Woman.'" *The Wordsworth Circle* 13, no. 4 (1982): 188–193.

Wordsworth, William. *Lyrical Ballads, and Other Poems, 1797–1800.* Edited by James Butler and Karen Green. Ithaca, N.Y.: Cornell University Press, 1992.

Wu, Duncan. *Romanticism. An Anthology.* 3rd ed. Oxford, Eng.: Blackwell, 2006.

—Robert C. Hale

## "Composed upon Westminster Bridge, September 3, 1802," William Wordsworth (1807)

Although it is one of his most famous sonnets, WILLIAM WORDSWORTH's "Composed upon Westminster Bridge" remains one of his most enigmatic works. Outwardly the facts are straightforward. Composed in 1802, it was first published in his 1807 *Poems in Two Volumes*. The poet stated that this piece was "composed on the roof of a coach on [his] way to France Sept. 1802." His sister DOROTHY WORDSWORTH, too, noted the occasion in her *Journal* (July 31, 1802): "The City, St Paul's, with the River and a multitude of little Boats, made a most beautiful sight as we crossed Westminster Bridge." The sun shone so brightly "with such a pure light," she continues, "that there was even something like the purity of one of nature's own grand spectacles."

A discrepancy in dating aside, the irony in finding the urban scene grander than nature is also the central idea of Wordsworth's poem: "Earth has not anything to show more fair" (l. 1); "This City now doth, like a garment, wear / The beauty of the morning" (ll. 4–5). Nonetheless, as the Wordsworth editor John O. Hayden has highlighted, such imagery has caused confusion among critics. Also, there are well-known verbal inconsistencies in the poem. It was later pointed out to Wordsworth that he describes the city both as clothed by beauty and as "bare" (l. 5). In reply he insisted that "the contradiction is in the *words* only (de Selincourt, II 182)—bare, as not being covered with smoke or vapour; clothed, as being attired in the beams of morning." Moreover, in the final line the speaker enigmatically refers to "that mighty heart" that "is lying still" (l. 14). First, what is "all that mighty heart"?: nature, God, the people, perhaps London itself? Second, in what sense might a "mighty" heart lay still—is it slumbering (as the houses are), is it hidden, is it perhaps even dead? A skeptic might read the poem as an attack on over-population. In such a reading the "smokeless air" (l. 8) registers the absence of human habitation, and the "beauty of the morning" can only exist when it is "silent, bare" (l. 5), rather than when it is bustling and peopled. Alternatively, one might read this sonnet as an attempt to transpose the transcendental teachings of nature onto the expanding cityscape. The speaker's soul has been educated by his observations of the sun in its "first splendour" (l. 10) so that now the observer can appreciate the world around him, whatever its appearance: "Ne'er saw I, never felt, a calm so deep!" (l. 11). In short, might this be a sonnet in praise of the city or a lament for the demise of the countryside? Is it a move beyond Wordsworth's obsessive poeting about nature or a failure to move on from his affective relationship with natural imagery?

## Further Reading

Wordsworth, Dorothy. *The Journals of Dorothy Wordsworth*. Introduction by Helen Dorbishire. Oxford: Oxford University Press, 1971.

Wordsworth, William, and Dorothy. *The Letters of William and Dorothy Wordsworth: The Later Years, 1831–1840*. 3 vols. Edited by Ernest de Selincourt. Oxford: Clarendon Press, 1939.

Wordsworth, William. *Select Poems*. Edited by John O. Hayden. London: Penguin, 1994.

Wu, Duncan, ed. *Romanticism: An Anthology*. 2nd ed. Oxford: Blackwell, 2000.

—Daniel Cook

## *Confessions of an English Opium-Eater*
### Thomas De Quincey (1821)

One of the most famous—or infamous—texts of the period, THOMAS DE QUINCEY's autobio-

graphical account of his addiction to laudanum (an alcoholic tincture of opium) is also one of the Romantic period's most influential in its discussion of ideas about selfhood and subjectivity. The book describes the course of the author's experience with opium from his first encounter at university in the early 1800s to his subsequent reliance on it though his adult life. The book began to take shape in 1820, when De Quincey arrived in Edinburgh to write for *Blackwood's Magazine*. He had a reputation for being unreliable and a scrounger, so few predicted the impact his new work would have. It was for John Wilson, *Blackwood's* editor, that De Quincey began what he termed the "Opium article." "Opium," he told William Blackwood, the publisher, "has reduced me for the last six years to one general discourtesy of utter silence. But this I shall think of with not so much pain, if this same opium enables me (as I think it will) to send you an article" (quoted in Walford Davies 269). In fact, what became *Confessions of an English Opium-Eater* was published not in *Blackwood's* but in the *London Magazine* in September and October 1821, then as a book in 1822, and again in 1856 in a revised version.

The book caused a sensation, largely because open discussion of addiction was unusual. De Quincey offered one of the first "literary" accounts of the physiological and psychological effects of drug addiction in a time where the negative side effects were little understood. The opening lines set out the book's aim: "I here present you, courteous reader, with the record of a remarkable period in my life: according to my application of it, I trust that it will prove not merely an interesting record, but in a considerable degree useful and instructive." In the section entitled "Preliminary Confessions" he tells the story of his childhood and the bleak period in which he lived alone in London as a homeless teenager in 1802–03, which sets the scene for account of his disturbed adult life. He originally took the drug for medicinal reasons (many doctors in the 18th and 19th centuries prescribed it), but the relief it offered was so great that he found it impossible to give it up.

In "The Pleasures of Opium" Da Quincey discusses the positive aspects of his experience (1804–12), and he extols the pleasures of "subtle" opium, which he argues can bring relief to all classes of society—"to the hearts of poor and rich alike, for the wounds that will never heal, and for the pangs that tempt the spirit to rebel, bringest an assuaging balm; eloquent opium! that with thy potent rhetoric stealest away the purposes of wrath; and to the guilty man, for one night givest back the hopes of his youth, and hands washed pure of blood" (1998; 49). However, in the section called "The Pains of Opium" he outlines in disturbing language the extremes of his addiction, including nightmares, visions, insomnia, and memory loss. Even as he walked round London, he forgot where he was: "Some of these rambles led me to great distances; for an opium-eater is too happy to observe the motions of time. And sometimes in my attempts to steer homewards, upon nautical principles, by fixing my eye on the pole-star, and seeking ambitiously for a north-west passage, instead of circumnavigating all the capes and headlands I had doubled in my outward voyage, I came suddenly upon such knotty problems of alleys, such enigmatical entries, and such sphinx's riddles of streets without thoroughfares, as must, I conceive, baffle the audacity of porters, and confound the intellects of hackney-coachmen" (De Quincey, 1998, 47).

Living in opium-induced stupors, De Quincey occupied a kind of hinterland between reality and hallucination, elation and depression, unable to separate dreams from reality or even recognise the passing of time: "The sense of space, and in the end, the sense of time, were both powerfully effected. Buildings, landscapes, &c. were exhibited in proportions so vast as the bodily eye is not fitted to conceive. Space swelled, and was amplified to an extent of unutterable infinity. This, however, did not disturb me so much as the vast expansion of time; I sometimes seemed to have lived for 70 or 100 years in one night; nay, sometimes had feelings representative of a millennium passed in that time, or, however, of a duration far beyond the limits of any human experience" (1998; 68). This last quote is a reminder that while De Quincey is remembered as the Romantic drug addict par excellence, he is also the "high priest of the shadowy world of dreams," writing 70 years before Sigmund Freud (Walford-Davies 275).

## Further Reading

Berridge, Virginia, and Griffith Edwards. *Opium and the People: Opiate Use in Nineteenth-Century England.* New Haven, Conn.: Yale University Press, 1987.

Hayter, Alethea. *Opium and the Romantic Imagination: Addiction and Creativity in De Quincey, Coleridge, Baudelaire and Others.* Wellingborough, Eng.: Crucible, 1988.

Lindop, Grevel. *The Opium-Eater: A Life of Thomas De Quincey.* New York: Taplinger, 1981.

De Quincey, Thomas.

———. *Confessions of an English Opium-Eater.* Edited by Grevel Lindop. Oxford: Oxford University Press, 1998.

Walford Davies, Damian. "Thomas De Quincey, Confession's of an English Opium-Eater." In *A Companion to Romanticism*, edited by Duncan Wu, 269–275. Oxford: Blackwell, 1999.

—John Hughes

## "Convict, The" William Wordsworth (1798)

WILLIAM WORDSWORTH is often described as the first great poet of the Romantic period, far more prolific than his friend SAMUEL TAYLOR COLERIDGE, with whom he worked. He is described as a mystic of nature, greatly influenced by the impressive beauty of the Lake District in the northwest of England, where he was born and where he lived for most of his life with his sister, DOROTHY WORDSWORTH, and then his wife Mary. The aptly named Wordsworth communicated with the calm, still waters of the lakes and with the contours of the landscape around them, bringing him a sense of time and place, a feeling of the presence and wisdom of the universe. The aim of Wordsworth's poetry was to share this communion with his readers, and he portrays a serene, a spiritual sublimity unparalleled in English poetry.

In this poem, written in 1796 and published in *Lyrical Ballads* (1798), Wordsworth is once more writing about and concentrating on apparently very ordinary concerns and sources involving nature; he is also scorning the pompous and epic style of some of his peers. His easily understood descriptions of the imprisoned man in the poem evokes the narrator's and thus the reader's compassion ("as a brother thy sorrows to share" [l. 48]) for the lack of freedom of the incarcerated individual—the awful predicament that has alienated him from the precious freedom that is essential to life. It is hardly surprising that the subject of freedom, or freedom from oppression in particular, is topical during this period of history, which was steeped in ideals of revolution. Notable is the quotation attributed to the French political philosopher JEAN-JACQUES ROUSSEAU (1712–78): "Man is born free, but everywhere he is in chains" (*The Social Contract,* 1762). As a young man, Wordsworth was a supporter of the revolutionary ideals in France; he visited the country in 1790 and again in 1791–92, when he witnessed meetings of the new National Assembly (see FRENCH REVOLUTION). He then turned from politics to poetry, albeit returning once more to France a couple of years later in 1795. It is thus possible to link "The Convict" with the common people in France who were oppressed by monarchy in prerevolutionary France and the nobles who constituted the ruling classes.

The convict in Wordsworth's poem has no name. He is one of a number of ordinary men—not a politician or a privileged subject in any way—and he is in prison; therefore he is to be pitied. He is a victim of conflict. One of the primary laws of nature (and human nature) is liberty, and it is significant that we are not informed of the nature of the convict's crime. Is he merely guilty of being an ordinary man? Is he, as a subject, a victim of circumstance? He is held in a dungeon and is an outcast for he has, against his will, been taken out of society as a punishment for his crimes against it, whatever they may have been. He obviously regrets his behavior; is suffering from a guilty conscience; feels steadily worse about his acts; and, given his predicament, wishing that he could "undo" them and go back into the past; or perhaps he is hoping that the past, before the political conflicts and upheavals, could come back to him.

It is perhaps significant that the poem's stanzas total 13, a number considered unlucky. The contrast between the outside and the inside of the prison is dramatic. Nature in all its splendor is described in lyrical terms, and we can detect easy symbolism in that autumn "precedes the calm season of rest" (l. 3), which could refer to winter and also to death. Dusk and the west indicate that night is falling, and spiritual darkness is to be perceived in the convict's quandary, for he is not free and suffers from regret and sadness; he is dejected and bound, his free will shackled. The glory and joy of nature is thus directly opposed to the convict's solitary confinement. The AMERICAN REVOLUTION had recently been fought in the west, and if we take up this symbolic reference, the essential passion of freedom is further stressed and exploited. It is clear from the start that liberty is wonderful as well as natural and that without it a person is helpless and hopeless. The easy, cushioned, ultimately privileged existence of the "monarch" (l. 26) is challenged by the images of battlefields in "dark synod" and "blood-reeking field" (l. 25). Wordsworth is speaking to us of actual imprisonment as well as of the right to free speech which, when quashed or suspended, injures a man's soul. His mention of "terror" (l. 40) is easily attributed to Reign of Terror, and "dull-clanking chains" (l. 37) to the aforementioned Rousseau quotation. Pain, oppression and imprisonment are both physical and psychological, real and spiritual.

This is a deceptively simple poem, with clear references; strong, evocative vocabulary; and powerful imagery. Wordsworth empathizes with all those who are oppressed in any way and regrets his own powerlessness regarding those who are prevented from experiencing the joys of freedom. Were the "arm of the mighty [Law]" (l. 51) his, he would probably allow the vox populi a reprieve. However, he seems to suggest that as a mere poet his powers are limited.

**Further Reading**

Gill, Stephen. *William Wordsworth: A Life.* Oxford: Oxford University Press, 1990.

Hartman, Geoffrey. *Wordsworth's Poetry, 1787–1814.* New Haven: Yale University Press, 1971.

Wordsworth, Jonathan. *William Wordsworth: The Borders of Vision.* Oxford: Oxford University Press 1982.

Wordsworth, William. *The Major Works: Including The Prelude.* Edited by Stephen Gill. Oxford: Oxford University Press, 2000.

—Isobel Heald

### Corsair, The  Lord Byron  (1814)

On February 1, 1814, LORD BYRON's *The Corsair* made literary history by selling out its entire run of 10,000 copies on the first day of publication. The poem is the third of a series of narrative poems published between 1813 and 1816, which came to be known collectively as the Turkish Tales. Building on Byron's first major success, CHILDE HAROLD'S PILGRIMAGE (1812), these tales take place in the Orient, playing into the popular predilection for romantic narratives set in exotic locations (see ORIENTALISM).

*The Corsair* tells the story of the pirate captain Conrad, the prototypical Byronic *homme fatal*, an unsympathetic hero who is eternally contemptuous of the world. In the poem's opening, Conrad decides to risk everything he has—including his crew and a comfortable life with his beloved wife Medora—in order to attack the sultan Seyd and steal his treasures. During the attack, Conrad frees the women in Seyd's harem, including his chief slave, Gulnare. As he does so, however, his crew is killed, and Conrad is captured by the sultan's men. Gulnare goes to see him in prison and promises to save his life in return for his having saved hers. Not long thereafter, Gulnare develops a plan for both Conrad and herself to escape from the sultan, but Conrad refuses to act deceitfully (in spite of the fact that his original attack on Seyd's court was initiated in disguise). Gulnare therefore kills Seyd herself and accompanies Conrad back to his home island. Upon their arrival, Conrad discovers that Medora has died from grief, having believed him to be dead. Crestfallen and brokenhearted, he rejects Gulnare's love and leaves the island alone.

The major themes of *The Corsair* include chivalry, masculinity, and the role of the hero. These themes are underscored by the poem's form. Unlike most of the other Turkish Tales, *The Corsair* is written in heroic iambs and includes numerous instances of dramatic dialogue, recalling JOHN MILTON's epic poem *Paradise Lost* (1667). Conrad is initially positioned as the definitive hero figure; he cannot even remain at home for an hour, always seeking his next adventure. As the tale unfolds, however, we begin to see inconsistencies in his concepts of chivalry and heroism, and thus, the poem concludes in the oft-quoted couplet "He left

a Corsair's name to other times, / Linked with one virtue and a thousand crimes" (canto 3, stanza 24).

The poem also has much to say about femininity by way of the disparities between its chief heroines, Medora and Gulnare. Medora is portrayed as beautiful, sweet, and refined—quite unlike the tougher, more masculinized Gulnare. Although Gulnare represents Conrad's female counterpart, he chooses to love only Medora. Along with Conrad's perpetual thirst for adventure, this suggests the deep lure of exoticism and fantasy, and it thus stands as a commentary on the heroic genre itself. What becomes particularly interesting in this regard, then, is the fact that the vast majority of Byron's reading public came to conflate the character of the Corsair (along with his other antiheroes) with the poet himself.

### Further Reading

Byron, George Gordon Byron, Baron. *Complete Poetical Works.* Edited by Jerome J. McGann and Barry Weller. Oxford: Clarendon Press, 1980.

Hull, Gloria T. "The Byronic Heroine and Byron's *The Corsair.*" *Ariel: A Review of International English Literature* 9, no. 1 (1978): 71–83.

Keegan, Abigail F. "*The Corsair*: A Pirate and a Homicidal Woman, Disrupting Sexual Difference." In *Byron's Othered Self and Voice: Contextualizing the Homographic Signature.* New York: Peter Lang, 2003, 113–128.

Kidwai, Abdur Raheem. *Orientalism in Lord Byron's "Turkish Tales": The Giaour (1813), The Bride of Abydos (1813), The Corsair (1814), and The Siege of Corinth (1816).* Lewiston, N.Y.: Mellen University Press, 1995.

Thorslev, Peter Larsen. *The Byronic Hero: Types and Prototypes.* Minneapolis: University of Minnesota Press, 1962.

Vitale, Marina. "The Domesticated Heroine in Byron's Corsair and William Hone's Prose Adaptation." *Literature and History* 10, no. 1 (1984): 72–94.

—Diana Koretsky

### Cowper, William  (1731–1800)

The poet, hymnist, and letter writer William Cowper (pronounced "Cooper") was born on

November 15, 1731, at Great Berkhamsted, Hertfordshire, England. His mother died giving birth to his brother John in 1737, bringing an end to Cowper's happy childhood, which he remembered as being filled with his mother's generous love (expressed in "On the Receipt of My Mother's Picture Out of Norfolk," 1798). Unfortunately, at the time of his mother's death Cowper was attending Dr. Pittman's School, where he was severely bullied by a boy of 15. This was the start of a mixed educational experience: At age eight he was sent to live with Mrs. Disney, an oculist (on account of damage to his eyes), before attending, from 1742, Westminster School in London, known particularly at this time for educating the sons of great Whig families. Cowper made several lifelong friends at Westminster and gained an excellent grounding in classical languages; he left able to read and write Latin verses (which he continued to do throughout his life). However, his "Tirocinium; or, a Review of Schools" (1785) tellingly suggests, "Great schools suit best the sturdy and the rough" (l. 341), not a likely description of the young boy.

When Cowper left Westminster, his father wished him to become a barrister; therefore, at age 18, reluctant to displease his family, he left for London to be apprenticed to a lawyer. He came to despise the law, but in 1752 he fell in love with his cousin Theodora Jane Cowper. The "Delia" poems of these years suggest an affair that was loving yet emotionally intense. Sadly, perhaps due to the combination of personal and professional difficulty, this period saw the first of Cowper's intense depressions; he described himself as "Day and night . . . upon the rack, lying down in horrors and rising in despair" (Cowper 1979–86, 1:8). Probably because of this instability, Theodora's father decided to intervene in the cousins' romance and withheld permission for their marriage, causing them to part in 1755. Some years later his uncle attempted to help Cowper by nominating him to a position of clerk at the House of Lords. However, this necessitated a public examination, and the prospect of such scrutiny caused a catastrophic sense of despair. Cowper's account of his mental torment, suicide attempt, and final belief in Christian redemption was published posthumously in 1816 as *Adelphi,* a conversion narrative that framed his experiences with references to the Bible, especially the books of Isaiah and the Psalms.

Cowper was admitted to an asylum for the insane, and in 1765, following his recovery, he moved to rural Northamptonshire, where he was to remain for the rest of his life, inspiring his famous conviction that "God made the country, and man made the town" (*The Task,* book 1, l. 749). Subsequently, his poetry was to adopt a loosely pastoral position, descended from the classical poet Horace, that used a rural location as a platform for satirizing the vice and folly of the age. However, in the immediate aftermath of his 1760s depression, Cowper sincerely embraced—in a manner not seen in his earlier work and letters—a new religious life, characterized by the earnest diligence and emotional enthusiasm of an evangelical dissenting Christian. Eventually, in 1779 (together with John Newton), he published the well-known and successful collection *Olney Hymns.* However, despite the peace and serenity of the countryside (and the vital development of a lifelong companionship—not marriage—with Mary Unwin), Cowper continued to be regularly afflicted with mental torment. The year 1773 saw an especially acute episode that ended with his conviction that he was irredeemable in the eyes of God. Although he continued to demonstrate Christian faith in his subsequent writing, its prominence was reduced, and he lost all confidence in public worship; he did not pray, partake in grace, or enter a church again. Instead, he pursued a quiet life of rural occupation, developing a particular passion for gardening and a heartfelt compassion for animals, many of which he domesticated in his garden at Orchard Side.

In 1782 Joseph Johnson published Cowper's first collection, *Poems by William Cowper, of the Inner Temple, Esq.* Although this was not especially successful, his subsequent work, *The Task,* a six-book poem published together with the comic ballad *The Diverting History of John Gilpin* in 1785, proved an enduring popular and critical success. Later attempts at Homeric translation and Miltonic epic were never to achieve these heights, but *The Task* was enough to secure his reputation and set the tone for much subsequent Romantic blank-verse writing.

In 1792 Cowper became acquainted with William Hayley (the patron of WILLIAM BLAKE), who cared for him in his final years of mental decline. Cowper eventually died on April 25, 1800, and he was buried beside Mary Unwin (who had died in 1796) at St. Nicholas Church in East Dereham.

The rather melancholy tone of Cowper's life may lead readers to expect pain and despair from his work. They would be surprised, therefore, to find Cowper's poetry and letters characterized by a gentle wit, enriching warmth, and passionate evocation of a domestic/rural life and landscape. Indeed, poetry was to prove a salve for Cowper's strife, its regular rhythms and lilting cadences proving an antidote to the wretched confusion of mental instability. This is not to say that darkness is entirely absent—his "sapphics" ("Hatred and vengeance my eternal portion," 1816) are chilling in their expression of a mind battling under the rod of desolation. Yet, particularly in his masterpiece, *The Task*—inspired by his friend Lady Austen, Cowper's poetry is designed to edify, often through delight. Earlier, in his light verse dedicated to animals ("Epitaph on a Hare," 1784), and later, in a series of broadsides written for the Committee for the Abolition of the Slave Trade, Cowper used rhyming verse to encourage compassion for the oppressed and cruelly treated (he was passionately antihunting), but in *The Task*'s blank verse he drew together his moving experience of the natural world with his righteous condemnation of greed, vanity, and corruption.

*The Task* is a poem in which Cowper "Roved far and gather'd much" (book 6, l. 1012), moving between political and social commentary (especially on the effects of early economic globalization), affectionate and detailed description of a familiar landscapes, personal meditation, childhood memory, and calls for emotional connections between people. It thus constitutes a significant precursor to WILLIAM WORDSWORTH's *The EXCURSION* (1814) and *The PRELUDE* (1850). Episodes such as that of "CRAZY KATE" in book 1 of *The Task* prefigure the damaged characters of Wordsworth's contributions to the *LYRICAL BALLADS*, as does Cowper's angry denunciation of economic damage wreaked on rural communities. Book 4's extended depiction of a winter's evening spent in contemplation before the fireside is strikingly revived in SAMUEL TAYLOR COLERIDGE's "FROST AT MIDNIGHT" (1798). Both Wordsworth and Coleridge especially admired what Coleridge termed Cowper's "divine Chit chat" (Coleridge 1:279), naming the fluency of regular meter matched to the varied rhythms of speech (a significant contribution to Romantic poetics). Indeed, although Cowper's life was quiet and without public incident, his poetry and letters (much admired by William Blake) are a rich source for tracing the historic and aesthetic conditions that contributed to British Romanticism. His is a unique, warm, passionate and, vitally, compassionate voice that reached far beyond his domesticated rural life. Furthermore, it is a voice whose expression of the emotional experience of nature, and the human effects of economic expansion and globalization, has much to offer us today.

See also "TO WILLIAM WILBERFORCE, ESQ."

**Further Reading**

Coleridge, Samuel Taylor. *Collected Letters of Samuel Taylor Coleridge*. 6 vols. Edited by Earl Leslie Griggs. Oxford: Clarendon Press, 1956–71.

Cowper, William. *The Letters and Prose Writings of William Cowper*. 5 vols. Edited by James King and Charles Ryskamp. Oxford: Clarendon Press, 1979–86.

———. *The Poems of William Cowper*. 3 vols. Edited by John D. Baird and Charles Ryskamp. Oxford: Clarendon Press, 1980–95.

———. *"The Task" and Selected Other Poems*. Edited by James Sambrook. London and New York: Longman, 1994.

Hutchings, Bill. *The Poetry of William Cowper*. London: Croom Helm, 1983.

King, James. *William Cowper: A Biography*. Durham, N.C.: Duke University Press, 1986.

Newey, Vincent. *Cowper's Poetry: A Critical Study and Reassessment*. Liverpool, Eng.: Liverpool University Press, 1982.

———. "William Cowper and the Condition of England." In *Literature and Nationalism*, edited by Vincent Newey and Ann Thompson, 120–135. Liverpool, Eng.: Liverpool University Press, 1991.

Nicholson, Norman. *William Cowper*. London: John Lehmann, 1951.

Pite, Ralph. "'Founded on the Affections': A Romantic Ecology." In *The Environmental Tradition in English*

*Literature*, edited by John Parham, 144–155. Aldershot, Eng.: Ashgate, 2002.

Spacks, Patricia Meyer. "Forgotten Genres." *Modern Language Studies* 18, no. 1 (1988): 47–57.

———. *The Poetry of Vision: Five Eighteenth-Century Poets*. Cambridge, Mass.: Harvard University Press, 1967.

Wu, Duncan, ed. *Romanticism: An Anthology*. 3rd ed. Oxford: Blackwell, 2006.

—Rhian Williams

## Crabbe, George (1754–1832)

George Crabbe is today an equivocal figure in Romantic poetry. On the one hand, his verse, with its evocations of English rural life, won him the admiration of poets as diverse as LORD BYRON, Samuel Rogers (1763–1855), and SIR WALTER SCOTT; on the other, the at-times pungent realism of his writings, a quality which distinguishes his poetry from the more idealized works of WILLIAM WORDSWORTH and SAMUEL TAYLOR COLERIDGE, has set him somewhat apart from the Romantic poets customarily studied today in academic institutions worldwide. However, Crabbe's early 19th-century work, in particular, deserves to be read within the context of British Romanticism, and he is long overdue a reassessment by the critical establishment.

Born on December 24, 1754, in the coastal village of Aldeburgh, Suffolk, in the east of England, George Crabbe was the son of a collector of salt duties, effectively a minor government official. Though his father's profession would have not made the poet unequivocally of gentlemanly birth, it would have assured for him the advantages of an education that would underpin his accession as a young man to one of the professions, albeit in an understated way. In 1768 Crabbe appears to have been apprenticed to a physician (though the 1992 *Concise Dictionary of National Biography* describes him disparagingly as merely a "servant to a country doctor" ["George Crabbe" 673]). He practiced medicine at Aldeburgh prior to 1780, possibly as an apothecary—a physician of lower social status than a doctor, and one more likely to have professional contacts primarily with the less wealthy. During his apprenticeship he met Sarah Elmy (the "Mira"

mentioned in his poems and journals), whom he married in 1783. He was widowed in 1813.

In 1775, during his apprenticeship, Crabbe published the three-part poem *Inebriety*, a tirade against the evils of alcohol. Though this work attracted no great critical notice, Crabbe traveled to London, where he initially struggled to make a reputation as a writer. In 1781, with the encouragement of EDMUND BURKE, he published *The Library*, a poem in the manner of Alexander Pope. Burke was instrumental in both introducing the poet to influential literary figures such as Dr. Samuel Johnson and in encouraging Crabbe to take holy orders within the Church of England. Ordination carried the advantage of an assured, though not large, income; the possibility of preferment and patronage; and duties that were in many cases hardly onerous once one had passed beyond the first years of a curacy. Crabbe returned to Aldeburgh as a curate in 1781 and was appointed chaplain to the duke of Rutland at Belvoir Castle a year later. He was the incumbent of several nonresidential benefices from 1783—that is to say, he was the vicar but employed curates to do his work—and he was finally appointed resident rector of St. James's Church, Trowbridge, Wiltshire, in 1814. Here he controversially identified himself with those impoverished and angered by the mechanization of the cloth industry (Rogers 96).

One of the two works for which Crabbe is now best remembered was written during his time as chaplain at Belvoir. His reputation was effectively established by *The Village: A Poem in Two Books* (1783), a comparatively pugnacious work in heroic couplets, incorporating revisions suggested by Burke and Johnson. This poem self-consciously set itself aside from the pastoral tradition, proposing for the reader a glimpse of "the real picture of the poor" (l. 5) rather than the poetic idealism of lovesick swains and fair maidens. Indeed, Crabbe's words scarcely conceal an impatience with the anachronism of late 18th-century poetic depictions of village life: "Fled are those times, if e'er such times were seen, / When rustic poets praised their native green; / No shepherds now in smooth alternate verse, / Their country's beauty or their nymphs' rehearse; / Yet still for these we frame the tender strain, / Still in our lays fond Corydons complain, / And shepherds' boys their amorous pains reveal, / The only pains, alas! they never feel" (ll. 7–14).

Crabbe's most popular works after *The Village* maintained the association with both village (or rural) life and a distance from pastoral idealism, though his next published work, *The Newspaper* (1785), was a satirical piece that may well have been derived from poetry written during his time in Aldeburgh and London. His 19th-century writings are the most frequently encountered of his works, other than *The Village*, today. His collected *Poems* appeared in 1807, with several revisions to *The Village* in particular, though it is important also for the first appearance of his narrative poem *The Parish Register*. This poem was structured on the motif of a country clergyman revisiting the entries in the parish's formal record of births, marriages, and deaths. Notable among the narratives is that of "Sir Eustace Grey"—the madhouse recollections of a man who has killed a sexual rival in a duel, and who suffers both guilt and hallucinations during his subsequent incarceration.

The poet's next major publication was *The Borough* (1810). Framed in 24 "letters," it chronicles events in a country town, conventionally identified with Aldeburgh. This identification is enforced particularly by the embedded narrative of Peter Grimes (Crabbe 2006, 22), an actual resident of Aldeburgh during Crabbe's time there. Whatever the truth behind the deaths of the "slave-shop" (l. 119) or workhouse boys who died in Grimes's employ, Crabbe's verse emphasizes the progressive social and mental isolation of the "hated" (l. 166) fisherman, and his collapse into a form of obsessive remorse, troubled by GOTHIC nightmares that might have unsettled Byron's more famous THE GIAOUR: "Wild were his dreams, and oft he rose in fright, / Waked by his view of horrors in the night— / Horrors that would the sternest maids amaze, / Horrors that demons might be proud to raise" (ll. 225–228). Madness follows Grimes's murders, and his delusions of persecution include visions of retributive, pale-faced ghosts and a ghostly father who does not pity but condemns. The account of Grimes's life concludes with a desperate scene of confession prior to the fisherman's tortured deathbed encounter with his nemesis. It is, without doubt, a more grim and Romantic narrative than the popular operatic revision of the tale by Benjamin Britten (1945).

Crabbe retained the episodic narrative framing of *The Borough* in the structure of his two subsequent collections, *Tales in Verse* (1812) and *Tales of the Hall* (1819). Neither, though, attracted the attention of *The Borough*. Further unpublished poems were discovered following his death on February 3, 1832, in Trowbridge, some of these being published in a collected edition in 1834. Crabbe's son, a Suffolk clergyman also christened George (1785–1857), published a biography of the poet in 1834. The inclusion of excerpts from *The Village* and *The Borough* in recent scholarly anthologies has done much to introduce Crabbe's work to a new generation of students. That new generation would be wise, though, to look beyond Peter Grimes and consider as well the possibilities presented by *The Parish Register* and some of the twenty-one *Tales in Verse*.

## Further Reading

Crabbe, George. "'Book 1' of *The Village: A Poem in Two Books*. Excerpted in *British Literature 1640–1789: An Anthology*, 3rd ed., edited by Robert DeMaria, Jr., 1,092–1,095. Oxford: Blackwell, 2008.

———. *The Complete Poetical Works.* 3 vols. Edited by Norma Dalrymple-Champneys and Arthur Pollard. Oxford: Clarendon Press, 1988.

———. "'Letter 22' of *The Borough* ('Peter Grimes')." Excerpted in *Romanticism: An Anthology*, 3rd edition, edited by Duncan Wu, 143–150. Oxford: Blackwell, 2006.

Crabbe, George, Jr. *The Life of George Crabbe, by His Son.* London: Cresset Press, 1947.

"George Crabbe (1754–1832)." In *The Concise Dictionary of National Biography.* 3 vols. Oxford: Oxford University Press, 1992, 1:673.

Pollard, Arthur, ed. *Crabbe: The Critical Heritage.* London: Routledge and Kegan Paul, 1972.

Powell, Neil, *George Crabbe: An English Life.* London: Pimlico, 2004.

Rogers, Kenneth, *The Book of Trowbridge.* Buckingham, Eng.: Barracuda, 1984.

Whitehead, Frank. *George Crabbe: A Reappraisal.* London: Associated University Presses, 1995.

—William Hughes

### "Crazy Kate"  William Cowper  (1785)

From Book 1 of WILLIAM COWPER's popular six-book poem *The Task,* the description of "Crazy Kate" (as the passage and character both came to be called) consists of 2 lines (534–55). The passage first appeared by itself as "Crazy Kate" in the *County Magazine* in 1786, inspiring many other sympathetic portraits of mentally impaired rustics, as the literary historian Robert Mayo has shown. Like GEORGE CRABBE has done in *The Village* (1783), Cowper's descriptions of rural life in *The Task* include desperate figures and challenge the idealized portraits of the poor, such as those Oliver Goldsmith depicts in "The Deserted Village" (1770). "Crazy Kate," therefore, exemplifies popular humanitarian poetry written by middle- or upper-class poets to express and elicit sympathy for the poor and destitute.

Cowper's vivid description of Kate, which includes such details as her "cloak of satin trimm'd / With lace" (535–36), her "tatter'd apron" (551), and her "bosom heav'd with never-ceasing sighs" (554), made her popular with illustrators of his poetry. The brief narrative also reveals that she was a servant who fell in love with a sailor who subsequently went to sea and drowned. Her madness apparently derives from her "delusive" (541) fancy that imagines his return and from her frustrated sexual desire for "transports she was not to know" (543). Although Cowper does not give deeper insight into her psychology—as WILLIAM WORDSWORTH would do with some of his destitute characters later—he does provide the fasci-nating detail that Kate begs for pins instead of food or warm clothing and "hoards them in her sleeve" (554), finally closing the passage with the powerfully blunt "Kate is craz'd" (556). It is worth noting that Cowper himself suffered from mental illness

The general scope, tone, and style of *The Task* inspired Wordsworth's failed epic project *The Recluse* and his autobiographical poem *The PRELUDE.* More specifically, Cowper's delicate portrait of Crazy Kate furnished Wordsworth with a model for a multitude of forsaken women who appear in such poems from *Lyrical Ballads* as "The THORN," and "The COMPLAINT OF A FORSAKEN INDIAN WOMAN." Cowper's description of her in blank verse also influenced similar portraits such as Wordsworth's Margaret in "The RUINED COTTAGE" and ROBERT SOUTHEY's "Hannah, A Plaintive Tale" (1797). *The Task* also was a favorite work of ROBERT BURNS and JANE AUSTEN.

### Further Reading

Mayo, Robert. "The Contemporaneity of the 'Lyrical Ballads.'" *PMLA* 69 (1954): 486–522.

Priestman, Martin. *Cowper's Task: Structure and Influence.* Cambridge: Cambridge University Press, 1983.

Richey, William, and Daniel Robinson, eds. *Lyrical Ballads and Related Writings.* Boston: Houghton Mifflin, 2002.

Sheats, Paul D. *The Making of Wordsworth's Poetry, 1785–1798.* Cambridge, Mass.: Harvard University Press, 1973.

—Daniel Robinson

D

## "Defence of Poetry, A" Percy Bysshe Shelley
(1821)

PERCY BYSSHE SHELLEY wrote "A Defence of Poetry," arguably his most important prose work, in direct response to THOMAS LOVE PEACOCK's "The Four Ages of Poetry" (1820). Written in 1821, the essay was never published during Shelley's lifetime but first appeared in the 1840 collection of his prose writings edited by MARY SHELLEY. "A Defence of Poetry," which considers the function and importance of poetry and the role of the poet in society, could be read usefully alongside WILLIAM WORDSWORTH's PREFACE TO LYRICAL BALLADS and SAMUEL TAYLOR COLERIDGE's BIOGRAPHIA LITERARIA. For Shelley, there is no separation between art and life, the aesthetic and the political. Thus, he argues that poetry directly affects social conventions and behaviors. More important, he suggests that poetry teaches us to be better human beings through empathy.

Among the most remarkable aspects of Shelley's argument is his strong emphasis on the significance of the self and subjectivity, which situates him in interesting ways between antiquity and modernity. While "A Defence of Poetry" ostensibly mirrors the ancient Greek philosopher Plato's "Ion" in its discussion of divine inspiration, the disparity between Plato's and Shelley's concepts of the origin of this phenomenon represents a significant shift from the classical to the Romantic understanding of human experience. For Plato, divine inspiration is just that—inspiration sent from the gods. In the Platonic sense, a poet is a mere vessel,

and he neither brings about nor even necessarily comprehends the full impact of the poetry that he produces. Throughout the "Defence," Shelley relies on language strikingly similar to Plato's in describing the process of creation. In one instance he refers to "the mind in creation" as "a fading coal, which some invisible influence, like an inconstant wind, awakens to transitory brightness" (Shelley 531). Of particular significance in this passage is the fact that "this power arises from within" (531). This internal force becomes the key to understanding Shelley's notions of subjectivity and, indeed, prefigures the intellectual approach of one of the key figures of modernity, Sigmund Freud.

In these terms, when Shelley refers to poetry creating a "being within our being" (533), he means that poetry allows us to access the hidden recesses of our minds. Shelley alludes to this process when he refers to the "divinity in man" (518), but the significance of the phrase becomes more fully comprehensible when read in Freudian terms. This constitutes the major distinction between Plato's notion of divinity and Shelley's. Moreover, it creates a dynamic view of humanity and subjectivity, for each individual becomes an entire universe of things unto him- or herself. This multidimensional view of individual experience, in turn, lends itself to the possibility of ethical improvement through another Freudian concept: identification. In "A Defence" and other writings, Shelley calls this love; in contemporary terms, we understand it to be empathy. Thus, poetry directly influences the political because it quite literally makes us better people; but because the empathetic impulse must arise from within the individual, the poet is not a public figure but writes behind closed doors ("The poet is a nightingale, who sits in darkness," 516). As such, the essay concludes with the oft-quoted axiom, "Poets are the unacknowledged legislators of the World" (535).

## Further Reading

Bonca, Teddi Chichester. *Shelley's Mirrors of Love: Narcissism, Sacrifice, and Sorority.* Albany: State University of New York Press, 1999.

Edmundson, Mark. *Literature against Philosophy, Plato to Derrida: A Defence of Poetry.* Cambridge: Cambridge University Press, 1995.

McDayter, Ghislaine, ed. *Untrodden Regions of the Mind: Romanticism and Psychoanalysis.* Lewisburg, Pa.: Bucknell University Press, 2002.

Peacock, Thomas Love. *Peacock's Four Ages of Poetry. Shelley's Defence of Poetry. Browning's Essay on Shelley,* edited by H. F. B. Brett-Smith, 52. Oxford: Basil Blackwell, 1923.

Plato. "Ion." In *The Collected Dialogues of Plato, Including the Letters,* edited by Edith Hamilton and Huntington Cairns, Princeton, N.J.: Princeton University Press, 1989.

Shelley, Percy Bysshe. "A Defence of Poetry." In *Shelley's Poetry and Prose: Authoritative Texts, Criticism,* edited by Donald H. Reiman and Neil Fraistat, 478–510. New York: Norton, 2002.

—Diana Koretsky

## *Deformed Transformed, The*  Lord Byron
(1822)

The drama *The Deformed Transformed* presents LORD BYRON's concern with disability, particularly its origin and its effects on the individual as portrayed by Arnold, the hunchbacked protagonist who sells his soul to the devil for a perfect body. In the disabled Arnold, an alter ego for the author himself, Byron gives his readers a distinctly 18th-century portrait of disability.

Like many of his other works, *The Deformed Transformed,* which is his only work to deal explicitly with disability, reveals Byron's skepticism about orthodoxy and his affinity for the darker realms of existence. It also reflects on such subjects as the supernatural, free will, determinism, and mind/body dualism. Byron chose to remain linked with the GOTHIC and various forms of superstition/supernaturalism that would have appeared unorthodox, skeptical, and defiant to the more pious among the British readership.

The drama opens with a dialogue between Arnold and his mother, Bertha, in which the latter calls her son a "hunchback." Bitter like Byron, Arnold responds to his mother's insult, "I was born so, mother" (1.1.2). The scene is reminiscent of an occasion in Byron's youth when his mother called him "a lame brat." By having Bertha display her disgust with her own son, Byron reflects on his own familial relationships. Bertha tells Arnold, "Call not thy brothers brethren! Call me not mother" (1.1.24). Both mothers condemn their sons for their respective disabilities; in response, both sons hate their mothers—and God, because it is from their creators that they received their disabilities. The epithet *hunchback* is also significant because it recalls the 18th-century poet Alexander Pope's disability, to which Byron was sympathetic. Occasionally Byron made attempts at imitating Pope's writing, for example, in the figure of the Stranger in *The Deformed Transformed.* The Stranger reveals the shape-shifting process: "From the red earth, like Adam, / Thy likeness I shape, / As the being who made him, / Whose action I ape (1.1.384–387). The Stranger, using fire (from Hell?), apes God's creation of Adam, which was finished by God's breathing life into Adam.

By having Arnold born disabled, Byron reiterates the ideas of determinism and damnation, because of which Arnold (perhaps like Byron himself) cannot be accepted fully in society. They also remain outcasts from their creator. Arnold's disability grows so unbearable that he almost attempts suicide by falling on a knife. Standing by a pool, he begins to contemplate a better world—one without his disabled self—and considers whether nature would be happier if it "sees no foul thing like / [Himself]" (1.1.68–69). However, he notices a disturbance in the pool: "The ripple of a spring change my resolve? / No. Yet it moves again! The waters stir . . ." (1.1.77–78). Suddenly the Stranger springs up from the fountain, and he subsequently convinces Arnold to reconsider ending his life. Believing the Stranger may be demonic, Arnold questions him as to whether he is human or spirit. The Stranger replies: "As man is both, why not / Say both in one?" (1.1.82–83). Moreover, he falsely assures Arnold that he is not the devil by claiming that if he were the devil, he would not have saved him from suicide. The Stranger asks Arnold how he would recognize the devil, the "cloven-footed terror"—a common description of Satan—and mocks Arnold's disability. Arnold responds, "Do you—dare you / To taunt me with my born deformity?" (1.1.101–102). The Stranger replies: "Were I to taunt a buffalo with this / Cloven foot of thing, or the swift dromedary / With thy sublime of Humps, the animals / Would revel in the compliment" (1.1.103–106). Then the Stranger offers Arnold the option of assuming any shape he desires with "no bond / But [Arnold's] own will" (1.1.150–151). The Stranger provides Arnold with the ability to alter his appearance—including his hunchback—by inhabiting the body of another person, whether it be that of Julius Caesar, or Socrates, or Achilles, among others. Before choosing, Arnold engages in a monologue through which he reveals his thoughts regarding the opportunity to have a perfect body: "Had no power presented me / The possibility of change, I would / Have done the best which spirit may to make / Its way with all deformity's dull, deadly / Discouraging weight upon me . . ." (1.1.327–331). Arnold chooses the beautiful, powerful Achilles as his new body.

Once Arnold has taken the body of Achilles, the Stranger inhabits Arnold's former body. The Stranger states, "I will be as you were, and you shall see / Yourself for ever by you, as your shadow" (1.1.448–449). After all the shape-shifting has occurred, Arnold and the Stranger go to "Where the World / Is thickest," or, as the Stranger informs him, "Where there is War" (1.1.493–495). Riding black horses, they travel to early 16th-century Rome, which is under attack from Constable Bourbon. The Stranger adopts the name of empire, Caesar—a name, as the Stranger claims, suited for "the devil in disguise"—while Arnold becomes Count Arnold (1.1.540). Count Arnold, however, is not immortal like Caesar. Caesar reminds him, "But though I have given thee the form of Thetis' son, / I dipt thee not in Styx"—an allusion to Achilles' birthright (2.2.19–20).

Caesar points out some blemishes related to Christianity and even Arnold's disability. For example, Caesar describes the orthodoxy he sees in Rome: "I see the giant / Abode of the true God . . ." (1.2.37–38). He remembers that such orthodoxy emanates from a city with a corrupt beginning: "I saw you Romulus (simple as I am) / Slay his own twin . . . / . . . and Rome's earliest cement / Was brother's blood . . ." (1.2.80–84). The capital of Christendom was established by an act of fratricide—Romulus's murder of Remus—that hearkens back to Cain's slaying of Abel. As Count Arnold/Achilles battles in Rome, he faces his old enemies—the descendants of the Trojans who claimed the life of the original Achilles by fatally wounding his heel, reiterating Byron's obsession with his clubfoot.

Though he has a new body, Arnold-as-Achilles remains mortal and, in the end, fails to win the heart of Olimpia, the beautiful aristocrat he saves during the battle. She tells him that her dead body "'tis all [Arnold] e'er shalt have of [her]!" (2.3.125.). While Arnold remains defeated. Caesar, in demonstrating his supernatural nature, stands as the victor of Arnold, Olympia, and all humankind. All humans are made of clay and are bound by physical bodies that will eventually decay. Emphasizing the conflict between body and mind and the depravity of both, Caesar states: "Heroes and chiefs, the flower of Adam's bastards! / This is the consequence of giving Matter / The power of Thought. It is a stubborn substance, / And thinks chaotically, as it acts, / Ever relapsing into its first elements" (1.2.315–319). Caesar's body is nothing but a "mask" that covers his spiritual body so that humans, who have mistakenly been given reason, can relate to him. The body itself seems to be the source of depravity, something which Arnold has misunderstood. The form of Achilles will no more bring happiness than his original body; it only brings about misunderstanding.

*The Deformed Transformed* focuses on the psychological struggle of its hero. The antagonist stands in complete defiance of orthodoxy, while the hero questions orthodoxy with much skepticism, illustrating the religious doubts that Byron continually experienced. Arnold fails at his quest because the whole venture is a rejection of God and his creation. In seeking perfection, Arnold sinks more firmly into his imperfection, which is now mental as well. The new body, given by Caesar, never brings Arnold happiness, only pain. Perhaps Byron drew on his own experiences with doctors who tried to correct his own deformed foot by having him wear painful shoes (which never could have corrected the foot). For Byron, like Arnold, the physical body brought, along with its limitations, mental anguish. Only through acceptance from others would Byron find the affirmation he sought.

### Further Reading

Byron, George Gordon Byron, Baron. *Byron: Complete Poetical Works.* Edited by Frederick Page. New York: Oxford University Press, 1970.

—Mark W. Westmoreland

## "Dejection: An Ode"   Samuel Taylor Coleridge (1802)

"Dejection: An Ode" was first published in the *Morning Post* on October 4, 1802, the day of WILLIAM WORDSWORTH's wedding as well as SAMUEL TAYLOR COLERIDGE's seventh wedding anniversary. Coleridge had Wordsworth in mind when he wrote the poem. The poet mourns the loss of his poetic faculty and looks back at his youth when he was full of hope and vigor. "Dejection: An Ode" is both an ode and a conversation poem. There are six surviving transcriptions of the poem—the letter to Sara Hutchinson (April 4, 1802), the transcription for William Sotheby (July 19, 1802), the *Morning Post* version (October 4, 1802), the transcription for the Beaumonts (August 13, 1803), the publication in the *Sibylline Leaves* (1817), and the *Poetical Works* version (1828, 1829, 1834)—and each version reveals psychological insights into the poet's mind.

The published poem is a profound psychoanalytical account of the poet's mental and emotional state. It begins with a motto from "The Ballad of Sir Patrick Spens"—an indication of the fact that the moon, a symbol of his visionary powers, has gone: "Late, late yestreen I saw the new Moon, / With the old Moon in her arms; / And I fear, I fear, My Master dear! / We shall have a deadly storm."

The moon in "The Ballad of Sir Patrick Spens" is an indicator of approaching storms and the speaker in "Dejection: An Ode" wishes fervently for a storm to erupt, as only that can cure his numbness. In "Dejection: An Ode" the moon takes on a strange appearance that presages the coming of a storm. The speaker says that he feels only a "dull pain," (l. 20) "a grief without a pang" (l. 21)—a constant deadening of all his feelings. Speaking to the "Lady" (l. 25), he admits that he has been gazing at the western sky all evening, able to see its beauty but unable to feel it. The soul itself must provide the light by which we may hope to see nature's true beauty—"we receive but what we give" (l. 47). He calls the Lady "pure of heart" (l. 59) and says that she has the joy which is so vital. Joy, he says, binds us to nature, thereby giving us "a new Earth and new Heaven, / Undreamt of by the sensual and the proud" (l. 69).

The speaker insists that there was a time when he was full of hope, when "fancy made me dreams of happiness" (l. 79). But now that his troubles press him, he does not mind the loss of mirth, but he cannot bear the degeneration of his imagination, the source of his creativity. Hoping to escape the "viper thoughts" (l. 94) that coil around his mind, the speaker turns his attention to the wind blowing outside. He thinks of the world as an instrument played on by a musician, who spins out of the wind a "worse than wintry song" (l. 106). This melody first calls to mind the rush of an army on the field and then evokes a young girl, all alone. It is midnight, but the speaker has "small thoughts" (l. 126) of sleep. However, he hopes that his friend, the Lady, will be visited by "gentle Sleep" (l. 128) and that she will wake with joyful thoughts and a "light heart" (l. 132). Overall, the poem appears unrelieved in its gloom, particularly if it is read as a lament for the loss of poetic creativity. However, there are also hints that the "dejection" suffered by the poet is not necessarily final. The poet is able to engage with the people and wish them well.

### Further Reading

Benthall, R. A. "New Moons, Old Ballads, and Prophetic Dialogues in Coleridge's 'Dejection: An Ode.'" *Studies in Romanticism.* 37 (1998): 591–614.

Bouslog, Charles S. "Structure and Theme in Coleridge's *Dejection: An Ode.*" *Modern Language Quarterly* 24 (1963): 42–52.

Daniel, Robert. "Odes to Dejection" *Kenyon Review* 15: 129–140.

Matlak, Richard E. *The Poetry of Relationship: The Wordsworths and Coleridge, 1797–1800.* London: Macmillan, 1997.

Parrish, Stephen Maxfield. *Coleridge's Dejection: The Earliest Manuscripts and the Earliest Printings.* Ithaca, N.Y.: Cornell University Press, 1988.

—Nishi Pulugurtha

## De Quincey, Thomas (1785–1859)

Best known for his CONFESSIONS OF AN ENGLISH OPIUM-EATER, Thomas De Quincey also wrote numerous other essays for periodicals, enough to fill 21 volumes in the latest edition of his collected works. He was born Thomas Quincey in Manchester, England, on August 15, 1785, the son of a prosperous merchant who died of tuberculosis when Thomas was not yet eight. His mother, who sought to move in high society, added the "De" to the family name after her husband's death and moved the family to Bath, where De Quincey attended the grammar school. She later transferred him to Manchester Grammar School, but he was so unhappy there that at the age of 16 he ran away and spent four months traveling in Wales, followed by another four on his own in London. Reconciled briefly with his family, he entered Oxford University's Worcester College in 1803, remaining there until 1808, but he fled the university in the middle of his final examinations and never received a degree.

During this time De Quincey discovered the writings of WILLIAM WORDSWORTH and SAMUEL TAYLOR COLERIDGE, having read the first edition of LYRICAL BALLADS soon after it came out. He was impressed by its seemingly new sort of poetry, especially Coleridge's "The RIME OF THE ANCIENT MARINER" and Wordsworth's poetry generally. He thought he might become a poet himself, but in fact never wrote much poetry. Indeed, until he was in his 30s he wrote little at all. He did, however, make the acquaintance of several leading Roman-

tics, writing a letter of appreciation to Wordsworth, who wrote back to invite De Quincey to visit him at Grasmere. Too timid to accept the invitation at first, De Quincey instead contrived to meet Coleridge and CHARLES LAMB, but in the end he did travel to the Lake District and ended up staying with the Wordsworth family. He later rented Dove Cottage when they moved out of it, and for several years he was an intimate of the family and an assistant to Wordsworth, traveling to London in 1809 to see a political pamphlet of his through the press. His own first publication was an appendix to the pamphlet, yet although his companions thought he had great potential, he wrote virtually nothing over the next dozen years. This was in part perhaps because of his discovery of opium, a legal drug at the time, which he took at first for pain. In addition to relieving pain, he found that the drug made him euphoric and stimulated his dreams and visions. He thought at first it was the key to happiness, but eventually he became addicted.

In 1818–19 De Quincey took on the position of editor of the *Westmorland Gazette* and wrote various articles for it, but he never again held a steady job and soon descended into poverty, supported by an allowance from his mother and gifts and loans from friends. Meanwhile, he had married a local woman in the Lake District, much to the dismay of the Wordsworths, who thought her uneducated and beneath him. Eventually he had eight children to support, which he attempted to do through freelance writing for various magazines, including *Blackwood's*, *Tait's*, and the *London Magazine*. Initially he was dilatory at this endeavor, failing to produce promised work despite the urgings of his friend, John Wilson, the editor of *Blackwood's*. However, when threatened with arrest for debt, he finally set himself to writing a long-promised article on opium, which he combined with autobiographical revelation to produce the famous *Confessions of an English Opium-Eater*, which appeared in two installments in *London Magazine* in 1821.

The *Confessions* won De Quincy acclaim, and he began to write much more regularly, becoming a master at producing reviews and essays, but he remained in financial difficulties and was several times arrested and once imprisoned for debt. He also spent several years in the debtors' sanctuary at Holyrood Palace in Edinburgh. Because he was frequently on the run from creditors, De Quincey could not always refer to his books or find a quiet place to write, but he still managed to produce a number of highly regarded works in addition to more ephemeral journalism and reviews. Next to the *Confessions,* he is most highly praised for his essay "The English Mail-Coach" (1849), an evocation of the stagecoach era, combined with dream visions. Dream visions also dominate his semiautobiographical *Suspiria de Profundis,* which appeared in installments in 1845. His humorous essay "On Murder Considered as One of the Fine Arts" (1827, 1839), inspired in part by Jonathan Swift's *Modest Proposal,* has been much praised, as has his piece of Shakespearean literary criticism entitled "On the Knocking at the Gate in *Macbeth*" (1823). De Quincey also wrote a series of autobiographical sketches, along with biographical articles, literary reminiscences, and literary criticism of his fellow Romantics, notably Wordsworth and Coleridge. He is an important source of personal anecdotes concerning these two, though at the time Coleridge's family and the Wordsworths were much annoyed with his revelations about their personal lives. Wordsworth even called him a "pest."

Thomas De Quince died on December 8, 1859. Though he is sometimes referred to as transitional figure between the Romantics and the Victorian age, and he is even compared to 18th-century writers like Jonathan Swift and Lawrence Sterne because of his digressiveness, De Quincey is generally considered one of the Romantics. His emphasis on the self, his interest in dreams and visions, his focus on emotions and the sublime rather than on form—all align him with the Romantic tradition. His impassioned style is sometimes seen as the prose equivalent of Romantic poetry, and the emphasis on personal development in the *Confessions* is often compared to Wordsworth's similar emphasis in *The Prelude,* a poem De Quincey was allowed to read in manuscript before it was published.

De Quincy's writing was admired by such writers as Edgar Allan Poe; Ralph Waldo Emerson; and Charles Baudelaire, who translated him into French. He has sometimes also been seen as a forerunner of 20th-century modernist writers like Marcel Proust and Virginia Woolf for his conjuring up of the past and his interest in free association. Recently there has been an upsurge of critical interest in him, with literary critics exploring his political and social views, and at the beginning of the 21st century a new edition of his works appeared in 21 volumes.

**Further Reading**

De Quincey, Thomas. *The Works of Thomas De Quincey.* 21 vols. Edited by Grevel Lindop. London: Pickering and Chatto, 2000–03.

Lindop, Grevel. *The Opium-Eater: A Life of Thomas De Quincey.* New York: Taplinger, 1981.

Lyon, Judson S. *Thomas De Quincey.* New York: Twayne, 1969.

Morrison, Robert, and Daniel Sanjiv Roberts, eds. *Thomas De Quincey: New Theoretical and Critical Directions.* New York: Routledge, 2008.

Snyder, Robert Lance, ed. *Thomas De Quincey: Bicentenary Studies.* Norman: University of Oklahoma Press, 1985.

—Sheldon Goldfarb

## "Despondency: An Ode" Robert Burns (1786)

This poem, written at a time when ROBERT BURNS's relationship with his future wife, Jean Armour, was under much stress, is indicative of the depressive phases that plagued his life and surfaced in many other similar pieces, such as "The Lament" or "MAN WAS MADE TO MOURN: A DIRGE," as well as in his correspondence. Here the double "burden" of "grief" and "care" (l. 1)—reflected both in the repetition of the word *oppress'd* and in the same iambic monotony as that of THOMAS GRAY's "*ELEGY WRITTEN IN A COUNTRY CHURCH-YARD*" or Oliver Goldsmith's "The Deserted Village"—crushes the speaker and brings him to a halt, where he can only "sigh" (l. 3) in a conventional melancholy posture. Out of step with the tradition of "rural retreat" ranging from JOHN MILTON's 'Il Penseroso' to the Graveyard poets (whose works often focused on aspects of mortality and other gloomy topics), the "[l]istless, yet restless" (27) persona obviously does not relish his alienated, condition. On the contrary, he envies those "bustling, and justling" (l. 25) "[h]appy . . . sons of Busy-life" (l. 15) from whom he feels estranged. He envies, too, the "Solitary's lot" (l. 19) in particular the hermit's peaceful, sheltered seclusion inside his cave. The speaker yearns for the latter's condition of spiritual fulfillment (ll. 40, 42) and enjoyment of nature's abundance (ll. 33, 34, 36), a state akin to those "enviable, early days" (l. 57) of childhood innocence, "To Care, to Guilt unknown!" (ll. 58–59). A sense of doom prevails at the very end of the poem, the threat now being "dim declining *Age!*" (l. 70).

The rhyming scheme is important to the poem's mood and meaning. While the sustained phonic contrast between plosives (/p/, /b/, /d/, /t/, /k/) and fricatives (/s/, /z/, /f/) throughout the first stanza heightens the poem's expressiveness, the relentlessly repetitive iambic rhythm induces a sense of "doom" (l. 12)—with "ev'ry sad returning night / And joyless morn the same!" (ll. 22–23)—which culminates in the echoing *"tomb" "closing"* (l. 14) in on the poet, as suggested by the polyptotonic repetition of "close" (l. 13), itself bound up with "woes" through the internal rhyme. The poem's speaker, referred to first at the beginning of line 3 and then and the end of line 6, is literally trapped within the prison of his own self (note the stasis brought on by the two consecutive stresses on "I here" [l. 55]) and further qualified by privatives (words connoting such "unfitted" (l. 23), "joyless" (l. 24), and so on. Yet it can also be argued that the poem is more playful than first appears. Each stanza most often divides into two clearly defined and balanced rhetorical periods of 10 and four lines, thus conveying an impression of poise and symmetry which, in itself, stems the unruliness of the depressive mood. Unexpected changes of tempo and rhythm suggest a lightheartedness that will ultimately defeat the speaker's melancholy.

## Further Reading

Burns, Robert. *The Canongate Burns. The Complete Poems and Songs of Robert Burns.* Edited by Andrew Noble and Patrick Scott Hogg. Edinburgh: Canongate, 2003.

———. *The Letters of Robert Burns.* 2nd ed. 2 vols. Edited by J. De Lancey Ferguson. Revised by G. Ross Roy. Oxford: Clarendon Press, 1985

—Dominique Delmaire

## *Don Juan* Lord Byron (1819–1824)

LORD BYRON's epic poem *Don Juan* was begun in 1819, and at the time of the poet's death in 1824 it comprised 16 cantos of varying lengths and fragmentary pieces of another canto. In marked contrast to Byron's most famous poem, CHILDE HAROLD'S PILGRIMAGE, which catered to the Romantic public and its craving for exoticism and sentimental journeys, *Don Juan* follows the satirical tradition of the Renaissance and 18th-century NEOCLASSICISM. Written in ottava rima and modeled on the comic poems by the Italian Renaissance poets Ludovico Ariosto and Francesco Berni, *Don Juan* should be read in terms of a deconstruction of Romanticism and a revitalization of Augustan concepts of poetry. Thus, the poetological commandment "Thou shalt believe in Milton, Dryden, Pope / Thou shalt not set up Wordsworth, Coleridge, Southey" (Canto 1, stanza 205, ll. 1,633–1,634) clearly reflects the poem's anti-Romantic bias and shows to what extent Byron is indebted to 17th- and 18th-century notions of the mock heroic and the parodic.

What fits into the context of the parodic is the fact that, unlike the hallmarks of epic poetry, the poem is marked by a conspicuous lack of heroes in an age in which newspapers and emergent popular culture spawn short-lived heroes in inflationary abundance: "I want a hero, an uncommon want / When every year and month sends forth a new one" (1:1:1–2). Byron's choice of the 17th-century libertine Don Juan, however, raises expectations in the reader that are constantly thwarted and conducive to parodic effects. Thus, Don Juan is no longer the erotic overreacher and scoffer of love that he was in Tirso de Molina's and Mozart's dramatizations of the character. In Byron's poem he has been turned into an antihero buffeted around by fate, bullied by his hypocritical mother ("Morality's prim personification" [1:16:125] and waylaid by lascivious and greedy women.

While Romantic poetry cherishes the idea of man in tune with and sheltered by nature, Byron seems to share John Hobbes's and Jonathan Swift's anthropological pessimism when, in canto 2, he shows Don Juan and his tutor Pedrillo within a motley group of survivors of a shipwreck. Possibly influenced by Théodore Géricault's oil painting *Le radeau de Méduse* (1817), Byron broadens the satirical scope of the poem into a grim antitheological allegory of 19th-century man's deterioration: After the loss of the ship (suggestively called *Trinidada*), it takes the men huddled in the longboat seven days to pervert God's creation and to gradually turn into cannibalizing beasts. Reducing man to "a carnivorous production" (2:67:529), Byron thus challenges the Romantic myth of man's divine descent when, one generation prior to Charles Darwin, he has the shipwrecked not only fall "ravenously" (2:68:543) on their provision but also slaughter Pedrillo, the clergyman, who is the least fit in the bestialized microcosm of the boat.

Even though the most voracious among the cannibals are punished by madness and eventually die "with hyena laughter" (2:79:632), it is evident that time-honored concepts of poetic justice and morality have been replaced by notions of randomness and absurdity. Thus, what paradoxically saves Juan from becoming the next victim of cannibalistic desires is the simple fact that he contracted a venereal disease in Cadiz ("a small present made to him at Cadiz, / By general subscription of the ladies" [2:81:647–648]). In a world in which the Romantic symbol of the unifying rainbow has been trivialized into "a heavenly chameleon" (2:92:729), the reader is alerted to the fact that Juan's rescue is anything but providential; rather, it is the outcome of a sequence of accidents and fatal mishaps, which govern the protagonist's life. Thus, the short-lived pastoral idyll with Haidée (cantos 2–4), which follows the calamitous shipwreck, is as arbitrary as all the other adventures into which Don Juan, as the parodist of John Bunyan's pilgrim, is flung.

As the impotent victim of freakish fortune, Don Juan is sold at a slave market, dressed up as a girl in a harem to gratify the sensual needs of the sultana (cantos 5–6) and eventually thrust as a mercenary soldier into battle at the siege of Ismail (cantos 7–8). Almost at the same time that Goya was painting *Los desastres de la guerra*, Byron depicts war no longer in terms of a holy mission but as a further step in man's dehumanization, as an anthropological disease in which the cannon throw up their emetic and cause "a bloody diuretic" (8:12:91). Wavering between hero and buffoon, between "half-demon and half-dirt" (7:55:436), Byron's soldiers aimlessly wallow in blood; destroy

life and; due to the absence of the light of reason and taste, deflower 70-year-old spinsters.

Having escaped the horrors of war, Don Juan is finally admitted into the amorous favors of the Russian empress Catherine, and from there he is sent to England, where, on the "chessboard" of society (13:89:705), he is allotted his position. Seen from Byron's satirical perspective, Regency England is shown as an impeccably polished facade beneath whose monkish habit of virtue is—as in the case of the Duchess of Fitz-Fulke in the disguise of the haunting friar (canto 16)—an unfathomable reservoir of hostility, decadence, and suppressed sexuality.

Exposing British society to his relentlessly probing view, Byron vindictively tried to show his home country for what it was: a "superb menagerie" (12:24:192) in which human cattle endlessly chewed the cud of "abominable tittle-tattle" (12:43:343). But what must have exasperated Romantics like JOHN KEATS, who is said to have hurled the book to the ground in disgust, is the fact that, behind the mask of a digressive 18th-century hack writer, Byron dealt a death blow to Romanticism and to its ideals of Platonism and transcendentalism. Using provocative rhymes like *Plato* / *potato* and *pathetic* / *emetic*, Byron defines poetry as a constant struggle to aspire to the Icarian heights of sublimity, which is then invariably succeeded by the fall into the depths of sordid and trivial reality. While the Romantics clung to the notion of literature as a kind of epiphany with the poet as a priest, Byron expresses his idea of poetry using the image of an upward race which Pegasus seems to be winning, when suddenly the horse "sprains a wing and down we tend, / Like Lucifer when hurled from heaven for sinning" (4:1:4–5). More than any other poem of the Romantic period, *Don Juan* is thus meant to be a large-scale descent into the tragicomic hell of the human condition, which leaves the reader puzzlingly exposed to what Byron called "horrid glee" (2:50:398).

## Further Reading

Barton, Anne. *Byron: Don Juan*. Cambridge: Cambridge University Press, 1992.

Beatty, Bernard. *Byron's Don Juan*. Totowa, N.J.: Barnes & Noble Books, 1985.

Bone, Drummond. *Byron*. Tavistock, Eng.: Northcote House, 2000.

———. "Childe Harold IV, Don Juan and Beppo." In *The Cambridge Companion to Byron*, edited by Drummond Bone, 151–170. Cambridge: Cambridge University Press, 2004.

—Norbert Lennartz

### "Drum, The" John Scott (1782)

Written in 1782 as an antiwar poem, "The Drum" remained extremely popular during the 1800s and particularly during the time of the Napoleonic Wars (see BONAPARTE, NAPOLEON). The beating drum was regularly used in villages and towns to recruit men to the army, the belief being that to patriots its very sound would be "spirit-stirring," as William Shakespeare put it in *Othello*. Born in Hartfordshire, England, John Scott (1731–83) was a pastoral poet, friend of Samuel Johnson, social reformer, and a Quaker—and thus opposed to all types of violence. The poem's opening lines—"I hate that drum's discordant sound / parading round, and round, and round"—indicate Scott's anger at the cynical appeal to patriotism deployed by the army to ensnare "thoughtless youth" (l. 3), naive young men who are persuaded "To sell their liberty" (l. 5). *Liberty* is a key word for Scott: It is to be guarded, and its loss is something to be mourned. The drumbeat seems to have a hypnotic appeal (something captured in the rhythm of the poem), but to Scott its sound is not all pleasing but rather "discordant," a despoiler of the tranquil English town—in a way that a police siren is today. Yet for the young men the drum helps conjure up an attractive picture of army life. The "charms / Of tawdry lace and glittering arms" (ll. 5–6) are powerful, and the dormant sense of "Ambition" (l. 7) awakened in them is enough to make them sign up, little knowing they will not only "march, and fight . . . in foreign lands" but "fall" as well (l. 8).

Although it begins with the same two opening lines as the first stanza, the poem's second stanza is intended to contrast with the first. Rather than the glamorous vision of overseas service sold to the young men, the poet spells out what the sound of the drum evokes for him. To him, it "talks of ravaged plains, / And burning towns, and ruined swains / And mangled limbs, and dying groans" (ll. 11–13). War, he argues, brings nothing but destruction and the death of sons and fathers; its aftermath is not glory but "widows' tears, and orphans' moans" (l. 14), the sound of which replaces that of the drum across the battlefield. Whereas the young men in the first stanza are lured by "Ambition's voice" (l. 7), in the second, the poet sees nothing but "Misery's hand" (l. 15) at work. He seems to hint that the two are connected; that wanting more than you have been given does not bring satisfaction—just the opposite. The last lines of the first and second stanzas also seem to suggest that there is a moral message at work, the lines hinting at a kind of cause-and-effect relationship. The first stanza ends "To march, and fight, and fall in foreign lands" (l. 8). The second ends "To fill the catalogue of human woes" (l. 16)—as if one action leads irrevocably to another.

The poem is important not least because, as Betty T. Bennett notes, "War was the single most important fact of British life from 1793 to 1815. The poetry of the major Romantic writers concerned with the war—Blake, Wordsworth, Coleridge, Byron, and Shelley—reflects this imperfectly because their war poetry constitutes only a part of the total poetic response."

See also "BATTLE OF BLENHEIM, THE."

### Further Reading

Bennett, Betty T. *British War Poetry in the Age of Romanticism 1793–1815*. Edited by Orianne Smith. Available online. URL: http://www.rc.umd.edu/editions/warpoetry/intro.html. Accessed on August 1, 2009.

Perman, David. *Scott of Amwell, Dr. Johnson's Quaker Critic*. Ware: Rockingham Press, 2001.

—Andrew Maunder

**"Ecchoing Green, The" William Blake** (1789)
The title of this poem from SONGS OF INNOCENCE
AND OF EXPERIENCE refers to an idyllic rural location where children play happily, innocent and
untrammeled by the social conventions and strictures of adult worldliness and experience. This
scene of rustic pleasure is, however, undermined
by a sense of foreboding and infused with ominous,
even disturbing, portents. The cyclical structure
of "The Ecchoing Green" reinforces this impression of unease, charting a progression from day to
night. The movement between these binary opposites opens up this deceptively simple yet complex
poem to a multiplicity of interpretations. Day to
night can equally be perceived as the journey from
life to death, the evolutionary shift from childish
innocence to adult experience or the social and
cultural impact of the drift from a rural economy
to a largely urban way of life.

The first stanza represents morning, when
"The sun does arise" (l. 1). The light and quick
rhythm of Blake's verse and playful misspelling of
"chearful" (l. 8), as an untutored child might write
it, reflects the energy, joy, and liberation of youth.
The young enjoy their "sports" (l. 9), and the only
sounds to be heard are the "birds of the bush" (l.
6) and the "merry" and "chearful" peal of church
bells (ll. 3, 8). Note here that the presence of the
church is viewed positively—a herald of "Spring"
(l. 9) even—rather than as an agency of social
control. In this country setting the church appears
to be untainted by the rigid rules and hypocrisy
that characterizes its portrayal in the London of

"HOLY THURSDAY" and "The CHIMNEY SWEEPER."
The first of WILLIAM BLAKE's integral artworks
for the poem emphasizes an environment of traditional rustic simplicity: A man and three women
with toddlers at their knees sit under a shady oak
(symbolic of strength and protection) and look on
indulgently as two older boys dance and play.

The slow, assonantal rhythm of the second
stanza denotes a marked change of pace that is sustained throughout the remainder of the poem as the
brightness of the morning and sprightliness of youth
slows and fades toward old age and night. The
impetus from youth to age, light to dark, is further
accentuated by subtle shifts in narrative viewpoint.
In the first half of the verse, "Old John" (l. 11) and
the "old folk" (l. 14) "laugh at our play" (l. 15), the
use of "our" suggesting that the narrator is a youthful participant in the revelry. In the poem's 17th line
it is one of the senior citizens who reminisces "Such
such were the joys," recalling "our youth time" (l.
19) when, as "girls & boys" (l. 18) they capered on
"the Ecchoing Green" themselves (l. 20).

The somber tone of the final stanza is reflected
in the melancholy assonance of its rhythm. With
the "little ones weary" (l. 21), the "sun does
descend" (l. 22), putting an end to "our sports" (l.
23). There is an ambiguity here as to the narrative
viewpoint, suggesting perhaps a greater universality of consensus, an "our" in which all, both young
and old, are implicated. Death is a fact of life; it
comes to everyone. Aside from physical expiration,
though, there may be allusions to societal demise.
There is finality in the closing couplet as "sport" is

"no more seen" on "the darkening Green" (ll. 29–30). The "darkening" could denote the imminent end of a traditional, rural way of life, giving way to the corruption of city living in the wake of rapid urban expansion.

Indeed, the anxiety that underpins the closing stanza is reinforced by the second of Blake's integral artworks, which contains some notably sinister elements. As a group of men, women, and children file off to the left, a girl hangs back, reaching up to take a bunch of grapes from an impish male character reclining on the overhanging branch of a tree. The image carries connotations of sexual temptation and the biblical fall of Eve, but Blake's depiction of the tree also suggests an impulse toward a more constricted and manufactured society. The tree here is not the solid English oak but a cultivated and trained specimen with an ornate, twisted stem, reminiscent of those seen in formal landscape gardens. The illustration gives a powerful impression of nature defiled and contaminated with artifice.

Although there is no eponymous counterpoint poem to "The Ecchoing Green" in *Songs of Experience,* it may fruitfully be read in conjunction with "The GARDEN OF LOVE." In the latter work "the green" has been "filled with graves."

## Further Reading

Ackroyd, Peter. *Blake.* London: Sinclair-Stevenson, 1995.

Blake, William. *Songs of Innocence and of Experience.* Edited by Geoffrey Keynes. Oxford: Oxford University Press, 1970.

Eaves, Maurice, ed. *The Cambridge Companion to William Blake.* Cambridge: Cambridge University Press, 2003.

Myrone, Martin. *Seen in My Visions: A Descriptive Catalogue of Pictures by William Blake.* London: Tate Publishing, 2009.

Roberts, Jonathan. *William Blake's Poetry.* London: Continuum Publishing, 2007.

—Diane Mason

## Edgeworth, Maria (1767–1849)

Critics have nominated Maria Edgeworth as the Irish JANE AUSTEN and the female WALTER SCOTT. High praise indeed; however, Edgeworth needs no comparison to any other writer. Not only has she earned her own place in the canon of Romanticism, she forged the way for new literary styles that would become the hallmark of Romantic fiction, including those of Austen and Scott.

Edgeworth was born in Black Bourton, Oxfordshire, on January 1, 1767, the second of her father's 21 children (by four wives). When she was still a child, she and her family removed from England to their estate in County Longford, Ireland. Edgeworthstown was the family's seat given to them by James I in 1619 during his campaign to implant Protestants in Ireland. Her father, Richard Lovell Edgeworth, was a well-known author and inventor who counted ANNA LAETITIA BARBAULD among his friends. Mr. Edgeworth fostered his daughter's abilities by preparing her to become the estate's property manager and collaborating with her on his writing projects. Besides innovations to his own tenant system, he and his daughter initiated many education reforms and advanced their theories on how to raise children. The latter measures were in keeping with the Romantics' view of treating children as children instead of as miniature adults (see CHILDHOOD).

On the heels of MARY WOLLSTONECRAFT's *A VINDICATION OF THE RIGHTS OF WOMAN* (1792), Maria Edgeworth published *LETTERS FOR LITERARY LADIES* in 1795, arguing that women were just as rational as men and thus deserved equal education, a theme she would address later in *BELINDA.* The next year she completed *The Parent's Assistant,* a children's book that grew into six volumes and was the first of many that could be read, understood, and enjoyed by children, also an innovation during the Romantic period. With her numerous siblings, a significant audience was provided for her on which to try out these books. The work that made her famous, though, is *CASTLE RACKRENT: An Hibernian Tale Taken from Facts, and from the Manners of the Irish Squires before the Year 1782,* published in 1800.

Often claimed to be Ireland's first regional novel, *Castle Rackrent* is told in the Irish vernacular, reflects local color, and uniquely depicts the complicated and volatile class struggle in Irish tenantry. Its narrator, Thady Quirk, is a loyal steward who tells about the masters he has served, beginning with Sir Patrick, who drank himself to death. His heir, Sir Murtagh, is a "great lawyer" who refused "out of honor" to pay Sir Patrick's debts. His last master was Sir Kit, who, because of gambling debts, was forced to sell his estate to Thady's son. This novel led the way for family sagas, and it was one of the first with an "unreliable narrator" who was an observer rather than a character. Shortly before its publication, an introduction, glossary, and footnotes were added, written in the voice of an English narrator.

In 1800 the Irish dialect became politically unacceptable, a byproduct of the Act of Union that year, which merged the Kingdom of Ireland into the United Kingdom (which included England and Scotland). The Edgeworths were for colonial rule, believing that Britain could bring Ireland out of what they perceived a backward state, and therefore the annotation was a covert expression of British colonization over the Irish. Nevertheless, *Castle Rackrent* inspired Scott to write WAVERLEY, which began his famous series of historical novels set in Scotland. In his 1829 preface, Scott explained that he meant to do for Scotland what Edgeworth had done for Ireland. By telling stories of the Highlanders' noble past, he validated the Scottish experience, which had long been suppressed by the colonization by Britain.

Although often concerned with English oppression, Edgeworth's novels more consistently reveal her anxiety about the bondage of women. Edgeworth herself was a strong woman of independent means, commanding more money for her novels than anyone before her, until Scott published *Waverley*. She did receive an attractive proposal from a man who was her intellectual equal but declined to marry him. Projecting herself into her novels, she wrote of heroines faced with having to make tough decisions that cost great personal sacrifice. They challenge gender norms, with texts affirming their acumen, courage, and integrity. The most striking example is Lady Davenant in Edgeworth's last novel, *Helen* (1834). A powerful, intelligent woman with political clout abroad and in England, Lady Davenant is able to evoke beneficial social and political changes, thus refuting the idea that politics is not part of women's sphere. The Edgeworthian heroine was not only

steel-braced with moral rectitude; she found ways to mend immoral ruptures, including those outside her domestic realm. Impressed with its well-written moral lessons, the critic John Ruskin once said that he read Edgeworth's *Patronage* (1814) more often than any book other than the Bible.

Edgeworth remained unmarried, running her father's estate and devoting her entire life to writing. Like many of her contemporaries, she believed she could change the world for the better through her pen. Four of her novels, *Ennui* (1809), *Ormond* (1817), *Rosam und* (1821), and *Vivian* (1856), attempted to further educate the world about Irish culture. The ABSENTEE (1812) decried the exploitation of the Irish by British absentee landlords. Still, Edgeworth always held to the feudalistic idea that the nobility should rule with merit and benevolence, a belief in noblesse oblige shared by many Romantics who idealized the medieval past. Her books therefore often chastised the gentry for not living up to its responsibilities. With her emphasis on refined dialogue among the gentry, interaction of characters, and didacticism about how the upper class should behave, she paved the way for Austen's novels.

During the worst of the potato famines, Edgeworth worked unceasingly for the relief of the starving. Her first efforts were to try to persuade farmers to diversify their crops, and toward that end she purchased and distributed seed and built mills to grind flour. As starvation mounted, she convinced countless friends in America to send flour and rice, and she wrote *Orlandino* (1848), giving its proceeds to the Irish poor. Dying of a heart attack on May 22, 1849, she did not live to see the end of the Great Irish Famine. She was buried in the family's vault at St. John's Church in Edgeworthstown. Her nephew was THOMAS LOVELL BEDDOES.

## Further Reading

Butler, Marilyn. *Maria Edgeworth: A Literary Biography.* Oxford: Clarendon Press, 1972.

Edgeworth, Maria. *The Novels and Selected Works of Maria Edgeworth.* 10 vols. Edited by Marilyn Butler, et al. London: Pickering and Chatto, 1999–2003.

———. *Castle Rackrent and Ennui.* Harmondsworth, Eng.: Penguin, 1993.

———. *Belinda.* Oxford: Oxford University Press, 1999.

———. *Ormond, A Tale.* Harmondsworth, Eng.: Penguin, 2001.

Harden, Elizabeth. *Maria Edgeworth.* Boston: G. K. Hall, 1984.

Hollingworth, Brian. *Maria Edgeworth's Irish Writing: Language, History, Politics.* New York: St. Martin's Press, 1997.

Hurst, Michael. *Maria Edgeworth and the Public Scene: Intellect, Fine Feeling and Landlordism in the Age of Reform.* Coral Gables, Fla.: University of Miami Press, 1969.

Kaufman, Heidi, and Christopher J. Fauske. *An Uncomfortable Authority: Maria Edgeworth and Her Contexts.* Newark: University of Delaware Press, 2004.

Nash, Julia. *New Essays on Maria Edgeworth.* Aldershot, Eng.: Ashgate Publishing, 2006.

—Brenda Ayres

## "Eighteen Hundred and Eleven" Anna Laetitia Barbauld (1812)

ANNA LAETITIA BARBAULD's poem "Eighteen Hundred and Eleven," published in January 1812, is a powerful critique of British imperialism (see EMPIRE) and Great Britain's role in the Napoleonic Wars (see BONAPARTE, NAPOLEON). Barbauld's thematic concerns situate her within the context of Romantic revolutionary ideals. She paints a grim portrait of a fallen Britain for much of the poem, pointing out that no nation is immune to the caprices of time and destiny.

In 1811 England was suffering from numerous crises, including the war with France, economic hardships, and increasing strife with America and the illness of King George III (see MONARCHY). According to Barbauld, these crises resulted from Britain's imperialist and colonialist ambitions, which she criticizes throughout the poem. She begins with a stark critique of Britain's war with France. As she moves through each stanza, Barbauld details how the war has devastated the once-great nation. Her vision of England's decline demonstrates how nations with strong, intelligent leaders fail because of a lack of inspiration from the "Genius," a concept Barbauld uses throughout the text to represent liberty. This Genius is variously depicted as a "vagrant Power" (l. 259), "mighty impulse" (l. 272), and "awful form" (l. 324) to show its potential as a capricious, destructive, and ultimately liberating force. However, Barbauld's repetition of the words *if* and *perhaps* indicates that England may yet avoid its fate as a fallen nation. By returning to the literature of authors such as JOANNA BAILLIE and William Shakespeare, Britain may begin the healing process and turn away from the destructive practices of war and colonialism. Colonial exploitation and constant warring are signs that the "Genius" will soon turn from "Europe's desolated shores" (l. 322).

At the end of the poem, Barbauld predicts that the seat of power will shift from Britain to America and refers to a series of South American countries that were throwing off colonialism. Barbauld criticizes the luxury and materialism that is encouraged by repressive colonialism and shows how this luxury leads to the demise of the grandeur and privilege Britain had achieved by exploiting its colonies in the Americas. Although British conservatives viewed revolution as a threatening force, Barbauld portrays it as a tool to rid a fledgling nation of its former oppressor and to seize control of that oppressor's possessions. The cycle of revolution and renewal thus begins anew, as the old power of Europe weakens and crosses the ocean to America.

Incisive reviews by critics such as John Wilson Croker damaged Barbauld's literary reputation, and after the publication of "Eighteen Hundred and Eleven," she ceased publishing. Her apocalyptic vision of England's inevitable decline irritated conservative critics, and even Barbauld's friends, the diarist Henry Crabb Robinson and the novelist MARIA EDGEWORTH, hesitated to defend a poem with such radical sentiments. Moreover, Barbauld's intrusion into the masculine arena of war and politics clashed with popular notions of a private, domestic sphere for women. More than 150 years later, however, Barbauld's poem is finally receiving critical appreciation.

## Further Reading

Hadley, Karen. "'The Wealth of Nations,' or 'The Happiness of Nations'? Barbauld's Malthusian Critique in 'Eighteen Hundred and Eleven.'" *CLA Journal* 45, no. 1 (September 2001): 87–96.

Keach, William. "A Regency Prophecy and the End of Anna Barbauld's Career." *Studies in Romanticism* 33, no. 4 (Winter 1994): 569–577.

—Sara Dustin

## *Elegiac Sonnets and Other Poems*
### Charlotte Smith (1784)

CHARLOTTE SMITH's *Elegiac Sonnets*, first published in 1784 as *Elegiac Sonnets and Other Essays* and in subsequent editions as *Elegiac Sonnets and Other Poems*, is often credited with the revival of the sonnet form at the end of the 18th century. The number of sonnets grew at every stage of publication, with a second volume of the ninth edition appearing in 1797. *The Poems of Charlotte Smith* edited by Stuart Curran (1993) provides the definitive modern text and helps to cement Smith's position in the constellation of Romantic and proto-Romantic poets of the time. As Curran says, "Charlotte Smith was the first poet in England whom in retrospect we would call Romantic" (Smith xix). *Elegiac Sonnets* is perhaps most notable for Smith's choice of the sonnet form, the description of her sonnets as "elegiac," and her place in current discussions of the boundaries of Romanticism.

Smith's adoption of the sonnet form contravened the received wisdom among Samuel Johnson and other critics of the 18th century that English was a poor language for the sonnet, making hers one of the first volleys in a debate about whether the English sonnet (whether in Shakespearean or Spenserian guise) was an acceptable variation on the so-called legitimate sonnet, the Italian (or Petrarchan). The Augustan (18th century) consensus honored JOHN MILTON (by imitating him in the heroic couplets he detested) and bowdlerized Shakespeare; it also rejected the English sonnet and suggested the Italian sonnet could not be well written in English. MARY ROBINSON appealed to Milton and the idea of legitimacy to deflect criticisms of her Petrarchan sonnets as imitative and alien to English. Smith instead defined the sonnet broadly, as SAMUEL TAYLOR COLERIDGE would (in his *Sheet of Sonnets*), drawing the ire of staunch Petrarchan sonneteers such as ANNA SEWARD. Whatever their positions on the respective merits of the Italian and the English sonnet, women writers such as Smith, Robinson, and Seward defied the prevailing contemporary Augustan ethos to open a vibrant new front in the literary wars of succession to names such as Milton, Edmund Spenser, William Shakespeare, and Sir Philip Sidney. The title *Elegiac Sonnets*, like WILLIAM WORDSWORTHs and Coleridge's subsequent and more famous *Lyrical Ballads*, would have seemed paradoxical to its original audience, as the literary critic Daniel Robinson has explained. Robinson points out that, in the era of THOMAS GRAY's "ELEGY WRITTEN IN A COUNTRY CHURCH-YARD," the term *elegiac* designated the unity of brooding or morbid theme with alternately rhymed (heroic or elegiac) quatrain or heroic couplet form. "Smith's 'illegitimate' sonnet," says Robinson, "consists of three elegiac quatrains and a couplet, thus combining both English elegiac meters" (2003, 189). Smith's sonnets diverge from the accepted Italian model, but this is according to a pattern then thought fit for the themes of suffering and loss that pervade her works. This pattern is corroborated by Smith's longer works, such as "Ode to Despair," included with *Elegiac Sonnets* from the first edition and written in stanzas containing two heroic quatrains each; or "Elegy," also included in *Elegiac Sonnets* and written in heroic quatrains. Wordsworth echoes this usage with his "Elegiac Stanzas," a series of heroic quatrains written in 1807.

One excellent example of Smith's use and revision of the sonnet tradition is Sonnet 15 ("Where the green leaves exclude the summer beam"), one of several described as "From Petrarch." In Smith's verse, repetition of sounds binds lines together and establishes rhythm at least as much as the meter. While "bend as balmy breezes blow" (l. 2) may seem a bit too alliterative, the balance is better in what follows: "the lucid stream / . . . is heard to flow" (ll. 3–4) with "liquid lapse" (l. 3). The lapse/laps pun and repeated stress on *l* words work together with other aural effects to create a wavelike, languid rhythm suited to the dream vision it sets up. At times Smith may focus on sound to the detriment of meter. In the first line of Sonnet XV, for example, "Green" and "leaves" both take sufficient stress that it is better to read "Where the" as a pyrrhic foot and "green leaves" as a spondee. On this reading, the line is accentual pentameter rather than iambic. Whether Smith's frequent use of this effect (replacing a pair of iambs with a pyrrhic and a spondee) is a weakness or an innovation is a matter of critical priorities. Certainly, strict adherents to sonnet form would have to demur at Smith's choice of an alexandrine for the final line of Sonnet XV (and several others).

The importance of Smith's *Elegiac Sonnets* for the ongoing reassessment of the nature and boundaries of English Romanticism has been hinted at already. Stuart Curran, as noted, suggests that Smith is the first writer in what was subsequently called the Romantic tradition, while Daniel Robinson has pointed out the stylistic innovation declared in her title, in a manner that strongly resembles the later *Lyrical Ballads*. The precedent of Smith's appeal to Milton and Shakespeare against the Augustan consensus was not lost on Wordsworth and Coleridge. While Wordsworth's sonnets (such as "LONDON, 1802") show considerably more influence of the Petrarchan model than the English, PERCY BYSSHE SHELLEY's sonnets (such as "TO WORDSWORTH") have much more in common with Smith's "elegiac" sonnets than with Seward's "legitimate" sonnets. JOHN KEATS, perhaps the most highly regarded sonneteer among the later Romantics, wrote sonnets almost exclusively after the English model; Wordsworth, for one, would suggest that Smith deserves much of the credit for this.

In addition to *The Poems of Charlotte Smith*, Stuart Curren's articles "Charlotte Smith and British Romanticism" and "Mothers and Daughters: Poetic Generation(s) in the Eighteenth and Nineteenth Centuries" are indispensable for the student of *Elegiac Sonnets*, as is Daniel Robinson's "*Elegiac Sonnets*: Charlotte Smith's Formal Paradoxy." Brent Raycroft's "From Charlotte Smith to Nehemiah Higginbottom: Revising the Genealogy of the Early Romantic Sonnet" reads Smith against Coleridge and others, thus "writing Charlotte Smith back into the history of the early Romantic sonnet" (Raycroft 363). While the boundaries of English Romanticism remain the subject of intense debate, the place of Smith's *Elegiac Sonnets*, as an early and important member of that larger constellation

where *Songs of Innocence* shines alongside *Lyrical Ballads*, is assured.

See also "PARTIAL MUSE, THE"; "TO THE SOUTH DOWNS."

**Further Reading**
Curran, Stuart. "Charlotte Smith and British Romanticism." *South Central Review* 11, no. 2 (Summer 1994): 66–78.

———. "Mothers and Daughters: Poetic Generation(s) in the Eighteenth and Nineteenth Centuries." *Huntington Library Quarterly* 63, no. 4 (2000): 575–590.

Raycroft, Brent. "From Charlotte Smith to Nehemiah Higginbottom: Revising the Genealogy of the Early Romantic Sonnet." *European Romantic Review* 9, no. 3 (1998): 363–392.

Robinson, Daniel. "*Elegiac Sonnets*: Charlotte Smith's Formal Paradoxy." *Papers on Language and Literature* 39, no. 2 (Spring 2003): 185–220.

———. "Reviving the Sonnet: Women Romantic Poets and the Sonnet Claim." *European Romantic Review* 6, no. 1 (Summer 1995): 98–127.

Smith, Charlotte, *The Poems of Charlotte Smith*. Edited by Stuart Curran. New York: Oxford University Press, 1993.

Weisman, Karen A. "Form and Loss in Charlotte Smith's *Elegiac Sonnets*." *Wordsworth Circle* 33, no. 1 (Winter 2002): 23–27.

—Peter Epps

## "Elegy Written in a Country Church-Yard"
### Thomas Gray (1751)

"Elegy Written in a Country Church-Yard" is a meditative and didactic poem in heroic quatrains written by THOMAS GRAY. It was published in 1751, but Gray is said to have begun writing it some years earlier following the death of his close friend, Richard West, in 1742. Early praise came from Samuel Johnson, who said: "The *Church-Yard* abounds with images which find a mirror in every mind, and with sentiments to which every bosom returns an echo" (II. 418).

"Elegy" begins with an anonymous speaker entering a deserted country churchyard. As dusk falls, he meditates on questions of mortality, fame, and the lives of the rural poor; he celebrates their simple lives, which consist of the happiness of work and family. The speaker concludes that, in death, everyone is alike despite differences in class and birth. He praises the villagers who are buried here while contemplating whether there are any famous occupants ("mute inglorious Milton," "Some Cromwell" [ll. 59, 60]). He ends with an epitaph for himself, in which he reveals his anxiety about his poetic fame after his own death.

"Elegy" is composed in the heroic quatrain, also known as the elegiac stanza. This is a four-line stanza in lines of iambic pentameter, rhyming *abab*. The slow, stately pace created by this rhyme scheme confers a dignity on the poem itself, one that befits the subject of human mortality. Gray also uses the favored 18th-century literary device of personification, also known as conferring human characteristics to abstractions. Examples are "Chill Penury" (l. 51), "Flattery" (l. 44), and "Honour" (l. 43). Onomatopoeia, or the use of words to imitate sounds, is another poetic device used. Examples are "tolls" and "knell" (l. 1), both suggesting the ominous sound of a bell rung slowly, often to commemorate a funeral; and "cool sequester'd vale" (l. 75), a skilful evocation of greenness and shade. Alliteration, the repetition of consonants or stressed syllables, is also used many times, heightening the poem's aural quality. Examples are "haply some hoary-headed swain" (l. 97) and "listless length at noontide" (l. 103). Such devices give the "Elegy" a particularly sonorous quality that, in turn, made it a favorite for recitation among schoolchildren in the 19th and early-20th century.

"Elegy" works as a memento mori, a Latin phrase meaning "Remember that you are mortal." Throughout the poem, the speaker reminds the reader that death is inevitable and cares little for social distinctions. The use of the word *elegy* in the title is revealing: Whose elegy is this? The speaker does not appear to know the dead; this is one reason why he hypothesizes who they might be. At one level it commemorates everyone who is dead, while another reading would suggest that it is a lament for the rural poor. Finally, it could be an elegy for the poet's own mortality, both corporeal as well as in poetic reputation.

The choice of a churchyard is also important to understanding Gray's poetic intent. A churchyard is a boundary, or a liminal space between one form of existence and another, namely life and death. The fact that this is a country churchyard underlines the boundary between city and country, and between the hollow pleasures of a city existence and the simple joys of the country. Also, the poem begins at dusk, itself the boundary between "parting day" and nightfall.

In terms of genre, "Elegy" can be classified as a pastoral elegy. Celebrated examples in this genre include JOHN MILTON's "Lycidas" (1637) and PERCY BYSSHE SHELLEY's "Adonais" (1821). In a typical pastoral elegy, the poet's lament is expressed against the background of a pastoral scene, generally involving nymphs, shepherds, and swains. Nature laments with the poet, who is also accompanied by a procession of mourners. Gray uses many of these conventions, especially the choice of a rural setting, the reference to the old man as a "hoary-headed swain," and a rustic muse who creates epitaphs for the dead.

"Elegy" also works within many of the conventions of the georgic, a genre of didactic poetry celebrating rural life and work. Lines 25–32, in particular, bemoan that the dead are bereft from the simple pleasures of work, such as plowing the fields, that constitute "the short and simple annals of the poor."

Finally, "Elegy written in a Country Church-Yard" ends with a reflection on the place of poetry and the role of the poet. The speaker imagines that he is buried in the same churchyard, remembered only by the "hoary-headed swain." At one level, Gray's anxiety about his own poetic reputation is projected here. By asking the reader to remember the speaker, Gray may be requesting that his poetry not be forgotten after death. Just as the speaker of the "Elegy" has been "mindful of th' unhonour'd dead" (l. 93), Gray asks that the reader remember his poetry even if it does not achieve posthumous fame. His own literary career was not particularly productive, and his published work consists of only about a thousand lines of writing. From the poem's epitaph is clear that he perceived himself as "a youth to fortune and to fame unknown," not knowing that the "Elegy" would outlive him and ensure his poetic fame for centuries.

"Elegy" is notable for bridging the gap between the didacticism of neo-Augustan poetry and the individualism and emotional quality of Romanticism. By focusing on obscure villagers ("rude Forefathers of the hamlet" [l. 16]) and the death of an anonymous author, "Elegy" centers on the celebration of the unknown and uncelebrated individual who later became qualified as "Romantic." Gray's perfect phrasing and measured quatrains are exemplary of 18th-century poetry, but the inner emotions he examines are typically Romantic. As such, "Elegy written in a Country Church-Yard" is a product of a unique historical moment and straddles two literary periods with panache.

## Further Reading

Hutchings, Bill, and William Ruddick, eds. *Thomas Gray: Contemporary Essays.* Liverpool, Eng.: Liverpool University Press, 1993.

Johnson, Samuel. *The Lives of the English Poets.* 2 vols. London: J. F. Dove, 1826.

Kaul, Suvir. *Thomas Gray and Literary Authority: A Study in Ideology and Poetics.* Stanford, Calif.: Stanford University Press, 1992.

Mack, Robert L. *Thomas Gray: A Life.* New Haven, Conn.: Yale University Press, 2000.

Sells, Arthur Lytton. *Thomas Gray: His Life and Works.* Boston: Allen & Unwin, 1980.

—Devjani Roy

## Emigrants, The  Charlotte Smith  (1793)

In *The Emigrants*, CHARLOTTE SMITH meditates on the ramifications of exile, for both the French exiles arriving on British soil and an unjust British society, in this blank-verse epic written in two parts, which she called books. The first book, set on the Sussex cliffs overlooking the English channel in November 1792, chronicles the arrival of these emigrants, focusing on six emblematic figures ranging from an ambitious priest mourning the riches and promotion he lost as a result of the FRENCH REVOLUTION to the deposed nobility, including a mother who is "lost in melancholy thought" as she looks back, literally and figura-

tively, to her homeland. Smith argues for British tolerance and compassion for these figures victimized by the REVOLUTION, reflecting a hope that the egalitarian ideals championed by revolutionaries might inspire brotherhood in a British populace that typically reviled the French.

Book 2 opens on the same Sussex cliffs several months later and reflects the hopelessness associated with the Reign of Terror for those who sympathized with the Revolution. The emigrants are no longer the focus, as the speaker begins to articulate the personal connections between the injustices felt in the world and the institutional injustices embedded in British society. In verses often seen as almost completely autobiographical, the speaker invokes and subverts typical sources of Romantic solace, especially nature and the idyllic country life, "where youthful dreams / See the Arcadia that Romance describes" (ii, 177–78). Smith argues that Nature can have no power to recompense the "Woes such as these" resulting from the "Pride, Oppression, Avarice, and Revenge" (ii, 434) of a selfish society unwilling to care for its own. The speaker criticizes imperial policy, war, rural poverty, and a whole host of other social ills that plague Britain, carefully asserting that, if not amended, such an environment may lead to rebellion as well.

Smith's aggressive commentary on politics, economics, and social norms places her within a tradition of the female poet, according to Susan Wolfson, who traces how Smith both situates herself within and subverts a long tradition of male British poetry. Reworking imagery used by JOHN MILTON, Alexander Pope, and other similarly canonized male poets, Smith argues for a place within that canon while also demonstrating a deferential respect for them, as evidenced by her effusive preface dedicated to the poet WILLIAM COWPER. Wolfson concentrates on how Smith's gendered depiction of war, with the "widow and the orphan's peril" at its center, "brings the 'male' world of warfare into the 'female' world of the home" (Wolfson 53). Michael Wiley argues that Smith depicts the emigrants, and society at large, as a group that must move beyond institutionally inscribed borders and "reorient themselves according to the national-political geography" (57) that she presents within *The Emigrants* (Wiley ). Smith's consistent call for an England characterized by the values of freedom, peace, and equality once espoused by the French Revolution elevates *The Emigrants* to the realms of Romantic educational, political, economic, and social philosophic thought, a position rarely attributed to works written by women.

## Further Reading

Smith, Charlotte Turner. *The Emigrants: A Poem, in Two Books.* London: T. Cadell, 1793.

Wolfson, Susan J. "Charlotte Smith's *Emigrants:* Forging Connections at the Borders of a Female Tradition." *Huntington Library Quarterly: Studies in English and American History and Literature* 63, no. 4 (2000): 509–546.

Wiley, Michael. "The Geography of Displacement and Replacement in Charlotte Smith's *The Emigrants.*" *European Romantic Review* 17, no. 1 (January 2006): 55–68.

—Caralyn Bolte

## *Emma*  Jane Austen  (1815)

*Emma*, JANE AUSTEN's penultimate and arguably most complex and artistically satisfying novel, is centered on the perceptions and sensibilities of Emma Woodhouse. Readers live in Emma's consciousness, eavesdrop on her thoughts and feelings, and see through Emma's eyes what she sees—or what she should have seen. And what a heroine she is: imaginative, playful, and well-intentioned, but also snobbish, vain, willful, and occasionally inconsiderate and hurtful. Emma has grown up "spoiled" by a governess whose "mildness of temper had hardly allowed her to impose any restraint" (Austen 2005, 3) and an extraordinarily inactive and withdrawn father. Austen famously declared that she "was going to take a heroine whom no one but myself will much like"; instead, of course, generations of readers have fallen in love with Emma. Indeed, critics such as Tony Tanner, Lionel Trilling, Claudia Johnson, Nancy Armstrong, and Marilyn Butler have each advanced sophisticated arguments as to why readers love Emma. Perhaps the best and simplest explanation is that Austen's artful use of free indirect speech promotes a reader's identification with Emma; thus, her weaknesses, fears, and triumphs become our own. It becomes apparent that Emma simply cannot help herself, that her barbed playfulness is not fundamentally malicious, and that she feels honest remorse when she does wrong. At a deeper level, readers perceive and sympathize with the underlying boredom and emptiness at the heart of Emma's life; she meddles in part because she does not have anything else to do. Card and supper parties with her father and village women do not constitute a meaningful life.

Emma is, indeed, a failed leading lady in village society. By virtue of her wealth and position she should be the social leader in Highbury. She desires and asserts the prestige of that position, but she is uncomfortable with that role and frequently neglects her community responsibilities. Other Austen novels focus more on familial interactions, but it is *Emma* that best embodies Austen's declaration that "three or four families in a country village is the very thing to work on" (Austen 1995, 275). In *Emma* one sees the intersection of a range of social roles and characters: emerging medical and legal professionals (Mr. Perry, John Knightly), trade families reaching for gentry status (the Coles and the Westons), upward striving clergy (the Eltons), prosperous yeomanry (the Martins), a girl of uncertain parentage (Harriet Smith), a genteel spinster (Miss Bates), an impoverished governess (Jane Fairfax), an impulsive and not quite solid scion of wealth (Frank Churchill), and the lord of the manor (Mr. Knightly). Interactions with Emma define these supporting characters and, in turn, establish Emma's own character.

Indeed, *Emma* is an implicit study of woman's roles in early 19th-century England. Earlier Austen heroines faced the question of whom they should marry, but nowhere else in Austen is there a fundamental questioning as to what women should *be*. Should Harriet Smith be a genteel hanger-on, or is it more meritorious to be a farmer's wife? Emma—wealthy, talkative, and indolent—stands in direct contrast to the poor, quiet, and industrious Jane Fairfax, and various characters, including Emma herself, note and ponder this contrast. The "mommy" role of Emma's sister, Isabella, seems somewhat flat and unfulfilling, but is clearly preferable to that of the name-dropping and social-climbing Mrs. Elton. And Miss Bates, simultaneously admirable in her impecunious integrity and friendship and a point of fun in her wandering volubility, reminds us of the difficult fate of unmarried women who serve as social glue in their communities.

True to Austen's didactic instincts, *Emma* is concerned with how one should behave. Action is typically followed by reflection: Emma takes up Harriet Smith, and in a following chapter Mr. Knightly and Mrs. Weston offer contrasting opinions of Emma's behavior; Emma induces Harriet to turn down Mr. Martin, and Mr. Knightly and Emma subsequently argue about the wisdom of the action; Frank Churchill sends letters of apology for his actions, and Emma and Mr. Knightly present their own character assessments based on these letters; Emma famously insults Miss Bates, and Mr. Knightly's rebuke and her own self-recriminations follow. We, as readers, implicitly provide a second level of judgment as we judge the judgers.

The novel's underlying symmetrical architecture supports the sequence of action and reflection. Chapters typically end with epigrammatic last lines that reflect character judgments—for example, Mr. Knightly's comment that "a man of six or seven-and-twenty can take care of himself" (Book 1, chapter 1), or Emma's assessment that Harriet "might very well be conquered by Mr. Elton's admiration" (Book 1, chapter 4). Indeed, chapters of action often alternate with chapters of assessment and reflection, as with the assessments of Emma's and Frank Churchill's behavior mentioned above. And at the highest level the novel is similarly organized into three books of 18 or 19 chapters: Book 1 records a cycle of action, misjudgment, and remorse primarily concerning Emma's misjudgments regarding Mr. Elton and Harriet; Book 2 develops Emma's delusions and misjudgments regarding Frank Churchill and Jane Fairfax; and Book 3 psychologically culminates with the resolution of Mr. Knightly's and Emma's mutual misunderstandings as to each other's romantic inclinations. Indeed, Emma's repeated cycles of character misjudgment, improper action, understanding, and repentance challenge the traditional path to learning of early Jane Austen heroines, such as Catherine Morland, Elizabeth

Bennet, and Marianne Dashwood, who progress in self-knowledge and in control of their own behavior as they reach toward marriage. Marilyn Butler, for one, argues that Emma has traversed the same trajectory. But perhaps Emma, already a confirmed repeat offender, will instead irrepressibly continue to cyclically misjudge, err, and feel remorse: to continue to be, in Mr. Knightly's words, "faultless in spite of all her faults" (Austen 2005, 472). One feels that she is simply too vital and too charmingly imaginative and mischievous to defer to Mr. Knightly's wisdom and judgment for long. It is this continued "likeable" human fallibility that arguably makes her Austen's most human leading lady.

See also MANSFIELD PARK; PERSUASION; PRIDE AND PREJUDICE; SENSE AND SENSIBILITY.

**Further Reading**

Austen, Jane. *Emma.* Eds. Richard Cronin and Dorothy McMillan. Cambridge: Cambridge University Press, 2005.

———. *Jane Austen's Letters.* 3rd ed. Edited by Deirdre Le Faye. Oxford: Oxford University Press, 1995.

Butler, Marilyn. *Jane Austen and the War of Ideas.* Oxford: Clarendon Press, 1975.

Tanner, Tony. *Jane Austen.* Cambridge, Mass.: Harvard University Press, 1986.

—Gary Simons

## empire

The Romantic period saw the rise of a series of powerful European empires that dominated territories throughout the world. The legacy of these empires continues to be felt in the geopolitics of the 21st century.

Before 1760, as Linda Colley notes in *Captives,* "the major European powers and their overseas settlers had rarely viewed empire as something of which people of their sort, Christian, Western, and white, were uniquely capable" (Colley 171). But the massive colonial gains and losses of the Seven Years' War in Europe (1756–63), combined with the decline of the old Ottoman [Turkish], Mughal, and Chinese empires, led the European powers to become newly aware of the potential gains that could be made by their merchants and military forces. Believing that their time for imperial conquest had come, European nations focused on expanding their international territorial acquisitions. The British Empire was one of the largest and most powerful European empires to emerge. It is important to remember, however, that during this period Great Britain was in constant competition with other imperial powers—France, Spain and the Netherlands, among others—as well as with other countries, including the United States, which harbored imperial ambitions of its own. Discussions of empire circulated internationally and had relevance to more than just the citizens of the British Empire.

Britain leaped to the forefront of the European imperial powers during the Seven Years' War, in which the nation engaged in a global struggle with Spain and France. Its excellent navy allowed it to extend its military power more effectively than its opponents, and by the conclusion of the war it had captured a huge amount of territory: Florida, Canada, West Africa, Grenada, and Bengal are just a few of its new acquisitions. Ironically, the Seven Years' War also indirectly cost Britain its greatest colony: the American War of Independence was triggered, in part, by colonists' refusal to pay the taxes Britain levied in order to pay down its war debt.

Before the American Revolution, Britain's empire had been primarily a maritime and commercial one. Its focus was on establishing trade outposts rather than conquering territory, and much of Britain's imperial expansion was driven not by its state government but by chartered companies like the East India Company. Britons were taught to take pride in their Protestant empire, which was portrayed as standing for liberty, and despise what the historian Maya Jasanoff refers to as "the land empires of Catholic Europe, 'the Orient,' and even ancient Rome, which were widely critiqued as tyrannical, despotic and autocratic" (Jasanoff 10). But the territorial gains made in the Seven Years' War transformed Britain into a land empire, while the rebellion of the American colonies challenged Britons' self-image as the empire of liberty. The AMERICAN REVOLUTION also created in Britain a new appreciation for the capacity of military units to control colonial possessions.

The FRENCH REVOLUTION (1789) triggered a new series of wars between Britain and France, which would result in Britain climbing to the top of the European imperial hierarchy. As Jasanoff notes, the Napoleonic Wars were explicitly imperial: "For the French revolutionaries, conquest formed part of an imperial *mission civilistrice*, or 'civilizing mission,' designed to spread republican and Enlightenment ideals across Europe" (120). Britons, on the other hand, saw their role in the war as less of a civilizing mission and more of a restoration of order; however, in order to fight the French, they had to draw on the resources of the British colonies as never before.

By the end of the Napoleonic Wars, Britain had not only acquired more overseas territory but also had built a stronger identification between its citizens and the empire. By 1850 the British Empire looked very much like one of the autocratic land empires Britons used to criticize. A transcontinental entity that ruled millions of foreigners in areas won by military conquest, the British Empire of 1850 covered a quarter of the globe and claimed one in five people in the world as its subject. It would also "come to turn domination over non-white, non-Christian peoples into its mission and justification" (Jasanoff 121), a goal that had not been stressed in 18th-century conceptions of empire.

Not all Britons were happy with the growth of their empire. Maintaining Britain's overseas territories came at a high financial and military cost. Britain did not have a large population and thus had to make up its numbers by impressing (kidnapping and forcing) British men with some nautical ability to serve as sailors in its navy, though this ceased in 1815. Citizens affected by impressments understandably objected to them and to the colonial wars they saw as causing unnecessary harm to Britons. Imperial practices also came under attack from moralists who attacked the cruelty of such economic systems as the African slave trade (see SLAVERY). African slaves were bought with the wealth generated by Britain's colonies and were shipped to the West Indies, where they were forced to produce still more goods for British trade. Slavery thus played an important role in the maintenance of Britain's imperial system until its abolition in 1833.

Discussions of empire in relation to Romantic literature have been guided by works such as Edward Said's *Orientalism* (1978), which argues that Western texts about the East are permeated with imperial biases that legitimate domination of Eastern peoples. These texts portray the East as an irrational, weak, despotic and feminized "Other" and contrast it with a rational, strong, masculine West that provides the proper standard for civilization. Said also wrote *Culture and Imperialism* (1993), which examines the way in which seemingly domestic novels such as JANE AUSTEN's *MANSFIELD PARK* are implicated in the British imperial system. Other works that examine the relationship between Romantic literature and empire include Saree Makdisi's *Romantic Imperialism: Universal Empire and the Culture of Modernity* (1998), which argues that Romanticism itself is a response to imperialism; and Katie Trumpener's *Bardic Nationalism: The Romantic Novel and the British Empire* (1997), which analyzes the imperial role of fiction that celebrated cultural memory in England's "British colonies" (Scotland and Ireland) and its colonies overseas.

**Further Reading**

Colley, Linda. *Captives.* New York: Pantheon Books, 2002.

Fulford, Tim, and Peter J. Kitson. *Romanticism and Colonialism: Writing and Empire, 1780–1830.* Cambridge: Cambridge University Press, 1998.

Jasanoff, Maya. *Edge of Empire: Lives, Culture, and Conquest in the East, 1750–1850.* New York: Knopf, 2005.

Makdisi, Saree. *Romantic Imperialism: Universal Empire and the Culture of Modernity.* Cambridge: Cambridge University Press, 1998.

Said, Edward W. *Orientalism.* New York: Vintage Books, 1979

———. *Culture and Imperialism.* New York: Vintage Books, 1994.

Trumpener, Katie. *Bardic Nationalism: The Romantic Novel and the British Empire.* Princeton, N.J.: Princeton University Press, 1997.

—Siobhan Carrol

## *Endymion* John Keats (1818)

In *Endymion*, JOHN KEATS retells the classical love story between the shepherd Endymion and the immortal goddess of the moon, Cynthia. The poem, which consists of four books of approximately 1,000 lines each, is written rhyming couplets of iambic pentameter. In Book 1, following a joyous celebration of the god Pan, the despondent Endymion tells his sister, Peona, the dream he has had of an immortal lover and his desire to find her. In Book 2, supernatural forces guide Endymion to Venus, the goddess of love, and Adonis, a mortal. The couple are engaged in an immortal/mortal love affair, and they encourage the shepherd. By the end of the book, Endymion kisses an immortal woman, though her identity is not revealed to him because it is dark. The third book finds Endymion underneath the ocean, where he meets Glaucus, who relates his own story of lost love, after which Glaucus is reunited with his love, Scylla. Together, they take Endymion to the palace of Neptune, ruler of the oceans, who, like Venus, encourages Endymion to be patient. The final book introduces the Indian Maid, a mortal woman with whom Endymion falls in love and eventually chooses over the immortal lover he has been searching for since the beginning of the poem. After he does so, the Indian Maid transforms into the goddess Cynthia, and the lovers finally unite with a kiss.

*Endymion* begins with the famous line "A thing of beauty is a joy forever," and the poem explores this concept as it relates to the beauty of love. At the same time, the poem contrasts the values of mortal and immortal life. In Book 1, Endymion removes himself from the earthly festival of nature and tells his sister that he longs for his immortal lover, as that relationship must surpass any mortal love as well as anything on earth. Measured against the divine, Endymion believes "all the pleasant hues / Of heaven and earth" (1:691) fade in comparison. As Endymion journeys, he discovers the enduring nature of love through both his encounter with Venus and Adonis as well as with Glaucus, who has waited over 1,000 years to be reunited with his beloved. Endymion's growth displays itself in the final book when he chooses the mortal love of the Indian Maid: He recognizes that the attainable pleasures of the world offer more than divine pleasures that remain beyond the grasp of humans. The Maid's transformation into Cynthia suggests that the human acceptance of earthly beauty leads to immortality, thus tying Endymion's story to the concept introduced in the poem's first line.

*Endymion* is in part a pastoral poem, as evidenced by the shepherd-hero, the rustic setting of Book 1, and the focus on natural beauty, especially the moon. Additionally, the poem shares many aspects of an epic poem in that it includes supernatural forces, a questing hero, and elevated language. Finally, Keats's choice of Endymion and his interactions with gods and goddesses exemplifies the revived Romantic interest in classical culture and its myths.

See also *SAPPHO AND PHAON*.

**Further Reading**

Keats, John. *Complete Poems.* Edited by Jack Stillinger. Harvard University Press, 1978.

—Ken Bugajski

## *England and Spain* Felicia Hemans (1808)

FELICIA HEMANS's second book, published when she was 14, was as negatively reviewed as her first publication, *Poems* (1808). A long political poem, *England and Spain, or, Valour and Patriotism* expresses Hemans's adolescent interest in the political state of her nation during the Napoleonic Wars. Despite the unfeminine nature of her engagement with politics, Hemans justifies her views in a letter to her aunt, dated December 18, 1808, as stemming from her concern for her two brothers and prospective husband, who were fighting in the war, and her sympathy for "the noble Spaniards" whose freedom the French have breeched (quoted in Chorley 18–19). The poem also represents her initial support for the political and social conditions of the early 19th century, which she indirectly criticizes in her subsequent publications.

In her poem Hemans repeatedly personifies freedom and directly addresses it while condemning the French for ruining it. She denounces the despotism France has been exercising in the early 19th century with its attempts to dominate not only Europe but the whole world. The poem repeatedly juxtaposes NAPOLEON BONAPARTE's destruction and violence with British and Spanish bravery. Hemans's descriptions give a detailed account of past European glories, viewing the present heroism as comparable to legendary heroes such as "Wallace" and "Tell" (l. 38). However, these praises implicitly favor the English for their comparability to the ancient Romans, who instilled peace and prosperity (l. 71), and to the brave Spartans (l. 73). Hemans also praises older European heroes—Alfred the Great, Richard the Lionheart, the Spanish hero of Granada Gonsalvo, King Ferdinand V of Spain, and others—and compares their noble actions to those of British and Spanish patriots. She supports her views by describing the qualities of British soldiers and their noble motives of defending their homeland and instilling global freedom. She also praises the honest means by which the British have gained their goods, through "Commerce" (l. 93) rather than through the dishonest means of French tyrants who unfairly dominated other nations and appropriated their exotic goods. She ends the poem with praying for and blessing "British heroes" (l. 549). Despite PERCY BYSSHE SHELLEY's mistaken disappointment at her supporting "war" in his letter of March 13, 1811 (Hermans 2002, 20), Hemans actually devotes the final three stanzas to addressing "sweet Peace" (l. 567) again and begs it to return, denouncing the prevalent violence.

An interesting digression in Hemans's poem on war and freedom is her sixth stanza, in which she personifies genius as an ethereal being that lives in the skies (perhaps heaven). She begs it to descend to earth and instill its noble existence, rather indirectly emphasizing her wish for peace, which she repeats more explicitly at the end of the poem. She indirectly raises genius as a substitute for the destructive worldly ambition that unfortunately prevails. Hermans depicts these political views again, but more eloquently and embedded within a domestic content, in the title poem of her next successful publication, *The Domestic Affections* (1812).

**Further Reading**

Aaron, Jane. "'Saxon, Think not All Is Won': Felicia Hemans and the Making of the Britons." *Cardiff*

*Corvey: Reading the Romantic Text* 4 (May 2000). Available online. URL: http://www.cf.ac.uk/encap/journals/corvey/articles/cc04_n01.pdf. Accessed on January 12, 2009.

Chorley, Henry Fothergill. *Memorials of Mrs. Hemans: With Illustrations of Her Literary Character from Her Private Correspondence.* Philadelphia: Carey, Lea & Blanchard, 1836. Available online on Google Books.

Eubanks, Kevin. "Minerva's Veil: Hemans, Critics, and the Construction of Gender." *European Romantic Review* 8, no. 4 (1997): 341–359.

Hemans, Felicia Dorothea Browne. *Felicia Hemans: Selected Poems, Prose, and Letters.* Edited by Gary Kelly. Toronto, Ont.: Broadview Press, 2002.

———. *Poems; England and Spain; Modern Greece. 1808.* Edited by Donald H. Reiman. New York: Garland, 1978.

—Mariam Radhwi

## "England in 1819" Percy Bysshe Shelley
(1819)

"England in 1819" was published in one of the greatest years of literary production in the Romantic era. For PERCY BYSSHE SHELLEY—confirmed idealist, self-asserted atheist, and skeptical revolutionary—it was a year that would engender a series of overtly political works which he had intended for publication in one volume but which, due to the legal foresight of LEIGH HUNT, was not published. Shelley, then in self-exile in Italy, sent the sonnet "England in 1819," one of the works in this collection, to Hunt, his accompanying letter commenting: "What a state England is in! But you will never write politics" (LPBS 2:166). The first 12 lines of the sonnet catalogue that very state.

The first line uses haunting assonance and consonance as well as meter, which resolves at the end of the line to emphasize the fact of King George III's impending death: "Old, made, blind, despised, and dying king" (see MONARCHY). Sometimes loved by his people, but victim of the unfortunate and hereditary disease of porphyria, George III was given to bouts of pain and paralysis as well as fits of madness. Declared unfit to rule, he was

ensconced in Windsor Castle until his passing in 1820. His eldest son, then Prince of Wales ("Prinnie"), began serving as regent in 1811. "Prinnie" was not beloved by his people; rather, he was caricatured and lampooned by a public fed up with his dissipation and hypocrisy in his personal as well as his political life, from his marriage to the Catholic Mrs. Fitzherbert (1785) to his dissolving of that marriage by Parliament on legal grounds in order to assist in his paying off personal debt; his marriage to his cousin, Caroline of Brunswick, and his questionable deportment during that marriage and attempts to divorce her on untenable grounds of adultery—all to the disgust of the English people, who in large part came to her defense in such manner that the case was dismissed. "Prinnie" was no doubt the primary referent in Shelley's sonnet: "Princes, the dregs of their dull race, who flow / Through public scorn—mud from a muddy spring" (ll. 2–3).

Shelley's scorn moved through the king and his son-regent to the ruling class, which he characterized as exerting authority in a manner tantamount to the behaviour of literal blood-suckers who feed off the life of the country until satiated: "Rulers, who neither see nor feel nor know, / But leechlike to their fainting country cling / Till they drop, blind in blood, without a blow" (ll. 4–6). It was this very ruling class who turned a blind eye to the government-incited massacre of not only men but also women and children peaceably demonstrating in St. Peter's Field, Manchester, on August 16, 1819, which the press called the PETERLOO MASSACRE. It is likely that Shelley reacted to news of this event in the lines concerning "An army, whom liberticide and prey / Makes as a two-edged sword to all who wield" (ll. 8–9), indicating that the wielders of the swords could find themselves at the receiving end.

The three lines prior to the closing couplet observe the decay of law and religion, the latter of which he characterizes as "Christless, godless" (l. 11). Laws which both "tempt" and "slay" are both "Golden and sanguine" (l. 10), referring possibly to their draw of money and goods to the drawing of blood. "A senate, Time's worst statute unrepealed—" (l. 12) remains ambiguous due to its syntax. The statute seems to be the appositive of the senate, the body that would create the statute. The statute that remains unrepealed has been commonly thought to refer to Catholic Emancipation, but the scholar James Chandler contests that notion, interpreting it rather as a reference to Parliament as "a form of tyranny posing as a form of self-rule" (30).

Here, after 12 lines rhyming *abababcdcdcc,* the predicate of the sentence ends, and the verb is stated: *are.* All things detailed thus far in the poem "Are graves" (l. 13). And from the death of the king, the draining dregs of his offspring, the dropping off of the leechlike ruling class, the murder of innocents, and the decay of law and religion—the "graves"—a "glorious Phantom may / Burst, to illumine our tempestuous day" (ll. 13–14). The critical attention this poem has received has tended to focus on the word *may* in the penultimate line as indicative of Shelley's doubts concerning the probability of social and political reform. The power and meaning of the closing couplet of this Elizabethan sonnet may be read against his other work of this period. Specifically, Chandler points to Shelley's "An Address to the People on the Death of Princess Charlotte" (1817), in which Shelley writes of a "'glorious Phantom'" which is "'the Spirit of Liberty'" (25).

## Further Reading

Bamford, Samuel. *Passages in the Life of a Radical.* Oxford: Oxford University Press, 1984.

Bennett, Betty T., and Stuart Curran, eds. *Shelley: Poet and Legislator of the World.* Baltimore: Johns Hopkins University Press, 1996.

Bloom, Harold. *The Visionary Company: A Reading of English Romantic Poetry.* Ithaca, N.Y.: Cornell University Press, 1971.

Chandler, James. *England in 1819. The Politics of Literary Culture and the Case of Romantic Historicism.* Chicago: University of Chicago Press, 1998.

Curran, Stuart. *Shelley's Annus Mirabilis: The Maturing of an Epic Vision.* San Marino, Calif.: Huntington Library, 1975.

Reid, Robert. *The Peterloo Massacre.* London: Heinemann, 1989.

Scrivener, Michael. *Radical Shelley: The Philosophical Anarchism and Utopian Thought of Percy Bysshe Shelley.* Princeton, N.J.: Princeton University Press, 1982.

Shelley, Percy Bysshe. *The Complete Poetry of Percy Bysshe Shelley.* Edited by Donald H. Reiman and Neil
Freistat. Baltimore: Johns Hopkins University Press, 2000.

———. *The Letters of Percy Bysshe Shelley.* 2 vols. Edited by Frederick L. Jones. Oxford: Clarendon Press, 1964.

———. *A Philosophical View of Reform, Now Printed for the First Time.* Edited by T. W. Rolleston. London: Oxford University Press, 1920.

———. *The Poetical Works of Percy Bysshe Shelley.* 4 vols. Edited by Mary Shelley. London: Edward Moxon, 1839.

Wasserman, Earl R. *Shelley: A Critical Reading.* Baltimore, Md.: Johns Hopkins University Press, 1971.

—Donna Berliner

## "Eolian Harp, The" Samuel Taylor Coleridge (1796, 1834)

This poem is one of SAMUEL TAYLOR COLERIDGE's famous conversation poems, intimate, blank-verse poems written to close friends about serious subjects but in an informal style (including "THIS LIME-TREE BOWER MY PRISON," "FROST AT MIDNIGHT," and "FEARS IN SOLITUDE"). Coleridge wrote the poem during his engagement to Sara Fricker, and he addresses her directly in the opening stanza as they gaze on the beautiful landscape of Somersetshire. He creates a calm, pensive, pleasant feeling by appealing to the sense of touch (Sarah's "soft cheek"), sight ("white-flowered jasmin" and "the star of eve"), smell ("scents . . . from yon beanfield"), and sound ("the stilly murmur of the distant sea") (ll. 1–11).

At the beginning of the second stanza, Coleridge shifts attention to the Eolian harp, the poem's central trope. Named after the Greek god of wind, Aeolus, Eolian harps are wooden boxes with guitar-like strings that create mystical sounds when the wind blows through them. The first compares the sound of the harp to the voice of a "coy maid" flirting with her lover (l. 16), which suggests that the focus of the poem is romantic love; however, he then compares the harp's sound to "the witchery of sound" that elves make at twilight (ll. 21–22), suggesting that his true interest is the wind's different effects on the harp and how it stimulates the imagination. In lines 26–33 (which Coleridge added in 1817), he becomes more philosophical and compares the wind he had been discussing to the "one life within us and abroad" (l. 27). This life force exists in nature and within each human being and makes it "impossible / not to love all things" (ll. 31–32).

In the third stanza, Coleridge compares himself to the Eolian harp. As he stands on a hill looking into the noonday sunlight with "half-closed" eyes (l. 37), images of nature flow through his mind and stimulate his imagination just as the wind blows through the harp to create a magical sound. At the beginning of stanza 4, he again turns overtly philosophical and speculates that all human beings might be "organic harps" (l. 46) that are inspired by "one intellectual breeze," which is "the Soul of each, and God of All" (ll. 48–49).

However, the "more serious eye" of Sara chastises Coleridge (l. 50), and he abruptly ceases his heretical, pantheistic speculation. She brings him back to a more conventional, Christian mind-set, and he realizes that he has been "vain" in his philosophizing (l. 58), and that he should remember that God through Christ has "saved" and "healed" him, and that he has been blessed with peace, his home, and his "heart-honoured Maid" (ll. 62–65). Coleridge's abrupt shift from metaphysical pantheist as expressed in the first three stanzas to more conventional Christian in the last stanza strikes many readers. Ronald C. Wendling argues that the poem expresses Coleridge's belief that his philosophical thoughts are "potentially enervating" but that humankind needs "human and Christian" love to live life. William Scheuerle asserts, alternatively, that the poem is "not inconsistent" because "Only through a 'Faith that inly feels' can [Coleridge] realize the 'one Life,' which, in turn, will grant him the purity of the selfless loving heart that enables him to find the peace he celebrates at the end of the poem" (Scheuerle 598). Whether or not the conflict is resolved, most readers see the poem as beautifully rendering the struggle between the philosophical and personal sides of Coleridge's world view.

**Further Reading**

Coleridge, Samuel Taylor. *Samuel Taylor Coleridge.* Edited by H. J. Jackson. New York: Oxford University Press, 1985.

Scheuerle, William H. "A Reexamination of Coleridge's 'The Eolian Harp.'" *SEL: Studies in English Literature, 1500–1900* 15, no. 4 (1975): 591–599.

Wendling, Ronald C. "Coleridge and the Consistency of 'The Eolian Harp.'" *Studies in Romanticism* 8 (1968): 26–42.

—Robert C. Hale

## "Epistle to J. Lapraik, an Old Scottish Bard"
### Robert Burns (1786)

The "Epistle to J. Lapraik, an Old Scotch Bard" is one of the most celebrated poems of ROBERT BURNS' first volume, *Poems Chiefly in the Scottish Dialect* (Kilmarnock, 1786), where it was dated "April 1st, 1785." John Lapraik was a tenant farmer imprisoned for debt in Ayr (he was released in 1785) whose poetry (composed in prison) was published in his *Poems on Several Occasions* (1788). Burns's epistolary poem addresses such Romantic issues as the category of "natural" or uneducated genius, and the relationship between the tradition that is available to the self-taught Scots poet with the alternative poetic models provided by the English/neoclassical tradition.

The poem consists of 132 lines of "standard habbie" (stanzas of six lines that are sometimes referred to as "Burns stanzas," in which the first three lines and the fifth contain four stresses and the fourth and sixth lines contain two stresses, with the rhyme scheme *aaabab*). The poem's speaker describes his attendance at a social gathering one Shrove Tuesday evening ("On Fasteneen we had a rockin") when he encounters a song that "thirl'd the heart-strings thro' the breast, / A' to the life" (ll. 16–17); wondering whether it could be by Pope, Steele or Beattie he discovers that it originates from "an odd kind chiel / About *Muirkirk*" (ll. 23–24). Rejecting "a' jargon o' your Schools, / Your Latin names for horns an' stools" (ll. 61–62) the speaker instead implores: "Gie me ae spark o' Nature's fire, / That's a' the learning I desire; / Then tho' I drudge thro' dub an' mire / At pleugh or cart, / My Muse, tho' hamely in attire, / May touch the heart" (ll. 73–79).

Hence, having rejected poets who "Confuse their brains in *Colledge-classes*" (l. 68) and who "think to climb Parnassus / By dint o' Greek!" (ll.

71–72), the poem privileges an alternative tradition possessing the "natural" spark ("spunk") of genius of Allan Ramsay, Robert Fergusson, and Lapraik. This is, then, an expression of the same belief that genius is inherent rather than taught, and it is found in the common and native, inspiring such Romantics as WILLIAM BLAKE, WILLIAM WORDSWORTH, and SAMUEL TAYLOR COLERIDGE. Increasing critical attention has been paid in recent years, however, to the artifice involved in this profession of faith that genius is artless/authentic and to the extent to which even Burns' dialect poems have "standard features" (Fairer 181). Since Burns knew and admired the works of the English poets his speaker seems to reject, and he was an able practitioner of their verse forms, this artifice is perhaps less than surprising.

In the poem, Lapraik is praised as having "ingine" (l. 28)—"genius" or "ingenuity," we would say; the word *genuine* is (in standard English, anyway) from the same etymological root. The speaker wants to be a "real" (l. 86) and "true" (l. 89) friend to Lapraik. Yet while the speaker claims to "hae to learning nae pretence" (l. 51), and the very list of Scots poets in his alternative tradition gives the lie to this. Even the "Burns stanza" in which the poem is written was no such thing but Burns's appropriation of a verse form known as the "standard Habbie," after the piper-poet Habbie Simpson (1550–1620) and popularized by another poet, Robert Sempill (1595–1659).

The poem ends with the speaker's invitations to the addressee to meet with him at "Mauchline Race or Mauchline Fair" and with amiable professions of friendship. Burns included a second poem to Lapraik in *Poems, Chiefly in the Scottish Dialect,* entitled "To the Same" and dated 21st April 1785.

**Further Reading**

Burns, Robert. *Burns: Poems and Songs.* Edited by James Kinsley. London: Oxford University Press, 1969.

Douglas, Hugh. *Robert Burns: The Tinder Heart.* Stroud, Eng.: Sutton Publishing, 1996.

Fairer, David. *English Poetry of the Eighteenth Century, 1700–1789.* Harlow and London: Longman, 2003.

Roe, Nicholas. "Authenticating Robert Burns." *Essays in Criticism* 46 (1996): 195–218.

—Steve Van Hagen

## "Epistle to William Wilberforce" Anna Laetitia Barbauld (1791)

"Epistle to William Wilberforce" is characteristic of ANNA LAETITIA BARBAULD's political poems, in which she speaks from her position as a Dissenter to criticize the establishment's moral failings. The poem pays tribute to the work of the reform campaigner William Wilberforce and his supporters, just after the parliamentary defeat of their bill to abolish slavery in 1791. Like WILLIAM BLAKE, Barbauld takes the stance of an Old Testament prophet, fusing poetic inspiration with moral indignation (the "muse" of line 11) and denouncing the nation in a tone of despair and disgust. Her choice of form reflects her classical education, using the heroic style with elevated language, heroic couplets, and Hellenic references (for example, Astrea, the goddess of justice) to lend authority to her subject. Yet she redefines the "heroic" by celebrating effort rather than attainment and humane self-restraint rather than conquest. While some contemporaries regarded such a tone as inappropriately masculine, the literary historian Marlon B. Ross regards her stance as feminine in that, like HANNAH MORE, she considers it a woman's duty "to bring her finer sentiment to bear in order to restrain the ruder tendencies of man's conquesting desire" (Ross 221–222).

Although many women wrote for the abolitionist cause, this is not actually an antislavery poem. That slavery is a gross injustice is taken for granted, not argued. Barbauld's purpose is to indict the values of a nation that has failed to amend this evil and to prophesy its doom. She points out the failure of appeals to sympathy for the slave's 'groans' and 'constant tear', (ll. 5, 6) whose effect is dulled by the deep-seated cynicism of those with vested interests in the trade. Barbauld condemns not racism but greed as the root of slavery, an aggressive materialism that extends to Britain's colonial exploitation of India ("the gay east" [l. 86]) and provides the female domestic consumer with luxury goods, much like the slave owners themselves. Barbauld was unusual among abolition writers in thus linking the slave trade to Britain's wider imperial project (see EMPIRE). In a move anticipating much later critics of empire, Barbauld points to the savagery at the heart of a civilization that measures progress only by material criteria, as "the Scythian and the Sybarite" (l. 62) monstrously unite in the greedy exploiter. There is a strong puritan tone to her condemnation of the desire for exotic luxuries, contrasted with the "sober pomp of elder days" (l. 95) and its civic virtues. This adds a classical flavor to the Christian self-denial enjoined in the "palm" (l. 113). Barbauld is also concerned for the erosion of national identity as the ancient British values of "Simplicity," "Independence," and "Freedom" (ll. 100, 102, 103) are threatened by the country's new dependence on "foreign wealth" (l. 104).

In keeping with her Unitarian theology, the doom that Barbauld foresees is delivered, not by supernatural intervention but through the natural logic of colonial operations. She prophesies the moral and cultural decay of the oppressor, by which Africa and India are avenged. Her use of the terms *contagion* and *corruption* (ll. 87, 96) has been read by some critics as "xenophobic," promoting a notion of "racial contamination" (Richards on 463). But Barbauld nowhere suggests that these are qualities of the enslaved or colonized peoples. The corrupt values operating in the colonies spread back into the heart of the nation itself.

**Further Reading**

Barbauld, Anna Letitia. *Anna Letitia Barbauld: Selected Poetry and Prose.* Edited by William McCarthy and Elizabeth Kraft. Peterborough, Ont., and Orchard Park, N.Y.: Broadview Press, 2001.

Ellison, Julie. "The Politics of Fancy in the Age of Sensibility." In *Re-Visioning Romanticism: British Women Writers, 1776–1837,* edited by Carol Shiner Wilson and Joel Haefner, 228–255. Philadelphia: University of Pennsylvania Press, 1994.

Richardson, Alan. "Slavery and Romantic Writing." In *A Companion to Romanticism,* edited by Duncan Wu, 460–469. Malden, Mass.: Blackwell, 1998.

Ross, Marlon B. *The Contours of Masculine Desire: Romanticism and the Rise of Women's Poetry.* New York: Oxford University Press, 1989.

—Rebecca Styler

## epistolary fiction

The epistolary novel is told in a series of letters written by one or more characters. Critics distinguish between three different narrative forms of epistolary fiction: Monologic epistolary writing presents the letters of one character; the dialogic epistolary novel consists of the correspondence between two characters; and polylogic epistolary fiction juxtaposes the letters of three or more characters, frequently adding suspense by documenting the correspondence between both the sympathetic protagonists and the villains.

The tradition of epistolary fiction can be traced back to classic literature—for instance, to Ovid's series of verse letters *Heroides* and to the letters of Cicero, Pliny, and Seneca. An important early example of epistolary fiction is the sentimental novel *Cárcel de amor* (*Prison of Love*, 1492) by the Castilian writer Diego de San Pedro (ca. 1437–ca. 1498). The plot of the novel is propelled by the love letters between the protagonists Leriano and Laureola. San Pedro's work ends on a rather tragic note, which is, however, extremely effective in magnifying the pivotal importance of the epistle in the lovers' relationship: Separated from Laureola, Leriano commits suicide by drinking a potion made of his lover's shredded letters.

One of the earliest English epistolary novels that gained enormous popularity was Aphra Behn's (1640–89) *Love Letters between a Nobleman and his Sister* (1684). Behn's three-volume novel, set against the backdrop of the Monmouth Rebellion (a 1685 attempt to overthrow King James II), deftly experiments with the formal possibilities of the genre. While the first volume consists entirely of the exchange of letters between Sylvia and her lover and brother-in-law Philander, the second and third volume insert a panoply of letters of different authors into a third-person narrative that chronicles the fortunes of the lovers and contemporaneous historical events. Behn's second volume especially exploits the multi-perspectivity of the epistolary genre by introducing various forgeries, frauds, and interceptions that heighten the story's suspense.

Epistolary fiction rose to unprecedented acclaim and popularity in the 18th century, when writers of diverse literary backgrounds adapted the genre to various purposes and different topical concerns. Probably the most famous 18th-century author of epistolary fiction is Samuel Richardson (1689–1761), who wrote, among other sentimental epistolary novels, the extremely successful *Pamela: Or, Virtue Rewarded* (1740); *Clarissa: Or, the History of a Young Lady* (1748); and *The History of Sir Charles Grandison* (1753). In contrast to the latter two novels, which include letters of several characters, *Pamela* focuses exclusively on the diary entries and letters the eponymous heroine sends to her parents. The novel germinated in a manual of "familiar letters" in which Richardson provided model letters for everyday purposes. Among formal recommendations, introductory letters, and consolation epistles he also included a set of letters sketching the story of a virtuous and naive servant girl who successfully struggles against her master's resourceful attempts to seduce her until he makes her his legitimate wife. The larger scope of the epistolary novel *Pamela,* which sprang from these letters, allowed Richardson to develop the thoughts, doubts, hopes, and uncertainties of his eponymous heroine with great psychological realism. Pamela's letters are explicitly private and personal, and they produce the illusion of intimacy between character and reader. Richardson amplified the dramatic immediacy of his narrative by reducing the intermission between Pamela's experiences and her writing as much as possible. Henry Fielding (1707–54) famously burlesqued this technique of writing "to the moment" in his parody *Shamela* (1741), which shows the heroine in bed, scrawling on the paper, "I hear him coming at the Door," as her master enters the room.

*Clarissa* is widely regarded as Richardson's masterpiece. Besides four major letter writers—the long-suffering protagonist Clarissa Harlow and her friend Anna Howe against the libertine rake Lovelace and his associate, John Belford—Richardson brings to life a huge group of socially diverse minor correspondents. Generations of critics have celebrated the novel for its complex treatment of issues of class and gender, authority and trauma. However, while Richardson's *Sir Charles Grandison* was a perennial favourite with JANE AUSTEN (1775–1817) and George Eliot (1819–80), modern readers and critics have been less enthusiastic about his didactic story concerning the love trials of the notoriously good and gallant protagonist.

Although the epistolary form, which grants unparalleled access to the feelings and thoughts of the characters, had a particular affinity with the sentimental novel, the genre was appropriated by a wide spectrum of writers. Tobias Smollett's (1721–71) picaresque and highly comical *The Expedition of Humphry Clinker* (1771), for instance, records a family journey from Wales to Scotland in a series of 82 letters by six different letter writers. FANNY BURNEY's (1752–1840) EVELINA (1778), consisting of the letters of the title heroine to her clerical mentor, anticipates the novel of manners that would be popularized by Austen and MARIA EDGEWORTH (1767–1849) a few decades later. Epistolary fiction enjoyed similar success on the Continent. JEAN-JACQUES ROUSSEAU's (1712–78) *Julie, ou la nouvelle Héloïse* (*Julie, or the New Heloise,* 1761), Pierre Choderlos de Laclos's (1741–1803) *Les liaisons dangereuses* (*Dangerous Liaisons,* 1782), and JOHANN WOLFGANG VON GOETHE's (1749–1832) *Die Leiden des Junges Werther* (*The SORROWS OF YOUNG WERTHER,* 1774) were immediate best sellers and achieved wide dissemination beyond their countries of origin.

Toward the end of the 18th century, the popularity of epistolary fiction gradually waned. Austen experimented with the epistolary form in her juvenile work (see LOVE AND FRIENDSHIP) and in *Lady Susan* (1793–94). *Ellinor and Marianne* (1796), an early draft of SENSE AND SENSIBILITY (1811), was intended to be an epistolary novel. *Sense and Sensibility* still incorporates 21 letters, but the weight of plot development is carried by the novel's narrative sections. While there are few full-fledged epistolary novels in 19th-century literature, letters continue to figure in significant ways in the plots of a wide range of novels from Edward Bulwer Lytton's (1803—73) *Falkland* (1827) to Anne Brontë's (1820–49) *The Tenant of Wildfell Hall* (1848). Following MARY SHELLEY's (1797–1851) novel FRANKENSTEIN (1818), which is framed by an epistolary narrative, later 19th-century works of detective and gothic horror fiction, such as Wilkie Collins's *The Woman in White* (1859) and *The Moonstone* (1868) and Bram Stoker's *Dracula* (1897), use the multi-perspectivity of the epistolary form to explore problems of representation and truth.

### Further Reading

Beebee, Thomas O. *Epistolary Fiction in Europe 1500–1850.* Cambridge: Cambridge University Press, 1999.

Bray, Joe. *The Epistolary Novel: Representations of Consciousness.* London: Routledge, 2003.

Carnell, Rachel K. "Clarissa's Treasonable Correspondence: Gender, Epistolary Politics, and the Public Sphere." *Eighteenth-Century Fiction* 10, no. 3 (1998): 269–286.

Cook, Elizabeth Heckendorn. *Epistolary Bodies: Gender and Genre in the Eighteenth-Century Republic of Letters.* Stanford, Calif.: Stanford University Press, 1996.

Singer, Godfrey Frank. *The Epistolary Novel: Its Origin, Development, Decline, and Residuary Influence.* New York: Russel & Russel, 1963.

Zaczek, Barbara Maria. *Censored Sentiments: Letters and Censorship in Epistolary Novels and Conduct Material.* Newark: University of Delaware Press, 1997.

—Katharina Boehm

## *Essay on the Principle of Population*
### Thomas Malthus (1798)

The first edition of Thomas Malthus's *Essay on the Principle of Population* was published anonymously in 1798. Malthus (1766–1834), a scholar and Anglican clergyman, meant the pamphlet to be a polemical counterblast to what he saw as the naive and dangerous optimism of those revolutionary-era writers, particularly WILLIAM GODWIN, who saw human history as a progression toward individual and social perfectability. The *Essay* proved to be more influential, successful, and controversial than its author could have anticipated. Not only did it establish political economy as perhaps the most significant influence in public life throughout the first half of the 19th century and influence government policy for a generation, it also helped to discredit idealistic theories of nature's benevolence and proved to be a crucial factor in the development of evolutionary theory.

Throughout the 18th century it had been widely assumed that a rapidly increasing popula-

tion was a sign of a nation's greatness, and that the large families of the laboring classes were one of England's strengths. Malthus, however, interpreted the burgeoning population in quite different terms, identifying it as a significant and immediate threat to standards of living. The basic principle underlying this analysis was his assertion that population increases geometrically while food production increases arithmetically; in other words, population would inevitably, and quickly, outstrip the amount of food that could be produced, leading to famine, death, and disease, all of which were necessary and inevitable brakes on population growth.

Malthus would go on to revise his *Essay* repeatedly, publishing seven editions, all but the last of which appeared in his own lifetime, but the most significant changes were made between the first and second editions. The only options for population control that he could see in the first edition were birth control, abortion, and infanticide, which he condemned as being, respectively, unreliable, dangerous, and immoral. By the second edition, which he published under his own name in 1803, he felt himself able to offer a way out of this gloomy impasse, preaching a system of "moral restraint" by urging couples to marry later in life, have fewer children, and refrain from having any children at all until they were financially able to support them.

Even with this slight concession to free will tempering what had previously seemed to be a largely mechanistic view of human life, Malthus's essay proved to be highly divisive. In particular, the leading literary figures of the age were highly critical. SAMUEL TAYLOR COLERIDGE and WILLIAM HAZLITT argued that Malthus ignored the ways in which reasoned self-consciousness and fellow-feeling might contribute to the maintenance of social stability, and LORD BYRON criticized "moral restraint" in canto 12 of *DON JUAN*: "Without cash, Malthus tell you—'take no brides.' / So Cash rules Love." This literary animus continued through the century; in *Oliver Twist* (1838), for example, Charles Dickens condemns the New Poor Law (a piece of legislation that was conceived of and championed by the Utilitarians, who were greatly influenced by Malthus's theories), and in

*Our Mutual Friend* (1864–65) the convinced Malthusian Podsnap sees the deaths of the poor as inevitable and part of Providence.

Malthus's ideas met with greater favor in the economic and scientific communities, however, and his vision of the human race involved in a struggle for limited resources would influence the three major proponents of a theory of evolution in Victorian England: Herbert Spencer, Charles Darwin, and Alfred Russel Wallace.

**Further Reading**

Connell, Philip. *Romanticism, Economics and the Question of "Culture."* Oxford: Oxford University Press, 2001.

Malthus, Thomas. *An Essay on the Principle of Population.* Edited by Geoffrey Gilbert. Oxford: Oxford Worlds Classics, 2008.

—David McAllister

## *Essays of Elia* Charles Lamb (1823)

In an undated 1821 letter, CHARLES LAMB wrote to his friend SAMUEL TAYLOR COLERIDGE and signed himself not "C. Lamb" or "C. L.," as was his wont, but rather "Elia." It is the first instance in which he did so, but not the last. Writing under the pseudonym Elia, Lamb had begun publishing essays in the newly established *London Magazine* the year before. In 1823 he collected the essays he had contributed to the magazine and published them as a single volume entitled *Essays of Elia.* This was followed by a second volume of essays, *The Last Essays of Elia,* which appeared in 1833.

The first essay in this series is called "The South Sea House." Appearing in September 1820, the essay was a recollection of the place where Lamb first worked upon leaving school as a young man. Written in a lively and lighthearted tone, it incorporates a personified description of the building itself as well as brief biographical sketches of several of the men with whom Lamb worked within its walls. The polished tone, vivid descriptions, and mingled sense of fun and nostalgia inherently present in Lamb's writing style rendered the essay popular with the *London Magazine*'s readers. He went on to write and publish such essays almost every month for the next three years, then contributed more sporadically until the *London Magazine* finally folded in 1825.

The *Essays of Elia* are marked by their convivial, familiar tone. Where the modern critical essay is intended to be objective and to focus on a specific subject, the familiar essay is subjective and digressive, at once about the writer and about a chosen subject that the writer finds interesting or significant. Lamb drew the ideas for his essays from personal experiences—his childhood, his education, his relationships with friends and family members, his travels—and from his observations of the people and places around him. His style is polished, humorous, and conversational. Friends and family members could often find themselves written about in his essays, but although he could occasionally be critical, he was never hurtful or spiteful in his prose, and his chief source of humor was his own self-deprecation. Although Lamb himself suffered from bouts of depression and madness, in addition to living with and caring for his mentally unstable older sister Mary (in the essays referred to as "Bridget") throughout the whole of his adulthood, he was able to incorporate a keen sense of the absurd into his writing. Also notable is his stylistic control, which he masterfully parlays into a bittersweet tone—the essays of Elia are at once nostalgic and cynical, lighthearted and bitter—showcasing Lamb's own complicated personality.

At once endearingly personal and enticingly enigmatic, the essays reflect not only Charles Lamb's own views, prejudices, and philosophies, but also the society in which they were produced. A friend of Romantic writers, including Coleridge and WILLIAM WORDSWORTH, Lamb could not dissociate himself entirely from the sociopolitical ideas espoused by his peers. As a result, several of the essays reflect ideas of EMPIRE, nationalism, and nostalgia inherent in the writing of the Romantic movement.

**Further Reading**

Barnett, George Leonard. *Charles Lamb: The Evolution of Elia.* Bloomington: Indiana University Press, 1964.

Lamb, Charles. *The Essays of Elia.* London: Hesperus Press, 2009.

———. *Letters of Charles Lamb, Vol. 1 & 2.* Edited by William Macdonald. New York: E. P. Dutton & Co., 1903.

Prance, Charles A. *Companion to Charles Lamb: A Guide to People and Places, 1760–1847.* London: Mansell, 1983.

—Melissa A. Elmes

### *Eugene Onegin* Aleksandr Sergeyevich Pushkin (1823–1833)

Eugene Onegin took Aleksandr Pushkin a long time to write, and he published fragments of it throughout the 1820s before its first appearance as a complete work in 1833. In the early stages of writing *Eugene Onegin,* Pushkin (1799–1837) commented that he was "writing the motley strophes of a Romantic poem" (quoted in Pushkin 1964, 70); elsewhere he referred to the book as "a novel in verse in the manner of Byron's *Don Juan*" (quoted in Pushkin 1998, xv). Certainly the influence of Byron's mock-epic poem is pronounced in the satiric characterization of the protagonist, essentially a Russian Byronic hero.

In the first of eight cantos, or chapters, Pushkin introduces Onegin, a young St. Petersburg dandy who affects a pose of world weariness, on his way to the country to visit his dying uncle. "Like Childe Harold, ill-humored, languid" (1964, 112) he befriends a local landowner, Vladimir Lensky, who incarnates a more idealistic, lyrical Romanticism. The emotive Lensky writes poetry and adores the ordinary, coquettish Olga Larin. Onegin finds Olga insipid by contrast with her older sister, Tatyana, a moody introvert immersed in Samuel Richardson's and JEAN-JACQUES ROUSSEAU's sentimental writings. Pushkin treats all four main characters ironically, but even as he makes Tatyana the dupe of romantic fictions, he also embodies in her some of his own cherished ideals. Passionate and imaginative, her dreaminess reminiscent of Svetlana (the title character of a GOTHIC ballad by the earlier Romantic poet V. A. Zhukovsky), Tatyana is the novel's heroine—despite her youthful naïveté in becoming infatuated with Onegin, regarding him as her Byronic hero and writing him a heartfelt declaration of love. Not rake enough to take advantage of her feelings, Onegin nevertheless reveals his emptiness in a cold, condescending lecture to her about appropriate suitors.

The intrusive narrator's ironic stance toward the two couples alternates with a range of other tones, not just in verses about Tatyana but throughout the novel. Indeed, so prominent are the narrator, his concerns, and his varying moods that he becomes the third young man of the story, a protagonist more artistic than Lensky and more mature than either Lensky or Onegin. His commentary—a rich amalgam of satiric observations on worldliness, lyrical descriptions of nature, melancholy reflections on the passage of youth, appreciative catalogues of country traditions—constitute a full third of the novel. Identifying himself in canto 1 as Onegin's friend through his poetry, dislike of the north (Pushkin was exiled to the north for writing subversive poetry), and treatment of Tatyana as his muse, he soon emerges as his author's alter ego. He, Tatyana, and their creator unite in balancing principles with the imperatives of the heart.

Pushkin's flawed hero, on the other hand, betrays friendship as well as love. Cantos 5 and 6 show him at his worst as he maliciously flirts with Olga at Tatyana's name-day party, accepts the jealous Lensky's challenge to a duel, and then kills his comrade from sheer passivity even as he regrets the folly of their confrontation. In an ironic twist of fate rather than literature, Pushkin himself died in 1837 in a duel that, like aspects of *Eugene Onegin,* demonstrated his residual allegiance to Romantic—and aristocratic—values. Years later, in Moscow, Onegin falls in love with a sophisticated, beautiful society hostess—only to discover that she is Tatyana, now the wife of an elderly general. In the neoclassical symmetrical closure, Onegin writes her a passionate letter begging her to leave her husband for him; despite still loving him, Tatyana rejects him because she plans to remain faithful.

Most critics of *Eugene Onegin* join Roman Jakobson in seeing "the two leading lyrical motifs of the whole work" as "the ideal image of Tatyana" and "the theme of vanishing youth, which is always irretrievable" (Jakobsen 48). Adapted into an opera by Pyotr Ilich Tchaikovsky in 1879, the novel offers a unique fusion of Romanticism, romantic parody, neoclassical elegance, and realist representation of the 1820s that makes it, as Pushkin's contemporary the critic Vissarian Belinksy believed, a ritual encyclopedia of Russian life.

## Further Reading

Bethea, David M., ed. *The Pushkin Handbook.* Madison: University of Wisconsin Press, 2005.

Clayton, J. Douglas. *Ice and Flame: Aleksandr Pushkin's Eugene Onegin.* Toronto: University of Toronto Press, 1985.

Hoisington, Sona Stephan, trans. *Russian Views of Pushkin's Eugene Onegin.* Bloomington: Indiana University Press, 1988.

Jakobson, Roman. *Pushkin and His Sculptural Myth.* Translated and edited by John Burbank. The Hague: Mouton, 1975.

Pushkin, Aleksandr. *Eugene Onegin.* Translated and introduced by James F. Falen. Oxford: Oxford University Press, 1998.

———. *Eugene Onegin.* Translated by Vladimir Nabokov. Princeton, N.J.: Princeton University Press, 1964.

—Margaret Bożenna Goscilo

## evangelicalism

As members of a Protestant religious movement that influenced the Romantic movement, evangelicals stressed the supremacy of Scripture over the authority of the church and individual religious experience over ceremony. A belief in original sin (that mankind inherited sin from the Fall), in justification by faith (that good works or sacraments were unnecessary for salvation), and in new birth (the immediate regeneration of the sinner's nature at the point of conversion) were the key tenets of the movement's theology. Evangelicalism began sometime in the 1730s, but it was the Methodist leaders—John Wesley (1703–91) in England and George Whitefield (1714–70) in Wales—who embodied the movement's enthusiasm for sharing the gospel by introducing an open-air, itinerant preaching style that attracted large crowds. Wesley alone preached more than 40,000 sermons, and the daily conversions of listeners, when confronted with both the full weight of their sins and the opportunity to be permanently released from

them, were charged with characteristic evangelical emotion. At a time of great apathy, when many Church of England clergy did not reside in the parish from which they drew a living, evangelicalism's personal, enthusiastic, and social nature brought new converts to the Baptists, Congregationalists, and Methodists (and created a group within the Anglican Church that was later termed the Low Church). Wesley ensured Methodism's longevity and fostered a sense of community by introducing a routine of prayers, meetings, and church services and by involving the laity in church governance.

The pervasiveness of evangelicalism and the power of its laity had many social implications. Women and lower-class men were appointed to positions within the church (such as steward, trustee, or class leader) and were even permitted to preach. Because of their strong belief in the primacy of Scripture, Evangelicals created Sunday schools and Bible classes, bringing literacy and church doctrine to a wide range of people. In burgeoning urban settings such as Birmingham, England, evangelical churches fostered a much-needed sense of community, and church members were expected to come to each other's aid in times of sickness or financial difficulty. However, this close-knit, regulated community produced strict accountability. As the historians Leonore Davidoff and Catherine Hall argue, evangelicalism redefined the popular Georgian concept of manhood. Instead of drink, blood sports, and sexual escapades, Christian men were to be men of feeling, following Christ's example in submission and stewardship.

In politics, evangelicals were divided between the main political parties—Tory and Whig—because they could not join either comfortably: Their middle-class and poor members disliked Tory politics, and no evangelical could approve of liberal Whig politics. Evangelicals were also split on the subject of reform. Wesley continually supported the government, while the Clapham Sect, evangelical Anglicans who included the abolitionist William Wilberforce, fought for children's rights, an end to SLAVERY, and prison reform. During the FRENCH REVOLUTION, HANNAH MORE, the most popular evangelical author of the time, wrote government-funded tracts encouraging submission to the authorities. However, evangelicalism's importance was most felt by passage of the Repeal Act (1828). This watershed legislation stopped the marginalization of the Dissenters and led to an increase of religious tolerance and working-class rights.

## Further Reading

Bebbington, D. W. *Evangelicalism in Modern Britain: History from the 1730s to the 1980s*. Florence, Ky.: Routledge, 1988.

Clark, J. C. D. *English Society, 1688–1832: Ideology, Social Structure, and Political Practice during the Ancien Regime*. Cambridge: Cambridge University Press, 1985.

Davidoff, Leonore, and Catherine Hall. *Family Fortunes: Men and Women of the English Middle Class, 1780–1850*. 1987. Reprint, London: Routledge, 2002.

Jarvis, Robin. *The Romantic Period: The Intellectual and Cultural Context of English Literature, 1789–1830*. Harlow, Eng.: Longman/Pearson, 2004.

Watts, Michael R. *The Dissenters. Vol II: The Expansion of Evangelical Nonconformity*. Oxford: Clarendon Press, 1995.

—Diana Powell

## *Evelina* Frances Burney (1778)

*Evelina; or, The History of a Young Lady's Entrance into the World* presents fashionable London life as seen through the eyes of ingenue Evelina Anville. She is the daughter of Sir John Belmont, who secretly married Evelina's mother and has been absent from Evelina's life since her mother's death. While Evelina's guardian, Reverend Arthur Villars, and others working on her behalf try to convince Belmont to claim Evelina as his daughter, she travels to London with her friend Maria Mirvan and Maria's family. The story of an innocent abroad, Evelina's ignorance of polite customs causes her to make continual mistakes in her social interactions. Despite her missteps, however, she wins the heart of Lord Orville, who decides to marry her even before her father makes her his heir.

Orville's love for Evelina's inherent worth rather than her monetary worth supports the Romantic view of merit residing within individuals rather than socioeconomic classes. This emphasis on the importance of individuality also helps to dismantle the importance of other characters. For instance, Sir Clement Willoughby may possess social status and money, but his rudeness and scheming make him clearly unfit to be Evelina's partner. Individuality veers into oddness in some of the more comic characters, including the rough-mannered Captain Mirvan, who hates the French. Evelina's grandmother, Madame Duval, is an aged, Frenchified coquette who shows an inappropriate interest in clothing and makeup, and she continuously fights with Captain Mirvan. Evelina's brash, uncouth cousins, the Branghtons, reveal their lack of decorum by preferring low-bred entertainments such as the White-Conduit coffeehouse (which Evelina describes as full of gaudy, pert people) to the more refined pleasures of opera.

Yet Evelina's charm comes partly from her own quirks. She cannot stifle her laughter at the fop Mr. Lovel, and she is so sympathetic to the woes of the melancholy Mr. McCartney that she manages to save him from beginning a career as a highwayman. The brooding Mr. McCartney, who experiences emotion keenly, functions as a precursor to the Romantic solitary artist. A poet, Mr. McCartney is revealed to be Evelina's brother; his flowing emotions and poetic aspirations also provide shades of Romanticism in the novel. Later in the action, Evelina travels westward to Bristol Hotwells, where her chaperone brings her into high society. Lord Orville is also at Bristol, and he and Evelina get to know each other well enough there for them to discover how they have both been misled by Sir Clement. Sir Clement's attempts to keep Orville and Evelina apart fail, since this man of deception did not expect Orville and Evelina to deal honestly with each other. Evelina's honesty and artlessness are a large part of what causes Orville to want to marry her.

*Evelina* contains characteristics of a traditional 18th-century novel as well as Romantic work. However, its inclusion of such Romantic themes as the artificiality of social codes and the emotional sensitivity of poets paved the way for more canonical Romantic novelists, including Jane Austen, who was influenced by Frances Burney's novels.

**Further Reading**

Bilger, Audrey. *Laughing Feminism: Subversive Comedy in Frances Burney, Maria Edgeworth, and Jane Austen.* Detroit: Wayne State University Press, 1998.

Burney, Frances. *Evelina.* Oxford: Oxford University Press, 2002.

Doody, Margaret Anne. *Frances Burney: The Life in the Works.* Cambridge: Cambridge University Press, 1988.

Gallagher, Catherine. "Nobody's Debt: Frances Burney's Universal Obligation." In *Nobody's Story: The Vanishing Acts of Women Writers in the Marketplace 1670–1820.* Berkeley and Los Angeles: University of California Press, 1994, 203–256.

Straub, Kristina. *Divided Fictions: Fanny Burney and Feminine Strategy.* Lexington: University Press of Kentucky, 1987.

Thaddeus, Janice Farrar. *Frances Burney: A Literary Life.* New York: St. Martin's, 1999.

—Kathryn Strong

## "Eve of St. Agnes, The"  John Keats (1820)

As Jack Stillinger's invaluable landmark work *Reading The Eve of St Agnes* (1999) shows, there are countless interpretations of JOHN KEATS's most anthologized and, many would argue, greatest narrative poem. When the poem was first published in July 1820 in Keats's second collection, *Lamia, Isabella, The Eve of St. Agnes, and Other Poems,* "The Eve of St. Agnes" received mostly favorable reviews, but the poem was referred to in purely aesthetic terms. CHARLES LAMB described it as "almost a Chaucer-like painting" and the *New Monthly Magazine* saw in the poem "a soft religious light . . . shed over the whole story" (quoted in Hayden, 197). Since then, critics have argued over different interpretations of the poem—as a discussion of the Christian versus old religion; as a reinterpretation of the GOTHIC genre; as a reinvention of *Romeo and Juliet* and the sleeping beauty motif; as a celebration of love; and, in contradictory readings, as an insistence on the limitations of romance. Most frequently, the poem is viewed as a commentary on the imagination process and the conflict of reality versus desire. One of the most innovative interpretations of the poem is by James Twitchell,

who discusses Porphyro as a vampyric figure. The interpretations are endless—for every critical reading, there is most certainly a counterinterpretation, but the poem is insistently enigmatic, and therefore, as Jack Stillinger argues, all "are in some reasonable sense right" (Stillinger 3).

The interpretation that seems most closely linked to Keats's beliefs is the reading of the poem as a condemnation of a fruitless Christianity in favor of Keats's own religion of beauty and art. He uses history spanning 1,500 years as a means of marking a progression from spirituality as defined through Christian values of absolute reverence to God and physical purity, to spirituality as defined through art and beauty. Keats began writing the poem during a trip to the town of Chichester in West Sussex, a town that boasts the magnificent medieval 12th-century Chichester Cathedral; the visual stimulus for his adverse response to Christianity would have been right before his eyes. The poem begins outside the castle with the line "St. Agnes' Eve—Ah, bitter chill it was." This first line, which locates the poem in terms of season and the past, also significantly suggests through the dash that this poem will be a rewritten definition of the eve of a spiritual event. Therefore, from the first line, Keats suggests that this poem is a poetic reevaluation of religious devotion. Yet on this "St. Agnes's Eve," "silent was the flock in wooly fold" (l. 4), who are barred from the warmth of the castle. St. Agnes's natural legacy through her God-given name (meaning "lamb") are seen as still and uncommunicative outside the action of the castle, suggesting that St. Agnes is not a player in the events to come. Later on, Madeline is described as "hoodwink'd with faery fancy; all amort, / Save to St. Agnes and her lambs unshorn" (ll. 70–71), which is interesting because she is dreaming of a holy virginity represented by the lambs, when in truth "the lambs unshorn" are silent and frozen in the harsh reality of the January outdoors—and are not representative of the fantasy she desires or experiences.

The first stanzas are governed by imagery of cold, silent, and unproductive Christian spirituality and death at the bottom of the castle. Like St. Agnes's lambs, the Beadsman, hired to pray for members of the castle is also freezing with "numb

. . . fingers" and "frosted breath" (ll. 5, 6). The Beadsman is the character who carries on the spiritual legacy of St. Agnes and is the closest to a martyr figure in this poem, praying for others until he surrenders to fatigue and dies: "The Beadsman after thousand aves told, / For aye—unsought slept among his ashes cold" (ll. 377–378). He is also immediately associated with the worship of St. Agnes's virginity, for he walks "Past the sweet Virgin's picture" (l. 9). Though Keats admires his attempt at some form of devotion, calling the Beadsman "this patient, holy man" (l. 10), he portrays him as "meagre, barefoot, wan" and "slow" (ll. 12, 13), wasting a life praying for those who will not pray for themselves. To make the scene more tragic, the Beadsman's prayers have obviously not secured the members of the house places in heaven, for he is praying amid the "sculptur'd dead" (l. 14) of another age, which are "Emprison'd in black, purgatorial rails: / Knights, ladies praying in dumb orat'ries" (ll. 15–16). The "sculptur'd dead" are artistic images of Christian death, and yet there is no peace for them, for they are eternally in "dumb orat'ries," which suggest a silent and fruitless spirituality; they are in purgatory—frozen in prayer for eternity. The "knights, ladies" also suggest the future of the "argent revelry" (l. 37), whose silver color will eventually fade into stone.

Yet for Keats, this whole scene is also an artistic purgatory of lifeless art that cannot reach beyond the ages. The Virgin's picture, which fails to speak to the "revelry" upstairs, is an older form of art, described without color or detail. Similarly, the "sculptur'd dead" are artistic forms expressing eternal repression, and it is significant that the first color in the poem is "black" (l. 15), suggesting a dark and unproductive form of spirituality and a lack of art and creation within this part of the poem.

Porphyro is the figure in the poem who brings passion, art, and beauty into Madeline's castle. His name is derived from the Greek word *porphura*, meaning "purple pigment," and though his name signals numerous traits, including his passion and wealth, Keats's name can be taken quite literally, for in a sense Porphyro is the color purple, the richest of colors desiring to "blendeth" with the rose to create a new form of sexualized and spiri-

tual art. From the first image of him, it is as though he melts the frozen quality of the castle, for "across the moors, / Had come young Porphyro with heart on fire / For Madeline" (ll. 74–75), and later in the poem he is also described as "burning Porphyro" (l. 159). He moves up in the castle, following Angela "through a lowly arched way, / Brushing cobwebs with his lofty plume" (ll. 109–110), and in so doing he seems to brush the decay away from the castle with his decorative feather. Porphyro experiences disgust at the thought of Madeline's dream on St. Agnes's Eve, for "he scarce could brook / Tears, at the thought of those enchantments cold / And Madeline asleep in laps of legends old" (ll. 133–135). Porphyro sees her "asleep in lap of legends old" as tainting her purity, for it is a sexualized image which implies quite overtly that Madeline is being ravished by a decrepit form of unproductive spirituality—what the critic Ronald Sharp refers to as "a sterile conception of love" (Sharp 41). Significantly, after the expression of these fears, the poem increases its use of color, for "sudden a thought came like a full-blown rose" (l. 136), and "his pained heart/Made purple riot" (ll. 137–138). His thought of sexual consummation with Madeline is like a "full-blown rose," for he wants her to not be a bud again and reach a higher form of fulfillment with him. Yet it is obvious that Madeline is working at cross-purposes with Porphyro: She desires to experience a sexual consummation without becoming a "full-blown rose" for she is "Blinded alike from sunshine and from rain, / As though a rose should shut, and be a bud again" (ll. 242–243). Porphyro realizes the deathlike quality of this sterile sexuality based in past ages, and Keats makes it impossible not to choose between sunshine and rain in the end, for in the last lines of the poem they have "fled away into the storm" (l. 371). In addition, since the "pained heart" makes "purple riot," one immediately hears "painted heart," and it is clear that Porphyro's suffering is described in terms of color, because the world of depth of emotion and truth is one of art.

As Madeline enters her chamber, it is apparent that art, rather than St. Agnes and her Christianity, has transformed her room into a holy dwelling. Keats spends several stanzas marking the rich detail of the casement, which appears to be like a stained-glass window with opening doors on one wall of her room. Keats describes "A casement high and triple-arch'd there was / All garlanded with carven imag'ries," which is "diamonded with panes of quaint device" (ll. 208–209, 211). The casement is imbued with a positive religiousness not found in the "sculptur'd dead," for it is colorful, "Innumerable of stains and splendid dyes" (l. 212), as well as being "active" art. The "triple-arch'd" casement inevitably alludes to the holy trinity, and art is made a substitute for traditional religion in this part of the poem. Unlike the cold chapel, devoid of color or action, the casement in combination with the virgin moon conspires to bless Madeline with color creating a higher aesthetic religious experience. The casement and the "wintry moon, / threw warm gules upon Madeline's fair breast" (ll. 217–28), and in a sense Madeline becomes art as well by holding the shadows of the art upon her. She is bestowed with the rose color she is identified with throughout the poem as the "Rose-bloom fell on her hands, together prest" (l. 220), and color brightens the holy action and transforms it. In a similar image, in which "on her silver cross soft amethyst" (l. 221) falls, it is as if Porphyro and his "purpleness" are already melting into her, shading the idolatrous Christian image into a new holy picture represented by Porphyro and his violet religion of beauty. Like the amethyst shading the silver cross, Madeline's sleep foreshadows the sexual union of Madeline and Porphyro and her possible desire for such an action, for her "blanched linen" is "lavender'd" (l. 263), foretelling Porphyro's imminent presence in her sheets and the coloring of her white purity with a richer purple.

Yet Porphyro is simultaneously a heroic and a Satanic figure. There are numerous negative Miltonic (see MILTON, JOHN) allusions in the poem, which the critic Lucy Newlyn thoroughly and convincingly traces back to *Paradise Lost* (1667). As she writes, "Narrative expectations set him up as Romeo, while allusions suggest repeatedly that he is Satan" (Newlyn 175). Many critics, including Jack Stillinger in "The Hoodwinking of Madeline," have suggested that this foreshadows Madeline's rape by Porphyro. Like Satan, who steals into Adam and Eve's paradise and, importantly, Eve's dream, Porphyro is also stealing into Madeline's paradisial space and in a sense tricking her in the same way by melting "Into her dream" (l. 320), as Satan does in Book 5 of *Paradise Lost*. However, in transforming Porphyro into both a hero figure as well as a Satan figure, Keats proves his point that the highest religion is one of art and beauty rather than that of Christianity, for Porphyro's Satan-like actions create art, which is what, for Keats, matters in the end. Like SAMUEL TAYLOR COLERIDGE and PERCY BYSSHE SHELLEY, he also saw Satan as the hero of Milton's epic.

The sexual union between Madeline and Porphyro is a holy event, not only because, as Ronald Sharp writes, "it is beautiful," but because the imagery used suggests a spiritualized creation of art. Porphyro's sexual desire makes him not only a Satan figure or a Peeping Tom but an otherworldly figure, "Ethereal, flush'd, and like a throbbing star / Seen mid the sapphire heaven's deep repose" (ll. 318–319). The image of him as a "throbbing star" is certainly sexual, but it is also an image of the color and light he intends to give to Madeline. When they finally make love, it is likened to the mixing of distinctly colored flowers, creating not only a new color but a new scent; it is a sensuous creation of a new art through their lovemaking. Yet even in the midst of their sexual union, as Sharp points out, they are surrounded by a darker reality to which they must return. The "pattering" of "the sharp sleet / Against the window-panes" of the casement (ll. 323–325) suggest a shattering of an ideal; however it is also suggestive of the way in which one cannot be "Blinded alike from sunshine and from rain" (l. 242), for within beauty lies the frightening as well, and in a sense they escape into a sublime landscape. As we are told: "And they are gone: ay, ages long ago / These lovers fled away into the storm" (ll. 370–371). Keats does not let the reader know the future of Porphryo and Madeline. Perhaps the lovers successfully escape and live in Porphyro's castle, but this seems unlikely. Instead, it would make more sense if the lovers did freeze in the storm, for that is the only way to preserve the ideal of the love and the beauty that they have created. Into the storm, they are images of an eternal beauty frozen in time. They transcend the "sculptur'd dead" because they have reached a higher plane—and in the end, perhaps death within nature is the only avenue that allows them to reject the possible future of becoming the ordinary "knights and ladies" behind "purgatorial rails" in favor of reaching a higher aesthetic spirituality.

**Further Reading**

Hayden, John. *The Romantic Reviewers: 1802–1824.* Chicago: The University of Chicago Press, 1968.

Newlyn, Lucy. *Paradise Lost and the Romantic Reader.* Oxford: Clarendon Press, 1993.

Sharp, Ronald. *Keats, Skepticism, and the Religion of Beauty.* Athens: University of Georgia Press, 1979.

Stillinger, Jack. *Reading the Eve of St Agnes: The Multiples of Complex Literary Transaction.* New York: Oxford University Press, 1999.

Twitchell, James. *The Living Dead: A Study of the Vampire in Romantic Literature.* Durham, N.C.: Duke University, 1981.

—Lucy Morse

## *Every One Has His Fault* Elizabeth Inchbald (1793)

In structure and overall tone, ELIZABETH INCHBALD's *Every One Has His Fault* shares marked similarities with early 18th-century sentimental comedies. Indeed, Inchbald's acclaimed 1793 play forgoes the ribald humor that had been de rigueur in Restoration comedies for a gentler wit, and its fifth-act resolution benefits from a blending of emotional poignancy and relaxed jocularity. However, though some sentimental comedies contain satirical elements, they largely lack *Every One Has His Fault*'s political thrust and sardonic bite.

Operating within *Every One Has His Fault* is a multivalent social critique motivated by Inchbald's reformist politics, which are very much of their time. Obscured by the play's disarmingly orthodox facade, Inchbald censures the institution of marriage, hierarchical class structures, and patriarchal sovereignty. In the play's earlier acts, we are introduced to four male characters representing diverse ideological arguments on marriage: Mr. Solus is desperate to wed, having fathered several illegitimate children without ever enjoying the comforts of a lawful marriage; Mr. Placid is desperate to dispose of his wife, a decidedly nonplacid compan-

ion; Mr. Irwin has married a lady of superior rank for love but in doing so has destroyed her familial connections and financial security; and Sir Robert Ramble is enjoying restored bachelorhood after his extramarital affairs compelled his wife to seek a divorce. Inchbald makes it clear that while these men (with the exception of the penniless Irwin) possess the means to improve their situations, they lack the requisite resolve. In contrast, the women of the play are endowed with considerable resolve and negligible agency. Ramble's ex-wife, Miss Wooburn, was clever enough to legally obtain a divorce from her neglectful husband, and yet it is her guardian, Lord Norland, who holds her marital fate (and substantial dowry) in his hands. Similarly, after being disowned by her father for her marital misalliance, Lady Eleanor Irwin can only humbly petition former acquaintances for financial help as her husband slips further into despair. While *Every One Has His Fault* never advocates the complete abandoning of marital rites or proposes alternatives to patriarchal or aristocratic entitlements, it does urge for widespread sociopolitical reform.

While interdependent structures of class and gender impede the ambitions of some characters and facilitate others, it is through the artful manipulations of Mr. Harmony that old flames are rekindled (Ramble and Miss Wooburn) and wounds inflicted by family feuding are healed (the Irwins and Lord Norland). Though scholarship on *Every One Has His Fault* traditionally disregards Mr. Harmony as a conciliatory figure armed only with white lies and good intentions, recent work by Katherine S. Green suggests Harmony's deeper functionality, particularly given Inchbald's Jacobin proclivities and the play's premiere at Covent Garden only eight days after Louis XVI's execution in Paris (see FRENCH REVOLUTION). Harmony's profitable duplicity, a rejection of the period's ideal of absolute truth, resonates with increased meaning when considered within the political context of British diplomacy during the period.

**Further Reading**

Bolton, Betsy. *Women, Nationalism, and the Romantic Stage: Theatre and Politics in Britain, 1780–1800.* Cambridge: Cambridge University Press, 2001.

Green, Katherine S. "Mr. Harmony and the Events of January 1793: Elizabeth Inchbald's *Every One Has His Fault*." *Theatre Journal* 56 (2004): 47–62.

Inchbald, Elizabeth. *Selected Comedies*. Introduction and notes by Roger Manvell. Lanham, Md.: Univ. Press of America, 1987.

Jenkins, Annibel. *I'll Tell You What: The Life of Elizabeth Inchbald*. Lexington: University Press of Kentucky, 2003.

—Meredith Conti

## *Excursion, The*   William Wordsworth  (1814)

For much of the 19th century, this long dramatic poem was considered to be WILLIAM WORDSWORTH's major work. It eclipsed the reputations of *Lyrical Ballads*, his odes, and the posthumously published autobiographical poem *The* PRELUDE, which is now generally considered to be his masterpiece.

Although it was first published in 1814, recent scholarship has shown the poem's composition to have been the result of a series of intense bursts of activity, with much of the first two books composed as early as 1806. Wordsworth's original plan was for *The Excursion* to form part of *The Recluse*, the monumental epic that he was writing—or, at least, thinking about writing—from 1798 until the end of his life. *The Recluse* was to have a tripartite structure, with sections "on Man, on Nature, and on Human Life." *The Excursion*, which was to be the narrative "human life" section of this ambitious scheme, was the only part of *The Recluse* to be published in Wordsworth's lifetime.

The first of the poem's nine books incorporates "The Story of Margaret," or "The RUINED COTTAGE," which was originally written as a separate fragment, after which the poem advances largely through a series of debates among its four main speakers: the Poet, the Solitary, the Wanderer and the Pastor. The Poet, a younger man, is traveling with the Wanderer, a philosophically minded pedlar who takes him to meet his friend the Solitary in the secluded mountain vale where he lives. The Solitary is a former soldier and revolutionary preacher who has been thrown into despondency following the deaths of his wife and children and the destruction of his political hopes in the bloody aftermath of the FRENCH REVOLUTION.

The Wanderer and, to a lesser extent, the Poet gently reprove the Solitary for his misanthropy, his withdrawal from society, and his irreligious views, and the Wanderer suggests that an imaginatively apprehended faith in God could cure him of his despondency. The three men then travel to a secluded churchyard among the mountains, where they meet with the Pastor, who joins in their debate, drawing examples of the harmonizing effects of virtue and religion from the histories of the dead parishioners who are buried in his churchyard.

*The Excursion* has often been condemned (or worse, ignored) by critics who, while acknowledging the great beauty of some of its passages, have nevertheless seen it as overly didactic—a poem that tells readers, at some length, what to think and why they should think it. In recent years, however, more sympathetic critics have emphasized the poem's performative aspects, reading it as a work that foregrounds problems of reading and ideology while refusing definitively to endorse the philosophical position of any of its characters.

**Further Reading**

Bushell, Sally. *Re-reading The Excursion: Narrative, Response and the Wordsworthian Dramatic Voice*. Aldershot, Eng.: Ashgate, 2002.

Hickey, Alison. *Impure Conceits: Rhetoric and Ideology in Wordsworth's 'Excursion.'* Stanford, Calif.: Stanford University Press, 1997.

Reed, Mark L. *Wordsworth: The Chronology of the Middle Years, 1800–1815*. Cambridge, Mass.: Harvard University Press, 1975.

—David McAllister

# F

## "Factory, The" Letitia Elizabeth Landon
(1835)

Designed as a piece of social criticism and a product of the new industrial age (see INDUSTRIALISM), this emotive poem was published in LETITIA ELIZABETH LANDON's sixth collection, *The Vow of the Peacock and Other Poems* (1835). Its melancholy tone will be familiar to readers of Landon's other poetic works. The poem begins indignantly ("'Tis an accursed thing!—"), and the speaker describes how the smoke from the factory serves to block out the sun, throwing the unnamed town into a permanent state of darkness and gloom. What exactly the factory is manufacturing is never stated, but the smog from its chimneys wraps the town in "[a] dark funereal shroud" (l. 3), whose presence serves "as a type and sign" to sensitive observers of the "despair" that engulfs the community (ll. 7, 8). The beauties of nature—the moon, the sunset— are things of the past, no longer visible, though as the poet notes, the people ("Heavy with care, and pale with fear" [l. 16]) are too worn-down to think about what they are missing anyhow.

In line 18, the poet's senses switch from visual to aural; she hears a sound being carried in the breeze, "a low appealing cry" (l. 19) of children being put to work in the factory. The "cry" is the only way the children can "appeal" to the reader (they have no other way of articulating their misery). However, the poet hints that it is in vain, and "[a] thousand children are resigned / To sicken and to die!" (ll. 20–21). There is a sense here that Landon is very deliberately playing on her audience's familiarity with the shocking newspaper reports about inquiries into factory conditions taking place in the 1830s. The poet goes on to reflect how people shudder and "sicken" when they read in the Old Testament of the ritual child burning that formed part of the sacrifice to the Hebrew god Moloc, but when it is happening in their own country they feel nothing and even choose to ignore it. What is happening now is far worse. Whereas, the "heathen" Old Testament sacrifices were swiftly carried out today's child labourers face a lifetime in the factory fires of a Christian country: "—our idol, Gain, / Demands a living grave!" (ll. 28–29).

In the poem's second half the poet laments the fact that these children will never have the memories of a happy home to comfort them when they encounter unhappiness in adulthood. The importance of "home" makes itself felt in other Landon poems, as does its importance in the nurturing of children. Childhood is supposed to be an idyllic state for the child, a place where "Love is around him, and his hours / Are innocent and free" (ll. 38–39). However, in this town "the order is reversed, / And infancy, like age, / Knows of existence but its worst, / One dull and darkened page;— / Written with tears, and stamp'd with toil" (ll. 50–54). The child's inquiring mind, eager for knowledge, is "Crushed from the earliest hour" (l. 55) and is never allowed to grow. Landon uses the idea of the child as a delicate plant, which needs nurturing lest it "droops" and dies. These children are like "Weeds darkening on the bitter soil" (l. 56). The long hours in the factory mean that they can never rest. "Look," the poet commands her readers, pointing out a child whose "knees are bow'd with pain" and who "mutters from its wretched bed, / 'Oh, let me sleep again!'" (ll. 58–61). Despite its still being dark, the child's mother must force him to get up, and lighting her lantern, she takes him to work, where like an automaton "the little hands / Their task accustom'd ply" (ll. 70–71). Among the rows of children, "daily, some mid those pale bands, / Droop, sicken, pine, and die" (ll. 72–73). "Good God!" expostulates the poet, how can this be possible? It is surely unnatural to deny these children all the pleasures associated with growing up, to pile the cares of work on their heads. These children have "no childish days" (l. 75); instead, their "English home" is "One long and living tomb" (ll. 84–85). God seems unable to grant them "mercy"; he even seems to have forgotten them. But so, too, have the British population. Despite her colonies, her seeming prosperity and her much-publicized disavowal of slavery, Britain deserves to be cursed. How can she be "great and free" when her own population "pine like slaves" (ll. 90, 91)?

The poem thus ends on this indictment of the wealthier sections of the British population: those who benefit from the country's powerful trade routes and increasing industrial strength but are ignorant—or neglectful—of progress's victims. For a woman poet the subject matter (exploitation of children and the destruction of domestic nurturing) is carefully within the limits of what she might write about. Useful comparative readings could be made with ANNA SEWARD's "Colebrook Dale" (1810) and ANNA LAETITIA BARBAULD's "Inscription for an Ice-House" (1825). In Landon's poem there is no political solution put forward, and although there are some small hints that there will come a time when the oppressed will decide to rise up, the poem endorses the (feminine) virtues of pity and charity as fitting responses to the scene described. The questioning of God's interest in the children is potentially controversial, but the poem gets round this by suggesting that it is God's other children who should step in and help.

**Further Reading**

Lootens, Tricia. "Receiving the Legend, Rethinking the Writer: Letitia Landon and the Poetess Tradition." In *Romanticism and Women Poets: Opening the Doors of Reception,* edited by Harriet Kramer Linkin and Stephen C. Behrendt, 242–259. Lexington: University Press of Kentucky, 1999.

Stephenson, Glennis. *Letitia Landon: The Woman Behind L.E.L.* Manchester, Eng.: Manchester University Press, 1995.

—Paul Houseman

## "Fall of Hyperion, The"  John Keats  (1819)

JOHN KEATS composed "The Fall of Hyperion—A Dream" between July and September 1819. Like "HYPERION: A FRAGMENT," it was never completed, and it was not published until 1857, almost four decades after Keats's death. As in "Hyperion," the argument is based on the legend of the overthrow of the Titans by the gods of Mount Olympus. However, in the second version the disappearance of the Titans is announced in the title, and the poem begins long after their fall. Moreover, the poem takes a far more personal tone than *Hyperion,* with a first-person narrator who shares his emotions and his progress with the reader.

The first of two cantos draws on the Italian Renaissance poet Dante (ca. 1265–1321) and opens with an introduction that creates an opposition between fanatics and dreamers, and concludes by challenging posthumous readers to decide for themselves whether the text they are about to read is indeed poetry. The speaker is established from the start as a poet, through whose consciousness the plot will unfold. Canto 1 relates a process of initiation: The speaker first finds himself in a luxurious setting where he finds an abundance of tempting food, which he eats before drinking from a vessel containing an unknown beverage. The drink makes him lose consciousness, and he awakens to find himself in a sanctuary, where a sacred image is being worshipped by a "veiled shadow." He then hears words telling him that if he cannot ascend the steps leading to the altar, he will die where he is. He ascends the steps with great difficulty, thereby experiencing physical suffering, and eventually meets the shadow, who will prove to be the goddess Moneta.

The central part of poem is a dialogue between the poet-speaker and the goddess, in which the goddess states the famous distinction between poet and dreamer: "Art thou not of the dreamer tribe? / The poet and the dreamer are distinct, / Diverse, sheer opposite, antipodes, / The one pours out a balm upon the world, / The other vexes it" (1:198–201). This distinction echoes Keats's earlier anguished speculations about the status of the poet, especially compared with the philosopher, as in "LAMIA," for instance. Moneta then allows the speaker "to see as a God sees" (1:304) and to have access to the story of the fallen Titans. The poem repeats lines from the beginning of "Hyperion," focusing on Saturn and Thea, before being interrupted shortly after the beginning of the second canto and the introduction of Hyperion.

Thus, "The Fall of Hyperion," although similar to the earlier poem with regard to the overall argument, differs from it by concentrating on the poet's duty to humanity. It tries to place the Titans' fall within a wider context. Critics have underlined the parallel between the poem and Keats's concept of life as "the vale of soul-making," (Rollins 2.102) expressed in a famous letter to his brother George. However, like "Hyperion," the poem remains incomplete, perhaps because Keats still felt unable to express faith in the potential good of loss.

**Further Reading**

Bate, Walter Jackson. *John Keats.* London: Chatto & Windus, 1979.

Keats, John. *Complete Poems.* Edited by Jack Stillinger. Cambridge, Mass.: Belknap Press, 1982.

———. *The Letters of John Keats, 1814–1821.* 2 vols. Edited by Hyder Edward Rollins. Cambridge, Mass.: Harvard University Press, 1976.

Motion, Andrew. *Keats.* London: Faber & Faber, 1997.

Roe, Nicholas. *Keats and the Culture of Dissent.* Cambridge: Cambridge University Press, 1997.

Sperry, Stuart M. *Keats the Poet.* Princeton, N.J.: Princeton University Press, 1973.

—Sylvie Crinquand

## *Faust: A Tragedy*  Johann Wolfgang Von Goethe (1832)

Critics generally agree that there is a biographical element in nearly all the works of JOHANN WOLFGANG VON GOETHE (1749–1832), and the poetic drama *Faust: A Tragedy,* is no exception. Goethe, like many of the German Romantics, believed that one should engage the sciences as well as the arts. Thus, in addition to poetry, fiction, and drama, he published articles on physics and the natural sciences. In his day his scientific work was better received than much of that written by his peers, and critics today generally recognize it as ahead of its time. His *Faust,* which was begun in 1773 and revised right up to his death in 1832, well reflects the engagement of the sciences and pseudosciences that characterized his middle and later years and German Romanticism as a whole.

The title character is based on John Faustus, a late 15th-century German alchemist who reportedly offered his soul to the devil in exchange for forbidden knowledge. The popular subject of numerous literary and musical works, Faust—in Goethe's version—is peculiar to his creator and the scientific climate of his creator's age. Like FRIEDRICH VON SCHILLER and ERNST THEODOR AMADEUS HOFFMANN, Goethe embraced the antideterministic precept of *Naturphilosophie.* A conventionally German Romantic protagonist, Faust struggles between acceptance of an organically interconnected world and the lure of scientific exploits that promise to reveal its secrets. He chooses the latter position, and the broader implications of this choice are symbolized in his rejection of Gretchen, a human embodiment of the earth mother, and pursuit of Helen of Troy, in a womblike environment deep in the earth. Having destroyed Gretchen, it is only through the supernatural agency of Mephistopheles that he will possess Helen, albeit temporarily. Even the unnatural fire spirit Faust and his student conjure into being understands the principles of life better than his creators. A symbol of the interconnectedness of all life as Goethe saw it, the fire spirit is welcomed to, and united with, the ocean. In comparison, Faust, representing natural man, sees the ocean as a force to be mastered. This perception reflects the disregard for the principles of *Naturphilosophie* later symbolized by his blindness.

At the drama's conclusion, the alchemist, who was earlier rejected by the earth spirit, now imagines himself a Neptunist God of creation, evoking new life in the receding water of the marshes. Ironically, as life is organic and cyclical, the pit being dug in the earth is not a path out of primordial slime but one in which Faust must return, as a fossil, to the womb of the earth he once sought to master. Through Faust's ruin, Goethe offers his age a warning: Anyone who sees one's relationship with nature as that of conflicting power dynamics will be disconnected from the generative force within the body, the soul, and the natural world.

**Further Reading**

Brown, Jane K. *Goethe's Faust: The German Tragedy.* Ithaca, N.Y.: Cornell University Press, 1986.

Cotterill, H.B. *The Faust Legend and Goethe's Faust.* London: Hesperides, 2006.

Ford, Mary Hanford. *Goethe's Faust: Its Ethical Symbolism.* Whitefish, Mont.: Kessinger, 2006.

Goethe, Johann Wolfgang Von. *Faust I & II.* Translated by Stuart Atkins. Princeton, N.J.: Princeton University Press, 1994.

McCarthy, John A. *Remapping Reality: Chaos and Creativity in Science and Literature.* Amsterdam: Rodopi, 2006.

—Priscilla Glanville

## "Fears in Solitude" Samuel Taylor Coleridge
(1798)

"Fears in Solitude," written in April 1798, is a "conversation poem." Though it is structured as an interior monologue during the course of a walk, the poem arose from SAMUEL TAYLOR COLERIDGE's conversations with his friends at Nether Stowey, Somerset, about the war with France. The poem is an important statement of his political ideas on contemporary issues. "Fears in Solitude" begins and ends in retirement and addresses a public audience directly. Coleridge referred to the poem as *sermoni propriora* ("proper for a sermon").

The poem begins with a description of a dell: "A green and silent spot, amid the hills, / A small and silent dell!" (l. 1). The speaker lies down in this wonderful place and the "sweet influences" of nature "trembled o'er his frame" (l. 2). He hopes to find in this state "Religious meanings in the forms of Nature!"—(l. 24) but his senses are "gradually wrapt / In a half sleep" (ll. 25–26). Thus removed from the immediate present, he meditates on the state of English society and its relation to his own hopes and desires.

In Coleridge's other conversation poems, the audience is generally the common domestic circle of friends and family, but this poem is addressed to his country: "Oh Britons! Oh my brethren!" (151) and "Oh dear Britain! Oh my Mother Isle!" (173) The poem's first 28 lines conform to the distinctive features of conversational style. The idea of retirement is indulgently suggested—"In a half sleep, he dreams of better worlds." (26) Here Coleridge tries to collate his commitments in relation to a public audience. The poem was subtitled "Written in April 1798, during the Alarm of an invasion [by France]." In "FRANCE: AN ODE," Coleridge tried to justify his opposition to war, in "Fears in Solitude" the attack is based on his firm convictions: "We have offended, Oh! My countrymen! / We have offended very grievously, / And been most tyrannous" (41–42). He attacks Britain's colonialism and says, "have we gone forth / And borne to distant tribes slavery . . ." (48–49). Parliamentary corruption, state religion, and popular war mongering come under attack: "Secure from actual warfare, we have loved / To swell the war-whoop passionate for war!" (88–89).

Coleridge builds up to a climax of an ideal nation and a great family but this ideal is threatened by reality. He calls for thwarting invaders, "repel[ling] an impious foe," and putting an end to all factional strife. The poem rises to a passionate expression of the poet's love for his country and concludes with an account of his homecoming. He returns to Nether Stowey and its church, to Thomas Poole's house, to the trees, to his own cottage, and to Sara and their son Hartley. The poem thus moves back into the serenity and assurance of the pastoral landscape and the retirement mood. Coleridge is able to sustain the public mode because the poem supposes the usual conversational audience, his family and friends, on a larger, national scale.

## Further Reading

Everest, Kelvin. *Coleridge's Secret Ministry: The Context of the Conversation Poems 1795–1798.* Hassocks, Eng.: Harvester Press, 1979.

Jones, Chris. "John Newton and Coleridge's 'Fears in Solitude.'" *Notes & Queries* 41(1994): 339–341.

—Nishi Pulugurtha

## "Female Exile, The" Charlotte Smith (1797)

This poem, concerning the hardships suffered by refugees from the upheavals of the FRENCH REVO-LUTION, is a reworking of a passage originally contained in CHARLOTTE SMITH's blank-verse poem *The EMIGRANTS* and was first written in Brighthelmstone (modern-day Brighton) on the south coast of England in 1792.

While the first stanza provides the poem's rather inauspicious setting with a description of the hostile weather conditions and with rhyming words such as *howling* and *scowling* (ll. 1, 3), the other eight stanzas can be grouped according to their focus on different figures present in the scene the speaker observes. Stanzas 2, 3, and 4 are concerned with the titular figure of the poem, a "fair stranger" (l. 5) who comes to the beach every day, anxiously scanning the horizon in expectation of news from the country (and the husband) she has had to leave behind. The woman's present despair and destitution appear all the more poignant when the poem's speaker imagines what her life must have been like in happier times.

Stanzas 5, 6, and 7 turn toward the French lady's children, blissfully unaware of the sorrows affecting their mother. Their toys and games are described in great detail in order to heighten the contrast between their ignorance and their mother's acute awareness of the "multiplied miseries that wait on mankind" (l. 24), and they are described as "victims" (l. 23), a word echoing two lines from THOMAS GRAY's "Ode On a Distant Prospect of Eton College," a poem mourning the passing of childhood innocence: "Alas, regardless of their doom, / The little victims play." By way of the mother's thoughts on watching her children "with anguish" in stanza 7 (l. 25), the reader is gradually brought back to her point of view.

Stanza 8 depicts the arrival of a boat, which gives rise to "hopes" and "terrors" (l. 29) on the mother's part since she has no way of knowing whether it is good news or bad that this boat brings. The end of the stanza sees the lady "half expiring with fears" (l. 32), and this is how the poem's speaker leaves her, in order to turn from describing the group of exiles to addressing them directly in the final stanza.

It is this final stanza which, by means of the transition from description to direct address, foregrounds the person of the speaker in a way that is central to the overall meaning of the poem. While the previous stanzas dwell on the plight of the French lady and the blissful ignorance of her children, stanza 9 is concerned with the speaker's emotional involvement in the scene she surveys, thus introducing the important aspect of her sympathy for the exiles. She would, the speaker says, gladly "alleviate the woes" she sees, if only her own "hard fate" had left her in a position to do so (ll. 34–35). This final stanza establishes a complex empathic relationship among the exiles, the poem's speaker, and its readers: The mother, according to the critic Jacqueline M. Labbe, "feels her children's woe for them" (Labbe 89); she herself is pitied by the noble-hearted speaker, who is in turn pitied by her readers.

## Further Reading

Labbe, Jacqueline M. *Charlotte Smith: Romanticism, Poetry and the Culture of Gender.* Manchester, Eng.: Manchester University Press, 2003.

Smith, Charlotte. *The Poems of Charlotte Smith.* Edited by Stuart Curran. New York and Oxford: Oxford University Press, 1993.

—Patrick Gill

## femme fatale

The femme fatale (fatal woman) in literature became remarkably visible and versatile in the final years of the 18th century. Her presence fascinated and perplexed Romantic writers who struggled to explain her ambiguous sexuality, her distance from the domestic realm, and her disruptions of familiar romance plots. At once innocent and cunning, supernatural and sensual, the Romantic femme fatale inhabited a seductive body and an exotic landscape. As an embodiment of mystical forms of knowledge, she also prolonged erotic longing and narrative resolution. By revealing the artificial and arbitrary nature of gender, race, and class, the elusive fatal woman challenged their conventional interpretation throughout the 19th century.

The Romantic femme fatale was a driving force in two of this period's most popular and experimental forms: the GOTHIC novel and the ballad. Gothic novels, traditionally populated by exotic gypsies, sorceresses, or demons in disguise, accentuated the powers of fatal female characters who distract, deceive, and warn characters of dangers they will ultimately fail to heed. The femme fatale's appearance in these novels not only intensified the suspense of the gothic plot but also increased the need for distance and disguise. MATTHEW LEWIS's The MONK (1796) and SIR WALTER SCOTT's The Monastery (1820), for example, introduce femmes fatales who appear in human form but sing ballads that isolate them from the events they control from behind the scenes. The reigning femme fatale of The Monk orchestrates extravagant, fantastical situations that lead to the incorrigible monk Ambrosio's horrific demise. Similarly, the fatal women of Scott's novels serve as foils to his pining, one-dimensional Gothic heroines. In The Monastery, the White Lady of Avenel is the keeper of alternative, even deviant, forms of knowledge, yet while she is clearly invested in the lives of Scott's characters, she remains continuously suspended above the miraculous events she oversees.

The femme fatale was also an especially compelling character of gothic-Romantic ballads. The first English translation of GOTTFRIED AUGUST BÜRGER's "Lenore" (1774), an extravagant tale of eternal female longing and haunting, launched the most extensive period of balladry in English history. It also strengthened the popularity of the ballad's most compelling female character: the Romantic fatal woman. Bürger's tale (translated into English as "Leonora") inspired the eerie, primitive landscapes of gothic novels more than 50 years after its British inception. Gothic novel-

ists including Horace Walpole, ANN RADCLIFFE, and Matthew Lewis imagined both female and male protagonists whose powers were often as enigmatic as they were invincible.

Bürger's German-Romantic model of a domineering ghost-witch in maiden's clothing also informs subsequent ballads by Scott, SAMUEL TAYLOR COLERIDGE, and JOHN KEATS. Coleridge's "CHRISTABEL" (1816) and Keats's "LA BELLE DAME SANS MERCI" (1819), for example, feature supernatural temptresses whose narrative and erotic control cause both excitement and discomfort, exploring moments when desire and dread clash violently in the seductive gaze of the fatal female lover. Both writers, uncertain how to frame, clothe, and control female sexuality, highlight the need to monitor and contain this character's indistinct and transformative features. Coleridge's "Christabel" locates its femme fatale, Geraldine, somewhere between the shadowy borders of body and mind, pain and sympathy, even male and female. Geraldine's serpentine features fit easily into the loose narrative of the traditional ballad: Its repetitive, experimental form and anonymous narrator leap from one thought to another, then linger without explanation. Geraldine's undressing scene at the end of part 1 reveals curiosity about the powers of female seduction that is ultimately suppressed by a stronger anxiety about containing gothic excess, specifically in the form of female sexuality turned monstrous.

Keats's tale of fatal seduction begins where Coleridge's ballad leaves off. In "La Belle Dame Sans Merci" it is the dressing-up of the femme fatale rather than her undressing that disguises the gathering of feminine power and mystique. Keats's ballad-romance expresses competing desires for liberation and containment of the femme fatale. "La Belle Dame" explores the seductive powers that "Christabel" reveals "live upon [the] eye" (l. 547) rather than the ears or lips. Keats's merciless maiden, like Coleridge's serpentine Geraldine, undermines assumptions of power maintained by the courtly love tradition. Keats, however, reverses Coleridge's undressing of Geraldine, having his unwary knight adorn La Belle Dame and distance her visually from the wild world in which she thrives. The knight is unaware that his attempts to dress up La Belle Dame only strengthen her powers to enthrall him. She quietly accepts his feminine gifts of "a garland for her head, / And bracelets too, and fragrant zone" (l. 21–22) while leading him further into her lair of love with a "language strange" (l. 27). La Belle Dame, like Geraldine, gains control through passivity by allowing her assured knight to "set" her where he pleases and dress her in distinctly exotic garb.

Even after the ballad's popularity began to fade in the 1820s and 1830s, the Romantic femme fatale's archaic modes of speech, androgynous features, and arcane powers of foresight endured well into the early 20th century. The Romantic fascination with gothic prophecy and narrative disruption, however, was dramatically revised and moderated within the domestic romance plots of midcentury poetry and novels. The femme fatale, while emerging early in the century as a wandering Romantic muse, became dangerously more earthbound and articulate in such popular genres as the sensation novel and vampire tale. Her ethereal, otherworldly features, though gradually replaced by the more worldly flesh-and-blood heroines of Victorian novels, could no longer be safely confined to the literary realm.

## Further Reading

Bürger, Gottfried August. "Lenore." In *An Anthology of German Literature of the Romantic Era and Age of Goethe*, translated by Klaus-Peter Hinze and Leonard M. Trawick, 11–29. New York: Edwin Mellen, 1993.

Coleridge, Samuel Taylor. "Christabel." In *Romanticism*, edited by Duncan Wu, 475–490. Oxford: Blackwell, 2000.

Keats, John. "La Belle Dame Sans Merci." In *Romanticism*, edited by Duncan Wu, 1,054–1,056. Oxford: Blackwell, 2000.

Lewis, Matthew. *The Monk: A Romance.* Introduced by Hugh Thomas. New York: Modern Library, 2002.

Scott, Walter. *The Monastery.* Edited by Penny Fielding. Edinburgh: Edinburgh University Press, 1995.

Tennyson, Alfred. "Merlin and Vivien." In *Idylls of the King and a Selection of Poems.* New York: Signet, 2003, 126–152.

—Heather Braun

## Fleming, Marjory (1803–1811)

Though she died unpublished in 1811 at age eight, the Scottish writer Marjory Fleming nevertheless left behind a trove of poems and diaries that would earn her Victorian best-seller status and the distinction of being the youngest member of the *Oxford Dictionary of National Biography*. The third child in the middle-class family of James and Isabella Fleming, Marjory Fleming was born on January 15, 1803, in Kirkcaldy, Fife. The affection between Fleming and her teenaged maternal cousin, Isabella (Isa) Keith, resulted in her spending the majority of her sixth, seventh, and eighth years at the Keiths' socially connected Edinburgh home. It was here, according to her second posthumous editor, John Brown, that she became the cherished friend of SIR WALTER SCOTT, though there is little evidence to support this claim. Nonetheless, Fleming was inspired by the works of Scott, as well as those of Alexander Pope, THOMAS GRAY, Jonathan Swift, and William Shakespeare, all of which she found in the Keith's library. Under Isa Keith's tutelage, she wrote as voraciously as she read. During the final two years of her life, she filled three blank copybooks with a total of 9,000 words and also wrote 560 lines of poetry in a variety of forms, including accurate historical narrative (Johnson 1994, 85).

Due to the fact that Keith assigned journal writing simply to improve Fleming's penmanship, the journals are relatively unmediated, providing a rich cache of evidence for cultural historians, scholars of life-writing, and emerging interests in the study of CHILDHOOD. Fleming provides a rare glimpse into the more quotidian elements of early 19th-century life, as well as a depiction of childhood that is unromanticized by the hindsight that would characterize an adult's account. She describes "the horrible and wret[ched] plaege that my multiplication gives me you cant conceive it—the most Devilish thing is 8 times 8 & 7 times 7 it is what nature itselfe cant endure" (Fleming 1934, 46–47), and she reveals an emerging sexuality in styling herself as a "loveress" of "well made Bucks" (37, 49). Her frequent vows to more closely heed the religious instruction given to her by family, books, and ministers sheds light on the process of socialization as well as the mores of her time. "A

Melancholy Lay," the elegy for dead turkey chicks that is perhaps her most famous poem, reveals a child processing life's brutality as well as its pathos and humor, and is worthy of quoting in its entirety as a sample of her work:

> Three Turkeys fair their last have breathed
> And now this worled for ever leaved
> Their father & their mother too
> Will sigh & weep as well as you
> Mourning for thre osprings fair
> Whom they did nurse with tender care
> Indeed the rats their bones have cranched
> To eternity are they launched
> There graceful form & pretty eyes
> Their fellow pows did not despise
> A direful death indeed they had
> That would put any parent mad
> But she was more than usual calm
> She did not give a singel dam
> She is as gentel as a lamb
> Here ends this melancholy lay
> Farewell poor turkeys I must say. (Fleming 1934,
>    29–30)

Other often-anthologized Fleming poems are typically referred to as "Here Lies Sweet Isabel in Bed," "O Lovely O Most Charming Pug," and "On Jessy Watsons Elopement," though it should be noted that Fleming rarely titled her poems herself. Her final poem, "Address to dear Isabella on the Authors recovery," describes her recuperation from a potentially fatal case of measles. In a sad twist of fate, Fleming died of meningitis the following day, December 19, 1811.

After her death, Fleming's family put her papers away in domestic obscurity until her youngest sister, Elizabeth, shared them with the London writer H. B. Farnie almost 50 years later. Under Farnie's editing, excerpts of Fleming's journals went to press in 1858. This first publication altered or excised significant amounts of Fleming's own text in favor of Farnie's sentimental editorializing about the dead child. Her second and third editors, John Brown and Lachlan MacBean, repeated this pattern to lessening degrees, until in 1934 unexpurgated notebooks were released in both facsimile and typeset editions following

acquisition of the manuscripts by the National Library of Scotland.

The fact that Fleming is relatively unknown in the 21st century renders it difficult to conceive just how popular she was among Victorian and early 20th-century audiences. Robert Louis Stevenson and Algernon Charles Swinburne were among her devotees, and Mark Twain dedicated an entire essay to her praise. In 1905 Andrew Lang claimed that "It is superfluous to quote from [John Brown's 1863] essay on Marjorie Fleming; every one knows about her and her studies . . ." (Lang 73). Fleming's journals and poetry have been published in various forms by six editors, and she has inspired two semibiographical novels and a song cycle.

The critic Judith Plotz argues that Fleming provided a rare embodiment of the Romantic child, a construction of innocent childhood genius that remained relevant amid the Victorian veneration of children as moral exemplars. Yet despite her editors' saccharine tributes and bowdlerization, from her first audience Fleming has been beloved for her frank observations on the adult world. While she has retained little of her Victorian renown, the emergence of several critical articles and the 1999 edition of her work released by Mercat Press suggest that Marjory Fleming's precocity will continue to engage readers into the 21st century.

## Further Reading

Brown, John. "Marjorie Fleming." In *Marjorie Fleming,* edited by L. MacBean, 155–203. New York: G. P. Putnam's Sons, 1904.

Fleming, Marjory. *The Complete Marjory Fleming: Her Journals, Letters, and Verses.* Edited by Frank Sidgwick. London: Sidgwick and Jackson, 1934.

———. *The Journals, Letters, and Verses of Marjory Fleming in Collotype Facsimile from the Original Manuscripts in the National Library of Scotland.* Edited by Arundell Esdaile. London: Sidgwick and Jackson, 1934.

———. *Marjory's Book: The Complete Journals, Letters, and Poems of a Young Girl.* Edited by Barbara McLean. Edinburgh: Mercat Press, 1999.

Fleming, Marjory, and Richard Rodney Bennett. *A Garland For Marjory Fleming: Five Songs for Soprano and Piano.* London: Novello, 1986.

Johnson, Alexandra. "The Drama of Imagination: Marjory Fleming and Her Diaries." In *Infant Tongues:*

*The Voice of the Child in Literature,* edited by Elizabeth Goodenough, Mark A. Heberle, and Naomi Sokoloff, 80–109. Detroit: Wayne State University Press, 1994.

———. *The Hidden Writer: Diaries and the Creative Life.* New York: Doubleday, 1997.

Lang, Andrew. "Rab's Friend." In *Adventures among Books.* New York: Longman, Green, and Co., 1905, 57–78.

MacBean, L. "Marjorie Fleming: The Story of Pet Marjorie Together with Her Journals and Her Letters." In *Marjorie Fleming,* edited by L. MacBean, 1–153. New York: G. P. Putnam's Sons, 1904.

Malet, Oriel. *Marjory Fleming.* London: Faber and Faber, 1946.

Plotz, J. "The Pet of Letters: Marjorie Fleming's Juvenilia." *Children's Literature Association Quarterly* 17, no. 4 (1992): 4–9.

Stephen, Leslie. "Fleming, Margaret (1803–1811)." In *Dictionary of National Biography.* London: Smith, Elder & Co., 1889. Available online. URL: http://www.oxforddnb.com.libproxy.lib.unc.edu/view/olddnb/9707. Accessed on November 30, 2008.

Sutherland, Kathryn. "Fleming, Marjory (1803–1811)." In *Oxford Dictionary of National Biography,* edited by H. C. G. Matthew and Brian Harrison. Oxford: Oxford University Press, 2004. Available online. URL: http://www.oxforddnb.com.libproxy.lib.unc.edu/view/article/9707. Accessed on November 30, 2008.

Twain, Mark. "Marjorie Fleming, the Wonder Child." In *The Complete Essays of Mark Twain,* edited by Charles Neider, 455–465. Garden City, N.Y.: Doubleday, 1963.

Van Gelder, Robert. *Marjory Fleming: the Youngest Genius.* New York: Dodd, Mead, and Company, 1940.

—Katherine L. Carlson

## "France: An Ode" Samuel Taylor Coleridge (1798)

Written and first published in 1798, "France: An Ode" recounts SAMUEL TAYLOR COLERIDGE's disillusionment with mass political action, and particularly the FRENCH REVOLUTION, as a means of achieving human liberty. The ode has five enumerated stanzas and follows a general pattern familiar to readers of the Romantic odes: an apostrophe to nature with a rising movement, which gives rise to some reflection and an inner conflict, followed by a crisis and a falling movement, concluding with the speaker's discovery of a new resolution.

In the first stanza the speaker invokes natural emblems of "divinest Liberty," beginning with "Ye Clouds!" (l. 1) and descending to the forest floor before ascending through "Waves," "Forests high," "Clouds," "rising Sun," and "blue rejoicing Sky" (ll. 15–17). The second stanza applies this imagery to France, whose "giant-limbs" (l. 22) vehemently assert freedom in "air, earth, and sea" (l. 23). In the process, learning gives way to violence in France and in the European powers who oppose her. The speaker, though unwilling to be unpatriotic, still serves as an apologist for France.

The third stanza voices this apology for France, particularly in terms of the vehement irreligion the speaker sees played out in the Revolution. Rather than defending France to others, however, the speaker seeks to resolve his own cognitive dissonance, "to soothe my soul" (l. 49) and silence "fears that would not flee" (l. 58). He almost convinces himself that, given a society devoted to liberty, "Love and Joy" will inevitably prevail. The fourth stanza dramatizes the failure of these hopes: from "bleak Helvetia's icy caverns" (l. 66) come Freedom's cries (the Blake editor David Perkins notes that the poem responds to the French invasion of Switzerland). The poet can only beg, "Forgive me, Freedom!" (l. 64).

In the fifth stanza the speaker repudiates his ill-founded hopes but seeks to recover a natural sense of "divinest Liberty" as developed in the first stanza. He now asserts that all people are "Slaves by their own compulsion" (l. 86) who bind themselves even more firmly with their misconceptions of "Freedom." The spiritual themes set aside throughout the poem now assert themselves: Imagining that Liberty has cast off both "Priestcraft's harpy minions" (l. 95) and "Blasphemy's obscener slaves" (l. 96), the speaker stands "with temples bare" (l. 102) of hat and idols alike and returns to the "sea-cliff's verge," to the "pines" and the "earth, sea, and air," to discover freedom (ll. 99–100).

Even this resolution is tinged with inherent violence. The speaker's imaginative projection "through earth, sea, and air" (l. 103) reprises France's blow that "smote air, earth, and sea" (l. 23). The speaker claims to be "Possessing all things," which could be read in terms of grasping wealth or of a spirit's seizing a body (l. 104). There is room to question the purity of the "intensest love" the speaker claims, here. Coleridge continues to rework this relationship of nature and spirit throughout his career, in poems and prose; his insistence that spirit be thought of as active and creative, rather than passive and receptive, is the distinctive contribution that he, even more than WILLIAM WORDSWORTH, has made to the Romantic intellectual arsenal.

See also "FEARS IN SOLITUDE."

## Further Reading

"France: An Ode." In *English Romantic Writers*, 2nd ed., edited by David Perkins, 538–540. Fort Worth, Tex.: Harcourt Brace, 1995.

—Peter Epps

## *Frankenstein*  Mary Wollstonecraft Shelley (1818)

First published in a three-volume edition in 1818, *Frankenstein; or, The Modern Prometheus* represents a late flowering of both the Romantic and the first-phase GOTHIC traditions. The story as printed is the direct descendant of one told orally by PERCY BYSSHE SHELLEY at a gathering of Romantic writers in Switzerland during the rainy summer of 1816. Influenced by German ghost stories, Percy, MARY WOLLSTONECRAFT SHELLEY, LORD BYRON, and Byron's physician JOHN WILLIAM POLIDORI each narrated an original tale. Polidori's work was published as "The VAMPYRE" (1819); Byron published his own "Fragment" alongside *Mazeppa* (1819), in part to distance himself from his physician's work, which was repeatedly attributed to his own pen. Mary Shelley prefaced the first edition of *Frankenstein* by connecting the novel to a greater literary tradition as well as to the 1816 gathering "in the environs of Geneva." Her preface to the third edition of 1831 represents a significant retrospective to both this initial foreword and to the novel as a whole.

*Frankenstein* is nominally EPISTOLARY FICTION, a novel framed by the recollections of Robert Walton, an English explorer travelling to uncharted Arctic wastes. Walton's letters to Mrs. Saville, his sister in England—dated only through a vague chronology that locates the action in the 18th century—embody the recollections of the eponymous Swiss scientist Victor Frankenstein. These, in turn convey the life history told to him by the essentially nameless Creature, which—in popular, post-Hollywood culture—is so often mistakenly known by the surname of its creator. The narrative, which like many gothic texts is preoccupied with the importance of documentation and the credibility of witnesses, concludes with an encounter between Walton and the creature. Though the whole story may seemingly be simply a traveler's tale similar to those that have inspired Walton, his closing conversation with the dignified and regretful creature across the body of the dead scientist serves rhetorically to confirm both *Frankenstein*'s incredible story and its moralistic fable of responsibility and toleration.

Walton's function in the narrative is not merely one of providing a convenient frame for the novel through his fascinated attention to Victor Frankenstein's autobiographical progress from medical student to pioneer surgical experimenter. He is himself the type of enthusiast that Frankenstein once was, and he is as preoccupied with the legends of the unexplored arctic as much as the medical student had been with the archaic natural science of Albertus Magnus and Paracelsus. Frankenstein's enthusiasm and self-justification are tinged with a reflective quality that essentially warns Walton against such excesses as those that had led ultimately to the Swiss savant's downfall. The novel's subtitle, which evokes Prometheus as the independent spirit who stole fire from the gods, inevitably suggests also the punishment meted out to those who overreach and transgress boundaries. In the absence of gods, and in a secular age characterized by atheistic scientists such as Frankenstein, punishment may well come from the consequences of a reckless engagement with one's speculative discipline—a turning, as it were, of the object of devotion on the misguided devotee. There is as much persecution in *Frankenstein,* as much obsession with the preservation of secrets and occluded knowledge, as there is in CALEB WILLIAMS (1794), by Mary Shelley's father, WILLIAM GODWIN.

The Creature's origins are obscure. Frankenstein admits to being active in charnel houses (bone depositories) and graveyards, a practice that may link him to the so-called resurrection men who supplied the British medical profession with cadavers suitable for dissection. Though the grave holds no terrors for the atheistic natural scientist, the Creature's lack of bodily integrity poses an interesting theological question. Given that the Creature is implicitly composed of more than one body and may possibly incorporate organs from both sexes, and even components from animals, the question of a soul or spiritual identity becomes crucial to anyone with the most nominal attachment to Christianity. Does the Creature have one soul or many, selected from the souls of those who have contributed to his present state? If the former, then in which organ does the soul persist? Has that soul, indeed, been wrested from Paradise, denied a heaven or taken from a hell to which its previous existence has destined it? More blasphemous, perhaps, is the suggestion that the Creature might have a new and innocent soul, one granted it because of the act of creation and not dependent on a previous bodily existence. This would make Frankenstein, effectively a god, worthy of the devotion and worship that his egotistical tirades prior to the act of creation suggest he craves. If the Creature has no soul, however, and is truly secular, then there can be no heaven, or no eternal punishment, waiting at the end of its life—no fearful threat, as it were, to temper its desire or ambition. Frankenstein, as an atheist, behaves himself as one who has no soul, assuming that no fitting retribution may come as a result of his actions. Though the novel admits no divine retribution, the systematic doubling of Creature and creator mythologizes an appropriate punishment for a crime which is not merely against nature, or even an affront to the Deity, but which has a personal and individual effect on the agent of Frankenstein's destruction, the Adam who has become his Satan, the once-beautiful fallen angel rejected by his deity.

Hollywood mythologies have for the most part premised the Creature's savagery on some physiological disorder in his body parts, or on some malfunction in the scientific midwifery that brings him to life. In Shelley's *Frankenstein* there is no Igor to drop the donor brain, leaving it compromised with painful glass shards; there is no murderer's head containing a brain with criminal propensities; no partially rotted organ that will blight the morals of the body into which it is inserted. The anonymous Creature of the novel embodies a brain that is, mentally, a tabula rasa, or blank slate. In a Rousseauan sense (see ROUSSEAU, JEAN-JACQUES), the Creature is created innocent, a "noble savage," and his manners, morals, and destiny are progressively shaped by his encounters with those around him. Being of large brain, he learns abnormally fast and rapidly gains new language skills rather than finding, as Hollywood so often insists, residual ones being reclaimed from the donor organ.

Hollywood's evasion highlights one of the most unpalatable messages of the novel: that human behaviour is seldom altruistic, is often irresponsible and self-centred, and rarely displays the liberal toleration that is associated with Enlightenment posturing. The Creature is traumatically rejected by its creator on the gothic night of its creation. It is subsequently driven away by villagers fearful of its immense size and grotesque appearance. It finds toleration only in the person of a blind man, the elder De Lacey (or De Lacy), who is pleased with its educated and temperate conversation and ignorant of its physiological abnormality. His family, however, are gifted with sight and again reject the Creature without consideration or compassion. From this point his encounters with humanity are driven by revenge and resentment, and this includes his significant and early slaughter of young William Frankenstein. The Creature is aware of this: "[M]isery made me a fiend," it confides in the second chapter of volume 2. "Make me happy and I shall again be virtuous." Frankenstein, of course, declines to act on this request, largely because it is associated with the Creature's demand for a similarly constructed mate; in consequence, the creature progressively strips his creator of family and friends. Ultimately, they have only each other, and each pursues his respective nemeses until the novel's conclusion in the sterile arctic wastes. There is a mythic grandeur here that directly emulates the fateful relationships between God and Adam, and between God and Satan, in JOHN MILTON's *Paradise Lost*, one of the works which the creature comes to both understand and apply to his own situation when residing near the house of the De Lacey family in the seventh chapter of volume 2.

*Frankenstein* is many things. It is a meditation on human education and development and a fearful reflection on the shallowness of Enlightenment idealism. It is as much an experiment in protoscience fiction as it is an embodiment of the contemporary scientific ideals of Luigi Galvani (1737–98) and Benjamin Franklin (1706–90). It is an implicit commentary on the respective importance of the sexes in the construction of a balanced character. Most of all, though, it is the cardinal expression of one of the most enduring Romantic myths, one that persists into the 21st century. Mystery and myth, as it were, remain potent even in the world of secularity triumphant. If the Creature is a product of science, his revenge—and his reflection on that vengeful process—still recall the mythologies characteristic of a tumultuous age.

**Further Reading**

Byron, George Gordon, Lord. "Fragment of a Story." In *Vampyres: Lord Byron to Count Dracula*, edited by Christopher Frayling, 126–130. London: Faber and Faber, 1991.

Eberle-Sinatra, Michael. "Readings of Homosexuality in Mary Shelley's *Frankenstein* and Four Film Adaptations." *Gothic Studies* 7, no. 2 (November 2005): 185–202.

Lloyd Smith, Allen. "'This Thing of Darkness': Racial Discourse in Mary Shelley's *Frankenstein*." *Gothic Studies* 6, no. 2 (November 2004): 208–222.

Marshall, Tim. *Murdering to Dissect: Grave-Robbing, Frankenstein and the Anatomy Literature.* Manchester, Eng.: Manchester University Press, 1995.

Polidori, John. "The Vampyre." In *Vampyres: Lord Byron to Count Dracula*, edited by Christopher Frayling, 107–125. London: Faber and Faber, 1991.

Schoene-Harwood, Berthold. *Mary Shelley: Frankenstein—A Reader's Guide to Essential Criticism.* Cambridge: Icon, 2000.

Schor, Esther, ed. *The Cambridge Companion to Mary Shelley.* Cambridge: Cambridge University Press, 2003.

Shelley, Mary. *Frankenstein; or, The Modern Prometheus.* Edited by J. Paul Hunter. New York: W. W. Norton, 1996.

—William Hughes

## French Revolution (1789–1799)

Of all the events of the 18th and 19th centuries, the French Revolution arguably had the greatest impact on European history, literature, and politics. In 1780s France, members of the lower and middle classes witnessed their economic plight worsening. The excesses of the clergy and upper classes were increasingly vilified, and resentment against these two classes continued to fester. The French Revolution emerged in May 1789 with the convening of the Estates-General—or assembly—which represented the classes of the clergy, nobility, and commoners. The commoners, otherwise known as the Third Estate, had little success in countering the combined power of the clergymen and the nobles. However, the seeds of revolution were planted when the Third Estate convened its own meeting later in June 1789 and christened itself the National Assembly. Just one month later, on July 14, 1789, Parisians stormed the infamous Bastille prison, widely regarded as a symbol of the monarchy's repressive regime. Many members of the middle class (the bourgeois) and the urban lower classes (the sansculottes), especially the Parisians, had grown critical of the monarchy, and they readily supported a change in the so-called ancien regime.

In August 1789 the National Assembly undertook two important events: It eliminated feudalism with the August Decrees and composed the Declaration of the Rights of Man and of the Citizen, which was inspired by the U.S. Declaration of Independence. The declaration's writers denounced the hereditary monarchy system and advocated freedom and liberty. Within the very first article, the writers declared that "men are born and remain free and equal in rights," a revolutionary statement in a country with a long tradition of hereditary privilege. To symbolize the equalizing force of the Revolution, supporters adopted the popular slogan "Liberty, Equality, Fraternity." Indeed, it was this spirit of universal brotherhood that galvanized the Revolution in France and popularized it among liberals in England. In fact, the declaration would later influence important political writings by MARY WOLLSTONECRAFT and THOMAS PAINE. In addition, WILLIAM WORDSWORTH's homage to the language of the common man in the PREFACE TO LYRICAL BALLADS could certainly owe its inspiration to the French declaration.

During the early years of the French Revolution, liberal writers such as Wordsworth, PERCY BYSSHE SHELLEY, and WILLIAM GODWIN enthusiastically applauded the Declaration of the Rights of Man and the storming of the Bastille in 1789. The Romantic poets in general regarded the Revolution as a liberating, purifying force that would transform the landscape of European politics. Referring to the early years of the French Revolution, William Wordsworth wrote, "Bliss was it in that dawn to be alive" (Prelude 109), echoing the sentiments of poets such as Shelley and WILLIAM BLAKE, who used the Revolution to stimulate their imaginations and envision an apocalyptic change for nations and their governments. When the conservative member of Parliament EDMUND BURKE, in his *Reflections on the Revolution in France* (1790) condemned the Revolution for its radical overthrow of the traditional monarchial system and cautioned the English public that the same events could transpire in England, he was soundly rebuked in two famous responses: Mary Wollstonecraft's *A VINDICATION OF THE RIGHTS OF MEN* (1790) and Thomas Paine's *The RIGHTS OF MAN* (1791–92).

When scholars examine the treatment of the French Revolution during the Romantic era, they generally focus on the ideas of Wordsworth, Shelley, and their male contemporaries. Such studies help us to understand why Romanticism is consistently associated with revolutions. However, texts by lesser-known authors such as ANNA LAETITIA BARBAULD, HELEN MARIA WILLIAMS, MARY ROBINSON, CHARLOTTE SMITH, and Eliza Daye, among others, have been largely overlooked in these discussions of Romantics and the historical change of the French Revolution. As the events in France

began to escalate, women writers in England witnessed fascinating accounts of Frenchwomen's involvement in the Revolution. In fact, it would be fair to say that Frenchwomen played a key role in shaping the Revolution from 1789 to 1793. Political leaders such as Madame Roland and MME. ANNE-LOUISE-GERMAINE DE STAËL took the public stage, and women's clubs such as the Society of Revolutionary Republican Women became more common. Helen Maria Williams, in particular, contributed to contemporary understanding of the Revolution with her widely read *LETTERS FROM FRANCE* (1790–96) after a visit that year. Williams relocated to Paris in 1792 and ardently supported the ideals of the Revolution; her letters were an eyewitness account of the most important revolutionary events. Wordsworth, too, visited France during the early years of the Revolution and recorded his initially favorable impressions in *The PRELUDE*.

As regards the revolutionary rhetoric of the Romantic era, both male and female writers used similar images and language—fire, the shattered soldier, famine, tyranny, freedom, battlefields, NAPOLEON BONAPARTE—and followed similar trends from their generally positive response to the initial outbreak of the Revolution to the antiwar sentiments that followed the revolutionary excesses from 1792 onward. The September Massacres of 1792, which saw the executions of thousands of French citizens, certainly disenchanted revolutionary enthusiasts. A year later, the so-called Reign of Terror, instigated by Maximilien-François-Marie-Isidore de Robespierre and the Committee of Public Safety, further horrified previous supporters of revolutionary change as thousands of French citizens were executed at the guillotine for treasonable activities. Conservatives in England, worried that similar events could transpire in their own country, decried the execution of Louis XVI and Marie Antoinette in 1793.

By 1799 the Revolution had run its course. The Directory regime, which acted as a legislature, was pulled apart by internal dissention and public dissatisfaction with the Directory's often ruthless methods of compliance. In November 1799 the French army's general, Napoleon Bonaparte (1769–1821), staged a coup. The people of France, tired of the continual violence of the Revolution, welcomed Bonaparte's leadership, and in a short time he established a dictatorship that would eventually lead to his crowning as emperor in 1804. However, the effects of the Revolution would reverberate through the 19th century as other countries were seized by revolutionary fervor. Spain, Portugal, Greece, and Poland all staged various rebellions, and in 1848 Europe experienced a wave of revolutions. Popular fascination with the French Revolution still remains today, and scholars continue to analyze the complex effects of the Revolution on Romantic-era writers.

**Further Reading**

Bainbridge, Simon. *British Poetry and the Revolutionary and Napoleonic Wars: Visions of Conflict.* Oxford and New York: Oxford University Press, 2003.

Haywood, Ian. *Bloody Romanticism: Spectacular Violence and the Politics of Representation, 1776–1832.* Basingstoke, Eng.: Palgrave Macmillan, 2006.

Hunt, Lynn. *Politics, Culture, and Class in the French Revolution.* Berkeley: University of California Press, 1984.

Yarrington, Allison, and Kelvin Everest, eds. *Reflections of Revolution: Images of Romanticism.* London: Routledge, 1993.

—Sara Dustin

## "Frost at Midnight"  Samuel Taylor Coleridge
(1798)

A blank-verse poem, "Frost at Midnight" was composed by SAMUEL TAYLOR COLERIDGE in February 1798 and published in the quarto pamphlet entitled *Fears in solitude: written in 1798 during the alarm of an invasion: to which are added France, an ode; and Frost at midnight.* "Frost at Midnight" is part of a group of Coleridge poems traditionally known as his "conversation poems." These include "The EOLIAN HARP," "Reflections on Having Left a Place of Retirement," "THIS LIME-TREE BOWER MY PRISON," "FEARS IN SOLITUDE," "The Nightingale," "DEJECTION: AN ODE," and "To William Wordsworth." All of these poems are intimate meditations, "poems [that] have a remarkable and touching intimacy, a revelation of personal feeling

and circumstance," as J. R. Watson tells us (Watson 151). George Maclean Harper writes that "even when they are soliloquies the sociable man who wrote them could not even think without supposing a listener" (Harper 189).

"Frost at Midnight" is concerned with the poet's thoughts while he is in his Nether Stowey (Somerset) cottage at night, his "cradled infant" (Coleridge's firstborn son, HARTLEY COLERIDGE) by his side: "The inmates of my cottage, all at rest, / Have left me to that solitude that suits / Abstruser musings" (ll. 4–6). The poet feels isolated by the silence and stillness of the cold winter night, imprisoned in his thoughts and separated from the natural world by "the secret ministry" (l. 1) of the frost that covers his windowpanes. The poem traces the poet's movement of mind, the "fluttering" of the fire upon the grate akin to the poet's own restless thoughts: "Methinks its motion in this hush of nature / Gives it dim sympathies with me who live" (ll. 17–18).

The fire on the grate reminds the poet of his childhood, and in the next part of the poem he remembers the mysterious beauty and power of his boyhood imaginings: ". . . I dreamt / Of my sweet birthplace, and the old church-tower / Whose bells, the poor man's only music, rang / From morn to evening all the hot Fair-day, / So sweetly that they stirred and haunted me" (ll. 28–32). The poet's recollection of the "townsman, or aunt, or sister more beloved / When we both were clothed alike!" (ll. 43–44) brings his thoughts around to the love of his child.

The final section of the poem begins with this apostrophe: "Dear babe, that sleepest cradled by my side" (l. 45). The poet thinks about his own childhood, "For I was reared reared / In the great city, Pent 'mid cloisters dim" (ll. 52–53) and contrasts it to what he hopes his child will experience: "But thou, my babe! shalt wander like a breeze, / By lakes and sandy shores" (ll. 55–56). The poet's love for his baby fully releases his creative powers. The poem's final lines are a benediction in which the poet imagines for his son a paradisial world. The "secret ministry of frost" that had divided the poet from the natural world is now reimagined as the agent of eternal unity and divine beauty, and has now become identified with the poet's own shaping powers: "Therefore all seasons shall be sweet to thee, / Whether the summer clothe the general earth / With greenness ... / Or if the secret ministry of frost / Shall hang them up in silent icicles, / Quietly shining to the quiet moon" (ll. 66–75).

This final blessing was not always the end of Coleridge's poem. The original ending of the poem had six additional lines: "Like those [icicles], my babe! which, ere tomorrow's warmth / Have capp'd their sharp keen points with pendulous drops / Will catch thine eye, and with their novelty / Suspend thy little soul; then make thee shout / And stretch and flutter from thy mother's arms / As thou woulds't fly for very eagerness." Coleridge's decision in 1828 to cut these final lines has been both celebrated and criticized as diminishing the political tenor of "Frost at Midnight." Preeminent among those scholars who argue for the original 1798 ending is Paul Magnuson in his important article "The Politics of 'Frost at Midnight,'" in which he suggests that the poem should be read in the contexts of Coleridge's other poems and the political debates taking place in the 1790s. Since the publication of Magnuson's essay, many Romanticism anthologies now print the original version of the poem or both the 1798 and 1828 texts. In either version, Romanticists generally agree that, as Matthew Vanwinkle states, "Frost at Midnight" is "the culmination of Coleridge's achievement in his most influential lyric form, the conversation poem" (Vanwinkle 583).

**Further Reading**

Harper, George Maclean. "Coleridge's Conversation Poems." In *English Romantic Poets: Modern Essays in Criticism*, ed. by M. H. Abrams, 188–201. Oxford University Press, 1960.

Magnuson, Paul. "The Politics of 'Frost at Midnight.'" *The Wordsworth Circle* 22, no. 1 (Winter 1991): 3–11.

Vanwinkle, Matthew. "Fluttering on the Grate: Revision in 'Frost at Midnight.'" *Studies in Romanticism* 43, no. 4 (Winter 2004): 583–598.

Watson, J. R. *English Poetry of the Romantic Period, 1789–1830*. New York: Longman, 1985.

—Deborah Morse

# G

## "Garden of Love, The," William Blake
(ca. 1794)

WILLIAM BLAKE's "The Garden of Love" was drafted without title in his *Notebook* and etched for *Songs of Experience* (1794) as plate 44. The etching depicts a boy and a girl kneeling at an open grave; a tonsured monk by their side holds a book. Two worms are to the right of the writing, and the grave mound covered with briars is shown beneath.

As with many other poems from *Songs of Experience*, "The Garden of Love" is an allegorical representation criticizing tyrannical morality. In the poem, Blake looks on the garden as originally a symbol of Edenic innocence and love. The poem's speaker returns to a primeval garden to find that a chapel has been erected in it and taboos have been inscribed on it. The chapel's gates are shut, and "Thou shalt not" is written over the door (l. 6). The garden itself is no longer filled with fragrant flowers but turned into a desert full of briars, graves, and tombstones among which priests are walking their rounds. On an allegorical level, prohibition and prescriptive morality have imposed themselves upon innocence. As a human-made bulwark, the chapel here becomes emblematic for the encroachment of the church over the simple joys of life; it is an unnecessary mystification of the natural. Similarly, the garden's flowers, symbolic—as elsewhere in the *Songs*—of love and innocent happiness, are metamorphosed into briars, binding the speaker's "joys and desires" (l. 12). The Edenic state has become infected with a restrictive moral law, represented by the priests walking in it as agents of repression. As such, "The Garden of Love" directly attacks the institutionalized mechanisms of the church, separating the individual from God (the chapel's closed door) and prohibiting natural desires through doctrines and prescriptive moral codes ("Thou shalt not" written over it).

The theme of a prescriptive moral code that interferes between the individual and God runs throughout Blake's writing. Love is falsely tabooed, and thus sexuality becomes a sin, provoking feelings such as shame and envy. For Blake these mechanisms are clearly symptomatic of the fallen world and responsible for the suppression of natural desires and the individual. Throughout the prophetic books, this is exemplified by tyranny that gives rise to perverse taboos and represses life as such (see, for example, Blake's *Europe: A Prophecy* [1794], plate 15. "Over the doors thou shalt not: & over the chimneys Fear is written" [Blake 218]). The idea of the garden as a paradise perverted recurs in *JERUSALEM* (1804–20), where the evil character Vala turns it into a garden of taboos, death, and cruelty.

See also *Songs of Innocence and of Experience*.

### Further Reading
Ackroyd, Peter. *Blake: A Biography.* New York: Knopf, 1996.

Behrendt, Stephen C. *Reading William Blake.* New York: St. Martin's Press, 1992.

Blake, William. *William Blake's Writings.* 2 vols. Edited by G. E. Bentley. Oxford: Clarendon Press, 1978.

Bloom, Harold. *Blake's Apocalypse: A Study in Poetic Argument.* Garden City, N.Y.: Doubleday, 1963.

Eaves, Morris. *The Cambridge Companion to William Blake.* Cambridge: Cambridge University Press, 2003.

—Andrea Rummel

## Gardiner, Marguerite (Countess of Blessington) (1789–1849)

When Marguerite Gardiner is mentioned today, it tends to be in connection with two men: GEORGE GORDON, LORD BYRON; and Alfred, Count D'Orsay. Her own biography has traditionally proved difficult to write, entwined as it is with a series of myths and reinventions. The bare facts are these. Born on September 1, 1789, into an Irish Catholic landowning family, Gardiner survived an early marriage (age 14) and spent several years as the mistress of an army captain before becoming a celebrated society beauty and high-society hostess. Her marriage to Charles Gardiner, earl of Blessington, in 1818 allowed her to spend lavishly at their mansion in St. James's Square, London, where she entertained many of the leading politicians and writers of the day, including THOMAS MOORE (1779–1852) and John Galt (1779–1839). Such was her success that by 1838 Henry Chorley could describe her as "the grace and ornament of the literary world" (Charley 30).

Blessington started to publish during the 1820s. *The Magic Lantern; or Sketches of Scenes in the Metropolis* appeared in 1822, followed the same year by a travel diary, *Journal of a Tour through the Netherlands to Paris, in 1821.* The most famous of these nonfiction works stemmed from her meeting with Lord Byron in Genoa in 1823. This was A JOURNAL OF CONVERSATIONS WITH LORD BYRON (1834), an enterprise that revealed a shrewd sense of the public's appetite for celebrity gossip. It was a best seller and made Gardiner famous.

Gardiner's works tended to be anecdotal, and their tone was light and sophisticated. Although she had an eye for picturesque detail, her main qualifications were, according to the editor Ernest Lovell, seen to be her "feminine elegance of mind and high rank in society" (in Blessington 12). She was therefore a natural editor (from 1834) of the *Book of Beauty,* one of the most popular anthologies of poetry, engravings, and fiction (see ANNUALS AND GIFT BOOKS), and she made a similar success of editing *The Keepsake,* another annual. Thereafter she turned her hand to poetry and fiction, doing so with an energy that belied her reputation as a lady of leisure. There were 10 volumes of the former, most with such (clichéd) titles as *Flowers of Loveliness* (1835), *Gems of Beauty* (1836), *and The Belle of a Season* (1840). In terms of fiction, from *Grace Cassidy, or The Repealers* (1833) to *Country Quarters* (1850), there were at least 12 novels as well as three volumes of short stories and sketches. Many fall into the category of "silver fork" novels—that is, fiction detailing the glamorous lives of members of the upper classes. Some of them—for example, *Strathern* (1845)—contains loosely disguised portraits of real people (in this case the novelist and politician Edward Bulwer Lytton) and thus seemed to offer readers a titillating insight into how their "betters" lived and loved.

Despite being estimated to earn between £2,000 and £3,000 per year from her writing (an enormous sum for those days), Gardiner was constantly in financial difficulties. "The truth is," she wrote, "the numerous family of father, mother, sister, brother, and his six children, that I have to provide for, compels me to write" (quoted in Hawkins and Klaver xvi). But part of her problems were self-inflicted. She was notoriously extravagant. Eventually, in April 1849 she and Count D'Orsay—by this time her stepson-in-law as well as being (it was rumoured) her lover—fled to Paris to escape their creditors. Gardiner died there from a stroke two months later, on June 4, 1849, and gradually disappeared from histories of Romanticism. She has tended to be dismissed as a woman whose wealth and privilege allowed her to dabble amateurishly in fiction and poetry and whose private life is more interesting than either. There is some justification in this, but she has also been recognized as an important figure in Byron studies, and her interviews remain important sources for biographers. Her work as a novelist has been reevaluated (she is seen, for example, as a writer who "challenged social mores" [Hawkins and Kraver xxvi]), and as we discover more about the impact of women's writing and the 19th century magazine market, she looks set to be reinstated as an important player.

**Further Reading**

Blessington, Marguerite, countess of. *Lady Blessington's Conversations of Lord Byron.* Edited by Ernest J. Lovell, Jr. Princeton, N.J.: Princeton University Press, 1969.

Chorley, Henry. *Authors of England.* London: Tilt, 1838.

Feldman, Paula. *British Women Poets of the Romantic Era: An Anthology.* Baltimore: John Hopkins University Press, 1997.

Foulkes, Nick. *Last of the Dandies: The Scandalous Life and Escapades of Count D'Orsay.* New York: Little Brown, 2003.

Hawkins, Ann. "Delectable Books for Delicate Readers: The 1830s Gift Book Market, Ackerman and Co and the Countess of Blessington." *Kentucky Philological Review* 16 (March 2001): 20–26.

Hawkins, Ann, and Jeraldine Kraver, eds. *Marguerite Countess of Blessington: The Victims of Society.* London: Pickering and Chatto, 2005.

Jump, Harriet. *"The False Prudery of Public Taste": Scandalous Women and the Annuals 1820–1850."* In *Feminist Readings of Victorian Popular Texts,* edited by Emma Liggins and Daniel Duffy, 1–17. Brookfield, Vt.: Ashgate, 2001.

—Andrew Maunder

## George III   See MONARCHY.

## *Giaour, The*   Lord Byron (1813)

Subtitled "A Fragment of a Turkish Tale," *The Giaour* marks the first of LORD BYRON's four "Oriental Tales," the others being *The BRIDE OF ABYDOS, The CORSAIR,* and *Lara.* In May 1813 Byron was counseling the Irish poet THOMAS MOORE to "stick to the East," and in this instance he was following his own advice. The poem's title is taken from the Arabic word for "infidel" and is pronounced with a "j"; its pronunciation is determined by the poem's end-rhyme scheme with "power" (quoted in McGann 36). Byron composed the poem between September 1812 and March 1813 and published the first edition of nearly 700 lines in June 1813. During the subsequent seven editions printed in 1813, the poem reached its final length of 1,334 lines.

The work's form and structure are intriguing. The poem represents Bryon's only use of the popular Romantic form known as the fragment poem. Structurally, he uses three narrators whose distinct stories are linked loosely together to recall the Giaour's doomed love affair with a slave girl, Leila, and subsequent revenge against her master, Hassan, who drowns her to punish her infidelity. In piecing together these narrative threads, the poet fails to follow a strict chronology, using instead a combination of times and tenses to create a richer and more complex tale.

The poem opens with an elegy for ancient Greece and its heroes. This is closely followed by a call for the present-day Greeks to remember that distant past and to muster the courage to fight their Turkish oppressors—a mission Byron himself would follow. The narrator then offers his reader the "mournful tale" of the Giaour and his vengeance. The tale opens with the Giaour riding from Hassan's home, which, because of its owner's sin, has fallen into ruin and been transformed from a palace to a tomb. The story then flashes back to the reason for, and circumstances of, the battle between these two men. Hassan, wrongly believing that Leila has given herself sexually to the Giaour, orders that she be sewn into a sack, taken out to sea, and drowned. Learning of her death, the Giaour goes in search of Hassan and enters into battle. He kills his foe and avenges his lost love, but unlike Hassan, whose death in battle against an infidel promises a heavenly reward, the Giaour is cursed to live like a vampire, cut off from all he knows and loves. The poem concludes with a monk recalling the Giaour's final years of isolation in a monastery, where, on his deathbed, he confesses his deed and is haunted by a ghostly vision of Leila. Upon the Giaour's death, nothing is left to mark his grave or his life except for this tale.

Aside from offering analyses of its links to Romantic ORIENTALISM, contemporary critics have read the poem through the lens of feminist and queer theory. The relationship between Hassan and the Giaour is certainly suggestive: Is the important relationship the one that exists between the two men, rather than between the men and the woman? Leila herself seems merely a passive victim, an object even, to be handed back and forth between the more powerful males.

## Further Reading

Butler, Marilyn. "The Orientalism of Byron's *Giaour.*" In *Byron and the Limits of Fiction*, edited by Bernard Beatty and Vincent Newey, 78–96. Liverpool: Liverpool University Press, 1988.

Lew, Joseph. "The Necessary Orientalist? *The Giaour* and Nineteenth-Century Mysogyny." In *Romanticism, Race, and Imperial Culture, 1780–1834*, edited by Alan Richardson and Sonia Hofkosh, 173–202. Bloomington: Indiana University Press, 1996.

McGann, Jerome. *Byron and Romanticism.* Cambridge: Cambridge University Press, 2002.

Schneider, Jeffrey L. "Secret Sins of the Orient: Setting a Homotextual Context for Byron's *Oriental Tales.*" *College English* 65 (2002): 81–96.

Seed, David. "'Disjointed Fragments': Concealment and Revelation in *The Giaour.*" *Byron Journal* 18 (1990): 13–27.

—Jeffrey L. Schneider

## *Glenarvon* (The Fatal Passion)  Caroline Lamb (1816)

Released in England on May 9, 1816, *Glenarvon* was marketed as a true-to-life account of CAROLINE LAMB's chaotic 1812 love affair with LORD BYRON. The book was enormously popular, running to numerous editions, including a republication in the 1860s, albeit with a new title: *The Fatal Passion*. In actuality, the novel is not the torrid recollection of one of Regency England's most sensational scandals but, rather, a genre-bending tale of love, deception, and hypocrisy set during the Irish Revolution of 1798. Nonetheless, most of the characters in the novel are, in fact, thinly veiled depictions of various important figures in Lamb's social circle, the pinnacle of upper-class society of the period. As such, both *Glenarvon* and its author were blasted by critics, many of whom found the book "unreadable." Indeed, until the end of the 20th century, the novel was rarely considered by literary scholars except as a source for Byron stud-

ies. Nevertheless, *Glenarvon* is an interesting piece of literature, and despite nearly two centuries of negative attention, it has reemerged in criticism as an exemplar of early feminist writing, as well as a study of the dynamics of celebrity culture and the politics of revolution in the Romantic period. The book also has much to say regarding the aesthetics of the Romantic novel, and lends itself quite well to psychoanalytic interpretation.

The book's central plotline tells the story of Calantha, a naive aristocrat who becomes enamored of the mysterious rebel Glenarvon, the novel's Byron figure. Over the course of the novel, Glenarvon "ruins" numerous women, including Calantha and two others, Alice and Elinor. Collectively, these three heroines may be read as representations of Lamb herself. Alice and Calantha die of broken hearts after Glenarvon leaves them, but Elinor's death is far more interesting, and constitutes one of the story's major feminist aspects. Through much of the novel, Elinor is dressed up like a male soldier and joins Glenarvon in his political pursuits. She even delivers an incendiary revolutionary address to a gathering of rebels, formerly Glenarvon's followers, just before committing suicide by riding off a cliff on a horse—a characteristically masculine Byronic image. Likewise, Calantha and Alice resurface at the end of the book to underscore this feminist slant. Though the narrative plays with conventions of the GOTHIC throughout, in the book's only overtly supernatural scene, the spirits of Calantha and Alice return to torture Glenarvon and ultimately kill him. Thus, the novel has much to say about the role of femininity in the Regency period. To that end, *Glenarvon* also presents harsh criticisms of Lamb's social circle, most notably of Lady Melbourne, Byron's confidante and the mother of Lamb's husband, William. Indeed, by virtue of its form as well as its subject matter, Lady Caroline Lamb's *Glenarvon* offers readers a commentary on many pertinent social, political, and artistic issues of the day in ways that are sometimes unexpected in Romantic writing.

## Further Reading

Clubbe, John. "Glenarvon Revised—and Revisited." *Wordsworth Circle* 10 (1979): 205–217.

Graham, Peter. *Don Juan and Regency England*. Charlottesville: University of Virginia Press, 1990.

Kelsall, Malcolm. "The Byronic Hero and Revolution in Ireland: The Politics of *Glenarvon*." *Byron Journal* 9 (1981): 4–16.

Lamb, Caroline, Lady. *Glenarvon*. Edited by Frances Wilson. London: Everyman Paperback Classics, 1995.

McDayter, Ghislaine. "Hysterically Speaking: Lady Caroline Lamb's *Glenarvon* and the Revolutionary Voice." In *Romantic Generations: Essays in Honor of Robert F. Gleckner*, edited by Ghislaine McDayter et. al, 155–177. Lewisburg: Bucknell University Press, 2001.

—Diana Koretsky


## Godwin, William (1756–1836)

William Godwin was born on March 3, 1756, in Wisbech, Cambridgeshire, England. He was one of six children born to John Godwin, a minister, and Ann Hull, both of whom were Calvinists. Despite scant nurturing from his parents, Godwin was able to read in his infancy, although he was confined to pious literature. He was sent to school at age eight, and at 11 he was tutored by Reverend Samuel Newton, who practiced a strict form of Calvinism called Sandeminianism. When Godwin's father died, his mother sent him to the progressive Hoxton Academy, a Dissenting school where, serious and somewhat unpopular, he nevertheless flourished as a scholar and debater. Dedicating himself to the pursuit of truth, he began to read widely, and his interest in the French philosophes caused him gradually to lose his faith (though under SAMUEL TAYLOR COLERIDGE's influence he later turned to deism).

Godwin was appointed minister at Stowmarket, Suffolk, in 1779. He upset neighboring ministers over an issue of church doctrine and was shunned by them until he resigned and moved to London. Rejected from another ministerial post, he set himself up as a writer. His early output included biographies (*History of the Life of William Pitt Earl of Chatham*, 1783), sermons (*Sketches of History*, 1784), a spoof (*The Herald of Literature*, 1784), several plays (never staged) and three romances, all published in 1784: *Imogen; Italian Letters;* and *Damon and Delia,* a novel in the popular style with a character based on Godwin, who shows the wretchedness of life as an impoverished writer.

Godwin primarily wrote literary reviews, and through the *English Review* he met his life-long friend THOMAS HOLCROFT. In 1784 he was employed at the *New Annual Register,* and he subsequently became a successful political journalist, writing analysis for the *Political Herald.* He was courted by booksellers and dined with authors and politicians; however, his pursuit of truth at any cost hampered the fame he craved.

True to the Dissenting tradition of political and religious liberty, Godwin was a supporter of the FRENCH REVOLUTION in its early bloodless years. His response to the deterioration of the situation in 1791 was to write a treatise on political principles to steer humankind's progress back on track. *An Enquiry Concerning Political Justice and Its Influence on General Virtue and Happiness* (1793) has the pursuit of truth at its heart, arguing that government being essentially corrupt, politics will be supplanted by the scrupulous exercise of individual judgment policed by fearless criticism from others. Institutions such as marriage are rejected in favour of each "[consulting] his own understanding" (Godwin 1971; 16). It was a best seller, making Godwin the hero of radical political and literary circles; his many disciples included the future lions of literature WILLIAM WORDSWORTH and Coleridge. *Political Justice* was followed in 1794 by *Things as They Are; or, The Adventures of Caleb Williams* (see CALEB WILLIAMS), in which Godwin disseminated his ideas in fictional form to the wider reading public. Like *Political Justice,* it avoided the government's censure of inflammatory publications, and it went to 26 international reprints in Godwin's lifetime. A diluted stage version entitled *The Iron Chest* ran in London for decades.

Godwin practiced the reasoned and impartial action his philosophy advocated. After Holcroft's arrest for high treason, he wrote an article that influenced the court to drop the charges ("Cursory Strictures on the Charge Delivered by Lord Chief Justice Eyre to the Grand Jury, October 2, 1794"). In 1795 he and the feminist radical writer MARY WOLLSTONECRAFT began an unconventional courtship according to their principles, but they married in 1797 out of necessity when Mary became pregnant.

In September 1797 Mary Wollstonecraft died in childbirth. She left Godwin a daughter, Mary (see SHELLEY, MARY WOLLSTONECRAFT), and a stepdaughter, Fanny. Grief-stricken, he rushed out two books to honor his wife's memory: her *Posthumous Works,* and *Memoirs of the Author of a Vindication of the Rights of Woman,* a groundbreaking, frank biography that shocked the country, fueling the anti-Jacobin backlash in which Godwin and Wollstonecraft were cast as national villains. In response, Godwin published *St. Leon, A Tale of the Sixteenth Century* (1799), a fashionably GOTHIC-style novel in which he recants (with sincerity) his former views on marriage. He revised *Political Justice* twice during the turbulent 1790s.

In 1801 Godwin began an affair with a writer neighbour, Mary Jane Clairmont. Like Wollstonecraft, she was an unmarried mother, and Godwin married her when she became pregnant. She had a son, William, in 1803. With five children between them, the Godwins were always to struggle financially.

At the century's end, concluding that political reform was inseparable from the development of wider cultural activity (explored in *The Enquirer: Reflections on Education, Manners and Literature* [1797]), Godwin turned his attention to English literature. He wrote several (unsuccessful) plays and, hoping to benefit from the public's romantic interest in England's medieval past, a *Life of Chaucer;* his hopes were disappointed. He tried again with *Fleetwood, or the New Man of Feeling* (1805) inspired by Henry Mackenzie's famous novel of sentiment *The Man of Feeling* (1771). Like *St. Leon,* it was a financial failure if (moderate) critical success. However, a children's book of *Bible Stories* (1802) published anonymously did sell, and the Godwins opened a children's bookshop, selling more anonymous works. Despite the success of many of its publications—*Pantheon or Ancient History of the Gods of Greece and Rome* (1814) became a school textbook (a favourite of Keats's), while CHARLES and MARY LAMB's *Tales from Shakespeare* (published by Godwin) is still in print, as is *Swiss Family Robinson,* Godwin's 1816 translation of a German novel—the business never made money.

In 1812 Godwin struck up an exciting relationship with a young aristocratic devotee, PERCY BYSSHE SHELLEY, who raised money for Godwin's business. But as well as running away to France with the funds, took Godwin's daughter Mary, who, in the spirit of the New Philosophy, had become Shelley's lover; Mary's stepsister, Claire, also went with them. Godwin suffered further grief when his stepdaughter Fanny committed suicide in 1816. When Shelley and Mary were finally married (after Shelley's wife's suicide), Godwin and Shelley were reconciled, but in 1818, when the Shelleys emigrated to Europe, the relationship collapsed again. Throughout, Godwin importuned Shelley for money.

In 1817 Godwin wrote *Mandeville,* using familiar themes: the novel was praised by Shelley and WILLIAM HAZLITT. He was to write two further novels, *Cloudesley* (1830) and *Deloraine* (1833), although these were less successful.

In 1820 Godwin wrote an answer to the economist Thomas Malthus (1766–1834), with whom he had a lifelong dispute, entitled *Of Population: An Enquiry Concerning the Power of Increase in the Numbers of Mankind.* In 1822 the Godwins were evicted, from their home in Scinner Street, Finsbury and in 1825 the business went bankrupt. Godwin, in failing health, nonetheless worked on, supported by his son William (also a writer, who was to die suddenly in 1832). When Shelley's death brought Mary home, Godwin's life improved; in addition, a new generation of writers and artists were seeking his company.

In 1833 Godwin became a civil servant. The salary eased his troubles, and he continued to work, writing *Lives of the Necromancers* in 1834 and editing a novel by his late son (*Transfusion,* 1835). His last book, *The Genius of Christianity Unveiled* (published in 1873), is considered one of his best. He died on April 7, 1836, and was buried with Mary Wollstonecraft; in 1851 their bodies were moved to rest with Mary Shelley in the graveyard at St. Peter's Church, Bournemouth.

Although Godwin's work is not much read today, its influence on the writers and thinkers of the 1790s and early Romantic period cannot be overestimated. Shelley's poetry contains much of Godwin's political thought, and Mary Shelley's

FRANKENSTEIN shows the influence of her father's novels. Godwin was immortalized by Hazlitt in *The SPIRIT OF THE AGE*.

## Further Reading

Godwin, William. *The Anarchist Writings of William Godwin.* Edited by Peter Marshall. London: Freedom Press, 1986.

———. *Caleb Williams.* Oxford: Oxford University Press: 2009.

———. *The Collected Novels and Memoirs of William Godwin.* Edited by Mark Philp. London: Pickering and Chatto, 1992.

———. *Damon and Delia.* Gwynedd, Wales: Zena Publications, 1988.

———. *The Enquirer. Reflections on Education, Manners and Literature in a Series of Essays by William Godwin.* New York: Augustus M. Kelley, 1965.

———. *Enquiry Concerning Political Justice.* Edited by K. Coddeu Carter. Oxford Clarendon Press, 1971.

———. *St. Leon: A Tale of the Sixteenth Century.* Oxford: Oxford University Press: 1994.

Monro, D. H. *Godwin's Moral Philosophy: An Interpretation of William Godwin.* Westport, Conn.: Greenwood Press, Inc., 1978.

Philp, Mark. *Godwin's Political Justice.* London: Gerald Duckworth & Co., 1986.

St Clair, William. *The Godwins and the Shelleys: A Biography of a Family.* Baltimore: Johns Hopkins University Press, 1991.

Tysdahl, B. J. *William Godwin as Novelist.* London: Athlone Press, 1981.

—Maria Purves

## Goethe, Johann Wolfgang von (1749–1832)

Johann Wolfgang von Goethe was a poet; novelist; and writer of ballads, folk stories, science, and verse drama. His masterpiece, *FAUST: A TRAGEDY*, is a pivotal literary achievement, as are his novels *WILHELM MEISTER'S APPRENTICESHIP* (1795–96) and *The SORROWS OF YOUNG WERTHER* (1774), which has often been cited as a central Romantic bildungsroman, or story of growth and development. His plays have been said to express the zeitgeist and have a significant connection to the turbulent age in which he lived.

Born in Frankfurt, Germany, on August 28, 1749, Goethe experienced the French occupation of his homeland. He attended Leipzig University, where he fell in love, neglected his studies, and wrote poetry. He studied law at Strasburg and met the influential philosopher and literary critic J. G. Herder, who turned his attention to folk songs. In 1775 Weimar became Goethe's home, and he served as an administrator for the duke of Saxe-Weimar-Eisemach for more than a decade. Thereafter he devoted his life to literature. He died in Weimar on March 22, 1832.

Goethe sets forth his generation's spirit in *The Sorrows of Werther,* the confessions of an idealistic youth. This is a psychological novel that reveals the inner life and spiritual process of Werther, a lonely young man, who seeks solace in nature. Werther is a character of yearning and dreams who associates with children and simple folk, and yet has difficulty in the outer adult world. His passion for the universal spirit, nature, and higher things is shadowed by a self-destructive malaise. Werther expresses the tragic state of the Romantic individualist. Goethe shows in this character a man of emotional energy facing loneliness and unable to find his way in a world that has lost its spiritual focus. In all, Goethe wrote five novels, including *Werther,* as well as numerous short stories and tales. *Wilhelm Meister's Apprenticeship* is a novel of education and was often imitated as a model of fiction. NAPOLEON BONAPARTE was an admirer.

In his ethics Goethe implicitly rejected Immanuel Kant's moral imperative (the idea that human beings are rational and that reason dictates action) as too rigid a moral commandment, and he advocated humanistic ideals as well as freedom of spirit in harmony with the community of other people. In response to the fixed forms of French classicism, he argued for the inward form that is organic and alive. He was deeply interested in natural phenomena and the natural sciences. Goethe held that human life, nature, and art are one and the same. In his aesthetics he recognized that form is always changing but that in the creative desire to give form, the artist expresses the unity of life and nature.

Goethe's plays often developed from literary models such as Shakespeare, the Greeks, or the

French classicism of Racine. His first play, *Gotz von Berlichingen* (1773), emerged out of the sturm und drang (storm and stress) tradition. His characteristic plays include *Iphigenie auf Tauris* (1787), *Egmont* (1788), *Torquato Tasso* (1790), and *Faust* (1808/1832), which all carry elements of *bildung*, a culture in growth and process. Goethe's Iphigenia, the character based on Euripedes' play, has been called "a humane ideal" who reconciles body, nature, and spirit. The stages of *Faust* display Goethe's concern with ethical issues and values and with human passions. Feeling, values, and crisp poetic images are hallmarks of Goethe's literary style.

**Further Reading**

Boyle, Nicholas. *Goethe: The Poet and the Age.* Oxford: Oxford University Press, 1992.

Richards, Robert. *The Romantic Conception of Life: Science and Philosophy in the Age of Goethe.* Chicago: University of Chicago Press, 2002.

Sharpe, Lesley. *Cambridge Companion to Goethe.* Cambridge: Cambridge University Press, 2002.

Steiner, Rudolf. *Nature's Open Secret: Introductions to Goethe's Scientific Writing.* New York: Steiner Books, 2000.

Ugrinsky, Alexej. *Goethe in the Twentieth Century.* Westport, Conn.: Greenwood Press, 1987.

Williams, John R. *The Life of Goethe.* Oxford: Blackwell, 2001.

—Robert McParland

# gothic

The term *gothic* originally referred to the architectural style of the mediaeval period, particularly the great cathedrals of northern Europe. By the mid-18th century, however, it was also a literary term used to refer to a specific sensational style of imaginative writing. According to the literary historian David Punter, gothic fiction demonstrates "an emphasis on portraying the terrifying, a common insistence on archaic settings, a prominent use of the supernatural, the presence of highly stereotyped characters and the attempt to deploy and perfect techniques of literary suspense" (Punter 1). The first gothic novelist is generally reckoned to be Horace Walpole (1717–97), whose novel *The Castle of Otranto* was published in 1764. He helped establish many of the elements of gothic fiction that would become familiar to readers, including spooky setting (mansions, abbeys, castles); nightmare visions of the home; secret passages; locked rooms; a feeling of mystery and suspense; an emphasis on madness and disordered states of mind; omens, portents, visions, and the supernatural; and tortured family relationships often involving persecution of the female—all of which work to threaten the reader's sense of what is "normal."

By the 1790s CHARLES ROBERT MATURIN (1782–1824), CLARA REEVE (1729–1807), MATTHEW GREGORY LEWIS (1775–1818), Sophia Lee (1750–1824) and ANN RADCLIFFE (1764–1823) had emerged as the best-known gothic novelists, and they were joined from time to time by writers as diverse as SIR WALTER SCOTT, JANE AUSTEN, SAMUEL TAYLOR COLERIDGE, THOMAS LOVE PEACOCK, MARY SHELLEY, and JOHN WILLIAM POLIDORI. There was also a strong European tradition, notably in Germany, where GOTTFRIED AUGUST BÜRGER and ERNST THEODOR AMADEUS HOFFMANN were among the writers working in this mold. Gothic conventions also exerted a strong, if at times unacknowledged, influence both on more "serious" contemporaries, such as MARY WOLLSTONECRAFT and WILLIAM GODWIN (whose respective novels *MARIA, OR, THE WRONGS OF WOMAN* (1792) and *CALEB WILLIAMS* (1794) overtly politicize the conventions of the gothic romance), and the upcoming generation of Romantic poets, such as JOHN KEATS who claimed to have written his poem "The EVE OF ST. AGNES" (1819) under the influence of "Mother Radcliff" (Keats 283). Recent critics have attempted to analyze these examples of gothic writing in more detail, with the result that it is impossible to make distinctions between "male gothic" on the one hand and "female gothic" on the other. In the former, the supernatural terrors are generally real, the result of the emergence of the past into the present. In the latter, the heroine has often been deceived into thinking the supernatural real when in fact it is an illusion or a trick. Her terror is often increased by her own (female) susceptibility to imagining the worst. At the same time, these distinctions between male and female are often blurred. Both draw from the same fund of images.

Keats's comment above is a reminder that in Britain the most consistently popular gothic novelist was Ann Radcliffe, and it is worth considering her use of the tropes of gothic fiction. In 1789 Radcliffe anonymously published *The Castles of Athlin and Dunbayne* (subtitled *A Highland Story*). In this novella she updated the gothic novels of Horace Walpole, Clara Reeve, and others by combining the generic figures associated with this literary mode (the supernatural, ruined and sublime castles, mysterious individuals, assassins, violent storms) and peopling it with the sensitive and virtuous heroes and heroines of contemporary sentimental fiction.

In her second novel, *A Sicilian Romance* (1790), Radcliffe used a continental Renaissance setting for the first time and offered extended and sublime descriptions of the landscape, heavily influenced by paintings by Salvator Rosa, Gaspar Poussin, and Claude Lorrain. Well received critically, this and successive novels thematized intergenerational conflict, challenged the exploitation of women in the marriage market, and supported companionate marriages. The critic Robert Miles has suggested that Radcliffe can also be credited with the introduction of a "new hermeneutics of reading" in which the reader is invited to piece together, though is often allowed to misinterpret, mysterious events as they unfold through discovered and half-destroyed documents, snatches of conversation, and the inexplicable actions of protagonists (Miles 129–148). *A Sicilian Romance* features the first instance of Radcliffe's use of the "explained supernatural," where she provides a rational, if not wholly convincing, explanation of apparently supernatural events. In the heated political atmosphere of the 1790s, the triumph of reason over superstition dramatized in Radcliffe's novel was incongruously interpreted as expressive of both political radicalism and a patriotically English anti-Catholic sensibility.

Radcliffe's most recent biographer, Rictor Norton, argues that it is in her third novel *The Romance of the Forest* (1791) that Radcliffe achieves the most successful balance of characterization, description, sentiment, and mystery (Norton 89). Modern critics have also remarked upon Radcliffe's judicious use of allusion to and epigraphs from Shakespeare's plays and from the Graveyard School of poetry. This group of 18th-century poets made frequent use of dark, gloomy imagery often centering on death and mortality. Notable examples include Thomas Gray and William Cowper. In Radcliffe's case, such allusions were a strategy to legitimate her literary authority and thereby elevate the status of her work. This strategy seems to have been a successful one as contemporary critics praised her novels for their "solemn and decorous terrors" with one critic, Nathan Drake, lavishly declaring Radcliffe to be "the Shakespeare of Romance Writers" (quoted in *New Monthly Magazine;* Clery 51).

Uniquely, Radcliffe's assured critical reputation was mirrored in the commercial success of her novels. For her fourth novel, *The MYSTERIES OF UDOLPHO* (1794), she received the unrivaled amount of £500 as an advance, and the novel went on to be the world's first best seller. The impressive sales and universal critical acclaim that it garnered suggested something of the genre's commercial possibilities. In this novel, Radcliffe developed the aesthetic vision of gothic fiction by combining SENSIBILITY, terror, mystery, and sublime descriptions of the landscape to reenergize the generic conventions. In the context of the revolutionary 1790s, Radcliffe's use of gothic tropes such as the supernatural, a ruined and sublime castle with labyrinthine passages, assassins, cloistered religious orders, murderous passions, and violent storms seemed peculiarly attuned to contemporary political events, and commentators were quick to read the shocks and terrors administered in *Udolpho* as a response and reaction to the events of the FRENCH REVOLUTION. Significantly, on reading the novel, the diarist and writer HESTER LYNCH PIOZZI commented that "people are gaping for Wonders of every kind, and expect Marvels in the Natural World to keep Pace with the strange Events observed in the *Civil & Political World*" (quoted in Norton 90). Modern critics have also identified further revolutionary aspects to the novel in its dramatization of the triumph of middle-class values over aristocratic ambition and in its support of Enlightenment rationality over unenlightened superstition.

Set in Renaissance France and Italy, the novel follows its intelligent and "elegant" heroine, Emily

St. Aubert, from her idyllic life with her parents through her persecution at the hands of Montoni at Castle Udolpho, her thwarted love for the young aristocrat Valancourt and her discovery and unraveling of dark and tragic family secrets. By framing her heroine in the uncanny gothic world of Udolpho, Radcliffe achieves a more provocative and darker representation of female experience and subjectivity than that found in contemporary sentimental fiction. The literary historian Emma Clery has suggested that the gothic novel "displayed in the form of the romance the real contradictions and dangers which every gentlewoman of the period potentially faced," thus dramatizing the fears of the middle classes, whose social standing was most unstable and who were consequently as a group "most attentive to the taboos surrounding femininity" (Clery 23). Radcliffe's vision of a nightmarish world that threatens but ultimately fails to engulf Emily has also led the critic Robert Miles to describe her art as one that explores "transgressive borders without crossing them" (Miles 55).

While *The Mysteries of Udolpho* soberly warns against the dangers that an excessive sensibility pose to a young woman, equally the novel seems to revel in the darkly psychosexual fantasies with which Emily responds to traumatic situations. Her father tells her not to indulge in "pride of fine feeling," but his warning against "becom[ing] the victim of our feelings" is forgotten by Emily whose cruel treatment at Montoni's hands leaves her so vulnerable that she wrongly begins to speculate that her father has committed adultery, that Montoni poses a sexual threat to her, and twice that she has discovered the body of a murder victim (Radcliffe 70–80). Radcliffe's interest in darker states of mind, criminality, and the immoral is typical of gothic fiction and can also be read in the character of the passionate and brooding villain Montoni, described as "unprincipled, dauntless, cruel and enterprising; equally a stranger to pity and to fear; his very courage was a sort of animal ferocity" (358). In her next novel *The Italian*, Radcliffe would deepen the psychological character of the villain Schedoni to the extent that his character completely eclipses the novel's virtuous hero and heroine. Clearly, both the characters of Schedoni and Montoni can also be seen to have influenced

the brooding guilt of the Byronic heroes that followed them.

In *The Mysteries of Udolpho* Radcliffe continues to use "the explained supernatural," a strategy that she deployed in her earlier novels, and the rational explanation that she gives, for example, of a ghostly voice that haunts Emily ultimately dramatizes the triumph of reason over superstition. Gothic fiction has also been seen in the context of the French Revolution and the fact that English revolutionaries like THOMAS PAINE accused conservatives of a superstitious dread of monarchical authority. In *Mysteries* such an investment on Radcliffe's part in reason over superstition led to accusations of political radicalism being made against her (Miles 154). Radcliffe's celebration of middle-class values and their remodeling of both feudal society and the inequalities of aristocratic primogeniture were also read as politically provocative because controversially the novel seemed to favor the political enfranchisement of the middle classes, which in the revolutionary decade of the 1790s potentially represented a newly powerful political body.

Stylistically, the novel shows how gothic writers tended to offer extended descriptions of the landscape. In even the least receptive of Radcliffe's characters, sublime landscapes induce reverential awe and religious enthusiasm, and their response to nature is read as an index to a character's virtue. In this sense the gothic vision can also be said to have been shaped by EDMUND BURKE's 1757 account of the sublime (*A PHILOSOPHICAL ENQUIRY INTO THE ORIGIN OF OUR IDEAS OF THE SUBLIME AND BEAUTIFUL*), both in his assertion that the sublime originates with the feeling of terror and that sublimity in art is achieved through obscurity (Burke 53–55). In Burkean mode, the narrator of *Udolpho* proclaims that "[t]o the warm imagination, the forms which float half-veiled in darkness afford a higher delight than the most distinct scenery the sun can show," and frequently Emily's terror is exacerbated by the inability to be able to see things clearly (Radcliffe 72, 322).

The main literary influences on the novel were JOHN MILTON's *Paradise Lost*, the uncanny vision of the supernatural animated in Shakespeare's *Macbeth*, and the meditative and melancholy emotions at work in poems by the Graveyard

Poets William Collins (1721–59), James Thomson (1700–48), and James Beattie (1735–1803). Significantly, Radcliffe's interspersing of *Udolpho* with epigraphs from and allusions to the work of these male poets and dramatists, as well as her inclusion of her own original poems in the novel, was a way by which gothic novelists sought to legitimate and elevate their own literary productions by invoking the cultural authority of preceding (male) poets.

## Further Reading

Burke, Edmund. *A Philosophical Enquiry into the Origin of Our Ideas of the Sublime and Beautiful.* Oxford: Oxford University Press, 1998.

Clery, E. J. *Women's Gothic, from Clara Reeve to Mary Shelley.* Tavistock, Eng.: Northcote House and the British Council, 2000.

Dobrée, Bonamy. "The Genesis of Gothic Fiction." In *The Cambridge Companion to Gothic Fiction*, edited by Jerrold E. Hogle, 21–39. Cambridge and New York: Cambridge University Press, 2002.

Keats, John. *Selected Letters and Poems.* Edited by Douglas Bush. Boston: Houghton Mifflin, 1959.

Massé, Michelle. *In the Name of Love, Women, Masochism and the Gothic.* Ithaca, N.Y., and London: Cornell University Press, 1992.

Miles, Robert. *Ann Radcliffe, The Great Enchantress.* Manchester, Eng.: Manchester University Press, 1995.

"Mrs Radcliffe's Posthumous Romance." *New Monthly Magazine and Literary Journal* 16 (1826): 145.

Norton, Rictor. *Mistress of Udolpho: The Life of Ann Radcliffe.* Leicester, Eng.: Leicester University Press, 1999.

Punter, David. *The Gothic.* Oxford: Blackwell, 2004.

Radcliffe, Ann. *The Mysteries of Udolpho.* Edited by Bonamy Dobrée. Oxford: Oxford University Press, 1980.

—Sondeep Kandola

## *Grasmere Journals* Dorothy Wordsworth (1800–1803)

For several years at the start of the 19th century, DOROTHY WORDSWORTH lived with her brother, WILLIAM WORDSWORTH, in Dove Cottage, a former inn in the Grasmere Valley, Cumbria. Between May 1800 and January 1803, she kept a series of journals which have come to be known as the *Grasmere Journals.* Because of their attention to detail, the journals provide an invaluable account of the personal life of a major poet. They also reveal Dorothy Wordsworth as a keen observer and writer in her own right.

Dorothy began the journals in large part for William's benefit, noting in her first entry that she will "give Wm Pleasure by it when he comes home again" (1971; 31). Toward their end, the journals include travel accounts meant to be shared with friends. It can therefore be argued that the *Grasmere Journals* were never intended as private, introspective documents, and indeed there are only rare occasions when Dorothy turns her observations on herself.

Unsurprisingly, given Dorothy's joy at finally achieving a home life with her brother, the journals display her tenderness toward William, with many descriptions focusing on the quiet intimacy of sharing a cottage: "The fire flutters & the watch ticks I hear nothing else save the Breathings of my Beloved & he now & then pushes his book forward & turns over a leaf" (March 23, 1802). However, she is more than capable of rejecting sentimentality in favour of prosaic honesty; in the first sentence, she does not merely state that William and their brother John "set off into Yorkshire" but notes that they carried "cold pork in their pockets" (1971; 31). This opening indicates that her motivation for beginning to keep a journal may have been prompted by William's departure, and that writing for him was a way to maintain their emotional connection. It may also be the case that she felt her thoughts were only of value if used to amuse her brother or support his work, which it did by serving as a memory aid for William, who drew on its details of rural life and nature when writing his poems.

Her insights into the natural world, her brief sketches of beggars and local personalities, and her depictions of SAMUEL TAYLOR COLERIDGE all demonstrate that Dorothy Wordsworth was far more than a helpmate to her brother, and that she does not deserve the dismissive indulgence with which she has been treated by many critics. Colette Clark, for instance, began her 1960 introduction to the edited journals with the opinion that "Dorothy Wordsworth was one of those sweet characters whose only life lies in their complete dedication to a man of genius" (in Wordsworth 1960, ). Certainly Dorothy Wordsworth set great store by family life, having lacked it for most of her childhood, but to state that serving her brother and his family was her only function deprives her of personal importance. Unfortunately, because of her lack of introspection, it is difficult, if not impossible, to use the contents of the journals to determine whether Dorothy regretted that she never married, had children, or sustained her own financial independence for the majority of her life.

The *Grasmere Journals* as they are known today are incomplete. The notebook covering the period between December 22, 1800, and October 9, 1801, has been lost, and there are missing pages in the existing notebooks. Additionally, there are periods when Dorothy did not write entries or when a retroactive account provides only scanty information. In August 1802, for instance, she and William traveled to Calais, but in recounting the journey afterwards, she failed to include the specific details that were common in earlier entries.

Only recently have the Journals been published in their full extant form. Excerpts were included in an 1851 memoir of Wordsworth and a biography in the late 1880s. Their first publication in their own right occurred in 1897, but the editor, William Knight, deleted Dorothy's references to health issues and many allusions to the relationship between her and William. In 1941 Ernest de Selincourt edited all of Dorothy's journals, marking the first complete publication of the *Grasmere Journals*. However, it was not until 1958 that text from the entry of October 4, 1802, was included; this had been scored out, either by Dorothy herself or by a later reader, and was only deciphered when the editor Helen Darbishire used infrared technology. Interpretations of the deleted words were incorrect, however, until Pamela Woof's 2002 edition.

In spite of the dearth of explicit personal statements by Dorothy, literary critics have found the journals to be fruitful sources for biographical investigations. Most recently, Frances Wilson based her entire study of Dorothy around this material.

**Further Reading**

Wilson, Frances. *The Ballad of Dorothy Wordsworth.* London: Faber & Faber, 2008.

Wordsworth, Dorothy. *The Grasmere Journals.* Edited by Pamela Woof. Oxford and New York: Oxford University Press, 1991.

———. *Home at Grasmere: Extracts from the Journal of Dorothy Wordsworth, Written between 1800 and 1803, and from the Poems of William Wordsworth.* Edited by Colette Clark, Harmondsworth, Eng.: Penguin, 1960.

—Tracey S. Rosenberg

## "Grave of a Poetess, The" Felicia Hemans (1827)

This poem was first published in the *New Monthly Magazine* (July 1827) and later appeared in a slightly revised format as the final poem in FELICIA HEMANS's RECORDS OF WOMAN, WITH OTHER POEMS (1828). A footnote to the poem claims that it was inspired by the grave of "the author of *Psyche*," the Anglo-Irish poet MARY TIGHE. The note describes the surrounding village and churchyard in PICTURESQUE terms, suggesting that the poem will be a reverie inspired by contact with a historic location. In fact, Hemans had not visited the site. She would do so only after writing this poem and was disappointed by what she found. The poem, then, is really about an imaginary grave site; by not naming Tighe specifically, Hemans can generalize about female poets and posterity.

It is common in elegies to follow a pattern of grieving for the loss of the dead and then finding comfort in the dead person's release from pain. Hemans follows a similar structure by first noting the beauties of spring and conflating the speaker's grief with the loss experienced by the dead poetess, who can no longer appreciate such scents, sights, and sounds. Then, in the eighth stanza, the speaker finds comfort in knowing that the dead poetess is in heaven, enjoying even lovelier surroundings. The speaker finishes by noting the poetess's sorrow in life, which death has transformed to peace and joy. The final two lines suggest an interesting conflict, however. The speaker distinguishes between "the woman's heart" and "the poet's eye." One way to read this is as reinforcement of the literary establishment's belief that poetry was a masculine domain: A poetess might versify about love or domestic subjects, but she could never achieve the sophisticated standard of a poet. In this case, the only way for a female poet to reconcile her "woman's heart" and "poet's eye" is to die. Yet Hemans herself was often celebrated by reviewers for her "womanly" or feminine qualities; like Tighe, Hemans was classified a "poetess." Modern critics tend to see her using the case of Tighe to celebrate her own status as a poet(ess) whose grave might inspire pilgrimages. In a culture that viewed her poetry as insubstantial when compared to that of her male peers, this is a defiant statement.

The poem exemplifies several Romantic trends: reflections on mortality inspired by a graveyard or historically significant site, connections made between the sensual stimuli of nature and emotions, and self-reflective contemplation on the nature of the poet. The poem is more notable for its engagement with issues of gender, celebrity, and authorship. Her use of "poetess" is problematic because of its association with diminution. The term first appeared in Britain during the Romantic period and was used by male critics to designate writers of sentimental and inferior poetry. Hemans uses the conventions of the elegy to articulate the tensions inherent in being a woman and a poet. While celebrating the poetess, the speaker cannot help but anxiously note the distinction between woman and poet.

## Further Reading

Labbe, Jacqueline. "Re-Making Memory, Posterity, and the Memorial Poem." In *Memory and Memorials, 1789–1914: Literary and Cultural Perspectives,* edited by Matthew Campbell, Jacqueline Labbe, and Sally Shuttleworth. 132–146. London: Routledge, 2000.

Mandell, Laura. "Introduction: The Poetess Tradition." *Romanticism on the Net* 29–30 (February–May 2003). Available online. URL: http://www.erudit.org/revue/ron/2003/v/n29-30/007712ar.html. Accessed on July 24, 2008.

Matthews, Samantha. *Poetical Remains: Poets' Graves, Bodies, and Books in the Nineteenth Century.* Oxford: Oxford University Press, 2004.

Sweet, Nanora, and Julie Melnyk, eds. *Felicia Hemans: Reimagining Poetry in the Nineteenth Century.* New York: Palgrave Macmillan, 2001.

Westover, Paul. "Imaginary Pilgrimages: Felicia Hemans, Dead Poets, and Romantic Historiography." *Literature Compass* 2, no. 1 (January 2005). Available online. URL: http://www.blackwell-synergy.com/doi/full/10.1111/j.1741-4113.2005.00112.x. Accessed on November 14, 2008.

—Terri Doughty

## Gray, Thomas (1716–1771)

Best known for his "ELEGY WRITTEN IN A COUNTRY CHURCH-YARD" (1751), Thomas Gray has been seen both as a poet who bridges the gap between the 18th-century Augustans and the Romantics and, less flatteringly, as one who falls uncomfortably—and inconsequentially—into that gap. Gray was born on December 26, 1716, in London, where his mother, Dorothy, kept a milliner's shop. His father, Philip, was a strict disciplinarian and stern husband, and Gray grew up in a home filled with marital discord. To release him from this, Dorothy in 1725 paid for her son to attend Eton College, where her brother Robert was a master. The young Gray was an intellectual child who thrived on learning. In 1734 he left Eton to enroll at Peterhouse College at Cambridge University, where his associates included Horace Walpole. Gray accompanied Walpole on a "Grand Tour" of Europe in 1739, during which he immersed himself in French and Italian culture. On his return, Gray took up residence at the university again, and this remained his main home for the rest of his life. Gray had a private income and did not have to work but instead lived in the college following his own path of study, particularly classics. Gray's slender poetic output (he only published 14 poems in his lifetime) was famously attributed by the Victorian critic Matthew Arnold to his having been a "man born out of date . . . whose full spiritual flowering was impossible" (Arnold, 200–201). But to see Gray as nothing more than a poet born into a prosaic age that lacked the stimulating circumstances of the Romantic era is to underestimate the influence that this cautious, precise figure had on the poets who followed him.

The "Elegy Written in a Country Churchyard," which has become one of the best-known poems in the language, was written in 1750 and circulated among Gray's friends in manuscript before it was published anonymously, and to great acclaim, in 1751. Its tone of moral seriousness and its portrait of a doomed poet-figure would both be developed in the Romantic era. But Gray's reputation as a precursor of Romantic poetry rests on several other of his attributes: his deep appreciation of the natural world, particularly the rugged, mountainous landscapes of the Scottish highlands and the English lakes; his insistence on the importance of the poet as a public, national figure; his use of domestic rather than classical or exotic subjects of poetic inspiration; and his role in developing the ode as a suitable form for poetic experimentation.

After a trip to the Scottish highlands in 1765, Gray became increasingly interested in wild landscapes, and he traveled extensively in Britain in search of the PICTURESQUE. During a 1767 trip to the Lake District, he wrote a journal (in the form of a series of letters to his friend Dr. Thomas Wharton) that was published posthumously with an edition of his poems in 1775. His detailed descriptions of the landscapes he encountered and of the journeys that he made to find the best "stations" from which the views might be appreciated helped establish the late 18th-century vogue for nature tourism and contributed to a new perception of wild and mountainous regions as sites of sublimity and inspiration, rather than desolation and waste, which would prove to be enormously significant with the Romantics.

Gray also helped to stimulate poetic interest in Britain's "Celtic fringe," breaking new ground that was later to be explored by others, including JAMES MACPHERSON and THOMAS CHATTERTON. He became engrossed in early British poetry, an interest that fed directly into his Pindaric ode "The Bard," in which a heroic poetic figure confronts the tyrannical king, whom he denounces, and then throws himself off a mountain in a triumphant act of suicide.

Gray's poetry suggested that even if classical forms (those inspired by the ancient Greek and Roman poets) continued to dominate English verse, there was a deep well of local and national subject matter from which poets could draw the inspiration to write serious verse without reverting to classical subjects. In this he partly anticipated WILLIAM WORDSWORTH's poetic projects, although he lacked the formal iconoclasm of the Romantic poets. Wordsworth, however, singled out Gray's poetry in the PREFACE TO LYRICAL BALLADS as an example of the sort of excessively elaborate diction that he wished to reject. Gray, a shy man, never married and moved in restricted social circles. He died at Pembroke on July 30, 1771, and was buried alongside his mother at St. Giles Church in Stoke Poges.

**Further Reading**

Arnold, Matthew. "Thomas Gray." In *Complete Prose Works of Matthew Arnold*, vol. 9, *English Literature and Irish Politics* edited by R. H. Super, 189–204. Chicago: University of Michigan Press, 1973.

Gray, Thomas. *Thomas Gray's Journal of His Visit to the Lake District in October 1769*. Edited by William Roberts. Liverpool, Eng.: Liverpool University Press, 2001.

Gray, Thomas, Charles Churchill, and William Cowper. *Selected Poems of Thomas Gray, Charles Churchill and William Cowper*. Edited by Katherine Turner. London: Penguin Classics, 1998.

Mack, Robert L. *Thomas Gray: A Life*. New Haven, Conn.: Yale University Press, 2000.

—David McAllister

## *Guy Mannering; or, The Astrologer* Sir Walter Scott (1815)

Advertised as being by "the author of *Waverley*," which became the marketing tag used for most of SIR WALTER SCOTT's novels, *Guy Mannering* followed hard on the heels of *WAVERLEY* Scott's first "hit." Reputedly written in just six weeks and published on February 24, 1815, the first edition of 2,000 copies sold out in a day. The novel reached 11 editions in Scott's own lifetime and would remain massively popular throughout the 19th century. There were stage adaptations and ships were named after it, and the novel is also credited with introducing the famous phrase "blude's thicker than water; she's welcome to the cheeses and the hams just the same." The novel has also been suggested as an inspiration for the American author James Fenimore Cooper's *The Pioneers* (1823). Both Scott and Cooper show countries and communities in transition in which modern "civilized" values clash with those of an older, less obviously refined way of life.

The main action of *Guy Mannering* is set at the time of the AMERICAN REVOLUTION; the book depicts a Scotland set in its ways but at the same time becoming advanced—a fragmented country where people are displaced and struggling with different stages of progression. The novel is located chiefly in Galloway, in the southwest of Scotland. It opens when Guy Mannering, a young Englishman who has been touring the Lake District and southwestern Scotland, gets lost after sketching some PICTURESQUE ruins. Eventually he finds shelter at Ellangowan, a large house on an estate. By way of thanking his hosts for their hospitality, Mannering, who dabbles in astrology, draws up a chart for Harry Bertram, the young heir of Ellangowan, who has just been born. This predicts that when he reaches five years of age, misfortunes will befall him. A gypsy woman passing through the estate gives a similar prophecy as well as other predictions, the coming to fruition of which makes up the action of the rest of the novel. Thus, at age five, Harry is kidnapped by the smuggler Dirk Hatteraick and spirited off to Holland. Hatteraick is acting in collusion with the Bertrams' lawyer, Gilbert Glossin, who hopes to acquire the family property in the absence of a male heir. Adopted by a Dutch merchant, Harry Bertram is kept in ignorance of his true identity and brought up under the name Vanbeest Brown; meanwhile, his father dies and the debt-ridden estate is sold.

From the very start, Scott sets up the Scottish border region as an uncanny, spookish environment where strange things happen. According to his son-in-law, J. G. Lockhart, Scott took the basis of the story from events told to him by Joseph Train, a Galloway amateur historian and collector who supplied him with various tales of gypsies, including the tale of an astrologer who predicted the dangers that would happen to a child yet to be born. Other critics suggest Scott's main source was his sister-in-law, Elizabeth McCulloch Scott, an expert on Scottish folklore.

When Harry Bertram is reintroduced into the novel, he is a soldier in India and in love with Guy Mannering's daughter, Julia. Mannering imagines that the attentions paid to his daughter are directed at his wife. He wounds Bertram in a duel and leaves him for dead. On recovery, Bertram finds that Julia has returned to Britain to tour Scotland and the Lake District. These tourist elements of the novel are interesting for the ways in which they link Scott and his characters with many of the Romantic ideas of the time, including those popularized by WILLIAM WORDSWORTH and the LAKE SCHOOL. For example, Julia writes of the Lake District as "the country of romance. The scenery is such as Nature brings together in her sublimest moods,—sounding cataracts; hills which rear their scathed heads to the sky . . ." (Scott 143–44). When Bertram (still known as "Brown") journeys back to Ellangowan for the first time since childhood, he takes a route through a wild Borders country that passes by Hadrian's Wall, the famous stone barrier between England and Scotland built by the Romans in the second century. The wall is a ruin, but it prompts a discussion of the splendor of Rome and the transitory nature of empires. Bertram then meets a farmer, Dandy Dinmont, whom he rescues from muggers. Dinmont introduces Bertram to fox hunting, badger baiting, and salmon fishing. The men spear the salmon at night with the aid of torches "or fire-grates filled with blazing fragments of tar-barrels . . . the principal party were embarked in a crazy boat . . . while others, like the ancient Bacchanals in their gambols, ran along the banks brandishing their torches and spears . . . the twinkling of a fin, the rising of an air-bell, was sufficient to point out to these adroit sportsmen in what direction to use their weapon" (214). Scott thus sets up a clash between civilized restraint and the primal energies of the hunt. Bertram finds it difficult to take part: "[T]hough he concealed feelings that would not have been understood [he did not like] being quite so near the agonies of the expiring salmon, as they lay flapping about in the boat which they moistened with their blood. He therefore requested to be put ashore, and, from the top of a . . . bank, enjoyed the scene much more to his satisfaction" (217). Rather than exhibiting blood lust, Bertram enjoys the less crude but more picturesque "effect produced by the strong red glare on the romantic banks under which the boat glided. Now the light diminished to a distant star that seemed to twinkle on the waters. . . . Then it advanced nearer, brightening and enlarging as it again approached" (214–217).

As in many of Scott's works, identity is a central theme for the novel's young hero, and at various points Bertram is forced to consider not just who he is but who he wants to be. Adopting an assumed identity, he resumes the search for Julia and traces her to the neighbourhood of Ellangowan. Gilbert Glossin, who is now the owner of Ellangowan, recognises Bertram and again plots with Hatteraick to kidnap him. However, Meg Merrilies, Bertram's gypsy nurse, recognizes him too, and with the help of Bertram and Dandie Dinmont, she stops their plot, but she pays for this with her own life. Glossin dies at the hands of his henchman, Hatteraick. Thanks to Meg's efforts before her death, Bertram is acknowledged as the heir and regains his estates, later marrying Julia.

Although the sales of *Guy Mannering* in 1815 were more than Scott had hoped for, the critics were more circumspect. The *Critical Review* claimed that the novel "is too often written in language unintelligible to all except the Scotch" (*Critical Review*, June 1815, 600–603). The *Quarterly Review* thought "the state of society, though peculiar, is vulgar. Meg Merrilies is swelled into a very unnatural importance. . . . The greater part of the characters, their manners and dialect, are at once

barbarous and vulgar, extravagant and mean. . . . The work would be, on the whole, improved by being translated into English. Though we cannot, on the whole, speak of the novel with approbation, we will not affect to deny that we read it with interest, and that it repaid us with amusement" (*Quarterly Review*, January 1815, 501–509). More recently, critics have been interested in Scott's use of dialect and also in the ways in which the novel gave readers a backward-looking view of the Scottish nation. Some critics argue that Scott opened up new ways of looking at Scotland, others that he entombed it, creating a falsely melodramatic and sentimental picture.

**Further Reading**

D'Arcy, Julian Meldon. *Subversive Scott: The Waverley Novels and Scottish Nationalism.* Reykjavik: Vigdís Finnbogadottír Institute of Foreign Languages & University of Iceland Press, 2005.

Dekker, George G. "Border and Frontier: Tourism in Scott's *Guy Mannering* and Cooper's *The Pioneers*. Available online. URL: http://www.oneonta.edu/~cooper/articles/ala/1997ala-dekker.html. Accessed on November 3, 2008.

Lincoln, Andrew. *Walter Scott and Modernity.* Edinburgh: Edinburgh University Press, 2007.

McCracken-Flesher, Caroline. *Possible Scotlands: Walter Scott and the Story of Tomorrow.* Oxford: Oxford University Press, 2005.

Scott, Sir Walter. *Guy Mannering.* London: Penguin, 2003.

—Claire Reynolds

# H

**Hamilton, Emma, Lady** (ca. 1765–1815)
Emma, Lady Hamilton was artist's model, live performer, and social celebrity who seemed to embody many Romantic ideals. From a humble country background, the young and beautiful Emma Lyon (later known as Hart) made her debut on the London scene in the hardly glamorous role of nursery maid. Made redundant by the sudden death of her charge, she remained in the city, where she made the most out of her striking looks and amiable disposition. Soon her self-proclaimed "giddiness" and accommodating nature secured her the affection and financial protection of the rich and reckless Sir Harry Fetherstonhaugh; she bore him a daughter in 1782. There followed the Hon. Charles Francis Greville and, later, his uncle, Sir William Hamilton (1731–1803), British ambassador to Naples, connoisseur, collector, and patron of the arts. Enchanted by Emma's classical beauty, Hamilton quickly arranged her relocation to Naples (1787).

Soon Emma was launched into Neapolitan society, in which she rapidly rose to become a personal friend of Queen Maria Carolina. To the besotted Hamilton, Emma was the enchanting flesh and blood embodiment of his ideal of antique beauty, a mystical transubstantiation of classicism that she contrived to exploit with highly theatrical and somewhat exhibitionistic gusto. As Emma polished her heretofore scarce social accomplishments, Hamilton first made her his mistress and then his wife (1791). Her expert management (or, rather, artistic coordination) transformed Palazzo Sessa, Hamilton's residence, into a performative space where she staged her celebrated "attitudes," or miming of the figures on the antique vases and classical statuary, of which JOHANN WOLFGANG VON GOETHE left a rapturous description. If lacking in scholarship, at least Emma's interpretations were in tune with the current theories of acting. Her live display of her own body, clad and coiffured in classical style, convincingly blended references to ancient pantomime with the staging of animated emotions.

The Neapolitan idyll, however, took an unexpected turn when HORATIO NELSON (1758–1805) arrived in Naples in 1798, saluted as the hero of the battle of Abu Qir. Emma adroitly flirted her way to the admiral's heart and she started an affair with him that escalated into a notorious and widely publicized ménage à trois. Amid scurrilous cartoons of the trio—the apparently unaware cuckold, the amorous hero, and the social-climbing seductress—that amused and scandalized London's polite society, Emma gave birth to Nelson's daughter, Horatia, in 1801. Hamilton's death and then Nelson's (killed in the 1805 Battle of Trafalgar) left Emma destitute and friendless. Loath to retrench, she ended up in the King's Bench debtors' prison. On January 15, 1815, she died an alcoholic in France, repudiated by her daughter Horatia.

Lady Hamilton was portrayed by many of the most distinguished artists of her age, from George Romney through Joshua Reynolds, each of whom in his or her unique way attempted to capture on canvas her charms, poise, and seductiveness. Her colorful and at times shadowy lifestyle has for many years proved too big a temptation for biographers who have focused on the more notorious aspects of her life. The result has been to deflect serious critical attention away from what some theatre historians see as her truly original—and in many senses pioneering—achievements in the area of performance art.

## Further Reading

Elyot, Amanda. *Too Great a Lady: The Notorious, Glorious Life of Emma, Lady Hamilton. A Novel.* New York: New American Library, 2007.

Fraser, Flora. *Beloved Emma: the Life of Emma, Lady Hamilton.* London: John Murray, 2003.

Williams, Kate. *England's Mistress: The Infamous Life of Emma Hamilton.* London: Arrow Books, 2007.

Wilson, Kathleen. "Nelson's Women: Female Masculinity and Body Politics in the French and Napoleonic Wars." *European History Quarterly* 37 (2007): 562–581.

—Francesca Saggini

## Hardenberg, Frederick von    See NOVALIS.

## "Haunted Beach, The"    Mary Robinson
(1800)

This poem by MARY ROBINSON was included in the collection *Lyrical Tales* (1800); it was first published in the *Morning Post*, of which Robinson was poetry editor, on February 28, 1800. SAMUEL TAYLOR COLERIDGE wrote to ROBERT SOUTHEY recommending its inclusion in his *Annual Anthology of Poetry*, drawn by the poem's appeal to the Romantic affinity for the uncanny.

Robinson's inspiration for the poem was an undated incident she witnessed, described in an anonymous appendix to her posthumously published *Memoirs*. From her window, she watched two fishermen bring a body ashore. The body was still there the next morning; bathers passed by it without interest, and the lord of the manor forbade its burial. Although horrified by the situation, Robinson was unwilling to offend those in power. She gave the fishermen some money, and they dragged the body to the cliff and unceremoniously covered

it with rocks. She was strongly affected by the incident and possibly by her unwillingness to insist on a decent burial for the corpse.

Robinson creates an eerie atmosphere from the beginning of the poem. The reader remains detached, merely an observer of the poem's images, much as Robinson was an observer of the body on the beach. In the first stanza, she highlights and personifies a fisherman's shed standing on the beach, stronger than the boats often broken to pieces on the rocks. The ocean is angry and full of turmoil. In contrast, the moon throughout is a serene observer of the criminal and ghostly events, connected to the reader's detachment from the poem's events and Robinson's detachment from the corpse incident.

A mariner, who placed fame and fortune ahead of caring for his crew, has been killed, but Robinson does not reveal whether he was murdered by humans or by the sea. His body lies beneath the old shed, his spirit resting uneasily. For 30 years he has had to suffer the torment of his guilt and visitations by his betrayed messmates. In the midst of this supernatural drama, Robinson emphasizes the observers' detachment through the cold, serene moon and the constancy of nature prevailing despite human dramas. Robinson's repetition of the phrase "where the green billows play'd" at the end of each stanza but the last highlights the idea that the waves will bury and swallow acts such as the mariner's death.

There was little critical interest in this poem before 1990, and there are still few scholarly studies devoted to it. Some dismiss it as simply an inferior version of Coleridge's "The RIME OF THE ANCIENT MARINER." However, many scholars, including Duncan Wu, agree with Coleridge's assessment "it falls off sadly to the last—wants Tale—& Interest; but the images are new & very distinct—that 'silvery carpet' is just is just . . . the metre—oy! that woman has an Ear!" (Letters 1: 575–576). Although there is certainly an affinity between Robinson's and Coleridge's mariners, they are not identical. The poem's very evident sense of detachment and guilt has prompted some to assume that Robinson was assuaging her own conscience by writing a poem drawing attention to the unclaimed corpse rudely buried on the beach.

## Further Reading

Coleridge, S. T. *Collected Letters*. Edited by Earl Lealis Griggs. Oxford: Clarendon Press, 1956.

Pascoe, Judith. "Mary Robinson and the Literary Marketplace." In *Romantic Women Writers: Voices and Countervoices*, edited by Paula R. Feldman and Theresa M. Kelley, 252–268. Hanover, N.H.: University Press of New England, 1995.

Stuart, Curran. "Mary Robinson's *Lyrical Tales* in Context." In *Re-visioning Romanticism: British Women Writers, 1776–1837*, edited by Carol Shiner Wilson and Joel Haefner, 17–35. Philadelphia: Pennsylvania University Press, 1994.

Wu, Duncan, ed. *Romantic Women Poets*. Oxford: Blackwell Publishers, 1997.

—Leah Larson

## Hays, Mary (1759–1843)

Born in London and raised in a culture of British dissent, Mary Hays found fame and notoriety as an author of feminist novels during the 1790s. Supporting herself by her poems and a friend of radical thinkers including WILLIAM GODWIN and MARY WOLLSTONECRAFT, she challenged assumptions about proper female behavior and argued for the education of women. *Memoirs of Emma Courtney* (1796), Hay's most famous novel, is written in the first-person voice of a woman torn between her reason and her passions as she pursues a man she cannot marry. Notoriously, the heroine of *Memoirs* first proposes marriage and, on being rejected, offers to have sex with her love interest anyway. Similarities between the relationship depicted in *Memoirs* and Hays's relationship with the Cambridge reformer William Frend (1757–1841) led some readers to conflate the author with her scandalous heroine. Hays's reputation suffered accordingly, and she was seen, along with Mary Wollstonecraft, as a woman whose crusade for equal rights had led her into sexual impropriety.

Hays followed *Memoirs* with *The Victim of Prejudice* (1799), a novel about the injustices facing a rape victim; and two nonfiction books, *Female Biography* (1802) and *Memoirs of Queens* (1821). She is also thought to have written *Appeal to the Men of Great Britain in Behalf of Women* (1798), an argument for the reform of female education that criticizes cultural belief in women's inferiority. Hays's later works are less radical. Her novels *The Brothers* (1815) and *Family Annals or The Sisters* (1817) seem staid and moralistic, and Hays, perhaps tired of the snide attacks on her reputation, no longer seemed to shock. She remained, however, a well-known figure in the literary world and counted CHARLES and MARY LAMB, ANNA LAETITIA BARBAULD, and WILLIAM BLAKE among her acquaintances. Never marrying, Hays struggled to support herself in later years, subsisting on a small inheritance. She died in London on February 20, 1843.

Hays's work is often compared unfavorably to that of Wollstonecraft, her friend and onetime mentor. Some modern feminists have, like Wollstonecraft, criticized Hays for her reliance on the encouragement of male intellectuals. Others, like Gina Luria Walker, see Hays as steering a different course to Wollstonecraft in her desire "to understand the conversation of her forefathers, not in order to interrupt it, but to learn how to construct a parallel, woman-centered discourse and, perhaps to create an entirely new kind of dialogue" (Walker 134).

## Further Reading

Adams, M. Ray. "Mary Hays, Disciple of William Godwin." *PMLA: Publications of the Modern Language Association of America* 55, no. 2 (1940): 472–483.

Binhammer, Katherine. "The Persistence of Reading: Governing Female Novel-Reading in Memoirs of Emma Courtney and Memoirs of Modern Philosophers." *Eighteenth-Century Life* 27, no. 2 (2003): 1–22.

Hays, Mary. *The Correspondence of Mary Hays (1779–1843), British Novelist*. Lewiston, N.Y.: Edwin Mellen Press, 2004.

———. *Memoirs of Emma Courtney*. Edited by Marilyn L. Brooks. Peterborough, Ont., and Orchard Park, N.Y.: Broadview Press, 1999.

———. *The Victim of Prejudice*. Edited by Eleanor Rose Ty. Peterborough, Ont., and Orchard Park, N.Y.: Broadview Press, 1994.

Walker, Gina Luria. *Mary Hays, (1759–1843): The Growth of a Woman's Mind*. Burlington, Vt.: Ashgate, 2006.

—Siobhan Carrol

## Hazlitt, William (1778–1830)

Born in Maidstone, Kant, on April 10, 1778, William Hazlitt was the son of an Edinburgh-educated, radical Unitarian minister. After a brief residence in the United States, he attended the New Unitarian College, founded by Joseph Priestley, at Hackney in London (1793–95). He then pursued portrait painting and wrote *An Essay on the Principles of Human Action* (1805), which addressed the aesthetic, intellectual, and moral questions of egotism, to which his essays and much Romantic and Victorian criticism often return. In 1798 Hazlitt was awed by SAMUEL TAYLOR COLERIDGE's sermon in Shrewsbury (at this time Coleridge was still considering entering the ministry), and befriended WILLIAM WORDSWORTH, as recorded in his essay "My First Acquaintance with Poets"; however, accusations of sexual misconduct against Hazlitt and of political apostasy against Wordsworth and Coleridge later fractured their friendships.

In 1812 Hazlitt began writing for the *Morning Chronicle*. In 1817 he published a collection of essays called *The Round Table* and—working from Coleridge's 1811–12 lectures on Shakespeare and in turn informing JOHN KEATS's notions of "negative capability"—*Characters of Shakespear's Plays*, which puns on character as both dramatis personae and the subjective individuality of a play as articulated by criticism. Hazlitt gave influential lectures on the English poets in 1818 and published *Political Essays* (1819), *Table Talk* (1821), and *The SPIRIT OF THE AGE* (1825). He married in 1808 but divorced in 1822 because of an emotionally disastrous affair he had with Sarah Walker, a woman of dubious character whom he had met in 1821. He fictionalized the affair in *Liber Amoris; or, The New Pygmalion* (1823), a significant successor to THOMAS DE QUINCEY's *CONFESSIONS OF AN ENGLISH OPIUM EATER* (1821) and other autobiographical Romantic works. In 1824 Hazlitt married Isabella Bridgewater, but they divorced 1827. His last book was the *Life of Napoleon* (1828–30), which analyzes the causes of the FRENCH REVOLUTION and argues for the importance of print for diffusing knowledge and power to "the people." He died in London on September 18, 1830.

Hazlitt was most influential as an essayist publishing in competing periodicals. His many essays include "What is the People," an argument against Burkean conservatism (see EDMUND BURKE); "On the Pleasure of Hating," in which he suggests that criticism should be a positive mode of "hating" political and aesthetic tyrannies. Other Hazlitt essays that engage the terms by which Romantic writers conceptualized themselves, their works, and their age and by which subsequent critics have studied and defined Romanticism include "On Reason and Imagination"; "On Egotism"; and "On Gusto," which describes an aesthetic intensity of interest diffused throughout texts and paintings, thus making them available to what Adam Smith, Coleridge, and others called "sympathetic imagination"—the process of imagining oneself into the circumstances of characters, works, or other people and thus approaching but never fully realizing knowledge of their feelings. "On Gusto" may have influenced Washington Allston's and T. S. Eliot's notions of "objective correlatives." Critics focus on Hazlitt's style, which employs paradox, aphorism, digression, and contrast to express oppositional ends. Its internal contradictions appealed to Romantic-period ideas of the sublime, genius, and imagination as syntheses of oppositional features and also to Hazlitt's ideals of freedom, individuality, and regeneration.

### Further Reading

Abrams, M. H. *The Mirror and the Lamp: Romantic Theory and the Critical Tradition.* New York: Oxford University Press, 1953.

Bromwich, David. *Hazlitt: The Mind of a Critic.* New York: Oxford University Press, 1983.

Hazlitt, William. *Selected Writings.* Edited by Ian Cook. Oxford: Oxford University Press, 1999.

Natarajan, Uttara, ed. *Metaphysical Hazlitt: Bicentenary Essays.* New York: Routledge, 2005.

Paulin, Tom. *The Day Star of Liberty: William Hazlitt's Radical Style.* London: Faber and Faber, 1998.

Ready, Robert. "Hazlitt: In and Out of 'Gusto.'" *SEL: Studies in English Literature, 1500–1900.* 14, no. 4 (1974): 537–546.

—Jonathan Farina

## *Heart of Midlothian, The*  Sir Walter Scott
(1818)

The seventh in SIR WALTER SCOTT's series of Waverley Novels (see WAVERLEY), *The Heart of Midlothian* was originally published in the second series of *Tales of My Landlord* on July 25, 1818. The novel is set roughly 60 years in the past and takes its title from the old Tolbooth prison in Edinburgh (at the heart of the county of Midlothian), which was destroyed in 1817. Scott's plan was to research and rework different events that had occurred in the vicinity of Edinburgh's most notorious place of punishment. Thus, the novel's heroine, Jeanie Deans, was based on the story of Helen Walker, a Dunfriesshire woman who had walked all the way to London to beg a pardon for her sister on a charge of infanticide.

Like many of the previous Waverley novels, Scott wrote *The Heart of Midlothian* quickly, writing deep into the night despite his uncertain health. In Scotland it was received with wild enthusiasm, "such as I never witnessed there on the appearance of any other literary novelty," recalled J. G. Lockhart (quoted by Parker in Scott 1956, v). A cargo boat was needed to ship copies of the novel to London when it was completed. It was advertised on its title page as being the work of "Peter Pattison," a schoolteacher in the fictitious town of Gandercleugh, and edited by a colleague, Jedediah Cleishbotham. Hardly anyone was deceived by this ruse, and *The Heart of Midlothian* was immediately recognized as the latest of Scott's historical novels. Like the others it was immediately popular, partly, as SAMUEL TAYLOR COLERIDGE claimed, because it offered readers escapism in troubled times. "This," Coleridge argued, "is an age of anxiety from the crown to the hovel, from the cradle to the coffin; all is anxious striving" (Coleridge, 2003, 172). He did not rate Scott's novels very highly, at least as pieces of intellectual work, and thus saw the Scottish writer as feeding the public what they wanted.

What made the novel so seductive was its blatant appeal to the romance of "heritage" and the textualization of the myth of Scotland, which became something of a national pursuit in the 19th century. Scott would not have disagreed, although he also had a serious purpose as well. As his biographer Harriet Wood notes of his novels: "History impinges forcibly on the present in Scotland. Passers-by still spit on the stones that mark the site of the original Heart of Midlothian, the old town jail" (Wood 37) Although most of the characters are invented, Scott wanted to make Scotland's social and political history understandable in human terms, and thus the work is a pertinent example of the way in which, through HISTORICAL FICTION, history tends to be seen through the struggles of a tiny minority who are forced to make judgments and decisions.

In this way *The Heart of Midlothian* plunges its characters into real-life events. The novel opens in 1736 in Edinburgh, the scene of the Porteous riots. A condemned smuggler, Andrew Wilson, has helped his accomplice "Robertson" (really the young nobleman George Staunton) to escape. Won over by this act of generosity, the crowd react with fury when Captain Porteous, the soldier in charge of the city guards at Wilson's hanging, treats him with great brutality. Stones are thrown from the crowd, in response to which Porteous fires, killing half a dozen people. Porteous is subsequently condemned for murder, but the punishment is postponed by order of Queen Caroline (wife of George II). A group led by Staunton attack the Tolbooth Prison, drag Porteous outside, and lynch him in the Grassmarket. Back in London, the queen and her ministers are furious with the Scottish people, and part of the novel is about the strained relations that exist between London and Scotland. Staunton had also hoped to liberate his lower-class lover, Effie Deans, who is awaiting trial for the murder of a child, but she refuses to escape.

Effie's story is taken up in the second volume and focuses on her trial and condemnation. Effie—spoiled, reckless, and lacking restraint—had been seduced by Staunton, and she had hidden her pregnancy from her sister, father, and employers. Since she does not have the child and has informed nobody of her pregnancy, the assumption is made that she murdered her child to cover up her sin. In fact, the baby had been abducted by Staunton's unhinged ex-mistress, Madge Wildfire, while Effie lay in a fever. When cross-examined in court, Effie's elder sister Jeanie faces a moral dilemma when asked whether Effie told her of the pregnancy. A lie could save Effie's life, but Jeanie—caught "between God's laws and man's laws"—cannot tell a falsehood, despite her sister's pleas. Effie receives the death sentence. The queen is unlikely to show clemency because of her anger over the Porteous riots.

The bid to save Effie forms the main storyline of volume 3. In what is a test of her love, courage, and Christian faith, Jeanie journeys to London. In the course of her quest she is accosted by highwaymen and meets both Madge Wildfire and her mother, Meg Murdockson, who has sold Effie's son to a traveler in revenge for Staunton's seducing Madge. (It has been suggested that Madge's subsequent descent into madness owes something to WILLIAM WORDSWORTH's poem "The THORN.") In London, with the help of the duke of Argyle (presented as a type of ideal nobleman), Jeanie manages obtain an audience with the queen. She speaks so well that Queen Caroline is moved by the story and, in a clear sign that there is a power above the mere letter of the law, promises to act for her. On the way back to Scotland, Jeanie sees Meg Murdockson executed for witchcraft at Carlisle. It is suggested that Meg is the victim of anti-Scottish sentiment and the primitive fears that still exist in parts of the kingdom.

The final volume covers Jeanie's marriage to the Presbyterian clergyman Reuben Butler and their life on the estate of the duke of Argyle. Effie, meanwhile, runs away with and marries Staunton, although the couple remain childless, and she is never really happy despite their wealth. Some years later Staunton, having discovered that his lost child may not be dead, is shot by the robber Donacha dhu na Dunaigh (Black Duncan), who turns out to be his own son. The son then sails to America and joins an Indian tribe; Effie joins a convent.

At the end of the novel (chapter 51), Scott addresses his audience: "Reader, this tale will not be told in vain, if it shall be found to illustrate the great truth, that guilt, though it may attain temporal splendour, can never confer real happiness; that the evil consequences of our crimes long survive their commission, and, like the ghosts of the murdered, forever haunt the steps of the malefactor;

and that the paths of virtue, though seldom those of worldly greatness, are always those of pleasantness and peace" (495). Such an address is unusual in Scott's novels although the sentiments are common. He rarely suggests that any character is pure evil; rather, there are good and bad qualities in everyone. What Scott did want to stress was the idea that those who act well, exercise self-discipline and moral strength, do the "right thing," and even suffer for it will eventually achieve happiness and contentment. Revenge, on the other hand, is self-destructive and brings misery, as does unregulated passion.

Recent critics often suggest that *The Heart of Midlothian* is one of the most important Waverley novels, although they agree with Scott's contemporaries in thinking the final volume unnecessary. The novel is melodramatic in places, folkloric, and and heavily reliant on coincidence. Scott's clever use of Lowland dialect and the way in which this is contrasted with standard English is one of the book's most striking aspects. So, too, is the way in which he manages to keep the reader's interest in Jeanie, who runs the risk of seeming a little too priggish and perfect. Critics have talked about novel's topography and its use of spaces—Jeanie's journey is one from the margins (Scotland) to the center (London). The depiction of mob violence is unusual in novels of this time, and the book's depiction of religion, Calvinism, and providence has also interested critics.

**Further Reading**

Coleridge, S. T. *Selected Marginalia.* Edited by H. Jackson. Princeton, N.J.: Princeton University Press, 2003.

Gottlieb, Evan. "'To Be at Once Another and the Same': Scott's Waverley Novels and the End(s) of Sympathetic Britishness." In *Feeling British: Sympathy and National Identity in Scottish and English Writing, 1707–1832,* 170–207, Lewisburg, Pa.: Bucknell University Press, 2007.

Maxwell, Richard. "The Historical Novel." In *The Cambridge Companion to Fiction in the Romantic Period,* edited by Richard Maxwell and Katie Trumpener, 65–88. Cambridge: Cambridge University Press, 2008.

Hardie, Kath. *Sir Walter Scott: An Illustrated Historical Guide.* Norwich, Eng.: Jarrold, 2001.

Scott, Sir Walter. *The Heart of Midlothian.* Edited by Claire Lamont. Oxford: Oxford University Press, 1999.

———. *The Heart of Midlothian.* Edited by W. M. Parker. London: Dent, 1956.

Wood, Harriet Harvey. *Sir Walter Scott.* Plymouth, Eng.: Northcote: 2006.

—Andrew Lawrence

## Hemans, Felicia (1793–1835)

Born in Liverpool on September 25, 1793, to Felicity Dorothea Wagner Browne and George Browne, an Irish merchant and banker, Felicia Browne was the fifth of seven children. She lived in the bustling city until 1800, when financial difficulties forced her father to move his family to Gwrych, near Abegele, a small town in North Wales. There the family occupied a picturesque mansion overlooking the Irish Sea and her mother tutored her in literature, music, art, French, Italian, and other languages. Encouraged by the local vicar, Felicia later learned Latin, as well, and began writing poetry, which led to the 1808 appearance of her first volume, *Poems,* an effort catalyzed by her family's increasingly dire pecuniary straits. *Poems* received scant press attention, although two of its more notable subscribers included an army friend of her brothers, the man who would later marry her, Captain Alfred Hemans; and Thomas Medwin, a cousin of PERCY BYSSHE SHELLEY. On hearing of Felicia Browne's beauty and lyrical gifts, Shelley tried to arrange a meeting with her, but he was rebuffed by Mrs. Browne, an action which, scholars have speculated, saved the young writer from a potentially disastrous elopement.

Indeed, Felicia's family, particularly her mother, remained the center of her existence for years, even as she continued writing and publishing lengthy poems on international subjects, including *England and Spain, or, Valour and Patriotism* (1808) and *War and Peace* (1812). In spite of the poet's productivity, her work failed to generate the capital necessary to continue living in Gwrych. Following her husband's departure in 1809 to seek his fortune in Quebec, Mrs. Browne moved the children to a smaller house, and there, undeterred, Felicia kept writing. In 1812, when she was 19, her third volume of poetry, *The Domestic Affections and Other Poems* (which belies the collection's attention to current international affairs) appeared, and she married Captain Hemans. Within six years, now writing under her married name, she published three more books: *The Restoration of Works of Art to Italy* (1816), *Modern Greece* (1817), and *Translations from Camoens and Other Poets* (1818). Her children appeared even more rapidly than her collections; by 1818 she had given birth to five sons. As the Hemans family grew, they continued to face external pressures as well—the captain having been discharged from the militia—and after a few years in their home they returned to living with Felicia's mother, who assisted her in raising their children. Shortly before the birth of their fifth son, Alfred Hemans left for Italy in an apparently amicable separation. Felicia never saw her husband again.

Scholars have speculated that Felicia Hemans's unforeseen independence led to her increasing productivity and poetic success, although certainly the presence of her mother, sister, and brothers allowed her to focus on her writing. Her 1819 poem "The Meeting of Wallace and Bruce on the Banks of the Carron" was published to acclaim in *Blackwood's Edinburgh Magazine,* and her collection *Tales and Historic Scenes* sold out on its appearance in 1819. In addition to composing longer works, in the 1820s Hemans began contributing more frequently to literary magazines and annuals, work that she would later cull for collections. She also tried her hand at playwriting, although *The Siege of Valencia* (1823) was never performed and *The Vespers of Palermo* (1823) originally closed after only one night, though it later had a successful one-season run.

But it was in the magazines, as well as ANNUALS AND GIFT BOOKS, anthologies of poetry marketed specifically for women readers, that Hemans made her mark on the national literary stage. *The Amulet, Friendship's Offering,* and *Blackwood's* all clamored for the poet's efforts as she garnered increasingly positive critical attention and, more important for her publishers (and her family's stability), sales. *The Forest Sanctuary,* a lengthy poem in Spenserian stanzas and her personal favorite work, appeared in 1825, and RECORDS OF WOMAN, WITH OTHER POEMS, her most famous book, appeared in 1828. The latter volume, which included portraits of women from history and around the globe, cemented Hemans's reputation as England's favorite "poetess," but as recent attention to the volume has underscored, it hardly offers an easy valuation of "the domestic affections." Once again, Hemans turns to violence, war, and persecution as themes, though in a specifically gendered context.

The bleakness of *Records of Woman* undoubtedly grew out of personal tragedies the poet faced at home. In 1827 Hemans lost her mother, her original and most steadfast support, while at the same time her sister was planning her own marriage and subsequent leave-taking. Looking for a new community, one where her sons and she could find intellectual stimulation and friendship, Hemans moved her family to Wavertree, a village outside of Liverpool. Although depressed and ill, the poet found fans, friends, and mentors—among them, WILLIAM WORDSWORTH, SIR WALTER SCOTT, and the poet and essayist Maria Jane Jewsbury (1800–33). Nevertheless, the strain of her family and her career took a more severe turn, and in 1831 she sent her two eldest sons to Italy to live with their father, while she moved to Dublin. She continued to write, publishing *Songs of the Affections* in 1830 and *Scenes and Hymns of Life* in 1834, dedicating the latter volume to Wordsworth. In 1834 she caught scarlet fever, which eventually led to her death at 41 on May 16, 1835, a few days after she composed her last poem, "Sabbath Sonnet."

Hemans's poetry grew even more popular after her death. Each of her volumes, as well as her collected works, went through several editions on both sides of the Atlantic, and up until the early 20th century, she was frequently included in anthologies; children memorized her most famous lyrics, "CASABIANCA" and "The HOMES OF ENGLAND," well until the 1930s. By the mid-20th century, however, the poet had become identified only with those works and a few others, the vast majority of scholars and readers forgetting she had ever written anything else. And as a number of critics have recently pointed out, those few poems were generally misread as embarrassing sentimental effusions rather than the taut, complex lyrics they are. The 1990s, however, witnessed a renewed appreciation for Hemans and saw the reappearance of a number of her lyrics in anthologies and, more importantly, her longer works as well as articles and books devoted to her output. Not only does reading Hemans offer a corrective to misconceptions of the poet herself (and women poets in general) ; it also leads to a deeper appreciation of the Romantic era as well as the process of canonization in the 20th century.

See also "ARABELLA STUART"; "GRAVE OF A POETESS, THE"; "IMAGE IN LAVA, THE"; "INDIAN WOMAN'S DEATH SONG, THE"; "LAST SONG OF SAPPHO, THE."

## Further Reading

Feldman, Paula R. "The Poet and the Profits: Felicia Hemans and the Literary Marketplace." In *Women's Poetry, Late Romantic to Late Victorian: Gender and Genre, 1830–1900,* edited by Isobel Armstrong and Virginia Blain, 77–101. Basingstoke, Eng.: Palgrave, 1999.

Hemans, Felicia. *Felicia Hemans: Selected Poems, Letters, Reception Materials.* Edited by Susan Wolfson. Princeton, N.J.: Princeton University Press, 2000.

Lootens, Tricia. "Hemans and Home: Victorianism, Feminine 'Internal Enemies,' and the Domestication of National Identity." *PMLA: Publications of the Modern Language Association of America* 109, no. 2 (March 1994): 238–253.

McGann, Jerome. "Literary History, Romanticism, and Felicia Hemans." In *Re-Visioning Romanticism: British Women Writers, 1776–1837,* edited by Carol Shiner Wilson and Joel Haefner, 210–227. Philadelphia: University of Pennsylvania Press, 1994.

Sweet, Nanora, Julie Melnyk, and Marlon B. Ross, eds. *Felicia Hemans: Reimagining Poetry in the Nineteenth Century.* Basingstoke, Eng.: Palgrave, 2001.

—Katherine Montwieler

## *Hernani* Victor Hugo (1830)

On February 25, 1830, VICTOR HUGO's play *Hernani* opened at Paris's Comèdie-Française, one of the bastions of dramatic neoclassical ideals remaining in Europe. The premiere notoriously incited 39 days of rioting, as Hugo's avant-garde claque sparred with reactionary theatergoers over *Hernani*'s romantic composition and its explicit subversion of the fundamental tenets of NEOCLASSICISM. Though the aesthetic authority of French neoclassicism had already weathered criticism by MME. ANNE-LOUISE-GERMAINE DE STAËL, August Wilhelm von Schlegel, and Denis Diderot, among others, it was Hugo's celebrated drama and its accompanying riots that compelled French artists (and audiences) to join Germany and England in incorporating romanticism into their national repertoire.

Set in 16th-century Spain (a clear departure from the Greek and Roman settings of neoclassical plays), *Hernani* boasts several intertwining plotlines that temper its pathos with a social critique of those who would abuse positions of power—a favorite theme of much Romantic drama. Three men of disparate rank—the bandit Hernani, the nobleman Don Ruy Gomez de Silva, and King Don Carlos—all have amorous designs on the beautiful Doña Sol, whose own affections are trained solely on Hernani. Despite being romantic rivals, Hernani and Ruy Gomez unite to prevent Don Carlos's ascension from Spanish king to Roman emperor. However, with his impending election the once-malevolent Don Carlos acquires a compassionate heart and pardons the murderous conspirators. Following the discovery of Hernani's noble bloodline, he and Doña Sol marry, but the couple's marital bliss is cut short on their wedding day by the vengeful Ruy Gomez, who collects on the bridegroom's honor-bound pledge to die by his own hand at the nobleman's command. The play concludes with the dramatic suicides of Hernani, Doña Sol, and their repentant tormenter, Ruy Gomez.

In his manifesto of the romantic movement, 1827's preface to *Cromwell*, Hugo renounces neoclassical form's structural inflexibility and emotional inexpressiveness and urges the playwright's expanded freedom to pen works unfettered by archaic rules and notions of decorum. Further inveighing against the idealized, noble characters preferred by neoclassicists, Hugo advocates coupling the SUBLIME with the grotesque (at once both monstrous and comical) in order to capture the true essence of man. Representing Hugo's most successful attempt at applying his romantic theories to playwriting, *Hernani*'s assault on the ideals of neoclassicism begins with language. Ostensibly adhering to the general guidelines of the alexandrine verse required of classical tragedians, Hugo discards the artificial rigidity of the 12-beat line in favor of rhymed alexandrines with metrical flexibility, employing stichomythia (single alternating lines or half lines) and caesuras to better imitate organic expressions of emotion.

As well as making innovative use of language, Hugo disregards the supremacy of the unities of time, place, and action. Plots satisfying the neoclassical tenet of verisimilitude could not exceed 24 hours in length, utilize multiple locations, or feature complex or illogical subplots. In direct opposition to plays of the neoclassical canon, *Hernani* moves freely through space and time, most notably shifting from the ornate portrait gallery of the de Silva castle to the GOTHIC crypts of Charlemagne's tomb between acts 3 and 4. Furthermore, neoclassicism prohibits characters from undergoing significant personal changes through the course of the play or speaking to themselves (or the audience) through soliloquies, while Hugo's romanticism defies such constraints, allowing the lascivious and violent Don Carlos to evolve into a magnanimous emperor in a mere hour of stage time, narrating his own rapid transformation through a scene-length soliloquy.

In *Hernani* spectacle and violence are welcomed back onstage to affect the audience's emotions, diverging significantly from the neoclassical ideal of *les bienséances,* or proprieties. Perhaps the play's most striking defiance of neoclassicism is its profound resistance to generic classification. Modeled on Shakespearean tragedies and Spanish *comedia de capa y espada* (cloak-and-dagger plays), Hugo's work is also linked to the melodramatic genre (a form particularly suited to Romanticism). By incorporating myriad tragic, comic, spectacular, and farcical elements, *Hernani* complicates any easy designation of genre. Don Carlos's concealment within a closet, for example, resembles the popular sight gags of Parisian boulevard theater farces, while Doña Sol's onstage death both echoes and mocks the demises of tragic heroines such as Racine's Phèdre.

Hugo further breached neoclassical notions of theatrical decorum in his staging of *Hernani* at the Comèdie-Française. The company's actors, accustomed to declaiming their lines from within a rigid semicircle around the prompter's box, were retrained by Hugo to move fluidly around the set, utilize the furniture, and speak directly to other actors, using natural intonations. The Romantic acting of Mademoiselle Mars as Doña Sol, who died onstage writhing on the floor and wringing her hands, proved particularly distasteful to bourgeois and elite theatergoers and thrilling to their bohemian counterparts. It was these two groups that assembled to witness Hugo's unequivocal condemnation of established dramatic aesthetics, voicing their respective outrage and elation throughout the play's premiere. Having refused the services of the Comèdie-Française's claque (a group of audience members paid by a theater to applaud its performances) in favor of a rowdy collection of fellow Romanticists, Hugo strategically ensured that the play's opening night would be contentious and memorable. Taking meticulous notes of audience reactions on his script, Hugo observed that the play was interrupted audibly by the disorderly audience nearly every 12 lines of dialogue; the playwright went so far as to classify the outbursts into four categories: laughter, noise, whistling, and agitation. The nightly rioting dwindled as Hugo's romanticism became acknowledged as a valid alternative to neoclassicism and was subsumed within the French dramatic canon.

**Further Reading**

Halsall, Albert W. *Victor Hugo and the Romantic Drama.* Toronto: University of Toronto Press, 1998.

Hugo, Victor. *Hernani.* In *The Longman Anthology of Drama and Theater: A Global Perspective,* rev. ed., edited by Michael L. Greenwald, Roger Schultz, and Roberto D. Pomo, 761–793. New York: Person Longman.

———. "Preface to *Cromwell.*" 1827. Available online. URL: http://www.bartleby.com/39/40.html. Accessed on November 30, 2008.

—Meredith Conti

# historical fiction

Works of historical fiction are set in a past age and seek to recover, to varying degrees of fidelity, the social conditions, manners, and spirit of a historical period. The Romantic period is widely regarded as a crucial moment in the emergence of a specific form of historicism. In the late 18th and early 19th centuries, unprecedented political ruptures, social change, large-scale imperial expansion, and rapid technological development restructured the human experience in profound ways. These processes gave rise to a new historical self-consciousness. The idea of the "spirit of the age"—of a particular concomitance of political, social, intellectual, and artistic events that gave birth to the unique spirit of the period—is ubiquitous in the contemporary literature, from WILLIAM HAZLITT's *The SPIRIT OF THE AGE* (1825) and John Stuart Mills's 1831 series of articles for the *Examiner,* also entitled "The Spirit of the Age," to Edmund Bulwer Lytton's *England and the English* (1833) and various poetical and prose writings of PERCY BYSSHE SHELLEY. The closing paragraph of Shelley's "A DEFENCE OF POETRY" (1821) exemplifies the feeling, widespread among Shelley's contemporaries, that the period through which they were living would be looked upon by posterity as a political and artistic movement and entity in its own right: "our own will be a memorable age in intellectual achievements, and we live among such philosophers and poets as surpass beyond comparison any who have appeared since the last national struggle for civil and religious liberty" (Shelley 117).

This self-fashioning of the age as being separated, in many ways, from the preceding decades and generations, altered the terms on which history itself was understood. The traditional, pre-Romantic view of history held that history's lessons worked by example, providing a range of historical precedents that encapsulated worthy or disreputable political or personal modes of behavior. However, history's morals could hardly speak to the Romantic subject, whose character and ideals were understood to be profoundly shaped by the momentous transformations convulsing the period. History, in the Romantic context, was endlessly referred to and drawn on to understand the dynamics of social and political change.

The decades between 1780 and 1830 witnessed the outpouring of thousands of historical works. Widely acclaimed multivolume works such as David Hume's *History of Great Britain* (1754–62) and John Lingard's *History of England* (1819–30) ran through numerous editions and were perpetually pirated and plagiarized.

Novelists, too, developed a strong interest in history and used it to diverse ends in their fiction. Historical periods, especially those of medieval Italy and Spain, supplied tantalizingly exotic backdrops for the suspenseful plots of many GOTHIC novels, including ANN RADCLIFFE's *The MYSTERIES OF UDOLPHO* (1794), Horace Walpole's *The Castle of Otranto* (1764), and MATTHEW GREGORY LEWIS's *The MONK* (1796). MARIA EDGEWORTH's pioneering regional novel *CASTLE RACKRENT* (1800) adopted the historical perspective to trace the decline, over four generations, of an Anglo-Irish family. THOMAS LOVE PEACOCK satirized the conventions of the romance genre in his mock-historical novels *Maid Marian* (1822) and *The Misfortunes of Elphin* (1829).

The rise of the historical novel as a genre in its own right, however, is intimately connected with the writings of the prolific Scottish author SIR WALTER SCOTT, who is often credited with the invention of the modern historical novel. Scott authored 23 novels, 20 of which were set in different historical periods of the past. His first novel, *WAVERLEY; or 'Tis Sixty Years Since*, anonymously published in 1814, brought him wide recognition as an author and was a phenomenal success with readers: The book's first edition sold within two days on publication. The novel is set during the 1745 Jacobite Rebellion, which attempted to restore the Stuart dynasty to the British throne. The central conflict and trajectory of *Waverley* illustrates the core of Scott's literary interest in the past: the friction between and competition of an archaic, regressive culture on the one hand and a modern, refined, and enlightened culture on the other.

While Scott's post-Enlightenment sympathies were clearly aligned with what he perceived to be the security and progressive civility of modernity, he astutely manipulated his audience's appetite for the romance and turmoils of the past. His highly sophisticated engagement with historical themes is extremely varied and often experimental. While *Waverley* is told from a conventional third-person perspective, Scott's second novel, *GUY MANNERING* (1815), is told through a wide range of texts—letters, journal entries, epigraphs—a technique that discards a secure ideological standpoint and gives voice to the diverging opinions of the historical characters. *Old Mortality* (1816) is remarkable for including a chapter in which the narrator explains how he collects and organizes the historical information that is used in the subsequent chapters to reconstruct the events of military campaigns against the Covenanters in the late 17th century. *Redgauntlet* (1824), Scott's most technically refined novel, begins as an epistolary novel (see EPISTOLARY FICTION) before it blends into a third-person narrative, interspersed with journal entries and inserted tales. But the work that made Scott's name on the international stage and turned the historical novel into a publishing phenomenon beyond Britain's borders was *IVANHOE: A Romance* (1819). *Ivanhoe* is set in 1194, when Richard I returned from the Third Crusade to banish his brother John, who had usurped Richard's power during his absence, from the English throne. Scott's mythical construction of the roots of British national identity strongly fueled the Victorian cultural fascination with the Middle Ages.

The first modern critic to reflect on Scott's achievement as an historical novelist was Georg Lukács, who devoted a section of his seminal *The Historical Novel* (1937; translated 1962) to Scott's works. While critics of the mid-20th century largely turned away from Scott, heightened critical interest in literary historiography and in literature as a nation-building project have reinvigorated scholarship on his writings in the late 20th and early 21st centuries.

## Further Reading

Brown, David. *Walter Scott and the Historical Imagination.* London: Routledge & Kegan Paul, 1979.

Buzard, James. *Disorienting Fiction: The Autoethnographic Work of Nineteenth-Century British Novels.* Princeton, N.J.: Princeton University Press, 2005.

Dennis, Ian. *Nationalism and Desire in Early Historical Fiction.* London: Macmillan, 1997.

Duncan, Ian. *Scott's Shadow: The Novel in Romantic Edinburgh.* Princeton, N.J.: Princeton University Press, 2007.

Lukács, Georg. *The Historical Novel.* Translated by Hannah and Stanley Mitchell. London: Merlin, 1962.

Shaw, Harry E. *The Forms of Historical Fiction: Sir Walter Scott and His Successors.* Ithaca, N.Y.: Cornell University Press, 1983.

Shelley, Percy Bysshe. *Selected Prose Works of Shelley.* Edited by Henry S. Salt. London: Watts & Co., 1915.

White, Hayden. *The Content of Form: Narrative Discourse and Historical Representation.* Baltimore: Johns Hopkins University Press, 1987.

———. *Metahistory: The Historical Imagination in Nineteenth-Century Europe.* Baltimore: Johns Hopkins, 1973.

—Katharina Boehm

## Hoffmann, Ernst Theodor Amadeus (E. T. A. Hoffmann) (1776–1822)

E. T. A. Hoffmann, a jurist, writer, composer, caricaturist, and painter, is best known as a writer of GOTHIC short tales. Born Ernst Theodor Wilhelm Hoffmann in Königsberg, Prussia, on January 24, 1776, he later adopted a pen name that replaced *Theodor* with *Amadeus*, in homage to the composer Wolfgang Amadeus Mozart. A gifted student of science, music, and art in his youth, Hoffmann studied law at the University of Königsberg. After marrying and graduating, he worked as a Prussian law officer, a conductor, and a stage director before turning to writing in the last—and most productive—10 years of his life.

Given his varied interests, it is not surprising that Hoffmann achieved his greatest success as a writer of short tales in the German Romantic tradition. Influenced by Georg Philipp Friedrich Freiherr von Hardenberg, the poet and Neptunist known as NOVALIS, Hoffmann shared the earlier poet's interest in a medium that fused the varied arts and natural sciences and blurred the boundary between measurable experience and the supernatural. While Novalis championed the then-new theories of degeneration and extinction of species, Hoffmann embraced the antideterministic pre-cept of Naturphilosophie, or philosophy of unity in nature. A defining feature of German Romanticism, especially pronounced in the writings of Hoffmann, FRIEDRICH VON SCHILLER, and JOHANN WOLFGANG VON GOETHE, Naturphilosophie also influenced such works as MARY SHELLEY's FRANKENSTEIN and Nathaniel Hawthorne's "Rappaccini's Daughter."

Writing at a time in which England, Germany, and France all embraced the gothic as a national genre, Hoffmann employed its characteristically German themes and conventions. Thus, his tales take place in contemporary settings instead of medieval ones, and he renders them phantasmagoric, or dark and dreamlike. Many of them engage the natural and pseudosciences and feature a protagonist's struggle between everyday life and the dark world of his dreams. For example, in "The MINES OF FALUN" (1819) we meet Elis Frobom, a young sailor who is corrupted by a supernatural agent in the form of an old miner. The miner quotes Novalis and other students of geology, glorifying science's power to reveal nature's hidden secrets, inspiring in Frobom a destructive lust for power. In "The Sandman" (1816) we meet Nathaniel, whose father, an alchemist seeking the secrets of life, dies while performing a chemical experiment with his friend, Coppelius. When, as an adult, Nathaniel meets Coppelius again, he becomes increasingly obsessed with the old man, dreaming of him evoking supernatural power through metalworking and thinking him the incarnation of a boogeyman from a childhood tale. He ultimately succumbs to madness, transferring his obsession to a mechanical female doll, thinking it a live person. Typical of Hoffmann's work and of German Romanticism in general, such characters find themselves unable to navigate the boundary between ordinary life and the world of fantasy that ultimately consumes them. Their psychic disintegration is often represented through the use of a doppelgänger, or alter ego, as they move between reality and fantasy or madness.

Nearly 60 years after his death on June 25, 1822, Hoffmann himself became the protagonist of a gothic Romantic story when he and his work—specifically "The Sandman," "Councilor Krespel," and "Adventures of a New Year's Night"—were immortalized in Jacques Offenbach's opera *The Tales of Hoffmann* (1881). This has proved a fitting tribute to the writer whose first creative outlet was music, who championed the fusion of the arts, and whose tale "The Nutcracker and the Mouse King," adapted by Alexander Dumas and then Pytor Ilyich Tchaikovsky, would become one of the best known masterpieces of Western ballet.

**Further Reading**

Hoffmann, E. T. A. *The Best Tales of Hoffmann.* Edited and translated by E. F. Bleiler. New York: Dover, 1978.

Knopf, David Glenn. *Authorship as Alchemy: Subversive Writing in Pushkin, Scott, and Hoffmann.* Stanford, Calif.: Stanford University Press, 194.

McGlathery, James. *E. T. A. Hoffmann.* London: Twayne, 1997.

—Priscilla Glanville

## Hogg, James (1770–1835)

James Hogg, known as the "Ettrick Shepherd," was a Scottish poet and novelist born at Ettrick Forest, Selkirshire, in the Borders country that would remain a literary inspiration for him throughout his career. The early years of his life were spent in virtual poverty following the bankruptcy of his father, a tenant farmer. Hogg himself had to leave school after only a few months to take on work as a farmhand and shepherd for various employers. Nevertheless, he eventually taught himself to read and write, assisted in this endeavour by one of his employers, who made his library available to Hogg and encouraged the precocious youth to explore it. Hogg began to compose little songs and verses, gaining a local reputation as "Jamie the Poeter," and by his early 20s he had anonymously published his first poem in the *Scots Magazine* (1794). His first collection, *Scottish Pastorals, Poems, Songs, Etc.,* was published in 1801 and received modest praise. In 1810 Hogg moved to Edinburgh and integrated himself into the literary establishment. Thus began a remarkable literary career that would culminate in one of the most astonishing novels in Scottish literary history—*The PRIVATE MEMOIRS AND CONFESSIONS OF A JUSTIFIED SINNER.*

Claiming to have the same birth date as ROBERT BURNS, Hogg also affected to be Burns's successor as "Heav'n-taught ploughman," rustic poet to the masses—a reputation that worked both for and against him in his career. He certainly could boast an intimate knowledge of the folk tradition of rural Scotland, abundantly manifest in his poems and tales. His knowledge of Scottish ballads was gained from his mother, and he shared many of these songs with WALTER SCOTT when the latter was scouring the Borders in search of materials for his MINSTRELSY OF THE SCOTTISH BORDER. For her part, Hogg's mother afterward complained to Scott that by printing the ballads he had effectively ruined them: "[T]here was never ane o' my sangs prentit til ye prentit them yoursell, an' ye hae spoilt them a'thegither" (quoted in Hogg 1972, 62). Hogg's introduction to Scott was both a blessing and a curse, and their relationship epitomized Hogg's uneasy status among the Edinburgh literati. Certainly Scott was immensely helpful to Hogg in advancing his career, but Scott's social condescension, and Hogg's defensiveness threatened the friendship at times. The tension in the relationship turned, as well, on literary issues, as the writers would eventually clash on the matter of historical representation in fiction.

Hogg began to write and publish in various genres, bringing out in 1807 a collection of ballad imitations (*The Mountain Bard*) and a sheep-farming manual (*The Shepherd's Guide*). In keeping with Burns, a daughter was born to him out of wedlock that year, followed by another daughter from a different lover a year later. He became increasingly indebted, and it was at this point that he decided to go to Edinburgh to become a professional writer. In 1810 he began a periodical called *The Spy*, most of which he wrote himself. An observer in the manner of Addison and Steel's "Mr Spectator," Hogg's "Spy" reveals gossipy details about Edinburgh's literary and social world. Containing poems, stories, and essays, this very experimental journal was reasonably successful, but it was discontinued after one year, in part because of concerns about its liberal tone and subject matter.

It was in Hogg's 43rd year that his literary reputation began to blossom, with the publication in 1813 of the book-length poem *The Queen's*

*Wake,* which included the extraordinary poems "The Witch of Fife" and "Kilmeny." The narrative "play" of the work, in which a series of tales is told within an overarching narrative, as well as the incorporation into the text of Hogg himself as a persona, introduced readers to the "postmodern" sensibility that would mark his later works. *The Queen's Wake* also revealed Hogg's originality, his command of the ballad form, and his keen sense of Scottish folk history and national themes. The popular work went through six editions in his lifetime, and it stands as one of the seminal works of British Romantic poetry. Upon its arrival, Hogg's name began to be mentioned in the same circles as those of LORD BYRON and Scott.

Hogg put his newfound celebrity to work by assembling a collection of poems by such luminaries as WILLIAM WORDSWORTH, ROBERT SOUTHEY, and Byron. When the luminaries declined the invitation to contribute, he decided to produce the collection anyway, and the result was *The Poetic Mirror, or, The Living Bards of Britain,* a series of inspired parodies, with his send-up of Wordsworth's *The Recluse* perhaps the high point. And in typical Hogg fashion, he did not neglect to parody himself. During this time he was given a farm at Altrive Lake, rent-free for life, from the duke of Buccleuch, and over the next several years he divided his time between there and Edinburgh and married Margaret Phillips, with whom he would eventually have one son and four daughters. In Edinburgh he also was the founding member of an ostensible debating society, the Right and Wrong Club, which appears to have been a glorified drinking club.

Hogg's most important literary connection in Edinburgh during these years was with *Blackwood's Edinburgh Magazine* (see NEWSPAPERS AND MAGAZINES). The "Maga" group included the publisher William Blackwood and contributors John Wilson and John Gibson Lockhart (Scott's son-in-law). The brashness of this journal was signaled by its first number, in which appeared something called the "Chaldee Manuscript." Mostly Hogg's idea, the "manuscript" was supposedly a translation of a newly discovered biblical text, but in fact it was a scathing satire on the Edinburgh literary scene—so offensive, in fact, that the issue had to be withdrawn. But the most interesting product of the "Maga" collaborators was the infamous *Noctes Ambrosianae,* a series of "conversations," mostly imaginary, that appeared in *Blackwood's Magazine* between 1822 and 1835. Though Hogg had a hand in writing the early sketches, before long Wilson was writing all of the Shepherd's speeches. Hogg figures in many of the conversations as the "Ettrick Shepherd," a not always flattering representation but a dominant and at times delightful one all the same. The relationship of the "shepherd" to Hogg and his career is a complicated one that has some bearing on understanding his literary motivations and techniques. This complexity is owing in part to the fact that Hogg played up the role of shepherd once he realized that the *Noctes* pieces were providing publicity in the marketplace. At the same time, he bristled at some of the characterizations, which could be very insulting, ridiculing not only his literary and social pretension but his physical appearance as well. He had to use all of his imaginative powers to maintain the upper hand in this relationship and turn the condescension to his advantage, which he accomplished in his work by exploiting this tension created by his ambiguous status as "author" and "shepherd."

Like Scott, Hogg eventually turned his talents to the novel, publishing *The Brownie of Bodsbeck* in 1818. This historical novel is concerned with the Covenanting revolution of 1679, also known as the "Killing Time" because of atrocities committed by government forces. As with much of Hogg's prose fiction, the novel has an unconventional approach to historical evidence reflected in unconventional narrative constructions. *The Brownie* gives rise to multiple voices telling their own stories, all of which are mediated by the kind of unreliable narrator typical of Hogg's fiction. It creates its sense of history not from the technique of historical verisimilitude or probability, but rather from a foregrounding of tradition and oral history through its multilayered and multi-voiced narration. So it was perhaps inevitable that Hogg's historical representation would become contested ground, particularly as its historical subject matter intersected with that of Scott's novel *Old Mortality* (1816). Scott upbraided Hogg for his delineation of the historical record, but with its assimilation of tradition and folk history, *The Brownie of Bodsbeck* arguably incorporates a certain historical value that surpasses Scott's more acclaimed representation. Certainly Hogg believed this was the case, informing Scott that, although he may have altered a few parts of his novel for narrative reasons, he remained faithful to the truth, which, he pointedly added, is "a great deal mair than you can say for your tale o' Auld Mortality" (Hogg 1972, 105–106).

Throughout the 1820s Hogg continued to write songs and stories and contribute to various periodicals, but he spent most of these years in financial distress, struggling to maintain his farm and his in-laws' household. His second work of fiction would turn out to be the very popular *Winter Evening Tales* (1820), a collection concerned with the oral storytelling of Hogg's locale. In 1822 he published his second novel, *The Three Perils of Man: or War, Women and Witchcraft*, a Border romance that, characteristically, interrogates the very basis of romance. This was followed in 1823 by *The Three Perils of Woman: or Love, Leasing and Jealousy*, a novel that incorporates an implicit critique of Scott's inaugural historical fiction, *WAVERLEY* (1814), in particular the curious elision in Scott's novel of the atrocities committed at the decisive battle of Culloden during the 1745 Jacobite Rebellion. In contrast to Scott's novel, the "third peril," or section, of Hogg's novel contains a hellish vision of a corpse-ridden countryside, where the roasted and decapitated bodies of women and children are uncovered in hastily dug graves.

In 1824 Hogg published his crowning achievement: *The Private Memoirs and Confessions of a Justified Sinner*, a remarkably original and innovative story that the writer Iain Crichton Smith calls "a towering Scottish novel, one of the very greatest of all Scottish books" (Smith 1). Hogg himself was sufficiently spooked by his own creation to publish it anonymously, declaring that, "it being a story replete with horror, after I had written it I durst not venture to put my name to it" (1972, 55). The contemporary reviews did not encourage him to soon change his mind on that score, as the author was criticized for narrative inconsistency, needless ambiguity, and indecency. The *Justified Sinner* incorporates many forms—GOTHIC

nightmare, psychological thriller, religious parable, comedy, mystery tale, and even historical fiction. Using the technique of the double narrative, Hogg combines historical actuality with the supernatural to produce a unique social, political, and literary critique hitherto unseen in Scottish letters. The "memoir" in question—the ravings of a tortured "sinner"—is in the hands of an Edinburgh "Editor," who is clearly intended to represent rational, post-Enlightenment Scotland as well as Scott on some level. The raw history of the manuscript, the Sinner's anguished attempt to confess his life of iniquity, is thereby mediated through the controlling frame narrative of the Editor, who goes to some length to explain and rationalize this disturbing and volatile "confession." However, in this enterprise the Editor is surely impeded by the figure of the Sinner's mysterious doppelgänger, Gil-Martin, a sinister shape-shifter with alarming control over the Sinner's actions, implicating him in rape, murder, and assorted other crimes. In the second narrative—that of the Sinner himself—Gil-Martin's frightening ambiguity is laid bare. It seems evident that Hogg intended Gil-Martin's character to be undecidable: he is both a diabolical "necromancer" (Hogg 2002, 126)—the devil himself—and Robert's projected "double," the externalization of Robert's tormented soul. André Gide refers to Hogg's portrayal of the devil as "among the most ingenious ever invented," for while his appearance is "always psychologically explicable," he is also seen by other characters (Gide xv).

In the Editor's final, brief narrative, a kind of coda, the novel's indeterminacies converge in a stunning crescendo. The Editor and his associates go in search of the Sinner's grave, whose existence they know of through a letter published in *Blackwood's Magazine* by James Hogg. Hogg's clever innovation was actually to publish this letter in *Blackwood's Magazine* the previous year and then incorporate part of it into his novel. He extends the joke by having a shepherd, "James Hogg," dismiss the Editor and his party when they seek directions to the grave: "I hae mair ado than I can manage the day, foreby ganging to houk up hundred-year-auld banes" (202, 170). His intertextual narrative play and his mockery of the Editor's aspirations afford him a last laugh on the Establishment that would confine him to the sheep pastures, unless they deign to invite him to their salons. But more than this, *The Private Memoirs and Confessions of a Justified Sinner* is a masterpiece that questions the very basis of history, narrative representation, and Enlightenment rationality. If Hogg wrote nothing else, he would be forever remembered for this stunning work.

Over the next 10 years Hogg continued to struggle financially, yet he managed to contribute stories and poems to a variety of periodicals. He spent the winter of 1832–33 in London, where he was enthusiastically celebrated on the literary circuit. In 1833, the year after Scott had died, he published *Familiar Anecdotes of Sir Walter Scott*, intended as a frank but warm tribute to his mentor but, characteristically, containing some indiscrete anecdotes, which greatly offended Scott's son-in-law, John Gibson Lockhart. However, as Douglas Mack points out, Lockhart's anger probably stemmed from the fact that a man of his "aristocratic pretensions" had to endure seeing his family "discussed in print by a man of Hogg's lowly background" (in Hogg 1972, xii). Such prejudices followed Hogg throughout his career and certainly contributed to his neglect in the years after he died (November 21, 1835). But while he did not achieve the greatness of Scott, Hogg's literary achievement offers a rich multiplicity of voices from Scottish society that convey attitudes and values not often represented in the grand narratives of historical fiction.

### Further Reading

Alexander, J. H. *The Tavern Sages: Selections from the Noctes Ambrosianae.* Aberdeen, Scotland: Association for Scottish Literary Studies, 1992.

Gide, André. Introduction to *The Private Memoirs and Confessions of a Justified Sinner,* by James Hogg, ix–xvi. London: Cresset Press, 1947.

Groves, David. *James Hogg: The Growth of a Writer.* Edinburgh: Scottish Academic Press, 1988.

Hogg, James. *The Brownie of Bodsbeck.* Edited by Douglas S. Mack. Edinburgh: Scottish Academic Press, 1976.

———. *Memoir of the Author's Life and Familiar Anecdotes of Sir Walter Scott.* Edited by Douglas S. Mack. Edinburgh: Scottish Academic Press, 1972.

———. *The Private Memoirs and Confessions of a Justified Sinner.* Edited by P. D. Garside. Edinburgh: University Press, 2002.

Hughes, Gillian H. "The Critical Reception of *The Confessions of a Justified Sinner.*" *Newsletter of the James Hogg Society* 1 (May 1982): 11–14.

Simpson, Louis. *James Hogg: A Critical Study.* Edinburgh: Oliver and Boyd, 1962.

Smith, Iain Crichton. "A Work of Genius: James Hogg's *Justified Sinner.*" *Studies in Scottish Literature* 28 (1993): 1–11.

Wilson, John. *Noctes Ambrosianae.* 4 vols. Edited by J. F. Ferrier. Edinburgh: William Blackwood, 1863.

—Ross MacKay

## Holcroft, Thomas (1745–1809)

Thomas Holcroft rose from absolute poverty to become an infamous and influential playwright, orator, political agitator, and novelist. He was born in London on December 10, 1745, the son of a shoemaker, and during his childhood and youth he worked variously as a peddler, stocking weaver, stable boy, cobbler, and tutor. At the age of 25 he became an actor, performing at the Haymarket in London and at theaters in Dublin and across England. In 1778 he produced his first play, *The Crisis, or Love and Fear;* his novel, *Manthorn, the Enthusiast* was published serially in the same year. In 1780 another novel, *Alwyn,* recounted Holcroft's experiences as a strolling actor, and he produced two pamphlets describing the anti-Catholic Gordon riots.

Between 1782 and 1784 Holcroft lived in Paris, gathering material for adaptations of contemporary French drama. His adaptation of Beaumarchais's *Mariage de Figaro* was performed at Covent Garden to great acclaim in 1784 as *Follies of a Day.* In that year Holcroft became intimate with a circle of radical thinkers including THOMAS PAINE, MARY WOLLSTONECRAFT, and Joel Barlow. In 1786 he met WILLIAM GODWIN, and over the course of the next decade, each man had a profound influence on the other's political thought. Both were "electrified" by the FRENCH REVOLUTION in 1789, and they declared themselves committed republicans. Holcroft joined a committee to publish the first part of Paine's *The RIGHTS OF MAN* (1791). He contributed to the radical *Monthly Magazine* in 1792 and joined the reformist Society for Constitutional Information that same year.

While Godwin set about systematizing his political ideals in *Political Justice* (1793), Holcroft believed that literary expression was the most effective means of disseminating radical ideas. In 1792 he published the epistolary novel *Anna St. Ives*, in which the enlightened heroine educates her rakish suitor in the principles of political justice. His plays *The School for Arrogance: A Comedy* (1791) and *The Road to Ruin: A Comedy* (1792) also espoused progressive views.

Holcroft's political activities brought him to the attention of government in 1794. One of a dozen reformers arrested on a charge of high treason, he was held for eight weeks at the Old Bailey, though he was never brought to trial. The first three defendants—Thomas Hardy, John Horne Tooke, and JOHN THELWALL—were acquitted, and the government's case collapsed. Holcroft's public reputation was damaged by the charge of treason, however. The publication of his second "Jacobin" novel, *Hugh Trevor* (1794), was interrupted by his imprisonment, the second half not appearing until 1797, and the five plays he produced between 1796 and 1798 generally met with a hostile reception.

In 1799 Holcroft left for the Continent, living in Hamburg and Paris until 1802. In Paris he again found inspiration in French drama. His adaptation of Pixérécourt's *Coelina* was performed in London as *A TALE OF MYSTERY* (1802). It was a great success and is credited as the first example of melodrama on the English stage. Holcroft produced another novel, *Memoirs of Bryan Perdue*, in 1805. He died in London on March 23, 1809, having dictated part of his autobiography. The work was completed by WILLIAM HAZLITT and published as *The Memoirs of Thomas Holcroft* in 1816.

## Further Reading

Barrell, John. *Imagining the King's Death: Figurative Treason, Fantasies of Regicide, 1793–1796*, Oxford: Oxford University Press, 2000.

Hazlitt, William. *The Memoirs of Thomas Holcroft*. In *The Complete Works of William Hazlitt*, vol. 3, edited by P. P. Howe. London and Toronto: J. M. Dent and Sons, 1931.

Holcroft, Thomas. *The Novels and Selected Plays of Thomas Holcroft*. 5 vols. Edited by W. M. Verhoeven. London: Pickering & Chatto, 2007.

Kelly, Gary. *The English Jacobin Novel, 1780–1805*. Oxford: Clarendon Press, 1976.

Rosenblum, Joseph. *Thomas Holcroft: Literature and Politics in England in the Age of the French Revolution*. Lewiston, N.Y.: E. Mellen Press, 1995.

—Mary Fairclough

## "Holy Thursday"  William Blake  (1794)

Like most of the poems published in WILLIAM BLAKE's collection *SONGS OF INNOCENCE AND OF EXPERIENCE*, "Holy Thursday" actually consists of two poems: one from an innocence perspective and one from that of experience. Published five years after its companion poem, "Holy Thursday" from *Songs of Experience* paints a very different picture of the Feast of the Ascension of Jesus at St. Paul's Cathedral than does its earlier, more innocent partner. (Holy Thursday in this case refers to the celebration of Jesus' ascension 40 days after Easter, rather than what Christians usually mean by Holy Thursday, celebrating the Last Supper before his crucifixion.) In the poem from *Songs of Innocence*, the children of the charity schools of London march into the cathedral, ready to celebrate the ascension under the watchful eyes of the elderly schoolmasters. The scene is one of innocent praise as these children, some of the poorest children in London, are shown "raising their innocent hands" during the service. But the angelic scene of this earlier poem is not seen in the "Holy Thursday" of *Songs of Experience*. Like much of Blake's poetry, "Holy Thursday" exemplifies the social concerns that many of the Romantic poets held about rapidly expanding industrial England and the poverty that such expansion brought along with it.

In the later poem, Blake reexamines the annual festival at Saint Paul's in light of the reality of the children's situation. The beauty and majesty of the ceremony are ignored, while the social implications of a church ceremony for the poor are examined closely. His eyes now opened and tinted by life's hard experiences, the narrator sees the children in a more realistic light. In a tone full of contempt and disgust, the poem claims, "Is this a holy thing to see, / In a rich and fruitful land, / Babes reduc'd to misery, / Fed with cold and usurous hand?" (ll. 1–4). In these lines, Blake is criticizing London society's attitude toward these young children; the upper classes felt that they "did enough" to help the poor of London by funding the charity schools and that, beyond this minor form of help, the wealth they had been blessed with did not need to be passed on to those of lesser fortune in England. Instead, the rich of London went to the Holy Thursday services so that they could receive their rightful thanks from the poor. Blake criticizes this attitude, accusing them of a warped sense of pride for their minor acts of charity. In the midst of the Industrial Revolution and the wealth it provided, these poor London children were living without proper food or clothing. In the innocence poem, the children are shown singing for joy as they enter St Paul's Cathedral. Instead of looking with approval upon the scene, the experience poem asks, "Can it be a song of joy?" (l. 6). The children's song is not joyful or angelic; rather, the experienced ear hears instead a child's cry of hunger and pain.

The poem continues with a brief portrait of the poor of London. The third stanza creates a dreary picture of barren fields and difficult paths. While most of the rich viewed England as a land of plenty, Blake describes a land of "eternal winter" (l. 12), painting images of a starving, barren land. Not only does the land currently hold no food for the poor children, but these children cannot see hope in their futures either, as the barren fields are now overgrown with thorns. Even though the upper classes of London were prospering and the middle classes were gaining prestige, this poem points out that these advancements failed to help the lower classes in any way.

Blake closes the poem with a plea to the rich: "For where-e'er the sun does shine, / And where-e'er the rain does fall, / Babes should never hunger there, / Nor poverty the mind appall" (ll. 13–16). The experience viewpoint of this poem hinges on this final stanza. Giving a minimal amount of financial support to charity schools was not enough

in the way of social welfare for the poor. Instead, Blake cried out for a type of socialism in which the wealth of the nation would be spread out and shared between rich and poor alike. To Blake, no civilized, industrious, and prosperous nation should allow any of its citizens to live in constant hunger and poverty, and he considered it the duty of the wealthier classes to correct the social injustices that plagued England at the time.

Today, many of Blake's works are seen as prophetic and inspired, with many of his works speaking out against the social and political injustices that infested his native London. However, this collection of poems as a whole was apathetically received by his contemporaries. Despite many of the poems' highly philosophical and socially critical nature, *Songs of Innocence and Experience* tended to be viewed as nothing more than a collection of children's nursery rhymes. ROBERT SOUTHEY, poet laureate from 1813 until 1843, thought Blake's verses simplistic and the work of a madman. In fact, most of Blake's contemporaries believed him to be insane, and this belief negatively affected the publications of many of his works throughout the early 1800s (his poem "The TYGER" was the only exception). It was not until the 1860s and the publication of Alexander Gilchrist's biography of Blake that the author's poems were studied with any seriousness by academics. Today, however, no study of the Romantic period would be considered complete without at least two or three examples of Blake's poetry.

**Further Reading**

Blake, William. "Holy Thursday (Experience)." In *British Literature 1780–1830*, edited by Anne K. Melloy and Richard E. Matlak, 300. Forth Worth, Tex.: Harcourt Brace, 1996.

Fairer, David. "Experience Reading Innocence: Contextualizing Blake's 'Holy Thursday.'" *Eighteenth-Century Studies* 35, no. 4 (Summer 2002): 535–562.

Ferber, Michael. *The Social Vision of William Blake*. Princeton, N.J.: Princeton University Press, 1985.

Gardner, Stanley. *Blake's Innocence and Experience Retraced*. New York: St. Martin's Press, 1986.

Gillham, D. G. *Blake's Contrary States: The Songs of Innocence and of Experience as Dramatic Poems*. Cambridge: Cambridge University Press, 1966.

Gleckner, Robert F. "Point of View and Context in Blake's Songs." In *Twentieth Century Views: Blake, A Collection of Critical Essays,* edited by Northrop Frye, 98–111. Upper Saddle River, N.J.: Prentice-Hall, 1966.

—Melissa Ann Greggs-West

## "Homes of England, The," Felicia Hemans (1827)

A celebration of domesticity and English nationhood, FELICIA HEMANS's often-anthologized poem "The Homes of England" was originally published in *Blackwood's Magazine* in 1827. The poem has contributed to Hemans's reputation as one of the quintessential female domestic poets, even when much of her other poetry complicates her culture's understanding of the domestic sphere and its relationship to history and politics. Indeed, a similar undercurrent might be found in "The Homes of England."

An initial reading of the poem presents a cohesive and idealized vision of England, one that is rooted in domesticity and love for the rural landscape. This vision unifies class divisions, announcing the home as the force that binds the nation together. Whether speaking of the aristocratic country estate or the poor country cottage, Hemans claims that the home, with its warm hearth and motherly affection (see stanza 2), unifies England. The poem omits much in its nationalistic representation, however, such as contemporary urban industrialization and class strife, both of which seem not to fit into the poem's vision. Nonetheless, the last stanza links freedom with the English home and celebrates its role in rearing "hearts of native proof . . . / To guard each hallow'd wall" (ll. 35–36). Hemans elevates the role of women and the domestic affections in the creation of English identity, using a romanticized vision of the home to evoke patriotic feeling and action.

Sensitive readers should ask why the home needs to be guarded. The epigraph from SIR WALTER SCOTT's MARMION (1808), which Hemans appended to the poem when it was published in volume form, also suggests that the English home is at risk: "Where's the coward that would not dare / To fight for such a land?" Hemans's original epigraph from JOANNA BAILLIE's play *Ethwald* (1802) does not provoke such anxiety. In many of Hemans's poems, including the popular "CASABIANCA" (1826), the failure or absence of the domestic influence results in tragic death. "The Homes of England" calls for greater protection and support of the home in English culture, implying a threat to domesticity.

Tension can also be seen in the poem's form. Like "Casabianca," "The Homes of England" might first appear to follow a rigid and formulaic form; however, subtle variation is at work in the rhyme and meter. The rhyme scheme of the first stanza (*aabacdcd*) initiates a pattern that later stanzas do not follow (*abcbdede*). The seven-syllable "homes of England" line beginning each stanza also reveals irregularity with the lines that follow it, alternating iambic tetrameter and iambic trimester (also subject to occasional variation). The first stanza, then, establishes a pattern that is broken, a stylistic feature that may help Hemans underscore the fragility of the domestic realm.

### Further Reading

Hemans, Felicia. *Felicia Hemans: Selected Poems, Letters, and Reception Materials.* Edited by Susan J. Wolfson. Princeton, N.J.: Princeton University Press, 2000.

———. *Felicia Hemans: Selected Poems, Prose, and Letters.* Edited by Gary Kelly. Peterborough, Ont., and Orchard Park, N.Y.: Broadview Press, 2002.

Lootens, Tricia. "Hemans and Home: Victorianism, Feminine 'Internal Enemies,' and the Domestication of National Identity." *PMLA* 109 (1994): 238–253.

Mellor, Anne D. *Romanticism & Gender.* New York: Routledge, 1993.

Sweet, Nanora, and Julie Melnyk, eds. *Felicia Hemans: Reimagining Poetry in the Nineteenth Century.* Houndsmills, Eng.: Palgrave, 2001.

—Albert Sears

## Hood, Thomas (1799–1845)

Born in London's Cheapside on May 23, 1799, in a flat above his parent's bookshop, Thomas Hood was surrounded by literature throughout his very early childhood until the death of his father forced him and his mother to move to Islington. It was here that Thomas studied under an influential schoolmaster who helped to spark an interest in learning. Soon after, he found work in a local counting house before ill health forced the young boy to move away from the city to live with relatives in Scotland. Hood's typically Romantic interest in the formative effects of childhood are evident in the poem "I REMEMBER, I REMEMBER" (1826). Invigorated by the fresh air and country living, he indulged in extensive reading, which soon led him to contribute humorous articles to local newspapers. Indeed, from 1815 to 1817 he found employment as a journalist in Dundee before moving back to London to begin work as an engraver.

After arriving in the capital, Hood did not work as an engraver for long. In 1821 the editor of the *London Magazine,* John Scott, was killed in a duel, which allowed Hood to be appointed as the new copy editor of this popular periodical. While working in his new editorial role, he found himself in close contact with some of the most prominent literary figures of the day, including THOMAS DE QUINCEY, CHARLES LAMB, and SAMUEL TAYLOR COLERIDGE. His own literary career was perhaps initially influenced by his contact with such people, and in 1825 he collaborated with his brother-in-law, John Hamilton Reynolds, on *Odes and Addresses to Great People* before going on to publish *Whims and Oddities* (1826–27) on his own.

Although from 1828 onward Hood regularly contributed to the *Athenaeum,* he was essentially defined as a humorist. Indeed, after publishing some of Alfred, Lord Tennyson's work in an annual called the *Gem,* he went on to take command of the *Comic Annual* (1830–42), whereby he portrayed many current events in caricature. Yet he also believed in the power of poetry to change minds and in the period that he worked as editor on the *Comic Annual,* he wrote possibly his most famous attacking poem, "The Song of the Shirt" (1843), which originally appeared anonymously in the Christmas edition of the magazine *Punch.* Hood used this poem to comment on the harsh reality of the life seamstresses and the immorality of exploiting the lower reaches of society for cheap labour. It was swiftly reprinted in the *Times* before being translated into various other languages for publica-

tion abroad. Moreover, it was adapted for the stage by the editor of *Punch* and even influenced the world of Victorian art, with pieces such as Anna Elizabeth Blunden's *The Seamstress* (1854) receiving widespread acclaim.

After a prolonged illness, which partly prompted him to write other socially conscious poems such as "The Bridge of Sighs" and "The Song of the Labourer" from his sickbed, Thomas Hood died on May 3, 1845.

See also "RUTH."

**Further Reading**

Ousby, Ian, ed. *The Cambridge Guide to Literature in English.* Cambridge: Cambridge University Press, 2003.

Wolfson, Susan, ed. *Selected Poems of Thomas Hood, Winthrop Mackworth Praed and Thomas Lovell Beddoes.* Pittsburgh: University of Pittsburgh Press, 2001.

—Jessica Webb

## Howitt, Mary (1799–1888)

A journalist, poet, and translator, Mary Howitt was born Mary Botham into a strict Quaker family in Coleford, Goucestershire, England, on March 12, 1799. Few books were permitted, and the young Mary made up her own stories and poems. In 1818 she married a fellow Quaker, William Howitt (1792–1879), and much of her writing career was linked with his. Despite being in a constant state of pregnancy, the young wife and mother found time to write poems and sketches which she managed to get published in a range of annuals (see ANNUALS AND GIFT BOOKS) and magazines. Her poetry collections *The Forest Minstrel* (1823) and *The Desolation of Eyam* (1827) did well and reflected her interest in natural history. The *Literary Gazette* suggested that the poems belonged to the "modern school," detailing not only the different shades in a single tulip but also "poring over bits of blades and tiny insects" (quoted in Woodring 12).

The Howitts were heavily influenced by WILLIAM WORDSWORTH. Like JOHN CLARE and WILLIAM COBBETT, they also felt nostalgic for rural England before the numerous Enclosure Acts running from 1750s through to the 1830s had led to the fencing and hedging of land and before

INDUSTRIALISM had started to make its mark on the landscape. Nottingham, where the Howitts lived in the 1820s, was a prime example of how a small weaving town could quickly become a major industrial centre. Mary Howitt's *Sketches of Natural History* (1834) was intended not only to record her impressions of the countryside but also to popularize the discipline of botany more generally and also to teach moral lessons. "The Sparrow's Nest" is a versification of the process of building a nest but also carries the moral that one can be happy even in the humblest of homes. The most famous poem in *Sketches,* "THE SPIDER AND THE FLY: AN APOLOGUE. A NEW VERSION OF AN OLD STORY," is cast as a tale of seduction and warns against vanity and falling into temptation.

As a couple, the Howitts were energetic literary producers. They were dependent on writing to make money and maintain their middle-class standard of living. In 1839 Mary published *Hymns and Fireside Verses* before taking over from LETITIA ELIZABETH LANDON as editor of the magazine *The Drawing Room Scrapbook,* for which she provided verses and ballads to illustrate engravings. By this time she had become slightly cynical about much of the writing she was doing, seeing it as hack work. "Many causes," she wrote, "have conspired to make literature what it is now, a swarming but insignificant breed; one being the wretched, degraded state of criticism; another is the annuals; and in fact, all periodical writing, which requires a certain amount of material, verse or prose, in a given time" (quoted in Woodring 34). One of the important functions of her work was to popularize less-educated readers, who found Wordsworth or PERCY BYSSHE SHELLEY heavy going, some of the central tenets of their ideas were: the return to nature, primitivism, and the poet's duty to encourage sympathy in his or her fellow beings. She did this by imitations—conscious and unconscious—and by tribute, admiring in particular the treatment of humble characters, as in Wordsworth's "The IDIOT BOY" and "The THORN"; her own poems reflect this admiration.

William Howitt, meanwhile, turned to criticism and journalism. His *Homes and Haunts of the Most Eminent British Poets* (1847) remains an important book, not least for its attempt to rehabilitate LORD BYRON's posthumous reputation. In his essay "The

Great Modern Poets Great Reformers," he touted SIR WALTER SCOTT, ROBERT SOUTHEY, THOMAS DE QUINCY, Wordsworth, and SAMUEL TAYLOR COLERIDGE as true radicals "and must forever be numbered amongst the greatest promoters of the freedom of opinion, and the spirit of liberty that so much distinguish this age" (quoted in Woodring 69).

By middle age Mary Howitt had become a respected literary figure. She was a prominent member of the London literary scene and the center of a number of varied networks. She knew Wordsworth, JOHN KEATS, JAMES HOGG, and MARY RUSSELL MITFORD. Observers described her as having an air of "amiability rather than of powerful intellect but which was much more attractive than her husband's rather more self-regarding personality" (quoted in Woodring 11). Like many other women writers of the age, Howitt organized her writing around the demands of home and family, working at a table in the dining room so that she could be easily found. Later works entailed several books for children, including *My Own Story, or the Autobiography of a Child* (1845), as well as the translation of works by the Swedish novelist Fredrika Bremer (1801–65), a project that lasted from 1842 to 1863. The preface to *Ballads and Other Poems* (1847), which contains the statement "The love of Christ, of the poor, and of little children always were and will be ruling sentiments of my soul," is a useful summary of Howitt's interests.

Mary Howitt died in Rome on January 30, 1888. Given her fame in her own day, her interests in women's rights and antislavery campaigns, and her role as a popularizer of Romantic ideas via her own verse, it is surprising that she is not better known.

## Further Reading

Dunicliff, Joy. *Mary Howitt.* London: Excalibur, 1992.

Howitt, Mary. *Ballads and other Poems.* London: Longman, 1847.

———. *Mary Howitt's Poems: Birds and Flowers.* London: T. Nelson, 1872.

———. *My Own Story, or the Autobiography of a Child.* London: Tegg, 1845.

Woodring, Carl. *Victorian Samplers: William and Mary Howitt.* Lawrence: University of Kansas Press, 1952.

—Andrew Maunder

## Hugo, Victor (1802–1885)

Born in Besançon, France, on February 26, 1802, Victor Hugo was variously a poet, novelist, and dramatist. His first collection, *Odes and Various Poems,* appeared in 1822, and for the next 60 years he was never without a writing project. His first historical romance—a genre for which he would become as famous as SIR WALTER SCOTT—was *Han of Iceland* (1823). *Cromwell,* his first verse play appeared in 1827, although it was deemed too long to stage. Hugo's plays were initially deemed shocking, particularly *HERNANI* (1830), a historical drama of doomed love and self-sacrifice containing the statement: "Romanticism, so often ill-defined, is only . . . liberalism in literature" (Hugo). "Liberty" is a key theme in his work and one taken up in his most famous novels, *Notre-Dame de Paris* (*The* HUNCHBACK OF NOTRE DAME, 1831) and *Les Misérables* (1862). Hugo produced novels, dramas, and poems that dealt with key political and philosophical questions of his time and were a product of the social turmoil of postrevolutionary France. He died in Paris on the May 22, 1885, by which time he was the grand old man of French literature and was given a state funeral.

### Further Reading

Frey, John Andrew. *A Victor Hugo Encyclopedia.* Westport, Conn.: Greenwood Press, 1999.

Halsall, Albert W. *Victor Hugo and the Romantic Drama.* Toronto: University of Toronto Press, 1998.

Hugo, Victor. *The Essential Victor Hugo.* Edited by E. H. Blackmore and A. M. Blackmore. Oxford: Oxford University Press, 2009.

Hugo, Victor. *Four Plays.* London: Methuen, 2004.

Robb, Graham. *Victor Hugo: A Biography.* New York: W. W. Norton & Co., 1999.

Porter, Laurence M. *Victor Hugo.* Boston: Twayne, 1999.

Ireson, J. C. *Victor Hugo: A Companion to His Poetry.* Oxford: Clarendon Press, 1997.

—Charles Richards

## humanism

First used in the 19th century to describe the Renaissance cultural movement, *humanism* is both a unique and complex term. The term is difficult to define, but it is rich in historical, literary, and political contexts. One way to understand humanism is as a worldview "that posits human values and concerns, rather than divine or supernatural values, as the central focus of life and thought" (Klages 11). German humanism, an important part of the political reforms that took place within the country around the time of the FRENCH REVOLUTION, saw special interest in ancient Greek culture. One of the main philosophical and political voices of this time was George Wilhelm Friedrich Hegel. Hegel was interested in the concept of the Hellenic ideal, where a "passion for freedom" would be the basis for future societal aspiration.

During the French Revolution, Germany, concerned about France's imperialist designs and supportive of Great Britain, came to influence British literature and philosophy. The Romantic period, seen as a response to both the Enlightenment and the French Revolution, would produce some of the most radical humanist thinkers of its time, including WILLIAM BLAKE, LORD BYRON, and PERCY BYSSHE SHELLEY. These Romantic sympathizers for the French revolutionary cause, with their distinctive imaginary talent and appreciation for the power of the human mind, best represent through their poetry and prose the type of humanism that was practiced during the Romantic period.

Blake uses biblical imagery and allegory in his poetry and artistic plates in ways that highlighted the extraordinary ability of the creative faculties of the human mind. For him, "salvation and damnation—and in fact all eternal creation—flow directly from humanity, not from an exterior agent" (Hoagwood 77). Blake referred to his final epic poem, *The Four Zoas,* as the "one grand story of mankind" (Blake 214).

The humanism of Byron and Shelley, second-generation Romantics, is more defiant and openly critical of Britain's politics and religion. The protagonist Cain in Byron's dramatic poem *CAIN: A MYSTERY,* for example, attempts to understand his fallen state by rebelling against a perceived tyrannical god figure. Cain continuously praises the natural world, admiring the beautiful "lights above . . . in the azure" (1.1.276) and adores his mortal wife-sister, Adah, so keenly that he would rather "bear all" than "see her weep" (1.1.327–330).

Cain's desire to appreciate and understand his world while also acknowledging the limitations of his human state is unique but very much a part of the tradition of the Byronic hero. Shelley's dramatic poem PROMETHEUS UNBOUND portrays Prometheus as an exemplary humanist who chooses to sacrifice his own autonomy in his attempt to improve the human condition. Intellectual pursuits that focused on human and social betterment were important to the Romantic period, and the visionary poets who recognized the potential value and goodness of humanity were the true advocates of humanism in the 18th and 19th centuries.

## Further Reading

Blake, William. *Blake's Poetry and Designs.* Edited by Mary Lynn Johnson and John Grant. New York: W. W. Norton & Co., 1979.

Byron, George Gordon, Byron, Baron. *Byron's Poetry.* Edited by Frank D. McConnel. New York: W. W. Norton & Co., 1978.

Davies, Tony. *Humanism.* 2nd ed. Abingdon and New York: Routledge, 2008.

Everest, Kelvin. *English Romantic Poetry.* Buckingham and Bristol, Eng.: Open University Press, 1990.

Hoagwood, Terrance Allan. *Prophecy and the Philosophy of Mind.* University: University of Alabama Press, 1985.

Kinney, Arthur F. "The Making of a Humanist Poet." *Literary Imagination* (2006): 29–43.

Klages, Mary. "Humanist Literary Theory." In *Literary Theory: A Guide for the Perplexed.* London and New York: Continuum International Publishing Group, 2006, 10–29.

Natarajan, Uttara. *The Romantic Poets.* Malden, Oxford, and Carlton: Blackwell Publishing, 2007.

Shelley, Percy. *Shelley's Poetry.* Edited by Donald H. Reiman and Neil Fraistat. New York: W. W. Norton & Co., 2002.

—Devon Pizzino

## Hume, David (1711–1776)

The empiricist philosopher and historian David Hume was born in Edinburgh on May 7, 1711. His treatise *On Human Nature* appeared in two volumes in 1739. In *An Enquiry Concerning Principles of Morals* (1751) and *An Enquiry Concerning Human Understanding* (1758), Hume argued that the origin of morality is within feelings. His perspective on moral virtue served as a reference point for the philosopher Jeremy Bentham's (1718–1832) utilitarian hedonistic view that identified virtue with pleasure and vice with pain. It also had an impact on the Scottish realist school and the work of the philosopher and economist Adam Smith (1723–90). The Scottish intellectual context expressed itself in "common sense" philosophy, marked skepticism, and a concern with history. Along with his philosophical work, Hume authored the expansive, multivolume *History of England* (1754–61).

As a young man, Hume encountered the influences of the British empiricists JOHN LOCKE (1632–1704) Francis Hutcheson (1694–1746), and Joseph Butler (1692–1752), who focused on empirical data and experience in contrast to the continental rationalists and their deductive method. Hume sought to apply Isaac Newton's experimental method to the human mind. His objective was to develop a science of human nature grounded in empirical data and experimental method. This would, he argued in *An Enquiry Concerning Human Understanding,* be "a complete system of the sciences, built on a foundation almost entirely new" (Hume 1978, xvi). It would sweep away rationalist claims.

Following John Locke's *An Essay Concerning Human Understanding* (1690), Hume asserted that there were no innate ideas and that people developed knowledge from experience: "All the perceptions of the human mind resolve themselves into indistinct kinds, which I shall call impressions and ideas" (Hume, 1978; 27). He called Locke's ideas of sense "impressions" and used the term *ideas* to designate those representations made by our imaginations or memories. Pushing empiricism and skepticism to their limits in Book 1 (parts 4 and 7) of the *Treatise on Human Nature* (1739), he argued against assumptions of cause and effect. There he distinguishes the "antecedent" and the "consequent." Antecedent reflects René Descartes's (1596–1650) method of doubt, which seeks a priori standards of judgment so one can decide what is trustworthy. Hume proceeds by consequent thinking, with empirical reasoning. Skepticism arises in Hume's argument about causal inference. He takes empiricism further than Locke with his concerns about matters of fact and relations of ideas. In this, he had an influence on Immanuel Kant's (1724–1804) synthesis of empiricism and rationalism, and also it has been suggested, in Walter Scott's historical novels.

Hume wrote effectively across several intellectual areas. His *History of England* shows an interest in the character of the Stuart kings and in human motivation. He mediated between Tory and Whig positions, remaining politically neutral. In his political writings he tended to maintain this neutrality, and in the area of political economy he rejected mercantilism and favored much the same system as would be advocated by Adam Smith. In chapters 10–11 of the *Enquiry Concerning Human Understanding,* he rejects evidence for miracles and asserts that they violate the laws of nature and the knowledge established through experience. He follows his critique of religious thought in *The Natural History of Religion.*

In his public life, Hume was judge advocate in an expedition to L'Orient, Brittany, in 1747 and to Vienna and Turin in 1748; he became advocate's librarian in Edinburgh in 1752. His history writing followed, beginning in 1754 with his volume on the Stuarts. He was secretary to the embassy in Paris from 1763 to 1765. From there he brought the work of JEAN-JACQUES ROUSSEAU to the attention of the British public. He became under secretary of state for the Northern Department in 1767–68. In 1768 he settled in Edinburgh, where he died on August 25, 1776. Hugely influential, Hume's philosophy also helped serve as a catalyst for the Romantic movement, and he confused and infuriated its adherents in equal measure.

**Further Reading**

Ayer, Alfred. *Hume: A Very Short Introduction.* Oxford: Oxford University Press, 2000.

Graham, Roderick. *The Great Infidel: A Life of David Hume.* London: Birlinn, 2006.

Hume, David. *An Enquiry Concerning Human Understanding.* Oxford: Clarendon Press, 1978.

———. *A Treatise on Human Nature: Being an Attempt to Introduce the Experimental Method of Reasoning into Moral Subjects.* London: Penguin, 2004.

—Robert McParland

## *Hunchback of Notre Dame, The* (*Notre-Dame de Paris*) **Victor Hugo** (1831)

VICTOR HUGO's historical novel *The Hunchback of Notre Dame* portrays the Gothic architecture of the cathedral as central to the lives of the characters. While English translations of the title emphasize the role of the bell ringer Quasimodo, Hugo's original French title, *Notre-Dame de Paris,* prioritizes the cathedral, and frequent interruptions to the narrative expound on the importance of architecture as an insight into the Middle Ages. The cathedral becomes symbolic of the religious, political, and social events during the time of its construction, and in its vastness it is compared to the 19th-century novel as a medium for artistic expression. The book's nostalgic perspective encouraged a revival of interest in the medieval period and initiated the cathedral's historical preservation and renovation.

Set in 1482, the narrative shifts between various characters whose story lines intersect with the attempted kidnapping of the young gypsy dancer Esmeralda by the archdeacon of Notre Dame, Claude Frollo, and his adopted son, Quasimodo. The kidnapping is told from the perspective of the poet Pierre Gringoire, whose death sentence, imposed by the king of the Truands, is reprieved by Esmeralda's pity. Despite marrying Gringoire to save him, Esmeralda is in love with Captain Phoebus, who foiled the abduction. Frollo's endeavours to gain access to Esmeralda are motivated by the conflict between his search for knowledge and his need for affection, and he emerges as a figure inspiring sympathy and contempt. Frollo frames Esmeralda for the attempted murder of Phoebus, foresees an attack on Notre Dame to force her from sanctuary and recruits the assistance of Gringoire, who misguidedly delivers Esmeralda into Frollo's hands. The source of Esmeralda's condemnation and her only opportunity for salvation from death is Frollo, whose propositions Esmeralda rejects.

Other characters have a genuine desire to protect and assist Esmeralda, but their actions contribute to her doom. Quasimodo's affection for Esmeralda, motivated by her kindness when he was in the pillory and in need of water, prompts his violent efforts to protect her from the Truands, the very people who could have rescued her. Hugo presents the passions and emotions of characters as unavoidable and ultimately the source of tragedy. Esmeralda's own desire for the dishonorable Phoebus results in her final capture, when, hidden by her newly discovered mother, she cannot help but call out to Phoebus when she hears his voice. Justice is delivered when Frollo is pushed from the towers of Notre Dame by Quasimodo, whose conflict between his love for Frollo and Esmeralda is resolved as Frollo laughs while watching Esmeralda's execution. Quasimodo's final gesture, dying with Esmeralda, becomes a poignant reminder of the tragedy and the transience of the past as the attempt to separate the two bodies causes his remains to crumble to dust.

The intricacy of Hugo's characterization releases his characters from GOTHIC stereotyping. Hugo presents individuals forsaken by society, with the majority of the main characters orphans or alone. For a novel set in and around a cathedral, there is no solace in religion, and Frollo's neglect of religion emphasizes the pursuits of the individual but warns of the consequences of unrestrained action. Esmeralda's natural and unfailing kindness contrasts against the shifting behaviors, intentions, and deeds of the other characters. In *The Hunchback of Notre Dame*, justice is tragic as individuals with extreme passions conflict with an inevitably corrupt society.

**Further Reading**

Hugo, Victor. *Notre-Dame of Paris.* Translated by John Sturrock. London: Penguin, 2004.
Robb, Graham. *Victor Hugo.* London: Picador, 1997.

—Tony W. Garland

## Hunt, Leigh (James Henry Leigh Hunt) (1784–1859)

Born in London on October 19, 1784, the son of lawyer-turned-clergyman Isaac Hunt and his wife Mary, James Henry Leigh Hunt was educated at Christ Hospital in London before working as a clerk in the war office and ultimately embarking on a writing career, primarily as a journalist. William Michael Rossetti, brother of Christina and Dante Gabriel Rossetti, wrote of his friend and contemporary: "Leigh Hunt is known to us all as a fresh and airy essayist, a fresh and airy poet, a liberal thinker in the morals both of society and of politics (hardly a politician in the stricter sense of the term), a charming, companion, a too-constant cracker of genial jacosities and of puns" (Rossetti, 1887, 21). A liberal and idealist, Hunt's political views led to several prosecutions and a two-year prison sentence for an unfavorable 1813 article on the Prince Regent (later George IV). His essays on politics and social reform, which first appeared in *The Examiner,* a weekly paper published by Hunt and his brother John, earned him a reputation as one of the most popular writers of his own time (see NEWSPAPERS AND MAGAZINES).

Hunt's importance to the Romantic movement lies chiefly in his friendship with and introduction to the larger literary world of JOHN KEATS and PERCY BYSSHE SHELLEY. Modern scholars are chiefly interested in his influence on and association with these writers, who have collectively come to be termed the "second-generation Romantics." His influence on younger writers in his later years was also notable; it is widely believed that Charles Dickens, a longtime acquaintance, based the character of the impecunious Harold Skimpole in *Bleak House* (1852–53) on Leigh Hunt. Hunt died on August 26, 1859.

See also: "TO ROBERT BATTY, M.D., ON HIS GIVING ME A LOCK OF MILTON'S HAIR."

**Further Reading**

Cox, Jeffrey. *Poetry and Politics in the Cockney School.* Cambridge: Cambridge University Press, 1998.
Hunt, Leigh. *The Autobiography of Leigh Hunt.* Whitefish, Mont.: Kessinger Publishing, 2007.
———. *Selected Writings: Leigh Hunt.* Edited by David Jesson-Dibley. New York: Routledge, 2003.
Roe, Nicholas. *Leigh Hunt: Life, Poetics and Politics.* London: Routledge, 2003.
Rossetti, William Michael. *The Life of John Keats.* London: Walter Scott, 1887.

—Melissa A. Elmes

## "Hyperion: A Fragment" John Keats (1820)

JOHN KEATS began to compose "Hyperion" in the last months of 1818 and abandoned it in April

1819; it was eventually published as a fragment in 1820. This epic poem, written in Miltonic verse, was to have staged a story of classical Greek mythology: the overthrow of the Titans by the Olympian gods, and Hyperion giving way to Apollo. However, Keats discontinued the poem at the beginning of Book 3, after introducing Apollo, and the original design was never completed. Despite its incomplete state, "Hyperion" ranks among Keats's masterpieces, if only because of the beauty of its opening lines, which establish an atmosphere of heavy sadness and loss: "Deep in the shady sadness of a vale / Far sunken from the healthy breath of morn, / Far from the fiery noon, and eve's one star, / Sat grey-haired Saturn, quiet as a stone, / Still as the silence round about his lair" (1:1–5).

Interpretations of the poem range from the biographical—Keats was nursing his brother Tom who died of tuberculosis as he was writing the poem—to the political, the poem being considered as Keats's comment on his own turbulent times and on the advent of Romanticism. Most critics, however, agree in seeing the poem as Keats's way of putting into verse his lifelong questioning about the meaning of beauty when confronted with loss and death. In a letter to J. H. Reynolds written in May 1818, Keats had favorably compared WILLIAM WORDSWORTH with JOHN MILTON, adding: "[This] proves there is really a grand march of intellect" (quoted in Strachan, 17). "Hyperion" may be seen as a poetical expression of this statement.

Book 1 is initially focused on Saturn's despair and on the attempts made by Thea, Hyperion's wife, to comfort him. When the fallen Titan at last utters a few words, he grieves the loss of his creativity, which has deprived him of his identity: "I am gone / Away from my own bosom: I have left / My strong identity, my real self, / Somewhere between the throne, and where I sit." (1:112–115) The poem then turns to Hyperion's anger at knowing that he, too, will fall, as Saturn has just fallen, and to his determination to resist his fate.

In Book 2 we discover several of the fallen Titans, who are joined by Saturn in a forlorn den and are trying to make sense of their fall. Here Keats uses his characters as a playwright would, making them utter contradictory points of view.

If Book 1 has often been appreciated for its poetical beauty, Book 2 is usually quoted for the Titans' theses, which echo thoughts expressed in Keats's letters. Thus, both Oceanus and Clymene clearly act as the poet's mouthpiece, because they both stress how beautiful the new gods are, insisting on the necessity of progress, as Oceanus does: "So on our heels a fresh perfection treads, / A power more strong in beauty, born of us / And fated to excel us, as we pass / In glory that old Darkness" (2:212–215) Death is justified because the new generation will be more beautiful, and this view is supported by Clymene, who describes the effect Apollo's music has had on her, thus underlining how beneficial the new god will be for humanity. These views arouse Enceladus's violent response, and he exhorts the Titans to rebel against their fate since Hyperion is still unvanquished. Book 2 ends with the arrival of Hyperion and with his sadness as he sees the state of his fallen friends.

Thus, while insisting on the necessity of evolution and progress, "Hyperion"'s first two books focus at length on the painful emotions triggered by the fear of death. Book 3 endeavors to change both focus and mood by introducing Apollo, who is just being transformed into a god by Mnemosyne. But the poem stops there, as though the poet had felt unable to depict the Olympian gods after his description of the mourning Titans.

The poem betrays Keats's ambivalence: His use of dramatic techniques enables him to express his own doubts as well as his faith in progress and development. More significantly, perhaps, Book 1 is clearly steeped in emotion, be it despair or anger, which Book 2 will try to channel more rationally through the Titans' speeches. As these feelings are central to Keats's poetry, they will be taken up again in the great odes of April and May 1819.

By focusing on the fallen Titans from the start, and by sympathizing with their emotions, the poet makes the sense of loss become so strong that it overcomes the more rational arguments about the necessity of progress. Setting out to write a poem depicting "the grand march of intellect" (letter to Reynolds, May 3, 1818), Keats becomes caught in emotion, and fails to complete the poem. In fact, the poem illustrates the tension between "consequitive [sic] reasoning" (letter to Benjamin Bailey,

November 22, 1817) and emotion, between Keats's intellectual beliefs and his deepest feelings, probably all the stronger since he was nursing his dying brother as he wrote the poem.

"Hyperion" purports to integrate the awareness of human suffering within a broader vision of humanity, whereas it actually portrays the intensity of human suffering when confronted with death. That is why even the arguments uttered by Oceanus and Clymene, designed to justify progress and to place their own fall within a grander scheme, fail to convince the reader. They are too strongly counterbalanced by the acuteness of pain, masterfully depicted from the opening lines by the poetic rhythm and sounds. Indeed, most of the beauty of "Hyperion" comes from the portrait of suffering it offers, which is hard to reconcile with the optimistic belief in progress it had set out to explore.

The clash between the original argument and the emotions expressed in the first two books of the poem accounts for Keats's inability to complete it, because he found it impossible to bring himself to rejoice in the Olympians' reign. The poem was, however, meaningful enough for Keats to try again a few months later with "THE FALL OF HYPERION."

## Further Reading

Bate, Walter Jackson. *John Keats.* London: Chatto & Windus, 1979.

Crinquand, Sylvie. *Lettres et poèmes de John Keats: portrait de l'artiste.* Dijon, Toulouse, France: EUD, PUM, 2000.

Keats, John. *Complete Poems.* Edited by Jack Stillinger. Cambridge, Mass.: Belknap Press of Harvard University Press, 1982.

———. *The Letters of John Keats, 1814–1821.* 2 vols. Edited by Hyder Edward Rollins. Cambridge, Mass.: Harvard University Press, 1976.

Motion, Andrew. *Keats.* London: Faber & Faber, 1997.

Roe, Nicholas. *Keats and the Culture of Dissent.* Cambridge: Cambridge University Press, 1997.

Sperry, Stuart M. *Keats the Poet.* Princeton, N.J.: Princeton University Press, 1973.

Strachan, John. *The Poems of John Keats. A Sourcebook.* London: Routledge, 2003.

—Sylvie Crinquand

# I

## "I Am" ("Lines: I Am") John Clare (1846)

"I Am" (or "Lines: I Am," not to be confused with "Sonnet: I Am") is JOHN CLARE's best-known lyric poem. Like many poems written which he was a patient at Northampton General Lunatic Asylum (1841–64), its exact date of composition is unknown. Clare's friend Thomas Inskip praised its "exquisite . . . beaut[y]" in a December 1846 letter, and it was first published in the *Bedford Times* on January 1, 1848. Composed of three six-line stanzas in regular iambic pentameter with an *ababab* (first stanza) and *ababcc* (second and third stanzas) rhyme scheme, "I Am" was transcribed by Clare's asylum steward, W. F. Knight, and contains numerous penciled deletions and additions. Printings after 1848 (1863, 1864, 1865, 1866) exhibit variant punctuation, stanza numbering, and word choices. No original manuscript in Clare's hand is known to exist.

"I Am" is Clare's elegant but resolute assertion of self-identity in the face of utter alienation, striking in its quiet anticipation of death and tonal equanimity. Early criticism identified Clare's profound loneliness during his asylum years as the source of his lament ("My friends forsake me like a memory lost" [l.2]) and emotional estrangement ("Even the dearest, that I love the best / Are strange—nay, rather stranger than the rest" [ll.11–12). But Clare's lifelong bouts of psychosis invited increasingly medicalized interpretations of the poem's metaphysical concerns with selfhood, enclosure, and isolation ("And yet I am, and live— like vapours tost / Into the nothingness of scorn and noise" [ll.6–7]), facilitating a range of clinical and critical diagnoses that included hereditary insanity, "addiction to poetical prosing" (as one doctor called it), and, posthumously, schizophrenia. For much of the 20th century this critical approach imposed the objectives of the medical case study onto Clare's proto-confessional poetry, reading the lucid lines of "I Am" as the cardinal symptom and diagnostic sign of Clare's central place in the Romantic literature of "madness."

More recent scholarship has recognized the limitations of such medico-biographical analysis—for example, the paucity of clinical documentation during Clare's institutionalization and lack of concordance between 19th-century and contemporary definitions of mental illness and therapy. Rather than a symptom of Clare's supposed schizophrenia, a literary reading of "I Am" evinces the speaker's acute consciousness of self-identification as an ongoing creative task. The opening iambic foot ("I am—") of the authoritative Knight transcript immediately establishes the speaker's recognition of being, but the en dash that follows emphasizes this statement's lack of completion in a striking aposiopesis (breaking off). Exactly *what* (not who) the speaker is, is left open, a blank to be filled by any one of Clare's "readers"—the public, his doctors, his family, and indeed perhaps even Clare himself. Clare once stated, "I was Byron and Shakespeare formerly. At different times you know I'm different persons—that is the same person with different names" (quoted in Claire, 1949; 43). Self-identification in "I Am" begins by acknowledging

192

the impossibility of asserting oneself as a static subject ("yet what I am, none cares or knows" [l.1]).

"I Am" exemplifies the quintessentially Romantic intersection of creativity, illness, and self-fashioning: a triad of phenomena essential to what the scholar Jennifer Ford calls the "medical imagination" epitomized by Romantic poets such as SAMUEL TAYLOR COLERIDGE. In Clare's case, whether the basis of his imagination was psychopathological is of little consequence. In its refusal to define in static terms exactly what—and who—"is" the speaker of "I Am," Clare's poem is less an assertion of identity than a reflexive critique of 19th-century intellectual discourses that sought to pathologize the literary imagination.

## Further Reading

Ball, Joanna. "The Tear Drops on the Book I Read": John Clare's Reading in the Northampton General Lunatic Asylum, 1841–1864." *Wordsworth Circle* 34 (2003).

Bate, John. *John Clare: A Biography.* London: Picador, 2003.

Clare, John. *Poems of John Clare's Madness.* Edited by Geoffrey Grigson. London: Routledge and Kegan Paul Ltd., 1949.

Ford, Jennifer. *Coleridge on Dreaming: Romanticism, Dreams and the Medical Imagination.* Cambridge: Cambridge University Press, 1998.

Porter, Roy. "'All madness for writing': John Clare and the Asylum." In *John Clare in Context*, edited by Hugh Haugton, Adam Phillips, and Geoffrey Summerfield, 259–278. Cambridge: Cambridge University Press, 1994.

—Andrea Charise

## "Idiot Boy, The"  William Wordsworth  (1798)

Composed in 1798 while WILLIAM WORDSWORTH was staying at Alfoxden, Somerset, "The Idiot Boy" was included in *Lyrical Ballads*. Like other poems in that collection, it is intended to represent the essential passions of the human heart and to show how a human being on the margins of society can still be of value.

The idiot boy is the much-loved son of Betty Foy, who lives in an isolated rural situation. When she finds herself alone one night, with responsibility for a seriously ill neighbor, she sets her son on a pony with instructions to ride to the nearest town to fetch a doctor. When the boy fails to return, Betty sets off on foot to look for him, anxiety for her missing son having superseded concern for her neighbour. On arriving at the doctor's house, she discovers that Johnny has not been seen at his appointed destination. In her distress she forgets to report her neighbor's illness to the doctor and embarks on a wider search for her son, whom she eventually finds, near to a waterfall in the moonlight, still with the pony, who is peacefully grazing. During Betty's absence from home, her sick neighbor recovers from her indisposition and, anxious about Betty and Johnny, goes out to meet them. As all three are walking home, Betty asks her son where he has been and what he has seen. His reply, indicative of his mental retardation, is that "The cocks did crow to-whoo, to-whoo / And the sun did shine so cold!" (ll.460–461). Throughout the poem, which comprises 463 lines, the poet himself interpolates, both as narrator and as inquisitor. He describes the landscape through which Johnny and his mother travel, delineating the boy's relationship with nature. He questions Betty's motives and her wisdom in sending her son on such an errand, but he does not pass judgment.

Wordsworth claimed to have composed this poem almost extempore without any ensuing correction, but the end result suggests careful crafting. The versification is well-wrought: Four stress lines have a rhyming pattern of *abccb*, most stanzas comprising five lines. The first stanza has one additional line and the final verse, containing seven lines, concludes with a rhyming couplet. These formal properties, together with the imagery, especially pertaining to the boy and pony in the moonlight, give this poem the haunting qualities of the traditional ballad, and it remained one of Wordsworth's favorite compositions. "The Idiot Boy" undeniably fulfils his intentions as set out in the PREFACE TO *LYRICAL BALLADS*, but these aims were in themselves a problem to many of his contemporaries, some of whom argued that the poem's "low" subject matter did not justify the poetic skill that went into the composition. Today the poem is regarded as a prime example of Wordsworth's work in the 1790s, partly for the subject matter, but also for the way in which the emotional journey of the main protagonists lends importance to the narrative.

**Further Reading**

Gill, Stephen. *Wordsworth and the Victorians.* 1998. Reprint, Oxford: Clarendon Press 2001.

Wordsworth, William and Samuel Taylor Coleridge. *Lyrical Ballads.* Edited by R. L. Brett and A. R. Jones. 1968. Reprint, London and New York: Methuen, 1984.

Woof, Robert, ed. *Wordsworth: The Critical Heritage.* Vol. 1, 1793–1820. London: Routledge, 2001.

—Irene Wiltshire

**"Image in Lava, The"** Felicia Hemans (1827)

First published in *New Monthly Magazine* in September 1827 and reprinted in *Records of Woman* (1828), FELICIA HEMANS's "The Image in Lava" mirrors both 19th-century ideals of womanhood and the Romantics' scorn of materialism. The poem describes the excavations at the site of Herculaneum, where an imprint of a mother embracing her baby was found. Hemans celebrates this image made by the eruption of Mount Vesuvius to simultaneously depict the vulnerability of the domestic to worldly threats and the power of the domestic woman to defy dangers and gain immortality.

Hemans establishes a rhetorical relationship between the visual object and abstract emotions. She starts the poem by directly addressing the remains and wondering at the power that has preserved them. She celebrates the maternal imprint's ability to resist time and destruction, outlasting icons of masculine power as demonstrated in "the proud memorials rear'd / By conquerors of mankind" (ll.11–12) whose "temple and tower" have mouldered (l. 5). The inanimate imprint comes to life with Hemans's address in the third stanza to both the "Fair babe" (l. 18) and its mother, who have gained eternity. The poet finally transforms the imprint into an abstract entity, which she addresses as "human love" (l. 36). Hemans's juxtaposition of the material with the immaterial asserts the physical trace of an ideal, motherhood, in the

ancient imprint. She thus transforms the death of the mother with her child into a paradoxically positive icon of domesticity, contradicting the prevalent notion of women's victimization by creating "female characters [who] attain a moral victory over patriarchal domination" (Lundeen 6).

Although Hemans emphasizes the persistence of domestic emotions throughout the poem, she reveals an uncertainty with her doubtful repetition in the final line, where she insists that human love must be permanent. The scholar Anthony Harding interprets such ambivalence by asserting that Hemans uses the image in lava to resolve the paradox of women as vital to the well-being of domesticity but subservient to men. The maternal imprint thus favors "'female' traits of love and parental affection over the impartial male order, symbolized by the 'temple,' 'tower,' and 'cities' now moldering in dust" (Harding 148). Isobel Armstrong further interprets the poem as a 19th-century warning against the social violence of the postrevolutionary era and as a warning against the commodity culture that was "blind to its own hedonism and brutally impervious to social suffering" (Armstrong 220).

The poem simultaneously emphasizes the relic's spiritual and physical permanence: Its spiritual permanence results from the immortality of emotions of motherhood that resisted destruction, while its physical permanence results from the literal inability to transport the imprint from its place. Hemans thus not only physically preserves the story of an ancient natural disaster and women's domestic experiences in the first century A.D., but also preserves her own comparable 19th-century experiences as a woman and a mother. The poem further emphasizes the prevalent male/female dichotomy by treating the mother/baby relic as a "natural, 'feminine' monument" (Armstrong 214) and by arguing that maternal affections are more permanent than masculine endeavors.

**Further Reading**

Armstrong, Isobel. "Natural and National Monuments— Felicia Hemans's 'The Image in Lava': A Note." In *Felicia Hemans: Reimagining Poetry in the Nineteenth Century,* edited by Nanora Sweet and Julie Melnyk, 212–230. Basingstoke, Eng.: Palgrave, 2001.

Harding, Anthony John. "Felicia Hemans and the Effacement of Woman." In *Romantic Women Writers: Voices and Countervoices.* edited by Paula R. Feldman and Theresa M. Kelley, 138–149. Hanover, N.H.: University Press of New England, 1995.

Hemans, Felicia Dorothea Browne. *Felicia Hemans: Selected Poems, Letters, Reception Materials.* Edited by Susan J. Wolfson. Princeton: Princeton University Press, 2000.

Lundeen, Kathleen. "'When Life Becomes Art'—on Hemans's 'Image in Lava.'" *Romanticism on the Net* 29–30 (2003). Available online. URL: http://www.erudit.org/revue/ron/2003/v/n29/007716ar.html. Accessed on December 12, 2006.

Scott, Grant F. "The Fragile Image: Felicia Hemans and Romantic Ekphrasis." In *Felicia Hemans: Reimagining Poetry in the Nineteenth Century,* edited by Nanora Sweet and Julie Melnyk, 36–54. Basingstoke, Eng.: Palgrave, 2001.

—Mariam Radhwi

## *Improvisatrice, The* Letitia Elizabeth Landon (1824)

Much celebrated at the time of its first publication, ELIZABETH LETITIA LANDON's *The Improvisatrice* engages a number of cultural and artistic issues and is set throughout a range of continents and historical periods. This long narrative poem is titled after its narrator, an Italian artist who is a musician, painter, and extemporaneous writer of poetry (the title is a feminized version of the more traditional "improvisateur," a spontaneous composer of music and lyric poetry). The poem relays this narrator's failed romance, the unfolding of which is interrupted by her sharing poems that also tell stories of failed romance.

At the poem's opening, the narrator states that she is a Florentine artist—a musician, painter, and poet. Her story is one of doomed love. She falls in love with Lorenzo, only to find out he is betrothed. Lorenzo's wife ultimately dies, releasing him from his obligation, but not before the narrator has also died from heartbreak. The poems within this larger poem include stories of Sappho throwing herself off a cliff in the misery of unrequited love, a "Moorish" bride who dies at sea with her lover, and a young

Indian bride who throws herself on her husband's funeral pyre. This series of melancholic narratives, all of which focus on tragic women, further emphasize the hopelessness of the narrator's own situation. The poem continues beyond the narrator's death, with an anonymous voice finishing the verse by describing Lorenzo watching over the improvisatrice's ashes and art objects.

*The Improvisatrice* sustains various themes and engages a number of cultural and artistic questions. The narrator's position as a visual, musical, and literary artist raises the issue of female artistic authority and the availability of expressive modes for female artists. Landon herself was a successful poet during a period when such success was markedly less common for women than men, and she seems to imagine with the Improvisatrice a space of even more varied artistic opportunity for women. The poem represents—and seems invested in emphasizing the similarities between—a numbers of different cultures. A woman of mixed Italian and Indian descent, an Indian bride, Sappho, and the Italian narrator herself all suffer the disappointment of failed romance, perhaps suggesting that the shared identity category of gender is more determinative than the disparate national identities. The fact of the tragic endings to all the improvisatrice's stories, as well as to her own, raises questions about the possibilities for female self-determination. None of the women in the poem are able to move beyond their impossible dreams, and the poem ends with the narrator's own voice having been removed and replaced by an observer who focuses on Lorenzo.

In terms of literary periods, *The Improvisatrice* is near the end of what is traditionally considered the Romantic period and, unsurprisingly, contains elements of both the Romantic and nascent Victorian poetic traditions. Landon was known for her richly descriptive poetry, of which "The Improvisatrice" is representative. The melancholic poem contains elaborate descriptions of natural settings, art objects, and psychological states, and in so doing it evokes the poetic styling of WILLIAM WORDSWORTH, PERCY BYSSHE SHELLEY, and JOHN KEATS. Landon's poem is concerned with the conditions of artistic production and the role of the artist in society, both of which are concerns of the major Romantic poets. Landon also evokes the tradition of GOTHIC fiction by setting her poem and narrator in Italy, a technique used by novelists such as ANN RADCLIFFE. At the same time, the poem's narrative structure and use of distant historical and cultural settings anticipates the techniques of such Victorian poets as Alfred, Lord Tennyson and Robert Browning, as does the use of various personas.

### Further Reading

Landon, Leticia Elizabeth. *Leticia Elizabeth Landon: Selected Writings.* Edited by Jerome McGann and Daniel Ress. Peterborough, Ont.: Broadview Press, 2002.

Montwieler, Katherine. "Laughing at Love: L.E.L. and the Embellishment of Eros." *Romanticism on the Net: An Online Journal Devoted to Romantic Studies* no. 29–30. (February–May 2003). Available online. URL: http://id.erudit.org/iderudit/007717ar. Accessed on June 30, 2008.

"Landon, Letitia Elizabeth." In *The Cambridge Guide to Women's Writing in English,* edited by Lorna Sage, 376. Cambridge: Cambridge University Press, 1999.

—Rachel Bowser

## Inchbald, Elizabeth (1753–1821)

An actress, playwright, critic, and novelist, Elizabeth Inchbald, née Simpson was born on October 15, 1753, in the small market town of Bury St. Edmunds, Suffolk, where her father was a farmer. He died in 1761, and his daughter was supported by a large extended family until 1770, when she sought work as an actress. Initially unsuccessful, she ran away to London the following year and married Joseph Inchbald, a widower who was also an actor. For the next five years she managed to get work with him in a variety of theatrical companies touring England and Scotland. Despite physical disadvantages that included short sight, a stutter, and delicate health, Elizabeth Inchbald proved herself a wide-ranging and capable actress, even playing Hamlet on one occasion.

Although she had always written, it was not until her husband died in 1779 that Inchbald began to make a living from her pen, going on to become, as her biographer Annibel Jenkins notes, "virtually

the playwright in residence at Covent Garden in the winter and at the Haymarket in the summer" (Jenkins 11). Her first play, *A Mogul Tale,* which satirized the craze for hot-air balloons, was performed in 1784, and thereafter she wrote at least 20 more. These include *The Midnight Hour* (1787); *Such Things Are* (1787); ANIMAL MAGNETISM, A FARCE (1788); and the risqué comedy-melodrama *Lovers' Vows* (1798), a toned-down and politically neutered adaptation of August von Kotzebue's play *Der kinde der Liebe.* In its own day Inchbald's play was very successful, running for 42 performances, but it is now most familiar via its appearance in JANE AUSTEN's MANSFIELD PARK, where it serves as a shorthand for unrestrained conduct and emotional excess.

Although it was unusual in the 18th century for women to write plays and get them performed publicly, Inchbald was not the novelty act that many predicted. She was hardly ever without a writing project and was so successful that she was christened "the Tenth Muse." She was one of a select band of what the literary scholar Elle Donkin terms "designated survivors" within a "tightly controlled" system run and organized by men, which "worked with remarkable efficiently to keep women voiceless, property less, and acquiescent" (Donkin 2–3). Although she is often put together with other women dramatists of the period, including Hannah Cowley (1743–1809) and JOANNA BAILLIE (1762–1851), Inchbald's plays are more difficult to categorize in terms of their genre. They tend to mix elements of tragedy, comedy, and farce in a way that confused contemporary critics who liked to classify the plays they saw according to recognizable generic rules. What links many of them is a serious attempt to engage with ongoing social issues, including *The Child of Nature* (1788) and EVERY ONE HAS HIS FAULT (1793)—the latter attacked for its apparent democratic and seemingly antiwar sentiments, opening just a week after the execution of the French king Louis XVI. Often Inchbald's works attack the pretentions and hypocrisies of fashionable society, as in *Such Things Are* (1787). Another play, *The Massacre* (1792), attacks the killing of royalist prisoners. Although the play is set in the 17th century, the parallels with revolutionary France were not hard to draw. This may be why it was not performed in Inchbald's lifetime—it was too inflammatory.

Inchbald's success had a great deal to do with her professionalism and her commitment to writing as a career. She also valued her independence and refused several marriage proposals, including one from WILLIAM GODWIN. In 1789 she retired from the stage completely to devote herself to literary work. In 1791 she published her most famous novel, A SIMPLE STORY, which was followed by Nature and Art in 1796. The success of these books (the former has never been out of print) was due to an acute sense of the literary field of the 1790s and readers' tastes for stories of sentiment, sensibility, and moral improvement, plus a smattering of infidelity. In A Simple Story the central character, Miss Milner, is kept in line by her guardian, Dorriforth, a young Catholic priest with whom she falls in love. It has been suggested that the novel is partially autobiographical (with Miss Milner a version of Inchbald, and Dorriforth a version of the famously upright actor JOHN PHILIP KEMBLE, with whom Inchbald had a close relationship). Stylistically, the theater's influence is very apparent: The action and characters are carefully visualized, the dialogue is emphatic and occasionally stagey, and it is populated by recognizable theatrical "types."

Like A Simple Story, Nature and Art is also interested in the clash between "feeling" and the controlled, rational side of man's nature, as well as in the power of educating for good or ill. In this case it takes as its central idea the different upbringings of two men: Henry, "a child of nature" who has grown up on an African island, and William, his cousin who has been educated in corrupt, artificial world of modern Britain. The idea of the so-called noble savage, unspoiled and morally pure, was one that intrigued radical educators of the time, including JEAN-JACQUES ROUSSEAU. Like Godwin's CALEB WILLIAMS, the novel also attacks the cruelty of the system and those who administer it, as well as the assumption that men of high rank are automatically nobler than those of low rank.

Although Inchbald's novels were successful (she received £200 for A Simple Story), her main interest was always the theater. After her play To Marry or Not to Marry (1793), she turned toward theater criticism, writing introductions to 125 plays collected as part of the series The British Theatre; or A Collection of Plays Which are Acted at the Theatres Royal, Drury Lane, Covent Garden, and Haymarket. With Biographical and Critical Remarks, by Mrs. Inchbald. By this time Inchbald no longer needed to work and lived quietly in the London village of Kensington, gaining a reputation as a recluse. She was nonetheless part of a wide social and intellectual circle that included SARAH SIDDONS, THOMAS HOLCROFT, ALDERSON AMELIA OPIE, and MARIA EDGEWORTH, and she also counted LORD BYRON and WILLIAM HAZLITT among her admirers.

Inchbald died in Kensington, London, on August 1, 1821. Her plays fell out of favour after her death, but recent reevaluations have begun to place her work back in the mainstream tradition of 18th-century and Romantic theater.

### Further Reading

Cox, Jeffrey, ed. The Broadview Anthology of Romantic Drama. Peterborough, Ont.: Broadview Press, 2003.

Donkin, Ellen. Getting into the Act: Women Playwrights in London, 1776–1829. London: Routledge, 1995.

Inchbald, Elizabeth. Nature and Art. Edited by Shawn L. Maurer. London: Pickering and Chatto. 1997.

———. A Simple Story. London: Pandora, 1987.

Jenkins, Annibel. I'll Tell You What: The Life of Elizabeth Inchbald. Lexington: University Press of Kentucky, 2003.

Littlewood, R. S. Elizabeth Inchbald and Her Circle. London: Daniel O'Connor, 1921.

—Andrew Maunder

## "Indian Woman's Death Song, The" Felicia Hemans (1828)

First published in FELICIA HEMANS's famous collection RECORDS OF WOMAN, WITH OTHER POEMS, this poem opens with 15 lines of blank verse in which the narrator describes a canoe speeding "leaf-like" (l. 5) down a river. Within that boat is an Indian woman with her baby sleeping in her arms. The woman's "dark hair wav'd / As if triumphantly" (ll.10–11), even though the woman is singing her "song of death."

In the next section, Hemans shifts the perspective to the Indian woman's and the form to four-line stanzas of iambic heptameter (also called fourteeners). The woman commands the powerful river to "Roll swiftly to the Spirit's land" (l. 16) and to carry her and her child to a peaceful heaven. She explains that her husband has taken another wife, that she is no longer first in his heart, and that she is not willing to be second best. She wishes for a "blessed fount" (l. 32) that will help her wash away her sadness when she arrives in the spirit land. However, the woman is not simply taking her own life in this poem, but that of her daughter, who she says was born "for woman's weary lot" (l. 36). She will spare her daughter the sad fate that is due all women—"to pine in aching love away" (l. 38)—and will carry her to heaven where she will never experience sadness.

One of the most striking features of this poem is the way Hemans portrays the woman's suicide almost heroically. As the scholar Paula Feldman suggests, death becomes the Indian woman's "salvation" (in Hemans xxi). From the beginning the narrator displays the woman's impending death as triumphant. When the woman herself speaks, she is fully in command. Even though she implicitly compares herself to a "weary bird that storms have tossed" (l. 18) and a "deer that hath the arrow's hurt" (l. 19), the bird does not fall but "seeks" the calm sunshine and the deer "flies" into the peaceful wilderness (ll.19–20). With both metaphors the vehicles (the bird and deer) actively seek their end instead of succumbing to the elements, just as the woman takes control of her end.

The complication of the poem is that the mother takes her daughter's life as she takes her own. She has no reservations about committing this act and is even cheerful about it. Kathleen Lundeen notes that "Hemans romanticizes the mother's violence by presenting it as an act of courage" (Lundeen 84). Clearly the mother believes her daughter would be much better off in heaven than in the patriarchal society of the Native American tribe. The poem would certainly resonate with but also shock women in England as it criticizes a sexist system where women have little power to control their lives and suggests that it is better for mothers to kill their daughters than allow them to live without freedom.

## Further Reading

Hemans, Felicia. *Records of Woman, with Other Poems.* Edited by Paula R. Feldman. Lexington: University Press of Kentucky, 1999.

Lundeen, Kathleen. "Who Has the Right to Tell: The Ethics of Literary Empathy." In *Mapping the Ethical Turn: A Reader in Ethics, Culture, and Literary Theory,* edited by Todd F. Davis and Kenneth Womack, 83–92. Charlottesville: University Press of Virginia, 2001.

—Robert C. Hale

## industrialism

Industrialism involves a broad and complex series of changes in a culture when the means of production no longer depend on hand tools but on power machinery. The first such cultural evolution occurred in Great Britain roughly between 1750 and 1850 and is commonly referred to as the Industrial Revolution.

The industrialization of Great Britain had its genesis in the agricultural changes that took place following the so-called Glorious Revolution of 1688, which deposed King James II and saw the accession of William III and his wife Mary II. This gave Parliament ascendency over the king, and since members of Parliament were mainly large landowners, they then controlled the government, at least until 1832, when the REFORM ACT redistributed some political power to the middle classes. As the landowners took charge, they began to experiment with more efficient and lucrative forms of agriculture, and they saw the old system of common lands and tenant farmers as standing in the way of their efforts. Under the old system, tenant farmers raised a variety of crops and livestock for their own subsistence, but the landowners wanted to devote large tracts of land to one crop or one form of livestock. To gain control of the common lands, they passed hundreds of enclosure acts between 1760 and 1820, which allowed them to remove tenant farmers from the open land. The lands were fenced off ("enclosed") so that each plot could be used for the same product. Instead of working for themselves, English country people became dependent on daily wages, working for the landlords as hired hands or working in their cottages at spinning and weaving for merchants in the towns. Because of the less labor-intensive nature of the new methods of agriculture, however, many people found themselves without work and without a place to live.

In the meantime, Great Britain was spreading its power over a colonial EMPIRE, developing a huge shipping network, and establishing new markets worldwide. To take advantage of these new markets, the nation needed more goods to sell, so with capital available from agriculture and commerce, businessmen began to invest in more efficient ways to produce goods. These innovations came from two areas: inventions in textile production and the development of steam power. In 1733 John Kay (ca. 1704–ca. 1780) invented the fly shuttle, a device that allowed a loom to be worked by one person instead of two, cutting labor and increasing the production of cloth. This increase in production raised the demand for yarn, and in the 1760s the invention of the spinning jenny mechanized the spinning wheel. At first these early inventions were used by hand in people's homes. In 1769 Richard Arkwright (1732–92) patented the water frame, which allowed for the simultaneous spinning of many threads. This device relied on water, but in the 1780s Arkwright switched to steam power, and because of the size of the heavy equipment involved, he had to assemble his machinery in large factory buildings called mills.

The steam power used in the textile industry came from developments related to the coal-mining industry. Because of a dwindling timber supply in the 17th century, England had to turn to coal for fuel. Originally, access to coal deposits was limited by water accumulating in mine shafts, but building on the work of Denis Papin (1647–1712), who in 1681 invented the first steam device, Thomas Newcomen (1664–1729) developed the first steam engine, which was used to pump water from coal mines, allowing for greater access to coal deposits, saving labor, and lowering production costs. Newcomen's engine, however, burned so much fuel that it could only be used in the coal mines and was too inefficient for use elsewhere. James Watt (1736–1819) later perfected the steam engine, and steam became widely used to power mills by

the 1780s, ships in the early 1800s, and locomotives by the late 1820s. From 1780 to 1830, Great Britain's chief manufactured product was textiles, principally cotton, because cotton production was a new industry and was easily mechanized. Since the wool industry was much older, resistance to mechanization was strong, but eventually it, too, became mechanized.

Because mills became mechanized with coal-fueled steam power, they tended to be built in towns near the coal mines in the Midlands. Towns including Manchester and Birmingham saw their populations explode as many of the English country people displaced by enclosure migrated to the towns to work in the mills. Many people who worked as hand weavers and spinners in their cottages lost their livelihoods to mechanization, so they, too, looked for work in the mills. Because town officials would not gain the authority to incorporate their cities until the Municipal Corporations Act of 1835, they lacked the power to manage the growth, so these new population centers were drab, disorganized, dirty, and blackened by coal smoke. Housing was poorly made and densely packed; sanitation and sewers were practically nonexistent. Since mill work was unskilled, wages were usually too low to support a family. Women and children were used extensively as laborers in the mills and in the coal industry. The laborers worked 14-hour days, and because there were many more people than jobs available, unemployment was rampant. Although low wages, long days, the employment of women and children, and high unemployment had been common conditions for the poor for centuries, industrial labor was much more tedious and oppressive, and living conditions in the towns were much worse than those in the country. While the agricultural revolution and industrialization brought great wealth to the upper and middle classes, the poor did not share in the economic improvements.

Most of the well-known commentary on the social aspects of the industrial Revolution, such as the work of Charles Dickens (1812–70), Friedrich Engels (1820–95), Elizabeth Gaskell (1810–65), and Alexis de Tocqueville (1805–59), described the plight of the urban poor in the middle of the 19th century. However, with the notable exception of

WILLIAM BLAKE and to some extent, LETITIA ELIZABETH LANDON, the work of most writers during the Romantic period tended to focus on the effects of the depopulation of the rural areas and the impoverishment and demoralization of the people who were left behind in the earliest phases of the industrial Revolution; this was true, for example, in the work of JOHN CLARE, WILLIAM COBBETT, and GEORGE CRABBE. As the traditional social order broke down, the poets turned to nature for a sense of communion in a new kind of order. The most famous poet of nature was WILLIAM WORDSWORTH, who described not just its beauty but also its humanizing power as a moral guide through poems such as "LINES WRITTEN A FEW MILES ABOVE TINTERN ABBEY," "NUTTING," and *The* PRELUDE. Other poems by Wordsworth glorified the lives of rural characters, like an old leech gatherer in "RESOLUTION AND INDEPENDENCE," a young female farm laborer in "The Solitary Reaper," a shepherd in "MICHAEL," and an old huntsman in "SIMON LEE." He also attacked new technology in the poem "SUGGESTED BY THE PROPOSED KENDAL AND WINDERMERE RAILWAY."

In poems like "The Village Minstrel" and "Helpstone," John Clare, himself a rural farm laborer, wrote of the beauty of the natural world and about how enclosure was severing the people's connection to it. PERCY BYSSHE SHELLEY wrote of the power of nature to inspire the poet, and in describing its beauty the poet could then humanize society in such poems as "ODE TO THE WEST WIND," "MONT BLANC," and "TO A SKYLARK." The works of other writers, such as SAMUEL TAYLOR COLERIDGE, ANNA LAETITIA BARBAULD, CHARLOTTE SMITH, JOANNA BAILLIE, MARY ROBINSON, and MARY SHELLEY also made reference to the power of nature and described rural people and settings as a way to find a harmony in the chaos of social disruption brought on by industrialization.

## Further Reading

Bate, Jonathan. *Romantic Ecology: Wordsworth and the Environmental Tradition.* London: Routledge, 1991.

Brown, Richard. *Society and Economy in Modern Britain, 1700–1850.* London and New York: Routledge, 1991.

Cloudsley, Tim. "Romanticism and the Industrial Revolution in Britain." *History of European Ideas* 12 (1990): 611–635.

Daunton, M. J. *Progress and Poverty: An Economic and Social History of Britain, 1700–1850.* Oxford and New York: Oxford University Press, 1995.

Palmer, R. R., Joel Colton, and Lloyd Kramer. *A History of the Modern World.* 10th ed. Boston: McGraw-Hill, 2007.

Stevenson, John. "Social Aspects of the Industrial Revolution." In *The Industrial Revolution and British Society,* edited by Patrick K. O'Brien and Roland Quinault, 229–253. Cambridge: Cambridge University Press, 1993.

Thompson, E. P. *The Making of the English Working Class.* New York: Pantheon, 1964.

—John H. Jones

## Interesting Narrative of the Life of Olaudah Equiano, or Gustavus Vassa, the African Equiano, Olaudah (ca. 1745–1797)

Olaudah Equiano was enslaved at age 11 in 1756 and taken from Benin, West Africa, to the Caribbean and then to Virginia. He was sold to a naval lieutenant, who renamed him Gustavus Vassa. Equiano was then sold again to a Quaker, Robert King, who gave him positions of responsibility in his trading company. He was also allowed to trade for himself and eventually managed to save 40 pounds with which to buy his freedom. In 1792 Equiano married an Englishwoman, Susanna Cullen, and had two daughters with her, settling in London. He died in London on March 13, 1797, leaving 950 pounds to his younger daughter Joanna. Equiano's autobiography, *The Interesting Narrative of the Life of Olaudah Equiano, or Gustavus Vassa, the African* (1789), recounts his childhood in Africa, his abduction from his village, and his enslavement in locales such as the West Indies, America, and England. As well as recording his travels by boat, Equiano's narrative also captures the horrors of SLAVERY. For example, he vividly describes the decks of the slave ship and its foul stench and endless human suffering. In simple, clear prose, the former slave depicts scenes of bondage from Africa, Montserrat, and Georgia. In this way his narrative allows reading audiences to compare and contrast a variety of institutions of bondage over multiple continents.

Published a year after the passage of the Dolben Act (1788), which initiated restrictions on the number of slaves that could be carried aboard ships, Equiano's story had a special urgency. Along with other antislavery advocates such as Granville Sharpe, William Wilberforce, Thomas Clarkson, Sir William Dolben, and many others, the former captive desired the abolition of the slave trade. Consequently, as well as informing the public, the *Interesting Narrative* also directly exposed the mistreatment of slaves and argued against the oppressive system of bondage.

Although the slave narrative as a genre tended to have recognizable ingredients (the recollection of early youth, religious conversion), Equiano's account has some unique attributes. Notable is his description of the "talking book." Upon witnessing white men and boys reading books, a youthful Equiano assumes that the book is talking to the reader. This is his attempt to understand literacy and its connection to the individual. Subsequently, he pursues education by soliciting friends to assist him. The resulting descriptions, phrasing, allusions to the Bible, inclusion of verse, and primary sources suggests that the former slave achieved his goal of self-expression. Echoing the talking books of his past, Equiano's *Interesting Narrative* spoke to the late 18th-century reader.

Also striking in the text is the representation of Africa. Whereas the master class, proslavery parliamentarians, and apologists depicted Africa as uncivilized, Equiano disputes these claims by simply telling his story. His youth was full of long standing traditions in the Ibgo tribe, which trained men and women warriors and engaged in agriculture. Equiano's Africa is a place with its own system of governance and a rich culture.

Finally, Equiano's *Interesting Narrative* establishes a formidable voice in the fight for antislavery. It could be a precursor to SAMUEL TAYLOR COLERIDGE's opposition to the slave trade and the revolutionary cries of the 1790s. Interestingly, during his lifetime, some contemporaries criticized Equiano's writing style and characterized the narrative as "uneven." Most recently, some scholars have debated the legitimacy of his African origins; the biographer Vincent Carreta suggests that Equiano many have been born in South Carolina.

Yet while there is a controversy about his place of birth, it is undeniable that Equiano's *Interesting Narrative* provides a voice for the many slaves that he encountered on his travels.

See also PRINCE, MARY.

**Further Reading**

Boulukos, George E. "Olaudah Equiano and The Eighteenth-Century Debate on Africa." *Eighteenth-Century Studies* 40 (2007): 241–257.

Carretta, Vincent. *Equiano the African: Biography of a Self-Made Man.* London: The University of Georgia Press, 2005.

Costanzo, Angelo. *Surprizing Narrative: Olaudah Equiano and the Beginning of Black Autobiography.* New York: Greenwood Press, 1987.

Dabydeen, David. "Eighteenth-Century English Literature on Commerce and Slavery." In *The Interesting Narrative of the Life of Olaudah Equiano, or Gustavus Vassa, the African. Written By Himself,* edited by Werner Sollors, 228–240. New York: Norton, 2001.

Equiano, Olaudah. *The Interesting Narrative and Other Writings.* London: Penguin, 2003.

McBride, Dwight. *Impossible Witnesses: Truth, Abolitionism, and Slave Testimony.* New York: New York University, 2001.

Walvin, James. *The Black Presence: A Documentary History of the Negro in England.* New York: Schocken Books, 1971.

—Marilyn Walker

**"Intimations Ode"**  See "ODE: INTIMATIONS OF IMMORTALITY FROM RECOLLECTIONS OF EARLY CHILDHOOD."

**"I Remember, I Remember,"  Thomas Hood (1826)**

THOMAS HOOD's best-known poem was first published in the journal *Friendship's Offering* in 1826 and collected in his 1827 volume *The Plea of the Midsummer Fairies.* Notable for its simplicity of diction and imagery, it is a quietly effective poem in honor of his lost childhood in Islington, which was at the time a suburb separated from London by green fields.

The anaphoric first line sets up a rhythmic pattern in which memories are explored as regular and knowable entities. Rooted in the "house where I was born" (l. 2), the peeping sun, so the speaker recalls, "never came a wink too soon" (l. 5). This is juxtaposed with his darker modern-day opinion: "But now, I often wish the night / Had borne my breath away!" (ll.7–8). The second stanza adopts the generic associations of flowers as mnemonic devices: "The roses, red and white, / The vi'lets, and the lily-cups" (ll.10–11). Not merely a common literary trope, the flowers elicit memories of events specific to the speaker: "And where my brother set / The laburnum on his birthday,—/ The tree is living yet!" (ll.14–16). Next, the third stanza utilizes ornithological imagery, another common poetic device. "I remember, I remember, / Where I was used to swing, / And thought the air must rush as fresh / To swallows on the wing" (ll.17–20). Now, as in the first stanza, in its distance from the present this memory creates unpleasant feeling: "My spirit flew in feathers then, / That is so heavy now" (ll.21–22). The final stanza brings together the associations and contrasts established throughout the poem: "I remember, I remember, / The fir trees dark and high; / I used to think their slender tops / Were close against the sky: / It was a childish ignorance, / But now 'tis little joy / To know I'm farther off from heav'n / Than when I was a boy" (ll.25–32). In this way, "I Remember, I Remember" ends with a series of irresolute positions. The speaker faintly damns his "childish ignorance," and yet this prior state has been displaced by a somber realization that now, as a man, "I'm farther off from heav'n / Than when I was a boy."

On the surface, then, the melodic flow of the lyric represents the sweet pleasantries of memory universally felt: the joy that comes from recalling our childhood home and youthful endeavours. But the act of remembering necessarily distances us. The images are vivid to both the speaker and the reader, but we cannot feel our own experiences as we once did. In some instances, such as the tree that "is living yet!" and the assuredness that the sun will continue to peep through our windows, nothing has changed. But at the same time, everything has changed. The flowers will continue to bloom, but those flowers we remember died many winters ago. Indeed, beneath the saccharine surface of the poem lies hidden the speaker's own mortality: "And summer pools could hardly cool / The fever on my brow!" (ll.23–24). Memories, however sweet, are finite and mutable. Such is life and art.

**Further Reading**

Jeffrey, Lloyd N. *Thomas Hood.* New York: Twayne Publishers, 1972.

Reid, John Cowie. *Thomas Hood.* London: Routledge & K. Paul, 1963.

—Daniel Cook

## *Irish Melodies* Thomas Moore (1808–1834)

During the Romantic era, a movement arose in which musicians and poets of England, Ireland, Scotland, and Wales sought to revive and preserve their national folk music, resulting in several collections; among the more familiar is SIR WALTER SCOTT's MINSTRELSY OF THE SCOTTISH BORDER (1802–03). In 1792 the musician Edward Bunting (1773–1843) attended a gathering of nine of the last oral-tradition Irish harpers, and after traveling through Ireland in search of additional melodies, he transcribed the music and published it under the title *General Collection of Ancient Irish Music* (1796). It was this collection that was thought to be the primary inspiration for THOMAS MOORE's interest in the movement, an interest that led to Moore's *Irish Melodies,* in which, like ROBERT BURNS in Scotland, Moore set lyrics for traditional national melodies. Other works he consulted were Joseph C. Walker's *Historical Memoirs of the Irish Bards* (1786) and Charlotte Brooke's *Reliques of Irish Poetry* (1789).

Moore—still stinging from FRANCIS JEFFREY's highly unfavorable review of his *Odes and Epistles* in the *Edinburgh Review* and from the unwelcome publicity following his abortive duel with Jeffrey—found, in the project of the *Melodies,* just the work that would restore his reputation. Hence, when he was approached by the music publisher William Power to write lyrics for the project in collaboration with the musician Sir John Stevenson, he readily accepted. Although the collaboration was often an uneasy one, for Stevenson's arrangements of the traditional music were far more stylized and "academic" than Moore thought germane to the project's purpose, the end product was a success. Moore took the *Melodies* "on tour," singing in varied venues in Ireland as well as across Britain.

The *Irish Melodies* were a great sensation in their day, due at least in part to the sensibilities of the time and its taste for intense emotion. Moore seemed to have had an unfailing instinct for the blend of music and lyrics as well as a talent for writing the songs to best showcase his voice and talent for delivery. Of the 124 *Melodies*, each of which project one dominant theme, 40 are love songs, and 30 or more concern Ireland, her troubled history and the love of her patriots for her. Other lyrics concern contemporary occurrences, meditations on life and the beauties of nature, and drinking. Aesthetically, the *Melodies* rely for much of their mythic qualities on Irish symbols such as the bard, his harp, the shamrock, and references to Irish legends.

It is slightly strange that Moore was able to sing of the troubles of Ireland at the hands of her oppressor without being charged with sedition at a time when England was not handing out such charges sparingly; after 1810, however, he was mindful to write increasingly in metaphor and allegory. The year 1798 saw an Irish revolt, for the most part Catholic, which led to a deepened chasm between the Irish and the English and between Irish Catholics and Irish Protestants. The British government's Act of Union of the English and Irish parliaments (1801) caused further Irish dissatisfaction; in 1823, the Irish politician Daniel O'Connell encouraged the nationalism that led to the founding of the Catholic Association.

Moore sang his *Irish Melodies* in drawing rooms across England, maintaining that the music was an integral part of the work. In 1841 he noted in an edition of his collected works that the printing of the collected *Irish Melodies* as lyrics without their accompanying music was an aesthetic blunder, for, as he reflected, poetry is composed and judged by very different standards than is song, especially when the poet sets lyrics to irregular airs. He was aware that his lyrics would be ill-judged by a posterity that would be reading them alongside the great Romantic lyric poems. Nevertheless, some of his songs are still performed regularly, such as "The Last Rose of Summer."

## Further Reading

DeFord, Miriam Allen, *Thomas Moore*. New York: Twayne Publishers, 1967.

Grobman, Neil R. "The Ballads of Thomas Moore's *Irish Melodies*." *Southern Folklore Quarterly* 36 (1972): 103–120.

Jones, Howard Mumford. *The Harp That Once: A Chronicle of the Life of Thomas Moore*. New York: Henry Holt and Company, 1937.

Jordan, Hoover H. "Thomas Moore: Artistry in the Song Lyric." *SEL: Studies in English Literature* 2 (1962): 403–440.

Moore, Thomas, and Daniel MacLise. *Moore's Irish Melodies: The Illustrated 1846 Edition*. Mineola, N.Y.: Dover Publications, Inc., 2000.

Kelly, Ronan. *Bard of Erin: The Life of Thomas Moore*. Dublin: Penguin Ireland, 2008.

Strong, L. A. G. *The Minstrel Boy*. Alfred A. Knopf, Inc., 1937.

Tessier, Thérèse. *The Bard of Erin: A Study of Thomas Moore's Irish Melodies (1808–1834)*. Salzburg, Austria: Institut für Anglistik und Amerikanistic, 1981.

Walker, Joseph C. *Historical Memoirs of the Irish Bards*. 1786. Reprint, New York: Garland, 1971.

Vail, Jeffrey W. *The Literary Relationship of Lord Byron and Thomas Moore*. Baltimore: Johns Hopkins University Press, 2001.

—Donna Berliner

## "Isabella; or, The Pot of Basil"  John Keats (1820)

JOHN KEATS's third volume of poems, *Lamia, Isabella, The Eve of St. Agnes, and Other Poems*, was published in July 1820. Keats wrote "Isabella" because of two suggestions; one came from his friend John Hamilton Reynolds, who wanted to collaborate with Keats on a book of verses based on Giovanni Boccaccio's *Decameron* (1353). The other suggestion came indirectly from WILLIAM HAZLITT on February 3, 1818. Attending his lecture "On Dryden and Pope," Keats heard Hazlitt proclaim, "I should think that a translation of some of the other serious tales in Boccaccio and Chaucer, as that of

Isabella, the Falcon, of Constance, the Prioress's Tale . . . if executed with taste and spirit, could not fail to succeed" (quoted in Cox 429). Keats chose Boccaccio's fifth story of the fourth day, the tragic love affair of Isabella and Lorenzo, and began writing in late February or early March 1818; he had finished the poem by April 27, 1818.

Boccaccio's story, in brief, is that Isabella loves Lorenzo, a man who works for her three brothers in Messina. She is observed by one of her brothers when she visits Lorenzo at night in his bedroom. Her three brothers believe that Isabella will bring shame on the family if the affair is discovered, so they kill Lorenzo, bury his body, and tell everyone that he is away on business. Isabella deeply laments her lover's absence, but one night he comes to her in a dream to reveal that her brothers murdered him. Isabella goes to Lorenzo's burial site, finds his body, severs his head, wraps it in a fine cloth, and goes back to her home. She cries over Lorenzo's head, washing it with her tears; she then puts it in an herb pot, covers it with earth, and plants Salerno basil in the pot. Weeping over the pot of basil, the plant flourishes and Isabella never lets it out of her sight. Her brothers, however, become suspicious of her behavior. They steal the pot away from her without her knowing, discover Lorenzo's head, and flee Messina, never to return. In the absence of her basil pot, Isabella pines away for her lover and dies.

Keats was familiar not with Boccaccio's original story in Italian but with an edition from 1684, a translation published originally in 1620 by the writer John Florio. Florio stripped the story of its sexual overtones completely, and in his version, instead of the shame that the brothers feel about their sister's behavior with Lorenzo, they are merely displeased with the affair. In Boccaccio's story the brothers' shame give them impetus for murder, but in Florio's version the brothers choose to murder Lorenzo rather than let the affair continue. In Keats's "Isabella; or, the Pot of Basil," he reduces the three brothers to two, moves the narrative from Messina to Florence, and gives the brothers a stronger reason to murder Lorenzo; as merchants, they want their sister to marry well so that they can benefit financially from her marriage. For his narrative verses Keats chose ottava rima, a rhyming style made popular by Italian writers, including Boccac-

cio. This is a stanza consisting of eight lines, rhyming *abababcc* and using iambic pentameter. Ottava rima was used by other Romantic poets, such as LORD BYRON for *Beppo* (1818), which Keats would probably have read as it was published just as he was beginning "Isabella."

In "Isabella" Keats imbues his tale with a narrative depth that does not exist in Boccaccio's original tale or Florio's translation. Moreover, he spends time developing details of the poem that have no counterpart in the original source. One such instance is when he describes Isabella's two brothers as "Enriched from ancestral merchandize" (l. 106) and goes on to detail how many men died while working for them and in what ways that they died. Keats writes: "For them the Ceylon diver held his breath, / And went all naked to the hungry shark . . . / . . . for them alone did seethe / A thousand men in troubles wide and dark" (ll.113–118). His emphasis on the brothers' need to make money, no matter the cost to humanity, shows why they are able to kill Lorenzo so easily. Critics have noted that Keats's descriptions of people and physical places in the poem are very realistic. His imagery is sharp and vivid, but not overly emotional. This is shown when Isabella discovers Lorenzo's burial site and unearths his body. Keats writes: "Upon the murderous spot she seem'd to grow, / Like to a native lily of the dell . . . / . . . At last they felt the kernel of the grave, / And Isabella did not stamp and rave" (ll.365–376). Although Isabella's grief is intense, Keats prefers to save her outward emotional turmoil for later in the poem when she is washing her basil pot with tears; here she is calm and self-possessed at her lover's murder site. In Keats's rendition of Boccaccio's simple narrative, he creates a complex and interesting poem about "human suffering" and love (Stillinger 1971, 44).

Keats initially did not want "Isabella" to be published with the other poems in the 1820 volume, referring to it in hindsight as "mawkish" and in a letter to his friend and literary advisor Richard Woodhouse, as "A weak-sided Poem" (quoted in Cox 410). However, he finally relented when his friends declared "Isabella" to be an important and beautiful poem. For most of the 19th-century, literary critics regarded "Isabella" with good favor and placed this poem on the level of the other romances in the volume, "LAMIA" and "The EVE OF ST. AGNES." CHARLES LAMB published a review in the *New Times,* July 18, 1820, calling "Isabella" "the finest thing in the volume," and his review was not unique (quoted in Cox 515). However, most 20th-century critics have completely disregarded the poem; instead, it has been viewed as one of transition for Keats, a sign of his immaturity as a poet because of what has been viewed as an overly sentimental tale of tragic love. Most notable was Amy Lowell's scathing critique, in which she claimed that in "Isabella," "Keats descends to tortured similes and forced metaphors to an extent that sets one's teeth on edge" (Lowell 624). More recently, however, literary critics have begun to see "Isabella" as having a prominent place in the history of Keats's writing and in his evolution as an important Romantic poet.

**Further Reading**

Boccaccio, Giovanni. *The Decameron.* Translated by Richard Aldington. New York: Garden City Books, 1949, 228–230.

Cox, Jeffrey N., ed. *Keats's Poetry and Prose: Authoritative Texts, Criticism.* New York and London: W. W. Norton & Company, 2009.

Keats, John. *John Keats: Complete Poems.* Edited by Jack Stillinger. Cambridge, Mass.: Belknap Press, 2003.

Kipperman, Mark. "John Keats." In *Dictionary of Literary Biography: British Romantic Poets 1789–1832,* vol. 96, edited by John R. Greenfield, 179–219. Detroit: Gale Research, 1990.

Lowell, Amy. *John Keats.* Boston and New York: Houghton Mifflin, 1925.

Ridley, M. R. *Keats' Craftsmanship: A Study in Poetic Development.* New York: Russel & Russel, 1962.

Stillinger, Jack. *The Hoodwinking of Madeleine and Other Essays on Keats's Poems.* Urbana: University of Illinois Press, 1971.

—Barbara Tilley

## *Ivanhoe* Sir Walter Scott (1819)

*Ivanhoe* was the fifth of SIR WALTER SCOTT's Waverley novels, a series of historical novels that dealt with the major themes of social progression and religious or cultural tolerance. The series drew its name from the first novel in the series, WAVERLEY, which was published anonymously in 1814. After its great success, Scott published his later novels with the phrase "by the author of *Waverley,*" even after it was widely known that he was the author. Although all the early Waverley novels dealt with the history of Scott's native Scotland, *Ivanhoe* broke from this tradition by following the reign of the 12th century king Richard I, sometimes known as "the Lionheart."

Set during the Crusades, *Ivanhoe* is a mythical story of Middle Ages chivalry, maidens in distress, and romance against all odds. The characters range from the lofty Prince John to the humble servant Wamba, portraying Christians and Jews alike in a moral light. This historical novel was seen as such a soul-moving rendition of the romanticized medieval age that most of Scott's contemporaries credited him with initiating the medieval revival that swept England during the Romantic period. The story itself revolves around the life of Sir Wilfred of Ivanhoe, son of the Saxon Cedric of Rothwood, and his love of two women, the Lady Rowena and the Jewess Rebecca.

Prior to the start of the tale, Cedric has disinherited his son for supporting the Norman king Richard; he is also upset that Ivanhoe has fallen in love with Cedric's ward, the Lady Rowena, who has been promised to the Saxon lord Aethelstane so that royal Saxon blood can be preserved. However, Rowena has returned Ivanhoe's affections, and the two are determined to consummate their eternal love through marriage. After leaving his father's house, Ivanhoe joins King Richard to fight with the Crusaders in the Holy Land. As the story opens and progresses, he returns from the Crusades to defend the honor of King Richard against the scheming Prince John, who seeks to unseat his brother from the English throne. However, after angering many members of the Order of the Knights Templar at a tournament hosted by Prince John, Ivanhoe is wounded in the fight and carried off to the home of Isaac of York, a Jew. His daughter Rebecca cares for Ivanhoe and convinces her father to bring the wounded knight back to York.

While traveling back to their home, Isaac, Rebecca, and Ivanhoe, abandoned by their servants, cross paths with Cedric's homebound group. Lady Rowena convinces her guardian to allow the group safely back to York, to which Cedric complies. Before reaching York, Maurice de Bracy, infatuated with Rowena's beauty, captures the entire group and leads them off to the Castle of Torquilstone. While trapped within the castle, Rowena is forced to fight off the advances of Bracy, while Rebecca is equally pursued by Bri-ande Bois-Guilbert. Their rescue comes through the Black Knight, who is Richard the Lionheart in disguise. Aided by Robin Hood and his merry men, Richard storms the castle and rescues all inside, except Rebecca.

Bois-Guilbert flees the castle with Rebecca, expecting that the Templars will allow him to leave England with his maiden. However, the Grand-Master sees Bois-Guilbert's passion for Rebecca as sinful and a sign of her witchcraft. Through a biased trial, Rebecca is tried and convicted of witchcraft. She manages to secure a trial by combat, forcing Bois-Guilbert to fight to prove her guilt. Ivanhoe arrives on the scene to fight for Rebecca's innocence. After the Templar falls to Ivanhoe's blow, Rebecca is declared innocent in the eyes of God. Nevertheless, she and her family flee the country, fearing further persecution. Ivanhoe and Rowena are married, with Cedric's blessing, and live a long and happy life together, although the end of the tale suggests that Rebecca came to Ivanhoe's mind far more often that Rowena would have wished.

Throughout the story, the focus remains on the interactions between Norman/Saxon (opposing cultures) and Christian/Jew (conflicting religions). The opening scenes of the story place these conflicts before the reader, and they continue on throughout the text. Interestingly, *Ivanhoe* paints the Jews in a positive light, an act uncommon during the Romantic period. Despite the widespread emancipation of Jews and the restoration of religious liberties during the 1800s, many of England's citizens were still hostile toward "the rejected people." The healing arts that Rebecca practiced in the novel were often viewed as satanic by the British, and outbreaks of fever or plague were often blamed on the Jews, primarily because the latter were rarely affected by the outbreaks.

However, some critics do fault Scott's story for its minor historical inaccuracy. While the author does an excellent job of differentiating languages within the text (see Bossche), his characters often use terms and spout concepts that would not yet have entered England during the medieval period. The term *lingua franca*, for instance, would not enter the English language until the 1600s, and the burning of witches was condoned by the church until the time of the Spanish Inquisition (ca. 1478), though burning for witchcraft continued for another 200 years. Additionally, many historians feel that Scott's novel exaggerates the hostility that existed between Saxons and Normans.

*Ivanhoe* continued to be well-liked and influential throughout the 20th century. Contemporary portrayals of Robin Hood (including those seen in the 1973 Disney film) are derived primarily from Scott's novel. He was the first individual to term Robin Hood's followers as "Merry Men," and many of Robin's physical and sporting attributes come directly from *Ivanhoe*'s text. The popularity of the story itself also led to the 1952 release of a color film, starring Elizabeth Taylor as Rebecca, Joan Fontaine as Rowena, and Robert Taylor as Ivanhoe. While the film did diverge from the novel's original story line, deleting several characters and reducing the plot's complexity, the acting and costumes led to three Oscar and two Golden Globe nominations.

See also HISTORICAL FICTION.

## Further Reading

Bossche, Chris R. Vanden. "Culture and Economy in Ivanhoe." *Nineteenth-Century Literature* 42, no. 1 (June 1987): 46–72.

Chandler, Alice. "Sir Walter Scott and the Medieval Revival." *Nineteenth-Century Fiction* 19, no. 4 (March 1965): 315–332.

Lincoln, Andrew. *Walter Scott and Modernity.* Edinburgh: Edinburgh University Press, 2007.

Ragussis, Michael. *Figured of Conversion: "The Jewish Question" & English National Identity.* Durham, N.C.: Duke University Press, 1995.

Scott, Walter. *Ivanhoe.* New York: Oxford University Press, 1998.

—Melissa Ann West

## "I Wandered Lonely as a Cloud" William Wordsworth (1804)

This is one of the most famous poems of British Romanticism. WILLIAM WORDSWORTH's verses on the daffodils were composed in 1804, at a time when the poet was about to complete the first version of The PRELUDE. The incident that inspired the poem is recorded in DOROTHY WORDSWORTH's journal entry for April 15, 1802. While Dorothy gives the reader an accurate, albeit prosaic, description of the myriad flowers on the western shore of Ullswater, her brother takes the biographical incident merely as a point of departure to write a programmatic and self-referential poem on nature as a source of inspiration.

In the very first two lines of the poem, the speaker fashions himself as a typically Romantic individual who, in a state of melancholy dislocation, aimlessly rambles about the countryside. The idea of being in a vacuum is also stressed by the fact that the poet compares himself to an insubstantial cloud that "floats on high o'er vales and hills" (l. 2). What puts an end to this feeling of inanity and loneliness is the unexpected encounter with a "host" of golden daffodils (l. 4). Reminiscent of the hosts of angels in the Psalms, the vast number of daffodils suddenly makes him aware of the fact that there is a deeper meaning to life, which is waiting to be revealed and to give a new direction to his erratic wanderings in self-imposed isolation. The rhythmic movement of the flowers ("Fluttering and dancing in the breeze" [l.6]) amply shows him that he, as an individual, is participating in a universal dance which links the daffodils both with the countless stars that "twinkle on the milky way" (l. 8) and with the waves that "beside them [the daffodils] danced" (l. 13).

This poem highlights, more than any other, what in the context of Wordsworth's poetry is referred to as the mystic "spots of time." Closely related to the "plastic power" (Prelude 2:362) which enables the Romantic poet to reveal the world as a system of intricate correspondences, the speaker's sudden confrontation with the daffodils can be understood in terms of a momentary quasireligious experience of sacred affinities, a sort of epiphanic encounter with the sublime framework of existence. Redeemed by nature from his feelings of dissociation, the poet sees himself transported into "a jocund company" (l. 16) that not only revitalizes his spirits and restores his gaiety but also brings him invaluable "wealth" (l. 18) in ontological and poetological respects.

In particular, the poem's last stanza illustrates Wordsworth's poetological concept and gives insight into the way the poet should deal with "the spontaneous overflow of powerful feelings," which is one of the key terms in the PREFACE TO LYRICAL BALLADS (1798). Contrary to the myth of the Romantic poet as an enraptured genius who immediately acts upon his inspiration and thus defines poetry as a kind of écriture automatique (literally, "automatic writing"), Wordsworth leaves the reader in no doubt that the inspirational "show" (l. 18) of the daffodils, the unfiltered act of gazing, must be succeeded by recollections in tranquility. Recapturing the moments of epiphany in "vacant or in pensive mood" (l. 20), the poet makes it clear that rational distance and reflection are elements that are not incompatible with Romantic philosophy but are rather essential in the poet's mnemonic faculties ("that inward eye" [l.21]) and in bringing about what is the extreme opposite of loneliness and dejection: "the bliss of solitude" (l. 22).

Concluding the melodious poem with the image of the heart "danc[ing] with the daffodils" (l. 24), the poet underlines the fact that, in marked contrast to neoclassicist ideas of literature as the reflection of a mechanistic clockwork universe (see NEOCLASSICISM), Romantic poetry recreates and gives shape to man's contact with the sublime, with the cosmic rhythm that affiliates each Romantic individual with animated nature.

### Further Reading

Abrams, M. H. Natural Supernaturalism. Tradition and Revolution in Romantic Literature. New York: W. W. Norton & Company, 1973.

Gardiner, Alan. The Poetry of William Wordsworth. Harmondsworth, Eng.: Penguin, 1990.

Gill, Stephen, ed. The Cambridge Companion to Wordsworth. Cambridge: Cambridge University Press, 2003.

—Norbert Lennartz

# J

## "January 1795" Mary Robinson (1795)

One of MARY ROBINSON's best-known poems, this is a superb example of what the scholar Stuart Curran calls her "experiments in poetic montage," a lively collage of images that captures the contemporary scene. First published in London's *Morning Post* newspaper in the month of its title, "January 1795" has a journalistic quality, being an assessment of the contemporary state of society. The poem consists entirely of a list of descriptive phrases, most relying on a well-chosen adjective or participle to characterize a particular social group. Each line comprises one phrase, sometimes two, that creates an energetic rhythm. This is increased by the relentless trochaic tetrameter, which is, unusually, not relieved by shorter alternate lines. The poet does not stop for breath in her rush to encapsulate the whole of the social scene.

Robinson presents the vices of society in a range of situations, political and domestic. She compresses an entire social practice into a terse, suggestive phrase. "Wives who laugh at passive spouses" (l. 9) and "Arrogance o'er merit soaring" (l. 23) provoke the knowing reader to recognize the scenario to which she alludes. The satire often works by the juxtaposition of incongruities: "Lords in ermine, beggars freezing" (l. 2) is a pithy summary of an entire, irrational system of social inequality. The recurring social ills that are evoked are the absence of meritocracy, the deception wrought by appearances both in love and in state matters, a maladministered war (with reference to the British war against Revolutionary France),

and the unrewarded artist. Scattered references to "Authors who can't earn a dinner" (l. 17) voice a self-referential plea for the proper recognition of writers as important contributors to society, a complaint which Robinson develops elsewhere (for example, in her 1796 preface to SAPPHO AND PHAON).

The poem largely follows the earlier 18th-century satirists Jonathan Swift and Alexander Pope, in which the poet is social critic. Like them, Robinson finds fault with human nature as much as with the social institutions that corrupt it, the line more typically taken by Rousseau-influenced Romantics (see ROUSSEAU, JEAN-JACQUES). The theme of greedy self-advancement unites many of the disparate complaints. Yet the poem implies an underlying commitment to democratic values and a subtle critique of the authorities of the day, revealing Robinson's radical sympathies. "Gallant soldiers fighting, bleeding" (l. 8) may seem only sympathetic, but with the later jibe "Generals only fit for nurses" (l. 38), and the final stanza's regret of "peace retarded" (l. 43), an antiwar theme emerges. Through the same cumulative effect, there is an antiaristocratic stance, since the "Titled" are "gluttons" or "Lordlings empty and insipid," while "Merit" looks on the scene "deploring" (ll.3, 32, 24). The establishment is pictured as one run by the incompetent privileged.

The form, too, is classical in its balanced phrases, rhyming couplets, and tendency toward axiom—"Many a subtle rogue a winner" (l. 18) is one of several lines that ring like a proverb. Still, the regular form is enlivened by conversational idiom and feminine rhyme throughout (each line ends with an unstressed syllable). This achieves, as it later did for LORD BYRON, a buoyant, witty tone. The satire remains light, evincing a certain pleasure in the variety and energy of human activity, albeit seedy, and entertaining by its sheer poetic display.

**Further Reading**

Curran, Stuart. "Romantic Poetry: The I Altered." In *Romanticism and Feminism,* edited by Anne K. Mellor, 185–207. Bloomington: Indiana University Press, 1988.

Behrendt, Stephen C. "British Women Poets and the Reverberations of Radicalism in the 1790s." In *Romanticism, Radicalism and the Press,* edited by Stephen C. Behrendt, 83–207. Detroit: Wayne State University Press, 1997.

Robinson, Mary. *Selected Poems* of Mary Robinson. Edited by Judith Pascoe. Peterborough, Ont.: Broadview Press, 2000.

—Rebecca Styler

## Jeffrey, Francis (Lord Jeffrey) (1773–1850)

Francis Jeffrey was born on October 23, 1773, in Edinburgh and educated at Glasgow and Queen's College, Oxford. He edited the *Edinburgh Review* from the fourth through the 98th issue (1803–29). The *Edinburgh Review* was reformist from its inception, but Jeffrey's 1808 article entitled "Don Pedro Cevallos on the French Usurpation of Spain" decisively signaled its Whig partisanship, prompted SIR WALTER SCOTT to cancel his subscription and stop contributing, and thus instigated the inception of the Tory *Quarterly Review* in 1809.

Jeffrey wrote approximately 200 articles for the *Edinburgh Review,* but in terms of Romanticism, his most important contributions were his vitriolic reviews of WILLIAM WORDSWORTH's *Poems in Two Volumes* (1807), which Jeffrey called "trash"; *The EXCURSION* (1814), of which he infamously said, "This will never do"; and "The White Doe of Rylstone" (1815). He also dismissed SAMUEL TAYLOR COLERIDGE's "CHRISTABEL" (1816) as "utterly destitute of value" (quoted in Flynn, 152) and despised

ROBERT SOUTHEY's *Thalaba* (1802), which first names the LAKE SCHOOL of poets, of which Jeffrey insisted that the standards of poetry, like religion, "were fixed long ago, by certain inspired writers, whose authority it is no longer lawful to call in question" (quoted in Flynn, 153) and should not be perverted by "*dissenters* from the established systems in poetry and criticism." LORD BYRON's "English Bards and Scotch Reviewers" thus lampoons Jeffrey as a "Self-constituted judge of poesy," for writing of poetry as if it were a legal matter.

Admitted to the Scottish bar in 1794, Jeffrey was a career advocate and politician, serving as rector of the University of Glasgow (1820, 1823); dean of the Faculty of Advocates (1829); member of Parliament (MP) for Perth and Lord Advocate (1830), as which he introduced the Scottish Reform Bill (1831); MP for Edinburgh (1832–34); and Law Lord in the Court of Session (1834). While he legislated political reform, he reacted against literary reform and wrangled poetry for the discursive authority to determine taste, morality, truth, and the objects and subjects of poetics.

Jeffrey overemphasized the "peculiar system" that Wordsworth mentions, but does not fully delineate, in the PREFACE TO *LYRICAL BALLADS,* as if it were a fixed "manifesto" of "method" (quoted in Flynn, 152). He often describes passages of beauty and genius, but he interprets them as marks of potential genius repressed by unnatural and vulgar adherence to "system," which was a byword for British xenophobia (quoted in Flynn, 154). Jeffrey took offense to the disavowals of Alexander Pope, poetic language, and the emphasis on the lower classes. To these stylistic deviations, Jeffrey ascribed associations of French invasion and theory; Jacobinism; immoral German sentimentalism; the antiestablishmentarianism of JEAN-JACQUES ROUSSEAU and WILLIAM GODWIN; Methodism; and political, social, and poetic leveling. These associations are significant for modern criticism and history, but Jeffrey's reviews are more facetious than earnest defenses of Augustan poetics and reactionary politics. His vitriol earned him criticism in Coleridge's BIOGRAPHIA LITERARIA, but the *Biographia* agrees with many of Jeffrey's assessments, insists he was an honorable man when he was not reviewing, and suggests that he had memorized much of *Lyrical Ballads.* Jeffrey openly admired Scott, Thomas Campbell, Byron, JOHN KEATS (probably because rival journals disparaged him), and GEORGE CRABBE. "The severest of critics," as WILLIAM HAZLITT put it in *The Spirit of the Age* but "the best-natured of men" (quoted in Flynn, 176). Jeffrey may have affected to hate poems and poets that he loved. He died on January 26, 1850.

See also NEWSPAPERS AND MAGAZINES.

**Further Reading**

Flynn, Philip. *Francis Jeffrey.* Newark: University of Delaware Press, 1977.

—Jonathan Farina

## Jerusalem: The Emanation of the Giant Albion William Blake (1804, 1820)

Divided into four chapters, *Jerusalem* focuses on the actions of three main characters: Jesus Christ (who represents humanity in its divine form), Albion (the universal human whose initial error lies in his failure to recognize Jesus as one who will eventually lead him to his salvation) and Los (the poet-prophet and the embodiment of creative imagination, the instrument through which human salvation would become a possibility). The poem is not, it should be pointed out, Blake's shorter work "Jerusalem," which was later set to music and comes from the preface to MILTON: A POEM (1804–11).

The literary scholar Northrop Frye points out how the chapters into which Blake divides his epic can be viewed as a drama in four acts: a fall; man's struggle in the fallen world; his redemption by the divinity embodied in Jesus; and, finally, the Apocalypse. In the first chapter, addressed "To the Public," Blake announces his objective and recreates his mythological universe. He then dramatizes the principal conflict in which Albion dismisses Jesus as a "Phantom of the overheated brain!" In the ensuing chapters, Blake identifies "Errors" that prevent Albion from uniting with Jesus to achieve spiritual salvation. In chapter 2 addressed "To the Jews," the physically repressive elements of Judaism are condemned because an emphasis on the negation of one's physical being—focus on sin, divine

punishment, and absence of purity in the human body—takes the place of a celebration of humanity. In chapter 3, the mental degeneration of his contemporaries, symbolized by a worldly code of scientific rationalization of the existence of God, a ruthless system of moral laws, and a hankering after material possessions are detailed. In chapter 4, Blake vehemently criticizes "the Christians" for falsifying a religion of love and forgiveness and distorting it into one of sin and retribution. *Jerusalem* concludes with an apocalypse, Albion's final affirmation of the divinity of Christ, and his resurrection into "Humanity Divine" (4:23).

That Blake locates the conflict as well as its resolution within the mind of man is not merely a structural and poetic device. The scholar Clint Stevens has suggested that in *Jerusalem* thought should not be conceived as an approximation of the objective or unknown reality (240–241). Blake's primary focus is on the mind of man and human imagination. The failure and corruption of imagination through worldly influences—pride, envy, self-centeredness, an obsessive indulgence in physical and material needs, moral absolutes, religious dogmas, mechanically pursued scientific attitude, and the Female Will, or sexual manipulation on the part of women—subvert both man's awareness as well as pursuit of spiritual salvation. Unleashing of imagination alone can lead to the elimination of worldly influences, to spiritual victory and appropriation into infinity. Thus, Blake, would have us believe that both spiritual liberation and eternity are a state of the mind.

Blake created *Jerusalem* through his personally devised techniques of "illuminating printing" in which "pages" were etched on plates and individually colored. Each copy of a work was separately produced. *Jerusalem,* Blake's longest work, runs to 100 etched, illustrated, and hand-painted plates with about 400 lines of text. The single extant color copy of *Jerusalem* is in the possession of Yale University. *Jerusalem* was long considered a work of much obscurity, made more complex by Blake's use of personal mythology and political and religious content of which has been much debated. An attitude of contemptuous dismissal has given way to responsible, painstaking scholarship that has sought to interpret, explain, and restore the authorial intent as well as identify the merits of the poem. A broad pattern of resemblance between Blake's epic and the Book of Ezekiel is easily noticed. David Erdman's remark of 1970 ("the problem may be only that the poem has not had accurate and close readers as yet" [in Blake 928]) is accompanied by useful suggestions as to the poem's structure ("... each [of the four chapters] depends for its progression on a dialectical struggle of contraries" [ ]) and the meaning ("The immediate theme is ... war and peace, or better yet, peace without vengeance" [ ]).

## Further Reading

Ahearn, Edward J. *Visionary Fictions: Apocalyptic Writing from Blake to the Modern Age.* New Haven, Conn.: Yale University Press, 1996.

Blake, William. *The Complete Poetry and Prose of William Blake.* Edited by David V. Erdman. Berkeley: University of California Press, 2008.

Frye, Northrop. *Fearful Symmetry: A Study of William Blake.* Princeton, N.J.: Princeton University Press, 1974.

Paley, M. D. *Energy and Imagination: The Development of Blake's Thought.* Oxford: Clarendon Press, 1970.

Stevens, Clint. "William Blake's Golgonooza and Jerusalem: A Conversation in Visionary Forms Dramatic." *European Romantic Review* 20, no. 3 (2009): 289–307.

—G. R. Taneja

## *Journal of Conversations with Lord Byron, A*
**Marguerite Gardiner countess of Blessington**
(1834)

Initially published via instalments in the *New Monthly Magazine* (July 1832–December 1833), MARGUERITE GARDINER's account of her meetings with LORD BYRON (April–June 1823) has traditionally been seen as a valuable record of the enigmatic poet. In March 1833 a reviewer for *Fraser's Magazine* told readers: "Since the publication of Boswell's Life *of Johnson*, nothing of the kind so good ... has appeared" (quoted by Lovell in Blessington 6). Biographers of Byron—of which there have been large numbers—have drawn extensively on it, taking Gardiner's recollections as a reason-

ably accurate record of what Byron was really like. This is not to say that the book has not had some detractors ready to question its validity. Early on, Byron's final mistress Teresa Guiccioli claimed that the book should have been called "Imaginary Conversations" (in Blessington 7).

The context for the book is well known. Gardiner had known Byron before his self-imposed exile in Europe, and they had many friends in common. She was confident of being able to charm him when she set sail for Europe in August 1822. Certainly the couple were close, at least for a brief period. After Gardiner's arrival in Genoa on March 31, 1823, they saw each other several times a week, and it is these conversations and the brief letters exchanged that form the basis for the *Journal*.

Initially Gardiner did nothing with her material, but by the early 1830s she was in desperate need of money, and there was still plenty of interest in the (now-dead) scandal-ridden poet. By the time Gardiner wrote the *Journal*, her attitude to Byron had altered, and there is a good deal of sympathy for him, which helps create a sense of objectivity. However, some of the *Journal* seems antagonistic. The poet is described as overly "sensitive, jealous and exigent" and is presented as flippant, snobbish, and quick to cast off friends on a whim (Blessington 227–228). Yet the *Journal* also conveys something of Gardiner's own attraction to Byron, and she clearly wanted to do him justice. "I am glad ... the Conversations ... give you a better opinion of Byron," she told WALTER SAVAGE LANDOR. "He had arrived at that period in human life when he saw the fallacy of the past without having grasped the wisdom of the future" (quoted in Chew 234).

What is most important about the version of Byron given in the *Journal* is the complexity of his personality. Gardiner recognized the different dimensions of the poet's achievements as well as the difficult and often open-ended questions he provoked. That there has always been and still remains a difficulty in pinning down Byron is also apparent. Gardiner conveys the tension that existed—and still exists—between Byron's roles as aristocrat and democrat, selfish egotist and self-sacrificing freedom fighter. So while the slipperiness that Gardiner identifies in her subject has been formulated in many ways by biographers, hers is one of the first books to do so in any detail.

## Further Reading

Blessington, Marguerite, countess of. *Lady Blessington's Conversations of Lord Byron*. Edited by Ernest J. Lovell, Jr. Princeton, N.J.: Princeton University Press, 1969.

Chew, Samuel. *Byron in England. His Fame and After-Fame*. London: John Murray, 1924.

Harriet Devine Jump. "Marguerite Blessington, Teresa Guiccioli and the Writing of the Conversations with Byron." *Byron Journal* 31 (2003): 51–60.

Soderholm, James. *Fantasy, Forgery and the Byron Legend*. Lexington: University of Kentucky Press, 1996.

—Andrew Maunder

# K

## Kean, Edmund (1787–1833)

Impresario, actor, and Shakespearian scholar, Edmund Kean set new standards for interpretation of the emotions onstage. He was born out of wedlock in London on March 17, 1789, the son of Ann Carey, an itinerant actress, and Edmund Kean, possibly an architect's clerk. He first appeared on the stage at the age of four, and after a peripatetic early life that included a stint as a cabin boy at sea, he returned to the theater under the tutelage of his uncle, the entertainer Moses Kean, and the actress Charlotte Tidswell. By his teens he had become a Shakespearean actor and had learned music, dancing, and fencing. As a young man he appeared onstage with SARAH SIDDONS and married the actress Mary Chambers, who bore him two sons, one of whom subsequently died.

When Kean made his debut on the stage of a failing Drury Lane Theatre in the role of Shylock (1814), his direct competitor was without doubt the actor-manager JOHN PHILIP KEMBLE (1758–1823), the self-proclaimed true heir to the Shakespeare legacy. At the time tragedy, the only genre in which Kean ever worked, was widely regarded as the most intellectual and generically pure of dramatic forms, supposedly dissociated from spectacle and the entertainments that thrived in the strolling circuits and the capital's lower-class theaters. Kemble's statuesque onstage presence, his majestic movements, and his dignified delivery had established themselves as canonical, in particular as regards the Shakespearean tradition. Conversely, Kean had reached the Bard in catholic fashion, after his irregular theatrical upbringing had connected him to the fringe world of mimic and animal entertainments (at the beginning of his career he had made himself a name as Harlequin). The innovative brand of acting he exported onto the stage was quintessentially Romantic—aggressive, explosive, physical, irresistibly natural in mode, disconcertingly hybrid in form. Kemble's difference from Kean could thus not appear more marked in presence, acting, and lifestyle. Where the former was dignified and stately the latter's acting had the effect of "*reading* Shakespeare by flashes of lightening" (quoted by Davis, 937), in SAMUEL TAYLOR COLERIDGE's oxymoronic definition. The theatrical and cultural phenomenon of Edmund Kean contributed significantly to widening the rift between critical respectability and public popularity, and as a consequence he arguably bolstered the establishment of the Romantic dramatic ideology, ousting a more populist theater.

Undoubtedly, it was in the dark, Shakespearean roles that Kean's fire most vividly burnt—in Iago as well as Othello, in Richard III as in Macbeth, all of them played at times with bravado, against the custom of his thespian rivals. From a scholarly point of view, however, his most significant contribution was the attempted restoration of the original tragic ending to *King Lear*, altered in 1681 by Nahum Tate according to the neoclassical theories of poetical justice (see NEOCLASSICISM). Kean was also celebrated for giving life to an array of melodramatic, shadowy, and charismatic roles, such as Sir Edward Mortimer and Octavian in

George Colman the Younger's *The Iron Chest* and *The Mountaineers;* Barabas in Christopher Marlowe's *The Jew of Malta;* and, above all, Sir Giles Overreach in *A New Way to Pay Old Debts* by Philip Massinger, a role in which he triumphed.

Kean's attack on dramatic purity—that is, of the accepted form of tragedy—condemned him to unrelenting critical contempt. This was unfortunately coupled with well-publicized overindulgence in private life—a typically Regency passion for gambling, drink, and women, which indelibly marred his public persona and cost him the support of his public. In a culture that still equated artistic merit with private probity, the audiences' favour, quickly gained, was bound to be as quickly lost. After a very public and ruinous affair with a Mrs. Cox in 1825, the audience turned against him. Drunkenness made his memory embarrassingly unreliable and his body lame; his 11-year long sway over Drury Lane ended. Morally biased biographical accounts allege that he collapsed during a performance of *Othello* as he uttered the line, "Villain, be sure, you prove"—an impressive dramatic farewell as much as an indictment of guilt.

Kean died on May 15, 1833, two months after his histrionic demise, but this event was only to mark the beginning of his cultural afterlives. His on- and offstage overreaching quickly transformed him into the epitome of an ostensibly fast-living, pleasantly excessive, and commercially viable incarnation of Romanticism. Alexandre Dumas père chose him as the subject of a drama, *Kean* (1836), which was later reworked into a comedy by Jean-Paul Sartre (*Kean,* 1954), recently revived in London. In the 1960s Kean's flamboyancy reached the American shores with the Broadway fictionalization of his life, *Kean.* It is highly ironic, yet very significant, that in this latest musical foray, fact and myth inextricably blur into each other, with the latter having once more the upper hand, just as the actor might have wished.

## Further Reading

Bratton, Jacky. "The Celebrity of Edmund Kean: An Institutional Story." In *Theatre and Celebrity in Britain, 1660–2000,* edited by Mary Luckhurst, and Jane Moody, 90–106. New York: Palgrave Macmillan, 2005.

Davis, Tracy. "'Reading Shakespeare by Flashes of Lightning': Challenging the Foundations of Romantic Acting Theory." *English Literary History* 62 (Winter 1995): 933–954.

Kahan, Jeffrey. *The Cult of Kean.* Aldershot, Eng.: Ashgate, 2006.

Oya, Reiko. *Representing Shakespearian Tragedy: Garrick, the Kembles, and Kean.* Cambridge: Cambridge University Press, 2007.

Page, Judith. "'Hath Not a Jew Eyes?': Edmund Kean and the Sympathetic Shylock." *Wordsworth Circle* 34 (2003): 216–219.

—Francesca Saggini

## Keats, John (1795–1821)

While now considered to be one of the most important of the Romantic poets, John Keats was overlooked for a considerable time until Richard Monckton Milnes's monumental *Life, Letters, and Literary Remains of John Keats* (1848) helped arouse critical interest in the second half of the 19th century.

Born in London on October 31, 1795, Keats was the eldest of five children born to Thomas Keats and Frances Jennings Keats. His father managed a livery responsible for the hiring of horses and coaches to travelers, and the family lived adjacent to the stables in North London. Keats's family was clearly in "trade," and later Keats would be denigrated by some contemporaries as a "Cockney" poet, as he was described in *Blackwood's Magazine, The Quarterly Review* and *The British Critic* (see COCKNEY SCHOOL). Keats, it seems, was caught in a class slippage, something which was brought home further when Thomas Keats died in April 1804 after falling from a horse and fracturing his skull. Two months later, Frances married again, this time to a clerk, William Rawlings, but by all accounts the marriage was not happy. The Keats children were sent to live with their maternal grandparents, and when Frances's second marriage broke up she joined them, leaving the livery stables in the hands of her unscrupulous new husband. The death of Frances's father led to more financial problems, and the family existed in straightened circumstances. They moved to a much smaller house in Enfield, where Keats and his brothers attended Charles Cowden Clarke's academy, learning history, science, classics, and French.

The teenage Keats was athletic though famously short (he stood barely five feet tall), and initially there were thoughts of a career in the army. However, in 1811 he became apprentice to a surgeon, Thomas Hammond. In 1815, after completing his apprenticeship, he enrolled at Guy's Hospital in London, passing his exams a year later, when he also became licensed by the Society of Apothecaries. By this time Keats had lost enthusiasm for his medical career (he was reputedly upset by having to assist at operations in the days before anaesthetics). He had also become interested in literature and decided take it more seriously than a hobby. The publication of his first poem in *The Examiner* was followed in 1816 by "ON FIRST LOOKING INTO CHAPMAN'S HOMER," a poem inspired by his prodigious reading of the classics. The *Examiner*'s editor, LEIGH HUNT, met and encouraged him and then helped with the publication of his first volume of poems in 1817. The book was virtually ignored, but Keats continued writing, working on ENDYMION during most of 1817. By now his brother Tom was starting to show signs of consumption (tuberculosis), which ran in the family (their mother had died of the same disease in 1810), and Keats spent most of the next year caring for him until Tom's death in 1818, while also working on "HYPERION." Keats himself also began to suffer from ill health about this time, though whether it was the beginnings of consumption or venereal disease (as has been suggested) is unclear.

By now Keats's work was beginning to attract notice—though not all of the responses were favorable. This was also the period during which he met Fanny Brawne (1800–65), a neighbor whose widowed mother decided to rent half of Wentworth Place, the house in Hampstead in which Keats was living. Fanny was 18 when the couple met and had no pretensions to be intellectual. Instead, her normality seems to have been the attraction. The couple's many letters suggest a stormy and often tortured relationship stemming from Keats's jealousy over Fanny's flirtations with other men and his own idealization of womanhood more generally. "I am certain I have not a right feeling towards Women—at this moment I am striving to be just to them but I cannot—Is it because they fall so far beneath my Boyish imagination?" (Rollins, i, 341) he wrote in July 1818. However, he decided he wanted to marry, and the couple became unofficially engaged, although Keats's lack of income was a barrier.

This was also a period of uneven productivity on Keats's part, despite or because of Fanny. "The EVE OF ST. AGNES" was written in early 1819, but after this Keats fell into depression, and the next few months saw little output. In late April, however, he began writing "LA BELLE DAME SANS MERCI," a poem that testifies to his long-held fascination with love, death, and art. A flurry of great poems followed: "ODE ON A GRECIAN URN," "ODE TO A NIGHTINGALE," and "ODE ON MELANCHOLY." "Ode on Indolence" was written in June, followed by "ODE TO PSYCHE." This amazing burst of creativity in the final year of Keats's life has been much commented on. Partly it was prompted by a wish to earn money so that he and Fanny could marry. He also turned his hand to playwriting. *Otho the Great* was written over the summer, and this was followed by an attempt at a second, *King Stephen,* intended for the celebrated actor EDMUND KEAN, but neither play was produced. In autumn 1819 Keats was beginning to set great store by a new poem, "LAMIA," and began to prepare a new volume of poems for publication in which he planned to include all his recent works as well as "ISABELLA; OR, THE POT OF BASIL" (1818) and "Hyperion."

Keats's need to earn money at this time is significant for more than just biographical reasons. As the biographer John Barnard has suggested, he represented a new "middle class" writer infiltrating the realm of the gentleman author. With Keats's training in medicine rather than Greek mythology in mind, one reviewer snobbishly insisted, "It is a better and wiser thing to be a starved apothecary than a starved poet; so back to the shop Mr John" (quoted in Brainerd, 4), Keats's cause was not helped by Leigh Hunt's ill-judged account of his humble origins in his *Lord Byron and Some of his Contemporaries* (1828). Keats sought to disassociate himself from Hunt, but it proved a futile endeavour. Indeed, his literary agent had more immediate success with another of his clients, the so-called peasant poet JOHN CLARE. Keats's lack of commercial success is all the more striking given that today his works are so familiar. His well-wrought phrases hang in the air, from the optimistic "a thing of beauty is a joy for ever" to the lush "Seasons of mists and mellow fruitfulness" ("To Autumn")—phrases epitomizing his unsurpassed grasp of assonance and sound.

Amid the rapid maturation of his genius, Keats, in his poem "Sleep and Poetry" (1816), not unreasonably, asked, "Oh, for ten years, that I may overwhelm / Myself in poesy" (11.96–97). But by February 1820 he was not only taking laudanum (a mixture of alcohol and opium prescribed as a painkiller) in large quantities but had begun to cough blood—the first visible signs of the tuberculosis that would kill him. According to Charles Brown (1787–1842), one of the poet's closest friends, Keats's words after his first hemorrhage were: "I know the colour of that blood; it is arterial blood. I cannot be deceived in that colour, that drop of blood is my death warrant. I must die" (quoted in Motion, 496). His health deteriorated over the next year, although he carried on working in brief periods of recovery and taking exercise. Some observers thought that some of his symptoms were as much psychological as physical—the product of a highly wrought personality—despite his emaciated physical state being evidence to the contrary.

In June 1820 Keats's spirits were lifted by the positive reaction to his new volume of poems, and sales were good as well. This was gratifying, but it was too late. He was given accommodation by Leigh Hunt and then by the Brawnes, and it was from their house that in September 1820 he sailed to Italy (a popular destination for invalids), accompanied by the painter Joseph Severn. The desperate hope was that the warmer climate might prolong his life. He also wanted to ensure that Fanny—who had refused to give him up—would not have to nurse him at the very end. After a long and uncomfortable journey, first by ship and then by carriage, Keats and Severn settled in Rome, where Keats was attended by an English doctor named Clark. Despite periods of calm, however, there was little Clark could do. Tuberculosis was not very well understood, and there was no cure.

Keats became progressively worse, worn down by successive hemorrhages, and after a painful final few months, he died on February 26, 1821, at age 25.

Keats died believing he was a failure. Yet almost immediately he was lauded as a neglected genius in "ADONAIS" (1821), an elegy composed by his friend PERCY BYSSHE SHELLEY. Among other things, this poem promoted the idea that bad reviews of *Endymion* (1818) had hastened his untimely death. The delicate and therefore ethereal image of the poet became a common one. Yet, as commentators have increasingly understood, Keats moved in prominent, largely liberal intellectual circles, even if many such thinkers were (at the time) marginalized by conservative society. Not only did he receive a thorough, liberal education under the tutelage of Charles Cowden Clarke at Enfield, he frequently met with Shelley, WILLIAM WORDSWORTH, CHARLES LAMB, B. R. Haydon, and a host of exciting and learned men and women.

Keats was particularly stimulated by the critic WILLIAM HAZLITT, whose *Lectures on the English Poets* (1818) influenced some of his most accomplished poems, such as "The Eve of St. Agnes," a richly medieval and sensual piece. These poems engaged with the great and challenging questions that had long fascinated English poets: What is the role of art in our lives? What are the effects of life on art? Not only the gore of medicine but the deaths of his close family by tuberculosis, the wasting sickness that eventually consumed him as well, was offset against his desire to live beyond the physical world. This is captured beautifully, and hauntingly, in what many critics still consider one of his greatest works, "Ode to a Nightingale," which lushly combines the mourner's stupor with harsh uncertainty: "Was it a vision, or a waking dream? / Fled is the music;—Do I wake or sleep?" (ll.79–80). Such tensions were obscured by the championing of Keats by sentimental Victorians, for whom the neglected genius embodied the aestheticist's creed—"art for art's sake.'" On the contrary, it was the harsh realities of life that spurred Keats on to his greatest accomplishments.

More recently, the brutal honesty and acute sense of failure in what might be termed Keats's skeptical HUMANISM has gained new critical attention. In this regard, works that were long considered failures or merely juvenile pieces have received greater scrutiny. Prominent contemporaries, such as Hazlitt, complained that *Endymion* in particular was "soft and fleshy, without bone or muscle" (quoted in Aske, 69). This Keats lacked manliness, but today these "soft" works, along with what are sometimes treated as intrinsically feminized language and rhyme schemes, has been considered anew, especially by feminist and new historicist critics.

In such a way, Keats's poetry, as much as the poet himself, have become politicized, caught between revisionist and formalist critical approaches. Many readings place Keats in his immediate intellectual environment, while others wish to read his poems solely as poems. The greatest challenge in reading Keats today, then, is to prioritize one approach over the other. One might attempt a "literal archaeology" (Roe ix) in order to revisit the original nuances of his writings in an historical context, though this inevitably leads to problems associated with the limited purview of the poet's contemporaries. Or one might wish simply to celebrate the unique stylistic and linguistic qualities of this highly sensual body of work. Another approach would be to consider the development of Keats's works as historical phenomena—as a series of ongoing projects, as well as failures, that capture different moods and concerns, whether knowingly political or inwardly aesthetic. He embraced the fundamental paradoxes of art and life, permanence and mutability, beauty and death. At turns virtuosic in his achievements and overcome by his failures, he vented his frustration with the limits of the sonnet form, among other things, in such poems as "If by dull rhymes our English must be chained." Perhaps, too, one might add that the limits imposed by overly political readings of his life and works, on the one hand, and overly formalist ones, on the other, tarnish the extraordinary body of writings produced by this young poet. In the end he fulfilled at least one of his aims: "I think I shall be among the English Poets after my death."

See also "WHEN I HAVE FEARS THAT I MAY CEASE TO BE."

## Further Reading

Aske, Martin. *Keats and Hellenism.* Cambridge: Cambridge University Press, 1985.

Barnard, John. *John Keats.* Cambridge: Cambridge University Press, 1987.

Bate, Walter Jackson. *John Keats.* London: Chatto and Windus, 1979.

Bennett, Andrew. *Keats, Narrative and Audience: The Posthumous Life of Writing.* Cambridge: Cambridge University Press, 1994.

Blades, John. *John Keats: The Poems.* Basingstoke, Eng.: Palgrave, 2002.

Keats, John. *Complete Poems and Selected Letters of John Keats.* Edited by Edward Hirsch. New York: Modern Library Classics, 2001.

Keats, John. *The Letters of John Keats 1814–21.* 2 vols. Edited by Hyder E. Rollins. Cambridge, Mass.: Harvard University Press, 1958.

Motion, Andrew. *Keats.* London: Faber and Faber 1998.

Roe, Nicholas. *John Keats and the Culture of Dissent.* Oxford: Clarendon Press, 1997.

Turley, Richard Marggraf. *Keats's Boyish Imagination.* London: Routledge, 2004.

Walsh, John Evangelist. *Darkling I Listen: The Last Days and Death of John Keats.* New York: St. Martin's, 1999.

Watts, Cedric. *A Preface to Keats.* 5th ed. London and New York: Longman, 1996.

Whale, John. *John Keats.* Basingstoke, Eng.: Palgrave Macmillan, 2005.

Wolfson, Susan J. *The Cambridge Companion to Keats.* Cambridge: Cambridge University Press, 2001.

—Daniel Cook

## Kemble, John Philip (1757–1823)

The younger brother of the celebrated actress SARAH SIDDONS, and rival of EDMUND KEAN, John Philip Kemble became famous for his portrayal of tragic roles, particularly in Shakespeare. Kemble was born on February 1, 1757, into a theatrical family (his parents ran a touring company), and despite his father's intention that his son should train as a Catholic priest, there was a certain inevitability in Kemble's adult stage debut in 1776 (he had already performed small parts as a child). His family connections were clearly an advantage, and he had a rapid rise to stardom. After touring in the provinces, where he numbered ELIZABETH INCHBALD among his colleagues (she would later use him as the model for Dorriforth in *A Simple Story* [1791]), Kemble made his London debut as Hamlet at Drury Lane in 1783. He did not "electrify" theatergoers as his sister had done, but the performance was respectfully received and led to other leading Shakespearean roles: Richard III, Shylock, and King John. As was the custom, all were carefully edited to showcase the leading actor's particular strengths.

Kemble developed new readings of classic roles based on his idiosyncratic—declamatory— acting style: speaking slowly and deliberately, pausing after every second or third word so that the audience could catch every bit of the verse. For one anonymous reviewer in *The Thespiad* (1809), this made him seem boring, passionless, and even robotic, when compared to rivals: "Stiff, pompous, stern, each haggard feature groom'd: / Each step predest'd ... Precise in passion, cautious ev'n in rage, Lo Kemble comes, the Euclid of the stage: Who moves in given angles, squares at start, / And blows his Roman beak by rules of art" (quoted in Kelly 193). LEIGH HUNT noted: "He never pulls out his handkerchief without a design upon the audience" (quoted in Rowell 11). Sarah Siddons, who often acted opposite her brother, complained that even in "impetuous outbursts" Kemble was "always careful to avoid any discomposure of his dress or deportment" (quoted in Findlater 66).

In 1784 Kemble repeated the role of Hamlet before essaying one of his most famous parts, Cato in Joseph Addison's play of the same name. He had a particular penchant for playing stern heroes of ancient Rome (Coriolanus was another favorite role), partly because he was tall and considered himself fetching in a toga, but also because he was interested in classical models of heroism and in the opportunity for oratory that such parts offered. His declared aim was to display the leading passions of each hero, but he was also an innovator backstage, taking rehearsals very seriously, and was interested in spectacle and accurate visual details, as evidenced in a famous and lavish extras-filled production of Shakespeare's *Henry VIII* in which he played Cardinal Wolsey. Special scenery was commissioned, and costumes were designed that had a vague sense of historical accuracy. At other times Kemble's sense of period detail failed him, and he followed the convention of performing in whatever modern dress was to hand. Thus, he performed as Othello dressed in the uniform of an army officer of the day.

In the early days people recognized and appreciated Kemble's avowed seriousness. Leigh Hunt was one of his early admirers, noting that "were it not for Mr Kemble's exertions the tragedies of our glorious bard would almost be in danger of dismissal from the stage: and it does him infinite credit to have persevered in his exertions in spite of comparatively thin houses; to have added to the attractions of his poet by a splendour of scene as seasonable as well-deserved; and to have evidence so noble an attachment, and helped keep up so noble a taste, in an age of mawkishness and buffoonery" (quoted in Findlater 54).

By 1788 Kemble could claim to be the leading actor in London. He took over the management of the Drury Lane Theatre, planning to turn it into a shrine to Shakespearean drama, which would celebrate the Bard as the repository of patriotic, conservative English values. This artistic policy did not always sit easily with the reformist, revolutionary mood of the time, nor did Kemble's own lofty, quasi-aristocratic attitude to his (often rowdy) audiences, which some observers claimed indicated contempt for them.

In 1802 Kemble withdrew from Drury Lane, and the following year he became manager of the Covent Garden Theatre. Highly strung and prone to depression—both of which he sought to alleviate by excessive drinking—he also tended to be financially hard up. Then, as now, the business of production was costly, and he suffered a disaster when, in September 1808, Covent Garden caught fire and burned. By now he had a one-sixth share, and so he was liable for some of the costs. When the theater reopened the following year, there followed the so-called old price riots following the decision to raise prices for the pit and boxes and reduce the capacity of cheaper gallery by adding extra boxes. The mood of the audience was often resentful and violent, and catcalls increased. Kemble became a figure of ridicule—even hatred—not least when on one occasion he sent for the police to restore order and was rumored to have hired professional fighters to attack demonstrators. His nickname, "Black Jack," seemed to fit, and he became associated with figures of tyranny and authority. Eventually he was forced to climb down over the ticket pricing, although he tried unsuccessfully reinstate them the following year until riots broke out again. The public were very much in charge.

By 1815 Kemble was obviously a man in decline, especially when faced with the success of Edmund Kean with his more dangerous and unpredictable—sparky—style of acting, which made Kemble look like a relic. Leigh Hunt, who had come to dislike Kemble's monopoly of the London stage, called him "a teacher of elocution rather than an actor and not a good teacher on that account" (quoted in Findlater 67). Those who appreciated him recognized his limitations but realized that he was best when portraying outsized figures rather than in plays where naturalism was called for. But naturalism was never Kemble's aim. LORD BYRON called him "the most supernatural of actors," and this is a useful description. Kemble aimed for dignity. "The distinguishing excellence of his acting," wrote WILLIAM HAZLITT, "may be summed up in one word—*intensity*; in the seizing upon some one feeling or idea, in working it up, with a certain graceful consistency, and conscious grandeur of conception, to a very high degree of pathos or sublimity."

Kemble made his final appearance as Coriolanus on June 23, 1817, before settling in Lausanne, France, where he died on February 26, 1826. Since then his reputation has suffered. He was not as talented as his sister, and in comparison with Kean he has always seemed something of fossil.

## Further Reading

Donohue, J. *Dramatic Character in the English Romantic Age.* Princeton, N.J.: Princeton University Press, 1970.

Findlater, Richard. *Six Great Actors.* London: Hamish Hamilton, 1957.

Hazlitt, William. *Complete Works.* Edited by P. P. Howe. 21 vols. London: J. M. Dent, 1934.

Kelly, Linda. *The Kemble Era.* New York: Random House, 1980.

Rowell, George. *Victorian Dramatic Criticism.* London: Methuen & Co., 1971

—Martin Harris

## "Kubla Khan" Samuel Taylor Coleridge (1816)

"Kubla Khan," with its subtitle, "or, A Vision in a Dream, a Fragment," remains one of the best-known poems of English Romanticism, despite its often obscure—and much-debated—meaning. It is the most striking example of SAMUEL TAYLOR COLERIDGE's primary concern with the creative power of the imagination (which he was to discuss in *BIOGRAPHIA LITERARIA*) and the model for what would become a cliché of Romanticism: writing inspired by opium addiction.

The poem was first published in 1816 at the request of LORD BYRON, but it has not been possible for critics to fix a date of composition for it, although dates between 1797 and 1798 are often suggested. Coleridge called it a "fragment"; its genesis was related by the author himself, who added a preface in which he explained that the lines had originated from an opium-induced dream, implicit in the subtitle, in the autumn of 1797 at a farmhouse near Exmoor. Under the influence of an opium-based drug, he fell asleep while reading Samuel Purchas's *Purchas His Pilgrimage* (1613), a survey of world religions, and in particular a passage on the emperor Kubla Khan and the wonderful summer palace he commanded to be built. (Marco Polo's description of Shangdu palace from his work *Il Milione* was also included in Purchas's book.) A dream came to Coleridge and, once awake, he tried to report it in poetic form. The reason for claiming the poem to be a fragment was perfectly aligned with the Romantic aura of the period. Coleridge claimed that a visitor had interrupted him while he was writing it down, and while he "still retained some vague and dim recollection of the vision," much had passed away like "the images on the surface of a stream into which a stone has been cast, but alas! Without the after restoration of the latter" (quoted in Milne, 18).

Most critics are skeptical about the author's account of how the poem was composed. Yet the preface, which presents the fragment as a dreamlike vision, though misleading in some respects, should be regarded as an integral part of the poem's fictional world, as far as it reveals the main themes of the work in advance. It should be read as a kind of manifesto on the way of working of the Romantic poetic mind—namely, as the product of the unconscious (stimulated in this case by the use of laudanum) necessarily submitted to the constraints of artistic re-creation, which cannot be limited to the mere rendering of the voluptuous, disordered content of a vision.

The general outline of the landscape described in "Kubla Khan," though clear, has been the cause of widespread speculation on the meaning of its imagery, some insisting on a theme or purpose, some believing it to be a poem stressing the beauty of creation, and others reading sexual allusions throughout. The poem opens with an enigmatic but precise description of the emperor's palace in Xanadu. It is portrayed as "a stately pleasure-dome" (l. 2) located in an enchanted, savage spot where a woman cries for her lover and Alph, the sacred river, springs up violently, then meanders before plunging through caverns into a sunless sea. Suddenly the imagery concerning the dome disappears, and a new vision is abruptly introduced, apparently having no logical link to the previous lines. The poet wishes to recall the vision he once had of an Abyssinian maid playing a musical instrument and singing. If he could have done so, he would have been able to recreate the pleasure-dome in the air, but he laments his inability to capture the lost vision. Finally, in the poem's last lines, Coleridge portrays the prophet-bard who was to become popular in the Romantic period and was seen as different from the common human beings for his prophetic qualities and capability to penetrate the divine.

The poem reflects the contemporary taste for the exotic, and there are several allusions to various mystic traditions involving exalted and trance states that are also conveyed by opium addiction. Coleridge offers a symbolic representation of the brief moment of vision, when the poet can see through the imagination into the real life of things. The heavenly dome can be considered the result of human artistic creation, a combination of the sacred and profane, of nature and artifice, a symbolic site where all opposites may be reconciled. The river Alph appears to be an appropriate image of the divine life force operative in the poet. Emerging out of the earth, out of the unconscious regions of the human mind, its flow signifies the visionary moment of human contact with the life force. However, its origin from an intermittent fountain stands for the discontinuous nature of poetic inspiration. In general terms, the wild and tumultuous part concerning the river's running evokes the process of creation. It hints at the deep recesses of the Romantic mind in a fit of powerful creation. The disappearance of the river thus indicates the end of vision, when humanity is again confronted with the world of external phenomena, with the world as a "lifeless ocean" (l. 28). The abrupt introduction of the new vision thereinafter becomes the starting point for a second poetic experience inasmuch as it recalls the heavenly dome, images of spiritual quiet and harmony, and a regained Paradise where all opposites may be unified. Yet the poet's inability to revive the harmonious whole created by the music of the maid becomes the ground for the thwarting of the Romantic genius, who is unlikely to render the prodigious act of poetic creation as a whole. This is one reading. Nevertheless, all interpretations of "Kubla Khan" are to some extent conjectural, and there is always ample room for disagreement and new proposals, which simply affirm the poem's Romantic, unbounded nature.

## Further Reading

Beer, John. *Coleridge, the Visionary.* London: Chatto & Windus, 1959.

Corti, Claudia. "Visionary Aesthetics and Opiate Texts in British Romanticism." In *Inspiration and Technique. Ancient to Modern Views on Beauty and Art,* edited by John Roe and Michele Stanco, 217–241. New York: Lang, 2007.

Lowes, John Livingstone. *The Road to Xanadu: A Study in the Ways of the Imagination.* Boston: Houghton Mifflin, 1927.

Milne, Fred. "Coleridge's 'Kubla Khan': A Metaphor for the Creative Process." *South Atlantic Review* 51, no. 4 (1986): 17–29.

—Valeria Pellis

# L

## "La Belle Dame Sans Merci" John Keats
(1820)

This famously stylized ballad poem was written during the last year of JOHN KEATS's life, when he already knew he was fatally ill. It was published posthumously in the *Indicator* on May 10, 1820, but the original—slightly different—version has been traced to a letter written by Keats to his brother George, dated April 21, 1819. The same letter also contains other well-known poems, including "To Sleep," "On Fame," and "ODE: TO PSYCHE." With exception of the last, Keats claimed that all the other s had been "dash'd of[f] . . . in a hurry" (quoted in Scott, 294).

The title of the poem comes from a poem by the medieval writer Alain Cartier and translates as "the beautiful lady without pity." It is written in imitation of a folk ballad in 12 short stanzas of four lines, where the second and fourth lines rhyme. The poem begins with an unnamed passerby meeting a knight who is "haggard" and "woe-begone" (l. 6) beside a woodland lake in late autumn. The passerby cannot see any reason for the knight's "loitering" (l. 2) in such a place; the grass "has wither'd / And no birds sing (ll. 3– ). Yet even so, not all life is extinct; the squirrel has stored his winter food, and the natural world continues (ll. 7–8). Thus, there is a suggestion of an alternative lifestyle that the knight could choose.

From his appearance, however, the knight, seems to be dying. In stanza 3 his pallor is compared to the whiteness of a lily (a symbol of death) and then to a rose (a symbol of beauty). The rose is "fading" and "fast withereth" (ll. 11–12). In stanzas 4–6 the knight describes what has happened. He explains that he has been in love with and deserted by a mysterious lady—"a faery's child" (l. 14). He ignores warning signs—the fact that she has "wild" eyes and that she gives him "wild" honey (ll. 16, 26). Instead, he set her on his horse, and she took him to her "elfin grot" (l. 29), where she "wept, and sigh'd full sore" (l. 30). He was entranced by her, while "she look'd at me as she did love" (l. 19), and he "nothing else saw" (l. 22). Gradually the knight becomes more passive and the lady more dominant. In stanza 9, we hear how she "lull'd" him to sleep and he "dream'd" (ll. 33–34). During his dream he had a vision of "pale kings and princes" (l. 37), seemingly powerful men who cried, "La Belle Dame sans Merci / hath thee in thrall!" (ll. 39–40). These were the woman's former lovers, now her slaves, and now he too was one of them. The knight woke to find himself on the same "cold hill's side" (l. 36) on which he must wait "palely loitering" (l. 46).

Because Keats is imitating the folk ballad, he uses simple language. Earlier, his poem *ENDYMION* had been criticized for its over-complex language, and so in the letter to his brother, Keats draws humorous attention to his restraint now: "Why four kisses—you will say—why four because I wish to restrain the headlong impetuosity of my Muse—she would fain have said 'score' without hurting the rhyme—but we must temper the Imagination as the Critics say with Judgment. I was obliged to choose an even number that both eyes might have fair play; and to speak truly I think two a piece quite sufficient—Suppose I had said seven; there would have been three and half a piece—a very awkward affair—and well got out of on my side" (Scott, 285).

"La Belle Dame" focuses on a single event, provides little elaborative detail, and offers no moral judgment. The details are a mixture of the realistic and the strange/supernatural, which helps to create a sense of mystery, something which the long long/stressed syllables at the ends of lines emphasize (for example "no birds sing" in lines 4 and 48). The love described in the poem seems to be deathly and the woman a femme fatale whose powers are destructive. Yet, paradoxically, the message seems to be that love is the reason for living, and it is this reading that has contributed to the popular image of Keats—and the Romantic poet generally—as a dreamer, someone for whom love is everything and who will suffer for love.

An alternative reading has been to start with the anonymous passerby and suggest that he is perhaps not as reliable a witness as he presents himself. Perhaps the knight is not really miserable? Is he really pale and haggard? Is there really a knight? Is the poem the speaker's hallucination? Is he unbalanced? A further way of interpreting the poem is to say that the lady and her powers represent enchantment or imagination. Her "song" represents art and the lady, symbolizing imagination, transports the knight (poet?) to an ideal world. The knight becomes caught up in the delights of the imagination ("and nothing else saw all day long" [l. 22]). But this kind of experience is transitory—man cannot only live on this single level. The knight's refusal to relinquish the pleasures of the imagination is self-destructive, and he can no longer function in the real world. Other questions to be asked are: What is the meaning of the knight's experience? What is the meaning of the dream? What happened to the knight's horse?

## Further Reading

Barnard, John. "Keats's Belle Dame and the Sexual Politics of Leigh Hunt's Indicator." *Romanticism: The Journal of Romantic Culture and Criticism* 1, no. 1 (1995): 34–49.

Blades, John. *John Keats: The Poems.* Basingstoke, Eng.: Palgrave, 2002.

Conti Camaiora, Luisa. "Keats's La Belle Dame sans Merci: The Story of Two Versions." *Anglistica Pisana* 2, nos. 1–2 (2005): 9–30.

Grant, John E. "Discovering 'La Belle Dame Sans Merci.' In *Approaches to Teaching Keats's Poetry,* edited by Walter H. Evert and Jack Rhodes, 45–50. New York: Modern Language Association of America, 1991.

Keats, John. *Selected Letters of John Keats.* Edited by Grant Scott. Cambridge: Harvard University Press, 2002.

Rankin-Handlang, Sandy. "Keats, Ecstasy and the Feminine Psyche." *Publications of the Arkansas Philological Association* 22, no. 1 (1996): 43–60.

Scott, Grant F. "Language Strange: A Visual History of Keats's 'La Belle Dame Sans Merci.'" *Studies in Romanticism* 38, no. 4 (1999): 503–535.

Weissman, Judith. "'Language Strange': 'La Belle Dame Sans Merci' and the Language of Nature." *Colby Library Quarterly* 16 (1980): 91–105.

—Tom Richardson

## Lake School

The writers comprising the so-called Lake School poets are usually said to be SAMUEL TAYLOR COLERIDGE (1772–1834), ROBERT SOUTHEY (1774–1843), and WILLIAM WORDSWORTH (1770–1850) although a female writer such as ISABELLA LICKBARROW (1784–1847) might also fall into this category. The three men knew each other extremely well, at times even living together, and sometimes critiquing each other's writing in private and in public. Coleridge and Southey first met at Oxford University in 1794. Attracted to each other's philosophical and political leanings, they became close friends and "sketched out the scheme of a society in which all possessions would be held in common and . . . all incentives to evil and unhappiness removed" (Perry 17). Coleridge created a term for this way of living: *pantisocracy.* Southey and Coleridge planned to take their new political ideas to America, specifically "'the banks of the Susquehannah' (in Pennsylvania)," where they would create a settlement and recruit others to their scheme (Perry 19). However, this never materialized, and eventually Coleridge had a falling-out with Southey over their different political agendas, though they still remained friends. Coleridge and Southey were also brothers-in-law, having married two sisters, Sara Fricker and Edith Fricker, respectively.

Coleridge and Southey first met Wordsworth in 1795. All three men liked each other immediately, but it would be Coleridge and Wordsworth who developed a more meaningful friendship over time. Coleridge was deeply attracted to Wordsworth's poetry and his ideas about nature. Wordsworth, in turn, found Coleridge to be an invaluable critic of his poetry. Along with DOROTHY WORDSWORTH, William's sister, Coleridge was his most intimate friend, one who believed Wordsworth to be "a very great man . . . the only man, to whom *at all times* & in *all modes* of excellence I feel myself inferior" (quoted in Perry 41). The close ties through politics, family, and poetry are what drew Coleridge, Southey, and Wordsworth together initially. Another important factor that drew these poets together and kept them associated with one another was their proximity to each other. All three resided in the Lake District in the northwest of England: "Wordsworth moved to the Lake District in December 1799; Coleridge followed in 1800; Southey arrived in September 1803" and stayed until he died in 1843 (Chandler 35). Living in the same region, an area that was considered wild and fairly uninhabitable at the time, contributed to the general perspective among reviewers of their work that there was something distinctly different about these three men.

In 1802 a writer for the *Edinburgh Review,* FRANCIS JEFFREY, is supposed to have first identified and attacked Coleridge, Southey, and Wordsworth as "Lake School" poets. Writers studying these poets have long claimed that Jeffrey's review, in which he examined Southey's poem *Thalaba* and Wordsworth and Coleridge's LYRICAL BALLADS, was the defining moment when a new school of poetry was named. However, it is unclear how this piece of "fact" was born because upon looking back at the review, there is no mention of "Lake School" or any sort of "Lake" reference. However, what we do know is that Jeffrey called this group "a *sect* of poets . . . *dissenters* from the established systems in poetry and criticism" and a "fraternity"

(quoted in Hickey 305). In 1807, however, Jeffrey did come somewhat nearer to an association of the Lake District and the poets who lived there when he wrote that "[Wordsworth] is known to belong to a certain brotherhood of poets, who have haunted for some years about the Lakes of Cumberland" (quoted in Chandler 35). In 1809 an anonymous writer in the *Satirist* proclaimed Coleridge, Southey, and Wordsworth "The Bards of the Lake," coming even closer still to the idea of a special group of poets particularly associated with a region in England. But it was not until 1816 that THOMAS MOORE used the term *Lake School* in a review of Coleridge's poem "CHRISTABEL."

Although Coleridge, Southey, and Wordsworth never thought of themselves as a group of similar writers, nor did they see themselves as a "school" of anything, critics have insisted on calling these three writers by such descriptions as Lakeland Poets, Lake Writers, Lake Poets, Lakers, Lake School, and the Lake School of Poetry. The term *Lake School,* originally used as a term of derision, has now come to represent to literary critics and readers alike a certain type of poetry that predominantly focuses on writing about the realism of nature and humanity. Instead of trying to tame or elevate nature, the Lake Poets wrote about nature from a new perspective, one that captured the details of the land around them and, especially, man's humble position in nature. An important component of the Lake School poetry was its tone, which had a conversational element to it. To critics who were used to the lofty poetry of JOHN MILTON or Alexander Pope, which elevated the poet and his voice to a godlike status, the poems written by Coleridge, Southey, and Wordsworth were predominantly about the common man or sometimes even simply about themselves.

The poetry of the Lake School was an attempt "to write about nature, emphasizing the romantic and the imaginative" and "to write about 'matter-of-fact' subjects" (Davies 102). Most reviewers found it uninteresting because the subjects were about everyday people and places. The first edition of *Lyrical Ballads* (1798), Coleridge and Wordsworth's collaboration, was slow to sell and in some ways proved disconcerting to reviewers and readers alike. In "WE ARE SEVEN" Wordsworth writes about a meeting with a little girl; the poem is very simple in its tone and subject matter. He writes, "I met a little cottage girl: / She was eight years old, she said; / Her hair was thick with many a curl / That clustered round her head (ll. 4–8); his language is simple and direct. In the second edition of *Lyrical Ballads* (1802), Wordsworth attempted to address the tone and style of the poems that had been criticized previously by reviewers. In the PREFACE TO *LYRICAL BALLADS*, he insisted that he was writing for the reader of "superior judgment" and that although he might have written in language that was "too familiar," readers should be aware that the poems were meant as experiments in language, style, and tone.

Ironically, the poets who elicited such negative reviews have become some of the most loved and revered by readers of Romantic poetry. Writing about nature and realistic scenes of peoples' lives has long been attributed to the genius of the Lake School poets. Coleridge, Southey, and Wordsworth were all interested in the human element of existence; for example, Coleridge wrote about his own opium addiction in his poem "Pains of Sleep" (1816). Moreover, he tried to capture the "universal motion of things in Nature": In one of his many notebooks in which he recorded his impressions of nature, he describes the movement of "Starlings in vast Flights, borne along like smoke, mist . . . still expanding, or contracting, thinning or condensing, now glimmering and shivering, now thickening, deepening, blackening!" (quoted in Perry 58). Coleridge shows the birds in flight as he *sees* them moving, not how he imagines them to be.

Southey, too, often began a poem with a sense of immediacy as if one was standing and looking at what he saw. In his poem "God's Judgment on a Wicked Bishop" (1799), he writes: "The summer and autumn had been so wet, / That in winter the corn was growing yet, / 'Twas a piteous sight to see all around / The rain lie rotting on the ground" (ll. 1–4). Like Coleridge and Wordsworth, Southey's focus is often on the reality of the moment and bringing the reader into the poet's vision of the world.

For the Lake School poets, the aim was to describe people and places as they were seen in the very moment that they were experienced—though they would later come to realize the difficulties of doing this as they revised, crafted, and revisited their poems. They were also interested in philosophical, political, and emotional ideas of their time, and it is for these reasons that their poetry remains a source of interest even to 21st century readers.

See also "PANTISOCRACY."

**Further Reading**

Cook, Peter A. "Chronology of the 'Lake School' Argument: Some Revisions." *Review of English Studies* 28, no. 110 (May 1977): 175–181.

Chandler, David. "The Early Development of the 'Lake School' Idea." *Notes and Queries* 52 March (2005): 35–37.

Davies, Hunter. *William Wordsworth*. London: Frances Lincoln Ltd., 2009.

Goldberg, Brian. *The Lake Poets and Professional Identity*. Cambridge: Cambridge University Press, 2007.

Hickey, Alison. "Coleridge, Southey, 'and Co.': Collaboration and Authority." *Studies in Romanticism* 37 (Autumn 1998): 305–349.

Madden, Lionel, ed. *Robert Southey: The Critical Heritage*. London: Routledge and Kegan. Paul, 1972.

Perry, Seamus. *Samuel Taylor Coleridge*. London: British Library, 2003.

—Barbara Tilley

## Lamartine, Alphonse-Marie-Louis de Prat de (1790–1869)

Alphonse de Lamartine is widely considered the father of French Romantic poetry. Building on the foundation laid by prose writers such as JEAN-JACQUES ROUSSEAU, Vicomte Chateaubriand, and MME. ANNE-LOUISE-GERMAINE DE STAËL, Lamartine breathed new life into France's rich poetic tradition, thereby wielding an incalculable influence on writers of his own generation as well as those to follow. First and foremost, however, he considered himself a statesman, and like the Roman orator Cicero, he wrote most of his works during times when he was unable to participate in politics. In Lamartine we find a striking conjunction of emotional and intellectual genius—one of those rare writers who have the chance as well as the ability to put their dreams and ideas into action.

Lamartine was born on October 21, 1790, one year into the FRENCH REVOLUTION, to a family of the lower aristocracy. Despite being of noble birth, he grew up in a rather modest home in Milly, a tiny village in the countryside of Burgundy. There he developed a deep connection with nature and a lifelong kinship with the common people. Due to his family's opposition to NAPOLEON BONAPARTE, Lamartine was prevented from pursuing a diplomatic career until the end of the emperor's reign. He thus spent this restless period reading, traveling, and composing his first attempts at verse and drama. In 1816, after years of poor health, he was sent by his family to the thermal baths at Aix-les-Bains. This sojourn would inspire his first and most enduring literary legacy. In the background lay nature, in the foreground a woman. Her name was Julie Charles, and the two connected immediately. When forced to part ways, they planned to meet again the following September, but while Lamartine returned, Julie was far too sick to travel. Knowing that she would not live much longer, Lamartine sat down on the banks of Lake Bourget, and his grief took form in the elegiac ode "The Lake" ("Le Lac").

Following Julie's death, Lamartine placed more attention on his poetry, which was well received in the Parisian salons. Though worried about the negative effect it could have on his career prospects, he published "The Lake," along with 23 other poems, in March 1820. The collection, entitled *Poetical Meditations (Méditations poétiques)*, made Lamartine, like LORD BYRON before him, a national sensation overnight. While highly indebted to the tradition of 18th-century verse, the *Meditations* helped usher in a new era of French poetry. The themes of love and life, suffering and hope—sung in a deeply personal and musical voice—moved his readers, instilling a sense of poetic enthusiasm that France had not witnessed in a long time.

Following this literary success, Lamartine secured the diplomatic post he had sought for years. He also married an Englishwoman named Marianne Birch, and together they had a son and daughter, neither of whom lived past childhood.

Over the next decade, as his career took him to Naples and Florence, he published a large number of literary works, including the *New Poetical Meditations* (1823), *The Death of Socrates* (1823), *The Last Canto of Childe Harold* (1825), and *Poetical and Religious Harmonies* (1830). While these works met with great success, none of them were considered equals to the first *Poetical Meditations.*

When the Bourbons were overthrown during the July Revolution of 1830, Lamartine retired from diplomacy in protest of Louis-Philippe's accession to power. Over the next few years he published a series of key texts on politics and poetics (*On Rational Politics*, 1831; *On the Destinies of Poetry*, 1834). He also made a long journey to the Middle East (1832–33), captured in his famous *Voyage in the Orient* (1835). Following his return, he accepted his nomination to the Chamber of Deputies, thus commencing an extraordinary career in national politics. Proving himself a master orator, Lamartine quickly became a predominant voice in the chamber, advancing a highly progressive social agenda that included extending suffrage and workers' rights, protecting orphans, advocating the separation of church and state, constructing the first railways, and fighting for the abolition of SLAVERY and the death penalty.

While away from Paris, Lamartine spent most of his time at his picturesque estates at Saint Point and Monceau in his native Burgundy. There he hosted many notable artists of the day, including VICTOR HUGO, George Sand, Franz Liszt, Frédéric Chopin, and Alfred de Musset. Motivated in part by financial troubles, Lamartine took time away from politics to write. The literary texts published in this period (*Jocelyn*, 1836; *The Fall of an Angel*, 1838; *Poetical Contemplations*, 1839) show a development in his religious, philosophical, and poetical thought. In 1847 one of his most famous works appeared: *The History of the Girondists (Histoire des Girondins)*, which examines the ideals and excesses of the first French Revolution. In addition to bringing Lamartine much acclaim, this historical study gave considerable impetus to the revolution of 1848.

During the tumultuous period of 1848, Lamartine served as minister of foreign affairs under the provisional government and essentially assumed the role of its leader. Several important laws were passed at this time—due in no small part to Lamartine's efforts—including the abolition of slavery and the adoption of universal suffrage. Yet despite his prodigious and celebrated efforts in the early months of the revolution, his popularity quickly waned, and this was punctuated by a landslide loss to Louis Napoleon in the presidential election. As Lamartine faded from the political spotlight, he turned his attention toward publishing historical studies and periodicals aimed at educating the newly sovereign people of France. He also found time to write several more literary texts, including his memoirs *The Confidential Disclosures* (*Confidences,* 1849), a play on Toussaint Louverture (1850), the semiautobiographical novels *Raphael* (1849) and *Graziella* (1852), and *The Stonemason of Saint Point* (1851), the last of which is a masterpiece of simplicity and profundity. Following Louis Napoleon's coup d'état in 1851, Lamartine formally retired from politics.

The final years of Lamartine's life were marked by financial troubles and a decline in popularity. No stranger to the suffering of a debtor and ever the optimist, he persevered and produced an incredible volume of writing. The most important work that dates from this period is his *Familiar Course in Literature,* a monthly periodical he published over the last 14 years of his life. Totaling more than 10,000 pages, the *Course* demonstrates the immense breadth of Lamartine's learning, his great capacity for insight, and his devotion to sharing with his fellow citizens the artistic and cultural heritage of Europe, Asia, America, and the Middle East. After a sharp decline in health, he died on February 28, 1869.

Lamartine's literary reputation steadily diminished over the course of his lifetime and has never seen a strong revival. Today, while he is universally recognized as a key figure in literary history, his writing—with few exceptions—is considered hackneyed and overly sentimental. The eclipse of Lamartine's star is intimately linked to the rise of modern modes of criticism, and it may be the case that, as literary theorists and critics reconsider the social, ethical, and spiritual dimensions of art, Lamartine's work will be esteemed not only for its historical significance but for its artistic quality as well.

**Further Reading**

Birkett, Mary Ellen. *Lamartine and the Poetics of Landscape.* Lexington, Ky.: French Forum, 1982.

Fortescue, William. *Alphonse de Lamartine: A Political Biography.* New York: St. Martin's Press, 1983.

Hillary, David. *Lamartine: The Méditations poétiques.* Durham: University of Durham, 1993.

Ireson, J. C. *Lamartine: A Revaluation.* Hull, Eng.: University of Hull, 1969.

Lamartine, Alphonse de. *Poetical Meditations/Méditations poétiques.* Translated by Gervase Hittle. New York: Edward Mellen Press, 1993.

———. *Jocelyn.* Translated by Hazel Patterson Stuart. New York: Exposition Press, 1954.

Lombard, Charles M. *Lamartine.* New York: Twayne, 1973.

Whitehouse, Remsen H. *The Life of Lamartine.* Boston: Houghton Mifflin, 1918.

—Peter J. Hutchings

## Lamb, Caroline (1785–1828)

Lady Caroline Lamb is perhaps most famous for her tempestuous affair with LORD BYRON in 1812, which inspired her roman à clef, GLENARVON. Until the late 20th century, Lamb had largely been viewed as a footnote in the life of Byron, and her role in Romantic literature had not been considered apart from her involvement with the poet. However, Lamb is also a fascinating figure in her own right, and her work raises important questions about authorship, fame, and feminism in the early 1800s.

Lamb was born Caroline Ponsonby on November 13, 1785, in London. She was the third child of Frederick Ponsonby, Viscount Duncannon, later the earl of Bessborough, and his wife, Henrietta Elizabeth Ponsonby. A member of the aristocracy, Caroline grew up in Devonshire House and became close to her mother's sister, Georgiana, duchess of Devonshire. In a household atmosphere that was generally liberal and free from restraint, Caroline was extremely well-educated and exhibited great aptitude for the arts and humanities at an early age. However, she was also prone to nervous illness, which intensified in her adolescence following a fever. Despite this, she was formally presented to society in 1802, when she was 17.

That year, Caroline met William Lamb, second son of Lord and Lady Melbourne, and she married him 1805. William was a Whig politician who would eventually become prime minister under Queen Victoria, though Caroline would not live to see this. The couple's life together was turbulent. After two miscarriages, Caroline produced a son, Augustus, who was mentally disabled. She and William fought often and both had extramarital affairs. Then, in 1812, just after the publication of CHILDE HAROLD'S PILGRIMAGE, Caroline met Byron, and the two began a very public, though short-lived, affair. By September of the same year, Byron had moved on to Lady Oxford, once Caroline's good friend, but Caroline continued to cling madly to the poet. Before the year was over, her family dragged her to their estates in Ireland in an effort to prevent further embarrassment. While there, she wrote Byron scandalous letters. The biggest scandal of all, however, was the 1816 publication of *Glenarvon*. The book was widely read and enormously popular, though Caroline herself was shunned by virtually everyone she knew.

Caroline continued to write, publishing *Don Juan: A New Canto* (1819) and *Gordon: A Tale* (1821), both having to do, in one way or another, with Byron. She also produced two more novels, *Graham Hamilton* (1822) and *Ada Reis* (1823). In 1824 she was again confronted with Byron when she unwittingly encountered his funeral procession near her home. She never wrote again. By 1827 her health had severely declined and she was under the care of a full-time physician. Though she and William had officially separated, he returned from overseas to be at her side when she died on January 25, 1828.

## Further Reading

Cass, Jeffrey. "Irish Girls Gone Wild: *Glenarvon*, Regency Hypocrisy, and Spartan Virtue." *CEA Critic* 68, nos. 1–2 (Fall 2005–Winter 2006): 126–138.

Douglass, Paul. *Lady Caroline Lamb: A Biography.* New York: Palgrave Macmillan, 2004.

Lamb, Caroline, Lady. *Glenarvon.* Edited by Frances Wilson. London: Everyman Paperback Classics, 1995.

Soderholm, James. *Fantasy, Forgery and the Byron Legend.* Lexington: University Press of Kentucky, 1996.

Wilson, Frances. "'An Exaggerated Woman': The Melodramas of Lady Caroline Lamb." In *Byromania: Portraits of the Artist in Nineteenth- and Twentieth-Century Culture,* edited by Frances Wilson, 195–220. New York: St. Martin's Press, 1999.

———. *Literary Seductions: Compulsive Writers and Diverted Readers.* New York: St. Martin's Press, 2000.

—Diana Koretsky

## Lamb, Charles (1775–1834)

An essayist, critic, and occasional poet, Charles Lamb is best known for his collection of essays, ESSAYS OF ELIA, and for his collaborative work with his sister, MARY LAMB, on the children's volume *Tales from Shakespeare.* Born in London on February 10, 1775, Lamb was educated at Christ's Hospital, where he met and befriended the future poet SAMUEL TAYLOR COLERIDGE. Upon leaving school and after a short stint as a clerk in an examiner's office, he obtained a position as a clerk for the East India Company, where he worked for the next 33 years. Hereditary insanity, now commonly believed to have been a form of bipolar disorder, ran on his father's side of the family, and at the age of 20 Lamb suffered his first instance of insanity and spent six weeks in an asylum. His sister Mary also suffered from the disease, and in significantly greater fashion. A year after Lamb's own bout with insanity, Mary suffered a breakdown during which she murdered their mother with a kitchen knife. This incident had a profound impact on Lamb, who had Mary remanded to his own care following a year in the asylum, and he subsequently spent the rest of his life caring for her. The need for financial security in order to support them both during periods of wellness and to pay for treatment during Mary's insane spells forced Lamb to remain in his position with the East India Company rather than devoting himself to writing full-time, and his sense of responsibility concerning his sister's care prevented him from marrying and setting up a home of his own. He and his sister did, however, adopt a daughter, Emma Isola, and befriended a wide circle of influential writers and thinkers, which led to his second career as a popular essayist.

Despite his own depression and corresponding alcoholism, his constant concern for his sister, and the many hardships they faced as a result of their hereditary disorder and financial straits, Lamb as a person was widely respected and admired. His friendship with men such as Coleridge, WILLIAM HAZLITT, LEIGH HUNT, and WILLIAM WORDSWORTH not only afforded him a degree of normalcy and camaraderie in an otherwise difficult life—it also provided him with the opportunity to write and publish his own work. Four of Lamb's sonnets appeared in Coleridge's first publication, the 1796 *Poems on Various Subjects.* From there he went on to publish a romance, *A Tale of Rosamund Gray,* as well as several poems in a collaborative effort with his friend Charles Lloyd, entitled *Blank Verse.* These early poetic efforts met with little success, however, and it is his collaborative effort with his sister, the 1807 publication *Tales from Shakespeare,* that gave Lamb his first real success as a writer. The prose retelling of Shakespeare's plays for children, for which Lamb wrote out the tragedies and his sister the comedies, was so popular that it led to his reworking of Homer's *The Odyssey,* the 1808 *Adventures of Ulysses.* It was in 1808 as well that Lamb expanded his writing career by taking on the task of editing an anthology entitled *Specimens of the English Dramatic Poets Who Lived about the Time of Shakespeare.* His critical work in this anthology was well-received, and he subsequently published numerous critical essays in newspapers such as Leigh Hunt's *Reflector.*

Although his writings for children provided his early success as a writer and his critical work was widely admired, it was Lamb's series of familiar essays, written for the *London Magazine* between 1820 and 1825 under the pseudonym Elia (a name taken from one of his early coworkers at the examiner's office), that led to his widespread popularity as a writer. Later published in two volumes, *Essays of Elia* and *The Last Essays of Elia* dealt with Lamb's own experiences, thoughts, and emotions concerning all aspects of his life. He wrote about his childhood, his friends and relations, literature and the theater, the behaviors of men and women, and his own retirement from the East India Company, among many other topics. These essays were funny, intimate, and stylish, and they sealed Lamb's reputation as a writer. Observations such as "The human species, according to the best theory I can form of it, is composed of two distinct races, the men who borrow and the men who lend" ("The Two Races of Men") demonstrate his powers of observation concerning general human traits, while statements like "Lawyers, I suppose, were children once" ("The Old Benchers of the Inner Temple") and "I have been trying all my life to like Scotchmen, and am obliged to desist from the experiment in despair" ("Imperfect Sympathies") speak to his own prejudices and those prevalent in the London of his time. Further, his self-deprecating tone in statements like "Books think for me" ("Detached Thoughts on Books and Reading") and "Sentimentally I am disposed to harmony; but organically I am incapable of a tune" ("A Chapter on Ears") render the essays both funny and deeply human. In style, form, and substance the *Essays of Elia* continue to be regarded as among the best examples of English essay writing available for study.

In addition to *Tales from Shakespeare, The Adventures of Ulysses, Essays of Elia,* and his critical and poetic work, Lamb kept up a copious correspondence with friends such as Coleridge, Hazlitt, Wordsworth, and ROBERT SOUTHEY, and his letters display the same self-deprecating tone, stylish flair, and penchant for humor found in his published works. In one letter to Coleridge following a description of him written by the poet, Lamb famously wrote: "For God's sake, don't make me ridiculous any more by terming me gentle-hearted in print. . . . Please to blot out *gentle hearted,* and substitute drunken dog, ragged head, self-shaven, odd-ey'd, stuttering, or any other epithet which truly and properly belongs to the Gentleman in question" (letter of August 14, 1800, in Lamb 1903, I, 143). It is this combined sense of humor and humility for which Charles Lamb—who died on December 27, 1834—continues to be appreciated today.

**Further Reading**

Barnett, George Leonard. *Charles Lamb: The Evolution of Elia.* Bloomington: Indiana University Press, 1964.

Blunden, Edmund, *Charles Lamb: His Life Recorded by His Contemporaries.* Philadelphia: R. West, 1977.

Lamb, Charles. *The Essays of Elia.* Iowa City: University
    of Iowa Press, 2003.
———. *Letters of Charles Lamb, Vol. 1 & 2.* Edited by
    William Macdonald. New York: E. P. Dutton & Co.,
    1903.
———. *Selected Writings.* New York: Routledge, 2003.
Lamb, Charles, and Mary Lamb. *Tales from Shakespeare.*
    London: Wordsworth Editions, 1994.
Prance, Charles A. *Companion to Charles Lamb: A Guide
    to People and Places, 1760–1847.* London: Mansell,
    1983.

—Melissa A. Elmes

## Lamb, Mary (Mary Anne Lamb) (1764–1847)

Born on December 3, 1764, Mary Anne Lamb was
the older sister of the poet and essayist CHARLES
LAMB. Although she was an avid reader, she had
little formal schooling, and until she was 31 she
worked from home as a seamstress in order to
support and care for her invalid mother. Like her
brother, Mary seems to have suffered from bipolar
disorder, and in 1796, during one of her bouts of
insanity, she fatally stabbed their mother with a
kitchen knife. She was never tried for the murder
but was pronounced insane by a coroner's court
and confined to a madhouse for a year, after which
she was released into her brother's care and sent
to live with a caretaker. After the death of their
father in 1799, Mary came to live permanently
with Charles. With the exception of short periods
of insanity during which she resided in asylums, she
spent the rest of her life in the care of her younger
brother, a situation that profoundly impacted
Charles's life, causing him to forego plans to marry
and to continue to hold a position as a clerk at the
East India Company in lieu of pursuing a formal
writing career in order to support his sister.

In 1806 WILLIAM GODWIN, the widower of
MARY WOLLSTONECRAFT, asked Charles Lamb
to write a volume for a juvenile literature series
he was publishing. Working together, Charles and
Mary Lamb penned *Tales from Shakespeare,* a prose
retelling of Shakespeare's plays, with Charles writing out the tragedies and Mary the comedies. Mary
went on in 1808 to write *Mrs. Leicester's School,* an
epistolary novel (see EPISTOLARY FICTION) consist-

ing of letters written by fictional orphaned girls and
centering around Mary's own issues of grief and
loss. Her friend and fellow writer SAMUEL TAYLOR
COLERIDGE praised her book as a lasting contribution to English literature. Although *Mrs. Leicester's
School* never obtained the lasting status of an English classic foretold by Coleridge, *Tales from Shakespeare* continues to be popular with children and is
still in print today.

In 1823 Mary and Charles adopted an
orphaned girl, Emma Isola, and Mary began a
private class in their home for Emma, WILLIAM
HAZLITT's son, and a second girl, Mary Victoria
Novello, teaching the children Latin and reading to them from *Tales from Shakespeare.* Her love
of literature had a lasting influence on her pupils.
Emma married Edward Moxon, a publisher and
poet, in 1833, while Mary Victoria published a
*Concordance to Shakespeare* in 1844, influenced
strongly by the Lambs' *Tales from Shakespeare.*

Upon Charles's death in 1834, Mary's mental
health worsened, and she lived in and out of mental institutions for the remainder of her life. She
died on May 20, 1847, and was buried next to her
brother at All Saints' Church, Edmonton, London. Modern scholarship on Mary Lamb tends to
focus on her involvement with her brother's circle
of friends, which included Coleridge, Hazlitt, and
LEIGH HUNT, and on her insanity and its effects on
her own writing and that of her brother.

### Further Reading

Lamb, Charles and Mary Lamb. *The Letters of Charles
    and Mary Anne Lamb.* Edited by Edwin W. Mars.
    New York: Cornell University Press, 1975.
———. *Tales from Shakespeare.* London: Wordsworth
    Editions, 1994.
Watson, Kathy. *The Devil Kissed Her: The Story of Mary
    Lamb.* New York: Penguin Group, 2004.

—Melissa A. Elmes

## "Lamia" John Keats (1819)

Written in 1819, "Lamia" is the last of JOHN
KEATS's narrative poems and was included in his
second collection of poetry published in 1820.
The opening poem of *Lamia, Isabella, and The Eve*

*of St. Agnes,* it was received with enthusiasm as "decidedly the best" (*Eclectic Review,* 1820, 163).

"Lamia" is based on an anecdote Keats took from Robert Burton's *Anatomy of Melancholy* (1660), itself drawing on *De Vita Apollonii* by Philostratus (ca. A.D. 170–247). It centers, as do the two previous texts, on the love story between a young philosopher and a beautiful enchantress, or lamia. In Keats's poem, however, the earlier stories are significantly transformed. While in Burton, as well as in Philostratus, the lamia-woman is clearly branded as "evil," in Keats the valuations become more ambiguous. As Keats links the story with his habitual themes of beauty, the imagination and the confusing interdependence of dream and reality, its moral judgment becomes uncertain.

Keats's version of the love story between Lycius and Lamia opens with a mythological first part in which the classical Greek god Hermes encounters Lamia in the form of a serpent and metamorphoses her into a beautiful woman. As a fair gentlewoman, Lamia then meets Lycius, a young philosopher from Corinth, who falls in love with her. Both retreat to a fairy palace which Lamia conjures up in Corinth, invisible to and sheltered from the outside world. Lycius, however, yearns to make their love public and begs Lamia to marry him in great ceremony. At their wedding feast, the old philosopher Apollonius appears uninvited and, with his cold and rational gaze, names Lamia a serpent, thus exposing her and destroying the illusion of the fairy woman; Lycius dies of grief.

Throughout the poem, Lamia is associated with positive romantic values such as the imaginary and beautiful, clearly contrasted by the cold rationality of the philosopher and the outside reality. The struggle between these opposites recalls themes familiar from Keats's "LA BELLE DAME SANS MERCI:" the gap between real and ideal becomes insurmountable as beauty and the imagination, embodied in the figure of the female love object or FEMME FATALE, are increasingly seen as something dreamlike and elusive and remain incompatible with reality. In both poems, beauty no longer reliably references eternal truth as in "ODE ON A GRECIAN URN's" famous "Beauty is truth, truth beauty." In "Lamia" it is the "cold philosophy" of Apollonius that gains the upper hand

over the imaginary beautiful that Lamia and Lycius create. At the same time, "Lamia" brings to mind poems such as THOMAS LOVE PEACOCK's "Rhododaphne": As Lamia hovers between enchantress figure and positive ideal, the moral valuations are increasingly uncertain, and the whole poem remains steeped in ambiguity as to where the reader's sympathies should lie.

**Further Reading**

Anon. "Keats's 'Lamia,' 'Isabella' and Other Poems." *Eclectic Review* 4 (1820): 158–171.

Cox, Jeffrey. "'Lamia,' 'Isabella,' and 'The Eve of St. Agnes.'" In *The Cambridge Companion to Keats,* edited by Susan J. Wolfson, 53–68. Cambridge: Cambridge University Press, 2001.

Keats, John. *'Lamia,' 'Isabella,' 'The Eve of St. Agnes,' and Other Poems.* 1820. Reprint, Otley, Eng.: Woodstock, 2001.

Strachan, John, ed. *A Routledge Literary Sourcebook on the Poems of John Keats.* London: Routledge. 2003.

—Andrea Rummel

## Landon, Letitia Elizabeth (L. E. L.) (1802–1838)

Born in Chelsea, London, on August 14, 1802, Letitia Elizabeth Landon was the first of three children of John Landon, a retired navy midshipman and an army agent, and Catherine Jane Bishop Landon. Like much of Landon's life, details about her childhood are sketchy, though we know she began attending day school at five years old, when she began her studies of literature and French. When she was seven, Landon's family moved to a country house at Trevor Park in East Barnet, where her cousin Elizabeth oversaw her education, which Letitia supplemented with her own reading in Homer, Petrarch, and, her particular favorite, SIR WALTER SCOTT. Financial problems forced the Landons to move to a smaller home in London in 1814 and again in 1816. Always a voracious reader, the young Landon turned her attention to writing, an action her parents approved of, in the hope that their daughter's work could supplement the family income. In 1820 William Jerdan, a family neighbor and editor of the *Literary Gazette,* published

Landon's poem "Rome," under the initial *L*. The first effort was succeeded by several others—and Landon's lyrics—or, as Jerdan termed them, "Poetical Sketches" (now published under "L.E.L.")—in turn inspired a host of admiring poems addressed to the writer, who, Jerdan claimed (falsely) was "yet in her teens!"

Landon's first lengthy effort, *The Fate of Adelaide, a Swiss Romantic Tale; and Other Poems*, appeared in August 1821, but in spite of garnering good reviews and sales, the book failed to earn money for the writer and her family as the publisher went bankrupt shortly after the volume's debut. She persevered nevertheless, and although her second book, *The Improvisatrice and Other Poems*, met with several rejections before Hurst and Robinson finally published it in July 1824, it was an immediate, staggering success, earning the writer £300 and going through six editions in the first year alone. L.E.L.'s star was on the rise.

Landon's publishing success could not have come at a better time for her family. Her father's unexpected death in 1824 left the poet the sole breadwinner for her household, which still included her mother and brother (her younger sister had died at the age of 13). Jerdan encouraged her continued involvement in the *Literary Gazette*; in addition to poems, Landon contributed book reviews and essays, eventually serving as head literary reviewer. But it was the appearance of her second volume, *The Troubadour, Catalogue of Pictures and Historical Sketches*, in July 1825 that cemented her literary and popular standing, going through four editions and earning the writer £600. The following year her third volume of poetry, *The Golden Violet, with its Tales of Romance and Chivalry; and Other Poems*, was published to wide sales. Throughout these years, Landon continued to contribute her work to the *Gazette* as well as to ANNUALS AND GIFT BOOKS, outlets critics have speculated that were particularly appropriate given her most popular subjects and images.

Those subjects, as the titles of her early volumes attest, were generally young women, often artists, and their unfortunate experiences with love, which nearly invariably led to tragedy, most often their own death. Combined with Landon's style, which she claimed was spontaneous and effusive, and her verse form of choice (usually couplets, some more metrical than others), critics and her more general audience were quick to associate the poet with her literary creations. Jerdan and Landon encouraged the association, marketing the poet as LORD BYRON's young feminine heir. However, as her new works continued to trace the same territory (often haunted by the same flowers, moonlight, and tears), Landon's critical reputation suffered. Her detractors accused her first promoter of puffery and, later, worse sins, including his seduction of the young poetess. In print, Landon and her allies rallied to her defense, claiming that single, poor, and therefore unprotected, she had no choice but to suffer such slanderous accusations.

Nevertheless, Landon's poetic subjects continued to focus on the tragic consequences of love, though her 1829 collection, *The Venetian Bracelet, The Lost Pleiad, a History of the Lyre, and Other Poems*, exhibited a marked sophistication in tone and perspective that distinguished this later work from her earlier productions. In the 1830s she wrote poems for at least 15 annuals and edited two, *Fishers Drawing Room Scrap Book* (1832–39) and *Heath's Book of Beauty* (1833).

Her private life was no less full. Surprising to her contemporaries, Landon had moved away from her mother's home in 1826 and chosen to live by herself, in spite of continuing to support her family financially. Even more indecorous were her relationships with Jerdan, the artist Daniel Maclise, the novelist and politician Edward Bulwer-Lytton, and the journalist and publisher William Maginn. Publicly, Landon and her admirers described all of these friendships as platonic, though scandalous rumors, undoubtedly based in part on her chosen subject matter, continued to circulate. Personal disaster apparently struck her in 1834 when she became engaged to John Forster, the friend and future biographer of Charles Dickens. He confronted her about her relationship with the married Maginn, and although Landon maintained her innocence, she broke off their engagement. That same year witnessed the publication of her second novel, *Francesca Carrara*, which followed the earlier three-volume *Romance and Reality* (1831). Though Landon's silver-fork novels were popular among both her established audience and critics, they were soon all but forgotten, including during the rediscovery of her works in the 1990s, which focused on her poetry. However, F. J. Sypher's recent reissuing of Landon's novels may lead to a more complete scholarly reappraisal of the writer. The complexity and acerbic wit of these books and her final *Ethel Churchill* (1837) offer another perspective on the reigning feminine "poetess." Her work—which spans poetry, novels, literary essays, and reviews—and the different voices she adopts depending on form and audience (sentimental, sharp, educated, and erudite) is anything but one-dimensional. She continued to explore diverse genres as well, publishing her sixth collection of poetry, *The Vow of the Peacock and Other Poems,* in 1835 and *Traits and Trials of Early Life,* stories for children that may or may not have been autobiographical, in 1836.

That year Landon met George Maclean, the governor of Cape Coast Castle, a major English outpost on the Gold Coast of West Africa (contemporary Ghana). They became engaged in December, though rumors about both Maclean's and Landon's prior indiscretions circulated. Apparently either coming to a mutual agreement or dismissing the gossip about Landon's affairs with married men and Maclean's "native" African mistress, the two married in June 1838. One month later they left England for Africa, arriving at Cape Coast Castle in August. Just two months later, Landon died of an overdose of prussic acid, and although the inquest termed her death "accidental," rumors of her suicide or murder have continued to persist to this day. Her play *The Triumph of Lucca* was published posthumously.

If rumors about Landon's death led a dimension of intrigue to the recovery of her work in the 1990s, Cynthia Lawford published an even more surprising addendum to the poet's biography in *The London Review of Books* in 2000. Landon, Lawford relayed, had had at least three children out of wedlock; William Jerdan, her initial admirer and publisher, 20 years her senior, had fathered them between 1822 and 1829. Lawford speculated that Landon's two daughters and son never lived with either of their parents but were well aware of their genealogy and in correspondence with their father if not their mother. Because so much of the recov-

ery of Landon's work in the 1990s was based on the perception of her as a wrongly accused innocent adrift in London (the image she herself promoted), the impact of Lawford's unearthing of this aspect Landon's life is yet to be measured. At the very least, it shows the dangers of reading a writer's work autobiographically or with the assumption that a work—or even a body of work—will reveal a writer's complete story.

See also "FACTORY, THE"; *IMPROVISA-TRICE, THE;* "STANZAS ON THE DEATH OF MRS. HEMANS."

**Further Reading**

Landon, Letitia Elizabeth. *Letitia Elizabeth Landon: Selected Writings.* Edited by Jerome McGann and Daniel Riess. Peterborough, Ont.: Broadview Press, 1997.

Lawford, Cynthia. "Thou Shalt Bid Thy Fair Hands Rove: L.E.L.'s Wooing of Sex, Pain, Death and the Editor." *Romanticism on the Net: An Electronic Journal Devoted to Romantic Studies* 29–30 (2003). Available online. URL: http://www.erudit.org/revue/ron/2003/v/n29/index.html. Accessed on June 30, 2008.

Lootens, Tricia. "Receiving the Legend, Rethinking the Writer: Letitia Landon and the Poetess Tradition." In *Romanticism and Women Poets: Opening the Doors of Reception,* edited by Harriet Kramer Linkin and Stephen C. Behrendt, 242–259. Lexington: University Press of Kentucky, 1999.

Stephenson, Glennis. *Letitia Landon: The Woman Behind L.E.L.* Manchester, Eng.: Manchester University Press, 1995.

Sypher, F. J. *Letitia Elizabeth Landon: A Biography.* Ann Arbor, Mich.: Scholars' Facsimiles and Reprints, 2004.

—Katherine Montwieler

## Landor, Walter Savage (1775–1864)

A poet and essayist, Walter Savage Landor was born on January 30, 1775, in Warwick, England, the eldest son of Walter Landor, a doctor, and his second wife, Elizabeth Savage Landor. The family was wealthy (Elizabeth Savage was an heiress), but their son quickly established himself as unconventional and rebellious. In 1793 he enrolled at Oxford University where he was considered a "mad" revolutionary because his hair was unpowdered. Argumentative and quarrelsome, he was expelled in 1794 for shooting another student. After an affair with a Welsh woman, Nancy Jones, with whom he fathered an illegitimate child, Landor quarreled with his father. The year 1795 saw the publication of *The Poems of Walter Savage Landor,* and, in pamphlet form, the anonymous *A Moral Epistle.* It was in 1796, while staying on the Welsh Coast that Landor met 17-year old Rose Aylmer, the inspiration for his later poem "ROSE AYLMER" (1806). But the poem that made his reputation was "Gebir" (1798), based on the story of Charoba, queen of Egypt.

Landor tried his hand at journalism, getting a position on *Morning Chronicle,* but he did not stick at it, and in 1808 he attempted to raise a regiment to fight NAPOLEON BONAPARTE in Spain. This failed, and it depleted his considerable inheritance. He had already squandered vast sums trying to renovate Llanthony Abbey, his property in Wales. Advised to marry, he chose Julia Thuillier, the daughter of a bankrupt Swiss banker. The couple moved abroad, living variously in France and then Italy, where Landor remained until 1829, when he left his family and returned to England.

By this time Landor's literary career had begun to take off. His tragedy *Count Julian* (1812) had been much admired, and he was an expert classicist, having produced numerous poems modeled on classical Greek and Roman works. Other shorter poems were also popular, the best known of which are perhaps "Ianthe" (1831) and "The Maid's Lament" (1834). His greatest, success, however was his series of essays entitled *Imaginary Conversations* (1824–29), which imagined conversations between historical figures, including Henry VIII and Anne Boleyn (in which Anne protests her innocence), Leofric and his wife Godiva (who also justifies her actions), and Lord Brooke and Sir Philip Sidney, as well as classical figures, such as the statesman Pericles and playwright Sophocles. As Landor himself explained: "When I was younger . . . [a]mong the chief pleasures of my life, and among the commonest of my occupations, was the bringing before me such heroes and heroines of

antiquity, such poets and sages, such of the prosperous and unfortunate as most interested me . . . [and e]ngaging them in conversations best suited to their characters" (I, vi). The collection helped establish Landor as one of the leading essayists of the age, and for much of the 19th century he was held in high regard by those like his friends ROBERT SOUTHEY and Charles Dickens, who could overlook his bad temper and irascible nature. Critically, he was much admired. To C. H. Herford, in 1897, it appeared that "Landor was . . . on the whole the greatest prose-writer of the age of Wordsworth; and, after Wordsworth, Coleridge, Byron, Shelley and Keats, he was its greatest poet" (Herford 283). Nowadays Landor is no longer regarded as a "major" figure, but he was clearly a dynamic man and an experimental writer.

Landor's final years were sad ones. He fell out with his children, to whom he had already gifted their inheritance, and, virtually penniless, he was cared for in Italy by Robert Browning. He died there on September 17, 1864.

**Further Reading**

Herford, C. H. *The Age of Wordsworth.* London: J. Hales, 1897.

Landor, Walter Savage. *Selected Poetry of Walter Savage Landor (1775–1864).* Representative Poetry Online. Available online. URL: http://rpo.library.utoronto.ca/poet/193.html. Accessed on July 22, 2009.

*Imaginary Conversations.* 2 vols. London: Taylor, 1824/1829.

Super, R. H. *Walter Savage Landor: A Biography.* Westport, Conn.: Greenwood Press, 1954.

—Tom Matthias

## *Last Man, The* Mary Wollstonecraft Shelley (1826)

Published in 1826, MARY WOLLSTONECRAFT SHELLEY's three-volume novel *The Last Man* is part of an apocalyptic strand in late Romantic culture which, in the wake of LORD BYRON's poem 'Darkness' (1816) and culminating in John Martin's monumental painting *The Last Man* (1849), focused on mankind's extinction and on the dilapidation of the civilized world.

Although there is no denying that there are strong autobiographical references in the text, the novel cannot be dismissed as a simple roman à clef or "study of grief" (Stafford 224) motivated by the death of the author's husband. Conceived of as a manuscript found in "the murky subterranean passages" (Shelley 3) of the Cumaean Sibyl's Cave, the preface to the novel stresses the mantic (prophetic) quality of Romantic literature. But in contrast to PERCY BYSSHE SHELLEY's image in "Ode to the West Wind" (1820) of the poet as the "trumpet of a new prophecy" (69), *The Last Man* shuns all affiliations with Romantic millenarianism and, instead, gives a dystopian view of the world in the remote period from 2073 to the beginning of the 22nd century.

From the perspective of the novel's first-person narrator Lionel Verney, initially an uncouth and vindictive pariah, we learn that England has lost its monarchy and that the lawful successor to the throne, Adrian, has retired to Windsor to lead a life in pastoral seclusion. Meant to be an idealized portrait of Shelley, Adrian is invested with Christological qualities, in particular when he humanizes Verney and "touches [his] rocky heart with his magic power" (28). Although Lord Raymond, a Faustian character and philhellenist modeled on Byron, brings the state close to civil war by challenging "the commercial spirit of republicanism" (61) with his ideas of leadership, the first part of the novel revolves around a five-year idyll of peace and matrimonial harmony and, thus, nostalgically conjures up notions of Shakespearean Arcadia. As if adopting Byron's poetic method of creating paradisiacal places only to destroy them afterwards, Shelley depicts this spell of Arcadian beauty only to subject it to ruthless deconstruction. Haunted by "presentiment[s] of ill" (93), Perdita, a character ironically evocative of the female protagonist in Shakespeare's *The Winter's Tale,* is the first to sense that the idyllic situation is ephemeral and that loss and deprivation will soon be paramount. While idealists like Adrian still revel in ideas of "an universal spring" (220), the news of the plague spreading from the east suddenly confronts the community of late 21st-century Romantics with the pervasiveness of death. At first confined to Constantinople, the infection reaches London in 2094 and brings about not only the dissolution of time-honored patterns of order, but also a riotous form of hedonism that makes people "banish thought and opiate despair" (278).

In anticipation of modern man in T. S. Eliot's "The Waste Land," people at first begin to dread spring—the plague being "the companion of spring, of sunshine, and plenty" (316)—and to long for the icy stagnation of winter. But when the "mower's scythe" (284) is heard everywhere, and death even disrupts performances in the theater or in Westminster Abbey, Adrian's advice is eventually acted upon, and a group of Ahasuerian wanderers embarks on "a bitter, joyless, hopeless pilgrimage" (361). This dead-end voyage shows to what extent John Bunyan's 17th-century idea of life as a religious journey has been replaced by the image of man erratically and vainly flying from the horrors of mortality. No matter how quickly they proceed to the South, the plague as an elemental force of arbitrary destruction is omnipresent: Even the sublimity of "the glorious Alps" (419), once the Romantic epitome of soul-expanding grandeur, is now one of the hotbeds of disease and consequently seen in terms of a backdrop to the spectacular twilight of humankind, the "fitting costume to our last act" (425). When the plague comes to an abrupt end, the loneliness of the last four survivors blatantly contrasts with the deserted cultural riches of Rome, Venice, and Greece. In order to intensify Verney's isolation and to show the ruthlessness of man's fate, he is eventually compelled to put up with the loss of his companions in a shipwreck episode, which, in the end, leaves him as "that monarch of the waste—Robinson Crusoe" (448).

Having been deprived both of his fellow creatures and of the readers of his apocalyptic chronicle, the first-person narrator is not only meant to reduce WILLIAM WORDSWORTH's "bliss of solitude" ("Daffodils," 1804) to absurdity, he is also instrumental in deconstructing the Keatsian belief in the longevity of art. Compared to JOHN KEATS's notion of art as an everlasting "friend to man" ("ODE ON A GRECIAN URN," 1819) Mary Shelley's novel stresses the meaninglessness of all arts, when, in the face of the total annihilation of humankind, the last man in the world selects a few books by Homer and Shakespeare but forms "no expectation of alteration for the better" (469).

## Further Reading

Lennartz, Norbert. "Apocalyptic Voices: Mary Shelley's The Last Man and the Romantic Idea of Decadence." In *Romantic Voices, Romantic Poetics: Selected Papers from the Regensburg Conference of the German Society for English Romanticism,* edited by Christoph Bode and Katharina Rennhak, 167–176. Trier, Ger.: WVT, 2005.

Mellor, Anne K. *Mary Shelley: Her Life, Her Fiction, Her Monsters.* New York: Routledge, 1989.

Paley, Morton D. 'The Last Man: Apocalypse without Millennium.' In *The Other Mary Shelley: Beyond Frankenstein,* edited by Audrey A. Fisch, Anne K. Mellor, and Esther H. Schor, 107–123. New York: Oxford University Press, 1993.

Shelley, Mary. *The Last Man.* Oxford: Oxford University Press, 1998.

Stafford, Fiona. *The Last of the Race: The Growth of a Myth from Milton to Darwin.* Oxford: Clarendon, 1997.

—Norbert Lennartz

## "Last Song of Sappho, The"  Felicia Hemans
## (1831)

One of FELICIA HEMANS's late poems, published in *Blackwood's Edinburgh Magazine* (January 1831) and reprinted in *National Lyrics and Songs for Music* (1834), "The Last Song of Sappho" documents the tragic story of the ancient Greek poet Sappho, whose fame persisted in spite of most of her poems being lost. In his *Epistles,* to Roman poet Ovid (43 B.C.–ca. A.D. 17) documented her story of unrequited love for the boatman Phaon, which ended in Sappho's suicide. Hemans editor Susan J. Wolfson also lists some Romantic writers, including HME. ANNE-LOUISE-GERMAINE DE STAËL, LETITIA ELIZABETH LANDON and MARY ROBINSON, whose works expressed the popular interest in Saphho's anguish (Hemans 2000, 465)—for example, Robinson's SAPPHO AND PHAON.

Intrigued with this story, Hemans adopts Sappho's persona to describe her agony moments before her suicide. Hemans identifies with Sappho's plight, suggesting Hemans's depression caused by her mother's death in 1827 and her own increasing illness, which, according to Gary Kelly, rendered her "virtually an invalid" by the following year

(Hemans 2002, 88). Hemans' semiautobiographic hints return at the poem's end with Sappho's hope of reunion with her loved ones upon her death. The poem also describes the plight of female genius that paradoxically victimized women given the 19th-century conservative ideals limiting and discouraging female outlets. Thus, genius turned into a weapon that marked such women as outsiders and deprived them of emotional satisfaction.

Like other Romantic writers who sought relief from their agonies in turning to natural elements, Hemans's Sappho turns for emotional and physical relief to the "dark, unslumbering sea" (ll. 1, 13). She identifies with the sea's roaring "moan," which becomes her "dirge" (l. 2), carrying her own cries. She wonders whether its "secret caves" can relieve her (l. 7). She laments the grief humans have caused her, admitting that she loved the world but her disappointments were greater. She dies heartbroken because her excessive emotions were misdirected as if toward the transient "desert sands" (l. 24). She admits her fame, which she will pass to the sea, and asks in return for a place to rest and be hidden. The poem ends with Sappho's begging the sea for the last time for her much wished-for "peace" (l. 40).

## Further Reading

Hemans, Felicia Dorothea Browne. *Felicia Hemans: Selected Poems, Letters, Reception Materials.* Edited by Susan J. Wolfson. Princeton, N.J.: Princeton University Press, 2000.

———. *Felicia Hemans: Selected Poems, Prose, and Letters.* Edited by Gary Kelley. Peterborough, Ont.: Broadview Press, 2002.

Linley, Margaret. "Sappho's Conversions in Felicia Hemans, Letitia Landon, and Christina Rossetti." *Prism(s): Essays in Romanticism* 4 (1996): 15–42.

Ross, Marlon B. *The Contours of Masculine Desire: Romanticism and the Rise of Women's Poetry.* Oxford: Oxford University Press, 1989.

Scott, Grant F. "The Fragile Image: Felicia Hemans and Romantic Ekphrasis." In *Felicia Hemans: Reimagining Poetry in the Nineteenth Century,* edited by Nanora Sweet and Julie Melnyk, 36–54. Basingstoke, Eng.: Palgrave, 2001.

—Mariam Radhwi

## "Leech Gather, The"  See "RESOLUTION AND INDEPENDENCE."

## *Letters for Literary Ladies*  Maria Edgeworth (1795)

This was the first published work by the Anglo-Irish novelist MARIA EDGEWORTH and is a plea for reform in women's education. Edgeworth, aged 27 in 1795, came from a cultivated and highly educated family. Her father, Richard Lovell Edgeworth, had a keen interest in education (he was an admirer of JEAN-JACQUES ROUSSEAU and ANNA LAETITIA BARBAULD) and had encouraged his obviously intelligent daughter to immerse herself in works of literature and history. Under her father's eye, Maria began a translation of a French text, Félicité de Genlis's fictionalized educational work *Adèle et Théodore* (1782), with a view to publishing it. However, this project proved short-lived after a family friend and man of letters, Thomas Day, managed to persuade Mr. Edgeworth that authorship was an unseemly activity for a young woman. The increasing number of women writers emerging at this time—not all of them free from the whiff of scandal—seems to have been partly responsible for this view. This moratorium on Maria's literary activities remained until Day's death in 1789.

*Letters for Literary Ladies* is a witty response to this ban on literary activity. If she cannot write or even procure herself an education, Edgeworth asks, what is a young woman to do? The discussion takes the form of letters between two gentlemen in which they debate (among other things) "the habits and virtues essential to the perfection of the female character" (1). The first gentlemen believes that educating women too highly is wrong because it will encourage her to become a "literary lady" and thus neglect womanly (domestic) duties; such a woman will not make a good wife and mother. Edgeworth's other gentleman offers his own defence of educated women: "Do not, my dear Sir, call me 'a champion for the rights of women' . . . I am more anxious for their happiness than ambitious to enter into a metaphysical discussion of their rights. . . . (29) "I do not desire to make my daughter a musician, a painter,

or a poetess; I do not desire to make her a botanist, a mathematician, or a chemist; but I wish to give her the habit of industry and attention, the love of knowledge and the power of reasoning; these will enable her to attend to excellence in any pursuit of science" (20).

The gentleman who argues against the education of women suggests that the very idea of the "feminine" is dependent on innocence—and by implication ignorance—of the world and its controversies: "We [men] mix with the world without restrain, we converse freely with all classes of people, with men of wit, of science, of learning, with the artist, the mechanic, the labourer, every scene of life is open to our view . . . we see things as they are; but women must always see things through a veil, or cease to be women" (2–3). Significantly, the second gentleman in arguing against this position does not go so far as to suggest that women should use their rational faculties to gain positions in the professions or workplace but rather to make them fitter companions for their husbands, who lack opportunities to keep up to date with new developments. For many men, "the understanding is but partially cultivated; and general literature must be neglected by those who are occupied in earning bread or amassing riches for their family. . . . The other sex [women] have no such constraint upon their understandings; neither the necessity of earning their bread, nor the ambition to shine in public affairs, hurry or prejudice their minds; in domestic life they have leisure to be wise" (27). Women do not have to work and therefore have more time to study. At the same time, when men realize that they don't have to go and seek intellectual companionship in their club or coffee houses, society itself will begin to be reformed.

Edgeworth's book can usefully be read alongside MARY WOLLSTONECRAFT's *VINDICATION OF THE RIGHTS OF WOMAN* and Barbauld's "The RIGHTS OF WOMAN," protofeminist discussions of similar topics.

## Further Reading

Butler, Marilyn. *Maria Edgeworth.* Oxford: Clarendon Press, 1972.
———. "Maria Edgeworth." In *A Dictionary of British and American Women Writers 1660–1800,* edited

by Janet Todd, 110–112. London: Methuen & Co., 1987.

Edgeworth, Maria. *Letters for Literary Ladies.* Edited by Claire Connolly. London: Everyman, 1993.

Narain, Mona. "A Prescription of Letters: Maria Edgeworth's *Letters for Literary Ladies* and the Ideologies of the Public Sphere." *Journal of Narrative Technique* 28, no. 3 (Fall 1998): 266–286.

—Julie Hardgreaves

## *Letters from France*  Helen Maria Williams
(1790–1796)

The eight volumes of HELEN MARIA WILLIAMS's *Letters from France* depict the FRENCH REVOLUTION as romance and espouse passionate politics. When Williams began her eyewitness account with *Letters Written in France in the Summer of 1790,* English readers were eager for information about the Revolution. But political writing was a masculine preserve, and even a well-known poet like Williams risked censure for unladylike engagement with public events. Emphasizing personal observation, she grounded her report in the narrator's love of liberty and deeply felt experience of the sublime and sometimes tragic spectacle of Revolution. *The Letters* use informal epistolary travel narrative, interweaving description, anecdote, and commentary to appeal to readers' imaginative sympathies. This form enables Williams to speak as a heroine of sensibility, identifying herself with female images of liberty to become the natural voice of the people.

Residence in France gave Williams access to important characters in the revolutionary drama: She was a close friend of Madame Roland (Marie-Jeanne Roland de la Platière, 1754–93) knew Maximilien Robespierre (1758–94), and met NAPOLEON BONAPARTE (1769–1821). Buoyed by idealism, Williams's early *Letters* downplay revolutionary violence or excuse it as a legacy of tyranny. Throughout the *Letters,* her focus on female victims and heroines shows women as worthy to be citizens and arouses sympathy for their plight. In the second series she emphasizes her role as a true disciple of JEAN-JACQUES ROUSSEAU, whose values have been betrayed by a villainous Robespierre.

In the 1790 *Letters* Williams blends domestic and public scenes to create an episodic romance. Her account of the du Fosse family, which could be seen as an allegory of the Revolution, moved contemporary readers and influenced WILLIAM WORDSWORTH's tale of Vaudracour and Julia in *The PRELUDE.* The second volume of *Letters* portrays the Revolution's chivalry while warning that France is outstripping Great Britain in pursuit of liberty. By the time the next two volumes were published anonymously in 1793, Britain was at war with France and a reaction against sensibility and revolutionary values had begun. In these volumes Williams's feelings about the Revolution are divided, metaphors of storm and darkness abound as she laments a lost golden era of revolutionary idealism. Letters by male observers make up most of volume 3 and about one third of volume 4, framing moments of sensibility with a more detached perspective.

The four volumes of the second series, published in 1795–96, depict the Reign of Terror and its aftermath, ending with William's ambivalent response to the establishment of the Directory. Her narrative of her own imprisonment inspired FELICIA HEMANS's "Prisoners' Evening Service." In this series Williams compares Madame Roland and Charlotte Corday to virtuous Roman women while she makes Robespierre a GOTHIC villain and associates the Jacobins with madness, disease, monstrosity, and cannibalism. Here she combines documentary and melodrama with vignettes of sensibility to create a tragic interlude ending with a renewal of hope when Robespierre falls. Despite the imperfections of the Revolution, Williams remains faithful to the imaginative and deeply felt belief in its possibilities that inspired a generation of Romantic writers.

### Further Reading
Williams, Helen Maria. *Letters from France.* Facsimile Edition of vols. 1–4. 2 vols. Delmar, N.Y.: Scholar's Facsimiles and Reprints, 1975.

———. *Letters Written in France in the Summer of 1790 to a Friend in England.* Edited by Neil Fraistat and Susan S. Lanser. Peterborough, Ontario: Broadview Press, 2001.

—Linda Mills Woolsey

## Letters Written during a Short Residence in Sweden, Norway and Denmark Mary Wollstonecraft (1796)

*Letters Written during a Short Residence* is a book of love, betrayal, and tragedy. It is a central document in the historiography of Romanticism as MARY WOLLSTONECRAFT provides a public account of the despair, anger, and suicidal depression that she experienced following the breakdown of her relationship with the American author and businessman Gilbert Imlay (1754–1828). An emotional appeal to an absent and neglectful lover and a travelogue describing the topography of a remote and isolated part of Europe, *Letters* is also a political treatise denouncing the harmful effects of trade and commerce and the baneful consequences of monarchical government and imperialism.

Wollstonecraft met Imlay in Paris in 1793 and fell madly in love with him. Following the birth of their daughter, Fanny, in 1794, the relationship cooled, and in 1795 a distraught Wollstonecraft attempted suicide. In the aftermath of this, Imlay appointed Wollstonecraft as his business agent responsible for seeking reparation for a lost vessel in which he had invested, and she set out on her four-month Scandinavian journey on June 9, 1795. *Letters* describes a profoundly cathartic experience in which Wollstonecraft, "musing almost to madness," tries to come to terms with her life without Imlay. Her wounded sensibility finds expression as she reflects on Imlay's betrayal, but it is the hybrid quality of *Letters* that makes it so appealing. Her melancholia is soothed by the beauty and sublimity of the Scandinavian landscape, culminating in her memorable account of the waterfall near Fredericstadt, Norway, which has all of the qualities of a Wordsworthian "spot of time."

Wollstonecraft's detailed descriptions of the manners, customs, diet, and dress of the peoples of Scandinavia adds great color and gusto to her epistles, but it is perhaps her interest in the political life of the countries that is of most significance. Norway was heavily under the dominion of Denmark, but Wollstonecraft saw the seeds of liberty and independence breaking forth. She considered Sweden and Demark to be corrupted and polluted by the effects of monarchy, despotism, and the voracious practices of merchants and speculators,

but in Norway she saw the "independent spirit" of a "manly race" (78–79). Norway is, she declares, "the most free community I have ever observed" (102), and she enthusiastically notes their fervent support for the French Republic established in the wake of the FRENCH REVOLUTION. These political observations frequently coincide with her bitter declamations against the humanitarian and ecological impact of capitalism. Her anger at a system whereby "the interests of nations are bartered by speculating merchants" reaches a crescendo in letters 23 and 24 as she inveighs against the "sordid accumulators of *cent per cent*" (195). The political and personal merge, however, as she turns from her invective against the capitalist marketplace to point a finger directly at Imlay, himself a businessman and speculator, accusing him of being "strangely altered, since you have entered deeply into commerce." Imlay has been has morally corrupted by his pursuit of wealth, and this, she suggests, was the cause of his betrayal.

A sense of tragedy surrounds Wollstonecraft's *Letters*. It was her last publication before her premature death in childbirth in 1797, and her daughter, Fanny Imlay, who accompanied her on the journey, was to commit suicide in 1816 at the age of 22. The personal sadness that envelops *Letters* and its introspective, confessional qualities combine with Wollstonecraft's independent, restless spirit and her fundamental political radicalism to create a work that captures the very essence of English Romanticism.

**Further Reading**

Favret, Mary A. "*Letters Written during a Short Residence in Sweden, Norway and Denmark:* Traveling with Mary Wollstonecraft." In *The Cambridge Companion to Mary Wollstonecraft,* edited by Claudia L. Johnson, 209–227. Cambridge: Cambridge University Press, 2002.

Nyström, Per. *Mary Wollstonecraft's Scandinavian Journey.* Translated by George Otter. Gothenburg, Sweden: Kungl. Vetenskaps-og Vitterhets-Samhället, 1980.

Todd, Janet. *Mary Wollstonecraft: A Revolutionary Life.* London: Columbia University Press, 2000.

Wollstonecraft, Mary. *The Works of Mary Wollstonecraft.* 7 vols. Edited by Janet Todd and Marilyn Butler. London: William Pickering, 1989.

Wollstonecraft, Mary, and William Godwin. *A Short Residence in Sweden, Norway and Denmark; and Memoirs of the Author of The Rights of Woman.* Edited by Richard Holmes. London: Penguin, 1987.

—Stephen Burley

## Lewis, Matthew Gregory (Mark Lewis)
(1775–1818)

On May 16, 1818, passengers and crew of the ship *Sir Godfrey Webster* bound for England from the West Indies gathered on deck to witness the burial of one of their number: Matthew "'Monk" Lewis, a plantation owner who had once been an author and MP but who had died suddenly at the age of 43 from taking an emetic as part of his treatment for yellow fever. In keeping with naval custom, his improvised coffin was lowered into the water, weighted down with chains, but as the ship prepared to make sail, the chains broke off and the coffin burst up out of the depths of the ocean and bobbed off in the direction of Jamaica. Back home in England among those who paid tributes were Lewis's friends: the writers THOMAS MOORE; ROBERT SOUTHEY; SIR WALTER SCOTT; Theodore Hook; and, in Italy, where Lewis had stayed the previous year, JOHN POLIDORI, PERCY BYSSHE SHELLEY and LORD BYRON. The latter expressed the thoughts of many when, in a double-edged tribute, he suggested that Lewis "was a good man—a clever man—but a bore—a damned bore—one may say" (quoted in Leask 639). The *London Courier* also expressed the general feeling when he suggested that if Lewis were remembered at all (which seemed unlikely), it would be solely as a man who had wasted his talents, who "had devoted the first fruits of his mind to the propagation of evil" becoming "a reckless defiler of the public mind; a profligate" rather than for any worthwhile literary endeavours (quoted in Peck 174–177). Were they around today, his acquaintances would no doubt be surprised at the interest Lewis begun to generate. Prompted largely by his influential best-seller *The MONK* (1796), claims for his greatness have appeared in a multitude of settings, and his most famous novel continues to be read and studied today.

Despite a great deal of detailed biographical attention, Matthew Gregory Lewis remains a fairly indeterminate and often obscure figure. What, then, do we actually know about him? He was born on July 9, 1775, into a modest English home in London, where his father, also called Matthew, was a civil servant for the British government as well as being part of a wealthy family of Jamaican plantation owners; his mother, Frances was poorly educated and frivolous but a talented musician and dancer. Apparently young Matthew was an intelligent, precocious child, with a love of the theater and literature and devoted to his mother, and the scandal of his parents' separation and attempted divorce in 1783 on the grounds of his mother's adultery shook him. By 1790, however, he had entered Christ Church College at Oxford University as a student of classics, though he did little in the way of studying, preferring to travel around Europe and study French and German drama, in particular the "sturm und drang" plays that were all the rage then. By this the time the ambitious, quick-witted Matthew had transmogrified into a fully fledged literary man, completing his first play *The Epistolary Intrigue* in 1791 and a second, *The East Indian* in 1792.

When, in 1792, Lewis left university for the summer, he dutifully obeyed his father's wish that he follow a diplomatic career, traveling to Germany to learn the language but also soaking up Weimar's rich literary atmosphere, including a meeting with JOHANN WOLFGANG VON GOETHE. After graduating in 1794, he went to Holland for more diplomatic experience, financially supported by his generous father. In his spare time (of which he had a great deal), he took on literary work, including another play, *The Twins* (1793), poetry (which his mother tried to sell to magazines on his behalf), and the book that would become *The Monk*. In September 1794 Lewis wrote to his mother from the Hague: "What do you think of my having written, in the space of ten weeks, a romance of between three and four hundred pages octavo? I have even written out half of it fair. It is called 'The Monk,' and I am myself so pleased with it, that, if the Booksellers will not buy it, I shall publish it myself" (quoted in Peck 19). Although the speed of the book's composition has been questioned, no one doubted its success when it appeared anonymously in March 1796.

Early reviews were positive, although SAMUEL TAYLOR COLERIDGE, reviewing the book for the *Critical Review*, warned that it was a novel "which if a parent saw in the hands of a son or daughter, he might reasonably turn pale," and the work left "the most painful impression . . . of great acquirements and splendid genius employed to furnish a *mormo* for children, a poison for youth, and a provocative for the debauchee" (quoted in Peck 25). It was in this capacity, though, that Lewis's literary career took off, encouraged more than held back by the controversy his work generated. The *Monthly Review* judged the book "totally unfit for general circulation," while the *Monthly Magazine* thought it the kind of book to encourage "voluptuous revelry" especially in those of a weak-minded or sensitive disposition (Peck 27). The reading public rushed to buy the book, among them HESTER LYNCH PIOZZI, who recorded how "there is a Book in the World called the *Monk* which surpasses in Horror every possible—& every Impossible Tale" (quoted in Peck 29). Nine months after its publication, ANNA SEWARD wrote that she was still struggling to obtain a copy, such was the demand. The piece was rushed onto the stage, and in 1798 JAMES BOADEN's version of the play, *Aurelio and Miranda*, was premiered at Drury Lane Theatre with the leading actor of the day, JOHN PHILIP KEMBLE, agreeing to take the role of the monk, with disappointing results.

Notwithstanding the attention given *The Monk* and the lengthy spell in which Lewis all but disappeared from the literary canon, invariably judged as a "one-hit wonder," his literary output is more impressive and various than we are often given to understand. His first performed play, *Castle Spectre*, with Kemble and Dorothea Jordan in the leading roles, opened at Drury Lane in December 1797, "the outstanding example of British Gothic melodrama" added £18,000 to the theater's takings (Leask 637). Lewis's commitment to drama meant that each year between 1797 and 1809 he was hardly ever without a play being premiered: *Adelmorn the Outlaw*, another GOTHIC drama was performed in 1801, followed by a historical tragedy *Alfonso, King of Castile* (1802); a monodrama, *The Captive* (1803); a melodrama *Rugantino, or, the Bravo of Venice* (1805); the spectacular melodrama *The Wood Daemon, or, The Clock Has Struck* (1807);

another historical verse drama, *Adelgitha, or, The Fruits of a Single Error* (1807); *Venoni, or, The Novice of St. Mark's* (1808); and *Temper, or, The Domestic Tyrant* (1809). Lewis's biggest hit was the equestrian drama *Timour the Tartar* (1811), which had live horses on the stage. Elsewhere, his diverse output included *Tales of Wonder* (1802), a collection of eerie ballads with contributions from WALTER SCOTT, ROBERT SOUTHEY, and John Leyden, partly inspired by the success of German equivalents such as GOTTFRIED AUGUST BÜRGER's long poem *Lenore* (1773). The quality of these works varies enormously, but the diversity of these achievements is a reminder that Lewis is a figure who cannot be conveniently classified with a single label.

Lewis's literary career ended in 1812 on the death of his father, upon which he found himself a rich man. By all accounts his vanity and pomposity increased, and he became renowned as a snob whose main interest was himself. His collection *Poems* (1812) was his last, and he proceeded to devote himself to family business, including management of two slave plantations in Jamaica. In 1815 he set out to inspect his property—"to suck his sugar canes," as Byron put it (quoted in Peck 152)—and also to review the treatment of the slaves. Lewis's "ownership" was a source of considerable disagreement with some of his acquaintances, notably MME. ANNE-LOUISE-GERMAINE DE STAËL. He was not a supporter of the antislavery campaign, despite advocating humane treatment and making attempts to improve the lives of those living on his own estates. It was during his return from a second visit that he died, on May 16, 1818, amid rumors that he had been poisoned by other plantation owners, disgusted at the changes he was making, or by the slaves themselves.

As with the list of Lewis's works given above, the different interpretative frameworks through which he can be examined is a reminder of the breadth of his achievements and the complex and often open-ended questions his work provokes. That there has always been and still remains a difficulty in pinning down Lewis owes much to the tension that exists between his roles as orthodox and conservative supporter of the status quo and writer of garish portrayals of evil and sexual obsession. The ambiguity that critics and biographers—

and even Lewis's own friends—have identified has been formulated in many ways, but it includes the tensions between Lewis's seemingly orthodox public persona and his rumored homosexuality, the emphasis in the novels on disguise and the double life, and the schism within a writer who writes of the past while pushing the boundaries of what can be said in the present.

## Further Reading

Irwin, Joseph James. *M. G. "Monk" Lewis.* Boston: Twayne, 1976.

Leask, Nigel. "Matthew Gregory Lewis." *Oxford Dictionary of National Biography.* Oxford: Oxford University Press, 2004, 635–640.

Macdonald, D. L. *Monk Lewis: A Critical Biography.* Toronto and Buffalo: University of Toronto Press, 2000.

Peck, Louis F. *A Life of Matthew G. Lewis.* Cambridge, Mass.: Harvard University Press, 1961.

—Ben Harding

## Lickbarrow, Isabella (1784–1847)

The Quaker poet Isabella Lickbarrow was born in November 1784 in Kendal, Westmorland, in the picturesque northwest of England. Her parents died when she was young, but her keen intellect was nurtured by the support of close friends and family, most notably her aunt, Deborah, mother of the eminent scientist John Dalton (1766–1844). When her father died, Isabella, now 20, faced a life of poverty such were the limited opportunities for a middle-class woman to earn her own living. With her first volume of poetry, entitled POETI-CAL EFFUSIONS (1814), Lickbarrow sought to create a fund "to assist the humble labours of herself and her orphan sisters which would increase their family comforts and better their condition in life" (Lickbarrow 1994, ). The list of subscribers to this collection included notable literary figures such as WILLIAM WORDSWORTH, ROBERT SOUTHEY, and THOMAS DE QUINCEY. In 1818 Lickbarrow appeared as the author of another volume of poetry, *Lament upon the Death of Princess Charlotte, and Alfred, a Vision.* At the same time, she wrote prolifically for the *Westmorland Advertiser* between

1811 and 1815, as well as for the *Monthly Repository* (1818), the *Lonsdale Magazine* (1820), the *Westmorland Advertiser and Kendal Chronicle* (1820–23), and the *Kendal Mercury and Westmorland Advertiser* (1837–40).

Lickbarrow was much admired by her contemporaries, though her outwardly conventional works have fared less well over the last two centuries. Until Constance Parrish's recent collection of her works, which includes an invaluable biographical introduction, little was known about the poet. No likenesses of her survive, and there remain notable gaps in her life story. In addition to Parrish's book and further articles, leading Romanticist scholars such as Duncan Wu and Stuart Curran have contributed important accounts of her life and works.

It is possible that Lickbarrow's poems advocating the abolition of the slave trade will help garner great interest in Romantic studies. But, although this represents one of many intellectual attractions in her works, her technical ingenuities and verbal vigor must not be overlooked. While she might become a historical test case of specific interest—no doubt through her connections with an important geographical region apropos the Romantics—it is important to maintain her identity as an accomplished poet. She was, as Parrish is at pains to stress, a lifelong devotee to her Muse, her "Belov'd companion of my early years! / My friend in solitude, my secret joy!" ("Introductory Address—To the Muse"). She offers an attractive corollary to familiar Romantic ideals of the inspired poet: "And to immortalize his song, / Harmonious language, rich and strong, / Should in spontaneous numbers flow, / And ev'ry thought with beauty glow." As the title of this poem—"On the Difficulty of Attaining Poetic Excellence"—attests, a common obsession with Romantics such as JOHN KEATS, Wordsworth, and SAMUEL TAYLOR COLERIDGE was how to capture the exertions of the fleeting imagination within the artifice of poetry. As Jonathan Wordsworth has suggested in his preface to a facsimile of *Poetical Effusions,* her writing "is compelling": "We are asked to adapt to each new metre, listen to the beat that draws us in," such as in "A Ballad": "Where is the youth, the youth so lovely, / Who rode to-day on the dappled steed? / Over the moors he rode so briskly, /

Scarce could the fleet hounds match his speed." The results of Lickbarrow's ambitions are plain to see, evidenced in a substantial body of beautiful, quietly effective and highly accomplished verse. Despite these achievements, the final years of Lickbarrow's life were especially harsh. Her sisters became patients in the Lancaster Asylum in 1820. She herself wrote on, in poor health, and died of tuberculosis in 1847. (*See also* LAKE SCHOOL.)

**Further Reading**

Curran, Stuart. "Isabella Lickbarrow and Mary Bryan: Wordsworthian Poets." *Wordsworth Circle* 27, no. 2 (1996), 113–18.

Lickbarrow, Isabella. *Collected Poems.* Edited by Constance Parrish. Grasmere, Eng.: Wordsworth Trust, 2004.

———. *Poetical Effusions.* Edited by Jonathan Wordsworth. Oxford and New York: Woodstock Books, 1994.

Parrish, Constance. "Isabella Lickbarrow: An 'Unlettered' Poetess." *Charles Lamb Bulletin* 106 (1999): 66–77.

———. "Isabella Lickbarrow, Lakeland Quaker Poet: More Facts." *Notes and Queries* 45, no. 2 (1998): 200–202.

———. "Isabella Lickbarrow's Relationship to John Dalton." *Notes and Queries* 46, no. 1 (1999): 34.

———. "Isabella Lickbarrow to Lord Lonsdale: A Newly Discovered Letter." *Notes and Queries* 46, no. 4 (1999): 448–449.

———. "Postscript on Isabella Lickbarrow, the 'Unlettered Poetess.'" *Wordsworth Circle* 28, no. 1 (1997): 70–72.

Parrish, Constance, and Duncan Wu. "Isabella Lickbarrow: A Romantic Rediscovered." *PN Review* 30, no. 1 (2003): 64–69.

Wu, Duncan. "Isabella Lickbarrow and the Westmorland Advertiser: A Literary Partnership." *Wordsworth Circle* 27, no. 2 (1996): 118–126.

—Daniel Cook

## "Lines Written a Few Miles above Tintern Abbey, on Revisiting the Banks of the Wye, during a Tour, July 13, 1798" ("Tintern Abbey") William Wordsworth (1798)

The poem more commonly known as "Tintern Abbey" is one of the central texts of British Romanticism. Like other examples of what the scholar M. H. Abrams has named "the greater Romantic lyric," this poem powerfully affirms, on the one hand, the possibility of a deep connection between the human mind and "Nature," while staging, on the other, the "sad perplexity" of doubt and anxiety that attends the speaker's sense of losing precisely this connection (ll. 122, 60). Written in 1798, at the end of the annus mirabilis of collaboration between WILLIAM WORDSWORTH and SAMUEL TAYLOR COLERIDGE that produced their landmark collection *Lyrical Ballads,* "Tintern Abbey" appears as the final poem in that book and marks a new departure for Wordsworth (and for the book) into the autobiographical blank verse that would later distinguish his greatest poem, *The* PRELUDE. Inspired by Coleridge's experimental "conversation poems," Wordsworth invites the reader to overhear an intimate, inner colloquy of observation and personal memory that modulates from ode-like apostrophes to the power of the surrounding landscape and statements of faith in an achieved oneness with nature; through striking admissions of doubt and elegiac mourning over loss; to a final, impassioned address to the speaker's silent companion, his "dear, dear Sister" Dorothy (l. 121) (see WORDSWORTH, DOROTHY). These modulations of tone and genre, combined with the poet's command of flowing blank verse, create an artful impression of spontaneity and emotional authenticity, even as they raise several interpretative cruxes that have kept this poem at the center of critical discussions of Romanticism.

Wordsworth's long title alludes to the 18th-century practice of "PICTURESQUE travel" made popular by such works as William Gilpin's 1782 guidebook *Observations on the River Wye . . . Relative Chiefly to Picturesque Beauty; Made in the Summer of 1770.* This book, along with paintings of the period, focuses in particular on the picturesque qualities of the ruins of Tintern Abbey, which Wordsworth both invokes and distances in his title by naming a location "a Few Miles above Tintern Abbey"—farther "inland" (l. 4)—where the abbey is no longer visible. This explains why the abbey itself does not appear in the poem (a subject of much critical debate) and reduces its symbolic value to a mere suggestion of a lost and violent past, or perhaps of values (such as GOTHIC superstition or Gilpin's picturesque) that the poem implicitly supersedes. Instead, as the author David Miall has shown, Wordsworth situates his poem upriver, where the "wild secluded scene" (l. 6) combines the natural sublime of "steep and lofty cliffs" (l. 5) with such human elements as "pastoral farms" and "wreathes of smoke" (ll. 16–17) to symbolize the poet's newer understanding of the way nature includes, and resonates with "The still, sad music of humanity" (l. 91). The title also announces, with the phrase "on Revisiting the Banks of the Wye," the poem's affinity with the 18th-century genres of the locodescriptive "prospect" and topographical elegy, but here too, as Mary Jacobus and others have pointed out, Wordsworth does more than just measure change by describing and interpreting a revisited landscape. Drawing on the model of Coleridge's "conversation poems," he adapts the traditional modes of allegorical description, elegy, and nostalgia to a new genre of personal memoir that narrates an evolution of consciousness (Jacobus 104 passed). Thus, the title's precise, diary-like dating and the opening phrase "Five years have past" encourage biographical critics to point out the strong contrast between the poet's "present pleasure" in the landscape (l. 63) and his first visit in 1793, when Wordsworth was indeed "like a man / Flying from something that he dreads" (ll. 70–71), having narrowly escaped the violence of the FRENCH REVOLUTION and fearing persecution at home for his radical views. The opening verse paragraph is thus a tour de force of locodescriptive verse, not only because it enacts in both form and figure the inter-penetration of imagination and landscape ("little lines / Of sportive wood run wild" [ll. 15–16]), but also for its doubling of emotional perspectives in such phrases as "Thoughts of a more deep seclusion" (l. 7), in which the speaker's former need to escape "alone" into the "houseless woods" (ll. 22, 20) is overlaid by his present desire to share a peaceful experience of contemplative self-transcendence with a fellow "worshipper of Nature" (l. 152).

This evolution of consciousness is explicitly developed in the central section of the poem as a narrative extending from "boyish days" (l. 73) through "thoughtless youth" (l. 90) to the present "joy / Of elevated thoughts" (ll. 94–95), and while the poem is for the most part a celebration of this

process, it is nevertheless marked by an countervailing tone of doubt, "loss," and "decay" (ll. 87, 113). For example, lines 42–49 describe a state of ecstatic, heightened awareness almost suggestive of Eastern contemplative practices: "that serene and blessed mood / In which . . . we are laid asleep / In body, and become a living soul" (ll. 41–46). Yet the confident assertion that in such a state "We see into the life of things" (l. 49) is immediately retracted: "If this / Be but a vain belief . . . " (ll. 49–50), a skepticism underscored by the speaker's elegiac intuition that he must "Suffer [his] genial spirits to decay" (l. 113). This tension is typical of "the greater Romantic lyric," in which the (male) speaker's quest for an integration of self and other, past and present, personal and social, is fraught by a pervasive modern sense of dislocation and alienation, in this case inspiring Wordsworth to adopt an ode-like pattern of transitions that, as the scholar Heidi Thomson notes, are often "abrupt, sharp, and dialectical in form" (Thomson 537).

The conclusion of "Tintern Abbey" is no exception. Taking many readers by surprise, the speaker suddenly turns to address his sister, in whom he glimpses a version of his "former heart" (l. 117), and with whom he shares a "chearful faith that all which we behold / Is full of blessings" (ll.133–135). With this move the poem transcends the ruminations of an isolated subjectivity in favor of an intersubjective exchange that is part of the speaker's sense of "recompense" for his loss of a more immediate, but more self-centered, relation to nature. Thomson shows how this "Address to Dorothy" does not so much resolve the problems posed by the poem as stress the importance of a "shared knowledge of nature" to any lasting evolution of consciousness (Thomson 545). Or, as Ralph Pite has put it, "Wordsworth seeks a relation to nature that . . . will re-establish or preserve community" (quoted in Miall). In this way, "Tintern Abbey" remains both central to the urgent concerns of Romanticism and freshly relevant to the challenges of our own day.

**Further Reading**

Abrams, M. H. "Structure and Style in the Greater Romantic Lyric." In *The Correspondent Breeze: Essays on English Romanticism,* 44–75. New York: Norton, 1984.

Jacobus, Mary. "Tintern Abbey and the Renewal of Tradition." In *Tradition and Experiment in Wordsworth's Lyrical Ballads 1798*, 104–130. Oxford: Oxford University Press 1976.

Miall, David S. "Locating Wordsworth: 'Tintern Abbey' and the Community with Nature." *Romanticism on the Net* 20 (November 2000). Available online. URL: http:www.erudit.org.revue/ron/2000/v/n20/00549ar.html. Accessed on July 7, 2009.

Thomson, Heidi. "'We Are Two': The Address to Dorothy in 'Tintern Abbey.'" *Studies in Romanticism* 40, no. 4 (Winter 2001): 531–546.

Wolfson, Susan. *The Questioning Presence*. Ithaca, N.Y.: Cornell University Press, 1986.

—Robert Lapp

## "Little Black Boy, The" William Blake (1789)

"The Little Black Boy" is a poem from WILLIAM BLAKE's seminal collection SONGS OF INNOCENCE AND OF EXPERIENCE (1789, 1794). This book juxtaposes qualities such as youth and maturity to demonstrate their complementary nature and function in the world. Specifically, "The Little Black Boy" depicts a precocious black boy seeking guidance from his mother and the Heavenly Father. The child's innocence lies in his lack of knowledge and his passive acceptance of racial dichotomies. The black boy of the "southern wild" bemoans his racial and social standing: "I am black, but O! my soul is white, / White as an angel is the English child: / But I am black as if bereav'd of light" (ll. 1–4). This opening stanza undermines contemporary arguments against the sensibility of Africans. These lines are especially poignant due to the slave-trade debates of the late 18th century. In parliamentary debates, newspaper accounts, and published journals, Africans were consistently characterized as unfeeling property. In Blake's rendering, the social construct of race that justified the slave trade and SLAVERY is acknowledged and places a negative connotation on blackness. Subsequently, the little black boy initially accepts the binaries of black and white. On the other hand, the speaker also claims "my soul is white" (l. 1). This phrase alludes to the child's emotional purity and his lack of guilt in regard to oppressing other human beings. His internalization of racism illustrates the effects of bondage on its youngest victims.

Whereas the little black boy assumes that his skin tone is "bereav'd of light" (l. 4), he seeks intellectual and spiritual enlightenment in from his mother and God. In terms of his maternal relationship, she is his first teacher. She is a conduit for connecting the child with Mother Nature and God. "Underneath a tree" (l. 5), she directs him toward the sun, clouds, and God. Beams of light, flowers and trees become representatives for the Supreme Being. Simultaneously, the youth receives the love of a parent and a holy education through his sylvan surroundings. By the poem's conclusion, the little black boy is no longer comparing himself to the English child but envisioning his dark body as a receptor of the love of God. "The Little Black Boy" is a Romantic predecessor to other depictions of black children in 19th-century abolitionist verse.

### Further Reading

Beer, John. *William Blake: A Literary Life*. New York: Palgrave Macmillian, 2005.

Blake, William. *Songs of Innocence and of Experience: Shewing the Two Contrary States of the Human Soul*. London, 1789.

Dyson, A. E. "'The Little Black Boy'; Blake's *Songs of Innocence*." *Critical Quarterly* (1959): 44–47.

Echeruo, Michael J. "Theologizing underneath the Tree: An African Topos in Ukawsaw." *Research in African Literatures* 23 (1995): 4–11.

Gleckner, Robert F. "Blake's Little Black Boy and the Bible." *Colby Library Quarterly* 18 (1982): 205–213.

Henry, Lauren. "Sunshine and Shady Groves: What Blake's 'Little Black Boy' Learned from African Writers." *Blake* 29 (1995): 4–11.

—Marilyn Walker

## "Little Girl Found, The" "Little Girl Lost, The" William Blake (1794)

WILLIAM BLAKE produced "Little Girl Found," one of poems in his SONGS OF INNOCENCE AND OF EXPERIENCE (1794), in his characteristic multimedia mode—the illuminated printing method that combined text with etching on copper plate followed by coloring of images.

"The Little Girl Found" is a sequel to "A Little Girl Lost" from *Songs of Experience*. The first two stanzas of the latter poem act as introduction to both poems. Despite their apparently simplicity of form and design, the poems in *Songs of Innocence and Experience* respond to deeper investigations. These two poems also echo one of Blake's major concern that he dealt with in his prophetic books: the prophetic vision sees in future "That the earth from sleep . . . Shall arise and seek . . . And . . . the Desert wild / Become a garden mild" ("A Little Girl Lost," ll. 3–8). In "The Little Girl Found," once the lost child is found, humans live happily among the beasts who had cared for the lost girl until her parents found her.

In the dialectic context of *Songs of Experience and of Innocence*, "The Little Girl Found" seems to project Blake's view that sexual repression is worse than loss of freedom. The little girl lost is found first by the beasts who "Loosed her slender dress, / And naked they conveyed / To caves the sleeping maid" ("A Little Girl Lost, ll. 50–52). When the distraught parents finally find the girl, she is in the care of the beasts. The little girl is "lost" only to her childhood and is now growing up. The newly awakened emotions in her, especially the emotion of love and sensual passions, are symbolized by the beasts who take charge of her. But she suffers no harm in their custody. She is "found" in the sense that her parents are able to understand and accept her new self with her grown-up body and mind.

The illustration to "A Little Girl Lost" shows two young human figures standing under a willow tree. A female, her body contours visible through her thin clothes, embraces a young, curly-haired nude male with her right arm. The illustration to plate 1 of "The Little Girl Found" shows a young, gowned female reclining on the grass, while in the second plate Blake shows a nude young female sleeping front of the other figures, including those of a lion, a lioness, and small children.

## Further Reading

Blake, William *The Complete Poetry and Prose of William Blake,* edited by Harold, Bloom, David Erdman, and Sir William Golding. University of California Press, 2008.

—G. R. Taneja

## Locke, John (1632–1704)

The philosopher John Locke's powerful influence on Romantic thinkers emerges from his epistemology and his political thought. Locke was active a century before the Romantic period, but his rejection of innate ideas and his emphasis on arriving at knowledge through sensation and building by association from simple to complex ideas provided a basis for psychological theories and the development of ideas about the imagination. Reactions against Locke were significant among the Romantics. The idealist reaction to Locke's empiricism, following the philosophy of Bishop George Berkeley (1685–1753), himself an empiricist, involved skeptical doubt about the external world and material reality. Romantics held that with keen perception they saw and heard the world and thereby experienced meaning and beauty. Following Locke and the work of David Hartley (1705–59), SAMUEL TAYLOR COLERIDGE asserted that the imagination actively constructed the world. WILLIAM WORDSWORTH responded to the empirical tradition of Locke by affirming that the observer with all of his or her senses is linked to the world. However, he reacted against the empirical tradition in his poem *The EXCURSION*, calling it "Dull and inanimate . . . Chained to its object in brute slavery" (4:1,251–1,263).

From Locke's *Essay Concerning Human Understanding* (1690), English thinkers from Hartley and DAVID HUME (1711–76) to Jeremy Bentham (1748–1832) and WILLIAM GODWIN (1756–1836) held that there were no innate ideas and that people learn from experience within their environments. Consequently, one could create good citizens by creating a good environment. Thus, Locke's epistemology had implications for education. In *Some Thoughts Concerning Education* (1693), he insisted that children should be given reading material different from that of their elders, which would help them to become familiar with experience and factual problems. Locke did not include imaginative literature or children's stories such as fairy tales, adventure stories, or romances, for these were held to be contrary to his emphasis on experience and reason. He stressed rationality in childhood education while focusing on rewards of praise and corrections of shame. His goal was to help children toward becoming rational, self-directed adults (see CHILDHOOD).

Locke's two treatises on government were written to justify the Glorious Revolution of 1688, when James II was deposed and James's daughter Mary and her husband William of Orange were invited by Parliament to become England's king and queen. The *First Treatise on Government,* written in 1689, argues against the divine right of kings and Robert Filmer's (1588–1653) argument for this in *Patriarcha.* The *Second Treatise on Government* starts with a reflection on the state of nature and proceeds to discovering the law of nature. All men and women are bound in the state of nature to preserve peace and to avoid harm to one another. Locke's view, in contrast with that of Thomas Hobbes, is that the state of nature is benevolent, that men and women turn to the social contract for convenience, and that man can know the principles of morality by his use of reason. In Locke's view, humanity of the past had existed in a state of nature endowed with inalienable rights. However, humanity violated the rights of the other and so its members joined in a social contract of mutual defense to protect those natural rights. If government rested on the consent of the governed, then it was legitimate. If not, those living within this structure had the right to abolish the government and to create a new one. Locke held that the best form of government was a constitutional monarchy with legislative power in a constituted parliamentary assembly elected by the people. If the monarch violated the public trust, he may be deposed.

Locke's influence was considerable not only in Britain but also in France and the United States. His empiricism countered the rationalism of the philosophers René Descartes (1596–1650), Gottfried Wilhelm Leibniz (1646–1716), and Benedict de Spinoza (1632–77). He asserted the potential of empiricism and experimentation. His political thought may have contributed to the FRENCH REVOLUTION. We see Locke's influence on Thomas Jefferson's formulation of "inalienable rights" to "life, liberty and the pursuit of happiness" in the Declaration of Independence and on the social and political thinking of Alexander Hamilton, among others.

## Further Reading

Dunn, John. *Locke: A Very Short Introduction.* Oxford: Oxford University Press, 2003.

Locke, John. An *Essay Concerning Human Understanding.* Abridged by Pauline Phemister. Oxford: Oxford World's Classics, 2008.

———. *John Locke: Political Writings.* Edited by David Wootton: Indianapolis: Hackett, 2003.

———. *Two Treatises on Government.* Birmingham, Ala.: Palladium Press, 2000.

—Robert McParland

## "London" William Blake (1794)

WILLIAM BLAKE wrote "London" in 1792 and included it in his publication of *Songs of Experience* in 1794. The poem invites the reader to take a tour of London in 1792. You will see many unpleasant things, but most of all, you are asked to listen. Notice the acrostic in the third stanza: The first letter of each line forms the word *hear* (first noted by the scholar Nelson Hilton). You will especially hear the cries of children in the last three stanzas.

The street and river Thames are "charter'd" (ll. 1, 2), requiring one to pay tolls before continuing, a reminder that passage in England is not free, as well as a reminder of THOMAS PAINE's *RIGHTS OF MAN,* published in 1791–92. Everyone is talking about Paine's work, the bloody FRENCH REVOLUTION, and the democracy in America after its revolution. Paine mentions the Magna Carta of 1215 that "charter'd" rights for English citizens, but then Paine also says, "It is perversion of terms to say that a Charter gives rights. It operates by a contrary effect, that of taking rights away. Rights are, inherently, in all the inhabitants; but Charters, by annulling those rights in the majority, leave the right, by exclusion, in the hands of a few" (179) Londoners should enjoy freedom of speech, but Mr. William Pitt, the prime minister, has banned literature that might be seditious ("in every ban," l. 7). (In fact, Blake was charged with sedition in 1803 but later acquitted.) Nothing and no one is free in London.

The government of 1792 fears revolution. On top of that, NAPOLEON BONAPARTE invaded

Austria, and now Prussian soldiers are all over London (l. 11) because George III has formed an alliance with Prussia, which is sure to lead the country into a major war with Napoleon. If so, indeed blood will run "down Palace walls" (l. 12); this explains why Blake originally wrote "German-forged links." However, as the reader-observer, you are thinking about other types of manacles (l. 8) especially when you hear "How the Chimney-sweepers cry" (l. 9). You know that the church often forces poor children into this job because they are so thin and can fit down chimneys, a job that often kills them.

The last thing you see are all of the young prostitutes. You "hear" the "curse" (ll. 13–14), which you know means venereal disease, which is passed to the men who pass it to their wives, and you know that both prostitute and wife give birth to children who are going to die from it (hence the "Marriage hearse" [l. 16]).

Just as Blake's poem is illustrated with an old man on crutches helped by a waif, all of the images in the poem are metaphorical. Blake is expressing his concern that if the political and social institutions (symbolized by the old man) that have had their way for centuries continue to "blacken" London and keep it in manacles or is kept itself in "mind-forg'd manacles" (l. 8) that resist reform, then they will be like prostitutes passing on disease and death to future generations.

See also "CHIMNEY SWEEPER, THE"; SONGS OF INNOCENCE AND OF EXPERIENCE.

## Further Reading

Clark, Steve, and David Norralls, eds. *Historicizing Blake.* Basingstoke, Eng.: Macmillan, 1994.

Erdman, David V. "Infinite London." In *Twentieth Century Interpretations of Songs of Innocence and of Experience,* edited by Morton D. Paley, 49–57. Englewood Cliffs: N.J.: Prentice-Hall, 1969.

Morris, Eaves, ed. *Cambridge Companion to William Blake.* Cambridge: Cambridge University Press, 2006.

Paine, Thomas. *The Rights of Man.* Edited by Gregory Claeys. Indianapolis, Ind.: Hackett, 1992.

Thompson, Edward P. "London." In *Witness against the Beast: William Blake and the Moral Law.* London: Cambridge University Press, 174–94.

Verdonk, Peter. "Poetic Artifice and Literary Stylistics." In *Linguistics and the Study of Literature,* edited by Theo D'haen, 42–53. Amsterdam: Rodopi, 1986.

—Brenda Ayres

## "London, 1802"  William Wordsworth  (1802)

In this sonnet addressed to the 17th-century poet JOHN MILTON, WILLIAM WORDSWORTH claims that England needs Milton to restore the qualities that the nation once represented. She is atrophying into a condition of moral, political, and social degeneracy. This degeneracy has affected society in all four realms: religion ("altar"), military prowess ("sword"), education and intellectual life ("pen"), the home ("fireside") (ll. 3–4). England has become "a fen / Of stagnant waters" (ll. 2–3), an image suggesting decay, stagnation. Milton, with his innate qualities of moral purity and grandiose vision, would be able to uplift the English nation at a time of such crisis. In life, Milton was a visionary ("Thy soul was like a Star" [l. 9]) and fearless, never seeking the approval of society. These qualities are missing from present-day England, Wordsworth argues.

Wordsworth also draws in the nation's economic status by his reference to the "ancient English dower" (l. 5). The word *dower* connotes the portion of a dead husband's wealth left to his widow; it also carries suggestions of dowry, the property that a new bride brings to her matrimonial home. Wordsworth replaces these economic meanings with a more patriotic one. He claims that the English "Have forfeited their ancient English dower / Of inward happiness" (ll. 5–6), meaning that they have relinquished the quintessential qualities of Englishness—namely, "manners, virtue, freedom, power" (l. 8). While these qualities have no monetary value, they are, as a legacy of English nationhood, priceless. English traditions, as represented by "the heroic wealth of hall and bower" (l. 4), can be restored only by Milton's messianic second coming.

Wordsworth argues that England needs Milton's "cheerful godliness" (l. 13) and his spiritual purity ("Pure as the naked heavens" [l. 11]) to bring society to rights. The sonnet's last three lines appear also to draw on the final line of Milton's own sonnet, "On His Blindness": "They also serve who only stand and wait." The central argument of both sonnets is the same: that performing one's duty for the larger good of society is better than moral inertia.

The Milton that Wordsworth seeks is not so much the real-life Milton as the "idea" of Milton: a public poet who speaks fearlessly on social issues. In addressing him, Wordsworth also suggests a parity between Milton's society and his own. Both are afflicted by political crises that, in turn, affect civic life: the English Civil War and the fall and rise of monarchy during the 17th century; the FRENCH REVOLUTION and the European revolutionary wars of the 18th century.

The political context against which Wordsworth composes is critical to understanding the sonnet. In March 1802 the Treaty of Amiens was signed by England, France, Spain, and the Netherlands, thereby ending the nine-year Napoleonic Wars for a peace of 14 months. It was a short-lived peace, but under the terms of the treaty, England recognized the authority of the new French Republic. The year 1802 was also an important one for Wordsworth personally: Accompanied by his sister, DOROTHY WORDSWORTH, he visited his (former) mistress, Annette Vallon, and their daughter Caroline in France, but in October he married Mary Hutchinson.

"London, 1802" adheres to the form and convention of the Petrarchan sonnet, modeled after the sonnets of Petrarch, the Italian Renaissance poet. Thus, there are 14 lines in iambic pentameter consisting of an eight-line octet followed by a six-line sestet. The octet poses a central argument or "question" that the sestet "answers" or resolves. The rhyme scheme generally followed is *abbaabba* (octet) and *cdecde* (sestet). Interestingly, in May 1802 Wordsworth's sister Dorothy is said to have read Milton's sonnets to him, which, in turn, inspired Wordsworth's extensive sonnet writing that year. The terse simplicity of the sonnet form allowed him to create a political poem that is stark and powerful despite its brevity.

Wordsworth's choice of Milton is both interesting and prophetic. Milton supported the republican cause during the English Civil War (1642–51).

Throughout his life, he was a tireless activist for religious, domestic, and civil liberties. He continued writing political pamphlets even after the restoration of the monarchy in 1660, despite being fined and arrested and suffering the onset of blindness. By choosing to address his sonnet to Milton, Wordsworth posits the earlier poet as a visionary figure who will lead England out of its sociopolitical morass. Milton is one of English poetry's luminary figures and known for his strongly nationalistic bent; hence, it is fitting that Wordsworth should turn to him for poetic guidance. While Milton is addressed as a messiah, his unorthodox and controversial religious affiliations are overlooked. Instead, Wordsworth paints him as the harbinger of a secular faith, one that unified the English nation. The choice of Milton is also prophetic in signaling Wordsworth's poetic turn away from the overt lyricality of his early poetry toward a more political and, ultimately, conservative voice. It is also a case of conscious self-fashioning. By addressing Milton directly, Wordsworth nominates himself the poetic conscience and moral arbiter of the nation and, thus, Milton's worthy successor.

"London, 1802" contributes to the Romantic movement's aim of presenting itself as the poetry not merely of feeling and emotion, but also of action. It marks the first-generation Romantics' growing disenchantment with the French republican cause, one that Wordsworth himself had promoted enthusiastically in *Lyrical Ballads* (1798) and *The PRELUDE* (1799). The liberty espoused by the French Revolution had given way to a republic that supported NAPOLEON BONAPARTE's violent self-aggrandizement. In time, Wordsworth began to see England as the repository of the ideals that the French Revolution had once upheld. In "London, 1802" he seeks to defend these ideals, calling out to a poet who, like him, had done so in the past. By using his poetry for social influence, he moves away from the aestheticism of early Romanticism and seeks also, subliminally or perhaps deliberately, to establish himself as the next Milton.

**Further Reading**

Barker, Juliet R. V. *Wordsworth: A Life.* New York: Ecco, 2005.

Fay, Elizabeth. *Becoming Wordsworthian: A Performative Aesthetics.* Amherst, Mass.: University of Massachusetts Press, 1995.

Gill, Stephen, ed. *The Cambridge Companion to Wordsworth.* Cambridge: Cambridge University Press, 2003.

—Devjani Roy

## "London's Summer Morning" Mary Robinson (1800)

In this poem, MARY ROBINSON demonstrates her talent for bringing a social scene to life, as she does in "JANUARY 1795," but here without the satiric purpose. This poem, first published in the *Morning Post* (August 1800) and collected in the posthumously published *Poetical Works of the Late Mrs Robinson* (1806), is a celebration of "the quotidian," finding richness and variety within the everyday (Curran 190). Robinson indeed "paints" the scene of a genre picture, drawing attention to the sounds, sights, textures, and energies of the everyday city. She employs a rich vocabulary and syntactic variety to briskly depict a wide range of activities. She also handles blank verse deftly, using frequent enjambment and caesura to create the naturalistic tone that WILLIAM WORDSWORTH aspired to, although some classical influence lingers in word inversion ("clouds impervious" [l. 9]) and the heavy use of adjectives.

At least 20 different occupations are depicted in an invigorating atmosphere of industry and purpose. The emphasis is initially on the sounds that accost the poet's ears as she wakes up, the milkmaid and dustman discernible only by the noises made by their work. Such individual details balance the more summary lists of tradespeople who create this human dawn chorus. From line 15, the poet has moved position and is now viewing the scene. She expands the range of senses so that light effects, textures, and movement are noted. The traders become characters in a minor drama, interacting with each other by "Annoying" (l. 19), admiring, purchasing, and, in the case of the clothes man who underpays for stolen goods, exploiting. This vice is conveyed without judgment, simply observed as another feature of the urban economy, with goods rather comically disappearing into "the green abyss" of his bag (l. 39). The poet herself becomes part of the drama, turning from enthusiastic observation to her own trade in the final line, to "paint" using her word tools (l. 42). Robinson has a talent for the well-chosen phrase that suggests much, such as the "dingy face" of the chimney-boy (l. 4), whose facial coloring tells the nature of his work; the housemaid who "twirls" her mop (l. 18), a dynamic visual image that also compliments her efficiency; the "limy snare" (l. 28) of the pastry glaze, which tempts the reader as well as the envious insect. Many miniature narratives are captured, making up the city's life.

Within this lively description, the poem pays tribute to the industry of those who keep the city going and recognizes their interconnectedness in the urban economy. Subtle differences of socioeconomic status are presented, in the "neat girl" (l. 19) and the "passenger" (l. 25) who are separated from the rest by their purchasing power. There is also a dramatic dimension. Even without using the first person, the poet's presence is felt, guiding her reader through the scene with a running commentary. The bracing opening rhetorical question, and the repeated "Now" that punctuates the poem, calls the reader's attention to appreciate the vitality within the mundane.

As did many women writers of the period, Robinson celebrates the common experience and locates herself firmly within it, rather than claiming an elevated position above it. Unlike Wordsworth or WILLIAM BLAKE, she presents the city as an invigorating place. As did many other women poets, she finds poetic sources within the immediate world around her, rather than in transcendence.

### Further Reading

Curran, Stuart. "Romantic Poetry: The I Altered." In *Romanticism and Feminism,* edited by Anne K. Mellor, 85–207. Bloomington: Indiana University Press, 1988.

Robinson, Mary. *Selected Poems of Mary Robinson.* Edited by Judith Pascoe. Peterborough, Ont.: Broadview Press, 2000.

—Rebecca Styler

### *Love and Friendship* Jane Austen (1790, 1922)

This parody of sentimental fiction is JANE AUSTEN's best-known juvenile work. Written in 1790, when she was only 14, it did not appear in print until 1922.

Austen's novella—which Austen intentionally titled *Love and Friendship*—is a mock epistolary romance consisting of 15 letters written by a woman named Laura to the daughter of her friend. In her first letter, Laura uses rhetoric typical of novels of sensibility when she offers to give an account of "the fortitude with which I have suffered the many Afflictions of my past Life" in the hopes that it will provide the girl with "a useful Lesson" (75). Through Laura's narration of her own early adventures, Austen sends up the emotive heroines, stilted diction, and pseudo-didacticism of sentimental novels. The witty story can be read as a moral satire to the extent that it exposes the spuriousness of Laura's claims to virtue and, by extension, the dubious morality of much sentimental fiction.

Austen makes fun of the idealized heroines of romance by having Laura begin her narrative by describing how beautiful, accomplished, and virtuous she was at 18. By her own account, her only flaw was a "sensibility too tremblingly alive" (76). The first incident in her story is the arrival of a mysterious young man at her parents' cottage. The noble youth, named Edward, has run away from home because he scorns to marry the woman his father has chosen for him: "Never shall it be said that I obliged my Father" (79). Edward declares his passion for Laura, and they are married at once. This episode ridicules two conventions of sentimental fiction: the portrayal of tyrannical parental authority and the formation of sympathetic bonds between characters. The second of these sentimental tropes is parodied again when Edward and Laura move in with Edward's friend Augustus and his wife Sophia. Laura describes her first meeting with Sophia as follows: "We flew into each others arms and after having exchanged vows of mutual Friendship for the rest of our Lives, instantly unfolded to each other the most inward Secrets of our Hearts—" (83–84).

The household is broken up when Augustus is sent to debtors' prison and Edward disappears. Laura and Sophia travel to Scotland to seek assistance from Sophia's relations. Laura explains in passing that they could not take refuge with her parents, as they had died some time earlier. With this fleeting remark, Austen exposes the hypocrisy of Laura, who, for all her tender sensibility, has little real compassion. The death of Laura's parents also affords Austen the opportunity of mocking the well-worn literary cliché whereby an orphaned heroine is discovered to be of high birth. At an inn, Laura and Sophia meet an elderly gentleman who readily acknowledges both as his long-lost granddaughters. After this providential reunion, the heroines proceed to the home of Sophia's cousin, Macdonald, where they convince his daughter to break her engagement with a suitable young man, because "he had no soul" and his hair was not auburn (91). After they help her to elope with a fortune hunter and are caught stealing banknotes, Macdonald throws them from the house.

As the heroines sit by a stream, they witness a carriage overturn. The passengers, who lie "weltering in their blood," are none other than Edward and Augustus. Laura explains that upon making this discovery, she and Sophia lose their senses: "Sophia fainting every moment and I running Mad as often" (96). The coup de grace of Austen's parody of the sentimental heroine occurs when Sophia's acute sensitivity proves fatal. As a consequence of having fainted repeatedly "in the open Air as the Dew was falling" (98), Sophia catches a cold, never to recover. On her deathbed, she gives her friend the following advice: "Run mad as often as you chuse; but do not faint—" a lesson (99), that serves as the ironic moral of Laura's tale.

*Love and Friendship* introduces themes that Austen developed more fully in novels such as SENSE AND SENSIBILITY (1811) and NORTHANGER ABBEY (1798, 1818). Stylistically, it offers an excellent early example of Austen's deft use of irony. It is also important for the way its critique of romance set precedents for the realism that came to characterize her approach as a writer.

### Further Reading

Austen, Jane. *Catharine and Other Writings.* Edited by Margaret Anne Doody and Douglas Murray. Oxford: Oxford University Press, 1998.

—Natalie Neill

## "Lucy Gray" ("Solitude")  William Wordsworth (1800)

"Lucy Gray," first published in the 1800 edition of *Lyrical Ballads,* is sometimes associated with the so-called "Lucy poems," which share its theme of response to the loss of a beloved female figure. However, "Lucy Gray" stands apart from the Lucy poems in that it is based on a supposedly real-life "circumstance," in WILLIAM WORDSWORTH's words, "told me by my Sister" of a "little girl" who vanished in "a snow-storm" (Wordsworth 385). Wordsworth told his friend Isabella Fenwick that his "spiritualising of the character" illustrates "the imaginative influences which I have endeavoured to throw over common life" (385). Indeed, his poetic retelling of this "incident" (385) has a mystical quality enhanced by his use of the quasi-archaic ballad form and his later alternative title, "Solitude" (added in 1815). Yet Wordsworth's "imaginative influences" may ultimately distract readers from "common life." "Lucy Gray," like several of the *Lyrical Ballads,* unsettles the poet's repudiation of GOTHIC sensationalism in the preface to the 1800 edition (see PREFACE TO LYRICAL BALLADS) blurring the line between the natural and supernatural, living and dead. In this particular lyrical ballad, Wordsworth's exploration of what he calls the "fluxes and refluxes of the mind" (745) is subordinated to the spooky question of whether "sweet Lucy Gray" (l. 59) can really still be "seen" (l. 12).

Wordsworth both distances the story from readers and makes it more immediate by supplying framing stanzas from the point of view of an unspecified narrator, whose reliability, like that of the narrator of "The THORN," seems to lessen as the tale unfolds. The speaker's initial claim that he has glimpsed the "solitary" girl (l. 4) soon becomes puzzling. Foregrounding problems of knowing, the third stanza seems to contradict the first one by asserting that "Lucy Gray / Will never more be seen" (ll. 11–12). The poem then segues abruptly into the suspenseful, fast-moving brief narrative of what turns out to be Lucy's last day alive. The four stanzas before the account of her disappearance slide between ominous anticipation of the "stormy night" (l. 13) and Lucy's "wanton" pleasure (l. 26) in her wintry surroundings. The speaker does not directly state that Lucy died in the snowstorm, although her "wretched Parents" (l. 33) seem to accept the fact of her death—"In Heaven we all shall meet!" (l. 42)—before finding apparent confirmation of it. The certainty of loss is modified by the revival of hope as the parents—and readers—follow the child's "foot-marks small" (l. 46) to the "middle" (l. 55) of a "Bridge" (l. 52), but Wordsworth does not describe the parents' reaction to this evidence of their bereavement, complicating his statement in the preface that his poems privilege "feeling" over "action and situation" (746). The final two framing stanzas vacillate over whether the allegedly "living Child" (l. 58) still exists, setting up a tension between Lucy's parents' consoling idea of encountering her again in a Christian afterlife and the implicitly more consoling—yet also potentially more sinister—suggestion that Lucy survives as a ghost, continuing to play and sing in the "Wild" (l. 60).

### Further Reading

Wordsworth, William. *Lyrical Ballads and Other Poems, 1797–1800.* Edited by James Butler and Karen Green. Ithaca, N.Y.: Cornell University Press, 1992.

—Kim Wheatley

## Luddites

The Luddite revolts were a series of machine-breaking riots in England from 1811 to 1816, affecting the hosiery and lace industries of the Midlands, the woollen industry of the West Riding of Yorkshire, and the cotton industry of Lancashire and Cheshire. Machine breaking as a form of protest against exploitation or against new machinery had a long tradition in Britain, yet the riots of the Regency era stand out due to their intensity and because they coincided with other protests such as food riots and political reform movements.

The name *Luddites* refers to the alleged leader of the revolts, Ned Ludd, or General Ludd. Threatening letters to manufacturers and proclamations, usually to the British government, were often signed with this name. However, there is little evidence to suggest that such a general controlling an army of machine breakers ever existed. The leaders of different groups more probably assumed this identity because of its symbolic power.

The Luddite revolts must be regarded against the background of the economic situation in Britain during the Napoleonic Wars: The hostilities with France intensified the problems of INDUSTRIALISM, namely poverty and unemployment due to the slow destruction of the home industries. When France and the United States blocked British trade, British industry suffered greatly. Wages for the workers dropped, while the price of bread rose. As many families faced starvation, it was no surprise that riots broke out. Yet the first Luddite revolts were not directed against new machinery: Rather, the protest focused on the frame-knitters' manifold exploitation by some of their masters and on the undermining of the hosiery trade by low-quality products. Therefore, during the first and second wave of riots in Nottinghamshire in spring and winter 1811, only the frames of unpopular hosiers were attacked, while those of employers who tried to maintain certain standards in employment and products remained untouched.

When the riots spread to other areas and trades, however, they became increasingly violent, and not only because common criminals seized their chance in a time of public unrest. In Yorkshire, for example, the cloth manufacturer William Horsfall, who used new shearing frames in his mill, was shot by four Luddites in 1812, just a few days after the attempted assassination of another mill owner, William Cartwright. Charlotte Brontë later immortalized him as Robert Gérard Moore in her novel *Shirley* (1849).

The general public was at first sympathetic with the plight of the workers. Thus, the authorities trying to stop the revolts received little help. Furthermore, the Luddites had taken an oath of secrecy, and upon their arrest only a few betrayed their comrades. Eventually spies were used to infiltrate their ranks, and these informers brought about several arrests. In February 1812 Parliament passed a bill that made machine breaking punishable by death. It was violently opposed by LORD BYRON in his maiden speech in the House of Lords, yet the rich and the titled remained largely unmoved by the poor's situation. Several executions and increasing military pressure finally brought an end to the Luddite revolts.

## Further Reading

Jones, Steven E. *Against Technology: From the Luddites to Neo-Luddism*. New York: Routledge, 2006.

Liversidge, Douglas. *The Luddites: Machine-Breakers of the Early Nineteenth Century*. London: Franklin Watts, 1972.

Thomis, Malcolm I. *The Luddites: Machine-Breaking in Regency England*. New York: Schocken Books, 1972.

—Sandra Martina Schwab

## *Luxima, the Prophetess: A Tale of India*

See MISSIONARY, THE.

## *Lyrical Ballads, With A Few Other Poems*
### William Wordsworth and Samuel Taylor Coleridge (1798; 1800)

This collection of 23 poems was published on October 4, 1798, in a print run of 500 copies. The volume was published anonymously because, according to Coleridge, "Wordsworth's name is nothing—[and] to a large number of persons mine *stinks*" (Coleridge 1, 412). On October 4, 1798, *Lyrical Ballads* appeared under the imprint of J. & A. Arch (Butler and Green 10). While its status as a landmark collection aiming to offer a new kind of poetry is now recognized, initial sales were slow. Writing in *Table Talk*, some years later, Coleridge remembered his publisher had told him that most of the sales had been to sailors who, seeing "THE RIME OF THE ANCIENT MARINER," positioned as the first poem in the volume, thought it a book of seafaring songs (Gardner, 21). Conversely, Wordsworth, the dominant partner (he also supervised the printing), thought the same ballad was putting other people off buying the volume.

As critics have noted, the title of the collection is significant, referring as it does to two important traditions in English poetry. By putting them together Wordsworth and Coleridge were trying to highlight that this was a revisioning of existing forms. This also helps explain the fact that the title is slightly misleading. There are few actual ballads in the collection—seafaring or otherwise—apart from "The THORN," Goody Blake and Harry Gill," and "The IDIOT BOY." Others, such as "The Female Vagrant," "WE ARE SEVEN," and "SIMON LEE," have been described as narrative poems, while "The Forsaken Indian Woman" and "The Mad Mother" have been classed as "songs" (Jones, 15). The most famous poem, "LINES WRITTEN A FEW MILES ABOVE TINTERN ABBEY" (more generally known as "Tintern Abbey"), is usually described as a "lyric." Thus as A. R. Jones and William Tydeman put it: "The volume is unified . . . not by any prevailing type of poetry represented, in spite of the expectations aroused by the title, but by the uniformity of poetic style and the attempt not merely to write in a new way but to discover the appropriate medium for a fresh apprehension of the truth" (15). This is well documented, not least in Wordsworth's "PREFACE TO THE *LYRICAL BALLADS*" accompanying the second (two-volume) edition of 1800. Wordsworth writes that the poets aimed to "make the incidents of common life interesting by tracing in them, truly, though not ostentatiously, the primary laws of our nature. . . . Low and rustic life was generally chosen. . . ." (Wordsworth and Coleridge 1988, 244–245). The advertisement for the collection likewise announced that "It is the honourable characteristic of Poetry that its materials are to be found in every subject which can interest the human mind" and that readers would receive a series of "experiments" written "chiefly with a view to ascertain how far the language of conversation in the middle and lower classes of society is adapted to the purposes of poetic pleasure" (Wordsworth and Coleridge 1988, 7).

One of the poems which encapsulates what Wordsworth and Coleridge were trying to do is "The Thorn." Like "Simon Lee," this poem experiments with traditional folk storytelling combined with a more sophisticated, ironic position on the part of the poet that we may think of as "lyrical"— the insight imparted to the reader is not necessarily discernible in the narrative itself. In the 1798 "Advertisement" to *Lyrical Ballads*, Wordsworth advises the reader that the narrator, or speaker, of the poem "is not supposed to be spoken in the author's own person: the character of the loquacious narrator will sufficiently shew itself in the course of the story" (Wordsworth and Coleridge 1988, 8). The story of "The Thorn" involves a woman named Martha Ray who, after being deserted by her lover 22 years ago, is still seen grieving by the thorn tree and thus is the subject of much curiosity and gossip in the rural community. The narrator's involvement in her story stems only from accidentally encountering her while seeking shelter from the storm. The narrator reports that he has heard the woman was pregnant at the time of her lover's departure and that some villagers speculate that she murdered the baby. The outline of the narrative thus owes much to the ballad "The Lass of Fair Wone," translated by William Taylor from the German of Gottfried August Bürger, which appeared in the April 1796 *Monthly Magazine*.

Again, like "Simon Lee," the story itself—the ballad—is slight. The poem explores instead the effect of superstition on the imagination and on the narrator's ability effectively to see, to interpret, and to explain. Perhaps in response to Robert Southey's complaint about the poem in the *Critical Review* of October 1798 that "he who personates tiresome loquacity becomes tiresome himself" (quoted in Wordsworth and Coleridge 1988, 319), Wordsworth, for the second edition of *Lyrical Ballads* (1800), added a lengthy note in which he describes the narrator as a retired "Captain of a small trading vessel" who has become "credulous and talkative from indolence" and "prone to superstition" (Wordsworth and Coleridge 1988, 288). The poem consists of 23 11-line stanzas, beginning with the narrator's description of the thorn itself in the first four stanzas. The language emphasizes the subjectivity of the narrator's perspective and the way he associates ideas and images. Well before he reveals the story of Martha Ray, Wordsworth's narrator, in the sixth stanza, he describes the "heap of earth o'er grown with moss" next to the thorn as "like an infant's grave in size" (ll. 56, 61)—a telling comparison given the revelations to come, one that seems to accord with Wordsworth's stated intention in the suggestion that the narrator's simile is perhaps subconsciously conditioned by his credulity. As the poem proceeds, the narrator imagines his listener's interlocutions and questions, revealing the limits of his knowledge in replies such as "I cannot tell; I wish I could" (l. 89) and "I'll give you the best help I can" (l. 111). The woman's story itself is also marked by equivocations such as "'tis said" and "some say." The poem thus explores the way this narrator has uncritically absorbed the community's gossip and speculation and how it has colored his perspective and insidiously damaged a woman's reputation.

Recently, poet Andrew Motion, formerly Britain's Poet Laureate, named *Lyrical Ballads* as one of his icons. As he puts it: "*The Lyrical Ballads . . .* is one of the defining documents of the Romantic movement. Not only because it has a wonderfully democratic range of subjects and interests, but also because it arises from the kind of self-consciousness we recognize as being modern. The book is more than two hundred years old now, but still feels wonderfully fresh and new: it's a beacon, as well as an icon." In 1798 the volume seemed odd, rather than modern, and was slow to catch on. Indeed, Sarah Coleridge, Coleridge's wife, noted that the poems "were laughed at and disliked by all with very few exceptions" (quoted in Jones and Tydeman, 15). WILLIAM HAZLITT recognized what the poets were trying to do but was not impressed, while Wordsworth, in particular, was bitterly hurt by Southey's review. While admitting Wordsworth's and Coleridge's talents as a poet, Southey had singled out "The Rime of the Ancient Mariner," "The Thorn," and "The Idiot Boy" for special censure, suggesting that the "'experiment'" "to ascertain how far the language of conversation in the middle and lower classes of society is adapted to the purpose of poetic pleasure" had failed because of its "uninteresting subject matter" (quoted in Wordsworth and Coleridge 1988, 319).

While the volume was not an overnight success, it was not a disaster either. Sales gradually increased, thanks partly to the support of MARY ROBINSON, who drew attention to it in *The Morn-*

*ing Post* in her role as that newspaper's poetry editor (from 1799). A new edition was commissioned in 1800 to include a second volume of new poems, and a substantial new preface. Wordsworth's "The Convict" was withdrawn, and in its place Coleridge's "Love" was inserted, as well as Wordsworth's "LUCY GRAY," "NUTTING," and "MICHAEL." A third edition of *Lyrical Ballads* appeared in June 1802 and was this time attacked by FRANCIS JEFFFREY in the *Edinburgh Review* (October 1802). In 1805 a fourth and final authorized edition of *Lyrical Ballads* was published (Graver 15).

See also "ANECDOTE FOR FATHERS"; "TO MY SISTER"; "THERE WAS A BOY."

**Further Reading**

Coleridge, Samuel Taylor. *Collected Letters*. Vol. 1. Edited by Earl Leslie Griggs. Oxford: Clarendon Press, 1956.

Graver, Bruce. "Preface." *Lyrical Ballads*. Electronic Edition. Available online. URL: http://www.rc.umd.edu/editions/LB/preface.html. Accessed July 23 2009.

Jacobus, Mary. *Tradition and Experiment in Wordsworth's Lyrical Ballads*. Oxford: Clarendon, 1976.

Jones, Alun, and William Tydeman. *Wordsworth. Lyrical Ballads: A Casebook*. London: Macmillan, 1972.

Motion, Andrew. "Icons." Available online. URL: http://www.icons.org.uk/nom/my-icons/the-lyrical-ballads. Accessed July 23, 2009.

Parrish, Stephen Maxfield. *The Art of the Lyrical Ballads*. Cambridge, Mass.: Harvard University Press, 1973.

Wordsworth, William, and Samuel Taylor Coleridge. *Lyrical Ballads*. Edited by R. L. Brett and A. R. Jones. London: Rutledge, 1988.

———. *Lyrical Ballads. An Electronic Scholarly Edition*. Edited by Bruce Graver and Ron Tetreault. With a Preface by James Butler and Karen Green. Available online. URL: http://www.rc.umd.edu/editions/LB/. Accessed January 9, 2010.

—Daniel Robinson

# M

## Macpherson, James (1736–1796)

A poet and fraudster, James Macpherson was born on October 27, 1736, in Ruthven, in the Spey valley, Scotland, the son of a poor farmer. Details of his early life are slightly vague. Educated at the Badenoch Parochial School, he probably finished his secondary education near Inverness. At the end of 1752, he settled in Aberdeen and matriculated at King's College, Aberdeen, at the beginning of the following year. Macpherson was an average student, but since he was unable to afford his tuition, he left college with no degree after two years. He stayed at Marischal College (later the University of Aberdeen) for some time and later became a student of divinity at the University of Edinburgh, which he also left with no degree. In 1756 he returned to Ruthven and started teaching at the local charity school.

During his years as a student, Macpherson had written numerous poems. He managed to publish several of them in the neoclassical vein, including *The Highlander* (1758) which heralds some of the themes later expounded in the more famous epic poem *Fingal* (1761). Apparently disappointed by his own productions, he managed to persuade his publisher to destroy all the remaining copies of his first works. Acknowledging the fact that his literary career had made a rather inauspicious start, he decided to venture into more unusual poetic territory.

Proud of the rich Celtic oral tradition of his native region, Macpherson started visiting villages and listening to the village elders, who recited Gaelic verses, although Gaelic was not his native tongue. He decided to transcribe the few fragments he had gathered from various oral sources but did not do so immediately. In 1758 he left Ruthven to return to Edinburgh, where he planned to become a writer or at least to widen the scope of his literary relations. He started by working as a copy editor for an Edinburgh publisher, but a recurring lack of money prompted him to supplement his income by acting as a tutor to the children of wealthy Scottish families. His first pupil, the son of the laird of Balgowan, apparently enjoyed Macpherson's lessons and his company so much that the family decided to take him on a tour of Scotland. On this occasion, Macpherson was introduced to the philosopher Adam Fergusson, who shared his taste for Gaelic poetry and introduced him in turn to the poet and dramatist John Home, whose play *Douglas* was already a success. Intrigued by Macpherson's fragments of poetry, Home asked him for samples of his collection. Macpherson gave him a poem in English entitled *The Death of Oscar*, which Home decided to show Hugh Blair, then professor of rhetoric and belles lettres in Edinburgh and member of a Scottish literary club called the Select Society.

Now supported by the most prominent Edinburgh literati, including the philosopher David Hume and the philosopher and economist Adam Smith, Macpherson managed to publish his *Fragments of Ancient Poetry, Collected in the Highlands of Scotland* anonymously in 1760. That same year, he also received a grant that enabled him to travel to the islands of Scotland's west coast in order to look for more samples of Gaelic verses.

In 1761 MacPherson was able to produce two epic poems purportedly written by Ossian, a third-century bard, to celebrate the heroic deeds of his father, Fingal. Publication followed with *Fingal: An Ancient Epic Poem* in 1761, and with *Temora* in 1763, alongside other poetic pieces. That same year, an enthusiastic Hugh Blair published a *Critical Dissertation of the Poems of Ossian* and dubbed Ossian "the Homer of the North" despite growing suspicions—especially in England and Ireland—about the poems' authenticity. Those who believed they had been forged denied them any literary value for this very reason, while others insisted on their intrinsic quality, regardless of their authenticity. *The WORKS OF OSSIAN,* published in 1765, included *Fingal, Temora,* several other shorter poetic pieces, and Blair's *Critical Dissertation.* The debate on the fragments lasted several years, the controversy being fueled by the publication of Samuel Johnson's *A Journey to the Western Islands of Scotland* in 1773 and by the negative conclusions of the report published more than 10 years later, in 1805, by the Highland Society of Scotland.

Despite all this, Macpherson had nonetheless succeeded in becoming the famous writer he had always dreamt of being. He had also become the protégé of John Stuart, third earl of Bute. A few years before his poems were proved a forgery, the political situation in Great Britain prompted his political patron to send him to America. In 1764 he became secretary to George Johnstone, the new governor of West Florida. However, this appointment was only temporary, and Macpherson was soon sent back to Britain, where he became deeply involved in political life as a political pamphleteer, writing for Lord Shelburne (prime minister, 1782–83) and later for Lord North (prime minister, 1770–82). Macpherson now pursued a new, highly successful career, even reaching a certain degree of fame with a pamphlet against the American Declaration of Independence (1776). In the meantime, he had also started writing historical essays such as *An Introduction to the History of Great Britain and Ireland* (1771), soon followed by *Original Papers Containing the Secret History of Great Britain from the Restoration to the Accession of the House of Hanover* and *History of Great Britain from the Restoration to the Accession of the House of Hanover* (1775).

The success of his essays and the concomitant publication of the fourth edition of the poems of Ossian confirmed Macpherson's popularity as a writer in England and abroad. Despite the controversy, the forged poems were translated into many European languages, from Spanish to Russian, and greatly influenced writers, painters, and composers across continental Europe, including the poet and playwright JOHANN WOLFGANG VON GOETHE and the composer Friedrich Mendelssohn. *Fragments of Ancient Poetry,* translated into French, was even said to be among NAPOLEON BONAPARTE's favorite readings on the battlefields. Macpherson's supposedly pure, unsophisticated epic corresponded to a general search for the ancient, so-called authentic, regional roots of many national cultures, and appealed to nationalistic pride and poetic sensitivity alike across the continent.

In 1777 Macpherson was back on the political scene when he agreed to defend the financial interests of Mohamed Ali, nawab of Arcot, who owed vast sums to the East India Company. As part of his lobbying campaign in favour of the prince, Macpherson published *The History and Management of the East India Company* in 1779 and bought himself a seat in the House of Commons the following year. Thanks to the emoluments of his Indian client, he had finally become a rich man, to whom the British government granted the lands of Ewen of Cluny, former chieftain of his clan, whose lands had been forfeited after the Jacobite defeat of Culloden. Macpherson declined the estate but hired the famous architect Robert Adam to build the Villa Belleville on a tract of land he had purchased in his native region of the Spey Valley. Highly successful but in poor health, he died on February 17, 1796, and was buried in Westminster Abbey, as he wished.

**Further Reading**

Curley, Thomas M. "Samuel Johnson and Truth: the First Systematic Detection of Literary Deception in James MacPherson's Ossian." *The Age of Johnson: A Scholarly Annual* 17 (2006): 119–196.

DeGategno, Paul J. *James Macpherson.* Boston: Twayne Publishers, 1989.

Duncan, Ian. "The Pathos of Abstraction: Adam Smith, Ossian and Samuel Johnson." In *Scotland at the Borders of Romanticism,* edited by Ian Duncan, Leith David, and Janet Sorensen, 38–56. Cambridge: Cambridge University Press, 2004.

Gaskill, Howard, ed. *The Reception of Ossian in Europe.* London: Thoemmes, 2004.

Hall, Stephen T. "James Macpherson's Ossian: Forging Ancient Highland Identity for Scotland." In *Constructing Nations, Reconstructing Myth: Essays in the Honour of T. A. Shippey,* edited by Andrew Wahrn, Graham Johnson, and John Walter, 3–26. Turnhout, Belgium: Brepols, 2007.

Haywood, Ian. *The Making of History: A Study of the Literary Production of James Macpherson and Thomas Chatterton in Relation to Eighteenth Century Ideas of History and Fiction.* Rutherford, N.J.: Fairleigh Dickinson University Press, 1986.

Manning, Susan. "Henry Mackenzie's Report on Ossian: Cultural Authority in Transition." *Modern Language Quarterly* 68, no. 4 (December 2007): 517–539.

Moore, Dafydd, ed. *Ossian and Ossianism.* 4 vols. London: Routledge, 2004.

—Sylvie Kleiman-Lafon

## Malthus, Thomas   See ESSAY ON THE PRINCIPLE OF POPULATION.

## *Manfred: A Dramatic Poem*   Lord Byron (1817)

Famously described by CAROLINE LAMB one of his many lovers, and seen by much of his age, as "Mad, bad and dangerous to know," LORD BYRON (1788–1824) achieved major celebrity status. Since Byron's best-received protagonists share his many excesses, he soon inspired an infamous and wildly popular literary type: the Byronic hero. This persona takes center stage in Byron's conventionally Romantic closet drama *Manfred, a Dramatic Poem,* which was begun in 1816.

A typical Byronic hero, Manfred is isolated from the human race he rejects, even loathes, by his extensive knowledge and capacity for feeling.

In the chain of human relationships, he tells us, he had but one link, one individual whom he recognized as a peer: his sister (Byron 195). She committed suicide, and he cares for nothing except her forgiveness, which he must seek beyond the grave. Because Manfred feels himself superior to conventional society, he also rejects its norms and constraints. A typical theme in GOTHIC and darker Romantic works, and reflective of Byron's rumored incestuous relationship with his half sister, Augusta Leigh, the siblings had engaged in a sexual relationship. Such is a common occurrence in Romantic literature, as incest offers the most narcissistic of protagonists a means of loving a near image of themselves while flouting the rest of society and defying its conventions. Unlike Augusta Leigh, Manfred's sister ended the affair by taking her own life, as Manfred himself will do at the drama's conclusion. Another common motif, suicide had been glorified in Romantic literature ever since JOHANN WOLFGANG VON GOETHE published his enormously influential novel *The SORROWS OF YOUNG WERTHER* in 1774.

Also characteristic of Gothic and darker Romantic works is Manfred's interest in magic and the supernatural. In order to conjure the spirit of his dead sister into being and beg her forgiveness, he will use charms and spells to master the elements and bargain with the prince of darkness. In this sense he is much like Goethe's Faust (see *FAUST: A TRAGEDY*), who attempts to master the hidden forces of nature and trades his soul for forbidden knowledge. The dangers of using science to uncover forbidden knowledge or master natural forces are commonly treated in 19th-century literature, as the age's Naturphilosophers championed a philosophy of a unified natural world, while alchemy, mesmerism, and geology sought to uncover or classify nature and its hidden forces. Thus, it is not surprising that Goethe, the writer and Naturphilosopher whose work Byron admired, joined his peers in praising *Manfred,* noting that he could "not sufficiently admire" its genius (quoted in Bone 252).

While many Romantic heroes are similar to Shakespeare's tragic figures in that they initially have altruistic motives and morals, Manfred is not heroic in the conventional sense. As Peter

Thorslev and other critics have suggested, lacking "heroic virtue" in the traditional sense, he is instead motivated by "titanic passions, his pride, and his certainty of self-identity" (Thorslev 187). In this, Manfred has less in common with Hamlet than with NAPOLEON BONAPARTE, whom Byron admired. Like Bonaparte, Manfred simultaneously inspired the age's loathing and admiration. His willfulness, his lack of restraint, and his superhuman ambitions are designed to make one uncomfortable, even as one admires his uncompromising will.

**Further Reading**

Bone, Drummond, ed. *The Cambridge Companion to Byron.* Cambridge: Cambridge University Press, 2005.

Byron George, Gordon Baron. *Lord Byron: The Major Works.* Edited by Jerome J. McGann. New York: Oxford University Press, 2000.

Grosskurth, Phyllis. *Byron: the Flawed Angel.* Boston: Houghton Mifflin, 1997.

Thorslev, Peter. *The Byronic Hero: Types and Prototypes.* Minneapolis: University of Minnesota Press, 1962.

—Priscilla Glanville

## *Mansfield Park* Jane Austen (1814)

JANE AUSTEN's third published novel continues her characteristically ironic study of courtship, manners and marriage among the rural gentry established in her earlier novels SENSE AND SENSIBILITY (1811) and PRIDE AND PREJUDICE (1813). *Mansfield Park* follows the sentimental tradition of 18th-century novels such as Samuel Richardson's *Pamela* (1740) and culminates in the happy union of the heroine to the man she loves, leaving some scholars to question Austen's placement within the Romantic movement. Indeed, even more so than her earlier novels, *Mansfield Park* appears to endorse conventional morality and to reject the Romantic rebellion of earlier heroines like Marianne Dashwood and Elizabeth Bennet. Yet, in the novel's privileging of the English countryside and rural life, critique of aristocratic artfulness and decadence, and concern over SLAVERY in the British colonies, *Mansfield Park* explores common Romantic themes and encourages critical conversations about the integrity of the term *Romantic* as a stable category.

The novel centers on the life of Fanny Price, niece of the wealthy Sir Thomas and Lady Bertram. Immediately it makes clear the importance for women of a "good" marriage—or what society views as such. Unlike her sister Lady Bertram, Fanny's mother did not marry advantageously, and upon the advice of Mrs. Norris, Mrs. Price's other sister, the Bertrams invite Fanny to live with them out of charity. At Mansfield Park, Fanny grows accustomed to upper-middle-class society, though her snobbish cousins Tom, Maria, and Julia make clear her dependent position. Only in the Bertrams' younger son, Edward, does Fanny find friendship, and she grows up to be shy, retiring, and levelheaded.

When Sir Thomas visits his plantations in Antigua, important plot developments unfold: Discipline in the household starts to vanish; Maria becomes engaged to the wealthy Mr. Rushworth; glamorous siblings Mary and Henry Crawford befriend Fanny and the Bertrams; and John Yates, a friend of Tom's from school, visits Mansfield Park. The Bertram children compete for the affections of the Crawfords, Fanny anxiously watches her beloved Edward fall in love with Mary, and Yates proposes the scandalous performance of *Lover's Vows,* a play by ELIZABETH INCHBALD. The notion of "performance" and masquerade is central to the novel generally. When Sir Thomas unexpectedly returns from Antigua, order is temporarily restored. Edward postpones proposing to Mary because of her apparently immoral behavior, and Maria marries Rushworth. Trouble resumes, however, when Fanny rejects Henry's proposal of marriage and incurs the wrath of Sir Thomas for declining such a fortunate marriage. She is sent to visit her parents' home, where she realizes the extent of her alienation from her parents' less prosperous existence. Meanwhile, things go dreadfully awry with the Bertrams: Tom's debauched lifestyle has left him gravely ill, Maria has left her husband to run away with Henry, and Julia has eloped with Yates. Upon her return to Mansfield Park, Fanny finds herself newly appreciated by the older Bertrams as well as Edward, who finally realizes his deep love for her.

Criticism of the novel often stems from Fanny's sometimes infuriating goodness and the novel's seemingly conservative positions on theatrical performances, women's desire, and social custom. Edward Said also sees Austen quietly endorsing British imperialism and slavery through the Bertrams' interests in Antigua, where Austen's own family held various investments. On the other hand, some critics conclude that Austen explicitly critiques Sir Thomas's tyranny both at home and abroad. The title *Mansfield Park* could directly reference the 1772 Mansfield judgment, which ruled that James Somerset, a black slave brought from Virginia, was a free man in England and could not be forced to return to slavery. Additionally, Austen's letters reveal that she was impressed with the work of the abolitionist Thomas Clarkson. This debate about the novel's position on slavery is indicative of larger critical discussions about how to read *Mansfield Park*. If Austen is not condoning middle-class comforts at the expense of enslaved others, then perhaps readings of the novel's moral judgments also should be reconsidered. Notwithstanding this controversy, *Mansfield Park* remains a central text in Romanticism and in Austen studies.

## Further Reading

Auerbach, Nina. "Jane Austen's Dangerous Charm: Feeling as One Ought about Fanny Price." In *Jane Austen: New Perspectives*, edited by Janet Todd, 208–223. New York: Holmes and Meier, 1983.

Austen, Jane. *Mansfield Park*. Oxford: Oxford World's Classics, 2003.

Greenfield, Susan C. "Fanny's Misreading and the Misreading of Fanny: Women, Literature, and Interiority in *Mansfield Park*." *Texas Studies in Literature and Language* 36 (1994): 306–327.

Fraiman, Susan. "Jane Austen and Edward Said: Gender, Culture, and Imperialism." *Critical Inquiry* 21 (1995): 65–92.

Said, Edward. "Jane Austen and Empire." In *Culture and Imperialism*, 80–97. New York: Knopf, 1993.

—Esther Godfrey

## "Man Was Made to Mourn: A Dirge"
### Robert Burns (1786)

Written in summer 1785, "Man Was Made to Mourn" ("Originally a song to the tune of Peggy Bawn") was first published in the Kilmarnock edition of ROBERT BURNS's *Poems, Chiefly in the Scottish Dialect* (1786). Gilbert Burns shed some light on the poem's composition, observing that his brother sometimes wrote to "bring forward some favourite sentiment of the author. He [Robert] used to remark to me, that he could not well conceive a more mortifying picture of human life, than a man seeking work. In casting about in his mind how this sentiment might be brought forward, the elegy *Man was made to Mourn* was composed . . ." (quoted in Burns 1801, 3, 384). The poem is thus uncompromisingly bleak and the plight of the unemployed man pivotal.

The poem begins on a November evening in Ayrshire when the young speaker meets an old man, "the rev'rend Sage" (l. 10). After enquiring whether the younger man is interested only in "youthful Pleasure" (l. 12) or has a "thirst of wealth" (l. 11)—unlike the old man himself, who has all too swiftly become "prest with cares and woes" (l. 13)—he becomes overtly critical and political, noting that "hundreds" (l. 19) have to work the land for "a haughty lordling's pride" (l. 20). The old man then elaborates on the time-honored contrast between the "licentious Passions" (l. 30) of youth and the "Cares and Sorrows" (l. 38) that have worn him down. In stanza 6, this contrast is extended to the wealthy, who are the "few [who] seem favourites of Fate" (l. 41) and the vast numbers of poor everywhere, "the crouds in ev'ry land, / All wretched and forlorn" (ll. 45–46). The regular rhyme and rhythm throughout and the fact that stanzas 3–6 all build up to the climax, "Man was made to mourn," make this conclusion all the more compelling. The focus subsequently shifts from man's "num'rous Ills" (l. 49) to the yet more debilitating "Regret, Remorse and Shame" (l. 52) and ultimately produces the slightly different and hence more emphatic conclusion that "Man's inhumanity to Man / Makes countless thousands mourn!" (ll. 55–56).

The image of the desolate unemployed man, "so abject, mean and vile" (l. 58), in stanza 8 is both stark and unforgiving. As the scholar Thomas Crawford notes, this is not just about a small-time tenant farmer facing eviction, but about all unemployed people who are not "give[n] leave to toil" (l. 60). The old man next questions why he has been given independence of mind and yet is still to be "yon lordling's slave" (l. 65). The rhetoric here underlines the fact that this is a critique of oppression and exploitation in any context (Thomas Crawford 22). After a moment's respite in stanza 10, when the old man reasons that he may be prejudiced and life must have some pleasures, the final stanza is explicitly and emphatically overwhelmed by death. Although there is a contrast between how the rich and poor perceive death—"a blest relief" (l. 87) and "welcome" (l. 83) for the poor and old, and "fear[ed]" (l. 85) by the rich—it is nonetheless evident that death, as the consummate leveller, comes to all.

Although not especially popular in the Burns canon, "Man Was Made to Mourn" does deal in a human way with man's plight, a common Burnsian (and Romantic) theme. It may not have the verve and vivacity of Burns's vernacular Scots poems, but the use of regular form, alliteration, assonance, and repetition makes the poem's pessimism all the more rhetorically powerful and fails to undermine the heartfelt sincerity of its bleakness.

## Further Reading

Carruthers, Gerard. *Robert Burns.* Tavistock, Eng.: Northcote House, 2006.

Crawford, Robert. *The Bard Robert Burns: A Biography.* Princeton, N.J.: Princeton University Press, 2008.

———, ed. *Robert Burns and Cultural Authority.* Edinburgh: Polygon, 1999.

Crawford, Thomas. *Burns: A Study of the Poems and Songs.* Edinburgh and London: Oliver & Boyd, 1960.

Burns, Robert. *The Letters of Robert Burns.* 2nd rev. ed. 2 vols. Edited by J. De Lancey Furguson and G. Ross Roy. Oxford: Clarendon Press, 1985.

———. *The Poems and Songs of Robert Burns.* 3 vols. Edited by James Kinsley. Oxford: Clarendon Press, 1968.

———. *The Works of Robert Burns.* 2nd ed. 4 vols. Edited by James Currie. London, 1801.

Rodger, Johnny, and Gerard Carruthers, eds. *Fickle Man: Robert Burns in the 21st Century.* Dingwall, Scotland: Sandstone Press, 2009.

Simpson, Kenneth. *Burns Now.* Edinburgh: Canongate Academic, 1997.

———, ed. *Robert Burns.* Aberdeen: Association for Scottish Literary Studies, 1994.

—Shona Allan

## *Maria, or, The Wrongs of Woman* Mary Wollstonecraft (1797)

MARY WOLLSTONECRAFT is generally celebrated for her visionary and universally acknowledged essay VINDICATION OF THE RIGHTS OF WOMAN. On a more personal level, she is remembered as the wife of WILLIAM GODWIN and the mother of MARY SHELLEY. But she is more seldom known for her novelistic skills. *Mary, a Fiction* was written in 1788, but in 1798 it was edited and published posthumously as a fragment by Godwin as *Maria, or, The Wrongs of Woman.*

The story of *Maria* centers on a woman whose tyrannical husband has put her into an asylum. As with so many variations of her own feminine self—Mary, Maria—Wollstonecraft's heroines speak (and write) in the name of female independence, embodying the political claims of their sex and long-time struggle for equal rights and opportunities. More than just fiction, this story of male "domestic tyranny" (Wollstonecraft 53), insensitive to the pangs of motherhood, is a powerful statement on what a modern woman is and, by empathy, on what a better man for that woman should be: "She [Maria] found however that she could think of nothing else; of, if she thought of her daughter, it was to wish that she had a father whom her mother could respect and love" (16). Wollstonecraft's ambition hits hard on the reader's consciousness as she articulates a link between society and sexual identity: "I am ready to allow, that education and circumstances lead men to think and act with less delicacy than the preservation of order in society demands from women. . . . Various are the cases, in which a woman ought to separate herself from her husband; and mine, I may be allowed empathically to insist, comes under the description of the most aggravated" (118). With this clear purpose in mind, the fictional tale that follows allows Wollstonecraft to impose her feminist manifesto without depriving her readership of the exoticism of an uncanny world and its share of sensational thrills.

This philosophical tale is built around the misfortunes of an 18th-century woman who is too insightful and emancipated for her age, with clear echoes of the GOTHIC: "Abodes of horror have frequently been described, and castles, filled with specters and chimeras, conjured up by the magic spell of genius to harrow the soul, and absorb the wondering mind. But formed of such stuff as dreams are made of, what were they to the mansion of despair, in one corner of which Maria sat, endeavouring to recall her scattered thoughts" (1). Wollstonecraft's talent is such that the extravagance of her "romantic fancy" does not in any way limit the extent of her social commitment. She shows her readers how her heroine experiences "the crushing hand of power, hardened by the exercise of injustice" (5).

Daringly for the time, Wollstonecraft makes a call for sexual equality that includes a woman's right to physical pleasure. In a candid speech, the novelist makes the point that: "When novelists and moralists praise as a virtue a woman's coldness of constitution and want of passion, I am disgusted. Truth is the only basis of virtue; and we cannot, without depraving our minds, endeavour to please a lover or husband, but in proportion as he pleases us. Men, more effectually to enslave us, may inculcate this partial morality, but let us not blush for nature without a cause!" (76). Wollstonecraft does not want to over-fictionalize the truth when it comes to the future well-being of an entire generation of repressed women. She writes, of course, about her own experience but also gives a voice to so many others of her educated contemporaries. In the novel, Maria, craving for intellectual substance, is as comfortable reading John Dryden and JOHN MILTON as she is translating JEAN-JACQUES ROUSSEAU from the French. This is how wide her reading is, and how menacing she would thus be to a narrow-minded husband.

In *Maria* Wollstonecraft joins fellow women writers, such as MARY HAYS and even ELIZABETH INCHBALD in *Nature and Art,* in denouncing all the excesses of female subordination. Against male influences and tastes, a radical school of women's writing is therefore born out of the depths of forced silences. Gathered around a "great moral purpose," and in reference to the hardships of her brave characters—Maria, but also Jemima—Wollstonecraft relies on the mixed powers of intellect and sensibility to "exhibit the misery and oppression, peculiar to women, that arise out of the partial laws and customs of society" (Wollstonecraft 125).

**Further Reading**

Elfenbein, A. "Mary Wollstonecraft and the Sexuality of Genius." In *A Cambridge Companion to Mary Wollstonecraft,* edited by Claudia Johnson, 228–45. Cambridge: Cambridge University Press, 2002.

Johnson, C. L. "Mary Wollstonecraft's Novels." In *A Cambridge Companion to Mary Wollstonecraft,* edited by Claudia Johnson, Cambridge: Cambridge University Press, 2002.

Tomalin, Claire. *The Life and Death of Mary Wollstonecraft.* Rev. ed. London: Penguin, 1992.

Wollstonecraft, Mary. *Maria, or the Wrongs of Woman,* in *The Posthumous Works of the Author of A Vindication of the Rights of Woman.* Edited by William Godwin. Mineola, N.Y.: Dover Publications, 2005.

—Caroline Bertonèche.

## "Marie Antoinette's Lamentation in Her Prison of the Temple" Mary Robinson (1793)

The execution by guillotine of the French queen Marie Antoinette (in Paris, October 16, 1793) prompted a deluge of memorial verses, drawings, and engravings. Despite the antimonarchist sentiments of many Romantic poets, the execution shocked many of those who had favored the revolutionary cause, and consequently revolutionary fervor cooled in Britain. Among Romantic writers, MARY ROBINSON was one of the few to have actually come into contact with the French king and queen (another was EDMUND BURKE). She describes the 1783 meeting in her memoirs as a "*grand couvert,* at which the King acquitted himself with more alacrity than grace, afforded a magnificent display of epicurean luxury. The Queen ate nothing. . . . She appeared to survey, with peculiar attention, a miniature of the Prince of Wales, which Mrs Robinson wore on her bosom, and of which, on the ensuing day, she commissioned the duke of Orleans to request the loan" (Robinson 1801, 2:94–95). The royal couple is presented as being on display, as is Robinson herself, and her memoirs make great play of her being a leader of British fashion, almost royal herself, thanks to her close relationship with the prince.

Robinson's sense of sympathy with the French queen makes itself felt in this poem, which was published in the *Monthly Magazine* in May 1793. The background to the poem is that Marie Antoinette had been imprisoned in the Temple prison in August 1792, together with her two children—Louis XVIII (who was seven), and his sister, Marie Thérèse. Marie Antoinette was accused of having incestuous relations with her son. The poem takes the form of a dramatic monologue spoken by the queen as she sits desolate in her cell. The warm "ruby" light (l. 1) of the setting sun should feel warm, but it seems to "mock" her "weary woes" (l. 4). This is "because on my sad breast appears / A dreadful record—WRITTEN WITH MY TEARS!" (ll. 5–6). Throughout the poem, certain phrases are capitalized as if to double their emphasis, as if the words themselves are not enough. The lamentation stresses the queen's pain-racked body; her broken health is tied up with her shattered life. Nighttime brings no release: While the poorest children of the country manage to sleep, the woman who was once at its head is denied this luxury. In an image that capitalizes on the popular idea of the queen as victim-martyr, it is explained that hers is a bed of thorns.

The dawn of each new day brings not hope but yet more sorrow. Nor do the sleeping figures of her children provide any comfort. The queen is haunted by the "dread" that their lives will be short; they are "CHERUBS ON THEIR FUNERAL BED!" (l. 24) The queen knows that "inhuman hands" will shortly separate the mother from her children; she begs that "BARBARITY" will "yet spare awhile / The sacred treasures of my throbbing breast; . . . their infant hearts, untouch'd by guile, . . ." (ll. 31–33) Where once the queen was adorned with rich jewels, her children are now her most valuable possessions, delicate plants that require nurture. Invoking the symbol of the fleur-de-lis—the lily traditionally associated with the French monarchy—she begs that "GALLIAS's LILIES" be allowed to "bloom" and "to deck with sweets A DUNGEON's GLOOM!" (ll. 35–36) She vows to protect her children from the "SAVAGE TIGER" that is revolutionary France. Her words have a certain tragic quality to them; in our role as Robinson's readers, we know—as the queen does not—that this will not be possible.

The second part of the poem focuses on the sounds the queen can hear from her cell. The contrast between the joyful church bells outside and the place in which she has been cast is striking. The prison is a place "Where MEAGRE GRIEF and SCOWLING HORROR DWELL!" (l. 54) The sound of the mob and their cannons make her panic, only to be laughed at by her "TYRANT JAILER" (l. 60). Deep in her heart, the queen knows she will die and begs that her "soul" will be able to "meet the keen lance of death with steadfast eye" (ll. 60–61). There is no escape; physically and psychologically she is trapped: "Where'er I turn, a thousand ills appear' / Arm'd at all points, in terrible array / PALE, HOOD-WINK'D MURDER, ever lurking near / And COWARD CRUELTY that shuns the day" (ll. 67–70). They have already killed her "Lord"—a reference to her murdered husband, whose show trial and public death is akin to that Jesus Christ. As king, Louis XVI, too, was divinely appointed, something his tormentors chose to ignore. His widow, meanwhile, can only wait in a state of uncertainty not knowing when her time will come. She hopes that after death her soul will find "sweet OBLIVION's dream" and find "some more peaceful shore" (75–76).

The woman drawn by Robinson is not the "scarlet woman" or "demi-rep" of antimonarchist propaganda but a "victim." Like other women poets of the time, such as FELICIA HEMANS, tended to do, Robinson domesticates her heroine; devoid of the trappings of monarchy, her feelings are those of every other wife and mother. The woman-centered subject matter is one of the ways in which Robinson differs from other male poets who wrote about the FRENCH REVOLUTION: Her interest is not in politicians but, rather, those who are so caught up in events that they cannot control its turmoil. There is perhaps a suggestion, too, that although one of the goals of the Revolution is "liberty," at least half the population (women) will never be free; theirs are lives destined to be lived out in servitude.

## Further Reading

Robinson, Mary. *Impartial Reflections on the Present Situation of the Queen of France.* London: John Bell, 1791.

———. *Memoirs of the Late Mrs Robinson, Written by Herself.* 4 vols. Edited by M. E. Robinson. London: R. Phillips, 1801.

———. *Selected Poems.* Edited by Judith Pascoe. Peterborough, Ont.: Broadview Press, 2003.

—Andrew Maunder

## *Marmion* Sir Walter Scott (1808, 1833)

Shortly after the success of his first romantic tale, the long poem *The Lay of the Last Minstrel* (1805), SIR WALTER SCOTT began writing his second tale, *Marmion.* Scott's publisher was so certain that the new tale would sell that he bought the copyright for 1,000 guineas (approximately 10 times the annual wage of a skilled laborer) before it had even been written. Scott began writing the poem late in 1806 and finished the piece in 1807. However, the edition of the tale that is currently used in academic studies is Scott's 1833 revision, which contained minor additions and linguistic corrections to the original text.

*Marmion* is the story of young Lord Marmion; his mistress, the nun Constance; the rich Clara de Clare; and Clara's lover, Sir Ralph de Wilton. The tale is delivered in six cantos, each beginning with a letter to one of Scott's friends. The letters do little to further the plot of the tale, but they do provide a historical backdrop for the story: the Battle of Flodden Field, which took place on September 9, 1513, between King James of Scotland and the English earl of Surrey. The Scottish suffered a horrible defeat at this battle, their king slain during the fight, although they maintained their honor with the French by diverting British troops from the war in France. While the battle serves as the setting for this tale, the story itself is only slightly affected by the war and its outcome.

At the start of the tale, Lord Marmion lusts after the rich Clara, even though he knows she is betrothed to Sir Ralph De Wilton. Assisted by his mistress Constance, Marmion writes a letter that implicates De Wilton in treason, forcing De Wilton to duel with Marmion for his honor. When De Wilton loses the duel, he is found guilty of treason and is forced to go into exile. Constance believes that her actions will again earn her the love of Marmion; instead, her lover abandons her, and she is walled up alive inside a convent as punishment for breaking her vows. Meanwhile, Clara attempts to clear De Wilton's name by producing documents that prove his innocence. When these documents are given to the earl of Angus, De Wilton is once again knighted and allowed to defend his honor against the vile Marmion. However, before he is able to seek his revenge, the Battle of Flodden Field occurs, and in the course of the battle, Marmion is killed. De Wilton, on the other hand, is proven to be a valiant hero, regaining both his honor and the hand of Clara.

Despite the popularity of *Marmion* with the reading public (partially due to the public's love for Scott), the author's literary contemporaries disliked the tale. Several individuals, including LORD BYRON, felt that the poem was less a work of literary genius and more a simplistic retelling of history. Additionally, many critics, both past and present, have difficulty correlating Scott's introductory letters with the actual text of the poem, with some going so far as to claim the letters are dishonest. As a whole, the poem is often difficult to follow, and there are several subplots that have little to do with the tale's main action. The most significant criticism of the work, however, centers on Scott's use of Marmion as the tale's hero. While he fits the pattern of the Byronic hero, Marmion is so fatally flawed by human desires and lusts that few critics have much good to say about him. Some have tried to claim De Wilton as the tale's true hero, an interpretation that has tended to be more acceptable despite Scott's obvious intentions against such a reading.

Although much of this poem is unknown to the modern reader, at least two portions of the tale are still read and memorized in the contemporary college classroom. Canto 5, often known as the Lochinvar passage, is still published in most college English anthologies. Also, one of the most famous quotations in the English language is found in canto 6, lines 332–333: "O, what a tangled web we weave, / When first we practise to deceive!" These lines are a specific reference to the fate of Constance following her misguided attempt to condemn De Wilton, but they can also been read as the moral to Scott's tale.

## Further Reading

Alexander, J. H. *Marmion: Studies in Interpretation and Composition.* Salzburg, Austria: Institut fur Anglistik und Amerikanistik, 1981.

Lincoln, Andrew. *Walter Scott and Modernity.* Edinburgh: Edinburgh University Press, 2007.

Raleigh, John Henry. "What Scott Meant to the Victorians." *Victorian Studies* 7, no. 1 (September 1963): 7–34.

Scott, Sir Walter. *Marmion.* Honolulu: University Press of the Pacific, 2001.

—Melissa Ann Griggs

## *Marriage of Heaven and Hell, The* William Blake (1793)

*The Marriage of Heaven and Hell* begins with "The Argument," rendered in irregular, unrhymed verse. The main text comprises 22 plates in the form of parables, aphorisms, "fancies," emblems, bitter denunciations, impassioned criticism, and quite often plain and simple statements of WILLIAM BLAKE's own views. It is followed by "A Song of Liberty" in three plates. The historical allusions in "The Song of Liberty" suggest that it was not composed before 1792, while it is generally accepted that *The Marriage of Heaven and Hell* was not begun until 1790.

*Marriage* is Blake's first attempt at deliberate and systematic formulation of the beliefs that were to shape his future writings. It is in this work that those beliefs find coherent, cogent, and powerful expression. *Marriage* contains, first of all, Blake's enunciation of what the critic M. D. Paley characterizes as the "ethic of liberation" through the cultivation of boundless springs of energy, which would overthrow restraints imposed on man by the strangulating "reason" and the false codes of morality supported by conventional religion (Paley). Blake denies the dualism of the body and the soul; maintains that divinity rests within each man, and, dialectically inverting the values of good and evil, castigates the sterile moral code that evolved out of this conventional dichotomy between these two forces. He lays bare the repressive nature of what is conventionally regarded as "good" and praises what is normally considered "evil" for its quality of ener-

getic rebellious opposition. Above all, in *Marriage*, he develops the doctrine of the "contraries."

Plate 1 of *Marriage* sets the scene, reveals the nature of the major concerns that would dominate this work, and introduces the main characters. It is with plate 2 that the narrative begins. Rintrah, who symbolizes Blake's wrath, the anger of the poet prophet, "roars, and shakes his fires in the burdened air / Hungry clouds swag on the deep" (ll. 1–2). Through his unmitigated anger, the poet-prophet seeks to chastise the society for its total degeneration into a state of sterility, passivity, lack of energy, and imagination that in Blake's view characterized the society of his day. "The Argument" as a whole implies that false religion has obscured the path of truth. In plates 3 and 4 Blake proclaims the emergence of a new Heaven—"eternal Hell," the revolutions in America and France—that marked the resurgence of the spirit of energy, rebellion, revolution, and an end to passive acceptance of the conventional values.

The literary scholar Harold Bloom points out how the concept of the "contraries" is at work in *Marriage* even before the poet announces the doctrine in plate 3. In Plate 1 we find that the roses are planted where the thorns still grow, and honeybees sing even though the heath remains barren. Blake opposes cliff to the river, tomb to the spring, and the bleached bones to the red clay. The meek man is later turned into an angry prophet. Blake states his dialectic thus: "Without contraries there is no progression. Attraction and Repulsion, Reason and Energy, Love and Hate are necessary to human existence" (plate 3, ll. 7–9). In the context of human existence, Blake maintains, there can be no progression without the stimulus and provocation of opposing forces. It is active opposition that channels static human existence into creativity.

It is significant that by the "marriage" of such contrary forces as heaven and hell, Blake implies that we have to cease valuing one contrary above the other. The "marriage" thus does not signify a state of unification, comingling, or mutual annihilation yielding a new whole. Rather, it suggests a reorganization of the contraries into a state of tension so that they give life to each other. Blake's use of the metaphor of *marriage*, though not rare among the Romantic poets, is the most daring and complex.

Blake maintains that it is the materialistic and rationalistic Lockean apprehension (see LOCKE, JOHN) which is inadequate because it fails to see the truly positive nature of opposing forces. It is in the light of this principle that he seeks to reexamine conventional opposition and the implicit value judgment involved in the two apparently contradictory concepts of good and evil. The conventional moral code places them as negating each other. Blake advances the view that when good embodies the sterile moral code, this is in fact evil. Evil, when embodying energy and revolution, freedom and imagination, should in fact be considered good.

Blake then goes on to analyze the errors of conventional religion. The body and the soul, he maintain, are not distinct from each other. The body is that part of the soul which is perceived through the limited sense perception of man. Also, it is wrong to attribute energy, which is generally associated with evil, to the body and then reason to the soul—and thus conclude that reason is superior to energy. To the conventional belief that the Christian God will torment man in eternity for following his energies, Blake boldly proclaims his view that "Energy is eternal delight" (plate 4, l. 29). According to Blake, the 17th-century poet JOHN MILTON, author of *Paradise Lost*, celebrates superiority of energy over reason because he created Satan, who is endowed with energy and thus has greater attraction. Milton was culpable as he had created a God who symbolized tyranny and who was more like a despot than like a friend among men.

The next four plates deal with the "Proverbs of Hell." Blake seeks to offer approval of energy, action, and defiance and expresses contempt for the weak and the passive. The sexual symbolism of some of the proverbs seeks to belittle the conventional restraints upon senses that for Blake are a major source of energy. Some deal with the question of perception, and a few others seeks to define the nature of action. But the more significant ones celebrate energy. The closeness of true humanity and the godhead is enunciated. The concepts of the Divine Humanity is one of the fundamental concepts of Blakean thought.

*The Marriage of Heaven and Hell* achieves its finale in the triumphant and prophetic tones of "A Song of Liberty," celebrating the resurgence of revolutionary activity in America and France. The "Song" begins with the groaning Enitharmon, as the eternal female transforms herself in Blake's later writings. Though "Albion's coast is sick" (l. 3) and "the American meadows faint" (l. 3), the "shadows of prophecy shiver along the lakes and the rivers and mutter across the ocean" (ll. 5–7). As Enitharmon is in labor with Orc, revolution is imminent. Blake calls upon the nations of the world to rise in rebellion. The spirit and champion of revolution, Orc—the fiery youth—is another figure that is developed much more fully later and appears in most of Blake's later poems, from *America* to *Vela*.

It is, of course, a commonplace of Blake scholarship that his canon is "Bible-soaked." The Bible remained an all-pervasive influence on the poet's mind, and his thinking always expressed itself in terms of a story of fall and resurrection. Underlining the rich and varied mosaic patterns of *Marriage* is the essential biblical ethos and progresses through various episodes that have their correspondences in biblical episodes. The mixture of the prose and poetry owes something to the vogue of this style in Blake's day in collections of proverbs and aphorisms as well as popular primers such as John Newbery's *A Little Pretty Pocket Book* (1744)—pious little books that contained woodcut illustrations, short poems designed to teach alphabets ("In Adam's Fall / We sinn'd All"), dialogues, hymns, proverbs, catechisms, the Lord's Prayer, the Ten Commandments, and so on. Blake was not only familiar with such primers, he may have executed engravings for them. He seems to have modeled some of his illustrations in *Marriage* after some of the standard illustrations found in the primers. A common frontispiece to primers is the "Tree of Knowledge," sometimes showing a figure in a tree knocking alphabetic fruit to a figure below. It has an unmistakable parallel with an illustration in plate 2 of *Marriage* where a figure in the tree hands down fruit to another figure below.

The amount of bitterness, the sting of irony, and the unrelenting satire that mark *The Marriage of Heaven and Hell* align Blake to the tradition to which also belong authors including Desiderius Erasmus, Henry Fielding, François Rabelais, and Jonathan Swift. The triumph of Blake's satiric art lies in the fact that he achieves a mixture of intellectual satire and prophecy, and thus he fuses the classical and the biblical tradition. In spite of the obvious debt that this work owes to various influences on its form as well as its content, the essential uniqueness of its design and structure and the perennial timeliness of its message remain unparalleled. If the salvation of man, spiritually and politically, was Blake's primary concern throughout his life, that concern finds its most appropriate expression in *The Marriage of Heaven and Hell.*

**Further Reading**

Blake, William. *Poetry and Prose of William Blake.* Edited by David Erdman and Harold Bloom. New York: Doubleday Anchor, 1965.

Damon S. Forster. *A Blake Dictionary: The Ideas and Symbols of William Blake.* Providence, R.I.: Brown University Press, 1965.

Paley, M. D. *Energy and Imagination: The Development of Blake's Thought.* Oxford: Clarendon Press, 1970.

Taylor, G. J. "The Structure of *The Marriage,* A Revolutionary Primer." *Studies in Romanticism* 13 (1974): 141–146.

—G. R. Taneja

## Martineau, Harriet (1802–1876)

Born in Norwich, England, on June 12, 1802, Harriet Martineau, was allowed by her parents to enjoy a similar education to that of her three brothers, at least before they were sent to university. She became an extraordinarily prolific and popular writer for the ordinary reading public on questions of social reform, economics, politics, religion, education, and women's role in society. Though she wrote a great deal of nonfictional prose—essays, reviews, translations, how-to manuals, travelogues, biographies, and histories—she is best known for publishing a series of social instruction novels, using fiction to expound on the principles of political economy.

Martineau got the idea of using narrative to teach political economy by reading Jane Marcet's 1816 book *Conversations on Political Economy,* but while Marcet addressed middle classes, Martineau addressed "*my great pupil,* the public" (quoted in Hunter, 39). So she told publisher William Tait. First published serially at an incredible rate of one volume per month, *Illustrations of Political Economy* (1834), a best-selling collection of 25 lengthy stories, was also inspired by the parliamentary blue books on the state of the country vis-à-vis INDUSTRIALISM, the greatest happiness principle of Jeremy Bentham and James Mill, Adam Smith's writings on laissez-faire, Thomas Malthus's ESSAY ON THE PRINCIPLE OF POPULATION, and David Ricardo's attack on the Corn Laws and approbation of free trade. The different expository stories that make up the *Illustrations* dramatize one or more economic theory. "Weal and Woe in Garveloch," for example, articulates in narrative Malthus's theory that the only means to decrease the suffering of the poor is to decrease the number of poor, who have to compete with each other for scarce jobs and resources. "A Manchester Strike" stages liberalism's vehement condemnation of factory legislation.

But Martineau should not be understood simply as an ideologue for industrial laissez-faire or an apologist for middle-class social ascendancy. Aside from the fact that she altered her views throughout her life, she was in many ways a social and political radical in the spirit of some of the first generation of Romantic poets and thinkers. In "Weal and Woe" she advocates late marriage and increased prudence, and perhaps implies the need for birth control, "the preventive check." Such a position coming from a woman—and one who was unmarried—had critics such as George Poulett Scrope in writing *The Quarterly Review,* "It is quite impossible not to be shocked, nay disgusted, with many of the unfeminine and mischievous doctrines on the principles of social welfare. . . . Poor innocent! She has been puzzling over Mr Malthus's arithmetical and geometrical ratios, for knowledge which she should have obtained by a simple question or two of her mama. . . . A *woman* who thinks child-bearing a *crime against society!* An *unmarried woman* who declaims against *marriage* . . ." (Scrope 423–425).

Though she had a faith in science, rationalism, progress, and the social order that was decidedly anti-Romantic, Martineau's fierce dedication to the abolition of SLAVERY, women's rights, and political activism aligns her with THOMAS PAINE and WILLIAM GODWIN, both of whom she admired greatly. As Deborah Anna Logan states in her introduction to the *Illustrations,* Martineau "participate[d] in the 'democratization' of knowledge encouraged by the Romantic writers, in turn establishing the foundation for the reform literature of the 1830s and paralleling the rise in literacy among the masses" (in Martineau 2004, 31). Harriet Martineau died in Ambleside, Cumbra, on June 27, 1876.

**Further Reading**

Hill, Michael, and Susan Hoecker-Drysdale, eds. *Harriet Martineau: Theoretical and Methodological Perspectives.* New York: Routledge, 2001.

Hunter, Shelogh. *Harriet Martineau.* Aldershot, Eng.: Scholar Press, 1995.

Logan, Deborah. *The Hour and the Woman. Harriet Martineau's "somewhat remarkable" Life.* DeKalb: Northern Illinois University Press, 2002.

Martineau, Harriet. *Harriet Martineau's Autobiography.* 2 vols. 1877. Reprint, London: Virago, 1983.

———. *Illustrations of Political Economy: Selected Tales.* Edited by Deborah Anna Logan. Peterborough, Ont.: Broadview Press, 2004.

Scrope, George Poulett. "Review." In *Illustrations of Political Economy: Selected Tales,* edited by Deborah Anna Logan, Peterborough, Ont.: Broadview Press, 2004.

—Rob Breton

## "Mary, the Maid of the Inn"  Robert Southey (1796)

This is one of a number of ballads written by ROBERT SOUTHEY in the 1790s and published in his *Poems* of 1797. The ballads (others include "Donica," "Rudiger," and "The Witch") took their inspiration from "real life" tales and folklore.

In this poem, Southey adapts the tale of Mary Clarkson, who was said to have gone to the Kirkstall Abbey ruins at night to collect a branch of the alder tree and saw three men carrying a corpse. The wind lifted the hat from one of the men, and it landed at Mary's feet. She took the hat back to the inn, where she discovered it belonged to her sweetheart, William Bedford (this name is Richard in the ballad). Eventually the three men were arrested, tried, and hanged. According to Southey: "The story of the following ballad was related to me, when a school boy, as a fact which had really happened in the North of England. I have adopted the metre of Mr. [Matthew] Lewis's 'Alonzo and Imogene'—a poem deservedly popular" (Southey 1989, Warter 2181). Southey's own "paltry ballad" as he described it, was equally successful—more so than his other so-called serious works, to his annoyance. As he noted: "[I]n my own mind it values little; yet how popular it has become! and where one person reads the 'Hymn to the Penates,' unquestionably the best piece in the volume, fifty can repeat that foolish ballad" (Warter I 69). Later, in 1809, he reported with a mixture of pride and disdain the poem's adaptation into "a melodrama . . . at one of the Strand theatres. . . . I verily believe that at least half my reputation is owing to that paltry ballad, which is bad enough to spoil a very fine story. The strolling players recite it here about the country (Warter 2, 181).

Yet while Southey wrote disparagingly of his "Balladings which I . . . look upon as the cask droppings—cheese parings & candle ends," he enjoyed hunting out old stories, and his efforts in this genre are sophisticated examples of the form. "Mary, the Maid of the Inn" is an eerie piece of writing that uses the form of the broadside ballad—that is to say, a printed set of verses (with or without music) usually relating in ghoulish fashion the adventures or misfortunes of a criminal or his or her victim and published for mass consumption. The poem opens with a question travelers often ask as they pass by the inn: "Who is she, the poor Maniac, whose wildly-fix'd eyes / Seem a heart overcharged to express? / She weeps not, yet often and deeply she sighs, / She never complains, but her silence implies / The composure of settled distress" (ll. 1–5). The poet then goes onto the explain the reasons for this; he takes the reader / listener back to the time to when Mary was a carefree, pretty young girl, delighting her customers and ready for fun: "The Traveller remembers who journeyed this way / No damsel so lovely, no damsel so gay / As Mary the Maid of the Inn" (ll. 13–15).

One evening, challenged to a wager by two guests, Mary agrees to visit an old haunted abbey on a stormy night (despite rumors about the ghosts of the monks who roam there). She sets off confidently: "O'er the path so well known still proceeded the Maid / Where the Abbey rose dim on the sight, / Thro' the gate-way she entered, she felt not afraid / Yet the ruins were lonely and wild, and their shade / Seem'd to deepen the gloom of the night" (ll. 56–60). Arriving at the abbey, and notwithstanding her fear, she plucks a branch from the bough of the elder tree as she has been asked to do. Suddenly she hears voices. Hiding, she sees two men carrying a body and realizes that her fiancé Richard is a body snatcher. Narrowly missing discovery when the wind blows off the hat of one of the men, she runs back to the inn with the hat, which she has seized: ". . . with wild speed, she rush'd in at the door, / She gazed horribly eager around, / Then her limbs could support their faint burthen no more, / And exhausted and breathless she sunk on the floor / Unable to utter a sound" (ll. 91–95). She is about to reveal what she has seen when the realizes she has brought the hat with her: "Her eyes from that object convulsively start, / For—oh God what cold horror then thrill'd thro' her heart" (ll. 98–99). The shock sends Mary mad.

Returning to the present, the poet notes in the final stanza that Mary cannot tell her own story but that the night's aftermath can be seen in the traces of execution: "His gibbet is now to be seen. / Not far from the road it engages the eye, / The Traveller beholds it, and thinks with a sigh / Of poor Mary the Maid of the Inn" (ll. 102–105). The incident has also left its mark on Mary; her life is ruined by the events, and she inhabits her own world.

Taken as a whole, the poem reveals Southey's early interest in German-influenced stories of horror popularized by GOTTFRIED AUGUST BÜRGER, MATTHEW GREGORY LEWIS, ANN RADCLIFFE, and others. Mary is very much the passive female victim, an object of desire and then of curiosity. At the same time, Southey was also interested in WILLIAM WORDSWORTH's work, and there are evident parallels with the tragic, isolated figures portrayed in "The THORN," "The Mad Mother," and "The COMPLAINT OF A FORSAKEN INDIAN WOMAN."

**Further Reading**

Geoffrey Carnall, *Robert Southey and His Age*. Oxford: Clarendon Press, 1960.

Southey, Robert. *New Letters of Robert Southey*. 2 vols. Edited by Kenneth Curry. New York and London: Columbia University Press, 1965.

———. *Poems*. 1st ed., 1797. Reprint, Oxford: Woodstock Books, 1989.

Warter, John Wood. *Selections from the Letters of Robert Southey*. 4 vols. London: Longman, 1856.

—Paul Smith

## *Mary Stuart: A Tragedy*   Friedrich Schiller (1800)

"*Mary Stuart: A Tragedy*" is a verse drama first performed in Germany at the Weimar Court Theatre on June 14, 1800; an English translation by John Mellish, the British ambassador in Hamburg, appeared in the same year. Initially, the play received a lukewarm response, but soon multiple productions were taking place all over Germany. Audiences shared FRIEDRICH VON SCHILLER's interest in the dramatic potential of the jealous relationship between Mary, Queen of Scots, and her cousin Elizabeth I, a rivalry that ended with Mary's trial and execution for treason in 1587.

Historians have always seen Mary as an enigmatic figure: Was she a schemer? a victim? a martyr? Schiller, having immersed himself in numerous histories of England, is no exception. His play focuses on the last part of Mary's life; the preceding events are only presented indirectly via dialogue and reportage, largely in act 1. In her short reign Mary revealed herself to be a self-indulgent, weak, and impressionable ruler, prone to losing the support of her cleverest advisors. She had been forced to abdicate in favor of her baby son, James, in 1567 and fled to England, throwing herself on Elizabeth's mercy in the expectation that, as another female monarch, she and Elizabeth would share a special bond. Elizabeth's response was to keep Mary under virtual house arrest in a series of castles for the next 19 years, unsure of what to do with her. Mary, a Catholic, proved a massive irritant to Elizabeth, a rallying point for people disaffected with Elizabeth's Protestant reign, and there were numerous conspiracies in which Mary's involvement was suspected but never proved. Matters came to a head in 1587 when the Catholic nobleman Sir Antony Babington devised a plot to assassinate Elizabeth and put Mary on the throne. Spies in Mary's household intercepted incriminating correspondence with Babington, which, for Elizabeth's advisers, was enough secure her guilt. Mary was tried at Fotheringay Castle—the location of the play's opening scene as her jailers search Mary's belongings for further evidence of treachery.

The play operates on several levels, and considerable use is made of contrasts and oppositions. The audience gains a very clear impression of the different political and religious attitudes represented by Elizabeth and Mary. Debates about legitimacy (Mary's supporters believed that she had a better claim to the English throne than Elizabeth, who was the offspring of Henry VIII's hasty marriage to Anne Boleyn) and of the laws of God versus the laws of man loom large. Mary naively believes that the supposed links between God and royalty will protect her despite examples to the contrary—Anne Boleyn being one of them. The atmosphere is one of intrigue and suspicion, which, Schiller implies, is what politics is really like: a smooth politeness disguising a ruthless and grubby reality. Mary's prison is itself a place of politicking and scheming and acts as a kind of microcosm for the wider world. Despite knowing of Mary's mendacity, Elizabeth is afraid to have her executed for fear of international reprisals from other Catholic states, notably Spain. The play taps into a feeling increasingly prevalent in Romantic writing, that of uncertainty—a sense that political regimes are unstable, that even anointed rulers are not safe.

Contemporary audiences familiar with the FRENCH REVOLUTION might have gained an impression that history simply repeats itself in a never-ending cycle of bloodshed and power struggles. Onstage, the tensions reach a climax with the face-to-face meeting between the two queens in act 3, scene 4, a meeting engineered by their respective advisers but which in real life never actually happened. Although the women actually have a lot in common, they fail to reach any common ground. On seeing Elizabeth for the first time,

Mary's initial response is that hers is "a face without a heart" (Schiller 73), while Elizabeth finds not a "humbled" broken woman but a "viper," unduly "proud, undaunted by misfortune" (76; 74). After a bitter exchange, Elizabeth leaves, angered at the lack of respect shown to her as victor.

Although the play's basis is the rivalry between the two queens, its political dimensions are often implied rather than overt. Part of the rivalry between the two women is sexual: Both compete for the affection of the earl of Leicester, Elizabeth hiding her deepest feelings under a mask of steely determination that is becoming tiring. Mary is more open and expressive. The literary critic E. L. Stahl has argued that the play's main theme is "the development of the heroine's [Mary's] character and her attainment of spiritual freedom" (Stahl 107). In act 5 Mary accepts her execution not as Elizabeth's right but as divine punishment for her involvement in the earlier murder of her second husband, Henry Darnley. Some critics see Mary's offering herself to God as evidence of spiritual grace and regeneration, but others suggest that she remains very self-aware in her actions and that her penitence strikes a false note, as if she is simply playing the role of martyr, conscious of creating her own legend.

### Further Reading

Schiller, Friedrich. *Two Plays by Schiller.* Translated by David MacDonald. Birmingham, Ala.: Oberon Books, 1987.

Stahl, E. L. *Friedrich Schiller's Drama.* Oxford: Clarendon, 1954.

—Andrew Maunder

### "Mask of Anarchy, The" Percy Bysshe Shelley (1819)

Occasioned by the deaths of those workingmen, women, and children who had assembled for a peaceful demonstration in St. Peter's Field near Manchester, England, on August 16, 1819, this poem is an expression of moral outrage and a call to political action. The demonstrators had come to hear the reformer Henry Hunt and to call for a repeal of the Corn Laws as well as parliamentary reform (universal suffrage, annual parliaments, and vote by ballot). The customary fear of gatherings by the working class—the "mob"—prompted the government to send in troops to break up the gathering, claiming the action was done to preserve law and "order." In the process, 11 people were killed and 421 seriously injured. News of the so-called PETERLOO MASSACRE reached PERCY BYSSHE SHELLEY on September 6 in Italy, where he was writing his verse drama *The Cenci*.

Shelley was horrified. In a letter to THOMAS LOVE PEACOCK, he wrote: "The tyrants here, as in the French Revolution, have first shed blood. May their execrable lessons not be learnt with equal docility!" (*Letters*, II, 119). Later he recorded how "the torrent of my indignation has not yet done boiling in my veins. I wait anxiously to hear how the Country will express its sense of this bloody murderous oppression of its destroyers. 'something must be done . . . What yet I know not.' (Shelley 1840, 2:117). Fired up by anger, he wrote a vigorous polemical poem in response to the events. The resulting piece of political protest is in ballad form and uses language that is direct and vigorous and proceeds in strong rhythmic verse. The "mask" of the title refers to the masques or pageants associated with upper-class entertainment but also refers to the mask worn by a thief or conspirator as disguise. In the context of the poem, *anarchy* means not simply chaos but misrule. In almost surreal fashion, the poem depicts a "ghastly masquerade" (l. 27) and what Shelley believes are England's repressive laws. From these come anarchy.

The poem presents itself as a dream experienced by the poet ("I") and which he has been called upon to write: "As I lay asleep in Italy / There came a voice from over the Sea, / And with great power it forth led me / To walk in the visions of Poesy" (ll. 1–4). In the dream he sees allegorical figures—Murder, Fraud, Hypocrisy, and a series of unidentified Destructions. Via these figures Shelley libels leading politicians of the time: "I met Murder on the way— / He had a mask like Castlereagh— / Very smooth he looked, yet grim; / Seven bloodhounds followed him" (ll. 5–8), fed by their master with human hearts. Shelley then goes on to describe the victory of Anarchy ("On a white

horse, splashed with blood; / He was pale even to the lips, / Like Death in the Apocalypse" (ll. 31–33). The irony here is that Anarchy comes associated with the forces of order and control: "I AM GOD, AND KING, AND LAW!" are the words he utters (l. 37). Shelley's point, of course, is that these are the institutions responsible for this chaos and upheaval.

This is not, then, merely a topical poem. While it was occasioned by a specific event, the poem argues for freedom and against tyranny in all places and at all times. Shelley asserts the need to reform social injustice without allowing one's fighting against it to become violent. The attitude of this poem matches his prose essay "The Philosophical View of Reform," insisting on hope and a spirit of reconciliation. Shelley goes on to examine how justice is deformed and how people are oppressed by poor conditions. One of his points is that England of 1819 declares itself free, but SLAVERY still exists thanks to the people who are kept down by economic conditions. What is slavery, he asks: "Tis to work and have such pay / As just keeps life from day to day" (ll. 160–161). The workers are mere cogs in a system that enriches others: "So that ye for them are made / Loom and plough and sword and spade / With or without your own will bent / To their defence and nourishment" (ll. 164–167).

During the poem, Shelley acidly criticizes the actions of the politicians Lord Castlereagh, Viscount Sidmouth, Lord Eldron, and other state dignitaries, holding that their complacency and their policies lie behind the demonstrators' death and injury. He asserts that lawyers and bishops have forgotten their true selves and their roles in administering justice, which, instead, have become murder, robbery, and fraud. The speaker of this poem imagines crowds falling under the trampling feet and swords of a tyrant's armies, and their blood will provide for regeneration. He recommends that the crowd learn endurance to overcome repression. For Shelley, the opponents of this repressive regime are heroes. The crowd should make a solemn vow to declare their rights, to overcome the oppression through nonviolent resistance. People would stand with folded arms in defiance of repressive tyranny, and through love they would become stronger, aiming toward the good. In resistance would be martyrdom. However, this would prompt an increase of the fervor of many toward justice and against injustice. "Light" would come as creativity, love, motion, and freedom.

In the poem, Hope, a "maniac maid" (l. 90) prevents the progress of anarchy. As Anarchy rises on a horse, the maid lies down in the street in front of Anarchy's parade. Suddenly, a misty light comes, and all behold it. At this point Anarchy has been overcome. Hope speaks to the "Men of England, heirs of Glory." The poem becomes an exhortation, seeking to encourage England to the level of the democratic liberation movements occurring in other areas of Europe at this time, such as Greece and Spain. He urges them: "Rise like lions after slumber / In unvanquishable number" (ll. 151–152). The poem celebrates freedom and the possibilities that are present in the men and women of England.

The poem was not published during Shelley's lifetime. If it had been, it probably would have made him notorious. LEIGH HUNT, previously incarcerated for seditious libel, declined to publish the poem because he did not want to return to jail for doing so; therefore, he held onto it until 1832, the time of the REFORM ACT, upon which he published the poem as a pamphlet.

## Further Reading

Bennett, Betty T., and Stuart Curran, eds. *Shelley:Poet and Legislator of the World*. Baltimore, Md.: Johns Hopkins University Press, 1996.

Bieri, James. *Percy Bysshe Shelley: A Biography*. Baltimore, Md.: Johns Hopkins University Press, 2008

Hendrix, Richard. "The Necessity of Response: How Shelley's Radical Poetry Works." *Keats-Shelley Journal* 27 (1978): 45–69.

Shelley, Percy Bysshe. *Shelley's Poetry and Prose*. 2nd ed. Edited by Donald H. Reiman and Neil Fraistat. New York: Norton, 2002.

———. *Essays, Letters from Abroad, Translations and Fragments, by Percy Bysshe Shelley*. 2 vols. Edited by Mary Shelley. London: Edward Moxon, 1840.

Vargo, Lisa. "Unmasking Shelley's Mask of Anarchy." *English Studies in Canada* 13, no. 1 (1987): 49–64.

—Robert McParland

## Maturin, Charles Robert (1782–1824)

Born in Dublin on September 25, 1782, Charles Robert Maturin was an Anglo-Irish Protestant clergyman who achieved literary fame through his GOTHIC novels and dramas. After graduating from Trinity College, Dublin, Maturin entered the church and was appointed as curate to the parish of Loughrea, a village in Galway. In 1806 he became curate of St. Peter's in Dublin, a position he held until his death. Curates tended to be poorly paid, and Maturin's experience was little different. His salary was just £100, and following his marriage to a singer, Henrietta Kingsbury, he needed to boost his income to provide for her and their growing family. Initially, he set up a tutorial college in Dublin, which initially brought in an income of £500–1,000 a year. However, in 1807 he was forced to give it up and turned instead to writing.

Maturin's first novels were in a gothic vein following the fashion set by ANN RADCLIFFE and MATTHEW GREGORY LEWIS. These were *The Fatal Revenge; or, the Family of Montorio* (1807); *The Wild Irish Boy* (1808), which seemed also to nod to SYDNEY OWENSON's *The WILD IRISH GIRL* and *The Milesian Chief* (1812). As Maturin feared ridicule and censure, all these were published under the pseudonym of Dennis Jasper Murphy. The novels did indeed attract mockery, but their style impressed SIR WALTER SCOTT, who admitted in the *Quarterly Review* that he was "at times impressed with no common degree of respect for the powers of the author" (Quarterly Review 3.6 [1810], 342).

Scott and Maturin began a correspondence that continued for the remainder of Maturin's life. It was through Scott that Maturin's five-act tragedy BERTRAM, OR, THE CASTLE OF ST. ALDOBRAND came to the notice of LORD BYRON and in turn to the management at Drury Lane Theatre, who produced the play in 1816 with EDMUND KEAN in the leading role. Though it was a huge popular success, the play was attacked in the *Courier* by SAMUEL TAYLOR COLERIDGE, who deplored the depraved public taste that sanctioned this kind of drama. However, his anger was in part because his own play, *Zapolya* (1817), had been sidelined in favour of *Bertram*. (Coleridge's comments on Maturin can be read in the appendix to his BIOGRAPHIA LITERARIA.)

Encouraged by *Bertram*'s financial success, Maturin spent extravagantly, but his later plays *Manuel* (1817), *Fredolfo,* and *Osmyn the Renegade* (1819) were failures, and he struggled to recapture this form. His most successful novels were *Women* (1818) and the text that is generally reckoned his masterpiece: *Melmoth the Wanderer* (1820). This novel, which involves the Faustian pact of John Melmoth, is structured as a series of stories-within-stories whose characters are all connected, despite their varied geographical settings, by their experiences with the hero, whose status as a "wanderer" would come to hold a particular fascination for later generations of writers. The French Romantics in particular were drawn to it, including Honoré de Balzac (1799–1850), who wrote a sequel, *Melmoth Reconcilié* (1835); and Charles Baudelaire (1821–67). JOHANN WOLFGANG VON GOETHE also attempted to translate the novel into German. In Ireland and England, however, Maturin's church superiors were outraged, and in the *Quarterly Review* John Wilson Croker claimed that *Melmoth the Wanderer* made "the most violent assaults, not merely on common sense and the English tongue . . . but on decency, and even religion" (Croker, 304). The character of Melmoth also gave Oscar Wilde (Maturin's great-nephew) a pseudonym after his release from Reading Gaol in 1897.

The final years of Maturin's life saw him struggle to maintain a literary career; He died in Dublin on October 30, 1824. His influence, however, has been considerable. Like those of MARIA EDGEWORTH, his works can be seen within the context of the Irish literary tradition and the national novel, and there are ambivalencies regarding revolution, particularly when translated into a Catholic or Irish-colonial setting. His work extends the gothic tradition and draws on and reinvigorates figures such as the Byronic hero. It also taps into Romantic ideas about identity and selfhood.

## Further Reading

Croker, John Wilson. *"Melmoth the Wanderer."* By the author of *Bertram: Quarterly Review* 48 (January 1821): 303–311.

Hansen, Jim. "The Wrong Marriage: Maturin and the Double-Logic of Masculinity in the Unionist Gothic." *Studies in Romanticism* 47, no. 3 (2008): 351–369.

Knox, Melissa. "Charles Robert Maturin (1780–1824)." In *British Writers: Supplement VIII,* edited by Jay Parini, 197–210. New York: Scribner's, 2003.

Kramer, Dale. *Charles Robert Maturin.* Boston: Twayne, 1973.

Lougy, Robert. *Charles Maturin.* Bucknell, Pa.: Bucknell University Press, 2001.

Maturin, Charles. *Melmoth the Wanderer.* Edited by Victor Sage. London: Penguin, 2004.

Scott, Walter. *"Fatal Revenge, or the Family of Montolia: A Romance." Quarterly Review* 3 (May 1810): 339–347.

Pearson, Jacqueline. "Masculinizing the Novel: Women Writers and Intertextuality in Charles Robert Maturin's *The Wild Irish Boy." Studies in Romanticism* 36, no. 4 (1997): 635–650.

—Paul Roberts

## *Maurice, or, The Fisher's Cot* Mary Wollstonecraft Shelley (1820)

This novella was originally written by MARY SHELLEY as a gift for Laurette Tighe, the daughter of Mrs. Mason (Lady Mount Cashell), one of the Shelleys' acquaintances in Pisa and a former pupil of Mary Shelley's mother, MARY WOLLSTONECRAFT. Denied publication by Shelley's father, WILLIAM GODWIN, for his Juvenile Library, the story remained unpublished until it was discovered in 1997 by descendants of Laurette Tighe.

Written in three "volumes" in imitation of the popular novels of the day, and employing a modified version of the frame narrative Shelley had used in her well-known novel FRANKENSTEIN, *Maurice, or The Fisher's Cot,* tells the story of its title character, who is introduced at the beginning of the story participating in the funeral of Barnet, an old fisherman. A traveler who witnesses the funeral learns about young Maurice and is then introduced to him. Maurice explains his decision to leave his parents because his supposed father, Daddy Smithson, had cruelly mistreated him. Changing his name from Henry to avoid detection, Maurice decides to go to make his own way and not return until he can support himself. His travels have taken him to the recently widowed Barnet, who agrees to have

Maurice live with him in exchange for some minor chores and, more importantly, companionship. Maurice quickly becomes a favorite of the village, assuming in some ways the late Dame Barnet's position in the community by reading from the Bible and teaching other children how to read. After Maurice completes his story, the traveler tells him about the kidnapping, some 11 years earlier, of his own son, for whom he spends two months each year looking near the area of his disappearance. After Maurice's status as the traveler's son is confirmed, aided by Dame Smithson's remorseful confession of Henry's kidnapping, father and son return to Windsor, though Henry's father purchases Barnet's cottage and the two continue to visit the village for two months every year. After an extended absence, a grown Henry returns one day to discover that the cottage has collapsed. He builds a new house near the old location and offers it to another poor fisherman's family in remembrance of kind old Barnet.

The most commonly identified characteristics of Shelley's novella are the recurring themes of loss, suffering, and alienation. In this context, biographical parallels are particularly significant, especially in terms of the loss of a child. By the time she began to compose the story, Shelley had already endured the deaths of three children. Mrs. Mason had to surrender her claims to her seven children by her first husband when she left him for George Tighe. For both women, therefore, the painful separation from one's offspring would have been a very meaningful subject. Throughout his history, however, Maurice's experiences of mistreatment and uncertainty fail to diminish his innate goodness, diligence, and compassion. In this regard, the novella can also be seen to contribute to the nature/nurture debate. In contrast to the creature in Shelley's *Frankenstein*, for example, who is portrayed as good until society's abuse causes him to become violent, Maurice never loses his original fine qualities, despite the suffering he endures. As in her novel, Shelley also incorporates discussion of the therapeutic values of nature, a theme widely treated in the literature of the Romantic period. Here, both Henry and his father appreciate the wonders of nature, though it is this appreciation, ironically, that originally led to Henry's kidnapping,

which occurred after his father and mother took a walk along a river, leaving their son in the hands of a nurse who promptly fell asleep, giving Dame Smithson her opportunity.

**Further Reading**

Markley, A. A. "Lost and Found: Mary Shelley, *Maurice, or the Fisher's Cot: A Tale*. Edited with an Introduction by Claire Tomalin." *Romanticism on the Net* 15 (August 1999). Available online. URL: http://www.erudit.org/revue/ron/1999/v/n15/005868ar.html. Accessed on July 27, 2009.

Mekler, L. Adam. "Placing *Maurice* within the Shelley-Godwin Circle." *CEA-MAGazine* 14 (2001): 23–33.

Shelley, Mary Wollstonecraft. *Maurice, or The Fisher's Cot: A Tale*. Edited by Claire Tomalin. New York: Knopf, 1998.

—L. Adam Mekler

## "Michael: A Pastoral Poem" William Wordsworth (1800)

Composed and published in 1800, "Michael: A Pastoral Poem" relates the story of an old shepherd forced by debt to send his only son, Luke, to the city, to avoid having to sell off his only property, the piece of land inherited from his father. Luke, however, falls into dishonor and leaves the country. Mad with pain, the old man still pretends to work at the sheepfold he had planned to build with his son.

This "homely" tale exemplifies WILLIAM WORDSWORTH's wish, as related in the famous PREFACE TO *LYRICAL BALLADS* (second edition, 1800), that his verse should portray "incidents and situations from common life, . . . in a selection of language really used by men." It also illustrates the quick transformation of the English countryside at the time, and how the young frequently left it for what often proved to be a worse existence in the city.

There is something deeply tragic about this poem, which is enhanced by its double biblical hypotext: the parable of the prodigal son and the sacrifice of Isaac by Abraham. But whereas the prodigal son eventually comes back, and Isaac is finally spared by his father, Luke never comes back after Michael chooses to send him to the city. The decline of the family then reads as an allegory of the extinction of the shepherd's lifestyle, as hinted by the name of his house "the Evening Star" (ll. 139, 478). Like Abraham, Michael was given a son, though he and his wife were relatively old, but unlike him, his descendants will not be as numerous as the stars.

"Michael" forms a diptych with another poem, "Repentance—A Pastoral Ballad," in which a heedless peasant sells his land and is devoured by regret. Both poems tackle the contemporary issue of land enclosures but endowing it with a symbolic weight by recalling at once the biblical Fall with its loss of innocence and the disappearance of the state of nature conjectured by philosophers in the 18th century. Between 1727 and 1815, the British Parliament adopted more than 5,000 bills on the enclosures of commons and land consolidation (reunion of small pieces of land into large, economically more lucrative ones), a process that deprived numerous peasants of their use of common lands. While "Repentance" describes the psychological consequences of this rural transformation on the peasantry, "Michael" shows the impossibility of putting an end to the process (in the absence of an heir, the property will be dismantled) and its unavoidable consequence: the drift of younger generations toward cities, where former peasants were turned into cheap workforce. This was often depicted in the works of JOHN CLARE.

The characteristics of this poem also belong to the list of Wordsworthian tales of forsaken parents and women—for example, "The RUINED COTTAGE," whose decay mirrors Michael's unfinished sheepfold; "The THORN"; "The Affliction of Margaret"; and "The Childless Father." The end of the first long stanza dedicates the poem to "youthful Poets, who among these Hills / Will be my second self when I am gone" (ll. 38–39), establishing a parallel between poet and character in their common worry regarding their heritage.

**Further Reading**

Averill, James H. *Wordsworth and the Poetry of Human Suffering*. Ithaca, N.Y., and London: Cornell University Press, 1980.

Butler, Marilyn. *Romantics, Rebels and Reactionaries: English Literature and Its Background, 1760–1830*. Oxford: University Press, 1981.

Hartman, Geoffrey. *Wordsworth's Poetry 1787–1814*. New Haven and London: Yale University Press, 1971.

Wordsworth, William. *The Major Works*. Edited by Stephen Gill. Oxford: Oxford World's Classics, 2000.

———. *The Poetical Works of William Wordsworth*. Edited by Ernest de Selincourt and Helen Darbishire. 2nd ed. 5 vols. Oxford: Clarendon Press, 1958.

———. *The Prose Works of William Wordsworth*. 3 vols. Edited by W. J. B. Owen and J. Worthington Smyser. Oxford: Clarendon, 1974.

—Aurelie Thiria-Meulemans

## Milton, John (1608–1674)

Despite having lived more than a century prior to the recognized start of the Romantic movement, the London-born poet and prose writer John Milton had a tremendous impact on writers of the Romantic age. This was evidenced in works such as JOHN KEATS's ENDYMION, MARY SHELLEY's FRANKENSTEIN, WILLIAM WORDSWORTH's MILTON: A POEM, PERCY BYSSHE SHELLEY's PROMETHEUS UNBOUND, and WILLIAM BLAKE's The MARRIAGE OF HEAVEN AND HELL—poems, novels, and works of drama that mimicked the style and preferred forms used by Milton, reflected on shared themes, and sometimes took Milton as their very subject. Like the Romantics, John Milton lived during an age of revolution and was in disagreement with social and moral standards of the times. In works such as *Of Reformation*, *Areopagitica*, and *Of True Religion*, he expressed his displeasure and his desire for change, presenting what were then considered heretical religious views and radical opinions on issues such as divorce, censorship, and republicanism versus the monarchy. His views were considered so controversial that he was jailed in 1660 during the Restoration, and his books were destroyed.

While Milton's works of social and political concern remain highly visible due to their provocative and progressive nature, his poetry is considered equally as dynamic. The author is perhaps best known for his composition of *Paradise Lost*, an epic poem in blank verse that was written, quite remarkably, after the loss of his eyesight. The poem, published in 1667, told the story of the fall of Satan and the subsequent Fall of Man. It was hailed not only for its aesthetic merits but also for its clever presentation of the author's political and religious views. Romantic writers were largely influenced by this work in particular. They would find an example in Milton's use of literature as a protest device, and they would draw inspiration from his focus on the concept of the hero, his reference to the GOTHIC, his emphasis on the SUBLIME, and his illumination of the significance of imagination. Both the poetry and the prose works of the 17th-century author also seemed to encapsulate the concept of the potential of the individual and the concept of strength in nationalism, which would become key themes in Romantic literature more than 100 years later.

Milton has often been cited as Britain's greatest poet, but critical response to his work has fluctuated, reaching a low point during the 20th century when writers such as Ezra Pound and T. S. Eliot criticized the form and themes of his work. Despite such criticism, Milton's works, which are now studied the world over, remain highly influential and are most frequently examined in conjunction with those works of the Romantic age that exhibit traces of its influence.

See also "LONDON, 1802"; "TO ROBERT BATTY, M.D., ON HIS GIVING ME A LOCK OF MILTON'S HAIR."

**Further Reading**

Harding, Anthony John and Lisa Low, eds. *Milton, the Metaphysicals, and Romanticism.* Cambridge: Cambridge University Press, 1994.

Milton, John. *The Complete Poetry and Essential Prose of John Milton.* Edited by Stephen M. Fallon, William Kerrigan, and John Rumrich. New York: Modern Library, 2007.

—Jennifer Banach Palladino

## *Milton: A Poem* William Blake (ca. 1804–ca. 1811)

This poem, with the 17th-century poet JOHN MILTON as its hero, was originally planned as an epic in 12 books, perhaps modelled on Milton's *Paradise Lost.* The date on the title page reads 1804 but Blake used his distinctive arrangement of etched text and illustrations supplemented by watercolor to print a new version in early 1811.

In the Blake canon, references to John Milton occur as early as 1784–85 (in "An Island in the Moon," for example) and can be found in *The MARRIAGE OF HEAVEN AND HELL, The Four Zoas,* and *JERUSALEM: THE EMANATION OF THE GIANT ALBION;* in his notebooks and annotations, in descriptive catalogues, advertisements and letters; and even in a public address of about 1810. Blake illustrated almost the entire Milton canon and created his portraits. A Miltonic influence spans the whole of Blake's literary career, life, and philosophy to a degree that must be considered remarkable. Blake was also the first to realize and elucidate the symbolic significance of Milton as a poet and did not treat Milton's greatest work, *Paradise Lost,* merely as an expression of the biblical view of history.

Blake's fascination with Milton as a Protestant poet-prophet and revolutionary was not merely dumb admiration. He demanded explanations, offered interpretations, drew conclusions, and indulged in blatant accusations. Blake, like Milton, sought to internalize the Apocalypse and believed that paradise was to be found within man. But his divergence from Milton's views on a number of issues ran a parallel course. Blake's advocacy of complete freedom of love and disregard for ceremony (Milton would support divorce only on grounds of incompatibility), his opposition to the "old religious order" (as elaborated in *De Doctrina Christiana,* [1823]) or his castigation of the Miltonic ideal of chastity (Blake dates its beginning by quoting from Milton's "Hymn on the Morning of Christ's Nativity") are among many examples of his iconoclastic attitude to the elder poet. He found Milton's Puritan theology repugnant. Milton was suspicious of passion and senses, emphasized the sinister "female will," and treated women with hostility and fear. Above all, he regarded reason as man's supreme faculty.

Blake felt that the spread of Puritanism, to which Milton had contributed, had smothered the spirit of true poetry, led to the humiliation of artists, and brutalized the people with an unforgiving system of impossible callous ethical and religious ideals. Politically, too, Puritanism had led England into internecine wars (the English Civil War of 1640–45, which led to the execution of King Charles I).

It is in *Milton: A Poem* that Blake creates a "fictional" context and opportunity for the older poet to purify his erroneous ways. He uses Milton as a character who is shown returning to earth in the form of Blake to correct his earlier mistakes. *Milton* is also about Blake where Blake is confronted with a tempting Satan. His choice is either to surrender the prophetic function of a poet or to emulate Milton's heroic dedication to the mission he had set for himself as a poet. But Milton's errors must be purged before Blake can inherit and don the mantle of a poet-prophet.

*Milton: A Poem* is in two books. Book 1 opens with an epic invocation to the muses. Blake goes on to describe the activities of Los, one of his mythological characters, who creates a universe and populates it with other Blakean characters. There is a collective debate over the actions of Satan. Referring to the central doctrines of Calvinism, Blake asserts that humanity is divided into the "Elect," the "Reprobate" and the "Redeemed." Inverting Calvinist values, he insists that the "Reprobate" are the true believers, while the "Elect" are locked in narcissistic moral righteousness.

Milton appears and agrees to return to earth—"a mournful form double; hermaphroditic: male and female / In one wonderful body" (plate 14, 37–38)—to purge the errors resulting from his own Puritanical convictions. "A Bard's Prophetic Song" inspires him as he "walkd about in Eternity . . . Unhappy tho' in heav'n" (plate 2, 16–18). The poem concludes with a vision of a final blending in which internal and external reality merges. The living and the dead annihilate mutual discord. Male and female are integrated and a cleansing of all of human perception takes place. Much like *The Marriage of Heaven and Hell*, *Milton* establishes the link between visionary writing and political struggle: "I will not cease from Mental Fight, / Nor shall my Sword sleep in my hand" (Preface 13–14).

Long considered unreadable and impenetrable (so 19th-century critics thought), recent scholarship has found in *Milton* a work of great depth and profundity. Several aspects of the poem, such as its aggressive female sexuality and androgyny as serving patriarchal ends, have been noted. Bisexual bewilderment and homosexual tendencies as well as Blake's ambivalence toward oral and anal intercourse and homosexuality have been suggested as being present. Blake's verse has often been accused of retreating into a private world of myths and symbols, yet a deeper engagement with mainstream contemporary thought is another significant aspect of *Milton: A Poem*.

**Further Reading**

Blake, William *The Complete Poetry and Prose of William Blake.* Edited by David Erdman. Berkeley: University of California Press, 2008.

Ahearn, Edward J. *Visionary Fictions: Apocalyptic Writing from Blake to the Modern Age.* New Haven, Conn.: Yale University Press, 1996.

Ostriker, Alica. "Desire Gratified and Ungratified: William Blake and Sexuality." In *Critical Essays on William Blake,* edited by Hazard Adams, Boston: G. K. Hall & Co., 1991.

—G. R. Taneja

## "Mines of Falun, The" E. T. A. Hoffmann (1819)

This tale by Ernst Theodor Amadeus Hoffmann, a German Romantic of the Gothic strain, features Elis Frobom, a sad young sailor led by a demonic spirit, in the guise of an old miner named Torbern, to pursue the life of a Naturphilosopher. Under Torbern's influence, Frobom becomes increasingly obsessed with digging for the philosopher's stone, as well as the forbidden secrets of nature and existence, deep in the Mines of Falun: a hell-like setting clearly meant to be beyond the limits of human experience. What unfolds is a psychomachia, or battle for the soul, in which Torbern and the vengeful queen of the mines invade Frobom's dreams and consume his waking thoughts, overshadowing the healing influence of a young innocent girl, Ulla, who longs to marry and protect him.

Frobom is a recognizable type in Romantic literature. A sailor with a solitary and melancholic disposition, he is more comfortable with nature than with his fellow human beings. Thus, his fall, like that of other Romantic heroes, is conventionally tragic. He may call the old miner to him with thoughts of suicide—a common literary motif—but it is his initial love and respect for the natural world that makes him so attractive a prize for the demonic Naturphilosopher. Torbern echoes the sentiments of the German poet NOVALIS (Friederich von Hardenberg) when he speaks of the glory of the miner, "to whose knowledge, to whose unwearying toil Nature opens her most secret treasure hoards" (Hoffmann 40). This is the same forbidden knowledge that will later tantalize and destroy MARY SHELLEY's Victor Frankenstein, whose words will also echo those of Novalis (see *FRANKENSTEIN*).

As is typical in German Romanticism, the setting of the tale is phantasmagoric, or dark and nightmarish. The mines of Falun are described as a hellish labyrinth of chasms, veined with metals that creep up their stony walls like sharp, gleaming plants. Over this hell presides a phantom queen, a gothic inversion of the typically nurturing Romantic earth mother. Enraged by geology's aspiration to uncover her secrets, the vengeful spirit will possess Frobom's heart and soul, ironically tempting him with sensual dreams full of gemological imagery before turning him into a fossil. Frobom thus becomes his own aesthetic ideal: an embodiment of the fusion of the arts and natural sciences and thus of German Romanticism. As Evans Lansing Smith notes in "Myths of Poesis, Hermeneusis, and Psychogenesis," the machinations of Hoffmann's phantom queen, and "the metallurgical operations leading to the forging of the philosopher's stone in alchemy" both mirror "the creative processes of poesis" (Smith 228). Hoffmann's treatment of the natural sciences—particularly the explorations of regeneration, degeneration, and extinction featured in "The Mines of Falun"—were extremely prescient in their day. Well before Charles Lyell published his *Principles of Geology* and Charles Darwin published his *On the Origin of Species*, Hoffmann explored one of the most destabilizing themes of 19th-century literature and science: When one digs too deeply for the secrets of nature and existence, what they uncover is the possibility of their own extinction.

**Further Reading**

Hoffmann, E. T. A. *Tales of Hoffmann.* New York: Heritage, 1943.

McGlathery, James. *Mysticism and Sexuality: E. T. A. Hoffmann.* American University Studies 39. New York: P. Lang, 1985.

"Naturphilosophie." *Wikipedia, The Free Encyclopedia.* Available online. URL: http://en.wikipedia.org/wiki/ Naturphilosophie. Accessed on July 26, 2009.

Smith, Evans Lansing. "Myths of Poesis, Hermeneusis, and Psychogenesis: Hoffmann, Tagore, and Gilman." *Studies in Short Fiction* 34, no. 2 (Spring 1997): 227–236.

—Priscilla Glanville

## *Minstrelsy of the Scottish Border: Consisting of Historical and Romantic Ballads, Collected in the Southern Counties of Scotland; With a Few of Modern Date, Founded upon Local Tradition*
**Sir Walter Scott** (1802, 1803, 1812)

An enormous critical and commercial success, both in Britain and North America, *Minstrelsy of the Scottish Border* is a collection of historical and romantic ballads. They were collected in the 1770s and 1780s by SIR WALTER SCOTT and various helpers in the southern counties of Scotland who interviewed musicians, itinerant craftsmen, shepherds (including JAMES HOGG), and old folk of the Borders and the Southern Highlands, transcribing the folk songs and poems they recited. The project was in some ways similar to ROBERT BURNS's works on the Scottish song 10 years earlier (1786) and was also inspired by Bishop Thomas Percy's *Reliques of English Poetry* (1765), which was just one of a large number of such collections published in the 18th century (including THOMAS MOORE's *IRISH MELODIES*).

The background to the collection is linked to the process of rapid modernization that Scotland was then undergoing. Many of the population of the Scottish Border valleys were leaving their traditional farms, lured by the prospect of work for better pay promised by the hosiery industry emerging in towns such as Hawick and Langholm. The Border people were often descendants of the Border reivers (bandits) and had been told tales of the exploits of their forebears. However, these stories were rarely written down; rather, they were passed orally from one generation to the next. By 1790 it appeared that they would be lost forever, and it was this that prompted Scott to try and collect them. In the introduction to the *Minstrelsy*, Scott says that he has attempted to preserve a record of "popular superstitions, and legendary history, which, if not now collected, must soon have been totally forgotten" (70). He continues: "By such efforts, feeble as they are, I may contribute somewhat to the history of my native country, the peculiar features of whose manner and character are daily melting and dissolving into the those of her sister and ally [England]. And trivial as may appear such an offering, to the manes of a kingdom, once proud and independent, I hang it upon her altar with a mixture of feelings, which I shall not attempt to describe." However, these words also suggest more than one motive. As the literary scholar Joyce Huff notes, "Scott saw himself as continuing the process of preserving the tradition in his own writing. Through preserving its traditions, Scott hoped to define and recover the essence of Scotland as a nation-state" (Huff 70).

As a boy, Scott had become fascinated by Scottish history, including stories of the Border reivers, the Covenanter wars, the Jacobite Rebellion, and the longstanding and bitter feuding with England. Encouraged by his Aunt Jenny, he was drawn, too, to the balladry that brought this history to life, and the romantic tales of the Borders would form the inspiration for much of his later writing. The project that would lead to the *Minstrelsy* seems to have started around 1792, when Scott started making "forays," or field trips, to the Borders in search of material. A reunion with an old schoolmate—now a publisher—James Ballantyne encouraged him further, as Ballantyne was receptive to the idea of publishing a volume of ballads. J. G. Lockhart, Scott's biographer and son-in-law, described the process of putting together the ballads as "a labour of love if ever there was" (quoted in Oliver 19). In collecting the ballads Scott adopted an approach that would be regarded today as rather lax. He relied on instinct in judging whether a poem was genuinely old or not, and he was also happy to alter or "improve" those pieces he felt did not meet his particular standards, or to boost their Jacobite or conservative credentials. He inserted new verses, changed rhyme schemes, and sometimes wrote completely new poems based on an old story. This flexible approach to historical accuracy is typical of much of his output.

Initially, Scott planned to focus on ballads commemorating historical incidents, but the first two-volume edition of the *Minstrelsy* in 1802 contained 29 heavily annotated historical pieces plus 24 romantic ballads, together with some "imitations," most of which were penned by Scott. Straight after publication, he began planning a third volume to be filled with imitations of traditional ballad forms by present-day authors, including MATTHEW GREGORY LEWIS and ANNA SEWARD. One of the poems Scott planned to include but which grew too long was the GOTHIC romance poem *The Lay of the Last Minstrel*. In May 1803 a second (revised) edition of the *Minstrelsy* was published, along with the third volume. A larger edition with a rearranged order was published in 1806, revised again in 1810, and published in its final format in 1812, containing 96 ballads.

The tragedies, scandals, and stories of love, rivalry, enmity, and friendship which provide the subject matter for the ballads clearly struck a chord with contemporary readers. The "Ballad of Kinmont Willie" is an account of a deadly feud that continued through the Borders for centuries, involving one of the most notorious Scottish Border reivers of the 16th century, William Armstrong of Kinmont. The poems' subject matter—murder, sexual intrigue, betrayal—was clearly exciting, although, as has been noted, they were also edited in such a way as to offer moral lessons. For example, many of the problems in the poems are seen to arise out of the corruption of the family unit. "Hughie the Graeme" tells of the execution of a horse thief betrayed by his wife, Maggie: "Fare ye weel, fair Maggie, my wife! / The last time we came ower the muir, / 'Twas thou bereft me of my life, / And wi' the Bishop thou play'd the whore" (ll. 57–60). As the critic Susan Oliver puts it, "A suggestion of moral example drawn from history that is relevant to the early 19th century, when radicalism and revolutionary sentiments were associated with excessive passions and loose morals emerges" (Oliver 32) The women in other ballads, particularly the historical ones, tend to be more conventionally passive and better-behaved and appear as damsels in distress or prizes to be won. The emphasis is also on masculine bravery and chivalrous deeds of derring-do involving knights on horseback. "Sir Patrick Spens" emphasizes service to king and country on the part of an otherwise obscure nobleman. "Auld Maitland" narrates a bloody encounter between the English and the Scottish, in which the eponymous hero is besieged in his castle but escapes in disguise with his sons to take bloody revenge on the English invaders. As well as loyalty to one's clan and bravery in the face of death, another common feature is the deployment of recognizable gothic and PICTURESQUE descriptive conventions in order to flag up the wildness of the Border regions, in contrast to the lowlands.

Overall, there is some debate about how successful Scott actually was in his declared mission to preserve the old ballads. How authentic are these works? As Joyce Huff puts it: "In removing ballads from Scottish social life and re-presenting them as typical specimens of Scottish culture, however, Scott transforms them, they lose whatever significance they had in Scottish social life and take on new meanings as signifiers of Scottishness." Divorced from their original context, they are changed forever.

See also MARMION.

**Further Reading**

Huff, Joyce. "Cameos, Coins and Character: Sir Walter Scott and the Invention of the Ballad Tradition." Available online. URL: http://web.archive.org/web/20080501150641/. Accessed on January 29, 2009.

Oliver, Susan. *Scott, Byron and the Poetics of Cultural Encounters.* London: Palgrave, 2005.

Scott, Sir Walter. *The Minstrelsy of the Scottish Border.* Edited by Thomas Henderson. London: Harrap, 1931.

—Penny Matthews

## Missionary, The *(Luxima, the Prophetess: A Tale of India)* Sydney Owenson (1811)

*The Missionary: An Indian Tale* is an international novel exploring national identity, religious tolerance, and colonial imperialism through the romance of Hilarion, a 17th-century Portuguese Franciscan priest, and Luxima, a Brahmin priestess. *The Missionary* combines the genres of travel narrative, oriental tale, and novel of sensibility with footnotes to a cosmopolitan array of sources meant to give its exotic and sentimental scenes historical authority. While contemporary reviewers criticized SYDNEY OWENSON's style as extravagant and sometimes accused the novel of Jacobinism, impiety, and immorality, it sold well in England, France, and the United States, with seven editions between 1811 and 1817. In 1859 it reappeared, slightly revised, as *Luxima, the Prophetess: A Tale of India.* The 1806 Vellore uprising and the 1857 Indian Mutiny made both editions timely, topical, and controversial.

The cross-cultural dialogue between Hilarion and Luxima is reminiscent of MME. ANNE-LOUISE-GERMAINE DE STAËL's *Corinne: ou l'Italie* (1807), and it continues themes of national character, religious tolerance, and anticolonialism established in Owenson's Anglo-Irish writings. Nature and feeling are crucial values in *The Missionary,* as mystic love and human passion are pitted against bigotry, dogma, tradition, and reason. Both Hilarion and Luxima are aristocrats consecrated as religious leaders. Bound by vows of chastity, they wrestle with desire as their mutual attraction grows. While the Eurocentric narrator frequently describes Luxima's faith as error and superstition, her Hindu tolerance, truth to nature, and reliance on feeling ultimately undermine the exclusivity, rigidity, and rationality of Hilarion's Roman Catholicism. Accepting Christianity out of love for Hilarion, Luxima becomes an ambivalent convert. The novel's Edenic descriptions of Kashmir, idealization of Luxima, use of Miltonic echoes, and association of Hindu sati (suttee) with the Inquisition's auto-da-fé were central to its impact on other Romantic writers. PERCY BYSSHE SHELLEY saw Luxima as a perfect heroine, and the novel influenced the oriental tales of LORD BYRON, THOMAS MOORE, and MARY WOLLSTONECRAFT SHELLEY.

In *The Missionary,* passionate attraction to Luxima subverts Hilarion's religious confidence and sense of cultural superiority. Volume 1 sets Hilarion's missionary vocation in the context of Spanish domination of Portugal and rivalry between Spanish Jesuits and Portuguese Franciscans. Zeal and perfectionism drive Hilarion into the heart of Kashmir when an agnostic Pundit suggests that Luxima is the key to converting her people. The second volume opens with a "revolution" in Hilarion's feelings and climaxes in an avowal of love triggered by his jealousy of a Mughal prince. Despite this confession, when Hilarion baptizes the excommunicated Luxima, he vows to deliver her to a convent. The third volume recounts their perilous wilderness journey and reunion with a humanisitic civilization where Muslims, Hindus, Jews, and Christians coexist. Jesuit bigotry disrupts this tolerant world, denouncing Hilarion to the Inquisition. He escapes being burned at the stake when an insurrection is triggered by Jesuit violence toward Luxima, who has fled the convent, determined to share Hilarion's death. Fatally stabbed in the conflict, Luxima dies in Hilarion's arms. He ends his days a hermit of an ambiguous faith that merges Catholicism, Hinduism, and his devotion to the memory of Luxima.

See also ORIENTALISM.

**Further Reading**

Dean, Dennis R. Introduction to *The Missionary* (1811), by Sydney Owenson. Delmar, N.Y.: Scholar's Facsimiles and Reprints, 1981, v–x.

Lew, Joseph. "Sydney Owenson and the Fate of Empire." *Keats-Shelley Journal* 39 (1990): 39–65.

Owenson, Sydney (Lady Morgan). *The Missionary: An Indian Tale.* Edited by Julia M. Wright. Peterborough, Ont.: Broadview Press, 2002.

Sondeep Kandola

## Mitford, Mary Russell (1787–1855)

The poet, novelist, and dramatist Mary Russell Mitford was born in Alresford, Hampshire, on December 16, 1787, the only child of George Mitford and his wife, Mary Russell Mitford, an heiress.

Initially the family was wealthy, but George Mitford was a compulsive gambler, and his extravagance reduced them to poverty. The task of supporting the family fell on the daughter, and she pursued it with great success. Mary Russell Mitford's first published work, *Poems* appeared in 1810. It was followed by the equally popular *Poems on the Female Character* in 1813. Her tragedy *Julian* was performed at Covent Garden in 1823, followed by *Foscari* in 1826 and *Rienzi* in 1828.

Mitford gained a much wider reputation with a series of country sketches, drawn from her observations of her own village, Three Mile Cross. From 1819 the series *Our Village* was published in the *Lady's Magazine,* boosting its sales considerably. The sketches were much admired for their rambling charm and detailed descriptions of village life, customs, and country landscapes. They were often seen as comparable in spirit with the countryside writings of GEORGE CRABBE; ELIZABETH BARRETT BROWNING called Mitford "a prose Crabbe in the Sun" (quoted in Astin 12). Mitford was also credited with preserving for posterity a way of life that was fast dying out in the wake of the Industrial Revolution, which was causing rural communities to break up. The sketches were published in five volumes (1824–32). Typical of Mitford's gently seductive tone is "Cousin Mary" (1824), an uplifting tale of a penniless girl who leaves the countryside to become a governess in a polluted industrial town. Her goodness is eventually recognized by her employer, who marries her.

Mitford published other works, including a novel, *Belford Regis, or Sketches of a Country Town,* in 1835, but she never recaptured the success of *Our Village.* By the time of her death on January 10, 1855, the unmarried Mitford had become a literary celebrity, very popular in North America and much feted by a large circle of famous admirers, including Browning, JOANNA BAILLIE, FELICIA HEMANS, WALTER SAVAGE LANDOR, and Alfred Lord Tennyson.

**Further Reading**

Astin, Marjorie. *Mary Russell Mitford.* London: Noel Douglas, 1930.

Edwards, P. D. *Idyllic Realism from Mary Russell Mitford to Hardy.* London: Macmillan, 1989.

Mitford, Mary Russell. *Our Village: Sketches of Rural Life, Characters and Scenery.* London: 1824–32.

Raymond, Meredith, and Mary Sullivan, eds. *Women of Letters: Selected Letters of Elizabeth Barrett Browning & Mary Russell Mitford.* Boston: Twayne, 1988.

—Andrew Maunder

## monarchy

In the Romantic period, or the years 1789–1840, the popularity of the British monarchy was fluctuating at best. Britain's royal family often received a bad press at the hands of poets, radical papers, and magazines, as well as cartoonists such as James Gillray (1757–1815) and George Cruikshank (1792–1878). This had not always been the case. In the early part of his reign, George III (1738–1820; r. 1760–1820) was admired for his simple home-loving virtues and interest in country pursuits, which earned him the nickname "Farmer George." The king was not outstandingly intelligent, and some called him dull, but he was hardworking and religious. He brought to his court a piety and high moral tone that had been lacking in his predecessors. He also wanted to stop the power of the monarchy from slipping any further and did his utmost to ensure that his ministers were the ones he wanted—although this also led to factionalism and instability because king and Parliament often disagreed about who were the best men for the job. One of the biggest humiliations of George III's reign was the AMERICAN REVOLUTION and subsequent loss of the American colonies in 1776, for which he was widely criticized. His popularity picked up, however, when he appointed the 24-year-old William Pitt as prime minister. It was a shrewd move: Pitt was a safe pair of hands, the country slowly grew more prosperous, and from 1793 it withstood the long war with revolutionary France.

George III had made a sensible political marriage to a German princess, Charlotte of Mecklenberg-Strelitz. The couple produced 15 children and appeared a model family, respectable and devoted. However as they grew up, the sons—notably George, Prince of Wales (George IV, 1762–1830)—rebelled against the claustrophobic atmosphere of the royal court. Scandals and gambling debts mounted up.

The main crisis of George III's reign came in 1788 when he fell ill, exhibiting signs of madness (in one report he was said to have addressed a tree, talking to it as if it were the king of Prussia). He suffered convulsions, foamed at the mouth, and talked ceaselessly. Medical experts were baffled and resorted to straitjackets, blistering, and bloodletting to draw out poisonous elements. Modern medical diagnosis has suggested that the king was not "mad" at all but suffering from porphyria, a metabolic imbalance that affects the nervous system.

In spite of his medical treatment, the king seemed to recover, and there was considerable public rejoicing, not least because it meant that his debauched son would not be able to assume power as regent. George's survival was one reason why the British throne did not suffer the same fate as its French counterpart, despite the emergence of republican and revolutionary sympathisers. Nonetheless, as he got older, George's hold on power weakened. He suffered relapses in 1801 and 1804, but in face of parliamentary opposition he continued to decide who would serve as his government's ministers. In 1810, however, his illness seemed irreversible, and he spent the last decade of his reign blind and isolated in a set of rooms in Windsor Castle, unable to remember who he was. By this time George was an object of pity and some affection, not least because the public tended to compare his dutiful behaviour with that of his sons.

The crisis of the king's latest illness led the Prince of Wales to assume the role of regent—to all intents and purposes, acting as king. In youth the prince had been a handsome dandy. MARY ROBINSON, briefly one of his mistresses, wrote of "the grace of his person, the irresistible sweetness of his smile, the tenderness of his melodious but manly voice" (quoted in Clarke and Ridley, 50). However, years of overeating and drinking had taken their toil, and by the 1800s he was very fat, heavily rouged, bewigged and corseted, separated from his wife and daughter, and reliant on the advice of a bevy of elderly, grasping mistresses. In 1812 LEIGH HUNT wrote that the prince was "a libertine over head and ears in debt and disgrace, a despiser of domestic ties, the companion of demireps [prostitutes], a man who has just closed half a century without a single claim on the gratitude of his country" (quoted in Clarke and Ridley, 50). George's seemingly callous attitude to his father had shocked many observers, and his treatment of women generally—including his wife, Caroline of Brunswick, whom he had married in 1794, as well as Maria Fitzherbert (a Roman Catholic whom he was rumoured to have married before marrying Caroline)—made him the focus of early feminist antipathy. Caroline was by no means an innocent victim, but when, in 1820, George became king and attempted to divorce her in order to prevent her being crowned queen, Caroline became the focus of wider republican feeling against the Crown—not least for the sexual double standards at work. PERCY BYSSHE SHELLEY wrote the poem "A New National Anthem" and the play *Oedipus Tyrannus; or Swellfoot the Tyrant* in response to the events of 1820. A good deal of titillating evidence was heard in public about the relations between king and queen, but George was forced to drop divorce proceedings. Caroline was barred from attending the coronation and, conveniently for her husband, died soon afterward in 1821.

George IV was intelligent and cultured, a leader of fashion and elegance and a patron of the arts and architecture, albeit one associated with extravagance and excess at a time when many of the population were living in poverty. He admired SIR WALTER SCOTT and JANE AUSTEN; the fact that the latter's novels are often (indirectly) about bad government and paternal neglect seemed to have escaped him. Constantly in debt to the tune of thousands of pounds, he loved spectacle and pageantry. But he was also regarded as weak, indecisive, lazy, greedy, and untrustworthy, with little social conscience or political ability. As a young man he had allied himself with the Whig party, thus associating himself with the politics of reform, but this was largely to annoy his father, who was a Tory. As an older man, George was much more conservative, opposed, for example, to granting Roman Catholics emancipation, though the Catholic Relief act of 1829, allowing them to hold public office, was passed anyway.

For most of his reign George IV was a semirecluse, occupying himself with plans for new buildings rather than pressing government affairs. By the 1800s the outlook for the monarchy appeared bleak; its popularity was at low ebb (see "ENGLAND IN 1819"). George's only legitimate child, Princess Charlotte, regarded as the hope for the future, had died in childbirth in 1817, prompting an outpouring of national grief from poets and journalists alike (for example, Shelley's "An Address to the People on the Death of the Princess Charlotte"). George's own death in 1830 met with more indifference, and no expectations were raised when his brother William, duke of Clarence (1765–1837) succeeded him as William IV (r. 1830–37). As the complete opposite to his brother—bluff, unpretentious, frugal, and married—William proved a greater success, despite his nickname, "Silly Billy." The early part of his reign was associated with sweeping reform under the Whig government led by Lord Grey, notably the 1832 REFORM ACT, which widened the right to vote. Much of this reform was against William's natural inclinations, but he had little choice but to go along with it.

William IV also became preoccupied with the royal succession. He and his wife, Adelaide, were a devoted couple, and their marriage and relatively simple lifestyle contrasted favorably with the louche atmosphere surrounding George IV. However, none of the couple's children survived babyhood, although William had a large family of illegitimate children (known as the "Fitzclarences"), the result of a much earlier 20-year relationship with the actress Dorothy Jordan. Though in bad health, William was determined to live until his niece, Victoria (1819–1901) reached the age of majority. He succeeded dying on June 20, 1837, a month after her 18th birthday. Victoria reigned until her death in 1901, making her the longest-serving British monarch, and helped restore respectability and popularity to the throne.

See also NEWSPAPERS AND MAGAZINES.

## Further Reading

Clarke, John, and Jasper Ridley. *The Houses of Hanover and Saxe-Coburg Gotha*. London: Casell, 2000.

Sales, Roger. *Jane Austen and Representations of Regency England*. London: Routledge, 1994.

———. *Literature in History 1780–1830*. London: Hutchinson, 1983.

—Andrew Maunder

### *Monk, The* Matthew Gregory Lewis (1796)

MATTHEW GREGORY LEWIS's controversial and popular novel *The Monk* (1796) employed aspects of GOTHIC fiction as popularized by ANN RADCLIFFE, his contemporary. At the same time, Lewis shaped the convention of the guilty male outsider, as seen in later Romantic works such as LORD BYRON's MANFRED: A DRAMATIC POEM (1817) and MARY SHELLEY's FRANKENSTEIN (1818). A novel of sexual, gender, and religious transgression, *The Monk* startled some of its early readers, including SAMUEL TAYLOR COLERIDGE in *The Critical Review* in 1797. Although Coleridge admired the character of Matilda and the narrative of the bleeding nun, he was concerned about the immorality represented in the novel, especially in Ambrosio's sexual excesses.

With its multiple plots, subplots, and various narrators, the complex form of *The Monk* is noteworthy. In contrast with Radcliffe's style, *The Monk* participates in the male gothic tradition, in which there is an emphasis on unruly and dangerous male sexuality, exemplified by Ambrosio, the monk of the novel's title. Ambrosio's character shows similarities to the villain of Horace Walpole's early gothic novel, *The Castle of Otranto* (1765), especially in Walpole's villain, Manfred. In addition, the characterization of the villainous monk Schedoni in Radcliffe's *The Italian* (1797) reacts to Lewis's treatment of the gothic, reducing the sexual and supernatural themes.

Ambrosio, the austere monk who breaks his vows of celibacy, embodies *The Monk*'s fear of sexual repression, especially in Catholicism. His life story parallels that of Agnes and Beatrice de las Cisternas, the bleeding nun, both of whom are placed in convents against their wills; in these characters' circumstances, monastic life serves as an institution of unnatural sexual repression that results in murder and social upheaval. Although Lewis's novel participates in anti-Catholic sentiment, similar attitudes can be found in novels by Radcliffe and in PERCY BYSSHE SHELLEY's *The Cenci* (1819).

The character Matilda, who disguises herself as the monk Rosario, is one of the novel's most fascinating figures. With a character open to multiple interpretations, Matilda violates normal gender roles, at once becoming a powerful woman and a villain. Often represented as masculine and insensitive, Matilda seduces Ambrosio, causing him to rebel against his strict moral codes. Her alchemical research contrasts with Victor Frankenstein's pursuit of forbidden knowledge; unlike Victor, Matilda does not experience guilt and remains powerful, even after being captured by the Inquisition. When she renounces God for her liberty, the novel aligns her with radical, revolutionary forces that are also satanic. In the end, however, both Matilda and Ambrosio are sent to Hell for their transgressions, providing closure and punishment for their transgressions.

### Further Reading

Blakemore, Steven. "Matthew Lewis's Black Mass: Sexual, Religious Inversion in *The Monk*." *Studies in the Novel* 30 (1998): 521–539.

Ellis, Kate Ferguson. *The Contested Castle: Gothic Novels and the Subversion of Domestic Ideology.* Urbana: University of Illinois Press, 1989.

Heiland, Donna. *Gothic and Gender: An Introduction.* Oxford: Blackwell, 2004.

Lewis, Matthew. *The Monk.* Oxford: Oxford World's Classics, 1996.

Watkins, Daniel P. "Social Hierarchy in Matthew Lewis's *The Monk*." *Studies in the Novel* 18 (1986): 115–124.

Williams, Anne. Art *of Darkness: A Poetics of Gothic.* Chicago: University of Chicago Press, 1994.

—Albert Sears

### "Mont Blanc" Percy Bysshe Shelley (1816)

"Mont Blanc" (Subtitle: "Lines Written in the Vale of Chamouni") (1816) is a meditative poem on the power of landscape on the mind. It was composed by PERCY BYSSHE SHELLEY following his visit to the Alps. In a letter to the satirist THOMAS LOVE PEACOCK, Shelley wrote: "The immensity of these aerial summits excited, when they suddenly burst upon the sight, a sentiment of ecstatic wonder, not unallied to madness." Mountain scenery was also a popular subject in 18th-century art, and Shelley had seen paintings by Salvator Rosa and J. M. W. Turner.

"Mont Blanc" combines the inscrutable nature of the mountain, Mont Blanc, with the mind's capacity to allegorize nature. The poem begins by comparing the human mind with its stream of consciousness to the flow of the river through the ravine of Arve. In the second stanza the speaker claims that the ravine has entranced him, a fact that lends credence to nature's power to influence. Here, Shelley seems to build on the philosopher JOHN LOCKE's theory of knowledge: something that could be gained only by sensory experiences and one's reflections on them. The third stanza has a shift in poetic focus from the ravine to the mountain itself. Mont Blanc dominates the mountains that surround it and seems eternal in comparison. In the fourth stanza, nature is characterized as anthropomorphic: The earth is "daedal" (l. 86), the mountains are "primaeval" (l. 99), and "The glaciers creep / like snakes that watch their prey" (ll. 100–101). Shelley also introduces the Romantic concept of nature's capacity to instruct: Mont Blanc is "Remote, serene, and inaccessible" (l. 97) but still has the power to "Teach" (l. 100). Another Romantic concept introduced is the contrast between the timelessness of nature and humankind's mortality. The fifth stanza contains a meditation on the mountain's power and height. Yet the poem ends on a note of paradox, with Shelley stating that the human mind, as expressed by "The secret Strength of things / which governs thought" (ll. 139–140), reigns over the natural world and gives shape to it.

In "Mont Blanc" Shelley propounds the Romantic concept of a pantheistic nature, or a nature that is imbued with godlike qualities. Scholars have pointed out that the poem highlights the poet's own conflict of faith. This is particularly relevant since Shelley's reputation as an atheist was established upon his publication of the subversive pamphlet *The Necessity of Atheism* (1811), which, in turn, led to his expulsion from University College, Oxford, where he was an undergraduate student. Interestingly, in "Mont Blanc" it is nature, not established religion, that teaches faith. On this subject, critical discussions have centered on lines 76–83 in the Third stanza. In these lines, nature appears to speak in mysterious ways, teaching both doubt and a "solemn" and "serene" faith (l. 78),

depending on the belief of the recipient. Mont Blanc, far from being an inanimate part of the landscape, has "a voice" (l. 80) that can instruct and make moral decisions. Like God, the mountain is preternatural: There is no indication of when it was created; it is never-ending, powerful, and an "unsculptured image" (l. 27). In projecting these divine qualities onto Mont Blanc, Shelley works firmly within the Romantic tradition. The Romantics believed that formal religion had severed humankind from nature; in turn, nature had the capacity to teach morality.

Mont Blanc also builds on Shelley's theory of poetry, which he later expanded in his essay "A DEFENCE OF POETRY" (1821). This essay ends with his celebrated claim: "Poets are the unacknowledged legislators of the world." Shelley also states: "A Poet participates in the eternal, the infinite, and the one; as far as relates to his conceptions, time and place and number are not" (Shelley 1977, 513). This statement helps us understand the concept of Mont Blanc, not just as mountain but also as symbol. Mont Blanc is eternal and infinite, and it has the capacity to "Teach the adverting mind" (l. 100); this makes it a fitting subject for the poet.

"Mont Blanc" also draws on two traditions critical to the landscape aesthetics of the 18th century: the SUBLIME and the PICTURESQUE. In his essay *A PHILOSOPHICAL ENQUIRY INTO THE ORIGIN OF OUR IDEAS OF THE SUBLIME AND BEAUTIFUL* (1757), EDMUND BURKE states that the sublime is analogous to ideas of pain, danger, and terror. It is distinct from the beautiful in that it arouses feelings of admiration and awe, not love. The picturesque tradition, on the other hand, stresses that irregularity, ruggedness, and rusticity are qualities that make an attractive landscape. The impetus for the popularity of this tradition came from various sources, but primarily William Gilpin's *Three Essays* (1792), in which he states that a landscape is not naturally picturesque; however, its potential can be enhanced by the depiction of the artist. "Mont Blanc" contains elements of both traditions. In the ravine that creates "a trance sublime and strange" (l. 35), the poet clearly draws from Burke, whereas the "many-coloured, many-voicéd vale" (l. 13) with its "crags" (l. 14) and "ice-gulfs" (l. 17) has elements of the rugged irregularity that forms a part of the picturesque tradition.

"Mont Blanc" is one of the greatest of the landscape poems that make up the Romantic canon. Its strongest Romantic characteristic is its argument that nature contains traces of the divine and is imbued with godlike powers to teach. The poem forges a connection between the human mind and nature as represented by the external world. In other words, the poem asks: Is the human mind a passive recipient of sensory impressions, or does it actively construct reality? Like another famous landscape poem, WILLIAM WORDSWORTH's "LINES WRITTEN A FEW MILES ABOVE TINTERN ABBEY" (1798), "Mont Blanc" posits a mind that receives, abstracts, and renders sensory impressions. In this manner it contributes to Romanticism in two ways: first, in its celebration of the beauty of the physical landscape; and second, through its examination of the self, particularly as represented by the human mind, as creator of experience.

## Further Reading

Leighton, Angela. *Shelley and the Sublime: An Interpretation of the Major Poems.* New York: Cambridge University Press, 1984.

Morton, Timothy, ed. *The Cambridge Companion to Shelley.* New York: Cambridge University Press, 2006.

Shelley, Percy Bysshe. *Shelley's Poetry and Prose: Authoritative Texts, Criticism.* Edited by Donald H. Reiman, and Sharon B. Powers. New York: Norton, 1977.

—Devjani Roy

## Moore, Thomas (1779–1852)

Born on May 28, 1779, in Dublin, the son of John Moore, a Catholic grocer, and Anastasia Codd Moore, Thomas Moore came from origins that were ordinary, making the international fame he achieved as his country's preeminent poet seem all the more extraordinary. Moore's was a precocious talent. His first poems were published while he was still a young teenager, and by the time he entered Trinity College, Dublin, in 1795, he was a practiced writer. As a member of the Catholic community, Moore was a sympathizer with those who

wanted to overthrow Ireland's Anglo-Protestant rulers, and he gained a reputation as a man with strong political conscience. He was a close friend of Robert Emmet, one of those who were executed for treason following the Irish uprising of 1798.

Leaving the hothouse atmosphere of student life in Dublin, Moore moved to London in 1799, ostensibly to train as a lawyer, but he was aware that the capital also offered more opportunities for an aspiring writer. He found that his songs, which he often performed personally, went down well with the social elite, and his ability to charm made him much in demand. A contemporary, Elizabeth Rennie, described him as "a very well-dressed, bright, sparkling-looking little man" (Rennie i), but despite his fondness for singing, "his voice was weak, power he had none" (170). His *Poetical Works of the Late Thomas Little* (1801) was a hit in spite—or perhaps because of—the risqué nature of the some of its contents.

After some time working for the civil service in Bermuda as registrar of the admiralty court and then traveling in North America—an experience he vowed never to repeat—Moore returned to London in November 1804 and threw himself into literary work once again, His next collection, *Epistles, Odes and Other Poems* (1806), caused a frisson of excitement among the reading public, though FRANCIS JEFFREY, writing in the *Edinburgh Review,* called the collection "a public nuisance" and accused Moore of obscenity. Famously, Moore challenged Jeffrey to a duel, which was only prevented when officers of the law broke it up. A rumor ran through London that even if the duel had gone ahead, no one would have been hurt because the participants were both using bullets made with wound-up paper. Moore felt humiliated and later challenged LORD BYRON to a duel when the poet wrote about this rumor. Conveniently, Byron was out of the country, so the duel never took place.

The biggest boost to Moore's fortunes was the project that led to the publication of his series called *IRISH MELODIES* (1808–34). When he retreated to Ireland in 1806, he was invited to write a series of "typical" Irish airs to illustrate old customs and Celtic stories, which would then be set to pianoforte, with music arranged by John Stevenson. The results would be published as a series of six parts, each containing 12 melodies. Moore's sympathy with Irish nationalism helped sell the idea to him; he observed that "In our music is found the truest of all comments upon our history" (quoted in Tessier xv). Part of the aim was to foster a sense of national pride, and the resulting songs mixed stirring accounts of heroism with lamentation; a recurrent form is the "aisling," a poem that invokes Ireland in the form of a beautiful young woman ("Erin"). Moore's ability as a performer helped sell *Irish Melodies* in London drawing rooms; one observer described him as captivating: "[H]e seems to improvise words and music; his eye lights up, and his voice becomes in turn lively or slow, gay or plaintive" (quoted in Tessier 83). They were clearly in tune with the times in their evocation of romantic emotion and their calls for freedom and support of nationalism.

For the next 25 years the project provided Moore with a steady income, though he felt he had sold the rights to the Melodies far too cheaply. A companion series, *National Airs,* ran from 1818 to 1827 and were well-received. *Blackwood's Edinburgh Magazine* called Moore "the Burns of Ireland" (Tessier 92). For LEIGH HUNT he was a "poetical animal," while Byron told MARGUERITE GARDINER (Lady Blessington) that Moore would "go down to posterity by his Melodies," which "were all perfect," and SIR WALTER SCOTT—whose MINSTRELSY OF THE SCOTTISH BORDERS and *The Lay of the Last Minstrel* tapped into similar enthusiasms—was reported as saying "Moore beats us all at song" (all quoted in Tessier 122).

Although the *Melodies* were the source of his reputation, he was not the firework people predicted would soon burn out. Despite the weakness of his voice, Moore was by all accounts a mesmerising singer and a competent, energetic actor, good enough to work professionally in works such as Richard Brinsley Sheridan's classic comedy *The Rivals* and in his own satiric play *M.P., or, The Blue-Stocking* (1811). During the 1800s he developed a reputation as a pungent satirist, attacking reactionary Tory governments or arguing for an improvement in conditions in Ireland, as in his poems "Corruption: An Epistle" (1808) and "Intolerance" (1808), both written after the manner of the great 18th-century satirists, notably Alexander Pope. *Intercepted Letters, or The Two-Penny Post-Bag* (1814) took the form of a set of letters in verse, supposedly written by cronies of the unpopular Prince of Wales (see MONARCHY). So popular was Moore that the manuscript prompted a well-publicized bidding war between rival firms of publishers. *The Fudge Family in Paris* (1818), a set of verses ascribed to writers ranging from a young lad of fashion to an Irish nationalist, helped boost Moore's finances, which were generally in a desperate state. The costs of supporting his parents, his wife Bessy (whom he married in 1811), and their children, as well as the more considerable expense of maintaining a lifestyle commensurate with the elite social circles he moved in took their toll. Moore was often reliant on patrons, notably Lord Lansdowne, to help him out, as well as on publishers.

Matters took a turn for the worse when the colleague whom Moore had appointed as a locum in his Bermuda post disappeared, leaving Moore responsible for debts of £6,000. Imprisonment for debt was a possibility, and so he fled to Europe, first France and then Italy. Unable to settle, Moore found it difficult to write. He continued writing about the Fudge family in *Rhymes of the Road* (1823) and worked on verses which would later form the basis for *The Epicurean* (1827). The most significant thing to come out of these years was a meeting with Byron in Italy. Byron generously entrusted Moore with the manuscript of his memoirs, the idea being that Moore would benefit from them should Byron die before him. This proved to be the case, and Moore used them as collateral for a loan from Byron's publisher, John Murray. But the ownership of the manuscript proved a bone of contention with the Byron family. Thinking—probably rightly—that the memoirs would be embarrassing, Lady Byron sued Moore for their return. Moore and Murray burned them in Murray's fireplace, but not before Moore had used them as the basis for a biography, *Letters and Journals of Lord Byron* (1830). Despite—or perhaps because of—the private wrangling, the work was a hit, and Moore was seen to have captured the essence of the iconic poet.

In later life Moore rekindled his interest in Irish history and politics. He turned down the chance to become a member of Parliament but produced several works with Irish themes and settings: *Memoirs of Captain Rock* (1824), *Travels of an Irish Gentleman in Search of Religion* (1833), and *The History of Ireland* (4 vols., 1835–46). The first of these is an attack on English misrule in Ireland in which Moore argued that English incompetence and cruelty was the cause of Irish retaliatory violence. "Captain Rock" was the name given by the poor to a mythical leader of the land-reform movement in southern Ireland in the early 1800s, and Moore's work struck a chord with Irish readers. A slightly different work—but keeping with the theme of tyranny—was *The Epicurean: A Tale* (1827) which claims to be based on an ancient manuscript. The plot, which is set in the third century, centers on a young man who journeys out of Egypt in a search for immortality. He is converted to Christianity by monks but is killed on the orders of the emperor Valerian, becoming a martyr.

Moore's last years were blighted by misfortune. All of his four children predeceased him, and by the mid-1840s he had begun to suffer from the senile dementia that would eventually lead to his death. His financial worries were eased by a civil-list pension in 1850, but he was often dependent on the support of friends. Nonetheless, when he died on February 25, 1852, his work was still popular. He was seen as an important poet, and the *Irish Melodies* still sold well. Though his reputation declined in the 20th century, he remained known among Byron scholars for his association with the poet. His own work gradually fell out of print. There has been some attempt to rehabilitate his literary reputation—notably as an Irish poet—but despite being a prominent and much-loved figure in his own day, Moore has tended to be overshadowed by his contemporaries. His verse romance *Lalla-Rookh,* which he sold to Longman's for £3,000 but which faded from view, has started to attract notice again, largely because of a growing interest in ORIENTALISM as part of Romantic culture.

**Further Reading**

Davis, Leith. "Irish Bards and English Consumers: Thomas Moore's 'Irish Melodies' and the Colonized Nation." *Ariel* 24, no. 2 (1993): 7–25.

Gibson, Mary Ellis. "Poems of Mary Carshore: The Indian Legacy of L.E.L. and Tom Moore." *Victorians Institute Journal* 32 (2004): 63–79.

Jones, Howard Mumford. *The Harp That Once—; A Chronicle of the Life of Thomas Moore.* 1937. Reprint, New York: Russell & Russell, 1937.

Moore, Jane. "Thomas Moore as Irish Satirist." In *Scotland, Ireland and the Romantic Aesthetic,* edited by David Duff and Catherine Jones, 152–171. Lewisburg, Pa.: Bucknell University Press, 2007.

Rennie, E. *Traits of Character; Being Twenty-Five Years' Literary and Personal Recollections. By a Contemporary.* 2 vols. London: Hurst & Blackett, 1860.

Tessier, Therese. *The Bard of Erin. A Study of Thomas Moore's Irish Melodies.* Salzburg: Institute fur Anglistik und Amerikanistik, 1981.

Vail, Jeffrey. *The Literary Relationship of Lord Byron and Thomas Moore.* Baltimore: Johns Hopkins University Press, 2001.

———. "Thomas Moore in Ireland and America: The Growth of a Poet's Mind." *Romanticism* 10, no. 1 (2004): 41–62.

White, Terence de Vere. *Tom Moore the Irish Poet.* London: Hamilton, 1977.

—Andrew Maunder

## More, Hannah (1745–1833)

Known primarily for her efforts in philanthropy and in social and educational reform, Hannah More was a prolific writer whose wide-ranging publications included plays; poems; a novel; and numerous religious, moral, and educational treatises. She was born on February 2, 1745, to a schoolmaster of middling means who provided Hannah (along with her four sisters) a more rigorous education than was typical for girls during this period. Having established a budding literary reputation in her teens, she attracted the attention of the London literati upon her arrival there in the winter of 1773–74 and was warmly received by such luminaries as the famous thespian David Garrick, the author Samuel Johnson, the artist Sir Joshua Reynolds, and the reformer and literary critic Elizabeth Montagu. The public life of More, who never married, can be divided into three periods that directly reflect the progression of her private concerns: the earlier period of literary writing, the middle years of works concerned with social and moral reform, and the later years of devotional and spiritual writing.

Early in her career, More's friendship with Garrick resulted in his production of two of her plays, *Percy* (1777) and *The Fatal Falsehood* (1779), while her connection with Montagu brought her into the Bluestocking Circle, a group of learned literary women. This period of her life produced numerous dramatic and poetic works, leading Johnson to call her "the most powerful versificatrix in the English Language" (quoted in Clarke, 155). Following the death of her mentor and patron Garrick in 1779, More became increasingly disillusioned with urban and aristocratic life. Drawn to the growing evangelical movement (see EVANGELICALISM), she eventually took a place among the Clapham Sect, an influential group of evangelicals who included the abolitionist William Wilberforce and the clergyman and hymn writer John Newton. With their encouragement and support, More directed her writing to more social and political endeavors including the abolitionist movement (see SLAVERY). These works are particularly noteworthy in their scope, directed to audiences ranging from the laboring poor to the aristocracy. Among the works of this period are an antislavery poem, her series of *Cheap Repository Tracts* (1795–97), *Thoughts on the Importance of the Manners of the Great to General Society and An Estimate of the Religion of the Fashionable World* (1790), *Strictures on the Modern System of Female Education* (1799), and *Hints Towards Forming the Character of a Young Princess* (1805).

In 1808 More published her only novel, CŒLEBS IN SEARCH OF A WIFE, one of the best-selling novels in the period. The writings of her later years reflect her increasing religious devotion: *An Essay on the Character and Practical Writings of St. Paul* (1815), *Moral Sketches* (1819), and *The Spirit of Prayer* (1825). Remarkably, despite her lifelong battles with poor health, More lived to be 88; she died on September 7, 1833. Though considered by her contemporaries to be one of the most widely influential writers of her time, she has been largely forgotten until a recent resurgence of interest in minor women writers of the period. The demise of her popularity can be attributed in part to her later reputation as an outdated conservative and anti-

feminist religionist, particularly in comparison with her contemporary foil, MARY WOLLSTONECRAFT.

See also YEARSLEY, ANN.

**Further Reading**

Clarke, Norma. *Dr. Johnson's Women.* London: Hambledon and London, 2000.

Ford, Charles Howard. *Hannah More: A Critical Biography.* New York: Peter Lang, 1996.

Hopkins, Mary Alden. *Hannah More and Her Circle.* New York: Longmans, Green, and Co., 1947.

———. *The Works of Hannah More.* 2 vols. London: Adamant Media Corporation, 2001.

More, Hannah. *Selected Writings of Hannah More.* Edited by Robert Hole. London: William Pickering, 1996.

Stott, Anne. *Hannah More: The First Victorian.* Oxford: Oxford University Press, 2003.

—Karen Swallow Prior

## "Mortal Immortal, The"  Mary Wollstonecraft Shelley (1833)

This GOTHIC short story by MARY WOLLSTONECRAFT SHELLEY, the author of *FRANKENSTEIN: or, The Modern Prometheus* (1818), explores the implications of immortality. In the story, alchemy—or artifice—overrides natural law and makes the impossible dream of immortality possible. The story contains many of the motifs found in Shelley's famous novel, including a protagonist who impulsively and thoughtlessly moves forward with a scientific experiment, the effects of which he is ill-prepared to face. The story is narrated by the 323-year-old Winzy, who, as an aspiring scientist of 20, apprenticed himself to Cornelius Agrippa, a figure whose influence makes itself felt in *Frankenstein* as well. Tormented by the thought that his beloved Bertha holds him in contempt because of his poverty, Winzy imbibes a potion that Agrippa has described as "a philter to cure love" (75). Winzy does not realize that this is an "Elixir of Immortality" that will cure not only love but "all things" (78) through the distanced perspective of immorality.

Immediately after drinking most of the elixir, a heated disagreement between Bertha and her wealthy (but tyrannical) protectress convinces

Winzy that Bertha is in fact devoted to him. Bertha leaves her patron's home, rejecting the wealthier match the other woman has championed. Winzy and Bertha marry and are happy until it becomes clear to both them and the townspeople that, while Bertha is aging naturally, Winzy is not. The couple is ostracized, and when Agrippa is on his deathbed, the truth comes out. Winzy, horrified, realizes that he may, in fact, never die. He recounts the painful later years of his marriage, condemning his wife for her self-conscious affectations of youth while recognizing that, although his deception is not as obvious as Bertha's, he, too, lives a lie. He is by all appearances a young man of 23, even though he is well past 50. When an aged Bertha dies, severing Winzy's final connection to humanity, he becomes a "sailor without rudder or compass—tossed on a stormy sea" for centuries. The story closes with Winzy's proposed exploration of the Arctic, to find either death or glory.

With its emphasis on the natural supernatural, Shelley's story is in the gothic mode, but it strays from gothic conventions by setting the narrative in the present. Shelley also explores the typically feminine motif of being trapped in, and defined by, one's body, and, in her tormented narrator, reveals the psychological damage that can accompany this condition.

See also MAURICE, OR THE FISHER'S COT.

**Further Reading**

Shelley, Mary Wollstonecraft. "The Mortal Immortal." In *Nineteenth Century Short Stories by Women,* edited by Harriet Devine Jump, 73–83. London: Routledge, 1998.

—Anita Rose

## "Mouse's Petition, The" Anna Laetitia Barbauld (1773)

The simple balladic form and light comic tone of this poem belie its subtler ideas. Published in ANNA LAETITIA BARBAULD's popular 1773 collection of *Poems,* this is one of her many occasional poems that respond to a particular event. It is addressed to Joseph Priestley, a Unitarian, chemist, and mentor and family friend to Barbauld, who addresses his religious and political sympathies as well as his scientific interests. The mouse in question has been trapped for the purpose of Priestley's experiments into atmospheric gases.

In the voice of the mouse, Barbauld uses the language of SENSIBILITY to evoke sympathy for a suffering victim, with many appeals to the reader's "heart" and references to its "sighs" and "cries" (ll. 2, 4). But Barbauld uses a mock-heroic tone that comically elevates the mouse's predicament, its "forlorn" contemplation of its "impending fate" (ll. 5, 8). Barbauld draws on contemporary radical politics as she alludes to JEAN-JACQUES ROUSSEAU's ideas of natural freedoms, which an oppressive institutional power denies, and she reasons from the premises of universal rights in several "If . . ." clauses. "Pity" (l. 39) has democratic implications when it includes all creatures as "nature's commoners" (l. 23). As the critic Marlon Ross argues, for the first few stanzas it is ambiguous whether the poem is a parody of democratic politics, reducing them to the level of absurdity, or a genuine plea for universal liberties, which are playfully couched in the voice of the humblest. William McCarthy reads the poem as a feminist allegory, whereby, as in other poems by women of the era, the plight of the trapped animal is used as a displaced female protest against patriarchal tyranny. This reading would suggest Barbauld is more conscious of gender politics than she is usually considered to be.

Barbauld takes sensibility beyond a purely emotional response, and connects it to particular religious and philosophical ideas. Here she draws on her liberal education, unusual for a woman, though less so in the Dissenting circles in which she moved. Barbauld alludes to the Unitarian commitment to universal benevolence, which "feels for all that lives," whereby compassion is not merely an effusion but a rationally guided impulse extended equally to all. She also alludes to neoplatonic ideas of God as "mind," or "an impersonal life force," which dwells in all phenomena. This is comparable with SAMUEL TAYLOR COLERIDGE's "One Life" theory, which was also informed by Unitarianism, and by Barbauld's influence. An ecocritical perspective might see in this poem (as in Coleridge's "The RIME OF THE ANCIENT MARINER") a challenge to the constructed hierarchy that assumes human superiority to the rest of the natural world and the freedom to exploit it.

Barbauld ends the poem with the homely moral sentiment to "... *all* of life we share / Let pity plead within thy breast / That with *all* to spare," (38–40), and her combination of instruction with entertainment sets her in the tradition of neoclassical poets such as Alexander Pope. Like other female poets of the era, she finds her inspiration within the mundane, but her treatment of sensibility as a democratic impulse and her near-pantheism anticipate aspects celebrated in Coleridge and WILLIAM WORDSWORTH's collection *Lyrical Ballads*. As regards the mouse's fate, we are reassured by a contemporary of Barbauld that the petition was successful.

**Further Reading**

Barbauld, Anna Letitia. *Selected Poetry and Prose.* Edited by William McCarthy and Elizabeth Kraft. Peterborough, Ont.: Broadview Press, 2001.

McCarthy, William. "'We Hoped the *Woman* Was Going to Appear': Repression, Desire, and Gender in Anna Letitia Barbauld's Early Poems." In *Romantic Women Writers: Voices and Counter-Voices,* edited by Paula R. Feldman and Theresa M. Kelley, 113–137. Hanover, N.H.: University Press of New England, 1995.

Ross, Marlon B. "Configurations of Feminine Reform: The Woman Writer and the Tradition of Dissent." In *Re-Visioning Romanticism: British Women Writers, 1776–1837,* edited by Carol Shiner Wilson and Joel Haefner, 91–110. Philadelphia: University of Pennsylvania Press, 1994.

Wordsworth, John. *The Bright Work Grows: Women Writers of the Romantic Age.* Herndon, Va.: Woodstock Books, 1997.

—Rebecca Styler

## "Mrs. Robinson to the Poet Coleridge"
### ("To the Poet Coleridge") Mary Robinson
(1806)

Along with SAMUEL TAYLOR COLERIDGE's poem "A Stranger Minstrel, written [to Mrs Robinson] a few weeks before her death," "Mrs Robinson to the Poet Coleridge" was one of a number of literary exchanges between two leading Romantic figures: the erratic poet and philosopher Coleridge and MARY ROBINSON, one of the major "celebrity" poets and actresses of the period. Written in praise of Coleridge's haunting "KUBLA KHAN," "Mrs Robinson to the Poet Coleridge" appeared under the pen name of Sappho in the *Morning Post* on October 17, 1800, as well as in *Memoirs of the Late Mrs Robinson* (1801). Because of this, it is logical to compare the poems. However, recent critics have noted that there are numerous indicators that Robinson was wary of this impulse. As Tim Fulford observes, "Reading Kubla Khan, she is inspired to write, rather than reduced to being the wailing victim of a demon lover," while Susan Luther situates the literary exchanges within 18th-century sexual politics: In order to appreciate the relationship between Coleridge and Robinson as kindred poets, we must consider "the vexed borders between private and public expression, the complications ideological, personal and generic encountered ... when male or female artist responds verbally (or otherwise) to another artist of the opposite gender" (Luther 394).

Such gendered dynamics aside, Daniel Robinson has suggested that the poem would have befuddled readers of the *Morning Post*, since Coleridge's "Kubla Khan" would not be available in print for another 16 years (Robinson saw it in manuscript). Contemporary readers might have instead focused more on the formal aspects of the poem in front of them. "Mrs Robinson to the Poet Coleridge" itself presents a series of oppositions and contradictions. It is at once religious and secular, paradisiacal and bewitching. The hymnal phrasing of the verse is offset against the pagan allusions, and the "new paradise" is marked out as a literary fabrication, adopted from Coleridge's "Kubla Khan." Indeed, Robinson's vision of "thy new paradise" (l. 6) is constructed from quoted phrases—"sunny dome" (ll. 13, 31), "caves of ice" (ll. 14, 32, 65)—as well as nuanced reinscriptions of the damsel with the dulcimer and rivers and enclosures. This reminds us that the "airy dreams" have "a magic all thy own!" (l. 71) and thereby exclude Robinson from the creative process.

Nevertheless, it is a highly stylized poem in which Robinson infuses her considerable sexual energy, here manifesting itself as a sort of verbal onanism if not a lovemaking through correspondence ("The mystic fountain, bubbling, panting" [l. 10])—a paradox that indicates the necessary distinction between Coleridge (the "spirit divine" [l. 2]) and Robinson as a poet in her own right. In the beginning of the piece the speaker tells the "spirit divine" that "Rapt in the visionary theme" (l. 1), "with thee I'll wander" (l. 2). Together they will "trace the circling bounds / Of thy new paradise extended" (ll. 5–6). But this "extended" imaginary world, the speaker realizes, entails weaving a crown for the celebrated Coleridge, the "Genius of heav'n-taught poesy" (l. 51) who, "While op'ning to my wond'ring eyes, / Thou bid'st a new creation rise" (ll. 52–53). Thereby, alone, the speaker encircles what had seemed a "boundless space" (l. 28). Coleridge's song, in the mouth of a nymph, is "madd'ning sweet" (l. 66). The nymph "sings of thee, oh favoured child / Of minstrelsy" (ll. 68–69), the poet who is isolated by his own demonic magic. Such "wondrous witcheries of song" (l. 63) entice Robinson, but she remains true to her guise as the English Sappho in this valediction to Coleridge's overbearing influence on her own visions. Coleridge's song "Shall wake me in ecstatic measures" (l. 60), and her creative energy will prevail without boundaries.

## Further Reading

Fulford, Tim. "Mary Robinson and the Abyssinian Maid: Coleridge's Muses and Feminist Criticism." *Romanticism On the Net* 13 (February 1999). Available online. URL: http://id.erudit.org/iderudit/005842ar. Accessed on July 25, 2009.

Levy, Martin J. "Coleridge, Mary Robinson, and *Kubla Khan*." *Charles Lamb Bulletin* 77 (1992): 156–167.

Luther, Susan. "A Stranger Minstrel: Coleridge's Mrs Robinson." *Studies in Romanticism* 33 (1994): 391–409.

Robinson, Daniel. "From 'Mingled Measure' to 'Ecstatic Measures': Mary Robinson's Poetic Reading of 'Kubla Khan.'" *The Wordsworth Circle* 26, no. 1 (1995): 4–7.

Stelzig, Eugene. "'Spirit divine! With thee I'll wander': Mary Robinson and Coleridge in Poetic Dialogue." *The Wordsworth Circle* 35, no. 3 (2004): 118–122.

Vargo, Lisa. "The Claims of 'real life and manners': Coleridge and Mary Robinson." *The Wordsworth Circle* 26 (1995): 134–137.

—Daniel Cook

## *Mysteries of Udolpho, The* Ann Radcliffe (1794)

Lauded by SAMUEL TAYLOR COLERIDGE as "the most interesting novel in the English language," ANN RADCLIFFE's *The Mysteries of Udolpho* (1794) was perhaps the most influential novel of the 1790s. As the scholar Donald K. Adams rightly claims, "the history of popular fiction throughout the 1790s was largely a chronicle of novelists striving to shape their romances in Mrs. Radcliffe's successful mode" (Adams 49). Minerva Press was a prolific publisher of GOTHIC novels, and most of its productions were tame, sentimental rehashes of Radcliffe's female gothic formula as popularized in *Mysteries*. Her extraordinary contract of £500 for that work—probably the result of her husband William's astute legal advice—exactly doubled the highest known copyright fee for novels to that date. It helped both to raise the profile of the gothic, which had been previously viewed as an impassioned, subliterary form, and to gain women writers greater respect. *Mysteries* has been in print continually since its initial publication.

A unique fusion of gothic novel, sentimental fiction, and bildungsroman, *The Mysteries of Udolpho* established the format of the female gothic, a novelistic subgenre that calls women's limited roles and domestic ideals into question, explores the conjunction between love and terror, and contests property-related issues. Set against a backdrop of religious wars in 16th-century France, the novel chronicles the adventures of Emily St. Aubert following the bankrupty and successive deaths of her parents when she is forced to leave her idyllic rural French home and beloved, potential future husband, Valancourt. She accompanies her newly married aunt, Madame Cheron, to the Castle Udolpho, her home in the Appenines where her aunt's new husband, Count Montoni, assumes increasingly terrifying and tyrannical dimensions. He abuses his position as guardian and repeatedly threatens the young woman with a loveless, arranged marriage and disinheritance. As with Horace Walpole's *The Castle of Otranto* (1764), the theme of the contested castle plays a prominent role, almost becoming a character in its own right. The question of rightful inheritance, which has spiritual, ethical, and material aspects, becomes paramount.

As the example of Montoni suggests, fears and anxieties about sexuality and marriage, including questions about male loyalty within that institution, loom large on this journey. Emily's nagging concerns about Valancourt are magnified by the haunting memory of her father grieving over a miniature portrait of a mysterious woman. This and other mysteries are solved after a variety of adventures in the prison-like castle—an un-Christian, vice-ridden locale to which Emily feels her fate connected as if "by some invisible means" (Radcliffe 250). The prospects are daunting as Udolpho is figuratively littered with female corpses whose tragic, repressed histories are unearthed during the course of Emily's explorations. These include the wife of Montoni's servant, who was killed when some of the battlements of the north tower of the castle descended on her; Signora Laurentini, whose dead body, Emily fears, is actually located behind a picture covered by a mysterious black veil; Emily's innocent aunt, the poisoned marchioness, whose tragic betrayal and murder Emily uncovers only toward novel's end; and Madame Cheron, Emily's bad aunt who gets her just desserts when she is incarcerated and dies while under Montoni's care. These numerous spectral foremothers, especially those who have paid for violating the ideology of femininity, haunt Emily's journey. Their fates remind her of the gothic novel's foremost moral as originally articulated in the preface to the first edition of *The Castle of Otranto* that "the sins of fathers are visited on their children to the third and fourth generations" (Walpole 5).

Emily must follow a course laid out by her father before his death between excessive reason—the paramount characteristic of the heartless gothic villain—and excessive SENSIBILITY, a characteristic frequently attributed to young women of Emily's era, especially those who read countless romances. Sensibility, however, as demonstrated by one's response to such things as art and SUBLIME landscapes (of which there are many in *Mysteries*) remains the key moral index.

The female gothic novel is ever critical of cloistered, untested virtue and seems to be driven by the 17th-century poet JOHN MILTON's theory, expressed in *Aeropagitica,* that trial "by what is contrary" purifies us (Milton 514–515). Emily's theoretical education is, subsequent to the deaths of her parents, subjected to some fairly severe practical tests. While it is imperative that Emily put her familial past into perspective, learn to accept death as a natural phase of life, and renew her faith in God, purported supernatural sightings—represented as part and parcel of a superstitious Roman Catholic worldview—must be subjected to Radcliffe's innovative gothic convention of the "explained supernatural." Such phenomena are ultimately rationally explained as the products of an overstrained sensibility and overheated imagination and are, finally, laid to rest.

At the novel's end, Valancourt, after undergoing his own set of trials involving money and gambling, is reunited with and married to a more practical yet still-pure Emily who has held steadfast to his memory; gained self-assertiveness; tempered her sensibility; and become apprised of, and gained control over, her financial affairs. In keeping with the traditional closure in a novel of sensibility, therefore, Emily's virtue, in the form of her unshaken faith and fortitude, is rewarded by way of inheritance and companionate marriage. Valancourt is likewise proven to be worthy of Emily and rewarded at the novel's end in the form, in part, of his brother's estates. Although he succumbs to gambling while in the treacherously seductive city of Paris, he is ultimately redeemed as he games for benevolent purposes—namely, to aid people in financial distress.

Radcliffe has been called "a bride of romanticism" (Spector 5), and while her appeal to reason was not, as Robert Spector notes, what made her popular, she was nevertheless "wise enough to maintain an adulterous union with the rationalists" (5). Emily is an intriguing combination of a practical figure with a heroine of sensibility, and her final union with Valancourt is figured as both sensible and emotionally fulfilling, the type of equal, loving partnership advocated by MARY WOLLSTONECRAFT in *A VINDICATION OF THE*

*RIGHTS OF WOMAN.* With a new type of character and the female gothic, Radcliffe hit upon a winning formula that brought her unforeseen levels of critical and commercial success, as well as a slew of imitators. Her production of five gothic romances between the late 1780s and the 1790s—*The Castles of Athlin and Dunbayne* (1789); *A Sicilian Romance* (1790); *The Romance of the Forest* (1791); *The Mysteries of Udolpho* (1794); and *The Italian, or The Confessional of the Black Penitents* (1797)—sparked a gothic vogue that left an indelible mark on that genre's conventions and reception.

## Further Reading

Adams, Donald K. "The Second Mrs. Radcliffe." In *The Mystery & Detection Annual,* edited by Donald K. Adams, 48–64. Beverly Hills, Calif.: Donald Adams, 1972.

Ellis, Kate Ferguson. *The Contested Castle: Gothic Novels and the Subversion of Domestic Ideology.* Urbana: University of Illinois Press, 1989.

Milton, John. *Complete English Poems of Education, Areopagitica.* Edited by Gordon Campbell. London: Dent, 1990.

Poovey, Mary. "Ideology and *The Mysteries of Udolpho.*" *Criticism* 21 (1979): 307–330.

Radcliffe, Ann. *The Mysteries of Udolpho.* Oxford: Oxford University Press, 1980.

Rogers, Deborah. *Ann Radcliffe: A Bio-Bibliography.* Westport, Conn.: Greenwood Press, 1996.

Sedgwick, Eve Kosofsky. "The Character of the Veil Imagery of the Surface in the Gothic Novel." *PMLA* 96 (1981): 255–270.

Spector, Robert Donald. Introduction to *Seven Masterpieces of Gothic Horror,* edited by Robert Donald Spector, 1–11. Toronto, New York, and London: Bantam, 1970.

Wolff, Cynthia G. "The Radcliffean Gothic Model: A Form for Feminine Sexuality." *Modern Language Studies* 9 (1979): 98–113.

—Carol Margaret Davison

# N

## "Napoleon's Farewell" Lord Byron (1815)

LORD BYRON's poem "Napoleon's Farewell" first appeared anonymously, and untitled, in LEIGH HUNT's newspaper The *Examiner* in 1815. Along with several other pro-Napoleonic poems, also pretended translations "from the French," the poem was included in Byron's *Poems* of 1816, published by John Murray, and in pirated editions by William Hone and others.

Byron composed the poem in July 1815, at a low ebb in NAPOLEON BONAPARTE's fortunes: Routed at Waterloo earlier that summer, Bonaparte sat in British custody aboard the *HMS Bellerophon*, soon to be exiled to St. Helena. Across three stanzas of emphatic anapestic meter, the poem stages Napoleon speaking to the nation of France in a voice alternately proud, wistful and defiant with the optimism of a wily survivor. The poem's conclusion projects one more miraculous return to the fight: "Yet, yet I may baffle the hosts that surround us, / And yet may thy heart leap awake to my voice" (ll. 21–22).

An early hero of the poet's, Napoleon played a crucial role in Byron's self-imagination and in his public representation. The poem is best read as part of a series of Byron's poetic statements on Napoleon, including the "Ode to Napoleon Buonaparte" (1814); *CHILDE HAROLD'S PILGRIMAGE*, canto 3 (1816); and *DON JUAN* (1818–24). In the 1814 "Ode," Byron had expressed shock and dismay at Bonaparte's first abdication. Now, by writing in Napoleon's voice, Byron both aligns himself more sympathetically with the deposed emperor and avoids a direct statement on his situation.

In the first stanza, the poem underscores Bonaparte's larger-than-life, world-historical status in ambivalent terms. The deposed emperor bids farewell to the land "where the gloom of my Glory / Arose and o'ershadowed the earth"—the alliterative linking of "gloom" and "Glory" sounding an ominous note (ll. 1–2). France is charged with weakly abandoning the leader who made her great (l. 3), but Napoleon's narcissism modulates in lines that reveal Byron's continued admiration: "I have warred with a world which vanquished me only / When the meteor of Conquest allured me too far; / I have coped with the nations which dread me thus lonely, / The last single Captive to millions in war!" (ll. 5–8). By the final stanza, the emphasis has shifted from Bonaparte's own love of glory and hunger for conquest to the patriotic struggle of a personified "Liberty" against the old monarchies—a view of the Frenchman with currency in Byron's Whig circles. The poem's final lines dramatize Bonaparte's parting call to France to reawaken and "call on the Chief of thy choice!" (l. 24). Issuing this call through Napoleon's voice is a deliberately provocative gesture at a moment when Bonaparte was widely regarded as Britain's archenemy. "Napoleon's Farewell" acquired an additional personal charge after Byron's own departure from England in 1816, when it could be read against Byron's own poem of farewell to his wife, "Fare Thee Well!" (1816).

## Further Reading

Bainbridge, Simon. *Napoleon and English Romanticism.* Cambridge: Cambridge University Press 1995.

Byron, George Gordon Byron, Baron. *The Complete Poetical Works.* Vol. 3. Edited by Jerome J. McGann. Oxford: Clarendon Press, 1981.

Clubbe, John. "Between Emperor and Exile: Byron and Napoleon, 1814–1816." *Napoleonic Scholarship: The Journal of the International Napoleonic Society* 1, no. 1 (April 1997). Available online. URL: http://napoleon-series.org/ins/scholarship97/c_byron.html. Accessed January 6, 2010.

Erdman, David. "'Fare Thee Well'—Byron's Last Days in England." In *Shelley and His Circle, 1773–1822,* vol. 4, edited by Kenneth Neil Cameron, 638–655. Cambridge, Mass.: Harvard University Press, 1961.

Kelsall, Malcolm. *Byron's Politics.* Sussex, Eng.: Harvester, 1987.

—Eric Eisner

## Nelson, Horatio (1758–1805)

Arguably the most famous naval figure in British history, Horatio Nelson, first viscount Nelson, was an icon of the Romantic movement and is still revered. Born on September 29, 1758, he joined the Royal Navy at Chatham in 1770. Under the patronage of his uncle, Captain Maurice Suckling who became comptroller of the navy in 1775, he began life as an ordinary seaman before being appointed to midshipman.

Although Nelson suffered chronic episodes of seasickness, this did not prevent him from becoming a prominent officer in the Royal Navy. Indeed, on June 20, 1779, he was made post captain of the 28-gun frigate HMS *Hinchinbrook* before being given command of the HMS *Boreas,* in which he sailed to the West Indies in 1784 to enforce the Navigational Acts and prevent trade between the United States and Great Britain's colonies. It was during this tour of duty that he met and married Frances Nesbit on March 11, 1787, before returning home from the Caribbean.

Following a relatively quiet period, Nelson was recalled to service after the outbreak of war with revolutionary France, during which he impressively secured Corsica as a Mediterranean base for

the Royal Navy in 1794. Although he was struck by splinters and blinded in his right eye, this did not prevent him from returning to duty less than 24 hours later. It was, however, the 1798 Battle of the Nile that transformed Nelson into a national hero. He boldly executed a night attack on the French fleet at Alexandria, which left NAPOLEON BONAPARTE's army stranded in Egypt. Moreover, it was shortly after this battle that he again met EMMA, LADY HAMILTON, wife of the British ambassador at Naples, and began a scandalous affair with her, which led to criticism, public outrage, and estrangement from Frances.

Nevertheless, the scandal was soon forgotten after Nelson's most famous triumph aboard HMS *Victory* at Trafalgar in October 1805. Just as victory was assured, however, he was mortally injured and died October 21, just before the battle ended. His body was brought back to Britain and buried in St. Paul's Cathedral; a memorial column was later erected at Trafalgar Square to commemorate one of Britain's most charismatic heroes. ROBERT SOUTHEY's *The Life of Horatio, Lord Nelson* (1813) was one of a number of attempts to mythologize Nelson's heroism.

## Further Reading

Roger Knight. *The Pursuit of Victory: The Life and Achievement of Horatio Nelson.* London: Basic Books. 2005

—Jessica Webb

## neoclassicism

In the context of Romanticism, *neoclassicism* means specifically Greek classicism, or, as it is now commonly known, Hellenism. Eighteenth-century neoclassicism tended to follow Roman precedents, and its most famous practitioners emphasized linearity, formal rigidity and moral rectitude (perhaps in keeping with Roman art, but certainly not with Roman society). Toward the beginning of the 19th century, Greece began to outstrip Rome in the English imagination, thanks in large part to the influential writings of the Swiss-German art historian Johann Joachim Winckelmann (1717–68), who upheld the Greek example as an apotheosis of "noble simplicity and sedate grandeur" (Winckelmann 30). This transition from Rome to Greece was marked by public attention to archaeological discoveries, a revival of interest in Homeric biography, the creation of a "Grecian" or *à la grecque* style in the decorative arts (usually associated with the works of the ceramicist Josiah Wedgwood [1730–95]), and a Greek revival in architecture, among other developments.

Reinforced by the classical curriculum of England's grammar schools and by the European "Grand Tour" that was de rigueur for young men of social standing, Hellenism was a mass-cultural movement that incorporated literary and non-literary writing, as well as the production, consolidation, and study of art objects and antiquities in museums. England's 1816 purchase of sculptures removed by Lord Elgin from the Parthenon remains one of the most significant and controversial legacies of Romantic neoclassicism. The marbles elicited passionate responses from many of the country's best-known writers, including LORD BYRON, who contested their acquisition, and JOHN KEATS and FELICIA HEMANS, who supported it.

In addition to cultivating a Hellenist aesthetic, many Britons championed the political cause of modern Greece's liberation from a centuries-old Ottoman rulership. Most notably, PERCY BYSSHE SHELLEY and Lord Byron spoke out for the independence of Greece, with both writing extensively on the matter (see especially Shelley's *Hellas* and the second canto of Byron's *CHILDE HAROLD'S PILGRIMAGE*). Moreover, when the Greek insurgency gained momentum in the 1820s, Byron joined in the fight; he died of rheumatic fever in 1824 while encamped in Missolonghi and is widely regarded as a national hero in Greece.

**Further Reading**

Winckelmann, Johann Joachim. *Reflections on the Painting and Sculpture of the Greeks.* Translated by Henry Fuseli. London: A. Millar, 1765.

—Noah Comet

## newspapers and magazines

During the 18th century, the daily newspaper emerged as the dominant form of print culture.

The first was the *Daily Courant* (1702), published in London, but as the century progressed, readers could enjoy increasing choice, both in London and in the provinces. Literacy rates were improving, but newspapers were also read aloud in the family circle. By the 1780s the important newspapers included the *Morning Chronicle* (founded 1770); the *Morning Post* (1772); the first London Sunday newspaper, (Mrs.) *E. Johnson's British Gazette and Sunday Monitor* (1779); the *Morning Herald* (1780); and the *Daily Universal Register,* founded by John Walter in 1785, which became *The Times* on January 1, 1788. By 1790 there were 13 morning and one evening daily papers appearing. However, there were often restrictions on reporting, and there was no open reporting of Parliament until 1771. The ban was finally lifted in that year as a result of public support for the politician and journalist John Wilkes (1725–97), who had been prosecuted in 1763 for seditious libel after an article appeared in the *North Briton.*

One of the things that happened during the course of the century was the emergence of an educated middle class who were anxious to learn of current events, cultural as well as political. In 1709, with the launch of the *Tatler,* another new form of publication started to emerge, initially identical to newspapers but incorporating different kinds of content—an essay, a bit of news, some gossip, and some literary criticism—what we would recognize today as a magazine. When the *Tatler* collapsed, its founder, Joseph Addison (1672–1719), started the *Spectator,* one of the most influential of the early British journals. The term *magazine* is generally acknowledged to have come into usage with the publication in the 1730s of the *Gentleman's Magazine,* run by Edward Cave (1691–1754). Its initial intention was to attract an audience with stories of crime and romance, but the magazine also began to list all new books published and gradually began featuring book reviews, or "epitomes," as they were called. In this respect, the term *magazine* also began to be understood as a repository of different items that were often disparate and apparently unrelated. Another characteristic was that instead of news, it printed comment. By 1760 there were 30 London periodicals; by the end of the century there were 80 in England as a whole. In 1797 the circulation of the major monthly magazines ranged between 3,250 and 5,000, much higher than the average figures for a book, and prices ranged from sixpence to two shillings. In 1811 the editor Josiah Conder (1789–1859) noted: "It must be obvious to every attentive observer, that the number and character of critical Reviews is a striking peculiarity of the age" (quoted in Sullivan xvi).

Magazine publishing was, however, seriously affected by the pressure put on it by successive governments. Stamp duty (or tax) was used by governments to help suppress or bankrupt opposition or radical publications. These costs had to be passed onto readers, often putting prices out of the reach of many people. The tax was gradually increased until, in 1815, it had reached fourpence per copy. Some editors tried to get around the tax. In 1816 WILLIAM COBBETT (1763–1835) began selling his weekly POLITICAL REGISTER in the form of a pamphlet rather than magazine. He dropped the price to twopence, and its circulation shot up to 40,000. Other radical publishers decided to ignore the law. Jonathan Wooler's (1786–1853) satirical magazine, the Black Dwarf, was published unstamped and sold for fourpence. In 1819, realizing what was going on—and also in reaction to the PETERLOO MASSACRE in August that year—Lord Castlereagh, the leader of the House of Commons, and Lord Sidmouth, the Home Secretary, decided to change the law in an effort to suppress radical activity and reduce the circulation of radical newspapers and pamphlets. They persuaded Parliament to pass the Six Acts, one of which—the Newspaper and Stamp Duties Act—levied the fourpence stamp duty on all journals that sold for less than sixpence. As few people—certainly not workmen—could afford to pay sixpence for a newspaper, the tax restricted the circulation of most of these journals to people with fairly high incomes. This reduced the number of people who could afford to buy potentially subversive newspapers that sought to sow seeds of discontent by questioning, mocking, or attacking the government. The stamp duty was also levied on magazines judged to contain any (in the words of the act) "public news, intelligence or occurrences, or any remarks or observations thereon, or upon any matter in Church or State." It was intended that the stamp duty would prevent publications

that intended to "excite hatred and contempt of the Government and holy religion."

One of the victims of this mood of oppression was LEIGH HUNT's weekly journal, the Examiner, founded with his brother, John, in 1808. Radical and forward-thinking, it advocated "reform in Parliament" and "liberality of opinion in general." This included supporting Catholic emancipation, attacking government corruption, and most notoriously attacking the MONARCHY, in particular George, Prince of Wales, the prince regent, and it resulted in Hunt and his brother being imprisoned for libel because they had called the Prince of Wales "a violator of his word, a libertine over head and cars in debt and disgrace, a despiser of domestic ties (the companion of gamblers and demireps, a man who has just closed half a century without one single claim on the gratitude of his country or the respect of posterity)" (quoted in Clarke and Ridley, 50).

The Examiner did more to rile the conservative governments of the times than almost any other paper, but it was not simply political in its concerns. In keeping with its radical outlook, the Examiner was also notable for its support and publication of the work of several literary figures, notably PERCY BYSSHE SHELLEY, WILLIAM WORDSWORTH, and JOHN KEATS. Hunt printed Shelley's "OZYMANDIAS" and "TO A SKYLARK" as well as Keats's "O, Solitude," and on December 1, 1816, he published the notice "Young Poets," in which he numbered Keats among three "young aspirants . . . who promise[d] to help the new school [of poetry] to revive Nature and [t]o put a new spirit of youth into everything" (quoted in Matthews, 42). The magazine's support for these new poets led to its being seeing as a cheerleader for what was christened "the COCKNEY SCHOOL of poetry."

In the early 1800s the other main literary magazines were the Monthly Review, the Critical Review, the Gentleman's Magazine, the European Magazine and the British Critic. In 1802, things were shaken up when a group of young literary men based in Edinburgh—including Sydney Smith (1771–1845), Francis Horner (1778–1817), FRANCIS JEFFREY (1773–1850), and Henry Brougham (1778–1868)—launched the Edinburgh Review as a cutting-edge forum for the discussion of literary, scientific, and political subjects. The magazine was intended to be a vehicle for Whig (liberal) views, including the abolition of SLAVERY and opposition to the Napoleonic War and the Corn Laws (which it believed harmful to free trade). Such was the success of its format that seven years later, a group in London founded the *Quarterly Review*. This magazine, published by John Murray, was Tory in political sympathies, and the *Edinburgh Review* and *Quarterly Review* quickly became the dominant intellectual organs of the period as well as bitter rivals.

The Romantic movement was often a source of debate among them. Francis Jeffrey wrote most of the reviews in the *Edinburgh Review*, which, in its first issues, attacked the new Romantic writers for their use of common language to treat high ideals and condemned their "splenetic and idle discontent with the existing instructions of society" (quoted in Sullivan 141). Gradually the magazine took a more sympathetic attitude, especially toward LORD BYRON, Keats, and Leigh Hunt. The *Quarterly* took a slightly different stance: It supported the conservative ROBERT SOUTHEY and the aristocratic Byron (until his poetry became too risqué) and was anti–Leigh Hunt and Shelley (both radicals) and Keats (lower class). Literary criticism was thus politicized to a degree, but what linked the criticism to the writers was "a shared belief in mimesis, a close relationship between literature and human experience, as well as in the moral effect of that literature" (Sullivan xviii).

Throughout the period, external factors hindered the production of both newspapers and magazines. Paper could be in short supply, particularly as literacy began to rise at the end of the century and demand increased. In the 1780s printing technology was still a fairly basic (manual) process. When Lord Stanhope invented the iron printing press in 1798, this was the first major innovation to the printing process since the 15th century. The first papermaking machine was not introduced until 1807, and the first steam-powered printing press in 1814.

See also ANNUALS AND GIFT BOOKS.

**Further Reading**

Clarke, John, and Jasper Ridley. *The Houses of Hanover and Saxe—Coburg-Gaha*. London: Cassell, 2000.

Gilmartin, Kevin. *Print Politics: The Press and Radical Opposition in Early Nineteenth-Century England*. Cambridge: Cambridge University Press, 1996.

Brewer, John, and Iain McCalman. "Publishing." In *The Romantic Age: British Culture 1776–1832*, edited by Iain McCalman, 197–206. Oxford: Oxford University Press, 1999.

Matthews, G. M. *John Keats: The Critical Heritage*. London: Routledge, 1971.

Parker, Mark. *Literary Magazines and British Romanticism*. Cambridge: Cambridge University Press, 2000.

Sullivan, Alvin. *British Literary Magazines: The Romantic Age 1789–1836*. Westport, Conn.: Greenwood Press, 1983.

—Mark Hughes

## "Night"  William Blake  (1789)

This is one of the poems in WILLIAM BLAKE's *Songs of Innocence*. Late in the 19th century, the poet Algernon Charles Swinburne singled out "Night" as one of the finest of the *Songs of Innocence* for its "loftiest loveliness." The 20th-century literary critic F. W. Bateson called it the collection's "greatest" poem.

Several poems in SONGS OF INNOCENCE AND OF EXPERIENCE are plainly didactic, and Blake the thinker, the moralist, or the prophet is never far behind the apparently plain and simple lyrical constructs. But his composition of "Night" appears to have been motivated by no radical prophetic or visionary impulse. What marks the spirit of the song is a remarkable sense of acceptance of the world the Christian God has created and bequeathed to mankind.

"Night" begins with a quiet evocation of all the characteristic features marking the time of night—the descending sun, the evening star, the silent birds, and "The moon, like a flower / In heaven's high bower / With silent delight sits / smiles on the night" (ll. 5–8). The daytime agitation of activities of the nibbling lambs and bounding flocks, now over, are recalled. The angels go about quietly ("silent moves / The feet of angels bright" [ll. 11–12]), pouring balm over those who may be distressed and protecting the unprotected. But "When wolves and tigers howl for prey / They pitying stand and weep" (ll. 25–26) because the angels do not wish to interfere with the cycle of life and death. Blake visualizes a time when the savagery of the roaring lions will give way to "tears of gold," and "wrath" will be "driven away" (ll. 34, 37, 39). The acts of cruelty are the sickness of this world, which will be cured only through the intervention of Christ. But that will transpire according to the plan of God in afterlife. The essential import of the song appears to be that God's care and compassion is there for each one of his creatures, and an eternal life awaits all.

"Night" thus evokes a state of innocence. The absence of questioning of what is apparently referred to as acts of savagery, as well as the spirit of acceptance that marks the poem, belongs more to the innocent and trusting mind.

Blake's illustration accompanying the poem shows leafy trees and vines encircling the tree trunks. There are angelic figures among the trees and over a lion's den. A moon with stars is suggested through dots in the margin. The second plate shows five female figures standing in two groups, representing the angels of the text.

## Further Reading

Blake, William. *Selected Poems of William Blake.* Edited by F. W. Bateson. London: Heinemann, 1957.

———. *The Complete Poetry and Prose of William Blake.* Rev. ed. Edited by David V. Erdman. Berkeley: University of California Press, 2008.

—G. R. Taneja

## *Nightmare Abbey* Thomas Love Peacock (1818)

While *Nightmare Abbey* is now considered to be THOMAS LOVE PEACOCK's most famous work, it received surprisingly little notice at the time of its initial publication in 1818. The third in a series of satirical novels by Peacock that includes *Headlong Hall* (1815) and *Melincourt* (1817), it *Nightmare Abbey* draws on the GOTHIC tradition to mock the ideas and posturings of various Romantic intellectuals. In the words of its creator, it is a comic romance that tries, Peacock explained in a letter to Percy Bysshe Shelley, "to bring to a sort of philo-

sophical focus a few of the morbidities of modern literature" (quoted in Burns, 105). It possesses no discernible plot and is largely dialogue-driven.

Nightmare Abbey is home to the misanthropic Christopher Glowry, esquire, and his only son and heir, Scythrop, a brooding individual suitably named after a relative who hanged himself. In his Germanizing tendencies—as suggested by his acts of devouring German tragedies, composing a tragedy on the German model, and sleeping with a copy of Peter Will's gothic novel *Horrid Mysteries* (1796) under his pillow—the tower-dwelling Scythrop is modeled after Peacock's illustrious friend PERCY BYSSHE SHELLEY. Shelley, notably, applauded the portrait. Several of the abbey's guests are also identifiable Romantic figures: Mr. Cypress represents LORD BYRON and Mr. Ferdinando Flosky, "a very lachrymose and morbid gentleman, of some note in the literary world" (9–10), furnishes a scathing caricature of SAMUEL TAYLOR COLERIDGE.

Punctuated with sometimes ludicrous discussions about contemporary literature and other issues, *Nightmare Abbey* takes the unmarried Scythrop and his misfortunes in love as its main narrative focus. As such, this parody combines traditional gothic concerns relating to inheritance with the more female gothic preoccupation of marriage. Glowry's pressure on his son to marry for money threatens a reprise of his own bitter experience of a loveless marriage to an enterprising woman. Thus may the "sins" of the father be visited upon the son, a traditional gothic lesson dating from that genre's inception with Horace Walpole's 1764 novella *The Castle of Otranto.* With its secret passageways and hidden apartments, Nightmare Abbey provides a suitable backdrop for Scythrop's guests, who "lament the good old times of feudal darkness" (8); are all ghostseers; and, according to Flosky, inhabit a world of ghosts.

As a domain of haunting and mystery, Nightmare Abbey is also a fitting setting for Scythrop's exploration of possible love objects. Two options, with "minds and habits as remote as the antipodes" (82), present themselves: his penniless, orphan cousin, Miss Marionetta Celestine O'Carroll, a musically inclined sprightly conversationalist; and the mysterious "Stella," Celinda Toobad, an educated heiress who speaks German, worships the Illuminati, and wages a war against what she describes as her "sex's slavery" (80). In this work of comic gothic, Peacock brings the traditional castle motif nicely to bear on Scythrop's dilemma: "With Stella, he could indulge freely in all his romantic and philosophical visions. He could build castles in the air, and she would pile towers and turrets on the imaginary edifices. With Marionetta it was otherwise: she knew nothing of the world and society beyond the sphere of her own experience" (82). Almost predictably, the indecisive Scythrop, who loves both women, ends up with neither, as Celinda marries Flosky and Marionetta weds Listless.

The mysteries of Nightmare Abbey are likewise solved and its ghosts exposed. The spectral woman with a white shroud and bloody turban who stalks one of the galleries—a ghost strikingly reminiscent of MATTHEW GREGORY LEWIS's famous bleeding nun from his porno-gothic work *The* MONK (1795)—is not a ghost at all. Parody also seems to have its limits. Despite Peacock's mockery of Scythrop's guests and their nostalgia for feudal times, the "Manichaean Millenarian" Toobad takes a page out of classic gothic fiction and advances an unsettling critique of their purportedly "enlightened" era with its children perishing in factories and thousands transported or relegated to the workhouse.

### Further Reading

Burns, Brian. *The Novels of Thomas Love Peacock*. London: Croom Helm, 1985.

Butler, Marilyn. *Peacock Displayed: A Satirist in His Context*. London: Routledge, 1979.

Peacock, Thomas Love. *Nightmare Abbey*. Edited by Marilyn Butler. London: Folio Society, 1994.

—Carol Margaret Davison

## Nodier, Charles (1780–1844)

A poet, novelist, and critic, Jean-Charles-Emmanuel Nodier was born in Besançon, France, on April 29, 1780. He was the illegitimate son of Antoine Melchior Nodier (then mayor of Besançon) and Suzanne Pâris, who was 17 years younger. The couple finally married in 1791, and young Charles was officially declared to be legitimate. Nodier père moved in the intellectual circles of Besançon and

insisted that his son should receive a thorough classical education. In 1792, in spite of his age, Charles was made a member of the Société des Amis de la Constitution (also known as the Club des Jacobins) before which he had already presented two discourses.

In September 1793, when Charles was only 13, his father—who, following the outbreak of the FRENCH REVOLUTION, had been appointed president of the Tribunal Criminel—took him on a trip to the neighboring town of Ornans to see the guillotine in action. This terrifying spectacle was to haunt his imagination for the rest of his life. A few years later, he was sent to live for a year with a former engineer, Justin Girod-Chantrans, who presented him with volumes of Shakespeare and introduced him to natural sciences and more particularly to entomology. In 1797 Nodier founded his own club, La Société des Philadelphes, and a year later, he published *Dissertation sur l'usage des antennes dans les insectes* (Dissertation on the use of antennas in insects) and a tentative autobiography, modestly entitled *Moi-même* (Myself). He also published a libertine novel anonymously: *Le Dernier chapitre de mon roman* (The last chapter of my novel).

Having graduated from the École Centrale of Besançon, Nodier became assistant librarian at the school's library, a position he soon lost for political reasons. He moved to Paris for a year but finally managed to go back to his native town and to his former position. In 1801 he published *Pensées de Shakespeare* (Thoughts of Shakespeare) before going back to Paris, where he wrote minor literary works influenced by JOHANN WOLFGANG VON GOETHE (*Le Peintre de Saltzbourg* [The painter of Salzburg] and *Les Proscrits [The banished]* in 1803), and a noteworthy encyclopaedia on insects (*Petite bibliographie des insectes*, 1801). At that time, fiercely opposed to NAPOLEON BONAPARTE, he consorted with republicans and royalists who shared his hatred of the First Consul. A satirical poem entitled *La Napoléone* was enough to send him back to prison for a few days and again to Besançon, where he wrote *Essai d'un jeune barde* (Essay of a young bard, 1804).

Nodier's anti-Bonapartist activities forced him to hide in the mountains while most of his friends were arrested and jailed. He was finally allowed to come back under the protection of the *préfet* (police chief) of the Doubs. In 1806 he published a volume of tales, *Les Tristes, ou mélanges tirés des tablettes d'un suicidé* (The sad ones, or jumbled [thoughts] taken from the notebooks of a suicide victim) which contained his first piece of fantastic literature, a tale entitled *Une Heure, ou la vision* (One hour, or the vision). Two years later, he was allowed to hold public lectures on philosophy, belles letters, and natural history; married Désirée Charve in the small town of Dôle; and published *Dictionnaire raisonné des onomatopées françaises* (Analytical dictionary of French onomatopoeias). The couple soon moved to Amiens, where Nodier became secretary to Sir Herbert Croft, but the financial ruin of the British philologist prompted him to accept a position in Illyria. The couple, who now had a daughter named Marie (who was later to become Charles's biographer), settled in Ljubljana, where Nodier was both the director of a polyglot newspaper—*Le Telegraph Illyrien*, printed in four languages—and a librarian. In 1812, just before leaving France, he had also published a legal treatise, *Questions de littérature légale*, thus widening the scope of his already varied interests. Nine months later, the French troops evacuated Illyria, and Nodier returned to France.

When the French monarchy was restored in 1814, Charles Nodier swore allegiance to the new king, Louis XVIII, who made him officer of the Ordre du Lys, but upon Bonaparte's return from Elba, he was forced once again to leave the capital and stayed with his friend and protector, the duc de Caylus, in Normandy. He came back after the period known as Napoleon's Hundred Days and became a regular collaborator on the *Journal des débats* (Journal of debates). The relative political stability of the Second Restoration enabled him to acquire a literary reputation with the publication of *Jean Sbogar* in 1818, followed by two other novels, *Thérèse Aubert* (1819) and *Adèle* (1820); and by his adaptation for the stage of Cyprien Bérard's *Lord Ruthven et les vampires,* the continuation of JOHN WILLIAM POLIDORI's "The VAMPYRE." These works also illustrate his growing taste for British GOTHIC literature.

In 1821 Nodier published an article in the *Annales de la littérature et des arts* in which he coined the term *littérature frénétique* (frantic literature), which was subsequently used to describe the French fantastic literature of the 1820s and 1830s, exemplified by authors such as Jules Janin (*L'Âne mort et la femme guillotinée* [The dead ass and the beheaded woman]), and Petrus Borel (*Contes immoraux* [Immoral tales]). That same year, he also published two volumes of *Mélanges de littérature et de critique;* a general preface to a very successful series entitled *Voyages pittoresques et romantiques dans l'ancienne France* (Picturesque and Romantic Travels through Ancient France); a novel, *Smarra ou les démons de la nuit (Smarra, or the Demons of the Night)*—; the dramatic adaptation of CHARLES MATURIN's BERTRAM; and an account of his trip to Scotland with the painter Eugène Isabey (1803–86), *Promenade de Dieppe aux Montagnes d'Écosse* (Promenade from Dieppe to the Mountains of Scotland).

The death of his second son, Amédée (his first son, Thérence, had died in 1816) did not put a stop to Nodier's prolific production. Part of his importance lies in his introducing Romantic writers to a new audience and he prefaced the translation of LORD BYRON's works. He also published *Essai sur la théorie des langues* (Essay on the theory of languages), followed by *Infernalia,* a collection of supernatural tales, and *Trilby ou le lutin d'Argail* (Trilby, or the Goblin from Argail), a longer tale and probably his most famous work.

In 1824 Nodier was appointed head librarian of the Bibliothèque de l'Arsenal in Paris, while the comte d'Artois was crowned under the name of Charles X. Nodier held a noteworthy salon known as Le Cenacle in his apartment that was frequented by, among others, the novelist VICTOR HUGO, the critic Charles-Augustin Sainte-Beuve, and the poet Alfred de Musset. In 1829 he started to make regular contributions to a new journal, *La Revue de Paris.* The year after, he published another long tale, *L'Histoire du roi de Bohême et de ses sept châteaux* (The story of the King of Bohemia and his Seven Castles), which was strongly inspired by the British novelist Laurence Sterne's digressive prose. The marriage of his daughter and the accession of Louis-Philippe to the throne of France opened a more melancholic period in Nodier's life. Apart from various works such as

*De Quelques phénomènes du sommeil,* a treatise on sleep, he published several other tales—*Mademoiselle de Marsan, Histoire d'Hélène Gillet, Le Songe d'or, L'Amour et le grimoire (The Story of Hélène Gillet, The Golden Dream, Love and the Book of Magic)*—while Eugène Renduel (who published most of the French Romantics) started to publish the first volumes of his complete works.

In 1833 Nodier's new publications included *Hurlubleu, La Combe de l'homme mort (Hurlubleu, or the Dead Man's Vale* [a fantastic tale]), fables, and apologues (*L'Homme et la fourmi* [*The Man and the Ant*]), as well as a historical text, *Le Dernier banquet des Girondins (The Banquet of the Girondins).* That same year, he was elected a member of the Académie Française, but his physical condition had started to decline. In 1834 he founded the *Bulletin du bibliophile* and published two important fantastic tales, *Paul, ou la Ressemblance* (Paul, or the Resemblance) and *Inès de Las Sierras.* Charles Nodier died in the dreamlike sanctuary of the Arsenal, one of the historic Parisian libraries, on January 27, 1844, just before his last novel, *Franciscus Columna,* was published.

## Further Reading

Buttel, B. "Nodier et l'École frénétique." *Bérénice* 12, no. 30 (1990): 1–65.

Castex, P.-G. *Le Conte fantastique en France de Nodier à Maupassant.* Paris: José Corti, 1951.

Eldridge, B. "The Two Trilbys." *New York Review of Science Fiction* 12, no. 216 (August 18, 2006): 1, 8–12.

Fujita, T. "L'Idée Frénétique chez Charles Nodier." *Kwansei Gakuin University Humanities Review* 9 (2004): 59–84.

Grivel, Charles. "Nodier: Le Tour de Babel." *Romantisme: Revue du dix-neuvième Siècle* 136 (2007): 15–25.

Loving, M. "Charles Nodier, the Romantic Librarian." *Libraries and Culture: A Journal of Library History* 38, no. 2 (Spring 2003): 166–181.

Lowe-Dupas, H. *Poétique de la coupure chez Charles Nodier.* Amsterdam: Rodopi, 1995.

Poulosky, L. J. *Severed Heads and Martyred Souls: Crime and Capital Punishment in French Romantic Literature.* New York, Peter Lang, 2003.

Nodier, Charles. *Smarra and Trilby.* Cambridge: Dedalus European Classics, 2004.

Oliver, Alfred Richard. *Charles Nodier, Pilot of Romanticism.* Syracuse, N.Y.: Syracuse University Press, 1964.

Puleio, M.-T. "Aux Sources du voyage romantique français: *Promenades de Dieppe aux Montagnes d'Écosse de Charles Nodier." Studi di Letteratura Francese: Rivista Europea* 29–30 (2004–2005): 53–69.

—Sylvie Kleiman-Lafon

## *Northanger Abbey*  Jane Austen  (1798, 1817)

*Northanger Abbey* was JANE AUSTEN's first novel, completed in 1798 but not published until December 1817, after her death. Traditionally, the novel is considered a satire of the conventions of GOTHIC fiction as established by contemporaries such as ANN RADCLIFFE and MATTHEW GREGORY LEWIS, but the more frequent themes of Austen's later work, especially the hypocrisies of a rigidly hierarchical social system, are more dominant aspects of the book. However, *Northanger Abbey* also presents evidence that its protagonist, Catherine Moreland, learns valuable lessons from the very same systems that are being critiqued.

*Northanger Abbey* is a bildungsroman narrative that follows the progress of Catherine Moreland as she learns to negotiate a social world beyond her provincial hometown. The novel begins with her trip to the resort town of Bath, where her aunt and uncle seek to provide an entry into various social circles. Two families occupy the majority of Catherine's time: the Thorpes and the Tilneys. Isabella Thorpe becomes Catherine's confidant and occasionally aggressive mentor, while Henry Tilney becomes Catherine's romantic interest. The majority of the novel takes place in Bath, with Catherine making social errors and learning how to recover from them. For example, Catherine allows herself to be persuaded by Isabella to take a day trip with the Thorpes even though she had made a previous engagement with the Tilneys. Similarly, Catherine is slow to realize that Isabella's brother, John, is interested in her and awkward at discouraging his attention.

The final third of the novel takes place at the Tilneys' home, Northanger Abbey. Austen's parody of gothic fiction emerges during this section, as

Catherine, who is a fan of contemporary authors like Ann Radcliffe, is eager to imagine Northanger Abbey as the setting of a gothic novel. Catherine's speculations begin innocently, with her indulging in enjoyable suspense regarding locked furniture and long hallways, but they soon lead to more sinister conclusions, including the notion that General Tilney murdered his dead wife. While Catherine ultimately repents her presumptive readings of the Tilney family, General Tilney abruptly sends her home when he discovers her family to be less wealthy than he had thought. Ultimately, Henry repairs this social breach, and the two are married.

*Northanger Abbey* has a lighter tone than many of Austen's later novels while still engaging major social and cultural issues. Austen's parody of gothic fiction is not solely a critique of literary conventions, but also of naive or undiscerning readers. Similarly, the novel's action in Bath is largely an account of inadequate social behavior, and until Catherine becomes a more sophisticated reader of social cues and conventions, she continues to draw the wrong conclusions. At the same time, *Northanger Abbey* endorses the value of even careless reading. Catherine learns valuable lessons from her social mistakes and is eventually able to form judgments based on her exposure to a flawed social system; for example, she ultimately concludes that Isabella is an insincere friend. Similarly, while her uncritical appreciation of gothic fiction led her to the wrong conclusion about Mrs. Tilney's death, it led her to the right conclusion regarding General Tilney's being a self-interested and untrustworthy man.

*Northanger Abbey* contains a lengthy passage in which the narrator praises the 18th-century novel form for its ability to present the truths of life in an entertaining manner, while decrying the tendency of literary critics to consider poetry as a more serious genre. The narrator notes the extent to which this is a gender division, and that novels written by women are taken comparatively less seriously than those written by men. Austen's engagement with contemporary literary movements can also be seen in the fact that *Northanger Abbey*'s story is one of an individual trying to establish her individual identity apart from and in relation to her surrounding society, which is very much a domi-nant interest of Romantic poets such as WILLIAM WORDSWORTH and SAMUEL TAYLOR COLERIDGE.

**Further Reading**

Austen, Jane. *Northanger Abbey: With Lady Susan, The Watsons, Sanditon.* Oxford: Oxford University Press, 2002.

Fraiman, Susan, ed. *Northanger Abbey: Backgrounds and Criticism.* New York: W. W. Norton, 2004.

Hardy, John. *Jane Austen's Heroines: Intimacy in Human Relationships.* Boston: Routledge, 1984.

Williams, Michael. *Jane Austen: Six Novels and Their Methods.* London: Macmillan Press, 1986.

—Rachel Bowser

## Norton, Caroline (1808–1877)

Caroline Norton was born into an illustrious family on March 22, 1808; she was the granddaughter of the playwright Richard Brinsley Sheridan (1751–1816). Her political involvement in defense of the rights of wives and mothers often overshadows her literary career. She suffered in an incompatible marriage with the politician George Norton before she left him in 1835 amid rumors of his cruelty and infidelity. A great scandal followed when her husband initiated divorce proceedings, accusing Caroline of having an affair with the prime minister, Lord Melbourne, and suing for damages for alienation of her affection. The court found in Caroline's favor, but her husband refused her access to her children and legally claimed the proceeds of her writing. She thus became an outspoken campaigner for the reform of laws relating to child custody, divorce, and women's property rights. These issues are also raised in her poetry, two novellas, and three novels—a significant output that HARTLEY COLERIDGE likened to the work of LORD BYRON and ELIZABETH BARRETT BROWNING.

Norton's first major books of poems were *The Sorrows of Rosalie* (1829) and *The Undying One* (1830), both of which feature the sentimentally cloying figure of the tragic heroine deserted by a lover or ruined by a marriage of convenience. Her most acclaimed poems are in *The Dream and Other Poems* (1840), but her most ambitious is *The Child of the Islands* (1845), a lengthy didactic poem in

Spenserian stanzas. Her best-known novel is the sensational *Lost and Saved* (1863) an exposé of upper-class sexual mores. Norton herself is often compared to MARY WOLLSTONECRAFT in terms of political influence. Of the two, though, Norton is less radical; she believed women needed the protection of the law because of their inherent weaknesses.

Norton's popularity continued well after her death on June 15, 1877, a few months after marrying a longtime friend, William Stirling Maxwell. George Meredith modeled the witty and bold heroine of his novel, *Diana of the Crossways* (1885), after her.

### Further Reading

Chedzoy, Alan. *A Scandalous Woman: The Story of Caroline Norton.* London: Allison and Busby, 1992.

Norton, Caroline. *Selected Writings of Caroline Norton.* Edited by James O. Hoge and Jane Marcus. Delmar, N.Y.: Scholars' Facsimiles and Reprints, 1978.

—Vicky Simpson

## Novalis  (Friederich von Hardenberg)  (1772–1801)

The German poet and philosopher Friederich von Hardenberg, who used the pen name Novalis, is sometimes reckoned the most influential of the German Romantics. A onetime pupil of FRIEDRICH VON SCHILLER, FRIEDRICH VON SCHLEGEL, and Johann Gottlieb Fichte, Novalis took his pseudonym from "de Novali," the name his ancestors had used. He tends to be associated with a certain type of Romanticism that embodies an interest in mysticism and a world-weary desire for death.

Novalis was born on May 2, 1772, in Saxony (then a German state), where his father was the manager of a salt mine. His parents were respectable, God-fearing Protestants with a strict code of discipline against which their son chafed. As a young man, Novalis studied law at the University of Jena, and as a student he was heavily affected by the ideals behind the FRENCH REVOLUTION and by JOHANN WOLFGANG VON GOETHE's sensational best seller WILHELM MEISTER'S APPRENTICESHIP (1794), which he called the Bible for the "new

age." In spite of his rebellious tendencies, he settled into a fairly conventional path and joined the Civil Service. However, he also studied philosophy in his spare time, publishing his thoughts as *Fragmenten* (1798), and started to associate with some of the leading intellectual figures of the time, including Goethe and Johann Gottfried von Herder.

It was at this time that Novalis experienced the personal tragedy that would dominate the remainder of his life: His fiancée, Sophie von Kühn, died in 1797, age 15. He contemplated suicide but also wrote poems describing his sense of hopelessness. These were later published as *Hymnen an die Nacht* (*Hymns to the Night*, 1800). In order to reunite himself with his dead lover, Novalis believed that he needed to release his spirit from all material things, and to this end his poems contain mystical elements (a focus on the mother goddess) and strange symbolic imagery. This wish to cling onto and retain a link with Sophie was apparently one of the reasons for his engagement to Julie von Charpentier in 1798: He believed she made Sophie's presence clearer.

By now, however, Novalis' health was beginning to fail; he was already suffering the early stages of the tuberculosis that would eventually kill him. Nonetheless, he carried on writing, leaving behind two unfinished romances, *Die Lehrlinge zu Sais* (*The Novices of Sais*) and *Heinrich von Ofterdingen*, when he died on March 25, 1801. These romances encapsulate much of Novalis's appeal to his contemporaries. In *Henry von Ofterdingen* a young medieval poet, Henry, searches for an elusive "blue flower," which is unattainable no matter how hard one strives for it; it comes to represent what one can never have, and it became the central symbol of German Romanticism.

### Further Reading

Appleby, Carol. *German Romantic Poetry: Goethe, Novalis, Heine, Holderlin.* London: Crescent Moon Publishing, 2008.

Novalis. *The Birth of Novalis: Friedrich von Hardenberg's Journal of 1797, with Selected Letters and Documents.* Edited by Bruce Donehower. Albany, N.Y.: State University of New York Press, 2007.

———. *Henry von Ofterdingen.* New York: Waveland Press, 1997.

———. *Hymns to the Night.* New York: McPherson and Co., 1998.

———. *The Novices of Sais.* London: Archipelago Books, 2005.

———. *Philosophical Writings.* New York: State University of New York Press, 1997.

—Jane Foster

### "Nurse's Song, The"   William Blake (1794)

As in the case of several of WILLIAM BLAKE's poems, "The Nurse's Song" appears in two versions in SONGS OF INNOCENCE AND OF EXPERIENCE, which he put together in 1794 through his composite method of illuminated printing. In Blake's own words, the several pairs of songs were meant to illuminate "the contrary states of human soul," but perhaps we should remind ourselves that he did not value one contrary above the other, and that in the context of human existence, there can be no progression without the stimulus and provocation of actively opposing forces.

The denizens of the world of the first "Nurse's Song" (1789) are innocent in the most fundamental sense of the word: They are not devoid of experience, or inexperienced; they are themselves. Blake achieves this effect though avoiding adjectives that add extra dimensions to the characteristic nature of the subjects: Grass is only green, birds merely fly. There are no metaphors because Blake does not want to bring any extraneous element into the universe of this poem and thus draw our attention to it. In that sense, the poem delineates itself. Its world is not described through the overseeing "adult," or "experienced," eye.

The two versions of "The Nurse's Song" are clearly distinct. In *Songs of Innocence,* the even pace of the song echoes the happy laughter of the children against the total stillness of the evening hours. Their infectious joy is projected easily as they play against the backdrop of "the green" (l. 1), "the little birds" (l. 11), "the hills . . . all covered with sheep" (l. 12), and the setting sun and "the dews of night" (l. 6) that will soon arise. Children feel at one with nature and they want to remain there as long as the birds and the sheep are still around. The nurse, with her "heart . . . at rest" (l. 3), allows the children "to go and play till the light fades away" (l. 13). Children's joy derives as much from their playful hop and leap as from the attitude of the caring nurse. Blake's remarkable account of the children's laughter—"The little ones leaped, and shouted, and laughed, / And all the hills echoed" (ll. 15–16)—against his vivid depiction of the hills and nature when "everything else is still" (l. 4) is enchanting.

The nurse in the earlier song, who comes across as one with children, shares their joy. She is pleased to let them have their way to enjoy themselves as they bound away in the greens over the hills. Blake shows her among the children talking to them. Unlike her, the nurse in *Songs of Experience* is shown standing apart, anxious and reflecting that children waste their time, which could be meaningfully employed. The atmosphere is no longer one of happy conviviality. Instead of laughter, Blake refers to children's "voices" (l. 1) and their "whisperings . . . in the dale" (l. 2). The nurse's own youthful days, which "rise fresh in my mind" (l. 3) at the sight of children, were marked by activities that now embarrass her. "Whisperings" might suggest actions on the part of growing children that they wish to hide from their nurse. The atmosphere suggests an end rather than a continuing, cyclical promise. The setting of the sun does not promise a new day rising at the end of the night. The tinkling sound of the first poem gives way to disciplined silence in the second. A hint of repression contrasts with joyous freedom. The firm and unyielding world of the second poem presents a stark contrast to the world of innocence.

It is interesting that the innocence of the first poem as well as the repressed maturity of the second, both point to the nurse. In their feelings and behaviour, the children in both poems reflect the world as perceived and interpreted by the two nurses. Blake may be suggesting that it is the same nurse at different stages of her life, and thus he points to the inevitable growth and cyclical nature of life.

Blake's illustration on the plate shows the nurse sitting under the tree in the shadows in the foreground, looking larger than the children. The children, looking relatively small, are in the middle ground, standing in a circle and holding hands and playing. The leafy trees and vines and the yellow tint between the hills indicating sunset are supplanted, in the interlinear space, by much vegetation, leaves, vines, a weeping willow, birdlike shapes, and human figures reaching out to each other. Living elements are shown to populate the plate interlinearly. This profusion supplements the first song's feeling of abundant joy. The second plate shows the similar pastoral setting, but children are not shown playing, and the nurse appears to be ready to comb a boy's long hair. The image reminds one of controlled domesticity: An order has been imposed on the scene. Unlike the first song, the interlinear space in the second plate is relatively bare.

### Further Reading

Blake, William. *The Complete Poetry and Prose of William Blake.* Rev. ed. Edited by David V. Erdman. Berkeley: University of California Press, 2008.

—G. R. Taneja

## "Nutting"  William Wordsworth  (1798)

"Nutting" was first published in the second edition of LYRICAL BALLADS in 1800. It was written while WILLIAM WORDSWORTH was staying in Goslar, a small town near Hanover, Germany. During the winter of 1798–99 the poet wrote several passages for *The* PRELUDE, and "Nutting" was originally intended for that work; however, Wordsworth later decided to shorten this passage and print it as an independent poem. The long dash at the beginning of the first line marks the juncture with a long introduction that was discarded. This rejected section can be found in James Butler and Karen Greens Cornell edition (302–4).

The episode took place during Wordsworth's boyhood, in Hawkshead, in the Lake District, where he and his brothers lodged with Ann Tyson (the "frugal Dame" [l. 11]). It describes a visit to "some far-distant wood" (l. 8) where the young boy wants to gather hazelnuts. Having found a peaceful and, as yet, unvisited bower, "where not a broken bough / Drooped with its withered leaves" (ll. 17–18), he enjoys a moment of perfect harmony with the place and then violently tears down the hazel branches. The exultation at such a "wealth of kings" (l. 51) that the boy then feels is marred by his "sense of

pain" (l. 52) at having destroyed the "quiet being" (l. 48) of the trees. The last three lines are addressed to the "dearest Maiden" (l. 54; probably his sister Dorothy, who is the addressee of the poem's suppressed introduction), and they advise her to show more "gentleness" (l. 55) toward nature than her brother has, because a "spirit" (l. 56) lives there.

The moral at the end of the poem sums up the lesson that the episode has taught the poet: His materialistic vision of nature has been replaced by a spiritual one. The boy's vision of nature as a discrete series of material, dead things, a "banquet" (l. 25) to which he can help himself, turns into an understanding of the world as a continuous, conscious, living whole. This realization proceeds in two steps, first an intense but instinctive feeling of unity, then a conscientious reorganization of the experience. Here the poem follows the poetical structure recommended by Wordsworth in his PREFACE TO LYRICAL BALLADS—emotions recollected in tranquillity: It narrates a striking and sentimental episode from a temporal and analytical distance. The day stands out as a unique moment, one "that cannot die" (l. 3; the assonance *day–die,* unique and highly visible, emphasizes the event's primordial place). The core of this episode is what Wordsworth elsewhere calls a "spot of time" (in *The Prelude,* Book 12, ll. 208–218 of the 1805 edition): a moment of deep understanding remembered forever after, which retains its formative virtue. It is recounted on lines 21–43. It gives him intense pleasure, "with such suppression of the heart / As joy delights in" (ll. 22–23), a "sudden happiness beyond all hope" (l. 29). It also reveals to the boy these places in nature from which men are usually excluded, the place where flowers "unseen by any human eye" (l. 32) grow, "reappear / And fade" (ll. 31–32), the "murmuring sound" (l. 38) of the "fairy water-breaks" (l. 33). Ultimately, it connects him with his surroundings, turning stones into "a flock of sheep" (l. 37) and the boy into their shepherd, resting his cheek on one of them, "fleeced with moss" (l. 36), feeling powerful emotions; his "heart luxuriates" for a world of "indifferent things" (l. 41) and of "vacant air" (l. 43)—a world which for a fleeting moment he understands on its own terms, in its self-sufficient completeness, and not for what he can appropriate from it.

But this is only one half of the experience. What gives it its value, what makes it conscious and lasting, is the wilful destruction that follows and brings home the irreplaceable enchantment of the past moment. With annihilation comes realization: It is when the living trees that harbored him fall "silent" (l. 53) that the boy becomes aware of the "being" (l. 48) he has killed. This single and isolated moment is thus enshrined in the poet's memory forever: the boy realized it "even then" (48) and the poet still remembers it now, still feels the pain.

This line unmistakably reminds the reader that this powerful experience is recollected, is told from a distance that is both temporal and analytical: the boyhood visions are colored by the adult's awareness and the potential innocence or naïveté of the child are filtered through the more disturbing theories that the poet has acquired. This darker vision of humanity follows a biblical narrative: The natural scene, the coppice of hazel trees, is described as an uncorrupted paradise, brought to its fall through the boy's sins—in particular his lust and his gluttony. The quest for the nuts is a form of rape: The boy's forceful entry ("Forcing my way" [l. 16]) into the "dear nook / Unvisited" (ll. 16–17), eventually "deform[s] and sullie[s]" (l. 47) the "tempting" (l. 20) purity and "virgin scene" (l. 21) in a surge of violence evoked by the rapid drumming of occlusive monosyllables (l. 44). The contrast between the original and the corrupted states of the scene is reinforced by parallel quatrains that describe its discovery (ll. 16–21), and then its destruction (ll. 43–47). The same endings ("nook," "bough," "rose" and "rose," "nook," "bower") surround sentences that evoke, first, the completeness of the place (l. 17) and, further down, its complete destruction (l. 44). But the contrast in fact emphasizes the exceptionality of the first occurrence; the wholeness of the woods is expressed with negation: the nook is "un"-visited, and "not" one bough is broken. The threat of destruction, the potential corruption, is always there. Between these two moments the "voluptuous" (l. 24) boy, a perfect

epicurean, postpones his "banquet" (l. 25), "luxuriates" (l. 41) in the knowledge that, "fearless of a rival" (l. 24), his "joy [is] secure" (l. 40), and that he can take his pleasure when and how he decides. This moment of harmony between man and nature is actually contaminated, tainted by the boy's gluttonous (and even sadistic) drives.

The relationship between man and nature is neither an escape from social corruption nor a cruel display of human perversions. It should be considered as an element in a complex set of relationships. Here two human figures introduce and conclude the poem, and the poet relates his natural experience to them. The Dame "disguise[s]" him with "weeds" (l. 9) and a "Motley accoutrement" (l. 12), which allows the boy to join the "thorns, and brakes, and brambles" (l. 13) as one of them. In the conclusion, and more crucially—because it organizes the poem's linguistic medium—the lesson is shared with the Maiden: The relationship with nature might be a partial failure, might be somehow corrupted, but what matters is that it ensures a successful relationship between humans that allows the poet to communicate his experience to someone dear.

## Further Reading

Pirie, David B. *William Wordsworth, the Poetry of Grandeur and of Tenderness.* London and New York: Methuen, 1982.

Pite, Ralph. "Wordsworth and the Natural World." In *The Cambridge Companion to Wordsworth,* edited by Stephen Gill, Cambridge: Cambridge University Press, 2003.

Stallknecht, Newton P. *Strange Seas of Thought: Studies in William Wordsworth's Philosophy of Man and Nature.* Bloomington: Indiana University Press, 1966.

Wordsworth, William. *Lyrical Ballads, and Other Poems, 1797–1800.* Edited by James Butler and Karen Green. Ithaca, N.Y., and London: Cornell University Press, 1992.

—Samuel Baudry

## "Ode: Intimations of Immortality from Recollections of Early Childhood" William Wordsworth (1807)

Begun in 1802, this poem first appeared in the collection *Poems in Two Volumes* (1807). It is a key poem for showing how, as a member of the Romantic literary tradition, WILLIAM WORDSWORTH used memories of youthful experiences as a source for writing. At the center of "Intimations of Immortality" are ideals that highlight certain characteristics of Romanticism, which are revealed through imagination, emotion, and youthful experiences found in the poet's memory of nature. Memory serves as a tool that can transfer him between the past and the present sense of nature. He is then able to look on nature with a heightened sensibility and presents his poem as the foundation for his worldview.

For Wordsworth the object of his affection is found in CHILDHOOD, as he seeks to relive his pleasurable moments in nature. The poet asserts that "Delight and liberty, [are] the simple creed[s] / Of Childhood, whether busy or at rest" (ll. 139–140). Nature offers a way of escape and through the eyes of the childish soul nature becomes a high place of tranquility, celebration, freedom and immortality. The poet seeks to find pleasure in nature because his transition into adulthood has not offered him similar solace. He also laments how "[t]he things which I have seen I now can see no more" (l. 9). He is now an adult, but he is unable to conform to custom and tradition and it is his youthful soul which provides him with access to life-enhancing communion with nature. As he notes: "Heaven lies about us in our infancy! / Shades of the prison-house begin to close / Upon the growing Boy, / But He beholds the light, and whence it flows, / He sees it in his joy" (ll. 66–70). Wordsworth reveals the delight in being an innocent child, a state that allows nature to be fully seen and enjoyed.

It has been suggested that a psychoanalytic approach can be useful when unraveling the poem. Psychoanalysis taps into the realm of the unconscious versus conscious thought, while focusing heavily on the unconscious thought. Psychoanalysis also highlights fantasy and the repression of deep wishes that are in the unconscious mind. Segments of Wordsworth's "Ode: Intimations of Immortality" can seem to mirror Sigmund Freud's Oedipus Complex, most obviously if one thinks of nature as the mother figure and adulthood responsibility as the father figure. A psychoanalytic reading would note how hostile feelings toward the parent of the same sex produces a regression back to the maternal figure; therefore, nature, for Wordsworth, becomes a spiritual place, and he is reborn as he attempts to reconnect with the source of his pleasure, nature-as-mother. As he notes: "The sunshine is a glorious birth" (l. 16). As the sun is perhaps the nucleus of the nature's origin, Wordsworth sucks life out of the sunshine in order to fortify his access into the source of his pleasure; he reactivates his intimate connection with the mother figure. He must look toward the unconscious, the loves of his fading memory of nature in youth, to receive solace.

In this poem, as in others, Wordsworth's memory is the source of comfort, inspiration and enlightenment; he turns to his past in order to find comfort in his future, although he is filled with much grief in the notion that he may never be able to capture nature as seen in youth. Wordsworth's memory becomes the gateway into his unconscious wishes. There is a sense of panic as the questions himself: "Whither is fled the visionary gleam? / Where is it now, the glory and the dream?" (ll. 56–57). The adult Wordsworth lacks the earlier connection to and appreciation of nature, and the effect is life-denying. Some versions of the poem impress its message still further upon the reader by including an epigraph, "The child is father of the man / And I could wish my days to be / Bound each to each by natural piety." As always in Wordsworth's poems, childhood is the most powerful of formative experiences.

## Further Reading

Lau, Beth. "Wordsworth and Current Memory Research." *Studies in English Literature.* 42, no. 4 (Autumn 2002): 675–692. Available online. URL: http://www.jstor.org/pss/1556291. Downloaded on February 25, 2008.

Wordsworth, Dorothy. *The Grasmere and Alfoxden Journals.* Edited by Pamela Woof. New York: Oxford University Press, 2002.

Wordsworth, William. *William Wordsworth: The Major Works.* Edited by Stephen Gill. New York: Oxford University Press, 2000.

—Jasmine Leigh

## "Ode on a Grecian Urn" John Keats (1820)

A poetic response to a work of art, JOHN KEATS's poem is an attempt to breathe life through poetic means into the world of antiquity as captured on an ancient Attic (Greek) vase. In this observation on and reflection of the world eternally captured by the images on the urn, Keats illustrates the typical Romantic interest in the classical Greek world while simultaneously engaging in his own act of pseudo-nostalgia and sentimental reflection and asking the reader to reflect on modern views concerning immortality and the purpose and aesthetics of art. Making use of the newly reintroduced ancient poetic form of the ode, albeit in a more modern, stanzaic form, and through the employment of sensuous imagery, personification and apostrophe to bring his subject matter to life, Keats is able at once to visualize the ancient world and to filter modern sensibilities through his observations, rendering the work ultimately Romantic. The resulting poem is widely acknowledged as one of the finest examples of the ode produced during the Romantic era.

The poem is divided into four parts, dealing in the first stanza with the vase as a whole, then in stanzas 2–4 with the two scenes depicted on its surface, before returning at last in the fifth and final stanza to the whole shape and Keats's final observations on it. He begins with an apostrophe, addressing the urn itself: "Thou still unravished bride of quietness, / Thou foster child of silence and slow time, / Sylvan historian" (ll. 1–3) and asking a series of questions concerning the source of its images: "What leaf-fringed legend haunts about thy shape / . . . What men or gods are these? What maidens loth? / What mad pursuit?" (ll. 5–9). The use of personification in the apostrophe transforms the urn into a teacher of the ancient world, and in this fashion the series of questions becomes a Socratic inquiry. The exact answer to these questions is unknowable, and the reader must unravel the mystery of the images and discern the urn's message for himself: The teacher will not reveal any real answer, but instead will generate further questions and observations, leading the reader to formulate his own conclusions with the poem's progression.

Following the introduction, Keats continues with a description of the images on the urn that is finely juxtaposed with his reflections on their silence and ambiguity. He conveys the illustrations on the urn through words: ". . . ye soft pipes, play on . . . / Fair youth, beneath the trees." (ll. 12–15) indicates a scene in which a solitary, unnamed young man plays upon an instrument, and "Who are these coming to the sacrifice? / To what green altar, O mysterious priest / Lead'st thou that heifer . . . / What little town by river or seashore, / or mountain-built with peaceful citadel." (ll. 31–36) indicates that there is a second set of images in which an unnamed town or city of unknowable location takes part in a ritualistic sacrifice to some god on an unknown occasion. Keats as onlooker speculates that the ever-silent youth in the first scene is thinking of a lover not depicted in the scene, and commiserates with him over the eternally missing "She": "Bold Lover, never, never canst thou kiss, / Though winning near the goal" (ll. 17–18) before begging him to "not grieve" with the consolation that "She cannot fade, though thou hast not thy bliss / Forever wilt thou love, and she be fair!" (ll. 18–20). He is agitated by the silence of the townspeople in the second scene, mourning that the "little town, [thy] streets forevermore / Will silent be; and not a soul to tell / Why thou art desolate" (ll. 38–40) before bemoaning that the vase "dost tease us out of thought" (l. 44) with its ambiguous figures and stories. Overall, Keats conveys that he is both pleased at the beauty of the images on the vase and annoyed at the unsolvable mystery of their story.

Keats has both a personal and a collective response to the vase. Commiserating with the solitary youth depicted in the first image leads him to sympathize and empathize on a personal level as an individual who shares a young man's passions, and swept away by his imaginative retelling of this unknown story of eternal lovers, he rapturously declares: "More happy love! More happy, happy love!" (l. 25) and goes on sentimentally to imagine the physical delights and torments of an eternal love: "For ever warm and still to be enjoyed, / For ever panting, and for ever young; . . . That leaves a heart high-sorrowful and cloyed / A burning forehead and a parching tongue" (ll. 26–30). His response here is at once sentimental and nostalgic despite the fact that he is a modern onlooker with no connection to these events of the past. Wondering about the events of the second scene, Keats points out that it is representative of the eternal passage of time and serves as a symbol of the dichotomy between the immortality of the object and the mortality of the men and women who are depicted upon it and who use and observe it: "Cold Pastoral! / When old age shall this generation waste, / Thou shalt remain" (ll. 45–47). This is a more philosophical response than is his response to the first scene, indicating a more universal acknowledgement of the vase's overall mystery. The vase frustrates Keats—and thus his reader—

by demanding but not answering the question as to which is more preferable—nature, or ideal art; the warmth of mortality in a finite, human life; or the cold comfort of immortality in a work of art. The one comfort present in all of this, Keats points out, is that the vase as object, speaking for itself at the end of the poem, reminds us that "beauty is truth, truth beauty" (l. 49)—or, in other words, that it is through such arts as this vase and the poetry within which it has now been immortalized that man can find a link with his own basic humanity and begin to seek the answers to such questions for himself.

### Further Reading

Keats, John. *Ode on a Grecian Urn and Other Poems.* Whitefish, Mont: Kessinger Publishing, 2004.

Strachan, John, ed. *The Poems of John Keats: A Sourcebook.* London: Routledge Press, 2003.

Vendler, Helen. *The Odes of John Keats.* Cambridge, Mass.: Belknap Press, 2004.

—Melissa A. Elmes

### "Ode on Melancholy" John Keats (1819)

The 20th-century literary critic and poet William Empson, in his *Seven Types of Ambiguity* (1930), quoted this poem as an instance of the seventh type of ambiguity, which "occurs when the two meanings of the word, the two values of the ambiguity, are the two opposite meanings defined by the context, so that the total effect is to show a fundamental division in the writer's mind" (Empson, 192). Empson noted that "Keats often used ambiguities of this type to convey dissolution of normal experience into intensity of sensations" (214). It is true that melancholy is strangely associated with joy in this ode. Keats's aim is intensity of feeling, even if it implies going through the extremes of exhilaration and despair.

The poem consists of three stanzas, made up of 10 pentameters, mainly iambic, rhyming *abab cde cde.* The first stanza is negative; the second, starting with "But," comes in opposition to the first; the third is assertive. The first line, in the imperative, is brimming with negation, setting a series of alliterations in *n*, completed with the other liquid syllable, *l* in *Lethe,* the Greek river of hell and oblivion. The rhythm is broken, cut with several caesuras. Not only oblivion is forbidden, but also voluntary death, through aconite, a poison. The expression "poisonous wine" (l. 2) is ambiguous. The association of the movement of twisting with the compound adjective "tight-rooted" (l. 2) suggests an active stance rather than a passive indulging in death. Empson writes that "the sensations of joy and sorrow" are pounded together "till they combine into sexuality" (214). "Kiss'd," used in line 3, is connected with "nightshade," Proserpine's "ruby grape" (l. 4), a passionate precious tint, the colour of autumn, the rich season of carnal delight (Bacchus) and death. In these four lines red and dark combine passion and bereavement, pleasure and melancholy, which is black like the underworld to which Proserpine belongs.

A religious note crops up with the "rosary" (l. 5), which should not be made of the fruit of a death tree. The "death-moth" (l. 6) is a hairy insect with the evocation of a death's head on its body. As butterflies are usual symbols of the soul, it is no wonder that it should be associated with Psyche, Love's lover, but also the Greek name for "soul." The apparently negative word *sorrow* (l. 8) is enclosed in a pattern of positive notions ("partner," "downy" denoting help and protection). Even *mysteries* (l. 8) is a word that arouses curiosity rather than fear. Keats warns his interlocutor against temptation. No contrast means numbness ("too drowsily" [l. 9]), and the absence of sensation lays the soul low. Sleep and sinking are connected as they are in "ODE TO A NIGHTINGALE." Here the link is emphasized through alliteration and assonance ("drowsily" / "drown" [ll. 9, 10]), reinforcing the idea of an ineluctable process initiated by "shade to shade" (l. 9). Although paradoxical, the "wakeful anguish of the soul" (l. 10) is positive here and means life.

The second stanza starts with "But." As in the first stanza and as is usual with Keats, the similes and metaphors borrow from the natural world. In the first verse, the natural elements represented death and night; now they express renewal and fruition, spring and summer. The melancholic state, being compared to a shower of rain, is fruitful; it is endowed with an engendering power and, falling suddenly from heaven like manna or God's food, is highly positive. The weeping cloud, personified, sounds tenderly melancholy. The compound adjective *droop-headed* (l. 13) has an effect of visual accuracy. The positive and negative notions are closely entwined in line 4, in which April contrasts with autumn in stanza 1 and the "green hill" with the "shroud" (l. 14). The mystery also lies in these doubtful identities, in this overspread ambiguity, emphasized by the powerful expression "glut thy sorrow" (l. 15). "Glut" suggests intense satisfaction and gives "sorrow" an active part, implying that it can be creative and feed on a symbol of beauty and happiness, "a morning rose" (l. 15). The flower of spring and summer, connected with the "morning," opens a fresh beginning, a new hope.

These lines are brimming with sensual intensity and plenitude. The rainbow, a symbol of conciliation, gathers all the basic colors. The peonies recall profusion and fullness ("wealth" and "globed" [l. 17]). Sorrow is linked with all sorts of pleasures. It is no surprise that love should come next. With her "rich anger" and her "peerless eyes" (ll. 18, 20), the mistress is the "belle dame" of courtly love, "sans merci" perhaps (see "LA BELLE DAME SANS MERCI").

The pronoun *She,* at the beginning of stanza 3, refers to "thy mistress" (l. 18) in stanza 2 and announces the personified "Veil'd Melancholy" (l. 26), similar to the veiled goddess cherished by the Romantics, among them the German poet NOVALIS. Her sacred nature is revealed. Delight now involves a religious exaltation of the senses, yet still placed under the sign of contrast: beauty, and death; joy, and farewell; pleasure, and pain. Joy, which is male, has a body (a "hand" and "lips" [l. 22]). Physical sensation is emphasized through the hyperbolic image of the "bee-mouth" that "sips" (l. 24), an image which looks forward to the mid-19th century poet Emily Dickinson. There is also the suggestion that melancholy can be found in the very center of delight—connected with taste and absorption, with strength ("strenuous tongue" [l. 27]) and joyful violent destruction ("burst" [l. 28]). Taste is taken metaphorically, and the soul is given substance ("trophies"), which the adjective *cloudy* partly denies (l. 30). The end is particularly ambiguous since the "trophies" refer to hunting or war, and therefore to sacrifice, already suggested in "Can burst Joy's grape against his palate fine" (l. 28).

Overall, the whole poem has a dialectic, argumentative structure—negation, opposition, assertion—but the reasoning is anchored in reality through the appeal to all the senses (synaesthesia) and the deep understanding of the ambivalent character of life which is not the sign of a "division in the writer's mind," as Empson says, but of an attempt to reconcile the opposites and to tackle the negative from an existential viewpoint, in a dramatic embrace.

## Further Reading

Blades, John. *John Keats: The Poems.* Basingstoke, Eng.: Palgrave, 2002.

Empson, William. *Seven Types of Ambiguity.* New York: New Directions, 1966.

Keats, John. *Complete Poems and Selected Letters of John Keats.* Edited by Edward Hirsch. New York: Modern Library Classics, 2001.

Watts, Cedric. *A Preface to Keats.* 5th ed. London and New York: Longman, 1996.

Whale, John. *John Keats.* Basingstoke, Eng.: Palgrave Macmillan, 2005.

Wolfson, Susan J. *The Cambridge Companion to Keats.* Cambridge: Cambridge University Press, 2001.

Anne Mounic

## "Ode to a Nightingale" John Keats (1819)

For many, JOHN KEATS's "Ode to a Nightingale" epitomizes Romanticism because it brings together so many of its defining themes, formal gestures, and philosophical concerns. It is certainly typical of the canon of male Romantic poets in that it features a solitary male speaker on a kind of spirit-quest, seeking to transcend a world of painful imperfection by moving outward into a natural world that promises an experience of original purity, freedom, and authenticity. In terms of form, this prompts a turn to the ode, an elevated classical genre traditionally reserved for the praise of some extraordinary, often metaphysical, entity. In this case, the ode is addressed to an archetypal bird whose wordless music suggests powerful emotions beyond the reach of language, and also the possibility of an expressive art that is paradoxically "artless" or unselfconscious, directly inspired by the truth of nature. The speaker's longing to identify with this symbol of natural truth inspires a strong, self-conscious exercise of the imagination that ends by creating a paradox: on the one hand, the poem itself demonstrates the power of the poetic imagination to conjure, like the bird's song, an ideal world; on the other, it draws attention to the ontological instability of such products of the imagination and their uncertain relation to the physical world. The literary scholar Helen Vendler has shown how these themes and philosophical puzzles resonate throughout Keats's other odes; they also inform the central Romantic lyrics of WILLIAM WORDSWORTH, SAMUEL TAYLOR COLERIDGE, and PERCY BYSSHE SHELLEY, among others.

"Ode to a Nightingale" ends with a question—"Do I wake or sleep?" (l. 80)—that typifies the Romantic urge to explore categories of experience that disturb or exceed the boundaries imposed by reason, which the Enlightenment had enshrined as the arbiter of truth. In one of his letters, Keats posits that authors need "Negative Capability," or the capacity to remain "in uncertainties, Mysteries, doubts, without any irritable reaching after fact & reason" (quoted in Cox 109). Even his choice of the nightingale creates this sort of strategic uncertainty: Literary tradition dictates that this is an allusion to the tragic myth of Philomela, whose song is irreducibly "melancholy" (Vendler 81). Coleridge, however, had challenged this tradition in "The Nightingale," asserting (accurately) that the bird we hear is in fact a male, joyfully singing a mating call. Keats follows Coleridge by introducing a bird of "happiness" that sings "of summer in full-throated ease" (l. 10), but he characterizes it as mythic and female (a "light-winged Dryad of the trees" [l. 7]) and later describes its song as a "requiem" and a "plaintive anthem" (ll. 60, 75).

Day and night are also blurred in the poem: Tradition has it that Keats wrote it one morning in May 1819 (according to his friend Charles Brown [Strachan 145]), and the first stanza suggests the daylight setting of a "melodious plot / Of beechen green, and shadows numberless" (ll. 8–9). However, we soon find that the bird sings in a night world so dark that the speaker "cannot see what flowers are at [his] feet" (l. 41), thus invoking the 18th-century tradition of night poems in which the sense of sight—so crucial to Enlightenment modes of verification and certainty—is symbolically removed, forcing the mind to rely on other senses associated with nonrational modes of cognition, such as hearing ("Darkling I listen" [l. 51]) and the sense of smell ("what soft incense hangs upon the boughs" [l. 42]).

As in other night poems, the question "Do I wake or sleep?" is presented as a tension between a higher wakefulness or "vision" (l. 79) (epitomized for the Romantics by JOHN MILTON's blind, seerlike insight) and a less palpable, potentially delusory "waking dream" (l. 79). Typical of Keats, and poignantly inflected by his personal circumstances, this binary is mapped onto a spatial contrast between the "forest dim "of the invisible bird (l. 20) and the harsh realities of the "world" "here" (ll. 19, 24), where even "youth grows pale, and spectre-thin, and dies" (l. 26), an allusion perhaps to the recent death of his brother Tom from tuberculosis. The poem is thus structured around three urgent attempts to bridge the gap between the speaker's human "sorrow" (l. 27) and the bird's natural "happiness" (l. 6). First, he imagines drinking the wine of "Hippocrene" (l. 16), the fountain of truth for the classical muses, but this path is rejected, perhaps because intoxication is too much like the "drowsy numbness" that opens the poem (l. 1). Instead, the speaker strives to reach the nightingale on "the viewless wings of Poesy" (l. 33), trying to conjure its invisible world with his unaided imagination, but again "the dull brain perplexes and retards" (l. 34), and he is left wondering if perhaps the only way to become one with the bird's "ecstasy" is to die (l. 58). To "become a sod" (l. 60), however, would make it impossible to hear, and it is the nightingale's "voice" that makes it "immortal" (ll. 63, 61), because its song remains "the same" across the "generations" (ll. 68, 62).

In a third attempt to match the sublime music of the bird, the soaring, visionary tone of stanza seven conjures a series of vivid moments throughout history in which this song has been heard, even in the imaginary realm of "fairy lands forlorn" (l. 70). On that word *forlorn*, however, the poem pivots downward in a typical moment of Romantic "dejection," as the bird flies away and the speaker realizes that even his imagination (that "deceiving elf" [l. 74]) cannot permanently overcome a fundamental difference: Whereas the nightingale remains free of any awareness of death, the speaker cannot escape his human consciousness of a "sole self" immersed in time, mutability, and mortality (l. 72).

In the uncanny silence that follows the bird's departure, however, the question remains: Does this final retreat into a lonely awareness of mortality constitute an awakening to rational truth, or is it a kind of "sleep" that has lost touch with a higher truth revealed in brief epiphanies of the eternal? Some would say that in composing this unique 80-line ode, with its sonorous rhyme scheme and sonnet-like stanzas, Keats has forged an enduring record of such an epiphany that fruitfully unsettles any firm boundary between the imagined and the real.

## Further Reading

Cox, Jeffrey N., ed. *Keats's Poetry and Prose: Authoritative Texts, Criticism.* New York: W. W. Norton & Co., 2009.

Roe, Nicholas. *John Keats and the Culture of Dissent.* Oxford: Oxford University Press, 1997.

Strachan, John, ed. *The Poems of John Keats: A Sourcebook.* London: Routledge, 2003.

Vendler, Helen. *The Odes of John Keats.* Cambridge, Mass.: Harvard University Press, 1983.

Wolfson, Susan J., ed. *John Keats.* New York: Pearson Longman, 2007.

—Robert Lapp

## "Ode to Autumn" John Keats (1819)

For the seven-week period between August 12 and the end of September 1819, JOHN KEATS lodged in Winchester, a town 60 miles southwest of London near the port city of Southampton. He was depressed, frustrated by his lack of progress toward completion of a new revision of HYPERION, and weighed down by personal and professional concerns, including a time-consuming collaboration with Charles Brown on a verse drama, *Otho the Great,* as well as his brother George's and his own financial troubles. On Sunday evening, September 19, Keats went for a walk to clear his mind. On his return, he composed his final ode, "To Autumn," which he included in a letter, dated September 21/22, to his friend Richard Woodhouse. In a separate letter to J. H. Reynolds, dated September 21, Keats provides an account of the inspiration for its composition: "How beautiful the season is now—How fine the air. A temperate sharpness about it. Really, without joking, chaste weather—Dian skies—I never lik'd stubble fields so much as now—Aye better than the chilly green of the spring. Somehow the stubble plain looks warm—in the same way that some pictures look warm—this struck me so much in my sunday's walk that I composed upon it" (Keats 2002, 345).

"To Autumn" is the final of Keats's five "great odes" written between April and September 1819, which also include "ODE TO PSYCHE," "ODE TO A NIGHTINGALE," and "ODE ON MELANCHOLY." The last two, "Melancholy" and "Autumn," are strikingly similar in form. They closely follow the three-part structure of the classic Pindaric ode: Stanza 1 is the strophe, stanza 2 is the antistrophe, and stanza 3 is the epode. The rhythm of both poems is predominately iambic pentameter. Moreover, each poem's stanza structure is a variation on the sonnet. The 10-line stanza structure of "Melancholy" consists of a heroic quatrain (four-line unit with an alternating rhyme scheme) followed by a sestet (six-line unit). The 11-line stanza structure of "Autumn" employs a heroic quatrain and a septet (seven-line unit). Despite their formal similarities, "Ode to Autumn" is generally considered to be superior, surpassing the art of "Ode on Melancholy."

Throughout literary history, autumn has figured predominately as the season of old age, waning vitality, impending death. However, the beauty of autumn in Keats's ode is its life-sustaining, life-affirming qualities: Autumn is the season of fulfillment, repletion, and abundance. A closely associated word, *teeming*, is significant in Keats's poetry. In the sonnet "WHEN I HAVE FEARS THAT I MAY CEASE TO BE" (1818), he writes about the anxiety he feels upon contemplating the possibility that he may die before he is able to write all the poetry contained in his "teeming brain" (l. 2). In "Ode to Psyche," the word appears twice, in a pair of nearly identical lines in stanzas 3 and 4. In "Ode

to Autumn," Keats also owes some debt to Shakespeare's Sonnet 97, in which the poet speaks of "teeming Autumn" (l. 6) as a season of abundance and richness. This is not the time of year of Sonnet 73, the autumn that is closely associated with old age and languishing vitality. Quite to the contrary, the autumn of Keats's ode is more vital than either spring or summer, because it is fruitful: It is the time of reaping, of harvesting. And although Keats does not use the word *teeming* in this ode, the poem itself is teeming with the imagery of overflow and abundance.

However, one word that Keats does use in both "When I have Fears" and "Ode to Autumn" is *gleaned* or *gleaner*. In the former, *gleaned* is the past-tense verb that controls the objective phrase "my teeming brain." The verb conveys the autumnal image of gathering and binding grain, an image that Keats uses in the next two lines of the first quatrain to develop into a full analogy between gathering grain into sheaves and binding poetry into books. In the latter, the noun *gleaner* appears in the antistrophe and represents a personified Autumn who reaps and processes the fruit, which in the strophe has fully ripened "to the core" (l. 6). Moreover, the image of gleaning, coupled with the image of pressing apples for cider, conveys a sense of finality, of the end of ripeness and the clearing away of the last fruits of the season before they rot and lose their usefulness.

Thus, "Ode to Autumn" is an iconic poem in the sense that it acts out, and mirrors, through its art what it praises about its subject. It explores the theme of autumn's abundance by containing an abundance of rich imagery and diction. Even the additional line of the septet in each stanza conveys that sense of abundance, of overflow, of the teeming quality of both the season and the poem. The strophe establishes the vitality, the "fruitfulness" (l. 1), and "ripeness" (l. 6) of the season, while the antistrophe continues the natural process into the stages of reaping and consumption, and includes the role of human beings in that process. And finally, the epode (which literally translates as "sung after" and was chanted or sung in classical Greece) emphasizes music from the beginning: "Where are the songs of Spring?" (l. 23). The septet contains multiple references to song, from the "wailful choir" (l. 27) of gnats to singing crickets, bleating lambs, and twittering robins. Harold Bloom succinctly summarizes the content and provides an outline of the structure: "The sequence of the three stanzas then is pre-harvest ripeness, late-harvest repletion, and post-harvest natural music" (Bloom 94).

"Ode to Autumn" is the climax and finale of a flourish of literary output between April and September 1819. Critics now generally agree that Keats produced his best and most mature poetry during this period. Bloom hails "To Autumn" as "the subtlest and most beautiful of all Keats's odes, and as close to perfection as any shorter poem in the English language" (Bloom 94); Robert Gittings comments that it is "the most serene poem in the English language" (Gittings 186). Ironically, Keats himself viewed the year 1819 as one of profound disappointment and failure, both professionally and personally. He and his brother George continued to struggle financially, which put in doubt his future prospects with his beloved Fanny Brawne; his health began to fail, and he had decided to end his pursuit of a literary career after September in favor of a more stable source of income. On February 23, 1821, at the age of 25—17 months after the composition of "Ode to Autumn"—Keats died of tuberculosis. This ode remains as a testament to both the bounty of nature and the art of Keats's poetry.

## Further Reading

Bate, Walter Jackson. *John Keats.* Cambridge, Mass.: Harvard University Press, 1963.

Bewell, Alan. "'To Autumn' and the Curing of Space." In *Keats's Poetry and Prose,* edited by Jeffrey Cox, 634–642. New York: W. W. Norton & Company, 2008.

Bloom, Harold. "The Ode 'To Autumn.'" In *The Visionary Company: A Reading of English Romantic Poetry,* 421–425. Garden City, N.Y.: Doubleday, 1961.

Creaser, John. "From 'Autumn' to Autumn in Keats's Ode." *Essays in Criticism* 38 (1988): 190–214.

Fraser, G. S. *John Keats: Odes. A Casebook.* London: Macmillan, 1971.

Gittings, Robert. *John Keats: The Living Year, 21 September 1818 to 21 September 1819.* Cambridge, Mass.: Harvard University Press, 1954.

———. *Selected Letters of John Keats.* Edited by Grant F. Scott. Cambridge: Harvard University Press, 2002.

Perkins, David. "Affirmation of Process in 'Ode on Melancholy' and 'To Autumn.'" In *The Quest for Permanence: The Symbolism of Wordsworth, Shelley, and Keats.* Cambridge, Mass.: Harvard University Press, 1959, 282–294.

Shakespeare, William. Sonnet 97. In *The Complete Works of Shakespeare,* 3rd ed., edited by David Bevington, 1,600. London: Scott, Foresman, 1980.

Swinden, Patrick. "John Keats: 'To Autumn.'" *Critical Quarterly* 20, no. 4 (1978): 57–60.

—John S. Prince

## "Ode to Duty" William Wordsworth (1807)

"Ode to Duty" marks a clear shift in WILLIAM WORDSWORTH's thinking. Modeled on THOMAS GRAY's "Ode to Adversity," it was composed early in 1804 and published in *Poems, in Two Volumes* (1807). It had its immediate source, however, in a series of conversations with SAMUEL TAYLOR COLERIDGE in the New Year of 1804 on the subject of man's natural disinclination to do one's duty, and in Wordsworth's rereading of JOHN MILTON which began in 1802. Coleridge's notebooks betray a deep uneasiness at what he saw to be the impracticability of the German philosopher Immanuel Kant's ideas on human morality. In the light of his addiction to opium, love for Sara Hutchinson, and neglect of his duties as a father and husband, Coleridge had become acutely aware of the vast gulf between one's duty and one's will. In the aftermath of long conversations with his friend on the subject, Wordsworth composed a definitive response in the form of "Ode to Duty," which was inspired by Coleridge's accounts of Kantian ethics and by Milton's emphasis on rigorous self-discipline. Stoicism, Wordsworth declared, was the new moral standard by which he, and by implication Coleridge also, ought to live. Coleridge, however, remained unconvinced by the high idealism of Wordsworth's poem and expressed his dissatisfaction in his subsequent correspondence and perhaps most fully in *BIOGRAPHIA LITERARIA*. *Ode to Duty* can thus be interpreted as a poem that indicates the increasing divergence in the thought of Wordsworth and Coleridge.

Closely linked to poems such as "RESOLUTION AND INDEPENDENCE" and looking forward to the austerity of passages of *The* P*RELUDE* and *The* E*XCURSION*, as well as "The White Doe of Rylstone," "Ode to Duty" is a meditative, philosophic lyric that enacts Wordsworth's self-dedication to duty. The poem celebrates the beginning of a new life and relationship with nature. Paradoxically, "the spirit of self-sacrifice," which Wordsworth invokes, and the "denial and restraint" that are central to his new vision will create a purer sense of liberty and independence than the spontaneous, imaginative responses to the natural world on which much of his earlier poetry is based. As the often overlooked epigraph from the Roman philosopher Seneca's *Moral Epistles* (added in 1833) indicates, Wordsworth's life of stoical duty is based on the perfect harmony of the natural and moral worlds. True happiness, Wordsworth argues, is founded firmly on the performance of man's duty to his fellow humans. Although neatly blending a sense of Romantic individualism with ascetic Miltonic values, Wordsworth concludes that individual fulfilment, or self-realization, is achieved through strict obedience to the laws of nature dictated by man's innate conscience.

The philosophy of the Stoics, Kant, and Milton thus come together in *Ode to Duty* and usher in a new stage in Wordsworth's imaginative life. Far from being a retraction of his earlier poetic vision, of that which characterizes the crystalline purity of lyrics such as the "Lucy" poems or "The Solitary Reaper," "Ode to Duty" instead signals an adjustment, or rather an improvement to it. The instinctive responses of the youthful imagination are now to be complemented by a stricter mental regulation in accordance with the divine law of nature. This was to become the basis of Wordsworth's mature poetic vision.

## Further Reading

Gill, Stephen. *William Wordsworth: A Life.* Oxford: Clarendon Press, 1989.

Hartman, Geoffrey. *Wordsworth's Poetry, 1787–1814.* New Haven, Conn., and London: Yale University Press, 1964.

Moorman, Mary. *William Wordsworth: A Biography.* 2 vols. Oxford: Oxford University Press, 1957.

Stallknecht, Newton P. *Strange Seas of Thought: Studies in William Wordsworth's Philosophy of Man and Nature.* Durham, N.C.: Duke University Press, 1945.

Wordsworth, William. *Poems, in Two Volumes, and Other Poems, 1800–1807.* Edited by Jared Curtis. New York: Cornell University Press, 1983.

—Stephen Burley

## "Ode to Psyche" John Keats (1819)

J*OHN* K*EATS* included a copy of this poem in a letter he wrote to his brother and sister-in-law, dated February to May 1819 (Keats 282–333). Keats mentioned in his letter that the poem was inspired by the story of Psyche and Cupid from Apuleius's *Metamorphoses,* or *The Golden Ass,* as is the more common title. Apuleius lived in the early part of the second century A.D. in Roman North Africa. His work, and especially the part about Psyche and Cupid, has been read as a counter-doctrine to Christianity (xxxvii–xxxix). The Inquisition tried to destroy all known editions of *The Golden Ass* during the Middle Ages, and the work was largely lost to most readers from that time until 1566, when William Adlington translated the work into English (Slade). In Apuleius's version of Psyche and Cupid, Psyche's curiosity leads to her punishment of walking the world, alone and loveless. Eventually she is rescued by Cupid and transported to Heaven, where she bears a child named Pleasure. Because of the child's name, it is unclear in the tale whether Psyche is rescued by lust or by a higher love. Keats jokingly told his brother and sister-in-law that Psyche's late appearance in the catalogue of Roman gods increased his enthusiasm for writing the poem. As he said, "I am more orthodox than to let a heathen Goddess be so neglected," after which follows the poem (Keats 330).

Critics have speculated that Keats was inspired to read *The Golden Ass* because the popular Irish poet M*ARY* T*IGHE* had reworked Apuleius's story into her poem P*SYCHE, OR* T*HE* L*EGEND OF* L*OVE* (Weller xxiv, xv). This possible heritage for Keats's poem is particularly interesting because critics have usually concentrated on tracing influential patterns from male authors acclaimed for writing what has been traditionally classed as higher literature, but one of the most important influences may have been the work of an Irish woman who wrote popular lyrics (Bate 327).

In that same letter, Keats also described his reading interests at the time he wrote "Ode to Psyche." In particular, he was reading various works of history, including William Robertson's *History of America* (1777) and Voltaire's *Le siècle de Louis XIV* (1751), which compelled him to formulate his own ideas about faith and religion. Keats saw a connection between different religions. As he said, "For as one part of the human species must have their carved Jupiter; so another part must have the palpable and named Mediator and saviour, their Christ, their Oromanes, and their Vishnu" (Keats 328). He defined religious belief as a manmade artifice—it is in the world that we create our souls, the world that is the "vale of Soul-making"—and he described "Soul-making" in the following terms: "There may be intelligences or sparks of the divinity in millions—but they are not Souls till they acquire identities, till each one is personally itself. . . . How then are Souls to be made? . . . How but by the medium of a world like this?" (326).

Because Keats wrote most of his great odes over the spring and summer of 1819, critics have tried to read his odes as a single work, each consequent ode revising and commenting on the ideas that appeared in odes that he wrote previously, but "Ode to Psyche" has presented some problems for this interpretive approach. As W. J. Bate has cautioned, "No single interpretation of any of the odes—still less of the odes as a group—satisfies anyone except the interpreter" (Bate 486). "Ode to Psyche" does offer some of the general themes and moods present in his later odes, such as Keats's worship of the imagination, his celebration of love as a timeless human emotion, and its melancholic mood, but there are parts of this poem that stubbornly refuse to assimilate with Keats's other works.

The poem's overall movement, for example, is difficult to understand in terms of Keats's other odes. The speaker asks, in lines 5–6, whether he has actually seen Psyche "with awaken'd eyes," or whether this is simply a dream. By the end of the poem, the speaker offers to build a temple to Psyche in "some untrodden region of my mind" (l. 51), thereby avoiding a resolution of the earlier question by firmly situating his worship of the goddess in his mind. We travel from "wild-ridged mountains" (l. 55) to a very tame and culti-

vated garden, a "rosy sanctuary" complete with a "wreth'd trellis" and all the artifice "the gardener Fancy e'er could feign, / Who breeding flowers, will never breed the same" (ll. 59–63). The last lines of the poem move from this garden of artifice to the temple itself, illuminated by a "bright torch" and complete with a "casement ope at night, / To let the warm Love in!" (ll. 66–67).

In this fashion, the couple, Cupid and Psyche, whom the speaker may have seen "couchèd side by side / In deepest grass, beneath the whisp'ring roof / Of leaves and trembled blossoms" (ll. 9–11) disappear, and the speaker erects a temple of worship in which Psyche waits for Cupid, alone. This movement from an outdoor, public space to inside a private temple is difficult to interpret in terms of the concerns in "ODE ON A GRECIAN URN," for instance. Where that poem celebrates artifice, here, in "Ode to Psyche," much seems to be lost as the speaker takes control of what he sees and envelops the goddess inside the temple of his mind. Psyche is left, at the end of the poem, yearning for her lover, and, one might say, trapped inside the temple instead of being able to roam freely under the trees. The speaker's worship of Psyche seems to force her back into her state of loneliness, which, in Apuleius's version, is Psyche's punishment.

Tracing other possible poetic influences on Keats at this time has yielded some interesting interpretations of this movement. For example, Homer Brown has compared the moment when the speaker stumbles on this couple lovemaking in the woods to the moment that Satan spies Adam and Eve in the Garden of Eden in JOHN MILTON's grand epic *Paradise Lost* (1667). In Milton's poem, Satan is inspired by his jealousy of God's love for his human creations to travel from Hell in order to view the lovers for himself. During the time that he watches them, Satan realizes that Hell is not a place, a location, but is instead a prison of his own devising, a torture he carries about with him that he can never escape. Comparing Satan's voyeurism to the voyeurism in "Ode to Psyche" has led Brown to assert that one should not read the project of this poem as an uncomplicated celebration of the power of the human mind. As he says, "['Ode to Psyche'] runs the risk of being just as self-enclosed and solipsistic as Satan's egotistical Hell" (Brown 54).

On May 4, 1819, a copy of this poem was handed to John Hamilton Reynolds and copied into Richard Woodhouse's book of manuscripts. Along with Keats's other odes, it was printed by Keats's publishers Taylor and Hessey in April 1820 under the title *Lamia, Isabella, The Eve of St. Agnes, and Other Poems*. Keats's first volume of poetry had inspired lampoons in *Blackwood's Magazine* and such critical reviews in the *Quarterly Review* that PERCY BYSSHE SHELLEY and LORD BYRON both claimed the reviews killed Keats, but his second volume received much critical praise. CHARLES LAMB and FRANCIS JEFFREY both wrote laudatory reviews for this new work (Colvin 516–520), but it was too late for Keats, who was in the last throes of illness and died before the work's eventual success. This poem, among the others in this volume, thus began Keats's posthumous career and was often read as proof that the poet had had the hardest, but most glorious, of paths—or, as Shelley described in ADONAIS, "who bought, with price of purest breath, / A grave among the eternal" (ll. 57–58; referenced in Colvin, 517).

## Further Reading

Apuleius. *The Golden Ass.* Translated and introduced by P. G. Walsh. Oxford University Press, 1999.

Bate, Jonathan. "Tom Moore and the Making of the 'Ode to Psyche.'" *Review of English Studies* 41, no. 163 (August 1990): 325–333.

Brown, Homer. "Creations and Destroyings: Keats's Protestant Hymn, the 'Ode to Psyche.'" *Diacritics* 6, no. 4 (Winter 1976): 49–56.

Colvin, Sidney. *John Keats: His Life and Poetry, His Friends, Critics, and After-Fame.* London: Macmillan, 1920.

Jack, Ian. *Keats and the Mirror of Art.* Oxford: Oxford University Press, 1967.

Keats, John. *The Letters of John Keats.* Edited by H. Buxton Forman. London: Reeves & Turner, 1895.

Slade, Benjamin. *The Golden Ass.* Available online. URL: http://www.jnanam.net/golden-ass/. Accessed on July 31, 2008.

Weller, Earle Varle, ed. *Keats and Mary Tighe: The Poems of Mrs Tighe with Parallel Passages from the Works of John Keats.* New York: Century Co., 1928.

—Sarah Nash

## "Ode to the West Wind"  Percy Bysshe Shelley (1820)

"Ode to the West Wind," one of the best known of PERCY BYSSHE SHELLEY's lyrics, explores the relationship between the power of nature and the poetic mind. Shelley, a powerful voice of Romantic poetry, seeks to describe effect of the wind's strength on the world. He asks for the wind to enliven him as it does the natural world so that he may go forth and share that spirit through the language of poetry. The plight of the Romantic poet is the desire to transform the world—to bring inspiration and knowledge to an uncertain world.

While announcing itself as an "ode," the poem is made up of five terza rima sonnets. The traditional Pindaric structure is truncated. Instead, the poem divides itself rather neatly into a bipartite structure more like a sonnet, and the "turn" in the poem comes after the first three stanzas. Like the sonnet, the Pindaric ode is characterized by abrupt transitions and distinctive "turns" of voice between triads, which are central to understanding Shelley's ode. The primary difference between odes and sonnets, aside from the structural distinctions, is the extent to which the voice of the poem is public or private. Shelley's appropriation of different poetic forms calls attention to a central theme of the poem: how can the poetic voice connect with and affect a public audience?

The first three stanzas, or sonnets, observe the impact of the wind, invoked as an animating spirit in the poem's first line, on the natural terrain, specifically land, sky, and sea. The impact of the "Wild Spirit" (l. 13) on the landscape builds in each stanza through Shelley's frequent use of enjambment, which moves the reader through the poem with a sense of anticipation. In each of these stanzas, Shelley describes the natural phenomenon over the space of the four tercets before the concluding couplet's final declaration, "O hear!" We see this most clearly in the first sonnet, where, after moving through the poem rapidly, the reader pauses to reflect on the image at the "turn" of the sonnet: "Wild Spirit, which art moving everywhere" (l. 13). Another invocation to the spirit, this line encourages reflection on the impact of the "Wild Spirit" throughout the poem.

The force of the wind emerges in images of both destruction and preservation, as the first stanza's final couplet anticipates. The dialectical force of the wind on the stationary landscape appears increasingly apocalyptic as the poem builds toward the impact of the wind on the poet himself in the final two sonnets. The more a reader tries to envision a figure of unity, even in reliable images like heaven or ocean, the greater the force within that figure threatens to destroy its cohesion. It is Shelley's revolutionary and revisionary hope to unleash human vitality and energy, sometimes destructive, through poetry. However, the recognition of human limitation is famously referred to in line 54: "I fall upon the thorns of life! I bleed!" In spite of this realization, a plea to the "Wild Spirit" comprises the final sonnet; the poet's call for his words to be spread "among mankind" (l. 67).

**Further Reading**

Curran, Stuart. *Shelley's Annus Mirabilis: The Maturing of an Epic Vision.* San Marino, Calif.: Huntington Library, 1975.

Shelley, Percy Bysshe. *Shelley's Poetry and Prose: Authoritative Texts, Criticism.* Edited by Donald H. Reiman and Neil Frastat. New York: Norton, 2002.

Wasserman, Earl R. *Shelley: A Critical Reading.* Baltimore, Md.: Johns Hopkins Press, 1971.

Yost, François. "Anatomy of an Ode: Shelley and the Sonnet Tradition." *Comparative Literature* 34, no. 3 (Summer 1982): 223–246.

—Sarah Peterson

## "Old Beggar, The" Mary Robinson (1800)

"The Old Beggar" was first published in the *Morning Post and Fashionable World* in 1800 (less than a year before MARY ROBINSON's death). The 20-quatrain ballad appeared in volume 4 of the poet's posthumously published *Memoirs* (1806). The poem has a uniform rhyme scheme (*abab*) and systematically varying metrical pattern. The central figure is the eponymous "Old Beggar," while the central themes are the vicissitudes of fortune and unrequited love.

The poem opens with a direct address to the reader: "Do you see the old beggar who sits at yon gate, / With his beard silver'd over like snow? / Tho' he smiles as he meets the keen arrows of fate, / Still his bosom is wearied with woe (ll. 1–4). The internal near-rhyme ("meets" / "fate") suggests that fate is an important idea in the poem. In the next line, alliteration of the words *wearied* and *woe* heightens pathos. Wintry imagery in stanzas 1 and 3 and elsewhere emphasize the beggar's advanced age while also arousing pity in the reader. "In the bleak blast of winter he hobbles along," relates the poet, "O'er the heath, at the dawning of day; / And the dew-drops that freeze the rude thistles among, / Are the stars that illumine his way" (ll. 9–12). The poet also creates sympathy by juxtaposing such descriptions as this one with images of the beggar in his youth. In the lines above, the hoary wanderer is depicted hobbling through the winter storm, his eyes cast downward; stanza 5 moves back in time, presenting him as a young soldier dressed "in martial trim" (l. 17) who boldly "march[es] thro' the storms of the day or the night" (l. 19). A jubilant tone and vernal imagery make the contrast more pronounced in stanzas 6 and 7: The young man ("younker") is "valiant" and "gay" (l. 24); the girl whom he secretly loves ("the maid of his heart") leads the dance around the maypole (ll. 26–27).

An explanation is given in quatrains 12 and 13 for the gallant soldier's transformation into a woeful old beggar: The youth came back from a battle to discover that his beloved had wed another (ll. 45–48). Elucidates the poet: "From that hour, o'er the world he has wander'd forlorn" (l. 49). The final stanzas return the reader to the present: "See him now, . . ." the poet remarks; "See his habit all tatter'd, his shrivell'd cheek pale; / See his locks, waving thin in the air" (ll. 53, 57–58). Still heartbroken, the feeble beggar longs for death. The ballad concludes: "Perchance, ere the May-blossoms cheerfully wave, / Ere the zephyrs of summer soft sigh; / The sun-beams shall dance on the grass o'er his grave, / And his journey be mark'd—to the sky" (ll. 77–80). With its natural imagery, focus on the pastoral, and main character drawn "from common life" (Wordsworth 392, 408), Robinson's "The Old Beggar" is certainly indebted to *Lyrical Ballads*. The poem is one of many "beggar poems" written in the 1790s, including WILLIAM WORDSWORTH's "The Old Cumberland Beggar" (1800) and CHARLOTTE

SMITH's earlier work "The Dead Beggar" (1797). "The Old Beggar" particularly resembles Smith's elegy in that the beggar's death is presented as a merciful release from suffering. As in the poems by Wordsworth and Smith, Robinson's beggar poem calls attention to the plight of disenfranchised members of society. Unlike the other poems, however, Robinson attributes the misfortunes of her beggar to romantic loss, or "love gone wrong," which, according to Judith Pascoe, is a characteristic preoccupation of Robinson's poetry (in Robinson 2000, 60).

**Further Reading**

Robinson, Mary. *Mary Robinson: Selected Poems*. Edited by Judith Pascoe. Peterborough, Ont.: Broadview Press, 2000.

———. "The Old Beggar." In *The Poetical Works of the Late Mrs. Mary Robinson*, vol. 3, edited by M. E. Robinson, 306 310. London: Richard Phillips, 1806.

Wordsworth, William. "Preface to *Lyrical Ballads* (1802)." In *Lyrical Ballads and Other Writings*, edited by William Richey and Daniel Robinson, 390–411. Boston and New York: Houghton Mifflin, 2002.

—Natalie Neill

## Old English Baron, The *(The Champion of Virtue)* Clara Reeve *(1778)*

Thirteen years after Horace Walpole launched an aesthetic revolution in Britain with the publication of *The Castle of Otranto* (1764), the first GOTHIC novel, CLARA REEVE published a novel modeled after, yet critical of, *Otranto*. Originally entitled *The Champion of Virtue* (1777), it was republished in London a year later as *The Old English Baron* (1778). In terms of sales, editions, translations, and dramatizations, it was immensely popular. Its critical reviews were mixed, with some commentators faulting the novel for its hyperdidacticism and appeal to the superstitious, an ironic critique given that, in her manifesto-like preface to the second edition, Reeve vehemently chastised Walpole for an improbable use of the supernatural that rendered *Otranto* ridiculous rather than sublime. Walpole's description of *The Old English Baron* as a

*caput mortuum*, the popular Latin tag for the worthless residue in a flask after alchemical distillation, was no less scathing.

*Baron* is derivative of *Otranto* in terms of its basic plot of usurpation/disinheritance and restoration. Strong echoes of *Otranto* are evident in the story of the virtuous peasant Edmund Twyford's restoration as the heir of Lovel Castle and the exposure and punishment of the usurping murderer, Sir Walter Lovel, Edmund's kinsman. Edmund follows in the path of *Otranto*'s Theodore, who assumes his grandfather Alfonso's place as a morally upright prince. Reeve places great emphasis on Edmund's numerous trials prior to receiving his just rewards in a work that combines the gothic with the conduct book (an instructional manual telling people how to behave) and the novel of sensibility. In an instance of gothic "doubling," he is revealed to be his father's virtuous son. Strikingly unlike Manfred, however, Lovel remains an unrepentant villain despite being banished from England on an enforced pilgrimage to the Holy Land. He sets the stage for countless remorseless gothic villains to come.

In keeping with *Baron*'s enlightenment theme, Lovel's "deeds of darkness" (Reeve 148) are literally exposed to daylight as Edmund, near the novel's end, provides evidence of his mother's treacherous death and leads his astonished jury-style auditors to Castle Lovel's concealed closet with its "fatal secret" (98), a gruesome memento mori in the form of the skeleton of Edmund's murdered father, "which appeared to have been tied neck and heels together and forced into the trunk" (148). This "awful spectacle" provides the powerful moral lesson "that though wickedness may triumph for a season, a day of retribution will come!" (148–149), a message reiterated in the novel's final lines (165). The treacherous sins of Edmund's forefather, Walter, are thus exposed and punished, after which Edmund's violated parents are, finally, jointly buried. Deadly to the narrative in its detail and consuming almost a third of its pages, Reeve's painstaking delineation of the legal aspects of Edmund's inheritance renders her middle-class preoccupations tediously and anachronistically clear.

While *Baron* has been denounced as "a footnote to literary history" (Spector 98), it bridged the works of Walpole and Radcliffe. Reeve's use of the "restrained supernatural"—her groaning, accusatory ghost in armour lacks the outlandish excesses of Walpole's supernatural machinery—helped lay the groundwork for ANN RADCLIFFE's strategy of reconciling the marvelous and the probable by way of her unique technique of the "explained supernatural." *Baron* may lack *Castle's* dreamy atmospherics, but Reeve's showcasing of dreams as a providential device and her use of the gothic to reaffirm a Christian worldview made a considerable impact on the gothic tradition. Perhaps most importantly, Reeve's incorporation of the "merit in obscurity" creed from the novel of sensibility rendered the gothic more acceptable to respectable female readers and writers.

**Further Reading**

Reeve, Clara. *The Old English Baron.* In *The Old English Baron* by Clara Reeve and *The Castle of Otranto* by Horace Walpole, edited by Laura L. Runge, 39–165. Glen Allen, Virginia: College Publishing, 2002.

Spector, Robert Donald. *The English Gothic: A Bibliographic Guide to Writers from Horace Walpole to Mary Shelley.* Westport, Conn.: Greenwood Press, 1984.

Trainer, James. Introduction to *The Old English Baron,* by Clara Reeve, edited by James Trainer, vii-xxiv. Oxford: Oxford University Press, 2003.

—Carol Margaret Davison

## "On First Looking into Chapman's Homer"
**John Keats** (1816)

Unlike his classically educated (upper-class) contemporaries PERCY BYSSHE SHELLEY and LORD BYRON, JOHN KEATS could not read Greek. He probably acquainted himself with Homer through the popular translations of Alexander Pope, the 18th-century neoclassical poet with a penchant for heroic couplets. To Keats's romantic sensibility, Pope's translation may have seemed stilted and dull. After discovering a copy of George Chapman's 17th-century translation of Homer, Keats and his friend Charles Cowden Clarke read passages aloud to each other throughout the night. As he walked home at dawn, Keats began composing. When

Clarke sat down for breakfast at 10:00 that morning, he found before him a copy of "On First Looking into Chapman's Homer."

The poem, published in 1816, is an example of the Italian or Petrarchan sonnet, which is divided between eight lines (the octave) and six (the sestet). The rhyme scheme in the octave is *abbaabba;* in the sestet it is *cdcdcd* or some variant. The two sections usually represent a division in thought: The octave may present a situation and the sestet a comment; or the octave a question and the sestet an answer. In the octave, travel and exploration become extended metaphors for reading. Keats has "travell'd" in the "realms of gold" (l. 1). He has explored classical literature, and he has visited vicariously "many goodly states and kingdoms" (l. 2), including the "western islands" where poets pledge their loyalty to Apollo, the god of poetry; yet he has only been "told" of "one wide expanse" where "deep-brow'd Homer ruled" (ll. 5–6). He remains unmoved by the translations of Homer until he hears Chapman "speak out loud and bold" (l. 8).

In the sestet, Keats moves beyond exploration to discovery. Through the use of two similes, he conveys his emotion. Before, he could not "breathe" the "pure serene" of the work (l. 7) because the translation did not move him; now, he feels the experience: "Then felt I like some watcher of the skies / When a new planet swims into his ken [view]" (ll. 9–10). In the second simile, he likens himself to an early explorer: "Or like stout [brave] Cortez when with eagle eyes / He star'd at the Pacific" (ll. 11–12). Much critical debate has ensued about Keats's use of "Cortez" since it was Balboa who discovered the Pacific. Susan Wolfson assumes Keats intentionally used "Cortez" rather than "Balboa" since Cortez was not the first European to view the Pacific, just as Keats was not the first to read Chapman's translation (Wolfson 221). What is relevant, according to Vincent Newey, is that each, Cortez and Keats, responds to his discovery with "freedom of spirit and sublime exaltation" (Newey 184).

In the sestet, familiar elements of Romanticism emerge as Keats focuses on an emotion so overpowering that it renders the explorers speechless. The sonnet is not just about Keats's emotion when he discovers Chapman's translation; it is about the excitement that accompanies any discovery that changes one's universe. As a Romantic, Keats aptly moves from one to all, as he includes along with himself, the astronomer, the explorer and all men as they stand figuratively together, awe-struck, on "a peak in Darien" (l. 14).

## Further Reading

Keats, John. *John Keats: Complete Poems.* Edited by Jack Stillinger. Cambridge, Mass.: Belknap Press of Harvard University Press, 1982.

Newey, Vincent. "Keats, History, and the Poets." In *Keats and History,* edited by Nicholas Roe, 165–193. Cambridge: Cambridge University Press, 1995.

Wolfson, Susan. *The Questioning Presence: Wordsworth, Keats, and the Interrogative Mode in Romantic Poetry.* Ithaca, N.Y.: Cornell University Press, 1986.

—Beth Jensen

## "On This Day I Complete My Thirty-Sixth Year" Lord Byron (1824)

LORD BYRON wrote this poem on his birthday, January 22, 1824, in Missolonghi, Greece, where he had become part of the movement to liberate the Greeks from Turkish oppression. Most believe it was his last poem, as he had written no poetry since leaving Italy. For many decades, therefore, it appeared last in anthologies of his collected works and became one of his best-known lyrics. In fact, his final poem was "I watched thee when the foe was at our side," written later that day and unpublished until 1887. Besides sharing the same composition date, internal evidence in both poems indicates that they were inspired by Lukas Chalandrutsanos, a 15-year-old Greek youth who joined Byron at Argostoli and became the center of his emotional life.

The poem begins with Byron lamenting the loss of his powers of attraction: Lukas proved to be indifferent to his affections. The disappointment in failing to entice Lukas was bitter to one whom so many had loved, prompting Byron to write, "'Tis time this heart should be unmoved / Since others it has ceased to move" (ll. 1–2). Lukas was far more interested in riding at the front of the cavalcade of Byron's troops and in his gifts of expensive clothes, lavish pistols, and pocket money.

This poem is divided into 10 numbered stanzas, composed of four lines each of iambic tetrameter, with an interlocking rhyme scheme of *abab*. It begins with the personal complaints of aging: "My days are in the yellow leaf" (l. 5). In addition, Byron wishes for the dispelling of his emotional turmoil in being rejected by Lukas: "But 'tis not *thus*—and 'tis not *here* / Such thoughts should shake my soul, nor *now*" (ll. 17–18). He longs to "Tread those reviving passions down" (l. 29), believing that he should be "indifferent" to "the smile or frown of beauty" (l. 31). By the fifth stanza, Byron shifts gears, pushing away his more sensitive feelings in an effort to collect his passion for a nobler aim than mere mortal love. The poem ends as a stirring call to arms for himself and all of Greece as she embarks on her quest for freedom.

When contemplating his involvement in the Greek cause, Byron had cast himself in terms of American revolutionaries. His arrival on the scene, in fact, saw him heralded as a kind of messiah, complete with a 21-gun salute and crowds of Greeks and philhellenes cheering him ashore. His real role, however, was rather limited, and he encountered infighting among various political factions, which made it difficult to get anything practical accomplished. In this, he discerned the truth that his role was largely ornamental; the Greeks were not interested in him as a military leader, merely in the publicity value of his name. In this way Byron ultimately had an impact on the actual fighting as his name got the world interested and involved in the Greek cause. His death in Greece did even more for the war effort than his living presence.

It can be argued that this poem sees the poet pushing for a global campaign to rouse support for the cause. He urges philhellen to "Awake!" (l. 25). He sets the scene with vivid images—"The Sword—the Banner—and the Field" (l. 21)—and urges readers to "Glory and Greece around us see!" (l. 22). Byron's fervor reaches its apex with the closing lines: "Seek out—less often sought than found / A Soldier's grave—for thee the best, / Then look around and choose thy ground / And take thy rest" (ll. 37–40).

## Further Reading

Byron, George Gordon Byron, Baron. *Lord Byron: The Complete Poetical Works.* Vol. 7. Edited by Jerome J. McGann. Oxford: Clarendon Press, 1986.

Crompton, Louis. *Byron and Greek Love: Homophobia in 19th-Century England.* Berkeley: University of California Press, 1985.

Marchand, Leslie A. *Byron: A Biography.* Vol. 3. New York: Knopf, 1957.

———. *Byron: A Portrait.* Chicago: University of Chicago Press, 1970.

Moore, Doris Langley. *The Late Lord Byron.* Philadelphia: Lippincott, 1961.

Robinson, Charles E. "The Influence of Byron on America." *Byron Journal* 5 (1977): 50–66.

St. Claire, William. *"That Greece Might Still Be Free": The Philhellenes in the War for Independence.* London: Oxford University Press, 1972.

Wu, Duncan. *Romanticism: An Anthology.* Oxford: Blackwell, 2006.

—Denise Tischler Millstein

## Opie, Amelia Alderson (1769–1853)

Amelia Alderson Opie was especially well-known in the early 19th century for novels such as *Adeline Mowbray* (1804) and *Valentine's Eve* (1816) and antislavery poems such as "The Negro Boy's Tale" (1802) and "The Black Man's Lament; or How to Make Sugar" (1826). She was born on November 12, 1769, into a supportive family in Norwich, a market town in the east of England. Her father and mother influenced a young Amelia in a myriad of ways. Dr. James Alderson had liberal views and frequently attended poor patients, demonstrating a compassion that would provide an example for the fledging writer. Likewise, her mother, Amelia Briggs Alderson, had unconventional child-rearing methods. For example, upon witnessing a young Amelia's fearful reaction to an African man, Aboar, Mrs. Alderson insisted that her child befriend the man. Amelia's subsequent friendship with Aboar was a catalyst for her adult sympathy for enslaved peoples. Indeed her commitment to the abolitionist movement was an important factor in her literary work.

In 1798 Amelia Alderson married the painter John Opie, who encouraged her to write; he died nine years later. By the 1820s, she was taking a deep interest in the Anti-Slavery Society (Brightwell 189). She seems to have read the parliamentary debates on SLAVERY, and her responses to them permeated "The Black Man's Lament; or, How to Make Sugar" (Eberle 86). Her detailed discussion of sugar production in the West Indies, a comparison of the English peasant to the slave, and references to religious conversion demonstrate her knowledge of the political and economic terrain.

In "The Black Man's Lament," Opie depicts an enslaved man, providing him with the voice customarily denied a subordinate person or inanimate object. In her verse, Opie imagines a bondsman articulating the concerns of his community and responding to the pulse of the British debates. Spliced together in this single speaker are the presumed desires of actual slaves and her authorial agenda. In order to have the imaginary bondsman speak directly to the political climate of Britain, Opie had to insert her voice into this fictional being. This poetic ventriloquism attempted to provide insights into the bondsman's feelings, shaping his image to the liking of domestic readers. British women writers such as Opie were mindful of the widespread reservations about the emancipation of the colonial slave; therefore, they devised literary techniques such as vocal appropriation to appeal to their readership. Subsequently, as well as the ventriloquized enslaved man or woman, Opie would also represent slaves as yearning for religious teachings. Her moralistic themes were ideal for advocating the emancipation of slaves, and her literary contributions critiqued many of Romantic-era issues such as slavery, gender, and revolution. Amelia Opie published regularly throughout her life and befriended numerous other writers, including SIR WALTER SCOTT and MME. ANNE-LOUISE-GERMAINE DE STAËL. She died in Norwich on December 2, 1753.

See also "STANZAS WRITTEN UNDER AEOLUS'S HARP."

## Further Reading

Brightwell, Cecilia Lucy. *Memoir of Amelia Opie.* London: Religious Tract Society, 1855.

Eberle, Roxanne. "'Tales of Truth?': Amelia Opie's Antislavery Poetics." In *Romanticism Women Poets:*

*Opening the Doors of Reception,* edited by Harriet Kramer Linkin and Stephen C. Behrendt. 71–98. Lexington: University of Kentucky Press, 1999.

Ferguson, Moira. *Subject to Others: British Women Writers and Colonial Slavery, 1670–1834.* New York: Routledge, 1992.

Howard, Carol. "'The Story of the Pineapple': Sentimental Abolitionism and Moral Motherhood in Amelia Opie's *Adeline Mowbray.*" *Studies in the Novel* 30 (1998): 355–376.

Macgregor, Margaret Eliot. *Amelia Alderson Opie: Worlding and Friend.* Northampton, Mass: Smith College, 1933.

Opie, Amelia. "The Black Man's Lament; or How to Make Sugar." In *The Poetry of Slavery: An Anglo-American Anthology 1764–1865,* edited by Marcus Wood, 271–277. New York: Oxford University Press, 2003.

———. *The Collected Poems of Amelia Alderson Opie.* Edited by Shelley King. Oxford: Oxford University Press, 2008.

———. "The Negro Boy's Tale." In *The Poetry of Slavery: An Anglo-American Anthology 1764–1865,* edited by Marcus Wood, 266–270. New York: Oxford University Press, 2003.

—Marilyn Walker

## orientalism

The term *orientalism* refers to scholarly, cultural, literary, and artistic representations of the Middle East, South Asia, and other geocultural regions—for example, parts of the African continent and the south of Spain, which were included in the Orient. During the Romantic period, the relationship between Great Britain and the East was marked both by the substantial expansion of British colonial territories in the East and by rising numbers of Western travelers who journeyed eastward. An ever-growing number of travelogues, such as William Hodges's highly successful *Travels in India* (1793), Thomas Daniell's *Oriental Scenery* (1808), and James Forbes's *Oriental Memoirs* (1813), reported about the culture, customs, and traditions of oriental countries. Exhibitions such as the Venetian explorer Giovanni Belzoni's 1821 Egyptian Exhibition in London showcased historical treasures and oriental objects of curiosity to great public acclaim. Oriental fashion, music, architectural styles, commodities, and other cultural products came into vogue during this period and were imported, recreated, and consumed on an unprecedented scale. Academic chairs and research centers for oriental studies were founded across Europe. Eminent orientalists, notably Sir William Jones (1746–94) and Abraham-Hyacinthe Anquetil-Duperron (1731–1805), translated numerous works from Persian, Arabic, and Sanskrit and introduced European readers to the learning and thought of ancient Eastern cultures. The Royal Asiatic Society of Great Britain and Ireland was founded in 1823 and supplied the institutional framework for the Oriental Translation Committee, which sought to promote the translation of oriental works.

The profound influence of oriental scholarship is evident in the realism of the orientalist descriptions of many literary works of the period. Works such as WILLIAM BECKFORD's *VATHEK* (1786), Elizabeth Hamilton's epistolary novel *Letters of a Hindoo Rajah* (1797), and ROBERT SOUTHEY's narrative poems *Thalaba the Destroyer* (1801) and *The Curse of Kehama* (1810) included extensive scholarly footnotes and annotations. Probably the most influential Romantic writer of orientalist texts was LORD BYRON, whose *CHILDE HAROLD'S PILGRIMAGE* (1812) and a series of "Eastern Tales" (1813–16), inspired by his own travels in Turkey, Greece, and Albania, strongly shaped subsequent orientalist works. Byron's texts, like the orientalist narrative poems of PERCY BYSSHE SHELLEY and THOMAS MOORE, often follow a romance or quest plot and associate the Orient with erotic femininity. Conversely, works of late Romanticism such as THOMAS DE QUINCEY's *CONFESSIONS OF AN ENGLISH OPIUM-EATER* (1821) increasingly connect the Orient with guilt, terror, and the dangers of infection and madness.

In the 20th century a significant body of critical and theoretical work has grown around the concept of orientalism. In his influential study *Orientalism* (1978), Edward Said has correlated Western epistemological discourses of orientalism with the rise of colonial empires. Said views the Romantic period as formative for the attitudes of the West toward the East: "The difference between representations of the Orient before the last third of the 18th century and those after it . . . is that the range of representations expanded enormously in the later period. . . . Europe came to be known to the Orient more scientifically, to live in it with greater authority and discipline than ever before" (Said 1995, 22). Said's controversial concept of orientalism as "a Western style for dominating, restructuring, and having authority over the Orient" (3) has been scrutinized by many scholars in recent years who have suggested that cultural exchanges between Europe and oriental countries were more pluralistic and complex than Said's frequently ahistorical and essentialist argument concedes (see, for instance, Ballaster, Irwin, and Yegenoglu).

See also EPISTOLARY FICTION.

## Further Reading

Ballaster, Ros. *Fabulous Orients: Fictions of the East in England, 1662–1785.* Oxford: Oxford University Press, 2005.

Fulford, Tim, and Peter J. Kitson, eds. *Romanticism and Colonialism: Writing and Empire, 1780–1830.* New York: Cambridge University Press, 1998.

Irwin, Robert. *Dangerous Knowledge: Orientalism and its Discontents.* New York: Overlook Press, 2006.

Makdisi, Saree, and Felicity Nussbaum, eds. *The Arabian Nights in Historical Context.* Oxford: Oxford University Press, 2008.

Said, Edward. *Orientalism.* 1978. Reprint, Harmondsworth, Eng.: Penguin, 1995.

———. *Culture and Imperialism.* London: Chatto & Windus, 1993.

Weir, David. *Brahma in the West: William Blake and the Oriental Renaissance.* Albany: State University of New York Press, 2003.

Yegenoglu, Meyda. *Colonial Fantasies: Towards a Feminist Reading of Orientalism.* Cambridge: Cambridge University Press, 1998.

—Katharina Boehm

## Owenson, Sydney (Lady Morgan) (ca. 1776–1859)

Sydney Owenson used to tell an apocryphal story that she was born on the Irish Sea, halfway between England and Ireland, as her actor father brought his English wife back to his native land. In the context of Ireland's political union with mainland Britain (1800) and the often violent conflict that continued to rage between the Irish and the English into the 20th century, Owenson's emphasis on her mixed national heritage appears to have been a necessary strategy to win over English readers at a time when any sympathetic representation of the Irish was perceived as politically hazardous. That she chose to subtitle her third and most successful novel, *The WILD IRISH GIRL* (1806) was judged to be so politically contentious that she had difficulties in finding a publisher willing to take it.

Owenson's interest in Irish culture and politics was forged in the binational and bireligious household in which she grew up and which was visited by many of Dublin's prominent writers and politicians. After the collapse of her father's theater, she briefly worked as a governess before turning to writing as a means of supporting her family. *The Wild Irish Girl*, in which an English aristocrat falls in love with an Irish princess and learns to appreciate Irish people and culture, was the first of four highly successful and influential novels that she wrote about Ireland; The others were *O'Donnel* (1814), *Florence Maccarthy* (1818), and *The O'Briens and the O'Flahertys* (1827). Glorvina, the heroine of *The Wild Irish Girl,* so captured the public imagination that Owenson often appeared in polite society in Dublin and London to entertain guests in the guise of her fictional character. In 1811 she published *The Missionary,* an orientalist novel (see ORIENTALISM) that focuses on the love affair between a Portuguese missionary and an Indian priestess. Like *The Wild Irish Girl* before it, *The Missionary* seeks to resolve questions of empire and racial and cultural difference through a recourse to sentimental solutions. The novel was imitated by fellow Irish novelist CHARLES MATURIN and much praised both by Owenson's Irish compatriot THOMAS MOORE and by PERCY BYSSHE SHELLEY, who wrote his poem "Alastor, or The Spirit Of Solitude" (1816) under its orientalist influence.

In 1812, while in the household of the marquess of Abercorn, Owenson married the Abercorns' doctor Thomas Morgan, who later gave up his profession to help his wife with her writing;

he was later knighted. In total, Owenson produced 70 volumes, including poetry; travel books; sketches; articles; a biography of the painter Salvatore Rosa; a comic opera; and a feminist history, the unfinished *Woman and Her Master: A History of the Female Sex from the Earliest Period.* Her work was widely translated, and literary friends included Moore, the Scottish poet Thomas Campbell, the essayist CHARLES LAMB, and the novelist MARY WOLLSTONECRAFT SHELLEY. Despite the overt political coloring of her novels, it was her travel writing that generated the most controversy: Her book *France* (1817) saw conservative critics attack her for impiety and demand that her husband and brother-in-law have their titles revoked; and another book, *Italy* (1821), was seized and burned in the Austrian Empire and Owenson was banned from ever traveling there. Both politically controversial and strongly independent, Owenson kept control of her finances throughout her marriage, and in 1837 she was the first woman writer to be awarded a pension of £300 by the British government. She died in London on April 14, 1859.

**Further Reading**

Campbell, Mary. *Lady Morgan: The Life and Times of Sydney Owenson.* London: Pandora Press, 1988.

Williams, Julia McElhattan. *Love Beyond the Pale: Sydney Owenson's The Wild Irish Girl, Maria Edgeworth's The Absentee and the Boundaries of Colonial Power.* Boston: Northeastern University Press, 1991.

—Sondeep Kandola

## "Ozymandias" Percy Bysshe Shelley (1818)

This famous sonnet was written in 1817 and published in 1818. In it, a traveler comes across the remains of an enormous statue in the desert, evidently a tribute to a once-great Pharaoh. The inscription on the statue reads: "My name is Ozymandias, King of Kings: / Look on my works, ye mighty, and despair!" (ll. 10–11). But as the traveler realizes, these words are in vain for now there is "Nothing" to be seen and "Round the decay / Of that colossal wreck, boundless and bare, / The lone and level sands stretch far away" (ll. 12–14).

Evoking the work of the historians C. F. Volney and Edward Gibbon, PERCY BYSSHE SHELLEY's reflections on the remnants of the Ancient Egyptian ruler Rameses II's (1304–1213 B.C.) are reminders of the Romantic poets' interest in ancient civilizations. However they also associate this poem with the larger political preoccupations and anxieties of the late 18th century. In an age of burgeoning individualism and egoism, Shelley's sonnet offered a stark counterpoint to egotistical strivings and political tyrannies.

The poem resulted from a writing contest with his friend Horace Smith, who also produced a sonnet entitled "Ozymandias." Smith's sestet more directly relates the inevitable transience of empires to London's future fall. The fact that Shelley's narrator demonstrates volatility without directly including England in its apocalyptic observations either suggests that the irony between Ozymandias's ignorant boasts and the unanticipated transience and decline of his empire is eternal and transcultural, or that Great Britain, with its unacknowledged poetic legislators, might actually escape the fate of Ozymandias's misperceptions. This traveler's tale of a former, fallen empire can also be seen as a muted echo of ANNA LAETITIA BARBAULD's earlier "EIGHTEEN HUNDRED AND ELEVEN" in its call to recognize the limits of imperial powers (invoking France's transition and quietly implying the possibility of England's vulnerability). It is also reminiscent of the situation faced by the wedding guest in SAMUEL TAYLOR COLERIDGE's "THE RIME OF THE ANCIENT MARINER," who hears a tale of decline told by the traveling mariner. While Coleridge's wedding guest becomes a sadder and wiser man upon hearing the mariner's tale, we receive no such confirmation from the narrator of Shelley's sonnet, who simply relates the story to us without overtly judging the tale, its traveling teller, or its decayed subject. It is a composition about decomposition, a tale told in the spirit of Shelley's "ODE TO THE WEST WIND," which heralds winter but also quietly prophesies the coming spring renewal.

The exact critical stance of the poem has been a source of much debate. It was published in LEIGH HUNT's radical periodical the *Examiner,* and its attack on tyrannical rulers fits that paper's political stance. Additionally, its matter-of-fact tone challenges the subjective inspirations and vitality of WILLIAM WORDSWORTH's "LINES WRITTEN A FEW MILES ABOVE TINTERN ABBEY." In this sense, the Shelley poem has also been read as a challenge to the statements of earlier Romantic period writers, yet it also continues some of their work. WILLIAM BLAKE, Wordsworth, and Coleridge all commented upon imperial visions and kingly boasts as well. So although different in the degree to which it affirms Romantic preoccupations with uncertainty in this transitory period, Shelley's sonnet can also be linked to the work of his predecessors and peers via its preoccupations with tyranny, with the relationship between art and empire, and with the nature and function of art and the artist.

This last point is significant, as is Shelley's choice of the sonnet form. Choosing a sonnet invokes a long tradition of poetic excellence, a strong British literary history and a demonstration of the poet's mighty workmanship. Early sonnets by British authors such as Edmund Spenser and William Shakespeare often feature poet-speakers who brag about the immortalizing powers of their poetry. The ironies of using this form to reveal that "The best laid schemes o' mice and men / Gang aft agley" (ROBERT BURNS, "TO A MOUSE," ll. 39–40) raise further questions about the lasting value of poetry and poems. While the words on the statue's pedestal ironically reflect the temporality of Ozymandias's empire, this poem can also be said to call attention to the shelf life of poets, including Shelley himself: How long will they be remembered and celebrated?

A slightly different way of looking at the poem is to say that Ozymandias does in fact survive and inspire, though not in the ways that he intended to. It is the power of literary mediation, of storytelling, that transcends the powers of kings and sculptors. Shelley's sonnet, both in its form and subject matter, recognizes that the present stands on the decayed shoulders of past giants, like JOHN KEATS's poetic reaction in "On Seeing the Elgin Marbles." Shelley's sonnet also contains many of the same questions posed by Keats's "ODE ON A GRECIAN URN:" Both meditate on the relationship between poetry and the other arts, and both ulti-

mately affirm the ability of poetry to transcend the unnaturalness of cold images and sculptural stasis. "Ozymandias" additionally confirms the power of poetic narrative over the limited and limiting use of words on the pedestal (even though those words outlast both the ruler's kingdom and the sculptor's creative mockery).

Overall, Shelley's poem presents us with a compendium of artistic dialogues (the mocking hand of the sculptor, the storytelling traveler who comes across the ruin, and finally the sonnet's narrator) that outweigh the singular (and ultimately fallible) power of a selfish ruler who has become the subject of a collective story but not its author. Ozymandias's story is neither timeless nor about timelessness; it is an affirmation of poetic circulation and a record of Shelley's continual attempt to reinvigorate the sonnet form.

## Further Reading

Austin, Timothy R. "Narrative Transmission: Shifting Gears in Shelley's 'Ozymandias.'" In *Dialogue and Critical Discourse: Language, Culture, Critical Theory*, edited by Michael Macovski, 29–46. Oxford: Oxford University Press, 1997.

Brown, James. "'Ozymandias': The Riddle of the Sands." *Keats-Shelley Review* 12 (1998): 51–75.

Everest, Kelvin. "'Ozymandias': The Text in Time." *Essays and Studies* 45 (1992): 24–42.

Freedman, William. "Postponement and Perspectives in Shelley's 'Ozymandias.'" *Studies in Romanticism* 25, no. 1 (1986): 63–73.

Janowitz, Anne. "Shelley's Monument to Ozymandias." *Philological Quarterly* 63, no. 4 (1984): 477–491.

Johnson, Anthony L. "A Study in Romantic Form: Shelley's 'Ozymandias.'" *Textus: English Studies in Italy* 7 (1994): 133–162.

Shelley, Percy. "Ozymandias." In *The Complete Poetical Works of Percy Bysshe Shelley*, edited by Thomas Hutchison, 550. London: Oxford University Press. 1943.

Sng, Zachary. "The Construction of Lyric Subjectivity in Shelley's 'Ozymandias.'" *Studies in Romanticism* 37, no. 2 (1998): 217–233.

—Jon Saklofske

# P

## Paine, Thomas (1737–1809)

Thomas Paine was one of the most controversial and divisive figures of the early Romantic period. Born in rural Norfolk on February 9, 1737, to a Quaker corset maker and his Anglican wife, Paine went on to become a significant figure in both the AMERICAN REVOLUTION and FRENCH REVOLUTION and played a central role in the "revolution controversy" that erupted in England in the 1790s.

The crucial turning point in Paine's life occurred in September 1774, when he was introduced to Benjamin Franklin in a London coffee-house. Until this meeting, Paine's life had been rather undistinguished: He had been a corset maker, a sailor, a shopkeeper, an English teacher, and a customs official; his only published writing was a pamphlet inspired by his time as an exciseman, in which he bewailed the poor conditions in which he and his fellow officers had worked. It had not been a success, and Franklin persuaded him to emigrate to America. It was there that Paine's first significant work appeared. *Common Sense,* a pamphlet that was published anonymously in January 1776, was a strident blast against British rule in America. It called for the rejection of MONARCHY, the end of America's role as a colony, and the establishment of a constitutional republic. The widely pirated pamphlet sold more than 150,000 copies in its first year of publication and helped galvanize public opinion in favour of the American Revolution.

After a spell in the militia and service as secretary to the Committee on Foreign Affairs (1777–79), Paine eventually returned to England and then went from there to France, where, as a result of his friendship with the marquis de Lafayette, he became involved in the turmoil of the French Revolution. When EDMUND BURKE published his *Reflections of the Revolution in France* (1790), in which he condemned the Revolution and argued that the members of any society did not possess the right to overthrow their leaders, Paine responded with his masterpiece *The RIGHTS OF MAN.* Where Burke had asserted the importance of tradition and the necessity that the living generation respect the system of government laid down by their forebears, Paine argued for natural rights that emerge as a result of rational thought. He not only defended the French Revolution against Burke's condemnation but called for revolution in Britain and the establishment of a republic.

*The Rights of Man* was written in clear, uncluttered prose, designed both to contrast with Burke's more florid and oratorical style and to be accessible to as wide an audience as possible. The book was published in two parts to further reduce the cost to the reader, and it proved to be both enormously popular and controversial. Pitt's government made clear that they considered the book to be seditious and allowed Paine to flee to France in September 1792. Tried for sedition in his absence, he was banished from the country. He did not return to Britain again.

Much of Paine's final major work, *The Age of Reason* (1793, 1795) was written while he languished in a Parisian prison cell, where he was sent for falling foul of Robespierre and his Montagards in the intensely factionalized Paris of the Reign of Terror. *The Age of Reason* is a treatise on religion, in which Paine argues for the destruction of organized religion and against the infallibility of the Bible. He condemns Christianity as superstition but argues against atheism in favour of deism or natural religion. Having (by his own account) escaped execution at the guillotine only by an oversight, Paine survived the Terror and eventually returned to America, dying in New York City on June 8, 1809.

**Further Reading**

Ayer, A. J. *Thomas Paine.* New York: Atheneum, 1988.

Paine, Thomas. *Common Sense, The Rights of Man and Other Essential Writings of Thomas Paine.* London: Signet Classics, 2003.

—David McAllister

## "Pantisocracy" Samuel Taylor Coleridge
(1794)

Written in 1794 but not published until more than a decade after the poet's death, this early sonnet represents the hopes that SAMUEL TAYLOR COLERIDGE harbored for the plan he hatched with ROBERT SOUTHEY to form a utopian community, dubbed a "pantisocracy," in North America. The plan collapsed less than a year after this poem was written, as Coleridge and Southey found themselves unable to agree on the administration of the proposed community. The sonnet observes a regular Petrarchan pattern and is therefore a "legitimate sonnet" according to a canon of criticism already mostly abandoned by the time of its publication, but very much current when Coleridge wrote the poem. Its imagery of the "Visionary Soul" (l. 1) longing for "the moonlight Roundelay" (l. 7) and a "Holy Spell" cast by "Wizard Passions" (l. 8) would mark it as among Coleridge's earliest poems even if the date were less clearly fixed, though dreams and nightmares frequently appear throughout Coleridge's writings.

In the poem's octave (first eight lines), the speaker claims to renounce nostalgia and regret, traveling across the sea "Sublime of Hope" (l. 5)

toward a land where "Virtue calm" (l. 6) can prevail. The reference to sublimity here is striking, as the prevailing understanding of the SUBLIME at the time was that of EDMUND BURKE, who stated that the essential quality of the sublime was the dread it evoked. The vastness and unseen depths of the sea being key marks of this conception of the sublime, the speaker's rendering of the "Ocean swell / Sublime of Hope" (ll. 4–5) is a grand fiat of imagination, the "visionary soul" at work.

The sestet (final six lines) quickly recapitulates the progress of the octave, as grieving eyes find "Tears of doubt-mingled Joy" (l. 10) at the enlightenment to come in the New World. The final conceit in the sestet contemplates sleepers awakening from the "Precipices of distempered Sleep" (l. 11) to "see the rising Sun" (l. 13) whose rays pierce through "Fiends" (l. 12), whose "Revels" stand in sharp contrast to the "holy spell" woven by the "Wizard Passions" (l. 8). These "rays of pleasance" blend the archaic sense of "pleasance" found in the opening lines of Geoffrey Chaucer's medieval *Canterbury Tales* with the then-current sense of the term, used in architecture and landscaping. In this latter sense, the "Pleasance" (l. 14) reprises the "cottag'd Dell" (l. 5) in the octave.

The poem may also contain hints of the impending failure of the pantisocracy. The speaker begins by saying "No more" but proceeds to "dwell" for the entire first quatrain on that which he will forget. The imagined goings-on in the "cottag'd Dell" are less affecting than the "Shame and Anguish" that "weigh" on the speaker (ll. 3, 2), and the "Joys that were" (l. 2) have a reality for speaker and reader that the "doubt-mingled Joy" (l. 10) of the future still lacks. The imagined future seems real only in the speaker's enthusiastic assertions, compared to which even the actual experience of waking from a bad dream may seem solid. The poem remains, however, an important example of Coleridge's "visionary" verse, and of the optimism about the power of imagination and enthusiasm that characterized early Romantic verse.

**Further Reading**

Coleridge, Samuel Taylor. "Pantisocracy." In *English Romantic Writers,* 2nd ed., edited by David Perkins, 513. Fort Worth, Tex.: Harcourt Brace, 1995.

———. "Pantisocracy." In *Selected Poetry and Prose of Coleridge*, edited by Donald A. Stauffer, 88. New York: Random House, 1951.

—Peter Epps

## "Partial Muse, The" (Sonnet 1) Charlotte Smith (1784)

The first poem of CHARLOTTE SMITH's *ELEGIAC SONNETS AND OTHER POEMS*, "The Partial Muse" is a Shakespearean sonnet introducing the poetic persona of the volume as someone who has been given a particular SENSIBILITY toward suffering. While this apparent gift of sensibility bestowed on her by her muse is accepted by the speaker with a certain grace, it is also described as a curse, condemning her to unhappiness. In the course of its three quatrains and closing couplet, the sonnet develops into "a complex poem about the relationship between the poet, her muse, and her reader" (Robinson 203).

The first quatrain of the poem outlines how the speaker has been accompanied by her muse from her "earliest hours" (l. 1) on and offers the image of "garlands" (l. 4) that her muse fashions for her from "wild flowers" (l. 3). This early in the poem, the muse is not presented as particularly sinister. On the contrary, it should be noted that all the words bearing negative connotations ("rugged path," "doom'd" [l. 2]) refer to the speaker's life rather than any influence the muse has on it.

The second quatrain, however, introduces a different aspect of the speaker's poetic talents by contrasting her life with that of those who are not blessed with these talents and are "far, far happier" (l. 5) as a consequence. This vantage point is continued in the third quatrain, in which the speaker's empathic qualities are further outlined. The closing couplet offers a summary of the dichotomy outlined in the preceding verses by asking "how dear the Muse's favours cost" (l. 13) and then giving a line which, in a note on the text, Smith herself identifies as a reference to Alexander Pope's poem "Eloisa to Abelard." As with the other intertextual references—such as the "wild flowers" evoking the madness of Shakespeare's King Lear (Fletcher 47)—Smith is keen to position her own writing among earlier works concerned with human suffering and the pity with which it is met. In adapting the final line of Pope's poem, it is particularly noteworthy that her paraphrase substitutes the plural pronoun *those* for the masculine pronoun *he*, thus deliberately including a woman's voice in the discourse of empathy and suffering so prominent in 18th-century poetry.

Above and beyond the obvious aspect of sensibility and of empathy with the suffering of others, the representation of nature as the young persona's nurturing environment and the expression of a poetic creed heavily biased toward emotion are typical of pre-Romantic and Romantic poetry. It is because of its overriding concern with the poet and her role that "The Partial Muse" has been described as "self-dramatising and self-referential" since it takes "the writer and her writing as its principal subject" (Fletcher 48).

### Further Reading

Fletcher, Loraine. *Charlotte Smith: A Critical Biography.* London: Palgrave, 2001.

Robinson, Daniel. "*Elegiac Sonnets*: Charlotte Smith's Formal Paradoxy." *Papers on Language and Literature* 39 (2003): 185–219.

Smith, Charlotte. *The Poems of Charlotte Smith.* Edited by Stuart Curran. New York: Oxford University Press 1993.

—Patrick Gill

## Peacock, Thomas Love (1785–1866)

Thomas Love Peacock, the foremost prose satirist of English Romanticism, was born on October 18, 1785, in Weymouth, Dorset, England. His formal education ended early due to his family's reduced financial circumstances, and he was largely self-educated, indulging in literary pursuits at a young age. After a brief stint as a merchant clerk, Peacock traveled through England and Wales in 1806 to gather material for what became the book-length long poem *The Genius of the Thames* (1810). On his travels he met his future wife, Jane Gryffydh, a parson's daughter with whom he was to have three children.

During a spell of financial distress, Peacock's publisher and benefactor, Thomas Hookam, introduced him to PERCY BYSSHE SHELLEY (his junior by seven years), with whom he quickly became close friends. Through Shelley's mediation, Peacock made the acquaintance of other Romantic authors, such as LEIGH HUNT and JOHN KEATS, and developed an interest in literary satire, a genre in which he was to excel. *Headlong Hall*, the first of his acerbic conversation novels, was an immediate success when it came out in 1816. Peacock's second novel in this mold, *NIGHTMARE ABBEY*, was published in 1818. The latter book used his inside knowledge of English Romanticism to caricature the movement's most prominent poets—Shelley, SAMUEL TAYLOR COLERIDGE, and LORD BYRON. His essay "The Four Ages of Poetry" (1820) was a similarly trenchant comment on what he held to be the inferiority of Romantic poetry to the classical verse of earlier ages. This piece, perhaps his most frequently anthologized work, was part of a conversation with Shelley, who used it in "A DEFENSE OF POETRY."

In 1819 an engagement at the East India Company put an end to Peacock's financial troubles. His coworker at the company was James Mill (the father of John Stuart Mill), who introduced him to the leading philosophical radicals of the time, including the Utilitarian thinker Jeremy Bentham. Peacock's satiric romance *The Misfortunes of Elphin* (a reworking of several Welsh legends) appeared in 1829, and his celebrated *Crotchet Castle* (a cutting satire on the 19th-century belief in social and intellectual progress) in 1831. Absorbed in office work, he stopped writing in the 1840s, although he became friends with numerous leading Victorian literati, among them Benjamin Disraeli; William Makepeace Thackeray; Thomas Babington Macaulay; and George Meredith, who became his son-in-law. Peacock's later works are less quarrelsome and mostly look back to his involvement with the famous Romantic poets who were his friends. Most notable among these works are his *Memoirs of Percy Bysshe Shelley* (1858, 1860). Peacock tragically outlived his two daughters. His health badly shaken, he died in his sleep on January 23, 1866.

Perhaps the most reclusive among the English Romantics, Peacock had poetic gifts that are apparent in his few personal lyrics (which won praise from Shelley, Byron, and Edgar Allan Poe, and crucially influenced JOHN KEATS). He is best remembered, however, as the most outstanding satirist of English Romanticism, and his reputation has constantly risen over the course of the 20th century. His satiric romances and conversation novels—which combine verse and prose, flights of fancy and astute renderings of reality—stand as major innovations in the English novel tradition.

**Further Reading**

Butler, Marilyn. *Peacock Displayed: A Satirist in His Context*. London: Routledge & Kegan, 1979.

Dawson, Carl. *His Fine Wit: A Study of Thomas Love Peacock*. London: Routledge & Kegan Paul, 1970.

Mills, Howard. *Peacock: His Circle and His Age*. Cambridge: Cambridge University Press, 1969.

Peacock, Thomas Love. *The Works of Thomas Love Peacock*. 10 vols. Edited by H. F. B. Brett-Smith and Clifford Jones. London: Constable, 1924–34.

Sage, Lorna, ed. *Peacock's Satirical Novels: A Casebook*. London: Macmillan, 1976.

Van Doren, Carl. *The Life of Thomas Love Peacock*. New York: Russell & Russell, 1966.

—Benjamin Kohlmann

### *Persuasion* **Jane Austen** (1817)

*Persuasion* (1817, with an 1818 date on the title page) was published posthumously following JANE AUSTEN's early death at the age of 41 in July 1817. One of its central concerns is the imagination that can exist behind the façade of manners and etiquette. Anne Elliot, the quiet heroine, has an "elegance of mind and sweetness of character" that her family does not appreciate. At 29 she has almost passed the marriageable age for women, her looks seem to have faded, and she finds herself in the role of the spinster aunt whom everybody exploits but nobody listens to. When her father, Sir Walter, and her eldest sister, Elizabeth—devastating satires of aristocratic arrogance—need advice regarding the family's money crises, they reject Anne's retrenchment proposal, opting instead to lease the family home and take up lodgings in Bath.

As in other works, Austen is interested in the reason why marriages do or do not take place.

Seven years earlier, Anne had been engaged to Frederick Wentworth. Her godmother, Lady Russell, had persuaded her to break off the engagement due to his lack of fortune. Now, he returns to the neighborhood as a captain made wealthy from the Napoleonic Wars. The FRENCH REVOLUTION and the Napoleonic Wars were major Romantic-era concerns, and the conversations of the multitude of naval officers in *Persuasion* showcase Austen's knowledge of these military conflicts, as well as her approval of the self-made gentleman. Upon his return, Anne is convinced that Captain Wentworth no longer cares for her, as he seems to enjoy the flirtatious attentions of the young Louisa Musgrove. Anne travels to Bath, one of the country's centers of aristocratic leisure, with Lady Russell, and they are eventually joined by the Musgroves, Captain Wentworth, and Wentworth's family. Anne is surprised to discover that her father and sister have reunited with their cousin Mr. Elliot in Bath because the two branches of the family had not been on speaking terms since Mr. Elliot made an imprudent marriage. Now that Mr. Elliot has been widowed, Elizabeth—delusional but ambitious—revives the hope she once had of marrying the heir to her father's estate. Yet Mr. Elliot soon turns his romantic attentions towards Anne. Mrs. Smith, an impoverished acquaintance whose situation acts as a stark reminder of the fate single women can expect, warns Anne that Mr. Elliot is only doing so in order to prevent Sir Walter from marrying Elizabeth's companion, the young widow Mrs. Clay. Meanwhile, Anne discovers that Louisa is engaged to Captain Benwick, a solemn man with whom Anne had discussed contemporary literature in Lyme. In these conversations, some of the more explicit connections between Austen's novel and the work of her romantic contemporaries become clear, as Captain Benwick specifically references SIR WALTER SCOTT's MARMION and *The Lady of the Lake* as well as LORD BYRON's THE GIAOUR and *The BRIDE OF ABYDOS*.

Two separate conclusions to *Persuasion* have survived, and most contemporary editions of the novel publish both endings. The draft that appeared in the first edition of Austen's novel dramatizes a conversation between Captain Harville and Anne Elliot. Wentworth overhears Anne's proclamation that women love "longest, when existence or when hope is gone" (256), and he responds by writing her a passionate letter declaring his love. In Austen's first draft of the conclusion, which survives in manuscript form, the love plot culminates in a conversation between Anne and Wentworth that clears up misunderstandings between the two lovers. Both versions of the conclusion see Anne and Wentworth united in matrimony.

## Further Reading

Austen, Jane. *Persuasion*. The Cambridge Edition of the Works of Jane Austen. Edited by Janet Todd and Antje Blank. Cambridge: Cambridge University Press, 2006.

Deresiewicz, William. *"Persuasion*: Widowhood and Waterloo." In *Jane Austen and the Romantic Poets*. New York: Columbia University Press, 2004, 127–158.

Waldron, Mary. *Jane Austen and the Fiction of Her Time*. Cambridge: Cambridge University Press, 2001.

—Alice Marie Villaseñor

## Peterloo Massacre (Manchester Massacre, Battle of Peterloo) (1819)

Variously called the Manchester Massacre and the Battle of Peterloo, the Peterloo Massacre is the name most commonly given to a deadly assault on peaceful demonstrators at St. Peter's Fields in Manchester, England, on August 16, 1819. The Manchester Patriotic Union Society had organized the demonstration, and participants were prepared to protest for a repeal of the Corn Laws; for parliamentary reform (universal suffrage, annual parliaments, and vote by ballot; in 1819 Manchester had a population of 200,000 but no MPs); and for job security, as new machinery made for increasing rates of unemployment and poverty. It is estimated that 50,000–60,000 men, women, and children from all over the county of Lancashire gathered for the meeting, many of them wearing their Sunday clothes in expectation of a jubilant family affair and in order to exhibit their respectability (and perhaps thus their worthiness of the franchise). Speakers asked to address the crowd included the politician Henry Hunt (1773–1835), the political agitator Richard Carlile (1790–1843), and the reformer John Cartwright (1740–1824). However, William Hulton, the chairman of Manchester's 10 magistrates, saw the gathering as heralding revolution and potentially turning into a riot or rebellion. Under Hulton, the magistrates, viewing the growing crowd from a house overlooking the field, arranged for the professional army to be on hand, including the Hussars; they also called up the Manchester and Salford Yeomanry, a group of local, young, and inexperienced shopkeepers and tradesmen acting as mounted militia. Orders were given to arrest the leaders of the demonstration, and about 60 Yeomanry cavalrymen were sent in to assist in the arrests. Apparently drunk, and under the captaincy of Hugh Birley, they charged the crowd with sabers drawn, heading toward the speakers' platform and yelling, "Have at their flags!" Slashing their way forward, they killed nine men and two women, one of whom was pregnant. Between 400 and 600 others were injured, some trampled by horses, some beaten, and some slashed. When the Hussars arrived, Hulton ordered them to disperse the crowd, but most accounts confirm that they primarily proceeded to subdue the yeomanry. The speakers were arrested and jailed (including Cartwright, even though he had been unable to attend).

The Tory government of the day condoned the magistrates and the militia, and by the year's end legislation was introduced to contain and criminalize public demonstrations and radical publications. That legislation was to become known as the Six Acts. But the public, and not just working classes, reading newspaper accounts from journalists at the event, were horrified and angered by the massacre. Eventually, the term *Peterloo* emerged as an ironic play of word on *Waterloo,* a battle that for the English symbolized honorable victory. As the historians Glyn Williams and John Ramsden argue, England's working classes became more radicalized after Peterloo, creating an atmosphere that would see increasing numbers of illegal, unstamped periodicals and eventually the emergence of Chartism (Williams and Ramsden 213, 215). PERCY BYSSHE SHELLEY's "ENGLAND IN 1819" and "The MASK OF ANARCHY" are passionate, poetic responses to the Peterloo Massacre that capture not only the poet's anger but also the cruel chaos of the day. A graphic firsthand account of the massacre can be read in Samuel Bamford's *Passages in the Life of a Radical* (1893).

**Further Reading**

Bamford, Samuel. *Passages in the Life of a Radical.* 1893. Reprint, New York: Cosimo Classics, 2005.

Bloy, Marjorie. "The Peterloo Massacre, 16 August 1819: Primary Sources." A Web of English History. Available online. URL: http://www.historyhome.co.uk/c-eight/distress/peter3.htm. Accessed on July 8, 2009.

Reid, Robert. *The Peterloo Massacre.* London: William Heinemann Ltd., 1989.

Williams, Glyn, and John Ramsden. *Ruling Britannia: A Political History of Britain, 1866–1988.* London: Longman, 1990.

—Rob Breton

## *Philosophical Enquiry into the Origin of Our Ideas of the Sublime and Beautiful, A*
### Edmund Burke (1757)

EDMUND BURKE was a key voice in the development of modern conservatism. Born in Dublin, Burke studied classics at Trinity College. He went to London to study law but abandoned this for journalism. For 29 years he was a member of Parliament, in which role he responded vigorously to the issues of political life in England and worked to preserve what he believed was of lasting value in Britain's system of government. In 1758 he established the *Annual Register,* becoming its first editor.

Burke published A *Vindication of Natural Society* in 1756 and A *Philosophical Enquiry into the Origin of Our Ideas of the Sublime and Beautiful* in 1757. In this treatise, he formulated a psychological aesthetic theory that exerted considerable influence. By analyzing aesthetic experience in a self-reflective manner, he prompted a movement from classical formalism toward romanticism. Burke countered the view that great art must have great clarity, arguing that the boundless infinite and the imagination, which moved through obscurity, are most important in art.

Burke compared the harmonious and socially cultivating influences of the beautiful with the awe-inspiring fearful and wonder-provoking experience of the sublime. Equating beauty with order, he argued for moderation and against extremes in civil affairs. By Burke's time, the SUBLIME, which referred to an elevated style in classical rhetoric, had come to designate a natural phenomena or artwork that elicited wonder and spiritual awakening. Burke defined the sublime as whatever "is productive of the strongest emotion of which the mind is capable" (39). One could experience a "delightful horror, a sort of tranquility tinged with terror." The sublime is "Whatever is fitted in any sort terrible, or is conversant about terrible objects, or operates in a manner analogous to terror, is a source of the sublime; that is, it is productive of the strange emotions of which the mind is capable of feeling" (39). The sublime, for Burke, was darkness, awe, infinity, terror. The beautiful, in contrast, was brightness, color, harmony, smoothness, and order. The terms of Burke's treatise would have considerable influence on the Romantic poets.

### Further Reading

Burke, Edmund. *A Philosophical Enquiry into the Origin of Our Ideas of the Sublime and Beautiful.* London: Routledge, 2008.

Lock, F. P. *Edmund Burke. Volume I: 1730–1784.* Oxford: Oxford University Press, 2008.

O'Brien, Conor Cruise. *Edmund Burke.* London: Vintage: 2002.

—Robert McParland

## picturesque

The Enclosure Acts (1750–1850) of 18th- and 19th-century England gave landowners powers to enclose common land to improve agricultural profitability. The division of these commons into smaller fields allowed better control and grazing of sheep and cattle as well as intensive crop growing. Although the acts made theoretical provision for those who lost their rights of grazing or farming on the commons, the provision was rarely implemented. This led many to seek employment in urban areas (see INDUSTRIALISM).

Although the Enclosure Acts made the land more profitable for landowners, much of England began to lose its natural beauty. Some in society felt rural England was losing its identity, and with the help of landscapers and artists, they sought to preserve and reestablish its authenticity. Soon, artistic and literary works about the natural world permeated people's aesthetic ideals, and guidebooks suggested how one's personal landscape should look. This preoccupation with the land became known as the picturesque, an artistic and ideological movement that WILLIAM WORDSWORTH later diagnosed as "a strong infection of the age" (*The Prelude,* Book 12). Influential landscape artists and writers such as "Capability" Brown (1715–83) and William Gilpin (1724–1804) sought to recreate the natural landscape in Britain. In his *Essay or Prints* (1768). Gilpin envisioned a "kind of beauty which would look well in a picture" (quoted in Watson 11)—hence the picturesque, which became associated with anything that might look like it could be situated in a painting: striking interiors or unadulterated terrain—mountainous scenery, babbling brooks, rocky backdrops, and even personal libraries. In an attempt to recapture the authenticity of the natural world, artists like Brown and Gilpin were hired to create landscapes that, ironically, were felt to look untouched and natural. They sought to "frame" views of landscapes that would look like a painting: rustic, natural, and uncultivated.

The practice of tailoring landscapes in the likeness of Brown and Gilpin's tastes became a commonplace practice for landowners seeking to enhance the natural beauty of their own properties. As David Lowenthal and Hugh Price point out: "What is considered 'essentially English' is a calm and peaceful deer park, with slow-moving streams and wide expanses of meadowland studded with fine trees" (Lowenthal and Price 192).

### Further Reading

Lowenthal, David and Hugh C Price. "English Landscape Tastes." *Geographical Review* 55, no. 2 (April 1965): 186–222.

Watson, J. R. *Picturesque Landscapes and English Romantic Poetry.* London: Hutchinson, 1970.

—Sarah Fanning

## Piozzi, Hester Lynch  (Hester Lynch Thrale)
(1741–1821)

A salon hostess, literary muse, travel writer, poet, biographer, and journalist, Hester Lynch Piozzi was born Hester Lynch Salusbury on January 27, 1741, in Caernarvonshire, Wales. She was a member of a prominent landowning family, but after her father went bankrupt, she married the wealthy brewer Henry Thrale in 1763; the couple had 12 children. Although Henry was neither emotionally nor intellectually supportive, Hester felt free to associate with whom she liked, and their home in Streatham, London, attracted the cultural lions of the age (the so-called Streatham Worthies)—from the Irish writer Arthur Murphy to the English novelist FRANCES BURNEY, from the artist Sir Joshua Reynolds to the statesman and philosopher EDMUND BURKE, and most notably of all Dr. Samuel Johnson, with whom the Thrales became intimate in 1765 and who found with them total sanctuary: a supportive professional environment, a genial haven of erudite conversation, and the pleasures of social entertainment.

After Henry Thrale's death in 1781, Hester Thrale shunned the warnings of her advisers and married the Italian singer and musician Gabriel Mario Piozzi in 1784. This decision alienated the affections of many, including Dr. Johnson, whose death she was accused of having accelerated. Hester and Gabriel Piozza moved to Wales, where, unburdened from the well-meaning yet smothering encroachment of her relatives and former friends—who had for many years imposed on her a socially sanctioned cultural, generic, and familial straitjacket—she embarked on the most creative phase of her career. First was a contribution to the *Florence Miscellany* (1785), which was followed by the successful *Anecdotes of the Late Samuel Johnson* (1786) and later an edited collection, *Letters to and from the Late Samuel Johnson* (1788). Written in a candid, yet authoritative style, both of these works fueled the rivalry with Johnson's self-elected hagiographer, James Boswell, thus further contributing to the construction of her controversial contemporary reputation. Hester Piozzi's last work, *Retrospection* (1801), is a broad-ranging historical panorama, ambitiously subtitled "a Review of the Most Striking and Important Events, Characters, Situations and their Consequences which the last Eighteen Hundred Years have presented to the view of mankind." Once more her idiosyncratic voice resounded in a male-dominated genre, in a final challenge to the contemporary cultural restrictions imposed upon female authors. She died in Clifton, Bristol, on May 2, 1821.

Hester Lynch Piozzi's oeuvre testifies to her versatility and erudition. Translations from the French and Latin (such as the juvenile "Essay on Man," 1747; a translation of Racine's *Épitres sur l'homme*, or Boethius's *Consolations of Philosophy* with Johnson); the six-volume *Thraliana* (a unique autobiographical repository of anecdotes, verses, and snippets of private life from the period 1776–1809); an innovative travel journal in the present tense entitled *Observations and Reflections Made in the Course of a Journey through France, Italy, and Germany* (1789); and a lexicographical study, *British Synonymy* (1794). She also authored two unpublished plays, *The Adventurer* (1790) and *The Two Fountains* (1789).

### Further Reading

Clifford, James L. *Hester Lynch Piozzi: Mrs Thrale.* Rev. ed. Oxford: Clarendon Press, 1986.

Eger, Elizabeth, and Lucy Peltz. *Brilliant Women: Eighteenth-Century Bluestockings.* London: National Portrait Gallery Publications, 2008.

McCarthy, William. *Hester Thrale Piozzi: Portrait of a Literary Woman.* Chapel Hill: University of North Carolina Press, 1985.

Piozzi, Hester Lynch. *Thraliana: The Diary of Mrs. Hester Lynch Thrale (later Mrs. Piozzi), 1776–1809.* Edited by Katherine C. Balderston. Oxford: Clarendon Press, 1942.

Smith, Orinane. "Unlearned and Ill-Qualified Pokers into Prophecy: Hester Lynch Piozzi and the Female Prophetic Tradition." *Eighteenth-Century Life* 28 (Spring 2004): 87–112.

Watson Brownley, Martine. "'Under the Dominion of Some Woman': The Friendship of Samuel Johnson and Hester Thrale." In *Mothering the Mind: Twelve Studies of Writers and Their Silent Partners*, edited by Ruth Perry and Martine Watson Brownley, 64–79. New York: Holmes and Meier, 1984.

—Francesca Saggini

## "Poem on the Inhumanity of the Slave Trade" Ann Yearsley (1788)

This 425-line blank-verse narrative poem was published in 1788 and dedicated to ANN YEARSLEY's then-patron, the earl of Bristol. A competing text, "Slavery, A Poem," by Yearsley's former benefactress HANNAH MORE, was published in the same year. Both were ostensibly prompted by Sir William Dolben's proposal of a bill in the House of Commons to restrict the numbers of slaves who could be transported from Africa to Britain's West Indian colonies (see SLAVERY).

Whereas More largely condemns slavery generally, Yearsley particularizes and personalizes slavery's evils. Preempting later, more celebrated antislavery texts, such as Harriet Beecher Stowe's 19th-century *Uncle Tom's Cabin*, Yearsley emphasizes slavery's separation of families. As the literary scholar Mary Waldron notes: Yearsley's "dramatic blank verse is very different from More's stately couplets. Yearsley seems to have set out ... to make the reader feel rather than to think ..." (Waldon 170). The poem depicts the young Luco's separation from his parents and from his female companion, Incilanda. When the brutal Christian slave trader Gorgon cracks the whip against his cheek, Luco retaliates, striking Gorgon's forehead with a hoe. Luco is tied to a tree before the plantation's other slaves and burnt to death.

Yearsley's presentation of Luco seems to suggest the trope of the "noble savage." He is identified as "Indian" (l. 64), and yet he personifies a Western European ideal of chivalry. By Yearsley's time there was already a long tradition of describing the racial "other" in such culturally anomalous terms, occasionally accommodating European physiognomy as well, as in the case of Aphra Behn's century-old *Oroonoko* (whose title character Behn described as having a "Roman nose"). Although Yearsley's reading on the subject is uncertain, the idea(l) of the "noble savage" that stretched back at least to the French essayist Montaigne was revivified for the Romantic age by JEAN-JACQUES ROUSSEAU.

The poem's strident assertions that Christianity is irreconcilable with affronts to the rights of the weak and vulnerable are also notable (and constitute a recurrent theme in Yearsley's later work,

as in *Stanzas of Woe* [1790]). She asks Christians: "Is this your piety? Are these your laws, / Whereby the glory of the Godhead spreads / O'er barb'rous climes? Ye hypocrites, disown / The Christian name, nor shame its cause: yet where / Shall souls like yours find welcome?" (ll. 315–319). While such arguments appear widely in Romantic-period writing, they were prominent in the work of several laboring-class poets (as in the later poetry of James Woodhouse). This broaches the subject of whether Yearsley was conscious of her own humble origins and thereby intimates that slaves and the labouring classes are united in their exploitation by a society laying a false claim to be Christian. Such questions have been contentious, and Yearsley's poems, including this one, have received increasing critical attention in recent years.

### Further Reading

Ferguson, Moira. *Eighteenth-Century Women Poets: Nation, Class, and Gender.* Albany: State University of New York Press, 1995.

Waldron, Mary. *Lactilla, Milkwoman of Clifton: The Life and Writings of Ann Yearsley, 1753–1806.* Athens: University of Georgia Press, 1996.

Yearsley, Ann. *Selected Poems.* Edited by Tim Burke. Gloucestershire, Eng.: Cyder Press, 2003.

—Steve Van Hagen

## Poems Descriptive of Rural Life and Scenery John Clare (1820)

Published as *Poems Descriptive of Rural Life and Scenery. By John Clare, A Northamptonshire Peasant*, this was JOHN CLARE's first printed volume. It appeared in January 1820, published by John Taylor (a cousin of the bookseller Edward Drury, who undertook to find a home for Clare's work) and James Hessey. The book's success—it sold its original printing of 1,000 copies within two months, a second edition of 2,000 before the end of the year, and ran to a further edition in 1821—turned the unknown laborer from Helpstone into a well-known name.

The volume was introduced by Taylor, who depicted Clare as a type of the "natural genius" beloved of primitivism and (misleadingly, since he had read widely) emphasized his alleged innocence and naëveté: "They are the genuine productions of a young Peasant, a day-labourer in husbandry, who has had no advantages of education beyond others of his class; and though Poets in this country have seldom been fortunate men, yet he is, perhaps, the least favoured by circumstances, and the most destitute of friends, of any that ever existed" (Clare, 1820; vii). As the biographer John Lucas has observed, "Clare was being marketed—the term is not too strong—in a manner that was intended to fit him into the tradition of 'peasant poets.' Eighteenth-century taste had included a taste for the primitive, and tastes exist in order to be satisfied" (Lucas 10). Lucas's point is key—promoting Clare strenuously to appeal to the "taste" for the primitive which, as the success of THOMAS CHATTERTON, ROBERT BURNS, and ANN YEARSLEY shows, was strong in the Romantic period, helped arouse short-term interest in Clare. Tastes change, however, and when they did, Clare failed to build a long-term career.

The volume contained some 70 or so poems divided into three sections, headed (according to Clare's preference) "Helpstone," "Songs and Ballads," and "Sonnets." It included poems such as "Helpstone," "What is Life?," "Dawnings of Genius," the Burnsian "A Familiar Epistle to a Friend," "Patty," "The Primrose," "The Gypsies' Evening Blaze," "The River Gwash," and "The Meeting." Numerous poems (such as "My Mary" and "The Ways of the Wake")—or, in some cases, parts of them ("Helpstone")—were cut, either by Taylor's hand (to satisfy his habit of correcting Clare's grammar or his distaste for "dialect," or because the subject matter was deemed indecorous) or to please the patron Taylor found for Clare, the evangelical, antiradical Lord Radstock. Perhaps the book's best-known individual poem is its first, "Helpstone," Clare's homage to his native village. As the biographer and editor Jonathan Bate has argued, the volume is influenced by the "previous eighty years' poetry of sensibility," "peppered with" poems that are overwrought and moral, and utilizes a diction replete with "Latinate abstractions" (Bate 149–154). Yet "Helpstone" also embodies themes that Clare would repeatedly return to throughout his life, not least in its idea

of the Helpstone of his youth as a kind of Eden or Arcadia. Clare makes the political point even here that the enclosure of common lands (see PICTURESQUE) had eradicated this idyll (it was on political grounds that Radstock had insisted on cuts from the poem). Clare was nothing if not the poet of self as defined by his absorption in the local landscape and the experiences enjoyed and remembered there. Lines from the above passage could have served as a fitting epitaph.

While *Poems Descriptive* was received rapturously by many contemporary critics, there has been a tendency to reconsideration in recent years. Modern commentators have sometimes been inclined to privilege Clare's later works—the parts of his oeuvre neglected (or even unpublished) during his lifetime—such as The SHEPHERD'S CALENDAR, *The Midsummer Cushion*, and *The Rural Muse*. Bate, for instance, argues that "[i]n retrospect, we may say with confidence that each book [of Clare's] was better than the last. . . . As his work improved, it became less known" (150).

Critics have also tended to focus on the qualities of the many early poems omitted from *Poems Descriptive*, to intimate that they were often superior or just more interesting than those published, and to dwell on the reasons for John Taylor's original selection. Yet the poems that did appear contain many intimations of the later Clare, and in some cases they are well respected in their own right. If Clare was English Romanticism's ultimate "natural genius"—today he is certainly regarded as the finest laboring-class poet England has produced—then *Poems Descriptive of Rural Life and Scenery* will remain of permanent interest as the volume that introduced him to the world. In 1989 the poems (and many others that were unpublished from Clare's early period) were made available as Clare wrote them thanks to the monumental editorial labors of Eric Robinson and David Powell. The critical controversy over whether such presentation is warranted endures, as Jonathan Bate documents in pages 563–575 of his biography of Clare.

## Further Reading

Bate, Jonathan. *John Clare: A Biography.* New York: Farrar, Strauss and Giroux; London: Picador, 2003.

Clare, John. *The Early Poems of John Clare 1804–1822.* Vol. 1. Edited by David Powell and Eric Robinson. Oxford: Clarendon Press, 1989.

———. *Poems Descriptive of Rural Life and Scenery.* London: Taylor and Hessey, 1820.

———. *Selected Poems.* Edited by Jonathan Bate. New York: Farrar, Strauss and Giroux, 2003.

Lucas, John. *John Clare.* Plymouth, Eng.: Northcote House, 1994.

—Steve Van Hagen

## *Poetical Effusions* Isabella Lickbarrow (1814)

Little is known about the life of the Lake Poet ISABELLA LICKBARROW. The preface to her 1818 poem "Lament for Princess Charlotte" describes her as "young female in humble life, a native of Kendal . . . an orphan, unlettered, and of exemplary character." In *Poetical Effusions* readers are told how the poems were written secretly "after the domestic employments of the day . . . at intervals stolen from repose" (iii). Her intention in writing is "to assist the humble labours of herself and her orphan sisters' by establishing a fund "which would increase their family comforts and better their condition in life" (iii). Lickbarrow was initially published anonymously in a local newspaper, the *Westmorland Advertiser, or Kendal Chronicle.* The paper's editors, M. and R. Brathwaite, supported her efforts, and it was they who organized the publication of *Poetical Effusions.* The collection's frontispiece shows a long list of subscribers who paid in advance for a copy, including WILLIAM WORDSWORTH, THOMAS DE QUINCY, and ROBERT SOUTHEY.

Like her more famous Lakeland neighbors, Lickbarrow wrote about the local scenery and the beauties of the countryside. Some critics have seen similarities between the poems in *Poetical Effusions* and Wordsworth's works—a point Lickbarrow herself seems to have been sensitive about. In the collection's preface, the point is made that "She [Lickbarrow] wishes to disclaim every idea of plagiarism, but as the enlightened reader into whose hands these 'Poetical Effusions'—may fall, will soon discover where she may unwittingly have borrowed the expressions of others, or made use of similar language naturally arising from the contemplation of similar subjects, she hopes under these circumstances every candid allowance will be made" (iv). Some of the lines in "The Naiad's Complaint" do sound like Wordsworth's: "Nor greater pleasure could Columbus feel / When first beyond the transatlantic deep / His wandering eye beheld another world, / Than I, when in my wanderings I have found / Some sweet sequestered spot unknown before" (ll. 11–15). Lickbarrow shares Wordsworth's desire to capture the intensity of feeling evoked on seeing particular landmarks and beauty spots for the first time. As Duncan Wu puts it: "What distinguishes her treatment of the Lake District landscape she knew and loved is a mystical sense of being drawn into its heart" (Wu). Thus, "On Underbarrow Scar," which describes Lickbarrow's sighting of the limestone ridge high above Kendal, Cumbria, shows a wish to convey not only the sublimity of the scene but the poet's own sense of communion with nature: "Describe this vast stupendous pile of rock, / As rugged as the confines of the world, / Whence the huge masses far beneath it hurled / Seem severed by a mighty earthquake's shock; . . . / With what sincere delight I wander here; / When from the cares and toils of life set free, / I hail the blest return of liberty; / And these loved scenes my wearied spirits cheer; / At ease reclined upon this airy brow, / The prospect stretching wide, pleased I survey / The stony slope, the hanging woods below, / The ridges of the heath, the winding way" (ll. 23–26, 34–41). The poem is almost a love lyric to nature but celebrates nature, the life-giver.

Nature is also a source of inspiration, as becomes evident in "On Esthwaite Water." In a passage which shares something with Wordsworth's "There Was a Boy," a connection is makes between the lake as "bright reflector" (l. 16) and the poet's "yielding breast" (l. 22). Lickbarrow describes a moment where the lake appears perfectly still and calm, allowing the spectator to take in the beauty of the countryside reflected in it: "Inverted on the waveless flood, / A spotless mirror smooth and clear, / Each fair surrounding object shone / In softer beauty imag'd there. / Brown hills, and woods of various shades, / Orchards and sloping meadows green, / Sweet rural seats, and shelter'd farms, / Were in the bright reflector seen. / . . . / Struck with the beauty of the scene, / I cry'd, Oh! may my yielding breast / Retain but images of peace, / Like those, sweet lake, on thine imprest" (ll. 9–16, 21–24). The fear for the poet is that such inspiration as this gives may soon vanish. Soon: ". . . o'er Esthwait's tranquil lake, / A stronger gale full frequent blows, / The soothing prospect disappears" (ll. 33–35).

In addition to describing the wonders of nature, the collection also contains musings on the Napoleonic War ("Invocation to Peace"; "Written after the News of a Battle"), on explorations of the vulnerability of women ("Anna"; "The Lover's Resolution"), and on sexual desire ("On the Sprint at Garent Bridge" and "Lines Written on the Banks of the Eden near Kirkby Stephen"). There are also poems that question the difficulties of achieving success as a poet, notably "On the Difficulty of Attaining Poetical Excellence." The poem "To an Opening Rose" also speaks of a desire for public recognition that never seems to come. The poet wonders if she will be remembered in years to come but suspects not: "I, like the wild flowers of the mountains, / That unknown unheeded die, / Like them shall leave a name unhonour'd, / And like them forgotten lie" (ll. 41–44). For many years this was indeed the case. It is only recently that Lickbarrow has begun to receive the recognition she craved.

## Further Reading

Bennett, Andrew. *Romantic Poets and the Culture of Posterity.* Cambridge: Cambridge University Press, 1999.

Lickbarrow, Isabella. *Poetical Effusions.* Kendal: M. Braithwaite, 1814.

———. *Poetical Effusions* (1814). Available online. URL: http://digital.lib.ucdavis.edu/projects/bwrp/Works/LickIPoeti.htm. Accessed on September 30, 2008.

Wu, Duncan. "Out of Poverty, Riches." *Guardian* (August 6 2004). Available online. URL: http://www.guardian.co.uk/books/2004/aug/07/featuresreviews.guardianreview14. Accessed on September 30, 2008.

—Alison Bennett

## *Poetical Meditations* Alphonse de Lamartine (1820)

*Poetical Meditations (Méditations poétiques)* was the first and most famous collection of poetry written by ALPHONSE-MARIE-LOUIS DE PRAT DE LAMARTINE. The father of French Romantic verse, Lamartine published the *Meditations* in March 1820. Following the fall of NAPOLEON BONAPARTE, the Bourbon dynasty had recently been restored to power, and Paris was experiencing a period of artistic renaissance. Passing through half a dozen editions before the year's end, this small volume of poetry became an almost sacred text to young Parisians and went on to influence every French poet of the following generations. Alain Vaillant has suggested, and not without reason, that the appearance of the *Meditations* was perhaps "the only true literary event" (249) in modern French literature.

The collection originally consisted of 24 poems, the longest of which is around 300 lines. The arrangement follows no overarching narrative, though the juxtaposition of certain poems carries an apparent logic—for example, by positioning "Providence to Man" after "Despair," the second poem responds to the skepticism of the first. Apart from such instances, the *Meditations* examine an eclectic assortment of religious, philosophical, and personal subjects. While one of the text's primary innovations is the infusion of palpable and topical enthusiasm, sentiment, and sincerity into a poetic tradition that had long grown cold, Lamartine often deliberately casts the characters and settings in universal, transcendent terms. In this way he strikes a balance between subjectivity and universality. For example, he changed the title of the collection's most famous poem from "The Lake of B***" to "The Lake." The decision to remove the title's element of particularity serves, in part, to counterbalance the narrator's intimate expression of his own inner life.

Among the 24 poems, Lamartine explores a variety of timeless themes—including love and loss, transience and permanence, man and nature, faith and doubt—and modernizes them by speaking in a deeply personal, human voice. At the same time, he tempers this expressive lyricism with traditional form, diction, and imagery. As a result, he stands at the frontier between classical and romantic verse. Indeed, when the *Meditations* were first published, a young VICTOR HUGO deemed Lamartine "a classicist among the romantics" (Hugo 1820, 374). This phrase well captures Lamartine's poetic sensibility. Some have argued that his formal conservatism is due to a general lack of ability; others believe he was simply conforming to the royalist and Catholic tastes that prevailed in the Parisian salons of the time. It is also possible that Lamartine's balance between expressive innovation and classical form was a worthy and well-founded aesthetic choice. In any case, the contrast between form and content adds a unique and ambiguous dimension to the *Meditations*.

Though the collection's language and sentimentalism may now appear outdated, its historical importance remains indisputable. In addition, most critics recognize the musical genius of Lamartine's verse, as well as the depth and subtlety of his thought. "The Lake" remains by far the best-known poem in the *Meditations;* in fact, it is arguably the most famous poem in the French language, and its lines "O time! Suspend your flight; and you, kind hours, / Suspend your course" (ll. 17–18) are known by every French student. At the same time, the collection also contains several other lyrical and philosophical masterpieces, including "Isolation," "Man," "Evening," "The Valley," "Providence to Man," "Memory," "Faith," and "Autumn."

**Further Reading**

Birkett, Mary Ellen. *Lamartine and the Poetics of Landscape.* Lexington, Ky.: French Forum, 1982.

Fortescue, William. *Alphonse de Lamartine: A Political Biography.* New York: St. Martin's Press, 1983.

Hillary, David. *Lamartine: The Méditations poétiques.* Durham, N.C.: University of Durham, 1993.

Hugo, Victor. "Méditations Poétiques" *Le conservateur Littéraire* 10 (April 1820): 374–381. *Le conservateur Littéraire. Edition Critique.* Edited by Jules Marsan. Paris: Hachette, 1922, 190–198.

Ireson, J. C. *Lamartine: A Revaluation.* Hull, Eng.: University of Hull, 1969.

Lamartine, Alphonse de. *Poetical Meditations/Méditations Poétiques.* Translated by Gervase Hittle. Lewiston, N.Y.: Edward Mellen Press, 1993.

Vaillant, Alain. *La Crise de la Littérature: Romantisme et modernité.* Grenoble: ELLUG, 2005.

—Peter J. Hutchings

## "Poison Tree, A" William Blake (1794)

In "A Poison Tree," WILLIAM BLAKE indicts two aspects of human behavior that extend from excessive reason and experience—repression and hypocrisy. Ostensibly, these are connected to his larger fears regarding complete subservience to institutional (and scriptural) mores. The illustration to the poem in his *Songs of Experience* volume depicts a human figure lying with arms outstretched, crucifix-like. An extended tree branch surrounds the poem's text, forming a serpentine frame.

"A Poison Tree" suggests a tension within human consciousness thanks to the use made of absolute opposites such as "innocence/experience," "right/wrong." The poem questions whether things are ever that simple. In its ditty-like metrical scheme, its (mostly) iambic tetrameter lines present the message as one that is straightforward: "I was angry with my friend: / I told my wrath, my wrath did end. / I was angry with my foe: / I told it not, my wrath did grow" (ll. 1–4). But beneath its simplicity, the opening stanza's anaphoric strategy points to the complications to come, particularly because the first-person voice is at the heart of the poem's development. We can identify the speaker as the manifestation of a universal self; we all share the tendencies that the speaker reveals.

We can also consider the significance of the biblical Fall in relation to the poem's intention and its portrayal of the destructive agent. The transubstantiation of the speaker's rage into the poison tree of the title that "bore an apple bright" (l. 10)—which in turn destroys the foe—is a process heavily loaded with religious and ethical significances. It implies the possibilities of interpreting the speaker as the God of Creation, whose original forbiddance led to the Original Sin in a process that, in itself, makes possible the ultimate Christian sacrifice and salvation.

In the larger scheme of Blake's considerations of the convergence and aggregation of innocence and experience, this injunction at the center of the story of the Fall is indicative of the arbitrary institutional forces that limit the complete fulfillment of human kind's potential. At the same time, the image of an apple falling from a tree is at the center of a different myth with its own protagonist, Isaac Newton, being one of several figures for whom Blake shows great disdain. Both church doctrine and scientific discovery alike are sources of received knowledge that are representative of repressive, hypocritical, overextended—and often self-righteous—projections of human reason. This latter is a quality that Blake indicts throughout much of his poetry and prophetic writings; it also gives rise to the problems that come with experience.

See also SONGS OF INNOCENCE AND OF EXPERIENCE.

**Further Reading**

Blake, William. *The Complete Poetry and Prose of William Blake.* Edited by David V. Erdman. Berkeley: University of California Press, 1982.

———. *The Illuminated Blake: William Blake's Complete Illuminated Works with a Plate-by-Plate Commentary.* Edited by David V. Erdman. New York: Dover, 1992.

———. *Songs of Innocence and of Experience: Blake's Illuminated Books, Vol. 2.* Edited by Andrew Lincoln. Princeton, N.J.: Princeton University Press, 1991.

Gallagher, Philip J. "The Word Made Flesh: Blake's 'A Poison Tree' and the Book of Genesis." *Studies in Romanticism* 16 (1977): 237–249.

Hirsch, E. D., Jr. *Innocence and Experience: An Introduction to Blake.* Chicago: University of Chicago Press, 1975.

—Lim Lee Ching

## Polidori, John William (1795–1821)

Although he wrote a number of poems, plays, and stories, John Polidori remained a relatively marginal figure during the Romantic period and is known primarily in terms of his relationships with other more notable writers of the 19th century. His father, Gaetano Polidori, had served as secretary to the prominent Italian dramatist Vittorio Alfieri before moving in 1791 to London, where he married Anna Maria Pierce in 1793 and where his son John was born on September 7, 1795. In 1815, shortly before his 20th birthday, Polidori became the youngest student to graduate with a medical degree from the University of Edinburgh.

In early spring 1816, Polidori was hired as LORD BYRON's personal physician when Byron made his final departure from England. Their travels through Europe included a visit to the site of the Battle of Waterloo and, later that summer, Byron's residence in the Villa Diodati, Geneva. It was there that Polidori participated with Byron, PERCY BYSSHE SHELLEY, and Mary Godwin (later MARY SHELLEY) in the ghost-story writing contest that spawned FRANKENSTEIN. As indicated in his diary of the summer—apparently commissioned by Byron's publisher John Murray but not published until 1911, 90 years after Polidori's death—Polidori's interactions with the Diodati circle were characterized largely by his unsuccessful attempts to gain the respect of the rest of the group. The works he read to his colleagues were often met with ridicule, and he was frequently left behind with Mary Godwin and her stepsister, Claire Clairmont, when Byron and Shelley went out on excursions.

Although Polidori had left Byron's service by the end of the summer or 1816, his name became permanently associated with Byron's early in 1819 with the publication of "The VAMPYRE," his reworking of Byron's unfinished contribution to the ghost-story contest. According to Polidori, he had revised Byron's fragment in response to a female acquaintance's challenge that such a topic could not make a suitable foundation for a story. However, when it was published—without Polidori's knowledge—with Byron's name as the author, a vicious controversy ensued, resulting in a series of personal charges against Polidori, whose reputation was inalterably damaged. The work itself certainly bears Byron's influence, not simply in literary terms—allusions to his poetry appear throughout—but also in the title character, who takes his name, Ruthven, from a character in GLENARVON, Lady CAROLINE LAMB's fictional treatment of Byron published after the end of their brief but tumultuous relationship.

In the aftermath of the "Vampyre" controversy, Polidori continued to struggle to make a name for himself. Later in 1819, for example, he published the completed version of his entry in the ghost-story contest, *Ernestus Berchtold; or the Modern Oedipus,* a GOTHIC story inspired not only by Sophocles' play but also by the events of the FRENCH REVOLUTION and Napoleonic Wars, especially as they impacted the Swiss regions he had first visited in 1816. In this respect, he also demonstrates the influence of Byron's writings from the same period, including his "The PRISONER OF CHILLON" and "MANFRED: A DRAMATIC POEM." Polidori's situation quickly deteriorated following the publication of *Ernestus Berchtold,* though he continued to write and had a couple of shorter works published. He ultimately committed suicide by taking prussic acid, dying early in the morning of August 24, 1821.

### Further Reading

Barbour, Judith. "Dr. John William Polidori, Author of *The Vampyre." Imagining Romanticism: Essays on English and Australian Romanticisms.* Ed. Deirdre Coleman and Peter Otto, 85–110. West Cornwall, Conn.: Locust Hill, 1992.

Macdonald, D. L. *Poor Polidori: A Critical Biography of the Author of* The Vampyre. Toronto: University Of Toronto Press, 1991.

—L. Adam Mekler

## *Political Register, The* (1802–1835)

This weekly newspaper was founded and edited by WILLIAM COBBETT. Initially the paper was loyalist, but Cobbett grew disenchanted with the government's conduct during the war against France and critical of abuses of power. In 1809, during a growing atmosphere of government censorship, Cobbett was charged and found guilty of sedition, though he continued to publish the *Register* during his two-year term in Newgate Prison. The topics addressed seem a confusing and sometimes cranky amalgam: banking and paper money, corrupt elections, INDUSTRIALISM and the mistreatment of the urban worker, the ills of the potato diet, the neglect of the rural worker, government surveillance and oppression, the effeminacy of tea drinking, and the decline of traditional manly

sports such as boxing, among many others. Cobbett's style and structure were organic, however, and ultimately all of these topics were woven together into one master narrative: systematization and centralization—what Cobbett called "The Thing"—were ruining England. To modern readers, his frequent scapegoating of minorities and ethnic groups, such as Quakers, Jews, and the Irish, is unacceptable. Nonetheless, the persona "Cobbett" was presented in the *Register* as "the Poor Man's Friend," whose primary goal was parliamentary reform to better represent the voices of working men (none of the leading radicals supported votes for women).

The *Political Register* was a stamped paper, subject to taxation. In 1815 the government increased the stamp tax to fourpence per copy, making the *Register* too expensive. In 1816, then, Cobbett began publishing the lead articles of the *Register* as unstamped weekly pamphlets, priced only two-pence per copy. Critics promptly labeled the paper "two-penny trash" (a title Cobbett would later use for a series of articles), but circulation increased from about 1,000 copies sold weekly to approximately 40,000. With its broad distribution, the *Register* was an influential voice in early 19th-century radicalism.

From 1817 to 1819, Cobbett wrote the *Register* from North America, where he had fled fearing another arrest for sedition, making comparisons between England and America unflattering to the former. On his return, just after the PETERLOO MASSACRE, when the military and a force of special constables attacked an outdoor meeting of radical supporters, including women and children, at St. Peter's Field, Manchester, the *Register* continued its aggressive attacks on the government. In 1821 Cobbett began a series of articles in the *Register* challenging a government report on agricultural conditions. He recounted his own findings during various journeys throughout England; these were collected and published as *RURAL RIDES* (1830). Limited parliamentary reform came with the 1832 REFORM ACT, but Cobbett, though eventually elected to Parliament, continued to critique the system via the *Register* until his death.

Although the *Political Register* is not generally included among canonical Romantic texts, in its organic style and structure, its interest in rural/agrarian rather than urban/industrial values (including its treatment of landscape), and its resistance to socioeconomic oppression generated by liberal individualism, the paper shared many of the values associated with literary Romanticism, which is linked to a spirit of revolution or rebellion the *Political Register* certainly demonstrates.

See also NEWSPAPERS AND MAGAZINES.

## Further Reading

Dyck, Ian. *William Cobbett and Rural Popular Culture.* Cambridge: Cambridge University Press, 1992.

Fulford, Tim. *Romanticism and Masculinity: Gender, Politics, and Poetics in the Writings of Burke, Coleridge, Cobbett, Wordsworth, De Quincey, and Hazlitt.* Basingstoke, Eng.: Macmillan, 1999.

Gilmartin, Kevin. *Print Politics: The Press and Radical Opposition in Early Nineteenth-Century England.* Cambridge: Cambridge University Press, 1996.

Gunzenhauser, Bonnie J. "Reading the Rhetoric of Resistance in William Cobbett's Two-Penny Trash." *Prose Studies* 25, no. 1 (2002): 84–101.

Ulrich, John M. *Signs of Their Times: History, Labor, and the Body in Cobbett, Carlyle, and Disraeli.* Athens: Ohio University Press, 2002.

—Terri Doughty

## Polwhele, Richard    See "UNSEX'D FEMALES, THE."

## Preface to *Lyrical Ballads*    William Wordsworth (1802)

Whereas the first volume of *Lyrical Ballads*, published in 1798, opened with a rather short "Advertisement," the two-volume edition of 1800 was introduced by a long preface, which was extended in the 1802 edition and to which was then added an appendix on poetic diction. The Preface to *Lyrical Ballads* is signed by WILLIAM WORDSWORTH, but both its content and its very existence rest on Wordsworth's conversations with SAMUEL TAYLOR COLERIDGE. The latter convinced him of the necessity to explain the theoretical ground underlying the poems, which was, like the volumes themselves, the result of their collaboration and emulation.

The publication of the first edition of *Lyrical Ballads* marked the onslaught of the battle of taste that accompanied the first decades of the 19th century and the Romantic movement: Enthusiasm and fury crystallized around Wordsworth's simple poetry, and those who admired it opposed, sometimes violently, those who despised it. The Preface was Wordsworth's response to these fervent reactions. His text implies that the general reading public was unprepared for such revolutionary poetry, and that it had consequently been unfavorably received. It might be true that much in the first volume created unrest, but it nevertheless appeared at a time when popular ballads and unsophisticated poetic language were already fashionable, and the volume had enough success to grant a second, and extended, edition two years later, so that Wordsworth's claim of unpopularity might be overstated. Yet the two poets' formal and thematic inventions were such that they felt they had not been taken seriously enough and that there was more in their poetry than had been acknowledged. Their revolutionary tendencies had not been recognized, and the Preface was there to emphasize them. Wordsworth wanted to state the innovations of his poetry and justify them, and his argument—whether it was warranted or exaggerated—came to form the core of the Romantic literary ideology: Contemporary poetry was corrupted, and he and Coleridge renewed and purified it, but the public was not prepared and it took them time to accept this revolution.

Contemporary taste and successful poets "upon which general approbation is at present bestowed" (l. 42; the references to the line numbers are from the Butler and Green edition, pages 738–739 for the "Advertisement," pages 741–760 for the Preface, and pages 761–765 for the Appendix) with their "gaudiness and inane phraseology" (l. 7) are rarely explicitly targeted in the Preface, and Wordsworth reassures the readers that his goal is not to condemn these compositions to which they have "attached the endearing name of Poetry" (l. 669). He nonetheless hopes to show that his own poetry is clearly superior: It "give[s] other enjoyments, of a purer, more lasting, and more exquisite nature" (ll. 679–681); it is "genuine poetry" (l. 686), which "interest[s] mankind permanently" (l. 686) and improves "moral relations" (ll. 687–688). The 1802 Appendix identifies the shortcomings of contemporary poets: They have mechanically adopted the language of the earlier poets, those who invented a poetic language by listening to the language spoken by men in extraordinary occasions (Appendix, ll. 35–36) and have thus "constructed a phraseology" (l. 45) which has become an "extravagant and absurd language" (l. 65).

The new and improved poetry of Wordsworth and Coleridge is therefore bound to disturb the readers. They will need time and effort to become accustomed to it (Preface, ll. 635–652). Wordsworth singles out three threads of criticism that have been directed at *Lyrical Ballads* (which he had already anticipated in the 1798 "Advertisement") and that the Preface should justify in order to avoid further misunderstandings: the subject matter (chosen among common life), the language (which is not poetic diction), and his decision to write in verse (and not in prose).

Wordsworth's first and longest line of defense centers on the aims and subjects of the poems. These poems are "experiments" (Advertisement, l. 4; Preface, l. 2) in a quasiscientific sense: Their goal is to help understand the human mind better. His philosophical background comes from JOHN LOCKE (1624–1704) and David Hartley (1705–57): The basic unit of the mind is the sensation; as the individual develops, he or she learns to associate, group, and refine these sensations, which thus become more and more complex ideas. Wordsworth's goal is to expose these "primary laws of our nature" (Preface, l. 66)—that is, "to illustrate the manner in which our feelings and ideas are associated" (l. 120), "to follow the fluxes and refluxes of the mind" (ll. 121–122). His poetry thus endeavors to achieve some philosophical truth "not individual and local, but general, and operative" (ll. 341–343).

Two consequences follow from this elevated purpose, both of which have been strongly attacked by the readers of the first edition. First, to render the movements of the mind more distinct, the characters in the poems must be assailed by violent passions; they must be "in a state of excite-ment" (l. 120), and their minds must be "agitated by the great and simple affections of our nature" (123). This is why the poems' subject matter is so often violent and dramatic—and not to subscribe to the contemporary fashion for "frantic novels, sickly and stupid German Tragedies, and deluge of idle and extravagant stories in verse" (168–169). Second, the poems should depict "incidents of common life" (l. 65) and characters from the low society because they are in permanent contact with nature, "a better soil" (l. 69) on which passions grow more powerful, because there these emotions are "less under restraint" (l. 70), less deformed by social constraints, and because these emotions are expressed in a "a plainer and more emphatic language" (l. 70).

This linguistic simplicity is the second aspect Wordsworth has to defend in his Preface. The contemporary and conventional language of poetry—poetic diction, "the common inheritance of Poets" (l. 206)—is rejected on principle: It is stale and automatic, cut from human life. On the contrary, Wordsworth wants to use the "real language of men" (l. 4); he wants to give the reader "flesh and blood" (l. 188). The risk is that if the poems do without the obvious signs that tell the readers that they are reading poetry (the stock images and personifications of poetic diction), the poet might be accused of "prosaism" (l. 214) and his poems considered as no more than versified prose. However, this is precisely Wordsworth's point: There is, he claims, no essential difference between the language of prose and metrical composition (ll. 249–250) as "the same human blood circulates through the veins of them both" (ll. 259–260).

The similarity therefore begs the question: What is poetry (with or without meter) and how is it different from "vulgarity and meanness of ordinary life?" (l. 267). Wordsworth answers these questions in the 1802 edition. First, the language of poetry should be "a *selection* of the language really spoken by men" (ll. 265–266, my emphasis), and this selection must be made with "taste" and "feeling" (l. 266). Second, meter is superimposed. This last point leads to a long development on the necessity and function of versification, to which Wordsworth attributes two opposed but complementary actions. It has a soothing effect:

The depiction of violent and primal passions produces "an unusual and irregular state of the mind" (l. 498), which can become painful; meter, as it imposes a regularity to this turmoil, can temper and restrain these passions (l. 505) and make their contemplation pleasurable. Conversely, it also has an exhilarating effect: Meter will impart passion to the words because the readers are accustomed to connect particular rhythm with particular emotions, "chearful [sic] or melancholy" (l. 517). This dialectic of passion and restraint forms the core of Wordsworth's final topic, the role and psyche of the poet.

In the 1802 edition, Wordsworth wonders "what is meant by the word Poet?" (l. 294) and tries to elucidate the mechanism of creation. The poet is "a man speaking to men" (l. 296); he is different from other men only in degree, but not in kind (l. 431). He is simply endowed with more sensibility, enthusiasm and tenderness, and a greater knowledge of human nature (ll. 296–298): his passions, feelings and thoughts are the same but more intense. What is more, he possesses the capacity to conjure up these passions when they are absent (l. 303), "without immediate external excitement" (l. 311), as well as a greater power in expressing them (l. 434).

Wordsworth then delves deeper into the psychological mechanisms of this creative process, and this final analysis recapitulates two essential arguments of the Preface: Poetry is an ambiguous activity, both passionate and philosophical; the value of poetry is as high as, perhaps higher than, that of science. For even if poetry is the expression of a sensibility, "the spontaneous overflow of powerful feelings" (ll. 102–103), it has no value if it is not also "thought long and deeply" (l. 106). This dual process is later developed: "Poetry is the spontaneous overflow of powerful feelings: it takes it origin from emotion recollected in tranquillity" (ll. 537–538). First come passionate feelings; later, these are recreated ("emotion, similar to that which was before the subject of contemplation, is gradually produced" (ll. 439–441), and eventually distance and reflection allow the analysis and writing of these feelings. The results, the poems, are as valuable as the "labours of the men of Science" (l. 401); indeed, should science "create a material

revolution . . . in our condition" (l. 402), the poet will be at its side to guide us, to show us the values and dangers of these discoveries (ll. 406–410): to carry "sensation into the midst of the objects of the science itself" (ll. 405–406).

## Further Reading

Jordan, John Emory. *Why the Lyrical Ballads? The Background, Writing, and Character of Wordsworth's 1798 Lyrical Ballads.* Berkeley: University of California Press, 1976.

Purkis, John. *A Preface to Wordsworth.* London: Longman, 1970.

Wordsworth, William. *Lyrical Ballads, and Other Poems, 1797–1800.* Edited by James Butler and Karen Green. Ithaca, N.Y., and London: Cornell University Press, 1992.

———. *The Prose Works of William Wordsworth.* 3 vols. Edited by W. J. B. Owen and Jane Worthington Smyser. Oxford: Clarendon Press, 1974.

Wordsworth, William, and Samuel Taylor Coleridge. *Lyrical Ballads.* Edited by R. L. Brett and A. R. Jones. London and New York: Routledge, 1991.

—Samuel Baudry

## *Prelude, or Growth of a Poet's Mind, The*
**William Wordsworth** (1799, 1805, 1850)

Originally intended as a mere prologue to *The Recluse,* a much grander but ultimately unfinished project, WILLIAM WORDSWORTH's *The Prelude* eventually developed into a substantial epic of 14 books written in blank verse. Containing key elements of Romantic discourse—such as the decisive role of childhood experiences, subjectivity, introspection, nature, imagination, and the role of poetry itself—it represents a central text of the Romantic canon. Wordsworth's widow, Mary, suggested the poem's title. Wordsworth himself had addressed *The Prelude* to SAMUEL TAYLOR COLERIDGE and had therefore never thought of the text in any other way than as "The Poem to Coleridge."

The history of composition and publication of *The Prelude* is highly complex, with first drafts written in 1798 and last full-scale revisions made in 1839. There are 17 major manuscripts of the text. Wordsworth wrote the *Two-Part Prelude* in 1799 and then the *The Prelude* of 1805 (which was, however, not published until 1926). It consists of 13 books, including the five-book *Prelude* of 1804. The posthumously published *Prelude* of 1850, finally, is the outcome of various revisions. The episode of the lovers Vaudracour and Julia was omitted and Book 10 divided, as a result of which the poem consists of 14 books overall. As far as the style is concerned, the 1805 *Prelude* is thought by many scholars to be the version that represents Wordsworth at the height of his powers as a literary Romantic. *The Prelude* of 1850 is considered to be more orthodox, since the radical tone so characteristic of the earlier versions has been considerably moderated. This version reflects later Victorian influences on Wordsworth, such as traditional Anglican theology, and it tends to be more self-consciously literary and more conservative politically.

Influences on *The Prelude* include St. Augustine's *Confessions*; JOHN MILTON's epic *Paradise Lost* (1667); Mark Akenside's *Pleasures of the Imagination* (1744); and JEAN-JACQUES ROUSSEAU's *Confessions* (1782), in which Rousseau takes himself as his subject. In a letter to his friend George Beaumont dated May 1, 1805, Wordsworth apologetically observed of *The Prelude* that it was "a thing unprecedented in Literary history that a man should talk so much about himself" (quoted in Rehder, 44). Like Rousseau, the man Wordsworth portrayed was himself. Unlike Rousseau, he had a distinct and many-layered Romantic-era poetic agenda.

The Wordsworth scholar M. H. Abrams calls *The Prelude* the first "fully developed poetic equivalent" of the bildungsroman and the *Künstlerroman* (the German term for a novel in which the hero is an artist of some kind) (Abrams 586). Dealing with the poet's own childhood in the rural environment of Hawkshead, his student years in Cambridge, his hiking tour through the Alps, as well as his sojourn in France and eventual return to England, the poem documents Wordsworth's education and development. It depicts the development of an exemplary mind that learned to participate in the divine and would attest to the possibility of the same for all humankind. For Wordsworth, God speaks to us through the sanctity of His creation, and our interchange with nature implies a moral responsibility.

Rather than being a smooth and linear process, however, this development is characterized by various moments of crisis and failure. Repeatedly, the poet feels unable to fulfil his vocation and is afraid of losing his poetic powers. At the opening of Book 1, the reader is presented with a hesitant poet who is uncertain about what themes to write on. It is only in line 271 that Wordsworth properly begins his great epic of introspection with an account of several episodes from his early childhood. In Book 3, we witness a young Wordsworth who—after being full of anticipation for the education he hopes to gain at Cambridge—is increasingly disappointed by and critical of the system of institutionalized learning practiced at Cambridge, which, in his view, fails to stimulate his imagination. Finally, the poet experiences his greatest crisis when he feels that he has lost his imagination after being forced to return from France due to the Napoleonic Wars. His personal crisis thus coincides with the political one following the FRENCH REVOLUTION. According to the literary scholar Stephen Gill, it is precisely this correlation of personal and historical turmoil that makes *The Prelude* "a landmark in European literature," for "it records the coming into being of an individual consciousness at exactly the moment when European society was being tortured into extreme self-consciousness through the convulsion of the French Revolution and the Napoleonic war that followed" (Gill 1991, 3).

In these moments of crisis, the poet derives comfort from nature on the one hand and from the recollection of memories on the other. In the 1805 version in what is a clear reference to EDMUND BURKE's *A PHILOSOPHICAL ENQUIRY INTO THE ORIGIN OF OUR IDEAS OF THE SUBLIME AND BEAUTIFUL*, the poet claims to have been fostered by "beauty and fear" (1. 306) when roaming through "the presences of Nature" (l. 490). This view of the personified Nature as a parent is reinforced in Book 2, where she is increasingly presented as a substitute mother for the young boy, who had lost both his parents by the age of 13; and in Book 5, when her teaching is presented as ideal and contrasted with modern theories of education. Not surprisingly, therefore, it is during Wordsworth's summer holiday back at Hawkshead, when he is reintegrated into nature, that he considers himself to be a "dedicated spirit" who has been initiated into its secrets and chosen to translate them through his poetry for the public (4:344).

Besides Wordsworth's intimate relationship with nature, it is above all the recollection of "spots of time" experienced in his childhood that helps him to overcome his existential crisis. "Spots of time" are epiphanic moments during which the poet gains insight into an eternal truth from "isolated memories" (Jonathan Wordsworth 181). Imagination is identified as the power that succeeds in transforming an ordinary incident into a visionary experience. The recognition that the poet's mind is a "creator and receiver both" (2:273) and that imagination is superior to all other forms of knowledge becomes a poetic tenet during the poet's climactic ascent of Mount Snowdon described in the concluding chapter of *The Prelude*.

The center of *The Prelude* takes the reader through London—through an examination of Wordsworth's "present theme," "to retrace the way that led me on / Through Nature to the love of humankind" (1805, 8:425–427); through prerevolutionary, postrevolutionary, and Napoleonic France; and through Wordsworth's ideals for humanity, his struggles with Godwinian rationalism, and his moral crisis (Book 10), which, through failure to find answers to moral dilemmas, led him to immerse himself in the study of mathematics as an exercise of mind in which he finds certainty and a kind of factual, objective purity, "their clear / And solid evidence" (1805, 10:329–330), the poet having "yielded up moral questions in despair."

Book 11 reflects on man and nature, the dangers of reason, and other matters, punctuated by two exceptional passages of transcendental poetry. The first concerns "spots of time," which provide the spiritual and emotional sustenance for future years, "A renovating virtue" (1805, 11:208–210), often experienced through forms of nature, through which "our minds / Are nourished and invisibly repaired" (1805, 11:214–215).

In Book 12 Wordsworth's plea is for transcendent powers of perception that would allow him, along with other poet-seers, "to perceive / Some-

thing unseen before" (1805, 12:304–305) and wishing to have "A power like one of Nature's" (1805, 12:312). In the meditation on Salisbury Plain, Wordsworth envisions the ancient Druids and their abilities as seers guided by "the breath / Of music" (1805, 12:347–348). The poet connects himself to them, to "the pure spirit, and best power, / Both of the object seen, and eye that sees" (1805, 12:377–378).

Book 13, the ascent of Mt. Snowdon, is the culminating meditation of *The Prelude*. Wordsworth has climbed the mountain with a friend and a local shepherd and, at its summit, sees moonlight break through fog, shining upon "a huge sea of mist" (1805, 13:43) at their feet while roaring waters sounded from a "blue chasm" (1805, 13:56). From this recollection, he muses on the imagination and describes those who develop the faculty as those who are "quickened, roused, and made thereby more fit / To hold communion with the invisible world" (1805, 13:107–108), with abilities that have issued from God; they are able to understand eternal verities through interchange with nature.

After the descent, Wordsworth meditates on intellectual, or spiritual, love, from which come truth and beauty and which exists with imagination, again, leading one to "infinity and God" (1805, 13:205). He expresses hopes that he has written an "enduring" work, that Coleridge's health will return, and that in their collaborative literary endeavors, he and Coleridge, speaking as "Prophets of Nature" (1805, 13:446), will ensure that civilization will not devolve into the "old idolatry," "servitude," "ignominy and shame" (1805, 13:436–438), but that they will have contributed to civilization in a way that will help humanity understand the possibilities of imagination, "A lasting inspiration, sanctified / By reason and truth" (1805, 13:447–448), which can lead to an apprehension of divinity.

In view of the great significance of Wordsworth's poem, it does not come as a surprise that *The Prelude* has evoked strong critical response. Important voices include Harold Bloom, who defined *The Prelude* as one of the greatest examples of the internalized quest romance; and Geoffrey Hartman, who, in his influential essay "A Poet's Progress: Wordsworth and the *Via Naturaliter*

*Negativa*" (1962), questioned the widespread view that Wordsworth was a worshipper of nature. Hartman argues, instead, that Wordsworth did not write about nature "as an immediate external object" but rather considered it to be a stimulus for imagination, which, eventually, results in a transcendence of nature and a growing independence of imagination from Nature. Finally, Beth Lau's recent use of interdisciplinary memory research to show that in *The Prelude* Wordsworth intensely engages with processes of memory operation demonstrates that the work remains attractive and stimulating for readers to the present day.

Part Romantic conversation poem, part epic, part spiritual meditation and reflection, part narrative, but modern in its violation of strict chronology and the announcement of its own form, *The Prelude* asks the reader for intense participation. While it seems to follow the course of Wordsworth's life, the descriptions of events and recollections of the past are overlaid with the poetic development of the present. Events are described in retrospect by the poetically developed imagination not only as narrative in time but also as encounters with the SUBLIME and attendant transcendental moments and the ensuing apprehension they provide of the universe and God. Overall, the poem is a reminder that a major focus in the poetry of Wordsworth is the renovation of the human psyche and, ultimately, the preservation of moral civilization through a process involving interaction with nature, the remembrance involved in "spots of time," and the poetic activity of the Romantic creative imagination. In the most intense moments of *The Prelude*, the poet recollects the past—event and emotion—and observes and describes Nature, transforming perception to conception and conception to an apprehension of eternal truths. *The Prelude* describes the development of the mind of the poet—in this poem, Wordsworth himself—from childhood, culminating in the conviction that he has the imaginative vision to be the poet-seer who can understand and translate for the reader absolute verities through the imagination and its interaction with nature. Yet because of the irregular nature of its publication history, *The Prelude* influenced no other writers of Romanticism, save his sister, DOROTHY WORDSWORTH, and Coleridge,

to whom the poem was addressed and to whom it was read by Wordsworth in its entirety.

See also "ASCENT OF SNOWDON, THE."

## Further Reading

Abrams, M. H. "The Design of *The Prelude*: Wordsworth's Long Journey Home." In *The Prelude 1799, 1805, 1850*, by William Wordsworth, edited by Jonathan Wordsworth, M. H. Abrams, and Stephen Gill, 585–598. New York and London: W. W. Norton, 1979.

Barth, J. Robert. "The Temporal Imagination in Wordsworth's *Prelude*: Time and the Timeless." *Thought* 66, no. 261 (June 1991): 139–150.

Bloom, Harold, comp. "The Internalization of Quest-Romance." In *Romanticism and Consciousness. Essays in Criticism*, 3–24. New York and London: W. W. Norton, 1970.

———, ed. *Wordsworth's The Prelude*. New York: Chelsea House Publishers, 1986.

Gill, Stephen. *William Wordsworth: The Prelude*. Cambridge: Cambridge University Press, 1991.

———. *Wordsworth's The Prelude: A Casebook*. Oxford: Oxford University Press, 2006.

Hartman, Geoffrey. "A Poet's Progress: Wordsworth and the *Via Naturaliter Negativa*." *Modern Philology* 59, no. 3 (1962): 214–224.

Hodgson, John A. "Tidings: Revolution in *The Prelude*." *Studies in Romanticism* 31 (Spring 1992): 45–70.

Lau, Beth. "Wordsworth and Current Memory Research." *Studies in English Literature 1500–1900* 42, no. 4 (2002): 675–692.

Lindenberger, Herbert. *On Wordsworth's Prelude*. Princeton, N.J.: Princeton University Press, 1963.

Milnes, Timothy. *William Wordsworth—The Prelude*. London: Palgrave Macmillan, 2009.

Rehder, Robert. *Wordsworth and the Beginnings of Modern Poetry*. London: Croom Helm, 1981.

Ricks, Christopher. "Wordsworth: 'A Pure Organic Pleasure from the Lines.'" *Essays in Criticism* 21 (1971): 1–32.

Wordsworth, Jonathan. "William Wordsworth, *The Prelude*." In *Oxford Companion to Romantic Studies*, edited by Duncan Wu, 179–190. Oxford: Blackwell, 1998.

Wordsworth, William. *The Prelude 1799, 1805, 1850: William Wordsworth*. Edited by Jonathan Wordsworth, M. H. Abrams, and Stephen Gill. New York: W. W. Norton & Company, 1979.

———. *The Prelude.* Edited by Ernest de Selincourt, revised by Helen Darbishire. Oxford: Oxford University Press, 1959.

———. *The Thirteen-Book Prelude.* Edited by Mark L. Reed. Cornell University Press, 1992.

—Donna Berliner and Nicole Frey Büchel

## *Pride and Prejudice* Jane Austen (1813)

*Pride and Prejudice* stands as one of the most popular novels of all time. Other novels may be more artistically complex, describe a greater range of human experience, or more subtly illuminate the human heart, but for sheer delight and human warmth few works can compete with JANE AUSTEN's most popular novel. *Pride and Prejudice* eschews powerful Romantic effects, yet as a classically restrained small-*r* romance, it continues to thrill and engage. Other Austen heroines do, of course, find their soul mates, but Elizabeth Bennet and Mr. Darcy stand in select company with pairings such as Jane Eyre and Mr. Rochester and Romeo and Juliet, forming the quintessential love stories of English literature. Elizabeth is not a neglected stepdaughter, but there is a deeply satisfying Cinderella-like sweep to her romance.

Elizabeth Bennet arguably exemplifies the woman that many females would like to be and the one many confident men would like to marry. Generations of readers have validated Austen's own characterization of Elizabeth as being "as delightful a character as ever appeared in print" (Austen, 1995, 201). Intelligent and sensitive, attractive (but not defining herself through her beauty), responsible and discerning, loving to those who deserve her love, she carries her independence of thought and judgment up to, but normally not over, the line of incivility. "Lizzy" walks in the mud to support her ill sister, verbally spars with Caroline Bingley and Darcy, confides in her sister Jane and with her friend and foil Charlotte Lucas, is mortified by the inappropriate behavior of her own parents and younger sisters, questions her precipitate judgments, revises her incorrect opinions, and courageously confronts Lady Catherine—and she does this all with a sprightliness and a true decorum that transcends the superficial formal politeness of the times.

*Pride and Prejudice*'s heroine is surrounded by an inimitable and unforgettable cast of comic characters—most notably Mr. Collins, Lady Catherine, and Mrs. Bennet—who are imbued with life through Austen's extraordinary ear for and presentation of delicate shadings of pompous and foolish speech. Through contrast and comparison, these characters implicitly establish Lizzy's own good sense. Moreover, Austen's comedic figures are humorous without themselves being objects of malice; in her later works Austen's satire grew sharper and more judgmental, but the characters of *Pride and Prejudice* are more innocent than antagonistic in their failings and peculiarities, and, accordingly, the comedy in *Pride and* Prejudice is endearingly good-natured.

In fact, the novel's romance and the comedy are so effectively presented—in Austen's own words, the novel is "light, & bright, & sparkling" (Austen 1995, 203)—that some readers may give short shrift to the serious themes that inhabit Austen's text. Of course, the originally planned title, *First Impressions,* denotes one of the novel's themes: the inherent danger of making quick judgments of character. However, an equally significant thread on the importance of parenting runs through the book. Time and again the foolishness of Mrs. Bennet (putting Jane at risk by sending her to Netherfield in the rain; glorying in Lydia's disaster of a marriage) or the withdrawn nature of Mr. Bennet (not actively supervising his younger daughters; failing to successfully address Lydia and Wickham's elopement) is contrasted with the Gardiners' effective "parenting" of the Bennet girls. The financial dependency faced by women is, of course, also central to the novel, as manifested by the plot-driving potential disinheritance through entailment facing the Bennet women and the probing examination of Charlotte Lucas's decision to marry an officious buffoon for financial security.

Additionally, the discussions between Elizabeth, Caroline Bingley, and Darcy as to the nature of accomplishment for women, along with Elizabeth's inherent verbal assertiveness, have fueled differing assessments by critics such as Marilyn Butler and Claudia Johnson as to the level of conservatism or proto-feminism to be associated with the novel. Along similar lines, the contrast between Jane's (and Bingley's) simplicity and trustfulness and Elizabeth's (and Darcy's) complexity and skepticism regarding the motives and characters of others raises yet another central moral question of the novel: Is it better to be lovingly charitable or intelligently judgmental? Presumably most readers would rather be an Elizabeth than a Jane, yet Elizabeth's well-known comment to her sister that "Till I have your disposition, your goodness, I never can have your happiness" (339) subverts and ultimately questions Austen's supposed preference.

Those readers who become emotionally involved with the characters and the story line, or absorbed and intrigued by the underlying social and moral themes, risk underappreciating Austen's stylistic artistry and the clarity and precision of her language. The writing is so transparently effective that it often requires a close rereading to reveal its subtle excellences. Many critics have hailed the ironic and epigrammatic brilliance of the novel's first line: "It is a truth universally acknowledged, that a single man in possession of a good fortune, must be in want of a wife" (5). However, this novel does not always flaunt its articulateness, nor does it rely only on omniscient narratorial commentary. Indeed, much of it is revealed through dialogue in which wit and wisdom are irregularly conjoined but in which character is invariably revealed. One notes, for example, that Mr. Bennet's admission that his guilt regarding his parental failings will "pass away soon enough" simultaneously conveys his intelligence, his love of ironic wordplay, and his self-knowledge regarding initial error as well as his future escape from responsibility. Further, true to the novel's presumed epistolary roots in the 18th-century novel, Jane, Darcy, Lydia, Mr. Gardiner, and Mr. Collins all write plot-advancing letters in character-revealing voices. Even short descriptive narrative passages concisely and precisely convey nuances of character, action, and excitement. Indeed, despite its status as an extraordinarily well-loved novel, *Pride and Prejudice* paradoxically may still be underappreciated for its social and moral complexities and undervalued as a work of literature.

## Further Reading

Austen, Jane. *Jane Austen's Letters.* 3rd ed. Edited by Deirdre Le Faye. Oxford: Oxford University Press, 1995.

———. *Pride and Prejudice.* Edited by Carol Howard. New York: Baines and Noble, 2003.

Butler, Marilyn. *Jane Austen and the War of Ideas.* Oxford: Clarendon Press, 1975.

Johnson, Claudia. *Jane Austen: Women, Politics, and the Novel.* Chicago: University of Chicago Press, 1988.

Tanner, Tony. *Jane Austen.* Cambridge, Mass.: Harvard University Press, 1986.

—Gary Simons

## Prince, Mary (ca. 1788–?)

Mary Prince created a furore when her life story *The History of Mary Prince, a West Indian Slave* was published in London in 1831. Ghosted by Susanna Strickland but ostensibly written by Prince, it was the first account of the life of a black woman to be printed in Great Britain, was instrumental in raising awareness about the transatlantic slave trade, and played a part in forcing its eventual abolition.

The basic details of the life of Mary Prince are as follows. The daughter of slaves, she was born into SLAVERY at Brackish Pond, Bermuda, 600 miles from the coast of Virginia, in about 1788. She and her parents were the legal property of Charles Myners, and as was often the case, she was separated from her parents. When Myners died, Prince and her mother—both deemed saleable commodities—were sold to a Captain Williams. Prince presented this part of childhood as being "the happiest period of my life. . . . I was made quite a pet of by Miss Betsey [Williams] and loved her very much" (Prince 7). However, as she notes: "[I was] too young to understand rightly my condition as a slave" (7). A stark reminder of this came at age 12 when Prince was hired out to another plantation; Williams subsequently sold her on to another slave owner. Prince's account of her life at this time is full of details of casual cruelty. Minor offences were punishable by flogging, and she recalled: "To strip me naked—to hang me up by the wrists and lay my flesh open with the cow-skin, was an ordinary punishment for even a slight offence" (15).

In 1806 Prince was sent to work on the salt pans of Turk Island: "I was immediately sent to work in the salt water with the rest of the slaves. This work was perfectly new to me. I was given a half barrel and a shovel, and had to stand up to my knees in the water, from four o'clock in the morning till nine, when we were given some Indian corn boiled in water, which we were obliged to swallow as fast as we could for fear the rain should come on and melt the salt" (25). In 1818 she was sold to John Wood, a plantation owner who lived in Antigua. Now age 30, she began to suffer from rheumatism "and grew so very lame that I was forced to walk with a stick" (25). It was at this point that things began to change, albeit slightly. Prince began attending meetings held at the Moravian Church, where she was taught to read. It was in Antigua that she met a widower, Daniel Jones, an ex-slave who had managed to buy his freedom. Jones asked Mary to marry him, which she did in 1826. John Wood was furious and had her whipped.

A turning point came when, in about 1828, Prince accompanied John Wood and his wife to London. Overwhelmed with work and going blind, she reputedly walked out shortly after arriving and sought refuge at the Moravian Mission House in Hatton Gardens. She then found employment at the home of Thomas Pringle, the Methodist secretary of the Anti-Slavery Society. It was Pringle who, in 1831, helped her publish *The History of Mary Prince, a West Indian Slave* in order that "good people in England might hear from a slave what a slave had felt and suffered" (3). The book—a story of physical and psychological humiliation, poverty, hardship and murder—caused a sensation and provoked two libel actions. John Wood sued the publishers, claiming that Prince had "endeavoured to injure the character of my family by the most vile and infamous falsehoods" (Prince 2000, 44). He lost his case. Other readers found the accounts of sadistic employers and ritual violence against Prince too over-the-top to be believable. On one occasion Mrs. Pringle had to write to one group (the Birmingham Society for Relief of Negro Slaves) to confirm that she had seen the evidence on Mary, and the "whole of the back part of her body is distinctly scarred . . . chequered with the vestiges of severe floggings" (Prince 2000, 64). Later, two supporters of the British-American slave system—James MacQueen, editor of the *Glasgow Courier,* and the Reverend James Curtin, an English missionary—took up Wood's case and challenged

the veracity of Prince's narrative. In an article in *Blackwood's Magazine* they claimed that Prince's book contained a large number of lies. Prince and her publisher sued for libel and won. The case was heard in the same year that the Emancipation Bill was finally passed in British Parliament.

Some aspects of the book are evidently written so as to present Prince in a way that would not antagonize polite readers. The book also mimics other slave narratives of the period. The antislavery societies sought to win support by presenting slaves as pure and Christian victims. As the literary scholar Sarah Salih has pointed out, Prince's ghost writer, Susanna Strickland, followed a fairly typical pattern adopted by many abolitionists of censoring Prince's experiences and deliberately blurred parts of the story to suit the antislavery cause. At the libel court case brought by Mr. Wood, in March 1833, Prince appeared as a witness and freely admitted a sexual relationship with a [white] Captain Abbot and "Oyskman—a freedman" (ix). However, in the book Strickland had inevitably taken a tactical decision to omit these aspects. Salih explains that as part of the propaganda war, "it was important for the anti-slavery society to present Prince as sexually pure," or at least repentant (in Prince, x). In the same way, the *History* concludes with Prince thanking Mrs. Pringle for teaching her "daily to read the word of God . . . [and] the great privilege of being enabled to attend Church three times on the Sunday" (Prince, 36). Though the story is partial—in both senses of the word—at the same time it is an inspiring tale, an account of how trauma and hardship can be overcome and how an individual can be enslaved and yet not be a slave. As related in the text, Prince often runs away and has a very definite sense of her own worth, and it is only rarely that she gives way to feelings of absolute despair.

Despite her brush with notoriety, little is known of Prince's life after this time. It is generally thought that she stayed in England after 1833, probably working as a servant. Her *History* is an important contribution to early black writing, and it offers a glimpse into the lives of enslaved men and women whose life stories cannot be traced. In the introduction to her recent edition of the *History,* Sarah Salih points to examples throughout the account of Prince's resistance (marrying without permission and repeatedly defending herself and others, physically and verbally). She concludes: "Far from passively accepting the punishments meted out to her, Mary Prince protested against her treatment at every available opportunity. Her History is a culmination of this protest" (in Prince, xxx). Jak Beula, founder of Nubian Jak, the organization behind the Mary Prince commemorative plaque erected in Camden, London, in 2007, says Prince has always been overlooked because she is difficult to pigeonhole: "History has a problem with her as a genuine heroine because she wasn't educated and was very obviously reliant on the anti-slavery movement to represent her— unlike someone such as Mary Seacole, who was a self-made woman. She may not have been a poster girl for women's independence, but," he insists passionately, "she's an extraordinary symbol of tenacity and resilience" (quoted in Wajid). Prince's story also raises questions about how many other women took a similar route. Was Prince's an exceptional story?

See also EQUIANO, OLAUDAH.

**Further Reading**

Midgley, Clare. *Women against Slavery: The British Campaigns, 1780–1870.* London: Routledge, 1992.

Prince, Mary. *The History of Mary Prince.* Edited by Sarah Salih. London: Penguin, 2000.

Sharpe, Jenny. *Ghosts of Slavery: A Literary Archeology of Black Women's Lives.* Minneapolis: University of Minnesota Press, 2003.

Wajid, Sara, "They bought me as a butcher would a calf or a lamb." *The Guardian* (October 19, 2007). Available online. URL: http://www.guardian.co.uk/uk/2007/oct/19/race.historybooks. Accessed on January 26, 2009.

—Penny Hawkins

## "Prisoner of Chillon, The" Lord Byron (1816)

In summer 1816 LORD BYRON met PERCY BYSSHE SHELLEY and MARY WOLLSTONECRAFT SHELLEY in exile in Switzerland. At the end of June, the two poets undertook a visit to the medieval castle and prison of Chillon, where the Swiss religious figure Prior François Bonivard (1496–1570) was held for four years until 1536. Byron is said to have carved his name in Bonivard's cell, though some believe it is too high on the wall for this to be the case. Legend also tells us that Byron composed the poem in two days, virtually on the scene, inspired by Bonivard's Promethean example. Bonivard was originally thought to have been chained to one of the pillars in the dungeon, defying his oppressive captors for the sake of the people. Historical inaccuracies, like the fact that Bonivard was not held in the dungeon and was certainly never chained, do little to mar Byron's exquisite empathetic poem, a dramatic monologue divided into 14 parts that imagines what such a long imprisonment must have been like. The lines are each written in iambic tetrameter, with an irregular rhyme scheme.

The first part of the poem introduces the protagonist, rushes through his family history, and implies that Bonivard's punishment was unjust, adding a brief critique of despotism. The narrator then describes the dungeon, revealing that it is a perversion of nature, being unhealthy and dark. From there, he relates the deadening influence of his surroundings. After the deaths of his brothers, his prison becomes in a very literal way, "a living grave" (l. 114): Their corpses are not given the honor of burial and remain in the cell. Byron thus contrasts freedom and imprisonment with life and death. His younger brother's death marks the narrator's descent into total isolation.

Typical of a Byronic hero, imprisonment is a torture to Bonivard because he is naturally an active man, and being forced into stillness blocks his ability to interact with the world. This eventually leads to the loss of all feeling, until a bird lands near his window and sings, giving him a momentary release. However, this only lasts until the bird flies away: "And cheering from my dungeon's brink, / Had brought me back to feel and think" (ll. 277–278). Then Bonivard climbs to his window and looks out—but the scenes of nature he spies only remind him of his separation: "I did descend again, / The darkness of my dim abode / Fell on me as a heavy load" (ll. 359–361).

Eventually Bonivard cuts himself off from all externals and comes to find comfort in the emptiness. Once he is permanently freed from his cell, he makes the entire world a prison: "My very chains and I grew friends, / . . . I / Regain'd my freedom with a sigh" (ll. 391–394). In this final section, Bonivard has lost the taste for freedom, revealing the final horror: that man can be so broken by prison that even liberty loses its appeal.

## Further Reading

Byron, George Gordon Byron, Baron. *Lord Byron: The Complete Poetical Works.* Vol. 4. Edited by Jerome J. McGann. Oxford: Clarendon Press, 1986.

Hall, Jean. "The Evolution of the Surface Self: Byron's Poetic Career." *Keats-Shelley Journal* 36 (1987): 134–157.

Longford, Elizabeth. *The Life of Byron.* Boston: Little, Brown and Co., 1976.

Marchand, Leslie A. *Byron: A Biography.* Vol. 3. New York: Knopf, 1957.

Quennell, Peter. *Byron in Italy.* New York: Viking Press, 1941.

Rutherford, Andrew. *Byron: A Critical Study.* Stanford, Calif.: Stanford University Press, 1961.

Thorslev, Peter Larsen. *The Byronic Hero: Types and Prototypes.* Minneapolis: University of Minnesota Press, 1995.

—Denise Tischler Millstein

## *Private Memoirs and Confessions of a Justified Sinner, The* **James Hogg** (1824)

JAMES HOGG's *The Private Memoirs and Confessions of a Justified Sinner* is a uniquely chilling tale of religious fanaticism that combines GOTHIC conventions with a fascination with abnormal psychology. According to the critic Frederick Frank, *Confessions* exposes "a new and deeper vein of the gothic" to produce the darkest psychological narrative in that tradition (Frank 151). The literary historian Walter Allen doubts "whether a more convincing representation of the power of evil exists in our literature" (Allen 130). What renders *Confessions* particularly compelling is that this quintessentially Scottish Faustian tale is twice-told, each telling supporting a different reading of the source of Robert Wringhim's homicidal drives, madness, and suicide. Such a doubled narrative is apposite

given that the crux of the divergent interpretations and the pièce de résistance in Hogg's masterpiece is Wringhim's flattering, duplicitous double, who goes by the provocative and unusual name of Gil-Martin.

What the critic Rebecca A. Pope has characterized as the novel's "double-devil debate" (Pope 232) is determined on the basis of whether one believes Gil-Martin to be a projection of Wringhim's mentally disturbed imagination or the devil himself. The first account of Wringhim's crimes, provided by an apparently rational, objective editor, supports the former case while the second "inside story" version, narrated by the justified sinner himself, supports the latter. As such, *Confessions* is a type of psychological case study, one rife with perplexing disjunctions between its two accounts. It is on the basis of these discrepancies, according to the author André Gide, that Hogg's novel is titillating both to "those who are attracted by religious and moral questions, and, for quite other reasons, psychologists and artists, and above all surrealists who are so particularly drawn by the demoniac in every shape" (Gide ix). In blurring this boundary between the rational and the irrational and thus unsettling modern, rational certainties by way of the supernatural, *Confessions* holds true to gothic form. Notably, however, at the time of its anonymous initial publication, it was severely criticized as "extraordinary trash" (quoted in Hogg 256) that was flawed on two primary counts: first, for its poor representation of Gil-Martin, who was deemed neither SUBLIME enough to terrify the reader nor grotesque enough to be laughed at; and, second, for its very clumsy structure of presenting two divergent narratives chronicling the same events (257).

*Confessions* is set in Scotland between 1687 and 1712 when the country was experiencing internal strife and constitutional upheaval. Scotland was, many felt, a nation divided, a perceived division that intensified over the course of the 18th century when a split was increasingly fabricated between the Gaelic, backward, "gothic" Highlands and the English-speaking, "civilized" Lowlands. The figurative demonic union of the novel's two principal figures (Wringhim and Gil-Martin) takes place against this complex backdrop, key to which was the political union between England and Scotland (1707).

*Confessions* is a gothic tale of usurpation and disinheritance that commences with the unsuitable marriage between the laird of Dalcastle and Lady Rabina, an Antinomian Calvinist. Adherents of this extreme, heretical branch of Calvinism maintained that no action on the part of an elected ("justified") individual, even murder, would affect their election. After her unsuccessful attempts to convert the laird with the aid of her religious adviser, Robert Wringhim, Sr., Rabina gives birth to a son, George Colwan, who is recognized by the laird as his legitimate offspring. When the laird refuses to recognize her second son, however, Robert Wringhim senior assumes the role of the child's father and grants him his name. A boy of "ardent and ungovernable passions . . . [and] sternness of demeanour" (Hogg 19), Wringhim Jr. meets his spiritually healthy, morally upright half brother in young adulthood and persecutes him. George's subsequent murder, apparently by his companion, Thomas Drummond, leads to the premature death of his brokenhearted father and arouses the suspicions of his father's housekeeper, Arabella Logan, who assumes a detective-like role in seeking out the truth. She eventually secures evidence of Wringhim's involvement in the murder from Arabella Calvert, a prostitute and eyewitness to the events. By the time the officers are dispatched "to apprehend the monster" (92), however, Wringhim disappears. Thus ends, rather abruptly and mysteriously, the editor's narrative.

Logan's intense fascination with "the extraordinary being who accompanies" Wringhim (90) sets the stage for the second narrative. Wringhim's own account is a gothic spiritual autobiography that offers a far more harrowing version of events of his early years under the tutelage of "his reverend father" (107) when he lived in "terror" in the state of reprobation (99–100) and experienced regular "bodily chastisements" for his innumerable sins (108). His first meeting with Gil-Martin significantly coincides with Wringhim's discovery that he is one of the elect, a member of the "society of the just made perfect" (115), in which he assumes the rather dramatic role of a "two-edged weapon" that may "lay waste . . . [God's] enemies" (122).

The Gil-Martin-Wringhim relationship dramatically alters over time: Gil-Martin's early flattery and servility toward the spiritually proud Wringhim deteriorates into the provocative goading of his unwitting prey into murderous action and then reveling in his terror and anguish. Wringhim's final tormented days and desperate suicide while under Gil-Martin's "protection" suitably mirror the editor's recounting of George's persecution by Wringhim. The novel closes with the exhumation of the suicide's grave containing Robert's mummified corpse and tormented memoirs. A perplexed editor remarks that he does not "comprehend the writer's drift" (254).

Hogg's greatest innovation in *Confessions* is to figure Antinomian Calvinism as ideologically akin to a demonic secret society and to forge an equation between the Calvinist Covenant and a Faustian pact (see FAUST). With Gil-Martin, Hogg fashioned the most insidiously intimate double in the British gothic tradition, earning him the great praises of André Gide who called *Confessions* "a work, so singular and so enlightening" that "so voluptuously tormented" him (Gide ix, x). Hogg warns that monsters like Wringhim are being made nation-wide by reverend "fathers" disseminating perverse ideologies. Thus is MARY SHELLEY's monster-making motif and concern with unnatural parents and children brought brilliantly to bear on ideology. *Confessions* paved the way for such "heart of darkness"–style psychomachias as Nathaniel Hawthorne's "Young Goodman Brown" (1835), Edgar Allan Poe's "William Wilson" (1840), Robert Louis Stevenson's *The Strange Case of Dr. Jekyll and Mr. Hyde* (1886), and Henry James's *Turn of the Screw* (1898), each of which captures a sense of the provocative, penumbral frontier that is human psychology.

**Further Reading**

Allen, Walter. *The English Novel: A Short Critical History.* Harmondsworth, Eng.: Penguin, 1965.

Frank, Frederick S. *The First Gothics: A Critical Guide to the English Gothic Novel.* New York and London: Garland Publishing, 1987.

Gide, André. Introduction to *The Private Memoirs and Confessions of a Justified Sinner,* by James Hogg, ix–xvi. London: Cresset Press, 1947.

Hogg, James. *The Private Memoirs and Confessions of a Justified Sinner.* Edited by John Carey. Oxford: Oxford University Press, 1991.

Pope, Rebecca A. "Hogg, Wordsworth, and Gothic Autobiography." *Studies in Scottish Literature* 27 (1992): 218–240.

—Carol Davidson

## *Prometheus Unbound* Percy Bysshe Shelley (1820)

A lyrical drama in four acts published in 1820, *Prometheus Unbound* was never intended for the stage; rather, its dramatic structure serves to convey the fluidity and multivocality consistent with the poem's unfixing of mythologies. The mind of Prometheus, blending and merging as it does with the psyches of other characters, is symbolic of One Mind, of which, according to PERCY BYSSHE SHELLEY in "A DEFENCE OF POETRY," all other minds form the "co-operating thoughts" (Shelley 522).

In this poem, Shelley rewrote a lost play also entitled *Prometheus Unbound,* the original sequel by the ancient Greek dramatist Aeschylus to his extant *Prometheus Bound.* In the lost drama from the fifth century B.C., Prometheus allegedly repents his action of giving fire to mankind and so is forgiven by Jupiter for his transgression and released from his torments. Although Shelley chooses an ancient myth for his poem, he demonstrates that the original myth has no precedence or authority over the myths that stem from it. Shelley's Prometheus does not repent but inverts the Aeschylean theme by forgiving his oppressor, Jupiter, a thin disguise for the Judeo-Christian god and—typically for Shelley—every other form of earthly tyrant ever made in a tyrannical god's image: king, patriarch, and priest. Prometheus then achieves dominion over his oppressor in a triumph of love over hatred. Significant critical interpretations of the poem include Earl Wasserman's Platonic account of the evolution of Shelley's mind as embodied in the heroic figure of Prometheus, Harold Bloom's discussion of the titanic action being undercut by the poem's irony, and Carlo Baker's examination of the "Psyche-Epipsyche" theme on a cosmic scale. Barbara Gelpi's psychoanalytic reading, *Shelley's Goddess,* examines eroticized maternity in a Lacanian/Kristevan reading of the poem.

In act 1 we find Prometheus bound to a precipice in the Indian Caucasus with two ocean nymphs, Panthea and Ione, playing the traditional interpretive role of the Greek chorus and sympathizing with Prometheus's 3,000 years of torment. Prometheus repents his original curse against Jupiter, repeated back to him by a sorrowful "Spirit of Earth." Mercury, himself sympathetic to the titan but bound to obey Jupiter's orders, brings Prometheus new torments in the form of Furies who bombard him with tragic human truths of murder, hypocrisy, and cruelty. Prometheus's forgiveness of his enemy, however, sets in motion the process of his eventual liberation. At the end of act 1, a number of benevolent spirits arise and soothe Prometheus with a prophecy about him quelling Death. Prometheus responds that the only hope is in love, and he thinks of his exiled lover, Asia. The act ends with Panthea leaving to meet her.

Alone in a valley in the Caucasus, Asia has a premonition of her sister's arrival. Act 2 foregrounds the heroines of Prometheus's unbinding, Asia and Panthea, in a lyrical and nebulous world of dream. When the younger ocean nymph, Panthea, arrives, they tell one another dreams of beauty (Prometheus as sunrise) and love (a shared kiss). Asia sees a vision of Prometheus while looking into Panthea's eyes. Panthea and Asia then recall other dreams, both of which end with a voice saying "follow, follow." A symbolic merging of identities between the actors in the psychic drama occurs as the two sisters follow the echoing voices out of the vale. They arrive at the Cave of Demogorgon, "a mighty darkness" (2.4.2), where Asia asks many questions about the creation of the world, the progress of human history up to the moment, and the existence of god. The answers are occasionally straightforward (that Jupiter is the source of suffering) and sometimes enigmatic ("the deep truth is imageless" [2.4.116]). Demogorgon represents inexorable physical laws of the universe, the principle of necessity. The "Spirit of the Hour"—the hour of Prometheus's and indeed all humanity's liberation—arrives. Asia speaks her famous lyric, "my soul is an enchanted boat" (2.5.72), intimating the transformative power of love. Asia and Panthea depart in the chariot of the Spirit of the Hour to find and deliver Prometheus.

Act 3 begins with Jupiter on his throne proclaiming his omnipotence over everything but the soul of man. He awaits the arrival of Demogorgon triumphantly, but Demogorgon arrives only to drag him into the abyss, crying for mercy. Following a brief dialogue between Apollo and Ocean about a solar eclipse, the chariot, with Asia, Panthea, Ione, the Spirit of the Hour and Hercules in it, arrives. Hercules perfunctorily unbinds Prometheus, but Asia is more to be credited with Prometheus's release. Prometheus gives Ione a shell ("a voice to be accomplished" [3.3.67]) to blow into and create music all over the world. Earth describes the feeling of music being blown through her, and she sends the characters on a journey to a cave at the end of time. At the "cave of Prometheus," the Spirit of Earth greets Asia as her mother and tells her of the glorious transformation of humanity. The Spirit describes in detail a world transformed into a state of perfection, the veil torn aside, and man left "equal, unclassed, tribeless and nationless" (3.4.195).

Typically, act 4 receives less critical attention than the first three acts. It was appended to an earlier three-act version of the poem Shelley hoped to have published, and it appears extraneous to some readers. However, it moves the psychic drama beyond the confines of the individual mind to encompass a renewal and revelation of the cosmos. It also makes explicit a call to the reader for participation in the imaginative transformations symbolized in the earlier acts. Prometheus and Asia are absent from act 4, since their marriage, symbolizing the end of time, has already taken place. Panthea and Ione, still mediators of the vision, remain near the cave of Prometheus and listen to music from unseen spirits and hours singing in celebration of the end of evil and the triumph of love. The Moon and the Earth are joined in an eclipse which is a consummation. Demogorgon arises again from the earth and describes the apocalyptic present as a day which ends all tyrannies, and he proclaims Love the victor. He also offers a prescription for others to recreate this vision by imitating Prometheus's suffering, forgiveness, hope, and steadfastness: "These are the spells by which to reassume / An

empire o'er the disentangled Doom" (4.568–569). Demogorgon's words make explicit Shelley's optimistic interpretation of a tragic human history ending in liberation and joy.

The enormous scope and spiritual ambition of *Prometheus Unbound* led William Butler Yeats to call it "one of the sacred books of the world" (Yeats 65). A mythopoeic and utopian work, Shelley's poem lends itself to allegorical meanings on scientific, philosophical, biographical, historical, political, religious, psychological, and anagogic levels. The poem's place in literary history is probably undervalued either because it is difficult or because people take issue with one or more of Shelley's opinions. It blurs the boundary between kerygma, or sacred writing, and literature, and thus expresses Shelley's conviction in "A Defence of Poetry" that "poetry is indeed something divine" (Shelley 2002, 531). Many, including Shelley himself, consider *Prometheus Unbound* his greatest achievement.

**Further Reading**

Baker, Carlos. *Shelley's Major Poetry.* Princeton, N.J.: Princeton University Press, 1948.

Bloom Harold, *Shelley's Mythmaking.* New Haven, Conn.: Yale University Press, 1959.

Gelpi, Barbara Charlesworth. *Shelley's Goddess: Maternity, Language, Subjectivity.* New York: Oxford University Press, 1992.

Shelley, Percy Bysshe. "A Defence of Poetry." In *Shelley's Poetry and Prose,* edited by Donald Reiman and Neil Fraistat, 509–535. New York: Norton, 2002.

Wasserman, Earl R. *Shelley's Prometheus Unbound. A Critical Reading.* Baltimore: Johns Hopkins University Press, 1965.

Yeats, W. B. "The Philosophy of Shelley's Poetry." In *Essays and Introductions.* London: Macmillan, 1900.

—Monika Lee

## *Psyche, or The Legend of Love*  Mary Tighe (1805)

*Psyche* was published privately in an edition of 50 copies in 1805. Based primarily on the legend of Cupid and Psyche found in *The Golden Ass* by the Roman poet Lucius Apuleius (ca. 123/125–ca. 180) and written in Spenserian stanzas, the poem is made up of six lengthy cantos (each nearly 600 lines long), a sonnet dedication to the poet's mother, and a brief prose preface. After MARY TIGHE's premature death from tuberculosis, the poem was republished by her cousin along with many of her shorter poems, and soon after it was reprinted three additional times and published in the United States.

While the first two cantos follow Tighe's Latin source relatively closely, the second half of the poem draws far more from Edmund Spenser's *The Fairie Queene* (1590–96) and other allegorical writing. As in Apuleius's version, Psyche is the victim of Venus's jealousy of her beauty, and the goddess sends her son, Cupid, to punish her and demands that she be sacrificed. But Cupid has himself fallen in love with the pure Psyche, and he steals her away at the last minute. He insists that she never see her rescuer, but she sneaks into his room one evening, only to wake him by dripping wax from her candle on him as he sleeps. She is, again, banished, and her only chance of being reunited with her love is to make a quest to gain Venus's forgiveness. The second half of the poem describes this quest and makes several allusions to Spenser, with the inclusion of his villainous Blatant Beast.

Tighe's initial reviewers focused almost exclusively on her lush and sensuous language, which famously influenced JOHN KEATS's poetry. Like Spenser before her, she creates elaborate and rich bowers in her poetical world, frequently describing the flora in great detail. Additionally, the lovers' eroticism is clear: Tighe makes recurring references to lips and arms, panting and sighing. Keats's borrowings of this sensuous language were so extensive that in 1929 Earle Vonard Weller published an entire book that explored parallel passages in their works. More recently, however, critics have focused less on Tighe's language and more on a number of themes that the poet explores within it, particularly the complex gender issues and reversals in the text.

## Further Reading

Linkin, Harriet Kramer. "Romanticism and Mary Tighe's *Psyche*: Peering at the Hem of Her Blue Stockings." *Studies in Romanticism* 35, no. 1 (Spring 1996): 55–72.

———, "Skirting around the Sex in Mary Tighe's *Psyche*." *Studies in English Literature*, 42, no. 4 (2002): 731–752.

Tighe, Mary. *The Collected Poetry of Mary Tighe*. Edited by Paula R. Feldman and Brian C. Cooney. Baltimore: Johns Hopkins University Press, 2010.

Weller, Earle Vonard. *Keats and Mary Tighe: The Poems of Mary Tighe with Parallel Passages from the Works of John Keats*. New York: Modern Language Association, 1928.

—Brian Cooney

## Queen Mab: A Philosophical Poem Percy
Bysshe Shelley (1813)

*Queen Mab: A Philosophical Poem* (1813) is a fantastic dream vision in nine lengthy cantos with a radical, political message. It sports an unwieldy appendix of notes, longer than the poem itself, that are derived from PERCY BYSSHE SHELLEY's reading in French and Scottish Enlightenment philosophy, the Greeks, and the Roman poet Lucretius's *On the Nature of Things*. Consequently, the poem has often been read as "an overwrought didactic, political manifesto that summarizes Enlightenment philosophy and other source texts" (Lee 170).

With epigraphs from Voltaire, Lucretius, and Archimedes and a dedication to Shelley's first wife, Harriet, *Queen Mab* begins with an image of a sleeping Ianthe (the name of Shelley's infant daughter). A Fairy Queen, named for Shakespeare's Queen Mab from Mercutio's famous speech in *Romeo and Juliet* (1.4.53–94), arrives in a chariot and calls Ianthe's soul to awaken, separate from her body, and accept a gift. The Fairy will reveal the secrets of the past, the present, and the future to Ianthe's spirit, not again referred to as Ianthe but simply as "the Spirit" until she reenters her sleeping body at the end of the poem. This fact emphasizes her prototypical quality as the universal, undifferentiated human spirit in its purest form, unchained from "earth's immurement" (1.188). The poem is the narrative of Mab's teachings as she and the Spirit look down on the earth and view its past, present, and future scenes.

The fairy's chariot, or "car," flies over mountains and oceans to the her "etherial palace" (2.29) and the "Hall of Spells" (2.42), where Mab and the Spirit survey the earth, its inhabitants, and its ancient monuments, either ruined or someday to be ruined, to observe that human pride is foolish in its attempts to achieve immortality through art, architecture, and religion. A long speech of Lucretian science extols the physical universe and its invisible spirits. Mab shows a king as a hideous caricature of a human being, victim of his appetites and tormented by his vices. From this she generalizes about the misery of kings, the absurdity of being ruled by them, and the paradox of subjects who hate them succumbing to their authority. Kings will disappear altogether and only the virtuous man achieves immortality through "deathless memory" (3.165). Despite being out of step with natural goodness, ultimately mankind, too, will fulfill nature's perfection.

A night full of beauty gives way to a battlefield of slaughtered corpses destroyed by "kings, and priests, and statesmen" (4.80). There is nothing natural about war, Mab argues, but children are raised and coerced into accepting and idealizing it. Soldiers are merely "hired assassins" (4.169) and "bullies" of a king's fear (4.179). From this attack on the military, Queen Mab, increasingly Shelley's didactic mouthpiece in the poem, enumerates the evils of religion, used by the tyrant to cloak and excuse his crimes. Mab issues a warning to religious, military, and state leaders of the impending misery intrinsic to vice. Commerce is also cursed, because of gold's enslaving power, and fame is an idol. Alluding to THOMAS GRAY's "mute inglorious Milton" (l. 59) from "ELEGY WRITTEN IN A COUNTRY CHURCH-YARD," Mab asserts that many men of genius lie buried without accomplishment because of poverty. She says that even good things are corrupted into evil by commerce and the falsehood of religion. The heart of one good man is worth more than anything else. The rousing diatribe ends with Fairy Mab saying the time has come for selfishness to die (5.249–250).

In a parallel with Adam in Book 12 of JOHN MILTON's *Paradise Lost* speaking to the archangel Michael about an account of human history, the Spirit asks if there is hope. The Fairy echoes Michael in her reassurances that evil will destroy itself and the earth will be renewed, but without Michael's insistence on faith. In fact, Mab blames misery on Religion, a male "prolific fiend" (6.69). A history of Religion's personified life shows that he began innocently enough as a deist who used the word *God* as an abstraction from the wonders and beauties of the natural world. In middle age, Religion became a murderer, and now he is old and dying. Mab describes an everlasting spirit of life that animates all of nature, a "Soul of the Universe" (6.190) which is not God. The Spirit tells of seeing an atheist burned at the stake. Mab says the atheist was right, and the name of God is responsible for bloodshed and terror. She summons Ahasuerus, the Wandering Jew, who believes in an avenging Jehovah who created the world in seven days. According to Ahasuerus, humankind was created to fulfil that god's sadistic and self-aggrandizing purpose. Shelley parodies the Genesis stories and satirizes religious belief, with Moses, God's "murderer," and Christ as another function of God's malice, sent to save only a handful of followers and to give vent to God's cruel anger. Ahasuerus echoes Milton's Satan in his defiance and describes Christians massacring each other in the internecine wars. He rails against the hypocrisy of preaching love while practicing hatred. Reason, we are told, now begins to displace this God.

Canto 8 describes a future earth renewed with joy, hope, love, health, and freedom. Evil fades to become a distant memory. Ianthe's Spirit fills with joy at the description of fertile deserts and harmless predators. A feminine Earth is recreated with "consentaneous love" (8.108). The misery of man's former existence is emphasized and contrasted with his future: a vegetarian, feminist, proto-marxist utopia guided by happiness and science. "Omnipotence of mind" (8.236) will bring about this change. Queen Mab sings a song of celebration: The only heaven is a renewed earth. Time is fled. Reason and Passion are both freed, but Reason is the Queen of Passion. Death still comes, but mildly and without disease. Men and women are finally equal, and the palace of the King whispers of the death of SLAVERY and religion, its halls filled with the sound of children's playfulness. Queen Mab concludes that she has finished her task and returns Ianthe to the present corporeal body with encouragements about not fearing death, which is "but the voyage of a darksome hour" (9.174). Ianthe's spirit is thankful and blessed as she descends in the car, rejoins with her body, and wakes to see her lover, Henry, casting his looks of love on her.

Early influential studies of *Queen Mab* can be found in Kenneth Neill Cameron's *Young Shelley: Genesis of a Radical,* Carlos Baker's "Spenser, the Eighteenth Century and *Queen Mab*," and Ross Woodman's *The Apocalyptic Vision in the Poetry of Shelley.* For the most part, essays, such as David Worrall's and Neil Fraistat's, have focussed on the historical and political aspects of interpretation. Jessica Smith, Timothy Morton, and Allan Bewell provide analyses of topology and climatology, and Monika Lee positions the poem in the context of 18th- and 19th-century language theories.

*Queen Mab* may well be Shelley's most widely read and influential long poem. Pirated by the radical underground, it became a bible to the 19th-century Chartist movement and a huge influence on British Marxists, especially George Bernard Shaw. Although Shelley scholars have traditionally been sensitive to its shortcomings as a literary work, left-wing radicals have long embraced it as a treatise of working people's moral and political rights. Despite overzealousness and occasional heavy-handedness, in this poem, first composed when he was 18, Shelley shows his early skills in versification and metaphor. Moreover, he lays down the themes and poetic strategies developed in his later works, particularly in PROMETHEUS UNBOUND, a highly accomplished treatment of the utopian reformist optimism found in *Queen Mab*.

## Further Reading

Baker, Carlos. "Spenser, the Eighteenth Century, and Shelley's *Queen Mab*." *Modern Language Quarterly* 2 (1941), 81–98.

Bewell, Allan. *Romanticism and Colonial Disease*. Baltimore: Johns Hopkins University Press, 1999.

Cameron, Kenneth Neill. *Young Shelley: Genesis of a Radical*. New York: Macmillan, 1950.

Fraistat, Neil. "The Material Shelley: Who Gets the Finger in Queen Mab?" *Wordsworth Circle*. 33 (Winter 2002). Available online. URL: http://www.bu.edu/editinst/resources/wordsworth/index.html. Accessed January 10, 2010.

Lee, Monika H. "'Nature's Silent Eloquence': Disembodied Organic Language in Shelley's *Queen Mab*." *Nineteenth-Century Literature* 48, no. 2 (1993): 169–193.

Morton, Timothy. "*Queen Mab* as Topological Repertoire." *Romantic Circles* (August 1997). Available online. URL: http://www.rc.umd.edu/praxis/early-shelley/morton/morton.html. Accessed January 10, 2010.

Shelley, Percy Bysshe. *Shelley's Poetry and Prose*. Edited by Donald H. Reiman and Sharon B. Powers. New York: Norton, 2001.

Smith, Jessica. "Tyrannical Monuments and Discursive Ruins: The Dialogic Landscape of Shelley's *Queen Mab*." *Keats-Shelley Journal* 47 (1998): 108–141.

Woodman, Ross Greig. *The Apocalyptic Vision in the Poetry of Shelley*. Toronto: University of Toronto Press, 1964.

Worrall, David. "Kinship, Generation and Community: The Transmission of Political Ideology in Radical Plebeian Print Culture." *Studies in Romanticism* 43, no. 2 (Summer 2004): 283–295.

—Monika Lee

# R

## Radcliffe, Ann (1764–1823)

Ann Radcliffe was one of the most influential writers of her generation and has been called the "Shakespeare of romance." Little is known about Radcliffe's life. She was born Ann Ward in London on July 9, 1764, the only child of William and Ann Ward. Her father was a haberdasher, selling items used in the manufacture of clothing. The family was related to Thomas Bentley, the business partner of the celebrated pottery manufacturer Josiah Wedgwood. It was through this connection that Mr. Ward moved his family to Bath in 1772 to manage one of the firm's branches. Anne seems to have been educated at home, though it has been suggested that she may also have attended Sophia Lee's school for young ladies when her family moved to Bath. She spent much of her early youth in Bath at the home of her uncle Thomas Bentley, a Dissenting merchant. At his house, Ann Ward would have met various people of distinction, especially literary women like Elizabeth Montagu, Mrs. Ord, HESTER PIOZZI, and ANNA LAETITIA BARBAULD. It is possibly through these means that she became familiar with Shakespeare's tragedies and the "Graveyard School" of English poetry that are frequently quoted in her novels, as well as Lee's own sentimental historical novel *The Recess* (1785). In 1787 Ann married William Radcliffe, who was the proprietor of the *English Chronicle* and who encouraged her to write. They lived a seemingly happy life of seclusion and had no children. There is no account for why, at the age of 32, she

stopped publishing. Most critics believe she retired to avoid notoriety, but the lack of any of her correspondence prevents further inquiry into her reasons. She died in London on February 7, 1823.

Radcliffe published five GOTHIC novels—*The Castles of Athlin and Dunbayne* (1789), *A Sicilian Romance* (1790), *The Romance of the Forest* (1791), *The* MYSTERIES OF UDOLPHO (1794), and *The Italian* (1797)—and various works recounting her travel in England and on the Continent, including *A Journey Made in the Summer of 1794* (1795), before she stopped publishing. Her first novel appeared 24 years after Horace Walpole's *The Castle of Otranto* (1765). In a commentary on Walpole's fanciful tale, SIR WALTER SCOTT explained that Radcliffe altered the gothic romance by providing a rational explanation at the end of her novels for what were thought to be supernatural events. Although an admirer of Radcliffe, Scott felt himself cheated into sympathy with the terror in her novels and complained that the emphasis on rationality ruined the interest of a second reading. However, Radcliffe's novels were incredibly popular with the public; the biographer E. B. Murray points out that "she was willing to tinker with, but not ignore, rational limits of the 18th-century empirical psychology her readers were morally and esthetically conditioned to accept" (Murray 13). She did reuse, although in a more subdued manner, many gothic props found in Walpole's tale as well as in CLARA REEVE's *The* OLD ENGLISH BARON (1777) and Lee's *The Recess*—for example, a late medieval setting, victimized women and menacing men, medieval castles, labyrinthine passages, flickering candles, creaking doors, ghostly apparitions, superstition, and folklore.

Radcliffe's novels essentially mix the gothic romance with the novel of sensibility, which features a virtuous heroine and a courtship plot. In her best-known novel, *The Mysteries of Udolpho*, the recently orphaned Emily St. Aubert is separated from her betrothed, the hero Valancourt, when her aunt remarries a villainous man named Montoni. Montoni isolates Emily in Udolpho, a castle high in the Apennines, where he threatens her life, honour, and fortune. After much suffering, Emily escapes from Udolpho, the mysteries are explained, and Emily and Valancourt marry and return to live happily in her childhood home.

All of Radcliffe's heroines undergo an important lesson in the excess of sensibility: They must learn to resist the fancies of their imaginations and to use reason as a guide. Catherine Morland, the main character of JANE AUSTEN's *NORTHANGER ABBEY*, must learn a similar lesson. However, Austen's character's imagination is not provoked by apparently supernatural phenomena, but rather by a too assiduous reading of Radcliffe's novels. Thus, Austen ridicules the popularity of the gothic by contrasting its romance and terror with the normal realities of English life. More recent feminist critics, specifically Ellen Moers, see the value the gothic genre held for women writers and readers. In *Literary Women* (1976), Moers coins the term *heroinism* to describe the paradoxical freedom that the gothic heroine experiences while she is being persecuted by others: She explores abandoned corridors, hidden vaults, and locked rooms and often travels independently (or with an inefficient chaperone) far from her home.

Radcliffe's most striking characters, though, are probably her villains, whose calculated self-interest and diabolical natures inspired MATTHEW GREGORY LEWIS's lurid character of Ambrosio in *The MONK* (1796) and contributed to the development of the Byronic hero or outcast. Radcliffe's villains are almost always father figures whose threats of seduction, imprisonment, rape, or murder cause the flight of the daughter. The novels implicitly interrogate the distribution of power in a patriarchal society and demonstrate male

restrictions on female behavior, but Radcliffe is mainly conservative, especially when compared to MARIA EDGEWORTH or MARY SHELLEY, both of whom began publishing a few years after Radcliffe stopped. Nevertheless, as the biographer Robert Miles points out, Radcliffe's novels present a case for "a new, liberal order set up in opposition to a regressive, feudal (and in that respect) 'patriarchal' one" (Miles 5). She typifies the 1790s, a period of spirited questioning, political instability, and social transition, but few concrete conclusions.

Radcliffe's novels are admired, perhaps most of all, for their use of landscape, weather, and effects of light as a sort of theatrical stage upon which her plots could be enacted. She was influenced by her favorite painters, especially Salvator Rosa and Nicolas Poussin; their works are filled with dark caves, steep cliffs, barren crags, savage wildernesses, gloomy skies, and awesome mountain ranges. These natural scenes evoke a combination of pleasure and terror, of psychological and physiological effects, and these are the effects Radcliffe strives to attain with the depiction of nature in her novels. In this, she builds on EDMUND BURKE's theories in *A PHILOSOPHICAL ENQUIRY INTO THE ORIGIN OF OUR IDEAS OF THE SUBLIME AND BEAUTIFUL* (1757), a work she knew very well. Murray explains that "key descriptions and incidents in her novels first 'touch' on the imagination, but they are sufficiently distanced by vagueness or the lack of empirical details to keep curiosity unsatisfied. The reader's imagination is incited to probe but never to dissolve the darkness or to diminish the distance" (Murray 27). More detail on her method and the distinction she perceived between terror and horror is contained in "On the Supernatural in Poetry," a preface to *Gaston de Blondville* (published posthumously in 1833).

## Further Reading

Dekker, George C. *The Fictions of Romantic Tourism: Radcliffe, Scott, and Mary Shelley.* Stanford, Calif.: Stanford University Press, 2005.

Miles, Robert. *Ann Radcliffe: The Great Enchantress.* Manchester, Eng.: Manchester University Press, 1995.

Moers, Ellen. *Literary Women.* Garden City, N.Y.: Doubleday, 1976.

Murray, E. B. *Ann Radcliffe*. New York: Twayne, 1972.

Norton, Rictor. *Mistress of Udolpho: The Life of Ann Radcliffe*. London: Leicester University Press, 1999.

Radcliffe, Ann. Preface to *Gaston de Blondeville*. Edited by Frances Chiu. Kansas City: Valancourt, 2006.

———. *The Italian*. London: Penguin, 2001.

———. *The Mysteries of Udolpho*. London: Penguin, 2001.

—Vicky Simpson

## Records of Woman, with Other Poems
### Felicia Hemans (1828)

*Records of Woman, with Other Poems* (1828), the most popular collection of poems by England's most popular 19th-century woman poet, was penned by FELICIA HEMANS at the apex of her career. The volume, as its complete title suggests, is divided into two sections: the first, "Records of Woman," includes 19 poems; the second contains 38 briefer "Miscellaneous Pieces." The poems that comprise the first half of the volume are portraits of women that span the centuries and the globe, and their subjects include nameless peasant girls, North American Indians, European queens, and classical and contemporary writers and artists. While critics from Hemans's day to our own have focused on the representation of domesticity in "Records of Woman," the poems—particularly when read in the context of each other—also express a kind of dissatisfaction with women's conventional lot.

Hemans's subjects are linked by their gender and by their desire to transcend their personal situations, and they are also linked by being based on historical figures whose lives and accomplishments were first reported by earlier writers. The extensive notes and epigraphs that precede each poem clearly articulate the historicity of Hemans's project; by including lengthy introductory material, Hemans offers a specific context in which to read the poems. The notes and epigraphs, which appear in English, German, French, and Italian, demonstrate Hemans's own vast reading in languages, literature, and history, and the poems themselves show how the writer has improved on others' particular representation of events. By comparing the construction of texts and differences between historical and poetical accounts, as well as the fluid boundaries of history and literature, *Records of Woman* demands that its readers engage actively with the "literature" and the "history" before them and educate themselves through a dialectical process.

Thus, in form as well as in content, the collection complicates the notion of separate spheres even as it articulates them—whether they are femininity and masculinity, imperialism and domesticity, or history and literature. In the combination of epigraphs, notes, and poems, Hemans shows the making of literature and of history to be explicitly social, political projects indebted to the work of others, and she announces her familiarity with European liberal intellectuals (quoting LORD BYRON and MME ANNE-LOUISE-GERMAINE DE STAËL, among others), and she shows her audience that education is a process accessible to and attainable by women. Finally, in privileging often derided feminine emotions and experiences but recontextualizing them in an historical sphere, the volume shows its readers (particularly its women readers familiar with sentimental poetry and novels) that they have special insights into history, even as the collection also promotes critical reading with its acknowledgment that just as historical accounts are not mimetic fact, neither is poetry purely innocent inspiration.

Grounded in historical facts—often wars, rebellions, or other acts of destruction—the poems contextualize women not in an isolated sphere removed from the casualties and evils of the world, but sometimes in reaction to it and at others as its catalysts. For example, the first poem of the volume, "ARABELLA STUART," is a dramatic monologue that traces Stuart's fluctuations as she waits for her lover, William Seymour, alternately hopeful and despondent about whether they will meet again. Stuart's desire for a peaceful reunion with her lover is echoed throughout the collection by famous and ordinary women alike, and critics have generally seen this desire as indicating Hemans's own valuation of the home, tending to ignore the poems' political context. However, as the introductory note attests, it is Stuart's desire for marriage that instigates her imprisonment and death. The note and poem together offer an early rendering of the feminist insight that "the personal is political" and public, as well as its counterpoint, "the political is also personal" and often generated by "passions." Throughout *Records of Woman,* then, Hemans underscores the often political context of the private tragedies that have affected women throughout history, particularly the brutalities of war and its consequences. Women within the collection are not simply martyrs or victims: "The Bride of the Greek Isle," the subject of the volume's second poem, sets fire to the men who attack and kill her wedding party in a fierce act of revenge, and the mother of "The Indian City" leads an attack that takes the lives of hundreds. Neither does Hemans shy away from infanticide: "The INDIAN WOMAN'S DEATH SONG" precedes the title character's suicide and her murder of her forsaken children.

If death is a constant throughout the collection, another theme raised by Hemans throughout "Records of Woman" is women's relationship to art. One of the most anthologized poems of the volume, "Properzia Rossi," is another dramatic monologue in the voice of an artist whose abandonment by her lover catalyzes not only her eventual death but also her most beautiful and complex creations. The final record, "The GRAVE OF A POETESS," more explicitly recalls Hemans as an artist (even though its ostensible subject is the 19th-century Irish writer MARY TIGHE) and the tensions of her own professional life that may have led to her early death at 41, but also of course to her renown and subsequent literary canonization.

The second half of the collection includes some of Hemans's even more famous work, including "The HOMES OF ENGLAND," "The Landing of the Pilgrim Fathers in New England," and "The Graves of a Household," poems that were memorized and recited in both the United States and England throughout the early part of the 20th century. If, on one level, these poems can be read naïvely, on another they also point to criticism of violent national projects, including imperialism (see EMPIRE). The critical appreciation of Hemans that began in the 1990s nearly always draws attention to this ambiguity and tension within the poet's most complex works. Even in her pithy lyrics, the poet belies the seemingly sentimental valuation of nationality, femininity, and even, perhaps most surprisingly, Christianity, in her revelation of the potentially disastrous consequences of an oversimplified easy identification with any particular worldview.

## Further Reading

Cottingham, Myra. "Felicia Hemans's Dead and Dying Bodies." *Women's Writing* 8, no. 2 (2001): 275–294.

Hemans, Felicia. *Felicia Hemans: Selected Poems, Letters, Reception Materials.* Edited by Susan J. Wolfson. Princeton, N.J.: Princeton University Press, 2000.

———. *Records of Woman, with Other Poems.* Edited by Paula R. Feldman. Lexington: University Press of Kentucky, 1999.

Montwieler, Katherine. "Hemans and Home-Schooling: History, Literature, and Records of Woman." *Nineteenth-Century Feminisms* 2 (Spring–Summer 2000): 10–31.

Sweet, Nanora, Julie Melnyk, and Marlon B. Ross. *Felicia Hemans: Reimagining Poetry in the Nineteenth Century.* Basingstoke, Eng.: Palgrave, 2001.

—Katherine Montwieler

## *Red and the Black, The* Stendhal (1830)

Stendhal's (Marie-Henri Beyle's) novel titled *The Red and the Black* is the story of an ambitious young man's path from the provinces to worldly success as first the secretary and then the intended son-in-law of a Parisian nobleman—and finally to his trial and execution for shooting his first mistress. Notable for its balanced, ironically detached style, the novel is also early realist in its inspiration by newspaper accounts of an actual crime and its minute details of daily life in Restoration France. At its core, however, lies the Romantic worldview that its author developed while growing up in Grenoble, southern France, in his father's conservative, middle-class household, where he learned to despise mediocrity, conformity, and materialism.

The novel's hero, Julien Sorel, embodies such key Romantic values as individuality, passion, boldness, challenge to authority, and liberalism. Educated enough to enter the bourgeois home of the mayor of Verrières, Monsieur de Rênal, as a tutor, Julien masks his hero worship of NAPOLEON BONAPARTE. Although he dreams of emulating Bonaparte's rise to glory through the red uniform of the military, in a reactionary society that fears exceptional men and exploits, he redirects his "pursuit of happiness" (a quintessential Stendhalian priority) toward achievement in the clergy's black cassock. Both manipulative and naive, endowed with the inner nobility of the Romantic outcast, he elicits the sympathy of Madame de Rênal, whom he seduces in the calculating spirit of class warfare but grows to love. This affair with an older woman together with his fiery outrage against society's injustices, his sensitivity, and his withdrawals into nature for solitary brooding—especially on mountain heights that imply his moral elevation—give Julien a Rousseauistic aspect to counterbalance his Napoleonic aura (see ROUSSEAU, JEAN-JACQUES). Moreover, the incestuous overtones of the adulterous liaison not only typify Romanticism's taboo relationships but also belong to the Stendhalian motif—repeated in *The Charterhouse of Parma* (1839) and connected by critics to Stendhal's own childhood loss of his mother—of sons in oedipal alliance with mother figures against an oppressive patriarchy. As the literary scholar Peter Brooks notes, "All Stendhal's novels record the failure of authoritative paternity in his protagonists' lives" (Brooks, 76).

Although Stendhal persistently relies on an ironic narrative voice to underline Julien's egotism and obtuseness, he also firmly establishes his protagonist as a "man of spirit." In Book 1 the love of Madame de Rênal and her sons, ostracism by his uncouth peers at the Besançon seminary, and mentoring by its chief abbé proclaim Julien's superiority. In Book 2, despite making provincial faux pas in the marquis de la Mole's household and continuing to play "the resentful plebeian," Julien wins his employer's favor and the love of de la Mole's daughter, the arrogant Mathilde. This second liaison, a protracted battle of two strong wills to dominate each other, culminates in Mathilde's surrender to Julien's advances and then a pregnancy that sanctions his marriage into her aristocratic family.

But his creator provides a more exceptional fate for Julien by having Madame de Rênal write the marquis a jealous letter denouncing him as a social-climbing seducer. Julien's intense, spontaneous reaction—shooting Madame de Rênal in

church—expresses his author's commitment to *espagnolisme,* defined by Irving Howe as "the insubordinate freedom of an individual . . . the vitality of instinct and emotion which creates a valid order of its own, brushing aside both morality and convention" (Howe 34). And consistent with Stendhal's recurring theme of confinement leading to spiritual liberation, the imprisoned Julien grows tired of playing the part of a hero and recognizes that the weeks he spent with Madame de Rênal in a country retreat as the greatest happiness of his life. Overjoyed by her survival, forgiveness, and loving visits, he expresses his authentic self at last by purposely alienating his jury and going to the guillotine "with no illusions" (501). In the novel's supremely Romantic closure, Madame de Rênal dies three days afterward of a broken heart.

### Further Reading

Bloom, Harold, ed. *Stendhal.* Broomail, Pa.: Chelsea House Publishers, 2002.

Brooks, Peter. *Reading for the Plot: Design and Intention in Narrative.* New York: Vintage Books, 1985.

Howe, Irving. *Politics and the Novel.* New York: Columbia University Press, 1992.

Jefferson, Humphries. *The Red and the Black: Mimetic Desire and the Myth of Celebrity.* Boston: Twayne Publishers, 1991.

May, Gita. *Stendhal and the Age of Napoleon.* New York: Columbia University Press, 1977

Stendhal. *The Red and The Black.* Translated and edited by Catherine Slater, Oxford: Oxford University Press, 1991.

—Margaret O'Brien

## Reeve, Clara (1729–1807)

Clara Reeve was born on January 23, 1729, in the East Anglian port of Ipswich. She was the oldest daughter of William Reeve, an upper-middle-class Anglican rector and "oracle," as she described him, from whom she learned all she knew. Reeve, her mother, and two of her sisters moved to the provincial town of Colchester after her father's death in 1755. She eventually took her own lodgings and wrote to support herself, something she continued to do until the age of 71. She never married and died in Ipswich on December 3, 1807, at the age of 78.

A collection entitled *Original Poems*, in which Reeve openly combated existing prejudices against women writers, constituted her first publication (1769). *The OLD ENGLISH BARON* (1778), the work for which she is best known, was first published in 1777 under the title *The Champion of Virtue* and upheld a type of restrained supernaturalism. This GOTHIC narrative of usurpation featuring the themes of concealed identity and inward merit was written in part as a corrective to what Reeve considered to be Horace Walpole's egregious supernaturalism in the first work of gothic fiction, *The Castle of Otranto* (1764). Despite the mediocrity and even tedium ascribed to *Baron* by SIR WALTER SCOTT in his "Prefatory Memoir to Clara Reeve," the novel remained popular well into the 19th century. It rendered the gothic a more acceptable genre for female readers and writers and helped pave the way for ANN RADCLIFFE and her innovative convention of the explained supernatural.

Reeve's next work, *The Two Mentors: A Modern Story* (1783), was an epistolary, moralistic novel of sentiment and manners about upper-middle-class life that examined two pedagogical methods: private cultivation of the domestic and social virtues, and introduction into the fashionable world. It was followed by *The Progress of Romance* (1785), a rare 18th-century work of literary history and criticism penned by a woman. This study and defense of the development of prose romance is presented as a series of adversarial dialogues that consider the moral duties of novelists. Romance was, in Reeve's view, a way to imagine social transformations in the readers' world. The writer, she maintained, should combine moral purpose with an exciting story. Her dedication to her next novel, *The Exiles; or, Memoirs of the Count de Cronstadt* (1788), openly articulated her novelistic intention "to support the cause of morality, to reprove vice, and to promote all the social and domestic virtues" (I, iv) This work of EPISTOLARY FICTION about interclass marriage and the question of virtue featured inset memoirs penned by its three main characters. As illustrated by her historical novel, *Memoirs of Sir Roger de Clarendon* (1793),

Reeve did not shy away from political issues. She signaled her adherence to classical republicanism in this awkwardly constructed contribution to the debate on the FRENCH REVOLUTION.

Several explicitly didactic works closed off Reeve's literary career. *The School for Widows* (1791), which considered suitable marriages and attacked false sensibility, was followed by an epistolary sequel, *Plans of Education* (1792). This quasi-novel drew on the conduct book, an 18th-century form of instruction manual telling young women has to behave in polite society, and the tradition of feminist utopia to advance plans for socially useful projects, the education of girls and women, and the independence of unmarried women. It also underscored the importance of discipline and the need for ensuring accord between educational programs and social rank. Reeve's last novel, *Destination* (1799), undertook a similar subject in emphasizing the importance of matching childrens' unique dispositions to their career paths. That she should cap off her career with a fictionalized history for children—*Edwin, King of Northumberland: A Story of the Seventh Century* (1802)—is entirely in keeping with her lifelong engagement with education as a means of social and moral reform.

## Further Reading

Clery, E. J. "Clara Reeve and Sophia Lee." In *Women's Gothic: From Clara Reeve to Mary Shelley*, 25–50. Tavistock, Eng.: Northcote House Publishers, 2000.

Kelly, Gary. "Introduction: Clara Reeve." In *Bluestocking Feminism: Writings of the Bluestocking Circle, 1738–1785*, vol. 6, edited by Gary Kelly, et al., xxiii–xlix. London: Pickering & Chatto, 1999.

Reeve, Clara. *The Exiles; or, Memoirs of the Count de Cronstadt*. 2 vols. London: Hookham, 1788.

———. *The Old English Baron*. Edited by James Walt and James Trainer. Oxford: Oxford World's Classics, 2008.

———. *The School for Widows*. Edited by Jeanine Casler. Delaware: University of Delaware Press, 2003.

Scott, Sir Walter. "Prefatory Memoir to Clara Reeve." In *Sir Walter Scott on Novelists and Fiction*, edited by Ioan Williams, 94–101. London: Routledge & Kegan Paul, 1968.

Voller, Jack G. "Clara Reeve." In *Gothic Writers: A Critical and Bibliographical Guide,* edited by Douglass H. Thomson, Jack G. Voller, and Frederick S. Frank, 361–364. Westport, Conn., and London: Greenwood Press, 2001.

—Carol Margaret Davison

## Reform Act  (Representation of the People Act)
(1832)

The Representation of the People Act, also known as the First Reform Act, the Great Reform Act, and most commonly as the Reform Act of 1832, was declared by Parliament to be "An Act to amend the representation of the people in England and Wales." Scotland and Ireland had separate reform acts in the same year. Facing stiff opposition from the conservative Tory party in both the House of Commons and in the nonelected upper chamber, the House of Lords, the prime minister Lord Grey and his Whig party initiated the acts to reform the electoral system in the United Kingdom, correcting abuses and addressing corruption, increasing the size of the electorate by altering the rules for franchise qualification, and reapportioning parliamentary representation in a way fairer to the expanding cities of the industrial north. Without doubt, the Reform Act brought about change: More than 130 seats were stripped from 86 boroughs that had very small populations (what were called "rotten" or "pocket" boroughs); 130 seats were redistributed to counties, small towns, and the larger industrial centers such as Manchester, Birmingham, and Leeds; and the franchise was extended to any man owning a household worth £10, adding 217,000 voters to the electorate. After 1832, approximately one in five men had the right to vote.

However, many at the time were disillusioned by the act, and most historians today view it as a feeble anticlimactic gesture to punctuate the so-called Age of Reform and curb the social unrest that had been reaching a boiling point since the July Revolution in France (1830). Notwithstanding that the terms of the act were heavily compromised by two years of parliamentary debate, its achievements were moderate and in some ways even regressive. As the historian Dorothy Thompson

points out, the act "had defined more clearly than at any other time before or since in British history, and more clearly than had been done in any other country, a qualification for the inclusion in the political institutions of the country based entirely on the possession of property, and the possession of a regular income" (Thompson 27). The act also officially disenfranchised women. Parliament had slightly expanded the definition of the respectable classes but had angered many others by ignoring their demands for representation. The writer A. N. Wilson argues that those who hoped the act "would usher in an era of democracy, or even government by the bourgeoisie, were to find their hopes disappointed. Grey's Cabinet was almost entirely aristocratic" (Wilson 39). The historian G. M. Young documents that corruption was as rampant after the act was passed as it had been before: "[T]here was still much bribery, and more intimidation, and election day was still a carnival which usually ended in a fight. Open voting kept the tenant under his landlord's eye" (Young 45). Subsequent Reform Acts in 1867 and 1884 would address many of these issues, though women did not get the vote on the same terms as men until 1928.

If the history of English Romantic thought is to be seen as inextricably linked to and often dominated by the political events and revolutionary atmosphere of the period, then the Reform Act of 1832 can be seen as the culminating point of that thinking, though certainly less revolutionary than Romanticism itself. PERCY BYSSHE SHELLEY's "The MASK OF ANARCHY," deemed too subversive to be published in 1819, was finally published in 1832.

See also SWING RIOTS.

### Further Reading

Burns, Arthur, and Joanna Innes, eds. *Rethinking the Age of Reform: Britain 1780–1850.* Cambridge: Cambridge University Press, 2003.

Thompson, Dorothy. *The Chartists.* Aldershot, Eng.: Wildwood House, 1984.

Wilson, A. N. *The Victorians.* London: Hutchinson, 2002.

Young, G. M. *Portrait of an Age: Victorian England.* Annotated and edited by George Kitson Clark. London: Oxford University Press, 1977.

—Rob Breton

## "Resolution and Independence" ("The Leech Gatherer") William Wordsworth (1807)

Composed in 1802 as "The Leech Gatherer" and published in heavily revised form in *Poems in Two Volumes* of 1807, "Resolution and Independence" consists of 20 Chaucerian stanzas (iambic pentameters rhyming *ababbcc*). At the poem's opening, the poetic persona is enjoying a beautiful walk after the rain, when he starts worrying about his own future, lamenting over the sad destiny of poets who died in misery, particularly THOMAS CHATTERTON and ROBERT BURNS (stanzas 1–7). Marveling at the coincidence, the poet spots an old man on the moor, standing close to a pool whose water he is stirring with his staff, carefully looking for something. Questioned, the old man answers that he is looking for leeches, an activity that used to secure an honest living for him. Now the leeches have almost disappeared, but he keeps to his work, obstinately (stanzas 8–15). Unfortunately, the old man, repeatedly though implicitly compared to a prophet, makes such a strong impression on the poet that he is unable to listen and has to renew his question to the leech gatherer who kindly agrees to repeat the story of his life, three times in all, before he changes the subject (stanzas 16–19). Eventually the poet confesses his admiration for the old man's resolution and his shame concerning his former doubts (stanza 20).

The leech gatherer is one of the many solitaries the poet encounters in his walks through his native Lake District (others being "The Discharged Soldier" and "The Solitary Reaper"). DOROTHY WORDSWORTH's journal describes an actual meeting of the poet with a leech gatherer not far from their Grasmere cottage. According to the biographer Stephen Gill, by writing "The Leech Gatherer," Wordsworth was trying to fight the crisis of self-doubt that was overcoming SAMUEL TAYLOR COLERIDGE at the time. Gill believes the poem testifies to Wordsworth's capacity to seize on the outside world and find material for his poetry in experience, contradicting A. E. M. Conran's sarcastic interpretation of the poem as "the comedy of a solipsist face with something outside himself" (Conran 74). For Frederick W. Bateson, "Two voices turn out to be complementary instead of contradictory" in the poem—"the Wordsworthian

Sublime" and "the Wordsworthian Ridiculous" (Bateson 4). Albert Gérard, however, qualifies this judgment: "Through his ecstatic identification with the leech-gatherer, Wordsworth raises himself from puzzled recognition to mature acceptance of the positive value of suffering" (quoted in Jones 122). But the end of the poem can also be read as an attempt to put at a distance the old man/oracle, an ominous reminder of what the poet thinks he himself is becoming: one unable to find in nature what he used find there. "[W]ither is fled the visionary gleam?" Wordsworth asks in "ODE: INTIMATIONS OF IMMORTALITY FROM RECOLLECTIONS OF EARLY CHILDHOOD," published in the same collection. It is as if he, too, is bound therefore to repeat the story of his life over and over again (through the ceaseless revision of *The PRELUDE*). The poem thus encapsulates the turning point that the 1807 *Poems in Two Volumes* symbolized in Wordsworth's career: the end of his first decade as a published poet.

### Further Reading

Bateson, F. W. *Wordsworth: A Re-Interpretation.* London: Longmans, Green & Co., 1954.

Conran, Anthony E. M. "The Dialectic of Experience: A Study of Wordsworth's Resolution and Independence." *PMLA* 75 (1960): 66–74.

Gérard, Albert. "'Resolution and Independence': Wordsworth's Coming of Age." In *Wordsworth: The 1807 Poems: A Casebook,* edited by Alun R. Jones, 113–125. London: Macmillan, 1990.

Gill, Stephen. *William Wordsworth: A Life.* Oxford: Clarendon, 1989.

Wordsworth, William. *Poems in Two Volumes, and Other Poems, 1800–1807.* Edited by Jared Curtis. Ithaca, N.Y.: Cornell University Press, 1983.

———. *The Poetical Works of William Wordsworth.* Vol. 2. Edited by Ernest de Selincourt. Oxford: Clarendon Press, 1944.

—Aurelie Thiria-Meulemans

## "Reverie, A" Joanna Baillie (1790)

JOANNA BAILLIE originally published this poem anonymously in her experimental collection *Poems.* One of the collection's aims, according to the extended title, is "To point out, in some instances, the different influence which the same circumstances produce on different characters" (Baillie i). Along with the companion poems "A Disappointment" and "A Lamentation," "A Reverie" presents a character pining for a lover. Robin, a poor farmworker, longs to marry Nelly, the fairest maid in the land. As he works with his dog, Comrade, he drifts into the titular reverie and explains why he cannot marry her: "Ah! happy is the man whose early lot / Hath made him master of a furnish'd cot. / . . . Who toils not daily in another's field" (ll. 45–50). Robin longs for a higher status that would have enabled him to inherit a furnished home and his own farm so that he does not have to work "in another's field." He continues to lament his status and longs for material wealth to gain his neighbors' respect and to buy presents for Nelly. In the midst of his reverie, he effectively asks the rhetorical question: *Could you marry me, despite my poverty, even though love is the only dowry I can offer you?* Robin suggests her answer when he recounts a meeting in which he and Nelly had walked passed a rich neighbor's house and Robin "wish'd both cot and Nelly made for me" (l. 74). Nelly's "eyes" (l. 75) revealed then that she loves him and wants to marry him. Robin awakens from his reverie when he hears Nelly's voice as she approaches on a wagon. The poem ends with Robin and Comrade bounding to meet Nelly, and the conclusion implies that the two will marry despite Robin's poverty.

Like many of WILLIAM WORDSWORTH's poems in *LYRICAL BALLADS*, this poem focuses on the lives of the rural working class. Unlike Wordsworth's poems, Baillie here employs heroic couplets, a form in vogue with most neoclassical poets of the 18th century (see NEOCLASSICISM). Like Wordsworth, Baillie is interested in exploring human psychology, but she examines it by comparing Robin to the protagonists in "A Disappointment" and "A Lamentation"—lovers who are in similar situations, but whose characters cause them to react to their situations more negatively.

A comparison of "A Reverie" to "A Disappointment" also yields a comment on class. Even though Robin is frustrated that his poverty is an obstacle to marrying Nelly, Baillie suggests that love is more powerful than the lovers' economic disparity because when he hears Nelly's voice in the distance Robert "leaps with lightsome limbs th' enclosing" fence (l. 88) and cheerfully rushes to greet her. At the close of "A Disappointment," on the other hand, Sue abandons poor William for wealthy Rob, whose pockets are "line[d]" with "gold." Rob is so angry at the poem's close that he gives his dog an "an angry kick," and Baillie exposes a more bitter reality in which money and class are more important than love.

**Further Reading**

Baillie, Joanna. *Poems.* Edited by Jonathan Wordsworth. 1790. Reprint, New York: Woodstock Books, 1994.

—Robert C. Hale

## Rights of Man, The   Thomas Paine (1791–1792)

THOMAS PAINE's *The Rights of Man* was the most famous of all British radical political books published during the first years of the FRENCH REVOLUTION. In its style as much as its thematic content, it asserted that political sovereignty is the exclusive right of ordinary people and called for a popular political revolution in Britain.

The immediate context for Paine's book was the condemnation of the French Revolution in the well-received *Reflections on the Revolution in FRANCE* (1790) by EDMUND BURKE, a philosopher and member of Parliament. Of the more than 70 critical replies that Burke's book occasioned, Paine's exerted the most influence on international public opinion. Published on March 13, 1791, part 1 of the *Rights of Man* sold an unprecedented 50,000 copies by the time a sixth edition was released in May. Through many pirated and translated editions, it went on to become the single biggest-selling book of any variety to date.

If *The Rights of Man* earned Paine considerable esteem in radical political circles in Britain, it also provoked extreme hostility: He was burned in effigy by crowds; harassed by state agents; and, after the publication of part 2 in 1792, eventually convicted of seditious libel by the British government. He only escaped the consequences of the conviction by fleeing to France, where he was one of few non-Frenchmen to be appointed to the National Assembly. In principle, Paine saw the French Revolution as continuing the AMERICAN REVOLUTION, and in *The Rights of Man* he reiterates arguments he had already made in two pamphlets that had played an instrumental role in encouraging the American leaders to decisively declare independence from Britain and found a democratic republic, *Common Sense* and *The Crisis* (1776).

*The Rights of Man* argues that human rights are the first principle of politics, and that these rights are inalienable entitlements shared equally by all human beings regardless of the historically defined privileges of social class. Not only does Paine cite the full *Declaration of the Rights of Man and of the Citizen* accepted by the National Assembly of France, he also offers the first major explanation and defense of human rights in the English language. This egalitarian vision of rights became an irreversible, if not irresistible, part of the political discourse of British Romanticism and, after influencing the early political positions of WILLIAM WORDSWORTH and SAMUEL TAYLOR COLERIDGE, surfaces again most visibly in PERCY BYSSHE SHELLEY's Pamphlet *Declaration of Rights* (1812).

However, *The Rights of Man*, especially part 2, is not an abstract political philosophical treatise intended for specialists but, rather, an effort to effect an immediate revolution in Great Britain that would continue the work of those in America and France. Indeed, what truly alarmed the British government was that Paine wrote in a radically new, plainspoken style: Whereas Burke wrote the *Reflections* for his educated peers, *The Rights of Man* was written to be read by the same ordinary people who it declared were the principal actors in politics. That politics is for ordinary people is a message conveyed by every sentence in the book.

## Further Reading

Blakemore, Steven. *Burke and the Fall of Language.* Hanover, N.H.: University of New England Press, 1988.

Butler, Marilyn. *Romantics, Rebels and Reactionaries: English Literature and Its Background, 1760–1830.* Oxford: Oxford University Press, 1981.

Hitchens, Christopher. *Thomas Paine's Rights of Man: A Biography.* London: Atlantic Books, 2006.

Keane, John. *Tom Paine: A Political Life.* London: Bloomsbury, 1995.

Paine, Thomas. *Rights of Man, Common Sense, and Other Political Writings.* Edited by Mark Philp. Oxford and New York: Oxford University Press, 2008.

—Alastair Hunt

## "Rights of Woman, The" Anna Laetitia Barbauld (1825)

The most frequently anthologized poem by ANNA LAETITIA BARBAULD, "The Rights of Woman" was edited and published posthumously by her niece, Lucy Aikin, in *Works of Anna Leatitia Barbauld* (1825). Aikin places the poem as having been written some time after December 1792. Many critics read the poem as an example of Barbauld's antifeminism, claiming that it is a response to, possibly even a parody of, MARY WOLLSTONECRAFT's *A VINDICATION OF THE RIGHTS OF WOMAN* (January 1792), prompted by Wollstonecraft's criticism of Barbauld's "To a Lady, with Some Painted Flowers" (1773).

The poem's first two lines, a call to arms, have three exclamation points, suggesting an exaggerated and possibly ironic sympathy for "injured Woman" (l. 1). The poem appears to validate separate spheres, the idea that women are associated with the domestic realm only, and with emotion rather than reason. Stanza 3 presents feminine blushes and "soft, melting tones" (l. 11) instead of masculine tools of war. By the end of the poem, the speaker tells Woman that her pride will "give way" to love (l. 28); thus, she must "abandon each ambitious thought" (l. 29). The demand for women's rights is seemingly fruitless.

There is no contextual evidence, however, that Barbauld was offended by Wollstonecraft. Indeed, Aikin herself appears to have been motivated by the desire to present her aunt as a more conventional woman, to disassociate her from 1790s radical feminism, hence her inclusion of "The Rights of Woman" in the *Works*. Moreover, the poem is not as antifeminist as it appears; it certainly is not uncritical of men. The feminine "empire" of the heart (l. 4) is set against an "imperial foe" (l. 18), Man, who is described as "stubborn" and "treacherous" (ll. 18, 19). This links male dominance at home with male imperialism overseas. In keeping with the tenets of difference feminism which holds that men and women or essentially different, the poem celebrates women's distinctive qualities: Instead of feminine traits seen as inferior to those of men, they are here presented in positive images. Female purity and grace are set against male licentiousness, rudeness, and sullenness. Purity and grace are not women's only weapons, though, as the speaker also urges women to use wit and art, recognizing the strength of women's minds as well as their hearts.

The poem also seems to hope for a different relationship between women and men. Stanza 5 concludes that if Woman conquers Man, she "mayst command, but never canst be free" (l. 20). This is followed by two stanzas that explain how being worshipped or wooed by men cannot last, so any position that sets woman above man is precarious at best. The last line of the poem (l. 32) claims that "mutual love" will replace "separate rights," thereby suggesting that an equal relationship between the sexes is natural and good.

"The Rights of Woman" touches on themes frequently found in Romantic writings of the 1790s: justice, revolution, and emancipation. The speaker urges women to claim their rights and revolt against men, but to find freedom in equality rather than in moral authority.

## Further Reading

Bradshaw, Penny. "The Limits of Barbauld's Feminism: Re-reading 'The Rights of Woman.'" *European Romantic Review* 16, no. 1 (2005): 23–37.

Levasseur, Susan. "'All Monsters, All Prodigious Things': Anna Barbauld's 'Rights of Woman' and Mary Wollstonecraft's Revolution in Female Manners." *Nineteenth-Century Feminisms* 5 (2001): 10–36.

McCarthy, William. "A 'High-Minded Christian Lady': The Posthumous Reception of Anna Laetitia Barbauld." In *Romanticism and Women Poets: Opening the Doors of Reception*, edited by Harriet Kramer Linkin and Stephen C. Behrendt, 165–191. Lexington: University Press of Kentucky, 1999.

—Terri Doughty

## "Rime of the Ancient Mariner, The" Samuel Taylor Coleridge (1798)

The first version of this famous poem appeared in LYRICAL BALLADS (1798), where it was one of four poems by SAMUEL TAYLOR COLERIDGE. It was revised for the second edition in 1800 and revised again when it appeared in *Sibylline Leaves* in 1817.

The poem is modeled on the ballad form, which, as well as being ostensibly simple and direct, tends to deal with a single situation or event. There is often a startling or tragic incident or uncanny event. In this case it is a crime and its punishment. An old sailor with a "long grey beard" and "glittering eye" (the "ancient mariner"; l. 3) meets three young men on their way to a wedding feast (an event associated with celebration and friendship) and manages to waylay one of them. He proceeds to tell a long story—punctuated by interjections from the wedding guest—of how his ship was tossed toward the South Pole in a storm. The ship was stuck in ice: "The ice was here, the ice was there, / The ice was all round: / It crackd and growled, and roared and howled, / Like noises in a swound!" (ll. 59–62). Suddenly an albatross flew across the snow and emerged out of the fog to be greeted with cheers of joy: "As if it had been a Christian soul, / We hailed it in God's name" (ll. 63–66). The bird guided the ship for nine days, and eventually the ship was able to break through the ice. A southerly wind started up, and the ship was able to go north. However, the mariner—out of either boredom or cruelty—shot the bird. His fellow sailors protested at his having killed the bird since, as they believed, it "made the breeze to blow" (l. 94). The significance of the killing is such that it is referred to in every remaining section of the poem.

Initially it seemed that everything was returning to normal: The fog cleared, the sun shone, and the sailor became a hero, for the sailors, having changed their minds, said: "'Twas right . . . such birds to slay, / That bring the fog and mist" (ll. 101–102). By approving what the mariner had done, the sailors became implicated in his deed, and they too suffered the curse that settled over the ship. The vessel was driven north and became becalmed. The crew lacked food and water, despite being surrounded by it: "Water, water, every where / Nor any drop to drink" (ll. 121–122). As they starved, they again blamed the mariner (a "wretch"), accusing him of killing the bird, which they had decided was a good omen, and they hanged the corpse of the bird from the mariner's neck. Around the ship, nature, which was once represented by the magnificent bird, started to manifest itself in more horrible ways; and the beautiful albatross was replaced with "slimy things [that] did crawl with legs / Upon a slimy sea" (ll. 124–125). Some of the crew had nightmares in which the spirit of the South Pole was chasing their ship in order to exact revenge for the killing of the bird. One by one the crew died of starvation, with the mariner the sole survivor. He experienced a kind of living death for having broken the bonds that tie man with nature. As the ship rotted, the mariner was overtaken by various states of remorse, fear, and misery, haunted by "the curse in a dead man's eye" (l. 260). Significantly, Coleridge does not try to analyze the mariner's state of mind in depth; rather, he uses the description of the desolate landscape to convey it: "Alone, alone, all, all alone, / Along on a wide wide sea!" (ll. 232–233).

Nature plays an important part in the sense of desolation that pervades the poem and mirrors the characters' psychological state and the events that befall them. Left on the "phantom ship," the mariner was truly alone, finding himself unable to pray for help and, by implication, cut off from any comfort God might bring. As he recalls: "Oh Wedding-Guest! This soul hath been / Alone on a wide, wide sea: / So lonely 'twas, that God himself / Scarce seemed there to be" (ll. 597–600). The mariner remained in this state for seven days. Then, one night, he saw the water snakes playing in the water. An unexpected reaction took place: "A spring of love gushed from my heart, / And I blessed them unaware / . . . That self-same moment I could pray; / And from my neck so free / The Albatross fell off, and sank / Like lead into the sea" (ll. 284–290). The spell was thus broken, and the ship was brought back to land.

However, the mariner has not escaped. As penance he is sentenced to roam the world—a wanderer—doomed to repeatedly confess his guilt and teach by example, what he has discovered. His lesson is the importance of loving all God's

creatures: "He prayeth best, who loveth best / All things both great and small; / For the dear God who loveth us, / He made and loveth all" (ll. 614–617). For some, this moral sits awkwardly with the rest of the poem. Coleridge himself thought he had overdone it, later saying in 1830 that "the only, or the chief fault, I may say so, was the obtrusion of the moral sentiment so openly on the reader as a principle or cause of action in a work of such pure imagination" (Coleridge 1990, 1:149). Others have also criticized the poem for having a moral that might be seen as trite or too obviously didactic. However, the wedding guest is moved by it and, turning his back on the wedding feast, goes to the church to pray: "He went like one that hath been stunned, / And is of sense forlorn: / A sadder and a wiser man, / He rose the morrow morn" (ll. 622–625).

Coleridge's collaborator on *Lyrical Ballads,* WILLIAM WORDSWORTH, recalled that the genesis of the poem came about in the autumn 1797: "[H]e (Coleridge), my sister [DOROTHY WORDSWORTH], and myself started from Alfoxenden pretty late in the afternoon, with a view to visit Linton and the Valley of Stones near to it; and as our united funds were very small, we agreed to defray the expense of the tour by writing a poem to be sent to the 'New Monthly Magazine.' . . . Accordingly we set off, and proceeded along the Quantock Hills towards Watchet; and in the course of this walk was planted the poem of 'The Ancient Mariner' founded on a dream, as Mr Coleridge said, of his friend Mr [John] Cruikshank [Cruikshank had had a dream about 'a skeleton ship, with figures in it']. Much the greatest part of the story was Mr Coleridge's invention, but certain parts I suggested: for example, some crime was to be committed which should bring upon the Old Navigator, as Coleridge afterwards delighted to call him, the spectral persecution" (Wordsworth 1:107–108). How much Wordsworth really did influence the poem is uncertain—though living in close proximity, it is clear that the two poets had frequent discussions about what they were writing.

Coleridge also drew on his reading of books of sea travels and on his interest in medievalism. He worked on the ballad for four months before he showed it to the Wordsworths on March 28, 1798. The Wordsworths evidently approved, but when the poem appeared, initial reactions were mixed. CHARLES LAMB wrote that "the feelings of a man under the operation of such scenery dragged me along like Tom Piper's magic whistle" (Lamb 6:209). A reviewer for the *Analytical Review* deemed it "The extravagance of a mad German poet" (quoted in Garner, 119). The reference is perhaps to GOTTFRIED AUGUST BÜRGER, whose supernatural poem "Lenore" appeared in 1773. "The strangest story of a cock and a bull that we ever saw on paper ... a rhapsody of unintelligible wilderness and incoherence" was the verdict of another critic on "The Rime," while ROBERT SOUTHEY, a friend of Coleridge's, offered only halfhearted praise: "Many of the stanzas are laboriously beautiful; but in connection they are absurd or unintelligible." Southey claimed not to be able to understand the story and suggested that "Genius has here been employed in producing a poem of little merit" (quoted in Coleridge 1965, 21). Even Wordsworth worried that the poem was partly responsible for the poor sales of *Lyrical Ballads*, telling the publisher Joseph Cottle that it "has upon the whole been an injury to the volume. I mean that the old words and the strangeness of it have deterred readers from going on" (quoted in Jones and Tydeman, 13).

Since then, however, the poem has become one of the classics of English literature and provoked a variety of readings. For some the poem should be read as a restatement of Coleridge's view on the natural world and of "One Life." In a letter of 1803 he wrote that "nature has her proper interest, and he will know what it is who believes and feels that everything has a life of its own, and we are all One Life" (Coleridge 1956, 2:522). Others have read the poem alongside other supernatural works, notably Coleridge's "CHRISTABEL." There has also been much debate over the poem's symbolic and allegorical qualities. Is it a version of the Fall of man but also of his redemption and rebirth? Is it a retelling of the biblical story of Cain, who killed his brother? Is it really a story about literary creativity, with the albatross a symbol of inspiration? As long as the poem remains widely read and taught, these debates look set to continue.

## Further Reading

Bygrave, Stephen. *Samuel Taylor Coleridge.* Plymouth, Eng.: Northcote House in association with the British Council. 1997.

Coleridge, Samuel Taylor. *The Annotated Ancient Mariner.* Edited by Martin Gardner. New York: Clarkson N. Potter, Inc., 1965.

———. *Collected Letters of Samuel Taylor Coleridge.* Vol. 2. Edited by Earl Leslie Griggs. Oxford: Clarendon Press, 1956.

———. *Table Talk.* 2 vols. Edited by Carl Woodring. London: Routledge, 1990.

Garner, Michael. *Romanticism and the Gothic.* Cambridge: Cambridge University Press, 2000.

Jones, Alun, and William Tydeman, eds. *Wordsworth. Lyrical Ballads: A Casebook.* London: Macmillan, 1972.

Lamb, Charles. *The Works of Charles and Mary Lamb.* Vols. 6 and 7. Edited by E. V. Lucas. London: Methuen, 1905.

Wordsworth, Christopher. *Memoirs of Wordsworth.* 2 vols. London: Moxon, 1851.

—Keri Sullivan

## *Robbers, The* **Friedrich von Schiller** (1781)

Written in 1781 and influenced by William Shakespeare and JEAN-JACQUES ROUSSEAU, this play reflects FRIEDRICH VON SCHILLER's positive reaction to the literary novelties brought forth by the Sturm und Drang (storm and stress) movement, in which extremes of emotion were given free rein. It was by far the best-known play circulating in Europe during the Romantic period, and its high emotional charge has stirred the readers' interest ever since. Whether acclaimed enthusiastically by contemporary readers and audiences or fiercely rejected by the representatives of the era's reactionary politics, *The Robbers* had a reputation as a revolutionary drama, in terms of both its content and its language. The main themes, topical at the dawning of Romanticism, reflect the desire for freedom from moral and social repression, the problematic nature of freedom and the perils inherent in indulging in it, and the disavowal of moral and feudal tradition. The language is often "unliterary," burning with youthful fire and energy and often close to blasphemy, thus breaking all the literary and linguistic bonds that other Sturm und Drang poets had already challenged.

Generally seen as the prototype of the Romantic outlaw narrative, which was to follow its unparalleled popularity (as in the work of LORD BYRON), the play dramatizes the conflict between two aristocratic brothers. The elder, Karl Moor, leaves his family after being disinherited and becomes a robber, leading a group of rebellious students into the Bohemian forest. Whereas he fights for freedom and justice against corrupt, oppressive institutions, such as the church as well as the old aristocratic world represented by his evil brother, his followers become intoxicated by their own violence, degenerating into anarchy. Meanwhile, the Machiavellian Franz, the younger brother, schemes to inherit his father's considerable estate, bringing discredit on Karl's supposed criminal behavior. Returning to his father's castle in disguise, Karl finally sees that lawlessness is no answer to injustice and that terror is incompatible with idealism.

The play overflows with all the fury of youth. The character of Karl is drawn in a most powerful manner: romantic and heroic, he is the impetuous idealist, disregarding obsolete laws and opposing his brother's ruthless pragmatism.

The play's critique of social corruption and its affirmation of proto-revolutionary republican ideals astounded the original audience during its premiere in Mannheim in 1782, turning Schiller into an overnight sensation. People shouted and fell into each other's arms; women fainted. Since the play portrays the conflict between authority and the individual, age and youth (this may also allude to an ideal struggle between the anciens régimes ruling in Europe and the revolutionary wishful thinking that was to become a concrete reality during the political events in France of 1789), absolutism in the German states was experiencing its first underground tremors.

Romantic writers in England, especially SAMUEL TAYLOR COLERIDGE, admired Schiller's drama and greeted its theme of liberty with enthusiasm. *The Robbers* was translated at various times in Europe, the translators trying to get around censorship by hiding many of the play's subversive references in adaptations, which cer-

tainly reduced its impact but nonetheless evoked the original.

**Further Reading**

Mortensen, Peter. "Robbing *The Robbers:* Friedrich Schiller and the Politics of British Romantic Translation." *Literature and History* 11 (2002): 41–61.

—Valeria Pellis

## Robinson, Mary (Mary Darby, "Perdita") (1758–1800)

Mary Darby Robinson, a popular actress, feminist writer, and the subject of a late 18th-century scandal, was born on November 27, 1758, and raised in Bristol, along with her two sisters and three brothers. Her father, Nicholas Darby, was a sea captain and merchant of Irish origins; her mother, Hester, was an indulgent parent. Mary began her education at the Bristol school run by HANNAH MORE's sisters until her father made the disastrous decision, in 1765, to establish a fishing post on the coast of Labrador. The family was reduced to straitened circumstances, and Nicholas became estranged from his wife after settling with a mistress in Canada. Mary's education became sporadic; and in 1768 she was placed under the tutelage of the talented but alcoholic Meribah Lorrington in London. She subsequently pursued her learning with a Mrs. Leigh and taught briefly at a short-lived school established by her mother in 1771, before completing her education at a finishing school.

Mary soon decided to forge a career in the theater. She consulted the actor-manager David Garrick (1717–79) who, immediately impressed, planned her debut as Cordelia opposite his King Lear at the famous Drury Lane Theatre in Covent Garden. These plans were abandoned when Mary's mother pressured her into marrying Thomas Robinson, a clerk who claimed, untruthfully, to be the nephew of a wealthy Welshman. They were married in April 1773.

While her husband led an increasingly debauched lifestyle, Mary became a well-known socialite and attracted the attentions of noted libertines such as George Robert Fitzgerald (ca. 1746–86). In 1774 the Robinsons were forced to abandon London in order to escape Thomas's creditors. They settled briefly in Wales, at the home of Thomas's "family," where Mary gave birth to Maria Elizabeth (1774–1818). When they returned to London in May 1775, Thomas was arrested and taken to the Fleet prison, accompanied by Mary. It was during this imprisonment of nine months and three weeks that Mary Robinson published her first work, *Poems, by Mrs. Robinson* (1775), which gained little notice. She was supported by her patron, Georgiana Cavendish, duchess of Devonshire (1757–1806), to whom Robinson dedicated her second volume, *Captivity, A Poem: and Celadon and Lydia, A Tale* (1777).

Following their release on August 3, 1776, Mary returned to her earlier ambition of going on stage. She was engaged by Richard Sheridan (1751–1816), who had replaced Garrick as the manager of Drury Lane, and finally made her début as Juliet Capulet on December 10, 1776, playing opposite William Brereton's Romeo. Mary was warmly reviewed, and she continued her theatrical career with a wide range of parts, including Amanda in Sheridan's *The Trip to Scarborough*, Ophelia in Shakespeare's *Hamlet*, Araminta in Congreve's *The Old Batchelor*, and Octavia in Dryden's *All for Love*.

Robinson's portrayal of Perdita in *The Winter's Tale* led to the most notorious episode of her life. On December 3, 1779, the Prince of Wales, the future George IV (1762–1830), attended her performance and immediately afterward began to court her. By early 1780 they were lovers and had gained the nicknames "Perdita" and "Florizel." The prince convinced Robinson to abandon the stage, which she did on May 31, 1780, and financed her extravagant lifestyle. As early as December, however, his attentions had turned to the courtesan Elizabeth Armistead (1750–1842).

Distraught at having been cast aside, Robinson threatened to publish the prince's love letters. Newspapers eagerly followed each development in the scandal, and sides taken were expressed through caricatures and poems. Robinson eventually agreed to return the letters in return for £5,000 and an annuity. In October 1781, partly as an attempt to escape the scandal, she traveled to Paris, where she moved in fashionable society and

was said to have conducted at least one high-profile affair (with the duc de Lauzun) before returning to London two months later. She continued to be shadowed by gossip after beginning relationships with the politician Charles James Fox (1749–1806) and Colonel Banastre Tarleton (1754–1833). Her relationship with Tarleton, begun in 1782, lasted 15 years, until he married the heiress Susan Priscilla Bertie (1778–1864). During this time Robinson appears to have suffered a paralytic stroke brought on by a miscarriage.

From the early 1790s, Robinson began to fashion a new career as a writer, for which she eventually gained significant respect. This began with her association with the Della Cruscans, a movement that began in Florence in the mid-1780s and was led by the poet Robert Merry (1755–98). The group celebrated sensibility, Renaissance love poetry, and sensuality; their poems were also suffused with erudite references. Though not a central member of the group, Robinson began a poetic dialogue with "Leonardo" (Merry) in *The World* under the pseudonym "Laura."

Robinson's later works embraced a great variety of styles and concerns. Like so many writers of her generation, she sympathized with the aims of the FRENCH REVOLUTION but also with the fate of Louis XVI and Marie Antoinette (see "MARIE ANTOINETTE'S LAMENTATION IN HER PRISON OF THE TEMPLE"). She expressed her political views through poetry published under the pseudonym "Tabitha Bramble"; addressed the problem of social ranks in the novel *Vancenza, or, The Dangers of Credulity* (1792); and, as "Anne Frances Randall," placed feminist concerns center stage in *A Letter to the Women of England, on the Injustice of Mental Subordination* (1799). As a poet she attracted the notice of SAMUEL TAYLOR COLERIDGE, who communicated with her via the pages of the *Morning Post*, of which she became poetry editor in 1799. Robinson's admiration of Coleridge's and WILLIAM WORDSWORTH's *LYRICAL BALLADS* (1798) is apparent in her own *Lyrical Tales* (1800); evidence of this friendship is seen in "TO THE POET COLERIDGE." Her poem "LONDON'S SUMMER MORNING" is often compared to the poems by Wordsworth and WILLIAM BLAKE on the same subjects, as is another poem, "The OLD BEGGAR."

During this period of literary productivity, Robinson moved repeatedly between England and France, though plagued by ill health. She was never entirely free of financial difficulties and was arrested by a creditor only seven months before her death on December 26, 1800.

One of the most striking features of Mary Robinson's literary career is the diversity of the styles and personas she adopted. Her pseudonyms included Laura Maria, Julia, Portia, Sappho, Lesbia, Oberon, Anne Frances Randal, and Tabitha Bramble, in addition to being widely known, still, as Perdita. At first, Robinson may have used these names as a way of escaping the scandal surrounding her, but in her later works she often used a pseudonym before revealing her identity. She also learned that scandals were not necessarily detrimental to her work: Her first novel, *Vancenza*, sold out on the first day. Robinson had an acute understanding of the literary marketplace and reinvented herself in various ways depending on her audience (Pascoe 260), but also as an extension of her stage career.

It was perhaps this interest in theatricality that drew Robinson to the Della Cruscans, many of whom had also worked for the theater. "Ode to Della Crusca" (1791) is her most explicit response to the group. It celebrates "Della Crusca" (Merry) as the "Enlighten'd Patron of the sacred Lyre" (l. 1), whose magical spell gives her poetic inspiration. Robinson's self-representation as "untutor'd" (l. 35) is belied by the poem's complex alternation between octosyllabic and decasyllabic lines in imitation of classical Greek odes. Robinson also responded enthusiastically to Merry's "Laurel of Liberty" (1790) in her quarto poem 'Ainsi va le monde' (1790), which praises the democratic spirit behind the French Revolution and denounces tyranny through a range of literary and political references. The fierce denunciations of the Della Cruscans' affectation and radicalism, led by William Gifford (1756–1826) in 1791, contributed to Robinson's desire to distance herself from the group.

SAPPHO AND PHAON (1796), a series of 44 Petrarchan sonnets that stands as one of Robinson's most accomplished volumes, is "a central document in the poetry of sensibility" (McGann 55). Robinson's adept manipulation of the sonnet form adds to recent critical arguments that women writers were at the heart of the Romantic sonnet revival. The sonnets explore Sappho's damaging love for Phaon, who abandons her. Robinson identified with Sappho's passionate character; readers also saw parallels between her and Sappho, who, as Robinson stated in her preface to the work, "enlightened by the most exquisite talents, yet yielding to the destructive control of ungovernable passions" (Robinson 2000, 149). She admired the ancient Greek poet Sappho as a rare example of a widely known and admired female writer. Indeed, an important aspect of the work is its celebration of a female literary tradition.

Feminist concerns characterized much of Robinson's works. Her novels, for which she frequently drew on her own life, tend to combine GOTHIC plots with condemnations of female oppression. In *Walsingham, or, The Pupil of Nature* (1797), she tackles inheritance rights in a plot that shows a woman raised as a man by her mother in order to keep the family estate. In *The Natural Daughter* (1799), Robinson addresses the problem of illegitimate children and female employment through the heroine, who is accused by her husband of infidelity after she takes in an illegitimate child. The novel is also a warning against "misguided sensibility" (Ty 76). The nonfiction work *Letter to the Women of England* (1799) recasts the epistolary form, often associated with sentimental women's literature, as a polemical tool. The work reflects Robinson's admiration for her friend MARY WOLLSTONECRAFT (1759–97) and contains a powerful attack on sexual double standards.

Robinson's later works shed valuable light on Romantic literary collaborations. She began a literary relationship with Coleridge, principally through the pages of the *Morning Post*. In "Ode to the Snow-Drop" (originally printed in her novel *Walsingham*, reprinted in the *Morning Post*, 1800), she compares herself to the vulnerable flower: "I have known the cheerless hour, / Have seen the sun-beams cold and pale, / Have felt the chilling, wint'ry gale, / and wept, and shrunk like thee!" (ll 32–35). Coleridge responded directly with "The Snow-Drop" (originally written in 1797), in which he assures her that her "potent sorceries of song"

(l. 16) will give her immortality. Robinson's "To the Poet Coleridge" (1800) famously contains the first published reference to "KUBLA KHAN," which she had seen prior to its publication. In "Ode Inscribed to the Infant Son of S. T. Coleridge" (1800) she celebrates the birth of his child. She drew on "The RIME OF THE ANCIENT MARINER" (1798) in her poem "The HAUNTED BEACH" (1800), in which, against a ghostly background, a fisherman is doomed to waste "in Solitude and Pain, / A loathsome life away" for having committed murder (ll. 80–81). Robinson's *Lyrical Tales* (1800), which she considered, with some justification, her "favourite offspring" (Mary Robinson 1999, 54) offers numerous points of comparison with the works of Coleridge, Wordsworth, and ROBERT SOUTHEY.

Robinson began to write her memoirs shortly before her death; they were edited and published in 1801 by her daughter Maria Elizabeth as *Memoirs of the Late Mrs. Robinson, Written by Herself*. The autobiography, though incomplete, is one of her most powerful prose works. Robinson draws heavily on gothic conventions, from the setting (she was born next to a ruined monastery) to the recurrent theme of female virtue under attack ("he had a young and amiable wife in a sister kingdom, and . . . apprehended some diabolical stratagem for the enthralment of my honour" [Robinson 2007, 20]). Robinson insists throughout on her lifelong misery, describing her destiny as "dark" and the world as a place of "duplicity." Nevertheless, the work reveals an impressive self-awareness notably with its strong emphasis on disguise. It is also unusual as an example of early female literary autobiography that insists on both artistic "genius *and* domestic solicitude" (Peterson 48).

An account of Mary Robinson's reception must consider the numerous articles and caricatures that commented on her sexual relations in graphic ways. Early representations often stressed her sensuality, such as Thomas Gainsborough's 1781 portrait or the 1783 cartoon "Florizel and Perdita." However, Robinson also had her supporters (George Romney's 1781 portrait presents a far more respectable image, as does that of Sir Joshua Reynolds) and succeeded, eventually, in gaining respect for her writings. Nevertheless, her lifestyle contributed extensively to her neglect during the Victorian period. Along with many of her female contemporaries, Robinson was largely ignored until the mid-1990s, when an interest in rediscovering forgotten Romantic women writers began to grow. There has been as yet no full-length critical study of her writings, though new editions of her works have begun to accumulate. A best-selling biography, written by Paula Byrne, was published in 2005. Mary Robinson is now recognized as an important voice in British Romanticism who engaged with contemporary issues, interacted with—and influenced—some of the leading writers of her day, and explored self-performance in sophisticated ways.

See also "JANUARY 1795."

## Further Reading

Byrne, Paula. *Perdita: The Life of Mary Robinson.* New York: Random House, 2005.

Curran, Stuart. "Mary Robinson's *Lyrical Tales* in Context." In *Re-Visioning Romanticism: British Women Writers, 1776–1837,* edited by Carol Shiner Wilson and Joel Haefner, 17–35. Philadelphia: University of Pennsylvania Press, 1994.

McGann, Jerome. "Mary Robinson and the Myth of Sappho." *Modern Language Quarterly* 56, no. 1 (1995): 55–76.

Pascoe, Judith. "Mary Robinson and the Literary Marketplace." In *Romantic Women Writers: Voices and Countervoices,* edited by Paula Feldman and Theresa M. Kelly, 252–268. Hanover, N.H.: University Press of New England, 1995.

Peterson, Linda H. "Becoming an Author: Mary Robinson's *Memoirs* and the Origins of the Woman Artist's Autobiography." In *Re-Visioning Romanticism: British Women Writers, 1776–1837,* edited by Carol Shiner Wilson and Joel Haefner, 36–56. Philadelphia: University of Pennsylvania Press, 1994.

Robinson, Daniel. "Reviving the Sonnet: Women Romantic Poets and the Sonnet Claim." *European Romantic Review* 6, no. 1 (Summer 1995): 98–127.

Robinson, Mary. *Letter to the Women of England.* Edited by Sharon M. Setzer. Peterborough, Ont.: Broadview Press, 2003.

———. *Mary Robinson: Selected Poems.* Edited by Judith Pascoe. Peterborough, Ont.: Broadview Press, 1999.

———. *Memoirs of the Late Mrs. Robinson, Written by Herself.* Reissued as *Beaux and Belles of England.* London: Echo, 2007.

Ty, Eleanor Rose. *Empowering the Feminine: The Narratives of Mary Robinson, Jane West, and Amelia Opie, 1796–1812.* Toronto: University of Toronto Press, 1998.

—Juliette Atkinson

## *Rob Roy* Sir Walter Scott (1818)

One of a series of historical novels written by SIR WALTER SCOTT in the 1800s, this novel is constructed as a first-person narrative by Frank Osbaldistone, who writes down the adventures of his youth for his friend Will. The novel is set in Britain at the time of the 1715 Jacobite Rising (an attempt to restore the Stuart MONARCHY). The plot centers on Frank, a young Londoner, who dislikes working in his father's counting-house and is sent to Osbaldistone Hall, his uncle's estate in northern England. There, he falls in love with the mysterious Diana, a Catholic Jacobite, and unintentionally offends his cousin Rashleigh. When Rashleigh takes Frank's place in London, he retaliates for the offense by stealing important commercial papers. To retrieve these documents, Frank and Andrew, his servant, go north again— to Glasgow, where Frank meets Jarvie, his father's business partner, and to the Highlands, Rob Roy MacGregor's country. The papers restored, Frank is reconciled to his father and marries Diana.

Most of these characters and events are fictional. This enables Scott to use his historical novel to comment on early 19th-century Britain, when, notwithstanding the Union of 1707, the relationship between England and Scotland was strained. Thus, many critics read the novel in terms of (inner) colonial criticism, but Scott's primary aim is to mediate between England and Scotland.

The journey structure of the plot is devised to overcome prejudices. Still in England, Frank thinks of the Scottish as "a race hostile by nature to the more southern inhabitants" of Britain (Scott 95). In the north, only Rashleigh shows animosity; Frank's Scottish acquaintances even help him find the stolen papers. Jarvie, Scott's mouthpiece,

explains further that the Highlanders are violent out of necessity, not malice, since the economic conditions in the Highlands are dire. Still, Andrew's view of Scotland as a paradise infected by the English (117, 236) is not valid either. Scott ridicules this approach by presenting Andrew ironically. The irony starts with his surname, Fairservice, as the services he renders Frank are questionable. The gradual deconstruction of prejudices is mirrored in the figure of Rob Roy, who first appears in disguise but reveals more and more of his true self the closer Frank gets to the Highlands. How England and Scotland can cooperate beyond all prejudices is shown on a symbolic level. Diana is half Scottish. She appears wild (113) since she lacks friendly guidance (182). Scotland, too, desires friendship. So far, England has treated her sister kingdom as inferior and thereby provoked resistance. Like Diana, though, Scotland would show a friendlier face if England were to extend a friendly hand. The marriage between Frank and Diana marks an ideal world of union and compromise.

Rob Roy as a type has no place in this ideal world. Highland robbers belong to the past. Thus, Frank never sees Rob Roy again after his marriage (452). However, Rob Roy as an individual has only turned freebooter out of need, and he shares the values of the mercantile world. He is not hostile to Scott's concept of a peacefully unified Britain and thus does not meet the violent end predicted for him but eventually dies quietly of old age.

See also HEART OF MIDLOTHIAN, THE; IVANHOE; WAVERLEY.

**Further Reading**

Duncan, Ian. Introduction to *Rob Roy*, by Sir Walter Scott, vii–xxviii. Oxford: Oxford University Press, 1998.

Gordon, Robert C. *Under Which King? A Study of the Scottish Waverley Novels.* Edinburgh: Oliver & Boyd, 1996.

Lincoln, Andrew. "Scott and Empire: The Case of Rob Roy." *Studies in the Novel* 34, no. 1 (Spring 2002): 43–59.

Scott, Sir Walter. *Rob Roy.* Oxford: Oxford University Press, 1998.

—Vera Ruttmann

## "Rose Aylmer" Walter Savage Landor (1806, 1846)

"Rose Aylmer" is an eight-line lyric poem first published in the collection *The Simonidea* (1806). The collection as a whole reflects WALTER SAVAGE LANDOR's interest in ancient literature and his belief in the relevance of classical forms to modern life and writing. Landor was famous for his imitations of ancient poets, something which he saw as a way of anchoring his own work within a poetic tradition. This has also brought charges that he lacks the originality of famous contemporaries such as WILLIAM WORDSWORTH and SAMUEL TAYLOR COLERIDGE. In this case, the collection's title alludes to the Greek poet Simonides of Ceos (556–468 B.C.), who was famous for his simple elegies. The first three poems in the collection thus memorialize three recently deceased women: Harriet Lambe (the wife of Landor's friend, Dr. William Lambe); Nancy Jones (a young girl with whom Landor fell in love while visiting Tenby in 1795); and Rose Aylmer, the daughter of Welsh friends who lived in Carmarthen. Landor stayed with Rose's family several times in the 1790s. In 1798 Rose, age 19, journeyed to India by sea, accompanying her aunt, Lady Russell, whose husband had been made a court judge. Unable to survive the conditions, Rose died of cholera two years later on March 2nd 1800.

Landor does not seem to have been romantically involved with Rose; indeed, he later claimed that the memorial lines had come to him when he was brushing his teeth before bed. The lines were first published in 1806, and Rose's full name was withheld. In the first version the name *Aylmer* could refer either to a man or a woman: "Ah what avails the sceptred race, / Ah what the form divine! / What, every virtue, every grace! / For, Aylmer, all were thine" (ll. 1–4). When the poem was republished in 1846, Rose's full name was restored and the sentiments struck a stronger chord with readers familiar with mortality and premature death. As the scholar Keith Hanley notes: "The inclusion of the first name, Rose, previously omitted, adds a faintly touching individuality to the poem's overall effort . . ." and the name became "synonymous with recognisable configurations of feeling": melancholy, loss, regret, mourning, of things left unsaid (in Landor xxix–xxx). The opening line "Ah, what avails the sceptred race!" also recalls Rose's distinguished ancestors (her family claimed to be able to trace its lineage back to Edward I and King Alfred the Great), plus her own status as a flower of English womanhood possessing "every virtue, every grace" (l. 3). The poem's admirers included CHARLES LAMB, who told Landor that the poem possessed "a charm I cannot explain. I lived on it for weeks" (quoted in Super 232). In the aftermath of World War I, Frank Lambert was one of a number of composers who set the words to music, recognizing its appeal to those mourning the untimely deaths of millions of young people.

### Further Reading

Landor, Walter Savage. *Walter Savage Landor: Selected Poetry and Prose.* Edited by Keith Hanley. Manchester, Eng.: Carcenet Press, 1981.

Super, R. H. *Walter Savage Landor.* New York: New York University Press, 1954.

—Andrew Maunder

## Rousseau, Jean-Jacques (1712–1778)

Probably no greater influence on the genesis of European Romanticism exists than Jean-Jacques Rousseau, Genevan essayist, political theorist, Enlightenment philosopher, novelist, autobiographer, social scientist, and educational theorist. Brought up in Geneva, Rousseau led an itinerant existence doing a variety of menial jobs until he arrived in Paris in 1742, where he started to gain a reputation as an essayist. Although his specific connection to Romanticism is still hotly debated, that he influenced the movement and was even understood by many people to symbolize Romantic thought is undeniable. Many of the themes of Romanticism, if not initiated by Rousseau, were at least made widely known by him. An immense popularity, both offset and abetted by the virulence and vocality of his detractors (who attacked his domestic life including his abandoned illegitimate children), led to a Rousseaumania among readers of the late 18th century, the hallmarks of which were a cult of nature and a taste for sensibility. As the literary historian W. J. T. Mitchell writes, Rousseau's impact on the 19th century is similar to Sigmund Freud's or Karl Marx's on the 20th: no one had to read him to be influenced by him (Mitchell 644).

Rousseau's actual writings, however, are often misrepresented and oversimplified in multiple assessments of him as a symbol of Romanticism. These Romantic Rousseaus include the solitary exile, child of nature, sensitive soul, political revolutionary, opponent of the church, republican reformer, scapegoated exile, utopian idealist, champion of feeling, passionate lover of an unattainable woman, nostalgic dreamer, and visionary madman. Ideas expressed in his major writings—*Discourse on the Arts and Sciences* (1750); *Discourse on the Origin of Inequality among Men* (1755); *Emile, or On Education* (1762); *The Social Contract, or Principles of Political Right* (1762); *Julie, or The New Heloise* (1761); *Confessions* (1782, 1789); *Reveries of a Solitary Walker* (1782); and *Dialogues, Rousseau Judge of Jean-Jacques* (1780, 1782)—contribute significantly to these major Romantic prototypes, but are far more complex than the commonplace simplifications of his thinking suggest.

Rousseau's *Discourse on the Arts and Sciences* exploded on the Parisian literary scene in 1750 when it won the competition held by the Academy of Dijon and garnered him instant fame. In it he argues a counterintuitive claim that the development of the sciences and the arts are hallmarks of human society's corruption away from its more moral natural state. The first essay and his second, *Discourse on the Origin of Inequality among Men*, which extols the *bon sauvage* ("good savage," not "noble savage," a phrase he never used) so crucial to Romantic primitivism, lay the groundwork for some anti-Enlightenment strains of Romanticism. Misreadings of Rousseau's *bon sauvage* as some kind of pure moral being, rather than the relatively amoral person Rousseau described, became a touchstone for Romantic nostalgia and primitivism and formed the basis for Voltaire's satirical portrait in *Candide*. Nonetheless, Rousseau did praise nature in all his works and, more than any other writer, raised it to the level of the sacred or the sublime for a succeeding generation of artists.

Sometimes hyperbolically called the "Father of the FRENCH REVOLUTION," Rousseau espoused and championed political reform, republicanism, patriotism, and individual liberty. These became part of a larger continental movement preoccupied by issues of political equality and reform. *The Social Contract* challenged the idea of private property and has been linked to the development of Hegelian dialectic and Marxism. Despite many discrepancies between Rousseau's political theory and the aims of the French Revolution, his name became a byword for the revolutionary, possibly because of his notion of individual liberty.

Part 2 of the *Confessions* was published posthumously in 1789, thereby cementing popular associations of the scandals of Rousseau's personal life with the French Revolution. His novel *Julie, or The New Heloise* was one of the best-selling novels of the 18th century, and despite its lack of political content, it too became infamously read as an allegory of the French Revolution. The love story between Julie and her music tutor, St. Preux, threatened conservative notions of class and patriarchal control within marriage. English Jacobin writers in the 1790s—among them the political philosopher WILLIAM GODWIN, Reverend Joseph Fawcett, and MARY WOLLSTONECRAFT—were avid though not uncritical readers of Rousseau. William Godwin's most influential work, *An Enquiry Concerning Political Justice* (1793), is a derivative reworking of much of Rousseau's political philosophy in *The Social Contract*. Godwin responded to Rousseau's personality and ideas in his novels CALEB WILLIAMS, *St. Leon*, and *Fleetwood*. Mary Wollstonecraft challenged Rousseau's ideas on female education in *A VINDICATION OF THE RIGHTS OF WOMAN*, even while she admired his republican views and his sensibility; she imitated the themes and plot of *The New Heloise* in her novel *Mary*. The political idealism of the first generation of Romantic poets, WILLIAM WORDSWORTH, SAMUEL TAYLOR COLERIDGE, and ROBERT SOUTHEY, is reflected through this Rousseauian lens. MARY SHELLEY was reputedly reading the *Confessions* when she wrote *FRANKENSTEIN*, about a Genevan genius whose abandonment of his creature leads to self-torment. Shelley later wrote that Rousseau's abandonment of his five children was the primary reason behind his personal unhappiness (Mary Shelley 1839, 132).

LORD BYRON celebrates Rousseau in canto 5 of CHILDE HAROLD'S PILGRIMAGE. German writers indebted to Rousseau include JOHANN WOLFGANG VON GOETHE, FRIEDRICH VON SCHILLER, and FRIEDRICH VON SCHLEGEL. The French writers, MME. ANNE-LOUISE-GERMAINE DE STAËL, and ALPHONSE-MARIE-LOUIS DE PRAT DE LAMARTINE were also much influenced by reading Rousseau, especially by his sensitivity to nature and the cult of the individual.

The emerging autobiographical and confessional voices dominating poetry in Romantic texts (notably Wordsworth's The PRELUDE, PERCY BYSSHE SHELLEY's Alastor, Byron's Childe Harold's Pilgrimage, and JOHN KEATS's "The FALL OF HYPERION") are apparent heirs of Rousseau's self-analysis and introspection. Shelley's final poem, "The Triumph of Life," has Rousseau as a Virgilian guide to Shelley's Dante, both of whom can be seen "as multiple representations of a self-questioning Rousseau, who is, in turn, a projection or a figure for a self-questioning Shelley" (Lee 156). But individual references to Rousseau, though frequent in Romantic writing, blur and mask the scope of his singular impact, by stereotyping a figure whose paradoxes and complexities evolved through time into new ways of thinking about culture, government, and selfhood.

Jacques Voisine's J.-J. Rousseau en Angleterre l'époque romantique and Henri Roddier's J.-J. Rousseau en Angleterre au XVIIIe siècle discuss Rousseau's influence on English Romantic poets. Irving Babbitt's Rousseau and Romanticism is a diatribe that simplistically equates Rousseau and Romanticism with literary and political chaos. Edward Duffy's Rousseau in England: The Context for Shelley's Critique of the Enlightenment and Monika Lee's Rousseau's Impact on Shelley: Figuring the Written Self highlight the influence of Rousseau on Percy Bysshe Shelley, who proclaimed him "the greatest mind the world has produced since Milton" (P. B. Shelley 1968, 1:494). Paul de Man's Allegories of Reading examines the full implications in Rousseau's writing of a language and a self-figuration that tend toward nihilism. Samuel Taylor thinks Rousseau's relationship to Romanticism can mainly be defined as a problem of incoherence in the self stemming from antagonistic forces in the human psyche. Recent discussions of Rousseau and Romanticism have veered away from earlier simplistic assessments and emphasize instead the philosophical, linguistic, and psychological complexities in Rousseau's works.

## Further Reading

Babbitt, Irving. Rousseau and Romanticism. New Brunswick, N.J.: Transaction Publishers, 1991.

Claudon, Francis. The Concise Encyclopedia of Romanticism. Toronto: Omega, 1986.

de Man, Paul. Allegories of Reading: Figural Language in Rousseau, Rilke, and Proust. New Haven, Conn.: Yale University Press, 1979.

Duffy, Edward. Rousseau in England: The Context for Shelley's Critique of the Enlightenment. Berkeley: University of California Press, 1979.

Lee, Monika. Rousseau's Impact on Shelley: Figuring the Written Self. Lewiston, N.Y.: Edwin/Mellen Press, 1999.

Mitchell, W. J. T. "Influence, Autobiography, and Literary History: Rousseau's Confessions and Wordsworth's The Prelude." English Literary History 57 (1990): 643–664.

Roddier, Henri. J.-J. Rousseau en Angleterre au XVIIIe Siècle. Paris: Boivin, 1950.

Rousseau, Jean-Jacques. Oeuvres Complètes. 4 vols. Edited by Bernard Gagnebin and Marcel Raymond. Paris: Gallimard, 1959–69.

Shelley, Mary Wollstonecraft. Frankenstein; or, The Modern Prometheus. Peterborough, Ont.: Broadview Press, 1994.

———. "Rousseau." In Lives of the Most Eminent Literary and Scientific Men of France. London: Longman, 1839, 111–174.

Shelley, Percy Bysshe. The Letters of Percy Bysshe Shelley. 2 vols. Edited by F. L. Jones. Oxford: Oxford University Press, 1968.

———. Shelley's Poetry and Prose. Edited by Donald Reiman and Neil Fraistat. New York: Norton, 2002.

Taylor, Samuel. "Rousseau's Romanticism." In Reappraisals of Rousseau: Studies in Honour of R. A. Leigh, edited by Simon Harvey, Marian Hobson, David Kelley, and Samuel S. B. Taylor, 2–23. Totowa, N.J.: Barnes and Noble, 1980.

Voisine, Jacques. Rousseau en Angleterre l'époque romantique: les écrits autobiographiques et la légende. Paris: Didier, 1956.

Voltaire, François-Marie Arouet de. *Candide, or, Optimism/Voltaire.* Translated by Peter Constantine. New York: Modern Library, 2005.

Watson, Nicola. *Revolution and the Form of the British Novel, 1790–1825: Intercepted Letters, Interrupted Seductions.* Oxford: Oxford University Press, 1994.

Wollstonecraft, Mary. *Mary, A Fiction; and, The Wrongs of Woman.* Edited by Gary Kelly. London: Oxford University Press, 1976.

—Monika Lee

## "Ruined Cottage, The" Robert Southey (1799)

One of a number of "English eclogues"—blank-verse poems focusing on scenes, incidents, and histories involving rustic life and characters—"The Ruined Cottage" is now best known as the poem that ROBERT SOUTHEY purportedly plagiarized from WILLIAM WORDSWORTH, whose poem of the same name first appeared in 1798. Southey, however, claimed originality for his own poem, and in the preface to the collection in which the poem appeared, he announced: "The following eclogues, I believe, bear no resemblance to any poems in our language. This species of composition has become popular in Germany, and I was induced to attempt it by an account of the German idylls given me in conversation" (quoted in Smith). Southey's other eclogues are "The Old Mansion House," "The Grandmother's Tale," "Hannah," "The Sailor's Mother," "The Witch," "The Last of the Family," and "The Alderman's Funeral."

Southey's and Wordsworth's poems are certainly very similar. Both are intended to move the reader on an emotional level, and both highlight the ways in which people's lives can be ruined by events that are not their fault. Southey's elegiac poem begins when the poet/speaker and a friend, Charles, pass by a ruined cottage, and the poet observes that his friend is struck by the overgrown, empty dwelling with its "creeping weeds and nettles" (l. 5). The building's decrepit appearance seems to embody "melancholy thoughts" (l. 11); there is something almost tomblike about it. The poet then reveals that he has known this place since childhood, "this [having] been / My favorite walk even since I was a boy" (ll. 19–20). Moreover, despite its humble appearance, the cottage has a history which "should not be untold" (l. 45) Southey's speaker recounts the story of a humble widow who brings up her daughter, Joanna, a healthy girl with "red and white" cheeks (l. 69) in this cottage. The widow's modest ambition was for her daughter to gain "something better than a servant's slate" before her own death (l. 91). The mother's life was ruled by anxiety on her daughter's behalf, and she experienced a "pang / Like parting life to part with her dear girl" (ll. 92–93). Soon afterward, the daughter "by a villain's wiles seduced / Had played the wanton, and that blow had reached / Her mother's heart. She did not suffer long, / Her age was feeble, and the heavy blow / Brought her grey hairs with sorrow to the grave" (ll. 100–104). The mother's cottage quickly fell into disrepair, its sole function in the present being to act as a kind of memory prompt to the poet, reminding him of his ability to feel deeply and be moved—abilities that are the lifeblood of his power as a poet: "I pass this ruin'd dwelling oftentimes / And think of other days. It wakes in me / A transient sadness, but the feelings Charles / That ever with these recollections rise, / I trust in God they will not pass away" (ll. 105–109).

In many ways Southey's poem is a familiar one, a point made by CHARLES LAMB, who told Southey in a letter dated March 15, 1799, that he could "find no fault in [the poem] unless Joanna's ruin is a catastrophe too trite, and this is not the first time you have clothed your indignation in verse in a tale of ruined Innocence" (Lamb 1975, 1:131). Lamb preferred the mother ("a great a favourite with me"). He added: "I want to hear more of her, and of Joanna you have given us still less. But the picture of the rustics leaning over the bridge & the old Lady travelling abroad on summer evenings to see her garden water'd, are images so new and true, that I decidedly prefer this ruin'd cottage to any poem in the book." (Lamb 1975, 1:131).

The newness or otherwise of the poem is a topic that has fascinated critics ever since. The poem sits neatly alongside Southey's other works of the 1790s, notably in its scenic description and in its memorializing of the past and its peoples. Yet other similarities between Southey's poem and Wordsworth's seem a bit too close for comfort.

Both tell the story of a deserted cottage where domestic tragedy has occurred and where death has allowed nature to reinstate itself. Both also use the device of the poet recounting the story to a friend. The literary scholar Stuart Curran notes of the relationship that "Although [Southey's] plot is different from that of Wordsworth's poem—it concerns a mother's dissolution after the seduction of her lone daughter—the general theme of female betrayal and decline and a narrative frame through which the tale is imparted by an older man to an inexperienced male friend are sufficiently alike that it is scarcely possible to believe that the two poems were written in total independence one from the other" (Curran 23). At the time, however, Southey was then better known than Wordsworth, and the junior poet clearly felt disinclined to make much of it.

**Further Reading**

Curran, Stuart. "Mary Robinson's *Lyrical Tales* in Context." In *Re-Visioning Romanticism: British Women Writers, 1776–1837*, edited by Carol Shiner Wilson and Joel Haefner, 17–39. Philadelphia: University of Pennsylvania Press, 1994.

Jacobus, Mary. "Southey's Debt to *Lyrical Ballads* (1798)." *Review of English Studies* 22 (1971): 20–36.

Lamb, Charles, and Mary Lamb. *The Letters of Charles and Mary Anne Lamb*. 2 vols. Ithaca, N.Y.: Cornell University Press, 1975.

Smith, Christopher. "Robert Southey and the Emergence of *Lyrical Ballads*." *Romanticism on the Net*. 9 (February 1998). Available online. URL: http//www.erudite.org/revue/ron/1998/v/n9/005792al.html.

Southey, Robert. *Poetical Works, 1793–1810*. 5 vols. Edited by Lynda Pratt. London: Pickering and Chatto, 2004.

—Mark Harris

## "Ruined Cottage, The"  William Wordsworth
(1798)

First published in *Lyrical Ballads* and subsequently (redrafted to appear) in Book 1 of *The Excursion*, this poem is about how wisdom is gained via the remembrance of suffering. The version discussed here is that which appears in the *Lyrical Ballads*.

WILLIAM WORDSWORTH's notes on the poem's composition report: "All that relates to . . . the ruined cottage &c., was taken from observations made in the South West of England" (Wordsworth 1993, 81). The poet in this instance is a traveler who finds, in the midst of a natural setting "a ruined house, four naked walls / That stared upon each other" (ll. 31–32). The traveler meets an "aged Man / Alone, and stretched upon the cottage bench" (ll. 33–34), who narrates the story of Margaret, the "Last human tenant of these ruined walls" (ll. 490–492). This Pedlar, who "loved her / As my own child" (ll. 95–96), narrates Margaret's tale because he is able to reanimate invisible and absent "Things which you cannot see" (l. 68).

As a memory marker at a physical place and as a symbol of the preindustrial past, the cottage and its ruination, are revealed to be emblematic of the decline in Margaret's condition and her community's loss of vitality. In the *Journals of Dorothy Wordsworth* (1941), William Wordsworth's sister, DOROTHY WORDSWORTH, describes this relation between architecture, inhabitants, and human memory by writing how the decaying local area the Wordsworths visited "seemed to retain the memory of its connection with man in some way analogous to the ruined building" (l. 213). "The Ruined Cottage" captures this gradual decline. Two years after Margaret's husband "joined a troop / Of soldiers going to a distant land" (ll. 268–269) to combat "the plague of war" (l. 136) their hut was "As cheerful as before" (l. 306). Yet five years later it starts to "decay" (l. 477). The cottage gradually becomes "comfortless" (l. 402), as if "the better part were gnawed away" (l. 418) and this is because the social connections that bound people have been lost. This severance of connection between people and "a happy land" (l. 137) erodes a previous way of life. The village's labor force has been lost to military service while Margaret's community becomes reliant "for bread on parish charity" (l. 156) as its earlier agrarian traditions become unsustainable. The fate of "The Ruined Cottage" is thus bound up with the early 19th-century social and demographic changes accompanying INDUSTRIALISM.

The Pedlar recalls Margaret at her residence: "She is dead / And nettles rot and adders sun themselves / Where we have sate together" (ll. 109–111). He recalls her through her daily rituals (she drew water from her well for travelers) and personal artifacts denoting loss; she would never again draw water from the well's "useless fragment of a wooden bowl" (l. 91). Margaret is also memorialized by nature: the "group of trees," "clustering elms that sprang from the same root," stand "alone" (ll. 27, 28, 30). We also see how Margaret's memory is imprinted at this place because her suffering is attached to it. Nature witnesses her searching its landscape for the husband she hoped for but did not know "if he were dead / She knew not he was dead" (ll. 398–399). Because they understand her wish to be reunited, groves, streams, and hills mourn Margaret by speaking: "In these their invocations with a voice / Obedient to the strong creative power / Of human passion" (ll. 78–79). As the poem progresses, Margaret and place merge; we hear how she traveled farther from home and appeared almost spectral: "Her face was pale and thin, her figure too / Was changed" (ll. 338–339). When she transforms into a fleeting perception, evading the range of human sight, she becomes a genius loci (a spirit of a place). As Margaret puts it, "My tears / Have flowed as if my body were not such / As others are, and I could never die" (ll. 356–357). As a ghost of the past frozen in the latency of an "unquiet widowhood / A wife and widow" (ll. 446–448), Margaret's failure to find her husband (l. 351) and reawaken her life merges the human and nature at place into "one sadness" (l. 80).

Wordsworth's telling of Margaret's story is, as Kurt Fosso puts it "about the debt owed the dead" (Fosso 329). As an elegy, "The Ruined Cottage" joins the living and dead British people through remembrance; this has a pedagogical function of teaching readers moral truths associated with remembering. Remembrance is a panacea to the Pedlar's and the traveler's grief over Margaret's death: "That what we feel of sorrow and despair / From ruin and from change, and all the grief / The passing shews of being leave behind / Appeared an idle dream that could not live / Where meditation was" (ll. 520–524). Likewise, something good can come out of this: "But we have known that there is often found / In mournful thoughts, and always might be found / A power to virtue friendly" (ll. 228–230). The Pedlar's reminiscences perform the Wordsworthian tenet that mourning, conjoined to memory, potentially reveals the virtuous. The Pedlar identifies virtue in Margaret's past conduct—she drew "cool" water for passers-by (l. 100), and he is inspired by remembrance of her "cheerful hope" (l. 148). At the threshold of life/memory and death/forgetting, the cottage, like Margaret's "secret spirit of humanity" has "still survived" (ll. 503, 506).

### Further Reading

Fosso, Kurt, "Community and Mourning in William Wordsworth's 'The Ruined Cottage,' 1797–1798." *Studies in Philology* 92 (1995): 329–343.

Wordsworth, Dorothy. *Journals of Dorothy Wordsworth.* Edited by E. De Selincourt. New York: Macmillan, 1941.

Wordsworth, William. *The Fenwick notes of William Wordsworth.* Ed Curtis, Jared. Bristol Classical Press, London, 1993.

———. *William Wordsworth: Selected Poetry.* Edited by Stephen Gill and Duncan Wu. Oxford: Oxford World's Classics, 1998.

Wordsworth, William, and Samuel Taylor Coleridge. *Lyrical Ballads 1805.* Edited by Derek Roper. Plymouth, Eng.: Northcote House, 1987.

—Rachael Cameron

### *Rural Rides* William Cobbett (1830)

*Rural Rides* is a collection of essays recounting a series of journeys made via coach and horseback throughout the south of England. It was first published in WILLIAM COBBETT's radical weekly newspaper, the *POLITICAL REGISTER*, in the 1820s, then collected and published separately in 1830. His original full title indicates their purpose: *Rural Rides in the Counties of Surrey, Kent, Sussex, Hampshire, Wiltshire, Gloucestershire, Herefordshire, Worcestershire, Somersetshire, Oxfordshire, Berkshire, Essex, Suffolk, Norfolk, and Hertfordshire: with Economical and Political Observations relative to matters applicable to, and illustrated by, the State of those Counties respectively.*

Cobbett initially embarked on the journeys to challenge the conclusions of a parliamentary committee on agricultural distress. The rides are more than a fact-finding mission or a travelogue, however, as Cobbett uses them to exhort his readers to resist what he calls "the System," or "the Thing": modern urban, industrial socioeconomic structures. "The Thing" is centered on London, which Cobbett calls "the Great Wen," or tumor, figuring the city, the country's political center, as a disease. He angrily notes the emergence of new economic systems of stocks and paper money, various encroachments of the city into the countryside, changing relations for the worse between socially aspiring farmers and their laborers, and the impoverishment of laborers. It is easy to be amused by his attacks on tea drinking, pianoforte-playing farmers' wives, and potato-eating laborers (whom he contrasts with the bacon-and-bread-eating stalwarts of his memory). Nonetheless, he is not simply engaging in nostalgia for the past. Like Thomas Carlyle's 1829 essay "Signs of the Times," *Rural Rides* is an early entry into the 19th-century condition-of-England debate, raising serious questions about the costs of urbanization and industrialization (see INDUSTRIALISM). Cobbett argues that the existing stewards of the land are not doing their job and that the only way to change "the System" is to embrace universal suffrage (for men), which would reform Parliament, leading to the resolution of the ills diagnosed during the rides.

Cobbett's railing against "the System" has certain qualities in common with the Romantic challenge to established authority. He is much more materially focused than, say, WILLIAM BLAKE, but he shares the latter's distaste for bureaucracies of all kinds. Cobbett's nostalgia for a rural, agrarian world that is slipping away is also a value often associated with literary Romanticism. The rides are cyclical, both literally in Cobbett's loops throughout the countryside and figuratively in his return to scenes of past associations. They also display his organicism and insistence on human interdependence with the natural world, celebrating lives lived in accordance with traditional rural rhythms and good stewardship of the land. Just as WILLIAM WORDSWORTH and other Romantic poets use physical landscape as the inspiration for psychological landscape and formation of subjectivity, Cobbett uses the physical landscape as the inspiration for contemplation and the formation of a political identity. Despite appreciating the beauties of the natural world, he does not seek sublimity or even the picturesque in his landscapes: He always sees landscape in terms of the humans who have shaped it.

**Further Reading**

Benchimol, Alex. "William Cobbett's Geographies of Cultural Resistance in the Rural Rides." *Nineteenth-Century Contexts* 26, no. 3 (2004): 257–272.

Cobbett, William. *Rural Rides.* London: Penguin, 2001.

Mulvihill, James. "The Medium of Landscape in Cobbett's Rural Rides." *Studies in English Literature* 33, no. 4 (1993): 825–840.

Ulrich, John M. *Signs of Their Times: History, Labor, and the Body in Cobbett, Carlyle, and Disraeli.* Athens: Ohio University Press, 2002.

—Terri Doughty

## "Ruth" Thomas Hood (1829?)

THOMAS HOOD is best known for his satirical, whimsical, and comedic poems, yet he also penned a number of more serious and politically conscious works. The most famous of these is "The Song of the Shirt," which was published in *Punch* in 1843; it attacked the poverty and deprivation suffered by working-class female needleworkers. "Ruth" can be read as a poem about women's labor, but it is also a love poem, and its labor is pastoral, or at least agricultural. Unlike in "The Song of the Shirt," the expenditure of effort produces not upper-class luxury but a healthy and energized beauty—an "autumn flush" (l. 5) and "long lashes veil'd a light, / That had else been all too bright" (ll. 11–12)—that Ruth comes to portray in the poem.

But what kind of beauty is it? Ruth's portrait is not only physical—it emanates from her work, which reflects the morality of her character. As a retelling of the Old Testament story of Ruth, it becomes emblematic of the feminine ideal she embodies in the poem and for which she will be rewarded with the poetic persona's love. Hood's poem focuses on the moment that Boaz, though not named in the poem, falls in love with Ruth as he watches her work in his fields to support herself and her mother-in-law after her husband Mahlon's death.

The first three stanzas of the poem are interesting because of the way in which they portray Ruth in relation to the nature surrounding her. While the first stanza singles out Ruth from the field where she gleans (gleaning is the act of collecting any crops that have been leftover from the harvest proper, thus emphasizing her relative poverty), by stressing her otherworldliness as "the sweetheart of the sun" (l. 3), the following two stanzas focus on her face in order to emphasize how harmoniously she blends with the field. This correspondence between the female body and nature is a characteristic of Romantic poetry that Hood exploits for his own purposes.

Revealingly, Hood's poem follows a very different course from an encounter described by another Romantic poet who similarly comes across a woman working in a field, namely WILLIAM WORDSWORTH's "The Solitary Reaper" (1807). Whereas Wordsworth idealizes the solitary reaper at a distance—her very otherness allows him to imagine and objectify her identity—Hood sensualizes Ruth's labor by fastening on her facial characteristics, which are hidden behind her tresses as she works in the field. The major difference between Wordsworth's poem and Hood's is the absence of the poetic "I," which only emerges in the fifth and final stanza in order to address her not as an object of his desire but as a subject: "Sure, I said, Heav'n did not mean, / Where I reap thou shouldst but glean, / Lay thy sheaf adown and come / Share my harvest and my home" (ll. 17–20). In the Old Testament, Boaz does marry Ruth. What is notable though about Hood's ending is the exchange he proposes: Ruth is enjoined to give up her labor and to be simultaneously raised out of poverty by the labor of love. This is an egalitarian, selfless act by Boaz, but one which, in relatively conventional gendered terms, returns Ruth to the domestic sphere. After all, the reader only hears his voice in the poem and s/he is left to assume that Ruth takes up his offer to marry him.

**Further Reading**

Harris, Beth, ed. *Famine and Fashion: Needlewomen in the Nineteenth Century.* Aldershot, Eng.: Ashgate, 2005.

Hood, Thomas. *The Complete Poetical Works of Thomas Hood.* Edited by Walter Jerrold. London: Henry Frowde, 1906.

—Kyriaki Hadjiafxendi

# S

## Sade, Donatien-Alphonse-François, marquis de (1740–1814)

The marquis de Sade, most often remembered as the origin of the term *sadist*, was born on June 2, 1740, into a French aristocratic family. He was the only child of Comte Jean-Baptiste de Sade, a diplomat and rake, and Marie-Eléonore de Maillé de Carman, a lady-in-waiting of the princesse de Condé. Sade was born in the palace of the prince de Condé and lived there until he was four. He was educated by his uncle, a priest and scholar, and pursued a military career, serving in the Seven Years' War (1756–63) before marrying, at his father's insistence, Renée-Pélagie de Montreuil, the oldest daughter of a wealthy judge, in 1763. His reputation for violent, sexual mistreatment of men and women is a consequence of his pursuit of pleasure. His mother-in-law's desire to maintain respectability resulted in Sade spending nearly half of his life in a number of prisons and an insane asylum.

Prior to the FRENCH REVOLUTION, Sade's kidnapping and sexual and physical abuse of prostitutes resulted in a number of imprisonments in the 1760s and his exile to his chateau at La Coste. In the 1770s he fled to Italy with his sister-in-law after further mistreatment of prostitutes and committing sodomy with his manservant. His mother-in-law obtained a royal arrest warrant that was executed when de Sade returned to Paris to visit his fatally ill mother. He escaped the death penalty but was held in the Bastille, where he would write his masterpiece of sexual horrors and unchecked power,

*The 120 Days of Sodom.* After the storming of the Bastille on July 14, 1789 the work was believed lost but was later rediscovered hidden in De Sade's cell. Released in 1790 after the Constituent Assembly abolished the royal warrant, Sade was financially destitute, so he published novels and essays and attempted to stage plays. *Justine,* story of a virtuous woman who repeatedly suffers misfortunate in an unjust world and is finally killed by a thunderbolt, was revised for sale and published anonymously in 1791. *Philosophy in the Bedroom* (1795) combines the sexual corruption of a young woman with a critique of social morality in a dramatic dialogue. In *Juliette* (1797–1801), the sequel to *Justine,* Sade approaches the iniquities of civilization from the perspective of a prospering criminal.

Sade was divorced by his wife after being released from prison, and he met Marie-Constance Quesnet, who would remain with him for the rest of his life. Involved in revolutionary politics, he was elected to the National Convention in a party notorious for radical views, but he opposed convictions carrying the death penalty. The Reign of Terror was an uncertain time for Sade, who suffered further imprisonment and barely escaped the guillotine. During the regime of NAPOLEON BONAPARTE, he was arrested and imprisoned for publishing *Justine* and *Juliette.* When his family agreed to pay for his imprisonment, he was declared insane and moved to the insane asylum at Charenton, where his treatment varied from solitary confinement to enjoying the company of Constance and being encouraged to produce plays. In his final years, Sade conducted an affair with the young daughter of an asylum employee. Just before an order for his transfer to a state prison could be fulfilled, he died on December 2, 1814.

The majority of Sade's work, which covers novels, philosophical essays, dialogues, plays, and personal correspondence, was written while in prison without the expectation of publication, and a great deal of his work was destroyed by his surviving son after his death. *The 120 Days of Sodom* was not published until 1904. What remains is controversial and varied, erotic and disgusting, philosophical and melodramatic. Like many of his contemporaries, the marquis de Sade was a proponent of personal freedom who heavily criticized social and religious institutions, but his choice of extreme sexual content and the scandals of his life are irrevocably connected to his work.

## Further Reading

Airaksinen, Timo. *The Philosophy of the Marquis de Sade.* London: Routledge, 1995.

Gray, Francine du Plessix. *At Home with Marquis de Sade.* London: Hamish Hamilton, 1999.

Sade, marquis de. *Marquis de Sade, Justine, Philosophy in the Bedroom, and Other Writing.* Translated by Richard Seaver and Austryn Wainhouse. New York: Grove Weidenfeld, 1990.

Shattuck, Roger. *Forbidden Knowledge: From Prometheus to Pornography.* New York: St. Martin's Press, 1996.

Thomas, Donald. *The Marquis de Sade.* London: Allison and Busby, 1992.

—Tony W. Garland

## *Sappho and Phaon* (*Sappho and Phaon in a Series of Legitimate Sonnets, with Thoughts on Poetical Subjects, and Anecdotes of the Grecian Poetess*) Mary Robinson (1796)

In *Sappho and Phaon*, MARY ROBINSON constructs a sonnet sequence of 44 poems to relate a doomed love affair between Sappho, the ancient Greek poetess (who is the speaker of the sonnets), and Phaon, the ferryman with whom she falls in love. The first seven sonnets articulate Sappho's love for Phaon and the manner in which love dominates and renders useless her powers of reason. Sonnets

8 through 15 anticipate both physical and emotional intimacy with Phaon, as Sappho describes Phaon's great beauty and prays for the "tuneful maids" (Sonnet 8, l. 9) or the muses, to make her desirable to Phaon.

Beginning with "Delusive hope!" Sonnet 16 marks a change in tone that erases the optimism of the earlier sonnets. In Sonnet 18, the speaker asks, "Why art thou chang'd? O Phaon! tell me why?" (l. 1), but no answer comes forth, leaving Sappho alone and feeling betrayed. The following section details Sappho's despair at losing Phaon without explanation and chronicles the inability of anything—including the moon, philosophy, patience, and nature—to provide consolation. In sonnet 30, Sappho bids farewell to her home "to seek my Lover, or my Grave!" (l. 14). After a final prayer for Phaon's return, Sappho concludes that "Phaon is false!" (Sonnet 35, l. 5) and will not come back. She then prepares for death so that she can leave the pain of mortal life behind (Sonnets 36–40). The final four sonnets trace Sappho's accent to a "dizzy precipice" (Sonnet 43, l. 1) where she jumps into "the rocky deep" (Sonnet 42, l. 2).

One of Robinson's goals for the sonnet sequence is to place herself specifically and women writers generally into the classical literary tradition. The complete title of the text, *Sappho and Phaon in a Series of Legitimate Sonnets, with Thoughts on Poetical Subjects, and Anecdotes of the Grecian Poetess*, provides the first clue to this project. By writing Petrarchan sonnets—"legitimate sonnets," as she describes them in her prefatory comments and by which she means sonnets organized according the model popularized by the Italian poet Francesco Petrarch (1304–74)—Robinson draws on classical Italian literary models. She also notes that JOHN MILTON favored the Petrarchan sonnet, and in this way she links herself to both poets. Women's place in literary tradition is also at issue, especially near the end of the preface, where Robinson pays "tribute to the talents of my illustrious country-women; who, unpatronized by the courts, and unprotected by the powerful, persevere in the paths of literature" (Robinson 149). By calling attention to women's place in the literary tradition and in society, Robinson parallels 19th-century women and Sappho. Further, Sappho's experience, as related in the sonnets, becomes symbolic of all women whom men have wronged and betrayed. FELICIA HEMANS described another aspect in "The LAST SONG OF SAPPHO."

By writing about women and their place in society, Robinson's text reflects the 19th-century interest in women's rights that can be found in the works of many other writers, including MARY WOLLSTONECRAFT, MARY HAYS, ANNA LAETITIA BARBAULD, and MARY SHELLEY. Additionally, in writing about an ancient Greek poet and by drawing from Ovid's account of Sappho and Phaon, Robinson exemplifies the Romantic fascination with classical culture that can also be seen in writers such as JOHN KEATS, MARY TIGHE, and PERCY BYSSHE SHELLEY.

**Further Reading**

Robinson, Mary. *Selected Poems of Mary Robinson*. Edited by Judith Pascoe. Peterborough, Ont.: Broadview Press, 2000.

—Ken Bugajski

## Schiller, (Johann Christoph) Friedrich von
(1759–1805)

Friedrich von Schiller was a dramatist and a lyric poet whose works was chiefly concerned with freedom and social and moral responsibility. He was born on November 10, 1759, in Marbach, Württemberg (now in Germany) to Johannes Kaspar and Elisabeth Dorothea Schiller, part of a family of strict Lutheran Protestants. As a boy, Schiller was a pupil in the state military academy, where he studied law and medicine but was really interested in theology. In 1780 he was expelled from the academy after writing an essay on religion, "On the Relation Between Man's Animal and Spiritual Nature." Despite having no enthusiasm for military life, he was enrolled in his father's army regiment as a doctor.

Even as a child, Schiller was chaffing against the restrictions imposed on him, and it is no surprise that many of his works deal with the topic of freedom in one form or another. His play *Die Rauber* (The ROBBERS, 1781) was a principal work of German literature's *Sturm und Drang* (storm and stress) era. The play, with its themes of liberty and authoritarian rule, received admiring commentary from WILLIAM HAZLITT and SAMUEL TAYLOR COLERIDGE. In *Kabale und Liebe* (*Intrigue and Love,* 1784) Schiller turned to a critique of contemporary society, where the machinations of the state affected the love of a youthful hero and his girl. He turned to blank-verse drama with *Don Carlos* (1787), a play of political machinations set in the 16th-century court of Philip II of Spain that attacked political absolutism; and to historical tragedy with *Wallenstein* (1799). The second and third parts of this three-part play were translated into English by Coleridge in 1800. As the historical drama became a focus of Schiller's work, he produced MARY STUART: *A Tragedy* (1800) and *Die Jungfrau von Orleans* (*The Maid of Orleans,* 1801). He wrote the classical drama *Die Braut von Messina* (*The Bride of Messina,* 1803) with a chorus. His final notable play was *Wilhelm Tell* (1804).

In 1797–98 Schiller collaborated with JOHANN WOLFGANG VON GOETHE on a collection of ballads, at about the same time that in Britain WILLIAM WORDSWORTH and SAMUEL TAYLOR COLERIDGE were producing their *Lyrical Ballads* (1798). Schiller's "An die Freude" was later set to music by Beethoven in his *Ninth Symphony* as the "Ode to Joy." Several more Schiller poems have been set to music by other composers.

Schiller's deep interest in history led to his appointment as a professor of history in Jena, Germany. His historical writing included *The Revolt of the Netherlands* (1788) and *A History of the Thirty Years' War* (1798–1800). He also wrote dramatic criticism on the moral influence of the theater. With his interest in philosophical aesthetics, he was engaged in a study and critique of the aesthetics of Immanuel Kant that had an impact on the critical writings of August and FRIEDRICH VON SCHLEGEL. Schiller wrote *Briefe uber die aesthetische Erzeihung des Menschen* (*On the Aesthetic Education of Man,* 1795) and *Uber naïve und sentimentalische Dichtung* (*On Naïve and Reflective Poetry,* 1795–96). In the latter work, he offers a contrast of his own style and methods with Goethe's.

Schiller died of tuberculosis on May 9, 1805, age 45. Nonetheless, his influence on a new generation of writers was well established.

## Further Reading

Schiller, Friedrich. *An Anthology for Our Time, in New English Translation and the Original German. With an Account of His Life and Work by Frederick Ungar.* Translations by Passage, Jane Bannard Greene, and Alexander Gode von Aesch. New York: Ungar, 1959.

———. *Plays.* Edited by Walter Hinderer. New York: Continuum, 1983.

Sharpe, Lesley. *Friedrich Schiller: Drama, Thought, Politics.* Cambridge: Cambridge University Press, 1991.

Simons, John D. *Friedrich Schiller.* Boston: Twayne, 1981.

—Robert McPharland

## Schlegel, Friedrich von (1772–1829)

A German critic and philosopher, Friedrich von Schlegel is generally reckoned to be one of the most influential thinkers of the Romantic period, articulating the tenets of literary Romanticism. According to Schlegel, *romantisch* expresses emotionalism and spirituality in an imaginative form. Great creative writing is a bringing together of two elements: the "daylight" of reason and the unfathomable "night" of creation. Schlegel's ideas matched and inspired other well-known figures of the Romantic movement: WILLIAM WORDSWORTH, SAMUEL TAYLOR COLERIDGE, PERCY BYSSHE SHELLEY, JOHN KEATS, LORD BYRON in Great Britain, as well as Nathaniel Hawthorne, Edgar Allan Poe, and Walt Whitman in America.

Schlegel was born on March 10, 1772, in Hanover, Germany, the younger brother of the philosopher August Wilhelm von Schlegel. As a young man, he moved in German intellectual circles that included NOVALIS and LUDWIG TIECK, and he was heavily influenced by the philosophers Immanuel Kant, J. G. Fichte, and Georg Hegel, in particular their ideas relating to selfhood and free will. In 1797 Schlegel published *The Greeks and Romans,* which was followed by *The History of the Poetry of the Greeks and Romans* (1798). However, it was his editorial work with his brother August that helped publicize his philosophical and aesthetic ideas about Romanticism. The brothers founded the magazine the *Athenäum,* in which many of the central tenets of what would come to be accepted as Romanticism were articulated: an interest in mythology, folk stories, and fairy tales, as well as communion with nature and a belief that poetry should encompass every aspect of life and above all the sense of the "religion of art," as Schlegel termed it. Also important was the sense of writing across genres—what he called *Universalpoesie* (universal poetry). This is something which features in *Lucinde* (1799), his semiautobiographical—and at the time scandalous—novel, based on his affair with Dorothea Veit. The novel combines prose with letters, diary entries, and dreamlike sequences in a fragmentary narrative. It also offered a new model for relationships encompassing complete individual freedom and equal partnership between men and women—physical, spiritual, and intellectual.

Although Schlegel had advocated freedom in all things and extolled extramarital relationships in *Lucinde,* as he grew older he became more conservative. In 1808 he converted to Roman Catholicism. His work also took him to Austria—at that time a byword for repressive politics. In 1809 he was made court secretary in Vienna, although he continued to write and give lectures. His later works include *The Philosophy of History* (1829) and *The Philosophy of Life and Philosophy of Language in a Course of Lectures* (1828). He died in Dresden on January 12, 1829.

## Further Reading

Eichner, Hans. *Friedrich Schlegel.* New York: Twayne Publishers 1970.

Klaus, Peter. *Friedrich Schlegel.* Stuttgart: Metzler, 1978.

Schlegel, Friedrich. *The Æsthetic and Miscellaneous Works of Frederick Von Schlegel.* Charleston, S.C.: BiblioBazaar, 2008.

———. *Lectures on the History of Literature, Ancient and Modern.* 3 vols. Charleston, S.C.: BiblioBazaar, 2008.

———. *Lucinde.* New York: Bastian Books, 2008.

—Michael Smith

## science

Throughout the late 18th and early 19th centuries, a scientific revolution was taking place which coincided with revolutions of industry and culture. During this time, many Romantic writers, artists, and thinkers began reacting to a perceived mechanized view of the world reflected in scientific theories of the day. Literature and art of the period began to reflect on nature, presenting it in a light both terrifying and mysterious. Works such as MARY SHELLEY's FRANKENSTEIN emphasized the responsibility of society in the quest for scientific advancement and presented the belief that nature must be appreciated and respected rather than controlled. Other Romantic works shared this emphasis. The British poet WILLIAM BLAKE saw a connection between the imagination and theories of science, mathematics, and physics, *The Book of Urizen*, written in 1794, revealed a darker side of science. A parody of the theory of creation popular during the Enlightenment, it began with a description of the creation of the world based on Newtonian theories and geological formations—a rational, mathematical formation that was typical of Enlightenment thinking. The *Enlightenment* is term commonly used to describe a range of philosophers, scientists and movements active from the start of the 1600s through to the early 1800s. Though no movement is ever without its disputes (and the Enlightenment is no exception), the thinkers involved tended to stress the ability of individuals to achieve progress (social, scientific, political, technological) through the use of critical thinking and reason, and by turning their backs on old superstitions.

As studies in cognitive science and the life sciences gained momentum, many scientific theories during the Romantic period began to shift from the previous focus on Newtonian ideologies and the rational thinking, deductive reasoning, and mechanization of the universe prompted by the Enlightenment. JOHANN WOLFGANG VON GOETHE's research in optics sought to prove that the ability to see color was a result of internal human ability, not the result of a mathematical equation as Sir Isaac Newton's (1642–1727) theories had declared. The theories of the European scientists Sir Humphry Davy (1778–1829), Jean-Baptiste Lamarck (1744–1829), and John Dalton (1766–1844) reflected a deeper respect for nature and a further disconnect from the Enlightenment belief that nature could be understood by intellect alone.

Emphasis had previously been placed on physics and mathematics, but the study of biology—and of life itself—grew in importance during the Romantic period. The life sciences, including biology, organic chemistry, and psychology, were also considered to be areas of high importance. In 1801 Lamarck set out a theory of biology to separate the characteristics of living beings from the laws of physics, reinforcing the Romantic theory of organic nature. His main focuses were on botany, invertebrate zoology, and evolution, indirect reflections of his interests in poetry and nature. As a biologist, he theorized that nature created life and that the environment naturally drives the evolution of simple to complex organisms, beliefs that also later influenced Charles Darwin's (1809–82) famed evolutionary theories. Erasmus Darwin (1731–1802), grandfather of Charles Darwin and an English physician during the late 18th century, integrated interests in science and evolution, philosophy, and poetry. His poetry was largely admired by Romantic figures such as WILLIAM WORDSWORTH and SAMUEL TAYLOR COLERIDGE, as were his studies in cognitive science and neurobiology. His most famous work, *The Botanic Garden,* a set of two poems written in 1791, suggested a relationship between science and emotion while reflecting his interests in botany.

Davy, who discovered the chemical and electromagnetic affinity of molecules in 1807, also considered nature a force to be respected and understood. To Davy, this could be achieved not through attempts to control nature, but rather through attempting to connect with nature on an emotional and sentimental level in order to appreciate and live in harmony with it. Chemistry was not simply a study of individual elements; it was a study in how elements participated in complex chemical reactions to create an end result. Davy hoped that the changing views of science and nature could eventually lead to changes in society as a whole. The English chemist was also a minor poet, becoming good friends with Wordsworth and Coleridge. Coleridge endorsed the empirical method of data collection that was employed by the likes of Davy and hoped that chemistry and related fields of natural science would reconcile the opposing forces in nature and society. In 1807

Coleridge praised Davy's studies in a letter, saying that his theories did more to empower nature than Newton's theories. PERCY BYSSHE SHELLEY, another prominent Romantic poet, believed that mankind could change the courses and outcome of the world by understanding science and the cause-and-effect relationships man had with the natural world—a view also held by Davy.

In 1803 Dalton, an English chemist known for his work dealing with partial pressures, developed the atomic theory, which proposed that every element was made up of individual atoms distinct to that element and that elements can combine to form a distinct compound. In line with the thinking of Lamarck and Davy, Dalton's work was consistent with Romanticism's antireductionist theory, whereby individual parts are not as important alone as the whole they comprise.

Perhaps one of the most striking developments during the Romantic period was the integration of science and the arts. Despite the common assumption that all Romantics reacted against scientific progress, many maintained strong interests in scientific developments, holding their scientific peers in high regard.

### Further Reading

Fulford, Tim, Debbie Lee, and Peter J. Kitson. *Literature, Science and Exploration in the Romantic Era: Bodies of Knowledge.* Cambridge: Cambridge University Press, 2004.

Kipperman, Mark. "Coleridge, Shelley, Davy, and Science's Millennium—Samuel Taylor Coleridge, Percy Bysshe Shelley, Humphry Davy." *Criticism* (Summer 1998). Available online. URL: http://findarticles.com/p/articles/mi_m2220/is_n3_v40/ai_21182131/pg_1. Accessed on January 25, 2008.

Olsen, Richard. *Science and Scientism in Nineteenth-Century Europe.* Urbana: University of Illinois Press, 2007.

Poggi, Stefano, and Maurizio Bosso, eds. *Romanticism in Science: Science in Europe, 1790–1840.* Dordrecht and Boston: Kluwer Academic Publishers, 1994.

Richardson, Alan. *British Romanticism and the Science of the Mind.* Cambridge: Cambridge University Press; 2005.

—Julie Roy

## Scott, John   See "DRUM, THE."

## Scott, Sir Walter (1771–1832)

Sir Walter Scott was a Scottish poet and novelist who popularized HISTORICAL FICTION. Born on August 15, 1771, in Edinburgh, he was sent by his parents to his grandparents' home in the Borders region in 1773 in the hope that the lameness he suffered from due to a bout of polio would be ameliorated. Here, Scott was exposed to the rich folklore and culture of the Borders region, which he would use extensively in his first literary endeavors. In early 1775 he returned to Edinburgh, where he began his formal education, entering law school and eventually becoming a lawyer in 1792. In 1797 he married Margaret Charlotte Charpentier, with whom he had five children. In 1799 he received the post of sheriff-deputy of Selkirk County, and around this time be began to write some poems and ballads. He also did some translations from the German and entered into a business arrangement with the publisher James Ballantyne, a long relationship that eventually would end in financial catastrophe.

By Scott's own account, he was a voracious reader as well as a collector of folklore and ballads from the Borders region, where he undertook numerous expeditions. His first major publication, MINSTRELSY OF THE SCOTTISH BORDER (1802), was a collection of Scottish ballads that also included a great deal of introductory material, notes, and appendices, features that would become a hallmark of Scott's writing. The *Minstrelsy* eventually extended to three volumes and was very popular, selling well in North America as well as throughout Europe and receiving critical praise. Scott's antiquarian appetite was whetted by his work on this collection; its success encouraged him to turn his hand to writing his own poetry celebrating the Scottish past, and in 1805 he produced *The Lay of the Last Minstrel*. With a meter modeled on Coleridge's "CHRISTABEL," this six-canto ballad was intended, as the preface asserts, "to illustrate the customs and manners which anciently prevailed on the Borders of England and Scotland" (Scott, 1925, 3). It was immensely popular, going through six editions in the next three years and selling almost 30,000 copies, bringing instant fame to Scott. While the critical reception was equally as positive for the most part, the poem's many structural flaws did not go unnoticed. Nevertheless, the success of *The Lay of the Last Minstrel* inspired Scott to turn more seriously toward a career as a professional writer.

Scott followed up this achievement with a series of verse narratives: MARMION (1808), *The Lady of the Lake* (1810), *The Vision of Don Roderick* (1811), *Rokeby* (1813), *The Bridal of Triermain* (1813), *The Lord of the Isles* (1815), *The Field of Waterloo* (1815), and *Harold the Dauntless* (1817). Of these, *The Lady of the Lake* was the most commercially successful, selling 25,000 copies in the first eight months. The rest of these titles received a mixed reception, both critically and in the marketplace. Not surprisingly, so many titles in such quick succession resulted in some careless and weak compositions, as critics pointed out. Scott's inclination to mix historical and fictional figures and events surfaces in some of these poems, a method that was both praised for its novelty and criticized for its inaccuracies. Likewise, the scheme to publish anonymously was first attempted with the publication of *The Bridal of Triermain*. It appeared in the same year as *Rokeby,* and it was hoped that readers would assume it to be the product of an imitator and that the sales of both would benefit, something of a necessity for Scott as his business dealings and general financial situation were beginning to become complicated and strained. In any case, he eventually realized that, with the enormous success of LORD BYRON'S CHILDE HAROLD'S PILGRIMAGE (1810), the field of verse narratives was becoming crowded, and he decided to try his hand at novel writing.

Scott's first novel, WAVERLEY, was published anonymously in 1814, and the next 18 years saw the publication of some 27 novels set in periods ranging from the 11th century to his own era; these came to be known as the "Waverley novels." His decision to keep his authorship secret probably was motivated at first by a certain insecurity with respect to how his audience would react to their favorite author turning to a genre more associated with female writers, and later by marketing strategies intended to generate mystery and speculation among readers. Often considered the first historical novel, *Waverley* skillfully blends historical subject matter and romance elements, and was greeted by the critics as an extraordinary achievement that "cast the whole tribe of ordinary novels into the shade" (Jeffrey 208). *Waverley* and 10 other novels are all set in Scotland and thus came to be known as the "Scottish novels." These are: GUY MANNERING (1815), *The Antiquary* (1816), *The Black Dwarf* (1816), *Old Mortality* (1816), ROB ROY (1818), *The* HEART OF MIDLOTHIAN (1818), *The* BRIDE OF LAMMERMOOR (1819), *A Legend of Montrose* (1819), *St. Ronan's Well* (1824), and *Redgauntlet* (1824). These are generally considered Scott's best, if not always his most popular (IVANHOE holding that honor, by most accounts).

*Waverley* serves as a satisfactory paradigm for nearly all the other Scottish Novels. The structural similarities of Scott's novels are striking: Many of them contain such standard motifs as a confrontation between two characters, a journey, a contrast of cultures, two heroines, an uncle-nephew relationship, initiation rites, and historical personages. Furthermore, the narrative technique is similar in many of the novels, with the narrative proper of 14 of the novels beginning in the second chapter. The prefaces, postscripts, notes, and self-reviews, most of which were written after the fact for the Magnum Opus edition (1829), indicate that Scott saw *Waverley* as establishing the pattern for the following series of historical novels. On this level its narrative functions as a kind of manifesto for Scott's program of quasisocial realism as represented in the Scottish novels.

As historical fiction, *Waverley* has also enjoyed a generous reception among critics, including historical ones. In fact, it was not unusual for a Scott novel to be accorded the status of a history and Scott that of a first-rate historian. While the Scottish novels represent Scottish history within a romance structure, they attempt to reinforce the fundamental themes of the growth of historical consciousness and the progress of civil society. Accordingly, while the narrative must make concessions to romance conventions for purposes of storytelling, on balance the romance must be neutralized, contained, and finally rejected in the interests of the particular historical ideology that

Scott wishes to project. This ideology typically is a reflection of the prevailing intellectual tenets of Enlightenment and post-Enlightenment Scotland and frames "improvement" and "progress" as inherent and inevitable principles. Scotland's struggle to assume its rightful place among modern nations is tied up in this, and Scott's work goes some way toward constructing a "nationalist myth." Each of the Scottish novels leans in this direction.

*Waverley*, for instance, is ostensibly about the failure of romance to contend with the forces of what the narrator refers to as "real history," manifested specifically in the Jacobite Rebellion of 1745. Accordingly, the text manifests a conscious effort to "thematize" romance in preparation for its ultimate rejection. Waverley himself is depicted at first as a hopeless romantic whose impractical education makes him unfit for the enterprise he undertakes on behalf of the Jacobite rebels. A protagonist of "sneaking imbecility," in Scott's own words, Waverley is more acted upon than active, and he is swept along through a series of misadventures that are orchestrated by unseen hands. Inevitably, however, after his "adventure" in armed struggle, Waverley shakes off his idealism and comes to the famous insight that "the romance of his life was ended, and . . . its real history had now commenced" (Scott *Waverley* 1986, 283).

For Scott, "real history" is an anchor with which he hopes to secure the novel to a credible historiographical context. Indeed, just as Waverley must relinquish his romantic proclivities before he can begin his "real" life, the narrative itself must achieve historical verisimilitude in order to avoid the embarrassment of "mere romance." Arguably, however, when we examine Waverley's transformation we discover that, if anything, his life becomes more "enchanted" after his epiphany, as "real history" is absorbed into a romance of political restoration, symbolized by the grand reconciliation scene with which the novel closes, and underscored by the curious elision in the novel of the event that terminated the Jacobite rebellion, the battle at Culloden—which resulted in a general slaughter and the enforced breakup of the clan system in the Highlands. While we might think of this reconciliation, in the context of the novel at least, as a kind of wish fulfillment given the historical realities it

papers over, it originates in Scott's interpretation of two momentous events in England and Scotland's past, namely the Glorious Revolution of 1688 and the Union of the Crowns in 1707. As the scholar Douglas Mack points out, Scott conceived of both of these events as crucial "precursors of a rational, stable British settlement that secured the rights of men of property by establishing freedom, under the law, from arbitrary power" (Mack xxv)—perhaps also a kind of wish fulfillment on Scott's part. The other Scottish novels roughly follow a similar pattern to that of *Waverley*: Historical material is presented in rich detail, but this representation is skillfully controlled within the narrative, supported by the paratextual apparatus—the notes, prefaces, postscripts, appendices, essays, reviews, histories, journals, and letters—where much of the novels' historical detail is elaborated.

For all their romance excess, the Waverley novels can be seen as a grand shaping of the substance of Scottish history, a kind of aestheticization of history. These works had enormous influence on the literary as well as the historical consciousness of Scott's age. Arguably, questions of historical representation in fiction cannot be addressed adequately without considering the Waverley novels. One of Scott's admirers, Georg Lukács, praises Scott for his "historical faithfulness . . . making concretely clear the historical necessity of a concrete situation," which in Scott's case was "the authenticity of the historical psychology of his characters" (Lukácz 65). He admires Scott's ability in the novels to maintain a balanced view of history through the device of the "mediocre" or "middling" hero (32, 33), the character who seems able to be on both sides at once.

Scott's desire to effect a "middle-way" solution to historical crises in the novels probably reflects his politics. What can be pieced together—from his histories of Scotland and NAPOLEON BONAPARTE, his letters, and other biographical information—confirms Scott's Tory conservatism in social and political matters. He harbored a typical ruling-class suspicion of lower-class unrest and a distrust of any change that was not managed from above or that threatened established customs and institutions. In short, in the political sphere at least, it would not be an exaggeration to call Scott a reactionary, especially in relation to specific events such as industrial revolution or the FRENCH REVOLUTION, although this characterization has often been exaggerated by critics wishing to reject Scott's oeuvre. On the other hand, the novels often exhibit a sympathy for institutional and political reform, and they demonstrate that Scott understood the inevitability—the necessity even—of the kind of historical change that ameliorates the living conditions of what he calls the "lower orders." Nevertheless, like that of many of his fellow conservatives, Scott's fear of the politicization of the "lower orders" was often irrational, as numerous remarks in his nonfiction make clear. Consequently, on such contemporary issues as the REFORM ACT—by any standards a minimum response to poverty, destitution, and disfranchisement—Scott's reactions do not always reflect well on his otherwise well-intentioned efforts to construct a "civil society."

Scott's writing career was not confined to novels during this period, and his literary productivity has become the stuff of legends. In addition to 27 novels and 11 collections of poetry, he also wrote or edited a nine-volume biography of Napoleon (1827); a two-volume history of Scotland (1829–30); 12 volumes of historical stories for children (*Tales of a Grandfather*, 1828); a four-volume edition of *Lives of the Novelists* (1821–24); a 19-volume edition of *The Works of Jonathan Swift* (1814), including a biography; an 18-volume edition of *The Works of John Dryden* (1808), including a biography; dozens of short stories; and hundreds of essays, reviews, and letters. With such a prodigious output, errors of composition and other lapses were inevitable, and Scott was the subject of much criticism on that score.

Certainly Scott wrote for money, something of a necessity for him when he was faced with financial ruin. The crisis was brewing for many years, brought on by his purchase of an estate at Abbotsford and the prolonged, extensive renovations he undertook, not to mention the acquisition of hundreds of relics and artifacts. The financial demands of this venture seriously strained the Ballantyne publishing house, with which he was involved as a silent partner. After years of protracted struggle, the business finally succumbed to bankruptcy in 1826. It was generally recognized that this crisis

was Scott's folly, born of his antiquarian obsessions and aristocratic pretensions. Indeed, his friend JAMES HOGG asserted that "the only foible I ever could discover in the character of Sir Walter was a too strong leaning to the old aristocracy of the country. His devotion for titled rank was prodigious and in such an illustrious character altogether out of place. It amounted almost to adoration" (Hogg 95). (Perhaps the most extraordinary illustration of Scott's adoration was the famous 1822 royal visit to Scotland that he orchestrated. He managed to convince George IV that the king was not only a Stuart prince but a Jacobite Highlander as well, and he persuaded the rotund monarch to appear before his astonished subjects in full Highland regalia, an affair that came to be known as the "one and twenty daft days.") Scott's compatriot, Thomas Carlyle, was astounded that a writer of Scott's talents "must kill himself that he may be a country gentleman, the founder of a race of Scottish lairds" (Carlyle 3:173). Referring to Scott's financial ruin as "one of the strangest, most tragical histories ever enacted under the sun," Carlyle remarked that "to cover the walls of a stone house in Selkirkshire with knickknacks, ancient armour and genealogical shields, what can we name it but a being bit with delirium of a kind?" (3:173).

Determined to pay off his debts and perhaps hold on to Abbotsford, or at least avoid total ruin, Scott wrote furiously through serious illness, working on several projects at once. One of these was the million-word biography of Napoleon Bonaparte, and it is difficult to imagine that, as he wrote, he did not see a reflection of his own life in the image of the fallen Napoleon. It was at this time that he decided to lay "aside his incognito" as a novelist (Scott *Chronicles* 1827–28, xix), and reveal himself at last as the "Author of Waverley." However, he makes a virtue of necessity by insinuating that he was obliged to reveal his authorship "after the affairs of my publishers . . . unfortunately passed into a management different from their own" (xix), a euphemism for the fact that the revenues of both Scott and the Ballantyne Press were to be confiscated by a group of trustees comprised of their creditors. More probably, his decision to confirm his authorship—a fact, it should be noted, that was already generally known—probably had more to do with financially capitalizing on his fame at a time when he desperately needed every cent he could earn to pay off his considerable debts. In failing health after having suffered a stroke in 1830, and working feverishly to pay off his debts, Scott died at Abbotsford on September 21, 1832. Remarkably, because his novels continued to sell after his death, his debts were eventually paid off.

Scott is often described as the quintessential romantic, although this label may owe more to his role in establishing the novel as a literary form during the Romantic period than to any aesthetic characteristics that might associate him with the Romantics. In his prefaces he never does seem altogether comfortable with his role as a romancer, and he is even more uncomfortable with any suggestion that he has abused history. These constraints may partially explain his distancing effects: the anonymity and use of pen names; the creation of imaginary editors and antiquarians; and, most important, the contrived debates with these characters in which Scott himself, in the persona of the anonymous "Author of Waverley," engages in a vigorous defense of his artistic methods. All the same, certainly one value of his novels is their capacity to engage this tension between romance and realism and to illuminate problems of historical representation. On balance, however, Scott seems destined to suffer from mixed critical judgments concerning his achievement, and it is perhaps for this reason that he has been called Scotland's "greatest and most troubling writer" (Massie 13).

## Further Reading

Carlyle, Thomas. *Critical and Miscellaneous Essays*. 4 vols. London: Chapman and Hall, 1888.

Hogg, James. *Memoir of the Author's Life and Familiar Anecdotes of Sir Walter Scott*. Edited by Douglas S. Mack. Edinburgh: Scottish Academic Press, 1972.

Jeffrey, Francis. Review of *Waverley; or, 'Tis Sixty Years Since*, by Walter Scott. *Edinburgh Review* 24 (November 1814): 208–243.

Johnson, Edgar. *Sir Walter Scott: The Great Unknown*. 2 vols. London: Hamish Hamilton, 1970.

Lockhart, J. G. *Memoirs of the Life of Sir Walter Scott, Bart.* Edinburgh: Robert Cadell, 1842.

Lukács, Georg. *The Historical Novel*. London: Merlin, 1962.

Mack, Douglas. Introduction to *The Tale of Old Mortality*, by Walter Scott, Harmondsworth, Eng.: Penguin, 2000.

Massie, Allan. "Who Invented Scotland—and England?" Review of *The Origin of Scottish Nationalism*, by Neil Davidson. *Times Literary Supplement* (August 11, 2000): 13.

Scott, Walter. *The Antiquary*. Edited by David Hewitt. Harmondsworth, Eng.: Penguin, 1998.

*Chronicles of the Canongate*. Edited by Claire Lamont. Harmondsworth: Penguin, 2003.

———. *Heart of Midlothian*. Edited by Claire Lamont. Oxford: University Press, 1989.

———. *Ivanhoe*. Edited by A. N. Wilson. Harmondsworth, Eng.: Penguin, 1986.

———. *The Journal of Sir Walter Scott*. Edited by W. E. K. Anderson. Oxford: Clarendon Press, 1972.

———. *The Lay of the Last Minstrel*. Reprint, Cambridge: Cambridge University Press, 1925.

———. *Letters of Sir Walter Scott*. 12 vols. Edited by Sir Herbert Grierson. London: Constable, 1932–37.

———. *Life of Napoleon Buonaparte*. 9 vols. Edinburgh: Longman, 1827.

———. *Minstrelsy of the Scottish Border*. 4 vols. Edited by T. F. Henderson. Edinburgh: Oliver and Boyd, 1932.

———. *Old Mortality*. Edited by Angus Calder. Harmondsworth, Eng.: Penguin, 1985.

———. *Redgauntlet*. Edited by Kathryn Sutherland. Oxford: University Press, 1985.

———. *Rob Roy*. London: Dent, 1986.

———. *Waverley; or, 'Tis Sixty Years Since*. Edited by Claire Lamont. Oxford: University Press, 1986.

Welsh, Alexander. *The Hero of the Waverley Novels*. 1963. Reprint, with New Essays on Scott, Princeton, N.J.: University Press, 1992.

—Ross MacKay

## *Sense and Sensibility* Jane Austen (1811)

JANE AUSTEN was something of a social voyeur in the sense that she closely observed humans, and human nature, in civilized society. While it seems that she had some sympathy with the Romantics, she did object to excessive "sensibility." Austen believed that some people might use what she called SENSIBILITY in order to exaggerate their feelings. She felt that intense feelings in one individual would take precedence over the feelings of other individuals, which would lead the intensely feeling individual to renege on his or social duty, preventing them from following the rules of a civilised society.

In *Sense and Sensibility* Austen uses Elinor and Marianne Dashwood to explore the ideals and problems of Romanticism. Through her own situation, Austen was fully aware that excessive emotional display and societal constraints could not work in harmony together. As the critic Tony Tanner notes, Elinor and Marianne are presented as "slightly, but crucially different" characters (Tanner 378). Elinor "limits herself to fancy—an appropriate Coleridgean distinction" (Tanner 375) as she has intense feelings but keeps those within herself. Marianne has imagination, an open warmth of spirit, and intense appreciation of nature; arguably a more Wordsworthian distinction. Therefore, the division between them is not as stark as it may at first seem. The sisters are not polar opposites of each other, but rather more mirror images. Elinor's sense means that she conforms to society's unspoken "rules," even though those rules are constricting; Elinor understands that to survive she has to conform. This is not to suggest that Elinor does not feel or have feelings as intense as Marianne—she does, but she keeps those feelings to herself, so much so that even her closest relatives have no idea of how she suffers in loving the unattainable Mr. Ferrars. The result of her excessive restraint is that she sees Marianne's constant attempts to break out of society's mold, as far as Elinor is concerned, as necessarily disastrous. The authors Sandra Gilbert and Susan Gubar state that Austen "reflects on the dangers of the romantic celebration of personal liberty and self-expression for women who will be severely punished if they insist on getting out" (Gilbert and Gubar 154).

While Marianne's romantic nature urges her to "get out," Austen is also fully aware of the role women in society and how women are forced to conform to social falsehoods. Marianne's enthusiasm, her refusal to bow to conformity, and her spontaneity are very attractive; as Gilbert and Gubar note, she abhors the "polite lies of civility"

(156). There is, here, the suggestion that while Austen supports the sentiments of sincerity, she also realizes that sincerity and truth are not conducive to a harmonious society. As a result of this, she ensures that Marianne is forced to reach maturity in order to attain a balance between outward emotional display and conformity. Marianne's girlish excitement and enthusiasm have to be curbed so that she can achieve status through marriage. However, unlike so many other heroines, she does not die but rather experiences a "living death" through serious illness. Through this illness she realizes her "own abhorrence of [her]self," her "fretful selfishness" and "some duty neglected, or some failing indulged." Austen's lesson for Marianne is a harsh but totally necessary one that teaches her to appreciate the society in which she lives. In contrast to Willoughby, who willingly gives up his romantic sincerity for wealth, Marianne is forced to shed her spontaneous self, romantic ideals and sincerity for marriage, security and adherence to social "normality."

Austen's exploration of Romanticism through the Dashwood sisters allows us to see both introverted and extroverted emotional excesses. If Marianne is the extroverted emotional being, then Elinor is the introverted one. Elinor restrains all emotion until she realizes that Mr. Ferrars, is, after all, free to marry her. At this point she experiences a kind of breakdown of emotion and runs out of the room, but only then, behind closed doors, does she "burst into tears of joy," which sends Ferrars into a "reverie" (325). This suggests that Edward is unable to cope with such an outburst of emotion, particularly from someone he thought to be so restrained, but because her outburst is "hidden" behind the doors, she is easily forgiven for it. It is as though Austen herself saw the right that everybody has to express their inner feelings, and yet she understood very well the restraints imposed by a society that was slow to change and tolerate freedom of personality. Hence, she restricts Marianne's wildness by imposing a serious illness upon her, radically changing her character so that she conforms to society's norms and expectations. The critic D. W. Harding states that Austen was a "social critic" in search of "unobtrusive spiritual survival" (quoted in Drabble, 54). Arguably, Austen's *Sense and Sensibility* is the best demonstration of how to express controlled emotion while also showing consideration for one's fellow members of society.

### Further Reading

Austen, Jane. *Sense and Sensibility*. Edited by Ros Ballaster. Penguin Classics, London, 1995. With an appendix of the original Penguin Classics introduction by Tony Tanner (1986).

"Jane Austen." In *The Oxford Companion to English Literature*. Edited by Margaret Drabble. Oxford: Oxford University Press, 2000. 54.

Gilbert, Sandra M., and Susan Gubar. *The Madwoman in the Attic*. New York: Yale University Press, 1984.

Jane Austen Society of the United Kingdom. "*Sense and Sensibility:* Summary." Available online. URL: http://www.janeaustensoci.freeuk.com/pages/novels_ss.htm. Accessed on April 9, 2009.

—Pauline Guerin

## sensibility

With foundations in the 18th-century moral philosophy of DAVID HUME (1711–76) and Adam Smith (1723–90), the concept of sensibility was ubiquitous throughout late 18th-century literature and culture, and its traces can be felt within Romantic literature. Essentially, *sensibility* is an emotional response stemming from a person's innate virtue. Although there is some conflation between the terms *sensibility* and *sentimentality,* there are important distinctions to be made between them. *Sentimentality* can suggest the artificial display of fine feeling to the point of excess. Nonetheless, we can see that much literature of sensibility models for readers how to cultivate sensibility and moral character.

Throughout the literature of sensibility, gender is always an important facet; for example, the ability to feel emotion—even to shed tears, especially when one witnesses suffering—was considered acceptable female behavior. Indeed, scholars have recognized that female writers of the period gravitated toward the literature of sensibility, both fiction and poetry. Nonetheless, the period gave rise to the "man of feeling," a character exhibiting feminine characteristics who can be seen in many novels of the period, ranging from Laurence Sterne's *Tristram Shandy* (1759–67) to Henry MacKenzie's *The Man of Feeling* (1771) and FRANCES BURNEY's EVELINA (1778).

Sensibility is a staple in the GOTHIC novels of the period, especially as it distinguishes heroic and moral characters from those who are villainous. Several characters in CLARA REEVE's *The OLD ENGLISH BARON* (1778), especially Edmund Twyford and Sir Philip Harclay, exemplify sensibility as the outward expression of Christian virtue, particularly when they are easily moved to tears and trembling. Conversely, the villain of the novel, Sir Walter Lovel, feels no remorse for his crimes. The gothic novelist ANN RADCLIFFE also relies on sensibility to represent the moral qualities of her heroines, such as Emily St. Aubert in *The MYSTERIES OF UDOLPHO* (1794); in particular, Radcliffe's heroines are moved to heightened emotional responses at moments of terror or when they witness sublime natural scenery.

The late 18th-century obsession with sensibility gave rise to criticism of it, especially as an artificial behavior in women. HANNAH MORE's poem "Sensibility: A Poetical Epistle to the Hon. Mrs. Boscawen" (1782) distinguishes between false sensibility and that which is authentic and moral. For More, such false displays of feeling make sensibility vulgar. JANE AUSTEN's *SENSE AND SENSIBILITY* (1811) also mocks artificial displays of emotion, as when Marianne bids a contrived, emotional farewell to the trees and leaves when her family vacates Norland. Austen contrasts such behavior with sense or reason, as we see in Marianne's sister Elinor, who avoids a walk when the sky foretells a storm.

The role of sensibility is also important in poetry, such as in THOMAS GRAY's "ELEGY WRITTEN IN A COUNTRY CHURCH-YARD" (1751), in which we see reflective feeling in the poet as he contemplates mortality. In many later male Romantic poets, including PERCY BYSSHE SHELLEY and JOHN KEATS, the role of emotion in the process of writing is paramount, such as we see in WILLIAM WORDSWORTH's pronouncement about poetry and powerful feeling in PREFACE TO *LYRICAL BALLADS.* Sensibility, then, evolved throughout the Romantic period, in which can be seen a movement from the moral quality of emotional displays to its relationship to poetic creativity.

## Further Reading

Barker-Benfield, G. J. *The Culture of Sensibility: Sex and Society in Eighteenth-Century Britain.* Chicago: University of Chicago Press, 1992.

McGann, Jerome. *The Poetics of Sensibility: A Revolution in Literary Style.* Oxford: Clarendon Press, 1996.

Mellor, Anne D. *Romanticism and Gender.* New York: Routledge, 1993.

Novak, Maximillian E., and Anne Kostelanetz Mellor. *Passionate Encounters in a Time of Sensibility.* Newark: University of Delaware Press, 2000.

Todd, Janet. *Sensibility: An Introduction.* London: Methuen, 1986.

—Albert Sears

## Seward, Anna (1747–1809)

Dubbed "the Swan of Lichfield" after her "Elegy on Captain Cook" (1780) gracefully captured the public mood in the wake of explorer James Cook's death, Anna Seward was born on December 12, 1747. She was the daughter of Elizabeth Hunter Seward, whose father had taught the celebrated journalist and dictionary complier Samuel Johnson, and of Thomas Seward, prebendary of Salisbury and canon residentiary of Lichfield. Born in Eyan, Derbyshire, Anna resided in the Bishop's Palace in Lichfield from the age of seven until her death. Her relationship with John Saville, the married vicar-choral of Lichfield Cathedral, though devoted, was most likely entirely platonic. After his death, Seward ensured the security of his family. She never married, dying on March 25, 1809.

Seward's father had schooled her in English letters but admonished her against writing, an instruction she ignored. Among her literary associates were James Boswell and Samuel Johnson, whose opinions of her work were varied; William Hayley, highly celebrated as both a poet and a scholar in his time; Richard Lovell Edgeworth, whom her adoptive sister, Honora Sneyd, married in 1773; and SIR WALTER SCOTT, later the reluctant editor of her literary legacy. Through Seward's acquaintance with Lady Eleanor Butler and Sarah Ponsonby, a famous lesbian partnership known as "The Ladies of Llangollen," she considered variant interpersonal female relationships and wrote of them in *Llangollen Vale, with Other Poems* (1796).

Seward's *Louisa: A Poetical Novel, in Four Epistles* (1784), which went into five editions by 1792, anticipates the Romantic verse-narrative in form, and in subject matter it emphasizes the exploration of the psyche rather than the movement of plot. With CHARLOTTE SMITH, Seward helped revive the sonnet in British literature through her preface to and poems in her *Original Sonnets on Various Subjects; and Odes Paraphrased from Horace* (1799). This includes the frequently anthologized "TO THE POPPY." As a translator, she chose to adapt the meanings of the originals in English rather than adhere to their form.

Seward's literary mentor was Charles Darwin's grandfather, Erasmus Darwin (1731–1802), whose biography she wrote. It has been thought that she may have fared better as a poet without this mentorship, which encouraged the pretentious phraseology against which WILLIAM WORDSWORTH wrote in his PREFACE TO LYRICAL BALLADS. Her own eye for talent was good, and she particularly recognized the cutting-edge voices in modern poetry of her friend ROBERT SOUTHEY and of a young assistant editor to MARY ROBINSON at the *Morning Post*, SAMUEL TAYLOR COLERIDGE.

## Further Reading

Ashmun, Margaret. *The Singing Swan: An Account of Anna Seward and Her Acquaintance with Dr. Johnson, Boswell, & Others of Their Time.* 1931. Reprint, New York: Greenwood Press, 1968.

Labbe, Jacqueline M., "Every Poet Her Own Drawing Master: Charlotte Smith, Anna Seward and *Ut Pictura Poesis.*" In *Early Romantics: Perspectives in British Poetry from Pope to Wordsworth,* edited by Thomas Woodman, 200–214. Basingstoke, Eng.: Macmillan; New York: St. Martin's, 1998.

Monk, Samuel, "Anna Seward and the Romantic Poets: A Study in Taste." In *Wordsworth and Coleridge: Studies in Honor of George McLean Harper,* edited by Earl Leslie Griggs, 118–134. New York: Russell & Russell, Inc., 1962.

Webb, Timothy. "Listing the Busy Sounds: Anna Seward, Mary Robinson, and the Poetic Challenge of the City." In *Romantic Women Poets: Genre and Gender,* edited by Lilla Maria Crisafull and Cecila Pietropoli, 80–111. Amsterdam: Rodopi, 2007.

—Donna Berliner

## Shelley, Mary Wollstonecraft (1797–1851)

Born in Somers Town, London, on August 30, 1797, Mary Wollstonecraft Shelley was the only child of MARY WOLLSTONECRAFT, the educational theorist and pioneer for women's rights, and WILLIAM GODWIN, the anarchist philosopher and bookseller. Wollstonecraft died 11 days after giving birth to Mary. She was brought up with her mother's other daughter, Fanny, whose father was the American adventurer Gilbert Imlay. When Mary was three years old, Godwin married his next-door neighbor, Mary Jane Clairmont, who introduced her two illegitimate children into the household: Mary Jane, who became known as Claire, and Charles. Mary acquired another half sibling when Godwin's second wife gave birth to William. With her sister Fanny she attended a "Dame School," the popular name given to a certain type of infant school run—often haphazardly—by an elderly lady, and then, for seven months in 1811, Miss Caroline Petman's school at Ramsgate, where the daughters of Dissenters were educated. While at home, Mary had access to her father's library and tutelage, benefiting from the historical books he wrote for children. Visiting tutors gave her lessons in art and French, in which she became fluent. Other languages she acquired included Latin, Greek, Italian, and some Spanish.

In June 1812 Mary Wollstonecraft Godwin was sent to Dundee for her health and stayed at the home of William Baxter, who had supported her father during his opposition to the Treason Trials of 1794. The house at Broughty Ferry overlooked the romantic scene of a 15th-century castle. In the 1831 introduction to her most acclaimed novel, *FRANKENSTEIN,* she wrote that trees and mountains were where her imaginative works were fostered. Mary stayed with the Baxters, who became a second family, for 16 months. One of the daughters, Christina, made a return visit with Mary to the Godwins in London. The day after their arrival on November 11, 1812, they are believed to have met the young Romantic poet and aristocrat PERCY BYSSHE SHELLEY, who was accompanied by his wife, Harriet Westbrook, and her older sister. Mary resumed her sojourn in Scotland until March 1814 when, on returning to the Godwin household, she found that Shelley had established himself as a firm favorite with her sisters. He was also a disciple of the writings of their father, to whom he gave financial assistance, a circumstance later fictionalized in her short story "The Parvenue" (1836). The poet also revered Wollstonecraft (her mother, also a poet), whose works he and Mary are reputed to have read aloud at her graveside as their romance blossomed. William Godwin disapproved of their union as Shelley was still married and his wife was expecting their second child.

On July 28, 1814, the lovers eloped to France, taking with them Mary's half sister Claire. Mary later published a version of her journal account of their travels as the jointly authored *History of a Six Weeks' Tour through a part of France, Switzerland, Germany and Holland* (1817), which was also a travelogue of the inner Romantic journey. The impoverished trio wandered around Europe, which had been ravaged by the Napoleonic Wars, returning to England in September. On February 22, 1815, Mary gave birth to a premature daughter, who survived for just 11 days. In her journal she recorded a dream of the baby coming back to life. This ties in with the theme of reanimation, which characterized some of her fiction, most notably *Frankenstein.*

Between September 1814 and July 1815, the couple stayed in a series of lodging houses before settling at Bishopsgate on the edge of Windsor Great Park, which furnished in part the setting of Mary's third novel, *The LAST MAN* (1826). While living there, she gave birth to their son, William, in January 1816. The following May they departed for Geneva with Claire Clairmont to rendezvous with LORD BYRON, who was spending the summer in Switzerland. Their destination had been determined by the fact that Claire was pregnant with Byron's child and hoped, at the very least, for his paternal support. The convergence of Byron, his physician JOHN POLIDORI, and Shelley's party would lead to a cross-fertilization of literary production culminating in the publication of *Frankenstein; or, The Modern Prometheus* (1818).

As Mary Shelley explained in her introduction to the revised edition of *Frankenstein* in 1831, her inspiration for the novel had been the idea for members of the group to tell each other ghost stories of their own invention. According to Mary's anonymous account as given to THOMAS MOORE in his *Life of Lord Byron* (1835) the great poet had suggested that they should all contribute to a book, which his fame would help sell. This entertainment took place in 1816 at Villa Diodati at the side of Lake Leman in Geneva, Switzerland, during that "wet and uncongenial summer" (Shelley 1980, 7) as Mary wrote in the 1831 Preface to *Frankenstein*. These adverse weather conditions had come about due to the activity of Mount Tambora on the island of Sumbawa, south of Borneo, which proved to be the most violent volcanic eruption in recorded history. This had resulted in the coldest summer on record, which ironically precipitated the forging of *Frankenstein* from the heart of a volcano.

The night of the ghost-story writing proposed by Byron might have been June 13, when the group had been driven indoors by an electrical storm. Lightning has been associated in the popular imagination, mainly through film adaptations, with the genesis of Shelley's monstrous birth myth. In her 1831 introduction, she indicates how a conversation about galvanism had helped spark her creativity. Byron's guests diverted themselves by reading some German ghost stories translated into French, entitled *Fantasmagoriana, ou Recueil d'Histoires d'Apparitions de Spectres, Revenans, Fantômes, etc.; traduit de l'allemand, par un Amateur* (1812), which, according to the preface of the 1818 edition "excited in us a playful desire of imitation" (Shelley, 1980, 14). Two of these, "The Death-Bride," about a spectral lover, and "The Family Portraits," in which a portrait comes to life, influenced Mary's creation along with her "waking dream," which probably took place on June 16. Her tale of a creature created out of the parts of cadavers, which would seek vengeance upon its creator, would emerge as one of the most powerful and enduring myths to explode out of the GOTHIC tradition.

On returning to England, Mary lodged at 5 Abbey Churchyard in Bath, where she continued her plan of transforming her tale into a novel. While writing in October, she learned of the suicide of her half sister Fanny, who had died after taking laudanum at the Mackworth Arms in Swansea. The following December, there was more sad news. Percy Shelley's wife Harriet, whom he had left (though no official separation had taken place), had taken her own life by drowning in Hyde Park's artificial lake known as the Serpentine. The exact date of her death is disputed, but it freed him to marry Mary at St. Mildred's Church in London on December 30, 1816. In January 1817 Claire gave birth to Byron's daughter, Alba, known later as Allegra, and during the following September, Mary's second daughter, Clara Everina Shelley, was born.

By this time the Shelleys had been living at Albion House, Marlow, in Buckinghamshire for five months, and it was here that *Frankenstein* reached completion. The novel was published anonymously in three volumes on January 1, 1818. The author was assumed by some to be a disciple of William Godwin, to whom it was dedicated. WALTER SCOTT alighted on Percy Shelley as the obvious candidate; in fact, Shelley had only actually written the preface, though he had helped edit the novel. Mary's name appeared on the title page of the second edition, issued in 1823, the year after Percy's death. The person responsible for this publication was Godwin, who also made minor alterations from the first edition. In August that year, the story was dramatized by Richard Brinsley Peake as *Presumption: or, The Fate of Frankenstein*, which Mary Shelley saw performed at the Lyceum and the English Opera House in London. It proved highly successful, and a new version was staged in Paris.

In March 1818, the Shelleys set sail from Dover for the Continent, prompted by concerns for Percy's health and fears that after the Lord Chancellor gave custody of his children by Harriet to her family, the law would take away his children by Mary. The tragic loss of their children, however, came about in other ways. In September 1818 their two-year-old daughter, Clara, died from dysentery in Venice, and their three-year-old son, William, died of malaria, otherwise known as "Roman fever," in Rome in June 1819. Their fourth and only surviving child, Percy Florence Shelley, was born on November 12, 1819, in Florence. It was here that Mary Shelley started research work on a historical novel set in the 14th century, eventually called *Valperga, or, The Life and Adventures of Castruccio Castracani* (1823), the idea for which she had conceived in Marlow in 1817. It concerns the clash between tyranny and republicanism. Castruccio is a despotic warlord who is modeled on the actual feudal lord of Lucca. He is in love with Euthanasia, who rules the fortress of Valperga in a peaceful and conciliatory way according to the principles of reason and sensibility.

In January 1820 the Shelleys moved to Pisa. That year Mary Shelley wrote the mythological verse drama *Midas* and the children's story MAURICE, OR, THE FISHER'S COT, before settling, probably in the autumn, to the composition of *Valperga*, a task that occupied most of 1821. In April 1822, the first of more terrible losses for that year struck with the death of Clare's daughter Allegra. The news arrived while the Shelleys were at Casa Magni at San Terenzo, their summer residence. In June Mary narrowly escaped dying after a miscarriage, and in July Percy was drowned in a sudden storm while sailing back from Livorno to Lerici.

The death of her husband, followed by that of their friend Byron in 1824, prompted Mary Shelley to declare herself to be "the last relic of a beloved race" and to identify with the eponymous hero Lionel Verney of her apocalyptic novel *The Last Man* (1826). Verney is the last survivor of a plague that has wiped out the human race. This pessimistic vision was seen as unfeminine, and the book was blasted by one critic as an "elaborate piece of gloomy folly"; The book was even banned in Austria. Shelley was so disheartened by the criticism that she returned to the historical romance and wrote *The Fortunes of Perkin Warbeck*, set at the end of the 15th century. Warbeck had been a pretender to the English throne during the reign of Henry VII, and Shelley believed him to be the lost duke of York, long believed to have been murdered in the tower, reputedly on the orders of Richard III. The novel was eventually published in 1830 as an antimonarchical historical romance.

Financial distress also forced Shelley to start writing stories and essays for periodicals in 1823. For example, she published one story and two essays in *The Liberal* in 1823, and a year later there appeared, in *London Magazine*, "On Ghosts"; "Recollections of Italy"; and "The Bride of Italy," which was based on Percy's infatuation with Teresa (Emilia) Viviani. Mary also started submitting material to ANNUALS AND GIFT BOOKS, and between 1823 and 1839 she wrote more than 20 stories for gift books or periodicals; 16 of these stories were published in *Keepsake*. Examples include: "The Evil Eye" (1829), which evokes Albanian superstition, and "The Dream" (1831), set during the reign of Henry IV of France. She also published two well-known tales dealing with the supernatural: "Transformation" (1830), based on Byron's drama *The DEFORMED TRANSFORMED* (1824), which Mary Shelley had copied for him; and "The MORTAL IMMORTAL" (1833). She wrote most of the essays for the five volumes of the Rev. Dionysius Lardner's *Cabinet of Biography: Lives of the most Eminent Literary and Scientific Men of Italy, Spain and Portugal* (1835–37) and *Lives of the most Eminent Literary and Scientific Men of France* (1838–39).

For the third edition of *Frankenstein*, published in 1831, Shelley wrote a longer introduction and made extensive revisions. In this version, the portrayal of the hero, Victor Frankenstein, who is believed to be based partly on her late husband, was made more sympathetic. Victor is a Romantic scientist who isolates himself while carrying out nefarious experiments with the parts of dead bodies. His creation of a monstrous being, which he rejects, has been seen as an allegory of the child-parent relationship, drawing on the creation of Adam as derived from JOHN MILTON's *Paradise Lost*. As suggested by the novel's subtitle, *The Modern Prometheus*, Victor Frankenstein is an example of the Romantic overreacher, who transgresses boundaries between the human and the divine. The creature is motivated initially by the more ordinary desire for a family and eventually finds the idealized De Laceys, but they too reject him. In retaliation, he targets Victor's family members, including his youngest brother, William, and fiancée, Elizabeth, before disappearing into the Arctic wastes, ostensibly to destroy himself. Like her mother, Mary Shelley emphasized the importance of the domestic affections, and in *Frankenstein* she demonstrates how the neglect of family relations can trigger tragedy.

The search for, and return to, origins was the Romantics' Holy Grail, which Shelley pursued through the search for parentage. In her mythological drama *Proserpine* (composed 1820, published 1832), a mother searches for her daughter, who has been snatched by the god of the underworld. The heroine is described as a "child of light," a phrase that Percy Shelley had first used in allusion to his wife and her maternal heritage. Like Mary Shelley herself, several of her other heroines are motherless. In her second novel, *Mathilda,* composed in 1819, the heroine, whose mother dies shortly after giving her birth, forms a close bond with her father. She is troubled when he distances himself from her. The reason, as he eventually divulges, is because he has been harboring an unlawful and monstrous love for his daughter. Mary Shelley sent the manuscript to her father, who was so disgusted with the content that he refused either to publish it or return it to her despite repeated requests. It was not published until 1959.

In Shelley's sixth novel, *Lodore* (1835), the Byronic Lord Lodore abducts his daughter, Ethel, and takes her to the American wilderness to live in isolation. After he dies in a duel, Ethel is befriended by the intellectual and independent Fanny Derham (thought to be based on Shelley's friend Fanny Wright, an advocate for women's rights) and is eventually reconciled with her mother. Shelley reworked the father-daughter relationship for her short story "The Mourner" (1829), about a supposed parricide, and in her final novel, *Falkner* (1837). Here, Rupert Falkner forsakes his beloved Alithea for a life in India. When he returns he discovers that she has married another man, believing Falkner to be dead. She drowns trying to escape him. He adopts an orphaned girl, Elizabeth Raby, who falls in love with Alithea's son, Gerard Neville. Falkner tries to sever the relationship. He is convicted of the murder of Alithea but is finally freed and then forgiven by Gerard. Family values, particularly familial duty, was important to Mary Shelley both in and outside

of fiction. In 1837 she started work on writing her father's life and editing his papers, a task she never completed, and in 1839 and 1840 she produced multivolumed editions of her husband's poetry, which included previously unpublished poems and her own valuable biographical and contextual notes. In 1840 she published *Essays, Letters from Abroad, Translations and Fragments by Percy Bysshe Shelley* (2 vols).

Readers can find in Mary Shelley's work the Romantic themes of the wanderer, incest, suicide, nature, and the SUBLIME. Her writings grapple with the challenge of creating a society that endorses the values of collaboration, equality, education, and harmony with the natural world. Her final full-length work was her two-volume *Rambles in Germany and Italy, in 1840, 1842, and 1843* (1844), which was based on letters written during two journeys that she had taken with her son, who inherited the Shelley baronetcy upon his paternal grandfather's death in 1844, becoming Sir Percy.

Toward the end of her life, Mary Shelley went to live with her son and his wife, Jane, at her husband's boyhood home, Field Place in Sussex. Here she planned to write Shelley's biography, until illness intervened. For about two years the family lived at Field Place and at a house in Chester Square in London while Sir Percy was purchasing a new house near Bournemouth. When Mary Shelley knew that she was dying, she asked to be buried with her parents at St. Pancras. According to the literary historian Emily Sunstein, Shelley turned down Edward Trelawny's offer that she take his burial plot next to that of Percy Shelley in Rome, on the basis that it was too costly. She died on February 1, 1851, of meningioma (a type of brain tumor) at Chester Square. The bodies of her parents were exhumed and reburied on either side of their daughter in Bournemouth near Boscombe Manor, the home of her son.

## Further Reading

Blumberg, Jane. *Mary Shelley's Early Novels.* Houndmills, Eng.: Macmillan, 1993.

Eberle-Sinatra, Michael, ed. *Mary Shelley's Fictions: From Frankenstein to Falkner.* Houndmills, Eng.: Macmillan Press, 2000.

Fisch, Audrey, Anne K. Mellor, and Esther H. Schor, eds. *The Other Mary Shelley: Beyond Frankenstein.* New York: Oxford University Press, 1993.

Mellor, Anne K. *Mary Shelley: Her Life, Her Fiction, Her Monsters.* London: Routledge, 1988.

Morrison, Lucy, and Staci L. Stone. *The Mary Shelley Encyclopedia.* Westport, Conn.: Greenwood Press, 2003.

Seymour, Miranda. *Mary Shelley.* London: John Murray, 2000.

Shelley, Mary Wollstonecraft. *The Journals of Mary Shelley, 1814–1844.* 2 vols. Edited by Paula R. Feldman and Diana Scott-Kilvert. Oxford: Clarendon Press, 1987.

———. *The Letters of Mary Wollstonecraft Shelley.* 3 vols. Edited by Betty T. Bennett. Baltimore: Johns Hopkins University Press, 1980–88.

———. *Mary Shelley: Collected Tales and Stories.* 2nd ed. Edited by Charles E. Robinson. Baltimore: Johns Hopkins University Press, 1991.

———. *The Mary Shelley Reader.* Edited by Betty T. Bennett and Charles E. Robinson. Oxford: Oxford University Press, 1990.

———. *Mary Shelley's Literary Lives and Other Writings.* 4 vols. Edited by Nora Crook et al. London: Pickering & Chatto, 2002.

———. *Maurice, or the Fisher's Cot.* Edited by Claire Tomalin. London: Penguin, Viking, 1998.

———. *The Novels and Selected Works of Mary Shelley.* 8 vols. Edited by Nora Crook et al. London: Pickering and Chatto, 1996.

———. *The Original Frankenstein.* Edited by Charles E. Robinson. Oxford: The Bodleian Library, 2008.

———. *Frankenstein.* Edited by M. K. Joseph. Oxford: Oxford University Press, 1980.

Sunstein, Emily W. *Mary Shelley: Romance and Reality.* Boston: Little, Brown and Co., 1989.

I would like to acknowledge the invaluable assistance of Nora Crook.

—Marie Mulvey-Roberts

## Shelley, Percy Bysshe (1792–1822)

Born on August 4, 1792, to an affluent family, Percy Bysshe Shelley would reject the comforts of wealth and dedicate himself to a lifelong critique of the structures of power that he believed maintained the irreparable gap between the privileged and the impoverished. Throughout his life, Shelley inveighed against institutional powers that utilize mechanisms of oppression—chiefly the church, the state, and the educational system. He also urged a turn away from paper currency, traditional marriage, and meat-eating diets, all as part of his personal and poetic program designed to remove, or at least to evade, mechanisms and practices that he felt secured systems of oppression. Turning to poetry throughout his life, he wielded language as an instrument of truth and encouraged poets to create a liberated world by constructing such a place in their works. In "A DEFENCE OF POETRY" (1821), Shelley wrote that "Poets are the unacknowledged legislators of the world" (Shelley 2002, 513), and his life and career furnish proof of the ways in which his commitment to an intellectual revolution offered a vision of a world freed from the constraints of hierarchies of all kinds.

Shelley shocked his father, a member of Parliament, and his grandfather, a baronet, by being expelled from Oxford University following the publication of the pamphlet *The Necessity of Atheism* (1811), which he cowrote with his friend Thomas Jefferson Hogg. Later that same year, he eloped with Harriet Westbrook, with whom he would have two children, Charles and Ianthe. Living variously in Wales, Ireland, and England throughout the next year, he composed a number of antigovernment tracts and poems, which he and his associates distributed in the streets, making him an increasingly notorious enemy of tradition and order.

Late in 1812, Shelley met WILLIAM GODWIN, whose radical writing he had long admired. Shelley not only assumed Godwin's debt, which he managed for the rest of his life, but he also fell in love with Godwin's daughter, Mary, abandoning Harriet to elope with her in 1814 (see SHELLEY, MARY WOLLSTONECRAFT). Despite his belief in free love, Shelley and Mary were married in 1816, largely in hopes of securing custody of his children with Harriet, who had committed suicide weeks earlier. His elopement with Mary enraged Godwin, regardless of the fact that both he and his late wife, the well-known feminist writer MARY WOLLSTONECRAFT, had also advocated free love. Harriet's family, the

Westbrooks, prevailed legally and retained custody of Shelley's children, and Shelley and Mary went on to have four children of their own, only one of whom, Percy Florence, survived to adulthood.

Two of the most influential figures in Shelley's adult life were George Gordon Byron, the sixth LORD BYRON, and the critic, essayist, and poet LEIGH HUNT. Byron, the most popular poet of the day, befriended Shelley and had a child with Mary's half sister, Claire Clairmont. In summer 1816 he hosted the Shelleys at his home in Italy, Mary conceived the idea that would become her famous novel FRANKENSTEIN (1818). Shelley's relationship with Byron is immortalized in Shelley's "Julian and Maddalo: A Conversation" (1819), which examines the strikingly different attitudes of its title characters, the sensitive Julian (Shelley) and the cynical Maddalo (Byron). "Julian and Maddalo" offers a fascinating character study for those interested in the diverse personalities that comprise second-generation Romanticism. Hunt, a leading publisher of progressive political works, encouraged Shelley's radicalism and, with Shelley and Byron, planned a journal for the promotion of such thought, *The Liberal,* which folded after only four issues in the wake of Shelley's untimely death.

During the summer of 1822, the Shelleys took a home on the Bay of Lerici with their friends Edward and Jane Williams, and Shelley hired a sailing boat, the *Don Juan,* which he and Edward piloted to Pisa, where they met the Hunts. On July 8, 1822, as Shelley and Williams were returning home, the *Don Juan* was overtaken by a sudden storm, drowning both men and the cabin boy they had hired for the passage. Their bodies washed up on the shore and were immediately interred, as dictated by local quarantine laws. Byron accompanied Mary to the site of Shelley's temporary grave, where he, Hunt, and Edward Trelawney disinterred the body in order to cremate it. This incident is recalled in Louis Edouard Fournier's painting *The Funeral of Shelley* (1889), one of many Victorian-era representations of Shelley that contributed to a sanitizing of the poet's legacy, emphasizing his idealism at the expense of his controversial anti-traditional beliefs. The influential Victorian critic Matthew Arnold, for example, described Shelley as "a beautiful ineffectual angel beating in the void his luminous wings in vain" (Arnold, *Essays in Criticism, Second Series,* 1888). Such purely aesthetic appreciations effaced Shelley's ideological commitments and immortalized the radical poet as a glorious but ultimately failed visionary (see PROMETHEUS UNBOUND). This partial view of Shelley prevailed until his critical resurgence in the counterculture of the 1960s. Since then he has continued to be lauded by scholars who have studied his work from multiple perspectives, including Marxism, psychoanalysis, feminism, deconstructionism, and New Historicism.

Shelley has long been considered one of the six major Romantic poets, who may be grouped according to two generational lines. The first, or older, Romantics included WILLIAM BLAKE, WILLIAM WORDSWORTH, and SAMUEL TAYLOR COLERIDGE. The second generation included Shelley, Byron, and JOHN KEATS, whom Shelley deeply admired and for whom he wrote the elegy "ADONAIS" (1821) upon Keats's death from tuberculosis. While all Romantic writers share a dissatisfaction with the inequities of power and representation in the world (see, for example, "OZYMANDIAS," "SONG: TO THE MEN OF ENGLAND," and "ENGLAND IN 1819"), and while all advocate various means for removing impediments to universal freedom, the second-generation Romantics, who came to maturity after the collapse of the FRENCH REVOLUTION, may be distinguished from their predecessors by their advocacy of a more radical intellectual revolution, which proceeded from the sharing of ideas, chiefly in the poetry and prose of members of their generation.

The younger Romantics often regarded their elder statesmen with cynicism and disdain, and Shelley's sonnet "TO WORDSWORTH" (1816) examines the bases upon which the younger poet rejected his senior, lamenting the once-idealistic Wordsworth's fall into conservatism and the abandonment of his youthful ideals. Shelley's longer poem "ALASTOR: or, The Spirit of Solitude" (1815) described a failed Wordsworthian poet, a figure so selfishly dedicated to personal fulfillment that he loses sight of the world around him, dying alone as he gazes narcissistically into the river that takes him to his death. Shelley's continuation of Wordsworth's *Peter Bell,* titled *Peter Bell the Third*

(1819), extends his critique of the elder poet's fall from youthful promise and indicts Wordsworth's contemporary, Coleridge, for a similar ideological erosion.

For Shelley, the notion of revolution took on an entirely new meaning. He urged the gradual series of social improvements introduced in his own writings, believing these would be realized through legislative changes that would reconstruct the world according to the idealistic models their writings described. Perhaps the most accessible prose accounts of Shelley's belief in the power of human perfectability, which he thought would result from the gradual change brought by reform, may be found in the pamphlets and essays for which he is now less well-known, including *A Refutation of Deism* (1814), *A Proposal for Putting Reform to the Vote* (1817), *An Address to the People on the Death of Princess Charlotte* (1817), and *A Philosophical View of Reform* (1820).

In addition to his politically charged prose works, many of Shelley's poems contain prefaces and notes that articulate and examine his ideological commitments. The footnotes to his first major attack on social order, a long poem entitled QUEEN MAB (1813), pointed to religion, marriage, and diet as three practices that reinforced the social divisions and stratifications that underwrite the oppression of individuals and cultures. Six years later he composed "The MASK OF ANARCHY" (1819) in direct response to the government-ordered attack on a gathering of peaceful protesters at St. Peter's Field in Manchester (see PETERLOO MASSACRE). Shelley recounts this historical tragedy in the preface to his poem, which imagines a mythic contest between Liberty, who bears with dignity the oppressions forced upon her, and Anarchy, Shelley's symbol for a government so engorged with its own sense of power that it literally crushes beneath it any who question its ways. In the end, Liberty triumphs, offering one of many versions of a narrative model that attests to Shelley's belief in historical progression and human perfectability. Although he lamented that such universal liberation would not be realized in his own lifetime, he looked forward to what he posed as an historical inevitability, and here as elsewhere, he set his work in a mythic, transhistorical location to emphasize the placeless-

ness of such a utopian scenario. For Shelley, writing in mythic terms allowed him to leap out of his own time to imagine the perfection of the world in some distant future, as the hopeful final line of "ODE TO THE WEST WIND" (1819) implies: "If Winter comes, can Spring be far behind?"

Shelley often drew from historical situations for the bases of his imaginative work, as in "The Mask of Anarchy." Similarly, his underappreciated satire *Oedipus Tyrannus; or Swellfoot the Tyrant* (1820) lampoons the real-life controversy over the so-called Queen Caroline affair, in which King George attempted to bar his wife from claiming her place as queen by exposing her countless affairs—indiscretions of the very sort the king also enjoyed. Mocking such a hypocritical campaign, *Oedipus Tyrannus* reminds readers of the decadence that pervades government at all levels, highlighting erotic relationships as symbols of larger political problems. For Shelley, such relationships offer models for the liberation or the oppression of the entire human race, depending on whether those relationships are based on equality, as were the ideal relationships Shelley described in many of his works, or on inequality and contests for power, as he saw in the Queen Caroline affair.

Shelley addressed the problem of oppressive relationships in *The Cenci: A Tragedy, in Five Acts* (1819), which dramatized the plight of the members of a real-life 15th-century Italian family whose wealthy, sadistic patriarch used his power and influence to win absolution for his sins and who forced himself sexually on his daughter, Beatrice, the figure Shelley constructs as the play's hero. Refusing to give in to her father's repeated advances and disgusted by his ability to purchase forgiveness from the pope for his countless crimes, Beatrice is finally raped by her father, who tells her that the child she will bear will remind her forever of the act he has forced upon her. Beatrice hires two assassins, who kill Count Cenci, but in the end her plan is discovered, and she and her mother are sentenced to death for their roles in the assassination plot. In *The Cenci*, Shelley exposes the connections between two kinds of oppression, those specific to the private life of the family and those that pervade all of society. *The Cenci* also reminds his readers of the problems with relationships, like the one between Beatrice and her father, that are based on inequality and that demand the submission of one partner to the will of the other.

Shelley's use of individual relationships as models for larger social structures informs much of his work. "On Love," an essay written in 1818 but not published until after his death, extols the power of love to save an individual from the wreck of loneliness, isolation, and despair and to make available to him, or to her, a vision of the perfect self. Such a purifying relationship underwrites *Laon and Cythna; or, The Revolution of the Golden City: A Vision of the Nineteenth Century in the Stanza of Spenser* (1818), a 12-canto attack on MONARCHY and religion that poses the erotic couple as both emblem and agent for revolution. Hoping to outrage critics and, thus, to introduce an even wider audience to the ideas the poem examines, Shelley described the heroes of *Laon and Cythna* not only as lovers but as twins, an incest motif that led to the poem's suppression. At his publisher's insistence, he altered the relationship to exclude the incestuous connection, and the poem was reissued later that same year as *The Revolt of Islam,* a titular alteration that makes clear the equivalence to Shelley of political engagement (the focus of the new title) and personal relationships (the focus of the original).

Like *Laon and Cythna,* Shelley's best-known epic work, PROMETHEUS UNBOUND: A LYRICAL DRAMA IN FOUR ACTS (1820), centers the rebellion of the human race against the gods on the relationship between an erotic couple, Prometheus and Asia. Further, the poem underscores the power of language to reset relationships of power and to transform various contexts of oppression into the those of liberation: From the beginning, Prometheus has only to take back ("unsay") his curse on Jupiter to be released from the suffering Jupiter has imposed. By the poem's end, it is Prometheus's articulation of a vision of universal freedom, along with his unbounded love for Asia, whom he treats not only as his lover but as his equal, that leads to the creation of a new and wholly liberated world. *Prometheus Unbound* thus locates the birthplace of freedom in the cradle shared by language and love, and it reminds Shelley's readers of the significance of feminism—the total equality of men and women—to his model of liberation.

Shelley's belief in the potential for love to empower those so selflessly involved grew in part out of his advocacy of free love, which he defended in "Epipsychidion" (1821), writing that "True Love in this differs from gold and clay / That to divide is not to take away" (ll. 160–161). He composed "Epipsychidion" as a love offering to Teresa Viviani, a beautiful young woman whose father had imprisoned her in a convent because she refused to accept the husband he had chosen for her. At once praising her for demanding her own rights and attacking her father and the legal and religious structures that allowed him to oppress her, Shelley describes the power of love to break the bonds of tyranny, and he invites "Emily" to join him in a free-love community, a utopic "far Eden of the purple East" (l. 417). In the end, though, "Epipsychidion" closes with a lament, and Shelley admits that the escape from the convent he has imagined for "Emily" will not come to pass, in part because he has been unable to marshal language, his key instrument of revolution, to describe completely the better world that would allow for her escape. In the rhetorical collapse that closes the poem, Shelley admits both the possibility of freedom and the impossibility of its realization in his own day, leaving the reader to follow him in trusting the Romantic belief that, in the future, such a perfect world will indeed emerge.

See also "MONT BLANC."

## Further Reading

Behrendt, Stephen C. *Shelley and His Audiences.* Lincoln: University of Nebraska Press, 1989.

Bennett, Betty T., and Stuart Curran, eds. *Shelley: Poet and Legislator of the World.* Baltimore, Md.: Johns Hopkins University Press, 1996.

Bonca, Teddi Chichester. *Shelley's Mirrors of Love: Narcissism, Sacrifice, and Sorority.* Albany: State University of New York Press, 1998.

Brown, Nathaniel. *Sexuality and Feminism in Shelley.* Cambridge, Mass.: Harvard University Press, 1979.

Cameron, Kenneth Neill. *Shelley: The Golden Years.* Cambridge, Mass.: Harvard University Press, 1974.

———. *The Young Shelley: The Genesis of a Radical.* New York: Macmillan, 1950.

Curran, Stuart. *Shelley's Annus Mirabilis: The Maturing of an Epic Vision.* San Marino, Calif.: Huntington Library, 1975.

Gelpi, Barbara. *Shelley's Goddesses: Maternity, Language, Subjectivity.* New York: Oxford University Press, 1992.

Gladden, Samuel Lyndon. *Shelley's Textual Seductions: Plotting Utopia in the Erotic and Political Works.* New York: Routledge, 2002.

Holmes, Richard. *Shelley: The Pursuit.* New York: E. P. Dutton, 1975.

Jones, Steven E. *Shelley's Satire: Violence, Exhortation, and Authority.* DeKalb: Northern Illinois University Press, 1994.

Morton, Timothy. *Shelley and the Revolution in Taste: The Body and the Natural World.* Cambridge and New York: Cambridge University Press, 1995.

Scrivener, Michael Henry. *Radical Shelley: The Philosophical Anarchism and Utopian Thought of Percy Bysshe Shelley.* Princeton, N.J.: Princeton University Press, 1982.

Shelley, Percy Bysshe. *Shelley's Poetry and Prose.* 2nd ed. Edited by Donald H. Reiman and Neil Fraistat. New York: Norton, 2002.

Ulmer, William A. *Shelleyan Eros: The Rhetoric of Romantic Love.* Princeton, N.J.: Princeton University Press, 1990.

White, Newman Ivey. *Shelley.* 2 vols. New York: Knopf, 1940.

Wasserman, Earl R. *Shelley: A Critical Reading.* Baltimore, Md.: Johns Hopkins University Press, 1971.

Wroe, Ann. *Being Shelley: The Poet's Search for Himself.* New York: Pantheon, 2007.

—Samuel Lyndon Gladden

## "Shepherd, The" William Blake (1789)

"The Shepherd" is one of WILLIAM BLAKE's *Songs of Innocence* printed in his illuminated printing method in 1789 and included in the combined SONGS OF INNOCENCE AND OF EXPERIENCE in 1794. Blake made additional printings at later dates.

This short, eight-line poem describes the relationship between the shepherd and his flock as a supportive one, rather than one that is paternalistic or hierarchical. In the first stanza, the shepherd "strays," rather than directs, and he "follow[s] his sheep," rather than leads (ll. 2, 3). Also, his "tongue" is always "filled with praise" (l. 4) instead of scolding or chastisement. In the second stanza the shepherd merely "hears the lambs innocent call, / And hears the ewes tender reply" (ll. 5–6) and does not interject his own voice. This shepherd allows his sheep to go their own way but stays with them to keep them safe.

The image of the shepherd and sheep in the poem is allegorical of the biblical pastoral motif, representing at the same time the relationships between God and humankind, the church and parishioners, and the guardian and child. In the Bible, however, the shepherd is a spiritual guide and a figure who leads, while the sheep have a tendency to wander and even disobey, as in Psalms 23:2–3, Isaiah 40:11 and 53:6, Ezekiel 34:12, and Matthew 18:12. While the New Testament does emphasize the self-sacrifice of the shepherd, it also insists on guidance, as in John 10:16. If Blake's "The Shepherd" is an allegorical rendition of the biblical shepherd/flock motif, then this representation of a supportive and protective, rather than guiding and leading, shepherd critiques and undermines the traditional version. While the innocent speaker of "The Shepherd" may be describing the relationship between shepherd and flock incorrectly, according to biblical tradition and church teaching, Blake may be offering an alternative vision of that relationship through the innocent speaker. Indeed, the traditional view is shown in a negative light in such *Experience* poems as "The CHIMNEY SWEEPER," "The GARDEN OF LOVE," "The Little Vagabond," and "A Little Boy Lost."

Blake may also be indicating in "The Shepherd" that the speaker's view is naive and that such a contrary and idealized understanding of the shepherd/flock relationship cannot exist in the world of experience governed by church tradition. The repetition of the word *sweet* in line 1 may suggest an ironically cloying tone, and the fact that the shepherd strays only "From the morn to evening" (l. 2) makes some readers wonder whether the shepherd's takes on a more forceful, guiding role at night. Also, the poem indicates that the shepherd is watchful while the sheep "are in peace" (l. 7), but it makes no indication of what the shepherd does when the sheep are not in peace. Does he step in and scold his flock? The poem's illustration raises similar questions. Although the shepherd is shown turning his head to his right to listen to a lamb and making eye contact with it, he is positioned in the foreground with his back to the flock, suggesting that he is in a position of leadership; even his left knee is bent, as if he were about to take a step forward with his flock following behind. The poem and its illustration may be suggesting that the speaker's idea of how a shepherd should behave toward his flock is based on the naïveté of innocence and may overlook circumstances that only experience would help the speaker to understand.

Despite the innocent speaker's naïveté, Blake's "The Shepherd" offers a view of the shepherd/flock motif that stands as an alternative to that offered by the Bible and the church. Perhaps without knowing it, the innocent speaker challenges the conventional idea and offers a version that removes the paternalistic, hierarchical aspect of the relationship and places the sheep on equal terms with the shepherd.

## Further Reading

Blake, William. *The Complete Poetry and Prose of William Blake.* Rev. ed. Edited by David V. Erdman. Garden City, N.Y.: Anchor, 1982.

———. *The Illuminated Blake.* Edited and annotated by David V. Erdman. New York: Dover, 1992.

———. *Songs of Innocence and of Experience.* Edited by Andrew Lincoln. Princeton, N.J.: William Blake Trust/Princeton University Press, 1991.

Hirsch, E. D., Jr. *Innocence and Experience: An Introduction to Blake.* New Haven and London: Yale University Press, 1964.

Leader, Zachary. *Reading Blake's Songs.* London and Boston: Routledge and Kegan Paul, 1981.

Lindsay, David W. *Blake: Songs of Innocence and Experience.* Atlantic Highlands, N.J.: Humanities Press International, 1989.

Richardson, Alan. "The Politics of Childhood: Wordsworth, Blake, and Catechistic Method." *ELH* 56 (1989): 853–868.

Shrimpton, Nick. "Hell's Hymn Book: Blake's *Songs of Innocence and of Experience* and Their Models." In *Literature of the Romantic Period, 1750–1850,* edited by R. T. Davies and B. G. Beatty, 19–35. New York: Barnes and Noble, 1976.

—John H. Jones

## *Shepherd's Calendar, The*   John Clare (1827)

JOHN CLARE's third published volume, *The Shepherd's Calendar; with Village Stories, and Other Poems,* appeared in April 1827. It was written in response to a suggestion made in August 1823 by Clare's publisher, John Taylor, that he compose both a descriptive and a narrative poem about each month of the year. The delay of three and a half years between Taylor's suggestion and the volume's publication was caused by a mixture of editing problems and other practical difficulties. In 1825 Taylor split from his business partner, James Hessey, and his financial difficulties contributed to his later desire to publish a shorter work than had been envisaged. The stress that he was under also led Taylor to adopt an even more interventionist policy than usual with Clare's work, and the relationship between the two men became strained for a time. At one stage Taylor intended to drop the narrative poems for each month, although they were later restored because of the extensive cuts elsewhere (as detailed below). As the editors Eric Robinson and Geoffrey Summerfield summarize: "*July* was totally rejected and Clare submitted an alternative version; *December*, in contrast, was only reduced from 152 lines to 128 . . . the sequence as a whole was reduced from 3,382 lines . . . to 1,761 lines . . . and *July* was replaced by a completely new poem" (in Clare 1964, ix).

Apart from feeling a need to correct Clare's grammar, Taylor disliked Clare's poetry when it was "describing common things" and advised him to "raise your Views generally, & speak of the Appearances of Nature each Month more philosophically" (quoted by Robinson and Summerfield in Clare 1964, viii). The "Village Stories, and Other Poems" were added to the volume to pad it out after the cuts to "The Shepherd's Calendar" itself, and the "Other Poems" consisted of "nine poems that had been published in the London [Magazine] back in 1822 and 1823" (Bate 305). Clare's original text became widely available only with the Robinson and Summerfield edition in 1964, and then with the text edited by P. M. S. Dawson, David Powell, and Eric Robinson in 1996.

Clare's work takes its place in a line of English poems detailing the annual rural cycle that dates back at least to Edmund Spenser's poem of the same name although, as Jonathan Bate notes, in Clare's landscape, "there is always work to be done: the poems are peopled by woodmen, shepherds and milkmaids, all toiling and sweating, unlike the decorative figures of classical pastoral" (in Clare 2003, xvi) As one might expect, the poem deviates from its model (James Thomson's "The Seasons," one of Clare's favorite poems) in its "naturalistic" Romantic subject matter—Bate likens "January" to a "Dutch 'genre' painting" in which "cottage life is vividly realized through the careful placing of everyday objects" (in Clare 2003, xxv)—and in its fluctuating rhymes and meters, which include pentameter, tetrameter, blank verse, and couplets. Although Clare only occasionally lapses into the first person, he includes considerably more rustic vernacular than Thomson (or at least he did before Taylor's cuts).

A survey of each month's subject matter provides the truest sense of the poem's scope. "January: A Winter's Day" features perhaps more of an account of what the shepherd cannot do (because of the weather) than of what he can; it also depicts the shepherd's journey home. "January" stresses rural tales about "faireys" and witches' spells. "February" details the activities of ploughmen and shepherds and "The gossips" who "saunter in the sun," while long passages toward the end describe the natural world. "March" depicts sowing as well as hedging, ditching, and ploughing, and again arguably concentrates on the natural world itself as much as on the labor that takes place within it. "April," which dwells more than the rest of the poem on pastoral delights as traditionally conceived, details the laborers' optimism at the coming of spring and the flowers that are beginning to bloom. "May" describes schoolchildren, flowers, and the thresher whose occupation keeps him in the barn.

From "June" onward, the poem concentrates intensely on labor (hence Taylor's dissatisfaction with "July"). "June" begins with a passage about wheat and corn before describing mowing, ploughing, and—in a passage that would not look out of place in another poem that greatly influenced Clare, Robert Bloomfield's *The Farmer's Boy* (1800)—sheep shearing. Clare then returns to old rural customs, passages that should not be misconstrued as merely nostalgic; his purpose is also "a political one: the poetry is written in order to preserve the 'old customs' that were being destroyed by the march of economic 'progress'" (Bate in Clare 2003, xxv). In "July" (in Clare's original version, if not the version published in 1827), the emphasis on labor is maintained with opening passages on field work and a sustained focus on the sounds to be heard. Lines on shepherding are followed by those on reaping and turnip seed planting. The village evening is described, before passages on insects, the "horsboy," and a long digression on animals. An extract on "the weary thresher" follows before a passage describing the laborer relaxing in the pub in the evening sets his life within a wider context. "August" then builds on this focus on labor by describing reapers and gleaners and then general field work. "September" concentrates almost wholly on the harvesting and its conclusion. "October" deals mostly with nature; "November," including some notable attempts at conveying the sounds of rural life, is concerned with weather conditions, while "December" focuses predominantly on the rural community's festive customs.

The volume (as published) was not successful, and by 1829 only 400 copies were sold. As the biographer John Lucas observes, to quote from *The Shepherd's Calendar* without doing so at length "is practically impossible" because of its comprehensiveness; Clare "refuses to reject or scorn, and . . . won't select either" (Lucas 52). Yet Lucas also summarizes the gulf between Taylor's view and the critical reaction of many modern critics and readers: "Clare's original is a great poem. The only month that isn't up to much is 'April,' which comes closest to following Taylor's prescriptions" (51).

**Further Reading**

Bate, Jonathan. *John Clare: A Biography.* New York: Farrar, Strauss and Giroux; London: Picador, 2003.

Clare, John. *John Clare: Poems of the Middle Period, 1822–1837.* Vol. 1. Edited by P. M. S. Dawson, David Powell, and Eric Robinson. Oxford: Clarendon Press, 1996.

———. *John Clare: Selected Poems.* Edited by Jonathan Bate. New York: Farrar, Strauss and Giroux; London: Faber and Faber, 2003.

————. *John Clare: The Shepherd's Calendar.* Edited by Eric Robinson and Geoffrey Summerfield. Oxford: Oxford University Press, 1964.

Lucas, John. *John Clare.* Plymouth, Eng.: Northcote House, 1994.

—Steve Van Hagen

## "She Walks in Beauty" Lord Byron (1815)

LORD BYRON wrote "She Walks in Beauty" in June 1814, and in 1815 it appeared in *Hebrew Melodies,* a collection of Byron's lyrics that were written to accompany some authentic Hebrew airs that Isaac Nathan (ca. 1792–1864) had adapted from the music of the synagogues. Attracted to the poetry and music of the Hebrew Bible as well as the melancholy and haunting desolation that inform them, Byron undertook the project with enthusiasm. Though many of the lyrics are neither Hebrew nor Christian in theme, ranging from love songs to reflective lyrics, "She Walks in Beauty" in particular stands apart from the collection; even the love songs yield a despondent tone that is in keeping with the poems expressing grief for the lost Jewish homeland. Furthermore, most of the Hebrew melodies are spoken by narrators who do not necessarily reflect the author's own emotional states. "She Walks in Beauty," however, is rooted in Byron's own admiration of a particular "She," and we are allowed insight into the speaker's desire and appreciation through the gaze that directs the poem.

At a London party at Lady Sarah Sitwell's in June 1814, Byron saw for the first time the beautiful Anne Horton (who subsequently married Robert Wilmot, Byron's first cousin). She appeared in a mourning dress with spangles, and Byron was so overcome by the image of her pale skin against the dark outfit that he composed "She Walks in Beauty" the next day. Though this anecdote may serve to provide context for the poem, neither the dress nor any concrete depictions of the woman's physical appearance figure in Byron's narrative. Rather, the remarkable opening line "She walks in beauty, like the night" (l. 1) immediately sets up a comparison between the "beauty" that the woman emanates and "the night / Of cloudless climes and starry skies" (ll. 1–2), thus establishing the poem's

treatment of darkness and light. It is in the woman's appearance that the oppositions are reconciled, for "all that's best of dark and bright / Meet in her aspect and her eyes" (ll. 3–4). The coexisting presence of darkness and brightness in the beloved object's eye, and the desirability located there, is a typically Byronic practice. The enjambment, or continuation of one line into the next without pause, adds to the sense of mediation. The woman is here described in the language of classical artistic appreciation through the aesthetic category "beauty" and also through the speaker's admiration of the woman's "aspect" (l. 4). Without a doubt, we are viewing the woman through the speaker's gaze.

Though it might be tempting to view the speaker as merely admiring the woman's physical beauty, the awe which the woman inspires in the speaker goes beyond physicality. In effect, her appearance is an outward manifestation of her inner goodness and beauty. It is on her face that "thoughts serenely sweet express / How pure, how dear their dwelling place" (ll. 10–11). The woman is an emblem of mediating harmony, and she represents ideal beauty through the perfected balance of the oppositions presented in the poem. Through this woman, the "best of dark and bright" are "mellow'd to that tender light / Which heaven to gaudy day denies" (ll. 4–5). The meeting of dark and bright is so ideal, in fact, that "One shade the more, one ray the less" would "impair" the "nameless grace / Which waves in every raven tress, / Or softly lightens o'er her face" (ll. 7–10). The woman's gentle nature is illustrated through the vocabulary that Byron warmly employs throughout his carefully crafted stanzas: "tender," "grace," "softly," "serenely sweet," "pure," "dear," "soft," "calm," "goodness," "peace," and "innocent" are the designations that fashion the tone and world of the poem, giving an impression of the woman's nature. It is through the meeting of darkness and brightness, and the unity between what is best in each, that the beauty of the poem's object is illuminated. Byron goes beyond the self-consciousness inherent in most love poetry through not only elevating "A mind at peace with all below" (l. 17), but "A heart whose love is innocent!" (l. 18) and, thus, selfless.

## Further Reading

Ashton, Thomas L. *Byron's Hebrew Melodies*. Austin: University of Texas Press, 1972.

Byron, George Gordon Byron, Baron. *The Complete Poetical Works*. Vol. 3. Edited by Jerome J. McGann. Oxford: Clarendon Press, 1981.

Franklin, Caroline. *Byron: A Literary Life*. New York: St. Martin's Press, 2000.

Keanie, Andrew. *Lord Byron*. London: Greenwich Exchange, 2006.

Marchand, Leslie. *Byron's Poetry: A Critical Introduction*. Boston: Houghton Mifflin, 1965.

Payne, Geoff. *Dark Imaginings: Ideology and Darkness in the Poetry of Lord Byron*. Oxford: Peter Lang, 2008.

—Bailey Shaw

## "Sick Rose, The" William Blake (1794)

This poem, plate 39, appears ninth in WILLIAM BLAKE's 1794 version of SONGS OF INNOCENCE AND OF EXPERIENCE. Though Blake is known for rearranging the order and moving poems between *Innocence* and *Experience*, "The Sick Rose" is generally acknowledged as a permanent poem in the *Songs of Experience* collection. "Experience," for Blake, is "man's state when disaster has destroyed the initial bliss" (Damon 197); thus, a poem about a sick rose is appropriate for a collection of lyric poetry that addresses a state beyond innocence. The sick rose represents a love (often read within the parameters of heterosexual marriage) that is no longer ideal, pure, and innocent. A useful comparison is with ROBERT BURNS's use of the same flower in "A Red, Red Rose," also published in 1794. If the rose in Blake's poem is interpreted as a traditional symbol of love, as Burns's more clearly instructs his reader to interpret the rose as a metaphor for love, then the personified "Rose" in Blake's poem is not an ill person but a sick love and a state of corruption.

It is perhaps essential to consider Blake's illustration of "The Sick Rose" in conjunction with the text. Near the top of the plate, among the leaves on the thorny rose stems, two women lie dead after fighting and escaping a worm's grasp. The woman at the bottom of the frame is pictured emerging from the rose, coming into her sexuality, but is restrained by the worm that is wrapped beneath her breasts (a similar image appears in the representation of Oothoon in Blake's VISIONS OF THE DAUGHTERS OF ALBION [1793]). The woman partially enclosed within the rose at the bottom of the frame may be foul of form. She is visible only from the waist up, and the top portion of her body is voluptuous and seductive—arms held wide in a gesture of openness and welcoming. The bottom portion of the woman's body is not visible, which allows the reader to imagine the possibility that, beneath her skirts, she is monstrous, foul, and deformed. The rose is much greater in size than the worm, and it looks as though, at any moment, the rose could wholly enclose the worm. Still, the worm flies in the night, amid "howling storm" (l. 4) and is terrifyingly "invisible" (l. 2). This invisibility deprives the rose of any power against the worm because she may not realize he is there until he has already come into her and, at that, perhaps enters her violently with brutal force against her will. The sick rose may be read as a corruption of virginal purity by a phallic worm; sexuality may be read as a secretive seduction, the individual infected by culture. Additionally, the sick rose may be interpreted as a mother figure, and the worm a baby that feeds on her identity and is associated with death and the ground.

Blake's sick rose, arguably, dies in medias res. The complete ballad form, as it is indicated for this purpose, is four stanzas of four lines each. But "The Sick Rose," an incomplete ballad form, ends after two stanzas of four lines each. Ostensibly, the "missing" first half of "The Sick Rose" would describe the rose in a state of innocence—a state of beauty, strength, and purity.

## Further Reading

Blake, William. "Songs of Experience: The Sick Rose." In *Blake's Poetry and Designs*, edited by Mary Lynn Johnson and John E. Grant, 47. New York: Norton, 1979.

Damon, S. Foster. *A Blake Dictionary: The Ideas and Symbols of William Blake*. Providence: Brown University, 1965.

Frye, Northrop. *Fearful Symmetry: A Study of William Blake*. Princeton, N.J.: Princeton University Press, 1947.

—Elaine Wood

## Siddons, Sarah (1755–1831)

In her day, Sarah Siddons was universally hailed as one of England's greatest tragic actresses. Her style of acting is generally agreed to mark an important transition between a rejection of the older neoclassical emphasis on prescribed gestures and declamatory speech and the more fully Romantic vision embodied in the extremely passionate style of her rival actor EDMUND KEAN, with its emphasis on powerful feeling and expression of the emotions. Siddons's complexly layered portrayals of female characters were noted for their new psychic realism.

Siddons was born on July 5, 1755, into a traveling troupe of actors headed by her father, Roger Kemble, and mother Sarah (Sally) Kemble; it also included her famous actor brother, JOHN PHILIP KEMBLE, and the strolling actor William Siddons (whom she married in 1773). In 1775 Siddons made her acting debut at Drury Lane Theatre under David Garrick, but she was judged unremarkable and her contract was terminated. After several years of acting in the provinces, she returned to Drury Lane in 1782 in the title role of Thomas Southerne's *Isabella, or, the Fatal Marriage*. She played to a resounding triumph, launching an astonishing 20-year reign over the London stage.

Siddons's skill raised acting to the level of high art and made the acting profession respectable. In achieving such success, she surmounted a number of difficulties. For one thing, actresses in the 18th century had to work hard to overcome the default position that women enduring such public exposure for financial gain were unfeminine and morally suspect. Moreover, Siddons had to find ways of conducting a physically demanding profession onstage while in the advanced stages of pregnancy (she had seven children) and while separated from her young children on tour.

A tall and serious-looking beauty, Siddons exploited her regality in the creation of characters such as Desdemona, Belvidera, Calista, Rosalind, Ophelia, Queen Catherine, Volumina, and Jane de Monfort. She was most famous, however, for her interpretations of Lady Macbeth, whom she often played against her brother John's Macbeth. She invested her characters, even those riddled with crippling flaws or seeming evilness, with a certain nobility and grandeur.

Bringing an intense professional studiousness to the development of her roles, Siddons complicated her portrayals of women characters forced themselves to play femininity. In her notes to *Macbeth*, for instance, she described Lady Macbeth's character as having to be consciously squelched in sympathetic deference to her husband, "in gratitude for his [Macbeth's] unbounded affection, and in commiseration of his sufferings, she suppresses the anguish of her heart, even while that anguish is precipitating her to the grave which at this moment is yawning to receive her" (quoted in Campbell 129).

Siddons achieved incredible popularity, and a kind of Siddonsmania swept the country. Although cartoonists lampooned her intense style and derided her as Queen Rant, most of her adoring public preferred to agree with Sir Joshua Reynold's apotheosis of her as the *Tragic Muse* in his famous 1794 portrait. She died on June 8, 1831.

### Further Reading

Burroughs, Catherine B. *Closet Stages: Joanna Baillie and the Theater Theory of British Romantic Women Writers.* Philadelphia: University of Pennsylvania Press, 1997.

Campbell, Thomas. *Life of Mrs. Siddons.* London: E. Wilson, 1834.

Moody, Jane. *Illegitimate Theatre in London, 1770–1840.* Cambridge and New York: Cambridge University Press, 2000.

—Tammy Durant

## "Simon Lee: The Old Huntsman" William Wordsworth (1798)

WILLIAM WORDSWORTH was famously interested in rustic people and the countryside they inhabited. "Simon Lee," first published in *Lyrical Ballads* (1798), reflects both these interests. The 1798 version is the text discussed here. As a young man, Simon Lee is completely at one with nature, competing with it, reveling in it, and even overcoming it. This is in complete contrast to the solitary existence he and his wife are forced to live in their old age. The hectic, wild, "merry" days of his youth are over, and he finds himself fighting a losing battle as nature gradually takes back its control over him. Even his simple "moss-grown hut of clay" (l. 57) is symbolic of a grave slowly taking over; nature reclaiming the huntsman to the earth.

Simon Lee's "merry" demeanour and "cheek . . . like a cherry" (ll. 14, 16) are stereotypical characteristics of country people, but being red of cheek also suggests the flush that comes with drunkenness. We are told that the huntsman "reeled and was stone-blind" (l. 44) as though drunk, or even narcotically high, on the drug of nature. "[F]ull of glee" (l. 18), he is triumphantly joyful as he lives for the moment and the thrill of the hunt. He gains mastery over nature and his fellow huntsman, whom he all "could outrun" (l. 41) He cannot physically consume the countryside, but his reputation covers "four counties round" (l. 19). Wordsworth's mellifluous rhythm emphasizes the larger-than-life figure that is Simon Lee and creates an excitement akin to that felt by the huntsman himself: The bouncing rhyme reiterates the gallop of the horse and sheer joy and freedom of Simon's occupation.

As the poem progresses, a sense of intense melancholy emerges as the bold huntsman, who owes something to the chivalric knight of mediaeval romances, finally puts his horses and his livery to rest. Like the knights who jousted, he has "but one eye left" (l. 15), symbolizing not only the constant battles he faces but also the end of his usefulness. His dragons are foxes and other fauna, his army his hounds, his horse his constant companion. However, instead of retiring with a just reward, Simon has only his aged wife and a small amount of land for tillage left to him. The great "hall of Ivor" lies abandoned like the huntsman himself. It is a fact of nature that however much man tries to control it, and however big the man, nature will conquer him in the end.

In "Simon Lee" the past is romanticized, and nostalgia is cultivated "for its imaginative conceptions of the ideal and the heroic . . . as reflected in chivalric romance' (Drabble 872). The past is always rosier than the present, and things seem happier, more exciting. The Romantics often claimed to write their literature in opposition to rational thinking and restraint, allowing the emotions to overrule practicality, and this is certainly the case in "Simon Lee." With the sound of the hounds, Simon's "heart rejoices" (l. 46), projecting him back to his younger, carefree, happier days. Yet with the passing of time, the great man is now reduced to a bent, helpless figure with "tears [in] his eyes" (l. 97), who relies on a stranger to axe his tree. His "thanks and praises" (l. 98) emphasize his loss of pride in accepting help, and his effusive gratitude leaves the speaker "mourning" (l. 104) because as a young man Simon would never have had to utter such words to anyone. To reflect this mournfulness, the poem's velocity slows, taking on the dejection and gloominess that surrounds the huntsman's life in old age. Truly the earth will eventually reclaim him, reiterating nature's perpetual strength and man's ultimate weakness.

**Further Reading**

Gill, Stephen, ed. *The Cambridge Companion to Wordsworth.* Cambridge: Cambridge University Press, 2003.

Wordsworth, William. *Lyrical Ballads.* Edited by R. L. Brett and A. R. Jones. London: Routledge, London, 1991.

———. "Simon Lee." In *The Oxford Companion to English Literature.* Edited by Margaret Drabble. Oxford University Press, 2000, 872.

—Pauline Guerin

## *Simple Story, A* Elizabeth Inchbald (1791)

ELIZABETH INCHBALD's novel is a tale of two generations, and the narrative is split into two halves. The first part relates the story of Miss Milner and Dorriforth, the Catholic priest appointed by her dying father as her guardian. Inchbald's plot appears to conform to the principles of a literature of SENSIBILITY in which characters are governed by their feelings. As a result of her emotions, Miss Milner blushes, faints, and even falls ill. But A *Simple Story* transgresses both literary and social conventions. Miss Milner falls in love with Dorriforth, but he is forbidden to marry, and she is forced to conceal her sacrilegious feelings. But when Dorriforth's relative Lord Elmwood dies, he inherits an earldom and is released from his vows of celibacy in order to marry and produce an heir. Despite their contrasting characters, the earnest Dorriforth realizes his love for Miss Milner, and they become engaged. When Miss Milner refuses to submit to Dorriforth's authority, however, he calls off the engagement. He is only prevented from leaving for the Continent by his counselor, Sandford, previously Miss Milner's stern critic, who reconciles the couple, and they are married.

The second half begins 17 years later and recounts the relationship between Dorriforth, now Lord Elmwood, and his daughter, Lady Matilda. Here Inchbald draws much more explicitly on the conventions of GOTHIC fiction, as the firm Dorriforth evolves into a domestic tyrant. In the intervening years, Miss Milner, now Lady Elmwood, has had an adulterous affair while Lord Elmwood was abroad in the West Indies. On his return, Lady Elmwood fled, and he had vowed never to see her or the young Matilda again. On her deathbed, however, Lady Elmwood pleads with her husband to protect Matilda; he agrees only on the condition that she live confined in a secluded part of his estate and that they never meet. One day Matilda accidentally encounters Lord Elmwood, and after an overwrought emotional scene he banishes her. He only overcomes his resentment when Matilda is abducted by a rakish nobleman, Lord Margrave. Lord Elmwood rescues his daughter, they are reconciled, and the novel ends with her betrothal to Rushbrook, Lord Elmwood's nephew and heir.

Inchbald's conclusion to *A Simple Story* attributes the contrasting fates of her two heroines to Miss Milner's lack of "A Proper Education" (Inchbald 342), which left her unable to moderate her passions and her behaviour. This moral anticipates MARY WOLLSTONECRAFT's *A VINDICATION OF THE RIGHTS OF WOMAN,* published a year later, which argues that "the neglected education of my fellow-creatures is the grand source of the misery I deplore" (Wollstonecraft ). But *A Simple Story* does not conform to this moral. Wollstonecraft noted in her review of the novel in the *Analytical Review:* "It were to be wished . . . in order to insinuate a useful moral into thoughtless unprincipled minds, that the faults of the vain, giddy Miss Milner had not been softened . . . by such splendid, yet fallacious

virtues" (quoted in Inchald 2007, 381). Inchbald refuses to condemn Miss Milner. Though flirtatious and disobedient, she is sensitive and generous, and though she lacks a "proper education," she educates the stern Dorriforth by awakening his neglected emotions. In making her heroine a flirt, Inchbald offers a strong challenge to models of acceptable female behavior. Wollstonecraft argues that "the female mind [is] tainted by coquetish arts"; women should learn instead to "think and reason" (quoted in Inchbald 2007, 381). But Inchbald demonstrates that in the present state of society, women are often forced to resort to coquetry to assert any autonomy.

*A Simple Story* is not just concerned with the limitations of female power. Inchbald dramatizes the struggle for dominance in a domestic sphere, in which power becomes eroticized. Miss Milner rejoices that "the grave, the pious, the anchorite Dorriforth . . . is animated to all the ardour of the most impassioned lover—while the proud priest, the austere guardian is humbled . . . into the veriest slave of love" (Inchbald 172). She refuses his command not to attend a masquerade, declaring that "as my guardian, I certainly did obey him; and I could obey him as a husband; but as a lover, I will not" (186). The scholar Terry Castle notes that by compromising Dorriforth's domestic authority, Inchbald questions his claim to that authority: "He, just as much as his fiancée, seeks power and dominance; the only difference is that his narcissism is veiled by a mantle of patriarchal prestige" (Castle 307). Miss Milner's attendance at the masquerade assumes powerful significance. As Castle notes, the "subversive technical functions" of the masquerade are "implicit in the narrative as a whole" (294). Through Miss Milner's unbowed spirit, "Inchbald revivifies every aspect of the masquerade's utopian theatre of freedom: its moral and sensual fluidity, its anti-patriarchalism and celebration of female pleasure" (328). Even in the second half of the novel, Lady Matilda, though emotionally and physically confined to a far greater extent than her mother, overcomes the despotism not just of Lord Margrave but of Lord Elmwood himself.

The transgressive features of *A Simple Story,* as well as its intense emotional power, led immediately to comparisons with JEAN-JACQUES

ROUSSEAU's *Julie; ou La nouvelle Héloïse (Julie; or The New Heloise,* 1761), in which a young woman falls in love with her tutor. Inchbald's own politics were radical, and though she probably wrote most of *A Simple Story* before 1789, the novel's connections with Rousseau, in addition to its powerful critique of absolutism, anticipate many features of the debate over the FRENCH REVOLUTION conducted in fiction and nonfiction during the 1790s.

Inchbald was an experienced playwright, and *A Simple Story* demonstrates the influence of theater. The novel's two-part structure and its depiction of tyranny echo Shakespeare's *A Winter's Tale. A Simple Story* also generates much of its emotional effect through dramatic conventions, including the belief that gestures speak louder than words. The novelist MARIA EDGEWORTH wrote to Inchbald declaring, "I believed all to be real, and was affected as I should be by the real scenes if they had passed my eyes" (quoted in Boaden, 2, 152). Edgeworth praised the authenticity of Inchbald's presentation of "feeling," a feature of the novel that anticipates the finest Romantic work.

## Further Reading

Boaden, James. *Memoirs of Mrs Inchbald: Including her Familiar Correspondence with the most Distinguished Persons of her Time.* 2 volumes. London: Bentley 1833.

Byrne, Paula. "*A Simple Story*: From Inchbald to Austen." *Romanticism: The Journal of Romantic Culture and Criticism* 5, no. 2 (1999): 161–171.

Castle, Terry. *Masquerade and Civilization: The Carnivalesque in Eighteenth-Century English Culture and Fiction.* London: Methuen, 1986.

Inchbald, Elizabeth. *A Simple Story.* Edited by Anna Lott, Peterborough, Ont.: Broadview Press, 2007.

Kelly, Gary. *The English Jacobin Novel, 1780–1805.* Oxford and New York: Clarendon Press, 1976.

—Mary Fairclough

## slavery

Great Britain was neither the first nor the only country to engage in the enslavement of African peoples, but from the middle of the 17th century to the middle of the 19th century, it was the most prominent. The British involvement is usually said to have begun with the first successful slaving expedition to Africa by Sir John Hawkins in 1562, when 300 Africans were captured, but the slave trade did not become an important industry until 1640, when planters in the West Indies began to grow sugar. Prior to that time, European indentured servants did most of the labor in the tending of tobacco and cotton crops in the New World, but because sugar production required considerably more labor, the slave trade grew rapidly. Over the next 200 years, Great Britain controlled about one half of the slave trade, enslaving and transporting some 2 million Africans to the New World.

The slave trade took place along a triangular route. First, British merchants sent ships to the Gold Coast, where as many as 38,000–42,000 Africans per year were kidnapped or bought for up to £15 per head. The Africans were then shipped to the West Indies under horrific conditions. This part of the journey was known as the "Middle Passage"; 13 percent of those enslaved died en route, and another 33 percent died during the "seasoning" (break-in) period following delivery. In the West Indies the Africans were sold for £35 each on average, and they worked in the tobacco and sugar fields. Profits from the sale of Africans were used to purchase tobacco and sugar, which were then shipped to and sold in England and Europe for even higher profits.

The issue of trafficking in human beings divided the English nation like no other, except perhaps for the FRENCH REVOLUTION. Proponents of the slave trade were well organized and had strong political support from powerful figures, such Henry Dundas, first viscount Melville; the duke of Wellington; and King George III. Their arguments in favor of the slave trade came on two fronts. Some argued that slavery and the slave trade were morally justified because black Africans were inferior to white Europeans. In this view, blacks were non-Christian, incapable of rational thought, and unproductive, so they were unfit for freedom and in need of a benevolent master. Proponents also argued that slavery had always existed in Africa and that the conditions for slaves were better than those of the English factory worker. Others argued in favor of slavery and the slave trade on economic grounds. While Great Britain was the leader in the slave trade, France and Holland were beginning to make inroads into the market. Also, they said, the slave trade was necessary for the plantation system, and without it, port cities such as Bristol, Liverpool, and London, as well as the entire nation, would suffer. Proponents recognized the growing popularity of abolition, but they saw the nation's economic interest as more important, and they saw themselves as protecting that interest.

The abolitionist argument was also made on two fronts. Some abolitionists attacked slavery from a religious and philosophical perspective, arguing that it was a violation of Christian doctrine and the innate, natural rights of man. Others argued on a more personal and social level, claiming that slavery was a violation of domestic affections since it broke up families and exposed black women to the sexual abuses of white masters. Religious groups were deeply involved in the abolition movement. Quakers led the way on both sides of the Atlantic, influencing other groups, including the Methodists. Women were especially active in the abolition movement, providing leadership and numbers to various abolition societies, protests, sugar boycotts, the writing and distribution of thousands of books and pamphlets, and the gathering of thousands of signatures for hundreds of petitions. In order to overcome the powerful business and political interests supporting slavery and the slave trade, abolitionists focused their efforts on swaying popular opinion.

The abolitionists' efforts gradually brought about change, aided by a series of events. A leading lawyer and evangelical, Granville Sharp (1735–1813), brought two important cases before the powerful judge William Murray, Lord Mansfield (1705–93). The first was the case of James Somerset in 1772. Somerset, a slave, had been brought to England from the West Indies by his master, Mr. Stewart of Virginia. While in England, Somerset escaped, was recaptured, and was threatened with his return to the West Indies. When Sharp intervened, Lord Mansfield ruled that the master's colonial rights did not extend to England and ordered Somerset freed. In the second case, in 1781, Captain Luke Collingwood of the slave ship *Zong* threw overboard 132 plague-infected slaves as rotten cargo in order to save water and with the intent to collect insurance. Sharp's attempt to prosecute Collingwood was unsuccessful, but the publicity caused great outrage.

The 1790s were difficult years for the abolitionists, partly because of the increasingly conservative nature of Parliament in light of the French Revolution and partly because of the bloody slave uprisings of 1791 in Saint Domingue (now Haiti) led by Toussaint Louverture, which cost the lives of 40,000 French soldiers. As a result, many people came to see the abolitionists as radicals. During this time, William Wilberforce, an important member of Parliament, led the introduction of several bills to abolish slavery and the slave trade, but with no success until 1799, when the Slave Limitation Bill (also referred to as the Slave Carrying Bill) was passed, extending an earlier bill from 1788 that limited the number of slaves a ship could carry. From then, the abolitionists gradually were able to end the slave trade in 1807 and slavery in 1833. The fact that the slave trade was losing its economic importance to the nation also aided the abolitionist cause.

Because of the national focus on slavery, it is no surprise that it makes its way into the literature of the period. JANE AUSTEN's MANSFIELD PARK and MARIA EDGEWORTH's BELINDA contained characters who were West Indian planters. Edgeworth's novella *The Grateful Negro* argued in favor of the planters but criticized the abusive treatment of slaves. Slave narratives by Ottabah Cugoano, OLAUDAH EQUIANO, and MARY PRINCE gave firsthand accounts of those abuses and riveted the nation's readers. Thomas Day's "The Dying Negro" (1773) and WILLIAM COWPER's "The Negro's Complaint" and "Pity for Poor Africans" (both 1788) were especially influential abolitionist poems. A whole host of authors, including ANNA LAETITIA BARBAULD, SAMUEL TAYLOR COLERIDGE, HANNAH MORE, AMELIA ALDERSON OPIE, PERCY BYSSHE SHELLEY, ROBERT SOUTHEY, HELEN MARIA WILLIAMS, WILLIAM WORDSWORTH, and ANN YEARSLEY, all wrote against the inhumanity of slavery. In contrast, others, such as MATTHEW GREGORY LEWIS, owned plantations and the slaves who worked on them. Elsewhere, although WILLIAM BLAKE's poem "The LITTLE BLACK BOY" was not widely known until the 20th century, his illustrations for John Gabriel Stedman's *Narrative of Five Years' Expedition against the Revolted Negroes of Surinam* (1796) provided some of the most shockingly graphic visual depictions of the atrocities perpetrated by white owners against black slaves. Although most English abolitionist authors never actually got past the culture of "Anglo-Africanism"—that is to say, the notion that white European Christians were superior to black African non-Christians—their work made an important contribution to ending the abomination of slavery.

See also "EPISTLE TO WILLIAM WILBERFORCE"; "TO WILLIAM WILBERFORCE, ESQ."

## Further Reading

Antsey, Roger. *The Atlantic Slave Trade and British Abolition, 1760–1810.* Atlantic Highlands, N.J.: Humanities Press, 1975.

Brown, Christopher Leslie. *Moral Capital: Foundations of British Abolitionism.* Chapel Hill: University of North Carolina Press, 2006.

Craton, Michael. *Sinews of Empire: A Short History of British Slavery.* Garden City, N.Y.: Anchor, 1974.

d'Anjou, Leo. *Social Movements and Cultural Change: The First Abolition Revisited.* New York: Aldine de Gruyter, 1996.

Davis, David Brion. *The Problem of Slavery in the Age of Revolution, 1770–1823.* Ithaca, N.Y., and London: Cornell University Press, 1975.

Haywood, Ian. *Bloody Romanticism: Spectacular Violence and the Politics of Representation, 1776–1832.* Basingstoke, Eng., and New York: Palgrave Macmillan, 2006.

Lee, Debbie. *Slavery and the Romantic Imagination.* Philadelphia: University of Pennsylvania Press, 1999.

Mannix, Daniel P., and Malcolm Cowley. *Black Cargoes: A History of the Atlantic Slave Trade, 1518–1865.* New York: Viking, 1962.

Mellor, Anne K., and Richard E. Matlak. *British Literature, 1780–1830.* Fort Worth, Tex.: Harcourt Brace, 1996.

Walvin, James, ed. *Slavery and British Society, 1776–1846.* Baton Rouge: Louisiana State University Press, 1982.

Williams, Eric. *Capitalism and Slavery.* 1944. Reprint, New York: Russell and Russell, 1961.

—John H. Jones

## Smith, Charlotte (1749–1806)

Circumstances resulting from an unfortunate marriage, a dozen children, and a poorly written will made writing an economic necessity for Charlotte Smith. Because of her husband's financial recklessness, she sought publication for her first book of poetry, ELEGIAC SONNETS AND OTHER POEMS (1784), from debtors' prison. These poems and the novels and poetry penned over the next two decades often capitalize on Smith's personal experiences as a sensitive and intelligent woman wronged by a patriarchal and despotic society, as well as showing her importance—along with that of ANNA SEWARD—in the development of the sonnet in the late 18th century. Displaying contradictory Romantic propensities to withdraw from or engage with a society that too frequently disappoints one's ideals, Smith's brooding and rebellious works evoke sympathy for the oppressed and advocate reform in a turbulent period of revolution. Her writings sold well, and though she had to fight to keep her profits from her husband, Smith was a literary success in her lifetime. Stylistically and thematically, she influenced writers such as WILLIAM WORDSWORTH, JANE AUSTEN, and SIR WALTER SCOTT.

Born Charlotte Turner on May 4, 1749, to parents in the landed gentry, Smith enjoyed a comfortable childhood despite the early death of her mother and her father's overspending. She excelled in traditional female accomplishments at school; entered society at age 12; and, upon her father's remarriage to a wealthy heiress, acquiesced to an arranged marriage to Benjamin Smith, son of a West India merchant, when she was 15. The marriage was a disaster, marked by infidelity, physical abuse, and profligacy, though Charlotte remained with her husband for 22 years before leaving him and taking responsibility for their nine surviving children. Due to his son's known extravagance, Benjamin's father left his estate to Charlotte and her children, but the will was fraught with legal problems and the money remained frustratingly inaccessible during her lifetime, producing a legal quagmire that would inspire the infamous Jarndyce vs. Jarndyce case in Charles Dickens's novel *Bleak House* (1852–53).

Living on the edge of poverty while fighting to secure places for her children in middle-class society, Smith described herself as a "slave of the Booksellers" as she churned out 10 novels and three books of poetry. Drawing from her unique position outside yet within middle-class respectability, she made her name an important one in literary circles even though her resentment toward her husband's worthlessness often led her to qualify her surname *Smith* by drawing a line through it.

Themes from Smith's life appear thinly veiled throughout her novels, which follow the sentimental tradition while openly critiquing parental figures who orchestrate mercenary marriages, artful legal systems that promote fraud and injustice, and social inequities that stem from abuses of power. Unlike Smith, many of her characters manage to avoid the pitfalls she illustrates. In *Emmeline* (1788), her heroine narrowly escapes marriage to a charming yet destructive man, and in *The Old Manor House* (1793) a hidden will restores the rightful inheritor to his estate. Smith also engages contemporary political discussions. Like many British liberals, she supported the FRENCH REVOLUTION in its early stages, and her novel *Desmond* (1792) champions the revolutionary cause through the title character. Through the novel's romance plot, Smith also demonstrates how domestic cruelty mirrors governmental oppression, directly connecting the personal to the political.

Although her novels provided much-needed income, Smith considered them artistically inferior to her poetry. Even more so than in her fiction, her poems cross boundaries between literature and life, and she invites readers' comparisons of the narrators of her poems and herself by detailing the tragedies of her own life in her personal introductions to the collections. As LORD BYRON would do decades later, Smith marketed herself as a tortured artist, and in *Elegiac Sonnets*, the poems' personas frequently call upon sleep, forgetfulness, madness, and death to release them from their experience of loss, weariness, and sorrow. Gazing at bones washed from a graveyard positioned too close to the sea, the speaker in "SONNET: WRITTEN IN THE CHURCH-YARD AT MIDDLETON IN SUSSEX" (1789) covets the dead's repose: "While I am doom'd—by life's long storm opprest, / To gaze with envy on their gloomy rest" (ll. 13–14). Not only did the collection revitalize the sonnet form for later Romantic writers such as SAMUEL TAY-

LOR COLERIDGE, JOHN KEATS, and PERCY BYSSHE SHELLEY, it also standardized the Romantic interest in rural settings and attraction to melancholic temperaments.

Like other Romantic writers, Smith also struggled to reconcile her radical beliefs with her own middle-class affiliations. In *The EMIGRANTS: A Poem in Two Books* (1793), Smith identifies with the plight of the aristocrats who fled their properties in France; like them, she had grown up expecting a very different life from the one she found herself living. However, the poem does not exonerate the wealthy from their responsibility in their reversal of fortune. With a cynical perspective on individuals and society, Smith nonetheless pities those who suffer and recommends a therapeutic retreat from society into nature: "How often do I half abjure Society, / And sigh for some lone Cottage, deep embower'd / In the green woods" (ll. 42–44). Smith continues to explore the comforting, if not entirely restorative, qualities of nature in her posthumous *Beachy Head: With Other Poems* (1807). Influenced by the death of her favorite daughter, Anna Augusta, as well as pressing financial concerns and her own declining health, the title poem, "BEACHY HEAD," is hauntingly redolent of innocence lost and promises broken.

Charlotte Smith died on October 28, 1806, the same year as her estranged husband, after losing six of her 12 children, watching her family's fortune disappear in the hands of legal bureaucracy and exhausting herself to write her way free from her creditors. As with many Romantic women writers, her literary reputation faded throughout the 19th and 20th centuries, but renewed interest in the Romantic canon and in the sonnet form has encouraged a surge of recent scholarship. Readers today can appreciate Smith not only for the inspiration she gave to Romantic celebrities like Wordsworth, but also for her writings' poignant depictions of human endurance and suffering. Since the 1990s, when interest in Smith's contributions to Romantic literature revived, it has even been suggested that rather than her better-known male counterparts, it was Smith who was really the first Romantic poet in England.

See also "FEMALE EXILE, THE"; "TO THE SOUTH DOWNS."

## Further Reading

Fletcher, Loraine. *Charlotte Smith: A Critical Biography.* New York: Palgrave, 1998.

Fry, Carrol Lee. *Charlotte Smith.* New York: Twayne, 1996.

Labbe, Jacqueline M. *Charlotte Smith: Romanticism, Poetry, and the Culture of Gender.* Manchester, Eng.: Manchester University Press, 2003.

Smith, Charlotte. *Celestina.* Edited by Loraine Fletcher. Peterborough, Ont.: Broadview Press, 2004.

———. *Desmond.* Edited by Antje Blank and Janet Todd. Peterborough, Ont.: Broadview Press, 2001.

———. *Emmeline, the Orphan of the Castle.* Edited by Loraine Fletcher. Peterborough, Ont.: Broadview Press, 2003.

———. *The Old Manor House.* Edited by Jacqueline M. Labbe. Peterborough, Ont.: Broadview Press, 2002.

———. *The Poems of Charlotte Smith.* Edited by Stuart Curran. New York: Oxford University Press, 1993.

———. *The Young Philosopher.* New York: Garland, 1974.

—Esther Godfrey

## "Solitude"    See "LUCY GRAY."

## "Song: She Dwelt among the Untrodden Ways" ("Song") William Wordsworth (1800)

WILLIAM WORDSWORTH's "Song," a 12-line, three-stanza poem better known as "She Dwelt among the Untrodden Ways," appears in the significantly expanded second edition of Wordsworth's and SAMUEL TAYLOR COLERIDGE's LYRICAL BALLADS (1800). Written in late 1798 during Wordsworth's stay in Germany, this elegiac piece praises the beauty and laments the death of Lucy, a woman who lived and died "beside the springs of Dove" (l. 2) in a remote part of England. The poem, though, does not simply glorify its subject but instead depicts human sympathy as a phenomenon that allows the heart to transcend all distances, whether between parts of the world or between the living and the dead.

In the eyes of the narrator, Lucy's seclusion occasions a life of profound loneliness; thus, Lucy was "a Maid whom there were none to praise / And very few to love" (ll. 3–4). The second stanza offers imagery that amplifies the woman's loveliness and loneliness alike: "A Violet by a mossy Stone / Half-hidden from the Eye! / —Fair as a star when only one / Is shining in the sky! (ll. 5–8) Although Lucy lived an uncelebrated provincial life, her fate anguishes the speaker: "But she is in her Grave, and oh! / The difference to me" (ll. 11–12). This ongoing sense of loss, intensified by its immediacy, suggests not only "the capacity of the dead to provoke lingering grief in the living," as the scholar Kurt Fosso asserts (144), but also the combined power of memory and love to connect human souls across time and space. More than a cause of sorrow and regret, Lucy is a part of the speaker's being.

By virtue of its tone and subject, "She Dwelt among the Untrodden Ways" bears some relation to three other poems included in the 1800 *Lyrical Ballads*: "Strange fits of passion have I known," "A slumber did my spirit seal," and "Three years she grew in sun and shower." Despite variations in detail, all four pieces involve a speaker who foresees or mourns the death of a beloved young woman named Lucy (save in "A Slumber," which commemorates but does not name its subject). For this reason scholars frequently analyze the poems together, regarding each as a unique rendering of a single incident. Some Romanticists contend that a fifth piece, "LUCY GRAY," also belongs among these so-called Lucy poems (Fosso 141–145).

## Further Reading

Fosso, Kurt. *Buried Communities: Wordsworth and the Bonds of Mourning.* Albany: State University of New York Press, 2004.

Wordsworth, William. "Song." In *Lyrical Ballads, and Other Poems, 1797–1800,* edited by James Butler and Karen Green, 163. Ithaca, N.Y., and London: Cornell University Press, 1992.

—Tim Ruppert

## Songs of Innocence and of Experience: Shewing The Two Contrary States of The Human Soul William Blake (1794)

The first four lines of the "Motto to the Songs of Innocence & of Experience," from WILLIAM

BLAKE's notebook, assert that mankind requires experience as a counterforce to innocence, to counter mental passivity: "The Good are attracted By Mens perceptions / And Think not for themselves / Till Experience teaches them to catch / And to cage the Fairies & Elves." *Songs of Innocence and of Experience* thus liberates the mind from even benevolent-sounding tyrannies by compelling readers to consider the complex relationship between these "Contrary States."

Blake published *Songs of Innocence* in 1789, *Songs of Experience* in 1793–94, and the combined text in 1794. Though not composed at the same time, and *Songs of Innocence* was published separately, the two parts form a dialogue rather than discrete texts, which is underscored by how Blake moved poems from *Innocence* to *Experience*. While the poems of *Songs* are written in a direct, unornamented language, they raise provocative questions. There is the issue of there being no definitive text. The 28 surviving editions show 19 different arrangements of the poems within the two sections, although after 1815 Blake settled on an order, but later copies included a new poem, "To Tirzah." There is also the question of how the arrangement affects interpretation of the larger text and of individual poems. Significant, too, is the idiosyncratic punctuation, capitalization, and spelling and how this impacts on possible meanings.

Finally, there is the issue of how reading the poems without simultaneously viewing the plates upon which they were inscribed gives precedence to the verbal effect. Blake, however, devised a method of relief etching, which he called illuminated printing, that created a joint verbal-visual medium. Blake wrote the text of the poem and drew the design directly onto a copper plate with an acid-resistant varnish—in reverse; after the plate was exposed to acid, text and design were left in relief. A printed impression was then watercolored by hand, either by Blake himself or by his wife, Catherine. Unsurprisingly, he produced few copies of *Songs*.

The effect of this method was twofold. First, the inseparable image and text depend upon and inform each other. The images—not simply punctuating or underscoring meaning—signify, and readers should scrutinize them individually as well as noting motifs, such as trees, children, birds, and vines. Printed words and design merge such that the editions of *Songs* created by Blake were closer to illuminated manuscripts than to printed books. Second, he could control all aspects of producing and disseminating the text; we cannot separate the poet from the artist, printer, publisher, and bookseller. His printing method yoked two contraries—the mass-produced printed image and the unique work of art. Not only did Blake arrange the plates differently from one copy to the next (and further complicating matters, he produced different versions of several of the plates), but no two were ever water-colored alike: "What look like plants in one copy become flames in another; clear skies turn black and stormy; haloed figures lose their haloes" (Leader xix).

Opening *Songs*, the questions multiply. On the title page, beneath fluid swaths of flaming colors and letters swirling into the design, we see Adam and Eve covering their nakedness and shielding their prostrate bodies from flames. The image depicts the moment immediately after the Fall when they leave Eden. Yet before we succumb to the kind of dualistic thinking that sees experience as merely negating innocence, we should recall that the contrary states exist in a dynamic tension, which we see by contrasting this plate with the frontispiece and title page for *Innocence*. The former depicts a shepherd with a pipe, gazing upward at a child on a cloud; the latter, a seated mother or nurse instructing two young children, who gaze at a book opened on her lap. While these pastoral scenes evoke innocence, they and the poem "Introduction," which connects to the former image, also question our perceptions of this state. The poem introduces a figure "Piping songs of pleasant glee" (l. 2), at first spontaneously for himself and then at the behest of the child, who asks him to "Pipe a song about a Lamb!" (l. 5), to pipe it again, to sing it, and finally to write down his songs, "In a book that all may read" (l. 14). In response to the child's commands, the piper plucked a "hollow reed" from which he fashioned a "rural pen" and "stain'd the water clear" in writing down his "happy songs / Every child may joy to hear" (ll. 16–20).

Are the *Songs* meant for children, adults, or both? The title page for *Songs of Innocence* echoes children's literature, except that such literature sought to restrain the impulses of children and teach them to obey authority while *Songs* counters the pabulum fed to children and adults alike. And are the hymnlike poems music, text, or both? A hollow reed functions as a pen while also indicating a musical instrument (the shepherd's pipe and the mouthpiece of a reed instrument). Similarly multiple meanings of the "stain'd" water (l. 18) calls to mind the ink used by writing implements, the ink used to print from an engraved plate, and the watercolored plates. "Stain'd" recalls the joint verbal-visual medium while the taint it insinuates also suggests the contrary states *Songs* will show. The transition from spontaneous music to reproducible song to writing signifies a fall from innocence into experience. The title page, stressing the instability of innocence, reminds us of the inevitability of that fall. Above the open book, fruit hangs invitingly from a tree, implying that in attaining knowledge, each individual reenacts the story of the Fall.

In all aspects of his life, Blake challenged orthodoxies. Born in London in 1757, into a family of tradesmen who were also Dissenters, he was exposed to the religious debates fermenting in London at this time and to the radical intellectual and political milieus found there. Educated at home, he read the Bible intensely and in a manner influenced by radical dissent, especially its focus on the prophets. The iconography and language of the Bible exerted a deep influence on Blake, who had religious visions from early childhood. He shared with many of his contemporaries the valuing of imagination, creativity, feeling, and spontaneity against a cold rationality, and we can trace this bent at least as much to his contact with radical dissent as to his reading of, among others, Geoffrey Chaucer, JOHN MILTON, John Bunyan, Shakespeare, Dante, Paracelsus, and Volney. Blake initially sympathized with tenets of the Swedenborgian church but then, in disillusionment, penned *The MARRIAGE OF HEAVEN AND HELL,* a withering satire of it. We can also find connections, if not directly, to the writings of a German theologian and mystic, Jacob Boehme (1575–1624), who was highly influential in Dissenting circles. Boehme saw God as the unity of contraries, of light and dark, mercy and jealousy, the lion and the lamb.

In his dialectical thinking, positive and negative aspects obtain in all things, and their opposition is necessary. The scholar E. P. Thompson argues that Blake's rhetoric, vocabulary, and concepts are drawn largely from the antinomian tradition within religious dissent, which, asserting salvation by faith, proclaimed that Christians are released from adherence to the moral law and, for some antinomian offshoots, sin. The focus on sin was for Blake merely a strategy used by priests to control humanity. This antihegemonic tradition, which "challenged the entire superstructure of learning and of moral and doctrinal teaching as ideology," taught him to expose everything that rationalized power and oppression (Thompson 110).

Starting at age 10, Blake received drawing instruction, favoring then-unfashionable artists such as Michelangelo, Raphael, and Albrecht Dürer. Apprenticed at 14 to James Basire, engraver to the Society of Antiquaries and the Royal Society, he was admitted in 1779 to the Royal Academy of Art. Blake derived his income primarily from his illustrations, such as those produced for the publisher Joseph Johnson, who introduced Blake to his circle, which included such leading radicals as Joseph Priestley; THOMAS PAINE; Blake's friend Henry Fuseli; and MARY WOLLSTONECRAFT, whose *Original Stories from Real Life* he illustrated. In this same period, Blake began to publish his writing, *Poetical Sketches* appearing in 1783. The year before, he had married Catherine Boucher, and in 1784 he set up a printing and publishing business, which proved unsuccessful. In 1788 he invented his method of relief etching, and in the same year he printed his first illuminated books, *All Religions Are One* and *There is No Natural Religion.*

Though he lived in relative poverty and obscurity, he continued to write and produce illustrations, constructing a rich mythology in his more than a dozen books, until his death in 1827. *Songs,* the only text known by the 19th-century reading public, was first reprinted in 1839. Alexander Gilchrist's biography, *The Life of William Blake, Pictor Ignotus,* published in 1863, introduced Blake to a wider audience. Algernon Charles Swinburne's critical essay on Blake appeared in 1868, and Dante Gabriel Rossetti's edition of Blake's poetry was published in 1875.

The year in which *Songs of Innocence* was published was also the year of the FRENCH REVOLUTION, which Blake enthusiastically supported, as he did the AMERICAN REVOLUTION, but he was disheartened by counterrevolutionary response. The critic David Erdman writes, "The recurrent negative theme in the *Songs* is the mental bondage of Anti-jacobinism, manifest . . . in the lives of children and youth forced into harlotry and soldiery and apprentice slavery by the bone-bending, mind-chaining oppressions of priest and king" (Erdman 272). He was also disillusioned too by the Reign of Terror, which commenced in 1793. The scholar W. J. T. Mitchell recommends that we see in *Songs of Experience* "a code word for postrevolutionary consciousness—awareness of terror, guilt, alienation, apostasy, unrelenting tyranny, irony, and a kind of sober wisdom coupled with unrelenting utopian hopes" (Mitchell 42). Nonetheless, Blake's radical commitments never wavered. His writing depicted organized religion as tyranny, rejected the authority of the Crown, challenged conventional notions of chastity and marriage, condemned exploitation, and saw the human and divine as united. His sympathies with the oppressed extended to slaves, workers, children, and women. Viewing patriarchal authority as a repressive force akin to Crown and church, he opposed all that thwarted impulses, sexual and affective.

Reading the poems of *Songs* together reveals the complexities of point of view. Additional layers of meaning unfold by connecting individual poems to poems with which they resonate or form pairs. The poems of *Innocence* require us to note ironies while simultaneously appreciating their literalism, especially those in which the state of innocence seems least problematic, such as "Spring": "Little Lamb / Here I am. / Come and lick / My white neck. / Let me pull / Your soft Wool" (ll. 19–24). Of course, we understand the child and lamb as symbols of Jesus and hence, for Blake, of divine humanity, at the same time that we recognize the literalness of this idealized landscape: a green upon which the laughter of villagers echoes ("The ECCHOING GREEN"), a field of sheep tended by a watchful shepherd ("The SHEPHERD")—scenes of security, communal pleasure, and, significantly, even of robust sexuality ("Laughing Song"). Irony bubbles up from the cracks in the defenses of innocence, when the guardians charged with protection fail in their responsibilities. Thomas R. Frosch writes that in these cases, "Innocence is put back together with some little fiction or myth" (Frosch 75).

The irony inheres in recognizing the fictions the speaker does not; thus, many of the poems of *Songs of Innocence* are ironic, revealing the precariousness and limitations of the state of innocence. The speaker of "The LITTLE BLACK BOY" pleads that his "soul is white" (l. 2) in response to a racist perception of him as "bereav'd of light" (l. 4). His mother offers the well-meaning myth that his dark skin better helps him "to bear the beams of love" (l. 14) emanating from God. The boy consoles himself with the debilitating thought then when he dies, he will be able to shade a little English boy from these beams "till he can bear, / To lean in joy upon our fathers knee" (ll. 25–26). The pathetic fantasy that this act will make the little English boy "be like him" (l. 28) and therefore love him is painfully eroded by the image showing the English boy receiving God's love with no thought for the protecting touch on his back. Here we see innocence sustained by ideology, as with "The CHIMNEY SWEEPER" and "HOLY THURSDAY."

The self-deceiving speaker of "The Chimney Sweeper," failed by his father, who "sold" him when he was little more than an infant (l. 2), teaches a younger boy, Tom Dacre, to accept his slavelike servitude. Quieted down, Tom has a dream in which thousands of boy sweepers, "lock'd up in coffins of black" (l. 12; the chimneys that caused the death of so many) are set free by an angel, run to wash in a river, and then ascend upon clouds. This dream offers escape through a visionary imaginative act but only a momentary escape paid for with submission: "And the Angel told Tom, if he'd be a good boy, / He'd have God for his father & never want joy" (ll. 19–20). The pun of "want joy" suggests that if obedient, Tom will never want for joy because he will never want it. Tom learns to repress his impulses, and as recompense he is able to work through the cold morning and still be happy and warm. He yet retains a vivid imagination in contrast to the stale nostrums of the speaker—"So if all do their duty, they need not fear harm" (l. 24)—who elicits our compassion as we note his illusions.

Similarly, the children of "Holy Thursday" retain an innocence the speaker lacks. The poem describes the annual service of thanksgiving for charity-school children held at St. Paul's Cathedral in London. The children march to the church, preceded by "Grey-headed beadles" guiding them "with wands as white as snow" (l. 3). We question just how innocent these instruments of control are, especially when we compare the beadles to the shepherd of the poem of the same name, who follows rather than regiments his flock, and who raises his own voice in praise as he hears their bleats. The children, "with radiance all their own" (l. 6), sing to heaven like "a mighty wind" or "like harmonious thunderings" that shake "the seats of heaven" (ll. 9–10). yet their song seems not to unsettle "the aged men, wise guardians of the poor" (l. 11) who sit beneath the children literally and spiritually. The speaker reproaches adults to "cherish pity, lest you drive an angel from your door" (l. 12), but we sense a yearly ritual that aggrandizes the guardians rather than cherishes pity. One need not recall the cruel beadle of Charles Dickens's *Oliver Twist* (1838) to tease out the irony. "The Divine Image," which directly precedes "Holy Thursday," affirms that pity has "a human face" (l. 10), which calls into question the pity put on public display.

The plate for "Holy Thursday" shows a scene of repressive control: children paired by gender and the color of their uniforms, which contrasts with the plate for "The NURSE'S SONG," where boys and girls dance together in spontaneous joy. Resisting the calls of the nurse to return home, these children leap, shout and laugh: "And all the hills ecchoed" (l. 16). In contrast, the arid ritual at St. Paul's Cathedral fails to "love the human form" ("The Divine Image," l. 17), which "The Divine Image" tells us is where "Mercy, Love & Pity dwell" (l. 19) and hence where God dwells, too. The children's radiance exists despite false guardianship, to which the speaker—not himself an agent of oppression, for he celebrates the children's exuberant song—lends tacit support. Nonetheless, rationalizations do not erase innocence, nor nullify its shaming power.

The speakers of "The Chimney Sweeper" and "Holy Thursday" in *Songs of Experience* expose oppression. The morally indignant speaker of "Holy Thursday" holds no illusions about the benevolence of the beadles, asking rhetorically whether it is "a holy thing to see" (l. 1) in such a rich land—"Babes . . . Fed with cold and usurous hand?" (ll. 3–4). The child speaker of "The Chimney Sweeper," questioned about his mother and father, responds that his parents forced him to be a sweep: "Because I was happy upon the heath, / And smil'd among the winters snow, / They clothed me in clothes of death, / And taught me to sing the notes of woe" (ll. 5–8). He grasps how his parents self-servingly concluded that he would not suffer ("And because I am happy & dance & sing, / They think they have done me no injury" [ll. 9–10]) and hints at a sadistic wish to end his happiness. In nearly the same breath, the child reveals their collusion with oppressive institutions that hypocritically mask their cruelty, for his parents "are gone to praise God & his Priest & King / Who make up a heaven of our misery" (ll. 11–12), while insisting upon his continued happiness with desperate special pleading. If the sweepers of *Innocence* enjoy a fantasy of escape, the sweeper of *Experience* lacks even that release, which points to what Zachary Leader calls "a dominant theme of *Experience*: the blighting effect victimization has on victimizers as well as victims" (Leader 165). The state of experience also has its limitations, especially limited vision. The speaker of *Experience*'s "Holy Thursday" witnesses the rationalizations of power, yet he cannot see the radiance of the children. Indeed, his perceptions amount to abstract generalities, seeing only "Babes reduced to misery" and hearing only a "trembling cry" (ll. 3, 5).

Returning to the relationship between innocence and experience, we find that the states comment on each other: Northrop Frye writes, "The *Songs of Experience* are satires, but one of the things that they satirize is the state of innocence. They show us the butcher's knife which is waiting for the unconscious lamb. Conversely, the *Songs of Innocence* satirize the state of experience as the contrast which they present to it makes its hypocrisies more obviously shameful" (Frye 237). The satire leads, however, to stalemate rather than resolution. Experience jolts us out of the unsustainable myths of innocence—the title page, showing a boy and girl mourning dead parents, forcibly reminds us of death—yet experience also heralds distress, wrath, frustration, confusion, cynicism, selfishness, and resignation. Instead of the unrestrictive green, the landscape shrinks to a claustrophobic space of repression, as in "The GARDEN OF LOVE," where policing "Priests in black gowns were walking their rounds, / And binding with briars my joys & desires" (ll. 11–12). The simple, open affections of *Innocence* twist into shame, sadism, and masochism. The connectedness of *Innocence* disintegrates into alienation, and the plates often depict isolated figures. Frightening, punishing authorities preside over a fallen humanity, disciplined by repressive institutions and inhibitions, which equate sexuality with sin. The introductory stanza to "A Little Girl Lost" declares that *"Children of the future Age"* (l. 1) will find it hard to comprehend how *"in a former time. / Love! sweet Love! Was thought a crime"* (ll. 3–4). Leader argues that this speaker pointing toward the future is the same for *Experience*'s "Introduction," "The Little Girl Lost" (a poem separate from "A Little Girl Lost"), "Holy Thursday," and the concluding poem, "The Voice of the Ancient Bard," as well as for "The TYGER" and "LONDON." The bard promises liberation and yet, as we have seen, also misperceives, which creates the self-induced terror of "The Tyger." The boy's catechism in *Innocence*'s "The Lamb" ("Little Lamb who made thee? / Dost thou know who made thee?" [ll. 1–2]) reassures him, for he knows the answer, while the anxious speaker of *Experience*'s "The Tyger" overwhelms himself with his mounting questions about the act of creation that culminate with "Did he who made the Lamb make thee?" (l. 20). The speaker sees the world in a binary, hence limited, way. Paralyzed by the fire of his imagination rather than grasping it like the classical hero Prometheus (who gave fire to man but suffered torment from the gods for his trouble), the speaker projects those images into "forests of the night" (l. 2) outside of himself. The image of the tiger ironically deflates the speaker's fears: Seen by daylight, it is a paper tiger holding no terrors, resembling strongly the mild tiger in the plates of "The Little Girl Found," who plays nonthreateningly around Lyca. Yet this thrilling poem attracts us with its searing imagery, overpowering for the eye not yet prepared for prophetic vision, and with its questions that remain unanswerable within the state of experience. Recently Ronald Paulson has considered ways in which conservative rhetoric deployed "tyger" as a trope for feared revolutionary activity.

The speaker in "London," if not overpowered, is appalled—paled by what he "marks" in every face: "Marks of weakness, marks of woe" (l. 4). That doubling of *mark* as noun and verb suggests that he not only observes but also bears these marks. Something cloaks (covering with a pall) his sight, for those marks are the only things he sees; his perceptions are otherwise limited to hearing: the cries of adults, infants, and chimney sweeps, the sighs of soldiers and curses of harlots. The speaker prophetically blasts an entire profit-driven, hypocritical, corrupt, militaristic system and targets its institutions: The "charter'd" street and Thames (ll. 1, 2) suggests commerce—namely, the charters bestowed on companies. The cry of the chimney sweep "appalls" (shames and pales) every corrupt "blackning Church" for condoning exploitation (l. 10). The sigh of "hapless Soldiers" (l. 11) apocalyptically transforms into blood running down the "Palace walls" (l. 12) of monarchs whose lusts for empire demand human sacrifice. The "youthful Harlots' curse" (l. 14)—literal prostitution and the prostitution that is loveless marriage—blights the oxymoronic "Marriage hearse" (l. 16) with misery and disease. (That harlot is also the Roman Catholic Church, figured by religious dissenters as the whore of Babylon.) In another oxymoron, the speaker's hearing becomes visionary: "In every voice; in every ban. / The mind-forg'd manacles I hear" (ll. 7–8); he discerns in the proscriptions of institutions and authority figures the clink of self-imposed restraints. The speaker does not judge but commiserates with his fellow sufferers, and bearing those marks of weakness and woe himself, emphasized by the image of a decrepit old man led by a child, he can offer no alternate vision of healthy community, such as of "The Ecchoing Green."

Blake writes aphoristically in the third plate of *The Marriage of Heaven and Hell*, "Without Contraries is no progression." Thinking in contraries sunders mind-forged manacles; as the opening motto implies, we think not for ourselves until we undo binaries like innocence and experience. *Songs of Innocence and of Experience* simultaneously invites and frustrates inquiry in order to resist any reductive logic; thus, we uncover no key that will systematize its contraries. The poems generate ambiguities, which only multiply as we read and reread them, for we must continually grapple with the dialectical relationship of innocence and experience. Blake devised a dual text-and-image method to prevent any passive reception of the poems and to arouse the mind and senses jointly. Nonetheless, the regeneration of a fallen humanity and return of Earth that the bard in the "Introduction" vainly hoped would immediately commence appears in the concluding poem to be not far off yet not immediate. Still, a prophetic consciousness emerges that calls a "Youth of delight" to "see the opening morn, / Image of truth new born" ("The Voice of the Anciet Bard," ll. 1–3). Blake's later prophetic books will imagine that new Jerusalem.

See also "LITTLE GIRL FOUND, THE"; "NIGHT"; "POISON TREE, THE"; "SICK ROSE, THE."

## Further Reading

Blake, William. *Complete Poetry and Prose*. Edited by David Erdman. New York: Doubleday, 1988.

———. *Songs of Innocence and of Experience*. Edited by Andrew Lincoln. Princeton, N.J.: Princeton University Press, 1991.

Erdman, David V. *Blake: Prophet against Empire*. 3rd ed. New York: Dover Publications, 1991.

Frosch, Thomas R. "The Borderline of Innocence and Experience." In *Approaches to Teaching Blake's Songs of Innocence and of Experience*, edited by Robert F. Gleckner and Mark L. Greenberg, 74–79. New York: The Modern Language Association of America, 1989.

Frye, Northrop. *Fearful Symmetry: A Study of William Blake*. Princeton, N.J.: Princeton University Press, 1947.

Gleckner, Robert F., and Mark L. Greenberg. "Introduction: Teaching Blake's *Songs*." In *Approaches to Teaching Blake's Songs of Innocence and of Experience*, edited by Robert F. Gleckner and Mark L. Greenberg, x–xvi. New York: Modern Language Association of America, 1989.

Leader, Zachary. *Reading Blake's Songs*. Boston: Routledge & Kegan Paul, 1981.

Mitchell, W. J. T. "Image and Text in *Songs*." In *Approaches to Teaching Blake's Songs of Innocence and of Experience*, edited by Robert F. Gleckner and Mark L. Greenberg, 42–46. New York: Modern Language Association of America, 1989.

Paulson, Ronald. "Blake's Revolutionary Tiger." In *The Sister Arts from Hogarth to Tennyson*, edited by Richard Wendorf, 169–183. Minneapolis: University of Minnesota, 1983.

Thompson, E. P. *Witness against the Beast: William Blake and the Moral Law*. New York: New Press, 1993.

Viscomi, Joseph. "Illuminated Printing." William Blake Archive. Available online. URL: http://www.blakearchive.org/blake/. Accessed on January 29, 2009.

—Tara McGann

## "Song: To the Men of England" Percy Bysshe Shelley (1819)

This dynamic poem, written during PERCY BYSSHE SHELLEY's stay in Italy during 1819–20, is generally reckoned one of his most overtly political works. Writing to LEIGH HUNT, Shelley asked him "if you know of any bookseller who would like to publish a little volume of popular songs wholly political, and destined to awaken and direct the imagination of the reformers" (quoted in Foot 1). Given the oppressive political climate of the time, his friend was unwilling to get involved. The laws on publishing were designed to suppress all forms of "sedition" or "criminal libel," and this is perhaps why Shelley did not try harder to get his poems into the public domain. Thus, the collection was never published as Shelley intended. Only two of the poems, "Ode to Liberty" and "ODE TO THE WEST WIND," were published before Shelley's death in 1820. "Song: To the Men of England" did not appear until MARY SHELLEY published it in 1839.

Shelley was a man who, it is often suggested, felt himself to be an outsider (morally, socially, and culturally). As the literary scholar Ifor Evans has claimed, his was a "personality in revolt" (Evans 140). Shelley supported the idea of revolution. "The system of society as it exists at present must be overthrown," he once wrote (quoted in Wolfson 193). Accordingly, he approved of the execution of King Charles I in 1649 after the English Civil Wars, when Britain briefly became a republic. He also supported the FRENCH REVOLUTION and the guillotining of King Louis XVI in 1793. However, the immediate backdrop to Shelley's activism at this time was the PETERLOO MASSACRE of August 1819, at which a peaceful protest by workers had been attacked by soldiers. According to the critic Paul Foot, "Song: To the Men of England" is one of a handful of poems by Shelley that "are direct and deliberate appeals to the masses to rise up and trample their oppressors" (Foot 169). The poem (often described as an anthem) is addressed to the poverty-stricken working class who, relentlessly tyrannized and abused by the ruling class, have been ground down into apathy. The opening lines set the tone: "Men of England, wherefore plough / For the lords who lay ye low? / Wherefore weave with toil and care / The rich robes your tyrants wear?" (ll. 1–4). Shelley seems to be asking a question that is still relevant today: Who should profit from the world and its wealth? Whom does it belong to? Shelley, of course, was clear and strident in expressing his belief that the earth should belong to everyone, not just a few—in theory, at any rate—and he has been seen as a forerunner for the ideas articulated by Karl Marx later in the 19th century. Thus, he rages against the exploitation of those who work with the land: The laborers work the fields but are not allowed to keep what they sow. He likens the working classes to bees—insects that work their whole lives away so that the queen (or king) is exempt from having to do any work herself. The lines "Those ungrateful drones who would / Drain your sweat—nay, drink your blood?" (ll. 7–8) suggest there is something vampiric about them: They suck the lifeblood out of the workers, leaving them feeling weak and powerless.

While the poem can be read as a call to revolution, Shelley's attitude to the enslaved workers is sometimes difficult to fathom. He feels pity for them but is impatient with their apathy and almost scornful that that they allow themselves to be exploited by those in power. As the literary scholar Michael Scrivener has noted, the poem is unusual in its "uncompromising view on labour alienation" (Scrivener 232). While Shelley

acknowledges that the workers have their products and profits taken by the aristocracy, he urges that they take action rather than just complain about it. For Shelley the plan of action is straightforward: "Sow seed—but let no tyrant reap" and "Forge arms in your defence to bear" (ll. 21, 24) This call to arms, although defensive, encourages the workers to use physical force to defend their rights, and in the climate of the time it was a dangerous call, which could have left the poet open to charges of treason. Shelley, however, suggests that such a revolt is necessary since failure to do so will be even worse. Those who will not "shake the chains ye wrought" (l. 27) will have to put up with their "cellars, holes, and cells" (l. 25), leaving the halls that they have labored over for the benefit of others. The macabre idea that their very dwelling places are tombs (graves dug by themselves) and that they represent a kind of living death is made explicit. Some critics have suggested that Shelley, pessimistic and patronizing, is insulting the workers here. The poem's language has shifted from the softer "wherefores" in the beginning of the poem to more uncompromising monosyllabic sentences: "With plough and spade and hoe and loom, / Trace your grave, and build your tomb" (ll. 29–30). The effect is like a hammer or chisel being struck. The writer Stephen Behrendt observes that "Shelley concludes in a disturbing tone of bitter irony" (Behrendt 195). The poem's "argument," Behrendt notes, is "sceptical" about whether anything will change. Shelley, he writes, "did not consider the 'men of England' actually capable of so decisive an assertion. . . . Having presumably raised the audience's ire in the opening stanzas . . . Shelley's final lines are a calculated challenge to the audience to reject their subhuman images . . . and to assume their full status as human beings. The deluded masses fall into the habit of nursing their oppressors, literally 'giving them all they have,' rather than risk the destabilizing trauma of resisting this unjust arrangement" (196).

Critics are divided about the poem's effectiveness. Shelley seems to be an activist, but it has been suggested that he did not really know what it was like to be a worker and that his understanding of economic and political systems is naive at best. It has also been pointed out that he only intended his work to be read by a small (educated) audience, not distributed to the masses, so is his work nothing more than posturing? He was against the vote for women, so in that case he did not intend for them to rise up. According to Susan Wolfson, Shelley's "vision of social poetry retreats into a vision for a select society" (206), thereby challenging the idea that Shelley actually wanted to revolutionize society. However, in Shelley's defense, it has been pointed out that while he did little to put his ideas into practice, he was extremely forward-looking in his ideas and inspirational in the development of socialism and the challenge to capitalism.

See also "MASK OF ANARCHY, THE."

**Further Reading**

Behrendt, Stephen C. *Shelley and His Audiences.* Lincoln: University of Nebraska Press, 1989.

Clubbe, John, and Ernest J. Lovell, Jr. *English Romanticism.* DeKalb: Northern Illinois University Press, 1983.

Cox, Jeffery N. *Poetry and Politics in the Cockney School: Keats, Shelley, Hunt, and Their Circle.* Cambridge: Cambridge University Press, 1998.

Duff, David. *Romance and Revolution.* Cambridge: Cambridge University Press, 1964.

Evans, B. Ifor. *Traditions in Romanticism.* Hamden, Conn.: Archon Books, 1964.

Foot, Paul. *Red Shelley.* London: Bookmarks, 1984.

Scrivener, Michael. *Radical Shelley: The Philosophical Anarchism and Utopian Thought of Percy Bysshe Shelley.* Princeton, N.J.: Princeton University Press, 1982.

Shelly, Percy Bysshe. "A Song: Men of England." In *The Norton Anthology of English Literature,* 7th ed., vol. 2, edited by M. H. Abrams and Stephen Greenblatt, 727–728. New York: W. W. Norton, 2000.

Wolfson, Susan. *Formal Charges: The Shaping of Poetry in British Romanticism.* Stanford, Calif.: Stanford University Press, 1997.

—Peter Shaw

## "Sonnet on Seeing Miss Helen Maria Williams Weep at a Tale of Distress"
### William Wordsworth (1787)

This poem, the first published work of WILLIAM WORDSWORTH, appeared in the *European Magazine* of March 1787, when he was a 16-year-old schoolboy at Hawkshead. Wordsworth signed the poem "Axiologus," a Greek-Latin translation of his own name—literally, the "worth of words." The scenario that the poem describes is complete fiction, as Wordsworth did not meet the poet HELEN MARIA WILLIAMS until 1820. But in making Williams the subject of his sonnet, he positioned his work within a fashionable contemporary discourse of sentimental verse.

In 1786 Helen Maria Williams had published her own *Poems, in Two Volumes,* a collection which had brought acclaim from critics and fellow poets alike. Wordsworth's was just one of several poetic tributes to appear in the *European Magazine* in that year alone. He is clearly indebted to Williams in the style as well as the subject of his sonnet, which at several points echoes Williams's "To Sensibility" of 1786. Wordsworth's speaker is physically moved by the sight of Williams's tears: His blood flows "In languid streams through every thrilling vein" (l. 2), and "Life left my loaded heart" (l. 5). The speaker revels in this "dear delicious pain" of sensibility (l. 4), even the loss of selfhood that it provokes, because such suffering is a moral response, a sign of "virtue" (l. 9). Williams's "tear" (l. 9) acts as a guiding light to "cheer the wand'ring wretch" (l. 14), perhaps the speaker himself, and to guide him homeward. Wordsworth even echoes the poetic diction of Williams's own poetry: in "Life's purple tide" (l. 1) he adopts, as the scholar James Averill notes, Williams's "favourite epithet for blood" (Averill 34).

The "Sonnet" has been routinely dismissed by critics as imitative and conventional, and for Stephen Gill it is "as empty a confection as any poem could be" (Gill 31). The poem was never republished in Wordsworth's lifetime, suggesting that it did not fit the narrative that Wordsworth would construct of his own poetic development. As the critic William Richey notes, the sonnet employs the "elaborate poetic diction" that Wordsworth "would condemn in his Advertisement to *Lyrical Ballads*" (Richey 435), and its "lachrymose" sentiment has been read as at odds with the more robust humanitarian concerns of his later verse.

The "Sonnet" bears clear evidence of Wordsworth's sentimental reading, but the seeds of his later Romantic achievements are also present. The poem's title suggests that Williams herself will be the focus of the verse, but Wordsworth is interested in the effect of her suffering on the speaker himself. As Averill notes, this is typical of sentimental conventions: "the poem's complex, involuted structure reflects a sensitive mind working within a literature fascinated by emotional response" (Averill 34). But Wordsworth takes this sentimental scenario and works into it the psychological interest, the association between thought and feeling, that was to preoccupy him in later work. The "Sonnet" anticipates Wordsworth' statement in his PREFACE TO LYRICAL BALLADS (1800) that in his poetry "the feeling therein developed gives importance to the action and situation and not the action and situation to the feeling" (Wordsworth 1963, 248).

### Further Reading

Averill, James. *Wordsworth and the Poetry of Human Suffering*. London and Ithaca, N.Y.: Cornell University Press, 1980.

Gill, Stephen. *William Wordsworth: A Life*. Oxford: Clarendon Press; New York: Oxford University Press, 1989.

Richey, William. "The Rhetoric Of Sympathy in Smith and Wordsworth." *European Romantic Review* 13, no. 4 (2002): 427–443.

Wordsworth, William, and Samuel Taylor Coleridge. *Lyrical Ballads*. Edited by R. L. Brett and A. R. Jones. London: Routledge, 1988.

Wordsworth, William. *Wordsworth: Poetical Works.* Rev. ed. Edited by Thomas Hutchinson and Ernest de Selincourt. London: Oxford University Press, 1969.

—Mary Fairclough

## "Sonnet: Written in the Church-Yard at Middleton in Sussex" Charlotte Smith

(1789)

First published as the 44th poem in the 1789 edition of CHARLOTTE SMITH's collection *ELEGIAC SONNETS AND OTHER POEMS*, this poem characteristically presents the poet's alienated sensibility and the longing to escape a desolate emotional experience. The speaker is a lone wanderer in a landscape characterized by GOTHIC aggression as the sea assaults the passive, "shrinking land"

(l. 4) that cedes territory to its invader. The sea's uncontrolled power is conveyed in strong verbs such as *Drives, Tears,* and *breaks* (ll. 6–8) and the alliterated phrase *swelling surge* (l. 3). There is a sense of the SUBLIME, combining the awesome and the transgressive, as the sea breaks its permitted boundaries. This includes the bounds of sanctity, since it irreverently disrupts the "silent sabbath" (l. 8) of the church's graveyard and scatters human bones grotesquely among the shore's debris.

While the speaker of many of Smith's sonnets can be read as androgynous, this poem lends itself to a gendered reading. The speaker takes on the position of the helpless female victim of gothic literature (a genre that Smith employed in her novels, to feminist purposes), identifying with the land, which is passive before the male aggressor. The sea behaves as the gothic tyrannical male whose ego knows no boundaries. Smith makes this political by turning it into an allegory of "life's long storm" (l. 13), which assaults her, symbolically implying patriarchal oppression as the cause of her suffering. She expresses an internalized sense of profound infringement of her self.

In addition, the poet's relationship to the landscape can be read as gendered, as it is one of exclusion. She wanders secretly at night and cannot participate in the power of the scene. The critic Jacqueline Labbe suggests that such a pose symbolizes Smith's own sense of disenfranchisement, as a female, from the land (since she lost a long legal battle for her children's inheritance of her husband's estate), and more widely of female marginalization in society. In contrast with the authoritative "masculine" pose of the writer of the prospect poem, or of WILLIAM WORDSWORTH's epiphanies, in which the poet identifies with nature's power, Smith draws attention to her helplessness before a world order in which the female is "opprest" (l. 13). The alienation suggested in many of her poems is here conceptualized as victimization. As in Sonnet 5, "TO THE SOUTH DOWNS," Smith concludes with a wish to escape painful consciousness through death: With no reference to a Christian afterlife, she envies the dissolution, the "gloomy rest" (l. 14) of her fellows whose remains are dispersed on the shore.

However, the poem also demonstrates the composite poetic identity that Labbe claims for

Smith. The poet varies the Shakespearean sonnet form, retaining the four quatrains and couplet but employing an *abba* rhyme scheme instead of the usual *abab*. The speaker of the poem might be equated with the historical person of Charlotte Smith, since contemporary readers knew much of her life story. However, another speaker is heard in the marginal notes, which give factual information about the geographical setting at Middleton. This rational, detached voice counterpoints the poem's construct of the helpless female poet, suggesting that Smith is not merely pouring out emotion as poetesses were thought to do, but carefully crafting her poetic personae.

**Further Reading**

Labbe, Jacqueline. *Charlotte Smith: Romanticism, Poetry and the Culture of Gender.* Manchester, Eng.: Manchester University Press, 2003.

———. *Romantic Visualities: Landscape, Gender, and Romanticism.* London: Macmillan, 1998.

—Rebecca Styler

## Sorrows of Young Werther, The Johann Wolfgang von Goethe (1774)

Published anonymously in 1774 (revised 1787), and first translated into English in 1779, *The Sorrows of Young Werther* was JOHANN WOLFGANG VON GOETHE's most successful work, ultimately becoming a best seller all over Europe. Clearly a product of the 18th-century cult of sentimentalism (*Empfindsamkeit*), it touched a nerve, captured the mood of a generation, and proved highly influential for the emergent phenomenon of Romanticism. Germany was struck by an epidemic of Werther fever, especially among young men who felt an affinity with Werther's emotionality and love of nature. The novel spawned not only many literary imitations Europe-wide but also a fashion craze (for yellow waistcoats and hose and blue jackets), and apparently a number of copycat suicides.

The novel tells the story of a hypersensitive young man, Werther, who falls desperately but hopelessly in love with a young woman, Lotte, who is promised to another. For a while, Werther goes away to work in another town, but after being slighted by an aristocrat there, he returns to the town where Lotte and her now-husband, Albert, live. Utterly at the mercy of his overwhelming feelings for Lotte, Werther perceives death as his only escape, and he therefore borrows Albert's pistols and commits suicide.

Essentially EPISTOLARY FICTION, the novel presents only Werther's letters (from May 1771 until December 1772) to his friend Wilhelm. Werther is thus far more a monologue from an increasingly paranoid protagonist. This narrative perspective allows us as readers exclusive access to Werther's decline, and we are unavoidably drawn in as the protagonist's letters become more impassioned and eventually deteriorate to frenzied notes. As the critic Martin Swales notes, "we find ourselves buttonholed, cajoled, and harried because Werther seems to be addressing each of us individually. We may despise him or admire him—perhaps, more accurately, we do both. But we cannot remain indifferent" (Swales 8). Only when Werther has reached the point of no return and his disintegration is manifest even in his language does the editor step in dramatically to take control of the narrative. Although basically invisible for most of the novel, the editor does taint our vision from the outset with his prefatory note emphasizing that this is the story of "poor Werther." Naturally, this technique also both lures us into and distances us from the subsequent story.

Whatever we feel about Werther, we cannot fail to perceive the unmitigated deterioration of his tortured soul. It is simply all-encompassing in his relationships with art, literature, religion, love, and nature. Initially abundant and verdant, nature soon becomes associated with inevitable death; Homer is replaced by the elegiac lamentations of Ossian, and Werther's solipsism is blatant when he just cannot grasp why he cannot control Lotte's feelings.

It is interesting to note that Goethe himself had a cautious and rather ambiguous relationship to *Werther*. Choosing never to read from it in public, 50 years later he revealed that *Werther* consisted of "nothing but rockets" (quoted in Eckermann 559). Part of the power of the novel is, however, this very ambiguity: Is *Werther* is a dreadful warning about the dangers of excessive emotion or the very apotheosis of such passion?

## Further Reading

Blackall, Eric A. *Goethe and the Novel.* Ithaca, New York: Cornell University Press, 1976.

Eckermann, Johann Peter. *Gespräche mit Goethe in den letzten Jahren seines Lebens.* Edited by Otto Schönberger. Stuttgart: Reclam, 1998.

Goethe, Johann Wolfgang von. *Goethe: The Collected Works.* 12 vols. Edited by Christopher Middleton, et al. Translated by Michael Hamburger, et al. Princeton, N.J.: Princeton University Press, 1994–95.

———. *The Sorrows of Young Werther.* Translated by Michael Hulse. London: Penguin Red Classics, 2006.

Lillyman, W. J., ed. *Goethe's Narrative Fiction. The Irvine Symposium.* Berlin and New York: de Gruyter, 1983.

Sharpe, Lesley, ed. *The Cambridge Companion to Goethe.* Cambridge: Cambridge University Press, 2002.

Swales, Martin. *Goethe: The Sorrows of Young Werther.* Cambridge: Cambridge University Press, 1987.

—Shona Allan

## Southey, Robert (1774–1843)

Born in Bristol, England, on August 12, 1774, Robert Southey was one of the leading men of letters during the Romantic period in England. Aside from his poetry, he was also a prolific historian, letter writer, editor, translator, and biographer. Above all, he is perhaps best remembered as a leading figure in the so-called LAKE SCHOOL, along with WILLIAM WORDSWORTH and SAMUEL TAYLOR COLERIDGE, and as the apologist poet laureate of England from 1813 until his death. In addition to his grand epics and narrative poems, such as *Joan of Arc* (1796) and *Madoc* (1805), his most familiar contribution to literary history might be "The Story of the Three Bears"—printed in his book *The Doctor* (1837)—the original to the much-adapted Goldilocks story.

As a young man, Southey wrote extensively and displayed a strong and ambitious mind. After his early education at Westminster School in London, he entered Oxford University with a view to a career in the church. But like many young people of his generation, Southey's religious beliefs were unsettled by his reading of modern authors and works, such as Voltaire, JEAN-JACQUES ROUSSEAU, Edward Gibbon, and JOHANN WOLFGANG VON GOETHE's notorious *The SORROWS OF YOUNG WERTHER* (1774). Along with Coleridge, whom he had met in 1794, Southey devised the scheme of pantisocracy—the establishment of an idealist settlement in North America (see "PANTISOCRACY"). He had been reading WILLIAM GODWIN's recently published treatise on political justice and found its faith in the triumph of a society based on reason highly appealing. However, the young ideologues lacked funds, and as time went on, they became increasingly disenchanted with the project and with each other.

After a brief sojourn in Portugal, Southey embarked in earnest on his career as a professional man of letters. Ballads were popular, so he wrote them (see "MARY, THE MAID OF THE INN"). He also wrote poetry for the liberal *Monthly Magazine* and enjoyed the favorable reception that his *Joan of Arc* received. Encouraged by WALTER SAVAGE LANDOR's financial support, he produced *The Curse of Kehama* (1810), a romance in irregular verse that told a story of resilient endurance against the backdrop of Hinduism. This work was published two years after the outbreak of the Peninsular War, by which time early euphoria was increasingly displaced by a pervasive political unease in Britain. In this regard, Southey was eager to participate in a new and ambitious periodical, the *Quarterly Review.* Although deeply suspicious of the periodical's links with the government, he felt the public ramifications of war deserved urgent consideration.

In 1813 Southey became England's poet laureate—an appointment he regarded as an opportunity to offer much-needed leadership to a nation threatened by infighting and political uncertainty. For many skeptical observers it established him finally as part of the Tory establishment, in contradiction to his youthful radicalism. Outwardly, many of his odes dealt with occasional subjects, such as a royal marriage, but nevertheless he hammered home a political point when possible, usually from a conservative vantage. He lambasted the idea of negotiating with NAPOLEON BONAPARTE—for some a freedom fighter, for others a tyrant—and warned the nation against the factionalism and sedition advocated in the radical press.

Nonetheless, Southey's laureate career reached an unhappy climax with his misjudged *A Vision of Judgement* (1821), an elaborate poem that describes the triumphant entry into heaven of the late King George III. Somewhat rashly, Southey associated political opposition with satanism, and in the preface outlined what he pejoratively dubbed the emergent "satanic school" of poetry. LORD BYRON took this personally and, in his own hugely entertaining and evidently more popular *Vision of Judgment* (1821), offered his own interpretation of the events that was far less flattering to the late and notoriously mad king.

At this time, Southey faced numerous personal tragedies. His 14-year-old daughter, Isabel, died in 1826, and his wife suffered mental distress before she died in 1837. Despite the support of his new wife, Caroline Anne Bowles, he spent the last years of his life in a state of senility, a shadow of the former youth of enthusiasm and ideas. He died on March 21, 1843, with his reputation then, as now, uncertain. Attacks on his political apostasy from Byron, PERCY BYSHHE SHELLEY, and WILLIAM HAZLITT have long influenced our inherited ideas about this complicated man of letters.

See also "BATTLE OF BLENHEIM, THE"; "RUINED COTTAGE, THE."

**Further Reading**

Bolton, Carol. *Writing the Empire: Robert Southey and Romantic Colonialism.* London: Pickering & Chatto, 2007.

Curry, Kenneth. *Robert Southey: A Reference Guide.* Boston: G. K. Hall, 1977.

Pratt, Lynda. "Robert Southey, Writing and Romanticism." *Romanticism on the Net* 32–33 (2003–2004), Available online. URL: http://www.erudit.org/revue/ron/2003/v/n32-33/009255ar.html. Accessed on June 24, 2009.

———, ed. *Robert Southey and the Contexts of English Romanticism.* Aldershot, Eng.: Ashgate, 2006.

Speck, W. A. *Robert Southey: Entire Man of Letters.* New Haven, Conn.: Yale University Press, 2006.

Storey, Mark. *Robert Southey: A Life.* Oxford: Oxford University Press, 1997.

—Daniel Cook

## "Spider and the Fly, The: An Apologue. A New Version of an Old Story" Mary Howitt (1829)

MARY HOWITT's juvenile ballad "The Spider and the Fly" was originally published in *The New Year's Gift* in 1829. In contrast to later work—such as Howitt's novel *An Art Student in Munich* (1853), which was criticized in *John Bull* (June 18, 1853) for its mode of false sentiment—this poem's republication in book form in *Sketches of Natural History; or, Songs of Animal Life* (1834) made her name a household word with subsequent editions and reprints. As T. Nelson and Sons put it in their "Publishers' Note" to the 1873 edition, Howitt was "everywhere recognized as the Children's Favourite—as one of their happiest and most successful teachers; setting before them the highest truths and most graceful fancies with all the embellishment of a polished yet simple diction" (Howitt 1873, v).

The crafty spider and the self-satisfied fly are recurrent animal motifs in Romantic poetry published in women's magazines such as *The Lady's Monthly Museum* (1798–1806) and *La Belle Assemblée* (1806–68). They are invariably used in cautionary tales to dramatize the conflict between duty and pleasure, industry and idleness, freedom and safety (as in Howitt's "The Seasons: Summer"). Yet, Howitt's reworking of their symbolic significance differs, as the poem's subtitle, "A New Version of an Old Story," suggests, in terms of the way in which her poetic rhetoric imbues masculine craftiness—conveying both industry and deceit—with sexual meaning.

Howitt's poem "The Spider and the Fly" has seven stanzas, in the course of which the "cunning" Spider uses varied ploys to seduce the "sweet" Fly into his parlour (stanzas 1–5). Its opening line, "'Will you walk into my parlour?' said the Spider to the Fly," has become, in the author Bessie Rayner Belloc's words, a "classic phrase" (Bellac 83). It testifies to how the Spider's craft of sexual seduction is developed through a rhetorical pattern of question and answer, as a didactic means to caution the "dear little children" against the dangers of female vanity, which is revealed to be a greater vice than curiosity (stanzas 6–7).

In Howitt's "An Essay on Man—In Four Epistles," the Spider is given as an example of the most sensuous insects (Howitt "Essay," 29). In the first five stanzas of her poem, the Spider's masculinity is encoded in his physical dominance of space and manipulation of the Fly's gaze. While the space closes up on the "spying" Fly as the Spider extends his invitation from the parlor (stanza 1) to the bedroom (stanza 2) and the pantry (stanza 3), her gaze turns away from the unknown and unfamiliar territory to which her curiosity and affection for commodities have led her upon the looking glass in order to see, but not recognize in the mirror, her real enemy—not the flattering Spider but her own vanity (stanza 4).

Although the Fly is not completely ignorant of sexuality, which is associated with entrapment (stanza 1) and death (stanza 2), some sexual knowledge proves to be an inadequate safeguard against the Spider's sensuality: "'Will you rest upon my little bed?' said the Spider to the Fly. / . . . And if you like to rest awhile, I'll snugly tuck you in!'" (stanza 3). It is only in the last two stanzas that it is made evident that the Fly's innocence does not derive from ignorance but from her power to recognize the lures that await her so as to resist temptation and seduction.

While the Fly is given as an example of avoidance in stanza 6, children are directly warned against the deceptive power of language that prevents them seeing things as they are in stanza 7—that the Spider's parlour is not "pretty" but a "dismal den" and that the Fly is not "witty" and "wise" but foolish and "silly." This is an idea that Howitt also uses in her poem "The True Story of Web-Spinner," whose illustration by Giacomelli draws attention to how the Spider's web, in which the Fly and many others like her are caught, exceeds its representation to become one with the poem on the page.

What makes the seventh and final stanza of "The Spider and the Fly" stand out is not so much the didactic tone for which Howitt is so well known. (It is not coincidental, for instance, that the advertisement of Howitt's *Tales in Verse* in *Peter Parley's Annual* depicts a woman with a pointing finger telling a story to a boy.) Rather, it is the shift in the poem's rhythmic pattern, which, by becoming more prosaic, encourages its implied readers—the "dear little children"—to protect themselves from "hearing his [the Spider's] wily, flattering words" by making their senses dumb: "And now, dear little children, who may this story read, / To idle, silly flattering words, I pray you, ne'er give heed: / Unto an evil counsellor, close heart and ear and eye, / And take a lesson from this tale, of the Spider and the Fly." Howitt privileges the printed word that children may read over the Spider's verbal rhetoric of seduction. Her poem thus differs from the use of the spider and the fly motif to warn against the detrimental impact of literature on female imagination during the Romantic period. For example, in another poem from the *Sketches,* "Fable X. The Spider and the Bee," the mother in the poem, who is concerned by her Lydia's reading of fraudulent books, argues that such "inferior art" weaves its "snare" like a spider around their foolish female readers to become the replicas of the foolish characters they create: "art like nature forms the fly" (Howitt 1873, 24).

The innovative way in which Howitt makes the exposition of the seductive power of language the center of her poetics is illustrative to her "genius and steady industry" as a literary women through which, according to Bessie Rayner Belloc, she changed the landscape of British poetry (Belloc 79–80, 86). The new version of the old story of bygone innocence that Howitt's "The Spider and the Fly" would tell in the Victorian period is that of the fallen woman, whose only options were either death or prostitution.

## Further Reading

Armine. "The Apollonian Wreath. The Bee and the Fly. A Fable." *The Lady's Monthly Museum* (June 1, 1807): 280–282.

Belloc, Bessie Rayner. *In a Walled Garden.* London: Ward and Downey, 1895.

Howitt, Mary. "An Essay on Man.—In Four Epistles. To H. ST. John, Lord Bolingbroke. Epistle I. Of the Nature and State of Man with Respect to the Universe." *La Belle Assemblée* no. 40–48 (date unknown): 7–30.

———. "Howitt's Tales in Verse." *Peter Parley's Annual* (date unknown): 376.

———. "Poetry, Original and Select." *La Belle Assemblée* no. 23 (October 1, 1807): 218.

———. "The Seasons: Summer." *La Belle Assemblée* nos. 40–47 (date unknown): 160–78.

———. *Sketches of Natural History; or, Songs of Animal Life.* Written by Mary Howitt, and Illustrated . . . by H. Giacomelli. London: T. Nelson and Sons, 1873.

———. "The Spider and the Bee." *La Belle Assemblée* nos. 48–54. (date unknown): 24.

*John Bull* review. "An Art Student in Munich. By Anna Mary Howitt. In Two Vols.—London: Longmans, 1853." *John Bull* no. 1697 (June 18, 1853).

—Kyriaki Hadjiafxendi

## Spirit of the Age, The; or, Contemporary Portraits  William Hazlitt (1825)

*The Spirit of the Age* by WILLIAM HAZLITT consists of 25 character sketches of prominent Romantic figures. Hazlitt's representative figures include poets, printers, essayists, natural philosophers, judges, abolitionists, reformers, and more, with some in combined entries: LORD BYRON, SIR WALTER SCOTT, WILLIAM GODWIN, SAMUEL TAYLOR COLERIDGE, ROBERT SOUTHEY, WILLIAM WORDSWORTH, Jeremy Bentham, WILLIAM COBBETT, LEIGH HUNT and THOMAS MOORE, Elia (CHARLES LAMB) and Geoffrey Crayon (Washington Irving), FRANCIS JEFFREY, Sheridan Knowles, Thomas Campbell and GEORGE CRABBE, George Canning, the Reverend Edward Irving, Thomas Malthus, Sir James Mackintosh, William Gifford, Horne Took, Lord Brougham and Sir Francis Burdett, and Lord Eldon and William Wilberforce. The book started as a series of character sketches titled "Spirits of the Age" in the *New Monthly Magazine*. Such series were common at the turn of the 19th century, when modern celebrity culture was emerging: Coleridge, for example, published a series of "Sonnets on Eminent Characters" in the *Morning Chronicle* in the 1790s. John Stuart Mill wrote in his essay "The Spirit of the Age" (1831) that the notion of a spirit of the age, or zeitgeist, was "the dominant idea" of the age. Recent work by James Chandler recognizes this dominant idea as a symptom of the emergence of modern historicist consciousness, by which people were beginning to recognize their contemporaneous culture as discreet from past cultures and stages of civilization. They represented their contemporaneous culture with representative figures and their productions, whereas previous generations represented history as the doings of kings, queens, nobles, and militaries.

In 1826 Hazlitt defined "the spirit of the age" in his book *The Plain Speaker* as "the progress of intellectual refinement, warring with our natural infirmities," but many critics have noted that the zeitgeist articulated in *The Spirit of the Age* is definitively paradoxical and amorphous, if it is definable at all. Hazlitt's abstract sense of the spirit of the age is best considered as a *form* of character without any stable content: Every individual character is paradoxical, internally contradictory, dynamic, and individuated in contrast to other characters; and yet every character, however different from the next, is nevertheless "a pure emanation of the Spirit of the Age," as Hazlitt describes Wordsworth. The characters embody the age, but for writers like Hazlitt, character could never be fully or stably embodied because it was an abstraction that aggregated many features, feelings, memories, and thoughts that were always changing. By definition, character exceeded full representation, and so the spirit of the age exceeds each of its representative individuals. *The Spirit of the Age* is significant for Romanticism for its documentation of important historical figures, then, but also as evidence of a specifically Romantic method of representing culture as a character, a paradoxical identity representative of the aggregate life of contemporary people.

### Further Reading

Chandler, James. *England in 1819: The Politics of Literary Culture and the Case of Romantic Historicism.* Chicago: Chicago University Press, 1998.

Hazlitt, William. *Selected Writings.* Edited by Ian Cook. Oxford: Oxford University Press, 1999.

Kinnaird, John. *William Hazlitt: Critic of Power.* New York: Columbia University Press, 1978.

Mill, John Stuart. *The Spirit of the Age.* Edited by Frederick von Hayek. Chicago: Chicago University Press, 1942.

Mulvihill, James, "Character and Culture in Hazlitt's *Spirit of the Age.*" *Nineteenth-Century Literature* 45, no. 3 (1990): 281–299.

Park, Roy. *Hazlitt and the Spirit of the Age.* Oxford: Oxford University Press, 1971.

Story, Patrick. "Hazlitt's Definition of the Spirit of the Age." *Wordsworth Circle* 6 (1975): 97–108.

*The Plain Speaker.* Edited by Duncan Wu. Oxford: Blackwell, 1998.

—Jonathan Farina

## Staël, Mme. Anne-Louise-Germaine de
### (1766–1817)

Anne-Louise-Germaine Necker was born in Paris on April 22, 1766, the daughter of Jacques Necker, future finance minister to Louis XVI, and his wife, Suzanne. She was, however, no ordinary Frenchwoman, being of Calvinist Swiss descent, and she enjoyed being present at her mother's salons from an early age. A *salon* was the name given to regular gatherings of literary, political, and artistic peoples and often hosted by fashionable, leisured, women. Married at 19 to Baron Eric Magnus de Staël-Holstein, Staël soon set up her own salon in Paris, a tradition she continued when in exile at the family home in Coppet, Switzerland. She traveled widely in Europe and thus came into contact with many important writers and politicians, from Jean de Rond d'Alembert, Denis Diderot, and Benjamin Constant de Rebecque to LORD BYRON, JOHANN WOLFGANG VON GOETHE, FRIEDRICH VON SCHILLER, and August and FRIEDRICH VON SCHLEGEL.

Not surprisingly, Staël began writing early. The author of two novels—*Delphine* (1802) and *Corinne ou l'Italie* (1807)—as well as various novellas, plays, and literary treatises, she was immensely successful. According to the biographer Mario Fairweather, she was "the most remarkable and the most famous woman of her time, whose work was read all over Europe and who influenced many of her contemporary writers, including Byron" (Fairweather 1). "Essai sur les fictions" (1795) was translated into German by Goethe, and Schiller published extracts from "De l'influence des passions sur le bonheur des individus et des nations" ("The role of the Passions in the happiness of individuals and nations" [1796]) in *Die Horen*. In "De la littérature dans ses rapports avec les institutions sociales" ("On Literature" 1800), Staël radically suggested that literature should reflect the zeitgeist and first made a distinction between the literatures of the North and South, a distinction which formed the basis of her differentiation between Romanticism and Classicism. This distinction is investigated further in "De l'Allemagne" ("On Germany"; 1813), arguably her best and most influential work.

Despite its length, "De l'Allemagne" was an unprecedented success at introducing, promoting, and disseminating certain German Romantic ideas and cultural trends. Yet it almost did not make it into print at all: In 1810 NAPOLEON BONAPARTE ordered Staël, one of his fiercest critics, into exile again—she had already spent 1803–06 in exile—and the manuscript pulped. One copy survived, though, and was published simultaneously in English and French by the British editor John Murray. This chequered history and Staël's rather public private life (her outspokenness and somewhat public affairs) may have helped it to sell out in three days.

"De l'Allemagne" has nonetheless not escaped criticism—variously for its lack of originality, for its subjectivity and (lack of) femininity, for being too influenced by August Wilhelm von Schlegel, and for its glaring mistakes, mistranslations, simplifications and exaggerations. Yet, for all its debatable faults, it was a huge achievement: in a pre-Internet age, it made something exotic and otherwise inaccessible available to an eager public.

Although Staël certainly transcended geographical and intellectual boundaries—before 1813, there had never been anything quite like "De l'Allemagne"—she has often been underestimated and even neglected. By the time she died in Paris on July 14, 1817, however, she had indelibly marked the zeitgeist and played a pivotal role in the development of European Romanticism. Perhaps the duc de Berry had a point when he suggested that, at that time, there were "three great powers in Europe: England, Russia and Mme de Staël" (quoted in Furst 56).

### Further Reading

Balayé, Simone. *Madame de Staël: Lumières et Liberté.* Paris: Klincksieck, 1979.

Berger, Morroe. *Madame de Staël on Politics, Literature and National Character.* London: Sidgwick & Jackson, 1964.

Fairweather, Maria. *Madame de Staël.* New York: Carroll and Graf, 2005.

Furst, Lilian R. *The Contours of European Romanticism*. London and Basingstoke: Macmillan, 1979.

Isbell, John Claiborne. *The Birth of European Romanticism: Truth and Propaganda in Staël's 'De l'Allemagne,' 1810–1813*. Cambridge: Cambridge University Press, 1994.

Porter, Roy, and Mikulas Teich, ed. *Romanticism in National Context*. Cambridge: Cambridge University Press, 1988.

Staël, Germaine de. *Major Writings of Germaine de Staël*. Translated and introduced by Vivian Folkenflik. New York: Columbia University Press, 1987.

Winegarten, Renee. *Mme de Staël*. Leamington Spa, Eng.: Berg, 1985.

—Shona Allan

## Stagnelius, Erik Johan (1793–1823)

Erik Johan Stagnelius has long been recognized as an influential Swedish Romantic poet and dramatist. Central to his work is the exploration of metaphysical questions concerning the human condition and the nature of things.

Born on October 14, 1793, into a clergyman's family, in Gärdslösa, Öland, Stagnelius received his elementary education at home. After graduating from Uppsala University in 1814, he worked as a clerk in Stockholm. He often took long leaves of absence from work due to his poor health, traveling home to his family during such periods. Stagnelius apparently lived the life of a recluse, at least while in Stockholm. Although little is known about his life, the dearth of factual evidence has not prevented biographers from speculations of his alleged addiction to opium and alcohol. He died in Stockholm on April 3, 1823.

Although Stagnelius's production of dramas and epic verse is extensive, it is his lyric poetry that has received the most attention. This has shaped the image of him as a Romantic who, in formally exquisite verse colored by erotic desire, expressed the artist's inability to touch the object of his longing and the accompanying feelings of torment and anguish. Less consideration has been given to Stagnelius's satires, which cast the poet in a quite different light.

A feature of other poems is religion. Particularly dominant is the poet's despair over the lot of the heavenly soul that is trapped in its earthly prison, and death is seen as the soul's way back to its divine home. Other traits of this religious mysticism that are common themes in Stagnelius's poetry include the fall of the soul from the absolute, the dualism of the spiritual and material worlds, the opposition of good and evil, and love as a way to salvation.

While Stagnelius's poems often deal with matters of religious conversion, there is also a constant tension between religious asceticism and sensuality. Desire is sometimes more a matter of the poet's urge for poetic inspiration than a carnal drift. Women in the poems are often symbols of love, invariably advocating a chaste love and a general attitude of privation—one of the recurring themes in Stagnelius's work. "The Mystery of the Sighs" ("Suckarnes mystèr," 1821) is famous for the lines in which he describes human life as governed by the two principles of "the power to demand" and "the compulsion to deprive."

During his lifetime, Stagnelius published only one epic poem, *Vladimir the Great* (*Wladimir den store*, 1817); a collection of religious poems, *Lilies in Sharon* (*Liljor i Saron*, 1821); and one play, *The Bacchantes* (*Backanterna*, 1822). His fame came posthumously when his collected works, containing vast unpublished material, appeared in 1824–26.

### Further Reading

Henrikson, Paula. *Dramatikern Stagnelius*. Stockholm/Stehag: Symposion, 2004.

Lysell, Roland. *Erik Johan Stagnelius. Det absoluta begäret och själens historia*. Stockholm/Stehag: Symposion, 1993.

Stagnelius, Erik Johan. *Samlade skrifter af Erik Johan Stagnelius* Edited by Fredrik Böök. Stockholm: Bonnier, 1911–1919.

—Ljubica Miočević

## "Stanzas on the Death of Mrs. Hemans"
### Letitia Elizabeth Landon (1835)

This poem was first published in the *New Monthly Magazine* (May–August 1835), two months after the death of FELICIA HEMANS, and was based on a poem by Hemans entitled "Bring Flowers." LETITIA

ELIZABETH LANDON's poem appears as a conventional elegy for a fellow poet, urging that flowers be brought to honor her, but it expresses tension regarding competing versions of the woman poet. Hemans was reviewed as a "feminine" writer, decorous if rather sentimental, and certainly not straining against her proper place. Landon references this assessment by commenting on Hemans's life—"So pure, so sweet" (l. 13)—and her poetry—"yet subdued and sweet" (l. 38). Although the speaker briefly acknowledges Heman's incorporation of voices "from far and foreign lands" (l. 33), the emphasis is on connecting Hemans with the domestic and the everyday, repeating the word *common* in two stanzas. The poem also refers to Hemans's womanly modestly: "Did thou not tremble at thy fame / And loathe its bitter prize" (ll. 73–4). However, there is also a hint here that such fame is false, for it derives from a misapprehension of the woman poet.

In stanzas 6 and 7, the poem's tone shifts, addressing Hemans's sorrows. This could be a veiled allusion to Hemans's abandonment by her husband, but the speaker seems more concerned to make a connection between female poetic power and unhappiness: "A fated doom is hers who stands / The priestess of the shrine" (ll. 51–2). From this point on, Landon appears to be projecting her feelings onto the dead Hemans, bemoaning "the soul's fine chords . . . too highly strung" (ll. 58–9) and the "heart . . . too sensitive" (l. 61). The speaker emphasizes the bond between herself and Hemans, then claims that Hemans had been neither loved nor appreciated rightly. Finally, instead of finding solace in the peace that Hemans has found in death, the speaker turns attention to her own unassuaged pain: "But the quick tears are in my eyes, / And I can write no more" (ll. 111–2). The poem, under the guise of honoring Hemans, rejects the model of the safe, domestic woman poet exemplified by her and implicitly criticizes reviewers who have created this false image. Landon posits another type of female poet, a being who responds strongly to sensations and suffers intensely from lack of true sympathy.

The connection between suffering and poetry can be found in male Romantic poets from WILLIAM WORDSWORTH to JOHN KEATS. Suffering is viewed as part of the creative process: The poet experiences strong emotions and then transcends them through processing them in poetry. Such sensitivity to emotional stimuli is not sentimental, however, but rather an indication of sensibility, the capacity to feel strongly. Whereas Hemans was classified a sentimental poetess (the diminutive form signifying the inferiority of her work to that of male peers), Landon insists on the sensible capacity of the female poet. The elegy, with its focus on loss, grief, and consolation, is particularly suitable for exploring the relationship between gender, SENSIBILITY, and poetry. Landon uses the form and her subject to critique gender bias in constructions of the poet.

## Further Reading

Labbe, Jacqueline. "Re-Making Memory, Posterity, and the Memorial Poem." In *Memory and Memorials 1789–1914: Literary and Cultural Perspectives,* edited by Matthew Campbell, Jacqueline Labbe, and Sally Shuttleworth, 132–146. London: Routledge, 2000.

Leighton, Angela. *Victorian Woman Poets: Writing against the Heart.* Charlottesville: University Press of Virginia, 1992.

Morrison, Lucy. "Effusive Elegies or Catty Critic: Letitia Elizabeth Landon on Felicia Hemans." *Romanticism on the Net* 45 (February 2007). Available online. URL: http://www.erudit.org/revue/ron/2007/v/n45/015820ar.html. Accessed on December 5, 2008.

—Terri Doughty

## "Stanzas Written under Aeolus's Harp"
### Amelia Alderson Opie  (1795, 1802)

Amelia Alderson (later AMELIA ALDERSON OPIE) first published this poem in the *Cabinet* in 1795 as "To Eolus's Harp" (Feldman 532). A revised version, retitled "Stanzas Written under Aeolus's Harp," appeared in her collection entitled *Poems* (1802). As its titles indicate, the poem's principal trope is the Aeolian harp, a stringed instrument that produces haunting sounds when exposed to the wind. A familiar image in contemporary poetry, the instrument is also the subject of such works as James Thomson's "An Ode on Aeolus's Harp" (1748), SAMUEL TAYLOR COLERIDGE's "The EOLIAN HARP" (1795), and MARY ROBINSON's "To the Aeolian Harp" (1796).

Opie's Aeolian harp poem consists of 11 decasyllabic quatrains rhyming *abab*. In the opening stanzas, the poetic persona beckons her audience to gather around to listen to the harp: "Come, ye whose hearts the tyrant sorrows wound; / Come, ye whose breasts the tyrant passions tear, / And seek this harp, . . . In whose still-varying sound / Each woe its own appropriate plaint may hear. / Solemn and slow yon murmuring cadence rolls, / Till on the attentive ear it dies away, . . . / To your fond griefs responsive, ye, whose souls / O'er loved lost friends regret's sad tribute pay" (ll. 1–8). Anaphora gives a ceremonious, incantatory quality to the first two lines. Throughout, the poet's language mimics the sounds of the harp. Repeated words, alliteration, and enjambment replicate the instrument's harmonic drone. Ellipses in some lines imitate the fading away of sound, while slant rhymes and irregularities in meter suggest the manner in which the harp's "tones / In wild disorder strike upon the ear" (ll. 13–14). Describing the enthralling power of the instrument, the poet observes that even "the gay, the giddy and the vain" become "[s]ilent and breathless" when they listen (ll. 17, 19). In stanza 6, Opie emphasizes the ethereal, almost supernatural quality of the music by likening the rapt listeners to the ancient crowds that encircled the sacred statue of Memnon at Thebes (which at daybreak each morning emitted mysterious harp-like sounds).

The word *But* at the beginning of stanza 7 signals a turn in the poem: The harp does not simply respond to auditors' "sorrows" and "passions" (ll. 1, 2), the poet suggests; its "trembling strings" (l. 25) awaken the imagination. Fancy is personified as an "enchantress" (l. 26) who, upon hearing the harp, waves her wand, causing a "band of airy shapes" to materialize (l. 28). In the final two stanzas, the speaker addresses the harp itself as a source of poetic inspiration: "O breathing instrument! be ever near / While to the pensive muse my vows I pay" (ll. 37–38), for "Thy faintest breath can Fancy's pinions play" (keep the wings of fancy in motion) (l. 40). The poem concludes with an explicit comparison between the harp's music and the speaker's own poems, which implies that the harp is not merely a source of inspiration but also a figure for (lyric) poetry: The poet has been inspired by the lyre and hopes that her poems ("my

plaintive lays") will in like manner inspire and "enchant" others (l. 44).

Opie was an outspoken advocate of republicanism and abolitionism, and many of her novels, poems, and other literary works give expression to her progressive political beliefs. She composed "Stanzas Written under Aeolus's Harp" during the period when she was "most closely associated with British Radicals" WILLIAM GODWIN, MARY WOLLSTONECRAFT, and THOMAS HOLCRAFT (Eberle 72). While superficially the poem does not engage with contemporary politics, the repetition of the word *tyrant* in the first two lines and the shift, over the course of the poem, from images of passive listening to those of active creation hint that the poetic persona's "plaintive lays" may well be calls for social change and revolution. Interpreted this way, the work may be compared to the radical poet PERCY BYSSHE SHELLEY's "ODE TO THE WEST WIND" (1820), in which the speaker asks his muse, the West Wind, to make him its lyre (l. 57), so that he may spread his revolutionary ideas "among mankind" (l. 67).

**Further Reading**

Eberle, Roxanne. "'Tales of Truth?': Amelia Opie's Antislavery Poetics." In *Romanticism and Women Poets: Opening the Doors of Reception*, edited by Harriet Kramer Linkin and Stephen C. Behrendt, 71–98. Lexington: University of Kentucky Press, 1999.

Feldman, Paula R., ed. *British Women Poets of the Romantic Era: An Anthology.* Baltimore and London: Johns Hopkins University Press, 1997.

Opie, Amelia Alderson. "Stanzas Written under Aeolus's Harp." In *Poems*, 131–134. London: T. N. Longman and O. Rees, 1802.

Shelley, Percy Bysshe. "Ode to the West Wind." In *Shelley's Poetry and Prose,* 2nd ed., edited by Donald H. Reiman and Neil Fraistat, 298–301. New York and London: W. W. Norton & Co., 2002.

—Natalie Neill

# Stendhal (Henri Beyle, Marie-Henri Beyle)
## (1783–1842)

Stendhal was the pseudonym of the French writer Henri Beyle (or Marie-Henri Beyle), who is best known for his novels The RED AND THE BLACK (1830) and The CHARTERHOUSE OF PARMA (1839), about young men caught up in lives of passion, crime, and intrigue. He took an active role in the cultural disputes in France in the 1820s between classicism and Romanticism, taking the side of the latter, but he was too much his own man to be a reliable part of any movement or party, and some commentators have connected him more with the later movements of realism and naturalism and with 18th-century rationalism.

Born in Grenoble on January 23, 1783, just a few years before the FRENCH REVOLUTION, Beyle was devastated by the death of his mother when he was only seven. He never got along with his father and hated the aunt who acted as his stepmother, as well as the priest who was his tutor. Feeling that he was suffering under tyrannical rule within his family, he rejoiced at the execution of Louis XVI and became associated with liberal and radical causes. Some commentators say he was always a rebel or an adolescent at heart, though he is also described as becoming more conservative in his later years.

Beyle escaped from his family and what he considered the overly provincial life of Grenoble by winning a mathematics prize and a place at the École Polytechnique in Paris in 1799. Once in the capital, however, he ignored mathematics, hoping to establish himself as a writer. He had dreams of becoming a famous dramatic poet, but his attempts at writing plays in verse came to nothing, and his later successes came in almost all other spheres of writing except drama and poetry.

Thanks to a cousin, the would-be writer obtained a military commission in 1800 and later held various government positions. Over the next 14 years he served on various missions and expeditions, including NAPOLEON BONAPARTE's ill-fated invasion of Russia in 1812. But his most important expedition, in personal terms, was one accompanying Napoleon's army to Italy in 1800. He fell in love with Italy—its operas, its painting, its women, and the passion he saw there, in contrast to the coldness, greed, and hypocrisy he saw in his native France. He was especially taken with Milan, where he would live from 1814 to 1821; on his tombstone his epitaph describes him as a Milanese.

Despite being such an Italophile, Beyle chose the Germanic name Stendhal for himself, deriving it from the name of the Prussian town of Stendal, the birthplace of Johann Winckelmann, an art critic with whom he differed.

The fall of Napoleon meant the end of Stendhal's government career for a decade and a half. He could find no position under the restored Bourbon monarchy, and only after the Revolution of 1830 ousted the Bourbons in favour of Louis-Philippe did he once again obtain a government position, as consul to the small Italian town of Civitavecchia, in the Papal States. He was unable, however, to return to his beloved Milan, because the Austrian authorities who regained power there after Napoleon's fall regarded him as a dangerous revolutionary or Bonapartist.

Between 1815 and 1830 Stendhal made something of a name for himself with books on music (The Lives of Haydn, Mozart, and Metastasio) and painting (History of Painting in Italy). He also published a travel book (Rome, Naples, Florence) and an essay on the nature of love ("De l'amour"), the latter containing a celebrated description of love as a sort of crystallization. In the 1820s he published two pamphlets entitled Racine and Shakespeare, criticizing attachment to convention and tradition and calling for literature suited to the modern day. He famously contrasted Romanticism and classicism by saying that Romanticism consisted of literature that gives pleasure to people today, while classicism was literature that gave pleasure to their great-grandparents.

Stendhal became known as a brilliant conversationalist in the salons of Paris and engaged in many love affairs and unsuccessful would-be affairs. One commentator said that his two professions were women and writing, and his writings, including his first novel, Armance (1827), as well as The Red and the Black and The Charterhouse of Parma, are notable for their analysis of obsessive love.

Stendhal's analytical approach to passion, along with his disagreements with other Romantics, such as VICTOR HUGO, over whether art should focus on the ordinary and even the ugly (Hugo's view) or on the beautiful (Stendhal's) have led some commentators to see him as remaining closer in some ways to the views of the 18th-century

French Enlightenment than to Romanticism, and some have compared him to LORD BYRON, whom he met in Milan in 1816, another writer who has been seen as being in the Romantic movement but not entirely of it.

Stendhal was notorious for not finishing his works; he left several unfinished novels and plays, and worked on a life of Napoleon that he never completed. On the other hand, he dashed off *The Charterhouse of Parma* in less than two months. He never married or raised a family, and he did not rise far in government or society. Nor did he achieve great fame as a writer, though Honoré de Balzac praised *The Charterhouse of Parma* extravagantly. Stendhal predicted that he would not be appreciated for years after his death, until 1880 or the 20th century, and indeed he attracted much more attention after he died of a stroke on March 23, 1842, than he did in his lifetime. He is well regarded now as an important novelist, though whether he was a true Romantic is still open to discussion.

**Further Reading**

Gutwirth, Marcel. *Stendhal.* New York: Twayne, 1971.

Keates, Jonathan. *Stendhal.* London: Sinclair-Stevenson, 1994.

Stendhal. *Stendhal: Reading of The Red and the Black and The Charterhouse of Parma.* Edited by Roger Pearson. London: Longman, 1994.

Richardson, Joanna. *Stendhal.* London: Gollancz, 1974.

Wakefield, D. F. *Stendhal: The Promise of Happiness.* Bedford: Newstead Press, 1984.

Wood, Michael. *Stendhal.* London: Elek, 1971.

—Sheldon Goldfarb

## "Stepping Westward" William Wordsworth (1807)

Civilization throughout Europe during the late 18th century was very much affected by not only the Industrial Revolution and FRENCH REVOLUTION, but also the AMERICAN REVOLUTION. Politics was in confusion, so people turned toward their own country and their instincts. It was at this time that the Lake District and the LAKE SCHOOL poets came into their own. The term *Lake Poets*

was used by LORD BYRON at the beginning of his satirical poem *DON JUAN* (1819–24), and it was an unmitigated attack on them. However, this dedication was never published by Byron during his lifetime, although a couple of verses were published anonymously. The Lake Poets included WILLIAM WORDSWORTH, whose contribution to English literature is enduring. He is remembered now more than ROBERT SOUTHEY—SAMUEL TAYLOR COLERIDGE's brother-in-law, who became poet laureate in 1814. Wordsworth's profuse output, varying in quality, appeals to the heart and to the imagination—though it was not always a safe escape from the realities of the time.

Although not describing the Lake District, "Stepping Westward" contains everything that is typical of Wordsworth—attention to details of nature and mention of "sky," "lake," "ground," and "spiritual right." The setting of this poem in rhyming couplets is a solitary, wild place in Scotland. Roger Sharrock notes that whilst on a tour of the country in 1803 Wordsworth and his sister Dorothy were walking by the side of Loch Ketterine. The sun had just set, the sky was magnificent, and they came across two ("well-dressed") women, one of whom posed the rhetorical question "What, you are stepping westward?" (Sharrock, 132) This is the first line of the poem, and Wordsworth refers to the greeting in the title and in the third line of the second stanza. He uses the word *destiny* in the first and second verses; it is first "wildish" (l. 2) and then "heavenly" (l. 12). We can see that nature is winning him over. Inspired by the greeting in the first two stanzas, he goes back to a description of it in the third, finishing with a reference to eternal journeying through the world and symbolically through life. The last stanza, containing 10 lines as compared with the eight lines of the first and second ones, lends weight and finality to the story and its message.

**Further Reading**

Abrams, M. H., ed. *Wordsworth: A Collection of Critical Essays.* Englewood Cliffs, N.J.: Prentice-Hall, 1972.

Gill, Stephen. *William Wordsworth: A Life.* Oxford: Oxford University Press, 1990.

Gilpin, George H., ed. *Critical Essays on William Wordsworth.* Boston: G. K. Hall, 1990.

Hartman, Geoffrey. *Wordsworth's Poetry 1787–1814.* New Haven, Conn.: Yale University Press, 1971.

Wordsworth, William. *Selected Poems of William Wordsworth.* Edited by Roger Sharrock. Oxford: Heinemann, 1958.

———. *The Major Works: Including The Prelude.* Edited by Stephen Gill. Oxford: Oxford University Press, 2000.

—Isabel Heald

## "Storm-Beat Maid, The"  Joanna Baillie  (1790)

"The Storm-Beat Maid (Somewhat after the style of our old English Ballads)" appeared in JOANNA BAILLIE's first collection of *Poems.* As its subtitle suggests, "The Storm-Beat Maid" takes part in the 18th-century ballad revival. Instigated by the publication of Thomas Percy's *Reliques of Ancient English Poetry* (1765), the renewal of interest in traditional forms of literature found expression in such texts as WILLIAM WORDSWORTH and SAMUEL TAYLOR COLERIDGE's *Lyrical Ballads* (1798) and SIR WALTER SCOTT's MINSTRELSY OF THE SCOTTISH BORDER (1802).

"The Storm Beat Maid," with its sub-title "Somewhat after the style of our old English Ballads," was published at a time when Baillie had not yet achieved success as a playwright but was experimenting with the composition of new or revised adaptations of old English and Scottish songs. The poem ended up in her collection entitled *POEMS; wherein it is attempted to described CERTAIN VIEWS OF NATURE and of RUSTIC MANNERS; and also, to point out, in some circumstances, the different influence which the same circumstances produce on different characters.* (1790). The collection was not very successful, but its contents are significant as examples of the kind of work Wordsworth and Coleridge would later attempt. Baillie sought to capture what she termed "true, unsophisticated representations of nature" (Baillie 1840, v) and wanted to use a simpler, less ornate language by which to do so. She decided that the rural lives of the country village in which she lived were equally valid as subject matter, and she counseled: "Let one simple trait of the human heart, one expression of passion genuine and true

to nature, be introduced, and it will stand forth alone in the boldness of reality, whilst the false and unnatural around it, fades away upon every side, like the rising exhalations of the morning" (Baillie 1999, 7).

In other ways, Baillie's tale of love betrayed is a conventional ballad in many respects: The story is told chiefly through action and dialogue, and the theme is tragic (as described by J. A. Cuddon). Composed in ballad meter, it consists of 41 quatrains of alternating iambic tetrameter and trimeter lines, rhyming *abab.* Characteristic of literary ballads, the poem has an abrupt beginning: "All shrouded in the winter snow, / The maiden held her way; / Nor chilly winds that roughly blow, / Nor dark could her stay" (ll. 1–4). The metrically incomplete (catalectic) fourth line conveys the urgency of the eponymous maid's journey. The dropped syllable also suggests her troubled state of mind, which is confirmed when she pauses to weep (l. 8). The cause of her distress, however, remains a mystery for most of the poem. Supernatural imagery betrays the influence of GOTHIC ballads like GOTTFRIED AUGUST BÜRGER's "Lenore" (1773) and fosters an eerie, elegiac tone. The word "shrouded" in the opening line "suggests the death-like nature of the maid's journey" (Breen 153, n.1). Later, she is likened to a "ghost that thro' the gloom to stray, / Wakes with the midnight bell" (ll. 19–20), and when morning comes and she passes wraithlike though a village, old men shake their heads and "[wish] her spirit peace" (l. 36). The maid's "wav'ring pace; / Like spring's inconstant blast" (ll. 38–39) gives an early intimation of her madness. The critic Jonathan Wordsworth notes that despite her otherworldliness she is often "described in terms of the natural world" (Wordsworth xii).

In the 11th stanza, the maid arrives at her destination, a castle where a wedding feast for the young master is in progress. An unbidden wedding guest, she prefigures the title character in Coleridge's later ballad, "The RIME OF THE ANCIENT MARINER." Unlike the uncanny and loquacious mariner, however, Baillie's maid is ever silent. A "gentle page" (l. 69) takes pity on the poor girl and interrupts the feast to announce her arrival. In a series of nature similes, he compares her face to a dewy morn (ll. 89–90), her skin to a "sheeted torn" (a smooth, ice-covered lake) (l. 91), and her body to a bending willow (l. 94). Leaving his guests and jealous bride, the bridegroom hastens to the fair, wild maiden. Although she appears not to recognize the young man, she mutters his name repeatedly (ll. 131–132). Her madness is now apparent, and its cause finally revealed: Her heart has been broken because her love, the master of the castle, has married another. In the final quatrains, the remorseful bridegroom speaks. He curses himself for marrying for money and then, in a tragic echo of the wedding vows he has just made to his new wife, promises never again to forsake his true love, the storm-beat maid: "'I'll share the cold blast on the heath, / I'll share thy wants and pains: / Nor friend nor foe, nor life nor death, / Shall ever make us twain'" (ll. 161–164). Yet, as the jarring slant rhyme suggests, it is too late, for his marriage has already taken place and the poor maid has lost her mind.

Principally a dramatist, Baillie is best known for her series of *Plays on the Passions* (1798–1812). With its strong dramatic element and emphasis on feeling, "The Storm-Beat Maid" anticipates the plays. Due also to Baillie's reliance on natural imagery and use of everyday language, the *Poems* exerted an important influence on Wordsworth and Coleridge's more famous collection. As Jonathan Wordsworth observes of "The Storm-Beat Maid" in particular, "Baillie has written in 1790 what is by any standards a lyrical ballad" (xiii).

## Further Reading

Baillie, Joanna. Preface to *Fugitive Verses*. London: Moxon, 1840. v–xii.

———. *Selected Poems of Joanna Baillie*. Edited by Jennifer Breen. Manchester, Eng.: Manchester University Press, 1999.

Baillie, Joanna. "The Storm-Beat Maid." In *Poems; Wherein It Is Attempted to Describe Certain Views of Nature and of Rustic Manners*. London: J. Johnson, 1790, 97–107.

Cuddon, J. A. "Ballad." In *The Penguin Dictionary of Literary Terms and Literary Theory*. 4th ed. London: Penguin, 1999.

Slagle, Judith. *Joanna Baillie: A Literary Life*. Madison, N.J.: Fairleigh Dickinson University Press, 2002.

Wordsworth, Jonathan. Introduction to *Joanna Baillie: Poems, 1790*, by Joanna Baillie, i–x. Oxford and New York: Woodstock Books, 1994.

—Natalie Neill

## sublime

The sublime (from the Latin *sublimis*, [looking up from] under the lintel, high, lofty, elevated) holds a central place in Romantic aesthetic debates. The concept first appeared as a rhetorical term in the Greek treatise *Peri Hypsous (On the Sublime)*, purportedly written by Longinus in the first century A.D. After the French poet Nicolas Boileau-Despréaux (1636–1711) translated the treatise into French in 1674, the sublime was increasingly used to describe great thoughts, elevated feelings, and lofty images and figures in rhetorical diction. In the 18th-century, English and Scottish writers such as Joseph Addison (1672–1719), DAVID HUME (1711–76), John Dennis (1657–1734), and Anthony Ashley Cooper, 3rd earl of Shaftesbury (1671–1713), became interested in the sublime as an effect of overpowering emotive immediacy triggered by the experience of grand nature. Addison, Dennis, and Shaftesbury had all traveled across the Alps at the turn of the 18th century, and they later wrote about their feelings of awe and terror and the impressions of infinite vastness and greatness that the sight of the mountains had inspired in them.

EDMUND BURKE's highly influential *A PHILOSOPHICAL ENQUIRY INTO THE ORIGIN OF OUR IDEAS OF THE SUBLIME AND BEAUTIFUL* (1757) was the first study that distinguished between the aesthetic principles of the sublime and the beautiful. Burke (1729–97) associates the latter with "smallness," "delicacy," and "smoothness." The sublime, conversely, depends on "vastness," "obscurity," and "magnificence." While the contemplation of the beautiful, according to Burke, stimulates love and pleasure in the beholder, the sublime calls forth admiration, reverence, respect, and astonishment: "Whatever is fitted in any sort to excite the ideas of pain, and danger, that is to say, whatever is in any sort terrible, or is conversant about terrible objects, or operates in a manner analogous to terror, is a source of the *sublime*; that is, it is productive of the strongest emotion which the mind is capable of feeling" (Burke 39). He refers to the sublimity of oceans and mountains and cites JOHN MILTON's Satan in *Paradise Lost,* the mouth of hell in Virgil's *Aeneid,* and the Book of Job as examples for the literary sublime.

Burke's study influenced the German philosopher Immanuel Kant's engagement with the sublime in *Observations on the Feelings of the Beautiful and Sublime* (1764) and *Critique of Judgement* (1790). Kant (1724–1804) locates his discussion of the sublime within an investigation of the relationship between the faculties of imagination and reason. The experience of the sublime, according to Kant, first overwhelms the mind and then allows reason, upon recovering its balance, to perceive transcendental ideas of infinity and the absolute. Encounters between the gifted individual and sublime nature play a pivotal role in the works of WILLIAM WORDSWORTH, SAMUEL TAYLOR COLERIDGE, WILLIAM BLAKE, LORD BYRON, PERCY BYSSHE SHELLEY, and many other Romantic writers.

Although individual treatments of the concept differ vastly, the sublime is generally understood to provide an intuition of the transcendental grounds of existence and to challenge the conventions of literary representation. Burke's notion of sublime terror has also had a profound impact on the GOTHIC novel. The sublime has traditionally been associated with uncontrollable excess and the SENSIBILITY of the male poet. However, critics have begun to revise these positions by suggesting that the concept of the sublime was actually developed to regulate excess and by drawing attention to the highly complex gender ideologies implicated in the idea of the sublime.

**Further Reading**

Burke, Edmund. *A Philosophical Enquiry into the Origins of our Ideas of the Sublime and Beautiful.* Edited by James T. Boulton. London: Routledge & Kegan Paul, 1958.

Hancock, Stephen. *The Romantic Sublime and Middle-Class Subjectivity in the Victorian Novel.* New York and London: Routledge, 2005.

Kant, Immanuel. *Critique of Judgement.* Translated by James Creed Meredith. Oxford: Clarendon, 1952.

———. *Observations on the Feelings of the Beautiful and Sublime.* Translated by John T. Goldwaith. Berkeley: University of California Press, 1960.

Longinus, Dionysius. *On the Sublime.* Trans. William Smith. London: J. Watts, 1739.

Mellor, Anne. *Romanticism and Gender.* New York: Routledge, 1993.

Trott, Nicola. "The Picturesque, the Beautiful and the Sublime." In *A Companion to Romanticism,* edited by Duncan Wu, 72–90. Oxford: Blackwell, 1999.

Weiskel, Thomas. *The Romantic Sublime: Studies in the Structure and Psychology of Transcendence.* Baltimore and London: Johns Hopkins University Press, 1976.

Weisman, Karen A. "Provocaton and Person-Hood: Romanticism in Extremis." *European Romantic Review* 9, no. 2 (1998): 177–186.

—Katharina Boehm

## "Suggested by the Proposed Kendal and Windermere Railway" William Wordsworth (1844)

By 1844 WILLIAM WORDSWORTH (1770–1850) was an elderly man, seen by some to be out of touch with the modern era. He regarded nature as a living, animated force in danger of being overtaken by INDUSTRIALISM and believed that nature should be appreciated for its own sake, and not as a resource to be exploited by moneymakers. His fears about political tyranny were thus replaced by fears about the tyranny of the factory and of technology. Wordsworth was also protective of the Lake District in Cumbria, the source of so much of his inspiration. In 1844 the proposed Kendal and Windermere rail line threatened to violate the area, and the thought of hordes of tourists filled him with anxiety. In the first line of this poem he demands angrily: "Is there no nook of English ground secure from rash assault?"

Windermere, as the name suggests, is named after the famous Lake Windermere—the longest lake in England (12 miles long and 1 mile wide). Originally, Windermere was a tiny village named Birthwaite until the arrival of the railway, when the Kendal and Windermere Railway Company named the train station as Windermere to make it sound more appealing to tourists. The village soon began to expand thanks to a rash of building, including hotels, villas, shops—all designed to cater for the new influx of visitors. In 1844 Wordsworth's response to this was a press campaign against the proposed railway line. He wrote a series of poems and letters to the *Morning Post* soliciting the support of the public and lobbying members of Parliament and the government department responsible, the Board of Trade. In his first letter to the *Morning Post* (October 16, 1844), however, he misjudged the mood of the times. He claimed that as a nonindustrial area, the Lake District did not need a railway and then tried to overturn the much-vaunted argument that the railway was a force for good because it made the Lake District accessible to all classes of society. Wordsworth argued that members of the working class would not have the ability to appreciate the "beauty" and "character of seclusion and retirement" that the Lakes offered: "a vivid perception of romantic scenery is neither inherent in mankind, nor a necessary consequence of a comprehensive education." Furthermore: "Rocks and mountains, torrents and widespread waters, and all those features of nature which go to the composition of such scenes as this part of England is distinguished for, cannot, in their finer relations, to the human mind be comprehended, even very imperfectly conceived, without processes of culture or opportunities of observation in some degree habitual." He finished by suggesting that hordes of tourists would destroy the very sights they had come to see, and he urged: "Let then the beauty be undisfigured and the retirement unviolated" (Wordsworth 1970, 156).

This first letter was not well received. Wordsworth's attitude came across as snobbish and unnecessarily elitist. In a bid to salvage the situation, he followed it up with a second letter (December 9, 1844) in which he tried to explain—albeit in more measured terms—that the appreciation of nature is something was a gradually acquired taste. Above all, the Lakes needed to be protected. They were "temples of Nature, temples built by the Almighty, which have still higher claim to be left un-violated" (162). He finished the letter by pointing out that his were not self-inter-

ested motives: "I have now done with the subject. The time of my life at which I have arrived may, I trust, if nothing else will guard me from the imputation of having written from any selfish interests, or from fear of disturbance which a railway might cause to myself." He added: "If gratitude for what repose and quiet in a district hitherto, for the most part, not disfigured but beautified by human hands, have done for me through the course of a long life, and hope that others might hereafter be benefited in the same manner and in the same country, *be* selfishness, then, indeed, but not otherwise, I plead guilty to the charge" (165).

The sonnet "Suggested by the Proposed Kendal and Windermere Railway" is further expression of Wordsworth's frustration. "Must," he asks, the "Schemes of retirement sown / In youth, and 'mid the busy world kept pure" now "perish"? (ll. 2–4). "[R]andom" arguments about the greater good ("false utilitarian lure," l. 7) are thrown at him, to make him betray the "paternal fields" (l. 8) that have been his home and inspiration for so long. As he has done throughout his career, the poet invokes nature: "Baffle the threat, bright scene, from Orrest head / Given to the pausing traveller's rapturous glance / Plead for thy peace thou beautiful romance / Of nature" (ll. 9–12). Orrest Head is a famous vantage point high above the village which provides magnificent views of Lake Windermere. Perhaps, Wordsworth seems to suggest, if those in positions of power could see this sight, they might be moved to think again. If this does not work "and, if human hearts be dead" (l. 12), then more is needed: "Speak, passing winds," he urges, "ye torrents, with your strong / And constant voice, protest against the wrong!" (ll. 13–14).

This poem, then, can be read in the context of Wordsworth's reactions to the industrial and PICTURESQUE trespass on the landscape—the same landscape that has been his main object of worship and constant companion since earliest youth. In it we see traces of the sentiments that characterize many of Wordsworth's better-known poems (reverence for nature and nostalgia for a way of life under threat, a belief that the poet can and should champion unpopular causes). However, it has also been suggested that the poem has a special relevance to the 21st century. Wordsworth had some supporters, but as the author James Mulvihill notes, he—like other champions of ecology—was also "representing a minority, [and] he speaks with both a sense of his argument's limited popular authority, overriding sense of its rightness notwithstanding, and a desire to extend this authority as possible into the public sphere" (Mulvihill 311). For James McKusick, such writing is an example of how important lessons can be gleaned from "[a] re-examination of the environmental concerns of the English Romantic period" (McKusick 111). Wordsworth's anxieties are not so different from current "fears about environmental pollution" (110). Along with SAMUEL TAYLOR COLERIDGE, JOHN CLARE, and WILLIAM BLAKE, he saw the necessity in reestablishing "a vital, sustainable relationship between humankind and the fragile planet on which we live" (McKusick 110).

## Further Reading

Fry, David. "The First Locomotives." The Victorian Web. Available online. URL: http://www.victorianweb.org/technology/railway1.html. Accessed on March 30, 2009.

McCracken, David. Wordsworth and the Lakes District: A Guide to the Poems and Their Place. New York: Oxford University Press, 1984.

McKusick, James. Green Writing: Romanticism and Ecology. New York: St. Martin's, 2000.

Mulvihill, James. Consuming Nature: Wordsworth and the Kendal and Windermere Railway Controversy. Modern Language Quarterly 56, no. 3 (1995): 305–326.

Newsome, David. The Victorian World Picture. New Brunswick, N.J.: Rutgers University Press, 1997.

Simmons, Jack. The Victorian Railway. New York: Thames and Hudson, 1991.

Spence, Jeffrey. "The Social Effects of Victorian Railways." The Victorian Web. Available online. URL: http://www.victorianweb.org/technology/railway3.html. Accessed on March 30, 2009.

Thomas, Keith. Man and the Natural World: Changing Attitudes in England, 1500–1800. New York: Oxford University Press, 1983.

Wordsworth, Dorothy. The Grasmere Journal. Edited by Jonathan Wordsworth. New York: Henry Holt and Company, 1987.

Wordsworth, William. Complete Poems. London: Wordsworth, 1995.

———. Wordsworth's Guide to the Lakes. 5th ed. Edited by Ernest de Selincourt. London: Oxford University Press, 1970.

—Jane Browning

## "Summer Evening's Meditation, A"
### ("Hymn XI")  Anna Laetitia Barbauld  (1773)

Appearing as the capstone to her first collection of Poems (1773), this 128-line blank-verse meditation is ANNA LAETITIA BARBAULD's major contribution to the 18th-century "night thoughts" tradition epitomized by Edward Young's The Complaint; or, Night Thoughts on Life, Death, and Immortality (1742–45). This tradition emphasized the poet's sensibility to the SUBLIME mysteries of silence and darkness along with a yearning to communicate larger metaphysical realities. It thus laid the groundwork for such central Romantic lyrics as SAMUEL TAYLOR COLERIDGE's "FROST AT MIDNIGHT" (1798) and JOHN KEATS's "ODE TO A NIGHTINGALE" (1819).

In 1773 Barbauld was living with her family in the renowned Dissenting academy at Warrington in Cheshire, where she had acquired a superb education, and such poems as "A Summer Evening's Meditation," along with "Corsica" and "Address to the Deity," instantly established her reputation as one of the "Nine Living Muses of Great Britain" (according to Richard Samuel's widely regarded painting of 1779). Though this poem is neoclassical in diction and allusion (with its decorous gestures toward "Dian's bright crescent" [l. 7] and the "Hesperian gardens of the west" [l. 16]), its blank verse and heavy enjambement recall the work of JOHN MILTON and James Thomson's The Seasons (1726–30), and it looks forward to WILLIAM WORDSWORTH's The PRELUDE. The speaker's deliberate self-positioning out-of-doors in the silent darkness (where "but a scatter'd leaf, which rustles thro' / The thick-wove foliage" [ll. 33–34] is the only sound to "break the midnight air" [l. 35]) is also reminiscent of Anne Finch's "Nocturnal Reverie" (1713).

However, the poem's most important influence is "Night Ninth" of Young's Night Thoughts, one line of which forms the epigraph ("One sun by day, by night ten thousand shine"). As in Young's poem, the "dead of midnight is the noon of thought, / And wisdom mounts her zenith with the stars" (ll. 41–42). Like Young, Barbauld takes the reader on a sublime imaginative voyage, designed to inspire awe and faith, outward into the cosmos—first through the solar system, then on to the stars "of elder beam" (l. 75), and then beyond to the "dread confines of eternal night" (l. 84). Here Barbauld shows the influence of cutting-edge Enlightenment science in her willingness to imagine "embryo systems and unkindled suns / Sleep[ing] in the womb of chaos" (ll. 87–88). Unlike Young, however, and typical of the late-18th-century Unitarian theology that had shed its gloomier roots in Calvinism, Barbauld does not use her night poem to participate in the memento mori of the "graveyard school" of poets (who included young, THOMAS GRAY, and THOMAS CHATTERTON, among others), but instead calls in her coda on the "gentler voice" of God that "whispers comfort to the swelling heart" (ll. 100–101). This warmly affective tone of devotion marks the poem's affinities with the religious enthusiasm of her age that similarly inspired the young Coleridge in such poems as "Religious Musings" (1796).

Barbauld's Unitarian emphasis on the benevolence of God also distinguished her widely influential *Hymns in Prose for Children* (1781), in which "A Summer Evening's Meditation" reappears as "Hymn XI." Here, recast in the soothing cadences of the biblical Psalms, Barbauld's poem, in which the contemplation of nature leads to an experience of the divine, reached countless children throughout the 19th century.

## Further Reading

Barbauld, Anna Letitia. *Anna Laetitia Barbauld: Selected Poetry and Prose.* Edited by William McCarthy and Elizabeth Kraft. Peterborough, Ont.: Broadview Press, 2002.

McCarthy, William. *Anna Laetita Barbauld: Voice of the Enlightenment.* Baltimore, Md.: John Hopkins University Press, 2008.

Mee, Jon. *Romanticism, Enthusiasm, and Regulation: Poetics and Policing of Culture in the Romantic Period.* Oxford: Oxford University Press, 2003.

Miller, Christopher R. *The Invention of Evening: Perception and Time in Romantic Poetry.* Cambridge: Cambridge University Press, 2006

White, Daniel E. *Early Romanticism and Religious Dissent.* Cambridge: Cambridge University Press, 2006

—Robert Lapp

## Swing riots (1830)

Though the so-called Swing riots occurred at the very end of the Romantic period, they are important for the way they expose a telling gap between the Romantic idealization of the rural landscape and the harsh realities of life among the lowest class of agrarian laborers. The riots, sweeping through the southeast of England in autumn 1830, were the agrarian equivalent of the Luddite machine-breaking actions in the new factory towns, and they created the same shock of reactionary repression in the government at Westminster as the PETERLOO MASSACRE in 1819. Nevertheless, the Swing riots were also part of a larger series of events in the early 1830s that finally created the conditions for such historic measures as the REFORM ACT of 1832 and the Poor Law Amendment Act of 1834.

During the Swing riots, thousands of unemployed agricultural laborers in the southeastern counties of England, driven to desperation by high prices, falling wages, and the advent of threshing machines that were eliminating their jobs, engaged in well-organized, extensive acts of rioting, destruction of machinery, and incendiarism (in particular the nocturnal torching of hay ricks, creating fires that could be seen for miles). These riots were named after the mythical "Captain Swing" who "signed" the rioters' many petitions for higher wages, better benefits for the poor, and the destruction of the new threshing machines. At the local level, as the historian Peter Jones points out, the riots actually succeeded in creating change, with many parishes negotiating increased benefits to the poor and wages. At the national level, however, they caused a severe reaction based on the mistaken notion that the riots were part of a larger pattern of radical revolt that included the July Revolution in France.

Two literary representations of the riots stand out: MARY RUSSELL MITFORD's tale "The Incendiary," in her 1832 collection *Our Village,* and the final chapters of John Galt's political novel *The Member* (1831). Mitford's tale is remarkable for its turn from the otherwise idealizing tendencies of her rural vignettes that had made her a sentimental favorite among readers of the *Lady's Magazine.* Injecting a note of almost GOTHIC terror into her description of "that terrible time," she writes that women of the gentry "tasted of fear, the bitterest cup that an imaginative woman can taste, in all its agonizing varieties" (Mitford ). Her tale, however, elides the political issues by having the "incendiary" turn out to be the young lady of the estate (rather than the disaffected young schoolmaster, who at first seems to have joined the rioters), the fire being set accidentally during a lovers' tryst. John Galt, meanwhile, engages the political issues head-on in his slyly satirical novel. The first-person narrator is Archibald Jobbery, a blithely corrupt Tory member of Parliament who is actually mistaken for "Captain Swing" and briefly arrested, cleverly complicat-

ing the novel's political thrust. Moreover, though a Tory himself, Galt engages his effete narrator in a conversation with (once again) the local schoolmaster, Mr. Diphthong, whose astute analysis of the rioters' grievances accords almost exactly with Peter Jones's recent definitive treatment of this event.

**Further Reading**

Galt, John. *The Member* and *The Radical.* Edinburgh: Canongate Classics, 1975.

Edwards, P. D. *Idyllic Realism from Mary Russell Mitford to Hardy.* London: MacMillan, 1988.

Jones, Peter. "Swing, Speenhamland and Rural Social Relations: The 'Moral Economy' of the English Crowd in the Nineteenth Century." *Social History* 32, no. 2 (August 2007): 271–290.

Mitford, Mary Russell. "The Incendiary." In *Our Village: Sketches of Rural Character and Scenery.* Vol. 5. London: Whittaker, Treacher & Co., 1832. 5–23.

—Robert Lapp

# T

*Tale of Mystery, A* **Thomas Holcroft** (1802)
Thomas Holcroft's *A Tale of Mystery, A Melo-Drame* was performed at Covent Garden Theatre on November 13, 1802. It was a runaway success, and since then it has been credited as the first example of melodrama—a genre characterized by its extreme situations and expressions of emotion—to be performed in England. The play tells the story of Francisco, attacked and left for dead by his villainous brother, Romaldi. As a result of this attack, Francisco loses the power of speech. His long-lost daughter Selina is also the object of Romaldi's malice. *A Tale of Mystery* relates their struggle to reveal Romaldi's crimes without demanding retribution; it ends with a climactic confrontation between the three characters.

The subtitle "A Melo-Drame" does not just refer to the play's sensational plot. Holcroft's source was *Coelina ou l'enfant du mystère* (Coelina, or the child of mystery), by Guilbert de Pixérécourt, which exemplified a new genre that had evolved in France after the FRENCH REVOLUTION. Melodrama combined sentimental plots with musical passages and mime. In France the political resonance of melodrama was conservative, but it was a mixed genre, and in this combination of elements, Holcroft saw the potential for articulating radical views. The alterations he made to his source demonstrate his belief that the theater was the most powerful medium for spreading principles of truth and justice.

Holcroft makes language a central concern of his work. The theater historian Jane Moody notes that he "expunges much of the play's original dia-logue, and substitutes the silent dramaturgy of pantomime" (Moody 90). Francisco's dumbness is a formidable obstacle to his obtaining justice and represents the political censorship Holcroft seeks to criticize. But Francisco's speechlessness is given greater "moral power" than Romaldi's duplicitous words. As Moody notes, "rhetorical skill and linguistic power tend to connote duplicity and deceit" which "the poor and the wronged struggle to unravel" (88). Holcroft makes "the poor and the wronged" the moral center of his play, adding a scene in which Fiametta, a housekeeper, defies her master by demanding mercy for Francisco.

In Pixérécourt's play the Romaldi figure is finally captured by police, but Holcroft displays little faith in the law, and he has Romaldi removed by "archers" whose status is unclear. Religious belief is also problematized. As Romaldi flees, Holcroft removes the appeals to God that Pixérécourt has the character utter. The critic Simon Shepherd notes that instead of presenting "man in an unproblematic relationship to an assumed order of justice centred outside of himself," Holcroft makes Romaldi "tormented by his own mind" (Shepherd 509). The staging of the climactic finale further complicates notions of righteous punishment. It is a wordless spectacle in which Romaldi, Francisco, and Selina all plead for mercy. The audience is encouraged to pity Romaldi; as Moody notes, Holcroft "resists spectators' desire for moral judgements" (Moody 91).

Holcroft found a powerful medium for his political ideals in melodrama. As the critic Philip

Cox notes, it was "a form that could speak directly to the 'lower-class' audience he wished to reach but that . . . could be used to address in a serious manner issues of individual and social justice" (Cox xix). But as the 19th century progressed, melodrama became divorced from more "literary" dramatic forms, contributing to the critical neglect of Holcroft's work from which it has only recently recovered.

### Further Reading

Cox, Philip. *Reading Adaptations. Novels and Verse Narratives on the Stage.* Manchester: Manchester University Press, 2000.

Holcroft, Thomas. *The Novels and Selected Plays of Thomas Holcroft.* Vol. 5. Edited by W. M. Verhoeven. London: Pickering & Chatto, 2007.

Moody, Jane. *Illegitimate Theatre in London, 1770–1840.* Cambridge and New York: Cambridge University Press, 2000.

Shepherd, Simon. "Melodrama as Avant-Garde: Enacting a New Subjectivity." *Textual Practice* 10, no. 3 (1996):. 507–522.

—Mary Fairclough

## "Tam o' Shanter: A Tale"  Robert Burns
(1790)

Considered one of ROBERT BURNS's finest poems, "Tam o' Shanter" was written in November 1790 after a deal the poet struck with the artist and antiquarian Francis Grose. Following his two previous books on England and Wales, the latter aimed at writing a book of old tales for Scotland. Burns suggested that he should include a drawing of Alloway Kirk, a church located in the poet's hometown and associated in his imagination with the witch tales that Betty Davidson, one of his mother's cousins, used to tell him as a child. Grose welcomed the idea as long as Burns would give him a poem as a commentary for his illustration. Written in a day at Ellisland, the complete version of the poem was sent to Francis Grose on December 1, 1790. First published on March 18, 1791, in the *Edinburgh Herald*, the poem appeared a month later, in April, as footnote to the account of Alloway Kirk in the second volume of Grose's *Antiquities of Scotland*. It was included in Burns's own Edinburgh edition of his *Poems* on February 16, 1793.

Burns reinvents the threatened folk heritage and uses it in a "tale"—literally, an imaginative story—about a tail, a pun intended by the poet. The epigraph, a distorted quotation from Gawin Douglas's *Eneados*, a vernacular translation of the Roman poet Virgil's *Aeneid*, sets a reading frame for the whole poem. Burns's poetic strategy consists of following the literary tradition set by Virgil's Hades, Homer's *Odyssey*, and transferring it onto the Scottish stage; hence the allusion to Brownies and Bogillis. This childish language also reveals his parodic intention in the vein of 17th-century poet Alexander Pope's *The Rape of Lock* or *The Dunciad*.

"Tam o' Shanter" is characterized by its feeling of rapid movement induced by its mixture of Scots and English and its tetrametric rhyming couplets mimicking the rhythm of the ballad. The protagonist Tam is the epitome of speed as he swiftly changes places and crosses borders. Burns takes up the key image of the bridge ("key-stane," l. 69) used to describe human life in Joseph Addison's essay "Vision of Mirza" in order to convey universality. "Tam o' Shanter" functions as a bridge between languages, cultures, and histories.

The poem opens on a Scottish setting and immortalizes the alcoholic conviviality of a public house in the town of Ayr. Tam is presented as the archetypal social drinker wheeling around taverns to collect his intoxicating nectar; hence the recurrent image of the bee (ll. 55, 193) to convey the pleasures of a comforting honey-like drink. The male community ("we," ll. 5, 7; "our," l. 10) is opposed to the female society embodied by Tam's wife. Remaining offstage and confined home, Kate is depicted as a "sulky sullen dame" (l. 10). The alliteration of *s* and *l* sounds stresses her unwelcoming appearance, while the pun on "gathering" (l. 11) links Kate to Shakespeare's Katherina in *The Taming of the Shrew*. Like Odysseus, Tam has to win home to his untamed Penelope. Kate's harangue sounds like a medieval flyting (a dispute or exchange of personal abuse in verse form): "thou was a skellum, / A blethering, blustering, drunken bellum;" (ll. 19–20). "Kate's bl . . . bl . . . bl . . . is the characteristic noise of blabber," insists Robert Crawford in *Burns and Cultural Authority* (16). Women are gently mocked in the poem: Kate's prophetic warning (ll. 29–32, 201–204)—couched in indirect speech, and therefore weakened—proves wrong as Tam wins over his female-led pursuers. Besides, the address to the ladies is quickly swept aside with the abrupt words "But to our tale" (l. 37).

Swiftly moving from the "bleezing ingle" (l. 38) to the "bleeze" (l. 102) of Kirk Alloway, Tam leaves the fraternal male territory to enter the more frightening and hellish female land and witness a witches' Sabbath presided over by the Devil. Peeping Tam plays the part of a voyeuristic onlooker at a forbidden *Macbeth*-like ritual with its own satanic regalia listed in graphic details (ll. 129–142) and its legion of seminaked witches. This nocturnal phantasmagoria, be it an alcoholic hallucination or the figment of a superstitious mind, can be read as a journey into male conscience and a peep at masculine sexual fantasy. The disturbing sight of "auld and droll" (l. 159) female sexuality contrasts with Nannie's sexual attractiveness. The sexy bewitching mistress Nannie and the faithful horse-companion Maggie, linked by their homophonic names, stand for two opposite visions of the feminine. Taking place in the GOTHIC setting of a churchyard on a very stormy night, the orgy is imbued with superstitious thoughts and supernatural elements. Yet death becomes a literary game in which humor and playfulness win over the unfamiliar and the frightening. The Black Mass is presided by a comic "auld Nick" playing the bagpipes (l. 123), and Nannie's "cutty sark" (l. 171; a cutty sarte is a chemise) results from her grandmother's economizing on material (ll. 172–178).

"Tam o' Shanter" is also a comical odyssey, a parodic rewriting of epics. The mock hero Tam riding his heroic mare like Alexander the Great on his famous horse is engaged in an epic battle against the Fury-like Nannie, an earthly version of Scylla and Charybdis depicted in Homer's *Odysseus* or Ovid's *Metamorphoses*. The poem ends with a tongue-in-cheek moral since the deathly chase only leads to the cutting of the mare's tail which "left scarce a stump" (l. 222). The protective female is punished, whereas sinful Tam escapes unscathed. The parodic sexual climax is characterized by a joke-castration marking the reassertion of male power. The sexual pleasure is turned into

a poetic jubilation which transforms the "tale o' truth" (ll. 13, 219) into a Scottish joke. The twofold aspect of the poem, part-serious, part-laughing, arises from the narrator's multiple personae and voices—as an intrusive teller, secondary character, or philosopher—which provide various layers of interpretation to the reader: "Remember Tam o' Shanter's mare" (l. 224). The open ending urging the readers to remember Tam's nightmare unifies the whole poem around an act of recollection and announces future poems such as Edgar Allan Poe's "Lenore," SAMUEL TAYLOR COLERIDGE's "The RIME OF THE ANCIENT MARINER," and WILLIAM WORDSWORTH's "The IDIOT BOY."

**Further Reading**

Bold, Allan. *A Burns Companion*. London: Macmillan, 1991.

Burns, Robert. *Selected Poems*. Edited by Donald. A. Low. London: J. M. Dent, Everyman's Poetry, 1996.

Crawford, Robert. *Robert Burns and Cultural Authority*. Iowa City: University of Iowa Press, 1997.

Grant, Raymond J. S. *The Laughter of Love: A Study of Robert Burns*. Calgary, Alb.: Detselig, 1986.

Lockhart, John Gibson. *The Life of Robert Burns*. London: J. M. Dent & Sons, 1959.

Mackay, James A. *Burns from A to Z—The Complete Word Finder: Concordance of the Complete Works of Robert Burns*. Dumfries, Scotland: J. Mackay, 1990.

Noble, Jack and Andrew. *The Art of Robert Burns*. Totowa, N.J.: Barnes and Noble, 1982.

—Céline Sabiron

## Thelwall, John (1764–1834)

The most notorious radical orator of the 1790s and early 1800s, John Thelwall was variously a poet, journalist, lecturer, teacher and farmer. He was born in London on July 27, 1764, the son of a silk merchant, and for a time he worked with his father before trying his hand as a tailor and then as a lawyer. After several false starts and after the family business failed, he decided to seek work as a journalist. Largely self-educated, Thelwall became a lecturer via his involvement with learned societies, notably the Society for Free Debate, the Society for Constitutional Information, and the Friends of the People, all of which encouraged his reformist sympathies. This turned him into an atheist, republican, and free thinker and gave him confidence in public speaking, despite his suffering from asthma.

In 1792 Thelwall became a prominent member of the London Corresponding Society. He was a republican, and his speeches calling for an end to the war with France and a reform of the electoral system brought him to the attention of government agents and security services who viewed the young revolutionary idealist as a dangerously inflammatory figure. Thelwall's biographers have suggested that he was actually quite a moderate figure in his views, but this was not how he was perceived by the authorities. He was also famously indiscreet and famously compared George III to a cockerel on a farmyard dung heap (the "libel of the Bantam cock"). His publisher was charged with libel and sedition when the remarks appeared in printed form in *Politics for the People.* Yet, there was, Thelwall believed, no particular "mischief" in "royalty itself, it was in those who, having the Treasury at their backs, and corruption in their hearts, had introduced a system of spies and informers to stop the free use of a man's intellectual faculties . . . and who were endeavouring to wrest from the people their few remaining rights and liberties" (quoted by Wordsworth in Thelwall 2000, i).

Thelwall attracted large crowds and his calls for property reform, freedom of thought and expression and universal male suffrage struck a chord with many people—dangerously so. When the British government got it into its head that the members of the Corresponding Society were on the verge of demanding a new parliament (similar to the French revolutionary system), 12 of the leaders, including Thelwall, were arrested. He was confined in the Tower of London, and six months later he was charged with treason, an indictment carrying a capital penalty. All his papers were confiscated, and he never received them back. However, when tried at the Old Bailey in December 1794, he was triumphantly acquitted. His case was seen as a triumph of the jury system over a repressive state.

Thelwall's time in detention prompted him to write *Poems Written in Close Confinement,* a collection of sonnets, odes, and lyrics in which he cast himself in a tradition of English republicanism stretching back to JOHN MILTON, a favorite Romantic inspiration. The collection is peopled by different characters: "Tyranny," "Liberty," Pomp," "Luxury," "Power," "Oppression," "Anarchy," all battling it out for the hearts and minds of the population. "Sonnet II: To Tyranny" is typical. In it the poet addresses "Hell born, Tyranny" (l. 1), who "with aspect bland" (l. 3) wants "to lull to rest, / The sterner virtues that should guard the throne / Of Liberty" (ll. 4–6). This Tyranny is a cunning seducer: "Deck'd with the gaudy zone / Of Pomp, and usher'd with lascivious arts / Of glossing luxury, thy fraudful smile / Ensnares the dazzled senses, till our hearts / Sink, palsied, in degenerate lethargy (ll. 6–10). Explaining the poems, Thelwall noted that they were not intended as great literature, but "transcripts of the heart, rather than flights of the imagination . . . intended to rouse the patriotic feeling, than calculated to amuse the admirer of poetic enthusiasm" (iii).

Despite his tendency to play down his literary work, Thelwall had begun to make a reputation for himself as a creative writer. *The Peripatetic* (1793) is a mixture of prose and poetry, with a dash of autobiography, which in form is partly a throwback to an earlier Augustan satiric tradition of Jonathan Swift and partly modeled from Laurence Stern's *A Sentimental Journey* (1768). At the same time, it responds provocatively to many of the shared debates of the late 18th century about the rights of man, the evils of SLAVERY, and the dangers of commerce and capitalism. Thelwall attacks the "tyrant badges" of social distinction—which run counter to nature—and which make "pigmy slaves" of modern mankind—and he calls on Britain's population to emulate their American counterparts by rebelling against this "brazen yoke." There are evident similarities with WILLIAM BLAKE and his "mind forg'd manacles" (London, l. 8).

The narrator of *The Peripatetic* is Sylvanus Theophrastus, Thelwall's alter ego, who wanders around the country tourist-like, commenting on the places and people he meets. A frequent starting point for a discussion is to view a town, country estate, castle, or monastery from a higher vantage point (such as a hill), rather like WILLIAM WORDSWORTH's "COMPOSED UPON WESTMIN-

STER BRIDGE, SEPTEMBER 3, 1802." Each building is seen as representative of a particular social institution, which is then dissected. In a poem describing Eltham on the outskirts of London, then (1793) becoming a sprawling suburb, Thelwall writes about the new middling class, rich through trade, who have built their "snug retreat" "o'er Gothic splendour's fallen seat" before using the same GOTHIC images to condemn the long-existent practices of cruelty and oppression that still enable the rich to feed on the poor. Ownership is a recurrent theme in Thelwall's work—even in descriptions of rural idylls. As in Oliver Goldsmith's famous poem "The Deserted Village" (1770), there is anger about the removal of the peasantry from their homes in the name of "improvement" and the threats to community and the sanctity of the family unit when the country folk are forced to migrate to urban slums in "some increasing town."

It was these shared interests—including a belief in the restorative powers of the countryside—that brought Thelwall into contact with SAMUEL TAYLOR COLERIDGE and William Wordsworth. Following his trial, Thelwall stayed with the like-minded poets during their sojourn in the West country in July 1797, believing that "'twould be sweet, beneath the neighbr'ing thatch, / In philosophic amity to dwell" ("Lines Written at Bridgewater, ll. 1–2"). Often in Thelwall's poetry, rural life is constructed as idyllic—the antithesis of the life of political persecution experienced in the city. Although the visit to Coleridge and Wordsworth went well, the threesome's discussions were watched by a government informer, Thomas Jones, working in Wordsworth's house as a servant. He notified a government spy, James Walsh, who was deeply suspicious of Thelwall. When Walsh arrived a few days later, he expected to catch the three men engaged in seditious activities and arrest them, but Thelwall had already left. Following this incident, Thelwall seems to have been cold-shouldered by Coleridge, who was alarmed at his friend's notoriety and the "pantisocratic" community they had envisaged did not happen (see "PANTISOCRACY").

Thelwall did not settle nearby as planned but instead rented a farm in Llys-wen on the banks of the River Wye near Wales, hoping to support his family on its proceeds. The farm failed, and the persecution which had dogged Thelwall in London persisted, thanks to some of his neighbours. In order to support his family, he returned to writing. His novel *The Daughter of Adoption* appeared in 1801. This is bildungsroman traces the moral and sentimental education of the hero and heroine and owes much to the radical sentiments of Coleridge and MARY WOLLSTONECRAFT. This was followed by *Poems Written Chiefly in Retirement* (1801), which include the "Poems of 1797"—part of a conversation with Coleridge over the relative value of political activity and romantic escapism—together with another series of poems, "Paternal Tears," mourning the death of Thelwall's daughter Maria in 1799. In two longer historical poems, "The Fairy of the Lake" and "The Hope of Albion; or, Edwin of Northumbria," Thelwall laments the passing of heroic ideals and allegorizes the England of the 1790s via Anglo-Saxon settings. In his mood and message, critics have seen links with Wordsworth and Coleridge's *Lyrical Ballads* and PERCY BYSSHE SHELLEY's *PROMETHEUS UNBOUND*.

Back in London, Thelwall began teaching elocution and speech therapy, opening an institute in 1809. For a man who advocated free speech, this choice of career was not an accident. Speech therapy, as Thelwall remarked, had to do with the "enfranchisement of fettered organs" (Thelwall, 1810, 9). In the same vein he became editor of the radical *Champion* newspaper and led the paper's denunciation of the PETERLOO MASSACRE at St. Peter's Field in August 1819. The rest of his life followed the familiar pattern of journalism and lecturing. By this time his radicalism seemed rather tame when compared to newer orators such as Henry Hunt (1773–1835) one of the figures behind the St. Peter's Field demonstration. Thelwall died in Bath on February 17, 1834, while on a lecturing tour. Since his death he has generally been seen as a marginal poetic figure, but in his time he was at the very center of Romantic political activism and the extraordinary literary creativity this was capable of producing.

**Further Reading**

McCann, Andrew. *Cultural Politics in the 1790s: Literature, Radicalism and the Public Sphere.* London: Macmillan, 1999.

Roe, Nicholas. "Coleridge and John Thelwall: The Road to Nether Stowey." In *The Coleridge Connection*, edited by Richard Gravil and Molly Lefebure, 60–80. New York: St. Martin's Press, 1990.

Scrivener, Michael. *Seditious Allegories: John Thelwall and Jacobin Writing*. University Park: Pennsylvania State University Press, 2001.

Thelwall, John. *A Letter to Henry Cline. Esq on Imperfect development of the faculties mental and moral, as well as constitutional and organic and on the treatment of the impediment of speech*. London: Richard Taylor, 1810.

———. *The Peripatetic*. Edited by Judith Thompson. Detroit: Wayne State University Press, 2001.

———. *Poems Chiefly Written in Retirement*. Oxford: Woodstock, 1989.

———. *Poems Written in Close Confinement in the Tower and Newgate, under a Charge of High Treason*. Edited by Jonathan Wordsworth. Washington, D.C.: Otley, 2000.

—Mark Harris

## "There Was a Boy"   William Wordsworth
(1800)

"There Was a Boy" is a blank-verse, autobiographical poem about the awakening of the imagination, written by WILLIAM WORDSWORTH in Germany while accompanied by his sister, DOROTHY WORDSWORTH, and also his friend and sometime collaborator, SAMUEL TAYLOR COLERIDGE. First published in the second edition of LYRICAL BALLADS (1800), Wordsworth categorized it a "poem of the imagination" and an "extract from the poem on my own poetical education" (Wordsworth 1974, 3:39, 48–49). Wordsworth had initially intended the lines for use in *The Prelude* (1798–9), the epic poem on the growth of his mind and imagination. He did not use them but later revised the lines for inclusion as lines 389–413 of Book 5 of *The Prelude* of 1805. The version included in *Lyrical Ballads* is the text discussed here and illuminates how important tracking the development of the imaginative faculty was to Wordsworth.

"There Was a Boy" enacts the familiar Wordsworthian theme of the experience, in childhood, of a primary connection to nature and imagina-tion. This relationship is figured by the image of a solitary youth communing with nature by mimicking owl hootings (ll. 5–10). This dialogue stages the boy's internal subjective reality acting on, and reacting to, his external material reality; as Wordsworth put it in the PREFACE TO LYRICAL BALLADS, "man and nature a[re] essentially adapted to each other" (Wordsworth and Coleridge, 259). Through imaginative identification, "he hung / Listening" (ll. 18–19), the boy intuits that his sense of self and nature correspond. When nature does not respond to him—"The pauses of deep silence mocked his skill" (l. 17)—the boy receives the scene unconsciously; "the visible scene / Would enter unawares into his mind" (ll. 21–22). In Wordsworth's account, he internalizes "solemn imagery" (l. 23) of rock, wood, and lake as "the mind of man [is] naturally the mirror of the fairest and most interesting qualities of nature" (Wordsworth and Coleridge 34). In this poem's analogy for the boy's mind, which receives and retains—"carried far into his heart" (l. 20)—nature is "the steady lake" (l. 25). This reflective surface (Wordsworth 1974, 3, 4) is a medium on which symbols are implanted and a palimpsest in memory whose layers facilitate intimations of meaning.

The boy loses his profound connection to "cliffs / And islands of Winander (ll. 1–2) through death. A poet's "spontaneous overflow of powerful feelings" (Wordsworth and Coleridge, 246) then retrospectively reanimates this boy's personal past and commemorates his life.

Recent critics have demonstrated how Wordsworth uses memory to recall absences; for Geoffrey Hartman, memory's role in Wordsworth's poetry is tied to mourning. The witness is "Mute— looking at the grave" (l. 32), as he has lost with adult socialization the boy's profound link to imagination and nature. However, this vision of a living adult remembering a dead 10-year-old child is a record of loss that functions as a consolation. This remembrance consoles adult readers by enriching and nourishing their imaginations; they may perceive, via the boy's unconstrained primary relations, that "which before had been only imperfectly or unconsciously seen" (Wordsworth, 1974, 2:58). This occurs because it is through the imagination that "ordinary things are presented to the mind in unusual ways (Wordsworth and Coleridge 248). The dead boy is exemplary as he enacts a relation to nature and imagination that becomes lost to adults but may, occasionally, be glimpsed after it is recaptured, through memory.

## Further Reading

Cameron, Rachael. "Recuperating the virtual past through Recollection: Wordsworth's 'Immortality Ode.'" *Colloquy*, 9 (2005): Available online. URL: www.colloquy.monash.edu.au/issue009/cameron.pdf. Accessed on June 1, 2009.

Hartman, Geoffrey. *The Unremarkable Wordsworth*. London: Methuen, 1987.

Wordsworth, William. *The Prose Works of William Wordsworth*. 3 vols. Edited by W. J. B. Owen and J. W. Smyser. Oxford: Clarendon Press, 1974.

———. *The Prelude 1799, 1805, 1850.* Edited by Jonathan Wordsworth, M. H. Abrams, and Stephen Gill. New York: W. W. Norton & Company, 1979.

Wordsworth, William, and Samuel Taylor Coleridge. *Lyrical Ballads*. Edited by R. L. Brett and A. R. Jones. London: Routledge, 1963.

—Rachael Cameron

## "This Lime-Tree Bower My Prison" Samuel Taylor Coleridge (1797)

SAMUEL TAYLOR COLERIDGE's "This Lime-Tree Bower My Prison" was written in 1797 and addressed to his friend CHARLES LAMB. This conversation poem achieves an order and harmony through its imagery, blending all the diverse elements in an act of creative imagination. Between 1795 and 1798, Coleridge wrote a number of verses popularly known as the "conversation poems," which celebrate retirement; friendship; domesticity; happiness; and a move toward an understanding of the relation between man, the community, nature, and God. "This Lime-Tree Bower My Prison" begins with a sense of loss that the speaker has suffered. The poet is unable to join his friends on their walk due to a foot injury caused by his wife, Sarah, accidentally spilling boiling milk on his foot: "Well, they are gone, and here must I remain, / This lime-tree bower my prison! I have lost / Beauties and feelings" (ll. 1–3). The cottage's beautiful garden appears as a prison since the poet is unable to venture out with his friends on their walk. As he sits brooding in the bower, he vicariously traces the journey undertaken by his dear friends. It is this imaginative recreation of their walk that enables the poet to move from retirement and apparent loneliness to introspection, then to the joy that he feels and the ultimately enlivening response to nature. This joy is achieved as he imaginatively traverses the journey undertaken by his friends. The descent into the "dell" (ll. 9, 10) is a projection of his dark mood, which is changed the moment he emerges into the open sky. What the speaker achieves is a unity of vision with his friends that asserts a community of shared experience. He no longer feels imprisoned as he achieves this unity, and he celebrates the fact he shares with Lamb, an external influence on the mind of man that brings "deep joy" (138).

This poem attests to Coleridge's belief in the healing powers of nature. It also, according to the scholar Kelvin Everest, "manifests a full intensity in the potential of Coleridge's ideal retirement, which may perhaps have developed in part out of a growing sense of the actual shortcomings in his domestic life, the irritations that were to loom large in his life with Sarah" (Everest, 242–243). The happiness and joy that he achieves is a distinctive quality of Coleridge's experience of nature. The vivid and beautiful description of the play of light in the garden testifies to the poet's belief in the presence of an all-pervading spirit in nature. At the same time the poem is a celebration of the creative power that emerges through the poet's recreation of his experience: "A delight / Comes sudden on my heart, and I am glad / As I myself were there!" (ll. 43–45). The bower, garden, nature, were always there, but now the fact that he sees its unifying presence indicates something special on the part of the speaker's experience: "Henceforth I shall know / That Nature ne'er deserts the wise and pure" (ll. 59–60). The parallel between Coleridge's "imprisonment" in the bower and Lamb's reluctant return to London is suggestive of this.

The end of the poem has the poet returning to the garden and seeing nature directly. Imagination has assumed priority in his mind, and he sees the operation of this power in other minds as well. This makes him alive to the fact that probably the realities of the garden will attest to his imagination. His perception of nature changes, and nature seems to partake in the all-pervading joy of life. Joy is a condition that bears the whole thrust of Coleridge's social experience. The sense of connectedness with the human community is a result of the change of his mental state. Throughout Coleridge's poetry, joy is associated with the domestic circle. It has the connotation of personal relationships and a stable home. Joy is the result of an emotional participation, a sense of shared community. "This Lime-Tree Bower My Prison" serves as a consolation for Charles Lamb and also as a biographical document.

## Further Reading

Coleridge, Samuel Taylor. *Poetical Works of Samuel Taylor Coleridge.* Edited by Ernest Hartley Coleridge. London: Henry Frowde, 1912.

Engell, James. "Imagining into Nature: This Lime-Tree Bower My Prison." In *Coleridge, Keats and the Imagination: Romanticism and Adam's Dream: Essays in Honor of Walter Jackson Bate.* Edited by J. Robert Barth and John L. Mahoney. Columbia: University of Missouri Press, 1990.

Everest, Kelvin. *Coleridge's Secret Ministry: The Context of the Conversation. Poems 1795–1798.* Hassocks, Eng.: Harvester Press, 1979.

Mellor, Anne K. "Coleridge's 'This Lime-Tree Bower My Prison' and the Categories of Landscape." *Studies in Romanticism* 18 (1979): 253–270.

—Nishi Pulugurtha

## "Thorn, The"  William Wordsworth  (1798)

Supposedly born out of WILLIAM WORDSWORTH's observation of a thorny, gnarled tree one stormy day in March 1798, "The Thorn" was first published in September that year as a contribution to his and SAMUEL TAYLOR COLERIDGE's landmark poetry collection LYRICAL BALLADS. One of several poems by Wordsworth that suggests the supernatural, "The Thorn" also explores subjects such as the human psyche, the fallen woman of the late 18th century, and especially the reliability of narrator and reader's role in interpretation.

On the surface, "The Thorn" speaks of a woman, Martha Ray, who, after giving "with a maiden's true good-will / Her company to Stephen Hill" (ll. 106–107), discovers on what was to be their wedding day that Stephen is betrothed to another. Finding herself with child and mad with anguish, she retreats to a mountaintop, where she spends most of her days. However, though supposedly pregnant, no child is ever seen. It is unknown if the child is stillborn or murdered by Martha's own hand. The consequence of the pregnancy, though, appears to be Martha's final descent into insanity, and 20 years later she still frequents that hilltop and can be heard wailing, "Oh misery! oh misery! / Oh woe is me! oh misery!" (ll. 65–66, 76–77, 241–242). While the subjects presented here—which include infanticide, a "fallen" woman, and insanity—are enticing to the modern reader, an even greater complexity can be found within the narrator's role. Here we find a man, a newcomer to the area 20 years after the jilting of Martha Ray, who attempts to tell us the story. However, it becomes increasingly clear that neither the narrator nor the rest of the townsfolk really knows what happened to Martha Ray and her child—if, in fact, there even was a child in the first place.

Wordsworth adds a note to the second edition of *Lyrical Ballads* (1800) where he regrets his inability to include an "introductory" poem to "The Thorn," which would properly introduce the poem's speaker. In this note he describes his speaker as a middle-aged man who has retired to a village or country town of which he is not a native and who "having little to do, become[s] credulous and talkative from indolence" (quoted in Perkins 197). It becomes progressively clear that this retired older man is an incorporation of the female gossip so often portrayed in literature. As the speaker takes us through the narrative, he consistently reminds us that he does not really know what happened and "cannot tell" (ll. 203, 232) the story; yet he continues to repeatedly speculate, sharing the town's hearsay. Wordsworth goes on to say in this note that such a man as his narrator would be "prone to superstition" and "of slow faculties and deep feelings" (quoted in Perkins 197), thus indicating that, to Wordsworth, the narrator and his predilection for constructing narrative is the central issue in this poem rather than Martha Ray and her ghostly child.

The poem begins "High on a mountain's highest ridge" (l. 23) with the narrator's description of a thorn, a pond, and a moss heap (shaped exactly, he says, like a child's grave), where Martha still wails and laments. But none of these things—the thorn, the pond, the moss heap, or even Martha—is easy to classify. As the critic Toby Benis points out, this poem is a series of people and objects that occupy marginal positions (Benis 206). Martha is a native who becomes alien, the narrator is a stranger who becomes familiar, and the baby is dead yet powerful when he shakes the ground as the townspeople attempt to take Martha to justice. These allusive positions work to define the poem. According to Benis, "As Martha's behavior becomes more complex, . . . the narrative about her becomes more obscure" (207). Take, for example, the narrator's strange remark about Martha's face: "'I did not speak—I saw her face; / Her face!—it was enough for me'" (ll. 188–189). This ambiguous reference is never again mentioned, nor explained; the reader is left to determine what—if any—monstrosity afflicts Martha's visage. Yet while the reader is uncertain what is fact and what is imagination, the poem still manages to invoke an empathetic humanitarian concern.

Called a "deliberate experiment" by Wordsworth (quoted in Perkins 190), "The Thorn" occupies a pivotal spot in Romantic poetry in its ability to combine the lyric with narrative, to reveal the psychology of the human mind, and to disclose human nature.

**Further Reading**

Benis, Toby R. "Martha Ray's Face: Life during Wartime in 'Lyrical Ballads.'" *Criticism* 39, no. 2 (1997): 205–227.

Christensen, Jerome. "Wordsworth's Misery, Coleridge's Woe: Reading 'The Thorn.'" *Papers on Language and Literature* 16, no. 3 (1980): 268–286.

Fulford, Tim. "Fallen Ladies and Cruel Mothers: Ballad Singers and Ballad Heroines in the Eighteenth Century." *The Eighteenth Century* 47 (2006): 309–329.

Johnston, Kenneth R. *The Hidden Wordsworth: Poet, Lover, Rebel, Spy.* New York: W. W. Norton and Company, 1998.

Perkins, David. *English Romantic Writers.* New York: Harcourt Brace Jovanovich College Publishers, 1967.

Wu, Duncan. *Wordsworth: An Inner Life.* Oxford: Blackwell Publishers, 2002.

—Nicole Burkholder-Mosco

## Thrale, Hester Lynch   See PIOZZI, HESTER LYNCH.

## Tieck, Ludwig (1773–1853)

Ludwig Tieck, nicknamed the "king of Romanticism," was one of the most prolific and versatile German authors in the first half of the 19th century. He wrote novels, novellas, romantic fairy tales, theatrical satires, and fantasy plays, and he worked as a translator, editor, and dramaturge. In these capacities he was instrumental not only in introducing a wider German audience to the works of Shakespeare, but also in keeping the memory of German writers such as NOVALIS, Heinrich Wilhelm von Kleist, and Jakob Michael Reinhold Lenz alive. In many of his works Tieck combined the fantastic with the eerie, thereby influencing authors like ERNST THEODOR AMADEUS HOFFMANN and Edgar Allan Poe.

Born Johann Ludwig Treck in Berlin on May 31, 1773, the eldest child of a rope maker, Tieck benefited from recent economic and social reforms under Frederick the Great. His family had risen to the middle classes, and he attended school together with the sons of aristocrats and high-ranking officials, among them WILHELM HEINRICH WACKENRODER, who became his closest friend. In 1792 he left for university to read theology, first in Halle, then in Göttingen, where he decided to focus on literature instead. With Wackenroder, he spent the summer semester of 1793 in Erlangen, and together they visited Bayreuth, Nuremberg, and Bamberg. Here in southern Germany, they got their first glimpse of Catholic rituals and of medieval, Renaissance, and baroque art and architecture. With these influences, Wackenroder started working on a manuscript that was eventually published in 1796 (but with a date of 1797), with a few additions by Tieck, as *Die Herzensergiessungen eines kunstliebenden Klosterbruders (Outpourings of an Art-Loving Friar)*. This collection of essays is often regarded as the start of and inspiration for literary Romanticism in Germany.

Without a university degree, Tieck returned to Berlin in 1794 and worked for Friedrich Nicolai's *Straussfedern*. While his early writings still displayed the influence of 18th-century literary traditions, the new Romantic spirit became more apparent in works like his unfinished novel *Franz Sternbalds Wanderungen* (1798) and *Volksmährchen* (1797). The latter book, a collection of stories published under the pseudonym of Peter Lebrecht, contained Tieck's most famous fairy tale, "Der Blonde Eckbert" ("BLOND ECKBERT"). He became part of the literary salons of Henriette Herz and Rahel Varnhagen von Ense, and in 1798 he married Amalie Alberti, whom he had met in the house of her brother-in-law, the royal director of music Johann Friedrich Reinhardt.

For a short while Tieck was part of the Jena circle of early Romantics and became acquainted with August Wilhelm von Schlegel, FRIEDRICH VON SCHLEGEL, Johann Gottlieb Fichte, Novalis, and Clemens Brentano, as well as JOHANN WOLFGANG VON GOETHE, FRIEDRICH VON SCHILLER, and Johann Gottfried Herder. Yet due to pecuniary problems, Tieck and his family moved often, and they were dependent on the goodwill of Tieck's friends, publishers, and patrons—among them Henriette von Finckenstein, who eventually became his lover. Because of his tendency to live above his means and his many travels to England and elsewhere, Tieck's financial situation never improved, even when he had a steady income, first as a dramaturge in Dresden and then as councillor and reader to the Prussian king Frederick William IV. His later years were overshadowed by illness. He died on April 28, 1853.

## Further Reading

Lillyman, William J. *Reality's Dark Dream: The Narrative Fiction of Ludwig Tieck.* Berlin: Walter de Gruyter, 1979.

Paulin, Roger. *Ludwig Tieck: A Literary Biography.* Oxford: Clarendon Press, 1985.

Tieck, Ludwig. *Der gestiefelte Kater. Puss-in-Boots.* Edited by and translated by Gerald Gillespie. Austin: University of Texas Press, 1974.

———. *Des Lebens Überfluss.* Stuttgart: Reclam, 1983.

———. "Eckbert the Blond." In *Spells of Enchantment: The Wondrous Fairy Tales of Western Culture,* edited by Jack Zipes, 281–295. New York: Viking, 1991.

———. *Franz Sternbalds Wanderungen.* Edited by Alfred Anger. Stuttgart: Reclam, 1986.

———. *William Lovell.* Edited by Walter Münz. Stuttgart: Reclam, 1986.

Tieck, Ludwig, and Wilhelm Heinrich Wackenroder. *Herzensergiessungen eines kunstliebenden Klosterbruders.* Stuttgart: Reclam, 1979.

—Sandra Martina Schwab

## Tighe, Mary (1772–1810)

Mary Tighe was an Irish poet best known as the author of the long Spenserian epic PSYCHE, OR THE LEGEND OF LOVE. The poem was published privately in a limited edition of 50 copies given to family and friends, who included THOMAS MOORE and ANNA SEWARD. It was via this small network that Tighe's fame slowly began to spread. After her early death, traditionally attributed to tuberculosis, her brother-in-law published her work in 1811 under the title *Psyche, with Other Poems*. The volume reached its third edition in about a year and proved to be a success, reputedly influencing JOHN KEATS, who imitated Tighe's lush language and melancholy subject matter.

Mary Blachford was born to Theodosia (née Tighe) and William Blachford on October 9, 1772. Her father died the following May, leaving his daughter's education to his wife, who played a crucial role in influencing Mary's later poetry. The Tighes were a wealthy and cultured family whose interest in languages, science, and the arts meant that all their children were well-educated and instilled with a love of learning. Though Mary excelled in literary study, (particularly enjoying Edmund Spenser's *The Fairie Queene*), her mother's circle, including the theologian John Wesley, discouraged her from pursuing what they viewed as frivolous literature. The tension between spirituality and worldliness would become one of Tighe's most important themes; she frequently complained of what she called "syren Pleasure."

Throughout her youth, Mary had many suitors, but her aunt arranged a meeting between her and her cousin, Henry Tighe in 1788. Her family had hopes of a great match, but in 1793 she married Tighe. The couple settled in London, where Henry Tighe abandoned plans to train as lawyer for the life of a gentleman of leisure. By all accounts he admired his wife but was a controlling and possessive husband. Mary sought escape in fashionable society and in her writing. Her disappointment may have been the source of another of her most frequent poetic subjects, abandoned women, particularly in *Psyche* and another poem, "Hagar in the Desert."

*Pysche*, Mary Tighe's most famous poem, is an erotic, richly allusive allegorical romance running to 3,348 lines. It reenvisions the ancient story of Cupid and Psyche (as told in Apuleius's *The Golden Ass*) from a protofeminist perspective, setting out the notion of a female quest and drawing links between Psyche's life and the creative restrictions experienced by female poets; like Psyche, they are females who are punished for daring to look on that which is forbidden. The poem's interest in this topic is most evident in canto 5, in which Psyche considers a life among the women writers who live in the kingdom of Castabella (the Queen of Chastity). Tighe refused to publish the poem commercially, thereby submitting herself to "the mercy of the reviewers, Edinburgh *butchers*," as she later admitted: "I have not the nerves for it" (Tighe xxxiii).

As early as 1789, Tighe exhibited symptoms that led to a diagnosis of consumption, the term used in those days for tuberculosis. From 1804 her ill health started to curtail her writing. In spite of this, she left more than 85 unpublished sonnets at the time of her death on March 24, 1810, many of them meditations on the idea of female identity, repression, and selfhood. Many also bear traces of Tighe's extensive reading as she invokes poets of the past, including JOHN MILTON, Alexander Pope, and THOMAS GRAY. Her work also includes an unpublished novel, *Selena* (1803), which incorporates poetry as a way of highlighting the psychological states of characters. Besides these works, Tighe left behind other drafts, a number of which were gathered in *Mary, a Series of Reflec-*

*tions* (privately printed in 1811). While she has, until recently, not received due critical attention, her examinations of the loss inherent in urbanization, the contradictions between the spiritual and the worldly, and the position of women in society make her an important figure in the Romantic period. Verse tributes after her death came from Keats and from FELICIA HEMANS, whose "The GRAVE OF A POETESS" was the last poem in *Records of Woman* (1828).

**Further Reading**

Tighe, Mary. *The Collected Poems and Journals of Mary Tighe.* Edited by Harriet Kramer Linkin. Lexington: University Press of Kentucky, 2005.

—Brian C. Cooney

**"Tintern Abbey"**   See "LINES WRITTEN A FEW MILES ABOVE TINTERN ABBEY, ON REVISITING THE BANKS OF THE WYE."

**"To a Mountain Daisy"** Robert Burns (1786)
This poem is addressed to a flower the rural speaker has accidentally destroyed with his plow. In lamenting the fate of the daisy, the speaker soon draws comparisons to other more or less vulnerable entities, including himself. The destruction of the flower is thus taken as an occasion for the speaker to contemplate life and mortality.

The poem's main argument first proceeds from a direct address of the daisy to a recapitulation of its brief life, which includes a comparison between this wild flower and other more refined specimens growing in sheltered gardens. After once more lamenting the fateful encounter between the daisy and his plow, the speaker turns to other objects of comparison: first an "artless Maid" (l. 31) betrayed by her lover, then a "simple Bard" (l. 37) unable to steer the course of prudence "On Life's rough ocean" (l. 38). All such hapless victims of life's vicissitudes share the fate of maid and bard in that they can only set their hopes on the next life, where, hopefully, they will find rescue from "Mis'ry's brink" (l. 46). Already having introduced a poet figure in the shape of the bard, the speaker makes his own identification with that particular role even more unmistakable by addressing himself in the very last stanza of the poem: "Ev'n thou who mourn'st the *Daisy's* fate, / *That fate is thine*" (l. 50).

"To a Mountain Daisy" is particularly noteworthy for its representation of nature, the identification of a diverse cast of entities as fellow sufferers, and the speaker's realization of his own mortality. However, most critics seem to agree that all these aspects are treated rather more successfully in other examples of what the critic Carol McGuirk terms ROBERT BURNS's "poems of direct address" (McGuirk 11), most notably "TO A MOUSE." "To a Mountain Daisy," which the biographer Gerard Carruthers describes as "one of Burns's most extreme exercises in rural sentiment" (Carruthers 15), may follow "the same process by which a sensitive interpreter stoops to ponder some humble object—mouse, louse, daisy—that has captured his eye by chance" (McGuirk 7), but as an expression of sincere sentiment, it seems fairly problematic. Its language moves from Scots to English and back for no apparent reason, the introduction of both the bard and the speaker is a redundancy, the argument is occasionally sidetracked by ultimately irrelevant observations, and the daisy has to serve as "a symbol for too many things" (McGuirk 11)—to the point where it loses its effectiveness as an image.

Even if "[c]ritics have generally disliked" the poem (Carruthers 15), it nonetheless illustrates a number of predilections of early Romantic poetry rather well. Its speaker is at once a man of the common people who is interested in their concerns and a disseminator of ultimate truths. The *"Parent-earth"* (l. 17)—unadulterated nature—is valued above gardens and human-made structures, and a sensibility toward others' suffering—even that of a single flower—is seen as not just noble but ultimately as the only valid response, since it is in our suffering that we are all united.

## Further Reading

Burns, Robert. *The Complete Poems and Songs of Robert Burns.* Edited by Patrick Scott Hogg and Andrew Noble. Edinburgh: Canongate, 2001.

Carruthers, Gerard. *Robert Burns.* Tavistock, Eng.: Northcote, 2006.

McGuirk, Carol. *Robert Burns and the Sentimental Era.* Athens: University of Georgia Press, 1985.

—Patrick Gill

## "To a Mouse,"   Robert Burns   (1786)

The poem "To a Mouse, On turning her up in her Nest, with the Plough, November, 1785" (commonly known simply as "To a Mouse") was first published in the Kilmarnock edition of *Poems, Chiefly in the Scottish Dialect* (1786). The poem consists of 48 lines of standard habbie (stanzas of six lines that are sometimes referred to as "Burns stanzas," in which the first three lines and the fifth contain four stresses while the fourth and sixth lines contain two stresses, with the rhyme scheme *aaabab*). It has been widely recorded that ROBERT BURNS' was inspired to write the poem after turning up a fieldmouse whilst out ploughing and saved the mouse from being killed with a spade.

"To a Mouse" begins with the following address: "Wee, sleekit, cow'rin, tim'rous beastie, / O, what a panic's in thy breastie!" (ll. 1–2). Throughout, however, the poem is more focused on the human world than such a beginning may suggest. One of Burns's biographers, Hugh Douglas, emphasizing the poet's need at the time of its composition to assume family and working responsibilities after his father's illness and eventual death, suggests that "The panic lay in Burns' own breast, and the poem was a cry of fear for himself rather than for the mouse. . . . At the time he was on the point of a nervous breakdown" (Douglas 7).

The beginning of the second stanza, "I'm truly sorry Man's dominion / Has broken Nature's social union" (ll. 7–8), appears to reference Alexander Pope's "Essay on Man" (which urges, in 3:179, that man should go to the animal world and "Here too all forms of social union find"). The stanza seems to build toward a democratic expression of solidarity with the mouse, who the speaker describes as "thy poor, earth-born companion, / An' fellow mortal!" (ll. 11–12). The poem as a whole, however, builds toward a conclusion that might bear out Douglas's implication that "To a Mouse" is ultimately a human-centered work. The final two stanzas appear to suggest that the poem is an allegory about the lowly tenant laborer commonly at risk of being thrown out of his home and, like the mouse, losing the fruits of his labor: "But, Mousie, thou art no thy-lane, / In proving foresight may be vain: / The best laid schemes o' mice an' men, / Gang aft agley, / An' lea'e us nought but grief an' pain, / For promis'd joy!" (ll. 39–42).

The closing lines express sympathy with the creature's plight and yet, by trading on the traditional contrast between human beings who possess reason and animals who do not, suggest that the human laborer's sufferings are greater because of human consciousness of them. "Still, thou art blest, compar'd wi' me! / The present only toucheth thee: / But Och! I backward cast my e'e, / On prospects drear! An' forward, tho' I canna see, / I guess an' fear! (ll. 43–48). The poem is, therefore, only one of Burns's many Romantic protests against the plight of the laboring classes, and it has consistently been one of his most loved works.

### Further Reading

Burns, Robert. *Burns: Poems and Songs.* Edited by James Kinsley. London: Oxford University Press, 1969.

Douglas, Hugh. *Robert Burns: The Tinder Heart.* Stroud, Eng.: Sutton Publishing, 1996.

—Steve Van Hagen

### "To a Skylark" Percy Bysshe Shelley (1820)

In June 1820, PERCY BYSSHE SHELLEY and MARY SHELLEY took a walk from their home near Livorno in Italy, through a field populated by skylarks, "a small European bird that sings only in flight, usually when it is too high to be clearly visible" (Reiman and Fraistat in Shelley, 304, n1). The potential for symbolic exchange between a bird that sings unseen and a poet is not difficult to find, and soon after this walk, Shelley produced his 21-stanza poem "To a Skylark," published in September 1820. The first six stanzas describe not the invisible bird but its imagined flight. The next six attempt to describe the skylark through characterization: "What is most like thee?" (l. 32). The final section asks for inspiration from the skylark but acknowledges that its song is as beyond poetry as it is beyond earth: "Better than all measures /

Of delightful sound— / Better than all treasures / That in books are found— / Thy skill to poet were, thou Scorner of the ground!" (ll. 96–100). As this example shows, the poem's five-line stanzas have the rhyme scheme *ababb*. The meter for the first four is trochaic trimeter, with the final line in iambic hexameter, called an alexandrine.

"To a Skylark" echoes a number of texts, including SAMUEL TAYLOR COLERIDGE's "KUBLA KHAN," JOHN KEATS's "ODE TO A NIGHTINGALE," and Shelley's own "ODE TO THE WEST WIND," which trace the uneasy relationship between poetic inspiration and human fallibility. The poem begins with an apostrophe from the poetic speaker to the unseen subject of his discourse: "Hail to thee, blithe Spirit! / Bird thou never wert— / That from Heaven, or near it, / Pourest thy full heart / In profuse strains of unpremeditated art" (ll. 1–15). The opening lines highlight immateriality, approximation, and spontaneity. The skylark is a spirit, not ("never") a bird. Its song is celestial—maybe. A telling qualification locates the skylark, if not "from Heaven," then "near it" (l. 3). This condition of being neither of earth nor quite of heaven, but on the threshold of both worlds, Stuart Peterfreund argues, identifies this as a fundamentally equivocal poem and the speaker "not only as a less gifted poet than the skylark, but as a poet who will fail in the attempt to capture his subject with some justice, let alone to emulate that subject" (Peterfreund 272).

The bird thus looks like a figure for the romantic poet. Its song comes from its "full heart" out of which pour "strains of unpremeditated art" (ll. 4, 5). But Shelley's speaker seems to know that this is not how poetry is produced. Poetry is more than harmonious madness: It originates in mind as well as heart. The poet's final injunction echoes the end of "Kubla Khan," although Shelley's speaker is importunate where Coleridge's is wishful: "Teach me half the gladness / That thy brain must know / Such harmonious madness / From my lips would flow / The world should listen then—as I am listening now" (ll. 101–105). With these lines, the speaker recognizes the fallibility of his symbol. Even as he cannot quite say what the skylark is ("*Like a Poet*" [l. 36] or "a high-born maiden" [l. 41] or "a glow-worm golden" [l. 46], but not these things) or where it is, he cannot be the poet that the unseen singing bird represents. To do so, as Peterfreund argues, would be "to relinquish the order of the human brain, and thereby to create a poetry that is nothing other than 'harmonious madness' . . . striking and compelling, perhaps, but ultimately indecipherable" (274).

## Further Reading

Peterfreund, Stuart. *Shelley among Others: The Play of Intertext and the Idea of Language.* Baltimore, Md.: Johns Hopkins University Press, 2002.

Shelley, Percy Bysshe. *Shelley's Poetry and Prose.* 2nd ed. Edited by Donald H. Reiman and Neil Fraistat. New York: W. W. Norton and Company, 2002.

White, Newton Ivey. *Shelley.* New York: Octagon Books, 1972.

—Kristin Samuelian

## "To My Sister"   William Wordsworth   (1798)

WILLIAM WORDSWORTH initially titled "To My Sister" as "Lines Written at a Small Distance from My House, and Sent by My Little Boy to the Person to Whom They are Addressed" and published it under that title in LYRICAL BALLADS (1798). In the poem Wordsworth summons his sister, DOROTHY WORDSWORTH, to "come forth and feel the sun" (l. 12). For one year, William and his sister lived at Alfoxden House in Sumerset. The two of them had not lived together as little children; however, they became close friends in adulthood and would live together for many years.

The poem takes place during the spring, a time of rebirth, and reminds us of the motto *carpe diem.* There is no time to waste: William urges Dorothy to step into nature and seize the day. He tells her to "Put on with speed your woodland dress, / And bring no book, for this one day / We'll give to idleness" (ll. 14–16). She must hurry away from her everyday life in order to slow down and enjoy "The spirit of the season" (l. 28).

Throughout the poem, Wordsworth juxtaposes the notions of indoor/outdoor, culture and books/nature, and travail/idleness. He also appears to be concerned with time—the time of clocks and calendars and the time of nature itself. The latter is driven by the movement of the trees, the rustle of the leaves, the current of the streams, and the animation of the animals. Wordsworth wants to leave behind the values, norms, issues, and concerns of his contemporaries and sit idly in nature.

When Wordsworth wrote this poem, he was well aware of the sociopolitical events of England and France. He had just witnessed the FRENCH REVOLUTION, to which the people of France reset their calendars. In France the new year began on September 22, 1792, the inception of the Republic. Human life was structured around a new system of time, a system organized around political events. Wordsworth, who is against this new system, wants to base time on the personal moments of his "living calendar" (l. 18). He claims that now is "the hour of feeling" (l. 24), the hour of nature, and that this hour is worth more than "fifty years of reason" (l. 26)—years of culture and books. This day the two of them will learn from nature itself, and their lesson will change their hearts more than any human-made invention or custom can do. Here, Wordsworth appears to privilege sensibility over enlightenment, the voice of the woods over the voice of reason.

While some make promises and personal resolutions, or "silent laws" (l. 29), William and Dorothy are to find their well-being in the day itself. Wordsworth describes how their days will be numbered in accordance with the natural laws of this world and not the loud, bitter laws of the French Revolution. Remember: carpe diem. Their temper shall be in harmony with nature and filled with love. Thus, in "To My Sister," Wordsworth reveals how one may replace the joyless, uninspiring, and stagnant pattern of time that most people live by with the fruitful, blessed, and living passage of time found in the rhythm of nature.

## Further Reading

Wordsworth, William. *The Major Works: Including the Prelude.* Edited by Stephen Gill. Oxford: Oxford University Press, 2000.

———. "Preface to *Lyrical Ballads.*" In *The Critical Tradition: Classic Texts and Contemporary Trends,* 3rd ed., edited by David H. Richter, 304–318. Boston: St. Martin's Press, 2007.

—Mark W. Westmoreland

## "To Robert Batty, M.D., on His Giving Me a Lock of Milton's Hair" Leigh Hunt (1810)

JOHN MILTON's impact on writers of the Romantic era has long been recognized. Like the Romantics, Milton wrote during an age of revolution (the English Civil Wars, 1642–46) and was a harsh critic of his age. By the 1790s he had emerged from a period of neglect and had been recast as a heroic figure. As with any great literary figure of the past, admirers were keen to retrace their steps and see the places where they lived and walked. Shakespeare's birthplace at Stratford upon Avon had already become a tourist attraction, as were sites associated with Milton. JOHN KEATS's poem "Lines on the Mermaid Tavern" memorializes a visit to Milton's former London home in Bread Street, where Keats encounters "Souls of Poets dead and gone" (l. 23).

Another form of literary tourism was the collecting of mementos belonging to dead authors. LEIGH HUNT was one such collector, acquiring locks of hair. (The bulk of his hair collection is now held at the University of Texas.) One of Hunt's prize possessions was a lock of Milton's hair, though stories differ as to how he came by it. According to Hunt, it came to him via a strange literary genealogy: It had belonged to the journalist Joseph Addison, who passed it on to Samuel Johnson, who gave it to John Hoole (translator and dramatist), who passed it to Dr Batty's father-in-law and via this family it eventually came to Hunt, who later showed it to Keats and gave half of it to Robert and ELIZABETH BARRETT BROWNING. Another story is that Hunt obtained the lock of hair after a ghoulish ceremony of August 1790 in which Milton's body was exhumed for inspection. Accounts describe how the lead coffin was opened, the shroud unwrapped, and teeth, bones, and hair taken from the corpse.

Somehow, then, Hunt obtained an "authenticated" lock of the hair, which became a literary prize: "Perhaps he [Milton] pressed it once, or underneath / Ran his fine fingers when he leant, blank-eyed, / And saw in fancy Adam and his bride. / With their heaped locks, or his own Delphic wreath" (ll. 5–8). Like the pilgrim who prays before icons and chases after relics, Hunt views the lock of hair as a talisman, connecting the present with the past: "It lies before me there, and my own breath / Stirs its thin outer threads, as though beside / The living head I stood in honoured pride, / Talking of lovely things that conquer death" (ll. 1–4). The hair is a link "the gentlest, yet the strongest thread" (l. 10) to his great literary forebear, who was a man of dignity and principle who should be emulated. The lock is inspiring and strength-giving, but it is difficult not to notice how time has made Milton into a collection of body parts—a possession to be controlled or sold as the owner's mood takes him.

Keats's poem "Lines on Seeing a Lock of Milton's Hair" (1818) is another tribute to the dead poet.

### Further Reading

Anonymous. *A Narrative of the Disinterment of Milton's Coffin in the Parish-Church of St Giles, Cripplegate on Wednesday, 4th of August, 1790, and of the Treatment of the Corpse, During That, and the Following Day.* 2nd ed. London, n.p., 1790.

Hunt, Leigh. *The Poetical Works of Leigh Hunt.* Edited by Thornton Hunt. London: Routledge, Wane and Routledge, 1860.

———. *Selected Writings of Leigh Hunt.* 6 vols. Edited by Robert Morrison and Michael Eberle-Sinatra. London: Pickering and Chatto, 2003.

—Joe Parrish

## "To the Men of England" See "Song: TO THE MEN OF ENGLAND."

## "To the Poppy" Anna Seward (1799)

Probably composed in the late 1780s, ANNA SEWARD's "To the Poppy" appears as Sonnet 71 in her volume of 100 *Original Sonnets on Various Subjects* (1799). Seward was a strict formalist when it came to writing sonnets, usually preferring the Miltonic variation of the Italian or Petrarchan sonnet. Like JOHN MILTON, Seward used the difficult but traditional rhyme scheme for the first 8 lines—*abbaabba*—in most of her sonnets, and she elided the conventional division between the octave and the sestet. "To the

Poppy," however, initially has the feel of the Italian sonnet but reveals its own unique structure, rhyming *abbaabccdedeff*. While not strictly speaking an Italian sonnet, "To the Poppy" does show Seward's interest in more complicated interweaving lines than is found in the English or Shakespearean sonnet, a form that she denounced. She also greatly resented the popularity of the English sonnet—particularly as practiced by CHARLOTTE SMITH, whom critics praised as superior in the form to Seward's idol Milton. Seward felt that Smith's sonnets were "facile" and were "extolled far above those of real genius" (Seward 1811 2: 216). Citing the French critic Nicolas Boileau-Despréaux in a letter, she believed that the sonnet should be difficult and "a test of skill" (Seward 1811, 2:162). Playing on the sonnet's conventional associations with love poetry, Seward uses the intricacy of the form itself to expose the appeal of the poppy as opiate, implying the toll it takes on consciousness.

Closing with an address to the plant as "thou flimsy, shewy, melancholy weed" (l. 14), Seward's sonnet stresses the plant's delusionary qualities and ends with the plain fact that it is a common weed and therefore harmful. The sonnet opens with a contrast of the red poppy to glorious "Summer roses" that represent "Love and Joy" (ll. 1, 2), while it is "gaudy, yet wild and lone" (l. 5). While the poppy's narcotic may ease "grief and pain" (l. 12), the flower's juice nonetheless brings "false peace" (l. 12). As the critic Sam George suggests, Seward's personification of the flower as "a love-craz'd Maid" (l. 8) suggests a literary kinship with Erasmus Darwin's *Loves of the Plants* (1791) (Darwin was Seward's neighbor and incorporated some of her poetry in his poem); and she reveals an interest in botany shared by other women writers, especially Smith.

Other contemporary women poets such as Henrietta O'Neill and Maria Logan also celebrated the poppy. The subject also links Seward's sonnet to the more famous, supposedly opium-inspired "KUBLA KHAN," written by SAMUEL TAYLOR COLERIDGE close to the time at which Seward's volume appeared; and to THOMAS DE QUINCEY's CONFESSIONS OF AN ENGLISH OPIUM-EATER.

## Further Reading

Feldman, Paula R., ed. *British Women Poets of the Romantic Era: An Anthology*. Baltimore, Md.: Johns Hopkins University Press, 1997.

George, Sam. *Botany, Sexuality and Women's Writing, 1760–1830*. Manchester, Eng.: Manchester University Press, 2007.

Robinson, Daniel. "Reviving the Sonnet: Women Romantic Poets and the Sonnet Claim." *European Romantic Review* 6 (1995): 98–127.

Seward, Anna. *Letters of Anna Seward: Written Between the Years 1784 and 1807*. Vol. 2. Edinburgh: Archibald Constable and Co., 1811.

———. *Original Sonnets on Various Subjects; and Odes Paraphrased from Horace*. London: G. Sael, 1799.

—Daniel Robinson

## "To the South Downs"   Charlotte Smith   (1784)

This sonnet features as the fifth in CHARLOTTE SMITH's popular *ELEGIAC SONNETS AND OTHER POEMS* of 1784. Smith's place within the mainstream of Romanticism is largely due to her exploration of the individual's subjective world and the quest to create unity from fragmented experience.

In the first quatrain, the poet depicts CHILDHOOD as the ideal state, in harmony with nature. As do WILLIAM BLAKE and WILLIAM WORDSWORTH, Smith idealizes childhood as a stage of unself-conscious innocence, in which the inner life is perfectly fused with the outer scene, the subjective with the objective world: her "wild" garlands and "artless song" suggest this, as do the responding "echoes" of the hills (ll. 3, 4). In the 20th-century psychoanalytic terms of Jacques Lacan, this ideal self is a constructed image, a projection of Smith's desire for unity and wholeness in place of the fragmentation that she experiences as an adult.

The poem goes on to imply this inner fragmentation, as the poet's emotional life is characterized by "pain," "care," and "a breaking heart" (ll. 7, 12, 8). She suggests, but negates, the possibility of recreating a sense of personal wholeness by participation in the natural scene of her childhood. She believes, in theory, that nature's beauty has power to bring such peace and solace, and thus she can transcend her cares. But the rhetorical questions leave the possibility unfulfilled, even before the resounding "no!" of the final couplet. Self-unity is a theoretical ideal which is not achievable in practice. Her sensibility remains alienated, and nature an inaccessible "alterity" (Curran). SAMUEL TAYLOR COLERIDGE narrates a similar failure to create self-unity in "DEJECTION: AN ODE" when he mourns that "I see, not feel" nature's healing potential, and he likewise remains emotionally fragmented. As a consequence, Smith's speaker longs for "oblivion" (l. 12). As Scott Freer has noted, in psychoanalytic terms, since consciousness is painful, the poet seeks escape from it—that is, nirvana. This culminates in the death wish expressed in the final couplet. Death is sought, to provide the completion that is unavailable in life itself.

This sonnet follows the Shakespearian model, with its three quatrains, a final couplet, and a rhyme scheme of *ababcdcdefefgg*. While the form is traditional, Smith demonstrates her bold transformation of the sonnet's conventional stance—that is, the male speaker's complaint of unrequited love. Smith retains the theme of unfulfilled longing but converts it to a more universal, even existential concern: the absurd disparity between her longing for emotional wholeness and the impossibility of achieving it. Overall, the sonnet subverts the usual stance taken by the 18th-century "prospect poem," in which the poet typically surveys his scene with a sense of control, and interprets the landscape with authority. Smith alludes to this tradition in her quotation from THOMAS GRAY's "Ode on a Distant Prospect of Eton College"—"your turf, your flowers among" (l. 2). But her narrator struggles to interpret the landscape fruitfully, or to appropriate its power. This isolated SENSIBILITY, and the failure of the imagination to transcend its bounds, is a nightmare shared at times by other poets, including Coleridge, WILLIAM COWPER, and Anne Brontë.

### Further Reading

Curran, Stuart. "Charlotte Smith and British Romanticism" *South Central Review* 11, no. 2, (1994): 68–78.

Labbe, Jacqueline, *Romantic Visualities: Landscape, Gender and Romanticism.* London: Macmillan, 1998.

Robinson, Daniel. "Reviving the Sonnet: Women Romantic Poets and the Sonnet Claim." *European Romantic Review* 6, no. 1 (1995): 98–127.

—Rebecca Styler

### "To William Wilberforce, Esq." William Cowper (1792)

WILLIAM COWPER's "To William Wilberforce, Esq.," first published in the *Northampton Mercury* on April 16, 1792, is a sonnet addressed to William Wilberforce (1759–1833), a political and social figure widely recognized as instrumental in bringing about the abolition of SLAVERY in the British EMPIRE. This sonnet forms part of a large canon of antislavery poetry published in the Romantic era. More specifically, it illustrates the relationship between the evangelical movement, with which both Cowper and Wilberforce were aligned, and the abolitionist cause.

The central tension in the sonnet is between the "cruel men" (l. 2) who call Wilberforce a "Fanatic" for his abolitionist "zeal" (l. 3) and Wilberforce, who desires to free the slaves "From exile, public sale, and Slav'ry's chain" (l. 4). This tension continues throughout the poem as Wilberforce's "glorious cause" (l. 8) is contrasted with the "cold Caution" and "weav[ing] delay" (ll. 9, 10) of those who attempt to halt the abolitionist effort. Religious language is employed to distinguish the "impious" (l. 2) or unholy men who oppose the abolition from the Christ-like Wilberforce, a "Friend of the Poor, the wrong'd, the fetter-gall'd" who "loose[s] th' enthrall'd" (ll. 5, 3).

The resolution of the poem's conflict begins in line 6 when the speaker urges Wilberforce to "Fear not lest labour such as thine be vain," beckoning him to foresee "Peace for Afric" (l. 12) as "remunerat[ion]" for his "toils severe" (l. 11). The motif of expectancy is observed by the scholar Robert Mitchell to be a recurring feature of much 18th-century antislavery poetry because of its ability to provide "pleasure and feelings of virtue in the present by means of an *anticipation* concerning a future event" (Mitchell 106). Wilberforce is informed that "the better hour is near" (l. 10) and is encouraged to remain optimistic as "Hope smiles" and "Joy springs" (l. 9). This language of movement and life stands in contrast to that of "Caution," "pause," and "delay" (ll. 9, 10)—terms used by Cowper to describe antiabolitionism.

Ultimately, however, the poem's final resolution is not presented in abolitionist terms. Instead, the speaker suggests that Wilberforce has already "won" the prize that matters most, "esteem and love" from "all the Just on earth" and "all the Blest above" (ll. 13–14). In these lines the speaker elevates Wilberforce and his cause by associating them with both temporal justice and spiritual transcendence. From this perspective the poet identifies Wilberforce's cause as a matter not only of worldly importance but also as a matter of eternal significance, presenting it as part of a spiritual struggle against the immoral perpetrators and supporters of the slave trade.

**Further Reading**

Cowper, William. "To William Wilberforce, Esq." In *The Poems of William Cowper: Volume III, 1785–1800*, edited by John D. Baird and Charles Ryskamp, 182–183. Oxford: Clarendon Press, 1995.

Hartley, Lodwick C. *William Cowper: Humanitarian*. Chapel Hill: University of North Carolina Press, 1938.

Mitchell, Robert. *Sympathy and the State in the Romantic Era: Systems, State Finance, and the Shadows of Futurity*. New York: Routledge, 2007.

—Laura E. Ralph

**"To Wordsworth" Percy Bysshe Shelley** (1816)
Written in 1814 and published in 1816, "To Wordsworth" is a unique poem for two reasons. First, PERCY BYSSHE SHELLEY simultaneously expressed admiration and disgust toward his subject, WILLIAM WORDSWORTH; and second, the poem spawned a subgenre of poetry and literary antipathy toward Wordsworth, including Robert Browning's "The Lost Leader" (1845).

In "To Wordsworth," the admiration Shelley has for the poet is drawn from the political and aesthetic leadership that Wordsworth possessed, and that Shelley thought himself destined to grow into. Shelley is disgusted, however, by Wordsworth's gradual turning away from his early, idealized support of the FRENCH REVOLUTION to a patriotic conservatism: "In honoured poverty thy voice did weave / Songs consecrate to truth and liberty,— / Deserting these, thou leavest me to grieve, / Thus having been, that thou shouldst cease to be" (ll. 11–14).

There is an evolving identity of both narrator and subject within the poem that mirrors the fracturing of Romanticism from its founders such as Wordsworth and SAMUEL TAYLOR COLERIDGE to the younger radicals LORD BYRON and Shelley, who felt betrayed by the elder Romantics. Wordsworth inspired Shelley in "honoured poverty," a phrase that perfectly captures Shelley's conception of the ideal poet: maligned but unflinching, radical and uncompromising. It was the French Revolution's Reign of Terror that prompted Wordsworth, like ROBERT SOUTHEY and Coleridge, to reassess his philosophy. However, for Shelley, this compromise and moderation embodied the worst form of betrayal. It was Wordsworth who had acted the coward and divided them, and Shelley places Wordsworth's philosophical infidelity on the same line or level as the personal: "Deserting these [values], thou leavest me [Shelley]."

The line ending with the word *weave* creates a doubling and then trebling of meaning. It alludes to Wordsworth's artistry, which Shelley so admired, but it also suggests empathy with the toil of the working man. The changes facing the economic landscape of Britain were woven into the values of the French Revolution, the cry of "truth and liberty" that were ultimately rejected by Wordsworth. Finally, *weave* fits the rhyming scheme with *grieve*, but the latter is the act of the narrator. Grieving is as important as weaving (creating the poem) as the emotional response to poetry must be as pure as the writing itself. All Shelley can do is grieve because once one has stopped grieving, one accepts things. If Shelley was to accept Wordsworth's betrayal, he would subsequently accept that form of compromise and conciliation that Wordsworth has come to embody. This is something that Shelley could not stand, and subconsciously he feared it would make him less radical with age. Although Shelley never met Wordsworth, he thought of him as a poetic spiritual mentor, but by the end of the poem he has come to think the poet "shouldst cease to be." Wordsworth has "been" inspirational, but Shelley bitterly regards his ideological change as a dishonorable death. Thus, he has to disparage the older Wordsworth's work in order to contrast it with his earlier poetic greatness. This mixture of admiration and disgust allows him to inherit the role of Britain's most socially committed poet only after Wordsworth has deserted it in disgrace.

**Further Reading**

Hamilton, Paul. "Wordsworth and Romanticism." In *The Cambridge Companion to Wordsworth*, edited by Stephen Gill, 213–229. Cambridge: Cambridge University Press, 2003.

Holmes, Richard. *Shelley: The Pursuit.* London: Quartet, 1976.

Johnston, Kenneth R. *The Hidden Wordsworth: Poet, Lover, Rebel, Spy.* London: Norton, 1998.

Shelley, Percy Bysshe. *Shelly's Poetry and Prose.* Edited by Donald H. Reiman and Neil Fraistat. London: Norton, 2002.

—Steven Powell

## "Tyger, The" William Blake (1794)

"The Tyger" is one of WILLIAM BLAKE's best-known poems from his most popular collection, SONGS OF INNOCENCE AND OF EXPERIENCE. Included with the *Experience* poems, "The Tyger" has often been interpreted as the inconclusive and deconstructive counterpoint to the song of *Innocence* entitled "The Lamb," which offers a simple yet profound universal equation between lambs, children, God and Christ. The tiger, however, is an anomaly that stands apart from such holy company, and Blake's narrator asks: "Did he who made the Lamb make thee?" (l. 20). From this open-ended question, readers have suggested that Blake's tiger, a symbol of his Dissenting religious views, asks whether a benevolent Christian God is capable of authoring a fearful creative symmetry that includes sublime horrors as well as innocent beauty. Alternative views suggest that the tiger, like Victor Frankenstein's creature (see FRANKENSTEIN), is the offspring of a satanic, rebellious creator who possesses godlike power. To fully understand the implications of this, it must be noted that during the time of the *Songs*' collective production, Blake was also composing The MARRIAGE OF HEAVEN AND HELL, a philosophical attempt to redefine and celebrate evil as "the active springing from Energy" (Plate 3 Blake 1988, 34).

Like many of Blake's other symbols, it is difficult to understand what the tiger conclusively means. However, this uncertainty, stemming from the tiger's multiple associations, is the spark of its vitality, which demands active, not passive, interaction with this poem. For example, "burning bright" (l. 1), the tiger may carry some symbolic association with the philosophical and scientific illuminations of the Enlightenment, which would also connect it with the egalitarian energies and "deadly terrors" (l. 16) of the FRENCH REVOLUTION, which were forged from such ideas. However, this predatory animal is also created with a hammer, chain, furnace, and anvil, relating it to the nightmare products of another revolutionary dream: the Industrial Revolution, which was disrupting England's agrarian way of life with increased urbanity, inhuman economies, domestic slavery, and unnatural working conditions that stifled imagination and perception (see INDUSTRIALISM).

Yet the tiger is not the true subject of this poem. It is the visible and symbolic result of a mysterious authorship, and Blake uses this poem to primarily interrogate the identity, motivations and power of the tiger's author, who not only "could" (l. 4) create it, but "dare[s]" (l. 24) to create and frame (or contain) this beast—subtly comparing him to Icarus (l. 7) and Prometheus (l. 8). The implied answer to the question of who created the tiger is, of course, Blake, a rebellious and romantic author and a visionary inventor and illustrator, who can create the lamb and the tiger because he remembers that "all deities reside in the human breast" (Blake 1988, 28).

Finally, Blake's illuminated, engraved plate of the poem features a cartoonish tiger in nonsymmetrical profile. Just as "The Tyger" opposes and yet extends "The Lamb," so too does the illustration multiply the potential meaning of this poem, prompting us to ask further questions about the nature of language, images, authorship, meaning, and creative responsibility.

**Further Reading**

Blake, William. *The Complete Poetry and Prose of William Blake,* rev. ed., edited by David Erdman, 24. New York: Doubleday, 1988.

———. *The Tyger.* Edited by Winston Weathers. Columbus, Ohio: C. E. Merrill, 1969.

Eaves, Morris, Robert N. Essick, and Joseph Viscomi, eds. *The William Blake Archive.* Available online. URL: http://www.blakearchive.org. Accessed on March 30, 2008.

Frye, Northrop. *Fearful Symmetry: A Study of William Blake.* Princeton, N.J.: Princeton University Press, 1947.

Gardner, Stanley. *The Tyger, the Lamb, and the Terrible Desart: Songs of Innocence and of Experience in Its Times and Circumstance.* Madison, N.J.: Fairleigh Dickinson University Press, 1998.

Hagstrum, Jean H. *William Blake, Poet and Painter: An Introduction to the Illuminated Verse.* Chicago: University of Chicago Press, 1964.

Hirsch E. D., Jr. *Innocence and Experience: An Introduction to Blake.* New Haven, Conn.: Yale University Press, 1964.

Kaplan, Fred. "'The Tyger' and Its Maker: Blake's Vision of Art and the Artist." *Studies in English Literature, 1500–1900.* 7, no. 4 (Autumn 1967): 617–627.

Paley, Morton. "Tyger of Wrath." *PMLA* 81, no. 7 (December 1966): 540–551.

—Jon Saklofske

# U

## "Unsex'd Females, The"  Richard Polwhele
(1798)

"The Unsex'd Females: A Poem, Addressed to the Author of *The Pursuits of Literature*" (1798) is the work of the Reverend Richard Polwhele (1760–1838), an Anglican clergyman and unsuccessful poet. Polwhele attacks the radical political ideals and scandalous lifestyles of a group of women writers led by the "Amazonian" MARY WOLLSTONE-CRAFT. His title is taken from Thomas J. Mathias's *The Pursuits of Literature* (1798), which condemns the pernicious influence of Jacobin politics on literature. Polwhele develops Mathias's attack by making this question of politics dependent on gender difference. His poem also engages with radical texts, namely George Dyer's "Ode to Liberty" (1792), which asserted that "the most sensible women are more uniformly on the side of Liberty" (quoted in Guest, 64); and WILLIAM GODWIN's *Memoirs of the Author of A Vindication of the Rights of Woman* (1798). Polwhele largely conducts his critique in footnotes, which are 20 times the length of his verse.

For Polwhele, the greatest threat of the "unsex'd females" is their unprecedented and unnatural actions: "Survey with me, what ne'er our fathers saw. / A female band despising NATURE's law" (ll. 11–12). Violation of "NATURE's law" is the crime that unites political and sexual transgression. Polwhele notes: "Nature is the grand basis of all laws human and divine: and the woman, who has no regard to nature, will soon 'walk after the Flesh, in the lust of uncleanness, and despise government.'"

Polwhele undertakes a self-conscious act of canon formation, selecting "a groupe of female Writers; whose productions have been appreciated by the public as works of learning or genius" (15–16). He targets ANNA LAETITIA BARBAULD, MARY ROBINSON, CHARLOTTE SMITH, HELEN MARIA WILLIAMS, ANN YEARSLEY, MARY HAYS, and the painters Angelica Kauffman and Emma Crewe. He does not hesitate to praise Barbauld's "chaste and elegant" work, the "sweetly picturesque" effect of Smith's sonnets, even the "genius" of Williams. But each has transgressed propriety by becoming "a politician." In opposition, Polwhele praises female writers who are content to express themselves through a refined sensibility: Elizabeth Montagu, Elizabeth Carter, Hester Chapone, ANNA SEWARD, HESTER PIOZZI, FRANCES BURNEY, ANN RADCLIFFE, the painter Diana Beauclerk, and most importantly HANNAH MORE, who is "as a character, in all points, diametrically opposite to Miss Wollstonecraft" (35–6).

Wollstonecraft is the archetypal "unsex'd female." Polwhele's presentation reveals the contradiction in the phrase itself, for though Wollstonecraft is "Amazonian" (6), she also displays typical female weaknesses. Wollstonecraft is a woman "whom no decorum checks" (l. 64) and who thus exhibits an excess both of reason and of passion. Polwhele notes, "I know nothing of Miss Wollstonecraft's character or conduct, but from the *Memoirs* of Godwin" (28), on which his verse draws so closely that the critic Nicola Trott characterizes the poem as a "negative biography, shadowing Godwin's own" (Trott 35). Polwhele makes Wollstonecraft's "lascivious" behavior (l. 116) a symptom of moral and political depravity. Even her death in childbirth becomes a consequence of her radicalism: "[T]he hand of Providence is visible, in her life, her death, and in the *Memoirs* themselves . . . that the fallacy of her doctrines and the effects of an irreligious conduct, might be manifested to the world" (29). Ironically, the "fallacious" doctrines and behaviour of the women he condemns are only reason Polwhele is remembered.

## Further Reading

Craciun, Adriana, ed. *A Routledge Literary Sourcebook on Mary Wollstonecraft's A Vindication of the Rights of Women.* London: Routledge, 2002.

Guest, Harriet. "Eighteenth Century Femininity: 'A Supposed Sexual Character.'" In *Women and Literature in Britain 1700–1800,* edited by Vivien Jones, 46–68. Cambridge: Cambridge University Press, 2000.

Pascoe, Judith. "Unsex'd Females: Barbauld, Robinson and Smith." In *Cambridge Companion to English Literature, 1780–1830.* Cambridge: Cambridge University Press, 2004, 211–226.

Polwhele, Richard. *The Unsex'd Females.* 1798. Reprint, New York: Garland, 1974.

Stafford, William. *English Feminists and their Opponents in the 1790s: Unsex'd and Proper Females.* Manchester, Eng.: Manchester University Press, 2002.

Trott, Nina. "Sexing the Critic: Mary Wollstonecraft at the Turn of the Century." In *1798: The Year of the "Lyrical Ballads,"* edited by Richard Cronin, 32–67. New York: St. Martin's Press, 1998.

—Mary Fairclough

## "Vampyre, The" John Polidori (1819)

This GOTHIC tale originated during the ghost-story contest involving LORD BYRON, JOHN WILLIAM POLIDORI, PERCY BYSSHE SHELLEY, and MARY SHELLEY during the Geneva summer of 1816, which produced Mary Shelley's FRANKENSTEIN. Byron's fragment was never completed, and Polidori revised Byron's text to create this tale, which was published without Polidori's knowledge in Henry Colburn's *New Monthly Magazine* in April 1819, listing Byron as the author. Byron denied authorship, while Polidori wrote the publisher to identify himself as the author and to request the appropriate recognition and financial consideration. Unfortunately, despite his actions, Byron's name continued to be listed prominently on the title page, and Polidori was criticized, variously, as a plagiarist and a literary parasite.

The story, as originally published, centers on Lord Ruthven, a character who shares his name with the Byronic character in Lady CAROLINE LAMB's novel *GLENARVON*, written after her affair with Byron had ended. (Polidori would later change his titular character's name to Strongmore, though the majority of modern editions have retained the original appellation.) In Polidori's tale, Ruthven becomes the object of fascination for the young narrator, Aubrey, who embarks with Ruthven on a tour of the Continent after certain embarrassments require Ruthven's departure from England. In this way, the story parallels the circumstances under which Polidori and Byron had themselves become traveling companions in 1816. During their trav-

els, Aubrey becomes acquainted with Ruthven's immoral character, typified by his gambling and his seduction of several women. Subsequently, Aubrey and Ruthven part company, and Aubrey becomes enamored with a young Greek girl, Ianthe, who is murdered by what appears to be a vampire. In the aftermath, Aubrey falls ill and is nursed by Ruthven, with whom he resumes his travels despite Aubrey's suspicion that Ruthven is indeed the vampire who has killed Ianthe. When Ruthven falls victim to a robber's attack, he induces Aubrey to swear an oath that he will not tell anyone of his death for one year and a day. Shortly after his return to England, Aubrey is shocked to encounter Ruthven—now calling himself the Earl of Marsden—in the midst of a drawing-room crowd. Again overcome, and now suspected of mental instability, he is confined to his room. As the anniversary of Ruthven's "death" approaches and he foresees his liberation from his oath, Aubrey begins to recover, only to discover that his sister is to marry Ruthven/Marsden. Aubrey tries frantically to get his sister to at least postpone her nuptials for one day, but his outbursts are viewed only as insane ravings. He dies on the same night that his sister becomes Ruthven's final victim.

Polidori's short story marks an important shift in the way vampires were portrayed in literature in the 19th century and served to influence several subsequent vampire tiles, culminating in 1897 with the publication of Bram Stoker's *Dracula*. In previous treatments of the vampire, such as ROBERT SOUTHEY's *Thalaba the Destroyer* and Byron's *THE*

GIAOUR, the vampire is often a type of reanimated corpse, ghastly in its appearance and zombie-like in its actions as it is confined to its native land, compelled to feed off the blood of its former loved ones. In Polidori's tale, on the other hand, the title character is a traveling aristocrat, handsome, charismatic, and able to seduce many of the victims he eventually murders.

**Further Reading**

Bainbridge, Simon. "Lord Ruthven's Power: Polidori's 'The Vampyre,' Doubles and the Byronic Imagination." *Byron Journal* 34, no. 1 (2006): 21–34.

Polidori, John. *The Vampyre and Ernestus Berchtold; or, The Modern Oedipus.* Edited by D. L. Macdonald and Kathleen Scherf. Peterborough, Ont.: Broadview Press, 2008.

Skarda, Patricia. "Vampirism and Plagiarism: Byron's Influence and Polidori's Practice." *Studies in Romanticism* 28 (1989): 249–269.

Twitchell, James. *The Living and the Dead: A Study of the Vampire in Romantic Literature.* Durham, N.C.: Duke University Press, 1997.

—L. Adam Mekler

## *Vathek* William Beckford (1782)

WILLIAM BECKFORD wrote *Vathek* in 1782, when he was 21 years old. It is considered both an oriental tale and a GOTHIC novel, modeled on the popular forms of both *The Arabian Nights* and Horace Walpole's *The Castle of Otranto.* The novel's plot centers on Vathek, a young caliph (ruler) with enormous appetites for luxury and knowledge whose greedy and overreaching nature finally leads to his undoing. The novel is full of fantastic events and considerable violence and blood; Vathek sacrifices 50 children, having them thrown into a pit for the Giaour (an evil magician) to devour, and dead bodies pile up at several points in the plot. LORD BYRON claimed to have used Beckford's Giaour (the name means "infidel") as a model for his 1813 poem *THE GIAOUR.*

The caliph Vathek is a classic dark Romantic man; he is attractive and admired, "but when he was angry, one of his eyes became so terrible that no person could bear to behold it; and the wretch upon whom it was fixed instantly fell backward,

and sometimes expired" (Beckford 109). Vathek is "addicted to women and the pleasures of the table" (109), and he has the power and money to indulge all of his vices excessively. Perhaps his most important Romantic characteristic is his "insatiable curiosity" (124); it is ultimately his desire to gain forbidden knowledge and power that leads him to deny his religious faith (Islam) and seek answers in the occult. Vathek is aided on his quest for power and knowledge by his mother, the princess Carathis, who engages in occult rituals and human sacrifice to help her son. He also manages to engage the affections of Nouronihar, a beautiful daughter of a devout Islamic emir, despite the fact that she is already promised to her cousin Gulchenrouz, whom Vathek attempts to have killed. A true Romantic hero-villain, Vathek ends his novel having "sullied himself with a thousand crimes" and he and his companions become "a prey to grief without end, and remorse without mitigation" (194). Many critics, including R. B. Gill, read biographical connections between Beckford himself and his title character.

*Vathek's* particularly complicated publication history is a major focus of the critical discussion about the text. Despite the fact that his native language was English, Beckford originally wrote the novel in French. With the help of Samuel Henley, he translated his manuscript into English. For unclear reasons, Henley published his translation without Beckford's approval in 1786; shortly thereafter, Beckford rushed two French editions to press. Most versions of the novel include an extensive section of notes explaining cultural and historical references written by Beckford and Henley. Beckford also wrote but never completed several short oriental tales that were to be inserted into the text, and he planned several more. Known as *The Episodes of Vathek,* the draft versions of these tales are included in some modern editions of the novel (such as Kenneth W. Graham's 2001 edition from Broadview Press).

See also ORIENTALISM.

**Further Reading**

Beckford, William. *Vathek. Three Gothic Novels.* Edited by E. F. Bleiler. New York: Dover Publications, Inc., 1966.

Conant, Martha Pike. *The Oriental Tale in England in the Eighteenth Century.* Norwood, Mass.: Norwood Press, 1908.

Gill, R. B. "The Author in the Novel: Creating William Beckford in Vathek." *Eighteenth-Century Fiction* 15, no. 2 (2003): 241–245.

Roberts, Adam, and Eric Robertson. "The Giaour's Sabre: A Reading of Beckford's Vathek." *Studies in Romanticism* 35, no. 2 (1996): 199–211.

—Bridget M. Marshall

## *Vindication of the Rights of Men, A* Mary Wollstonecraft (1790)

MARY WOLLSTONECRAFT's *Vindication* is one of the important texts of the revolutionary controversy of the 1790s, which evolved with the FRENCH REVOLUTION and focused on "the rights of man." With the encouragement of the radical publisher Joseph Johnson, Wollstonecraft initially published her text anonymously as a letter responding to the criticism EDMUND BURKE directed in his *Reflections on the Revolution in France* (1790) against Richard Price's radical sermon *A Discourse on the Love of our Country* (1789). In replying to Burke, Wollstonecraft attacked his conservative antirevolutionary views, focusing on, as the scholar Gary Kelly notes, the French Revolution and its English supporters, "rights," state, religious establishments, the British constitution, the ruling class, and the poor (Kelley 88).

In Burke's earlier *A PHILOSOPHICAL ENQUIRY INTO THE ORIGIN OF OUR IDEAS OF THE SUBLIME AND BEAUTIFUL* (1757), Burke had identified the SUBLIME—an aesthetic category—with masculine qualities. In her *Vindication*, Wollstonecraft attacks not only his hierarchical political views but also his gendered aesthetics. Thus, she begins her text by making the sublime and the beautiful "less gendered and more equal" (Wollstonecraft 16). She argues that "truth, in morals, has ever appeared to me the essence of the sublime; and, in taste, simplicity the only criterion of the beautiful" (35). In addition to redefining these categories, she repeatedly rejects Burke's understanding of "Nature" and "Reason," which, she argues, favours "slavery" (64). She thus ridicules his assurances of the stability and perfec-

tion of the traditional order. Wollstonecraft also condemns Burke's notion of "birthrights" (35), which, she argues, fail to grant freedom and equality to all citizens and introduce classist structures, which prohibit the majority of citizens from exercising their natural rights. She traces the present unjust distribution of power back to the 14th century, when the nobility gained their power by force and theft.

Wollstonecraft relentlessly draws attention to alleged discrepancies between Burke's behavior and his idealized view of conservative politics. She repeatedly attacks his rejection of the French Revolution, which she, like other radicals, has hailed as a new period of freedom and equality. But she questions Burke's inconsistent attitude that condemns the freedom the French promote while having previously supported American independence from England. She repeatedly promotes Price's view of religious freedom, condemning the prevalent and ancient corruptions of established religion by repeatedly affirming people's natural right to subjectively choose and practice their faith.

The editors D. L. Macdonald and Kathleen Scherf assert that Wollstonecraft's focus is "men (and women), in society, and . . . the relations between different classes" (in Wollstonecraft 15). Despite the strength with which she wrote and reasoned, she was criticized for engaging in political issues and displaying unwomanly behavior. Various critics also disapproved of her disorganized argument, which may be explained by the fact that she wrote and published her text within a few weeks after the appearance of Burke's *Reflections*.

### Further Reading

Gunther-Canada, Wendy. "The Politics of Sense and Sensibility: Mary Wollstonecraft and Catharine Macaulay Graham on Edmund Burke's *Reflections on the Revolution in France*." In *Women Writers and the Early Modern British Political Tradition*, edited by Hilda L. Smith, 126–147. Cambridge: Cambridge University Press, 1998.

Johnson, Claudia L. *Equivocal Beings: Politics, Gender, and Sentimentality in the 1790s: Wollstonecraft, Radcliffe, Burney, Austen.* Chicago: University of Chicago Press, 1995.

Jones, Chris. "Mary Wollstonecraft's *Vindications* and their Political Tradition." In *The Cambridge Com-*

panion to *Mary Wollstonecraft,* edited by Claudia L. Johnson, 42–58. Cambridge and New York: Cambridge University Press, 2002.

Kelly, Gary. *Revolutionary Feminism: The Mind and Career of Mary Wollstonecraft.* Basingstoke, Eng.: Macmillan, 1992.

Wollstonecraft, Mary. *The Vindications: The Rights of Men, the Rights of Women.* Edited by D. L. Macdonald and Kathleen Scherf. Peterborough, Ont.: Broadview Press, 1997.

—Mariam Radhwi

## Vindication of the Rights of Woman, A
### Mary Wollstonecraft (1792)

Whereas WILLIAM WORDSWORTH has often been called the father of Romanticism, MARY WOLLSTONECRAFT is often seen as the mother of feminism. However, *A Vindication of the Rights of Woman* encouraged much more than the women's movement. It revolutionized writing in a way that later became known as Romantic. Wollstonecraft's famous prose illustrates those Romantic characteristics that one will find throughout the canon of Romantic works, even the ones published by the "second-generation" poets: JOHN KEATS, LORD BYRON, and PERCY BYSSHE SHELLEY.

Romanticism coincided with NEOCLASSICISM (1765–1830), but it revolted against the control, order, and reason venerated by the latter. Throughout *Vindication,* Wollstonecraft constantly disparages neoclassical manners, artificial grace, artificial feelings, "starched rules of decorum," "false refinement," "sickly delicacy," women who refused to be mothers to their children, misguided notions of virtue, children denied their childhood—all things counter to what the Romantics considered natural and healthy. Central to the new way of thinking, as Wordsworth argued, was "low and rustic life" because "in that condition, the essential passions of the heart find a better soil in which they can attain their maturity, are less under restraint . . . less under the influence of social vanity" (Wordsworth 1988, 245).

Wollstonecraft's *Vindication* balks at societal constraints, and in contrast to the many horrific pictures she depicts of the upper classes, her ideal hearkens to the halcyon past, as illustrated in this rustic scene: "I still recollect, with pleasure, the country day school; where a boy trudged in the morning, wet or dry, carrying his books, and his dinner, if it were at a considerable distance; a servant did not then lead master by the hand, for, when he had once put on coat and breeches, he was allowed to shift for himself, and return alone in the evening to recount the feats of the day close at the parental knee. His father's house was his home, and was ever after fondly remembered; nay, I appeal to many superior men, who were educated in this manner, whether the recollection of some shady lane where they conned their lesson; or, of some stile, where they sat making a kite, or mending a bat, has not endeared their country to them?" (Wollstonecraft 300).

Wollstonecraft disdained all forms of artificiality. Remarkably, her style models the very theory of writing it propounds. Her 13 chapters are anything but orderly. One writer for the *Critical Review* said that her language is "flowing and flowery; but weak, diffuse, and confused" (quoted in Wollstonecraft 1997, 447). Wollstonecraft would have agreed to this with approbation. Her introduction warns the reader of her determination to "disdain to cull my phrases or polish my style;—I aim at being useful, and insincerity will render me unaffected; for, wishing rather to persuade by the force of my arguments, than dazzle by the elegance of my language, I shall not waste my time in rounding periods, or in fabricating the turgid bombast of artificial feelings, which coming from the head, never reach the heart" (Wollstonecraft 112). Her narrative is not linear but, rather, nearly stream of consciousness. To use a Romantic word, it is organic. Additionally, there is much repetition. For example, she constantly accuses women for being too preoccupied with their physical appearance and skills in coquetry, but her refrain is as naturally redundant as butterflies on a long summer walk. One might see them once on a bush next to a stream, but to see them again in the middle of a dusty road is to see them in a different way. Thus, every time Wollstonecraft brings up the same subject, she casts it in a different light so that the reader can appreciate different aspects. Furthermore, she wants the idea, like the butterflies, to never leave the reader throughout the entire work.

Though she is certainly flowery, she is not so in typical neoclassical pompous and contrived fashion. Using the language of nature, which in the "Preface" to *Lyrical Ballads* (1800) Wordsworth called a plainer, more simplistic expression that conveys elementary emotions common to all, which are "more easily comprehended, and are more durable" (Wordsworth, 1965, 245), Wollstonecraft emphatically and clearly analyzes the state of being female: "The conduct and manners of women, in fact, evidently prove that their minds are not in a healthy state; for, like the flowers which are planted in too rich a soil, strength and usefulness are sacrificed to beauty" (Wollstonecraft 109). The passage continues the metaphorical conceit with "flaunting leaves," "fade, disregarded on the stalk" (109), and "barren blooming" (92).

Her writing also aimed to grasp the essence of a thing, as defined later by SAMUEL TAYLOR COLERIDGE in BIOGRAPHIA LITERARIA: "Essence, in its primary signification, means the principle of individuation, the inmost principle of the possibility of any thing, as that particular thing." Unlike many 18th-century writers, her goal was not to achieve verisimilitude in her writing; she meant to use what William Wordsworth would term a "colouring of the imagination" (Wordsworth, 1988, 244), calling upon the reader to apply all of the senses, including those that are spiritual in order to gain knowledge. One example is in this passage from chapter 7: "A shadowy phantom glides before us, obscuring every other object; yet when the soft cloud is grasped, the form melts into common air. Leaving a solitary void, or sweet perfume, stolen from the violet, that memory long holds dear. But, I have tripped unawares on fair ground, feeling the balmy gale of spring stealing on me, through november [sic] frowns" (256). Aside from these and so many other Romantic characteristics, *Vindication* qualifies as a revolutionary piece of literature that helped usher in Romanticism. Perhaps the most salient part is when Wollstonecraft called upon readers to "enlarge the soul" (113) and to provide an understanding that "enlarges the heart," an organic growth championed 27 years later by her son-in-law, Percy Bysshe Shelley, with this expectation, that poetry "awakens and enlarges the mind itself by rendering it the recep-

tacle of a thousand unapprehended combinations of thought" (340).

See also LETTERS FOR LITERARY LADIES; "RIGHTS OF WOMAN, THE"; SIMPLE STORY, A.

**Further Reading**

Coleridge, Samuel Taylor. *Coleridge's Principles of Criticism.* Edited by Andrew George. Boston; D.C. Heath, 1895.

Falco, Maria J., ed. *Feminist Interpretations of Mary Wollstonecraft.* University Park: University of Pennsylvania Press, 1996.

Johnson, Claudia L., ed. *The Cambridge Companion to Mary Wollstonecraft.* Cambridge and New York: Cambridge University Press, 2002.

Kelly, Gary. *Revolutionary Feminism: The Mind and Career of Mary Wollstonecraft.* New York: St. Martin's Press, 1992.

Taylor, Barbara. *Mary Wollstonecraft and the Feminist Imagination.* Cambridge: Cambridge University Press, 2003.

Thompson, E. P. *The Romantics: England in a Revolutionary Age.* New York: New Press, 1997.

Wollstonecraft, Mary. *The Vindications: The Rights of Men, the Rights of Woman.* Edited by D. L. MacDonald and Katherine Schelf. Peterborough, Ontario: Broadview, 1997.

Wordsworth, William and Samuel Taylor Coleridge. *Lyrical Ballads.* Edited by R. L. Breet and A. R. Jones. London: Routledge, 1988.

—Brenda Ayres

## *Visions of the Daughters of Albion* William Blake (1793)

*Visions of the Daughters of Albion* introduces readers to WILLIAM BLAKE's complex portrayal of women. Despite the strength of her will, Oothoon suffers in confronting her sexuality. The frontispiece of the illuminated book offers a useful frame for approaching the text. It shows the three primary characters—Oothoon, Theotormon and Bromion—bound together in their anguish within the confined space of a cave. The cave, a recurrent symbol in Blake's work, calls our attention to the mental imprisonment that his characters suffer in response to the influence of inherited systems of belief. In this text, we recognize criticism of several cultural institutions invoked by the conflict between Oothoon, Theotormon and Bromion: sexuality, religion, colonialism (see EMPIRE), and SLAVERY, among others. More specifically, we recognize the characters personifying examples of the sexual and social domination that manifest within these systems.

Formal elements of the work serve to guide the reading process. The poetic lines, as is typical of Blake's prophetic work generally, are written in free verse, and the paratext (framework) is also central to understanding the work both textually and thematically. The plural form deployed in the title—*Visions*—points readers to the text's presentation of multiple perspectives on the same event: Oothoon's rape. This central event is described briefly in the "Argument" and elaborated on in the section of the text headed "Visions," which provides three reflections, separated by the Daughters' chorus, on the conflict resulting from Oothoon's exploration of her desire. The motto, the poetic line included under the title, offers a more general entrance into the work's interest in the limits of sensory perception, and the visual images supplement the poetry by bringing attention to crucial themes and textual moments.

If the work's motto—"The Eye sees more than the Heart knows"—introduces a central theme of the text, then one entrance into the story of *Visions* is through the difference between sense perception and intuition or imagination. An investment in imagination connects Blake with the other Romantic poets, whose work otherwise differs dramatically in form and content. While acknowledging the supremacy of visual sight, Blake calls attention to the difference between modes of perception and ask readers to consider their differences within the text.

Similarly, if the "Argument" establishes the central features of this struggle from Oothoon's perspective, then we immediately learn several pieces of information. She was not ashamed of her love for Theotormon but did evade the sexual reality exposed by that love, and when she decides to give in to desire and embrace her sexuality, she is punished by being raped. The presentation of the argument suggests that the rape serves as the consequence of her willing acceptance of sexual desire.

As an external response to her desire, the rape is established by the "Argument" as the disappointing reality of a world where female sexuality is repressed and scorned. The consequences for Oothoon, who is punished for exploring the sensations of her body, and for Theotormon, who suffers from his lack of desire for sensual enjoyment, establishes the poem's central tension.

The text of the "Visions" section can be organized into three parts separated by the Daughters' chorus of echoing sighs. Each part develops a more nuanced perspective through the three characters' voices. The first vision describes the details of Oothoon's decision to "pluck the flower" of Leutha's vale, to confront her desire for Theotormon. Unfortunately, Bromion punishes her by asserting dominance over her body and naming her a harlot. Bromion's language of possession and violence situates Oothoon firmly within a system that views female enjoyment of sex as a crime. Her punishment is solidified by the introduction of Theotormon, who sits on the threshold of Bromion's cave, as seen in the frontispiece. In an attempt to appease her lovers' jealous woes, Oothoon, who "cannot weep" because she has embraced her sexual desire, simulates despair by howling and calling for eagles to prey at her flesh, a scene pictured on plate 3. Oothoon suffers in the hope that the desecration of her body will restore her physical purity, but rather than lament her torture, Theotormon smiles.

The second perspective includes a dialogue between Oothoon, Bromion, and Theotormon that uncovers the cultural systems of colonialism and empiricism behind the male domination in the poem. Oothoon appeals to Theotormon's jealousy in her attempt to make him understand her decision to accept sexual desire as a way of getting beyond the "narrow circle" she felt her "infinite brain" enclosed within. This theme of limitation, both physical and conceptual, is central to Blake's work. The inability to recognize how cultural systems restrain individuals, particularly women, is represented by Theotormon's inability to hear Oothoon's lament. Bromion, on the other hand, can hear her because he does not repress his instincts the way Theotormon does. However, he acts on his instincts to control others and reinforces the systems of domination Blake exposes through the figure of Oothoon. The two men respond to Oothoon's plea by calling on existing systems of thought, which punish expressions of female desire. The conflict over improved sensual enjoyment established by this dialogue point to the larger issues at stake in the poem and Blake's work more generally.

The final plates reveal Oothoon still seeking Theotormon's understanding, but through an articulation of his hypocrisy rather than an appeal to his jealousy. She tries to communicate a belief in selfless love and the possibility that joy exists in forms different from the systems of domination that have enslaved the Daughters of Albion and will not succeed in controlling her. Though she may suffer the "name of whore," Oothoon enjoys the freedom of knowing herself pure in soul, if not in body. For Blake and Oothoon, rather than make someone a slave, desire is an expression of a higher perception of the heart rather than the eye. This belief is framed in the language of religion, a system Blake sees as perpetuating selfish love and restraining desire. The lack of these emotions keeps Theotomoron from understanding Oothoon. In this way the poem positions his idleness and unrelenting scorn as the real tragedy situated against the background of Bromion's crime, represented throughout by the cavernous setting.

The work's final image of Oothoon depicts her soaring above the three Daughters of Albion from whom she has divided and progressively distanced herself throughout the text. The final chorus confirms that they too are ignorant of Oothoon's strength. With arms extended like wings, hair flying about her freely, she exemplifies the power of the human spirit to rise above the cultural domination. Having risen above the preying eagle of plate 3, released from the chains of plate 4, Blake concludes the poem by illustrating Oothoon's autonomy and release from the constraints binding those around her.

## Further Reading

Blake, William, ed. *Visions of the Daughters of Albion.* Edited by Robert N. Essick. San Marino, Calif.: Huntington Library, 2002.

Bruder, Helen P. *William Blake and the Daughters of Albion.* Basingstoke, Eng.: Macmillan Press; New York: St. Martin's Press, 1997.

Goslee, Nancy Moore. "Slavery and Sexual Character: Questioning the Master Trope in Blake's Visions of the Daughters of Albion." *ELH* 57 (1990): 101–128.

Ostriker, Alicia. "Desire Gratified and Ungratified: William Blake and Sexuality." *Blake: An Illustrated Quarterly* 16 (1982–83): 156–165.

Wilkie, Brian. *Blake's Thel and Oothoon.* Victoria, B.C.: University of Victoria, 1990.

—Sarah Peterson

## Wackenroder, Wilhelm Heinrich (1773–1798)

A critic, novelist, and thinker who became one of the most influential exponents of fledgling Romantic thought in Germany before his early death at age 25, Wilhelm Heinrich Wackenroder was the son of an influential civil servant who became minister of justice. Born on July 13, 1773, he studied for a semester at Erlangen and was enraptured by Bamberg and Nuremberg and by Albrecht Dürer's art. Sensitive and receptive, Wackenroder responded enthusiastically and intelligently to the great works of painting he saw on a visit to Dresden in 1796. He wrote three novels, *Die Unsichtbaren* (1794), *Der Demokrat* (1796), and *Das Schlo Montford* (1796), as well his most famous work, a collection of essays entitled *Die Herzensergiessungen eines kunstliebenden Klosterbruders* (*Outpourings of an Art-Loving Friar,* 1797). The last-named—which included contributions from Wackenroder's friend LUDWIG TIECK—contained the story of "The Remarkable Musical Life of the Musician Joseph Berglinger," narrating the experiences of a composer caught between the claims of art and life—a situation which has been seen to resemble something of Wackenroder's own life. It tells of Joseph Berglinger, shy and melancholy, who, after much agonizing and contrary to his father's wishes, follows his ambition of becoming a musician. However, once he has followed his dream, disillusionment sets in. In a mirror of Wackenroder's beliefs, Joseph rejects the old ideas of classicism and "reason" together with the idea that music can be seen as a science (reason). Rather, all art is divinely inspired. In a bid to break with the rational and reason-based intellectual past, Wackenroder stressed the importance of emotions and imagination and championed the "law" of feeling.

After Wackenroder's death on February 13, 1798, Tieck helped oversee the publication of his remaining writings.

### Further Reading

Thornton, Karin. *"Wackenroder's Objective Romanticism."* *Germanic Review* 37 (1962): 161–173.

Wackenroder, Wilhelm Heinrich, and Ludwig Tieck. *Outpourings of an Art-Loving Friar.* London: Ungar, 1975.

Zipes, Jack. *"W. H. Wackenroder: In Defense of his Romanticism."* *Germanic Review* 44 (1969): 247–258.

—Thomas Morgan

## *Wanderer, The* Frances Burney (1814)

*The Wanderer; or, Female Difficulties* (1814) begins mysteriously: In the middle of the night, strangers fleeing France on a boat must decide whether to allow a dirty stranger on board with them. The GOTHIC overtones of this opening weave themselves throughout the novel, which contains not only a suicide attempt in a graveyard but also a pool of blood in a lonely forest cottage. Despite these elements, *The Wanderer* is not a gothic novel. It details the struggles of Juliet Granville (the stranger wanting passage on the boat), Lord

Granville's daughter who was raised by a French bishop. Lord Granville wishes Juliet to remain outside of England to hide his union with her mother, so he arranges for her to have an inheritance if she remains in France after she marries. An unscrupulous agent of Robespierre discovers this and forces Juliet to marry him by threatening the life of the bishop. Juliet escapes after the marriage ceremony but before the legal transfer of her inheritance to her husband. Because she and the bishop are both in danger of being found by her husband, Juliet keeps her identity hidden for most of the novel, and even the reader does not know her real name for the majority of the book. Characters in the book call her Ellis (a corruption of the misheard initials "L.S.") or refer to her as an incognita.

Part of Juliet's struggles result from her attempts merely to survive. She loses her purse when she flees France, so she is penniless. To make her way in the world, she works as a companion, a music teacher, a milliner, a mantua maker, and a shop owner. FRANCES BURNEY's emphasis on sympathizing with the individual transcending her circumstances while performing difficult menial labor reflects this work's Romantic sensibilities. Juliet's struggles to earn enough money to live constitute the "female difficulties" of the novel's subtitle, painting the plight of women in a sympathetic light. The main title of the work also resonates with Romantic imagery: The solitary wanderer in nature is a staple of such canonical works as WILLIAM WORDSWORTH's "I WANDERED LONELY AS A CLOUD" (1804).

Eventually, Juliet's husband finds her, is jailed, leaves jail, returns to France, and conveniently dies. The bishop finds Juliet, reassuring her that her marriage was never legal. This frees her to marry Harleigh, whom she met on the boat that took her from France, and who loved and respected her regardless of her refusal to explain her situation. Harleigh is also beloved by Elinor Joddrell, a wealthy young woman who ardently supports the cause of women's rights as well as the revolution in France. Harleigh admires Elinor's intellect, but her atheism and extreme views—she seems almost a caricature of MARY WOLLSTONECRAFT—make it impossible for him to return her feelings. Because *The Wanderer* ultimately upholds the status quo

and reinforces the utility of social codes, it is not a stereotypically Romantic narrative. Yet Burney's intensely sensitive take on women's struggles make this novel an intriguingly Romantic work.

## Further Reading

Burney, Frances. *The Wanderer.* Edited by Margaret Doody et al. Oxford: Oxford University Press, 2001.

Epstein, Julia. *The Iron Pen: Frances Burney and the Politics of Women's Writing.* Madison: University of Wisconsin Press, 1989.

Gemmeke, Mascha. *Frances Burney and the Female Bildungsroman: An Interpretation of The Wanderer: or, Female Difficulties.* Frankfurt: Peter Lang, 2004.

Jones, Darryl. "Radical Ambivalence: Frances Burney, Jacobinism, and the Politics of Romantic Fiction." *Women's Writing* 10, no. 1 (2003): 3–25.

Sabor, Peter, ed. *The Cambridge Companion to Frances Burney.* Cambridge: Cambridge University Press, 2007.

White, Eugene. *Fanny Burney, Novelist: A Study in Technique: Evelina, Cecilia, Camilla, The Wanderer.* Hamden, Conn.: Shoe String, 1960.

—Kathryn Strong

## "Washing Day" Anna Laetitia Barbauld (1797)

First published in the *Monthly Magazine* in December 1797, ANNA LAETITIA BARBAULD's poem opens in mock-heroic mode. "Washing Day" invokes the "domestic Muse" (l. 3) to tell of the hard work and inconvenience involved in the weekly chore of doing laundry. In the 1980s, some feminist critics read this use of the mock heroic as a celebration of women's work. Although the mode is usually seen as undercutting the importance of the subject addressed, Barbauld uses humor to suggest that female heroism, particularly of those "who beneath the yoke of wedlock bend" (l. 9), is akin to that of saints undergoing martyrdom.

Another persistent pattern in the first section of the poem is a contrast between the poetic and the domestic. The beauties of nature are crushed by the weight of drying aprons and sheets, which seems to suggest that the poetic is overwhelmed by the domestic, a not very encouraging image for a female poet. Any anxieties generated by this are immediately dissipated, however, by the humorous image of the male guest (presumably a woman would know better than to visit on laundry day) who receives scant hospitality and "early slinks away" (l. 57).

The tone of the poem changes in the second stanza, moving away from the mock heroic and the comic to give a more serious treatment of the speaker's memories of her childhood, pondering the mysteries of washing day. In the end, the speaker compares the soap bubbles to the "Mongolfier" balloon (l. 82), or the hot-air balloon first launched by Joseph Montgolfier in France in summer 1783, which for her links child's play and adult work. She concludes by claiming that verse itself—and "this most of all"—is but a soap bubble (l. 86). This self-deprecation seems to be an apology for an ephemeral work, a common device of female poets who do not wish to seem too bold or ambitious. Yet the oppositions in the poem between the domestic and the poetic are in effect reconciled by the bubble in the end, which is both a product of work (the laundry) and inspiration for imagination (the fantastic balloon). Far from ephemeral, "Washing Day" suggests that creativity is nurtured in female space, where the child is told stories by the maids (shades of the gossiping muses of the first line), and women's work inspires the imagination. Unlike the hapless male guest, and even the husband who tries in vain to "kindle mirth" (l. 54), the speaker is at home amid the seeming disruption of the day.

"Washing Day" represents the Romantic notion of the quotidian SUBLIME, the idea that an ordinary, common sight or experience can generate a transcendent vision that encompasses the everyday and the universal. This can be seen in the work of poets like JOHN CLARE and WILLIAM WORDSWORTH, who seek inspiration in the specifities of the natural world. However, "Washing Day" has much more in common with the work of DOROTHY WORDSWORTH and FELICIA HEMANS, locating the quotidian sublime in domestic space and activities.

**Further Reading**

Bordo, Haley. "Reinvoking the 'Domestic Muse': Anna Letitia Barbauld and the Performance of Genre." *European Romantic Review* 11, no. 2 (2000): 186–196.

Kraft, Elizabeth. "Anna Letitia Barbauld's 'Washing Day' and the Montgolfier Balloon." *Literature and History* 4, no. 2 (1995): 25–43.

Landry, Donna. *Muses of Resistance: Labouring-Class Women's Poetry in Britain, 1737–1796.* Cambridge: Cambridge University Press, 1990.

Messenger, Ann. *His and Hers: Essays in Restoration and Eighteenth-Century Literature.* Lexington: University Press of Kentucky, 1986.

—Terri Doughty

## Waterloo (1815)

On June 18, 1815, allied British, Prussian, Belgian, and Dutch forces defeated NAPOLEON BONAPARTE's French army at Waterloo, ending a period of conflict that had gone nearly uninterrupted for 23 years. When news of the victory reached London on June 22, business was suspended and crowds celebrated in the streets. Mail coaches set out to spread the news, festooned with victory wreaths and garlands. The press presented the victory as a glorious British triumph, masterminded by the duke of Wellington.

Poetic tributes to Waterloo appeared almost immediately. FRANCIS JEFFREY wrote in the *Edinburgh Review* of December 1816 that "all our bards . . . great and small, and of all sexes, ages, and professions, from WALTER SCOTT and ROBERT SOUTHEY down to hundreds without names or additions, have adventured upon this theme" (quoted in Bainbridge, 155). Walter Scott in "The Field of Waterloo" (1815) and Robert Southey in *The Poet's Pilgrimage to Waterloo* (1816) were not the only major Romantic figures to contribute to these "numerous effusions on that victory" as the *Monthly Review* put it in June 1816 (quoted in Bainbridge, 155). WILLIAM WORDSWORTH composed his "Thanksgiving Ode" (1816) to mark the national day of celebration for the end of the war, and canto 3 of LORD BYRON's *CHILDE HAROLD'S PILGRIMAGE* (1816) was in part an elegy to Napoleon and to the dead on each side. Scott, Southey, and Byron all visited Waterloo in the year following the battle and contributed to a burgeoning tourism industry by gathering souvenirs from the field.

Each of these works demonstrates the difficulty of representing Waterloo in verse. Though the facts of the battle were recounted endlessly, the event passed almost immediately into mythic status. Poetic tributes were marked with claims for the "sublimity" of the battle, but as a SUBLIME event it seemed too much for the imagination to comprehend. These tributes thus not only addressed the difficulties of translating martial action into verse but, for the literary historian Philip Shaw, raised "larger questions concerning the nature of the nation state and the authority of the poet" (Shaw 18). The poet laureate Southey's *Pilgrimage*, as the critic Richard Cronin notes, proved much less popular than the bleaker vision of Byron, who articulated "the fractured responses of a nation that knew itself to be divided" (Cronin 90).

Wordsworth's and Southey's accounts present a providential historical model in which Waterloo is the closure of a struggle that had begun with the FRENCH REVOLUTION. But Waterloo could not simply be read as an end point. Visitors to the field noticed how quickly the passing seasons erased any sign of the battle. As Shaw notes, Waterloo "was sublime because it exceeded, even as it generated, the ascription of narrative closure" (Shaw x). Claims for national unity in victory were also unsettled by the suspicion that perhaps war alone had made it possible to unite against a common enemy. In *Pilgrimage* Southey anticipates postwar social unrest in Britain when he notes that it is "Easier to crush the foreign foe, than quell / The malice which misleads the multitude." Shaw points out that the triumphant celebration of Waterloo "also captures a moment of life-threatening fragility, the point where dreams of national perfection teeter on the edge of impossibility" (4).

## Further Reading

Bainbridge, Simon. *Napoleon and English Romanticism.* Cambridge: Cambridge University Press, 1995.

Chandler David. *Waterloo: The Hundred Days.* London: Penguin, 2002.

Cronin, Richard. *The Politics of Romantic Poetry: In Search of the Pure Commonwealth.* New York: St. Martin's Press, 2000.

Shaw, Philip. *Waterloo and the Romantic Imagination.* Basingstoke, Eng.: Palgrave Macmillan, 2002.

—Mary Fairclough

## *Waverley*  Walter Scott  (1814)

The writing and publication of *Waverley; or, 'Tis Sixty Years Since* represented the beginning of a new career in a new genre for its author, SIR WALTER SCOTT. At the beginning of the 19th century, Scott had enjoyed great success as a poet, having written the hugely successful poems *The Lay of the Last Minstrel* (1805), MARMION (1808), and *The Lady of the Lake* (1810). By 1814, however, his career as a poet was waning, mainly due to competition from the second-generation Romantic poets, in particular LORD BYRON, whose poetry appealed much more to the changing tastes of the reading public. Recognizing that he could no longer command the public's adulation—or, perhaps more significantly, its purse as a poet—Scott published *Waverley* anonymously and achieved the greatest success of his career. It established his fortune and spawned 25 subsequent novels that came to be known as the "Waverley novels."

In the 1829 preface to the Magnum Opus edition of the novels, Scott recalls the genesis of *Waverley*. He claims to have begun it as an experiment in 1805, only to abandon it after having completed the first seven chapters. He then insists he had forgotten it entirely until he rediscovered it in October 1813, when he went to look for some fishing tackle in an old desk. Upon rereading those chapters, he was determined to finish the novel. He completed volume 1 in December 1813 and the final two volumes during a three-week period in June 1814.

Scott's romanticized history of the novel's composition is far less significant than the consideration of the gendered implications of his decision to become a novelist. He begins the novel's preface by insisting that he is a "maiden knight" whose efforts may ultimately fail. If they do, then clearly he will be more maiden than knight; after all, when Scott began his career as a novelist, he would have been participating in a form of gender/genre masquerade. Ina Ferris's "Re-Positioning the Novel: *Waverley* and the Gender of Fiction" argues that Scott's contemporaries regarded novel writing and reading as particularly feminine vocations. Ferris, among other critics, examines how with *Waverley* Scott infused the novel with an authority and masculinity that transformed the genre and elevated it to the realm of poetry. His contemporary critics also recognized such a shift. FRANCIS JEFFREY in the November 1814 edition of the *Edinburgh Review* insists that *Waverley* is so superior to "ordinary novels" that it should take "its place rather with the most popular of our modern poems, than with the rubbish of provincial romances" (quoted in Ferris, 294).

Distinct from other 19th-century novels, *Waverley* establishes a new novelistic genre—the historical novel (see HISTORICAL FICTION). In his seminal 1937 study *The Historical Novel*, Georg Lukács contends that Scott's most significant accomplishment lies in his presentation of the forces of history erupting into and transforming the life of his protagonist, Edward Waverley. Set during the Jacobite Rebellion of 1745, the novel follows Waverley's shifting fortunes and allegiances as he becomes increasingly entangled in the historical events surrounding him. From a structural standpoint, Scott establishes that his hero exhibits a sense of ignorance that Waverley will come to recognize and overcome through his adventures. In this case, the narrative tells the story of our hero's (mis)education in romantic sentimentality and eventual reformation into the virtues of the British bourgeois culture.

The opening chapters detail Waverley's early years and education in romance, poetry, and Jacobite politics at his uncle's estate, Waverley-Honour. Upon securing a commission in the English army, he is stationed in Scotland in the period immediately before the 1745 rebellion. On leave, Waverley visits the baron of Bradwardine and his daughter, Rose, at their estate, Tully-Veolan. During his visit through a series of plot twists, he travels to the Highlands and eventually meets the chieftain Fergus MacIvor and his sister, Flora, both of whom are inveterate Jacobites determined to secure the English throne for Bonnie Prince Charles. Waverley becomes enamored with the romantic landscapes and adventures that MacIvor embodies but feels compelled by duty to return to his commission. While attempting to return, he is arrested and imprisoned for treason. Rose eventually rescues him, and against his better judgment, he decides to join the Jacobites. After their eventual defeat, Waverley is forced into hiding until

Colonel Talbot, whose life he had saved earlier, grants him a full pardon. The reader learns that Fergus MacIvor has been condemned to death and his sister Flora has entered a convent in France. After witnessing the devastating Scottish losses at the Battle of Culloden and the MacIvors' fates, Waverley has finally matured and is left "a sadder and a wiser man" (436). Having learned the hard lessons of life and abandoned the follies of youth, Waverley eventually comes to the realization that "The romance of his life was ended, and that its real history had now commenced" (436). Real history is represented by his entry into the realm of bourgeois masculinity—his return from Scotland, marriage to Rose, and birth of his son.

In this sense, *Waverley* is infused with what the critic Nancy Armstrong calls "imperialist nostalgia." Armstrong insists that, even though British colonialism is often thought of in terms of the conquest of the Americas, the East, and some parts of Africa, the same process went on within Britain itself in terms of cultural divisions of labor, class, and regions. Scott's insistence on the romance of Scotland's Jacobite past coupled with his rugged depictions of the untamed landscape create a sense of just such a divide between the Scottish and the English. Understood in these terms, *Waverley* embodies a confrontation between nostalgia for a heroic and romantic Scottish past and a necessary acceptance of the English national project. Such an acceptance required Scotland's inevitable assimilation into a new British identity ("Great Britain") and the loss of an independent Scottish national identity.

## Further Reading

Armstrong, Nancy. "Imperialist Nostalgia and *Wuthering Heights*." In: *Wuthering Heights* Case Studies in Contemporary Criticism. Edited by Linda H. Peterson, 430–450. Boston: Bedford, 2003.

Ferns, Chris. "That Obscure Object of Desire: Sir Walter Scott and the Borders of Gender." *English Studies in Canada* 22, no. 2 (1996): 149–166.

Ferris, Ina. "Re-Positioning the Novel: *Waverly* and the Gender of Fiction." *Studies in Romanticism* 28, no. 2 (1989): 291–301.

Lukács, Georg. *The Historical Novel.* Translated by Hannah and Stanley Mitchell. London: Merlin, 1962.

Zimmerman, Everett. "Extreme Events: Scott's Novels and Traumatic History." *Eighteenth-Century Fiction* 10, no. 1 (1997): 63–78.

—Jeffrey L. Schneider

### "We Are Seven" William Wordsworth (1798)

Written in ballad form, "We Are Seven," first published in *Lyrical Ballads* (1798), is based on the poet's meeting with a little girl of eight years old whom he met while out walking some five years previously. After the speaker inquires how many siblings she has, he and the little girl become embroiled in an argument in which he tries to get her to conform to his point of view—to convince her that she is only one of five and not seven children. To his adult mind two of the children are dead and are, therefore, neither present nor part of the family, but to the child their presence is felt in both her imagination and her spirituality. The speaker's adult logic sees death as final, whereas for the child their spirits live on through nature. She sees her dead siblings in a similar manner to those siblings who "at Conway dwell" (l. 19) or the two who have "gone to sea" (l. 20), they may not be physically present, but they are still part of the family; death, to her, is not final.

The child leads a solitary, rustic existence, living only with her mother in "the church-yard cottage," a mere "Twelve steps or more" from the children's graves (ll. 23, 39). This close proximity enhances the sense of the dead children's presence. No other children are mentioned in the poem, so she eradicates her solitude through her uncorrupted imagination. The euphonic rhythm of the poem suggests that she is at ease with this solitude, although she lives within the romance of fantasy; her feelings are channeled and focused. She is not sad; she merely addresses her dead siblings as though they are alive, which, to the child, is logical. These two, unlike her siblings who reside elsewhere, she can "see" because their graves are very visible, the green a living proof of those who lay beneath; in contrast to the other four, their presence is constant.

Indeed, it is the speaker whose passion and feelings are in danger of overflowing as his frustration with the child increases. As an adult, it is illogical that he should indulge in such an "undignified squabble" with a child of eight years old (Gill 184). It is as though the roles of child and adult are reversed as he bullishly tries to persuade her to adopt his adult logic that death is final, and that she is only one of five. However, her persistence belies a maturity in her absolute belief that she is one of seven; as a result, she adopts her stance with a quiet yet determined attitude. The speaker becomes more passionate as the poem progresses, culminating in his feverish declaration that "they are dead; those two are dead! / their spirits are in heaven" (ll. 65–66) as he vainly attempts to get her to see reason. For him, religious indoctrination decrees that the spirit is taken to heaven, and that is where the children now reside. His passionate outpouring of frustrated emotion places his maturity in question: Why is he so irritated by his inability to persuade a young child to see his point of view? He cannot understand her simplicity or the fact that her "rustic, woodland air" (l. 9) makes her a part of nature itself.

The speaker is selfishly oblivious to the hurt he may be causing the little girl by his insistence that her siblings "are in heaven" and therefore not spiritually present. Heaven, it seems, is too much for the child to comprehend, for heaven is not tangible; unlike the graves, it remains unseen. It is an unacceptable concept for her; she needs the power of nature and its raised green graves in order to cope with the deaths of her siblings. This is ironic given her close proximity to the church and its religious teachings. The speaker, however, is intent on attempting to shatter her illusions without considering the consequences, placing him in a position of ridicule. More than this, it is the speaker who is uncomfortable with the little girl's concept of death and her ability to keep her siblings alive in her imagination. She also feels no guilt at being the one sibling left, as it was God who chose to take the others and conjoin them with nature. She is a pantheist who believes that God is visible in everything, particularly the nature he created, hence her simple belief in the visibility of the graves.

Stephen Gill states that Wordsworth's poetry "is peopled with . . . haunted guilty men. The haunted, guilty one was the poet himself" (2). It is well known that Wordsworth himself fathered an illegitimate child in France at the age of 22 with Annette Vallon. The meeting with this little girl perhaps reminded him of his own abandoned daughter. Unlike the child, his own daughter has nothing tangible with which to comfort herself in her father's absence. For her, Wordsworth has effectively "gone to sea," over the water to England; he is alive, but absent. The children are dead, but present. His inherent guilt is underlined by the child's insistence that "we are seven" (ll. 64, 69), reminding him that actually he is three!

The child has found an idyllic life in her connections with nature, which is a typical Romantic metaphor for the human condition. Arguably, children are at one with nature until life experience, or indoctrination, teaches them otherwise, therefore this child is the perfect metaphor for Romanticism. As a result, the speaker appears to have lost his connection with nature, and thus he searches for meaning until he realizes that he is "throwing words away" (l. 67). Her will in believing that her siblings are still present is reiterated by nature's very strength in self-perpetuating life. Nature lives, and dies, in winter, but like her buried siblings, it can never actually go away.

See also CHILDHOOD.

## Further Reading

Gill, Stephen, ed. *The Cambridge Companion to Wordsworth.* Cambridge: Cambridge University Press, 2003.

Wordsworth, William, and Samuel Taylor Coleridge. *Lyrical Ballads.* Edited by R. L. Brett and A. R. Jones. London: Routledge, 1991.

—Pauline Guerin

## "When I have Fears that I may cease to be"
### John Keats (1818)

On December 21, 1817, JOHN KEATS famously wrote to his brothers, "I mean by *Negative Capability,* that is when a man is capable of being in uncertainties, Mysteries, doubts, without any irritable reaching after fact & reason" (Keats I 193). The Shakespeare-influenced sonnet "When I have Fears that I may cease to be," written only a month

later, testifies to the truth of his words; the sonnet embraces "uncertainties, mysteries, doubts," allowing the poet to deliberate inconclusively on what is beyond "fact or reason." In this sonnet, Keats questions whether he will be able to create poetry that will last even when the mortal man is gone. His lines are full of doubt, and Keats's seemingly morose sonnet becomes an inconclusive meditation on mortal and immortal time.

The poem was written as a postscript in a letter to his friend John Reynolds, which seems an unusual place for one of Keats's finest sonnets. Yet as the biographer Stephen Coote writes, "Reynolds in particular would have appreciated what Keats had achieved here," for "in the copy of Shakespeare that the two men shared, Sonnet 64 was heavily marked, and Keats's poem is his own variation on Shakespeare's theme of time the destroyer" (Coote 128). However, for Keats time is not necessarily the destroyer; instead, it is the elusive mystery of what is to come. The poem may be read in the same way as Shakespeare's sonnet, which is a meditation on the way in which time takes away all, including the speaker's love, but Keats's sonnet is much more subtle—and perhaps even hopeful. There is immortal hope in the notion of the time he represents. In fact, through his complex time imagery, Keats offers keen insight into the ideological notions of mortality and immortality, blurring the lines between the celestial and the temporal. The temporal imagery in the poem combines images of cyclical mortality in pastoral time similar to that which can be seen in his "To Autumn"—human-made time shown in his clock imagery and pictorial representations of divine time.

The first quatrain is the bleakest, for it is cluttered with images of mortality. The poet articulates his fears concerning the completion and immortality of his writing, beginning: "When I have fears that I may cease to be / Before my pen has glean'd my teeming brain" (ll. 1–2). Commencing his poem with the word *When* designates the entire sonnet as an enjambed thought process on time following the hypothetical "when," but in addition, the sonnet becomes a general question of "when"—when will his abilities and poetic legacy end? Therefore, it is important that in these lines the speaker purposefully entwines two forms of mortal time, time as defined by his writing with time as seen through the pastoral world. He does this through the image of a human-made writing implement "gleaning" his "teeming brain." Since *gleaning* means "to gather or pick up corn left by the reapers," there is a suggestion that he wants the fruits of his mind to be metaphorically harvested; yet it is not an image of lasting work, since the seasonal action leads to the eventual consumption and death of crops. He hopes for immortality in his work through the ability of his "pen" to capture what he knows lies in his fertile brain and create "high-piled books" (l. 3), but he paradoxically uses images of the harvest. Similarly, he fears that he will cease to be "Before high-piled books . . . / Hold like rich garners the full ripen'd grain" (ll. 3–4). Connecting his future literary endeavors to the pastoral image of "garners" holding "ripen'd grain" could suggest future bountiful literary achievements; yet the harvesting and enclosed garners actually imply inaccessibility and material that must eventually perish. In turn, this presents the idea that even the hope of the "high-piled books" is an image of the mortality of his work.

However, through the writing of the poem, Keats is showing that he is undefeated by his fear and is continuing to contribute to the "high-piled books." The poem itself is therefore an exercise in defiance. The biographer Andrew Motion argues that the poem is a response to LEIGH HUNT's criticisms of ENDYMION, and that it shows that "Keats felt his success as a poet depended on his acquiring material, rather than on using what was his birthright" (Motion 226), and the first quatrain seems to suggest this view. Yet Motion also adds that the "'high-piled books' reaffirms the durable consolation of art itself" (226)—Keats in writing "high-piled books" has created a truth to the construction of them. The critic Jamey Hecht sees Keats's fears in sonnet form as Keats's view that "just as time is scarce, the moment can be a bountiful one because it is so brief as to only accommodate a sonnet" (Hecht 115). However, whether time is scarce or not is not decided in the poem, and the figuring of the sonnet in a letter actually implies Keats's attempt to make the poem a "durable consolation," for he wants it to last within the memory of another.

In the second and third quatrains, the poet moves into ideas of celestial time, and the poem gains a new dimension through which the poet's time is judged—uniting mortal and immortal visions of time. The "huge cloudy symbols" "upon the night's starr'd face" (ll. 6, 5) which he thinks he "may never live to trace / Their shadows with the magic hand of chance" (ll. 7–8) forms an image of a celestial clock complete with a "face," "hand," and "symbols" judging "the fair creature of an hour" (l. 9)—his poetry—whose transcendent "faery power" he fears he may not "relish in" for long (l. 11). His darker self fears that he will not be able to write his name in immortal letters through his work, which reminds one of the line on his tombstone—"Here lies one whose name was writ in water." However, in this poem the celestial clock is present, suggesting the possibility of the eternal. This is similar to the way in which, perhaps, Keats's hope of immortality lasted in his desire for his friend Joseph Severn to inscribe "one whose name was writ in water" in stone. Also significantly, the "symbols of a high romance," which simultaneously represent the stars, the numerals of the celestial clock, and a blurred version of "the charactery" in the first quatrain, are "cloudy," for he cannot read what the celestial clock has in store for the "romance" between himself and his writing. It is furthermore important that the "fair creature of an hour" with "faery power" is a paradoxical image, for Keats pictures something mythically timeless with the restraints of time on it, showing that at the same time he is contemplating the loss of the immortal "faery power" experienced in his writing, he is claiming that there is an immortal quality in his own work. The image of the celestial clock therefore represents the chance that his poetry will outlive the temporal constraints of the "pen," "books," and pastoral threatening his work in the first quatrain.

The progression from ideas of mortal to immortal time in the poem shows the poet's unceasing desire for immortality even as he is expressing the possibility of ceasing to exist. The poem begins with the contemplation of mortal time seen in his writing, for he worries that he "may cease to be / Before my pen has glean'd my teeming brain." Then the imagery moves upward to the immortal time of "the night's starr'd face," then down to the equally immortal image of the sea—a complex image presenting the SUBLIME unknown. In his earlier sonnet "On the Sea," the ocean is pictured as a sublime—both terrifying and beautiful—force, which "keeps eternal whisperings around desolate shores" (l. 1) and perhaps holds the voices of immortal "sea nymphs" (l. 14). In "When I have Fears," though the sea could be seen as a place in which time ceases to exist in this poem—where "love and fame to nothingness do sink" (l. 14)—instead, Keats's portrayal of the sea is akin to the depiction in the earlier sonnet. The sea is a place of eternity and peaceful desolation at the end of the mortal world, for as the speaker says, "on the shore / Of the wide world I stand alone and think" (ll. 12–13). The "shore" is the final location in which one can muse on the meaning of time before one finds out what is beyond the "wide world." The alliteration and assonance in this line add to the feeling of peace in the speaker's immobility, for it is as if doubt has come to rest in the final couplet. The image of the speaker on the "shore / Of the wide world" also recalls the end of his sonnet "ON FIRST LOOKING INTO CHAPMAN'S HOMER," which ends with the line "Silent, upon a peak in Darien." As in "Chapman's Homer," in "When I have Fears," he is also on the edge of the world—solitary and facing an unknown sublime landscape. Though the last line, "Till love and fame to nothingness do sink," could suggest the obliteration of Keats's hopes, the critic M. A. Goldberg argues that "nothingness" is positive, suggesting a return to a "fellowship with essence" (Goldberg 127). Goldberg convincingly persuades one that "when love and fame sink in the final line of the sonnet, it is not their essence which is being rejected, but only the special and temporal elements which prevent man from entering into their essence" (128). Therefore, at the end of the poem Keats actually throws off the shackles of his fear of mortality, and as "love and fame" sink, he embraces the inevitability of human doubt and the unknown—which may or may not lead to the immortality he desires.

## Further Reading

Coote, Stephen. *John Keats: A Life.* London: Hodder and Stoughton, 1996.

Goldberg, M. A. "The 'Fears' of John Keats." *Modern Language Quarterly* 18, no. 2 (1957): 125–131.

Hecht, Jamey. "Scarcity and Poetic Election in Two Sonnets of John Keats." *ELH* 61, no. 1 (1994): 103–120.

Keats, John. *The Letters of John Keats: 1814–1821.* Vol. 1. Edited by Hyder Edward Rollins. Cambridge: Harvard University Press, 1972.

Motion, Andrew. *Keats.* New York: Farrar, Straus, and Giroux, 1998.

—Lucy Morse

## *Wild Irish Girl, The* Sydney Owenson (1806)

In *The Wild Irish Girl*, Sydney Owenson (Lady Morgan) fuses EPISTOLARY FICTION and the novel of SENSIBILITY to envision a fictional resolution to English prejudices against contemporary Ireland, Irish culture, and its people, which, as the novel's English hero Horatio admits, ultimately had allowed England to justify its political dominance of its "sister" state since the Renaissance period. Owenson's direct celebration of Irish culture and custom came at a time when Irish identity was under threat from the Act of Union of 1800 between Great Britain and Ireland, which meant that while Irish affairs were directly administered from London for the first time, many absentee English landlords continued to neglect the Irish estates they had acquired.

Owenson politicized the epistolary form by framing the novel as letters that the young aristocrat Horatio Mortimer writes on a visit to his father's Irish estates to his friend, an English Member of Parliament. Indirectly, both represent England's abdication of responsibility in Ireland. Horatio visits Ireland filled with prejudices about the apparent savagery, ferocity, and barbarity of the people, and yet his experience of meeting courteous and hospitable Irish peasants brings him to question the Irish stereotypes that he, in common with his countrymen believed in. On reaching his father's neglected estates, Horatio disguises himself to penetrate the household of the Irish prince of Innismore, who had been disinherited by Horatio's ancestors. While Owenson represents Horatio as the unwitting exemplification of England's historical abuse of Ireland, by contrast, the prince of Innismore's daughter, Glorvina, is an unequivocally positive embodiment of Irish culture. However, as a woman,

Glorvina is also used by Owenson to underscore Ireland's present lack of political agency and capacity for self-determination. Significantly, for Horatio, Glorvina's "natural impatience and volatility," "a union of intelligence and simplicity, infantile playfulness and profound reflexion" are "both *natural* and *national*" (Owenson 92, 120). While Owenson's celebration of the national natural character might have been as guilty of stereotyping the Irish as her English contemporaries were, the important difference is that, without exception, Owenson's stereotypes of the Irish are positive.

It is in Horatio's growing attraction and love for Glorvina and, by extension, Ireland that Owenson articulates the possibility of more harmonious and less exploitative relations between the two nations. However, although love between the two protagonists suggests a direct sentimental solution to political problems, the novel's ending militates against such a comfortable resolution as the sudden death of the prince leaves Glorvina with no choice but to marry Horatio. At this point the epistolary form is abandoned, and the novel closes with injunctions that Horatio's father makes to his son on how he might protect and care for his Irish tenants after he marries Glorvina. Provocatively, through the forthcoming marriage and Horatio's inheritance of his father's Irish estates, *The Wild Irish Girl* suggests that the domination of Ireland by the English continues unchecked and is only partially moderated by love.

**Further Reading**

Ferris, Ina. "Narrating Cultural Encounter: Lady Morgan and the Irish National Tale." *Nineteenth-Century Literature* 51, no. 3 (December 1996): 287–303.

Owenson, Sydney. *The Wild Irish Girl.* Oxford: Oxford University Press, 1999.

Wright, Julia M. *Ireland, India and Nationalism in Nineteenth-Century Literature.* Cambridge: Cambridge University Press, 2007.

—Sondeep Kandola

## *Wilhelm Meister's Apprenticeship* Johann Wolfgang von Goethe (1796)

"Let me put it quite succinctly: even as a youth I had the vague desire and intention to develop myself fully, myself as I am" (Goethe 78). So says the eponymous hero of this much-imitated novel by JOHANN WOLFGANG VON GOETHE, which is often seen as a follow-up to The SORROWS OF YOUNG WERTHER (1774) and credited with setting the pattern for the bildungsroman (novel of development) genre. It tells of how a merchant's son becomes obsessed by the magical world of the theater and tries to fulfill his ambition of becoming a successful dramatist and performer and escape the bourgeois restrictions upon his life. What follows is a journey of self-discovery.

Along his path Wilhelm becomes involved with a theater company, encountering strange characters such as Mignon, an androgynous child, and a brooding minstrel. The hero finds himself having to come to terms with feelings of love and desire and the need to establish a new relationship with his father, his development marked by a series of episodic educational encounters. While on his journey, Wilhelm is introduced to the works of Shakespeare, who becomes his substitute father, and inevitably becomes transfixed with *Hamlet,* a play that has the father-son relationship as its crux. When his own father dies, Wilhelm feels liberated.

Although the novel is given the label of bildungsroman, there is some question about how literally this label should be applied. It has been suggested that in fact the novel suggests a conflict between the priorities of self and society, a conflict between what Goethe termed *Vollen* (desire and its fulfilment) and *Sollen* (social obligation and its fulfilment).

A sequel, *Wilhelm Meister's Journeyman Years,* was published in 1821.

**Further Reading**

Goethe, Johann Wolfgang von. *Wilhelm Meister's Apprenticeship.* London: Aegypan, 2007.

—Perry Thomas

## Williams, Helen Maria (1761–1827)

A well-known poet of SENSIBILITY in 1780s London, Helen Maria Williams later gained an international reputation for her eyewitness commentary on events in revolutionary France. Born in London on June 17, 1761 (some sources say 1762), Williams, the daughter of an army officer, grew up in Berwick-upon-Tweed, strongly influenced by her mother's Presbyterian heritage. When the family returned to London in 1781, Doctor Andrew Kippis introduced them to his Dissenting circle, encouraged Helen Maria's writing, and found a publisher for her poetry. In the early 1780s she published *Edwin and Eltruda: A Legendary Tale, An Ode on the Peace,* and *Peru.* By the time her *Poems* (1786) was published, she had established a reputation as a poet of sensibility concerned with social and political reform.

Williams's London salon was popular with progressive liberals, and her friends included ANNA SEWARD and MARY WOLLSTONECRAFT. WILLIAM WORDSWORTH, longing to meet her, wrote a sonnet celebrating Williams's capacity for feeling (see "SONNET ON SEEING MISS HELEN MARIA WILLIAMS WEEP AT A TALE OF DISTRESS"). In 1788 Williams published *A Poem on the Bill Lately Passed for Regulating the Slave Trade,* and in 1790 she issued her only novel, *Julia.* Less directly political than her poems, *Julia* uses the heroine and her foil, Miss Melbourne, to contrast genuine romantic sensibility with affectation in a narrative influenced by conduct books (texts imparting advice on manners and behavior), JEAN-JACQUES ROUSSEAU's *Julie, or the New Heloise* (1761), and JOHANN WOLFGANG VON GOETHE's The SORROWS OF YOUNG WERTHER (1774).

A visit to France in the summer of 1790 changed the course of Williams' life as she began a series of *LETTERS FROM FRANCE* that provided a generation of readers with images of the FRENCH REVOLUTION. Williams returned to Paris in 1792 and became a French citizen in 1817. Although she was imprisoned for several months in 1793 and had to flee Paris when foreigners were expelled in 1794, she returned after Robespierre's fall. Her salon continued to attract an international group of Revolutionary sympathizers, although her alliance with John Hurford Stone, an English political refugee and entrepreneur, hurt her reputation in England.

The eight volumes of *Letters from France* appeared between 1790 and 1796, followed by *A Tour in Switzerland* (1798), *Sketches of the State of Manners and Opinions in the French Republic* (1801),

*On the Late Persecution of the Protestants* (1816), *A Narrative of the Events Which Have Taken Place in France from the Landing of Napoleon Bonaparte to the Restoration of Louis XVIII* (1819), and *Souvenirs de la révolution Française* (1827). Williams's translation of J. H. Bernadin de Saint-Pierre's *Paul and Virginia* was widely read. In 1823 she published a collection of *Poems on Various Subjects.*

Linking sentiment with moral responsibility, Williams wrote as a romantic heroine of sensibility, maintaining her faith in the Revolution, though its reality fell short of her ideals. Her cosmopolitanism is strongly colored by Girondist loyalties (that is, support of the French legislative assembly), distrust of the lower classes, and a passionate interest in women's rights. After Britain declared war in 1793, conservative reviewers mounted increasingly hostile attacks on Williams; by the last decade of her life readers had tired of revolutionary themes. Her reputation in both France and England was further damaged when an 1803 edition of Louis XVI's letters, which she had edited in good faith, was exposed as a hoax. Despite declining sales, her work reflected the Romantic expression of a passionate desire for revolution marked by strong feeling, heroic individualism, and imaginative sympathy. Except for visits to Switzerland and the Netherlands, she remained in France until her death on December 15, 1827 (some sources say December 14).

## Further Reading

Blakemore, Stephen. *Crisis in Representation: Thomas Paine, Mary Wollstonecraft, Helen Maria Williams and the Rewriting of the French Revolution.* Madison, N.J.: Fairleigh Dickinson, 1997.

Craciun, Adriana. *British Women Writers and the French Revolution: Citizens of the World.* London: Palgrave Macmillan, 2005.

Kennedy, Deborah. *Helen Maria Williams and the Age of Revolution, 1790–1827.* Oxford: Clarendon Press, 1993.

—Linda Mills Woolsey

## Wollstonecraft, Mary (1759–1797)

Mary Wollstonecraft was born on April 17, 1759, and died on September 10, 1797, of sepsis following childbirth. During her short life she published translations, numerous literary reviews, books of education, treatises on the FRENCH REVOLUTION, a travelogue, and a radical book vindicating the rights of women. Her life, her writing, and the fact she wrote at all were equally radical. Her unconventional lifestyle barred her from public discussion for nearly a century until the feminists of the early 20th-century revived her name, her works, and her history.

Wollstonecraft was the second child and first daughter of John Edward Wollstonecraft's and Elizabeth Dickson's six children. John Wollstonecraft inherited some money but spent it poorly. Due to his failing efforts to establish himself as a gentleman farmer, the family moved often throughout Wollstonecraft's childhood, from London to Wales to Beverley, Yorkshire. John Wollstonecraft was a brutal man who beat his dogs and terrorized his wife; years later, Wollstonecraft told WILLIAM GODWIN that she sometimes used to lie on the landing outside her mother's room, to protect her mother from her father.

Wollstonecraft's most important friend was Fanny Blood, the eldest daughter of a family whose father was not cruel but was lazy and dissipated. He made no efforts to provide for his family; of necessity, Mrs. Blood sewed by the light of a single candle until very late hours, and Fanny earned some money by painting. Wollstonecraft was infuriated by Mr. Blood's dissipation and appalled at how little money the women could earn by their blinding toil.

In 1778 Wollstonecraft left home to work as a companion to a widow in Bath. She chafed against the petty tyranny she suffered as a paid companion, and she disliked the fashionable lives of the Bath visitors. However, her time there was her first introduction to the lives of the richer classes. During her time in Bath, several celebrated women were also there, including Mrs. Montague, a famous intellectual; the novelist FRANCES BURNEY; and Catherine Macaulay, a known historian.

In 1780 Wollstonecraft was called home to her mother's deathbed. After her mother's death, she moved in with the Bloods, with whom she worked and lived on a starvation diet. Then, in November 1782, she was called to her married sister's house:

Eliza Bishop had just given birth and was evidently on the verge of insanity. She wanted to get away from her husband, who was cringing and violent by turns. To save Eliza, one day in January 1783 Wollstonecraft and Fanny abducted her; they escaped in two coaches to avoid detection, leaving the baby behind.

This abduction demonstrated Wollstonecraft's willingness to go against convention, and indeed everything that society held sacred, on the strength of her own convictions. Eliza was a wife and a mother—she had duties and obligations, affection for her daughter, and no means of sustaining herself. Wollstonecraft herself owed Eliza's husband 20 pounds (borrowed on behalf of the Bloods). Her abduction of her sister can therefore be read in many ways: as heroic, as foolish, as cruel, and as necessary. But however one reads it, the event clearly demonstrates Wollstonecraft's willpower, single-mindedness, and persuasiveness.

From her youth, then, Wollstonecraft learned severe lessons about poverty, cruelty, and the consequences of women's legal, financial, and learned dependence. Eventually, she came to link sex-based and class-based oppression together. As Marilyn Butler puts it in the introduction to *The Works of Mary Wollstonecraft*, "Wollstonecraft's special contribution is to apply to gender her contemporaries' insights into cultural politics" (Wollstonecraft 17). For context, note that in 1770 an act of Parliament was passed, punishing women for witchcraft if they "seduced" anyone into marriage through "scent, paints, cosmetics, washes, artificial teeth, false hair, Spanish wool, iron stays, hoops, high-heeled shoes, or bolstered hips" (Wardle 136).

On a tenuous thread of hope, Wollstonecraft, Fanny Blood, and Eliza decided to open a school, one of the few things they could do with their collected skills. The school failed in Islington but succeeded when they moved to Newington Green. Up to this point, Wollstonecraft had primarily educated herself through wide reading. Her education had been as limited as those of many women: Most of her schooling came from the day schools she attended in Beverley. In Newington Green, however, she came to know a set of highly intelligent people, including two leading liberal philosophers,

Reverend Richard Price and Joseph Priestley, and Dr. Samuel Johnson.

Wollstonecraft spent most of her life trying to pay the debts of friends and family—particularly her father. She was often extremely poor; the artist Henry Fuseli's biographer said that in the early 1790s Wollstonecraft wore a coarse black dress, was very thin, and had not eaten meat for years. She was constantly helping others when she had almost nothing for herself.

In 1785 Fanny finally married a long-indecisive suitor, and the pair moved to Lisbon. Fanny had suffered from tuberculosis for years, and Portugal was thought to be good for the condition. Wollstonecraft was desperately lonely, and her letters to George Blood (Fanny's older brother and Wollstonecraft's lifelong friend) are full of depression. She wrote that she had "'lost all relish for life—and my almost broken heart is only cheared [sic] by the prospect of death. I may be years a-dying, tho', and so I ought to be patient'" (quoted in Wardle 40–41). But it was Fanny who died. In late 1785 Wollstonecraft was called to Lisbon for Fanny's childbirth, and after an extremely stormy 13-day passage, she reached Lisbon four hours before the baby was born. Fanny rallied, but then died on November 29; the baby died shortly thereafter. When Wollstonecraft returned to London, she found the school failing, the Bloods asking for money, her sight dimming, and her memory faulty. In desperation, she composed a tract entitled *Thoughts on the Education of Daughters.* The book calls upon parents, and especially mothers, to cultivate goodness in their children by showing them more affection. She sold the work to the publisher Joseph Johnson, who became her lifelong friend and patron. With the proceeds from this book, she sent the Blood parents to Dublin, and George after them.

Again short of options, in 1786 Wollstonecraft accepted a position as a governess to the daughters of Lord Kingsborough in Ireland. Though she had to borrow money for clothes and travel, she was hopeful that her income would enable her to discharge her debts. Lady Kingsborough showed her three daughters little affection but much strictness, and Wollstonecraft was appalled at the cold practicality of the daughters' education. She wrote:

"I almost wish the girls were novel readers and romantic; I declare false refinement is better than none at all, but these girls understand several languages, and have read *cartloads* of history, for their mother was a prudent woman" (Paul 1:187).

During her time as a governess, Wollstonecraft read JEAN-JACQUES ROUSSEAU's *Emile* and wrote her first novel, *Mary: A Fiction.* Commentators have read much of her own life and psychology into this novel. In letters she wrote during her time in Ireland, Wollstonecraft stressed that she felt physically and nervously ill, and that she almost feared madness. She was harassed by a sense of her inadequate French, and she was distressed that the eldest girl's good heart should be destroyed by a harsh upbringing. She was also increasingly disgusted by the contrast between the suffering poverty of the peasants and the overdressed and undeserved ease of the Kingsborough family.

In 1787 Wollstonecraft was dismissed by the Kingsboroughs, making her again homeless and jobless. Joseph Johnson, who had purchased her *Thoughts on the Education of Daughters,* offered her sustainable writing work if she moved to London. She accepted, beginning a life as a self-styled "first of a new genus": the female writer. She began working as a translator of books and as a reader, reviewer, and editorial assistant for the new journal *Analytical Review.* In the evening she attended Johnson's salon, which included some of the most innovative minds of the day. At Johnson's she met Henry Fuseli, WILLIAM BLAKE, THOMAS PAINE, the mathematician John Bonnycastle, the physician George Fordyce, and the classics scholar George Anderson. By 1789 Johnson had published her original works *Mary* and *Original Stories from Real Life.* Wollstonecraft was an established writer.

In 1789 France exploded into revolutionary chaos. On November 1, 1790, EDMUND BURKE published his *Reflections on the Revolution in France.* Mary Wollstonecraft's A VINDICATION OF THE RIGHTS OF MEN was the first published response (anonymously, on November 18). On December 18, 1790, a second edition of *Vindication* was published under Wollstonecraft's name. This text argues that a frozen, classist society prevents all classes from developing their full humanity.

In the next year, Wollstonecraft applied some of the same observations to the plight of women, and in 1791 she began writing A VINDICATION OF THE RIGHTS OF WOMAN. It was published in 1792 and widely reviewed. *A Vindication of the Rights of Woman* is an impassioned treatise arguing that women should not be raised to be weak, beautiful, but useless objects; instead, they should be raised as rational creatures capable of contributing to the fulfillment of human virtue. To counter arguments that women are incapable of rationality, she challenges society to try the experiment by teaching them.

In 1792, after the publication of *Rights of Woman*, Wollstonecraft asked Henry Fuseli's wife if she might move in with them, platonically. Sophia Fuseli turned her away, and in December she went to Paris, going there in response to a broken heart, to improve her French, and to see the Revolution she believed in. By then the FRENCH REVOLUTION was turning bloody, and many were horrified by its irrationality and bloodshed. On February 1, 1793, France declared war on England, and in July the Reign of Terror began.

In Paris, Wollstonecraft met and fell in love with the American adventurer Gilbert Imlay (1754–1828). Imlay was a speculator from New Jersey who represented himself as a natural man fresh from the unspoilt mountains of Kentucky. Following her own theories about love and marriage, Wollstonecraft commenced an affair with him without marrying him. He registered her as his wife with the American Embassy, in order to protect her in France, but they were never officially married.

After a time in Paris, Wollstonecraft moved to a cottage in Neuilly to escape revolutionary violence. From there she wrote letters to Imlay, speaking of their domestic bliss but also chastising him for being distant and erratic. It is clear even from this early date that Imlay was feckless and unreliable; it is equally clear that Wollstonecraft was profoundly faithful and impassioned but troubled, erratic, and unpredictable.

The Imlay-Wollstonecraft affair, and the intense suffering evident in her letters, is perhaps the clearest evidence that, despite her uniqueness, Wollstonecraft was the product of contemporary education. As she herself says in A *Vindication of* the Rights of Woman: "Men and women must be educated, in a great degree, by the opinions and manners of the society they live in. In every age there has been a stream of popular opinion that has carried all before it, and given a family character, as it were, to the century" (Wollstonecraft 1997, 128). In the letters to Imlay, we see the struggles of intellect against feeling, and we see condensed all of Wollstonecraft's despair about miseducation.

In September 1793 a pregnant Wollstonecraft returned to Paris to be with Imlay. Shortly afterward, they moved to Le Havre, France, where their daughter, Fanny, was born in May 1794. Imlay left them and went to England. Wollstonecraft's book *An Historical and Moral View of the Origin and Progress of the French Revolution,* smuggled in pieces out of France, was published in London in December.

The next year Wollstonecraft went to London, where she discovered Imlay's unfaithfulness. She attempted suicide in May 1795, but Imlay prevented her and shortly afterward asked her to go to Scandinavia on business for him. She went with a nurse and one-year-old Fanny. In letters written during this trip, she produced a singular and moving travelogue; they were edited and published as LETTERS WRITTEN DURING A SHORT RESIDENCE IN SWEDEN, NORWAY AND DENMARK in 1796.

Before the publication of her *Letters,* however, Wollstonecraft attempted suicide again, soaking her skirts and jumping into the Thames River from Putney Bridge in October 1795. She was saved by strangers and later recounted to William Godwin the horrors of feeling water fill her lungs. By this point the relationship with Imlay was over, and she wrote him a poignant letter expressing her sense of his inadequacy. As the 20th-century author Virginia Woolf later described their relationship: "Tickling minnows he had hooked a dolphin, and the creature rushed him through the waters till he was dizzy and only wanted to escape" (Woolf 160).

Back in London, one of Wollstonecraft's new neighbours was Godwin. They had met years before at Johnson's but had not been impressed with one another. Now, in August 1796, she went to call on him—an unprecedented move. She invited him to call on her, too, and they began an affair that was as much an affair of words as of bodies. Their an intense courtship is reflected in their letters. He was saturnine and she sensitive with recent pain, but their intellects and love of writing were well matched, and on March 29, 1797, they were married. Wollstonecraft was pregnant, and for financial reasons a marriage would be useful. But their marriage caused an uproar, partially because both had declared themselves so much opposed to the institution, and partially because it proved Wollstonecraft had never in fact been married to Imlay. As a result, they lost some friends who refused to associate with a "fallen" woman. After the first discomfort, however, there was little disturbance to their lives: They maintained separate households, separate chambers, and all their careful independence.

On August 30, 1797, after a long and painful labor, Wollstonecraft gave birth to a daughter (MARY WOLLSTONECRAFT SHELLEY, the future author of FRANKENSTEIN). When her labor began, Wollstonecraft had been unconcerned; her first child had been born easily, and she had recovered extremely quickly. But this time the placenta was not expelled naturally, and it broke when a doctor tried to remove it. After a few days' apparent recovery, Wollstonecraft began to be poisoned by the placental remains. Godwin nursed her closely, and they laughed together over the puppies that were used to draw off her milk. Despite her newfound happiness and desire to live, however, she died on September 10, 1797.

After Wollstonecraft's death, Godwin published her unfinished works, including MARIA, OR, THE WRONGS OF WOMAN, and he wrote and published a heartfelt homage to her, *Memoirs of the Author of A Vindication of the Rights of Woman* (both in 1798). His honesty about her love affairs and his generous assessment of them proved that she had not conformed to the moral standards of the day. Though the female novelist George Eliot read and admired *A Vindication of the Rights of Woman* in the 1850s, only now has Wollstonecraft begun receiving the critical the attention she so richly deserves.

## Further Reading

Flexner, Eleanor. *Mary Wollstonecraft: A Biography.* New York: Coward, McCann & Geoghegan, Inc., 1972.

Godwin, William. *Memoirs of the Author of A Vindication of the Rights of Woman.* Edited by Pamela Clemit and Gina Lura Walker. Peterborough: Broadview Press, 2001.

Johnson, Claudia. *Equivocal Beings.* London: University of Chicago Press, 1995.

———, ed. *The Cambridge Companion to Mary Wollstonecraft.* Cambridge: Cambridge University Press, 2002.

Paul, Kegan. *William Godwin: His Friends and Contemporaries.* 2 vols. London: Henry S. King & Co., 1876.

Todd, Janet. *Mary Wollstonecraft: An Annotated Bibliography.* New York and London: Garland Publishing, Inc., 1976.

———. *Mary Wollstonecraft: A Revolutionary Life.* London: Weidenfeld and Nicholson, 2000.

Wardle, Ralph M. *Mary Wollstonecraft, A Critical Biography.* London: Richards Press, 1951.

Wollstonecraft, Mary. *The Works of Mary Wollstonecraft.* Edited by Janet Todd and Marilyn Butler. London: William Pickering, 1989.

———. *The Vindications. The Rights of Man; The Rights of Woman.* Edited by K. L. MacDonald and Kathleen Scherf. Peterborough: Broadview, 1997.

Woolf, Virginia. *The Common Reader, Second Series.* London: Hogarth Press, 1948.

—Helen Hauser

## "Woman and Fame" Felicia Hemans (1829)

The central conflict in FELICIA HEMANS's "Woman and Fame" is between worldly fame and the blessings of home, hearth, and longed-for love. Autobiographical elements may certainly be seen in this work because, although Hemans had attained a high degree of fame herself, becoming one of the most widely read and published poets in English in the 19th century, along with SIR WALTER SCOTT and LORD BYRON, she had, however, been left by Captain Alfred Hemans as a single mother with five sons. The "nothingness of fame," as she termed it, is shown in her works to exact an enormous price from women.

"Woman and Fame" is structured in sextains: six-line stanzas, with the quatrain, rhymed *abab*, setting out a premise concerning fame, and the last two lines, closed couplets, reversing the attributes of fame by describing what would better fulfill a woman. Throughout, the aesthetic vibrancy of the quatrains overshadows the wished-for complacency of the couplets. The first stanza begins with an apostrophe to "Fame" as a tempter with a "charmed cup" which "seems" to promise immortality. The narrator realizes fame's insidious enchantment and requests instead "Sweet waters from affection's springs" (l. 6). In the second stanza, Hemans describes fame in terms of laurel leaves, a "gift" for which "Heroes have smiled in death" (ll. 3–4), but in the closing couplet she asks for a different gift, again, for the woman: a flower. (In another poem, "Corinne at the Capitol," she contrasts the lesser happiness the laurel can bring with the far greater happiness of making "the humblest hearth / Lovely but to one on earth!" [ll. 47–48].)

The third stanza describes fame as that which, through its "voice" and "thrilling tone" (l. 13), can create a visceral response akin to the reaction to a trumpet "Calling the brave to meet" (l. 16). The voice she, as a woman, would rather hear and be blessed by speaks "words of home-born love" (l. 18). The fourth stanza is accusatory in tone, depicting fame as a poor substitute for love, and even as a kind of predator, finding victims in the emotionally vulnerable. Fame's song she characterizes as "hollow" and its eye as expressing "mockery" (ll. 19, 20), both aimed at the "sick heart" (l. 21) that longs not for fame but for loving support in the world ("kindly looks to cheer it on" [l. 23]) and for the sounds not of fame but for the voices of loved ones who have passed away; the "tender accents that are gone" (l. 24) may well refer to the recent passing of her mother.

The last stanza apostrophizes fame again, claiming that it cannot be that which sustains "the drooping reed," nor the "fresh fountain" that will "cool" the "soul's feverish need" (ll. 26–28). The poem's closing couplet asks, "Where must the lone one turn or flee?" (l. 29) and answers with the definitive "Not unto thee" (l. 30), which, on closer examination, becomes ambiguous in that it does not supply a substantive answer to the posed question.

Hemans addresses the issue of women in fame in other works, including "Properzia Rossi," "Corinne at the Capitol," and "Joan of Arc, in Rheims," In the first-mentioned, the narrative voice is that of the successful sculptress Properzia Rossi, who abjures fame in that it did not bring and could not bring her love. In the second, the narrator reenacts the possible scene wherein the famous Boetian poetess of antiquity received her laurels, couching it in the love-versus-fame conflict, advocating that the wife is happier than the laureled poetess. Her Joan of Arc has found that "too much of fame" has supplanted the real "paradise": "home with all its loves."

During the Romantic era, the public production of art, and certainly any achievement of fame, was still seen as a transgression against the strictures of female modesty. But advances in the technology of literary production and the proliferation of periodicals and ANNUALS AND GIFT BOOKS made it possible for women to earn a living by writing; poets like Felicia Hemans and her contemporary, LETITIA ELIZABETH LANDON, were partially accepted violations of the prevalent gender role boundaries with regard to publishing because they wrote not for public display but rather for a feminine domestic goal that was socially acceptable: to support oneself and one's family.

## Further Reading

Hemans, Felicia. *Felicia Hemans: Selected Poems, Letters, Reception Materials.* Edited by Susan J. Wolfson. Princeton, N.J.: Princeton University Press, 2000.

———. *Felicia Hemans: Selected Poems, Prose, and Letters.* Edited by Gary Kelly. Peterborough, Ont.: Broadview Press, 2000.

———. *Works of Mrs. Hemans, with a memoir by her sister.* 6 vols. Edited by Harriet Hughes. Edinburgh: William Blackwood & Sons; London: Thomas Cadell, 1836.

Wolfson, Susan J. "Domestic Affections and the Spear of Minerva." In *Re-visioning Romanticism: British Women Writers, 1776–1837,* edited by Carol Shiner Wilson and Joel Haefner, 128–166. Philadelphia: University of Pennsylvania Press, 1994.

———. "Men, Women, and Fame: Teaching Felicia Hemans." In *Approaches to Teaching British Women Poets of the Romantic Period,* edited by Stephen C. Behrendt and Harriet Kramer Linkin, 110–120. New York: Modern Language Association, 1997.

—Donna Berliner

## Wordsworth, Dorothy (1771–1855)

Dorothy Mae Ann Wordsworth, the sister of WIL-LIAM WORDSWORTH, was born in Cockermouth, Cumberland, on Christmas Day 1771. She was the only girl of the five children born to John and Ann Wordsworth. Her lifelong wish to be part of a family was irrevocably shaped by her disrupted childhood: Her mother died in 1778 and her father five years later. For much of her childhood and adolescence, Dorothy saw her brothers only during their school holidays. She initially lived in Halifax, the northern industrial mill town, with a second cousin whom she considered a substitute mother, attending a day school and reading books kept in the subscription library in her cousin's shop. In 1787 she was sent to stay with her maternal grandparents in Penrith. Although in later life she acknowledged their generosity, at the time it was a difficult period. Not only was she deprived of school and books, but she felt isolated and unfairly cast into the role of a poor relation. Thankfully, her uncle, William Cookson, married, and Dorothy moved south to Norfolk with the couple in 1788, helping them raise their quickly growing family.

Dorothy's plan to live with her brother William was initially difficult to fulfill because her uncle rejected William for his liaison with a French woman who had borne his illegitimate child. In 1794 Dorothy and William took a walking tour through the Lake District, after which she spent 15 months visiting various relatives. In 1795 Dorothy and William moved southwest to rent Racedown Lodge, a Georgian mansion in Dorset, which Dorothy welcomed as much for its permanence of living arrangement as for the fulfilment of her dream of a family life. Two years later they moved to Alfoxden House in Somerset to be closer to William's friend SAMUEL TAYLOR COLERIDGE. Dorothy kept a journal here and continued to do so when she and William moved to Dove Cottage in the Lake District in 1799; the journals she kept there, now known as the *GRASMERE JOURNALS*, are arguably her most famous work. She also experimented in poetry, as evidenced in "A COTTAGE IN GRASMERE VALE."

In October 1802 William married Mary Hutchinson. The details surrounding the wedding, as depicted by Dorothy in the *Grasmere Journals*, have raised questions among literary critics about the exact nature of the siblings' relationship. While charges of incest seem spurious, there seems to have been a deep connection between William and Dorothy, evidenced by the fact that on the night before the wedding, Dorothy wore the ring that William would be giving to Mary the next day. A crossed-out sentence, deciphered in the 1950s by the use of infrared technology, was initially interpreted to say that on the morning of the wedding, William put the ring back onto Dorothy's finger and "blessed [her] fervently," but this phrase was later clarified to be "as I [Dorothy] blessed the ring softly." After the marriage, Dorothy lived with the couple and helped them raise their children.

Apart from factual details, little is known about Dorothy's life after the Grasmere period. In 1805 she suffered both personally and financially when the ship *Earl of Abergavenny* sank; not only did her brother John drown, but she lost her investment in the ship's cargo. She suffered from dementia for the last 20 years of her life, with symptoms no doubt exacerbated by opium addiction, and gave way to frequent tantrums. She remained at Rydal Mount, the Cumbrian house to which the Wordsworths had moved in 1813, from 1835 until her death on January 25, 1855.

In spite of Dorothy's reputation as a meek helpmeet to her brother, she traveled widely both in Britain and on the Continent. With William, she traveled in Germany (1798–99), Scotland (1803), and Switzerland and Italy (1820). She also went to Calais in 1802, where she met Annette Vallon, William's former lover, and their daughter, Caroline. Her solo travel included another visit to Scotland (1822) and the Isle of Man (1828) and visits to relatives who lived along the border of Wales.

Apart from a silhouette and one portrait made late in her life, no pictures exist of Dorothy Wordsworth. Descriptions by Coleridge and THOMAS DE QUINCEY portray her as wild-eyed and full of energy, though her journals indicate that she was prone to devastating headaches and was toothless by the age of 40. Most early biographers and literary critics judged Dorothy's value solely in terms of William. This affected many early edited versions of her journals, which deleted descriptions about health (considered too mundane to be included) and the relationship between William and Dorothy.

The importance of Dorothy's observations on William's work cannot be denied, and her own writing does provide both a close personal view of his life and factual details that William used for his poetry. However, more recent studies of her letters and journals have considered her work for its own literary merit and have brought her out from the shadow of her brother's genius. Frances Wilson's *The Ballad of Dorothy Wordsworth* (2008), the first major biography of her in more than 20 years, reinterprets Dorothy and the *Grasmere Journals*, drawing out the personality that has only rarely been acknowledged.

See also "TO MY SISTER."

## Further Reading

Gittings, Robert, and Jo Manton. *Dorothy Wordsworth.* Oxford: Clarendon Press, 1985.

Wilson, Frances. *The Ballad of Dorothy Wordsworth.* London: Faber and Faber, 2008.

Wordsworth, Dorothy. *The Grasmere Journals.* Oxford and New York: Oxford University Press, 1991.

—Tracey S. Rosenberg

## Wordsworth, William (1770–1850)

William Wordsworth's importance to Romanticism cannot be overstated. To start with, it is he who, together with SAMUEL TAYLOR COLERIDGE, produced one of the first key texts of the period with the publication of LYRICAL BALLADS in 1798. Most of Wordsworth's contributions to the Romantic canon can be found in four publications: *Lyrical Ballads; Poems, in Two Volumes* (1807); *The EXCURSION* (1814); and *Poems* (1815). The humanist focus within his work on nature, children, common life, and strong personal sentiment provided a new perspective in poetry and contrasted sharply with the heroic subject matter commonly found in the genre and still being employed by his contemporaries. So different was his voice from other poetic voices of his time that he felt compelled to publish a manifesto defending his work against critics. In his PREFACE TO LYRICAL BALLADS, written for the rerelease of the *Ballads* in 1800, Wordsworth refutes the heretofore commonly held belief in a hierarchy of poetry in which the epic was the greatest and the

short lyric the meanest of poetic forms by claiming that common life, written about in common language, is the most proper subject matter for a true poet. He also rejects the idea that poetry should be about a higher nature and higher ideals, claiming rather that poetry, uniting man with nature, should deal in sincerity over artifice and simple truths expressed simply over decorum. Finally, the Preface states that the primary role of poetry is that of preserving what is essentially human in the face of an increasingly urban and industrial society. The Preface therefore outlines the scope of Wordsworth's oeuvre and continues today to be influential both as a guide to his own work and as a critical source for study and evaluation of the Romantic canon. In its own time the Preface, like Wordsworth's poems themselves, sparked a heated debate among his detractors (including WILLIAM BLAKE, FRANCIS JEFFREY, and MARY SHELLEY) and his followers, catapulting him into the public arena as a controversial poet-philosopher.

Wordsworth was born on April 7, 1770, in Cockermouth, Cumberland, in the Lake District of northern England, one of five children born to the attorney John Wordsworth and his wife Ann. His mother died in 1778 and his father in 1783, leaving Wordsworth orphaned at 13. Under the guardianship of his uncles, he attended St. John's College at Cambridge, earning his B.A. in 1791. Following his matriculation at Cambridge, he took a walking tour in France, where he began a relationship with a Frenchwoman, Annette Vallon, who bore him a daughter, Caroline. Although he never married Annette, Wordsworth returned to visit throughout his life and supported both her and Caroline financially.

Lack of funds and the growing hostilities between England and France forced Wordsworth to return alone to England in 1792, when he began writing poetry in earnest. He published his first two volumes, *An Evening Walk* and *Descriptive Sketches*, in 1793. In 1795, while living in Somerset, he met Samuel Taylor Coleridge, and the two developed a friendship that resulted in the cowriting of the first edition of *Lyrical Ballads*, which contained (among other great poems) Coleridge's "The RIME OF THE ANCIENT MARINER" and Wordsworth's "LINES WRITTEN A FEW MILES ABOVE TINTERN

ABBEY," two of the foremost works in the Romantic movement. Also included in the first edition were "The THORN," "Goody Blake and Harry Gill," "The IDIOT BOY," "The Female Vagrant," and "The COMPLAINT OF A FORSAKEN INDIAN WOMAN." In 1799 nostalgia for his childhood home prompted Wordsworth to move back to the Lake District, where he associated with Coleridge and also with ROBERT SOUTHEY; as a result, the three are often referred to as the LAKE SCHOOL poets. Although the relationship between Wordsworth and Coleridge was strained by Wordsworth's career path (specifically the publication of his poetic vision, which greatly differed from that of Coleridge, in the Preface to *Lyrical Ballads*) and by Coleridge's opium addiction, they later reconciled and remained lifelong friends.

Wordsworth married his childhood friend Mary Hutchinson in 1802; the couple had five children, two of whom died in childhood. In 1813 an appointment as distributor of stamps for Westmorland provided the family with a yearly income and financial security, but although Wordsworth continued to write and publish poetry until his daughter's death in 1847, little of his later work is as important as his earlier poetry, and the lifestyle change brought about by this financial windfall seems to have adversely affected his writing career. Still, he was awarded honorary degrees from Durham and Oxford Universities in 1838 and 1839, respectively, a government pension in 1842, and the title of poet laureate upon the death of Southey in 1843. Wordsworth died on April 23, 1850, and his final work, *The PRELUDE*, the earliest version of which dates from 1799, was published by Mary later that year.

Any serious study of Wordsworth's poetry must begin and end with "Tintern Abbey." As the W. L. Renwick notes: "It might be said, without too much exaggeration, that Wordsworth spent the rest of his life expanding, glossing, commenting upon that poem" (Renwick 158). This seminal poem in the Romantic canon encapsulates Wordsworth's primary themes: the permanence of nature and transience of human-made things, the stagnation and mobility in the lives of men, and the importance and ambiguity of the imaginative life. A nostalgic tone permeates throughout,

the voice of the poet ringing through the lines. Wordsworth's use of blank verse is a nod to JOHN MILTON and his ideas concerning belief, although "Tintern Abbey," unlike *Paradise Lost*, makes no mention of God: Wordsworth's belief is a humanistic one, grounded in the world around him rather than in any actual religion. As he returns on a walking tour to this place he last visited five years ago, the poet takes the reader through an imaginative tour of his own evolution. Regarding the ruined abbey below, he considers the nature of the world and of men through the changes he perceives in himself and in his own life. The ruins of the abbey, at once a permanent and ephemeral edifice, symbolize for him the ravages of time on humans and human-made things and yet the constant presence of humans in the world, while the situation of the abbey among natural elements eloquently portrays the deeper and more profound nature of humans' relation to that world. The nostalgia inherent in his memories, signified in particular by a fleeting image of his sister, DOROTHY WORDSWORTH, (referred to but not expressly named), juxtaposed with more concrete natural images, demonstrates most fully his commitment to his new poetic ideal.

The themes of humans' relationship with nature and of nostalgia run throughout Wordsworth's oeuvre and are present in many of his shorter works, especially "THERE WAS A BOY" (1799), "I WANDERED LONELY AS A CLOUD" (1807), "The World Is Too Much with Us" (1807), "Surprised by Joy" (1815) and "Mutability" (1822). In *Elegiac Stanzas* (1807) he draws on these themes effectively by contrasting the image of a castle beset by a storm as painted by Sir George Beaumont with his own rendition in words of a more tranquil tone, a harmony between man's castle and the natural world. Each of these poems is an example of the fact that Wordsworth primarily focuses not on a narrative technique but, rather, a series of sentiments and images in his work. He invites the reader to join him in an imaginative contemplation of ideas rather than drawing the reader along in a story. This is in keeping with his idea that epics and ballads are not the only great poetic forms; he deliberately avoids telling a tale in favor of showing a human characteristic.

Wordsworth's poetry also makes frequent use of images of childhood to access nostalgia. In "To a Butterfly" (1801) he exclaims: "Oh! Pleasant, pleasant were the days / The time, when in our childish plays / My sister Emmeline and I / Together chaced the Butterfly!" (ll. 29–32), while his 1807 "Ode" is subtitled "Intimations of Immortality from Recollections of Early Childhood." Poems such as these make use of the childhood motif to highlight the idea that people are closer to nature than the modern world considers them to be; through the innocence of children can be found the connection between their childish joy and wonder at the world and the joy and wonder nature can invoke in those who willingly submit to their emotions. Inherent in such poems is the idea that the urban and industrial nature of society has robbed humans of the simple pleasures of nature. The children and childhood memories in these poems serve as a bridge for the reader between person and nature, calling forth memories of and nostalgia for simpler days while underscoring the more serious, philosophical nature of the man recalling these things.

Many of Wordsworth's poems concerning children and childhood also deal with death, as in "There was a Boy," LUCY GRAY (1799), and "WE ARE SEVEN" (1798). This underscores yet again the transient nature of our place in the world. But although the deaths of children are sad, Wordsworth seems to feel that rather than mourning their deaths, it is better to celebrate their eternal youth and therefore their eternal link with the natural world. An example of this is found in "We Are Seven": When the narrator exclaims, "But they are dead, those two are dead! / Their spirits are in heaven" in response to the news that two of her siblings have died, the girl to whom he is speaking resolutely declares that this is not so: "The little Maid would have her will, / And said, "Nay, we are seven!" (ll. 65–69). Wordsworth here turns the innocent belief of a child in the immortal nature of her dead kin into a deeper exploration of the relationship between mankind and the world. Through the eyes of this child, we are in the world and of the world, dead or no, ever present as part of the natural order of things.

Much of Wordsworth's work also decries the influence of urban and industrial life and bad government on the nature of man. Poems such as "Lines Written in Early Spring" (1798), "Calais, August 1802," and "October 1803" decry the state of man in corrupt society. Wordsworth rails against the behavior of men who act on their baser motives, claiming that mankind is stripped of nobility, hope, and greatness by such behavior. He feels that men who act in association with one another under these conditions, rather than with nature, slowly destroy the earth along with one another. As he exclaims in "Lines Written in Early Spring," "Have I not reason to lament / what man has made of man?" (ll. 23–24). In contrast, he approves of revolution in the spirit of overthrowing such forces and seeking out a nobler face for mankind in poems such as "French Revolution" (1805) and "Thomas Clarkson on the Final Passing of the Bill for the Abolition of the Slave Trade" (1807); in the latter, he calls Clarkson a "firm friend of human kind" (l. 15) for his part in the fight to end SLAVERY. Wordsworth's message in such poems is clear: Men behaving as nature dictates are noble; men behaving as urban society requires them to are corrupted and have lost their innate nobility; and men who rebel against society therefore regain their natural, noble state.

Not all of Wordsworth's work is so philosophical in nature, although even his simplest poems are often deceptively deep in meaning. A large number of his poems deal with pastoral themes and are essentially written snapshots of the countryside and the nature and activities of the animals and people who inhabit it. Among these are included some of his best-known works, including "NUTTING" (1799), "The Green Linnet" (1803), "To the Cuckoo" (1804), and "To a Skylark" (1805). Many of these poems incorporate Wordsworth's themes of childhood, nostalgia, and people's place in the world, but in the main they are felicitous scenes of simple life and creature traits. In this category can also be found humorous tales of country folk, such as "Goody Blake and Harry Gill" (1798); and "Andrew Jones" (1800), in which Wordsworth displays his sharp wit as well as his poetic style. He deals more seriously with country folk and country life in slightly longer pastoral works such as "MICHAEL: A PASTORAL POEM" (1800); "ALICE FELL" (1801); and "RESOLUTION

AND INDEPENDENCE" (1807), a poem sometimes referred to as "The Leech Gatherer." Throughout all of these poems, whether short and humorous or long and serious in tone, Wordsworth employs a keen observation of nature and of human nature in his imagery.

*The Prelude,* which Wordsworth began in 1796 and continued to work on throughout his life, although not published in his lifetime, is now widely accepted as his most important work. It incorporates not only a self-reflective tone but also most of the themes that occupied him throughout his career—nature, the lives of common folk, revolution, and the place of humans in the history of the world. In many ways, *The Prelude* is an expansion on and a reworking of "Tintern Abbey" in terms of theme, although it is far greater in scope and in controversy, dealing as it does with socialist and Jacobite views as well as the poet's own psycho-biographical experience. The most important aspect of this poem for Wordsworth is its tone of hope: It outlines the foundations of how mankind might be were it to function in the spirit of community, a committed and strong relationship between self and society, in harmony with human beings' true nature as belonging in the world and of the world.

William Wordsworth's oeuvre is varied in style—he wrote pastorals, sonnets, ballads, and odes, among others—and in subject matter, ranging from children to historical events and persons, natural subjects, country life, love and death, and even adaptations of Geoffrey Chaucer's work for modern sensibilities. But throughout his poems he remains consistent in his poetic philosophy as put forth in his Preface to *Lyrical Ballads:* that great poetry deals with simple things in simple language, and that "the poet . . . considers man and nature as essentially adapted to each other, and the mind of man as naturally the mirror of the fairest and most interesting qualities of nature" (Wordsworth 2007, 292). Throughout his work he maintains the voice of one who observes, filters, and records the relationship between humans and nature with a keen understanding and awareness of the ephemeral and transient quality of the former in comparison with the permanence and intransience of the latter. This is the essence of his Romanticism.

Wordsworth's status as an important poet was unquestioned through the end of the 19th century, when he was widely read and studied, but by the centennial celebration of his death in 1950, academic interest in his work was relatively minimal. There has been a strong resurgence in interest in Wordsworth since that point, with a great deal of scholarly work produced in the second half of the 20th century. Modern studies focus on his relationship with fellow writers Coleridge and Southey, on his relationship with his troubled sister Dorothy, on his preoccupation with the self, on his work on politics and nationhood, and on environmental issues. Additionally, much recent work has been done on the linguistics of his poetry and on the association of his work with critical schools of thought, especially New Historicism and poststructuralism. His Preface to *Lyrical Ballads* is a cornerstone text in critical theory and serves as the basis for many important critical studies of Romanticism.

One of the founders of the Romantic movement, William Wordsworth continues to have a profound impact upon our understanding of Romanticism today, and the continued influence of his work is evidence for his own statement that "Poetry is the first and last of all knowledge—it is as immortal as the heart of man."

See also "LONDON, 1802"; "ODE TO DUTY"; "TO MY SISTER." For commentary by one of Wordsworth's contemporaries, see PERCY BYSSHE SHELLEY's "TO WORDSWORTH."

**Further Reading**

Abrams, M. H., ed. *Wordsworth: A Collection of Critical Essays.* Englewood Cliffs, N.J.: Prentice-Hall, 1972.

Gill, Stephen. *William Wordsworth: A Life.* Oxford: Oxford University Press, 1990.

Gilpin, George H., ed. *Critical Essays on William Wordsworth.* Boston: G. K. Hall, 1990.

Hartman, Geoffrey. *Wordsworth's Poetry, 1787–1814.* New Haven, Conn.: Yale University Press, 1971.

Renwick, W. L. *Oxford History of English Literature, Vol. 9: English Literature 1789–1815.* Oxford: Oxford University Press, 1963.

Wordsworth, Jonathan. *William Wordsworth: The Borders of Vision.* Oxford: Oxford University Press, 1982.

Wordsworth, Jonathan, Michael C. Jaye, and Robert Woof. *William Wordsworth and the Age of Romanti-*

cism. New Brunswick, N.J.: Rutgers University Press, 1987.

Wordsworth, William. *Complete Poetical Works.* Bartleby. com. Available online. URL: http://www.bartleby. com/145/wordchrono.html. Downloaded on January 4, 2008.

———. *The Major Works: Including the Prelude.* Edited by Stephen Gill. Oxford: Oxford University Press, 2000.

———. *Preface to Lyrical Ballads.* In *The Critical Tradition: Classic Texts and Contemporary Trends.* 3rd ed. Edited by David H. Richter. Boston: St. Martin's Press, 2007. 285–298.

—Melissa A. Elmes

## *Works of Ossian, The* James Macpherson (1765)

Published in two volumes in 1765, *The Works of Ossian* brings together several purported translations of poetry from the Gaelic language which includes *Fingal* (an epic poem first published in 1761), *Temora* (another epic poem, first published in 1763), several other shorter poetic pieces, and a "Critical Dissertation" by Hugh Blair (1718–1800). Immediately after their first publication, these poems created a controversy over the extent to which they were authentic translations of antique texts, unscrupulous rewritings of plundered traditional ballads, or original creations.

*The Works* were the culmination of several years of poetic activity on JAMES MACPHERSON's part. He had already published anonymously a collection of poems in 1760 *(Fragments of Ancient Poetry Collected in the Highlands of Scotland and Translated from the GAELIC or ERSE language),* which had been highly successful. It contained 15 short prose pieces presented in a preface (which might have been written by Blair) as the translations of "genuine remains of ancient Scottish poetry" composed in "the most remote antiquity . . . coeval with the very infancy of Christianity in Scotland" and which had been recited and preserved by "bards . . . , manuscript [and] oral tradition . . . incorrupted [sic] to this day" (Macpherson 5; the references are to the pages of the Gaskill edition). The preface explains that the translation

is "extremely literal" (6)—word for word, when possible. The result is thus very distinct from the poetry of the second half of the 18th century: no poetic diction, no rhyme, no lines, and unfamiliar and disturbing images. It consists of 16 fragmentary monologues and dialogues in poetic prose that chronicle various wars against invaders from Scandinavia, the "Strangers! Sons of the waves" (7). Yet they do not depict battles proper; rather, they focus on the returning soldier, alone because he is the only survivor ("I return; but I alone of my race" [9]), or the woman left behind ("sad on the sea-beat shore thy spouse looketh for thy return [10]). The fragments are either dialogues with ghosts or monologues grieving for departed friends ("My tears, O Ryno! Are for the dead; my voice for the inhabitants of the grave" [24]). At the end of each poem, only tombs and memories remain: "Thou askest . . . whose memory is preserved in these tombs? . . . Thou has heard this tale of grief . . . : shed on her grave a tear" [19–20]).

The *Fragments* also introduced the figure of Ossian, who was to play an essential part in Macpherson's next supposed discovery—*Fingal, an Ancient Epic Poem in Six Books* (1761); this is one of the texts included in the 2-volume works. The whole epic is told by Ossian, the son of Fingal, the main hero of these poems. He was a blind bard, said to have lived in the third century, "the last of the race of Fingal. Sightless are his aged eyes" (18), whose function was to "[lament] the dead" (18). Each of the six books is introduced by an argument that sums up the main action of the epic as well as the various interruptions where bards recall other heroes, other battles, other deaths. The main plot centers on the attempted invasion of Ireland by ships from Denmark led by Swaran. Cuchulin, "the general of the Irish tribes" (54), and his chiefs first debate whether they should fight immediately or wait for the arrival of Fingal, the "king of those Caledonians who inhabited the north-west coast of Scotland" (54). A ghost warns them of defeat, but they nonetheless decide to engage the enemy; eventually "the whole Irish army gave way" (64). At that moment Fingal arrives and leads his army against the invaders; he then fights and defeats Swaran in individual combat, but spares him and invites him to the victory feast. Yet no sense of victory prevails, only regret. However glorious the present might be, the past and the future are so saturated with death, failures, and shame ("One day the warriors must die, and the children see their useless arms in the hall" [92]) that even in the midst of joy the heroes and the bards lament their fate: "The fame of my former actions is ceased; and I sit forlorn at the tombs of friends" (104).

The other poems in the first volume of *The Works of Ossian* and *Temora,* in the second volume, further explore the lives and deaths of the characters introduced in *Fingal,* continuing the same themes of loss and tragic violence in the same alliterative prose.

The extraordinary success and influence of Macpherson's collections in Europe probably rest on the series of paradoxes they express: These paradoxes were precisely those that late 18th-century European societies were experiencing. Collecting, translating, and publishing regional ballads from oral recitation had begun in the 1750s, but Macpherson drew on this new taste for the primitive to propose an extreme case: a long and sophisticated epic—the highest form of poetry according to the 18th-century canon—of a remotely archaic origin, composed almost spontaneously, in a language that is both prosaic and mysterious. This allows the text to convey another contradiction of the century. The poems might celebrate martial and heroic virtues but they do so ruefully, remorsefully. Military merit is extolled at the same time as it is lamented, and finally courage is less celebrated than is SENSIBILITY.

The question of authenticity—the possibility or, rather, the necessity of asking that question and the complexities it raised, independent of its answer—was in itself a literary revolution. The first serious enquiry, in 1796 by the Highland Society of Scotland, concluded that *The Works of Ossian* were not a literal translation; but they were definitely based on traditional tales truly collected in the Highlands. The earlier attacks on Macpherson as a fraud and charlatan were partially unfounded; his work was no hoax (like THOMAS CHATTERTON's *Rowley,* for example). These conclusions have since

been confirmed. Macpherson's collections are not the exact translations of identifiable texts but a recombination of traditional sources. This reworking of existing and identified sources tells us much about Macpherson's (and his contemporaries') conception of what early poetry was all about. He wanted to restore what had been corrupted by time but not by following a philological or scientific approach. Rather, he acted like every other teller of the epic since Ossian and the beginning of the poem: He made the poem his and brought it to life for his audience. There is no doubt in any case that the debate encouraged the preservation of Gaelic manuscripts that had previously been considered of little value and initiated extensive research into early Gaelic literature and the way it is transmitted, translated, and appropriated.

The crossbreeding aspect is probably the most enduring one of Macpherson's texts. His attempt to link opposed cultures—the Gaelic and the English, the oral and the printed, the Highlands and the Lowlands, and (more crucially) the local and national on the one hand and the universal and the classical epic on the other—precipitated a cultural revolution that led to Romanticism.

See also BURNS, ROBERT; MOORE, THOMAS; SCOTT, SIR WALTER.

## Further Reading

Gaskill, Howard. *The Reception of Ossian in Europe.* London: Thoemmes Continuum, 2004.

Macpherson, James. *The Poems of Ossian and Related Works.* Edited by Howard Gaskill. Edinburgh: Edinburgh University Press, 1996.

Moore, Dafydd. *Enlightenment and Romance in James Macpherson's The Poems of Ossian.* Aldershot, Eng.: Ashgate, 2003.

———, ed. *Ossian and Ossianism.* 4 vols. London and New York: Routledge, 2004.

Stafford, Fiona. Introduction to *The Poems of Ossian and Related Works,* by James Macpherson, edited by Howard Gaskill, v–xiii. Edinburgh: Edinburgh University Press, 1996.

—Samuel Baudry

# Y

## Yearsley, Ann (ca. 1753–1806)

Ann Yearsley has been billed as one of Romanticism's "natural geniuses"—a Bristol milk seller better remembered until recently for her sensational dispute with a patron than for her poetry. Born Ann Cromartie on July 8, 1753, she was baptized at Clifton Hill, Bristol and married John Yearsley, a day laborer, in 1774. Over the next decade she bore six children; only four survived. In winter 1783–84, the Yearsleys became destitute but refused to accept parish charity; having lost their accommodation, they sheltered in a disused Bristol farm building. Yearsley's mother died, and the poet's own life was endangered before a passing gentleman stumbled upon and saved the family. Yearsley was then already writing verse, having read some Shakespeare as well as Edward Young's *Night Thoughts,* JOHN MILTON's *Paradise Lost,* Alexander Pope's "Eloisa to Abelard" and Virgil's *Georgics.* After HANNAH MORE's cook purchased milk from the passing Yearsley, she showed her mistress some of the latter's work.

More, a poet, dramatist, and novelist, enlisted support for a subscription, and Yearsley's *Poems, on Several Occasions* was published by Thomas Cadell in June 1785. The volume included "A Prefatory Letter to Mrs. Montagu. By a Friend," in which More presented herself beneficently while depicting Yearsley as a naive primitive. The poems comprised numerous professions of gratitude to patrons but also the notable "Clifton Hill," a brooding semiautobiographical, locodescriptive poem in which the landscape mirrors its characters' psychology. The subscription's success brought profits, and More and Yearsley argued about the latter's access to them. Yearsley obtained both her royalties and different patrons. In 1786 *Poems, on Several Occasions* reached a fourth edition, now published by G. G. J. and J. Robinson. Here Yearsley first published her "Autobiographical Narrative," stating her side of the story.

Yearsley's *Poems, on Various Subjects* was published in 1787. Its contents often show development from earlier work and include significant poems on writing ("To Mr. ****, an Unlettered Poet on Genius Unimproved"), "natural genius" ("Addressed to Ignorance, Occasioned by a Gentleman's desiring the Author never to Assume Knowledge of the Ancients") and religion ("On Jephthah's Vow taken in a Literal Sense"). Yearsley subsequently published "POEM ON THE INHUMANITY OF THE SLAVE TRADE" (1788), and "Stanzas of Woe" (1790). Her verse drama *Earl Goodwin* was performed in Bristol in 1789 and published in 1791, and she wrote two further plays (since lost).

In 1793 Yearsley opened a circulating library, and in 1796 she published her third poetic volume, *The Rural Lyre.* Arguably her most diverse and ambitious collection, it contains "Bristol Elegy," a macabre portrait of a Bristol riot that occasioned many deaths; and "The Indifferent Shepherdess to Colin," a proto-feminist engagement with the bucolic. She also published *The Royal-Captives,* a four-volume novel, in 1795.

Yearsley's husband died in 1803, and she followed three years later, on May 6, 1806. Her final years were spent quietly in Melksham, Wiltshire. After a century and three quarters of relative neglect, she has attracted increasing attention in recent decades, often from feminist, historicist, and materialist critics. While her class orientation has proved especially contentious, her poetry is now being increasingly reassessed.

## Further Reading

Cairnie, Julie. "The Ambivalence of Ann Yearsley: Laboring and Writing, Submission and Resistance." *Nineteenth-Century Contexts* 27 (Winter 2005): 353–364.

Christmas, William J. *The Lab'ring Muses: Work, Writing, and the Social Order in English Plebeian Poetry, 1730–1830*. Newark: University of Delaware Press, 2001.

Ferguson, Moira. *Eighteenth-Century Women Poets: Nation, Class, and Gender*. Albany: State University of New York Press. 1995.

Landry, Donna. *The Muses of Resistance: Laboring-Class English Women's Poetry, 1739–96*. Cambridge: Cambridge University Press, 1990.

Waldron, Mary. *Lactilla, Milkwoman of Clifton: The Life and Writings of Ann Yearsley, 1753–1806*. Athens: University of Georgia Press, 1996.

Yearsley, Ann. *Selected Poems*. Edited by Tim Burke. Gloucestershire, Eng.: Cyder Press, 2003.

—Steve Van Hagen

# CHRONOLOGY

| Date | Europe | Americas | Literature | Culture | Science and Technology |
|------|--------|----------|------------|---------|------------------------|
| 1775 | In Britain, Edmund Burke advocates conciliation with America. | War of Independence (to 1783): Battles of Lexington and Concord, Bunker Hill<br><br>To date, 5.5 million slaves have shipped to United States | Richard Sheridan's *The Rivals* performed; Samuel Johnson's *A Journey to the Western Islands of Scotland* published | Charles Lamb born<br><br>Jane Austen born<br><br>Joseph Turner born<br><br>Pierre Augustin Beaumarchais's *The Barber of Seville* is performed. | Alessandro Volta invents the electrophorus. |
| 1776 | Catherine the Great introduces government reforms in Russia.<br><br>Britain: Prohibitory Act imposes sanctions on trade with America. | Continental Congress issues Declaration of Independence, announcing freedom from British rule.<br><br>British hang Nathan Hale as a spy (without a trial).<br><br>Thomas Paine's *Common Sense* is published, urging American independence from Britain. It sells more than 100,000 copies in three months. | Published: Adam Smith, *The Wealth of Nations;* Edward Gibbon, first volume of *The Decline and Fall of the Roman Empire* | David Hume dies.<br><br>John Constable born<br><br>David Garrick gives farewell performance at Drury Lane. | James Watt and Matthew Boulton build first commercial steam engine. |

| Date | Europe | Americas | Literature | Culture | Science and Technology |
|------|--------|----------|-----------|---------|------------------------|
| 1777 | | British victory at Brandywine Creek<br><br>British troops surrender after Battle of Saratoga.<br><br>Congress specifies the design of the U.S. flag: 13 alternating red and white stripes and 13 white stars on a blue background. | Thomas Chatterton's *Poems, Supposed to have been written by Thomas Rowley* published posthumously | Richard Brinsley Sheridan's *The School for Scandal* opens at London's Drury Lane Theatre. | James Cook's *A Voyage towards the South Pole and Round the World* published |
| 1778 | France declares war on Britain<br><br>Britain: Catholic Relief Act | France allies herself with America. | Published: Frances Burney, *Evelina;* Thomas West, *A Guide to the Lakes* | William Hazlitt born<br><br>Jean-Jacques Rousseau dies.<br><br>Voltaire dies. | |
| 1779 | Britain: Movement for Parliamentary Reform founded | Spain allies herself with America and retakes western Florida and the Bahamas. | Samuel Johnson publishes *The Lives of the Poets.* | Thomas Moore born<br><br>Richard Sheridan's *The Critic* performed<br><br>Death of Captain James Cook in Hawaii | Severn Bridge, made of iron, is built in Britain.<br><br>Jan Ingelhousz shows that plants use carbon dioxide and produce oxygen. |
| 1780 | Britain: Led by Lord George Gordon, Protestants march on Parliament to present a petition against the Catholic Relief Act of 1778. Riots follow, and there are many deaths.<br><br>Death of Maria Theresa, Empress of Austria<br><br>Britain declares war on the Netherlands. | Pennsylvania abolishes slavery.<br><br>British forces capture Charleston and defeat southern American army.<br><br>U.S. population estimated at 2.7 million | Published: George Crabbe, *The Candidate,* Thomas Gilpin, *Observations on the River Wye* | Joshua Reynolds paints *Mary Robinson as Perdita.* | Samuel Williams observes an eclipse and details the spots of light along the Moon's edge.<br><br>Jean le Rond d'Alembert publishes final volume of *Opuscubs Mathematiques,* rethinking modern calculus. |

| Date | Europe | Americas | Literature | Culture | Science and Technology |
|------|--------|----------|------------|---------|------------------------|
| 1781 | Austria: Joseph II abolishes serfdom. | Articles of Confederation become law.<br><br>Battle of Yorktown: British army surrenders. | Jean-Jacques Rousseau, *Confessions* published posthumously | Immanuel Kant publishes *Critique of Pure Reason.*<br><br>Henry Fuseli paints *The Nightmare.* | William Herschel discovers the planet Uranus, although he supposes it to be a comet. |
| 1782 | Britain defeats France at the Battle of the Saints, regaining control of the Caribbean. | Spanish settlers found Los Angeles.<br><br>Loyalist Americans begin to leave United States for Canada. | William Cowper publishes *Poems.* | Friedrich von Schiller's play *The Robbers* is performed in Mannheim.<br><br>Susan Edmonstone Ferrier (Scottish novelist) born<br><br>Sarah Siddons triumphs at Drury Lane in *Isabella.* | Joseph and Jacques Montgolfier build air balloon.<br><br>Harvard Medical School opens. |
| 1783 | Russia annexes the Crimea. | Treaty of Paris ends the War of Independence; the United States is formed.<br><br>The Great Lakes and the Mississippi are recognized as the frontiers. | Published: George Crabbe, "The Village"; William Beckford, *Dreams, Waking Thoughts and Incidents* | Emergence of evangelical movement under Charles Simeon | Henry Cort refines the process for "puddling" iron. |
| 1784 | Britain: William Pitt wins the general election.<br><br>Britain India Act is passed, and Prime Minister Pitt declares British control in India.<br><br>Commutation Act reduces taxes on spirits and tea. | Andrew Ellicot surveys and extends the Mason-Dixon Line. | Charlotte Smith publishes *Elegiac Sonnets.* | Death of Samuel Johnson<br><br>Founding of the Methodist Church by John Wesley<br><br>Joshua Reynolds paints Sarah Siddons as *The Tragic Muse.* | Edmund Cartwright invents steam-powered loom, thus revolutionizing weaving.<br><br>Benjamin Franklin invents bifocal eyeglasses. |

| Date | Europe | Americas | Literature | Culture | Science and Technology |
|------|--------|----------|------------|---------|------------------------|
|      |        |          |            |         | First mail delivered by coach (London to Bristol in 17 hours) |
| 1785 | Russia: Catherine II passes law freeing nobles from taxation and giving them total sovereignty of their lands and peasants.<br><br>Britain: In defiance of the Royal Marriage Act, the Prince of Wales secretly marries Maria Fitzherbert, a Roman Catholic. | New York abolishes slavery.<br><br>Treaty of Fort McIntosh | Published: William Cowper, "The Task"; Robert Burns, "To a Mouse"; Ann Yearsley, *Poems*; Marquis de Sade, *The 120 Days of Sodom*; James Boswell, *Journal of a Tour to the Hebrides* | Thomas Love Peacock born | France: Charles-Augustin de Coulomb, French physicist, sets down relationship between electric charges (known as Coulomb's law).<br><br>Jean Pierre Blanchard and John Jeffries cross the English Channel by balloon to France. |
| 1786 | Death of Frederick the Great of Prussia<br><br>Britain acquires Penang (Malaysia) | Daniel Shays leads farmers' revolt protesting high taxes; the rebellion is crushed. | Published: Robert Burns, *Poems, Chiefly in the Scottish Dialect*; William Beckford *Vathek*; Hester Piozzi, *Anecdotes of Samuel Johnson* | Mozart composes the Symphony in D (Prague Symphony) and his opera *The Marriage of Figaro*. | First ascent of Mont Blanc by Jacques Balmat and Michel Paccard. |
| 1787 | Britain acquires Sierra Leone; freed slaves settle there. | U.S. Constitution passed, pending states' ratification<br><br>First cotton mill opens in Massachusetts. | Marquis de Sade is imprisoned and writes *The Adversities of Virtue*. | Mozart composes the opera *Don Giovanni*.<br><br>Mary Russell Mitford born | John Fitch launches the first steamboat on the Delaware River. |

| Date | Europe | Americas | Literature | Culture | Science and Technology |
|---|---|---|---|---|---|
| | | The Shakers settle in Mount Lebanon, New York. | Published: Friedrich von Schiller, *Don Carlos*; Mary Wollstonecraft, *Thoughts on the Education of Daughters* | Thomas Lord opens cricket ground in London. | |
| 1788 | Britain: Temporary insanity of King George III caused by porphyria prompts the "Regency crisis." First shipment of British convicts is transported to Botany Bay, Australia. Gustavus III of Sweden invades Finland (claimed by Russia). Denmark invades Sweden but is fought off. Trial of Warren Hastings, governor of India, for corruption | New Hampshire becomes ninth state to ratify the U.S. Constitution; the Constitution becomes law (June 21). | Published: Charlotte Smith, *Emmeline*; Mary Wollstonecraft, *Mary*; Elizabeth Inchbald, *Animal Magnetism* | Mozart composes the Symphony in G Minor. John Walter, founder of the *Daily Universal Register* (1785), relaunches it as the *Times*. Rules for the game of cricket are set down. George Gordon Byron, Lord Byron, born The Methodist Charles Wesley dies on March 29. | Andrew Meikle patents a thrasher for removing husks from grain. |
| 1789 | France: Louis XVI summons the Estates General (parliament) to review the country's impending bankruptcy. Clergy and nobility outvote the Third Estate (middle class), which then establishes a new National (Constituent) Assembly; it governs France to 1791. | George Washington inaugurated as president First Congress convenes in New York. Judiciary Act of 1789 A national day of thanksgiving is proclaimed (November 26). | Published: Olaudah Equiano, *The Interesting Narrative of the Life of Olaudah Equiano, or Gustavus Vassa, the African. Written by Himself*; William Blake, *Songs of Innocence* and *The Book of Thel*; Elizabeth Inchbald, *The Married Man* | James Fenimore Cooper born | Erasmus Darwin publishes part 1 of *The Botanic Garden* (1789–91). Gilbert White publishes *The Natural History of Selbourne*. |

| Date | Europe | Americas | Literature | Culture | Science and Technology |
|------|--------|----------|------------|---------|------------------------|
| | Storming of the Bastille in protest at rumors that Louis XVI plans to dismiss the National Assembly, which issues its charter, *Declaration of the Rights of Man.*<br><br>Britain: Mutiny on HMS *Bounty*;<br><br>King George III recovers his health. | | | | |
| 1790 | Sweden wins naval battle against Russia. The peace treaty leaves Finland under Russian control.<br><br>Britain: General election gives William Pitt an increased majority. | U.S. census records population as 4 million. Philadelphia is the second largest city and named as U.S. capital for a 10-year period.<br><br>Samuel Slater builds the first American steam-powered cotton-processing machines in Rhode Island, an event that marks the beginning of the Industrial Revolution in America. | Published: Ann Radcliffe, *The Sicilian*; Edmund Burke, *Reflections on the Revolution in France*; Mary Wollstonecraft, *A Vindication of the Rights of Men*; Joanna Baillie, *Fugitive Pieces*; William Blake, *The Marriage of Heaven and Hell* | Death of Benjamin Franklin<br><br>Mozart composes *Cosi fan tutte* (*All Women Are Like That*)<br><br>Adam Smith dies.<br><br>Alphonse de Lamartine born | James Watt invents the pressure gauge.<br><br>Opening of a 91-mile canal from Coventry to Oxford |
| 1791 | Britain: William Wilberforce's bill for the abolition of slavery is defeated.<br><br>France: Louis XVI and his family try to escape France but are captured and brought back. | Bill of Rights is ratified and becomes part of the U.S. Constitution.<br><br>Slave revolt in French-controlled Saint-Domingue (now Haiti), inspired by French Revolution; Toussaint Louverture emerges as leader of liberation campaign. | Published: Elizabeth Inchbald *A Simple Story*; Ann Radcliffe, *The Romance of the Forrest*; Robert Burns, "Tam o' Shanter"; James Boswell, *Life of Samuel Johnson* | Mozart's *The Magic Flute* performed<br><br>Joseph Haydn composes the *Surprise Symphony.* | Luigi Galvani publishes *De viribus electricitatis in motu musculari,* describing electrical stimulation of frog nerves. |

| Date | Europe | Americas | Literature | Culture | Science and Technology |
|------|--------|----------|------------|---------|------------------------|
| | | Constitutional Act divides Canada into French- or English-speaking. | | Thomas Paine's *Rights of Man* published in England, supporting the French Revolution and calling for an overthrow of the English monarchy.<br><br>Mozart dies, leaving *Requiem* (Mass for the Dead) unfinished. | |
| 1792 | Britain: Royal proclamation outlaws seditious writings.<br><br>Denmark forbids the slave trade.<br><br>France becomes a republic; Louis XVI and family are imprisoned.<br><br>France declares war on Austria and Prussia. Russian army invades Poland, which is still recovering from the partition of 1772. Prussia invades the country in turn. | The dollar is introduced as national currency.<br><br>Democratic-Republican Party is formed to oppose the Federalists.<br><br>U.S. Congress passes a national conscription act to require "each and every free able-bodied white male citizen of the republic" to serve in the U.S. militia. | Published: Charlotte Smith, *Desmond*; Mary Wollstonecraft, *A Vindication of the Rights of Woman*; William Blake, "A Song of Liberty" | *The Rights of Man* banned; Thomas Paine is charged with sedition and flees to France.<br><br>Baptist Missionary Society founded in London<br><br>Claude-Joseph Rouget de Lisle composes "La Marseillaise," the French national anthem. | Britain: First use of gas lights by William Murdoch |
| 1793 | France: Girondin faction takes power; King Louis XVI and Queen Marie-Antoinette are guillotined.<br><br>Committee of Public Safety established under Maximilien Robespierre, marking the start of the Reign of Terror (to 1794). | Federal Fugitive Slave Law<br><br>James Hoban begins building the White House. | Published: Charlotte Smith, *The Old Manor House* and *The Emigrants*; William Godwin, *An Inquiry Concerning Political Justice*; William Blake, *Visions of the Daughters of Albion* | Percy Bysshe Shelley born<br><br>David's *Death of Marat* or *Head of the Dead Marat* (portrays assassinated politician)<br><br>John Clare born | Alexander MacKenzie completes east-west crossing of Canada. |

| Date | Europe | Americas | Literature | Culture | Science and Technology |
|------|--------|----------|------------|---------|------------------------|
|  | France declares war on Britain, Holland, and Spain (the "Coalition" War).<br><br>First British settlers arrive in Australia.<br><br>India: Britain imposes a legal system organized according to their model. |  |  |  |  |
| 1794 | France: Fall of Robespierre and Danton; a new assembly elected<br><br>Britain: Suspension of habeas corpus means "radicals" can be kept in prison without being charged.<br><br>Treason trials (12 leading radicals tried) | U.S. Army defeats Native Americans at Fallen Timbers.<br><br>Neutrality Act forbids U.S. citizens to serve in the armies of foreign countries. | Published: William Godwin, *Caleb Williams;* William Blake, *Europe: A Prophecy, The First Book of Urizen,* and *Songs of Innocence and of Experience;* Ann Radcliffe, *The Mysteries of Udolpho;* Thomas Paine, *The Age of Reason* | Samuel Taylor Coleridge and Robert Southey plan a "pantisocracy," a commune to be set up in Pennsylvania.<br><br>Edward Gibbon dies. | Eli Whitney patents the cotton gin; cotton production and plantation slavery expand in U.S. South.<br><br>Erasmus Darwin posits a theory of evolution. |
| 1795 | Britain: Bread riots (over the price of bread)<br><br>"Gagging Acts": Seditious Meetings Act and Treasonable Practices Act (which bans mass meetings)<br><br>Warren Hastings, former governor of India, acquitted on corruption charges | Slave revolts in Jamaica and the Windward Islands<br><br>Jay Treaty averts threat of renewed U.S. war with Great Britain (June).<br><br>Treaty of Greenville: 12 defeated Ohio Indian tribes cede their lands. | Published: Johann Wolfgang von Goethe, *Wilhelm Meister's Apprenticeship* (1795–96); John Thelwall, *Poems Written in Close Confinement in the Tower and Newgate* | Thomas Paine publishes second part *The Age of Reason,* an attack on conventional Christianity.<br><br>Thomas Carlyle born<br><br>James Boswell dies. | First horse-drawn railway<br><br>Mungo Park explores Niger River. |

| Date | Europe | Americas | Literature | Culture | Science and Technology |
|------|--------|----------|------------|---------|------------------------|
|  | France: The "Directory" (made up of five men) governs France (to 1799).<br><br>Napoleon Bonaparte given command of a French army<br><br>Poland divided between Russia, Prussia, and Austria<br><br>France conquers Netherlands.<br><br>Netherlands renamed the Batavian Republic |  |  |  |  |
| 1796 | Napoleon's Italian victories; he plans to invade Ireland.<br><br>Britain takes Ceylon from the Dutch.<br><br>Princess Charlotte, daughter of the Prince of Wales (later George IV) born<br><br>Insurrection Act (Ireland)<br><br>Spain allies herself with France in the war against Britain. | John Adams elected U.S. president<br><br>Tennessee becomes the 16th U.S. state. | Published: Frances Burney, *Camilla*; Matthew Lewis, *The Monk*; Samuel Taylor Coleridge, *Poems on Various Subjects*; Ann Yearsley, *The Rural Lyre*; Edmund Burke, *Letters on a Regicide Peace* | Robert Burns dies.<br><br>James Macpherson dies. | William Jenner develops a smallpox vaccination. |
| 1797 | Britain defeats a Spanish fleet at Cape St. Vincent.<br><br>The British take Trinidad and St Lucia.<br><br>British government imposes an extra 1 penny tax on all newspapers. |  | Ann Radcliffe publishes *The Italian.* | Death of Edmund Burke<br><br>Death of Horace Walpole<br><br>Death of Mary Wollstonecraft<br><br>Joseph Haydn composes the *Emperor Quartet.* | One-pound notes (paper money) issued for the first time.<br><br>Thomas Bewick publishes *A History of British Birds.* |

| Date | Europe | Americas | Literature | Culture | Science and Technology |
|---|---|---|---|---|---|
|  | Frederick William III becomes king of Prussia (to 1840). | | | | |
|  | France orders the seizure of neutral ships if transporting British goods. | | | | |
| 1798 | Britain, Austria, and Russia form an alliance against France; Napoleon invades Egypt (to 1799); British navy led by Horatio Nelson defeats French at the Battle of the Nile. | In readiness for possible war with France, Congress passes the Alien and Sedition Acts, restricting freedoms granted by Bill of Rights. | Published: William Godwin, *Memoirs of the Author of A Vindication of the Rights of Woman*; William Wordsworth and Samuel Taylor Coleridge, *Lyrical Ballads*, including "Tintern Abbey" and "The Rime of the Ancient Mariner"; Charles Brockden Brown, *Wieland*; Coleridge, "Fears in Solitude" | Joseph Hadyn's *The Creation* performed | Joseph Malthus publishes *Essay on the Principle of Population*. |
|  | Irish rebellion at Vinegar Hill by activists wanting independence from Britain | Virginia and Kentucky Resolutions, which claim that those states have the right to nullify the laws of federal government, in particular the Alien and Sedition Acts, passed the same year | | Friedrich Schlegel defines Romantic poetry in his journal *The Athenaeum* | Jeremy Bentham publishes *Manual of Political Economy*. |
|  | Napoleon occupies Rome and announces the Roman Republic. | | Dorothy Wordsworth begins her journals. | | |
| 1799 | France: The Brumaire coup overthrows the Directory; a "Consulate" is established. | Fries Rebellion in Pennsylvania | Mary Hays publishes *The Victim of Prejudice*. | Ludwig van Beethoven composes First Symphony (C major). | The preserved carcass of an extinct mammoth is discovered in Siberia. |
|  | Second "Coalition War": Britain, Austria, Russia, Portugal, Naples, and the Ottoman Empire ally themselves against France (to 1802). | George Washington dies. | William Wordsworth writes the "Two-Part Prelude" of 1799. | Hannah More publishes *Strictures on the Modern System of Female Education*. | Discovery of the Rosetta Stone in Egypt |
|  |  | Russian-American Company takes over Russian trade in Alaska. | | | |

| Date | Europe | Americas | Literature | Culture | Science and Technology |
|------|--------|----------|------------|---------|------------------------|
| | | | Matthew Lewis edits *Tales of Terror*. | William and Dorothy Wordsworth settle into Dove Cottage, Grasmere.<br><br>John Galt born | |
| 1800 | Britain: Robert Owen runs New Lanark mills and advocates social reform.<br><br>Napoleon defeats Austrians at Marengo, Italy. | Washington, D.C., established as center of U.S. government<br><br>Gabriel's Rebellion (Richmond, Virginia); 35 slaves executed<br><br>U.S. census reveals a population of 5.3 million, including nearly 1 million slaves.<br><br>Thomas Jefferson elected president | Published: Maria Edgeworth, *Castle Rackrent*; Mary Robinson, *Lyrical Tales*; William Wordsworth, "Michael"; Friedrich von Schiller, *Maria Stuart*; Robert Bloomfield, *The Farmer's Boy* | Death of William Cowper<br><br>U.S. Library of Congress established<br><br>Death of Mary Robinson | Royal College of Surgeons founded in London<br><br>Invention of electric battery by Alessandro Volta<br><br>Alexander von Humboldt explores the Orinoco River in South America.<br><br>Eli Whitney makes muskets with interchangeable parts.<br><br>Early semaphore communication system piloted on hills between Boston and Martha's Vineyard, Massachusetts |

| Date | Europe | Americas | Literature | Culture | Science and Technology |
|---|---|---|---|---|---|
| 1801 | Britain: The United Kingdom of Great Britain (England and Scotland) and Ireland formed.<br><br>Census reports reveal a population in Britain of 11 million (75 percent rural).<br><br>Prime Minister William Pitt resigns because George III refuses to accede to Catholic emancipation; Catholics remain excluded from voting.<br><br>Paul I, czar of Russia, is murdered; Alexander I succeeds. | Toussaint Louverture seizes power in Haiti (to 1802).<br><br>U.S. ships launch an offensive against Algiers and Tripoli on the North African coast in an effort to defeat piracy. | Published: Maria Edgeworth, *Belinda*; Joanna Southcott, *The Strange Effects of Faith*; Amelia Alderson Opie, *Father and Daughter*; Robert Southey, *Thalaba*; James Hogg, *Scottish Pastorals*. | Ludwig van Beethoven writes the *Moonlight Sonata* and *Die Geschopfe des Prometheus*, his only ballet.<br><br>Union Jack becomes the official flag of the United Kingdom of Great Britain and Ireland. | Joseph Lalande publishes a catalog listing 47,390 stars.<br><br>Joseph-Marie Jacquard invents the punched-card loom.<br><br>The *Charlotte Dundas*, a steamship with paddle wheel, launched in Scotland |
| 1802 | Britain: Treaty of Amiens ends war with France for 14 months, allowing travel to Europe; many authors, artists, and politicians do so.<br><br>Health and Morals of Apprentices Act introduces protective factory legislation.<br><br>Napoleon declares himself "First Consul" for life. | The Spanish government overturns the rights of American traders to deposit goods for transshipment in New Orleans; this begins crisis that leads to the Louisiana Purchase.<br><br>United States Military Academy established at West Point | *Edinburgh Review* and William Cobbett's *Political Register* launched<br><br>Published: Samuel Taylor Coleridge, "Dejection: An Ode"; William Wordsworth, "Ode: Intimations of Immortality from Recollections of Early Childhood"; Walter Scott, *Minstrelsy of the Scottish Border* | Madame Tussaud exhibits waxworks in Britain. | William Paley publishes *Natural Theology: or, Evidences of the Existence and Attributes of the Deity, Collected from the Appearances of Nature.*<br><br>Matthew Flinders circumnavigates Australia, mapping its coastline (to 1803). |

| Date | Europe | Americas | Literature | Culture | Science and Technology |
|------|--------|----------|------------|---------|------------------------|
| 1803 | Britain returns to war with France.

Ireland: failed rising led by Robert Emmett

Britain at war with Maratha Empire of central India (to 1805) | Louisiana Purchase ($15 million) doubles the size of the U.S.

Ohio becomes the 17th state. | | Marquis de Sade committed to an insane asylum, where he uses the other inmates as actors in his plays | First use of paper-making machine in England |
| 1804 | France: Napoleon crowns himself emperor (to 1814).

Britain, Austria, Sweden, and Russia form new alliance against France and Spain aimed at containing Napoleon. | Thomas Jefferson reelected U.S. president.

Meriwether Lewis and William Clark begin journey to the West Coast (returning in 1806).

Haiti gains independence. | William Blake includes his poem "Jerusalem" in his book *Milton*. Published: Maria Edgeworth, *Popular Tales*; Friedrich von Schiller, *Wilhelm Tell* | Ludwig van Beethoven composes Symphony no. 3 and Piano Sonata in F Major despite being almost totally deaf. | Richard Trevithick builds first steam train.

Friedrich William Bessel calculates the orbit of Halley's comet. |
| 1805 | Napoleon proclaims himself king of Italy.

Battle of Austerlitz (Napoleon defeats Austrian and Russian forces)

Horatio Nelson's victory at Trafalgar ends threat of French invasion of Britain.

Mohammed Ali takes power in Egypt, challenging Ottoman rule. | U.S. forces capture Derna in North Africa, a base for Barbary pirates.

Virginia enacts a law requiring all freed slaves to leave the state. | Published: Mary Tighe, *Psyche*; Amelia Alderson Opie, *Adeline Mowbray*; Sir Walter Scott, *The Lay of the Last Minstrel*

William Wordsworth completes the 1805 version of *The Prelude*. | Friedrich von Schiller dies.

*Fidelio*, Ludwig van Beethoven's only opera, performed in Vienna | Joseph-Louis Gay-Lussac discovers water is composed of two parts hydrogen to one part oxygen. |
| 1806 | Napoleon dissolves Holy Roman Empire and invades Prussia.

Louis Bonaparte named king of Holland | South America: Wars of independence begin in the Río de la Plata. | Published: Sydney Owenson (Lady Morgan), *The Wild Irish Girl*; Lord Byron, *Fugitive Pieces*; | Death of William Pitt

Noah Webster publishes the first American dictionary. | Humphrey Davy uses electrolysis to isolate sodium and potassium. |

| Date | Europe | Americas | Literature | Culture | Science and Technology |
|---|---|---|---|---|---|
|  | Napoleon issues the Berlin Decree outlawing import of British goods into European countries allied with France; Britain's economy is sustained by Atlantic trade. Britain takes control of Cape Colony (South Africa) from the Dutch. |  | Ann and Jane Taylor, *Rhymes for the Nursery*, including "Twinkle, Twinkle Little Star" | Elizabeth Barrett [Browning] born |  |
| 1807 | Britain: Slave trade prohibited in British colonies Sierra Leone becomes a British colony. Napoleon defeats Russia at Friedland; invades Portugal Serfdom abolished in Prussia | U.S. Congress passes act prohibiting importation of slaves. Embargo Act forbids all trade with and travel to foreign ports. Chesapeake affair: British navy tries to board the USS *Chesapeake* moored off Virginia believing British deserters to be aboard. When permission is refused, British open fire, killing three and injuring 18. (The incident will be key factor in War of 1812.) | Published: Thomas Moore, *Irish Melodies;* Mme. de Stael, *Corinne;* Charlotte Smith, "Beachy Head;" Charles and Mary Lamb, *Tales from Shakespeare;* Sydney Owenson, *The Lay of an Irish Harp;* Lord Byron, *Hours of Idleness* | William Wilberforce publishes *A Letter on the Abolition of the Slave Trade.* Robert Morrison arrives in China to begin missionary work. Henry Wadsworth Longfellow born | Robert Fulton builds the first commercially successful steamboat in United States Georg Hegel's *The Phenomenology of Spirit* interprets history as the advance of the human mind, often through thesis, antithesis, and synthesis. Gas street lights used in London |
| 1808 | Napoleon attacks Spain, makes his brother Joseph king. Peninsular War follows, with British troops landing in Portugal under command of Arthur Wellesley (to 1814). | Osage Treaty cedes Sioux tribal lands in present-day Arkansas and Missouri. James Madison elected president | Published: Johann Wolfgang von Goethe, *Faust* (part 1); Walter Scott, *Marmion;* Felicia Hemans, *Poems* and "England and Spain" |  |  |

| Date | Europe | Americas | Literature | Culture | Science and Technology |
|------|--------|----------|------------|---------|------------------------|
| 1809 | Senegal, Martinique, and Cayenne captured by the British<br><br>Napoleon defeated by Austrian forces<br><br>Napoleon is excommunicated by the pope, whom he imprisons.<br><br>Napoleon divorces his wife Josephine. | Embargo Act repealed<br><br>Non-Intercourse Act passed | First publication of *Quarterly Review*<br><br>Hannah More publishes *Coelebs in Search of a Wife.* | Edgar Allan Poe born<br><br>Thomas Paine dies.<br><br>William Blake puts on one-man show of 16 paintings, including *The Ancient Britons*<br><br>Drury Lane Theatre destroyed by fire | |
| 1810 | Louis Bonaparte abdicates as king of Holland.<br><br>Mauritius and the Seychelles are annexed by Britain.<br><br>Napoleon marries Marie-Louise, daughter of Francis I of Austria.<br><br>George III declared incapable; George, Prince of Wales, becomes regent, beginning the "Regency Period." | Argentina gains independence. | Published: Sir Walter Scott, *Lady of the Lake*; Percy Bysshe Shelley, *Zastrozzi*; William Blake, *A Vision of the Last Judgment*; Jane Porter, *The Scottish Chiefs* | Death of Mary Tighe<br><br>Boxing: Tom Cribb beats Tom Molineaux in first international prize fight. | |
| 1811 | French retreat from Portugal.<br><br>Britain: Luddite riots (machine breaking) in the Midlands, protesting the mechanization of textile industry<br><br>Parliament declares slave trading a criminal offense.<br><br>Britain invades Java. | Venezuela, Paraguay, and Uruguay declare independence.<br><br>William Henry Harrison, governor of Indiana, defeats the Shawnee at the Battle of Tippecanoe.<br><br>Charles Deslandes leads Louisiana slave rebellion; troops kill more than 100 slaves. | Published: Jane Austen, *Sense and Sensibility*; Maria Edgeworth, *The Absentee* | Percy Bysshe Shelley is expelled from Oxford University for circulating his pamphlet *The Necessity of Atheism.*<br><br>Harriet Beecher Stowe born | Work begins work on the first U.S. federal highway. |

| Date | Europe | Americas | Literature | Culture | Science and Technology |
|---|---|---|---|---|---|
| 1812 | Napoleon begins invasion of Russia. The army of 500,000-plus captures Moscow, but bad weather and lack of supplies force a retreat; most French troops fail to make it back to France.<br><br>British win battle at Salamanca (Spain). | James Madison reelected U.S. president<br><br>United States and Britain go to war over British impressment of U.S. sailors and restriction of trade with France. | Published: Joseph and Wilhelm Grimm, *Fairy Tales* (vol. 1; later volumes follow in 1814 and 1822); Maria Edgeworth, *The Absentee;* Anna Laetitia Barbauld, "Eighteen Hundred and Eleven"; Lord Byron, first two cantos of *Childe Harold's Pilgrimage* | Ludwig van Beethoven composes Symphony no. 7<br><br>Charles Dickens born<br><br>Sarah Siddons retires from the stage. | |
| 1813 | France's dominance leads to the "War of Liberation," led by Prussia, with Britain, Russia, Austria, and Sweden.<br><br>Napoleon wins Battle of Dresden but is defeated at Leipzig.<br><br>British forces under Arthur Wellesley (later the duke of Wellington) victorious in Peninsular War | Battle of the Thames | Published: Jane Austen, *Pride and Prejudice;* Robert Southey, *The Life of Nelson;* Lord Byron, *The Giaour* and *The Bride of Abydos;* Percy Bysshe Shelley, *Queen Mab* | Robert Southey becomes poet laureate.<br><br>Leigh Hunt imprisoned for libel (1813–15) after the *Examiner* attacks the Prince Regent | A steam train, the *Puffing Billy,* is invented by William Hedley, in County Durham. |
| 1814 | Allied forces seize Paris; Napoleon is exiled to Elba.<br><br>Louis XVIII (brother of Louis XVI) becomes king of France (to 1824).<br><br>Congress of Vienna meets to discuss future boundaries of the European continent and reinstate monarchical system. | British troops burn Washington, D.C.<br><br>Treaty of Ghent ends the War of 1812.<br><br>Defeat of the Creek prompts removal of Native Americans from the South to the West. | Published: Jane Austen, *Mansfield Park;* Walter Scott, *Waverley;* Frances Burney, *The Wanderer;* Lord Byron, *The Corsair* and "Ode to Napoleon Bonaparte" | Edmund Kean makes his debut as Shylock at London's Drury Lane.<br><br>Francis Scott Key writes the poem that later becomes "The Star-Spangled Banner" during a British attack on Fort McHenry. | Steam-powered printing presses introduced at the *Times*<br><br>George Stephenson unveils his steam engine *My Lord.* |

| Date | Europe | Americas | Literature | Culture | Science and Technology |
|------|--------|----------|------------|---------|------------------------|
|  | Britain secures a declaration against the slave trade.<br><br>Britain acquires Guyana. |  |  |  |  |
| 1815 | Napoleon escapes Elba and retakes Paris (for 100 days).<br><br>Allied forces, under command of Wellington and Prussia's von Blucher defeat the French at Waterloo.<br><br>Restoration of Louis XVIII<br><br>Napoleon exiled to St. Helena<br><br>Britain: economic depression<br><br>Corn Law passed, bringing benefits to landlords<br><br>France prohibits the slave trade. | American troops defeat British forces at the Battle of New Orleans, despite the war having officially ended with the Treaty of Ghent. | Published: Lord Byron, *Hebrew Melodies*; Walter Scott, *Guy Mannering*; Philip Freneau, *A Collection of Poems on American Affairs* | David Ricardo publishes *An Essay on Profits*.<br><br>The waltz causes a sensation in Vienna. | Humphrey Davy invents the miner's safety lamp. |
| 1816 | Britain: Spa Fields riots over political reform | African Methodist Episcopal Church (AME) founded<br><br>Indiana admitted to the Union<br><br>Boom in cotton prices stimulates settlement of Alabama and Mississippi.<br><br>James Monroe elected president | Published: Percy Bysshe Shelley, "Alastor, or The Spirit of Solitude"; Samuel Taylor Coleridge, "Kubla Khan"; Jane Austen, *Emma*; John Keats, "On First Looking into Chapman's | Parthenon marbles purchased from Lord Elgin and exhibited in the British Museum.<br><br>John Nash rebuilds the Prince Regent's Pavilion in Brighton. | Leeds-Liverpool canal completed |

| Date | Europe | Americas | Literature | Culture | Science and Technology |
|------|--------|----------|------------|---------|------------------------|
| | | | Homer"; Thomas Love Peacock, *Headlong Hall;* Charles Robert Maturin, *Bertram;* Lord Byron, *The Prisoner of Chillon, and Other Poems;* Caroline Lamb, *Glenarvon;* Leigh Hunt, *The Story of Rimini* | The actor William Macready makes his Covent Garden debut. | |
| 1817 | Britain: Coercion Acts (extends the laws against "seditious" gatherings) following riots in London.<br><br>Princess Charlotte dies in childbirth (national mourning). | Mississippi admitted to the Union<br><br>Rush-Bagot Treaty<br><br>Founding of the American Colonization Society to return freed slaves to Africa<br><br>First Seminole War in Florida: Runaway slaves join Native Americans against the United States (to 1818). | Published: Thomas Moore, *Lalla Rookh;* Walter Scott, *Rob Roy;* Samuel Taylor Coleridge, *Biographia Literaria;* Robert Southey, *Wat Tyler;* Jane Austen, *Northanger Abbey* and *Persuasion;* William Cullen Bryant, *Thanatopsis* | Jane Austen dies.<br><br>Mme. de Stael dies.<br><br>Henry David Thoreau born<br><br>John Constable paints *Flatford Mill.*<br><br>John Kemble's farewell performance at Covent Garden | Gas used to light the Covent Garden theater |
| 1818 | Habeas corpus reinstated<br><br>Southern Africa: Zulus emerge as great military power, forming an empire under chief Shaka. | U.S.-Canadian border fixed along 49th parallel<br><br>José de San Martín leads Chile to independence. | Published: Mary Shelley, *Frankenstein;* Percy Bysshe Shelley, "Ozymandias"; John Keats, *Endymion;* Walter Scott, *The Heart of Midlothian* | | In *The World as Will and Idea,* Arthur Schopenhauer outlines a bleak view of the human condition.<br><br>John Ross makes unsuccessful attempt to discover the Northwest Passage. |

| Date | Europe | Americas | Literature | Culture | Science and Technology |
|------|--------|----------|------------|---------|------------------------|
| 1819 | Britain: Peterloo Massacre in Manchester (mounted troops charge a peaceful meeting of people campaigning for parliamentary reform, killing several). The Six Acts are passed, enabling suppression of "seditious" publications and large gatherings.<br><br>Birth of Princess Victoria (later queen), London<br><br>British establish Singapore as a free trade port. | Spain cedes Florida to the United States<br><br>Simón Bolívar leads independence movement in Colombia.<br><br>Boom in cotton prices, which stimulated settlement of the Southwest, ends. | Published: Washington Irving *Rip Van Winkle*; John Polidori "The Vampyre"; Percy Bysshe Shelley, "England in 1819" and *The Cenci*; Walter Scott, *The Bride of Lammermoor*<br><br>Lord Byron begins publication of *Don Juan* in installments.<br><br>John Keats produces series of odes ("To Psyche," "On a Grecian Urn," "To a Nightingale"). | | The *Savannah* is first steamship to cross the Atlantic; the first iron steamship, *Aaron Manby*, crosses from London to Paris.<br><br>Thomas Telford begins building the Menai Straits suspension bridge. |
| 1820 | Britain: Cato Street conspiracy to assassinate members of the government is uncovered.<br><br>George III dies; his son becomes George IV (to 1830).<br><br>Trial of Queen Caroline to prove adultery so that George IV can divorce her (he does not succeed).<br><br>Revolts in Spain and Italy against Bourbon rule<br><br>Zulus control most of southeast Africa and Natal. | Christian missionaries arrive in Hawaii.<br><br>U.S. Missouri Compromise admits new states to the Union, including Missouri as a slave state.<br><br>James Monroe is reelected president.<br><br>African-American population reaches 1.77 million; total U.S. population is 9.6 million.<br><br>Expansion of New England textile mills | Published: Percy Bysshe Shelley, *Prometheus Unbound* and "Ode to the West Wind"; Walter Scott, *Ivanhoe*; John Keats, "La Belle Dame Sans Merci"; Alphonse de Lamartine, *Poetic Meditations*; John Clare, *Poems Descriptive of Rural Life*; Robert Southey, *A Vision of Judgment*; Elizabeth Barrett, "The Battle of Marathon" | | Thomas Malthus publishes *Principles of Political Economy*. |

| Date | Europe | Americas | Literature | Culture | Science and Technology |
|------|--------|----------|------------|---------|------------------------|
| 1821 | Britain: George IV's coronation; Queen Caroline is excluded from the abbey. Greek war of independence from Turkish rule begins (to 1831). Napoleon dies on Saint Helena. | Simón Bolívar defeats Spanish army at Carabobo and secures independence of Venezuela. Mexico and Peru declare independence. U.S. occupation of Florida takes place. | Published: Walter Scott, *Kenilworth*; Percy Bysshe Shelley, "Adonais"; Thomas De Quincey, *Confessions of an English Opium-Eater* *The Spy*, a romance set in the American Revolution, establishes the reputation of U.S. author James Fenimore Cooper. | John Constable paints *The Hay Wain*. John Keats dies of tuberculosis in Rome, age 25. William Cobbett begins journey around England (later published as *Rural Rides*). | Michael Faraday invents an electric motor. Jean-François Champollion deciphers Egyptian hieroglyphics using the Rosetta Stone. |
| 1822 | Britain: Lord Castlereagh, foreign secretary, commits suicide. Congress of Verona Liberia established by abolitionists as a colony for freed American slaves | Brazil, Colombia, and Equador are liberated. Slave rebellion is suppressed in Charleston, South Carolina. | Published: Alexander Pushkin, *Eugene Onegin*; Caroline Bowles, *The Widow's Tale and Other Poems*; Thomas Lovell Beddoes, *The Bride's Tragedy*; Walter Scott, *The Pirate* | Percy Bysshe Shelley drowns in Italy, age 29. Royal Academy of Music founded in London Franz Liszt makes his debut in Vienna, age 11. Charles Fourier's *Traite de l'association domestique-agricole* argues that civilized man is artificial and ignores his natural side. | Charles Babbage designs a "difference engine," an early version of the modern computer. |

| Date | Europe | Americas | Literature | Culture | Science and Technology |
|------|--------|----------|------------|---------|------------------------|
| 1823 | Britain: The death penalty is abolished for more than 100 offenses.<br><br>Revolution in Spain is defeated. | Monroe Doctrine issued by United States, warning European states not to interfere in the Americas | Published: Mary Shelley, *Valperga*; Lord Byron, *Don Juan*, cantos 6–14; Charles Lamb, *Essays of Elia*; Mary and William Howitt, *The Forest Minstrel and Other Poems*; Felicia Hemans, *The Siege of Valencia*; Walter Scott, *Quentin Durward*; Caroline Lamb, *Ada Reis, a Tale*; James Fenimore Cooper, *The Pioneers* | Death of Ann Radcliffe<br><br>Lord Byron arrives in Greece to support the cause of Greek independence. | Charles Mackintosh patents system for waterproofing fabric. |
| 1824 | Britain: Combination Acts revoked, thus allowing workers to form trade unions.<br><br>Gaol Act assumes government responsibility for prison conditions.<br><br>Anglo-Burmese war begins to protect the trading interests of the East India Company (to 1826).<br><br>Dutch cede Malacca to Britain in return for Bengkulen in Sumatra.<br><br>Charles X becomes king of France (to 1830). | United States signs treaty with Russia agreeing on 50°40′ as the southern limit of Russian territory.<br><br>Establishment of the Bureau of Indian Affairs within the War Department.<br><br>John Quincy Adams elected president | Published: Mary Russell Mitford, *Our Village*; James Hogg, *Confessions of a Justified Sinner*; Letitia Elizabeth Landon, *The Improvisatrice*; Walter Scott, *Redgauntlet* | Ludwig van Beethoven composes Symphony no 9.<br><br>Lord Byron dies of a fever in Missolonghi, Greece, at the age of 36.<br><br>The National Gallery established in London | |

| Date | Europe | Americas | Literature | Culture | Science and Technology |
|------|--------|----------|------------|---------|------------------------|
| | Britain begins war against the Ashanti on the Gold Coast (Ghana) of Africa. | | | | |
| 1825 | Britain: Cotton Mills Regulation Act limits children under 16 to a 12-hour working day.<br><br>Russia: A rebellion following the death of Alexander I is put down. | U.S. Congress adopts policy of removal of eastern Indian tribes to territory west of the Mississippi River.<br><br>Frances Wright, establishes the Nashoba community in Tennessee.<br><br>Bolivia achieves independence. | Published: William Hazlitt, *The Spirit of the Age*; Felicia Hemans, *The Forest Sanctuary and Other Poems*; Maria Jane Jewsbury, *Phantasmagoria, or Sketches of Life and Literature*; Letitia Elizabeth Landon, *The Troubadour*; Walter Scott, *The Talisman* | John Nash redesigns Buckingham Palace. | First passenger train opens between Stockton and Darlington.<br><br>Opening of the Erie Canal, connecting the Great Lakes with the Atlantic Ocean |
| 1826 | Britain and Russia recognize Greece's right to independence.<br><br>Treaty of Yandabo gives Britain control of the Arakan Peninsula in Burma. | Haden Edwards leads unsuccessful rebellion against Mexican rule in Texas.<br><br>Brazil agrees to end the slave trade. | Published: Mary Shelley, *The Last Man*; Caroline Bowles, *Solitary Hours*; Benjamin Disraeli, *Vivian Grey*; Walter Scott, *Woodstock*; James Fenimore Cooper, *The Last of the Mohicans* | Felix Mendelssohn composes Overture to Shakespeare's *A Midsummer Night's Dream*.<br><br>University College, London, is founded to provide nonsectarian education.<br><br>John Constable paints *The Cornfield*. | First photographic image produced by Joseph-Nicephore Niepce<br><br>Zoological Society founded<br><br>American railroads built, powered by cable systems, horses, or sails<br><br>Foundation of the Society for the Diffusion of Useful Knowledge |

| Date | Europe | Americas | Literature | Culture | Science and Technology |
|------|--------|----------|------------|---------|------------------------|
| 1827 | George Canning becomes prime minister, hinting a possibility of reform.<br><br>Treaty of London: Britain, France, and Russia promise to guarantee Greek independence.<br><br>Battle of Navarino: France, Britain, and Russia defeat the Ottoman and Egyptian fleets. | U.S. Congress give the president the right to call out the militia.<br><br>The United States and Britain renew their agreement on joint occupation of Oregon for an indefinite period. | Published: Heinrich Heine, *Book of Songs*; Alfred, Charles, and Frederick Tennyson, *Poems by Two Brothers*; Thomas De Quincey, *On Murder Considered as One of the Fine Arts*; John Clare, *The Shepherd's Calendar*; Walter Scott, *The Life of Napoleon Bonaparte* | Ludwig van Beethoven dies in Vienna.<br><br>William Blake dies in London.<br><br>The first African-American newspaper, *Freedom's Journal*, begins publication in the United States | John Walker invents friction matches. |
| 1828 | Britain: Duke of Wellington becomes prime minister.<br><br>Repeal of the Test and Corporation Acts that kept non-Anglicans (Catholics and Dissenters) from holding public office and deprived them of other rights.<br><br>Zulu chief Shaka assassinated | Andrew Jackson elected president<br><br>The Georgia legislature abolishes tribal governments, allowing the breakup of the Cherokee lands.<br><br>Congress passes the "Tariff of Abominations."<br><br>Baltimore and Ohio Railroad chartered<br><br>Working Men's Party formed in Philadelphia, advocating social reform, free education, and nonimprisonment for debt | Published: Edward Bulwer Lytton, *Pelham*; Alexandre Dumas, *The Three Musketeers* | Joseph Grimaldi makes his final appearance at Sadler's Wells Theatre.<br><br>Connecticut lexicographer Noah Webster publishes the definitive scholarly edition of his two-volume *American Dictionary of the English Language* (see 1806). | |

| Date | Europe | Americas | Literature | Culture | Science and Technology |
|------|--------|----------|------------|---------|------------------------|
| 1829 | Ireland: Daniel O'Donnell campaigns to abolish the Act of Union between Britain and Ireland.<br><br>Britain: Catholic Emancipation Act<br><br>Robert Peel establishes a regular police force. | African-American abolitionist David Walker issues *David Walker's Appeal*, calling for slaves to revolt against their masters. | Published: Alfred, Lord Tennyson, "Timbuctoo"; Victor Hugo, *Marion Delorme*; Catherine Gore, *Romances of Real Life*; Gerald Griffin, *The Collegians* | | Invention of the typewriter<br><br>Louis Braille invents a reading system for the blind.<br><br>George Shillibeer introduces first omnibus to London streets. |
| 1830 | Death of George IV; his brother succeeds as William IV.<br><br>Charles Grey, 2nd earl Grey, becomes prime minister.<br><br>Swing riots in southern England against enclosures and new machinery<br><br>France: "July Revolution"; Charles X is overthrown, and Louis Philippe ("the citizen king") ascends the throne (to 1848).<br><br>Revolutions in Germany, Poland, Italy<br><br>The Gold Coast becomes a British protectorate.<br><br>Belgium proclaims independence from Netherlands. | First National Negro Convention meets in Philadelphia.<br><br>Congress passes the Indian Removal Act.<br><br>U.S. census shows a population of 12.8 million.<br><br>Joseph Smith establishes the Church of Jesus Christ of Latter-day Saints (the Mormons) in Fayette, New York | Published: William Cobbett, *Rural Rides*; Stendhal, *The Scarlet and the Black*; Alfred, Lord Tennyson, *Poems, Chiefly Lyrical*; Thomas Moore, *The Works of Lord Byron: With His Letters and Journals, and His Life*; Victor Hugo, *Hernani*; Oliver Wendell Holmes, "Old Ironsides" | Emily Elizabeth Dickinson born<br><br>Christina Rossetti born<br><br>Frederic Chopin performs Piano Concerto No. 2 in F Minor<br><br>*Godey's Ladies Book* founded | Charles Lyell publishes *Principles of Geology*.<br><br>Liverpool to Manchester railway opens with Robert Stephenson's locomotive *Rocket*. |

| Date | Europe | Americas | Literature | Culture | Science and Technology |
|---|---|---|---|---|---|
| 1831 | Britain: Lord John Russell introduces the "Great Reform Bill" (defeated but later passed in 1832, increasing voting population to 800,000). Britain has a population of 24 million; increasing by 1 million per year. Britain takes control of the state of Mysore, India. Jamaica: slave rebellion | New England Anti-Slavery Society is founded. Nat Turner leads slave revolt in Southampton, Virginia. *Cherokee Nation v. Georgia* Supreme Court case Samuel Francis Smith's hymn "America" is sung for the first time on July 4 in Boston. | Published: Ebenezer Elliott, *Corn-Law Rhymes*; Victor Hugo, *Notre Dame of Paris*; Thomas Hood, "The Dream of Eugene Aram"; Mary Prince, *History of Mary Prince, a West-Indian Slave*; Thomas Love Peacock, *Crotchet Castle*; Walter Scott, *Castle Dangerous*; Aleksandr Pushkin, *Boris Godunov* | | Charles Darwin begins HMS *Beagle* voyage (to 1836). First preparation of chloroform Michael Faraday discovers electromagnetic induction. English navigator James Ross plants the British flag at the North Magnetic Pole. |
| 1832 | Reform Act approved: New constituencies created in larger cities; pocket boroughs abolished; franchise includes all male owners of land or property worth £10 a year. | Andrew Jackson reelected U.S. president South Carolina Nullification Proclamation | Published: Johann Wolfgang von Goethe, *Faust*, part 2; Walter Scott, *Count Robert of Paris*; Percy Bysshe Shelley, "The Mask of Anarchy"; Douglas Jerrold, *The Factory Girl*; Sheridan Knowles, *The Hunchback*; Harriet Martineau, *Illustrations of Political Economy* (to 1834); Edward Bulwer Lytton, *Eugene Aram*; Marguerite Gardiner, Countess of Blessington, *Conversations of Lord Bryon* | Death of Johann Wolfgang von Goethe Death of George Crabbe Death of Sir Walter Scott Louisa May Alcott born | Sir Charles Wheatstone, English physicist, invents the stereoscope. New York & Harlem Railroad begins operating with the first streetcar. |

| Date | Europe | Americas | Literature | Culture | Science and Technology |
|------|--------|----------|------------|---------|------------------------|
| 1833 | Slavery abolished in British colonies.<br><br>Factory Act prohibits employment of children under age nine in factories.<br><br>East India Company's monopoly of trade in China ends. | American Anti-Slavery Society founded by abolitionist groups from New York and New England<br><br>Force Bill (March)<br><br>Texans vote to separate their territory from Mexico. | Aleksandr Pushkin, *Eugene Onegin* (first complete edition); Felicia Hemans, *Hymns on the Works of Nature; Sketches and Eccentricity of Col. David Crockett, of West Tennessee* | Hannah More dies.<br><br>Edmund Kean's final performance at Covent Garden, as Othello | Michael Faraday uses the terms *electrolysis, electrolyte,* and *cathode.*<br><br>Wilhelm Weber develops the electromagnetic telegraph. |
| 1834 | Tolpuddle Martyrs (Dorset laborers) transported for taking "unlawful oaths" when forming a trade union.<br><br>Report on Royal Commission on Poor Law, chaired by Edwin Chadwick<br><br>Alliance between Britain, France, Spain, and Portugal to protect sovereignty of the latter two<br><br>The South Australia Act permits the establishment of a colony. | National Trade Union begins to organize. | Published: James Hogg, *Songs by the Ettrick Shepherd;* Alexander Pushkin, "The Queen of Spades"; William Gilmore Simms, *Guy Rivers* (first of his series known as the Border Romances); Alexis de Tocqueville, volume 1 of *Democracy in America* (vol. 2 published in 1840) | Death of Samuel Taylor Coleridge<br><br>Britain: Houses of Parliament burn down. | A mechanical reaping machine is patented by Cyrus McCormick of Lexington, Virginia. |

**Bibliography**

Franklin, Fay, ed. *History's Timeline.* London: Ward Lock, 1981.

Kagan, Neil, ed. *National Geographic Concise History of the World: An Illustrated Timeline.* Washington, D.C.: National Geographic Society, 2006.

Stark, John. *Almanac of British and American Literature.* Littleton, Colo.: Libraries Unlimited, 1979.

*World History: An Illustrated Timeline.* London: Brown, 2007.

# SELECTED BIBLIOGRAPHY
## OF SECONDARY SOURCES

Abrams, M. H. *Correspondent Breeze: Essays on English Romanticism.* New York: Norton, 1984.

———. *Natural Supernaturalism: Tradition and Revolution in Romantic Literature.* New York: Norton, 1973.

Armstrong, Isobel. "The Gush of the Feminine: How Can We Read Women's Poetry of the Romantic Period?" In *Romantic Women Writers: Voices and Countervoices,* edited by Paula R. Feldman and Theresa M. Kelley, 13–32. Hanover, N.H.: University Press of New England, 1995.

Barker, Juliet. *Wordsworth: A Life.* New York: Viking, 2000.

Bate, Jonathan. *John Clare: A Biography.* London: Picador, 2003.

———. *Romantic Ecology: Wordsworth and the Environmental Tradition.* New York: Routledge, 1991.

Bate, Walter Jackson. *Coleridge.* New York: Macmillan, 1968.

———. *John Keats.* Cambridge, Mass.: Harvard University Press, 1963.

Bentley, G. E., Jr. *William Blake: The Critical Heritage.* London: Routledge Press, 1975.

Bloom, Harold, ed. *Romanticism and Consciousness: Essays in Criticism.* New York: Norton, 1970.

———. *The Visionary Company: A Reading of English Romantic Poetry.* Garden City, N.Y.: Doubleday, 1961.

Bradshaw, Michael. *Resurrection Songs: The Poetry of Thomas Lovell Beddoes.* Burlington, Vt.: Ashgate Press, 2001.

Brisman, Leslie. *Romantic Origins.* Ithaca, N.Y.: Cornell University Press, 1978.

Bromwich, David. *Disowned by Memory: Wordsworth's Poetry of the 1790s.* Chicago: University of Chicago Press, 1998.

Brown, Marshall. *Preromanticism.* Stanford, Calif.: Stanford University Press, 1991.

Butler, Marilyn. *Romantics, Rebels, and Reactionaries: English Literature and Its Background, 1760–1830.* New York: Oxford University Press, 1982.

Chamberlain, Robert. *George Crabbe.* New York: Twayne Publishers, 1965.

Chandler, James. *England in 1819: The Politics of Literary Culture and the Case of Romantic Historicism.* Chicago: University of Chicago Press, 1998.

Chase, Cynthia. *Decomposing Figures: Rhetorical Readings in the Romantic Tradition.* Baltimore, Md.: Johns Hopkins University Press, 1986.

Chernaik, Judith. *The Lyrics of Shelley.* Cleveland, Ohio: Press of Case Western Reserve University, 1972.

Chirico, Paul. *John Clare and the Imagination of the Reader.* New York: Palgrave Macmillan, 2007.

Christensen, Jerome. *Coleridge's Blessed Machine of Language.* Ithaca, N.Y.: Cornell University Press, 1981.

Coburn, Kathleen. *Experience into Thought: Perspectives in the Coleridge Notebooks.* Toronto, Canada: University of Toronto Press, 1979.

Colley, Linda. *Britons: Forging the Nation, 1707–1837.* New Haven, Conn.: Yale University Press, 1992.

Damrosch, Leopold. *Symbol and Truth in Blake's Myth.* Princeton, N.J.: Princeton University Press, 1980.

Deane, Seamus. *French Revolution and Enlightenment in England, 1789–1832.* Cambridge, Mass.: Harvard University Press, 1988.

De Man, Paul. *The Rhetoric of Romanticism.* New York: Columbia University Press, 1984.

Dickstein, Morris. *Keats and His Poetry: A Study in Development.* Chicago: University of Chicago Press, 1971.

Donaldson, Sandra, ed. *Critical Essays on Elizabeth Barrett Browning.* New York: G. K. Hall, 1999.

Donner, Henry Wolfgang. *Thomas Lovell Beddoes: The Making of a Poet.* Oxford: Blackwell, 1935.

Duffy, Edward. *Rousseau in England: The Context for Shelley's Critique of the Enlightenment.* Berkeley: University of California Press, 1979.

Edgecombe, Rodney Stenning. *Leigh Hunt and the Poetry of Fancy.* London: Associated University Presses, 1994.

Ellmann, Richard. *Yeats: The Man and the Masks.* New York: Norton, 1978.

Empson, William. *Seven Types of Ambiguity.* New York: New Directions, 1966.

Engell, James. *Creative Imagination: Enlightenment to Romanticism.* Cambridge, Mass.: Harvard University Press, 1981.

Erdman, David V. *Blake, Prophet against Empire: A Poet's Interpretation of the History of His Own Times.* Princeton, N.J.: Princeton University Press, 1954.

Ferguson, Frances. *Wordsworth: Language as Counter-Spirit.* New Haven, Conn.: Yale University Press, 1977.

Fletcher, Loraine. *Charlotte Smith: A Critical Biography.* New York: St. Martin's Press, 1998.

Frosch, Thomas R. *Shelley and the Romantic Imagination: A Psychological Study.* Newark: University of Delaware Press, 2007.

Fry, Paul H. *The Poet's Calling in the English Ode.* New Haven, Conn.: Yale University Press, 1980.

———. *Wordsworth and the Poetry of What We Are.* New Haven, Conn.: Yale University Press, 2008.

Frye, Northrop. *Fearful Symmetry: A Study of William Blake.* Princeton, N.J.: Princeton University Press, 1947.

———. *A Study of English Romanticism.* Brighton, England: Harvester, 1983.

Furst, Lilian, ed. *European Romanticism: Self-Definition: An Anthology.* London: Methuen, 1980.

Gilchrist, Alexander. *Life of William Blake, with Selections from His Poems and Other Writings.* Totowa, N.J.: Rowman and Littlefield, 1973.

Gill, Stephen. *William Wordsworth: A Life.* New York: Oxford University Press, 1989.

Gittings, Robert. *John Keats.* Boston: Little, Brown, 1968.

———. *Mask of Keats: A Study of Problems.* Cambridge, Mass.: Harvard University Press, 1956.

Griggs, Earl Leslie. *Hartley Coleridge: His Life and Work.* London: University of London Press, 1929.

Guyer, Sara Emilie. *Romanticism after Auschwitz.* Stanford, Calif.: Stanford University Press, 2007.

Halmi, Nicholas. *Genealogy of the Romantic Symbol.* New York: Oxford University Press, 2007.

Hartman, Geoffrey. *Wordsworth's Poetry, 1787–1814.* New Haven, Conn.: Yale University Press, 1971.

Hogle, Jerrold E. *Shelley's Process: Radical Transference and the Development of His Major Works.* New York: Oxford University Press, 1988.

Holden, Anthony. *The Wit in the Dungeon: A Life of Leigh Hunt.* London: Little, Brown: 2005.

Holmes, Richard. *Coleridge.* New York: Pantheon, 2000.

———. *Shelley: The Pursuit.* London: Weidenfeld & Nicolson, 1974.

Homans Margaret. *Women Writers and Poetic Identity: Dorothy Wordsworth, Emily Brontë, and Emily Dickinson.* Princeton, N.J.: Princeton University Press, 1980.

Hough, Graham Goulden. *The Last Romantics.* London: Duckworth, 1949.

Huchon, René. *George Crabbe and His Times, 1754–1832: A Critical and Biographical Study.* Translated by Frederick Clarke. London: J. Murray, 1907.

Janowitz, Anne F. *Lyric and Labour in the Romantic Tradition.* New York: Cambridge University Press, 1998.

Johnson, Edgar. *Sir Walter Scott: The Great Unknown.* 2 vols. New York: Macmillan, 1970.

Johnston, Kenneth. *Hidden Wordsworth: Poet, Lover, Rebel, Spy.* New York: Norton, 1998.

Johnston, Kenneth, ed. *Romantic Revolutions: Criticism and Theory.* Bloomington: Indiana University Press, 1990.

Keach, William. *Arbitrary Power: Romanticism, Language, Politics.* Princeton, N.J.: Princeton University Press, 2004.

Keach, William. *Shelley's Style.* New York: Methuen, 1984.

Labbe, Jacqueline M. *Charlotte Smith: Romanticism, Poetry, and the Culture of Gender.* New York: Palgrave, 2003.

Lauber, John. *Sir Walter Scott.* Boston: Twayne Publishers, 1989.

Leighton, Angela. *Shelley and the Sublime: An Interpretation of the Major Poems.* New York: Cambridge University Press, 1984.

Levinson, Marjorie. *Wordsworth's Great Period Poems: Four Essays.* New York: Cambridge University Press, 1986.

Lincoln, Andrew. *Walter Scott and Modernity.* Edinburgh, Scotland: Edinburgh University Press, 2007.

Liu, Alan. *Wordsworth: The Sense of History.* Stanford, Calif.: Stanford University Press, 1989.

Lovejoy, Arthur. "On the Discrimination of Romanticisms." *PMLA* 39, no. 2 (June 1924): 229–253.

Low, Donald A. *Robert Burns: The Critical Heritage.* London: Routledge, 1974.

Lowes, John Livingston. *Road to Xanadu: A Study in the Ways of the Imagination.* New York: Houghton Mifflin, 1930.

Lucas, E. V. *Life of Charles Lamb.* New York: G. P. Putnam's Sons, 1905.

Mahoney, Charles, *Romantics and Renegades: The Poetics of Political Reaction.* New York: Palgrave Macmillan, 2003.

Marchand, Leslie A. *Byron: A Portrait.* New York: Knopf, 1970.

Martin, Frederick. *The Life of John Clare.* London: Macmillan, 1865.

McFarland, Thomas. *Coleridge and the Pantheist Tradition.* Oxford: Clarendon Press, 1969.

———. *The Masks of Keats: The Endeavour of a Poet.* New York: Oxford University Press, 2000.

———. *Romantic Cruxes: The English Essayists and the Spirit of the Age.* New York: Oxford University Press, 1987.

McGann, Jerome. *Byron and Romanticism.* New York: Cambridge University Press, 2002.

———. *Don Juan in Context.* Chicago: University of Chicago Press, 1976.

———. *The Romantic Ideology: A Critical Investigation.* Chicago: University of Chicago Press, 1983.

McGuirk, Carol. *Critical Essays on Robert Burns.* New York: G. K. Hall, 1998.

Mellor, Anne K. *Romanticism and Gender.* New York: Routledge, 1993.

Mermin, Dorothy. *Elizabeth Barrett Browning: The Origins of a New Poetry.* Chicago: University of Chicago Press, 1989.

Monsman, Gerald Cornelius. *Confessions of a Prosaic Dreamer: Charles Lamb's Art of Autobiography.* Durham, N.C.: Duke University Press, 1984.

Moorman, Mary. *William Wordsworth: A Biography.* Oxford: Clarendon Press, 1965.

Najarian, James. *Victorian Keats: Manliness, Sexuality and Desire.* New York: Palgrave, 2002.

Notopolous, James A. *The Platonism of Shelley: A Study of Platonism and the Poetic Mind.* Durham, N.C.: Duke University Press, 1949.

Parker, Reeve. *Coleridge's Meditative Art.* Ithaca, N.Y.: Cornell University Press, 1975.

Pinch, Adela. *Strange Fits of Passion: Epistemologies of Emotion, Hume to Austen.* Stanford, Calif.: Stanford University Press, 1996.

Pollard, Arthur. *Crabbe: The Critical Heritage.* London: Routledge, 1972.

Pomeroy, Mary Joseph, Sister. *The Poetry of Hartley Coleridge.* Washington, D.C.: Catholic University of America, 1927.

Raine, Kathleen. *Blake and Antiquity.* Princeton, N.J.: Princeton University Press, 1977.

Rajan, Tilottama. *Dark Interpreter: The Discourse of Romanticism.* Ithaca, N.Y.: Cornell University Press, 1980.

Redfield, Marc. *The Politics of Aesthetics: Nationalism, Gender, Romanticism.* Stanford, Calif.: Stanford University Press, 2003.

Richards, I. A. *Coleridge on Imagination.* New York: Routledge, 2001.

Ricks, Christopher. *Keats and Embarrassment.* Oxford: Clarendon Press, 1974.

Roe, Nicholas. *Fiery Heart: The First Life of Leigh Hunt.* London: Pimlico, 2005.

Roe, Nicholas, ed. *Leigh Hunt: Life, Poetics, Politics.* New York: Routledge, 2003.

Said, Edward. *Culture and Imperialism.* New York: Knopf, 1993.

Saintsbury, George. *History of English Prosody, from the Twelfth Century to the Present Day.* New York: Russell & Russell, 1961.

Sperry, Stuart. *Keats the Poet.* Princeton, N.J.: Princeton University Press, 1994.

Spurgeon, Caroline Frances Eleanor. *Keats's Shakespeare: A Descriptive Study Based on New Material.* London: Oxford University Press, 1929.

Stabler, Jane. *Burke to Byron, Barbauld to Baillie, 1790–1830.* New York: Palgrave, 2001.

Stillinger, Jack. *The Hoodwinking of Madeline, and Other Essays on Keats's Poems.* Urbana: University of Illinois Press, 1971.

Storey, Mark. *Robert Southey: A Life.* New York: Oxford University Press, 1997.

Super, R. H.: *Walter Savage Landor: A Biography.* New York: New York University Press, 1954.

Sutherland, John. *The Life of Walter Scott: A Critical Biography.* Cambridge: Blackwell, 1995.

Sweet, Nanora. *Felicia Hemans: Reimagining Poetry in the Nineteenth Century.* New York: Palgrave, 2001.

Swinburne, Algernon Charles. *William Blake: A Critical Essay.* New York: Dutton, 1906.

Thompson, E. P. *Witness against the Beast: William Blake and the Moral Law.* New York: Cambridge University Press, 1993.

Thompson, James R. *Leigh Hunt.* Boston: Twayne, 1977.

Thorslev, Peter Larsen. *The Byronic Hero: Types and Prototypes.* Minneapolis: University of Minnesota Press, 1962.

Vendler, Helen. *Odes of John Keats.* Cambridge, Mass.: Harvard University Press, 1983.

Wasserman, Earl. *The Finer Tone: Keats' Major Poems.* Baltimore, Md.: John Hopkins University Press, 1953.

———. *Shelley: A Critical Reading.* Baltimore: Johns Hopkins University Press, 1971.

———. *Subtler Language: Critical Readings of Neoclassic and Romantic Poems.* Baltimore, Md.: Johns Hopkins University Press, 1968.

Weiskel, Thomas. *The Romantic Sublime: Studies in the Structure and Psychology of Transcendence.* Baltimore, Md.: Johns Hopkins University Press, 1986.

White, Terence De Vere. *Tom Moore: the Irish Poet.* London: Hamilton, 1977.

Wolfson, Susan J. *The Questioning Presence: Wordsworth, Keats, and the Interrogative Mode in Romantic Poetry.* Ithaca, N.Y.: Cornell University Press, 1986.

Woodring, Carl. *Politics in the Poetry of Coleridge.* Madison: University of Wisconsin Press, 1961.

Wordsworth, Jonathan. *Ancestral Voices: Fifty Books from the Romantic Period.* New York: Woodstock, 1996.

———. *Bright Work Grows: Women Writers of the Romantic Age.* Washington, D.C.: Woodstock Books, 1997.

Wu, Duncan. *Companion to Romanticism.* Oxford: Blackwell, 1998.

———. *Wordsworth: An Inner Life.* Oxford: Blackwell, 2002.

Zimmerman, Sarah MacKenzie. *Romanticism, Lyricism, and History.* Albany: State University of New York Press, 1999.

# INDEX

Page numbers in **boldface** denote main entries; page numbers followed by *c* denote chronology entries.

## A

abolitionism 515*c*, 526*c*, 527*c*
  "Epistle to William Wilberforce" 121
  *Interesting Narrative of the Life of Olaudah Equiano* 201
  Lickbarrow, Isabella 241
  More, Hannah 288
  Opie, Amelia Alderson 323
  slavery 417–418
  "To William Wilberforce, Esq." 464–465
Abrams, M. H. ix
  Byron, George Gordon Byron, Lord 53
  "Lines Written a Few Miles above Tintern Abbey" 242
  *Prelude, or Growth of a Poet's Mind* 346
absence 13–14
*Absentee, The* (Edgeworth) **1–2,** 107, 516*c*, 517*c*
accentual pentameter 110
Ackermann, Rudolph 11
acrostic poetry 246
Adams, Donald K. 291
addiction
  Coleridge, Samuel Taylor 83
  *Confessions of an English Opium-Eater* 87–88
  De Quincey, Thomas 100

Addison, Joseph 442
"Address to dear Isabella on the Authors recovery" (Fleming) 141
"Adonais" (Shelley) **2–3,** 521*c*
  Keats, John 216
  "Ode to Psyche" 318
"Ae Fond Kiss" (Burns) **3–5**
*Aella* (Chatterton) 65
Aeolian harp 437–438
*Aeropagitica* (Milton) 292
Aeschylus 355
Africa 201
*African Eclogues* (Chatterton) 65
African people 416
*Age of Reason, The* (Paine) 328–329, 509*c*
Aikin, Lucy 370
"Alastor" (Shelley) 405, 518*c*
alcoholism
  Coleridge, Hartley 80
  Kean, Edmund 214
alexandrine
  *Childe Harold's Pilgrimage: A Romaunt* 66
  "Elegy Written in a Country Church-Yard" 110
  *Hernani* 173
  "To a Skylark" 460
"Alice Fell" (Wordsworth) **5–6**
Allen, Walter 353
alliteration 111
Almqvist, Carl Jonas Love **6–7**
*Alwyn* (Holcroft) 180
ambiguity 310–312
*America: A Prophecy* (Blake) 7

American Revolution xii, **7–9,** 502*c*–504*c*
  *America: A Prophecy* 7
  Blake, William 35
  empire 115
  monarchy 281
  Paine, Thomas 328
  *Rights of Man* 370
Amiens, Treaty of 248, 513*c*
*Analytical Review* 373
anapestic meter 294
*Anatomy of Melancholy* (Burton) 230
"Anecdote for Fathers" (Wordsworth) **9–10**
*Anecdotes of the Late Samuel Johnson* (Piozzi) 335, 505*c*
*Animal Magnetism, a Farce* (Inchbald) **10–11,** 506*c*
*Anna St. Ives* (Holcroft) 181
*Annual* (Southey) 12
annuals and gift books **11–13**
  Hemans, Felicia 171
  Howitt, Mary 184
  Landon, Letitia Elizabeth 231
  Shelley, Mary Wollstonecraft 402
Anquetil-Duperron, Abraham-Hyacinthe 324
antifeminism 370
Antinomian Calvinism 354
*Antiquities of Scotland* (Grose) 449
antislavery. *See* abolitionism
antistrophe 314
*Anxiety of Influence, The* (Bloom) viii